Fodor's 91 Canada

Fodor's Travel Publications, Inc.
New York and London

 Published in the United States by Fodor's Travel Publications, Inc., a subsidiary of Random House, Inc., New York, and simultaneously in Canada by Random House of Canada Limited, Toronto. Distributed by Random House, Inc., New York.

ISBN 0-679-01888-3

Fodor's Canada

Editor: Kathleen McHugh
Associate Editors: Alison Hoffman, Holly Hughes
Contributors: Susan Bain, Suzanne Brown, Ray Chatelin, Andrew Coe, Robert Dreesen, Theodore Fischer, Allan Gould, Dorothy Guinan, Eve Johnson, Mary Kelly, David Laskin, Julia Lisella, Patricia Lowe, Peter Oliver, Alice Oshins, Paula Rackow, Linda K. Schmidt, Colleen Thompson, Julie Tomasz, Terri Wershler
Researchers: Cliff Gaw, James Meehan
Art Director: Fabrizio La Rocca
Cartographer: David Lindroth
Illustrator: Karl Tanner
Cover Photograph: Casimir/Leo de Wys, Inc.

Design: Vignelli Associates

Special Sales

Fodor's Travel Publications are available at special discounts for bulk purchases (100 copies or more) for sales promotions or premiums. Special editions, including personalized covers, excerpts of existing guides, and corporate imprints, can be created in large quantities for special needs. For more information write to Special Marketing, Fodor's Travel Publications, 201 East 50th St., New York, NY 10022. Inquiries from the United Kingdom should be sent to Fodor's Travel Publications, 20 Vauxhall Bridge Rd., London, England SW1V 2SA.

MANUFACTURED IN THE UNITED STATES OF AMERICA

10 9 8 7 6 5 4 3 2 1

Contents

Maps and Plans

Foreword

We wish to express our gratitude to those who helped prepare this guide: the Canadian Consulate General office in New York, particularly Lois Gerber and Barbara Cartwright; the Montréal Convention and Tourism Bureau, especially Mary Baker and Willow Brown in New York, and Marilyne Benson and Gilles Goselin in Montréal; the Québec Government House in New York, particularly Pierre Valiquette, Jovette Lieou, Christine Landry, and Brian LeCompte; the Québec City Region Tourism and Convention Bureau in Québec City, particularly Michel Gagnon and Patricia Germain; Steve Johnson of the Metropolitan Toronto Convention & Visitors Association; Tourism Vancouver, especially Elvira Quarin; and Whistler Resort Association, particularly Dan Thomas.

Chapters on Canada's more remote and less visited provinces—the Yukon, Northwest Territories, and Newfoundland and Labrador—were not completed in time to be included in this newly rewritten edition. They will be incorporated into *Fodor's Canada 1992*.

While every care has been taken to ensure the accuracy of the information in this guide, the passage of time will always bring change, and consequently, the publisher cannot accept responsibility for errors that may occur.

All prices and opening times are based on information supplied to us at press time. Hours and admission fees may change, however, and the prudent traveler will avoid inconvenience by calling ahead.

Fodor's wants to hear about your travel experiences, both pleasant and unpleasant. When a hotel or restaurant fails to live up to its billing, let us know and we will investigate the complaint and revise our entries where the facts warrant it. Send your letters to the editors of Fodor's Travel Publications, 201 E. 50th Street, New York, NY 10022.

Highlights'91 and Fodor's Choice

Highlights '91

On the economic front the Canadian dollar continues to climb and since 1987 has remained strong against the American dollar. Americans can expect to get less for their money, although bargains are still available; to get the most for your American dollar think clothing and antiques. The newly instituted 7% **Goods and Services Tax** will have an effect on prices across the board, but Americans and other foreign visitors can avoid the extra costs if they purchase their airline tickets and tour packages outside of Canada and apply for refunds on goods they buy while in Canada. The GST, alias Grab and Soak Tax, replaces other hidden taxes, but primarily affects Canadians, not visitors to the country.

In an effort to thwart inflation, Canada and the United States have recently designed a **free trade pact** intended to ease travel restrictions and boost tourism. The agreement eliminates most import taxes between the two countries immediately; within 10 years there will be no import tax.

Highlighting Canada's travel news is **Rail Canada's new fare system,** in which rates based on ridership have replaced rates based on distance traveled. Fares in the largest market have increased an average of 9%; in the eastern part of Canada prices remain unchanged, while elsewhere—where seasonal travel is popular—fares fluctuate. In this last category it is possible to save as much as 40% on a ticket, if you travel off-peak.

Canada's airlines have seen some changes this year in their on-flight smoking policies. Early in 1990 the Canadian government proposed a total **ban on smoking** on international flights, but protests by the two international carriers resulted in a phase-out plan that will eliminate 25% of the current smoking space each year through 1993. Since December 1989 Canada has prohibited smoking on domestic flights of six hours or less.

Toronto In fall 1990 Toronto welcomed the opening of **Terminal 3** (into which Canadian Airlines flies) at Pearson International Airport. Though flight delays and traffic jams are common at the over-used airport, this addition should relieve some congestion; meanwhile **Terminal 2,** which accommodates Air Canada, continues its two-year face-lift. **Midway Airlines,** based in Chicago, recently purchased Eastern's gates at Terminal 1 and is now flying between Toronto and several cities in the United States. In general, airfares continue to increase in Canada, due in part to **Wardair's** recent acquisition by Canadian Airlines International.

Other big news for Toronto was the mid-1990 completion of the **subterranean micro-city.** Pedestrians can walk the continuous path from Union Station on Front Street to Dundas and Yonge streets, enjoying more than 1,000 stores and services, without having to venture outdoors. The 11-kilometer-long (7-mile) underground mall is the second largest in North America.

Changing the look of the city in 1991 will be **BCE Place** (BC refers to Bell Canada), whose two new towers grace Toronto's skyline. Canada's five largest banks and two biggest trust companies will do business here. On the northwest corner of Front and Yonge streets stands the 1885 **Bank of Montréal.** After the restoration project ends (in 1992), the majestic building will be incorporated into one of the new, modern towers as home to the Hockey Hall of Fame.

Montréal Montréal prepares to celebrate its **350th anniversary** in 1992 amid a swirl of political controversy that would ground all activity in a less resilient city. But residents of the world's third-largest French-speaking metropolis have always been an optimistic lot. Now, unfazed by renewed talk of Québec's separation from the rest of Canada (*see* Québec Province, below), they forge ahead with birthday plans.

Change is most evident in the downtown core, where complexes, condominiums, and museums continue to sprout or spruce up for 1992. In 1991, however, the **Musée,** Montréal's museum of modern art, will move from its La Cité site, on the other side of Montréal harbor, into ultramodern quarters at Place des Arts, the city's performing-arts complex.

Eaton Centre, on rue Ste-Catherine Ouest, is ready for browsers. An expansion of Eatons, the well-known Canadian department-store chain, the new shopping complex also incorporates the popular tiered mall, **Les Terrasses.** Nearby, avenue du McGill College—a broad stretch connecting the campus of McGill University with the Place Ville-Marie complex—has been transformed into a flowery boulevard enhanced by such stylish architecture as that of Place Montreal Trust, with its up-market mall; the glass tower encasing the Banque Nationale de Paris; the new Ultramar headquarters; and the imposing granite Industrielle Vie high rise.

At press time the eagerly awaited **World Trade Centre,** built to attract more international business, was nearing completion. A patchwork combination of old and new buildings, it takes up almost an entire city block in historic Vieux-Montréal.

Nine new hotels are either on the drawing board or under construction, adding some 1,200 rooms by 1992. The plushest pair in the new lineup are the $70 million **Inter-Continental,** part of the World Trade Centre, and its neighbor, **Le Palais,** which is being built at a cost of $90 million farther east along rue St-Jacques. Both will provide five-star accommodations in the Vieux-Montréal quarter, which hasn't seen a deluxe hotel in decades. The most unusual of the new properties is the Holiday Inn's **Jardin Sinomonde,** which opens this year across from the convention center. In the heart of Chinatown, the 260-room property blends in with the surrounding architecture, and its Oriental theme extends to the lobby's Chinese garden and fountain. Also designed with the East in mind, the **Hôtel Furama,** at boulevard René-Lévesque and rue Hôtel de Ville, is scheduled to open in 1991.

Major municipal efforts have produced a wealth of new recreational attractions. Among them is the city's **first downtown beach,** which curves along the shore of Ile Notre-Dame Lake, at the heart of one of the islands that hosted the Expo '67 World's Fair. Thanks to a sophisticated water-filtration system—aided by 125,000 aquatic plants—the outdoor recreation center is open for swimming from late June through August and is landscaped to resemble beaches on the Laurentian lakes north of Montréal. It features a sandy shore, chalet-style restaurant, grassy picnic area, and boat rentals. Those who prefer sturdier vessels can hop aboard the new **summer ferry** that plies the St. Lawrence between Montréal harbor and the south-shore community of Longueuil.

At the east end of town, on rue Sherbrooke Est, the **Botanical Garden** has completed the landscaping of its Chinese Garden, one of the largest outside China. **The Olympic Stadium** across the street now has a tourist-reception building with a tour-bus depot, an information counter, a restaurant, and an auditorium presenting a multimedia show on Olympic Park history. Also on the former Olympic's site, the old Vélodrome has had its bicycle tracks demolished to make way for the **Montréal Biodôme,** slated to open in 1992. A unique natural-science museum, the Biodôme will replicate four different ecosystems in exhibition areas representing tropical jungles and northern forests, the St. Lawrence River and polar regions. There will also be new homes for the 500 residents of the current zoo and denizens of the Montréal Aquarium. All will be changing addresses sometime this year, so visitors are advised to check before setting off for either the zoo or the aquarium.

Québec City Although rich in history and traditional culture, Québec City does not lack the conveniences of a modern city. The hotels and restaurants are attuned to the needs of today's traveler. Two of Québec City's landmarks, the **Château Frontenac** and the **Hotel Clarendon,** will unveil their major renovations in 1991. The classic Château Frontenac spent $30 million in 1990 to enlarge and rejuvenate its facilities, including the installation of a garden on its roof, which is visible only from selected rooms within the hotel; a restoration of all guest rooms; and the addition of a new bistro. Around the corner the Hotel Clarendon, Québec City's oldest hotel, is undergoing $5.3 million of restoration as it enlarges and updates its facilities while preserving its Art Deco theme.

This year will also mark the completion of a three-year, $14 million project: **Manoir Victoria.** This promising new hotel is located in the heart of the Latin quarter. Since it opened its doors in 1988, the original 90-year-old Hotel Victoria has been transformed into a modern-day manor. Its aim is to please all, with everything from simple, brightly decorated rooms to elaborate suites with whirlpool baths for two. When completed, a downtown nightclub will be connected to the hotel.

The **Musée de Québec** will celebrate its "Grande Réouverture" in the spring of 1991 after undergoing $22.4 million of restoration. The museum is doubling its exhibition space by incorporating the space of an abandoned prison. Québecois and tourists alike are eager to visit this mysterious locale, which dates to 1867. The new museum will offer a diversion from its traditional Québec art by preserving a hallway of the original prison cells, with the iron bars and courtyard still intact. A permanent exhibit will portray a history of the prison; it was one of the first such institutions in Canada to introduce the communal philosophy to prison life. The original 1933 museum will be connected to the prison via the "Grande Hall," a bright hallway with a steepled glass roof, where the reception area, a restaurant with terrace facing the St. Lawrence River, and a boutique will be located.

Finally, **Place Royale** has embarked on a face-lift. The $9 million project was inspired by a 1990 fire that gutted two of the historic buildings. Luckily the two buildings destroyed by the blaze had not yet been restored. The final result is expected to be unveiled in 1992.

Vancouver Vancouver takes part in the PPG Indy Car World Series with the 1991 **Indy Vancouver,** one of 16 races worldwide. Over Labour Day weekend a 1.7-mile circuit through downtown streets will be run, during three days of racing.

Back in the city's spotlight is the former **Expo '86 site.** The 180 acres were sold to Hong Kong businessman Li Ka-Shing in 1987 but lay undeveloped for almost four years. This long strip of waterfront property adjacent to downtown Vancouver is now the largest urban-development project in North America. Building will be done in sections; the first was begun in late 1990, and the last will be finished in about 20 years. **International Village,** the first phase, abuts Chinatown and will consist of condominiums, townhouses, an office tower, hotels, parks, and commercial space. It was designed jointly by three prominent architectural firms from Vancouver.

Coastal British Columbia Leaving Vancouver and heading into British Columbia's interior was made easier this year, since the completion of

Highway 5 from Hope to Kamloops and with the new extension (**Highway 97a**) from Peachland, south of Kelowna, which cuts two hours of driving time from Vancouver to Okanagon. This will also make it easier for tourists following 1991's **Year of Music** festival (May–October) throughout the province. The event—designed with tourism in mind—will involve virtually every town, village, and city in British Columbia, as local and international performers present bluegrass, classical, rock, ragtime, and gospel shows on a five-month schedule.

Another cause for celebration is the 1990 opening of the **Native Heritage Centre,** in Duncan, on Vancouver Island. Devoted to the province's rich ethnic history, the establishment features interpretive presentations and exhibits that reflect the lives of the region's indigenous peoples.

Canadian Rockies In the Canadian Rockies, **Chateau Lake Louise** has undergone a major renovation and expansion, greatly improving the sprawling old hotel. Also renovated is the **Miette Hot Springs** resort, where almost a century ago prospectors soaked away their aches and pains. **Kananaskis Village,** which served as a base for the 1988 Winter Olympics, is now a full-service—and generally upscale—resort village.

With two new courses opened in the British Columbia Rockies in the last three years, the region has become increasingly attractive to golfers. For winter sportsmen, heli-skiing operators (most notably **Canadian Mountain Holidays**) have expanded operations considerably through the British Columbia Rockies in the last three years.

Manitoba, Saskatchewan, Alberta Two cities in the prairie provinces look forward to major openings in the near future. In summer 1991 Regina will welcome the new **Native Peoples Gallery** to the Saskatchewan Museum of Natural History. The gallery will focus on the province's Native heritage. In 1992 Edmonton expects to break ground for the new **City Hall,** across from the Edmonton Art Gallery.

Ontario Ontario's **sales tax** is now at an all-time high of 8%, but visitors should remember to apply for sales-tax rebates on goods purchased in Canada.

Québec Province After three years of deliberation concerning Québec's special status in the Canadian Constitution, the three-year attempt (called the **Meech Lake Accord**) to gain the province's signature was squashed. At press time (December 1990) the future relationship between Québec—which wants to freely promote the French language and culture—and Canada has not been decided. But Québec is determined to put its interests before those of the country, even if it means becoming a sovereign state. The province is expected to make a final decision in March 1991.

Nova Scotia Nova Scotia feeds tourists' hunger for soft adventure and a taste of the wilderness with its new national park, **Kejim-**

kujik Seaside Adjunct, which had been privately owned until the recent Parks Canada acquisition. The preserved land is still wild and remote, though hiking trails make it accessible to the public. Other national parks can be reached easily by car. Outfitters have been quick to respond to the demand, by developing all sorts of **package deals** that make it easy to enjoy the province's inexhaustible supply of natural adventures and opportunities.

Nova Scotia's developers have also responded to convention needs, and although Halifax is the major convention center, new **meeting facilities** such as those of Inverary Lodge, Baddeck, and White Point Beach Lodge Resort in Liverpool are now available for groups of 100 to 150 delegates.

But much of this development will be overshadowed in 1991 by the **Gathering of the Clans,** a spirited celebration that begins on July 1 with the big Tattoo in Halifax and continues all summer with a dozen or so clan gatherings around the province. One clan gathering spawns another, and it's a sure bet that the Nova Scotian countryside will resound with the skirl of the pipes and the camaraderie that accompanies the Highland games.

New Brunswick New Brunswick, too, is making great efforts to accommodate tourism, beginning with its provincial section of the **Trans-Canada Highway,** which is being upgraded. Other developments include Fredericton's new **Sheraton** (scheduled to open in August 1991), which will augment the city's previously scanty selection of lodgings. Additionally, bed-and-breakfast establishments continue to proliferate, as New Brunswick draws on its hospitable reputation. Kudos go to the **Malicete Indian Band** at Mactaquac, which has given up its ancient practice of netting fish, an activity that was endangering the Atlantic salmon (now on the comeback thanks to a concerned group of New Brunswick conservationists). To make up for the loss of their livelihood, the Malicete are receiving government help in erecting and operating a modern motel about 11 miles west of Fredericton.

Fodor's Choice

No two people will agree on what makes a perfect vacation, but it's fun and helpful to know what others think. We hope you'll have a chance to experience some of Fodor's Choices yourself in Canada. For detailed information about each entry, refer to the appropriate chapter.

Toronto

Attractions
Greektown, Toronto
Harbourfront, Toronto
Metro Toronto Zoo, Scarborough
Royal Ontario Museum, Queen's Park

Shopping
Eaton Centre
Hazelton Lanes
Kensington Market/Chinatown
Queen Street West
Yorkville Avenue/Bloor Street area

Cultural Events
Canadian Opera Company at the O'Keefe Centre
Concerts and symphonies at Roy Thomson Hall
National Ballet of Canada at the O'Keefe Centre
Theater at the Royal Alexandra
Theater at the St. Lawrence Centre

Restaurants
Le Bistingo (*Very Expensive*)
Nekah (*Very Expensive*)
North 44 (*Expensive*)
Pronto Ristorante (*Expensive*)
Avocado Club (*Moderate*)
BamBoo (*Moderate*)
Santa Fe Bar & Grill (*Moderate*)
Pearl Court (*Inexpensive*)

Hotels
Four Seasons Toronto (*Very Expensive*)
Chestnut Park Hotel (*Expensive*)
Windsor Arms (*Expensive*)

Montréal

Attractions
Le Centre Canadien d'Architecture
Montréal Botanical Garden
Musée des beaux-arts de Montréal
Place d'Armes
La Ronde

Shopping
Centre de Céramique de Bonsecours, Vieux-Montréal
Complexe Desjardins
Les Cours Mont-Royal
Faubourg Ste-Catherine
Notre-Dame Ouest for antiques

Marché aux puces, Vieux-Montréal
Les Promenades de la Cathédrale

Cultural Events Centaur Theatre
L'Opéra de Montréal
L'Orchestre Symphonique de Montréal
Théâtre du Nouveau Monde

Restaurants Les Mignardises (*Very Expensive*)
Milos (*Expensive*)
Les Filles du Roy (*Moderate–Expensive*)
Stash's (*Moderate*)
Xuan (*Moderate*)

Hotels Hôtel de la Montagne (*Very Expensive*)
Le Reine Elizabeth (*Very Expensive*)
Le Grand Hôtel (*Expensive*)
Château Versailles (*Moderate*)

Québec City

Attractions Château Frontenac
Citadelle
Musée de la Civilisation

Shopping Marché du Vieux-Port
Place Québec
Quartier Petit-Champlain

Cultural Events Bibliothèque Gabrielle-Roy
Grand Théâtre de Québec
L'Orchestre Symphonique de Québec

Parks Parc de l'Artillerie
Parc Cartier-Brébeuf
Parc des Champs-de-Bataille

Restaurants À La Table de Serge Bruyère (*Very Expensive*)
Le Saint-Amour (*Very Expensive*)
Aux Anciens Canadiens (*Expensive*)
L'Echaudée (*Moderate*)
Chez Temporel (*Inexpensive*)

Hotels Hilton International Québec (*Very Expensive*)
Manoir d'Auteuil (*Expensive*)
L'Auberge du Quartier (*Moderate*)
Hôtel Maison Sainte-Ursule (*Inexpensive*)

Vancouver

Attractions Dr. Sun-yat Sen Classical Garden, Chinatown
Granville Public Market, Granville Island
Museum of Anthropology, on University of British Columbia campus
Maritime Museum, Granville Island
Stanley Park Zoo

Shopping
Chinatown
Fourth Avenue (between Burrard and Balsam streets)
Pacific Center Mall
Robson Street

Restaurants
Chartwell (*Expensive*)
Tojo's (*Expensive*)
Kirin Mandarin Restaurant (*Moderate*)
Rubina Tandoori (*Moderate*)
Szechuan Chongqing (*Inexpensive*)

Hotels
Le Meridien (*Very Expensive*)
Pan Pacific (*Very Expensive*)
Wedgewood Hotel (*Expensive*)
Georgia Hotel (*Moderate*)
West End Guest House (*Moderate*)
Sylvia Hotel (*Inexpensive*)

Coastal British Columbia

Attractions
Anne Hathaway's Cottage, Victoria
Crystal Gardens, Victoria
Pacific Undersea Garden, Victoria
Royal British Columbia Museum, Victoria

Shopping
Chinatown, Victoria
Government Street, Victoria
Market Square, Victoria

Great Outdoors
Adams River Salmon Run, Okanagan Valley
Cathedral Provincial Park, Penticton
Inside Passage
Pacific Rim National Park, Vancouver Island
Queen Charlotte Islands

Restaurants
Sooke Harbour House (*Very Expensive*)
Larousse, Victoria (*Expensive*)
Corbett Lake Country Inn, Merritt (*Moderate*)
Old Mahle House, Nanaimo (*Moderate*)
Six-Mile-House, Victoria (*Inexpensive*)

Hotels
Hotel Grand Pacific, Victoria (*Very Expensive*)
Laurel Point Inn, Victoria (*Expensive–Very Expensive*)
Lake Okanagan Resort, Kelowna (*Expensive*)
La Coast Bastion Inn, Nanaimo (*Moderate–Expensive*)
Painter's Lodge, Campbell River (*Moderate–Expensive*)
Crest Motor Hotel, Prince Rupert (*Moderate*)
Lac le Jeune Resort, Kamloops (*Moderate*)
Craigmyle Guest House, Victoria (*Inexpensive–Moderate*)
Gables Country Inn and Tea House, Kelowna (*Inexpensive*)
The Greystone Manor, Comox (*Inexpensive*)
The Roadhouse Inn, Parksville (*Inexpensive*)

Canadian Rockies

Sights
The drive along the Icefields Parkway
The Banff Springs Hotel

The view from the Jasper Tramway
A boat cruise on Maligne Lake
Lake Louise and Moraine Lake

Sporting Activities Hiking through the national parks
Mountaineering around the Columbia Icefields and the Bugaboos of the British Columbia Rockies
Horse-pack trips in Kananaskis Country
Skiing at Lake Louise, Nakiska, and Panorama
Heli-skiing in the British Columbia Rockies

Romantic Hideaways Canoeing on Emerald Lake
Lake O'Hara Lodge

Restaurants Le Beaujolais, Banff (*Very Expensive*)
Post Hotel, Lake Louise (*Very Expensive*)
Le Beauvallon, Jasper (*Expensive–Very Expensive*)
One-Twelve, Revelstoke (*Expensive*)
Emerald Lake Lodge, Yoho (*Moderate–Expensive*)
Giorgio's, Banff (*Moderate–Expensive*)
Martha's Cafe, Canmore (*Inexpensive–Moderate*)

Hotels Chateau Lake Louise (*Very Expensive*)
Buffalo Mountain Lodge, Banff (*Expensive*)
Emerald Lake Lodge, Yoho (*Expensive*)
Post Hotel, Lake Louise (*Expensive*)
Prince of Wales Hotel, Waterton Lakes (*Moderate–Expensive*)
Storm Mountain Lodge, Banff (*Moderate–Expensive*)
Kilmorey Lodge, Waterton Lakes (*Moderate*)

Manitoba, Saskatchewan, Alberta

Attractions Alberta Science Centre/Planetarium, Calgary
Calgary Zoo
Devonian Gardens, Calgary
Manitoba Museum of Man and Nature, Winnipeg
Muttart Conservatory, Edmonton
University of Saskatchewan, Saskatoon
Wascana Waterfowl Park Display Ponds, Regina

Shopping Centre Four, Calgary
Strathcona Square, Edmonton
Portage Place, Winnipeg
Strathdee Shoppes, Regina
West Edmonton Mall

Parks Assiniboine Park and Zoo, Winnipeg
Fort Edmonton Park
Grand Beach Provincial Park, Winnipeg
Hecla Provincial Park, Winnipeg
Heritage Park, Calgary
Moose Mountain Provincial Park, Regina
Whiteshell Provincial Park

Restaurants Owl's Nest, Calgary (*Very Expensive*)
Unheardof Dining Lounge, Edmonton (*Very Expensive*)

Victor's, Winnipeg (*Very Expensive*)
Mieka's, Regina (*Expensive*)
Bistro Dansk, Winnipeg (*Moderate*)
Adonis, Saskatoon (*Inexpensive*)
Buzzards Wine Bar, Calgary (*Inexpensive*)
Chianti, Edmonton (*Inexpensive*)

Hotels Hilton International Edmonton (*Very Expensive*)
Westin Hotel, Calgary (*Very Expensive*)
Edmonton House (*Expensive*)
Place Louis Riel, Winnipeg (*Expensive*)
Sheraton Centre, Regina (*Expensive*)
Prince Royal Inn, Calgary (*Moderate*)
King George, Saskatoon (*Inexpensive*)
Sandman Inn, Regina (*Inexpensive*)

Ontario

Attractions Marineland, Niagara Falls
National Arts Centre, Ottawa
National Gallery of Canada, Ottawa

Sights Rideau Canal, Ottawa
View of Niagara Falls from Minolta, Kodak, and Skylon towers

Restaurants Rundles, Stratford (*Expensive*)
Le Soupçon, Ottawa (*Expensive*)
Café Henry Burger, Hull (*Moderate*)

Hotels Château Laurier, Ottawa (*Very Expensive*)
Queens Landing, Niagara-on-the-Lake (*Expensive*)
Raj Guest House, Stratford (*Expensive*)

Québec Province

Sights Basilica of Ste-Anne de Beaupre
Bonaventure Island, the Gaspé Peninsula
Jardin Zoologique, Granby

Restaurants L'Eau à la Bouche, Ste-Adèle (*Very Expensive*)
Chatel Vienna, Ste-Agathe (*Expensive*)

Hotels Auberge la Pinsonnière, La Malbaie (*Very Expensive*)
Hôtel Cap-aux-Pierres, La Baleine (*Very Expensive*)
Auberge la Maison Otis, Baie-St-Paul (*Expensive–Very Expensive*)

Nova Scotia

Sights The Citadel, Halifax
The Public Gardens, Halifax
Fortress Louisbourg, Cape Breton Island

Restaurants Clipper Cay, Halifax (*Expensive*)
Old Man Morias, Halifax (*Moderate*)

Hotels Chateau Halifax (*Very Expensive*)
Delta Barrington, Halifax (*Very Expensive*)
Halliburton House Inn, Halifax (*Expensive*)

Prince Edward Island

Sights Fort Amherst Port LaJoie National Historic Site, Rocky Point
Green Gables, Cavendish
Province House, Charlottetown

Restaurants The Griffon Room, Charlottetown (*Very Expensive*)
Claddagh Room Restaurant, Charlottetown (*Expensive*)

Hotels Dalvay-by-the-Sea, Grand Tracadie (*Very Expensive*)
Prince Edward Hotel and Convention Centre, Charlottetown (*Very Expensive*)
Shaw's Hotel and Cottages, Brackley Beach (*Very Expensive*)

New Brunswick

Attractions Kings Landing Historical Settlement, Fredericton
Market Square, Saint John
Reversing Falls Rapids, Saint John

Shopping Downtown Moncton
Madawaska Weavers, St. Leonard
Prince William Street, Saint John

Restaurants Benoit's, Fredericton (*Expensive*)
Fisherman's Paradise (*Moderate*)

Hotels Saint John Hilton (*Expensive*)

Canada

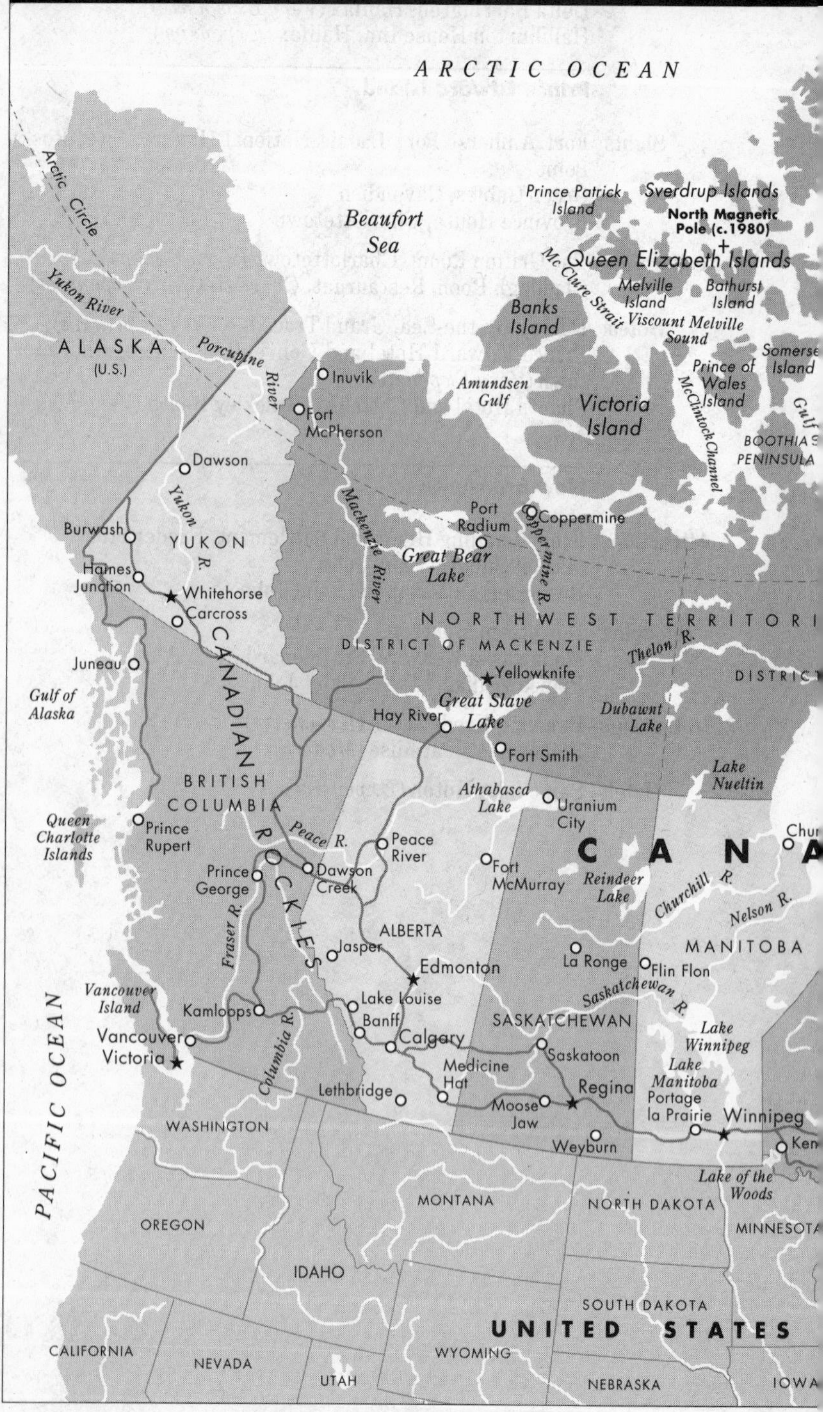
ARCTIC OCEAN
Beaufort Sea
Prince Patrick Island
Sverdrup Islands
North Magnetic Pole (c.1980)
Queen Elizabeth Islands
Mc Clure Strait
Melville Island
Bathurst Island
Banks Island
Viscount Melville Sound
Arctic Circle
Yukon River
ALASKA (U.S.)
Porcupine River
Inuvik
Fort McPherson
Amundsen Gulf
Victoria Island
Prince of Wales Island
McClintock Channel
BOOTHIA PENINSULA
Dawson
Yukon R.
YUKON
Burwash
Haines Junction
Whitehorse
Carcross
Mackenzie River
Port Radium
Coppermine
Coppermine R.
Great Bear Lake
NORTHWEST TERRITORI
DISTRICT OF MACKENZIE
Thelon R.
Yellowknife
Juneau
Gulf of Alaska
CANADIAN ROCKIES
Great Slave Lake
Hay River
Dubawnt Lake
Fort Smith
Lake Nueltin
BRITISH COLUMBIA
Athabasca Lake
Uranium City
Queen Charlotte Islands
Prince Rupert
Peace R.
Peace River
Dawson Creek
Prince George
Fort McMurray
Reindeer Lake
Churchill R.
Nelson R.
ALBERTA
MANITOBA
Fraser R.
Jasper
Edmonton
La Ronge
Flin Flon
Saskatchewan R.
Vancouver Island
Kamloops
Lake Louise
Banff
SASKATCHEWAN
Lake Winnipeg
Vancouver
Victoria
Columbia R.
Calgary
Saskatoon
Lake Manitoba
Medicine Hat
Regina
Portage la Prairie
Winnipeg
Lethbridge
Moose Jaw
Weyburn
PACIFIC OCEAN
WASHINGTON
Lake of the Woods
MONTANA
NORTH DAKOTA
MINNESOTA
OREGON
IDAHO
SOUTH DAKOTA
UNITED STATES
CALIFORNIA
NEVADA
WYOMING
UTAH
NEBRASKA
IOWA

ICELAND
Denmark Strait
GREENLAND (Denmark)
Ellesmere Island
Devon Island
Lancaster Sound
Baffin Bay
Baffin Island
Davis Strait
Prince Charles Island
Foxe Basin
Lake Amadjuak
Iqaluit
Lake Harbour
Southampton Island
Hudson Strait
KEEWATIN
Cape Chidley
Labrador Sea
Ivujivik
Coats Island
Mansel Island
Ungava Bay
Nain
Hudson Bay
NEWFOUNDLAND
Battle Harbour
D A
LABRADOR
Schefferville
Goose Bay
Belcher Islands
Fort Severn
Gander
Severn R.
Fort George
St. John's
QUEBEC
Newfoundland
James Bay
Sept-Iles
Anticosti Island
Lake Mistassini
Gulf of St. Lawrence
GASPÉ PENINSULA
ST. PIERRE AND MIQUELON (France)
Moosonee
ONTARIO
PRINCE EDWARD ISLAND
Rimouski
Chicoutimi
Sydney
NEW BRUNSWICK
Lake Nipigon
Québec City
Charlottetown
Cochrane
Ste.-Agathe-Des-Monts
Fredericton
NOVA SCOTIA
Thunder Bay
Timmins
Trois-Rivières
Saint John
Halifax
Lake Superior
Montréal
MAINE
Bay of Fundy
North Bay
Sudbury
St. Lawrence River
Sault Ste.Marie
Ottawa
N
ATLANTIC OCEAN
VT.
N.H.
Lake Huron
Toronto
Lake Ontario
WISCONSIN
Lake Michigan
Niagara Falls
MASSACHUSETTS
NEW YORK
R.I.
MICHIGAN
CONN.
0
400 miles
Lake Erie
N.J.
0
600 km
ILLINOIS
INDIANA
OHIO
PENNSYLVANIA

World Time Zones

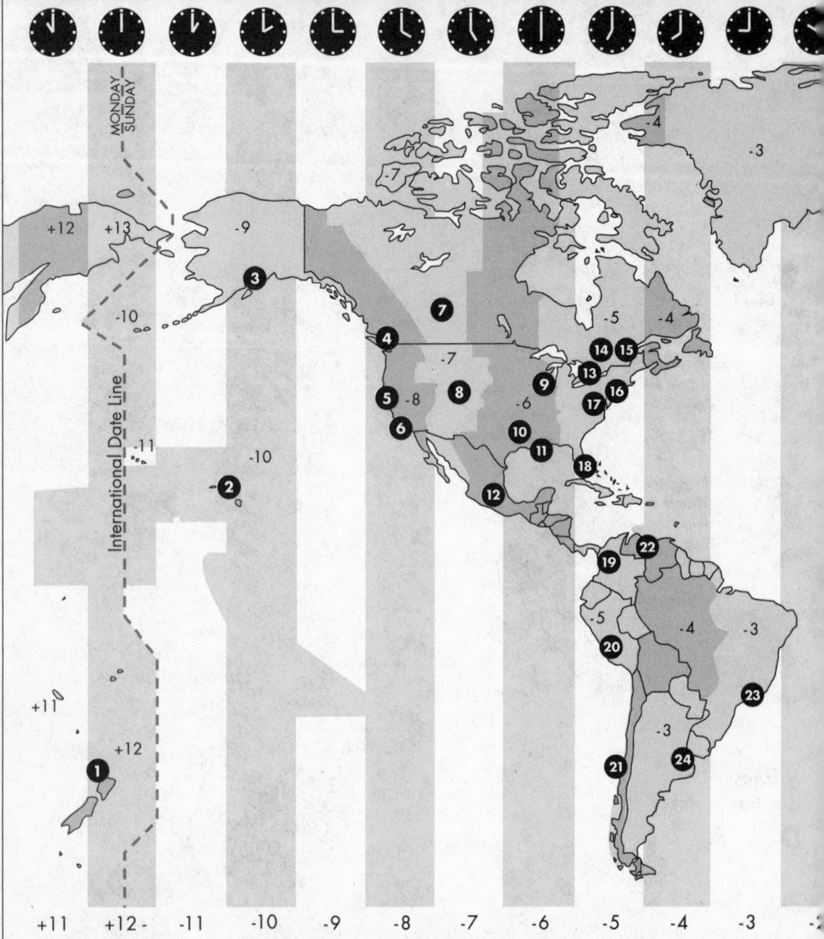

Numbers below vertical bands relate each zone to Greenwich Mean Time (0 hrs.).
Local times frequently differ from these general indications,
as indicated by light-face numbers on map.

Algiers, **29**
Anchorage, **3**
Athens, **41**
Auckland, **1**
Baghdad, **46**
Bangkok, **50**
Beijing, **54**

Berlin, **34**
Bogotá, **19**
Budapest, **37**
Buenos Aires, **24**
Caracas, **22**
Chicago, **9**
Copenhagen, **33**
Dallas, **10**

Delhi, **48**
Denver, **8**
Djakarta, **53**
Dublin, **26**
Edmonton, **7**
Hong Kong, **56**
Honolulu, **2**

Istanbul, **40**
Jerusalem, **42**
Johannesburg, **44**
Lima, **20**
Lisbon, **28**
London (Greenwich), **27**
Los Angeles, **6**
Madrid, **38**
Manila, **57**

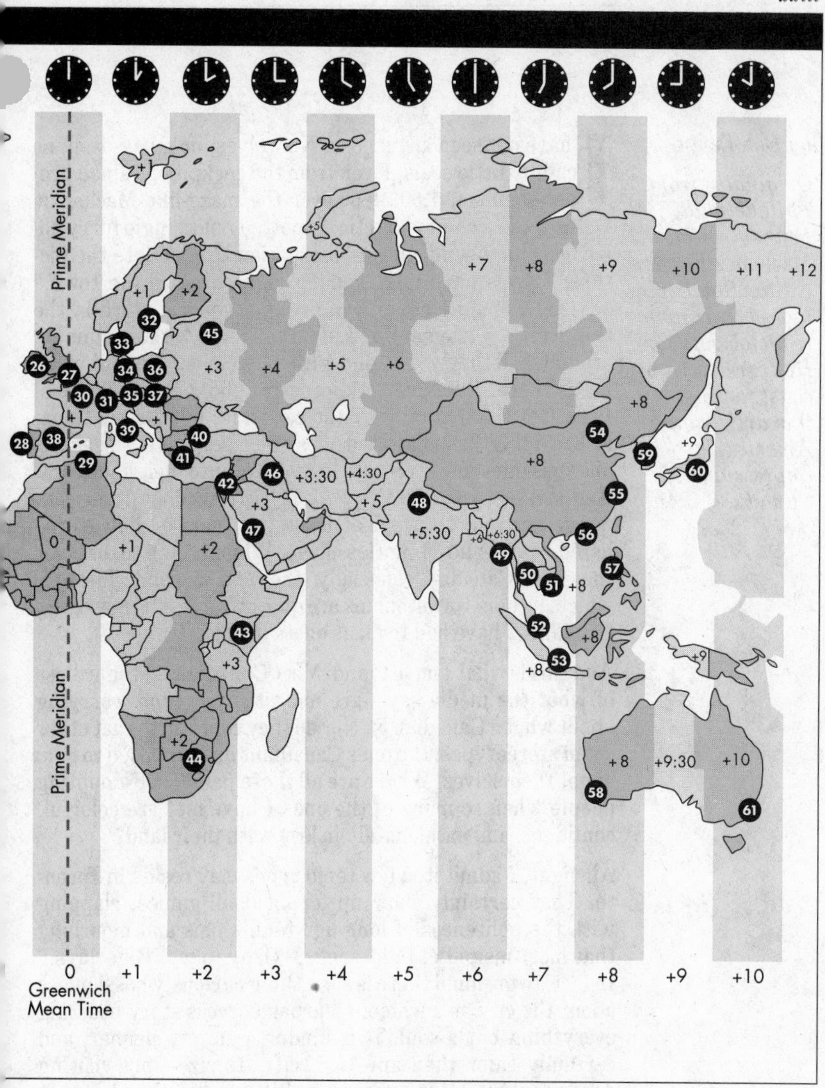

Mecca, **47**
Mexico City, **12**
Miami, **18**
Montreal, **15**
Moscow, **45**
Nairobi, **43**
New Orleans, **11**
New York City, **16**
Ottawa, **14**
Paris, **30**
Perth, **58**
Reykjavík, **25**
Rio de Janeiro, **23**
Rome, **39**
Saigon, **51**
San Francisco, **5**
Santiago, **21**
Seoul, **59**
Shanghai, **55**
Singapore, **52**
Stockholm, **32**
Sydney, **61**
Tokyo, **60**
Toronto, **13**
Vancouver, **4**
Vienna, **35**
Warsaw, **36**
Washington, DC, **17**
Yangon, **49**
Zürich, **31**

Introduction

by Bob Levin

Originally from Philadelphia, Pennsylvania, Maclean's *Foreign Editor Bob Levin moved to Toronto in October 1985. He traveled from coast to coast for this article on an American's impressions of Canada.*

I have not seen any moose. No wolves, no musk-oxen, no cuddly little seals. Even from the cockpit of a small propeller plane, 1,500 feet over the maze-like Mackenzie Delta in the icebound Arctic, I spotted not a single furry polar bear lumbering out of hibernation to complete the picture. "Foxes have been coming right up into the town," advised Ronald Knoller, who runs a general store in the tiny Arctic settlement of Aklavik. "You see them running around, and they've tangled with dog teams." But not when I was there. I did see an impressive elk in Banff National Park, trotting casually by the roadside, but for me Canada's wildlife has consisted mostly of squawking seagulls and mischievous raccoons in my Toronto neighborhood. And maybe that is just as well: It has forced an American, newly arrived, to avoid at least the "moose" half of the hated moose-and-Mounties cliché. While trying to discover the real Canada—especially the one beyond Toronto, which, as non-Torontonians are quick to argue, is not *really* Canada—I have had to focus on its people.

And this is what I have found: Most Canadians—regardless of what the media say—are not sitting around worrying about what a Canadian is. Nor do they conform to that other set of stereotypes, the ones Canadians are supposed to hold about themselves. Where are all those pallid, self-doubting people when so many of the ones I have met are colorful, confident, and passionately in love with their land?

All right, I admit it, a few tepid types may reside in Toronto. They certainly show up for baseball games, clapping with the politeness of long-ago tennis fans and mouthing that most insipid of fight songs, "Okay, okay, Blue Jays." In fact, to my mind there is something curiously passionless about the city as a whole, an urban success story boasting everything but a soul. It is kinder, gentler, cleaner, and certainly safer than any U.S. city its size—my visiting American friends invariably find it wonderful and cannot understand its New York–like, love-to-hate-it place in the Canadian national consciousness. My own feelings fall closer to the American view. But "I love Toronto" could never be the city's slogan—no, I *like* Toronto sums it up perfectly.

It has been on trips outside the city, to the more far-flung sectors of this most resolutely regional of nations, that I have found Canada at its more extreme, independent, quirky—even romantic, as un-Canadian a word as that is supposed to be. One snow-swept morning in Pouch Cove, a fishing-village-turned-suburb north of St. John's, Newfoundland, I visited William Noseworthy in his white clapboard house high on Noseworthy's Hill. Blue-eyed and ruddy-cheeked, Noseworthy sat in the kitchen by a wood stove, distractedly smoking a cigarette. He was 66 and had just retired the year before after four decades of fishing, but he still stared out the window at the North Atlantic. "There's something that draws you to it," he said in the rich accent of "the Rock."

His son, 31-year-old Barry, sipping a Labatt's beer, recalled that once, when he was 13, his father caught him whistling in a boat. "He was going to throw me overboard," said Barry. "It's just bad luck." William explained: "You don't whistle on the water. You wouldn't dare. You wouldn't launch your boat on Friday either. They're just superstitions, maybe. But several years ago, someone launched a big fishing trawler on a Friday, and she was lost on a Friday, and all the crew members, too." A minute later, William pulled out a shiny red accordion and played a jig, tapping his foot, but his eyes never left the water.

Newfoundland was also a place to sample Canadian regionalism at its most craggy and entrenched. The province's inshore fishermen claim that their very way of life is endangered by declining cod catches, which they blame on offshore trawling, often by foreigners. And they blame Ottawa for not looking out for their interests—even 40 years after joining Confederation, the old refrain still comes quickly to some residents' lips: "A Newfoundlander first, a Canadian second." But in a Pouch Cove twine store, where four diehard fishermen repaired their cod traps while country music drawled from a tape player, Frank Noseworthy, a slim, mustachioed cousin of Barry, said that he rejected the Newfoundlanders-first sentiment—and would far rather be Canadian than American. "In the States," he said, "them that's got it, gets more; them that don't, gets less. The Canadian government's more generous toward people that don't have."

Noseworthy has met many American tourists and he has not been impressed. "They come in their flashy cars," he said, "putting on airs. They seem to think they're a superior race, but I haven't seen one that's superior to me yet." He poked at the broken twine with his knife. He had one more thing to say, a point of both resentment and pride. "Some of the worst are Newfoundlanders who moved to the States. They forget their roots. They're sort of looking down their noses, instead of appreciating that there are people here trying to maintain their heritage."

Canada has hardly cornered the market on regionalism. A divided United States fought a horrific civil war in the 1860s, and as a northerner who has lived down South, I can attest to the fact that, to some southerners, the old resentments have not gone with the wind. But the United States also has the Melting Pot, the American Dream, the Pledge of Allegiance, the Hollywood-enhanced legends of Davy Crockett and even Ronald Reagan—an ever-enlarging collection of nationalistic symbols, myths, and heroes that bind the country together. Like glue, they may sometimes seem sticky and malodorous, but they do the job.

On the other hand, Canadians, writes Toronto author June Callwood, "have never created a myth that would unify them into nationhood"—except for Québec francophones. The question of Québec nationalism, heating up again over Premier Robert Bourassa's decision last December to prohibit English on outdoor commercial signs, has arisen wherever I have gone in Canada. Much of the sentiment seems to reflect that of Pouch Cove's William Noseworthy, who said, "They're always looking for special treatment—if they want to get out of Canada, let 'em get out."

In Montréal, there is no missing the passion behind the sign law. But in the office of Daniel Latouche, a political scientist and a former adviser to René Lévesque, the separatist Québec premier who died in 1987, I asked whether Québecers had a special affinity for Americans—whether, as Callwood implies, the two share a romantic vision of themselves. "There is a belief here," he replied, "that there are only two kinds of North Americans—Americans and Québecers. Two kinds of people who tried to build what North America is all about. One is much bigger, the other one lost. But both have a dream."

That is the kind of language an American can understand. But it may be a sign of American myopia that few people south of the international border, I suspect, would immediately include Québecers in such a continent-wide club of dreams. In fact, the Québec issue is quite literally foreign to Americans. The closest U.S. equivalent is the current push by Spanish-speakers in some states for official bilingualism; English-speakers have reacted heatedly, and 17 states have now declared English to be their official language. But the Hispanics are mostly recent immigrants, not a cofounding people like Québec francophones—and no American can seriously imagine Florida trying to secede from the union.

In a 37th-floor Montréal office looking out toward the frozen St. Lawrence, I asked commercial lawyer Ronald Montcalm whether there was anything binding the English and French together, any mutual myths or heroes. Montcalm thought about it and smiled. "Our hockey teams—boy, that's Canada's game." I would recall that answer on a plane the next day, when the Edmonton Oilers were on board and a steady stream of young autograph-seekers were interrupting their card game, and center Craig MacTavish talked about how "we're not the biggest country population-wise but we produce the best hockey players." But in Montcalm's office, hockey seemed more than just a sport—it was the great unifier. "At one point," the lawyer said, "Québec ultranationalists were talking about having our own team. The argument against that is, 'Hey, you've got to have Mario Lemieux and Wayne Gretzky on the same team or the Russians will beat us.' "

No Canadian region has left a more indelible impression on me than the North. The frontier is among the most enduring of American symbols, and while the American West was settled long ago, the Canadian North still lies empty and alluring—a distant dreamscape reachable by Boeing 737. Last March, I visited Inuvik, Northwest Territories, a government-built town on the east side of the Mackenzie Delta. It is a place of fur-trimmed parkas and brightly colored houses, with a church shaped like an igloo and a bar called The Zoo.

But, more traditionally, it also has an RCMP detachment, a CBC office and a Hudson's Bay Co. store. "Twelve hundred miles from anywhere," said Mayor John Hill, "and here's small-town Canada—at least the way the bureaucrats decided it would be." Which raises the question: How can a country whose government knows exactly what a Canadian town should look like—and can create one from scratch 200 kilometers (124 miles) north of the Arctic Circle—have such a famously chronic identity crisis?

For me, Inuvik aroused feelings of ambivalence as sharp as its −30°C (−22°F) cold. On the one hand, there is the exhilarating remoteness of the place and the upbeat attitudes of many immigrants to the area—prominent businesspeople who came originally from Scotland, Germany, Greece, even Lebanon. "You've got to have the balls to come and get started in business here," noted Hill, a British transplant. "But once you have, the competitiveness isn't as intense as it would be in, say, Edmonton."On the other hand, there is a local native population with profound problems. I am suspicious of snap impressions. I also know that Americans bear their own shame over their appalling treatment of natives, and I know that, for all the historic wrongs native people have suffered in Canada, they have now organized to elect legislators, fight for land claims, and combat social ills. But in the North, the despairing side of the picture is as obvious as stray beer cans. Inuvik's RCMP Cpl. John de Jong explained that at least 80% of local crimes are alcohol-related. "These are not what you'd call social drinkers," said de Jong. "They drink until the liquor is gone and then they search for more. Then we end up having to look after them one way or the other."

The natives' problems go beyond alcohol—the suicide rate among the Inuit of the Northwest Territories is four times the national average. "There's a lot of grief," confirmed Diane Nelson, a program coordinator with the Canadian Mental Health Association office in Inuvik. "This country is hard to live in, just trying to survive. People get drunk and wander off and die of hypothermia. They fall through the ice. There's a lot of tragedy in their lives." One Métis woman told me that her brother and sister had both died alcohol-related deaths—and that her father and several relatives had sexually abused her from the age of 6 to 17. "It puts you through hell," she said. However, she has managed to get on with her life—she is married and a college graduate.

The social workers and educators in town talked of culture shock—of native people thrust abruptly into the space age and paying the price emotionally; of old amusements like berry-picking and sliding and new ones like watching ever-present videos. In some places the old ways are still evident. One day I traveled the ice road, a slick, winter-only passage on the frozen Mackenzie, more than four feet thick, lined with scrubby bush and spindly black spruce—and speed-limit signs. The Richardson Mountains gleamed in the distance. The buzz of snowmobiles announced the onset of a town. Aklavik, a largely native settlement on the delta's west side, is a motley collection of wood houses, prone to erosion and flooding. Inuvik was designed to replace it, but many residents simply refused to leave. "This was supposed to be a ghost town," recalled Dorothy McLeod, a 59-year-old Métis. "But it's such a good place for hunting and trapping and fishing—you can almost live off the land. In Inuvik, you live out of the stores."

Maybe I was just seizing on hopeful signs; or maybe, like many whites, I tend to romanticize natives and their intense ties to the land. But later, when I thought of Aklavik, I thought also of the Newfoundland fishermen, clinging to a dwindling life in the boats, and of the French nationalists, fighting to preserve their language and culture—and I thought how they would have understood Dorothy McLeod, trying to hold on to the old ways.

Canadians share a collective guilt over the plight of the natives, but they take an often-justified pride in their treatment of other minorities. To an American, Canada's vaunted multiculturalism is, like Québec nationalism, simply a foreign concept. It is also an attractive one, although the gap between theory and practice is sometimes hard to ignore.

What is happening in Vancouver is a case in point. The trouble in Canada's Pacific paradise surrounds home-buyers from Hong Kong, which will become part of mainland China in 1997. The newcomers have cash on hand and have helped to drive up housing prices beyond the range of many Vancouverites, touching off a frenzied real estate boom. Never mind that the overwhelming majority of new British Columbians come not from Hong Kong but from such foreign locales as Alberta and Ontario—public perception has focused on the Asians. "There's always an element of anxiety about change," said Mayor Gordon Campbell. "But with a certain percentage there's clearly an element of racism as well."

Vancouver is undergoing a kind of tolerance test—one that, to some residents, lies at the very core of what it means to be Canadian. "I think Canada is developing some uniqueness," said Saintfield Wong, program co-ordinator of the Chinese Cultural Centre in Vancouver's Chinatown. "We're more receptive to new ideas—Canada's culture *is* multiculturalism." In his gift shop down the street, however, Harry Con expressed some doubts. The national president of Chinese Freemasons in Canada, Con maintained that multiculturalism keeps Canadians too tied to their old countries. "Everybody sends money home," he said. "Italians, Chinese. Whatever happens over there, people volunteer to help. But if the government here wants to raise taxes, we give them hell. So who loves Canada?"

Dwight Chan plainly does. Chan emigrated from Hong Kong in 1974 and now, at 39, he is a successful Vancouver real estate broker who understands the city's attractions to foreigners—the ocean and mountains, the mild climate, the patently laid-back lifestyle. I asked him, though, whether there is anything to tie newcomers to the country at large; even if current fears dissipate and the latest immigrants end up feeling as welcome as he does, is there, in American terms, such a thing as the Canadian Dream? After a moment's reflection, Chan said, "The Canadian Dream is probably a healthy, stable, and secure way of living, rather than the American Dream of big money. It's to have time to enjoy your life, to play, to travel. This country allows me to do all that, and that feels good to me."

Canada continues to defy easy definition. I have crossed and recrossed time zones, sampled caribou and cod's tongue, and gathered a startling variety of mental images that, like the country itself, may not add up to a coherent whole but certainly make a pretty picture. Canada is *not* the United States—that much is abundantly clear, even if Arctic-dwellers *can* watch Detroit news on television—and its ingrained regionalism is one of its most telling traits. Travel anywhere outside of Ontario, it seems, and over and over people say, as Vancouver's Mayor Campbell did: "We're very proud to be Canadians. But there is a strong sense that the central government does not recognize we're here." Americans say nasty things about Washington, too, but when their government launches an invasion of Grenada, they swiftly rally around.

In general, Canadians also strike me as more outward-looking than Americans. They did not, after all, grow up being told that they already live in the greatest country on earth. "Americans are like TV evangelists," maintained Roger Bill, an Indiana native who is now the Newfoundland-based Atlantic field producer for CBC Radio's *Sunday Morning* show. "They really believe theirs is the best way and everyone else should follow. Canadians aren't nearly so arrogant." They do, however, take a palpable pride in place, with a decided prejudice toward the small, friendly, and relaxed. "I wouldn't live in the States, or in Toronto or Montréal," said Richard Harvey, a high-school principal from Upper Gullies, Newfoundland. "You couldn't pay me enough." I have heard Inuvik people say the same about Yellowknife—and Aklavik people say the same about Inuvik.

I only wish Canadians would say it louder, that they would boast—with the kind of cheerful cockiness I saw at the Calgary Olympics last year—of a nation vast, varied, scenic, wealthy, safe, fair-minded, and infinitely appealing. I wish they would make an epic movie or two about it, one with endless prairies and dazzling mountains and heroic characters hell-bent on, say, building a railroad clear to the Pacific. I wish they would brag about the CBC and national health insurance, too, and I wish, if they really want to dispel the moose-and-Mounties image, that they would stop making that ubiquitous line of postcards picturing furry seals and polar bears and saying simply, "Canada." But then, I am afraid I sound very much like an American. Only a Canadian can really sum it all up. As Montréal lawyer Montcalm put it, "Funny country, eh?"

1 Essential Information

Before You Go

Government Tourist Offices

American visitors should contact the tourism department of the nearest **Canadian Consulate General** or **Canadian Embassy** for general information about travel to Canada:

United States 1 CNN Center, Suite 400, South Tower, Atlanta, GA 30303, tel. 404/577–6815; 3 Copley Pl., Suite 400, Boston, MA 02116, tel. 617/536–1730; 1 Marine Midland Center, Suite 3550, Buffalo, NY 14203, tel. 716/852–1345; 310 S. Michigan Ave., 12th floor, Chicago, IL 60604, tel. 312/427–1666; St. Paul Tower, 17th floor, 750 N. St. Paul St., Dallas, TX 75201, tel. 214/922–9806; 300 S. Grand Ave., Suite 1000, Los Angeles, CA 90071, tel. 213/687–7432; 701 4th Ave. S, Suite 900, Minneapolis, MN 55415, tel. 612/333–4641; Exxon Bldg., 16th floor, 1251 Avenue of the Americas, New York, NY 10020, tel. 212/768–2400; 50 Fremont St., Suite 2100, San Francisco, CA 94105, tel. 415/495–6021; 412 Plaza 600, 6th Ave. and Stewart St., Seattle, WA 98101, tel. 206/443–1777; 501 Pennsylvania Ave. NW, Washington, DC 20001, tel. 202/682–1740.

United Kingdom Canada House, Trafalgar Sq., London SW1Y 5BJ, England, tel. 071/629–9492.

If you know which province or city you plan to visit, contact the provincial or city tourism offices directly. They can offer more extensive information about special events, historic sites, and local accommodations. All except the Yukon office have toll-free numbers. (*See* Tourist Information in the individual chapters for addresses and telephone numbers.)

Tour Groups

With such an incredible number and variety of package tours to Canada, the only possible drawback is deciding how and when to go. You'll have to make up your mind whether you want to hook up with an escorted group tour, create your own itinerary by stringing together minihotel packages in various cities, follow a prearranged itinerary independently, hit the road with a fly/drive package, take to the rails on a train tour, spend several days exploring one city, or whip up a customized version of all of the above. Each option has advantages. To see as much as possible in a limited amount of time, think about a group tour. If freedom and flexibility are of primary importance, consider an independent package.

When evaluating any tour, be sure to find out (1) exactly what expenses are included—particularly tips, taxes, service charges, side trips, additional meals, and entertainment; (2) the ratings of all hotels on the itinerary and the facilities they offer; (3) the additional cost of single, rather than double, accommodations if you are traveling alone; and (4) the number of travelers in your group. Note if the operator reserves the right to change hotels, routes, or even prices after you've booked, and check out the operator's policy regarding cancellations, complaints, and trip-interruption insurance. Many tour operators request that packages be booked through a travel agent; there is generally no additional charge for doing so.

The operators and packages listed below represent a small sample of what is available. For additional resources, contact your travel agent or the national or provincial tourism office.

General-interest Tours

From the United States

Domenico Tours (751 Broadway, Bayonne, NJ 07002, tel. 212/823–8687 or 800/554–TOUR) and **Casser Tours** (46 W. 43rd St., New York, NY 10036, tel. 212/840–6500 or 800/251–1411) both tout a wide selection of escorted motorcoach tours and cruises to all major Canadian destinations. **Maupintour** (Box 807, Lawrence, KS 66044, tel. 913/843–1211 or 800/255–4266) offers a choice of nine tours, some of which combine rail, cruise, and helicopter flightseeing excursions. **Globus Getaway** (150 S. Los Robles Ave., Pasadena, CA 91101, tel. 818/449–0919 or 800/556–5454) and its budget-oriented affiliate, **Cosmos,** both tour the Canadian Rockies and Glacier National Park. **Tauck Tours** (11 Wilton Rd., Westport, CT 06881, tel. 203/226–6911 or 800/468–2825) has a variety of motorcoach tours to eastern Canada and the Canadian Rockies, as well as an all-helicopter adventure. **Brennan Tours** (4th Ave. and Battery Bldg., Suite 700, Seattle, WA 98121, tel. 206/441–8689 or 800/237–7249) specializes in tours of the Canadian Rockies, with the exception of one relatively new trip that covers the eastern part of the country. **Delta Dream Vacations** (tel. 305/522–1440 or 800/872–7786) offers "Canadian Adventure Circle" and "Heart of the Rockies" motorcoach tours.

From Canada

UTL Holiday Tours (2 Carlton St., 4th fl., Toronto, Ontario M5B 1J3, tel. 416/593–6777 or 800/387–2712) serves up more than a half-dozen motorcoach tours. Rocky Mountain golf and rail tours are also available.

From the United Kingdom

Bales Tours' (Bales House, Barrington Rd., Dorking, Surrey RH4 3EJ, tel. 0306/76881) offerings include a 15-day escorted tour of Canada from Montréal to Vancouver, taking in Québec, Toronto, and the Rockies; a nine-day spring or fall trip to Calgary, Lake Louise, Natural Bridge, Athabasca Glacier, and Jasper; and a 10-day tour of the Rockies, with two days spent exploring by helicopter. **Experience the Mountains** (Ambassador Suite 4, 341 London Rd., Mitcham, Surrey CR4 4TY, tel. 081/685–0344) specializes in vacations in the wilder regions of Canada, with an emphasis on sports and fitness, though fly/drive and bus tours are available. For example, the six-day "Bike the Big Country" cycle tour through British Columbia averages 50 miles a day, while the more sedate 15-day "Cariboo Trail," fly/drive tour begins and ends in Vancouver. **Kuoni Travel** (Kuoni House, Dorking, Surrey RH4 4AZ, tel. 0306/884609), has a wide variety of tours in Canada, including the 14-day "Arctic Adventure," the 18-day "The Trans-Canadian," and "City Stay" holidays in six major Canadian cities. **National Holidays** (Miry La., Wigan, Lancaster WN3 4AG, tel. 0942/821070) can arrange three- to four-day tours of the Rockies if you want to spend most of your holiday traveling independently but also want an overview of the region's spectacular scenery. It runs a number of city tours and motorhome tours as well. **Thomson Worldwide's** (Greater London House, Hampstead Rd., London NW1 7SD, tel. 071/387–8484) 13-night escorted "Rockies Trail" tour takes in Toronto, Calgary, Banff, Jasper, Kamloops, Whistler Resort, Victoria, and Vancouver.

Special-interest Tours

Adventure

Opportunities for rugged outdoor activities, such as camping, fishing, backpacking, guided canoe trips, white-water rafting, and backcountry skiing, are excellent in Canada. **Adventure**

Canada (920 Yonge St., Suite 747, Toronto, Ont. M4W 3C7, tel. 416/963-9163) leads wilderness expeditions throughout Canada and parts north, including a photo expedition near Churchill, Manitoba, in what's known as Polar Bear Country. **American Wilderness Experience** (Box 1486, Boulder, CO 80306, tel. 303/494-2992 or 800/444-0099) operates four backcountry canoe adventures along the Minnesota-Ontario Boundary Waters, the route followed by the French-Canadian voyageurs in birch-bark canoes. **Connections Canada** (1271 Howe St., Suite 204, Vancouver, B.C. V6Z 1R3, tel. 604/685-3381) operates fishing trips in British Columbia. **Tauck Tours** (*see* General-interest Tours, above) has eight-day journeys by helicopter through the Canadian Rockies. **Westwind Adventure Tours** (13292 Euclid Ave., Garden Grove, CA 92643, tel. 714/534-8630 or 800/223-7457) offers white-water rafting in the summer in the Rockies and skiing during the winter between Vancouver and Banff.

Cruises **Atlas Tours** (609 W. Hastings St., 5th floor, Vancouver, B.C. V6B 4W4, tel. 604/669-1332) heads up the coastal waters of British Columbia as far north as Alaska. Ships of the **Bermuda Star Line** (1086 Teaneck Rd., Teaneck, NJ 07666, tel. 201/837-0400 or 800/237-5361) cruise the waters around Nova Scotia and Prince Edward Island and down the St. Lawrence, with stays in Montréal and Québec City. **Royal Viking Line** (2 Alhambra Plaza, Coral Gables, FL 33134, tel. 305/447-9660 or 800/442-8000) tours Canada's eastern coast, calling at Charlottetown (Prince Edward Island), Halifax (Nova Scotia), and Montréal.

Fall Foliage In the peak leaf-peeping season, **Domenico Tours** (*see* General-interest Tours, above) heads to Montréal and the Laurentians, Nova Scotia, and Toronto. **Parker Tours** (98-12 Queens Blvd., Rego Park, NY 11374, tel. 718/459-6585) leads weekend and week-long tours through Québec and Ontario.

Package Deals for Independent Travelers

American Express Vacations (Box 5014, Atlanta, GA 30302, tel. 800/241-1700; in Georgia, 800/282-0800) has three-day packages to nearly a dozen Canadian cities, with an assortment of independent drive vacations also available. **UTL Holiday Tours** (*see* General-interest Tours, above) run a variety of independent tours to Alberta/British Columbia, Toronto/Montréal, Ontario/Québec, and the maritime provinces. You follow a set itinerary either by rental car or motorcoach, depending on the tour. **Delta Dream Vacations** (*see* General-interest Tours, above) offers four-day fly/drive packages to Vancouver, Montréal/Toronto, Calgary, and Edmonton.

When to Go

The sheer size of Canada—about half the area of the Soviet Union and almost as large as China—makes it difficult to generalize about the weather. When to go will depend on which part of the country you're visiting and what your interests are. In eastern Canada—which includes the maritime provinces of **Nova Scotia, New Brunswick,** and **Prince Edward Island**—temperatures are lower than inland. Winters, tempered by the Atlantic Ocean, are kinder here than in the rest of the country, though snow remains on the ground well into spring. Summers, too, benefit from the Atlantic air. Heavy sea fog is common much of the year. If you like your summers steamy and hot, head for the southern portions of **Québec** and **Ontario,** which border the Great Lakes and the United States. The summer sun shines in this region for eight to nine hours a day, though winters can be severe, with snow lasting from mid-December to mid-March. Farther west along Canada's southern border are the Canadian prairies that take in **Manitoba, Saskatchewan,** and **Alberta.** This is wheat-growing country. The summers are short but sunny, and marked by an occasional heavy shower. Winter snowfall in this area is light, but the winter temperatures aren't much higher than those recorded in the Arctic regions of the country. Unlike eastern Canada, which experiences blooming springs and brilliant autumns, the Canadian prairies move abruptly from summer to winter weather. For warmer winters and mild summers, head for western Canada, which includes the southern part of **British Columbia** and the western part of **Alberta,** within the Rocky Mountains. Though the weather fluctuates because of the two mountain ranges—the Coast Mountains and the eastern chain of the Rockies—generally, the coastal region has the country's mildest winters, with rainfall almost inevitable. Summers here are fairly sunny, but not as oppressively hot as parts of the prairie region. The best time to visit northern Canada is during its suprisingly warm summer. The area—which includes the northern parts of the provinces of **British Columbia, Alberta, Saskatchewan, Manitoba, Ontario,** and **Québec**—is marked by coniferous forest and Arctic tundra and makes up almost two-thirds of Canada. In winter, however, the weather in the north resembles that of Siberia, with devastating cold and dangerous windchills.

Climate The following are average daily maximum and minimum temperatures for a number of Canada's major cities.

Calgary

Jan.	23F	– 5C	**May**	61F	16C	**Sept.**	63F	17C
	2	–17		37	3		39	4
Feb.	29F	– 2C	**June**	67F	19C	**Oct.**	54F	12C
	8	–13		44	7		30	– 1
Mar.	34F	1C	**July**	74F	23C	**Nov.**	38F	3C
	14	–10		49	9		17	– 8
Apr.	49F	9C	**Aug.**	72F	22C	**Dec.**	29F	– 2C
	27	– 3		47	8		8	–13

Edmonton

Jan.	14F	–10C	**May**	63F	17C	**Sept.**	62F	17C
	– 3	–19		41	5		41	5
Feb.	22F	– 6C	**June**	69F	21C	**Oct.**	52F	11C
	4	–16		48	9		32	0
Mar.	31F	– 1C	**July**	74F	23C	**Nov.**	32F	0C
	13	–11		53	12		17	– 8
Apr.	49F	9C	**Aug.**	71F	22C	**Dec.**	21F	– 6C
	29	– 2		50	10		5	–15

Halifax	**Jan.**	33F	1C	**May**	58F	14C	**Sept.**	67F	19C
		20	−7		41	5		53	12
	Feb.	33F	1C	**June**	67F	19C	**Oct.**	58F	14C
		19	−7		50	10		44	7
	Mar.	39F	4C	**July**	73F	23C	**Nov.**	48F	9C
		26	−3		57	14		36	2
	Apr.	48F	9C	**Aug.**	73F	24C	**Dec.**	37F	3C
		33	1		58	13		25	−4

Montréal	**Jan.**	23F	−5C	**May**	65F	18C	**Sept.**	68F	20C
		9	−13		48	9		53	12
	Feb.	25F	−4C	**June**	74F	23C	**Oct.**	57F	14C
		12	−11		58	14		43	6
	Mar.	36F	2C	**July**	79F	26C	**Nov.**	42F	6C
		23	−5		63	17		32	0
	Apr.	52F	11C	**Aug.**	76F	24C	**Dec.**	27F	−3C
		36	2		61	16		16	−9

Ottawa	**Jan.**	20F	−7C	**May**	65F	18C	**Sept.**	68F	20C
		4	−16		44	7		49	9
	Feb.	23F	−5C	**June**	75F	24C	**Oct.**	57F	14C
		6	−14		54	12		39	4
	Mar.	34F	1C	**July**	80F	27C	**Nov.**	41F	5C
		18	−8		58	14		29	−2
	Apr.	51F	11C	**Aug.**	77F	25C	**Dec.**	25F	−4C
		33	1		56	13		12	−11

Québec City	**Jan.**	20F	−7C	**May**	62F	17C	**Sept.**	66F	19C
		6	−14		43	6		49	9
	Feb.	23F	−5C	**June**	72F	22C	**Oct.**	53F	12C
		8	−13		53	12		39	4
	Mar.	33F	1C	**July**	78F	26C	**Nov.**	39F	4C
		19	−7		58	14		28	−2
	Apr.	47F	8C	**Aug.**	75F	24C	**Dec.**	24F	−4C
		32	0		56	13		12	−11

Toronto	**Jan.**	30F	−1C	**May**	64F	18C	**Sept.**	71F	22C
		18	−8		47	8		54	12
	Feb.	32F	0C	**June**	76F	24C	**Oct.**	60F	16C
		19	−7		57	14		45	7
	Mar.	40F	4C	**July**	80F	27C	**Nov.**	46F	8C
		27	−3		62	17		35	2
	Apr.	53F	12C	**Aug.**	79F	26C	**Dec.**	34F	1C
		38	3		61	16		23	−5

Vancouver	**Jan.**	42F	6C	**May**	60F	16C	**Sept.**	65F	18C
		33	1		47	8		52	11
	Feb.	45F	7C	**June**	65F	18C	**Oct.**	56F	13C
		36	2		52	11		45	7
	Mar.	48F	9C	**July**	70F	21C	**Nov.**	48F	9C
		37	3		55	13		39	4
	Apr.	54F	12C	**Aug.**	70F	21C	**Dec.**	43F	6C
		41	5		55	13		35	2

WeatherTrak provides information on more than 750 cities around the world—450 of them in the United States. Dial 900/370–8728 to be connected to a computer, which is activated by a touch-tone phone. The call costs 75¢ for the first minute and 50¢ for each additional minute. The message instructs you to dial a three-digit access code for the destination you're interested in. The code is either the area code (in the United States) or the first three letters of the foreign city. For a list of all access codes, send a stamped, self-addressed envelope to Cities, Box 7000, Dallas, TX 75209, or call 214/869–3035 or 800/247–3282.

National Holidays

Though banks, schools, and government offices close for national holidays, many stores remain open. As in the United States, the move has been to observe certain holidays on the Monday nearest to the actual date, making for a long weekend.

New Year's Day (January 1), Good Friday (March 29), Easter Monday (April 1), Victoria Day (May 20), Canada Day (July 1), Labour Day (September 2), Thanksgiving (October 14), Remembrance Day (November 11), Christmas (December 25), and Boxing Day (December 26).

Provincial Holidays

Alberta: Heritage Day (August 5).

British Columbia: British Columbia Day (August 5).

New Brunswick: New Brunswick Day (August 5).

Manitoba, Northwest Territories, Ontario, Saskatchewan: Civic Holiday (August 5).

Québec: Epiphany (January 6), Ash Wednesday (first day of Lent), Ascension Day (May 9), St. Jean Baptiste Day (June 24), All Saints' Day (November 1), Immaculate Conception (December 8).

Festivals and Seasonal Events

No matter where or when you travel in Canada, you're likely to be traveling around the time of a festival or special event. Provincial holidays or "Discovery Days" are usually accompanied by local events. Victoria Day and Canada Day are celebrated in most places around the country. Winter is as active a time for Canadian celebrations as the summer. It's a good idea to pick up a local paper as soon as you arrive in a town. Listed below are only a select few of the provincial events. Some festivals, especially the music and dance festivals, may require tickets or reservations. It's best to contact the provincial tourist boards in advance for a complete listing of events and further details.

Alberta

January: Jasper Winter Festival in Jasper and Marmot Basin features dogsledding, skating, ice-sculpting, and other events. **February:** Calgary Winter Festival, with more than 200 events. **March:** Edmonton Annual International Autoshow. **April:** Silver Buckle Rodeo at Red Deer attracts cowboys from all over North America. **May:** Edmonton International Children's Festival draws professional musicians, mimes, jugglers, clowns, puppeteers, and singers worldwide; Red Deer Annual Westerner Spring Quarter Horse Show, where horses compete from Western Canada and the United States. **June:** Jazz City International Festival in Edmonton features 10 days of jazz concerts, workshops, club dates, and free outdoor events; Ponoka 53rd Annual Stampede professional rodeo attracts participants from across the continent. **July:** Ukranian Pysanka Festival in Vegreville celebrates with costumes, traditional singing and dancing; Calgary Exhibition and Stampede is one of the most popular Canadian events and includes 10 days of Western showmanship, hot-air balloon races, chuck-wagon races, agricultural shows, craft exhibits, and Indian dancing; Edmonton's Klondike Days celebrate the town's early frontier community with pancake breakfasts, gambling casinos, gold panning, and raft races. **August:** Fringe Theatre Festival, in Edmonton, is regarded as one of the largest festivals for alternative theater in North America.

British Columbia **January–February:** Skiing competitions take place at most alpine ski resorts throughout the province. **March–April:** Pacific Rim Whale Festival celebrates the spring migration of gray whales with guided tours by whale experts and accompanying music and dancing. **May:** Cloverdale Rodeo; Vancouver Children's Festival features free open-air stage performances by more than 20 companies. **June:** Each year, Harrison Festival of the Arts focuses on different ethnic music, dance, and theater, such as African, Caribbean, and Central American; Dragon Boat Festival, in Vancouver, includes entertainment, exotic foods, and the ancient "awakening the dragons" ritual of long, slender boats decorated with huge dragon heads. **July:** Vancouver Sea Festival celebrates the city's nautical heritage with sailing regattas, windsurfing races, and the Tunnel Hull speedboat race, with speeds of up to 200 kph (120 mph). **August:** Peach Festivals in various areas around Penticton; Squamish Days Loggers Sports Festival features loggers from around the world competing in a series of incredible logging feats; Pacific National Exhibition in Vancouver has parades, exhibits, sports, entertainment, and logging contests. **September:** Okanagan Wine Festivals occur in the Okanagan-Similkameen area.

Manitoba **February:** Festival du Voyageur, in St. Boniface, Winnipeg, celebrates the history of the region's early fur traders. **March:** Royal Manitoba Winter Fair in Brandon. **June:** Red River Exhibition, in Winnipeg, features lumberjack contests, body-building shows, and an international band festival. **July:** Winnipeg Folk Festival takes place in Birds Hill Park, 24 kilometers (15 miles) northeast of Winnipeg, and features performers singing country, bluegrass, folk, Acadian music, and jazz on 10 stages scattered throughout the park; Threshermen's Reunion, in Austin, features antique tractor races, sheep tying, and threshing contests; Northwest Roundup and Exhibition, in Swan River, includes professional rodeo events, chuck-wagon races, and stage shows. **August:** National Ukrainian Festival, in Dauphin, offers costumes, artifacts, exhibits, fiddling contests, dancing, and workshops; Icelandic Festival, in Gimli, gathers the largest Icelandic community outside of Iceland; Pioneer Days, in Steinbach, celebrates the heritage of the Mennonites with demonstrations of threshing and baking, a parade, a horse show, a barbecue, and Mennonite foods.

New Brunswick **June:** Jazz NB, in Moncton, features major national and international jazz artists performing around the city. **July:** Mirimachi Folk Song Festival, in Newcastle, features fiddling competitions, casinos, beer gardens, and a parade; Loyalist

Days, in St. John, celebrates the town's founding with parades, dancing, and sidewalk festivities; Lobster Festival, in Shediac, features lobster-eating contests and other entertainment. **August:** Foire Brayonne, in Edmundston, is the largest French festival outside of Québec; Festival By the Sea, in St. John, attracts more than 130 entertainers from across Canada and includes cultural and ethnic performances; Acadian Festival, at Caraquet, celebrates the region's Acadian heritage with folk singing and indigenous food.

Nova Scotia **June:** Apple Blossom Festival, in Annapolis Valley, includes dancing, parades, and entertainment. **July:** Highland Games, in Antigonish, display Highland dancing and marching bagpipers; Nova Scotia Bluegrass and Oldtime Music Festival at Ardoise. **August:** Annapolis Country Exhibition is Nova Scotia's biggest agricultural fair. **September:** Nova Scotia Fisheries Exhibition and Fishermen's Reunion serves up parades, schooner races, and seafood.

Ontario **January:** Ontario Winter Festival Bon Soo in Sault Sainte-Marie. **February:** Winterlude, in Bal de Neige, Ottawa, encourages ice-sculpting, snowshoe races, ice-boating, and other wintertime activities. **April:** Maple Syrup Festival in Elmira. **May:** Stratford Festival, in Stratford, features performances of many of Shakespeare's plays through June; Folk Arts Festival, in St. Catharines; Festival of Spring, in Ottawa, heralds the season with 3 million blossoming tulips. **June:** Metro International Caravan is an ethnic fair in Toronto; International Festival of Native Arts features dancers, crafts booths, and entertainment in Toronto; Changing of the Guard begins at Ottawa's Parliament Buildings (through September). **July:** Queen's Plate thoroughbred horse race takes place in Toronto; Blueberry Festival in Sudbury; Molson CART race in Toronto. **August:** Glengarry Highland Games, in Maxville, is North America's largest Highland Gathering; Six Nations Native Pageant is an Iroquois celebration and exhibit of the tribe's culture and history in Brantford; Caribana draws on the riches of Toronto's West Indian community for this Caribbean festival; Royal Canadian Henley Regatta, in St. Catharines, is the largest rowing regatta in North America; Canadian National Exhibition, in Toronto, features air shows, entertainment, and exhibits. **September:** Festival of Festivals is an international film festival in Toronto; Niagara Grape and Wine Festival, in St. Catharines, celebrates this fruit. **October:** Oktoberfest, in Kitchener–Waterloo, attracts more than half a million enthusiasts to its many beer halls and tents.

Prince Edward Island **June:** Irish Moss Festival in Tignish; Charlottetown Festival Theatre (through September) offers a series of concerts and musicals. **July:** Prince Edward Island Irish Heritage Festival in Mill River; Summerside Lobster Carnival & Livestock Exhibition, in Summerside, is a week-long feast of lobster. **August:** Highland Games, in Eldon, is a gathering of Scotsmen for games and celebrations; Annual Community Harvest Festival in Kensington.

Québec **February:** Winter Carnival, in Québec City, is an 11-day festival of winter sports competitions, ice-sculpture contests, and parades. **April:** Sugaring-off parties throughout the province celebrate the beginning of the maple syrup season. **May:** Festival des Cantons, in Sherbrooke, has hayrides, dancing, and contests; Benson & Hedges International fireworks competition is on Montréal's Île Sainte-Hélène. **June:** Molson Grand Prix, with some of the world's best drivers, takes place on the Gilles-Villeneuve Race Track, in Montréal; Festival Orford features international artists performing at Orford Park's music center (through August); International Jazz Festival in Québec; International Children's Folklore Festival takes place in Beauport, Québec. **July:** Festival international de jazz de Montréal features more than 1,000 jazz musicians from all over the world for this 10-day series; Québec International Summer Festival offers entertainment in the streets and parks of old Québec City. **August:** Montréal World Film Festival; Plein-Art (Arts and Crafts) Show in Québec City. **September:** Québec International Film Festival in Québec City. **October:** Festival of Colors, throughout the province.

Saskatchewan **March:** Winter Festival in Meadow Lake is a three-day festival with a minor hockey tournament, family snowmobile rally, dance, children's events, Jam Can curling, and sled races. **May:** Vesna Festival, in Saskatoon, is the world's largest Ukranian cabaret, with traditional Ukranian food and crafts; International Band and Choral Festival, in Moose Jaw, attracts 7,000 musicians, 100 bands, and 25 choral groups. **June:** Yellowhead Arabian Horse Show in Yorkton; Frontier Days, in Swift Current, is a community fair and exhibit with parades, horse show, and rodeo. **July–August:** Buffalo Days Exhibition, in Regina, features rides, a grandstand show, dancing, livestock judging, and horse racing.

What to Pack

Clothing How you pack for travel to Canada will depend more on the season in which you're traveling than on any Canadian customs. Layering is the best defense against Canada's cold, long winters; a hat, scarf, and gloves are essential. For summer travel, loose-fitting natural-fiber clothes are best. If you're planning to spend time in Canada's larger cities, pack both casual clothes for day touring and more formal wear for evenings out. If your visit includes a stay at a large city hotel, bring a bathing suit in any season to take advantage of the indoor pool.

Miscellaneous Like the United States, Canada has 110-volt, 60-cycle electric power. British visitors should bring an adaptor for their electric hairdryers, irons, razors, etc. An extra pair of glasses, contact lenses, or prescription sunglasses is always a good idea; it is important to pack any prescription medicines you use regularly, as well as any allergy medication you may need. A pocket calculator comes in handy to convert kilometers to miles, Celsius to Fahrenheit, and Canadian dollars to American dollars. If you plan on camping or hiking in the deep woods during the summer, especially in northern Canada, insect repellent is a must, especially in June, which is blackfly season.

Carry-on Luggage Airlines generally allow each passenger one piece of carry-on luggage on international flights from the United States. The bag cannot exceed 45 inches (length + width + height) and must fit under the seat or in the overhead luggage compartment.

Checked Luggage Passengers are generally allowed to check two pieces of luggage, neither of which can exceed 62 inches (length + width +

height) or weigh more than 70 pounds. Baggage allowances vary slightly among airlines, so check with the carrier or your travel agent before departure.

Taking Money Abroad

Currency Exchange Because U.S. dollars are more in demand in Canada than Canadian dollars are in the United States, you get the best rate at **Deak International** retail offices in Canada, located at the major airports and the downtown metropolitan areas. Call the Deak office in Toronto (tel. 416/863–1993) for exact locations. Offices are generally open weekdays 9–5. If your travel plans call for you to arrive at night or during the weekend, it's best to have $50 to $100 in Canadian funds before you leave. Most U.S. banks will convert American dollars into Canadian dollars. If your local bank doesn't provide this service, you can exchange money through **Deak International** (tel. 212/635–0515) or **Ruesch International** (tel. 800/424–2923). Deak has offices throughout the United States; Ruesch has offices in New York, Chicago, Washington, and Los Angeles, but can arrange for overnight delivery of funds or traveler's checks to other cities and rural areas.

Credit Cards and Traveler's Checks Major credit cards and traveler's checks are widely accepted. The most recognized traveler's checks are **American Express, Barclay's, Thomas Cook,** and those issued through major commercial banks, such as **Citibank** and **Bank of America.** Some banks issue the checks free to established customers, but most charge a 1% commission. Buying your traveler's checks in Canadian dollars will probably save you money. Remember to take the addresses of offices where you can get refunds for lost or stolen traveler's checks.

Getting Money from Home

There are at least three ways to get money from home: (1) Have it sent through a large commercial bank that has a branch where you are staying. The only drawback is that you must have an account with the bank; if not, you'll have to go through your own bank, and the process will be slower and more costly. (2) Have it sent through American Express. If you are a cardholder, you can cash a personal check or a counter check at an American Express office for up to $1,000; $200 will be in Canadian dollars, and $800 in traveler's checks. There is a 1% commission on the traveler's checks. You can also receive money through an American Express MoneyGram, which enables you to obtain up to $10,000 in cash. It works this way: You call home and ask someone to go to an American Express office—or an American Express MoneyGram agent located in a retail outlet—and fill out an American Express MoneyGram. It can be paid for with cash or with any major credit card. The person making the payment is given a reference number and telephones you with that number. The American Express MoneyGram agent calls an 800 number and authorizes the transfer of funds to the American Express office or participating agency where you are staying. In most cases, the money is available immediately on a 24-hour basis. You pick it up by showing identification and giving the reference number. Fees vary with the amount of money sent. For $300, the fee is $30; for $5,000, the fee is $195. For the American Express MoneyGram location nearest your home and a list of Canadian locations, call 800/543-4080. You do not have to be a cardholder to use this service. (3) Have money sent through Western Union, whose U.S. number is 800/325-6000. If you have a MasterCard or Visa, you can have money sent for any amount up to your credit limit. If not, have someone take cash or a certified cashier's check to a Western Union office. The money will be delivered to a bank where you are staying. Fees vary with the amount of money sent and the precise location of the recipient.

Cash Machines Virtually all U.S. banks belong to a network of ATMs (Automatic Teller Machines), which dispense cash 24 hours a day in cities throughout the country. Two of the largest systems—Cirrus, which is owned by MasterCard, and Plus, which is affiliated with Visa—have extended their automatic teller services to Canada. A recent study shows that travelers may actually save money by using ATMs—instead of commercial exchanges—to change money.

To receive a card for one of the ATM systems, you must apply for it. Cards issued by Visa and MasterCard may also be used in the ATMs, but the fees are usually higher than the fees on bank cards. There is also a daily interest charge on credit card "loans," even if monthly bills are paid on time. Each network has a toll-free number you can call to locate machines in a given city. The Cirrus number is 800/4-CIRRUS; the Plus number is 800/THE-PLUS. Check with your bank for information on fees and on the amount of cash you can withdraw on any given day.

Canadian Currency

The units of currency in Canada are the Canadian dollar (C$) and the cent, in the same denominations as U.S. currency ($1, $5, $10, $20, 1¢, 5¢, 10¢, 25¢, etc.). At press time (August 1990), the exchange rate was C$1.10 to U.S.$1 and C$2.10 to £1.

What It Will Cost

Note: Throughout this guide, unless otherwise stated, prices are quoted in Canadian dollars.

It's true that the U.S. dollar is worth some 10% more than the Canadian dollar, but this translates into upward of a 10% savings only when goods in both countries are sold at the same price. Because many goods and services are priced slightly higher in Canada than in the United States, the actual savings is closer to 10%. Food prices are higher in Canada than in the United States, but lower than in much of Western Europe. The biggest expense of the trip will be accommodations, but a range of choices, from economy to deluxe, is available in metropolitan areas, the country, and in resort areas.

Sample Prices 1991 The following prices are for Toronto; other cities and regions are often less expensive: Dinner at an Expensive restaurant, without tax, tip, or drinks, will cost $30-$40; Moderate, $20-$30; Inexpensive, under $20. A double room at an Expensive hotel costs $130-$185; Moderate, $80-$130; Inexpensive, under $80. A soda costs about 80¢; a glass of beer, $3; a sandwich,

$2.50; a taxi, as soon as the meter is turned on, $2, and 25¢ per every 287 meters; a movie, about $7.

Passports and Visas

Americans Because of the volume of border traffic between Canada and the United States (for example, many people live in Windsor, Ontario, and work in Detroit), entry requirements are fairly simple. Citizens and legal residents of the United States do not need a passport or a visa to enter Canada, but proof of citizenship (a birth certificate) and identity may be requested. U.S. citizens entering Canada from a third country must have a valid passport or an official U.S. travel document. If you return to the United States by air, possession of a passport can save a long wait in line. Naturalized U.S. citizens should carry a naturalization certificate or some other evidence of citizenship. Resident aliens should be in possession of their U.S. Ilien Registration or "green" card.

Britons All British citizens require a valid passport to enter Canada. British Visitors' Passports are not valid, however. Application forms are available from most travel agents and major post offices, or contact the **Passport Office** (Clive House, 70 Petty France, London SW1H 9HD, tel. 071/279–3434). Cost is £15 for a standard 32-page passport, £30 for a 94-page passport. All applications must be countersigned by your bank manager, or by a solicitor, a barrister, a doctor, a clergyman, or a justice of the peace, and must be accompanied by two photographs. British citizens do not require a visa or any innoculations to enter Canada.

Customs and Duties

On Arrival
Americans and Britons Clothing and personal items may be brought in without charge or restriction. American and British visitors may bring in the following items duty-free: 200 cigarettes, 50 cigars, and two pounds of tobacco; personal cars (for less than six months); boats or canoes; rifles and shotgun (but no handguns or automatic weapons); 200 rounds of ammunition; cameras, radios, sports equipment, and typewriters. A deposit is sometimes required for trailers and household equipment (refunded upon return). If you are driving a rented car, be sure to keep the contract with you. Cats may enter freely, but dogs must have proof of a veterinary inspection to ensure that they are free of communicable diseases. Plant material must be declared and inspected.

On Departure
Americans If you have brought any foreign-made equipment from home, such as cameras, it's wise to carry the original receipt with you or to register it with U.S. Customs before you leave home (Form 4457). Otherwise, you may end up having to pay duty on your return. You may bring home duty-free up to $400 in foreign goods, as long as you have been out of the country for at least 48 hours and you haven't made an international trip in 30 days. Each member of the family is entitled to the same exemption, regardless of age, and exemptions may be pooled. For the next $1,000 worth of goods, a flat 10% rate is assessed; above $1,400, duties vary with the merchandise. Travelers 21 or older may bring home one liter of alcohol, 100 cigars (non-Cuban), and 200 cigarettes. Only one bottle of perfume trademarked in the United States may be brought in. There is

no duty on antiques or art over 100 years old. Anything exceeding these limits will be taxed at the port of entry, and may be taxed additionally in the traveler's home state. Gifts valued at less than $50 may be mailed to friends or relatives at home duty-free, but you may not send more than one package per day to any one addressee, and packages may not include perfumes costing more than $5, tobacco, or liquor.

Britons On your return to Great Britain you may bring home: (1) 200 cigarettes or 100 cigarillos or 50 cigars or 250 grams of tobacco; (2) two liters of table wine and, in addition, (a) one liter of alcohol over 22% by volume (most spirits), (b) two liters of alcohol under 22% by volume (fortified or sparkling wine), or (c) two more liters of table wine; (3) 50 grams of perfume and ¼ liter of toilet water; and (4) other goods up to a value of £32.

For further information, contact **HM Customs and Excise** (Dorset House, Stamford St., London SE1 9PS, tel. 071/928-0533).

Traveling with Film

If your camera is new, shoot and develop a few rolls of film before leaving home. Pack some lens tissue and an extra battery for your built-in light meter. Invest about $10 in a skylight filter: It will protect the lens and reduce haze. Film doesn't like hot weather, so if you're driving in summer, don't store film in the glove compartment or on the shelf under the rear window. Put it behind the front seat on the floor, on the side opposite the exhaust pipe. On a plane trip, never pack unprocessed film in check-in luggage; if your bags get X-rayed, say good-bye to your pictures. Always carry undeveloped film with you through security and ask to have it inspected by hand. (It helps to keep your film in a plastic bag, ready for quick inspection.)

The old airport scanning machines, still in use in some countries, use heavy doses of radiation that can turn a family portrait into an early morning fog. The newer models used in all U.S. airports are safe for anything from five to 500 scans, depending on the speed of your film. The effects are cumulative; you can put the same roll of film through several scans without worry. After five scans, though, you're asking for trouble. If your film gets fogged and you want an explanation, send it to the National Association of Photographic Manufacturers (550 Mamaroneck Ave., Harrison, NY 10528), which will try to determine what went wrong. The service is free.

Language

It amuses Canadians to see how many visitors assume that "everyone will speak French to me." Canada is, indeed, a bilingual country, in that it has two official languages, English and French. And visitors are charmed, even fascinated, to see cereal boxes and road signs in both languages. Though English is widely spoken, it may be useful to learn a few French phrases if you plan to travel to the province of Québec or to the French-Canadian communities in the maritime provinces (Nova Scotia,

New Brunswick, and Prince Edward Island), northern Manitoba, and Ontario. Canadian French, known as Québécois or *joual*, is infused with English words. The result is an interesting mix called "franglais."

Canada, like the United States, has been settled by successive influxes of immigrants, from the British, Scotch, Irish, and French to the Germans, Scandinavians, Ukrainians, and Chinese. Many of these groups maintain their cultural identity through their native language, and ethnic daily and weekly newspapers are common. Immigration since the 1960s accounts for Asians, Arabs, East Indians, Italians, Hispanics, and Caribbean blacks. The native population of Canada now comprises less than 1% of the population, yet it is possible to hear the languages of Indians and Inuits where these groups reside.

Staying Healthy

Shots and Medications No special shots are required for entry into Canada. If you have a health problem that may require purchase of prescription drugs, ask your doctor to write a spare prescription for you using the drug's generic name, because brand names vary from country to country.

Dangers Recently, cases of "beaver fever," caused by an intestinal parasite known as *Giardia lamblia* and once considered quite rare, have been reported by backcountry hikers. Symptoms include diarrhea, gas, cramps, and vomiting. To avoid catching the parasite, be sure to boil stream, lake, and river water for more than one minute or filter it before drinking (filters are available at camping stores). If symptoms last for more than 24 hours, see a doctor. Mosquitoes and blackflies are also notorious pests in Canada's woods. Take along insect repellent on hiking trips, especially in June—the height of blackfly season.

Doctors The **International Association for Medical Assistance to Travelers (IAMAT)** is a worldwide organization offering a list of approved English-speaking doctors whose training meets British and American standards. Contact IAMAT for a list of physicians and clinics in Canada that belong to this network. **In the United States:** 417 Center St., Lewiston, NY 14092, tel. 716/754–4883. **In Canada:** 40 Regal Rd., Guelph, Ont. N1K 1B5. **In Europe:** 57 Voirets, 1212 Grand-Lancy, Geneva, Switzerland. Membership is free.

Insurance

Travelers may seek insurance coverage in three areas: health and accident, lost luggage, and trip cancellation. Your first step is to review your existing health and home-owner policies; some health insurance plans cover health expenses incurred while traveling, some major medical plans cover emergency transportation, and some home-owner policies cover the theft of luggage.

Health and Accident Several companies offer coverage designed to supplement existing health insurance for travelers:

Americans

Carefree Travel Insurance (Box 310, 120 Mineola Blvd., Mineola, NY 11501, tel. 516/294–0220 or 800/343–3553) provides coverage for emergency medical evacuation. It also offers 24-hour medical phone advice.

International SOS Assistance (Box 11568, Philadelphia, PA 19116, tel. 215/244–1500 or 800/523–8930) does not offer medical insurance but provides medical evacuation services to its clients, who are often international corporations.

Travel Assistance International (1133 15th St. NW, Suite 400, Washington, DC 20005, tel. 202/347–2025 or 800/821–2828) provides emergency evacuation services and 24-hour medical referrals.

Travel Guard International, underwritten by Transamerica Occidental Life Companies (1100 Centerpoint Dr., Stevens Point, WI 54481, tel. 715/345–0505 or 800/782–5151), offers reimbursement for medical expenses, with no deductibles or daily limits and emergency evacuation services.

Wallach and Company, Inc. (243 Church St. NW, Suite 100D, Vienna, VA 22180, tel. 703/281–9500 or 800/237–6615) offers comprehensive medical coverage, including emergency evacuation, for trips of 10 to 90 days.

WorldCare Travel Assistance Association (605 Market St., Suite 1300, San Francisco, CA 94105, tel. 415/541–4991 or 800/666–4993) provides unlimited emergency evacuation, 24-hour medical referral, and an emergency message center.

Britons We recommend strongly that you purchase adequate insurance to guard against health problems, motoring mishaps, theft, flight cancellation, and loss of luggage. Most major tour operators offer holiday insurance, and details are given in brochures. For free general advice on all aspects of holiday insurance, contact the **Association of British Insurers** (Aldermary House, Queen St., London EC4N 1TT, tel. 071/248–4477). A proven leader in the holiday insurance field is **Europ Assistance,** (252 High St., Croydon, Surrey CR0 1NF, tel. 081/680–1234).

Lost Luggage On international flights, airlines are responsible for lost or damaged property of up to $9.07 per pound (or $20 per kilo) for checked baggage, and up to $400 per passenger for unchecked baggage. If you're carrying valuables, either take them with you on the plane or purchase additional insurance for lost luggage. Some airlines will issue extra luggage insurance when you check in, but many do not. Insurance for lost, damaged, or stolen luggage is available through travel agents or directly through various insurance companies. Luggage loss coverage is usually part of a comprehensive travel insurance package that includes personal accident, trip cancellation, and sometimes default and bankruptcy.

Two companies that issue luggage insurance are **Tele-Trip** (Box 31685, 3201 Farnam St., Omaha, NE 68131, tel. 800/228–9792), a subsidiary of Mutual of Omaha, and the **Travelers Insurance Co.** (Ticket and Travel Dept., 1 Tower Sq., Hartford, CT 06183, tel. 203/277–0111 or 800/243–3174). Tele-Trip operates sales booths at airports, and also issues insurance through travel agents. Tele-Trip will insure checked luggage for up to 180 days and for $500 to $3,000 valuation. For one to three days, the rate for a $500 valuation is $8.25; for 180 days, $100. The Travelers Insurance Co. will insure checked or hand luggage for $500 to $2,000 valuation per person, also for a maximum of 180 days. Rates for one to five days for $500 valuation are $10; for 180 days, $85. Other companies with comprehensive policies include **Access America, Inc.**, a subsidiary of Blue Cross-Blue Shield (Box 807, New York, NY 10163, tel. 212/490–5345 or 800/284–8300); **Near Services** (450 Prairie Ave., Suite 101, Calumet City, IL 60409, tel. 708/868–6700 or 800/654–6700); **Travel Guard International** and **Carefree Travel Insurance** (*see* Health and Accident Insurance, above).

Before you go, itemize the contents of each bag in case you need to file an insurance claim. Be certain to put your home or business address on each piece of luggage, including carry-on bags. If your luggage is lost or stolen and later recovered, the airline will deliver the luggage to your home free of charge.

Trip Cancellation
Americans Flight insurance is often included in the price of a ticket when paid for with American Express, Visa, and other major credit cards. It is usually included in combination travel insurance packages available from most tour operators, travel agents, and insurance agents.

Britons *See* Health and Accident Insurance, above.

Renting and Leasing Cars

You'll have to weigh the added expense of renting a car from a major company with an airport office against the savings on a car from a budget company with offices in town. If you're flying into a major city or arriving by train and plan to spend a few days there before exploring the rest of the province, you can save money by touring the city on foot and by public transportation and also by arranging to pick up your car in the city when you're ready to head out. However, you could waste precious hours trying to locate the budget company in return for only a small financial savings. If you're arriving and departing from different airports, look for a one-way car rental with no return fees. Rental rates vary widely, depending on car size and model, number of days you use the car, insurance coverage, and whether drop-off fees are imposed. In most cases, rates quoted include unlimited free mileage and standard liability protection. Not included are the Collision Damage Waiver (CDW), which eliminates your deductible payment should you have an accident; personal accident insurance; gasoline; and a 7% sales tax.

Driver's licenses issued in the United States are valid in Canada. You must be at least 21 to rent a car.

To make sure you get the type of car you want, it's best to arrange a car rental before you leave home. Rental companies usually charge according to the exchange rate of the U.S. dollar at the time the car is returned or when the credit card payment is processed. **Avis** (tel. 800/331–2112), **Budget Rent-a-Car** (tel. 800/527–0700), and **Hertz** (tel. 800/654–3131) all have offices at major airports in Canada. If you are looking for a bargain or a recreational vehicle, try **Tilden Rent-a-Car,** 1485 Stanley St., Montréal, Québec H3A 1P6, tel. 514/842–9445, or in the U.S., call Tilden's affiliate, **National Rent-a-Car** (tel. 800/328–4567 for reservations throughout Canada; tel. 514/878–2771 for reservations in the Montréal area).

Rail Passes

Although **VIA Rail,** Canada's exclusive passenger carrier, has made considerable cuts in its services—specifically, dropping all of its special rail tours—it is still possible to travel coast to coast using VIA Rail. The railroad offers a Canrailpass to independent travelers of any age, and "social fares" to senior citizens and students. VIA train information is available in the United States by calling 800/665–0200, 800/387–1144, 800/361–3677, or 800/561–3949; in Hawaii call 808/922–5596; in Great Britain contact Compass Travel, 9 Grosvenor Gardens, London SW1W 0BH.

Student and Youth Travel

The **International Student Identity Card** (ISIC) entitles full-time students to rail passes, special fares on local transportation, student charter flights, and discounts at museums, theaters, sports events, and many other attractions. If purchased in the United States, the $10 cost of the ISIC card also includes $2,000 in emergency medical coverage, $100 a day for up to 60 days of hospital coverage, as well as a collect phone number to call in case of emergency. Apply to the **Council on International Educational Exchange** (CIEE, 205 E. 42nd St., New York, NY 10017, tel. 212/661–1414). In Canada, the ISIC is available for C$10 from the Association of Student Councils (187 College St., Toronto, Ont. M5T 1P7).

Travelers under age 26 can apply for a **Youth International Educational Exchange Card** (YIEE) issued by the **Federation of International Youth Travel Organizations** (FIYTO, 81 Islands Brugge, DK-2300 Copenhagen S, Denmark). It provides services and benefits similar to those provided by ISIC card. The YIEE card is available in the U.S. from CIEE (*see* above) and in Canada from the **Canadian Hostelling Association** (CHA, 333 River Rd., Vanier, Ottawa, Ontario K1L 8H9, tel. 613/476–3844).

An **International Youth Hostel Federation** (IYHF) membership card is the key to inexpensive dormitory-style accommodations at thousands of youth hostels around the world. Hostels aren't only for young travelers on a budget, though; many have family accommodations. Hostels provide separate sleeping quarters for men and women at rates ranging from $7 to $15 a night per person and are situated in a variety of facilities, including converted farmhouses, villas, restored castles, and even lighthouses, as well as specially constructed modern buildings. There are more than 5,000 hostel locations in 75 countries around the world. IYHF memberships, which are valid for 12 months from the time of purchase, are available in the United States through **American Youth Hostels** (AYH, Box 37613, Washington, DC 20013, tel. 202/783–6161). The cost for a first-year membership is $25 for adults 18 to 54. Renewal thereafter is $15. For youths (17 and under), the rate is $10; for senior citizens (55 and older), the rate is $15. Family membership is available for two adults traveling with up to two children for $35. Every national hostel association arranges special reductions for members visiting their country, such as discounted rail fare or free bus travel, so be sure to ask for an international concessions list when you buy your membership.

Council Travel, a CIEE subsidiary, is the foremost U.S. student travel agency, specializing in low-cost charters and serving as the exclusive U.S. agent for many student airfare bargains and student tours. CIEE's 80-page Student Travel catalog and "Council Charter" brochures are available free from any Council Travel office in the United States (enclose $1 postage if ordering by mail). In addition to the CIEE headquarters (205 E. 42nd St.) and branch office (35 W. 8th St.) in New York City, there are Council Travel offices in Berkeley, La Jolla, Long Beach, Los Angeles, San Diego, San Francisco, and Sherman Oaks, CA; New Haven, CT; Washington, D.C.; Atlanta, GA; Chicago and Evanston, IL; New Orleans, LA; Amherst, Boston, and Cambridge, MA; Minneapolis, MN; Portland, OR; Providence, RI; Austin and Dallas, TX; Seattle, Washington; and Milwaukee, WI.

The **Educational Travel Center** (438 N. Frances St., Madison, WI 53703, tel. 608/256–5551) is another student-travel specialist worth contacting for information on student tours, bargain fares, and bookings.

Students who would like to work abroad should contact CIEE's **Work Abroad Department** (205 E. 42nd St., New York, NY 10017, tel. 212/661–1414, ext. 1130). The council arranges various types of paid and voluntary work experiences overseas for up to six months. CIEE also sponsors study programs in Europe, Latin America, Asia, and Australia, and publishes many books of interest to the student traveler. These include *Work, Study, Travel Abroad: The Whole World Handbook* ($9.95 plus $1 book-rate postage or $2.50 first-class postage) and *Volunteer! The Comprehensive Guide to Voluntary Service in the U.S. and Abroad* ($6.95 plus $1 book-rate postage or $2.50 first-class postage). The Information Center at the **Institute of International Education** (IIE) has reference books, foreign-university catalogs, study-abroad brochures, and other materials, which may be consulted by students and nonstudents alike, free of charge. The Information Center is located on 1st Avenue between 45th and 46th streets in New York City (809 UN Plaza, New York, NY 10017, tel. 212/984–5413). It's open weekdays 10–4; closed on holidays. **Canadian University Travel Service Ltd.** (CUTS), sister organization of CIEE, serves as Canada's student travel bureau. CUTS has offices in about 28 locations throughout Canada, including Halifax, Montréal, Québec City, Ottawa, Toronto, Saskatoon, Edmonton, Victoria, and Vancouver. They are usually located on a university campus. To use CUTS services, you'll need an International card, available at CUTS offices (with proper ID) or at the addresses already mentioned above. CUTS helps you find student discount fares, sells European train passes for further travel, and can arrange working holidays and set up language courses. In addition, CUTS arranges tours and canoe trips and can help you with domestic flights. Their "Discount Handbook" lists more than 1,000 stores and service establishments that offer bargains to ISIC card carriers.

Traveling with Children

Publications ***Family Travel Times*** is a newsletter published 10 times a year by Travel With Your Children (TWYCH, 80 8th Ave., New York, NY 10011, tel. 212/206–0688). A one-year subscription costs $35 and includes access to back issues and twice-weekly opportunities to call in for specific advice.

Hotels Although most major hotels in Canada welcome children, the policies and programs they offer are usually limited to a free stay for children under a certain age when rooming with their parents. For example, the Sheraton Hotels worldwide offer a free stay to children under the age of 18. At Best Westerns, the age limit ranges from 12 to 16, depending on the hotel, because each Best Western operates independently. Babysitting services can often be arranged at the front desk of most hotels. In addition, priority for connecting rooms is often given to families. Inquire about programs and discounts when you make your reservation.

Home Exchange Exchanging homes is a surprisingly low-cost way to enjoy a vacation abroad, especially a long one. The largest home-exchange service, **International Home Exchange Service** (Box 3975, San Francisco, CA 94119, tel. 415/435–3497) publishes three directories a year. Membership ($35) entitles you to one listing in all three directories. Photos of your property cost an additional $8.50, and listing a second home costs $10. **Vacation Exchange Club, Inc.** (12006 111th Ave., Unit 12, Youngstown, AZ 85363, tel. 602/972–2186), publishes one directory in February and a supplement in April. Membership is $24.70 per year, for which you receive one listing. Photos cost another $9; listing a second home costs $6. **Loan-a-Home** (2 Park La., Mount Vernon, NY 10552) is popular with the academic community on sabbatical and businesspeople on temporary assignment. There's no annual membership fee or charge for listing your home; however, one directory and a supplement costs $30. Loan-a-Home publishes two directories (in December and June) and two supplements (in March and September) each year. All four books cost $40 per year.

Getting There On international flights, children under two not occupying a seat pay 10% of adult fare. Various discounts apply to children from age 2 to 12, so check with your airline when booking. Reserve a seat behind the bulkhead of the plane, because there's usually more leg room and enough space to fit a bassinet, which the airlines will supply. At the same time, ask about special children's meals or snacks; most airlines offer them. For more information about the children's services offered by 46 airlines, see TWYCH's Airline Guide, published in the February 1990 issue of ***Family Travel Times*** (*see* above; the guide will be published again in February 1992).

Ask the airline in advance if you can bring aboard your child's car seat. For the booklet ***Child/Infant Safety Seats Acceptable for Use in Aircraft,*** write to the Federal Aviation Administration (APA-200, 800 Independence Ave. SW, Washington, DC 20591, tel. 202/267–3479).

Hints for Disabled Travelers

The **Information Center for Individuals with Disabilities** (Fort Point Pl., 1st floor, 27–43 Wormwood St., Boston, MA 02210, tel. 617/727–5540) offers useful problem-solving assistance, including lists of travel agents who specialize in tours for the disabled. For a small fee, **Moss Rehabilitation Hospital Travel Information Service** (12th St. and Tabor Rd., Philadelphia, PA

19141, tel. 215/329–5715) provides information on tourist sights, transportation, and accommodations in destinations around the world. **Travel Industry and Disabled Exchange** (TIDE, 5435 Donna Ave., Tarzana, CA 91356, tel. 818/368–5648), for a $15 per-person annual-membership fee, provides a quarterly newsletter and a directory of travel agencies and tours to Europe, Canada, Great Britain, New Zealand, and Australia—all specializing in travel for the disabled.

Mobility International USA (Box 3551, Eugene, OR 97403, tel. 503/343–1284) is an internationally affiliated organization with 500 members. For a $20 annual fee, it coordinates exchange programs for disabled people around the world and offers information on accommodations and organized study programs.

Hints for Older Travelers

The **American Association of Retired Persons** (AARP, 1909 K St. NW, Washington, DC 20049, tel. 202/662–4850) has two programs for independent travelers: (1) the Purchase Privilege Program, which offers discounts on hotels, airfare, car rentals, RV rentals, and sightseeing; and (2) the AARP Motoring Plan, which furnishes emergency aid (road service) and trip-routing information for an annual fee of $33.95 per person or couple. (Both programs include the member and member's spouse or the member and another person who shares the household.) The AARP also arranges group tours, including apartment living in Europe and Australia, through **Olson-Travelworld,** (100 N. Sepulveda Blvd., Suite 1010, El Segundo, CA 90245, tel. 213/615–0711 or 800/421–2255). As of 1991, **American Express Vacations (Package Deals for Independent Travelers,** *see* above) will arrange tours. AARP members must be 50 or older; annual dues are $5 per person or per couple.

When using an AARP or other discount identification card, ask for reduced hotel rates at the time you make your reservation, not when you check out. At restaurants, show your card to the maître d' before you're seated, since discounts may be limited to certain set menus, days, or hours. When renting a car, remember that economy cars, priced at promotional rates, may cost less than cars available with your discount ID card.

Elderhostel (80 Boylston St., Suite 400, Boston, MA 02116, tel. 617/426–7788) is an innovative 16-year-old educational program for people 60 and older. Participants live in dorms on some 1,200 campuses around the world. Mornings are devoted to lectures and seminars; afternoons to sightseeing and field trips. Fees for two- to three-week trips, including room, board, tuition, and round-trip transportation, range from $1,700 to $3,200.

Saga International Holidays (120 Boylston St., Boston, MA 02116, tel. 800/343–0273) specializes in group travel for people over 60. A selection of variously priced tours allows you to choose the package that meets your needs.

National Council of Senior Citizens (925 15th St. NW, Washington, DC 20005, tel. 202/347–8800) is a nonprofit advocacy group with some 5,000 local clubs across the country. Annual membership is $12 per person or per couple. Members receive a monthly newspaper with travel information and an ID card for reduced-rate hotels and car rentals.

Mature Outlook (6001 N. Clark St., Chicago, IL 60660, tel. 800/336–6330), a subsidiary of Sears Roebuck & Co., is a travel club for people over 50, with hotel and motel discounts and a bimonthly newsletter. Annual membership is $9.95; there are currently 800,000 members. Instant membership is available at participating Holiday Inns.

Further Reading

Fiction Mordecai Richler is well known as the author of *The Apprenticeship of Duddy Kravitz,* a novel set in Montréal, which was made into a movie. His various collections of essays are also worth exploring. Margaret Atwood, a prolific poet and novelist, is also regarded as a stateswoman of sorts in her native Canada. Her most recent novel, *The Cat's Eye,* is set in northern Canada and Toronto. Alice Munro writes about small-town life in Ontario in *The Progress of Love. Northern Lights,* by Howard Norman, focuses on a child's experiences growing up in Manitoba and, later, Toronto. Howard Engel's mystery series features the adventures of Bennie Cooperman, a Toronto-based detective. *The Suicide Murders* is an especially compelling novel from the series. Jack Hodgin's *Spit Delaney's Island* is peopled with loggers, construction workers and other rural Canadians. *Peace Shall Destroy Many* is Rudy Wiebe's account of a Mennonite community in Manitoba. Joy Kogawa's first novel, *Obasan,* tells about the Japanese community of Canada during World War II. *Medicine River* is a collection of short stories by Native American writer Thomas King, who was one of the authors, along with Cheryl Calver and Helen Hoy, of *The Native in Literature,* about the image of Native Americans in literature.

Nonfiction *Canada North* is by Farley Mowat, as is *Never Cry Wolf,* his humorous account of a naturalist who goes to a remote part of Canada to commune with wolves. Andrew Malcolm gives a cultural and historical overview of the country in *The Canadians.* Stephen Brook's *The Maple Leaf Rag* is a collection of idiosyncratic travel essays. *My Country,* by Pierre Burton, is one of many of Burton's books about Canada worth reading for its personal look at Canada. *Short History of Canada,* by Desmond Morton, is a recent historical account of the country.

Arriving and Departing

From the U.S. by Plane

Be certain to distinguish among (1) nonstop flights—no changes, no stops; (2) direct flights—no changes but one or more stops; and (3) connecting flights—two or more planes, two or more stops.

Airports and Airlines Every major U.S. airline has nonstop flights to Canada. The major international hubs are Montréal (Mirabel), Toronto, and Vancouver, but international flights also fly into Halifax, Calgary, and Edmonton. From the U.S. nonstop service to Canada is available from New York, Hartford, Boston, Philadelphia, Pittsburgh, Washington, Baltimore, Atlanta, Miami, Tampa, Denver, Minneapolis-St. Paul, Indianapolis, Chicago, Cleveland, Columbus, Dayton, Seattle, San Francisco, Los Angeles, and Honolulu.

Flying Time
To Montréal From New York: 1½ hours; from Chicago: 2 hours; from Los Angeles: 6 hours; from London: 6½ hours.

To Toronto From New York: 1½ hours; from Chicago: 1½ hours; from Los Angeles: 4½ hours.

To Vancouver From Montréal: 6½ hours; from Chicago: 4 hours; from Los Angeles: 2½ hours.

Enjoying the Flight If you're lucky enough to be able to sleep on a plane, it makes sense to fly at night. Unless you're flying from Europe, jet lag won't be a problem. There is little or no time difference between the United States and Canada. Because the air on a plane is dry, it helps, while flying, to drink a lot of nonalcoholic beverages; drinking alcohol contributes to jet lag, as does eating heavy meals on board. Feet swell at high altitudes, so it's a good idea to remove your shoes at the beginning of your flight. Sleepers usually prefer window seats to curl up against; those who like to move about the cabin ask for aisle seats. Bulkhead seats (located in the front row of each cabin) have more legroom, but seat trays are attached rather awkwardly to the arms of the seat rather than to the back of the seat ahead. Generally, bulkhead seats are reserved for the disabled, the elderly, or parents traveling with infants.

Discount Flights The major airlines offer a range of tickets that can increase the price of any given seat by more than 300%, depending on the day of purchase. As a rule, the further in advance you buy the ticket, the less expensive it is and the greater the penalty (up to 100%) for canceling. Check with airlines for details. The best buy is not necessarily an APEX (advance purchase) ticket on one of the major airlines, because these tickets carry certain restrictions: They must be bought in advance (usually 21 days); they restrict your travel, usually with a minimum stay of seven days and a maximum of 90; and they also penalize you for changes—voluntary or not—in your travel plans. But if you can work around these drawbacks (and most travelers can), they are among the best-value fares available.

Consolidators Other discounted fares—up to 50% below the cost of APEX tickets—can be found through consolidators, companies that buy blocks of tickets on scheduled airlines and sell them at wholesale prices. Tickets are subject to availability, so passengers must have flexible travel schedules. Here again, you may lose all or most of your money if you change plans, but at least you will be on a regularly scheduled flight with less risk of cancellation than on a charter. As an added precaution, you may want to purchase trip-cancellation insurance. Once you've made your reservation, call the airline to confirm it. Many consolidators advertise in newspaper travel sections.

Travel Clubs Another option is to join a travel club that offers special discounts to its members. Several such organizations are **Discount Travel International** (114 Forrest Ave., Narberth, PA 19072, tel. 215/668–2182); **Moment's Notice** (40 E. 49th St., New York, NY 10017, tel. 212/486–0503); **Traveler's Advantage,** (CUC Travel Service, 40 Oakview Dr., Trumbull, CT 06611, tel. 800/648–4037); and **Worldwide Discount Travel Club** (1674 Meridien Ave., Miami Beach, FL 33139, tel. 305/534–2082). These cut-rate tickets should be compared with APEX tickets on the major airlines.

Air Couriers Travelers willing to put up with some restrictions and inconvenience, in exchange for a substantially reduced airfare, may be interested in flying as an air courier. A person who agrees to be a courier must accompany shipments between designated points. There are two sources of information on courier deals: For a telephone directory listing courier companies by the cities to which they fly, send $5 and a self-addressed, stamped business-size envelope to **Pacific Data Sales Publishing,** 2554 Lincoln Boulevard, Suite 275-F, Marina del Rey, CA 92091. ***A Simple Guide to Courier Travel*** is available for $12.45 from the Carriage Group, Box 2394, Lake Oswego, OR 97035.

Smoking If the airline tells you there are no seats available in the nonsmoking section, insist on one: Department of Transportation regulations require carriers to find seats for all nonsmokers, provided they meet check-in time restrictions. These regulations apply to all international flights on U.S. domestic carriers. Smoking is also banned on all Canadian commercial carriers on North American routes.

From the U.S. by Car

Drivers should have proper owner registration and proof of insurance coverage. U.S. motorists are advised to obtain a Canadian Non-Resident Inter-Provincial Motor Vehicle Liability Insurance Card, which is accepted as evidence of financial responsibility anywhere in Canada. It is available from any U.S. insurance company. You won't need an international driver's license; any valid one will do. If you are driving a rented car, be sure to have the vehicle registration forms, along with a copy of the rental contract, to indicate that use in Canada is authorized by the rental agency. If you are driving a car that is not registered in your name, you should carry a letter from the owner that authorizes your use of the vehicle.

The U.S. Interstate Highway System leads directly into Canada at 12 points: I–95 from Maine to New Brunswick; I–91 and I–89 from Vermont to Québec; I–87 from New York to Québec; I–81 and a spur off I–90 from New York to Ontario; I–94, I–96, and I–75 from Michigan to Ontario; I–29 from North Dakota to Manitoba; I–15 from Montana to Alberta; and I–5 from Washington state to British Columbia. Most of these connections hook up with the Trans-Canada Highway within a few miles.

From Alaska, take the Alaska Highway (from Fairbanks), the Klondike Highway (from Skagway), and the Taylor Highway (to Dawson City).

From the U.S. by Train, Bus, and Ship

By Train **Amtrak** (tel. 800/872–7245) has service from New York to Montréal, New York and Buffalo to Toronto, and Chicago to Toronto. Amtrak's "Montrealer" departs from New York's Pennsylvania Station at 8:30 PM and arrives in Montréal the next day at about 10:45 AM. Sleepers are highly recommended for the overnight trip, but must be booked well in advance. The "Montrealer" is the only Amtrak train to Canada that requires reservations.

A second Amtrak train to Montréal departs New York City from Grand Central Station in the morning and takes 9½ hours; New York to Toronto takes 11 hours and 45 minutes; Chicago to Toronto takes 10½ hours; and Buffalo to Toronto takes four hours. In addition to these direct routes, there are connections from many major cities.

By Bus **Greyhound** has a monopoly on bus service to Canada, but you can get from almost any point in the United States to any point in Canada on its extensive network. One of the longest routes, from New York City to Vancouver via Seattle, takes about 3½ days. If you plan to cover a lot of ground, look into the Greyhound Pass, which is valid for travel in the United States and Canada. A seven-day pass costs about $189, a 15-day pass about $249. For ticket information, contact your local Greyhound office.

By Ship You can take a car ferry between Seattle and Victoria (British Columbia) or Maine and Nova Scotia (*see* Essential Information in individual chapters). Many Canadian cities are also accessible by sea on private yachts and boats. Local marine authorities can advise you about the necessary documentation and procedure.

From the U.K. by Plane

Airlines The major carriers between Great Britain and Canada are **Air Canada** (tel. 081/759–2636), **British Airways** (tel. 071/897–4000), and **Canadian Airlines International** (tel. 0800/234444). Air Canada has the most flights and serves the most cities, with at least one flight a day to Toronto, Vancouver, and Montréal from Heathrow, and considerably more at peak periods. Air Canada also flies to Calgary, Edmonton, Halifax, and St. John's from Heathrow; to Toronto from Birmingham and Manchester; and to Calgary, Halifax, Toronto, and Vancouver from Prestwick (Glasgow). British Airways has as many as 23 flights a week to Canada from Heathrow, serving Montréal, Toronto, and Vancouver. Canadian Airlines International serves Calgary, Edmonton, Ottawa, and Vancouver from London Gatwick, though it also has at least one flight a day to Toronto and has service from Manchester to Toronto.

Fares The round-trip APEX fare from London to Toronto or Montréal is £448; economy is £630; business class is £1,618; and first class is £2,630. The round-trip APEX fare from London to Vancouver is £568; economy is £870; business class is £1,956; first class is £3,302.

Charters The leading charter company, **Globespan International** (tel. 0293/541541) offers daily flights from Gatwick to Toronto, as well as less frequent flights from Gatwick to Calgary, Edmonton, Halifax, Montréal, Ottawa, and Vancouver. It also offers weekly service from Birmingham, Cardiff, Manchester, Prestwick, and Stanstead to Toronto; and from Manchester and Prestwick to Vancouver. Fares are competitive: The round-trip fare from London to Toronto or Montréal, for example, is £294. Specialist ticket companies such as **Travel Cuts** (tel. 071/637–3161) sometimes have even lower fares, though not at peak periods and with absolutely no frills. Round-trip fares for London–Toronto, for example, can start from as low as £195. Check the advertisements in *Time Out* and the Sunday newspapers for other inexpensive fares.

From the U.K. by Ship

Gray Dawes Travel (Dugard House, Peartree Rd., Stanway, Colchester, Essex CO3 5UL, tel. 0206/762241) arranges passages on freighters to three Canadian cities: Halifax, Montréal, and Vancouver. The trip to Vancouver goes through the Panama Canal, then on to Los Angeles, Oakland, Portland, and Seattle. The sailing to Halifax leaves from Bremerhaven every week and can take 8 to 12 passengers; fares begin at £475 one way and the trip takes 8 to 9 days. The sailing to Montréal leaves from Antwerp every 10 to 14 days and can take 10 to 12 passengers; fares begin at £900 one way, and the voyage takes about two weeks. The sailing to Vancouver leaves from Fleixstowe or Hamburg once a month and can take 10 to 12 passengers; fares are from £1,700 one way, and the trip takes nearly a month. The demand for all these sailings is considerable, and you may have to book many months, even a year, in advance.

Staying in Canada

Getting Around

By Plane **Air Canada** (tel. 800/422–6232), the government-owned airline, operates in every province. The other major domestic carrier is the privately owned **Canadian Airlines International** (tel. 800/426–7000). Regularly scheduled flights to every major city and to most smaller cities are available on Air Canada or Canadian Airlines International or the domestic carriers associated with them: **Air Alliance** serves Québec; **Air Atlantic** flies in the Atlantic region; **Air British Columbia** serves British Columbia; **Air Nova** serves Atlantic Canada; **Air Ontario** serves the Ontario region; **City Express Airlines** flies between major cities in Ontario and Québec; and **First Air** includes a flight from Ottawa to New York. These airlines can be contacted at local numbers within each of the many cities they serve.

Canada is a huge country, but jet travel has shrunk it considerably—to fly from Montréal to Vancouver takes six hours. However, service to smaller cities is often only once or twice a day. Therefore, you may encounter long stopovers when trying to reach your destination.

In addition to the regular flights in the North, there are also a number of charter airlines and fly-in airports. Check with the territorial tourist agencies for charter companies and with the District Controller of Air Services in the territorial (and provincial) capitals for the locations of air bases that allow private flights and for regulations.

Smoking Smoking has been prohibited on Canadian commercial planes on North American routes since September 1988. The ban was extended to all Canadian flights, including flights to Europe and the Far East, on July 1, 1990.

By Train Transcontinental rail service is provided by **VIA Rail Canada.** If you're planning on traveling to several major cities in Canada, the train may be your best bet. Routes run across the country as well as within individual provinces, with the exception of the Northwest Territories and the Yukon.

You can choose either sleeping-car or coach accommodations on most trains. Both classes allow access to dining cars. Sleeping-car passengers can enjoy comfortable parlor cars, drawing rooms, bedrooms, and roomettes. First-class seats, sleeping-car accommodations, and Dayniter seats between Ontario, Québec, and the maritime provinces require reservations. Train information is available from the United States. (*See* From the U.S. by Train and Rail Passes, above). Each province also has a toll-free information number.

By Bus The bus is an essential form of transportation in Canada, especially if you want to visit out-of-the-way towns that do not have airports or rail lines. Two major bus companies, **Greyhound** (222 1st Ave. SW, Calgary, Alb. T2P 0A6) and **Voyageur** (265 Catherine St., Ottawa, Ont. K1R 7S5), offer interprovincial service. Greyhound's 7-, 15-, or 30-day pass (*see* From the U.S. by Bus, above) is good throughout North America. Voyageur offers similar package discounts. These options are often honored by Canada's many provincial bus lines.

By Car Canada's highway system is excellent. It includes the Trans-Canada Highway, which runs about 5,000 miles from Victoria, British Columbia, to St. John's, Newfoundland, using ferries to bridge coastal waters at each end. The second-largest Canadian highway, the Yellowhead Highway, follows the old Indian route from the Pacific Coast and over the Rockies to the prairie. North of the population centers, roads become fewer and less developed.

Speed limits vary from province to province, but they are usually within the 90–100 kph (50–60 mph) range outside the cities. The price of gasoline varies more than the speed limit, from 36¢ to 54¢ a liter. (There are 3.8 liters in a U.S. gallon, 4.5 liters in a Canadian Imperial gallon.) Distances are often shown in kilometers, and gasoline is usually sold in liters, although the Imperial gallon is still used in some places.

Foreign driver's licenses are valid in Canada. Members of the **Automobile Association of America** (AAA) can contact the **Canadian Automobile Association** (1775 Courtwood Crescent, Ottawa, Ont. K2C 3J2, tel. 613/226–7631) for travel information, itineraries, maps, and tour books. If you are a member of the AAA, you can also dial 800/336–4357 for emergency road service in Canada.

Telephones

Phones work as they do in the United States. Drop 25¢ in the slot (pay phones eagerly accept American coins, unlike U.S. phones, which spit out Canadian money) and dial the number. There are no problems dialing direct to the United States; U.S. telephone credit cards are accepted. For directory assistance, dial 411. To place calls outside Canada and the United States, dial "0" and ask for the overseas operator.

Mail

Postal Rates In Canada you can buy stamps at the post office or from automatic vending machines in most hotel lobbies, railway stations, airports, bus terminals, many retail outlets, and some newsstands. Within Canada, postcards and letters up to 30 grams cost 37¢. Letters and postcards to the United States cost 43¢ for up to 30 grams, 74¢ from 30 to 100 grams.

International mail and postcards run 76¢ for up to 20 grams, $1.20 for 20–50 grams.

Telepost is a fast "next day or sooner" service that combines the CN/CP Telecommunications network with letter-carrier delivery service. Messages may be telephoned to the nearest CN/CP Public Message Centre for delivery anywhere in Canada or the United States. Telepost service is available 24 hours a day, seven days a week, and billing arrangements may be made at the time the message is called in.

Intelpost allows you to send documents or photographs via satellite to many Canadian, American, and European destinations. This service is available at main postal facilities in Canada.

Receiving Mail If you plan to receive mail while in Canada, you can have it sent c/o General Delivery in the location you'll be visiting by using the following address: c/o General Office, Main Post Office, (city and province), Canada, postal code (may be obtained from the post office). Mail must be picked up within 15 days, or it will be returned to the sender.

Tipping

Tips and service charges are not usually added to a bill in Canada. In general, tip 15% of the total bill. This goes for waiters, waitresses, barbers and hairdressers, taxi drivers, etc. Porters and doormen should get about 50¢ a bag ($1 or more in a luxury hotel). For room service, $1 a day is sufficient ($2 in luxury hotels).

Opening and Closing Times

Stores, shops, and supermarkets are open at times similar to those in the United States: Monday through Saturday from 9 to 6—although in major cities, supermarkets are often open as early as 7:30 AM and stay open until 9 PM. Blue laws (enforced Sunday closings) are in effect in much of Canada, so don't expect to get much souvenir shopping done on Sunday. Retail stores are generally open on Thursday and Friday evenings; most shopping malls until 9 PM. Most banks in Canada are open Monday through Thursday from 10 to 3, and from 10 to 5 or 6 on Friday. Some banks are also open on Saturday morning. Many banks offer automated tellers at any hour. All banks are closed on national holidays. Drugstores in major cities are often open until 11 PM, and convenience stores are often open 24 hours a day, seven days a week.

Shopping

About five years ago, the exchange rate favored the U.S. dollar, so even though the price tags were the same in both countries you were always ensured a 25% discount. These days, Canadian prices don't exactly mirror those in the United States. With the current exchange rate, you can expect only a small "discount."

In some of Canada's provinces, a sales tax refund is available when goods are exported from Canada (or, in some cases, from the province). Ontario has a particularly good system for such refunds, provided that the tax you are claiming back equals at least C$7. Ask about tax refunds at the time of your purchase or inquire at your hotel before setting out to shop.

Antiques On the whole, prices for antiques are lower in Canada than in the United States, and each province has something to offer, although the serious antiques hunter will want to investigate the pockets of shops in Montréal and Toronto. Along Montréal's rue Sherbrooke O, the shops feature everything from ancient maps to fine crystal. For funkier finds, stroll through Vieux-Montréal, where antiques and collectibles range from Napoleonic-period furniture to 1950s bric-a-brac. Toronto's offerings are equally eclectic, although priced higher than elsewhere in Canada. (But for comparison's sake, consider that many Toronto antiques dealers send their wares to New York City, where the price is doubled before it goes on the sales floor.) The Yorkville area caters to interior designers, with its European collections, although the antiques markets at Lansdown and Harbourfront are livelier and have wider selections. Antiques shopping is a respectable pastime in downtown Vancouver as well, and Victoria offers some of the best buys in antique silver in its shops clustered on Front Street.

Arts and Crafts Sweaters, silver objects, pottery, and Acadian crafts can be found in abundance in New Brunswick. For pewter, head for Fredericton. For woven items, visit the village of St. Andrews. The Mennonite communities of Ontario sell their handmade quilts each May at the Mennonite Relief sale. Prices can run to $2,000 for a large quilt.

Fashion Canada's three major department stores—**The Bay, Simpson,** and **Eaton**—often called the Big Three, are steeped in more than a 100 years of tradition and are fixtures of shopping malls throughout Canada. The Bay—or if you're French-speaking, La Baie—specializes in moderately priced goods. Simpson has brought both American and Canadian designers to its stores. Eaton is the most sophisticated of the three and the most designer-oriented. Canadian designers featured at the Big Three and more exclusive boutiques include Alfred Sung, Wayne Clark, Simon Chang, Marilyn Brooks, and Lyse Spenard.

Canada's retail chains are all fairly hip and can offer some good buys. Consider **Roots** for casual, well-made clothes; **Club Monaco,** a chicer version of the Gap; **Au Coton,** for cotton-only clothes; **Thalie,** for inexpensive women's clothes; and **Heritage House,** for American and Canadian designers for the country-club set.

Fur You can buy a fur in any big city, but for the best prices, head to Toronto and Montréal, the wholesale fur districts of Canada. Mink is a good buy in Canada. You can also find fox coats, but fox is not a specialty of Canada. January is a particularly good time to shop for fur, since it is sale season. In the United States, fur garments must be labeled to distinguish farmed from trapped pelts. Canada's trapping business is legal and profitable, and the industry has resisted pressure from the United States to enforce a similar labeling system. If you are concerned about whether the animal was farmed or trapped, you'll have to ask the salesperson.

Indian Art For the best price and a guarantee of authenticity, purchase Inuit and other native crafts in the province where they originate. Many styles are now attributed to certain tribes and are mass-produced for sale in galleries and shops miles away from their regions of origin. For Inuit art and sculpture, head for the West Coast. Interest has grown for this highly collectible art, usually rendered in stone. The Canadian government has registered the symbol of an igloo as a mark of a work's authenticity. Be sure this Canadian government sticker or tag is attached before you make your purchase. Many galleries and shops in the west also carry work done by the Indians of the Northwest, who have revived their ancient art. They are known for their highly stylized masks, totem poles, and canoes. Themes and images from nature, such as whales, bears, wolves, and eagles, are prominent in their work. Bright colors and geometric patterns distinguish their woven products: blankets, wall hangings, and clothing.

In and around Calgary you can find ceremonial headdresses, clothing, and tools made by the nomadic Plains Indians. Algonkian and Iroquoian art survives mainly in the museums of Eastern Canada and in the gift shops of some of the reservations in Ontario.

Maple Syrup Eastern Canada is famous for its sugar maples. The trees are tapped in March, and the sap is collected in buckets to be boiled down into maple syrup. This natural confection is sold all year. Avoid the tourist shops and department stores; for the best prices and information, stop at the many farm stands and markets in the provinces of Québec and Ontario. A small can of syrup costs about $5.

Sales Tax

A country-wide sales tax of 7% (Goods and Services Tax) went into effect on Jan. 1, 1991.

Non-residents can get a full refund on the GST by submitting a rebate form within 60 days of leaving Canada. Forms may be obtained from certain retailers, from duty-free shops, and from customs officials; invoices must be attached for any goods taken out of the country. In some cases the GST tax is levied in addition to the provincial tax; in other cases it supplants it, promising a new and complicated system. All provinces, except Alberta, the Northwest Territories, and the Yukon, levy a sales tax from 4% to 12% on most items purchased in shops, on meals in restaurants, and, sometimes, on hotel accommodations. Alberta charges 5% tax on hotel rooms.

National Parks

Banff, the country's first national park, was established in 1885, and since then the national park system has grown to encompass 34 national parks and 79 national historic sites (for day use only). Because of Canada's eagerness to preserve its environment, new lands are continually being added to this network. Almost every park offers camping—either primitive camping or campsites with various facilities that can accommodate recreational vehicles. Hiking trails weave their way through each of the parks. Among the most popular parks are Fundy National Park in Nova Scotia and the several Rocky

Mountain parks. Environment Canada publishes two pamphlets: *Canada's National Parks* lists each of the parks and any activities and facilities available, and *Canada's National Historic Sites* provides descriptions of each of these parks and sites, including opening and closing times and some background information. Write to Inquiry Center, Environment Canada, Ottawa, Ontario K1A 0H3, tel. 819/997–2800.

Participant Sports and Outdoor Activities

Biking Eastern and Western Canada offer some of the best bicycling terrain. In the east, bikers favor the Gaspé Peninsula in Québec and the surrounding Atlantic provinces. The terrain varies from very hilly around the Gaspé to flat on Prince Edward Island, and varied in New Brunswick and Nova Scotia. A western tour might include the area around the Rocky Mountains and on through British Columbia. The plains of central Canada may seem attractive for level biking, but cyclists run the risk of blacking out on too many miles of endless flatland. Some cities, such as Vancouver and Ottawa, have bike trails marked throughout town. Write to the provincial tourist boards for road maps (which are more detailed than the maps available at gas stations) and information on local cycling associations.

Camping Canada's 2,000-plus campgrounds range from simple roadside turnoffs with sweeping mountain vistas to fully equipped facilities with groomed sites, trailer hookups, recreational facilities, and vacation village atmosphere. Many of the best sites are in Canada's national and provincial parks, with nominal overnight fees. Commercial campgrounds offer more amenities, such as electrical and water hookups, showers, and even game rooms and grocery stores. They cost more, and somehow defeat the point of camping: getting a little closer to nature. If all you need is a clear patch of ground to pitch a tent, then you can simply pull off the road on millions of square miles of Crown lands and set up camp. For listings of private and public campgrounds, contact the tourist office of the province you plan to visit. For brochures and other information on national parks, *see* National Parks, above.

Canoeing Your degree of expertise and experience will dictate where you will canoe. Beginners will look for waterways in more settled areas. The pros will head north to the streams and rivers that flow into the Arctic Ocean. The Canadian Government Travel Office offers maps, information, and advice for those in either category. Provincial tourist offices and the federal Department of Northern Development and Indian Affairs (Ottawa, Ont. K1A OH4, tel. 819/997–0002) can also be of assistance, especially in locating an outfitter to suit your needs.

Fishing Anglers can find their catch in virtually any region of the country, though restrictions, seasons, license requirements, and bag limits vary from province to province. You should inquire at provincial tourist offices (*see* Essential Information in individual chapters for tourist office addresses and telephone numbers). In addition, special fishing permits are required to fish in all national parks. The permits can be obtained at any national park site, for a nominal fee, and are valid in all the national parks across Canada. **Prince Edward Island** offers cod, mackerel, salmon, and sea trout in the Atlantic and speckled trout and rainbow trout in its other waters. The waters surrounding

Prince Edward Island have some of the best deep-sea tuna fishing. **Nova Scotia** has some of the most stringent freshwater restrictions in Canada, but the availability of Atlantic salmon, speckled trout, and striped bass makes the effort worthwhile. Salmon, trout, and black bass are abundant in the waters of **New Brunswick,** but many of the streams and rivers are leased to private freeholders, either individuals or clubs. The lakes of **Québec** hold trout, bass, pike, and landlocked salmon, called ouananiche (pronounced *Wah*-nah-nish). Just about every kind of North American freshwater game fish is available in some part of **Ontario. Manitoba** offers lake trout, brook trout, pike, grayling, walleye, Hudson Bay salmon, and smallmouth bass. It also offers a winter fishing season, but some areas require a guide. **Alberta** is considered a paradise for sportfishers, with its trout in streams; its pike, walleye, and perch in lakes; and its grayling, goldeye, and whitefish in rivers. **British Columbia** is unparalleled for salmon, but only two of the five species may be taken in nontidal waters.

Golf Every province has something for the duffer, but British Columbia and Ontario dominate the golf scene. Ontario has nearly 400 golf courses. British Columbia also has many golf courses, and Victoria's mild weather makes it especially appealing to golfers.

Hiking Miles and miles of trails weave through all of Canada's national and provincial parks. Write to the individual provincial tourist offices (*see* Essential Information in individual chapters) or contact the Inquiry Center for the Department of Parks (*see* National Parks, above).

Horseback Riding This sport is popular out West, especially in places like Banff National Park in Alberta, which has many outfitters that can arrange week-long trips on the park's trails. Contact the park's information center for more details (tel. 403/762–3324).

Hunting Canada is rich with a variety of game, including deer, black bear, moose, caribou, elk, and wild goose. As with fishing, hunting is governed by federal, provincial, and territorial laws. You will need a hunting license from each province or territory in which you plan to hunt. A federal permit is required for hunting migratory game birds and is available at most Canadian post offices. In many of Canada's provincial parks and reserves and adjacent areas, the entry of any type of weapon is forbidden. No hunting is permitted in Canada's national parks. Guides are required in many places and are available almost everywhere. Provincial tourist offices can provide specific information.

Mountain Climbing Offering mountain climbers a challenge are the summits of Banff and Jasper national parks in Alberta and the provincial park of Mt. Robson and Yoho National Park in British Columbia. Mountain climbing should not be undertaken lightly. Write to the Inquiry Center (*see* National Parks, above) for more information about these parks.

Sailing and Scuba Diving Sailing is common on both coasts, and rentals are available in many places. More than 3,000 ships are wrecked off the coast of Nova Scotia, making it particularly attractive to divers. The provincial Department of Tourism can provide details on the location of wrecks and where to buy or rent equipment.

Skiing Skiing is probably the most popular winter sport in Canada. For downhill skiing there are slopes in every province, but those in Québec, Alberta, and British Columbia are the best. Alberta and British Columbia also offer heli-skiing trips. For cross-country skiing, almost any provincial or national park will do.

Whale Watching The shores off British Columbia are some of the best places to observe whales, seals, and other natural wildlife. Day-long, and sometimes more extensive week-long, boat trips are offered. In the Pacific Ocean, along Vancouver Island, migrating whales pass on their way to California breeding grounds in the fall and back in the spring.

White-water Rafting There are opportunities for rafting in almost every province, but the white waters of Ontario and British Columbia are especially inviting for thrill seekers.

Winter Sports Canadians flourish in winter, as the range of winter sports attests. In addition to the sports already mentioned, at the first drop of a snowflake Canadians will head outside to ice skate, toboggan, snowmobile, dogsled, snowshoe, and ice-fish.

Spectator Sports

Baseball If you're missing a bit of Americana, don't fret. Baseball has been a favorite in Canada since the major leagues expanded into Montréal in 1969 with the Montréal Expos, and the Toronto Blue Jays formed a World Series-caliber club. Minor league teams compete in Vancouver, Edmonton, Calgary, Lethbridge, and Medicine Hat.

Curling For a true taste of Canadian sportsmanship you might want to watch a curling match, which is not unlike a bowling match on ice. Two teams of four players each compete by sliding large stones toward a mark in the center of a circle, or "house."

Football The Canadian Football League plays the game its own way, allowing three downs, a 110-yard field, and 12 players per team.

Hockey Officially, Canada's national sport is lacrosse, but tell that to Wayne Gretsky, who was a national hero until he defected to play hockey in Los Angeles. Ice hockey is played by children and professionals alike, with leagues and teams organized everywhere. The National Hockey League teams include the Vancouver Canucks, Calgary Flames, Winnipeg Jets, Stanley Cup Champion Edmonton Oilers, Toronto Maple Leafs, Montréal Canadiens, and Québec Nordiques. The season runs from October to April.

Rodeos and Horse Racing Alberta is rodeo country. Thoroughbred racing during the spring, summer, and fall takes place in Ontario, Manitoba, Saskatchewan, Alberta, and British Columbia.

Dining

The earliest European settlers of Canada—the British and the French—bequeathed a rather bland diet of meat and potatoes. But though there are few really distinct national dishes here, the strong ethnic presence in Canada makes it difficult not to have a good meal, especially in the larger cities, where Greek, Italian, Chinese, and Indian immigrants operate restaurants. In addition, each province is well known for various specialties. **Ontario** is famous for its cheeses. Seafood usually heads the menu at restaurants in **British Columbia, Nova Scotia, New Brunswick,** or **Prince Edward Island.** Leave your vegetarian tendencies at home when visiting **Alberta** and **Saskatchewan,** where the meals invariably center on thick steaks and roasts. In some areas of Canada, especially in the plains, you may be lucky enough to find some native Indian treats, such as venison, pheasant, and buffalo meat accompanied by fiddlehead ferns in the spring or wild rice. And vestiges of what the European settlers learned from the Indians is evident in the hearty ingredients that make up the French-Canadian cuisine, which thrives in **Québec.** To enjoy the best of the province's hearty meat pies and pâtés, head to Québec City; Montréal dining tends to be more classic French than French-Canadian.

Lodging

Aside from the quaint hotels of Québec, Canada's range of accommodations more closely resembles that of the United States than Europe. In the cities you'll have a choice of luxury hotels, moderately priced modern properties, and smaller older hotels with perhaps fewer conveniences but a bit more charm. Options in smaller towns and in the country include large full-service resorts; small, privately owned hotels; roadside motels; and bed-and-breakfast establishments. Canada's answer to the small European family-run hotel is the mom-and-pop motel, but even though Canada is as attuned to automobile travel as the United States, you won't find these motels as frequently. Even here you'll need to make reservations at least on the day on which you're planning to pull into town.

Chain Hotels There are two advantages to staying at a chain hotel. The first is that you'll be assured of standard accommodations, your own bathroom, and a range of services at the front desk. The second is the ease with which you can get information and make or change reservations, since most chains have toll-free booking numbers.

The major hotel chains in Canada include:

Best Western International: tel. 800/528–1234
CP (Canadian Pacific) Hotels & Resorts: tel. 800/828–7447
Delta Hotels: tel. 800/263–8255
Four Seasons Hotels: tel. 800/332–3442
Holiday Inns: tel. 800/465–4329
Howard Johnson Hotels: tel. 800/654–2000
Radisson Hotels: tel. 800/333–3333
Ramada: tel. 800/228–2828
Sheraton Hotels: tel. 800/325–3535
Travelodge: tel. 800/255–3050
Westin Hotels: tel. 800/228–3000

Room Rates Expect accommodations to cost more during the heavy, summer tourism season than off-season. But don't be afraid to ask about special deals and packages when making your reservations. Big city hotels that cater to the business traveler often offer a special weekend package on Friday and Saturday nights. If you're planning to visit a major city or resort area during the high season, make your reservations well in advance. Also be aware of any special events or festivals that may coincide with your visit. For resorts and lodges, consider the winter ski season high as well and plan accordingly.

Bed-and-Breakfasts One way to save on lodging and spend some time with a native Canadian is to stay at a bed-and-breakfast establishment. They are gaining in popularity and are located in both the country and the cities. Every provincial tourist board either has a listing of B&Bs or can refer you to an association that will help you secure reservations. Rates range from $20 to $60 a night and include a continental or a full breakfast. Because most bed-and-breakfasts are in private homes, you'll rarely have your own bathroom. And some B&B hosts lock up early. Be sure to ask about your host's policies. Room quality varies from home to home as well, so don't be bashful about asking to see a room before making a choice.

Country Vacations Farm vacations are one way to enjoy the Canadian countryside. Depending on the size of the farm and the farmers' preferences, you'll be able to observe and/or participate in the daily activities of a working farm. These stays include breakfast and some offer other meals and special family rates. For more information about country vacations (farms, seashore, or ranch), write to **Canadian Country Vacations Association,** Box 2580, Winnipeg, Manitoba R3B 4C3, tel. 204/475–6624.

Dorms and Hostels There are a few alternatives to camping for those on a budget. Among them are hostels, which are open to young and old, families, and singles (**Canadian Hostelling Association,** 333 River Rd., Tower A-3, Vanier City, Ottawa, Ont. K1L 8H9, tel. 613/748–5638); the YM-YWCA (**YMCA National Council,** 2160 Yonge St., Toronto, Ont. M4S 2A1, tel. 416/485–9447); or the university campuses, which open their dorms to travelers for overnight stays from May through August.

Resorts Most of the country's resorts and lodges are open year-round and focus on such sports activities as boating, golfing, hiking, or canoeing, and, of course, skiing. Ski resorts right outside the major cities tend to be elaborate and more expensive. Packages at many ski resorts are available well into spring, where there are still good snow conditions. At the fishing and wilderness lodges, you can expect accommodations in cabins, often with housekeeping units. Most big resorts offer full health and fitness facilities as well. A variety of meal plans are almost always available, from breakfast only to three meals a day.

Relais & Châteaux This prestigious association of small hotels and inns has 10 members in Canada. Many once served as private estates to the Canadian wealthy. One property is set in a wildlife preserve in the Algonquin Park in Ontario; another is in the countryside, just 30 minutes from Montréal. Reservations must be made directly with each property, though a list of the properties and other information about a Relais & Châteaux stay is available from **Relais & Châteaux Information,** tel. 713/783–8033. Expect to spend anywhere from $150 to $450 a night.

Provincial Ratings and Taxes There is no national government rating system for hotels, but many provinces rate their accommodations. For example, in British Columbia and Alberta, a blue Approved Accommodation decal on the window or door of a hotel or motel indicates that it has met provincial hotel association standards for courtesy, comfort, and cleanliness. Ontario's voluntary rating system boasts about 1,000 Ontario properties. Room taxes also vary greatly from province to province. For example, New Brunswick charges 11% on hotel rooms, British Columbia adds

8%, and where appropriate, another 2% municipal tax, while Ontario taxes hotel rooms at 5%.

Credit Cards

The following credit card abbreviations are used throughout this guide: AE, American Express; CB, Carte Blanche; D, Discover; DC, Diners Club; MC, MasterCard; V, Visa. It's a good idea to call ahead to check current credit card policies.

Nightlife

In large cities, such as Montréal and Toronto, the problem isn't what to do in the evening, but how to choose from among the hundreds of events and attractions. Theater thrives all over Canada, but especially in Toronto, Montréal, and Vancouver. Dance has a large following in Canada, with everything from classical to avant-garde dance companies in almost every large city. You can hear almost any kind of music in the metropolitan clubs. Pick up a local paper at your hotel or at a bookstore. If you're staying near a university, you're sure to find a paper or magazine with listings devoted to the local club or art scene.

If you're visiting a smaller town or resort area, activity will pretty much be centered on dinner. However, the summer is an especially active festival season and should provide you with plenty of entertainment.

2 Portraits of Canada

A Great Northern Paradox

by Robert Fulford

Longtime Toronto journalist and broadcaster, Robert Fulford was editor of Saturday Night, *the leading Canadian monthly for 19 years. His specialty is the arts and literature.*

A character in an early play by Robertson Davies, who was a playwright long before he became a novelist of international renown, remarks sadly that Canada is not really a country you love: "It is a country you worry about." As it happens, I do love Canada, and most Canadians I know share this love; but it remains as true now as it was when Davies wrote it 40 years ago, that Canada is first of all a country you worry about, puzzle over, diagnose. It is a country whose citizens are more or less incessantly taking its temperature, always expecting the worst. Publicly and privately, in English and in French, in Parliament and in the newspapers and universities, we worry about Canada's identity, its future, its place in the world, and above all, its chance of surviving as a political entity in its present form. In the minds of Canadians—those nervous, cautious people who joined the Organization of American States after considering it for 79 years—the most striking fact about our country is that at almost any given moment it seems, if you follow the rhetoric of its leaders, to be on the verge of ceasing to exist.

For as long as any of us can remember, Canada has lived a peculiar contradiction—it is boundlessly promising and simultaneously fearful of the future. To describe it is to sound as if you are describing a talented but troubled adolescent. In fact, we often speak of Canada as a young country, and it is common for visitors or newcomers to remark on the newness, the freshness, and sometimes the innocence of it. Taken literally, this is nonsense—Canada has been in business for a long time. French immigrants, a mixture of peasants and priests and nobles, created New France on the banks of the St. Lawrence River (now the province of Québec) in the 17th century; even earlier there were fishing villages in Newfoundland, the island province out in the Atlantic. In 1867, before Germany and Italy were countries, Canada came together as a new kind of nation, a "dominion" from the Atlantic to the Pacific that was linked to Britain and loyal to the British crown but was understood to be moving toward independence. That event, Confederation, defined the political shape of the country; it was completed in 1949 when Newfoundland became the tenth province.

But "completed" is probably the wrong word to use about any element of Canadian history—Canada is a place that is always in a state of becoming, always transforming itself, always redefining its goals and its nature. Everything is contingent, and nothing is ever thought to be completed. Other countries—the United States being the leading example—may work out a constitution and set of values and then spend centuries living by that constitution and those values, doing the job well or badly as the occasion permits. Canada, on the other hand, changes not just the circumstances of national life, but the very philosophical underpinnings of that life. In a few decades we change our national beliefs, ideals, and emotional connections.

In 1867 Canada was proud to call itself "a British Dominion," even though a large fraction of its population was French-speaking. For a long time Canadian statesmen paid elaborate homage to England and the English monarch. But in the 20th century that connection began to appear to most Canadians as both unnecessary and dangerous. In both world wars Canadians fought as part of the British Empire or, as it was called later, the British Commonwealth. A great many French Canadians resented the fact that they, a minority within Canada, were drawn into war by the English-speaking and British-descended majority.

Before the 20th century was half over, there arose the idea that Québec was in some ways a distinct part of Canada, requiring its own status and privileges within the Confederation. Although only a quarter of Canadians were French-speaking, they asserted their belief that they deserved separate rights. By the 1960s, there was a popular movement within Québec to withdraw from Canada and form a separate state. That movement is still very much alive and remains a major reason why Canadians worry about their country's survival. Were Québec to separate it would still be the major trading partner of Canadians on either side of it; but they would *be* on either side of it—two chunks of Canada, separated as Pakistan was at its birth with such tragic results. This is why the constitutional discussions that became a more or less permanent part of Canadian life in the 1980s are crucial. The federal government and the governments of the 10 provinces are engaged once more, as Canadian leaders so often are, in saving Canada from falling apart.

The federal government has been working hard to satisfy Québec for the last 40 years or so, sometimes with the enthusiastic support of English-speaking Canada, and sometimes against the wishes of those English-speakers who have traditionally been suspicious of French Canadians' demands. In this process, the country has changed fundamentally. In 1950, a French-speaking Québecker would feel a foreigner when visiting the national capital in Ottawa. Even though that city is poised on a river between Ontario and Québec, it was then still a British city, and if you phoned the House of Commons the telephone operator answered only in English. Today Ottawa is bilingual, in keeping with the federal law that Canada has two official languages of equal status; elsewhere in Canada you can find bilingualism in everything from customs offices to federally owned broadcasting stations.

While making these changes, the federal government slowly began eliminating the signs of British influence. Canada stayed within the British Commonwealth, and to this minute Queen Elizabeth is still, constitutionally, the Queen of Canada, our head of state. But to placate French Canada, Ottawa reorganized Canadian symbolism. In the 1950s the word "dominion" was quietly dropped, not because it was British in origin—in fact, Canada was the first country to use it as a national designation—but because British monarchs had taken to speaking of *their* "dominion beyond the seas," and because Rudyard Kipling, in a famous poem, spoke of Queen Victoria having "dominion over palm and pine." (We were the "pine," and some Canadians didn't like the sound of it after a while.)

In the 1960s Canada stopped using as its flag the Canadian ensign, which featured a British Union Jack, and got its own design: a simple maple leaf that betrayed no ancient allegiances, British or French. In the 1970s most other British symbols just faded away, usually without much announcement or mourning—the royal coat of arms disappeared off the mailboxes, for instance. A few decades ago Canadians were legally entitled to live and work in Britain at will, and the reverse was also true; today a Canadian is a foreigner in Britain, with less status than a Belgian or a citizen of any other EEC country. And in Canada, someone from Britain is treated like any other foreigner.

These symbols, these connections, are the outward signs of an inner progress toward a nationhood that always turns out to be something of a surprise. With each generation we re-imagine ourselves in unpredictable ways. We may feel secure at any given moment in our identity—whether it is based on a region, a city, an ethnic group, or a pan-Canadian appreciation of the whole country—but is our sense of identity the same one that our grandparents understood? Is it in any way similar to the one our grandchildren will experience? In the United States, many can answer both of those questions with a confident "yes." Similarly, many people in France today can say that, yes, fulfilling the goals of the French Revolution will likely seem as important to their grandchildren as it does to them. But Canadians can't answer with anything like that kind of confidence.

This lack of a firm ideological mooring is not purely negative by any means. For many people it is altogether positive. Last year, when the United States twisted and writhed over a Supreme Court decision that seemed to permit desecration of the Stars and Stripes, Canadians watched in astonishment. No Canadian could imagine for a moment getting excited about the fate of a piece of cloth or any other secular symbol; but then, we have no symbols going back to the 18th century, and even if we did, we wouldn't know what they signified. It would be impossible to imagine a Committee on UnCanadian Activities, because first it would have to determine what a Canadian activity is—and that argument would never end. For the same reasons, a Canadian Pledge of Allegiance, recited by schoolchildren across the country, is an impossibility.

What this means is that no political form is imposed on Canadians, and—for some of us at least—the cultural air therefore is easier to breathe. Outsiders are sometimes bemused by the fact that, in Canada, citizenship does not even require adherence to the idea of Canada itself. Citizens in Alberta or Québec or Newfoundland may openly declare themselves in favor of withdrawing their provinces from Canada or may publicly regret that they ever joined—even today there are many Newfoundlanders who frankly state that it was a mistake for Newfoundland to become a province of Canada in 1949. But these people, far from being shunned or exiled, are treated as perfectly good Canadians and may even find themselves filling certain jobs in the federal government. The late René Lévesque, a Québec premier who spent the last two decades of his life trying to uncouple Québec from the rest of Canada, was mourned as a national hero from sea to sea when he died. Why? Because he was honest and forthright, he represented his people as best he could, and he pursued his goals by democratic means. Certainly no one ever said Lévesque was unpatriotic just because he wanted to break up the country. No one in Canada says, "My country right or wrong." Canadians say, "My country, maybe" or "My country, if."

Even so, the late 1980s, as well as bringing us a constitutional crisis over the status of Québec, also produced the most passionate outburst of patriotism since the Second World War. This patriotism largely emerged in negative terms, specifically as anti-Americanism, but it is also true that the passion behind it was generated as a defense of Canada and its values.

The United States, of course, is perceived as the major external threat to Canadian independence, whether it recognizes itself in that role or not. The last time the United States and Canada actually went to war was in June 1812, the same month Napoleon attacked Russia. Britain, while conducting its war against Napoleon, had searched U.S. ships and partially blocked certain U.S. ports. In response, President James Madison attacked the British colonies to the north, which were still in the process of turning into Canada. The war eventually reached from the Atlantic provinces to what is now southwestern Ontario. Part of Toronto was burned, Montréal was attacked, and British troops defending Canada eventually penetrated as far south as Washington, D.C. After a peace treaty was negotiated in 1814, everyone's territory was returned and both sides claimed victory. They have done so ever since, and to this minute you can find quite different versions of the outcome given in the school textbooks used in Niagara Falls, New York, and, a hundred yards away, Niagara Falls, Ontario.

In the United States, save for a few border towns and some isolated university courses, Canada does not exist as a political and cultural entity: It is a source of evil weather, it is a large piece of geography, and for many it is a wonderful place for vacations. But neither the politics of Canada—which are entirely different from U.S. politics, being parliamentary—nor the culture of Canada, can even be glimpsed in the U.S. media or in U.S. education. The U.S. public was taken by surprise when the Free Trade Agreement (FTA) signed by the Reagan and Mulroney administrations in 1988 became the most important political issue in Canada in recent years. To some, the FTA seemed an entirely logical extension of a process that has been going on for more than half a century, the economic integration of North America. From the standpoint of the Mulroney government, the FTA was a way of ensuring markets for Canadian goods in the United States. But to a great many Canadians—including the Liberal Party, the New Democratic Party, and the majority of artists and intellectuals—the FTA looked like a way of allowing U.S. culture to swamp culture produced in this country.

It touched a national nerve—*the* national nerve, in fact—the fear of U.S. domination. As it turned out, Mulroney's forces rallied, the FTA was ratified, and so far Canada remains an independent country. But 1988 reminded everyone that Canadian feelings about the United States run deep. Canadians watch U.S. TV and movies, read U.S. magazines, enjoy U.S. baseball, eat at McDonald's, and yet believe in themselves as a separate nation with a history worth remembering and traditions worth preserving.

Of course, there are still those who say that "Canadian culture" is an oxymoron, that the country lacks anything but highly derivative forms of artistic expression. Arthur Erickson, who is often regarded as the best of Canadian architects, once said, "I am fortunate that I can stand in Canada, a country without a culture, and look at the world." Canadians, in other words, being culture-free as well as ideology-free, can glory in the spiritual mobility this gives them. In truth, they have been working for a long time on building a culture, or cultures, and with notable success.

French Canada has found it easier, in a way, because of the comparative isolation that language provides—Québec poetry, novels, plays, TV shows, and movies speak directly to their intended audience (and often to faraway audiences in France, as well) in a way that no other art can. In English-speaking Canada, on the other hand, the majority of culture—mass movies, TV, music, fiction—traditionally has been imported from the United States; in a sense, the Canadian audience for popular culture is an overflow basin for U.S. products.

This means that Canadians must fight for an audience in these fields; even when government-backed, our movies and TV shows rarely capture huge audiences. Canadian artists, for the most part, have shifted to the higher ground of painting, poetry, serious fiction, and nonfiction, and in these spheres have done well. Canada produces a good many artists who find mass audiences, but usually the audiences are found in the United States, and in the rest of the world via the United States. "America's Sweetheart" in silent movie days, Mary Pickford, was a Toronto girl, and Lorne Greene, the star of what for years was the most popular TV drama, "Bonanza," was from Ottawa. The man who created Superman and the woman who played the superhero's girlfriend in the movies, Margot Kidder, are both Canadians. The writer who dreamt up Rambo, the macho hero of the 1980s, is a professor from a small city in Ontario. Regularly, Canada sends a stream of stars and producers across the border—Michael J. Fox; Donald Sutherland in one generation and his son, Kiefer, in the next; the creators of SCTV and of "Saturday Night Live." In the United States these personalities are seen as near-natives, which in a sense they are, since most of them grew up watching U.S. TV. Quickly, the successful Canadians are lost in the great ocean of life in the United States, and only their fellow citizens back home remember that once they were considered part of "Canadian culture."

To outsiders, Canada must seem a paradox: the second-largest country in the world, thinly populated, rich in natural resources and arable land, next door to the best market on the planet—yet insecure, internally conflicted, and altogether uncertain about how to approach the future. We are a country with problems as large and as varied as our geography. And yet they are the problems of a lucky people, and of a people who, for the most part, understand how lucky they are to be born in Canada, or to end up here. I cherish a story that emerged from Ottawa in 1950, when the Chancellor of the Exchequer in Britain's Labour Government, Hugh Gaitskell, was visiting Canada. At that time, his opposite number in Canada, Finance Minister Douglas Abbott, was bedeviled by many problems typically Canadian, involving the sharing of tax revenues between the federal and provincial governments. Gaitskell's England, on the other hand, was still devastated by the Second World War bombing, everything from sugar to clothing was rationed, the British pound was the subject of laughter in the money markets of the world, and the Labour Government was widely regarded as a gigantic failure. When Gaitskell arrived in Ottawa, Abbott described the excruciating political problems of the Canadian federal system and then asked, "What would you do if you had my problems?"

Gaitskell looked at him for a moment. "Well," he said, "first thing, I'd get down on my knees and thank God."

Beyond Plain Vanilla: Immigration Has Accentuated Canada's Diversity

by Andrew H. Malcolm

Andrew H. Malcolm is the national affairs correspondent for The New York Times *and is author of several books, including* This Far and No More *and* Someday.

As the historical story goes, when Jacques Cartier, the French explorer, stepped ashore in 1535 at the rapids near what was to become Québec City, he confronted a band of curious natives. Looking around at the pristine countryside, he asked them in French and sign language what they called that place. The Indians, looking about their humble village, replied "kanata." It is the Huron-Iroquois word for "settlement."

Thus conceived in bilingual misunderstanding did the world's second-largest country get its name, Canada. There have been many such "kanatas" in Canada's history. The French-English split, highlighted by the failure of the Meech Lake accord, an attempt to draw Québec into accepting the country's eight-year-old constitution by acknowledging the French province as a "distinct society," is but the most dramatic.

Although from the outside its image is that of a vat of vanilla yogurt, Canada in fact has always consisted of many disparate pieces sprawling over a country so immense that its southernmost tip in Ontario is actually closer to the Equator than to the top of Canada.

This geography, harsh climate, different languages and divergent cultures often make that land seem less like a single nation and more like a conservative collection of feuding fiefdoms. Québec has its own vibrant culture and celebrities who are virtually unknown next door in Ontario and vice versa. Canada's politically under-represented West resents the economic dominance of central Canada, which is jealous of the West's oil and gas. Every region tells ethnic jokes about the residents of Newfoundland, Canada's newest province, where they refer to people from other provinces disparagingly as C.F.A.'s (Come From Aways).

Centrifugal forces are always at work in Canada, which was settled not by waves of immigrants moving inexorably from sea to sea, but by many ethnic groups recruited overseas to settle in particular places where the young country needed more people. Though efficient, this method did not create a population with a broad sense of the land. Canada's immigration laws help perpetuate these ethnic population pockets and identities by creating a special status called Landed Immigrant, which allows newcomers to become Canadian while keeping their old nationality.

Even native Canadians work to isolate themselves; the Indians and Inuit of the vast Northwest Territories plan to divide that 40% of Canada's geographic mass along racial lines into two pieces.

From the beginning, each segment looked out for its own. In 1867, under the threat of expansion by the United States, Britain finally persuaded Canada's disparate regions to become a single country. As the price of its assent, British Columbia insisted on a rail line to connect it with the rest of the vast new nation.

Even now, each group is striving to be heard. The required ratification of the Meech Lake accord by the 10 provincial legislatures was blocked not by an English- or French-speaker but by the filibuster of Elijah Harper, a Cree Indian in the Manitoba Legislative Assembly who wanted distinct recognition for native peoples.

Also awaiting special recognition were Canada's feminists, not to mention groups representing the mushrooming ranks of Canada's newer immigrants from Commonwealth lands in Africa, the Caribbean, Hong Kong, and East Asia. Today, nearly half the children in Vancouver's school system have English as a second language. The city of Toronto, Canada's largest, routinely sends out property tax notices in six languages—English, French, Chinese, Italian, Greek, and Portuguese.

But many Canadians now see a fraying of traditional civility into the kind of outspoken divisiveness that has characterized the mixed records of other bilingual countries. There has been vocal resentment in some areas over the impact of rich Chinese fleeing Hong Kong, bidding up Canadian real estate prices, and replacing traditional bungalows with mansions seen as ostentatious by neighbors. Shouting matches and racial slurs erupted in Calgary recently over a school board decision to allow teenage Sikh boys to wear their ceremonial daggers in school when other youths were not allowed even pocketknives. Earlier, the Federal Government decided that Sikhs who become Mounties can wear their turbans instead of the traditional trooper hat. Even though the number of such Sikhs may one day be counted on one hand, it was the kind of "foreign" symbol that now arouses some Canadians to raise their voices.

Québec has always taken the lead in separatist actions. The province's move in late 1988, in open defiance of a Supreme Court decision, to outlaw any outdoor English signs while continuing to demand special protections for French-speakers offended even many liberal Canadians elsewhere. It seemed to violate the unwritten agreement that Québec's minority English community would be protected. As one result, nearly 100 communities outside the province passed resolutions declaring themselves English only, a meaningless move since few had many French residents anyway.

Then there are the political divisions. Newfoundland, the other stumbling block to Meech Lake's ratification, is governed by Premier Clyde Wells, a close confidante of Pierre Elliott Trudeau, the former Liberal prime minister who has long opposed the accord.

Jean Chrétien, the newly elected leader of the opposition Liberals, calls Canada's current mood "a growing distemper."

"The world," he warns, "has known other serene communities that have come apart from internal tensions."

There is evidence, too, that while the specter of Québec's separation struck terror into the hearts of most Canadians before the defeat of a provincial referendum on the issue 10 years ago, the prospect of Canada and Québec falling out of love now draws fatalistic shrugs.

"It is," Peter C. Newman, an author and nationalist, said sadly, "as if Québec is growing out of Canada and the rest of the country says, 'Enough already with your constant demands for special this and special that.' "

The political price of all this unrest is likely to be steep for Prime Minister Brian Mulroney. He treated the high-pressure, high-stakes Meech Lake talks like the former labor negotiator he is, relying on last-minute concessions that did not come. And the three-year Meech Lake process allowed too much time for an initial consensus to erode. Mr. Newman likened it to 10 co-workers who agree to lunch together and then schedule an hour's debate on where to go.

"Nothing in life is unanimous," he said, "especially in Canada."

3 Toronto

Introduction

by Allan Gould

Author of a dozen books, including The Toronto Book *and* The New Entrepreneurs: 80 Canadian Success Stories, *Allan Gould has also written for many Canadian magazines and written and performed political satire and biographical sketches for radio and TV.*

A joke popular in the neighboring province of Québec between the wars went "First prize, one week in Toronto. Second prize, two weeks in Toronto. Third prize, three weeks in Toronto." And who could blame them for laughing? Toronto was a deadly city, right into the 1950s, at which time its half-million citizens used to rush off to Detroit (a four-hour drive to the southwest) and Buffalo (90 minutes to the south, around Lake Ontario) for a good time. Today, of course, the rushing is in the opposite direction.

What on earth could have happened in so short a period? And why was no one surprised (in Toronto, at least) when various participants at the 1982 International Conference on Urban Design, in Toronto, ran around spouting such superlatives as "This is the most livable city in North America" and "It is an example of how a city could grow."

Much of Toronto's excitement is explained by its ethnic diversity. Nearly two-thirds of the 3.2 million people who now live in the metropolitan Toronto area were born and raised somewhere else. And that somewhere else was often very far away. What this has meant to Toronto is the rather rapid creation of a vibrant mix of cultures that has echoes of turn-of-the-century New York City—but without the slums, crowding, disease, and tensions.

Still, to give to its burgeoning ethnic population all, or even most, of the credit for Toronto's becoming a cosmopolitan, world-class city in just a few decades would be a kind of reverse racism, and not totally correct, either. Much of the thanks must be given to the so-called dour Scots who set up the banks, built the churches, and created the kind of solid base for community that would come to such a healthy fruition in the three decades following World War II. Toronto is clearly this country's center of culture, commerce, and communications—"New York run by the Swiss," according to Peter Ustinov's marvelously witty description of the place.

Toronto has gained the nickname of "Hollywood North," because literally dozens of major films have been made in this city, especially over the past decade, from *The Black Stallion* to *Three Men and a Baby* and from David Cronenberg's *Dead Ringers* to such TV series as *Degrassi Junior High, Night Heat,* and many more. Indeed, it is hard to walk about the city nowadays without tripping over a movie crew and a number of famous people. A story is still told about one particular film made in the downtown area in 1987. Since it was a crime movie set in New York City, street signs had to be put up and several tons of garbage trucked in and spread around the city street. After filming all morning, the cast took a lunch break. When they returned barely an hour later, all the garbage had been cleaned up!

That's Toronto, in a nutshell: Clean. Safe. Orderly. Yet somehow dynamic and exciting. Groucho Marx sang an old vaudeville tune back in 1967 that went "It's better to run to Toronta/ Than to stay in a place you don't wanta." And he was right. But nearly a quarter-century later, we can honestly change the words to "It's best that you run to Toronta/There's no better place that you'd wanta."

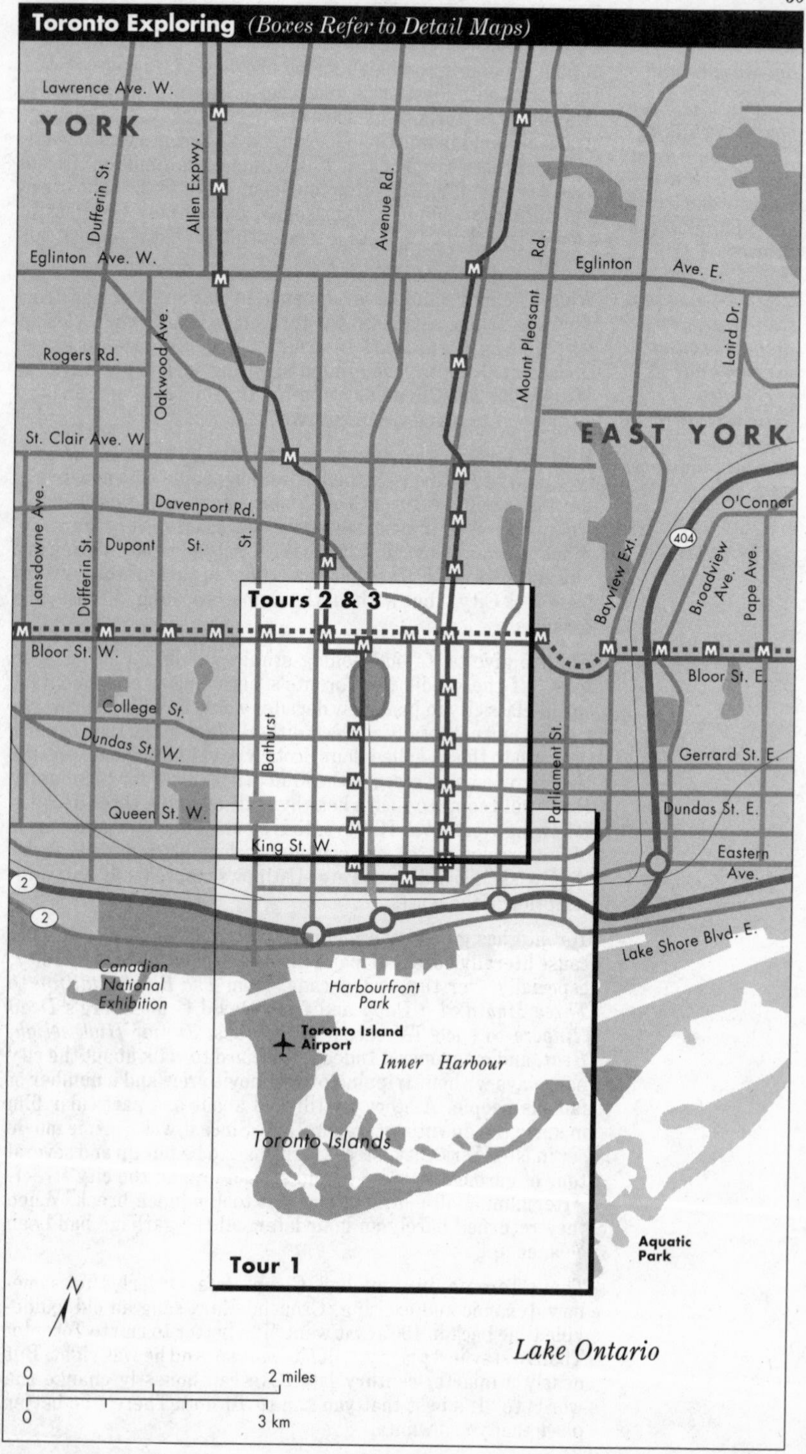
Toronto Exploring (Boxes Refer to Detail Maps)
Lawrence Ave. W.
YORK
Dufferin St.
Allen Expwy.
Avenue Rd.
Eglinton Ave. W.
Rd.
Eglinton Ave. E.
Mount Pleasant
Laird Dr.
Oakwood Ave.
Rogers Rd.
St. Clair Ave. W.
EAST YORK
Davenport Rd.
O'Connor
404
Lansdowne Ave.
Dufferin St.
Dupont St.
St.
Bayview Ext.
Broadview Ave.
Pape Ave.
Tours 2 & 3
Bloor St. W.
Bloor St. E.
College St.
Dundas St. W.
Bathurst
Parliament St.
Gerrard St. E.
Queen St. W.
Dundas St. E.
King St. W.
Eastern Ave.
2
2
Lake Shore Blvd. E.
Canadian National Exhibition
Harbourfront Park
Toronto Island Airport
Inner Harbour
Toronto Islands
Aquatic Park
Tour 1
N
Lake Ontario
0
2 miles
0
3 km

Essential Information

Arriving and Departing by Plane

Airports and Airlines

With a handful of exceptions—such as planes from Montreal, Ottawa, Buffalo, and Newark that land at Toronto's tiny **Island Airport**—flights into Toronto land at the **Lester B. Pearson International Airport,** so named in 1984 to honor Canada's Nobel Peace Prize–winning prime minister of a quarter-century ago. It's commonly called "the Toronto airport" or "Malton" (after the once-small town where it was built, just northwest of the city), but it's just as often called "impossible," since its terminals are inadequate for the number of travelers who use it. Waits for bags are often lengthy—although the free carts are a human touch—and Pearson can be dreadfully overcrowded, both coming and going. Terminal 1, which opened in 1964 to handle 3 million passengers, handled over *10 million* in 1989. The sorely needed Terminal 3 opened in late 1990 after many delays, and it is the only airline terminal in the world to ban smoking (with a few exceptions, such as in pubs).

There are three types of flights to Toronto: nonstop—no changes, no stops; direct—no changes but one or more stops; and connecting—two or more planes, two or more stops.

Toronto is served by **American** (tel. 800/433–7300), **Delta** (tel. 800/843–9378), **Eastern** (tel. 800/327–8376), **Midway** (tel. 800/621–5760), **Northwest** (tel. 800/225–2525), **United** (tel. 800/241–6522), **U.S. Air** (tel. 800/428–4322), **Air Canada** (tel. 800/422–6232), and **Canadian Airlines International** (tel. 800/387–2737).

City Express (tel. 416/360–4444 or 800/387–3060; 212/752–1160 in the New York City area) has inexpensive flights every day between Newark, New Jersey and the Toronto Island Airport, which is barely five minutes from the city's downtown area. In contrast, Toronto's major airport, Pearson International, is a half-hour drive from downtown; of course, it's a longer trip during rush hours. The catch? City Express's planes are Dash 7s and 8s, which are wonderfully reliable but still rather small and propeller-driven, with often limited luggage space.

Between the Airport and Center City

Although Pearson is not far from the downtown area (about 32 kilometers, or 18 miles), the drive can take well over an hour during Toronto's weekday rush hours (7–9 AM and 3:30–6:30 PM). Taxis and limos to a hotel or attraction near the lake can cost $30 or more. Many airport and downtown hotels offer free buses to their locations from each of Toronto's three terminals. Travelers on a budget should consider the express coaches offered by **Grey Coach** (tel. 416/393–7911), which link the airport to three subway stops in the southwest and north-central areas of the city. Buses depart several times each hour, from 8 AM to 11:30 PM. Fares average $6. Even better is the service to and from several downtown hotels, which operates every 20 minutes from 6 AM to midnight daily and costs approximately $9.

Should you be renting a car at the airport, be sure to ask for a street map of the city. Highway 427 runs south, some 3.6 miles to the lakeshore. Here you pick up the Queen Elizabeth Way (QEW) east to the Gardiner Expressway, which runs east into the heart of downtown. If you take the QEW *west*, you'll find yourself swinging around Lake Ontario, toward Hamilton, Niagra-on-the-Lake, and Niagara Falls.

Arriving and Departing by Train, Bus, and Car

By Train **Amtrak** (tel. 800/872–7245) runs a daily train to Toronto from Chicago (a 10-hour trip), and another from New York City (11 hours). From Union Station you can walk underground to many hotels—a real boon in inclement weather.

By Bus **Greyhound** (no 800 number; check with local information) and **Grey Coach** (tel. 416/393–7911) both have regular bus service into Toronto from all over the United States. From Detroit, the trip takes five hours; from Buffalo, two to three hours; from Chicago and New York City, 11 hours. Buses arrive at 610 Bay Street, just above Dundas Street.

By Car Drivers should have proper owner registration and proof of insurance coverage. There is no need for an international driver's license; any valid one will do.

Drivers may be asked several questions at the border crossing, none of them terribly personal or offensive: your place of birth; your citizenship; your expected length of stay. Beyond that, border guards will rarely go. Expect a slight wait at major border crossings. Every fourth or fifth car may be searched, and this can increase the wait at peak visiting times to 30 minutes.

The wonderfully wide Highway 401—it reaches up to 16 lanes as it slashes across Metro Toronto from the airport on the west almost as far as the zoo on the east—is the major link between Windsor, Ontario (and Detroit), and Montreal, Quebec. It's also known as the Macdonald-Cartier Freeway but is really never called anything other than "401." There are no tolls anywhere along it, but you should be warned: Between 6:30 and 9:30 each weekday morning and from 3:30 to 6:30 each afternoon, the 401 can become dreadfully crowded, even stop-and-go. Plan your trips to avoid these rush hours.

Those who are driving from Buffalo, New York, or Niagara Falls should take the Queen Elizabeth Way (fondly called the QEW or Queen E), which curves up along the western shore of Lake Ontario and eventually turns into the Gardiner Expressway, which flows right into the downtown core.

Yonge Street, which divides the west side of Toronto from the east (much like Manhattan's Fifth Avenue and Detroit's Woodward), begins at the Lakefront. Yonge Street is called Highway 11 once you get north of Toronto, and continues all the way to the Ontario-Minnesota border, at Rainy River. At 1,896.2 km (1,178.3 mi), it is the longest street in the world (as noted in the *Guinness Book of World Records)*.

From New York City 851 km (532 mi); from Washington, DC, 899 km (562 mi); from Miami 2,741 km (1,713 mi); from Montreal 558 km (349 mi); from Detroit 378 km (236 mi); from Chicago 854 km (534 mi); from St. Louis 1,310 km (1,023 mi); from Denver 2,485 km (1,553 mi); from Los Angeles 4,384 km (2,740 mi).

Getting Around

Most of Toronto is laid out on a grid pattern. The key street to remember is Yonge Street (pronounced "young"), which is the main north–south artery. Most major cross streets are numbered east and west of Yonge Street. In other words, if you are looking for 180 St. Clair Avenue West, you want a building a few blocks *west* of Yonge Street; 75 Queen Street East is a block or so *east* of Yonge Street.

At press time, the fare for buses, streetcars, and trolleys is $1.20. However, one can purchase eight adult tickets/tokens for $8, which lowers the price per journey a bit. All fares will undoubtedly rise at least a nickel during the first week of 1991; they invariably do. Two-fare tickets are available for $2.25. Visitors who plan to stay in Toronto for more than a month should consider the **Metropass,** a photo-identity card that costs $53 for adults, $34.50 for senior citizens. (And, yes, probably a few dollars more than that, as of January 1991.)

Families should take advantage of the savings of the so-called **Day Pass.** It costs $5 and is good for unlimited travel for one person, Monday–Saturday after 9:30 AM, and all day Saturday. On Sunday and holidays, it's good for up to 6 persons (maximum 2 adults), for unlimited travel. For information on how to take public transit to any street or attraction in the city call 416/393–INFO from 7 AM to 11:30 PM.

A very useful **Ride Guide** is published by the Toronto Transit Commission each year. It shows nearly every major place of interest in the city and how to reach it by public transit. These guides are available in most subways and many other places around the city.

The subways stop at 2 AM, but the Toronto Transit Commission runs bus service from 1–5:30 AM on most major streets, including King, Queen, College, Bloor, Yonge, and as far north as Sheppard, Finch, and Steeles.

By Subway There is little argument that the Toronto Transit Commission runs one of the safest, cleanest, most trustworthy systems of its kind anywhere. (It keeps winning international awards, which must mean something.) There are two major subway lines, with 60 stations along the way: the **Bloor/Danforth Line,** which crosses Toronto about three miles north of the Lakefront, from east to west, and the **Yonge/University/Spadina Line,** which loops north and south, like a giant "U," with the bottom of the "U" at Union Station. Tokens and tickets are sold in each subway station and at hundreds of convenience stores along the many routes of the TTC. Get your transfers just after you pay your fare and enter the subway; you'll find them in machines on your way down to the trains.

By Bus All buses and streetcars accept exact change, tickets, or tokens. Paper transfers are free; pick one up at the time that you pay your fare.

By Taxi The meter begins at $2, and includes the first 210 meters. Each additional 210 meters is 20¢—as is each additional passenger in excess of four. The waiting time "while under engagement" is 20¢ for every 35 seconds—and in one of our horrible traffic jams, this could add up. Still, it's possible to take a cab across downtown Toronto for little more than $5. The largest companies are **Beck** (tel. 416/467–0067), **Co-op** (tel. 416/364–8161), **Diamond** (tel. 416/366–6868), and **Metro** (tel. 416/363–5611).

By Car Seatbelt use is mandatory in the province of Ontario; unlike the response in the United States, where this is often seen as an infringement on one's right to die, the vast majority of Canadians welcomed this governmental move some years ago. The law applies to everyone in the car, and hefty fines have been known to be given. And that means infants as well; holding one upon the lap is as illegal as it is risky.

Pedestrian crosswalks are sprinkled throughout the city; they are marked clearly by overhead signs and very large painted Xs. All a pedestrian has to do is stick out a hand, and cars screech to a halt in both directions. And they must do it, too. Naturally, if you happen to be the pedestrian, don't be foolish; wait until the traffic acknowledges you, and begins to stop, before venturing into the crosswalk. You'll be amazed at your power.

Right turns on red lights are nearly always permitted, except where otherwise posted. You must come to a complete stop before making the turn.

Important Addresses and Numbers

Tourist Information The **Metropolitan Toronto Convention & Visitors Association** has its office at Queen's Quay Terminal (207 Queen's Quay W, Suite 509, M5J LA7, tel. 416/368–9821). Booths providing brochures and pamphlets about the city and its attractions, as well as accommodations, are set up in the summer outside the Eaton Centre, on Yonge Street just below Dundas Street, and outside the Royal Ontario Museum.

The **Traveller's Aid Society** is not just for the down-and-out. This is a nonprofit group whose 130 volunteers can recommend restaurants and hotels, and distribute subway maps, tourist publications, and Ontario sales tax rebate forms. *In Union Station, the socity is located in Room B23, on the basement level; tel. 416/366–7788. Open daily 9 AM–9 PM. In Terminal I at Toronto's Pearson International Airport, the society has its booth on the Arrivals Level, directly across from the exit, just past Customs, near Area B; tel. 416/676–2868. Open daily 9 AM–10 PM. In Terminal II, the booth is located between International and Domestic Arrivals, on the Arrivals Level; tel. 416/676–2860. Open daily 9 AM-10 PM.* (The location and phone at new Terminal III was unavailable at press time.)

Embassies The **Consulate General of the United States** (360 University Ave., just north of Queen St., M56 1S4, tel. 416/595–1700).

The **Consulate General of Britain** (777 Bay St., at the corner of College St., M56 2G2, tel. 416/593–1267).

For all other consulates—there are dozens of countries represented in Toronto—look up "Consulate Generals" in the white pages of the phone book.

Emergencies Dial 911 for **police** and **ambulance.**

Doctors and Dentists. Check the Yellow Pages or ask at your hotel desk. Also, call *Dial-a-Doctor* (tel. 416/492–4713), or the *Dental Emergency Service* (tel. 416/924–8041).

24-Hour Pharmacies. *Pharma Plus Drugmart* (Church St. and Wellesley Ave., about a mile from New City Hall, tel. 416/924–7760). *Luciff Place*, 700 Bay and Gerrard (tel. 416/979–2424). *Shoppers Drug Mart* (2500 Hurontario St., Mississauga, near the airport, tel. 416/277–3665).

24-Hour Pet Emergency Service. *Veterinary Emergency Clinic,* 201 Sheppard Ave. E, about a half-mile east of Yonge St., and a few blocks north of Highway 401, tel. 416/226–3663.

Road Emergencies. The *CAA* (the Canadian version of AAA) has 24-hour road service (tel. 416/966–3000).

24-Hour Gas Stations and Auto Repairs. *Texaco Stations,* at 153 Dundas St. W, behind New City Hall, near Bay St.; 333 Davenport, just south of Casa Loma; and 601 Eglington Ave. E, west of the Ontario Science Center. *Cross Town Service Center,* 1467 Bathurst St., at the corner of St. Clair Ave. W, is well-known and respected for both gas and repairs. *Jim McCormack Esso,* 2901 Sheppard Ave. E, in the Scarborough area, heading toward the Metro Zoo. *Guido's Esso,* 1104 Albion Rd., not far from the airport.

Poison Information Center. *The Hospital for Sick Children* (tel. 416/598–5900) or for the hearing-impaired (tel. 416/597–0215).

Guided Tours

Orientation

Toronto Harbour and Islands Boat Tours are provided by **Gray Line** (tel. 416/364–2412) on attractive, sleek, Amsterdam-style touring boats, with competent tour guides. The hourly tour visits the Toronto Islands, with lovely views of the Toronto cityscape. Boats leave from the Queen's Quay Terminal daily from late April through mid-October noon–5. Tours leave as late as 8:15 PM over the summer. Other boats depart from the Harbour Castle Westin. Prices are $8.95 adults, $6.95 senior citizens and students, $4.95 children ages 4–12.

Toronto Tours (tel. 416/869–1372 or 416/868–0400) also provides one-hour boat tours of the Toronto harborfront for similar prices from mid-May through October. They also run an informative 90-minute tour aboard a restored 1920s trolley car; it goes by both city halls, and through the financial district and the historic St. Lawrence area (*see* Special-interest Tours and Tour Groups, above).

Insight Planners (tel. 416/868–6565) has been providing creative and reliable tours, particularly to art galleries, since 1974.

Reception Ontario (tel. 416/636–0082) provides complete tour-planning services, including sightseeing tours, entertainment packages, hotel accommodations, and even guides in various languages.

Happy Day Tours (tel. 416/593–6220) runs half-day tours of Toronto for about $30 per person, which include admission to Black Creek Pioneer Village and visits to the mansions of Forest Hills, Casa Loma, Chinatown, Queen's Park, Yorkville, and Harbourfront. Book ahead.

Gray Line Sightseeing Bus Tours (tel. 416/393–7911) leave from the Bus Terminal (Bay and Dundas Sts.) and spend 2½ hours visiting such places as Eaton Centre, both city halls, Queen's Park, the University of Toronto, Yorkville, Ontario Place, and Casa Loma—the latter, for a full hour. Costs run about $16 for adults, $11 for children under 12.

Special-interest **Antours** (tel. 416/481–2862) provides several tours of Niagara-on-the-Lake, which include lunch and major performances at the Shaw Festival.

Art Tours of Toronto (tel. 416/845–4044) offers a series of fall and spring gallery and walking tours. Most tours include lunch, and range from $40 to $50 per person.

The **Toronto Stock Exchange** (tel. 416/947–4676) has tours of its exciting new facilities weekdays at 2 PM.

The **Bruce Trail Association** (tel. 416/690–4453) arranges day and overnight hikes around Toronto and environs.

Mysteriously Yours . . . should be of special interest to murder-mystery buffs. On Thursday, Friday, and Saturday evenings, a "despicable crime" is perpetrated at the Royal York Hotel. The mystery begins to unravel over cocktails at 6:30 and is solved after dinner, by 10. The complete dinner and mystery costs $50–$60 per person, including tax and tip. Call Brian Caws at 416/767–8687 or 800/NOT–DEAD.

Exploring Toronto

Orientation

Well, now you're in Toronto, and probably in the downtown area. It's rather confusing, isn't it? We're not talking Avenue A, B, and C here, or 33rd, 34th, and 35th streets, either, so already we're on somewhat shaky ground.

But once you establish that Lake Ontario runs along the south of the city, and that the fabulous Harbourfront complex is there, as well as the ferry to the lovely Toronto Islands, you are well on your way to orienting yourself.

It's a shame to turn your back on our now-blossoming waterfront but when you do, you meet the striking, often magnificent high-rise buildings that give Toronto so much of its skyline. Banks, banks, and banks: Yes, the church may have stood the highest and proudest in most Western towns since medieval times, but today it is the god Mammon who towers over what was once called (both mockingly and with reverence) Toronto the Good. (May we remind you that there were no movies shown on Sundays until the late 1950s and no Sunday newspapers until the late 1970s.)

Every one of the major banks of Canada, which are far wealthier and more powerful than most of their U.S. counterparts, has its headquarters in downtown Toronto, between University Avenue and Yonge Street.

This edifice complex first expressed itself in the black 54-story tower of the **Toronto-Dominion Bank** (T-D Centre), designed by the justly admired German-American architect Mies van der Rohe. There are four towers there now, eclipsed by I.M. Pei's silver and mirrorlike **Bank of Commerce** building, right across the street.

Only a few years later—and only a few feet away—came the **Bank of Montreal**'s tower, covered with handsome marble and now holder of the title "Tallest Building in the Whole British Commonwealth." In the end, Toronto's most stunning bank building would be not the tallest but the most extraordinary: the **Royal Bank Building,** designed by the very gifted Torontonian Boris Zerafa. Born in Cairo to parents of Italian and English descent—which is late 20th-century Toronto in a nutshell—Zerafa is also the designer of Toronto's Richmond-Adelaide Centre and the **Bank of Nova Scotia,** which opened in 1989.

The new **Scotiabank Tower** looks like another winner, but it would be hard to beat the Royal Bank for sheer beauty. Its golden exterior, coated with fully 2,500 ounces of real gold (purchased when it was only $100 an ounce) in order to keep the heat in and the cold out (or vice versa, depending on the season), truly defines the skyline of Toronto. It's "a palette of color and texture as well as mass," in Zerafa's own words; "it has a cathedral feeling, due to natural light." It is certainly worth a visit.

After seeing all the bank buildings, the next best place to get a sense of orientation would be, without doubt, the **CN Tower.** One local wag suggested that the 180-story, 130,000-ton structure was built to teach Canadian men humility. Perhaps. But for all its basic ugliness, the CN Tower is the ideal place to get a sense of the layout of Toronto. The food here is terrible, but those of you who enjoy an overpriced drink now and then should make a reservation and head up the tower any clear day between noon and five.

Back on terra firma, imagine the downtown area of Toronto as a large rectangle. The southern part is, as you already know, Lake Ontario. The western part, shooting north to Bloor Street and beyond, is Spadina Road, near the foot of which stands the CN Tower, Harbourfront, and the spectacular new SkyDome Stadium. On the east, running from the lakefront north for hundreds of miles (believe it or not), is Yonge Street, which divides the city in half. University Avenue, a major road that parallels Yonge Street, for some reason changes its name to Avenue Road at the corner of Bloor Street, next to the Royal Ontario Museum. A further note: College Street, legitimately named since many of the University of Toronto's buildings run along it, becomes Carlton Street where it intersects Yonge Street, then heads east.

Tour 1: Waterfront, the Financial District, and the Underground City

Numbers in the margin correspond with points of interest on the Tour 1 map.

Since, as we noted, Toronto has a waterfront as its southernmost border, it seems logical that we begin there. And it shouldn't be too hard to get there, since it's just south of Union Station, which is the terminus of both the University Avenue/Spadina Avenue and Yonge Street subways. Until quite recently, Toronto was notoriously negligent about its waterfront. The Gardiner Expressway, Lakeshore Boulevard, and a network of rusty rail yards stood as hideous barriers to the natural beauty of Lake Ontario.

Just over a decade ago the various levels of government—city, Metro, provincial (Ontario), and federal (Ottawa)—began a struggle to change this unfortunate situation. By that time, most of the area just south of the Gardiner Expressway and Lakeshore Boulevard was overflowing with grain silos, various warehouses, and unattractive (and unsweet-smelling) towers of malt, used by local breweries.

Part of the answer was the building of a very handsome hotel, the Harbour Castle Westin and an attractive tower of condominiums. The hotel has an exterior, glassed-in elevator that offers guests a view of the waterfront and the Toronto Islands.

Toronto Islands
❶

Just behind the giant Harbour Castle Westin is the debarkation point for ferries to the **Toronto Islands,** surely one of the highlights of any trip to the city—especially from May to October. It takes only eight minutes for the quaint little ferries to chug across the tiny bay. The islands make up one of the world's great parks.

The four thin, curved, tree-lined islands—Centre, Ward's, Algonquin, and Hanlan's Point—have been attracting visitors since 1833, four years before Victoria became queen and just a year before the town of York changed its name to Toronto. And the more than 550 acres of parkland are irresistible, especially during the hot summer months.

The beaches on Ward's tend to be the least crowded. They're also the cleanest, although there have been problems with the cleanliness of Lake Ontario's water over the past decade. Except for the hottest days in August, the Great Lake tends to be uncomfortably chilly, so bring appropriate clothing. You'll be wise to rent a bike for an hour or more and work your way across the interconnected islands.

If you are traveling with children, Centre Island is certainly the one to check out first. Signs everywhere read "Please Walk on the Grass," which should charm visitors to pieces, even before they begin to explore. A few hundred yards from the ferry docks lies **Centreville,** an amusement park that's supposed to be a turn-of-the-century children's village. The concept works wondrously well: True, the pizza, fries, and hot dogs are barely edible—pack a lunch!!—but on the little Main Street there are charming shops, a town hall, a little railroad station, and more than a dozen rides, including a restored 1890s merry-go-round with more than four dozen hand-carved animals. And there's no entrance fee to the modest, 14-acre amusement park, although you'll have to pay a nominal charge for each ride or buy an all-day pass. Perhaps most enjoyable for children is the free **Far Enough Farm,** which is near enough to walk to. It has all kinds of animals to pet and feed, ranging from piglets to geese, cows to birds. *Tel. 416/363–1112. Centreville is open 10:30–8 weekends only Apr. 30–May 15; daily Victoria Day (mid-May)–Labor Day; weekends again Sept. 10–25.*

All transportation on these islands comes to you compliments of your feet: No cars are allowed anywhere. Your nostrils will wonder at the lack of exhaust fumes, while your feet will wonder why you walked all the way along the boardwalk from Centre to Ward's Island (2½ kilometers, or 1½ miles).

There you'll find **Gibraltar Lighthouse,** built back in 1808, making it the oldest monument in the city that is still standing on its original site. Right next to it is a pond stocked with rainbow trout, and a concession for buying bait and renting rods.

Sandy beaches circle the islands, the best ones being those on the southeast tip of Ward's, the southernmost edge of Centre, and the west side of Hanlan's. There are free changing rooms near each of these areas, but no facilities for checking your clothes. Swimming in the various lagoons and channels is prohibited. The winter can be bitter cold on the island, but snowshoeing and cross-country skiing, with downtown Toronto over your shoulder, will be irresistible to many. In the summer, there are rowboat and canoe rentals, tennis courts, gardens, playgrounds, and a wildlife sanctuary.

The ferries run irregularly during the winter: every half-hour or so until 10 or 11 AM, and then every few hours thereafter. In the summer, the ferries leave three times an hour at the foot of Bay Street. The cost is $2 adults, 75¢ senior citizens, 35¢ children. For a recording giving the schedule and prices, call 416/392–8193; for other information, call 416/392–8186.

Harbourfront
❷

Back at the ferry docks on the mainland, your next move should be to **Harbourfront.** This is a trip that is well worth planning for—check *Now* and *Toronto Life* magazines, as well as daily newspaper listings, to see what concerts, dances, art shows, festivals, etc., are taking place there, and build your visit around them.

For many years, as we said, Toronto had good reason to be ashamed of its God-given, man-taken-away waterfront. Today, Harbourfront has become a 100-acre culture and recreation center, drawing more than 3 million visitors each year. Stretching from just west of the Harbour Castle Westin for nearly a mile to Bathurst Street, the complex has become the scene of fabulous entertainment, exquisite buildings, glorious attractions—a true match for San Francisco's Pier 39 and Baltimore's Inner Harbor.

Highlights are many. The **Queen's Quay** (pronounced "key") **Terminal** is a must: The 57-year-old food warehouse was transformed in 1983, at a cost of more than $60 million, into a magnificent eight-story structure with delightful specialty shops, eateries, and the handsome 450-seat Premiere Dance Theatre.

Contemporary art exhibits of painting and sculpture, architecture and video, photography and design, now take place at the **Power Plant,** just west of Queen's Quay. (The building started in 1927 as a power station for an ice-making plant; you can spot it by the tall red smokestack.)

York Quay Centre has concerts, live theater, readings, even skilled artisans at work in open craft studios. A shallow pond at the south end is used for canoe lessons in warmer months, and as the largest artificial ice-skating rink in North America in more wintry times. The Nautical Centre nearby has many private firms offering lessons in sailing and canoeing, and vessels for rent.

On **Maple Leaf Quay,** the very popular **Antique Market** takes place every day but Monday. The 70 dealers triple in number each Sunday.

Harbourfront is within walking distance of Union Station. Drivers should head for the foot of Bay Street or Spadina Avenue, and park in one of the many lots. For information, call 416/364–5665.

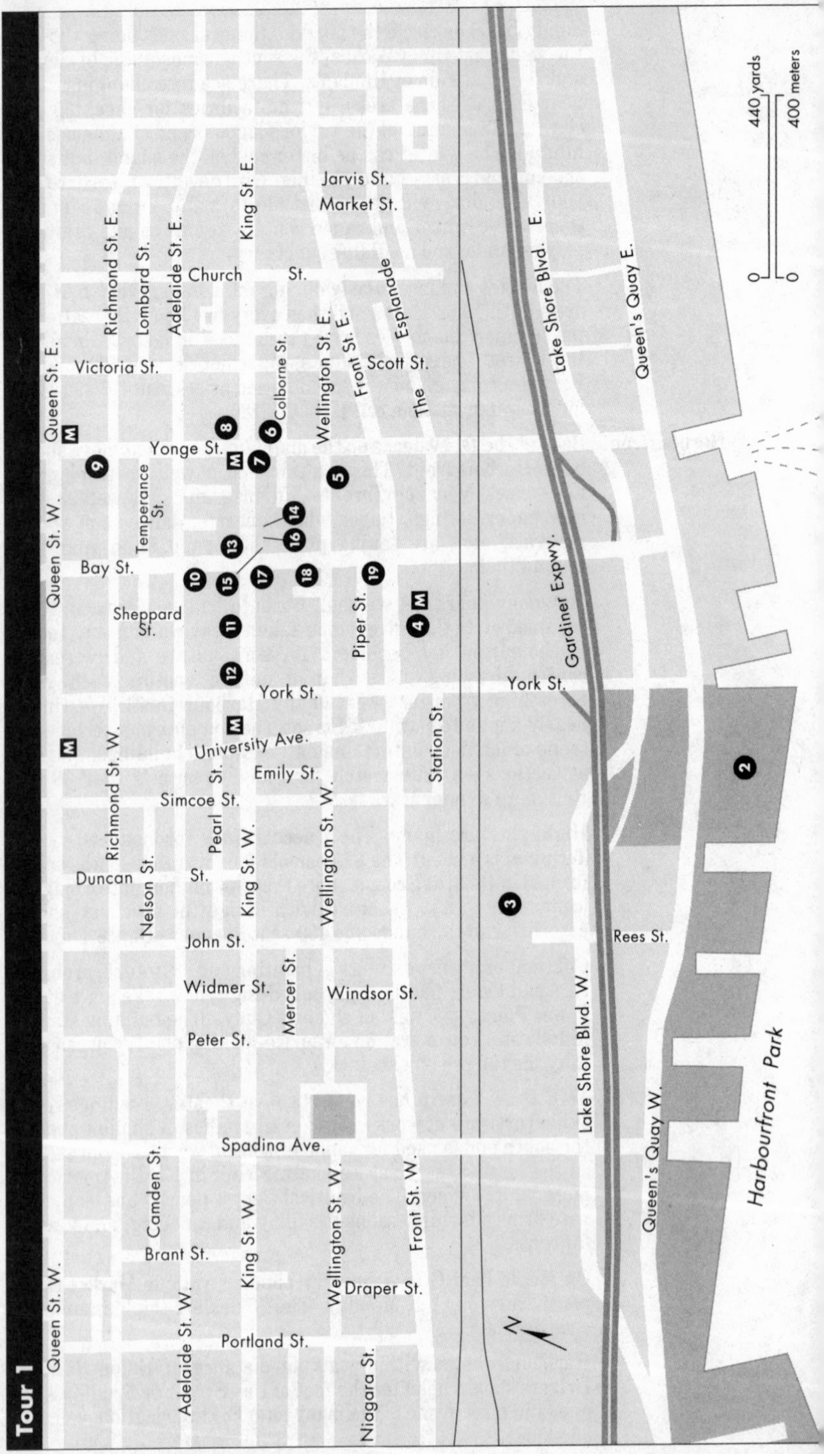
Tour 1
Queen St. W.
Queen St. E.
Richmond St. E.
Lombard St.
Adelaide St. E.
King St. E.
Jarvis St.
Market St.
Church St.
Victoria St.
Colborne St.
Wellington St. E.
Front St. E.
Esplanade
The
Scott St.
Yonge St.
Temperance St.
Bay St.
Sheppard St.
Piper St.
York St.
University Ave.
Richmond St. W.
Pearl St.
Simcoe St.
Emily St.
Station St.
Duncan St.
Nelson St.
King St. W.
Wellington St. W.
John St.
Widmer St.
Mercer St.
Windsor St.
Peter St.
Spadina Ave.
Camden St.
Brant St.
Adelaide St. W.
Portland St.
Draper St.
Niagara St.
Front St. W.
Lake Shore Blvd. E.
Lake Shore Blvd. W.
Gardiner Expwy.
Queen's Quay E.
Queen's Quay W.
Rees St.
Harbourfront Park
440 yards
400 meters
0
N
M

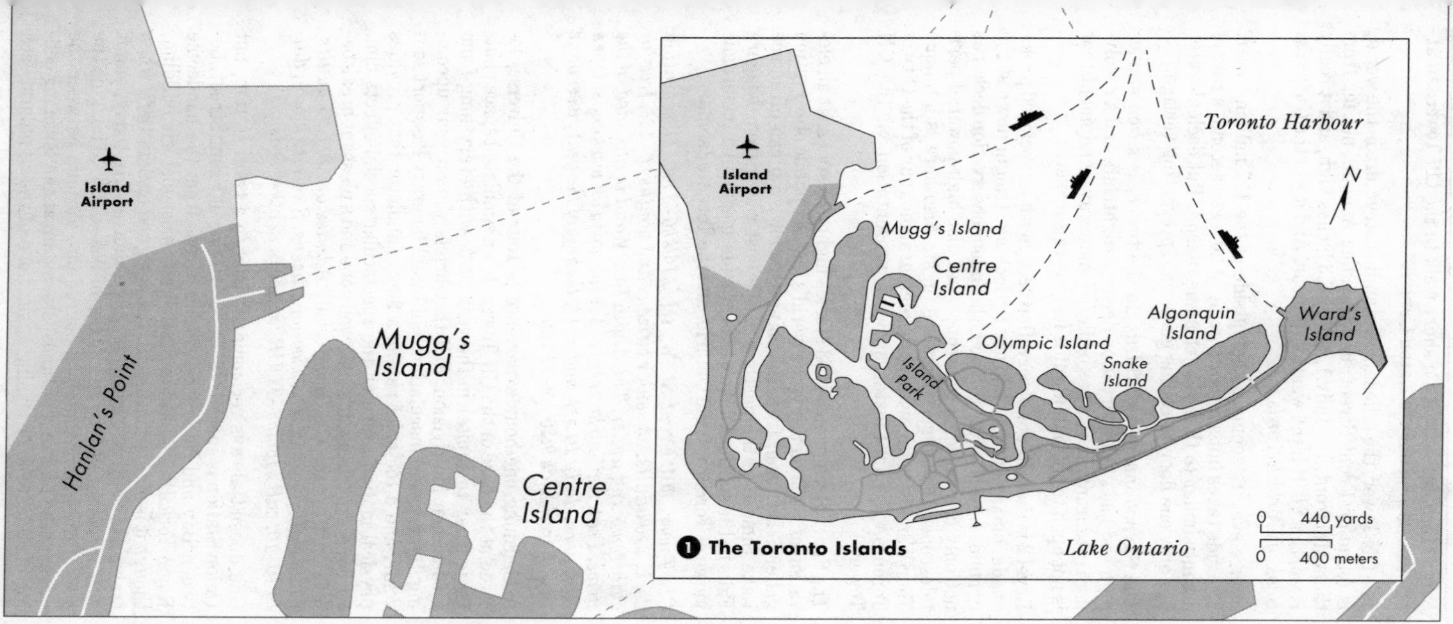

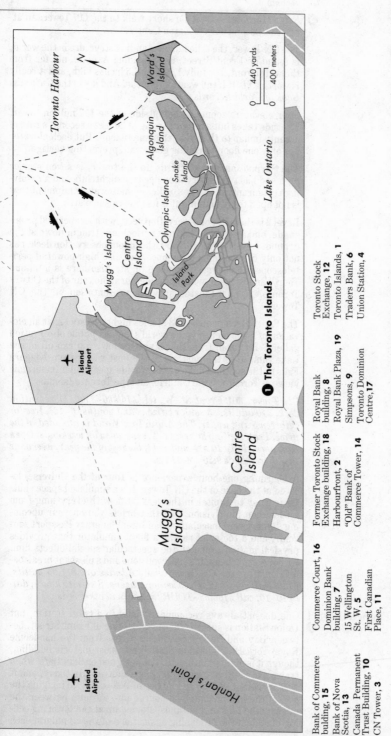

Bank of Commerce building, **15**
Bank of Nova Scotia, **13**
Canada Permanent Trust Building, **10**
CN Tower, **3**
Commerce Court, **16**
Dominion Bank building, **7**
15 Wellington St. W, **5**
First Canadian Place, **11**
Former Toronto Stock Exchange building, **18**
Harbourfront, **2**
"Old" Bank of Commerce Tower, **14**
Royal Bank building, **8**
Royal Bank Plaza, **19**
Simpsons, **9**
Toronto Dominion Centre,**17**
Toronto Stock Exchange, **12**
Toronto Islands, **1**
Traders Bank, **6**
Union Station, **4**

3 From Harbourfront, it's a short walk to the **CN Tower**, an attraction second only to Eaton Centre.

The CN Tower, the tallest free-standing structure in the world, is found on Front Street, near Spadina Avenue, not far from the waterfront. It's fully 1,815 feet, 5 inches high, and it really is worth a visit, if the weather is clear. And it's in the *Guinness Book of World Records.*

Four elevators zoom up the outside of the $57-million tower. The ride takes but a minute, going at 20 feet a second, a rate of ascent similar to that of a jet-plane takeoff. But each elevator has only one floor-to-ceiling glass wall, preventing vertigo.

The **Skypod**, about two-thirds up the tower, is seven stories high and has two observation decks, a nightclub, and a revolving restaurant. It also has oodles of microwave equipment that is not open to the public but is its true raison d'être.

Level 2 is the **outdoor observation deck,** with an enclosed promenade, and an outdoor balcony for looking straight down at the ground. Level 3 of the Skypod, the **indoor observation deck,** has not only conventional telescopes, but also high-powered peritelescopes that almost simulate flight. Also here is a unique Tour Wand System, which provides an audio tour of the City of Toronto. A mini-theater shows a presentation on the CN Tower.

The **Space Deck,** which is 33 stories higher, costs $2; at an elevation of 1,465 feet, it is the world's highest public observation gallery. But even from the Skypod below, you can often see Lake Simcoe to the north, and the mist rising from Niagara Falls to the south. All the decks provide spectacular panoramic views of Toronto, Lake Ontario, and the Toronto Islands.

CN Tower, 301 Front St. W, tel. 416/360–8500. Observation deck: $10 adults, $3 senior citizens and youths (6–16), free for children 5 and under. The Audio Tour Wand is included in the price. Peak visiting hours: 11–4, especially on weekends. Open summers, daily 10 AM–midnight; the rest of the year, weekdays 10–10, weekends 9:30 AM–11 PM.

A charming one-hour experience is **Tour of the Universe,** located at the base of the CN Tower. It's a simulated space shuttle journey to Jupiter in the year 2019, with everything from a 64-screen Multivision Wall that briefs you on your upcoming flight, laser "inoculation," an InterPlanetary Passport souvenir, and a too-brief ride in a flight simulator that provides physical motion to match the spectacular special-effects film. Although not cheap, it's very well done and a pleasant break before or after the CN Tower visit. *Admission: $11.95 adults, $5.95 children 3–12, $7.95 senior citizens. Summer hours, daily 10–10; call 416/363–TOUR for hours in other seasons.*

Financial District

One doesn't always recommend visits to a train station, but
4 **Union Station** is special. On the south side of Front Street, between Bay and York streets (and across from the handsome Royal York Hotel), Union Station is a most historic building, though it is of this century. It was designed back in 1907, when trains were still as exciting as space shuttles are today, and it was opened in 1927 by the Prince of Wales. Try to imagine the awe of the immigrants who poured into Toronto between the wars by the tens of thousands, staring up at the towering ceiling of Italian tile or leaning against one of the 22 pillars, each

one 40 feet tall and weighing 75 tons. Walk along the lengthy concourse and study the mellow reflection in its walls. Get a sense of the beauty of the light flooding through the high, arched windows at each end of the mammoth hall.

When you look up, you almost expect to see a rose window; instead, you can read the names of the towns and cities of Canada that were served by the two railroads that used Union Station when it first opened. Many of those places are no longer served by trains, which take too long in a world that now seems to travel at the speed of light. That the remarkable structure still remains is no thanks to the many local politicians of the 1970s who wanted it torn down. But once again, Torontonians rallied, petitioned, and won the day.

As you come out of Union Station, walk back to Yonge Street and the beautiful **Bank of Montreal** building, at the northwest corner of Front Street. Just steps north of it is a shabby row of shops, which are among the oldest surviving commercial buildings in the city. Many of the original Georgian facades have been drastically altered, but the one- and two-story buildings give you a sense of the scale of buildings from the 1850s and are the last remnants of the early business community of the then–brand-new city of Toronto.

5 Make a left turn at the first intersection, which is Wellington Street West. **Number 15** is the oldest building on this walk, an elegant stone bank designed in the Greek Revival style.

6 Head back a few steps to Yonge Street and go north again, away from Front Street. On the northeast corner of Yonge and Melinda streets, at 67 Yonge Street, is **Traders Bank,** the first "skyscraper" of the city when it went up in 1905–06, complete with an observation deck. The next building to the north (69 Yonge St.) was built in 1913, and it helped turn the intersection into a grouping of the tallest buildings in North America, outside of Manhattan. After more than 75 years, it is still owned by **Canadian Pacific,** the largest private employer in Canada (planes, trains, hotels, and more).

7 Just across the street, at the southwest corner of King and Yonge streets, is the **Dominion Bank building** (1 King St. W), erected in 1913 by the same architects who designed the voluptuous Bank of Montreal building we saw at Yonge and Front streets. It's a classic Chicago-style skyscraper and is well worth a visit inside. Climb the marble and bronze stairway to the opulent banking hall on the second floor, and enjoy the marble floor, marble walls, and the ornate plaster ceiling, which features the coats of arms of the then nine Canadian provinces.

8 On the northeast corner of Yonge and King streets (2 King St. E) is the original **Royal Bank building,** also put up in 1913. Note the distinctive cornice, the overhanging roof, the decorative pattern of sculpted ox skulls above the ground-floor windows, and the classically detailed leaves at the top of the Corinthian columns.

9 Walking several blocks farther north along Yonge Street, you reach the original **Simpsons** department store, on the northwest corner of Richmond Street West and Yonge Street (176 Yonge St.). Built in 1895, it was one of the city's first buildings with a steel-frame construction. There are attractive terra-cotta decorations in the section closest to Yonge Street, which

went up in 1908; the part along Richmond Street, near Bay Street, added in 1928, is a fine example of the Art Deco style, popular between the two world wars.

Continue a few steps west to Bay Street, a name synonymous with finance and power in Canada, as Wall Street is in the United States. Head south (left), back toward the lakefront. Just south of Adelaide Street, on the west side of Bay Street, is
10 the **Canada Permanent Trust Building** (320 Bay St.). Built in the very year of the stock market crash (and we don't mean the 1987 one), it's a skyscraper in the New York wedding-cake style. Look up at the ornate stone carvings both on the lower stories and on the top, where carved, stylized faces peer down to the street below. Walk through the imposing vaulted entrance, with its polished brass doors, and note that even the elevator doors in the foyer are embossed brass. The spacious banking hall has a vaulted ceiling, marble walls and pillars, and a marble floor with mosaic borders.

Turn right (west) along King Street, and you arrive at the first of the towering bank buildings that have defined Toronto's sky-
11 line over the past two decades. This is **First Canadian Place** (100 King St. W), built in the early 1970s. Its 72 stories were deliberately faced with white marble to contrast with the black of the Toronto-Dominion Centre, to the south, and with the silver of the Commerce Court Tower.

The second phase of the project, opened in 1983, houses the ul-
12 tramodern **Toronto Stock Exchange (TSE).** The Exchange Tower (2 First Canadian Pl.) has a Visitor's Center, where visitors can learn about the securities industry through colorful displays, or even join in daily presentations. The attractions are many: a 100-foot public gallery, a 140-seat auditorium, recorded tours, and a mini slide show of the TSE 300 Composite Index (an echo of the Dow Jones Average). *Tel. 416/947–4670. Admission free. Open weekdays 9:30–4. Public tour daily at 2.*

On the northeast corner of King and Bay streets (44 King St.
13 W) is the **Bank of Nova Scotia.** Built between 1949 and 1951, and partially replaced by the recently completed Scotia Tower just to the east, it has sculptural panels inspired by Greek mythology above the large, exterior windows. In the lobby, there are reliefs symbolizing four regions of Canada and a brightly colored gilded plaster ceiling. The original stainless steel and glass stairway with marine motifs is attractive, as are the marble counters and floors. The north wall relief depicts some of the industries and enterprises financed by the bank.

14 On the southeast corner of King and Bay streets is the **"Old" Bank of Commerce Tower,** which for a third of a century was the tallest building in the British Commonwealth. Its base has bas-relief carvings, and marvelous animal and floral ornamentation around the vaulted entrance. Because the top is set back, you must look up to see the huge, carved human heads on all four sides of the building.

15 The **Bank of Commerce building** (25 King St. W) was built in the two years following the stock market crash of 1929, but the hard times didn't prevent the creation of a stunning interior of marble floors, limestone walls, and bronze vestibule doors decorated with masks, owls, and animals. In the alcoves on each side of the entrance are murals that trace the history of transportation. The bronze elevator doors are richly decorated, the

vaulted banking hall is lit by period chandeliers, and each desk has its own lamp.

16 Just south of the "old tower," at 243 Bay Street, is **Commerce Court,** the bank's 57-story stainless-steel sister. And due west, just across Bay Street, also on the south side of King Street,
17 are the two black towers of the **Toronto-Dominion Centre,** the first International Style skyscrapers built in Toronto, thanks to the "less is more" man, Mies van der Rohe. The two towers went up in the mid-1960s, and they are starkly plain and stripped of ornament. The only decoration consists of geometric repetition and the only extravagance is the use of rich materials, such as marble counters and leather-covered furniture.

Immediately south of the T-D Centre towers, at 232 Bay
18 Street, is the **former Toronto Stock Exchange building,** which, for close to half a century, was the financial hub of Toronto. Built in 1937 of polished pink granite and smooth buff limestone, it's a delightful example of Art Deco design. The stainless-steel doors are a wonder, as is the wise and witty stone frieze carved above them. Don't miss the hilarious social commentary up there—the banker with the top hat marching behind the laborer, his hand sneaking into the worker's pocket.

Walk south another block, still heading toward Lake Ontario, to the northwest corner of Bay and Front streets: There, in all
19 its golden glory, is the **Royal Bank Plaza,** built only in 1976 but already a classic of its kind. Be sure to go into the 120-foot-high banking hall and admire the lovely hanging sculpture by Jesus Raphael Soto.

Underground City

The origins of Toronto's **Underground City**—purportedly the largest pedestrian walkway in the world, and more than four times the size of Montréal's, the world's second largest—go back over a generation, and it somehow all came about with very little assistance from the powers that be. As each major new building went up, the respective developers kept agreeing to interconnect their underground shopping areas, until it finally all came together. One can walk—and shop, eat, browse, etc.—without ever seeing the light of day, from beneath Union Station to the Royal York Hotel, the Toronto-Dominion Centre, First Canadian Place, the Sheraton Centre, Simpsons, the Eaton Centre, and the Atrium. Altogether, it extends through nearly three miles of tunnels and seven subway stops.

The Underground City has been called a must-see for visitors, but that's debatable; Toronto is so overflowing with attractions and first-class shopping that it's hard to recommend that one rush "downstairs." And, indeed, there are numerous other, but far smaller, underground retail passageways: beneath Bloor Street, running east of Yonge Street, and along College Street, between Yonge and Bay streets. And there are offshoots of the Underground City reaching all the way to the New City Hall and beyond. Enter the subterranean community from anywhere between Dundas Street on the north and Union Station on the south, and you'll encounter everything from art exhibitions to buskers (the city actually auditions young musicians and licenses the best to perform throughout its subway system and elsewhere) to walkways, fountains, and trees growing as much as two stories high. Because up to 50% of the complex lies underneath Toronto's multibillion-dollar Financial

District, you will keep bumping into men and women in business suits, browsing or on lunch breaks.

So don't see this so much as a walking tour but rather as a very pleasant option to escape sun, rain, snow, or heat. It's just another example of Toronto's architectural ingenuity—making a city that occasionally lacks a livable climate more livable.

Tour 2: From Eaton Centre to the City Halls and the Far and Middle East

Numbers in the margin correspond with points of interest on the Tours 2 and 3 map.

From the corners of Yonge and Queen streets, one can begin a tour that will include several of this city's most popular attractions, as well as some of its most interesting neighborhoods. Alas, one of these, Eaton Centre, is closed on Sunday, as of this writing, while others thrive on what is still considered the Lord's Day in the province of Ontario. Still, the following walking/driving tour should make for a very pleasant day in the central and western portions of Toronto's downtown.

Eaton Centre and City Hall

20 **Eaton Centre,** a 3-million-square-foot building that extends along the west side of Yonge Street all the way from Queen Street up to Dundas Street (with subway stops at each end), has quickly become the number-one tourist attraction of Toronto. Even people who rank shopping with the flu will still be charmed, even dazzled, for this is a very beautiful environment indeed. From its graceful glass roof, arching 127 feet above the lowest of the mall levels, to Michael Snow's exquisite flock of fiberglass Canada geese floating poetically in the open space of the Galleria, to the glass-enclosed elevators, porthole windows, and nearly two dozen long and graceful escalators, there are plenty of good reasons for visiting Eaton Centre.

Galleria Level 1 contains two food courts; popularly priced fashions; photo, electronics, and record stores; and much "convenience" merchandise. Level 2 is directed to the middle-income shopper, while Level 3, suitably, has the highest elevation, fashion, and prices. **Eaton's,** one of Canada's classic department-store chains, has a nine-floor branch here. At the southern end of Level 3 is a skywalk that connects the Centre to the seven-floor **Simpsons** department store across Queen Street.

Dozens of restaurants, from snack to full-service, can be found here. A 17-theater cinema complex—the initial unit of the now worldwide Cineplex chain—is located at the Dundas Street entrance. *Eaton Centre open weekdays 10–9, Sat. 9:30–6.*

Exit the Eaton Centre at Queen Street and walk just one long block west to Toronto's city halls. Yes, the plural is correct.

21 **Old City Hall** is the very beautiful building at the northeast corner of Queen and Bay streets, sweetly coexisting with the fu-
22 turistic **New City Hall,** just across the street, on the west side. The creator of the old one, which opened in 1899, was none other than E.J. Lennox, who would later design Casa Loma. It was considered one of North America's most impressive municipal halls in its heyday, and since the opening of its younger sister, it has been the site for the provincial courts, county offices, and thousands of low-cost marriages. Do note the hideous gar-

goyles above the front steps, which were apparently the architect's witty way of mocking certain politicians of the time. The great stained-glass window as you enter is attractive, and the handsome old structure stands in delightful contrast to its daring and unique sibling.

The New City Hall—humorously described by many as "a urinal for the Jolly Green Giant"—was the result of a massive international competition in 1958. The winning presentation by Finnish architect Viljo Revell was very controversial: two towers of differing height, and curved, yet! But there was and is a logic to it all: An aerial view of the New City Hall shows a circular council chamber sitting like an eye between the two tower "eyelids." Within months of its opening in 1965, the New City Hall became a symbol of a thriving city, with a silhouette as recognizable as, say, the Eiffel Tower.

Annual events at the New City Hall include the Spring Flower Show in late March; the Toronto Outdoor Art Exhibition early each July (the 29th annual one will be in the summer of 1990), and the Cavalcade of Lights from late November through Christmas each year, when more than 100,000 sparkling lights are illuminated across both city halls.

Tel. 416/392–7341 for details; for information on facilities for the disabled, 416/392–7732. Underground garage for 2,400 cars. Open to the public weekdays 8:30–4:30. Free 30-minute guided tours on weekdays. Cafeteria in the basement of the New City Hall open daily 7:30–4.

Chinatown and the Museums

Just north of the New City Hall begins Toronto's main **Chinatown,** which is the largest in all of North America. There are more than 100,000 Chinese living in the city, which is not bad, considering that just over a century ago there was only one—Sam Ching, who ran a hand laundry on Adelaide Street. Today, Chinatown covers much of the area of Spadina Avenue from Queen Street to College Street, running along Dundas Street nearly as far east as Bay Street.

One of the best times to explore Chinatown is on a Sunday, when, up and down Spadina Avenue and along Dundas Street, Chinese music blasts from storefronts, cash registers ring, abacuses clack, and bakeries, markets, herbalists, and restaurants do their best business of the week.

But whatever day you wander, we recommend that you start on Elizabeth Street, just north of the New City Hall, and walk north to Dundas Street, east toward Bay Street, and west to Spadina Avenue. You will be thrilled by the diversity, the excitement, the liveliness—the sheer foreignness of it all.

23 The **Shing Wah Daily News,** on Hagerman Street, near Bay Street, due north of the New City Hall (tel. 416/977–3745) will show you some of the 10,000 Chinese characters being typeset and printed, plus samples of Blondie and Dagwood speaking
24 Cantonese. **Mon Kuo Trading Co. Ltd.** (120 Elizabeth St., also just north of New City Hall) cultivates tens of thousands of bean sprouts under a sprinkler system in the basement, on their one-week growth to maturity.

On Dundas Street, you'll pass shops selling reasonably priced silk blouses and antique porcelain, silk kimonos for less than half the price elsewhere, lovely saki sets, and ladies' suits made
25 from silk. Huge Chinese characters hang over the **52nd Division**

Tour 2
Art Gallery of Ontario, **28**
Eaton Centre, **20**
52nd Division Police Station, **25**
Kensington Market, **29**
Mon Kuo, **24**
New City Hall, **22**
Old City Hall, **21**
Ontario College of Art, **26**
Shing Wah Daily News, **23**
Village by the Grange, **27**

Tour 3
Bloor and Yorkville, **44**
Campbell House, **30**
Colonnade, **45**
George R. Gardiner Museum of Ceramic Art, **41**
Hart House, **32**
Hazelton Lanes, **47**
Knox College, **34**
McLaughlin Planetarium, **42**
Medical Sciences Bulding, **35**
Metropolitan Toronto Library, **46**
Ontario Legislative Bulding, **38**
Parliament Bulding, **39**
Public and Community Relations Office, **36**
Queen's Park, **37**
Royal Ontario Museum, **40**
University College, **33**
University of Toronto, **31**
Sigmund Samuel Canadiana Collection, **43**

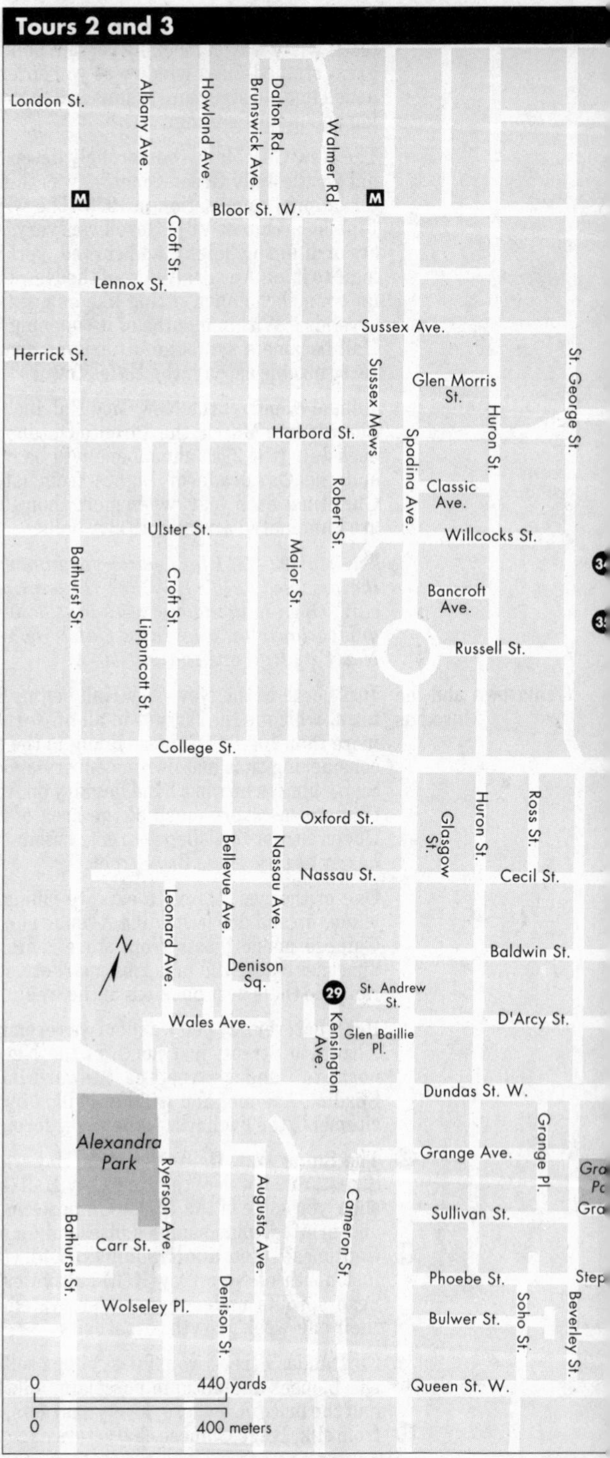

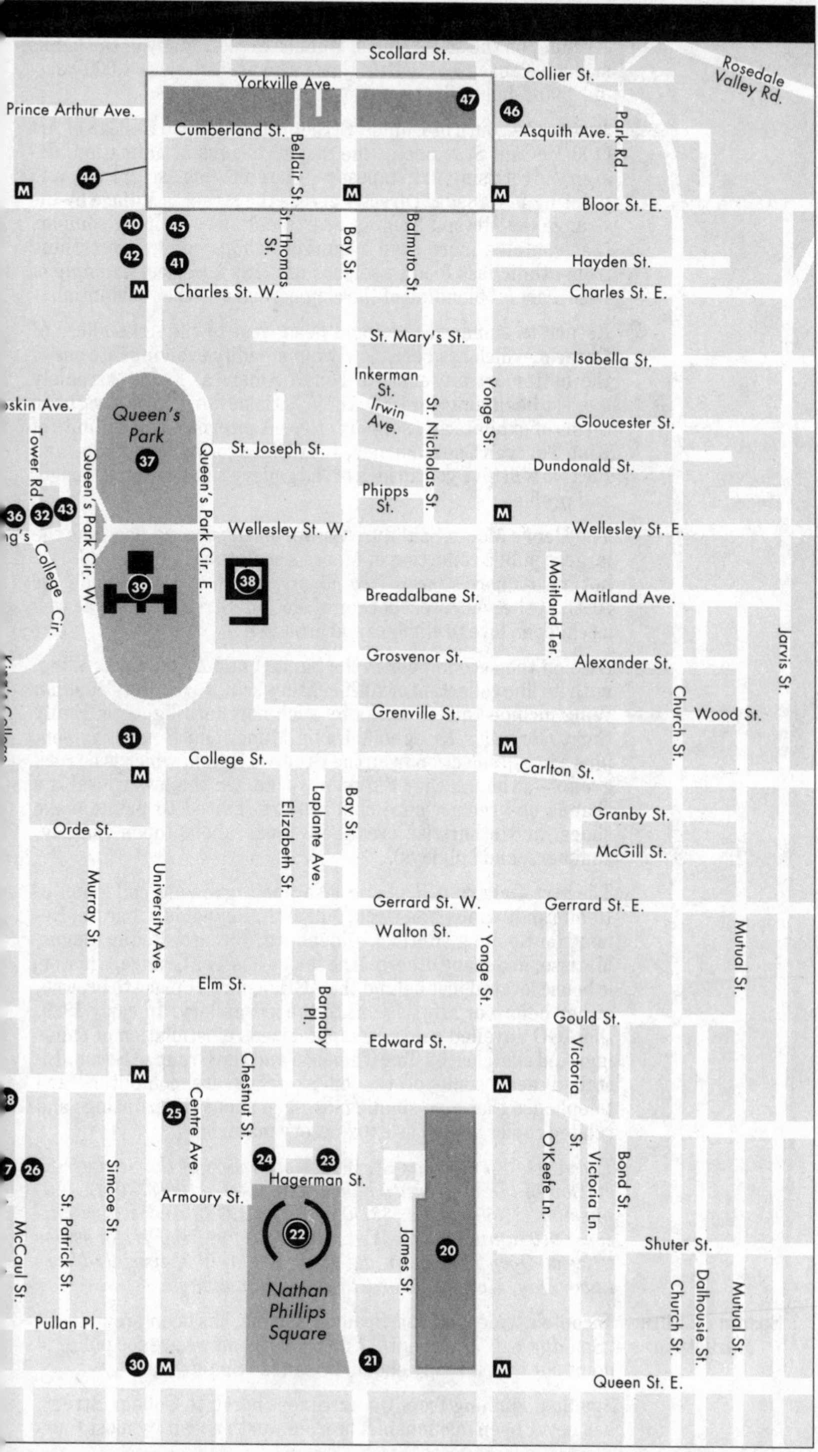
Scollard St.
Collier St.
Rosedale Valley Rd.
Yorkville Ave.
Prince Arthur Ave.
Cumberland St.
Asquith Ave.
Park Rd.
Bellair St.
Bloor St. E.
St. Thomas St.
Bay St.
Balmuto St.
Hayden St.
Charles St. W.
Charles St. E.
St. Mary's St.
Isabella St.
Inkerman St.
Irwin Ave.
St. Nicholas St.
Yonge St.
Gloucester St.
Queen's Park
Tower Rd.
Queen's Park Cir. W.
Queen's Park Cir. E.
St. Joseph St.
Dundonald St.
Phipps St.
Wellesley St. W.
Wellesley St. E.
College Cir.
Breadalbane St.
Maitland Ter.
Maitland Ave.
Grosvenor St.
Alexander St.
Jarvis St.
Church St.
Grenville St.
Wood St.
College St.
Carlton St.
Orde St.
Laplante Ave.
Elizabeth St.
Granby St.
McGill St.
Murray St.
University Ave.
Gerrard St. W.
Gerrard St. E.
Walton St.
Mutual St.
Elm St.
Barnaby Pl.
Gould St.
Edward St.
Victoria St.
Chestnut St.
Centre Ave.
O'Keefe Ln.
Victoria Ln.
Bond St.
Simcoe St.
Hagerman St.
Armoury St.
St. Patrick St.
McCaul St.
James St.
Nathan Phillips Square
Shuter St.
Dalhousie St.
Pullan Pl.
Queen St. E.

police station, a large building on the west side of University Avenue, on the south side of Dundas Street. Many of the banks still have abacuses, to help those who prefer to use 4,000-year-old "hand-held calculators" over the modern ones.

26 Just to the south of Dundas Street is the **Ontario College of Art** (100 McCaul St.), one of the major colleges of animation, design, advertising art, tapestry, glassblowing, sculpture, and
27 painting in Canada. Directly across the street is **Village by the Grange** (89 McCaul St.), an apartment and shopping complex that contains more than a hundred shops selling everything from ethnic fast food to serious art. It's a perfect example of wise, careful blending of the commercial and the residential.

28 Return to Dundas Street and head west to the **Art Gallery of Ontario,** which has been slowly but steadily evolving into one of the better art museums in North America. From extremely modest beginnings in 1900, the AGO is now in the big league in terms of exhibits and support. Recent international exhibits of King Tut, van Gogh, Turner, Judy Chicago, William Blake, and Picasso will give you an idea of the gallery's importance, image, and profile.

The **Henry Moore Sculpture Centre** on the second floor has the largest public collection of Moore's sculpture in the world. (Do not miss Moore's large *Two Forms,* which stands outside the AGO, at the southwest corner of McCaul Street. Adults as well as children love to climb in and around it.)

Also on the second floor is the **Samuel and Ayala Zacks Wing,** with its fine collection of 20th-century sculpture. The **Canadian Wing** includes major works by such northern lights as Emily Carr, Cornelius Krieghoff, David Milne, and Homer Watson, plus a broad selection from the Group of Seven, which is no rock group—although they *did* paint rocks. On the lower level is a "hands on" room where children are invited to paint, make slides, and otherwise creatively muck about (open Sunday, summers, and holidays).

The Art Gallery of Ontario also has a growing collection of Rembrandt, Hals, Van Dyck, Hogarth, Reynolds, Chardin, Renoir, de Kooning, Rothko, Oldenburg, Picasso, Rodin, Degas, Matisse, and many others. And it also has **The Grange,** a historic house located just behind the AGO, a perfect place to browse, either before or after a visit to the art gallery. In early 1989, the AGO unveiled a new, computerized reinstallation of paintings and sketches by Tom Thomson and the Group of Seven. Installed near some of the oil sketches are computers and telephones that give simple messages about the paintings and related topics as well as explanatory material.

The AGO, 317 Dundas St. W, 3 blocks west of the St. Patrick station of the University subway line; tel. 416/977–0414. Admission: $4.50 adults, $2.50 children 12–18 and senior citizens, $10 families. Free Wed. after 5:30 PM; free Fri. for senior citizens. Open Tues.–Sun. 11–5:30, Wed. until 9; also late-May–Labor Day, Mon. 11–5:30. Closed major holidays.

Spadina and the Marketplaces

Toronto's widest street, **Spadina Avenue,** has been pronounced "Spa-*dye*-nah" for a century and a half, and we are too polite to point out that it really should be called "Spa-*dee*-na."

Spadina, running from Queen Street north to College Street, has never been fashionable, or even worth a visit by most tourists. Way back, it was just a collection of inexpensive stores, factories that sold to you wholesale if you had connections, ethnic food and fruit stores, and eateries that gave you your 2¢ worth, usually plain.

And so it remains, with the exception of some often first-class, if modest-looking, Chinese restaurants sprinkled throughout the area. Each new wave of immigrants—Jewish, Chinese, Portuguese, East and West Indian, South American—added its own flavor to the mix, but Spadina-Kensington's basic bill of fare is still "bargains galore." Here you'll find gourmet cheeses at gourmet prices, fresh (no, not fresh-frozen) ocean fish, fine European kitchenware at half the price of that in stores in the Yorkville area, yards of remnants piled high in bins, designer clothes minus the labels, and the occasional rock-and-roll night spot and interesting greasy spoon.

For any visitor who plans to be in Toronto for more than four or five days, a few hours exploring the ins and outs of the garment district could bring great pleasure—and even greater bargains. Park your car at the lot just west of Spadina Avenue on St. Andrew's Street (a long block north of Dundas Street), or take the College or Queen streetcar to Spadina Avenue.

29 **Kensington Market** is a delightful side tour off Spadina Avenue. Here, the bargains are of the more edible kind. All your senses will be titillated by this old, steamy, smelly, raucous, colorful, European-style marketplace. Come and explore, especially during warmer weather, when the goods pour out into the narrow streets: Russian rye breads, barrels of dill pickles, fresh fish on ice, mountains of cheese, bushels of ripe fruit, and crates of chickens and rabbits that will have your children both giggling and horrified. Jewish and Eastern European stores sit side by side with Portuguese, Caribbean, Latin American, and East Indian stores—with Vietnamese, Japanese, and Chinese establishments sprinkled throughout. Most shops are open every day except Sunday, from as early as 6 AM.

Afterward, you can rest in **Bellevue Square** (corner of Denison Square and Augusta Place), a lovely little park with shady trees, benches, and a wading pool and playground for children.

Tour 3: Academia, Culture, Commercialism, Crassness

Numbers in the margin correspond with points of interest on the Tours 2 and 3 map.

University Avenue, running from Front Street for about three miles north to Bloor Street, where it changes its name to Avenue Road and continues north, is one of Toronto's few mistakes. It's horribly boring, with hospital after office building after insurance company after office building. Yet it is still an interesting start for a healthy walk, because it does have lovely flower beds and fountains in a well-maintained strip along its middle. Still, you may wish to drive this part of the tour.

30 One highlight is **Campbell House** (northwest corner of Queen Street and University Avenue), the stately Georgian mansion of Sir William Campbell, the sixth chief justice of Upper Canada. Built in 1822 and tastefully restored with elegant 18th- and early-19th-century furniture, it is one of Toronto's most charming "living museums." Costumed hostesses will tell you about

the social life of the upper class. *Tel. 416/597–0227. Admission: $2 adults, $1.25 students and senior citizens. Guided tours available. Open Oct.–mid May, weekdays 9:30–12:30 and 2:30–4:30; summers, weekdays 9:30–12:30 and 2:30–4:30, weekends noon–4:30.*

31 College Street is the southern boundary of the **University of Toronto.** It goes back to 1827, when King George IV signed a charter for a "King's College in the Town of York, Capital of Upper Canada." The Church of England had control then, but by 1850 the college was proclaimed nondenominational, renamed the University of Toronto, and put under the control of the province. And then, in a spirit of good Christian competition, the Anglicans started Trinity College, the Methodists began Victoria, and the Roman Catholics begat St. Michael's; by the time the Presbyterians founded Knox College, the whole thing was almost out of hand.

But not really: The 17 schools and faculties are now united, and they welcome anyone who can pass the entrance exams and afford the tuition. The architecture is interesting, if uneven. We recommend a walking tour. Enter the campus just behind the Parliament buildings, where Wellesley Street ends. Go under the bridge, past the guardhouse (whose keeper will not let you pass if you are encased in an automobile), and turn right, around King's College Circle.

32 At the top of the circle is **Hart House,** a Gothic-style student center built during the teens of this century by the Masseys—the folks who brought us Massey-Ferguson farm equipment, Massey Hall, Vincent Massey (a governor-general of Canada), and Raymond Massey, the actor. It was once an all-male enclave; today, anyone may visit the Great Hall and the library, both self-conscious imitations of Oxford and Cambridge. Check out the dining hall for its amazing stained-glass windows as well as its food, which is cheap and rather good.

As you continue around King's College Circle, you'll see on
33 your right the Romanesque **University College,** built in 1859.
34 Next is **Knox College,** whose Scottish origins are evident in the bagpipe music that escapes from the building at odd hours. It's been training ministers since 1844, although the building went up only yesterday—1915.

35 You may well wish to tip your hat to the **Medical Sciences Building,** which is no beauty but is where, in 1921, Drs. Banting, Best, and others discovered the insulin that has saved the lives of tens of millions of diabetics around the world.

There is lots more to see and do around the main campus of the
36 University of Toronto. Visit the **Public and Community Relations Office** (Room 133S, 27 King's College Circle, tel. 416/978–2021), across the field from Hart House, and pick up free maps of the school grounds. Guided one-hour walking tours are held on summer weekdays, setting out from the map room of Hart House at 10:30, 12:30, and 2:30 (tel. 416/978–5000).

Back at College Street and University Avenue, you can see the Victorian structure of the Parliament buildings to the north, with Queen's Park just north of them.

Queen's Park

There are a number of meanings to **Queen's Park,** for the native
37 Torontonian as well as the visitor. The term can refer to a charming circular park just a few hundred yards southeast of

the Royal Ontario Museum (on University Avenue, just below Bloor Street). This is a grand place to rest your feet after a long day of shopping or visiting the Royal Ontario Museum. But
38 Queen's Park also refers to the **Ontario Legislative Building,** which is the home of the provincial parliament. The mammoth building was opened back in 1893, a century ago, and is really quite extraordinary, with its rectangular towers, triangular roofs, and circular and oval glass.

39 The **Parliament Building** itself looks grotesque to some, with its pink exterior and heavy, almost Romanesque quality. But a close look will show the beautifully complex detail carved in its stone, and on the inside there are huge, lovely halls that echo half a millennium of English architecture. The long hallways are hung with hundreds of oils by Canadian artists, most of which capture scenes of the province's natural beauty. Should you choose to take one of the frequent (and free) tours, you will see the chamber where the 130 elected representatives from across Ontario, called MPPs (Members of Provincial Parliament), meet on a regular basis. There are two heritage rooms—one each for the parliamentary histories of Great Britain and Ontario—filled with old newspapers, periodicals, and pictures. And the lobby holds a fine collection of minerals and rocks of the province.

On the lawn in front of the Parliament buildings, facing College Street, are many statues, including one of Queen Victoria and one of Canada's first prime minister, Sir John A. Macdonald.

Tel. 416/965-4028. Guided tours from mid-May to Labor Day, daily on the hour 9-4, weekends every half hour 9-11:30 and 1:30-4; frequent tours the rest of the year; also at 6:45 PM when evening sessions are held. Queen's Park can be reached via the University Ave. subway; get off at College St. and walk north 1 block. If you drive, there are parking lots in the area, and metered parking around Queen's Park Circle.

40 Just to the northwest of Queen's Park is the world-class **Royal Ontario Museum.** Once labeled "Canada's single greatest cultural asset" by the Canada Council, the museum floundered throughout much of its existence, which began in 1912 (the same day the *Titanic* sank). It never stopped collecting—always with brilliance—reaching over 6 million items altogether. But by the 1970s, the monstrous building had leaky roofs, no climate control, and little space to display its glorious treasures. Today, thanks to a major fund-raising effort that brought in $80 million, the museum has the space it needs, and when expansion is completed sometime in the 1990s, the ROM will be the second-largest museum in North America, after New York's Metropolitan Museum of Art.

What makes the ROM so unique is the fact that science, art, and archaeology exhibits are all under one roof. The **Dinosaur Collection** will stun children and adults alike. The **Evolution Gallery** has an ongoing audiovisual program on Darwin's theories of evolution. The **Roman Gallery** has the most extensive collection of Roman artifacts in Canada. And the **European Musical Instruments Gallery** has a revolutionary audio system and more than 1,200 instruments dating back to the late 16th century. The **Discovery Gallery** allows children (over age 6) to handle objects from the ROM's collections and to study them, using microscopes, ultraviolet light, and magnifying glasses.

The **Bat Cave,** opened in early 1988, contains 4,000 freeze-dried and artificial bats in a lifelike presentation. Piped-in narration directs visitors on a 15-minute walk through a dimly lit replica of an eight-foot-high limestone tunnel in Jamaica, filled with sounds of dripping water and bat squeaks. Yes, the dinosaurs and mummies have a new rival in popularity.

ROM: 110 Queens Park, tel. 416/586–5549. Admission: $5 adults; $3 children, students, and senior citizens; $12 maximum for a family. Free Tues. for senior citizens, after 4:30 Thurs. for the general public. Open daily 10–6 (Tues. and Thurs. until 8). Closed New Year's Day. Discovery Gallery open Sept.–June, weekdays noon–4, weekends and holidays 1–5; July–Aug., weekdays 11 AM. To get there, take the University subway to the Museum stop; parking is expensive.

41 The **George R. Gardiner Museum of Ceramic Art** has now merged with the ROM, meaning that it costs not a penny more to visit a magnificent $25-million collection of rare European ceramics. The collection features 17th-century English delftware and 18th-century yellow European porcelain. *Located across the street from the ROM, on the east side of University Ave., just south of Bloor St. Same hours as the ROM.*

42 Next door to the ROM, to its south, is the **McLaughlin Planetarium,** which attracts some 250,000 visitors a year. There are four new 45-minute star shows each year. Open since 1986 is the **Astrocentre,** which has hands-on exhibits, computer terminals designed for both adults and children, and an animated model of the star system. *Tel. 416/586–5736. Admission: $4.50 adults; $2.50 children, students, and senior citizens. Senior citizens free on Tues. A combined admission ticket is available to ROM and planetarium, should you plan to visit both on the same day. Open same hours as the ROM, plus evening hours for the star shows. Tel. 416/586–5751 for a taped description of the current night sky.*

A five-minute walk due south of the planetarium will bring you
43 to the **Sigmund Samuel Canadiana Collection,** which is also part of the ROM and may be seen at no extra charge. Here is where you can view early Canadian furnishings, glassware, silver, and six settings of furniture displayed in typical 18th- and 19th-century homes. *14 Queen's Park Crescent W, on the northwest corner of University Ave. and College St. Open Mon.–Sat. 10–5, Sun. 1–5.*

After so much culture, you may wish to enjoy one of the most
44 dynamic and expensive areas of Toronto—**Bloor and Yorkville.**

Some call it Toronto's Rodeo Drive; others call it Toronto's Fifth Avenue. One thing is certain: These blocks are packed with high-price stores specializing in designer clothes, furs, jewels, specialty shops, ritzy restaurants, and more.

45 **The Colonnade,** on the south side of Bloor Street, a few doors east of University Avenue, has recently undergone a $10-million face-lift. In addition to several levels of luxury residential apartments and private offices, it also has more than two floors of stores selling quality leather goods, perfumes, jewelry, and European apparel.

Along the south side of Bloor Street are such stores as **Zoe,** with haute couture designs; **Creed's,** for more than seven decades the place for the latest fashions in furs, accessories, sportswear, lingerie, and shoes; **The Bay** (at the northeast corner of Bloor and Yonge streets), a department store with elegant, high-fashion designer clothes for men and women; **Holt Renfrew**, possibly the most stunning store in Toronto, with marble, chrome, glass, and glittering fashions for both sexes; and **Eddie Bauer**, selling sturdily made and cleverly designed clothing, equipment, and accessories for all sports.

A block north of Bloor and Yonge streets is the magnificent
46 **Metropolitan Toronto Library.** Arranged around a tall and wide interior atrium, the library gives a fabulous sense of open space. It was designed by one of Canada's most admired architects, Raymond Moriyama, who also created the Ontario Science Centre. Browsers will appreciate that fully one-third of the more than 1.3 million books—spread across 28 miles of shelves—are open to the public. The many audio carrels have headphones, which you may use to listen to any one of more than 10,000 albums.

The **Arthur Conan Doyle Room** will be of special interest to Baker Street regulars. It houses the finest public collection of Holmesiana anywhere, with records, films, photos, books, manuscripts, and letters. *789 Yonge St., just steps north of Bloor St., tel. 416/393–7000. Open May–Sept., Mon.–Thurs. 9–9, Fri. 9–6, Sat. 9–5; Oct.–Apr., Sun. 1:30–5. To get an answer to any question, on any subject, tel. 416/393–7131.*

Back on the east side of Avenue Road, two blocks north of Bloor Street and two blocks west of the Metro Library, is a real don't-
47 miss shopping area—**Hazelton Lanes** (416/968–8600). Offering everything from Swiss chocolates to Hermès silks and Giorgio Armani's latest fashions, this is a wonderful, magical paean to capitalism. And in 1989 it doubled, in size and glory, with the addition of some 80 new stores.

Casa Loma (1 Austin Terr.; on Spadina Rd., just south of St. Clair Ave. W and the St. Clair Ave. subway stop) is an honest-to-goodness 20th-century castle, with 98 rooms; two towers; secret panels; long, creepy passageways; and some of the best views of Toronto—all just a short distance from the heart of the city. The medieval-style castle was built shortly before the Great War by Sir Henry Pellatt, a soldier and financier who spent more than $3 million to construct his dream. Today, it's owned by the city of Toronto and has been operated by the Kiwanis Club of West Toronto since 1937, with profits going to aid its various charities.

Adults and children will be intrigued by the giant pipe organ; the reproduction of Windsor Castle's Peacock Alley; the majestic 60-foot-high ceiling of the Great Hall; and the mahogany and marble stable—reached by that long underground passage—with porcelain troughs worthy of Kohler. And architecture lovers will be fascinated by the rooms from English, Spanish, Scottish, and Austrian castles, which Sir Henry picked up during trips across Europe. The architect E.J. Lennox, who also designed Toronto's Old City Hall and King Edward Hotel, has created a remarkable structure; in a world of Disneyland-type plastic models, Toronto's "house on the hill" is a real treat.

There are no more guided tours of Casa Loma—you now get automatic tape recordings. That's all for the best, because you can drift through at your own speed while the children rush off to the stables or towers. You'll have walked a good mile by the time you're done, so wear sensible shoes. *Tel. 416/923–1171. Admission: $7 adults, $4 children 5–16 and senior citizens. Open daily 10–4. Closed Christmas Day and New Year's.*

What to See and Do with Children

Free Attractions

The **Hilton,** at University Avenue and Richmond Street, and the **Harbour Castle Westin,** at the foot of Bay Street, both have outdoor, glass-enclosed elevators, which provide hair-raising rides and spectacular views of the city. *See* Lodging, below.

The **ferry boat** to the **Toronto Islands** offers a stunning panorama of downtown Toronto. The islands themselves offer swimming and biking (bikes can be rented) in the summer, skiing in the winter, and the delightful **Far Enough Farm** in Centreville (*see* Tour 1, above).

Skating, skiing, and **tobogganing** are all available for free in most of the major Toronto parks and ravines. And, still thinking winter, don't forget the beautiful skating rink in front of the New City Hall and the often-terrifying hills at Winston Churchill Park, High Park, Earl Bales Park, and Riverdale Park.

The **David Dunlap Observatory** in Richmond Hill, just north of Metro Toronto, and the **McLaughlin Planetarium,** right next to the Royal Ontario Museum, both provide outer-space experiences for preteens and teens.

Harbourfront nearly always has free events and activities, from painting and sculpting to concerts and plays. Just being on the waterfront can be a thrill for children. Feeding the seagulls popcorn or hunks of bread is endlessly interesting, especially when the gulls catch the food in midair dives (*see* Tour 1, above).

Modestly Priced Attractions

Apple, strawberry, and **raspberry picking** are available within a short drive of downtown Toronto. Our favorite place is **Al Ferri's** (15 minutes west of the airport, near the corner of Mississauga Road and Steeles Avenue; tel. 416/455–8202). For a free list of places to pick fruits and vegetables in the vicinity of Toronto, call tel. 416/965–7701.

The **Art Gallery of Ontario** has a hands-on room that is marvelously creative and entertaining. Right behind it is the fascinating, historic **Grange** house. In front of the gallery is a Henry Moore sculpture that children love to climb (*see* Tour 2, above).

Casa Loma, that magical castle in the heart of Toronto, is much loved by all children. Even preschoolers will enjoy the great views from the towers and the long, creepy tunnel that leads to the stables (*see* Tour 3, above).

The Puppet Centre, near Yonge Street and Highway 401, has more than 400 puppets from all over the world.

More Expensive Attractions

The **Ontario Science Centre** is a must for children, especially age 5 and up; don't miss the free movies and the thrilling space, communications, laser, and electricity exhibits. *770 Don Mills Rd., about 11 km (7 mi) from downtown. By car, head west from the Eglinton Ave. exit on the Don Valley Parkway. By public transportation, take the Yonge St. subway from downtown to the Eglinton station and transfer to the Eglinton E bus.*

Get off at the Don Mills Parkway stop. Tel. 416/429–0193 for a recording, 416/429–4100 for further information. Admission: $5.50 adults, $4.50 youth, $1.75 children under 12, free for senior citizens, $12 for families. Weekdays are less crowded. Open daily 10–6; closed Christmas.

The **CN Tower** and the **Tour of the Universe** in its basement are not cheap, but they're a real treat for everyone, especially kids. (*see* Tour 1, above).

For theater and concerts, the **Young People's Theatre** (tel. 416/864–9732) often has excellent fare, and there are frequent performances for children at **Roy Thomson Hall** (tel. 416/593–4828) and the **Minkler Auditorium** (tel. 416/491–8877), which is up north, near Finch Street and the Don Valley Parkway.

The Metro Toronto Zoo

The Metro Toronto Zoo was built for animals, not people. The Rouge Valley, just east of Toronto, was an inspired choice of site when it was built in the 1960s, with its varied terrain, from river valley to dense forest, where mammals, birds, reptiles, and fish have been grouped according to where they live in the wild. In most of the regions, you'll find remarkable botanical exhibits in enclosed, climate-controlled pavilions. Don't miss the three-ton banyan tree in the Indo-Malayan Pavilion, the fan-shaped traveler's palm from Madagascar in the African Pavilion, or the perfumed flowers of the jasmine vines in the Eurasian Pavilion. The "round the world tour" takes some three hours and is suitable for any kind of weather, because most of the time is spent inside pavilions. It's been estimated that it would take four full days to see everything in the Metro Zoo, so study the map you'll get at the zoo entrance and decide in advance what you wish to see most.

For the younger children, there is the delightful Littlefootland, a special area that allows contact with tame animals, such as rabbits and sheep. In the winter, cross-country skiers follow groomed trails that skirt the animal exhibits. Lessons and rentals are available. There is an electrically powered train that moves silently among the animals without frightening them. It can accommodate wheelchairs (available for free, inside the main gate), and all pavilions have ramp access.

Located on Meadowvale Rd., just north of Highway 401, in Scarborough, a 30-minute drive from downtown. Or take Bus 86A from the Kennedy subway station; tel. 416/392–5901 for taped information, 416/392–5900 for human contact. For animal contact, visit the zoo. Admission: $8 adults, $5 children ages 12–17 and senior citizens, $3 children 5–11. Family rates available. Open daily except Christmas. Summer, daily 9:30–7; winter, daily 9:30–4:30.

Off the Beaten Track

Watching the Italian promenade. St. Clair Avenue West, running from Bathurst Street to Dufferin Street and beyond, remains the heart of this city's vibrant Italian community. On many evenings, especially Sunday, the street is filled with thousands of men and women promenading between *gelaterias*, eyeing each other, and generally enjoying their neighbors.

Greektown on a Sunday. The Danforth (Bloor Street east of the Don Valley Parkway) has great Greek restaurants, gift shops, and hundreds of Greek-Canadians promenading. Welcome to the Mediterranean!

There's no hotel more romantic than the **Guild Inn** (2010 Guildwood Pkwy., tel. 416/261–3331), and no view of Toronto more wonderful than from **Centre Island at sunset.**

Shopping

Toronto prides itself on having some of the finest shopping in North America; and, indeed, most of the world's name boutiques can be found here, especially along the Bloor Street strip (between Yonge Street and Avenue Road) and in the Yorkville area, which covers the three streets immediately north of and parallel to the Bloor Street strip.

Although some Canadians have traditionally frowned on the concept of discount stores as vulgar and beneath them, there are many moderately priced stores around the city and a lively off-price clothing trade.

Toronto has a large artistic and crafts community, with many art galleries, custom jewelers, clothing designers, and artisans. From sophisticated glass sculpture to native and Inuit art, the many beautiful objects you'll find are ideal for gifts or for your own home. Among traditional crafts, available at antiques and specialty stores, are quilts, wood carvings, and pine furniture.

Food items that are fairly easy to transport as gifts include wild rice, available in bulk or in gift packages, and maple syrup in jars or cans.

The biggest sale day of the year is Boxing Day, the first business day after Christmas, when nearly everything in the city, including furs, is half-price. In fact, clothing prices tend to drop even further as winter fades. Summer sales start in late June and continue through August.

Bargaining Toronto is *not* the Middle East, but one might haggle at flea markets, including the Harbourfront Antique Market, and perhaps in the Chinatown and Kensington Market/Spadina Avenue areas.

Refund Information Visitors, including Canadians from other provinces, can receive a refund on the 8% Ontario sales tax for purchases over $100, as well as on the 5% sales tax on hotel and motel bills, provided they leave within 30 days. It's worthwhile if you do a significant amount of shopping. There's a form to be sent in with your receipts after you leave Ontario. You can get the form at Pearson Airport, at visitors' information booths like the one outside the Eaton Centre, at Traveller's Aid in Union Station, or from the merchants themselves.

Shopping Districts

The **Yorkville Avenue/Bloor Street area** is where you'll find the big fashion names, fine leather goods, important jewelers, some of the top private art galleries, upscale shoe stores, and discount china and glassware. Streets to explore include Yorkville Avenue, Cumberland Street, and Scollard Street, all running parallel to Bloor Street, and Hazelton Avenue, running north from Yorkville Avenue near Avenue Road. Hazelton

Lanes, between Hazelton Avenue and Avenue Road, and the adjacent York Square are among the most chi-chi shopping areas in Canada, and they are headquarters for café society during the brief annual spell of warm weather.

On **Bloor Street** you'll find **Creed's** and **Holt Renfrew**—both very high end clothing stores (Holt's has men's and children's departments as well)—Harry Rosen for men, Georg Jensen, and shoe shops like Boutique Quinto and David's.

The **Eaton Centre** is a very large galleria-style shopping center downtown, on Yonge Street between Queen and Dundas streets. With scores of large and small stores and restaurants, all sheltered from the weather, it's one of the city's major tourist attractions. Generally speaking, the lower levels are lower priced and the higher levels are more expensive.

Queen Street West, starting just west of University Avenue and continuing past Spadina Avenue, creeping ever westward past Bathurst Street, is a trendy area near the Ontario College of Art. Here, you'll find young, hip designers; new and used bookstores; vintage clothes; two comic-book stores, including the biggest in North America (**Silver Snail,** No. 367; see also Dragon Lady Comic Shop at No. 200); and the more progressive private galleries.

Harbourfront includes an antiques market that's Canada's biggest on Sunday, when there are about 200 dealers. (390 Queen's Quay W, tel. 416/340–8377. Open Tues.–Fri. 11–6, Sat. 10–6, Sun. 8–6.) The **Queen's Quay Terminal** is a renovated warehouse that now houses a collection of unique boutiques, craft stalls, patisseries, and so on; it's a great place to buy gifts. There's a free shuttle bus from Union Station, or it's a fairly easy walk. Parking is expensive.

Spadina Avenue, from Wellington Street north to College Street, has plenty of low-price clothing for the whole family, as well as fur and leather factory outlets. **Winner's,** south of King Street, is a good discount outlet for women and children. **Evex Luggage Centre,** 369 Spadina Avenue, south of College, has good discount luggage, handbags, and leather accessories.

Downtown Toronto has a vast underground maze of shopping warrens that burrow in between and underneath the office towers. The tenants of the **Underground City** are mostly the usual assortment of chain stores, and the shopping is rather dull; also, directions are poorly marked. The network runs roughly from the Royal York Hotel near Union Station north to the Eaton Centre.

Department Stores

The major department stores have branches around the city and flagship stores downtown. They accept major credit cards and have liberal return policies. However, service tends to be very slow and uninformed compared with that of boutiques, and the stores generally lack the cachet of American chains like Bloomingdale's or Macy's. The big names are **Eaton's,** in the Eaton Centre; **Simpson's,** on Yonge Street between Queen and Richmond streets; and **The Bay** (The Hudson Bay Company), at Yonge and Bloor streets. Of the three, Simpson's is probably the most upscale, and The Bay the most downscale.

Specialty Shops

Antiques and Galleries

Yorkville is the headquarters of the establishment antiques dealers, including **Navarro Gallery** (33 Hazelton Ave., tel. 416/921–0031). There are several other pockets around town, including a strip along Queen Street East, roughly between Sherbourne and George streets.

The Allery (322½ Queen St. W, tel. 416/593–0853) specializes in antique prints and maps. **Art Metropole** (788 King St. W, tel. 416/367–2304) specializes in limited-edition, small-press, or self-published artists' books from around the world. **Ballenford Architectural Books** (98 Scollard St., tel. 416/960–0055) has Canada's largest selection of architectural titles and a gallery with usually interesting exhibits of architectural drawings and related work. **Jane Corkin Gallery** (179 John St., north of Queen St.; tel. 416/979–1980) specializes in photography. In the same building is **Isaacs Gallery,** owned by Av Isaacs, godfather of many of the established Canadian artists. The more avant-garde galleries include **Cold City** (30 Duncan St.), **YYZ** (1087 Queen St. W), and **Mercer Union** (333 Adelaide St. W). Also check out **Toronto Photographers Workshop** and the other galleries at 80 Spadina Avenue, where you'll usually find at least one opening on a Saturday afternoon. **Prime Canadian Crafts** (229 Queen St. W, tel. 416/593–5750) has an ever-changing array of merchandise. **Quasi Modo** (789 Queen St. W, next door to Dufflet Pastries; tel. 416/366–8370) has a quirky collection of 20th-century furniture and design. You never know what will be on display: vintage bicycles, Noguchi lamps, a corrugated cardboard table by Frank Gehry. **20th Century** (23 Beverley St., just north of Queen St.; tel. 416/598–2172) is for serious collectors of 20th-century design, particularly furniture, lamps, jewelry, and decorative arts. Many of the pieces are museum quality, and the owners are extremely erudite.

Books

Toronto is rich in bookstores selling new books, used books, best-sellers, and remainders. If you just need a current magazine or a paperback for the plane, there are the ubiquitous chains—Coles, Classic Bookshops, and W.H. Smith. Otherwise, we recommend:

The **Albert Britnell Book Shop** (765 Yonge St., just north of Bloor St.; tel. 416/924–3321) has been a Toronto legend since 1893, with a marvelous, British-like ambience and great browsing.

The **Book Cellar** (1560 Yonge St., above St. Clair Ave., tel. 416/967–5577; 142 Yorkville Ave., near Avenue Rd., tel. 416/925–9955) offers a fine choice of classical records, as well as international political and intellectual journals.

Book City has two locations (501 Bloor St. W, near Honest Ed's tel. 416/961–4496; and Carrot Common, 348 Danforth Ave., near Chester Station tel. 416/469–9997). It's strong on good remaindered books and has a knowledgeable staff.

Edward's Books and Art, one of the loveliest minichains in the city, now at four locations (356 Queen St. W, near Spadina Ave., tel. 416/593–0126; 2179 Queen St. E, in The Beaches tel. 416/698–1442; 387 Bloor St. E, at Sherbourne St. tel. 416/961–2428; and 2200 Yonge St., south of Eglington Ave. tel. 416/487–5431). It advertises huge discounts on bestsellers and remainders in every Saturday's *Globe and Mail*. All are open Sunday.

Longhouse Book Shop (recently relocated to 497 Bloor St. W, just west of Bathurst St.; tel. 416/921–9995) stocks only Canadian titles, handsomely shelved or piled high on pine tables: more than 20,000 back titles and new publications.

Bob Miller Book Room (180 Bloor St. W, just northwest of the ROM; tel. 416/922–3557) has the best literature section in the city and a staff that has been with Bob for decades.

Pages Books and Magazines (256 Queen St. W, tel. 416/598–1447) has a wide selection of international and small-press literature; fashion and design books and magazines; and books on film, art, and literary criticism.

This Ain't the Rosedale Library (483 Church St., south of Wellesley Ave.; tel. 416/929–9912) stocks the largest selection of baseball books in Canada, as well as a good selection of fiction, poetry, photography, design, rock, and jazz books.

Writers & Co. (2005 Yonge near Davisville, a few blocks south of Eglinton; tel. 416/481–8432) is arguably Canada's finest literary bookstore, with hard-to-find poets, essayists, and world novelists. If you have been looking for a rare Caribbean poetry collection, a Swedish play in translation, or an Asian novella, this is the one to visit. It's a marvelous place, and they'll be happy to order any book for you.

Clothing

Atomic Age (350 Queen St. W, tel. 416/977–1296) features the hottest young Toronto designers. (Also in the neighborhood are other stores for the young and zany: **Fab,** at No. 274; **290 Ion,** at No. 290; **B Scene,** at No. 352; **Fashion Crimes,** at No. 395; **Strange,** at No. 319; **Boomer,** for men at No. 309; **Metropolis,** at No. 265; and **I.X.L.,** at No. 198.)

Brown's (1975 Avenue Rd., south of Hwy. 401; tel. 416/489–1975) provides classic clothing for short men and women. There's also a store for men only (545 Queen St. W, tel. 416/368–5937). An offshoot is **Muskat & Brown** (2528 Yonge St., tel. 416/489–4005) for petite women.

Fetoun (97 Scollard St., tel. 416/923–3434) is one of the latest high-fashion emporiums for the nouveau riche. If you go to a lot of charity balls, this is the place to shop.

La Mode de Vija (601 Markham St., in Mirvish Village; tel. 416/534–6711) sells discount designer clothing with names like Anne Klein at good prices.

Sportables (Queen's Quay Terminal, tel. 416/360–6540) offers a good assortment of well-made casual wear in natural fibers.

Vintage Furs (39a Charles St. W, at Bloor and Bay Sts.; tel. 416/960–5020) sells secondhand furs for men and women.

Food Markets

Kensington Market (northwest of Dundas St. and Spadina Ave.; tel. 416/593–9269) is an outdoor market with a vibrant ethnic mix. Saturday is the best day to go, preferably by public transit, because parking is difficult.

St. Lawrence Market (Front St. and Jarvis St., tel. 416/392–7219) is best early on Saturday, when, in addition to the permanent indoor market on the south side of Front Street, there's a farmer's market in the building on the north side. The historic south market was once Toronto's city hall, and it fronted the lake before extensive landfill projects were undertaken.

Gift Ideas **The Back Store** (2111 Yonge St., tel. 416/482–0426) has everything for a friend with an aching spine.

Early Learning (387 Queen St. W, tel. 416/598–2135) sells European and Japanese playthings.

Filigree (1210 Yonge St., tel. 415/961–5223) has a good assortment of linens, as well as drawer liners, silver frames, and other Victorian pleasures. In the neighborhood are other gift shops selling fine glass and antiques.

Bragg (446 Queen St., west of Spadina Ave.; tel. 416/366–6717) has an amusing assortment of vintage bric-a-brac, china, cards, and jewelry.

Jewelry **Secrett Jewel Salon** (150 Bloor St. W, tel. 416/967–7500) is a reputable source of unusual gemstones and fine new and estate jewelry; local gemologists consider it the best in town.

Sports and Fitness

Participant Sports

A wide range of sports is available for each of Toronto's four distinct seasons. From Lake Ontario to the skiing hills just outside the city and the beautiful lakes and parks beyond, a thousand sports and recreational activities are at hand.

Contact the Ministry of Tourism and Recreation (Queen's Park, Toronto, Ont. M7A 2R2) for pamphlets on various activities. For information on sports activities in the province, call tel. 800/268–3735 from anywhere in the continental United States and Canada (except the Northwest Territories and the Yukon). In Toronto, contact Ontario Travel (tel. 416/965–4008).

A number of fine **conservation areas** circle the Metro Toronto area, many less than a half-hour from the downtown area. Most have large swimming areas, sledding, and cross-country skiing, as well as skating, fishing, and boating. Contact the Metro Conservation Authority (tel. 416/661–6600) and ask for their pamphlet.

Bicycling There are more than 18 miles of street bike routes cutting across the city and dozens more along safer paths through Toronto's many parks. Bikes can be rented on the Toronto Islands. The **Martin Goodman Trail** is a 12-mile strip that runs along the waterfront all the way from the Balmy Beach Club in the east end out past the western beaches southwest of High Park. Call the *Toronto Star* (tel. 416/367–2000) for a map.

Metro Parks Department (tel. 416/392–8186) has maps that show bike (and jogging) routes that run through Toronto parkland. **Ontario Cycling** (tel. 416/495–4141) has maps, booklets, and information.

Boating Grenadier Pond, in High Park, Centre Island, Ontario Place, Harbourfront, and most of the Conservation Areas surrounding Metro Toronto rent canoes, punts, and/or sailboats.

Fishing One does not have to go very far from downtown Toronto to catch trout, perch, bass, walleye, salmon, muskie, pike, and whitefish. Contact Communication Services, Wildlife Information, Ministry of Natural Resources (Queen's Park, Toronto M7A 1W3, tel. 416/965–4251).

Within Metro Toronto itself, fishing is permitted in the trout pond at Hanlon's Point on Toronto Island, as well as in Grenadier Pond in High Park. And the salmon fishing just off the Scarborough Bluffs, in Toronto's east end, is extraordinary!

There are more than 100 charter boats on Lake Ontario (about $60 for a half-day). Contact **Ontario Travel** (tel. 416/965–4008). Be warned, though: Some fish caught in this province have such high levels of mercury in them that you can take your temperature at the same time that you eat them. It's sad, but water pollution (including acid rain) has taken its toll upon the edibility of many fish in Ontario.

Golf The season lasts only from April to late October. The top course is **Glen Abbey** (tel. 416/844–1800), where the Canadian Open Championships is held. Cart and greens fees will cost up to $75 on weekends, but this course is a real beauty.

Less challenging courses—and much closer to the heart of the city—include the **Don Valley Golf Course,** just south of Highway 401 (Yonge St., tel. 416/392–2465); the **Flemingdon Park Golf Club** (Don Mills Rd. and Eglinton Ave., tel. 416/429–1740). For other courses, contact Metro Parks (tel. 416/367–8186) or Ontario Travel (tel. 416/965–4008).

Horseback Riding There are two stables within the city limits. **Central Don Stables,** in Sunnybrook Park (Leslie St. and Eglinton Ave.; tel. 416/444–4044), has an indoor arena, an outdoor ring, and nearly 12 miles of bridle trails through the Don Valley. **Eglinton Equestrian Club** (near Don Mills Rd. and John St., tel. 416/889–6375) has two indoor arenas.

Ice Skating Toronto operates some 30 outdoor artificial rinks and 100 natural-ice rinks—and all are free! Among the most popular are in Nathan Phillips Square, in front of the New City Hall, at Queen and Bay streets; down at Harbourfront, which has Canada's largest outdoor artificial ice rink; College Park, at Yonge and College streets; Grenadier Pond, within High Park, at Bloor and Keele streets; and inside Hazelton Lanes, that classy shopping mall on the edge of Yorkville, on Avenue Road, just above Bloor Street. *For details on any city rink, call 416/392–1111.*

Jogging The **Martin Goodman Trail** (*see* Bicycling, above) is ideal. Also try the boardwalk of The Beaches in the east end, High Park in the west end, the Toronto Islands, or any of Toronto's parks.

Sailing This can be a breeze, especially between April and October. Contact the **Ontario Sailing Association** (tel. 416/495–4240).

Skiing

Cross-country Try Toronto's parks and ravines; High Park; the lakefront along the southern edge of the city; Tommy Thompson Park; Toronto Islands; and, perhaps best of all, the inspired concept of Zooski, out at the stunning Metro Toronto Zoo, where one can ski past lions, leopards, and other furry friends. Check the yellow pages for ski equipment rentals; there are many places. Only Zooski charges a fee; all other places are free.

Downhill Although there are a few places where one can get a taste of this sport within Metro Toronto, such as **Earl Bales Park,** on Bathurst Street, just south of Sheppard Avenue, and **Centennial Park Ski Hill,** in Etobicoke (tel. 416/394–8754), the *best* alpine hills are a good 30–60 minutes north of the city. These include **Blue Mountain Resorts** (tel. 416/869–3799) in Collingwood, the **Caledon Ski Club** (tel. 416/453–7404) in

Caledon, **Glen Eden Ski Area** (tel. 416/878–5011) in Milton, **Hidden Valley** (tel. 705/789–2301) in Huntsville, **Hockley Valley Resort** (tel. 519/942–0754) in Orangeville, and **Horseshoe Valley** (tel. 705/835–2790) in Barrie. Call tel. 416/963–2992 for daily reports on lifts and surface conditions.

Sleigh Riding and Tobogganing **Black Creek Pioneer Village** (tel. 416/661–6610 or 416/661–6600), north of 401 along Highway 400, at Steeles Avenue, is open winter weekends 10–4 for skating, tobogganing, and horse-drawn sleigh rides. The best parks for tobogganing include **High Park,** in the west end, and our favorite, **Winston Churchill Park,** at Spadina and St. Clair avenues, just two blocks from Casa Loma. It is sheer terror.

Tennis The city provides dozens of courts, all free, and many of them floodlighted. Parks with courts open from 7 AM to 11 PM, in season, include the famous High Park in the west end; Stanley Park, on King Street West, three blocks west of Bathurst Street; and Eglinton Park, on Eglinton Avenue West, just east of Avenue Road. Call the **Ontario Tennis Association** (tel. 416/495–4215).

Hotel Health Facilities Nearly every major hotel in the Metro Toronto area has a decent indoor swimming pool; some even have indoor/outdoor swimming pools. The best include the **Sheraton Centre,** at Queen and Bay streets, and the **Inn on the Park,** at Eglinton Avenue near Leslie Street. Many also have health clubs, with saunas and Nautilus equipment.

Spectator Sports

Auto Racing For the past several years, the **Molson Indy** (tel. 416/595–5445) has been roaring around the Canadian National Exhibition grounds, including the major thoroughfare of Lakeshore Boulevard, for three days in mid-July. You'll pay more than $85 for a three-day "red" reserved seat, but general admission for the qualification rounds, the practice rounds, and the Indy itself, can be as cheap as $10–$20, depending upon the day. Considering that this ancient tradition began in only 1986, the Molson Indy has already become Toronto's international showcase to the motor-racing world. And with the cars reaching speeds of up to 200 mph, you'd better hurry down.

Less than a half-hour drive away is the **Cayuga International Speedway** (tel. 416/765–4461), where international stock-car races are held from May through September.

Baseball The **Toronto Blue Jays** have developed into one of baseball's most dynamic teams, and are all the more popular since their move into the SkyDome in the summer of 1989. *For ticket information, tel. 416/341–1111; to charge tickets, tel. 416/595–1362.*

Canoeing and Rowing The world's largest **canoeing and rowing regatta** is held every July 1, as it has been for more than a century, on Toronto Island's Long Pond. *Canoe Ontario, tel. 416/495–4180.*

Football Although the Canadian Football League has been teetering on the brink of dissolution, the **Toronto Argonauts** have, in recent years, developed into annual contenders. Americans might find the three downs and 110-yard field to be rather quaint, but the game is much like their own. *Tel. 416/595–1131 for tickets and information.*

Golf The permanent site of the **Canadian Open** golf championship is Glen Abbey, a course designed by Jack Nicklaus. This tournament is one of golf's Big Five and is always played in late summer. *Less than a 45-min drive west, along the Queen Elizabeth Way (QEW). Tel. 416/844–1800.*

Hockey The **Toronto Maple Leafs** play 40 home games each season (Oct.–Apr.), usually on Wednesday and Saturday nights, in the big, ugly Maple Leaf Gardens. There are always tickets available at each game—at least from scalpers in front of the stadium on Carlton Street, a half-block east of the corner of Yonge and College streets. Call the office (tel. 416/977–1641) at 9 AM sharp on the day of the game you wish to see.

Horse Racing

Harness Racing The **Greenwood** track, built in 1874, is where the best trotters and pacers do their stuff at three annual meetings. *Tel. 416/675–6110. Spring gathering runs Jan.–mid-Mar.; summer meeting, late May–Sept.; the brief winter meeting, the last two weeks in Dec.*

Thoroughbred Racing There are four major racetracks handled by the Ontario Jockey Club (tel. 416/675–6110)–two in the Toronto area; one down in Fort Erie, near Buffalo; and another about two dozen miles west of Toronto.

Greenwood Race Track is one of the premier harness tracks in North America and is the home of many of Canada's greatest trotting and pacing events, including the North American Cup. It is located in the city's east end, a 10-minute streetcar ride from downtown, at Woodbine Avenue and Queen Street East, near the lakeshore. *Tel. 416/698–3131. Winter meeting runs late Oct.–early Dec.; spring meeting runs mid-Mar.–late Apr.*

Woodbine Race Track is the showplace of Thoroughbred racing in Canada. *Located 30-min northeast of downtown Toronto, not far from the airport, at Hwy. 27 and Rexdale Blvd.; tel. 416/675–6110. Horses run late Apr.–late Oct.*

Mohawk is in the heart of Ontario's Standardbred breeding country, and it features a glass-enclosed, climate-controlled grandstand and other attractive facilities. *A 30-min. drive west of Toronto, along Hwy. 401, past the town of Milton; tel. 416/854–2255.*

Fort Erie, in the Niagara tourist region, is one of the most picturesque racetracks in the world, with willows, manicured hedges, and flower-bordered infield lakes. It has racing on the dirt as well as on grass, with the year's highlight being the Prince of Wales Stakes, the second jewel in Canada's Triple Crown of Racing. *Tel. 416/871–3200 from Toronto, 716/856–0293 from Buffalo.*

Royal Horse Show This highlight of Canada's equestrian season is part of the Royal Winter Fair each November. *The CNE grounds, Dufferin St., by the waterfront. Tel. 416/393–6400.*

Soccer Although Toronto keeps getting and losing and getting a professional soccer team, one can catch this exciting sport, as well as collegiate football, in the very handy **Varsity Stadium.** *Bloor St. W at Bedford, a block west of the Royal Ontario Museum and University Ave. Tel. 416/979–2186.*

Dining

by Joanne Kates

Restaurant critic for the Toronto Globe and Mail, *in 1988 Joanne Kates won both the best restaurant critic and best food writer awards in the Canadian food writing association. She is the author of four books, including her own cookbook and a Toronto restaurant guide.*

A decade ago visitors to Toronto enjoyed a varied mix of ethnic restaurants, but good food could not be found in the middle ground of gastronomy—between the Italian sandwiches and the Dover sole. Today, Toronto is a city of bistros.

The "bistroization" of Toronto is due in part to a new generation of chefs, the first wave of young people who are just now fanning out across the city, opening neighborhood restaurants that are a little cheaper, slightly less ambitious, and thus more accessible than those of their teachers.

What the bistros serve is another matter. That old tired imitation Continental menu, which Toronto's upper crust dined out on since before the Beatles, is finally dead. We are no longer stuck eating less than perfect imitations of what they do in Paris and Rome. The new bistros are eclectic, as likely to borrow from Bangkok as they are from Los Angeles. Furthermore, their clever mentors have taught the new generation of young chefs to do things that have heretofore been forbidden in kitchens—think for themselves, create dishes based on what dazzles them in the morning market, and use local ingredients and spontaneity of approach.

Highly recommended restaurants in each category are indicated with a star ★.

Category	Cost*
Very Expensive	over $40
Expensive	$30–$40
Moderate	$20–$30
Inexpensive	under $20

**per person without tax, tip, or drinks*

Bistros

Expensive ★

Brownes Bistro. In one night, you can count a dozen mink coats. Full-length dark ranch. What does a person who spends $17,000 on a coat want in a restaurant? Apparently she wants an impeccable bistro that avoids the tarted-up Paris look. Everything at Brownes is breathtakingly simple, from the white paper on the tables to the small black and white ceramic tiles. The monochromatic room is colored only by dark wood paneling and one fuchsia azalea at the bar. Lack of pretension is elevated to an art. Brownes's pizza may be the best in Toronto. The *gnocchi* are unexceptional. The bouillabaisse has perfect, sweet little fresh scallops, but a blandness of broth. There are seven main courses, and three of them are lamb. Brownes gives full glory to lamb's heretofore neglected parts, such as lamb shanks (braised till they soften like butter and served in their own heart-warming broth, slightly thickened, with fennel, potatoes, and carrots). A lemon curd and a darkly dense chocolate cake, served with crème fraîche and chocolate sauce, are both very fine. The price of under $70 for two, with wine—a real bargain—makes Brownes the hottest show in town. *2 Wood-*

lawn Ave. E, tel. 416/924–8132. Dress: casual. Reservations advised. AE, CB, DC, MC, V. Closed lunch, Sun.

Moderate ★ **Avocado Club.** The elegant Beaujolais closed for two weeks of frantic redecoration in 1990 and reopened as a sun-splashed fun spot, serving casual food that is also of the highest quality. The Avocado Club is light-hearted from the minute you walk through the door. Bright and sassy colors are everywhere. The devil's avocado, the restaurant's most popular starter, is warmed avocado with scallops and shrimps in a black bean chili sauce with Japanese cooking sake. Other appetizers refer, but always with chef Bob Bermann's light touch, to Thailand, Vietnam, and India, such as satay skewers, sweet/hot curried mussel salad. These days this type of cooking is as common as mosquitoes in a swamp, but rarely are so many culinary influences collected with such a gentle touch. *165 John St., tel. 416/598–4656. Dress: casual. Reservations advised. AE, MC, V.*

★ **BamBoo.** Inside a funky little inner courtyard decorated by a bohemian hand—fishnets on the walls, a stand of Muskoka bamboo, fading signs, all bordered by a thatched roof, à la South Pacific—is a relentlessly low-tech club-cum-restaurant that rebukes glitz-crazed Toronto with a smile up its sleeve. More and more ordinary people are going to the BamBoo for one purpose only: to eat food that jumps up joyously on the tongue. You can eat in the club area (240 seats, barnlike but warm) or in the small, funky dining room off to the right. On weekends guests line up for both the food and the live Caribbean music, which starts at 10 PM. Chef Wendy Young makes a hot and sour soup that has more oomph than anything in Chinatown. Much of the food is spicy. The callalloo, a creamed spinach and coconut soup, is the very weapon that blocked sinuses require. BamBoo's single most popular dish, Thai spicy noodles, comes in three modes—mild, medium, and wow! Mild is a superlative ungreasy wok-fry of rice noodles with peanuts, bean sprouts, chicken, shrimp, tofu, egg, Vietnamese fish sauce, chilies, sugar, garlic, and fresh lime juice. *312 Queen St. W, tel. 416/593–5771. Dress: casual. No reservations. AE, MC, V. Closed Sun.*

Brunch

Moderate ★ **Kensington Kitchen.** Its clientele is the self-consciously unchic University of Toronto people who live in the area and appreciate the ask-nothing ambience. The reigning sensibility belongs to Said Mukayesh, who leans heavily toward the healthy, so his interpretation of Middle East cooking includes whole-wheat pita; and if there's rice, it's brown. But none of this prevents Mukayesh from serving wickedly wonderful spinach-and-cheese ravioli in a dense cream sauce. Ingredients are fresh and always prepared with affection and care. Where else do you get velvety *baba ghannoush*, *lubya* (green beans in a thick sauce of cinnamon and cardamom), divinely garlicky fried eggplant, and assertive cream soups? The *tabbouleh* (cracked wheat salad with parsley, tomato, and cucumber) is delicate, and the falafel in pita is a class act. Two people could lunch splendidly for $10. *124 Harbord St.; south of Bloor St., tel. 416/961–3404. Dress: casual. Reservations not necessary. MC, V.*

Avocado Club, **16**
BamBoo, **10**
Brownes Bistro, **3**
Camarra's, **1**
Centro, **2**
Grano Cafe, **6**
Jerusalem, **7**
Kensington Kitchen, **9**
La Fenice, **14**
Le Bistingo, **12**
Le Cafe, **22**
L'Express Café, **13**
Nekah, **19**
New World, **23**
North 44, **5**
Oceans, **17**
The Parrot, **11**
Pearl Court, **20**
Pronto Ristorante, **4**
Renaissance Cafe, **8**
Santa Fe Bar and Grill, **15**
The Vegetarian Restaurant, **21**
Young Lok, **18**

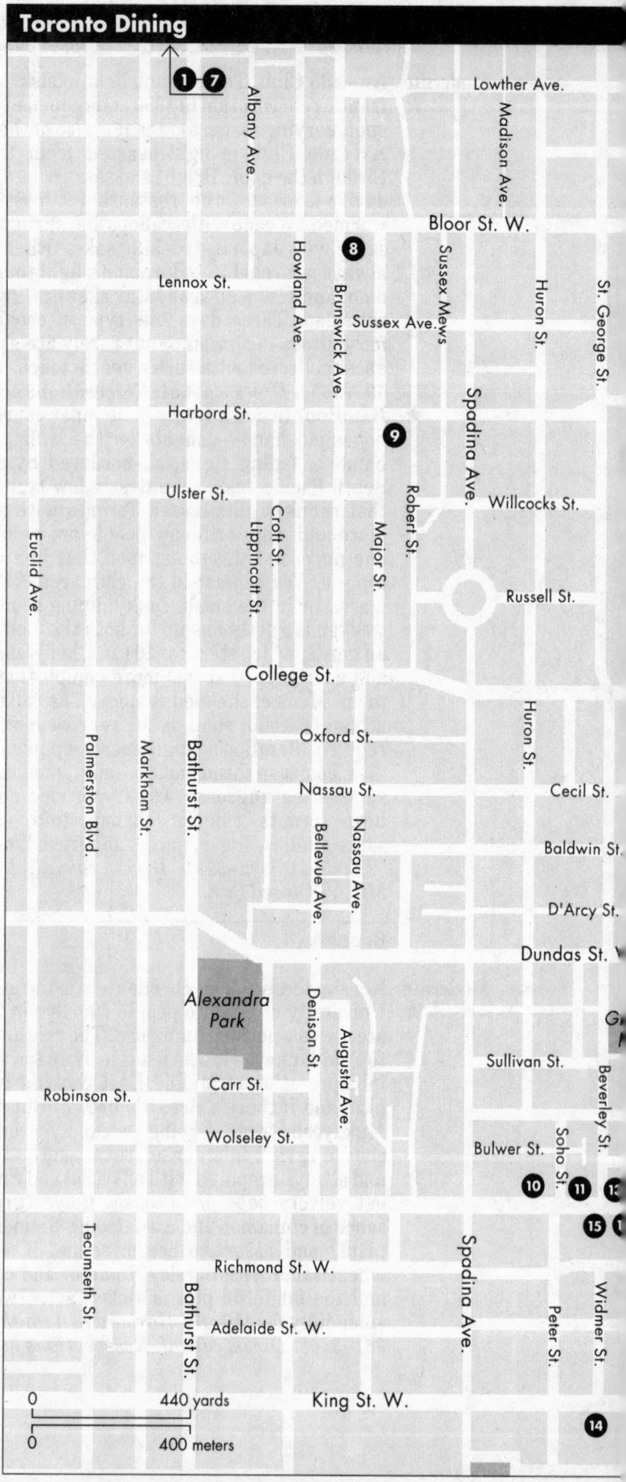

Hazelton Ave.
Scollard St.
Park Rd.
Rosedale Valley Rd.
N
Yorkville Ave.
22
23
Cumberland St.
Asquith Ave.
Bloor St. E.
Avenue Rd.
St. Thomas St.
Hayden St.
Charles St. E.
Church St.
Isabella St.
Queen's Park
Gloucester St.
St. Joseph St.
21
Dundonald St.
Queen's Park Cir. W.
Queen's Park Cir. E.
College Cir.
Wellesley St. W.
Wellesley St. E.
Jarvis St.
Breadalbane St.
Maitland Ave.
Grosvenor St.
Alexander St.
Grenville St.
Wood St.
College St.
Carlton St.
Carlton St.
Bay St.
Yonge St.
Allan Gardens
University Ave.
Gerrard St. W.
Gerrard St. E.
McCaul St.
Elizabeth St.
20
Pembroke St.
O'Keefe St.
Elm St.
Gould St.
George St.
Edward St.
Dundas St. W.
Dundas St. E.
St. Patrick St.
Simcoe St.
Chestnut St.
Victoria St.
James St.
Yonge St.
Mutual St.
18
Shuter St.
Jarvis St.
Church St.
Moss Gardens
Pullan Pl.
Nathan Phillips Square
Queen St. W.
Queen St. E.
Duncan St.
17
Richmond St. E.
Nelson St.
University Ave.
York St.
Adelaide St. E.
Bay St.
Pearl St.
King St. E.
19
Front St. E.
Wellington St. W.
Wellington St. E.

Cafés

Inexpensive **L'Express Café.** Just across from the charming Parrot bistro on Queen Street West, is a café that since the fall of 1987 has been serving good casual food with some dispatch. For under $5, they take the ordinary (chicken salad, ham and cheese) and annoint it with goat cheese or roasted red peppers in oil, laid lovingly between slices of impeccable Italian bread. The pizzas and savory tarts are enough to justify its existence. (The former is simple and robust; the latter, a texture of gossamer, thanks to the 35% cream.) The leek and *chèvre* tart with a touch of curry is one of the most inventive dishes. *254 Queen St. W, in walking distance of New City Hall; tel. 416/596–0205. Dress: informal. No reservations. AE, MC, V, for orders over $10. Closed Sun.*

Chinese

Moderate ★ **New World.** There is probably very little that could induce you to penetrate the wilds of Scarborough on a wintry night, but this place can. Again and again and again. Do not miss the New World's *shui kow* soup—a sea of fine stock afloat with freshly made dumplings of chopped shrimp, Chinese mushrooms, and barbecued pork—and the fresh abalone that comes in its shell accompanied by one pristine broccoli floret in a translucent sauce made from beef stock reduced with oyster sauce. It's not on the menu, but the password is, "Kam Wong said we could have it." New World is frankly Cantonese. There is a lick and a promise in the direction of Szechuan, but the cook's heart is on the sea. Big fat indelicate West Coast oysters come properly (barely) cooked in their own shells, dressed up with black beans, fresh coriander, and chives. Chicken cubes and scallops in phoenix nest are not to be missed. And I have never tasted fish so fresh in hot pots, nor eaten a hot pot crowned with soft shell crab and oyster. No reservations are taken for the hot-pot tables, so go early. This place is a treasure. *3600 Victoria Park Ave., tel. 416/498–1818. Dress: casual. Reservations advised on weekends. AE, MC, V.*

Young Lok. Upwardly mobile and still delicious, this is a handsome restaurant in the very attractive Village by the Grange. The menu is biblical in scope, ranging from tired old Cantonese clichés to the fiery stars of the Szechuan kitchen. The clear soups are great; the panfried pancakes with scallions is a bargain appetizer and wonderful: cheap, greasy, and oniony. The main courses are almost all terrific: Sautéed shrimp with ginger and scallion is crunchy on the outside, sweetly juicy on the inside. Fresh lobster in black bean sauce is a perfect juxtaposition of sweet flesh and salty beans. Vegetarians' hodgepodge, a Young Lok classic, has a variety of crunchy vegetables. Mandarin crispy duck is for all unrepentant grease lovers. *122 St. Patrick St., at Dundas St., just south of the Art Gallery; tel. 416/593–9819. Dress: casual. Reservations advised. AE, CB, D, MC, V. Dim sum weekends 10:30 AM–3 PM. Summer outdoor dining.*

Inexpensive ★ **Pearl Court.** This is the most recent of the good Chinese restaurants to hit the big time. Make sure you take a number as you join the crowd outside the door; by the way, you might end up sitting near the door, with its chilling draft. All this for superlative, barely cooked, fat, fresh oysters sizzling on a hot iron plate with black pepper and green onion. Or fresh kiwi clams, each one steamed with a half-teaspoon of minced garlic. Garlic is a central theme here. So is fresh coriander. Lemon grass accents the oxtail in a fine citrusy stew pot. Chicken in paper is a platter of little paper packets, each holding a little morsel of pink tender chicken steamed in soy with five-spice powder. Skip the soups, which are bland, and consider the oysters. *598 Gerrard St. E, near Broadview Ave.; tel. 416/463-8773. Dress: casual. V.*

French

Very Expensive ★ **Le Bistingo.** Certain gifts from Chef Claude Bouillet's kitchen are among the finest flavors Toronto can offer: His open ravioli filled with shrimp and scallops are astonishing—toothsome pasta sheets laid over and under with soft, sweet seafood, all bathed in the lightest of *blancs* thinned with fish stock. The house signature appetizer, duck liver sautéed until just pink and soft and napped in a very tart raisin sauce, is fabulous. Among main courses, the fish dishes shine. A perfectly cooked fat red snapper sits on a wondrously astringent bed of stewed endive, surrounded by beurre blanc cleverly thinned with vermouth. Those in the know order a hot dessert with dinner, and are thus seduced by fresh-from-the-oven buttery puff pastry cradling caramelized apples, then bathed in a foam of Calvados sabayon. As if that were not enough, there are sauternes by the glass (or real champagne) to wash it all down. *349 Queen St. W, tel. 416/598-3490. Dress: casual. Reservations required. AE, DC, MC. V.*

Italian

Expensive ★ **Centro.** Franco Prevedello spent blood, sweat, and $2 million on dreamlike art deco lighting, etched glass, 18-foot ceilings with fat white columns, oxblood leather armchairs, Rosenthal china worth $45 a plate, and the most exciting Italian wine cellar in Toronto. The food can be heavy and overcomplicated—*agnolotti* with too much cream; overcooked poached salmon—but every day it moves closer to inspired Italian country style, with such specialties as poached skate in a mustardy coriander vinaigrette; a fat, juicy roasted capon breast garnished with fresh pecans and lemon-pepper garlic mayonnaise; and espresso ice cream scented with Sambuca. *2472 Yonge St., tel. 416/483-2211. Dress: casual. Reservations advised. AE, MC, V. Closed lunch, Sun.*

★ **La Fenice.** This is the most authentic Italian restaurant in Toronto. Luigi Orgera is a ballerina in the kitchen, the Nureyev of the grill. Who else in Toronto has fresh *porcini* in October? Who else grates heavenly slivers of fresh white truffle on pasta? The antipasto trolley is more Rome than Toronto: mint-scented grilled eggplant; roasted zucchini; tangy salad of shrimps and squid; roasted sweet red peppers anointed in extra-virgin olive oil; and more. His *risotto al mare* is a tiny perfect stew of clams and mussels; the spaghetti is tossed with sweet chunks of sun-dried tomatoes, southern Italy incarnate. In fish, one can expect red and white snapper, yellowtail, and porgy, all as fresh as fish can be in this city. *319 King St. W, near John St.; tel. 416/585-2377. Dress: casual. Reservations required. AE, MC, V. Closed Sat. lunch, Sun.*

★ **Pronto Ristorante.** There's black mink, fat glistening pearls, and a conversation about Swiss bank accounts at the bar, where people with reservations at eight are waiting to be seated at nine. The mirrored ceiling and walls, the open kitchen, and the ceramic tile create a charming kaleidoscopic effect; it's so noisy and busy here that one is free to be casual. They make liberal use of the grill, charring red and yellow peppers, zucchini, summer squash, meat, and fish. One night, they grilled very fresh striped bass hot and fast till it was barely cooked, set it in a puddle of wonderfully astringent grapefruit butter, and painted on a rainbow of grilled vegetables. They grill salmon till it's pink perfection and toss it with roasted yellow peppers, cream, and *tagliatelle*. Pronto is a kitchen in superb control; even the waiters are charming. *692 Mount Pleasant Rd., south of Eglinton Ave.; tel. 416/486–1111. Jacket optional. Reservations required. AE, CB, D, MC, V.*

Inexpensive **Camarra's.** Pizza heaven, in northwest Toronto. The dough has always been high and soft, with the delightful bite of a leavened dough. And on top are only good ingredients—real Italian plum tomatoes, not the canned tomato sauce of too many Toronto pizzerias. Very casual. *2899 Dufferin St., 1 mi south of Hwy. 401; tel. 416/789–3222. Dress: casual. No reservations. AE, MC, V. Closed Sun. lunch, Tues.*

Mexican

Moderate ★ **Santa Fe Bar & Grill.** You wouldn't be able to find Santa Fe if you didn't know it was there. The only clue to its presence is a big turquoise lizard on the roof. The interior has all the southwestern elements—adobe walls, cowhide tub chairs, wooden chairs painted with a Georgia O'Keeffe palette, southwestern rugs on the walls. The kitchen has troubled itself to stock the staples of casual Mexican cuisine: *chipotles* (smoked jalapeños), *jicamas* (sweet crunchy white tubers), blue corn chips, corn husks, flour tortillas, and black beans. It's fun food. Sip a blue margarita in a huge highball glass with a little pizza or a platter of blue and gold corn chips. The more proper Mexican cooking is done with the right chilies and generosity of spirit. *129 Peter St., tel. 416/345–9345. Dress: casual. Reservations advised. AE, DC, MC, V.*

Nouvelle

Very Expensive ★ **Nekah.** Michael Stadtlander is probably the best cook in Canada. Other chefs copy; he creates. At Nekah, a spare and elegant room, he offers two six-course fixed-price menus for $60 each, and the menu changes nightly. Creamless vegetable purées come on handcrafted pottery bowls, crystalline consommés are served in black lacquer. Next there might be free-range chicken in fresh chervil jelly, or warm salad of raw oysters and barely grilled halibut, strewn with inoki mushrooms, white radish shred, and tiny tendrils of raw beet, in a barely there miso dressing. The silver is Rosenthal, the glasses are crystal, and the drinking water comes from an Ontario spring. Meat courses represent field and forest in the form of splendid venison, buffalo, and Toronto's best collection of wild mushrooms. Desserts are made-to-order extravaganzas—fresh fig fritters, warm puff pastries, glazed crepes with the house ice creams. Statdlander's technique is superb, his touch delicate. Nekah is the most exciting restaurant in Toronto this year. *32 Wellington St. E, tel. 416/867–9067. Dress: casual. Reservations advised. AE, MC, V.*

Expensive ★ **North 44.** Mark McEwan (formerly of Pronto) opened the most visually arresting dining room in Toronto in 1990. North 44, Toronto's longitude, is the restaurant's logo and an oft-repeated visual refrain. Everywhere you look there is another design statement. The message is metallic and modern; even the washrooms have the designer touch. One of the five best cooks in Toronto, McEwan's theme is southwest cuisine with a southeast Asian undertone, all afloat on a sea of beurre blanc and executed with finesse. McEwan dips fresh oysters in cornmeal, fries them crisp on the outside, melting on the inside, and sits them on a chili cream sauce. He pats together corn, potato and shrimp fragments into a pancake and fries it. Order the huge barely roasted scallops and you get grilled bok choy and creamed peppers. The fried rock snapper comes with gingered plum tomatoes and a McEwan introduction—french fried leeks, sophisticated kissin' cousin to onion rings. *2537 Yonge St., tel. 416/487–4897. Dress: casual. Reservations advised. AE, DC, MC, V.*

Oceans. Ponytails meet dark suits and diamonds rub shoulders with black jeans at Oceans. The oceans' reference is everywhere in the designer decor. This is a very luxe little room. Greg Couillard's signature dishes are Jamaican jump-up soup, Bangkok sauce, and his dazzling way of combining hot and sweet, often with peanut and coriander, to wake up tired taste buds. The tandoori salmon is divine, a wonderful lurid red, infused with flavor and still moist. The slash and burn grouper (tempura batter, stuffed) is also masterfully executed. The chicken Cheng Mai is all tied up in lemon grass and juicy in the sweet/hot/peanut mode. The splendour of the postmodern neonouvelle kitchen is its ability to borrow from Asia, India, China and points south. Greg Couillard does it with style to burn. *221 Richmond Street West, tel. 416/340–7620. Dress: casual. Reservations advised. AE, MC, V.*

Quick Meals

Moderate **Le Cafe.** Every hotel, even the Four Seasons, needs a coffee shop, but what other one serves freshly squeezed strawberry juice? The effect of the rough brick walls, gas lights, and greenery is calm, pastoral, and warm. The dinner menu goes from Spanish omelet and chicken salad to some real exotica, such as the salad of snow peas, shrimps, and baby corn with sesame oil; and squab brushed with Meaux mustard, grilled, and then baked with bread crumbs. Cold dishes and grilled foods are best; desserts from the hotel kitchen are wondrous, especially the luscious pastries. *21 Avenue Rd., just above Bloor St., tel. 416/964–0411. Dress: casual. AE, CB, MC, V.*

Inexpensive **Grano Cafe.** Franco Prevedello has served as godfather to a winner, helping a young couple, the Martellas, create a basic café—southern Italian style—the prettiest all-day café in Toronto. You order your meal at the bar, and Robert brings it. The soups and antipasti are dreams come true, the soups thick and strong, with fresh thyme and good stock. And some of the antipasti are as good as what you'd get in Bologna: Strips of zucchini are marinated with sweet oregano; a hint of caraway flavors the thin chewy strips of eggplant in oil. Grano's pizzas are so attractive because bread is the secret love at Grano (which means grain). All day the baker toils in the cellar under the café, and all day the breads come upstairs, fragrant and warm: The two most wonderful are the *foccaccia* and the oatmeal buttermilk bread. Avoid the steam-table stuff. *2035 Yonge St., below Eglinton Ave., tel. 416/440–1986. Dress: casual. MC, V. Closed Sun.*

★ **Jerusalem.** This is the ultimate family restaurant: the broadloom is dark red with a brown pattern, so accidents by children can go practically unnoticed. Service is fast. The bustle and noise are enough to camouflage the most unruly youngsters. And the food will not deliver a crisis to the taste buds. Jerusalem serves a rich variety of wonderful Middle Eastern foods—the most tender falafel in town, rich fried tomatoes with garlic, *sam bousek* (a deep-fried dough packet of ground meat and pine nuts), very sweet charcoal-grilled shish kebab, and ungooey baklava. *955 Eglinton Ave. W, tel. 416/783–6494. Dress: casual. AE, MC, V.*

Vegetarian

Moderate

★ **The Parrot.** For a long while, this was Toronto's only vegetarian restaurant serving very fine food; and although meat was added to the menu in 1983, superlative veggie meals continue to be offered. The *cappellini primavera* is a delectable rainbow of pasta and vegetables. Try the baked chèvre with olive oil and Parmesan fritters in tomato sauce. And the gnocchi are the finest I've ever eaten. *325 Queen St. W, near University Ave.; tel. 416/593–0899. Dress: casual. Reservations advised. AE, MC, V. Closed Sat.–Mon. lunch.*

Inexpensive

Renaissance Cafe. A modest restaurant with a limited but cosmopolitan menu—the likes of ratatouille and curries. The daily brunches are pleasant. *509 Bloor St. W, near Bathurst St.; tel. 416/968–6639. Dress: casual. Reservations advised. AE, MC, V.*

The Vegetarian Restaurant. For the uninitiated, there are lovely omelets, soups, and salads; for the adventuresome, soyburgers and soy pâté. It's now in a new location, in a cheerfully renovated Victorian house, with cafeteria-style service. *4 Dundonald St., just east of Yonge St.; tel. 416/961–9522. Dress: casual. No reservations. MC, V. Closed Sun. lunch.*

Lodging

Places to stay in this cosmopolitan city range, as one might expect, from luxurious hotels to budget motels to a handful of bed-and-breakfasts in private homes.

Prices are cut nearly in half over weekends and during special times of the year (many Toronto hotels drop their rates a full 50% in January and February).

Accommodation Toronto (tel. 416/596–7117), a service of the Hotel Association of Toronto, is an excellent source of finding the room and price you want. Don't forget to ask about family deals and special packages.

Highly recommended properties in each category are indicated by a star ★.

Category	Cost*
Very Expensive	over $175
Expensive	$125–$175
Moderate	$70–$125
Inexpensive	under $70

**All prices are for a standard double room, excluding optional service charge.*

Very Expensive

★ **Four Seasons Toronto.** It's hard to imagine a lovelier or more exclusive hotel than the Four Seasons, which is usually rated among the top two dozen hotels in the world and one of the top three in North America. The location is one of the most ideal in the city: on the edge of Yorkville, a few meters from the Royal Ontario Museum. The 379 units are tastefully appointed. Maids come twice a day, and there are comfortable bathrobes, oversize towels, fresh flowers, and a fine indoor/outdoor pool. Even the special family rates, however, will not drop the cost much below $200 a night. Yet during such slow months as January through March, sometimes into April, rooms on weekends have been offered for less than $80 per night (per person), and there is reason to believe that this tradition will continue into 1991. *21 Avenue Rd., M5R 2G1, a block north of Bloor St.; tel. 416/964–0411 or 800/332–3442. AE, CB, DC, MC, V.*

Harbour Castle Westin. This was a Hilton International hotel until 1987, when Westin and Hilton suddenly switched ownership of their major downtown Toronto hotels. A favorite with conventioners, it's located just steps from Harbourfront and the Toronto Island ferry. It's a bit inconvenient to the city's amenities except forthose directly on the lakeshore, but it enjoys the best views of any hotel in the city. There's a shuttle bus service to downtown business and shopping, and the swimming pool, squash courts, and health club are among the best in town. Its nearly 1,000 rooms are well-appointed and tastefully modern, and the frequent family and weekend rates help bring its regular price down by as much as a third. *1 Harbour Sq., M5J 1A6, tel. 416/869–1600 or 800/228–3000. AE, CB, DC, MC, V.*

Expensive

★ **Chestnut Park Hotel.** One of the newest—and biggest—additions to Toronto's hotel scene, this handsome 16-floor hotel with glass-enclosed atrium lobby could hardly be more convenient: just steps behind City Hall and a few short blocks from Eaton Centre. The 522 guest rooms, which include 21 for the disabled, are all well decorated, with finely crafted furniture and desks; many have queen- and king-size beds. Recreational facilities include a large heated indoor pool, sauna, Jacuzzi, health club and gymnasium, and a children's creative center. A business center makes the hotel attractive for executives. In addition, the Chestnut Hill will be connected by a walkway from the mezzanine level to a Museum of Textiles, where some 15,000 textiles from around the world will be displayed—the only museum of its kind in Canada. *108 Chestnut St., M5G 1R3,*

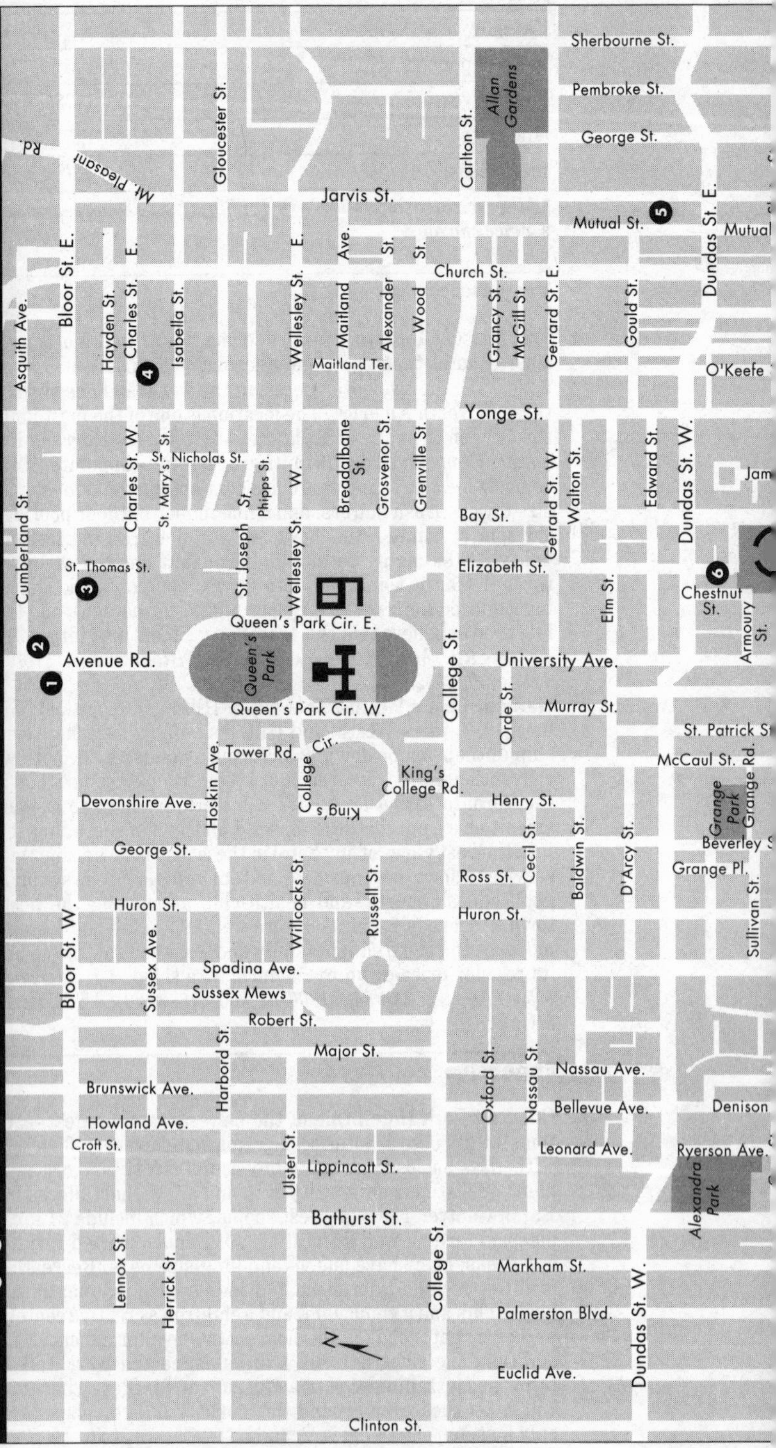
Sherbourne St.
Allan Gardens
Pembroke St.
George St.
Carlton St.
Gloucester St.
Mt. Pleasant Rd.
Jarvis St.
Mutual St.
5
Mutual
Dundas St. E.
Church St.
Bloor St. E.
Charles St. E.
Wellesley St. E.
Maitland Ave.
Alexander St.
Wood St.
Asquith Ave.
Hayden St.
Charles St.
Isabella St.
Wellesley St.
Maitland St.
Alexander St.
Wood St.
Grancy St.
McGill St.
Gerrard St. E.
Gould St.
4
Maitland Ter.
O'Keefe
Yonge St.
Cumberland St.
Charles St. W.
St. Mary's St.
St. Nicholas St.
St. Joseph St.
Phipps St.
Wellesley St. W.
Breadalbane St.
Grosvenor St.
Grenville St.
Gerrard St. W.
Walton St.
Edward St.
Dundas St. W.
Bay St.
St. Thomas St.
3
Elizabeth St.
Elm St.
6
Chestnut St.
Queen's Park Cir. E.
2
Avenue Rd.
1
Queen's Park
College St.
University Ave.
Armoury St.
Queen's Park Cir. W.
Orde St.
Murray St.
St. Patrick St.
Tower Rd.
College Cir.
McCaul St.
Hoskin Ave.
King's College Rd.
Devonshire Ave.
King's College Cir.
Henry St.
Grange Park
Grange Rd.
Beverley St.
George St.
Cecil St.
Baldwin St.
D'Arcy St.
Grange Pl.
Ross St.
Willcocks St.
Russell St.
Huron St.
Huron St.
Sullivan St.
Bloor St. W.
Sussex Ave.
Spadina Ave.
Sussex Mews
Robert St.
Major St.
Harbord St.
Oxford St.
Nassau St.
Nassau Ave.
Brunswick Ave.
Bellevue Ave.
Denison
Howland Ave.
Croft St.
Ulster St.
Leonard Ave.
Ryerson Ave.
Lippincott St.
Alexandra Park
Bathurst St.
Lennox St.
Herrick St.
College St.
Markham St.
Dundas St. W.
Palmerston Blvd.
N
Euclid Ave.
Clinton St.

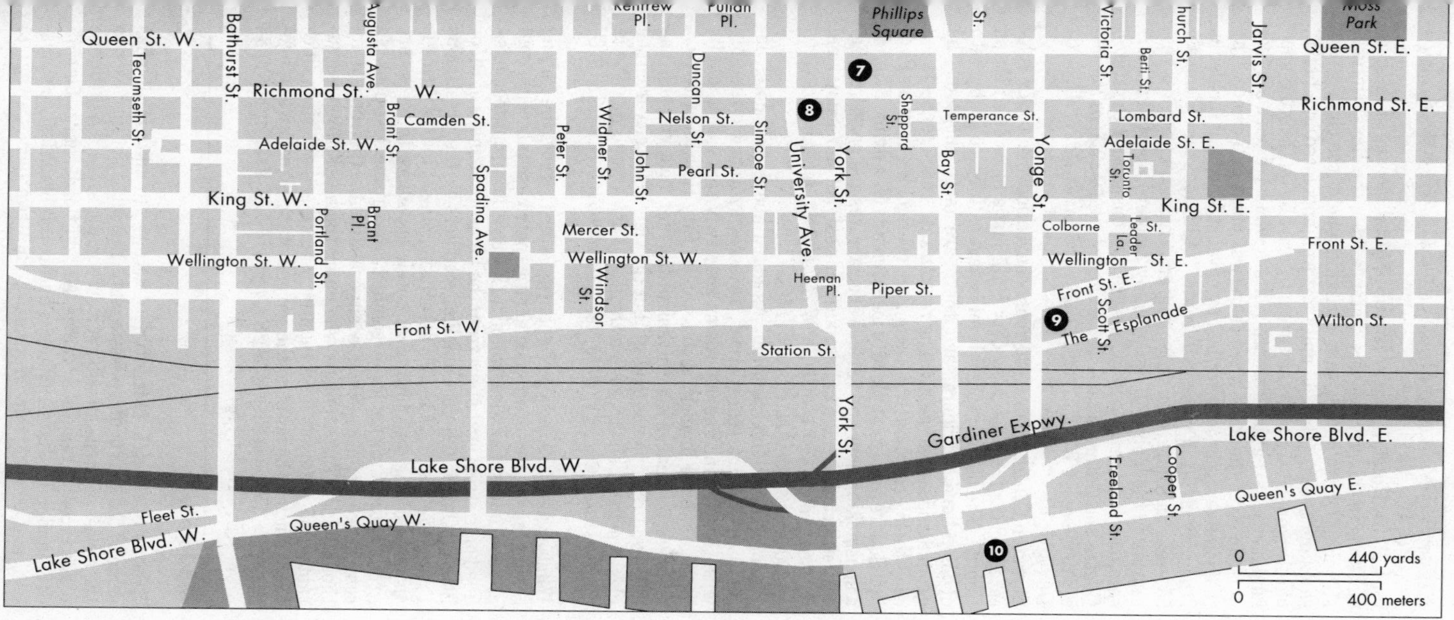

Brownstone Hotel, **4**
Chestnut Park, **6**
Four Seasons, **2**
Harbour Castle, **10**
Hotel Ibis, **5**
Novotel Toronto Centre, **9**
Park Plaza, **1**
Sheraton Centre, **7**
Toronto Hilton, **8**
Windsor Arms, **3**

just north of Nathan Phillips Sq.; tel. 416/977–5000. AE, CB, DC, MC, V.

Park Plaza Hotel. It may lack a pool, but it has one of the best locations in the city: a short distance from the Royal Ontario Museum, Queen's Park, and Yorkville (one of the city's great shopping areas). The 350 units are well-appointed in a plush, old-fashioned way, and they seem to coast by on their old-shoe familiarity to regular Toronto visitors who have been staying in them since the days when there was much less choice. The roof lounge was once described by novelist Mordecai Richler as "the only civilized place in Toronto." Additions now include a 550-seat ballroom, a business center, a palm court, and a restaurant in the lobby, all designed by Zeidler Roberts Partnership, the same architects who were responsible for the Eaton Centre and Ontario Place. *4 Avenue Rd., M5R 2E8, at the corner of Bloor St. W; tel. 416/924–5471 or 800/268–4927. AE, CB, DC, MC, V.*

Sheraton Centre. This 1,430-room conventioneer's tower is located across from the New City Hall, just a block from Eaton Centre. The below-ground level is part of Toronto's labyrinth of shop-lined corridors, and there are more shops on the ground and second floors. The restaurants' reach seems to exceed their grasp, but the Long Bar, overlooking Nathan Phillips Square, is a great place to meet friends for a drink. There's a nonsmoking floor and various special rates and packages. Facilities include a huge indoor/outdoor pool, hot tub, sauna, and workout room. *123 Queen St. W, M5H 2M9, tel. 416/361–1000 or 800/325–3535. AE, CB, DC, MC, V.*

Toronto Hilton International. As noted above, this hotel, located in the financial district, recently switched ownership with the Westin. The 600 rooms are newly renovated, and its nearness to the financial district, New City Hall, the CN Tower, and more makes it a convenient base for most visitors. The indoor/outdoor pool is modest, but the view of the city from the glass-enclosed elevators is a thrill. *145 Richmond St. W and University Ave., M5H 3M6, tel. 416/869–3456. AE, CB, DC, MC, V.*

★ **Windsor Arms.** Katharine Hepburn, Peter Ustinov, the Rolling Stones, and scores of other celebrities patronize this very small 81-room inn that nestles behind its ivy on a quiet, outdoor café–lined side street just steps from the high-ticket shops of Bloor Street. One of the 10 Canadian members in the prestigious French *Relais & Châteaux* association, the Windsor Arms is also one of the few downtown hotels anywhere to meet that group's standards for "calm, comfort, and cuisine." No pool. No conference facilities. Just a superb kitchen (patronized by thousands of Torontonians who enjoy the hotel's four restaurants) and rooms fit for a country inn. Rates have risen since 1988, placing the hotel on the top end of the Expensive category. *22 St. Thomas St., M5S 2B9, tel. 416/979–2341 or 800/668–8106. AE, CB, DC, MC, V.*

Moderate

Brownstone Hotel. This intimate hotel—110 units in all—has some of the charm of a private club. You could not be closer to the center of town and still get a quiet night's sleep. Ask for one of the recently renovated rooms. No additional charge for children under 14. Rates include Continental breakfast, newspaper, and membership in a health club two blocks away. *15*

Charles St. E, M4Y 1S1, tel. 416/924–6631 or 800/263–8967. AE, CB, DC, MC, V.

Novotel Toronto Centre. This moderately priced hotel—part of a popular French chain—opened in December 1987. There are 266 modest, modern rooms on nine floors in the heart of downtown, within walking distance of Harbourfront and the CN Tower. Facilities include an indoor pool, whirlpool, exercise room, and sauna. *45 The Esplanade, M5E 1W2, tel. 416/367–8900 or 800/221–4542. AE, CB, DC, MC, V.*

Inexpensive

Hotel Ibis. This recent hotel belongs to one of Europe's leading chains. It is centrally located just a few blocks from the New City Hall and Eaton Centre. As it proudly declares, "No bellhops, doormen, or concierges. No gushing fountains. And no room service with fancy silver trays." What it does have are 294 comfortable rooms with bare necessities (as well as 10 others specially designed and equipped for the disabled). There's no pool, but arrangements can be made with a nearby health club for a nominal fee. And there is a complimentary breakfast buffet. *240 Jarvis St., M5B 2B8, tel. 416/593–9400. AE, CB, DC, MC, V.*

Toronto Bed & Breakfast. More than two dozen private homes are affiliated with this service, most of them scattered across Metro Toronto. Rooms cost as little as $45 a night and include breakfast. *Tel. 416/961–3676.*

The Arts and Nightlife

The Arts

Toronto is the capital of the lively arts in Canada. True, Winnipeg has a very fine ballet, and Montréal's orchestra is superb. But in nearly every aspect of music, opera, dance, and theater, Toronto is truly the New York City of the North.

The best places to get information on cultural happenings are in the Friday editions of the *Toronto Star*, the Saturday *Globe and Mail*, the free weekly *Now* and *Metropolis* newspapers, and *Toronto Life*. For half-price tickets on the day of a performance, don't forget the **Five Star Tickets booth,** located in the Royal Ontario Museum lobby during the winter and, at other times, at the corner of Yonge and Dundas streets, outside the Eaton Centre. The museum booth is open daily 10–7, the Yonge and Dundas booth is open—in good weather—Monday–Saturday noon–7:30, and Sunday 11–3. Tickets are sold for cash only, all sales are final, and a small service charge is added to the price of each ticket. The booth outside the Eaton Centre also gives out piles of superb brochures and pamphlets on the city.

Concert Halls and Theaters

The **Roy Thomson Hall** (just below the CN Tower) has become since 1982 the most important concert hall in Toronto. It is the home today of the Toronto Symphony and the Toronto Mendelssohn Choir, one of the world's finest choral groups. It also hosts orchestras from around the world and popular entertainers from Liza Minnelli to Anne Murray. *60 Simcoe St., at the corner of King Street W, a block west of University Ave.; tel. 416/593–4828. Tickets $20–$50 (best seats rows H and J in the orchestra and row L upstairs). Rush seats are sold the day of a* *performance, beginning two hours before show time. Daily tours, highlighting the acoustic and architectural features of the stunning structure, take place Mon.–Sat. 12:30 PM (cost: $2). Tel. 416/593–4822 to confirm.*

Massey Hall has always been cramped and dingy, but its near-perfect acoustics and its handsome, U-shape tiers sloping down to the stage have made it a happy place to hear the Toronto Symphony, or almost anyone else in the world of music, for almost a century. The nearly 2,800 seats are not terribly comfortable, but it remains a venerable place to catch the greats and near-greats. *178 Victoria St. at Shuster, just a block north of Queen St. and a few feet east of the Eaton Centre; tel. 416/593–4828. Best seats are rows G–M, center, and in the balcony, rows 32–50.*

The Edward Johnson Building, in the Bloor Street/University Avenue area, houses the **MacMillan Theatre,** and it is an important place to hear avant-garde artists and the stars of the future. Because it's run by the faculty of music of the University of Toronto, the academic year also brings serious jazz trios and baroque chamber works—at little or no cost. *Located behind the McLaughlin Planetarium, just to the south of the Royal Ontario Museum subway exit; tel. 416/978–3744.*

The **O'Keefe Centre** has become the home of the Canadian Opera Company and the National Ballet of Canada. It is also home to visiting comedians, pre-Broadway musicals, rock stars, and almost anyone else who can fill it. When it was built in 1960, its 3,167 seats made it the largest concert hall on the continent. *1 Front St. E, a block east of Union Station; tel. 416/872–2262. Tickets $20–$50. Try for seats close to A47–48; avoid the very front rows, such as AA, BB, etc.*

About 50 yards east of the O'Keefe is the **St. Lawrence Centre for the Arts.** Since 1970, it has been presenting everything from live theater to string quartets and forums on city issues. The main hall, the luxuriously appointed **Bluma Appel Theatre,** hosts the often brilliant productions of the **Canadian Stage Company** and **Theater Plus.** Classical and contemporary plays are often on a level with the best of Broadway and London's West End. *Front St. at the corner of Scott St., a block east of Yonge St., two blocks from Union Station; tel. 416/366–7723. Tickets $15–$35. Try for rows E–N, seats 1–10.*

The other important theater in the city is the **Royal Alexandra,** which has been the place to be seen in Toronto since its opening in 1907. The plush red seats, gold brocade, and baroque swirls and curlicues all make theater-going a refined experience. It's astonishing to recall that all this magnificence was about to be torn down in the 1960s, but was rescued by none other than "Honest Ed" Mirvish of discount-store fame. He not only restored the theater to its former glory but also made it profitable. *Les Misérables*, which ran from March 1989 through May 1990, will return from early June 1991 through July, after a full year criss-crossing Canada. It's a marvelous production. *260 King St. W, a few blocks west of University, two blocks to the southwest of the CN Tower; tel. 416/593–4211. Tickets $30–$60. Student tickets can be as low as $12. Avoid rows A and B; try for rows C–L center. For musicals, try the first rows of the first balcony.*

Classical Concerts

The Toronto Symphony, now over 65 years old, is not about to retire. Since 1922, with conductors of the quality of Seiji Ozawa, Walter Susskind, Sir Thomas Beecham, and Andrew Davis, it has achieved world acclaim. Its new music director as of 1990/91 is Maestro Gunther Herbig. When the TS is home, it presents about three concerts weekly from September to May in Roy Thomson Hall and a mini-season each summer at Ontario Place. *60 Simcoe St., on King St., just west of University Ave.; tel. 416/593–4828. Tickets $16–$35.*

The **Toronto Mendelssohn Choir** often guests with the Toronto Symphony. This 180-singer group, going since 1894, has been applauded worldwide, and its *Messiah* is handeled well every Christmas (no, we couldn't resist that). *For program information, tel. 416/598–0422; for tickets, Roy Thomson Hall, tel. 416/593–4828.*

The **Elmer Isler Singers,** a fine group of nearly two dozen members, has also performed around the globe, and is a respected Toronto choir. *Tel. 416/482–1664.*

The **Orford String Quartet,** another world-class musical group, is based in Toronto at the Edward Johnson Building. *Tel. 416/978–3744.*

Opera

Since its founding in 1950, the **Canadian Opera Company** has grown into the largest producer of opera in Canada. From the most popular operas, such as *Carmen* and *Madame Butterfly,* usually performed in the original language, to more modern or rare works, such as *Jenufa,* the COC has proven trustworthy and often daring. Each year, at Toronto's O'Keefe Centre, more than 150,000 people attend their season of seven operas. The COC often hosts such world-class performers as Joan Sutherland, Grace Bumbry, Martina Arroyo, Marilyn Horne, and Canada's own Louis Quilico and Maureen Forrester. The COC also performs mini-operas in a tent during the summer, down at Harbourfront, on the shores of Lake Ontario. *Tel. 416/363–8231 or 416/393–7469.*

Dance

National Ballet of Canada made its official debut on the cramped stage of the old Eaton Auditorium on College Street in 1951. In less than four decades, the company has done some extraordinary things, with such principal dancers as Karen Kain, Frank Augustyn, Kevin Pugh, and Owen Montague all wowing the Russians at the Moscow competitions. *Performances Nov., Feb., and May at the O'Keefe Centre, at the corner of Front and Yonge Sts.; in summer at Ontario Pl. Office, tel. 416/362–1041, 416/872–1111 or 416/872–2277; O'Keefe Centre, 416/872–2262. Tickets $15–$55.*

Toronto Dance Theatre, its roots in the Martha Graham tradition, has created close to 100 works, more than a third using original scores commissioned from Canadian composers. It tours Canada and has played major festivals in England, Europe, and the United States. *Most performances are in the Premiere Dance Theatre, at Harbourfront, 235 Queen's Quay W; tel. 416/869–8444.*

Dancemakers is another important Toronto modern dance company, drawing on everyone from Martha Graham to Jose Limon and Merce Cunningham. It performs at both the Premiere Dance Theatre and Solar Stage (First Canadian Pl., on King St. near Bay St.; tel. 416/368–5135 or 416/535–8880).

Theater There are more than four dozen performing spaces in Toronto; we will mention only a handful of the most prominent.

The **Royal Alexandra,** the **O'Keefe,** and the **St. Lawrence centres** are described in Concert Halls, above.

The **Young People's Theatre** is the only theater center in the country devoted solely to children. But unlike purveyors of much of traditional children's fare, this place does not condescend or compromise its dramatic integrity. *165 Front St. E, near Sherbourne, 8 blocks east of Yonge St. Take the Yonge St. subway to King St. and then the King St. streetcar east, and walk down one block. Tel. 416/864–9732.*

Le Théâtre Française du Toronto, until recently known as Le Théâtre du P'tit Bonheur, has been providing French-language drama of high quality for many years. Its repertoire has ranged from classical to contemporary, from both France and French Canada. Recently it has moved to a marvelous location at Harbourfront, next door to the stunning Queen's Quay Terminal. In 1988, the theater performed a bilingual play, so English-speaking theatergoers could follow along. *The Du-Maurier Centre, 231 Queen's Quay W, tel. 416/534–6604.*

Toronto Free Theatre, although no longer free (and recently joining forces with the major Canadian Stage Company, which operates out of the St. Lawrence Centre), remains freewheeling and fascinating. This space has seen most of Canada's finest performers and playwrights showing their wares. *26 Berkeley St., just south of Front St. and 1 block west of Parliament St.; tel. 416/368–2856.*

The **Elgin** and **Winter Garden Theaters** are two of the newest/oldest jewels in the crowns of the Toronto arts scene. Both are old vaudeville places, stacked upon one another (The Elgin, downstairs, has about 1,500 seats, and is more suited for musicals; the Winter Garden, upstairs, is some 500 seats smaller, and more intimate; both are stunningly attractive.) Recently renovated, they have been used for jazz festivals, locally produced musicals *(The Wizard of Oz)*, and — a pleasant example — British actor/director Kenneth Branagh's Renaissance Theatre Company's productions of *King Lear* and *A Midsummer Night's Dream. 189 Yonge St., just north of Queen, tel. 416/872–5555.*

Second City, the Toronto version of the famous Chicago company, is the place where the inspired *SCTV* series had its genesis. Its revues tend to be the brightest, most reliable comedy in town. *The Old Firehall Theatre, 110 Lombard St., downtown, just east of Yonge St.; tel. 416/863–1162.*

There are many local productions of Broadway musicals and comedies presented in Toronto's numerous dinner theaters. These include **Harper's East** (38 Lombard St., downtown; tel. 416/863–6232) and **Limelight Dinner Theatre** (2026 Yonge St., just below Eglinton Ave.; tel. 416/482–5200).

Film Every September since 1976, Toronto has been holding a world-class film festival, called—with no great modesty—**The Festival of Festivals** (tel. 416/967–7371). Whether retrospectives of the films of Marguerite Duras, Jean-Luc Godard, and Max Ophuls, or tributes to the careers of Martin Scorsese, Robert Duvall, and John Schlesinger, this is the time for lovers of film.

Toronto is one of the film capitals of the world, and you can often catch a movie here that is not showing anywhere else—or even available on video. Foreigners will be either delighted or disappointed to discover that Toronto is still subject to the strange machinations of a provincial—in more ways than one—censor board, and therefore has no friendly neighborhood porno movies.

Fox Beaches (2236 Queen St. E, tel. 416/691-7330) is an old-style movie house that will flood anyone over 40 with warm nostalgia.

Reg Hartt Presents is one of the more delightful traditions of underground film in the city. On various days each month, in the Grapevine Room of the Diamond Club (410 Sherbourne St.), this movie-maniac maven will show such films as "The History of Animation" and "The Uncensored History of Warner Brothers Looney Tunes & Merrie Melodies." ("Warning: Many of these cartoons are sexist, racist, and as violent as a two-by-four in the face!" read his ads.) *Admission: $7–$10. Tel. 416/964–2739.*

Carlton Cinemas, part of the Cineplex chain, shows rare, important films from around the world in nearly a dozen screening rooms. *20 Carlton St., just steps east of the College St. subway; tel. 416/296–FILM.*

Ontario Film Theatre is in the Ontario Science Centre. A provincially funded film house, it is much admired for its foreign art films and retrospectives. *770 Don Mills Rd., near Eglinton Ave. E; tel. 416/429–4100.*

Nightlife

Jazz Clubs

For a romantic atmosphere, **Café des Copains** (48 Wellington St. E, near Yonge St.; tel. 416/869-0148) has a different solo jazz pianist every two weeks, playing every night but Sunday, from 8:30 PM to 12:30 AM. Two can enjoy the French-American cuisine for under $30. There is a bar, but this is no pickup place; people generally listen while the music is being performed.

A few blocks east of Eaton Centre is **George's Spaghetti House** (290 Dundas St. E, corner of Sherbourne St.; tel. 416/923-9887), the oldest continuously running jazz club in the city. The music starts at 8:30 PM, with the world-famous Moe Koffman (of "Swinging Shepherd Blues" fame) performing one week each month. (For Moe, and on weekends, you'll need reservations.) George's has a modest cover charge and a decent Italian menu. Closed Sun.

Chick 'n Deli has long been one of the great jazz places in Toronto. A casual atmosphere prevails, and the lack of a dress code helps with the neighborhood-bar ambience. There's a dance floor and dark wood everywhere, giving it a pub-like feel. It's also famous for wings and live music; the former half-price, Mon.–Tues. until 9, the latter playing at 9PM most nights, and 7:30 on Sundays. Check out the occasional earlier jazz shows, and the Sunday brunch — all you can eat for less than $10. *744 Mount Pleasant Rd., near Eglinton Ave,; tel. 416/489–3363 or 489–7931.*

Meyer's Deli is convenient to downtown and midtown hotels (69 Yorkville Ave., near Bay and Bloor Sts., tel. 416/960–4780). It is an attractive deli with solid, Jewish-style food and some of the better jazz to be experienced in Toronto. Here is where you can hear late-night sets Thursday, Friday, and Saturday.

Also in the downtown area is **Beaton's Lounge,** within Loew's **Westbury Hotel** (475 Yonge St., tel. 416/924–0611). Most evenings, the Lounge has top-40 bands and dancing, but on Sunday there's a jazz brunch from 11 AM to 3 PM. No jeans. The brunch costs about $20 for adults, $8 for children.

Rock and Popular Music

Most major international recording companies have offices in Toronto, so the city is a regular stop for top musical performers of today, whether Frank Sinatra, Billy Joel, Whitney Houston, Sting, Michael Jackson, or Bruce Springsteen. Tickets ($15–$40) can usually be booked through **BASS** (Best Available Seating Service); tel. 416/972–2262 or 416/972–2277.

Major venues include the **Sky Dome,** just west of the CN Tower, on Front Street, tel. 416/963–3513; **Maple Leaf Gardens,** 60 Carlton Street, a block east of Yonge Street and the College Street subway stop, tel. 416/977–1641; the **O'Keefe Centre,** Yonge and Front streets, tel. BASS, 416/872–2262; and **Exhibition Stadium,** at the CNE grounds, tel. 416/393–6000.

Ontario Place (tel. 416/965–7711) has pop, rock, and jazz concerts throughout its summer season, at no cost above that of admission to the park. This is one of the loveliest and least expensive places to see and hear a concert in all of Toronto.

Kingswood Music Theatre, next to Canada's Wonderland, also has important rock and pop concerts during the warmer months. *Located along Hwy. 400, 10 min north of Hwy. 401; tel. 416/832–8131. Admission usually only $7 above the cost of Canada's Wonderland.*

Since May 1989, **Superstars Niteclub** has been packing 1,700 people nightly into its giant room. Monday through Wednesday, it has professional acts, on the line of The Fixx, Jerry Seinfeld, and Sam Kinison, with prices ranging $10–$25. Thursday to Saturday is for dancing, with a cover of about $9. Hamburgers, chicken fingers, etc., provide the fuel. Laws banning liquor from being served on Sunday have freed the owners to use the place for children's and teen's concerts, featuring rap groups. *6487 Dixie Rd., 1 mi north of Hwy 401, and just west of the airport; tel. 416/670–2211. Open Mon.–sat. 7 PM–2 AM.*

Not far away is **Cameron Public House,** a small, eclectic place where the sounds alternate from jazz to hard rock to new wave: "alternative music," as they proudly call it. The Cameron gets a creative crowd, with many regulars. The suburbanite scene gets heavy on weekends, as do the crowds. *408 Queen St. W, tel. 416/364–0811.*

The **Diamond** has been described as "Toronto's premier live showcase room" and since this is where such international stars as Sinead O'Connor had their Toronto debut, you can understand what we mean. Music critics, musicians, agents, and recording producers make a point of dropping in to spot the next big act. Five bars provide the drinks, and the light, sound, and limited (700-seat) capacity all make for a magical night of rock 'n roll. *410 Sherbourne St., several blocks blocks east of Yonge; tel. 416/927–9010.*

Pop rock reins at the famous **Horseshoe Tavern,** also along the Queen Street strip. Good bands perform here, six days a week, with no food but lots of booze and a cover charge. It's a real tavern, with a pool table, lots of flannel-shirt types, mostly blue collar. Rock nostalgia lines the walls, and far more men than women line the bar. On weeknights, the ages range 25–40; on weekends, it's younger. *368 Queen St. W, corner of Spadina Ave.; tel. 416/598–4753. Closed Sun.*

A major showcase for more daring arts in Toronto has long been **The Rivoli,** along the Queen Street "mall." A place for new, local artists not yet established enough to have their own gallery showings, the back room functions as a club, with theater happenings, "new music" (progressive rock and jazz), comedy troupes providing very funny improvisations twice a month, and more. *332 Queen St. W, just west of University Ave.; tel. 416/597–0794. No dress code. Cover charge: $5–$10. Closed Sun.*

Reggae, Caribbean and More

Bamboo is listed in our restaurant section because its Thai/Caribbean food is remarkably delicious and just as remarkably reasonably priced. But this crazy old building, a one-time commercial laundry hidden behind the popular Queen Street strip, is where to find everything from reggae to calypso, Caribbean to African, and even jazz. The sightlines can be terrible, it's no place for a quiet conversation, but it's wildly popular: great eating, and great music. *312 Queen St. W, tel. 416/593–5771.*

Rhythm and Blues

The undisputed champion of R & B in Toronto is **Club Bluenote,** a few blocks north of the Yorkville area. It's quite unique, with many world-class musicians and singers frequenting it, and occasionally getting up and doing their stuff. A small dance floor, but who cares, with so much talent hanging around? The age range is 25–50, and the clientele is upper class. And this is no hit bar; people come here to listen to music in a serious way. When Whitney Houston, Sugar Ray Leonard, et. al. are in town, this is where they go. *128 Pears Ave., just north of Davenport Rd. and west of Avenue Rd.; tel. 416/924–8244. Usually closed Sun. Cover charge: $8–$10.*

Right next door is **Network,** an entertainment lounge specializing in name acts of the quality of The Stylistics, Junior Walker, and Goodman and Brown. It's a supper club and show, with the cover and buffet combined at a reasonable $20 or so. The only dress code is "No Jeans," and there is a dance floor. The clientele is urban professionals in their early thirties; the decor is modern—brass, black, polished oak. *138 Pears Ave., near Davenport Rd.; tel. 416/924–1768.*

Albert's Hall has been called one of the top 25 bars in all of North America, in spite of its shabby decor. It features top blues bands. The crowd is older and more laid-back than downstairs, in the Brunswick, but it's still noisy and friendly—and loud. *481 Bloor St. W, near Spadina Ave., tel. 416/964–2242. Cover charge on weekends; closed Sun.*

Black Swan was an old-time bar for three quarters of a century; today, its 120 customers nightly watch, listen and tap toes to wonderful, live rhythm and blues. Located out in the east end—where Bloor Street turns magically into "The Danforth," on the other side of the Don Valley Parkway—this spot will zap classic R & B lovers back into the 1960s. *154 Danforth Ave., tel. 416/469–0537.*

Chicago's, along the delightful Queen Street West strip, heading west from University Avenue, is a real charmer. Downstairs is a cowboyish bar and good hamburgers; upstairs is where you can see and hear the blues stars of tomorrow, and the day after. Dig the red neon sign in the shape of a beer cap. *335 Queen St. W, tel. 416/598–3301.*

Comedy Clubs

Bemelmans is all chandeliers, mirrors, marble, wood, and great beauty. The patio is lovely, but the real action is the crowded bar, where performers and artists pour in after their shows. (It doesn't hurt to have a 3 AM closing time, a rarity in this once staunchly WASP city.) And just a few hundred feet away from the heart of the city, Bloor and Yonge! *83 Bloor St. W, tel. 416/960–0306.*

Second City, just east of the heart of downtown, has been providing some of the best comedy in North America since its owner Andrew Alexander bought the rights to the name for one dollar. This converted fire hall has given much to the world, through both *Saturday Night Live* and the inspired *SCTV* series. Among those who have cut their teeth on the Toronto stage are the late Gilda Radner, Dan Aykroyd, Martin Short, Andrea Martin, Catherine O'Hara, and John Candy. Shows can be seen alone or as part of a dinner-theater package. *110 Lombard St., corner of Jarvis St., just a few blocks northeast of Front and Yonge Sts.; tel. 416/863–1111.*

Next to Second City, **Yuk-Yuk's Komedy Kabaret** has always been the major place for comedy in Toronto. This is where the zany comedian Howie Mandel and the inspired impressionist Jim Carrey got their starts, and where such comic luminaries as George Carlin, Rodney Dangerfield, Robin Williams, and Mort Sahl have presented their best routines. *1280 Bay St., just above Bloor St., 2335 Yonge St., just above Eglinton Ave. and 5165 Dixie, just above Eglinton; tel. 416/967–6425. No dress code. Cover charge: $7 and up. Yonge St. location closed Sun.*

Dancing

Berlin quickly became one of the most popular spots in Toronto, within a year of its opening in early 1987. There's no dress code, but people dress up for this upscale, European-style multilevel club. There is a Continental menu for dining and a seven-piece band for jazz, pop, and R & B. The crowd is 25–35 and very rich, and the club radiates a feeling of exclusivity. *2335 Yonge St., north of Eglinton Ave.; tel. 416/489–7777. Open Tues. and Thur. 6–2; Fri. and Sat. 6–3. $6–$12 cover.*

DJs play '60s music (downstairs) and '90s music (upstairs) in a four-story century-old funhouse named **Big Bop.** Drinks Wednesday nights cost $2.50; Thursday nights are Ladies' Nights, with no cover for women. In rebellion against the New York School of Glitzy, there is no chrome or mirrors—just a deliberate effort to be campy, vibrant, and unpretentious. The clientele is 18–25. It's a true meat market, but it doesn't pretend to be otherwise. Capacity is 800, and jeans are de rigueur. Many international stars walk in, but the owner insists that it's no big deal. (No big deal? Jack Nicholson. William Hurt. Matt Dillon!!) *651 Queen St. W, tel. 416/366–6699. Open weekends to 3 AM.*

An important after-hours club is **Club Z**, which is open weekends only for a young crowd that doesn't mind staying up way past its bedtime. Hours are 8 PM to 6 AM, Thursday to Sunday. No alcohol is served; music and dancing are the attractions. The music is funk, the crowd is young, and the soda pop flows like water. *11a Joseph St., one block north of Wellesley Ave. and Yonge St.; tel. 416/963–9430. Cover charge: $10 range. Dress: casual, but no sneakers or jeans on Sat.*

In the heart of Yorkville is **The Copa**, which has to be seen to be believed. The former warehouse is gigantic, with a capacity of 1,100! The crowd is in the 20–25 range and on the prowl. There's a zillion-dollar light show, with lasers and video screens. Tina Turner played for its grand opening; B.B. King and Ray Parker, Jr., have also performed here. The dance music is top 40; on Sunday nights, it gets funkier. *21 Scollard St., entrance off Yorkville Ave.; tel. 416/922–6500. Cover charge: $10.*

The Diamond is an art deco restaurant and dance club that continually brings in big acts, such as Kris Kristofferson and Pink Floyd. Acts range from jazz to country to rock; newcomers to the record scene will often showcase their talent here. Fridays and Saturdays are for dancing. The crowd is mostly early twenties; lots of students and young professionals. The many fashion shows appeal to the trendy downtowners. *410 Sherbourne St., north of Carlton, east of Yonge St.; tel. 416/927–9010. Cover charge. Line-up on weekends.*

Earl's Tin Palace has been described as the star attraction of the Yonge/Eglinton/Mt. Pleasant singles scene, and it does its job well: The fashionable, affluent people have made this place their home, and many arrive in groups. The decor is stunning: a big, airy tin palace with elaborate props, such as stuffed birds. The clientele dresses very well, with men even in (gasp) suits. The 35–40 crowd is better represented here than in most other clubs. *150 Eglinton Ave. E, not far from Yonge St.; tel. 416/487–9281. No cover.*

Back on Yorkville Avenue is **P.W.D. Dinkel's**, which has been attracting the trendies of the area for many years. The age range is 20–40, and regulars make up much of the crowd. The ratio of men to women is 50/50; the two stand-up bars are where the action is. A black and white dance floor has the usual mirrored ball and flashing disco lights nearby. Live bands play top-40–style, yet original, music. There's finger food and dinner at about $50 for two, with wine. *88 Yorkville Ave., tel. 416/923–9689. Open Mon.–Sun to 2 AM. Cover charge: about $9 on weekends.*

A bar/club called **StiLife** recently opened downtown and is very popular. It caters to an older (25–35) crowd and to rapidly aging 40-year-olds. The decor is metallic and modular, with all the furnishings custom-made. The art is aided by sophisticated lighting. No jeans or sneakers. A DJ provides dance music, and the clientele is Yorkville-ish, with many clothing designers, people who own other restaurants, etc. Check out the bathrooms—you'll find out why. *217 Richmond St. W, tel. 416/593–6116. Closed Sun. Cover charge: $6–$15.*

The most exciting '50s-type place is **Studebaker's**, in the University/King area. It's bright and colorful, with memorabilia, a jukebox, and a DJ. During the week, it attracts a business crowd, with far more males than females. On weekends, a younger, suburban crowd gathers after 8 or 9; expect a 60-minute wait. No T-shirts. *150 Pearl St., tel. 416/591–7960.*

Rockit has been described as "the mainstream dance crowd's terrestrial equivalent to rock 'n roll heaven." The pizza is dynamite, the wood-and-brass bar is gorgeous, and upstairs are the college kids in uniform (cool ties and designer jeans), dancing away to the Big Hits. *120 Church St., just east of Yonge, tel. 416/947–9555.*

Supper Clubs Long known as Toronto's "last elegant supper club," the **Imperial Room** of the Royal York Hotel recently dropped its policy of giving this city Tony, Ella, and Lena. Today, it's only dining and dancing to a live band with "a big band sound playing all your requests." The room is still a knock-out, and from 8–12, Tues.–Thurs., and 7:30–12:30, Fri and Sat., you can eat ($20–$30 each), dance and still enjoy one of Toronto's great spaces. *100 Front St. W, opposite Union Station, tel. 416/368–2511.*

Cafés **Chapter's Bookstore Cafe** is a wonderful Idea Whose Time Has Come. A sophisticated professional crowd (mid-30s–60s) fills the bar area, especially on weekend nights—although this is no pickup joint! The café upstairs is a cozy "bookloft," with a fireplace and reasonably priced food. There's an extensive magazine collection, which people at the bar sit and read. Every week a prominent author speaks in the upstairs café, followed by an informal conversation in the bar area. *2360 Yonge St., a block above Eglinton Ave., tel. 416/481–2472.*

The **Free Times Cafe** is a showcase for folk music, where singers nightly perform their own original work. The menu is "Kensington Canadian Cuisine," with both vegetarian as well as meat dishes; it's licensed and modestly priced. The decor is white stucco with stained-pine edging; the bar has café chairs with upholstered seats. Every six weeks, the original art changes. *320 College St., near Spadina Ave., on the edge of the University of Toronto campus; tel. 416/967–1078.*

Lounges Up on the 51st floor of the ManuLife Centre, **The Aquarius Lounge** is the highest piano lounge in the city, even before you take your first, expensive drink. The busy time in the summer is Thursday–Saturday after 8:30 PM, but there's a high turnover, so the wait is never too long. In the winter, the lines begin as early as 8 PM. This is not a place to meet people, and it is not trendy in the way that most bars in the Yorkville area are. But its romantic atmosphere makes this a marvelous place for a date. No shorts, but jeans are allowed. *55 Bloor St. W, at Bay St.; tel. 416/967–5225.*

In the Brownstone Hotel is **Notes,** an intimate bar/restaurant with a grand piano and a grand bar around it. It's done up in pink and beige tones, with black-lacquer furniture and antiques. You'll find no windows here, and the lighting is dim, but it's a good, quiet place to get to know someone. Dinner for two runs about $40–$50, including wine (their fresh sole is fine). A fine pianist entertains Tuesday–Saturday. *15 Charles St. E, tel. 416/924–7381.*

In the classy Four Seasons Hotel is **La Serre,** which looks like a library in a mansion: plush and green, with lots of brass and dark wood. It has a stand-up piano bar and a pianist worth standing for. Drinks, coffees, and teas are all expensive, but what can you expect in one of the costliest hotels in the country? Weekdays attract a business crowd, weekends bring out the couples. *Avenue Rd. and Yorkville Ave., tel. 416/964–0411.*

The **Park Plaza Roof Lounge** has been used as a setting in the writings of such Canadian literary luminaries as Margaret Atwood and Mordecai Richler. The decor used to be plush, in an older European style, with chandelier, marble tables, and waiters in red jackets. It remains an important hangout for the upper-middle class, businesspeople, professional, and, *bien sur*, literary types. Since 1990, it has been redone, but it's still gorgeous and tasteful. *In the Park Plaza Hotel, Avenue Rd. and Bloor St.; tel. 416/924–5471.*

The Twenty-Two has been a quiet meeting spot for Torontonians and tourists for more than a quarter-century. There's no dress code or cover, yet one can count on lovely live piano music nightly 5–8, and piano with singing 9 PM–1 AM. There are free hors d'oeuvres at 6 PM; if you're still hungry, dine at the excellent Courtyard Cafe, in the same building. Big deals and hot affairs go on here, but it's very discreet, possibly because of the dim lighting. Probably 90% are regulars who have good rapport with the staff. The decor is mostly tables for two, with beige-and-green chairs and walls and lots of wood. A sidewalk café has good seating capacity. If you've got something important to say to someone, this is one of the most pleasant places in the city to say it. *22 St. Thomas St., 1 block east and south of the ROM; tel. 416/979–2341.*

4 Montréal

Introduction

by Patricia Lowe

A former reporter and editor for the defunct Montréal Star, *Patricia Lowe is a native Montrealer.*

"Plus ça change, plus c'est la même chose," like other travel clichés, no longer applies to Montréal. For years, as Québec's largest city and the world's third-largest French-speaking metropolis, Montréal clung to an international reputation attained in the heyday of former Mayor Jean Drapeau, who brought his beloved hometown the 1967 World's Fair (Expo '67), the Métro subway, its Underground City, and the 1976 Summer Olympics. During his nearly three decades in power, Drapeau's entrepreneurial spirit added pizzazz to this transportation and financial capital at the gateway to the St. Lawrence Seaway.

But with the arrival of a nationalist provincial government in 1976, the mayor and Montréal were forced to rest on their laurels as the province agonized over its place in Canada. Separation from the rest of the country was seriously considered. The provincial government passed Bill 101, a controversial language act (still in force) making French the official language of business and public communication. For the city it was a wrenching ideological change; the only differences visitors saw were English or bilingual billboards and public signs replaced by French ones.

Nearly 60% of the province's population opted in 1980 to remain in the federal family; but a decade later, French-speaking Québeckers' old animosities regarding English Canada were rekindled when Prime Minister Mulroney attempted to unite all ten provinces through a constitutional agreement called the Meech Lake accord. The legislatures of two provinces voted not to accept the accord, so it was not ratified.

All this comes on the eve of Montréal's 350th anniversary, plunging residents into a passionate debate over their future as they prepare to celebrate their past. Nevertheless, Montréal continues to plan for the year-long party to mark its founding, on May 18, 1642, as a French missionary colony. Change is most evident in the downtown core, where complexes, condominiums, and museums continue to sprout or spruce up for 1992, turning the city into one vast construction site.

The melding of old and new is no more apparent than in the flamboyant office tower of Les Cooperants. Even though the design of this 35-story pink glass structure imitates the gothic-style Christ Church Cathedral it overshadows, it was not what the earnest French missionaries who founded Montréal envisioned. What today is a metropolis of 2.8 million—some 20% of other ethnic origin—began as 54 dedicated souls from France who landed on Montréal island in 1642. Led by career military man Paul de Chomedey, Sieur de Maisonneuve, they had come to this 32-mile-long island in the middle of the St. Lawrence to convert the Indians to Christianity.

They first set foot on a spot they called Ville-Marie, now Place Royale in Vieux-Montréal (Old Montréal). Although they were pioneer settlers, Place Royale had been named by French explorer Samuel de Champlain, who established a temporary trading post here in 1611.

Montréal Exploring *(Boxes Refer to Detail Maps)*

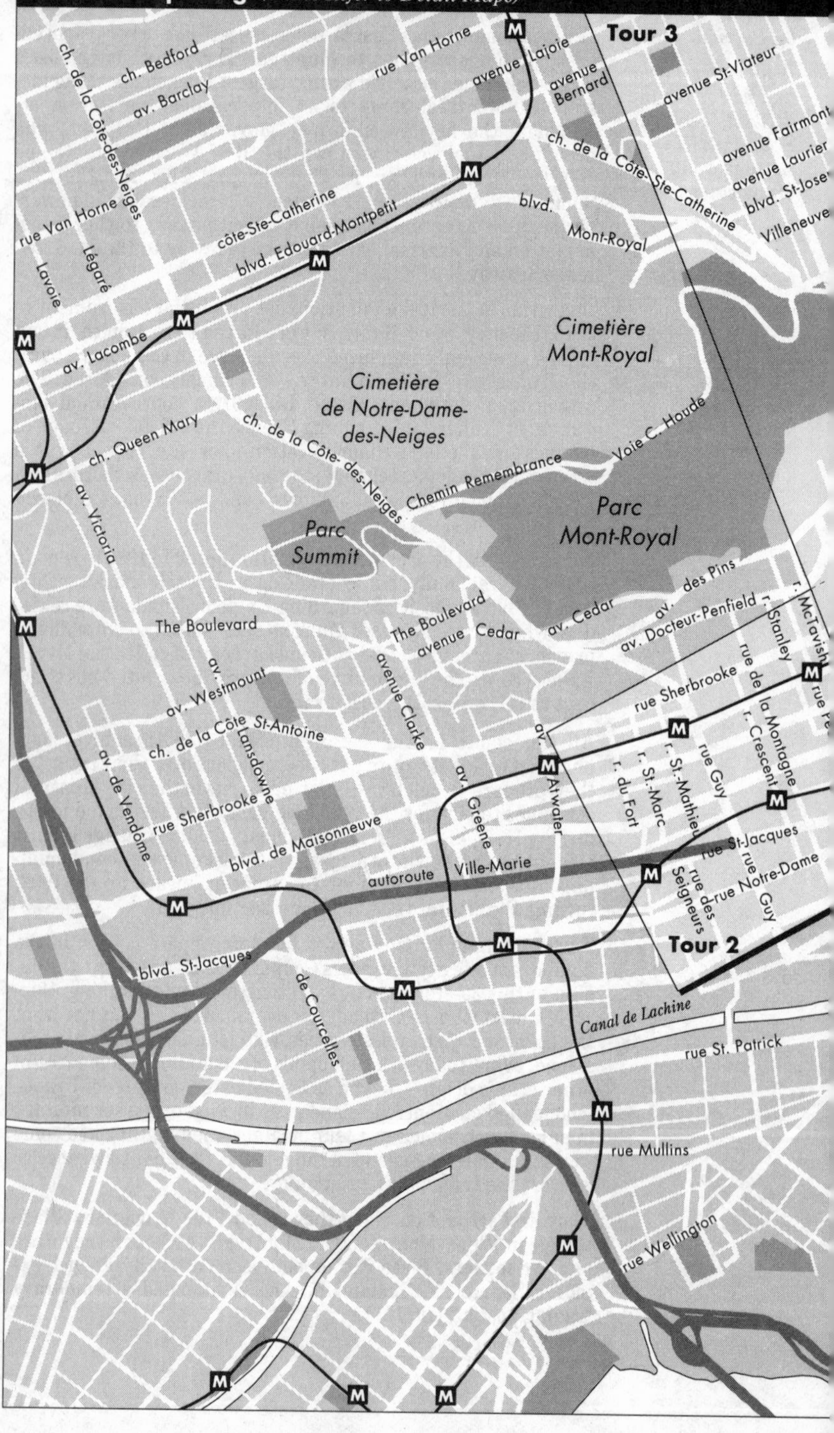
Tour 3
ch. Bedford
ch. de la Côte-des-Neiges
av. Barclay
rue Van Horne
avenue Lajoie
avenue Bernard
avenue St-Viateur
avenue Fairmont
avenue Laurier
blvd. St-Joseph
Villeneuve
ch. de la Côte-Ste-Catherine
rue Van Horne
côte-Ste-Catherine
blvd. Edouard-Montpetit
blvd. Mont-Royal
Légaré
Lavoie
av. Lacombe
Cimetière Mont-Royal
Cimetière de Notre-Dame-des-Neiges
ch. Queen Mary
ch. de la Côte-des-Neiges
Voie C. Houde
Chemin Remembrance
Parc Mont-Royal
Parc Summit
av. Victoria
av. des Pins
av. Docteur-Penfield
av. Cedar
The Boulevard
The Boulevard
avenue Cedar
r. McTavish
r. Stanley
rue de la Montagne
rue Sherbrooke
av. Westmount
av. Lansdowne
ch. de la Côte St-Antoine
avenue Clarke
av. Atwater
r. Crescent
rue Guy
r. St-Mathieu
r. St-Marc
r. du Fort
av. de Vendôme
rue Sherbrooke
av. Greene
blvd. de Maisonneuve
rue St-Jacques
rue Notre-Dame
rue Guy
rue des Seigneurs
autoroute Ville-Marie
Tour 2
blvd. St-Jacques
de Courcelles
Canal de Lachine
rue St. Patrick
rue Mullins
rue Wellington

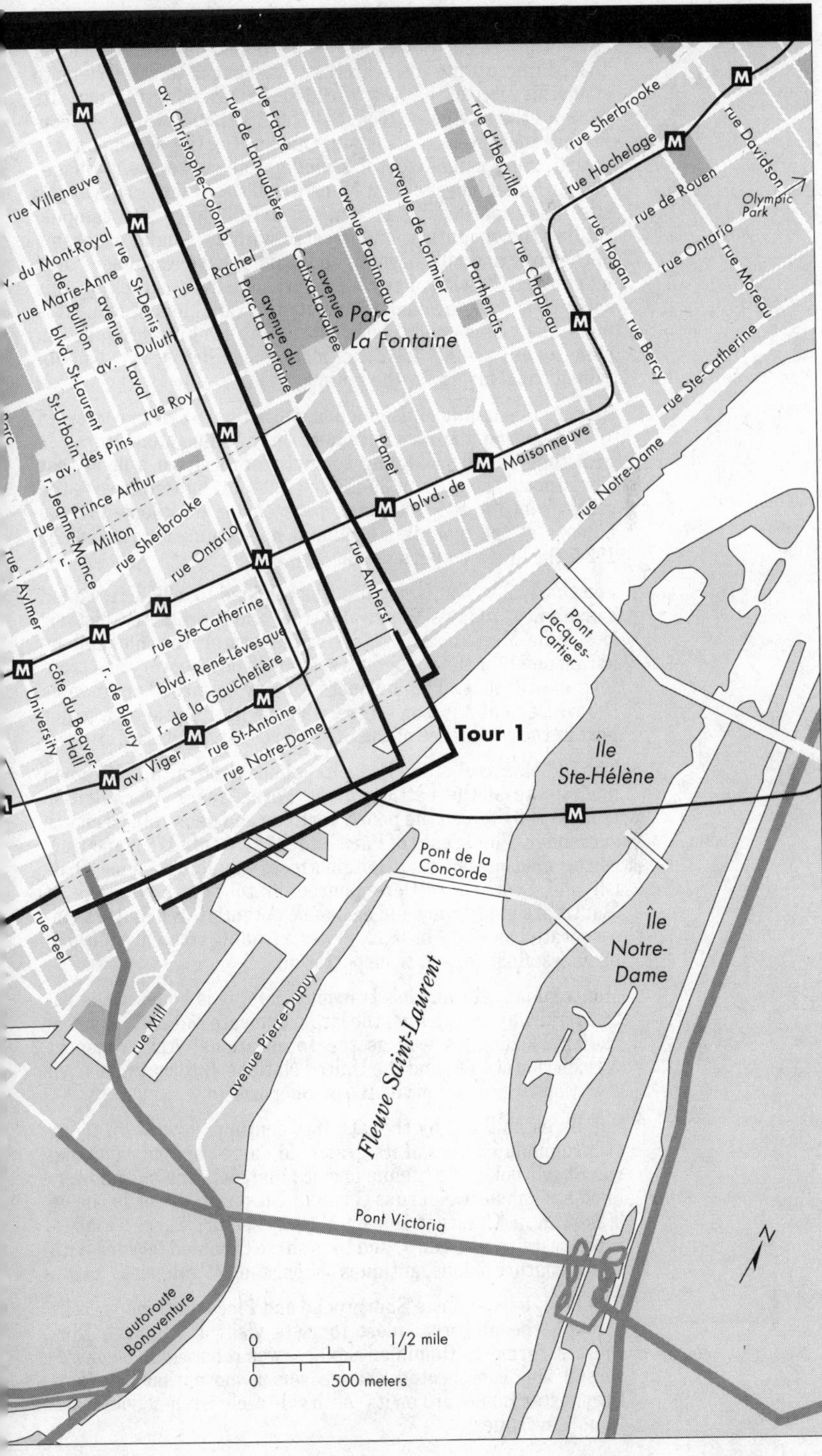

rue Sherbrooke
rue Davidson
rue Hochelage
rue de Rouen
Olympic Park
rue Ontario
rue Moreau
rue Hogan
rue Bercy
rue Ste-Catherine
rue d'Iberville
rue Chapleau
Parthenais
avenue de Lorimier
avenue Papineau
avenue Calixa-Lavallée
avenue du Parc La Fontaine
Parc La Fontaine
rue Fabre
rue de Lanaudière
av. Christophe-Colomb
rue Rachel
rue Villeneuve
av. du Mont-Royal
rue Marie-Anne
de Bullion
blvd. St-Laurent
avenue Laval
rue St-Denis
av. Duluth
St-Urbain
rue Roy
av. des Pins
rue Prince Arthur
r. Jeanne-Mance
r. Milton
rue Sherbrooke
rue Ontario
rue Aylmer
rue Ste-Catherine
blvd. René-Lévesque
r. de la Gauchetière
r. de Bleury
côte du Beaver-Hall
University
av. Viger
rue St-Antoine
rue Notre-Dame
Panet
blvd. de Maisonneuve
rue Notre-Dame
rue Amherst
Pont Jacques-Cartier
Tour 1
Île Ste-Hélène
Pont de la Concorde
Île Notre-Dame
rue Peel
rue Mill
avenue Pierre-Dupuy
Fleuve Saint-Laurent
Pont Victoria
autoroute Bonaventure
0
1/2 mile
0
500 meters
N
M

The first white man to see Montréal was Jacques Cartier, discoverer of the St. Lawrence, who stopped off on the island in 1535, interrupting his search for a shortcut to the Orient to claim this piece of the New World for France. Montréal owes its name to the navigator from St. Malo, although there are conflicting anecdotes on its origin. One has Cartier accompanying a welcoming committee of friendly Indians to their village, Hochelaga, supposedly on Mont Royal's southern slope at the site today marked by a cairn on McGill University campus. Scaling this mountain, and greeted with a splendid panorama of the river and hills beyond, he is said to have exclaimed "quel mont royal!" (what a royal mount). (Visitors can enjoy this same view from the chalet lookout atop Parc Mont-Royal.) It is more likely he named it later, at the French king's request, in memory of Cardinal Medici of Montreale (Sicily), who had obtained papal favors for the king.

A truer tale has de Maisonneuve, more than a century later, in 1643, planting a cross somewhere on the same Mont Royal, in gratitude for the fledgling colony's escape from a flood that Christmas. The present 30-meter (100-foot) lighted cross—the glare from its 158 bulbs can be seen for 64 kilometers (40 miles)—at the mountain's summit has commemorated, since 1924, the first wooden symbol.

For nearly 200 years, city life was confined to a 95-acre walled community, today's Vieux-Montréal and a protected historic site. Ville-Marie became a fur-trading center, the chief embarkation point for the voyageurs setting off on discovery and trapping expeditions. This business quickly upsurped re igion as the settlement's raison d'être, along with its role as a major port at the confluence of the St. Lawrence and Ottawa rivers.

The Old Montréal of the French regime lasted until 1759, when during one of the battles of the Seven Years' War, British troops easily forced the poorly fortified and demoralized city to surrender. The Treaty of Paris ended the war in 1763, and Québec became one of Great Britain's most valuable colonies. British and Scottish settlers poured in to take advantage of Montréal's geography and economic potential. When it was incorporated as a city in 1832, it was a leading colonial capital of business, finance, and transportation.

Montréal is still Canada's transport hub: It is home to the national railway and airline, the largest private rail company (Canadian Pacific), as well as the International Air Transport Association (IATA) and the United Nations' International Civil Aviation Organization (ICAO) on Sherbrooke.

Solidly established by the late 19th century, downtown today still reminds visitors of its grand old days, particularly along rue Sherbrooke, the lifeline of chic Montréal. The busy flower-lined stretch between rues Guy and University takes in the de la Montagne-Crescent-Bishop-Mackay sector, where sophisticated restaurants, cafés, and bars share canopied facades with haute-couture salons, antiques shops, and art galleries.

Rue Peel, between rue Sherbrooke and Place du Canada, rolls through the Montréal most tourists visit. Its Square Dorchester, formerly Dominion Square, was renamed in a controversial and complicated changeover, a move that also saw Dorchester Boulevard on its south side rechristened boulevard René-Lévesque.

Whatever the name, it has been the major tourist rallying point for more than 35 years. The recently renovated Dominion Square Building is the art deco home of tourism offices and information bureaus. Bus tours, taxi guides, and calèches (horse-drawn carriages) all depart from some point around this public park. The square's monuments and buildings are insightful commentaries on Montréal's multicultural history. Statues commemorate such varied personalities as heroes of the Boer War, poet Robert Burns, and Sir Wilfrid Laurier, a Québécois and Canada's Liberal prime minister from 1896 to 1911.

To the east, rue St-Denis and the surrounding Latin Quarter attract Francophiles, while a more ethnic flavor characterizes the Chinese, Greek, Jewish, Portuguese, and other districts around Prince Arthur's pedestrian mall, boulevard St-Laurent, and avenue du Parc.

A bohemian atmosphere pervades rue Prince Arthur, blocked off to traffic between rue St-Laurent and Carré St-Louis. What the mall's many restaurants sometimes lack in quality, they make up for in ethnic diversity—Chinese, Greek, Italian, Polish, Québécois, and Vietnamese—and price, especially at establishments where you supply the liquor (BYO). Some 12,000 Portuguese residents live in the area's St-Louis district, and their bright pastel houses and lush front gardens have contributed to the neighborhood's renaissance.

Early in this century, rue St-Denis cut through a bourgeois neighborhood of large, comfortable residences. After a period of decline, it revived in the early 1970s, and then boomed, largely as a result of the 1979 opening of Université du Québec's Montréal campus and the launch of the International Jazz Festival in the summer of 1980. Rows of French and ethnic restaurants, charming bistros, even hangouts for chess masters, cater to Franco- and Anglo-academics, while stylish intellectuals prowl the Québec designer boutiques, antiques shops, and art galleries.

Activity reaches its peak during the 10 days in late June and early July when some 500,000 jazz buffs descend upon the city to hear the likes of Dizzy Gillespie, Montréal-born Oscar Peterson, and Pat Metheny. Theaters hosting the 1,000 or so performers range from sidewalk stages to Place des Arts, the main performing arts center in downtown Montréal, Théâtre St-Denis, and the Spectrum.

The popularity of the jazz festival is rivaled only by August's World Film Festival, also featured near this area at Place des Arts and Cinéma Le Parisien on rue Ste-Catherine, among other venues.

Place des Arts and the adjacent Complexe Desjardins constitute another intriguing hive of activity. Soon to be joined by the new home of the Musée d'art contemporain, in October 1991, Place des Arts is really three separate halls built around a sweeping plaza overlooking rue Ste-Catherine.

One often-overlooked sector of the city requires a Métro ride but is worth the fare for a varied tour of Olympic and de Maisonneuve parks, the Château Dufresne Decorative Arts Museum, and the Botanical Garden—all located at or near the corner of boulevard Pie-IX (Métro station of the same name) and rue Sherbrooke est.

This triangle in the east end is distinguished by the flying saucer design of the Olympic Stadium, completed by the world's "tallest inclined tower." The stadium's latest attraction is the funicular cable car that speeds sightseers to its observation deck for a spectacular view of the island of Montréal.

Essential Information

Arriving and Departing by Plane

Airports Montréal is served by two airports: **Dorval International,** 22½ kilometers (14 miles) west of the city, handles domestic and most U.S. flights; **Mirabel International,** 54½ kilometers (34 miles) northwest of the city, is a hub for the rest of the international trade. A direct flight makes one or more stops before its final destination; a nonstop is just that; and a connecting flight means you will have to change planes at least once en route.

Airlines From the United States: **Air Canada** (tel. 800/422–6232) has nonstop service from New York, Miami, and Tampa; nonstop from Boston via Air Canada's connector airline, Air Alliance; direct service is available from Chicago, Los Angeles, and San Francisco. **American Airlines** (tel. 800/433–7300) has nonstop service from Chicago with connections from the rest of the United States. **British Airways** (tel. 800/247–9297) has nonstop service from Detroit to Montréal. **Canadian Airlines International,** formerly CP Air (tel. 800/426–7000) has a nonstop charter from Miami and direct or connecting service from Hawaii, Los Angeles, and Pittsburgh. **Delta Air Lines** (tel. 800/323–2323) has nonstops from Boston; Hartford, Connecticut; and Miami and connecting service from most major U.S. cities. **Eastern Airlines** (tel. 800/327–8376) has service from New York's La Guardia Airport. **Midway Airlines** (tel. 800/621–5700 has frequent nonstops from Philadelphia. **US Air** (tel. 800/428–4322) has nonstop service from Buffalo and Syracuse, NY and from Pittsburgh.

Flying Time From New York, 1½ hours; from Chicago, 2 hours; from Los Angeles, 6½ hours (with a connection).

Between the Airports and Center City The Dorval Airport is about a 20- to 30-minute drive from downtown Montréal, and Mirabel International is about a 45-minute drive away.

By Taxi A taxi from Dorval to downtown will cost $19. The taxi rates from Mirabel to the center of Montréal are $45, and you can count on about the same cost for a taxi between the two airports. All taxi companies in Montréal must charge the same rates by law. It is best to have Canadian money with you, because the exchange rate for U.S. dollars is at the driver's discretion.

By Bus **Aerocar** (tel. 514/397–9999) provides a much cheaper alternative into town from both airports. For $7 from Dorval or $9 from Mirabel, an Aerocar van will take you into the city, with stops at the Sheraton Center, the Château Champlain Hotel, Le Reine Elizabeth hotel (next to Gare Centrale), and the Voyageur bus station. Service between the two airports is $9. Aerocar buses leave Dorval every 20 minutes on weekdays and every half-hour on weekends. From Mirabel buses leave hourly or every half-hour between 2 PM and 8 PM.

Arriving and Departing by Train, Bus, and Car

By Train The Gare Centrale (Central Station), on rue de la Gauchetière between rues University and Mansfield (behind La Reine Elizabeth—Queen Elizabeth Hotel—on boulevard René-Lévesque Ouest), is the rail terminus for all trains from the United States and other Canadian provinces. It is connected by underground passageway to the Métro's Bonaventure stop (schedule information, tel. 514/871–1331).

Amtrak (tel. 800/USA–RAIL) reinstated the all-reserved overnight *Montrealer* in July 1989, giving travelers in the Northeast the option of day or night transportation. The *Montrealer* begins in Washington, DC, and stops in Baltimore, Philadelphia, Newark, New York (Pennsylvania Station), Stamford, New Haven, Amherst, and Montpelier, Vermont. It has a dining car with snacks, full dinners, and evening entertainment. Sleepers are available and advised because the reclining seat-footrest combination is not conducive to a good night's sleep. Make sleeper reservations well in advance, since they book early. The unreserved *Adirondack* departs New York's Grand Central Terminal every morning and takes 9½ hours to reach Montréal. It has a snack car but no dinner service or sleepers. A round-trip ticket on either train is cheaper than two one-way fares, except during major holidays.

VIA Rail (tel. 800/361–3677 or 514/871–1331) connects Montréal by train with all the major cities of Canada, including Québec City, Halifax, Ottawa, Toronto, Winnipeg, Calgary, and Vancouver.

By Bus **Greyhound** has coast-to-coast service and serves Montréal with buses arriving from and departing for various cities in North America. **Voyageur** and **Voyageur-Colonial** primarily service destinations within Québec and Ontario. **Vermont Transit** (tel. 800/451–3292) also serves Montréal, by way of Boston, New York, and other points in New England. Both lines use the city's downtown bus terminal, Terminus Voyageur (tel. 514/842–2281), which connects with the Berri-UQAM Métro station in downtown.

By Car Travelers can reach Montréal by a number of highways. It is accessible from the rest of Canada via the Trans Canada Highway 401, which connects from the east and west via Highways 20 and 40. The New York State Thruway (I-87) becomes Highway 15 at the Canadian border, and then it's 47 kilometers (30 miles) to the outskirts of Montréal. U.S. I-89 becomes two-lane Route 133 at the border, which is Highway 10 at Iberville. From I-91 from Boston, you must take highways 55 and 10 to reach Montréal. At the border you clear Canadian Customs, so be prepared with proof of citizenship and your vehicle's ownership papers. On holidays and during the peak summer season, expect waits of a half-hour or more at the major crossings.

Once you're in Québec, the road signs will be in French, but they're designed so you shouldn't have much trouble understanding them. The speed limit is posted in kilometers; on highways the limit is 100 kph (about 62 mph). There are extremely heavy penalties for driving while intoxicated, and drivers and front-seat passengers must wear over-the-shoulder seat belts. Gasoline is sold in Imperial gallons (equal to 1.2 U.S. gallons), and lead-free is called *sans plomb*. If you're traveling in the depths of winter, remember that your car may not start on extra-cold mornings unless it has been kept in a heated garage. All Montréal parking signs are in French, so brush up on your *gauche* (left) and *droit* (right). And you might see more of the city if you leave your car in a garage and hop aboard Montréal's extensive, excellent rapid transit system, the Métro.

You should be aware that, as of spring 1989, Montréal police have instituted a diligent tow-away and fine system for cars double-parked or stopped in no-stopping zones in downtown Montréal during rush hours and business hours. Penalties include a $35 ticket. If your car is towed away while illegally parked, it will cost an additional $35 to retrieve it. New York State residents should drive with extra care in Québec. Traffic violations in the province are now entered on their New York State driving record (and vice versa), since the passage of a traffic accord in July 1988. Especially with the downtown construction boom causing the temporary closure of many streets or the rerouting of traffic onto side streets, police are being extremely vigilant about ticketing Montréalers and visitors alike for parking infractions. Remember: Seat belts, back and front, are mandatory.

Getting Around

By Métro and Bus Armed with a few maps, you don't need a car to see Montréal; public transit will do quite well, thank you. The Métro is clean, quiet (it runs on rubber wheels), and relatively safe, and it's heated in winter and cooled in summer. Métro hours are from 5:30 AM to 12:30 AM (11 PM on the new Blue Line), and the trains run as often as every three minutes on the most crowded lines. It's also connected to the 15 kilometers (9.3 miles) of the Underground City, so you may not need to go outside during bad weather. Each of the 65 Métro stops has been individually designed and decorated; Berri-UQAM has stained glass, and at Place d'Armes a small collection of archaeological artifacts is exhibited. The recently opened stations between Snowdon and Jean-Talon on the Blue Line are worth a visit, particularly Outremont, with its glass-block design. Each station connects with one or more bus routes, which cover the rest of the island. The STCUM (Société de transport de la Communauté urbaine de Montréal) administers both the Métro and the buses, so the same tickets and transfers are valid on either service. You should be able to go within a few blocks of anywhere in the city on one fare. The 1990 rates are: adult fare, $1.25; children, 55¢; six tickets, $6; monthly pass, $32.75.

Free maps may be obtained at Métro ticket booths. Try to get the *Carte Réseau* (system map); it's the most complete. Transfers from Métro to buses are available from the dispenser just beyond the ticket booth inside the station. Bus-to-bus and bus-to-Métro transfers may be obtained from the bus driver.

By Taxi Taxis in Montréal all run on the same rate: $2 minimum and 70¢ a kilometer (at press time). They're usually prompt and reliable, although they may be hard to find on rainy nights after the Métro has closed. Each carries on its roof a white or orange plastic sign that is lit when available and off when occupied.

Montréal Metro

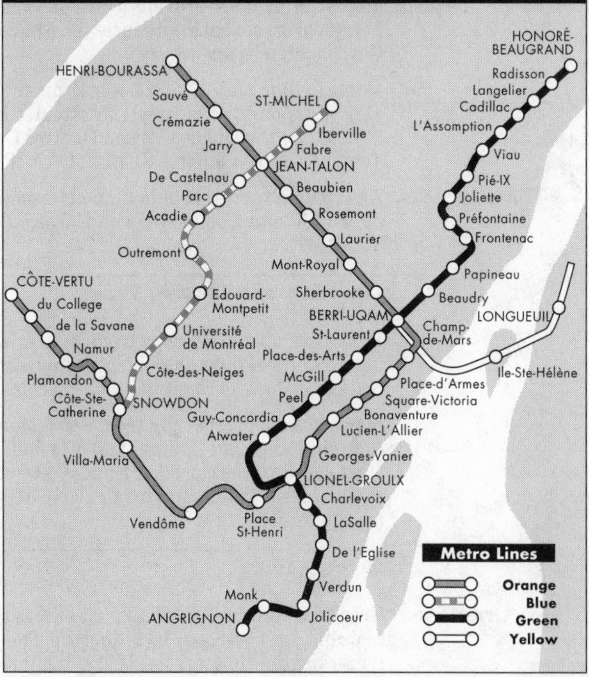

Important Addresses and Numbers

Tourist Information

Greater Montreal Convention and Tourism Bureau, 1555 rue Peel., H3A 1X6 Montréal, Québec (514/844–5400 or 800/363–7777) or **Tourisme-Québec** (514/873–2015).

Stop by the new downtown headquarters for Info-Touriste, the new home of Tourisme-Québec, on the north side of Square Dorchester. Run by the Greater Montreal Convention and Tourism Bureau, it is open June 12–September 2, Monday–Saturday 8:30–7:30, Sunday 9–5; September 3–June 11, daily 9–5. Tel. 800/443–7000, eastern United States; 514/873–2015 Montréal; 800/361–5405 Québec Province. Info-Touriste also operates two smaller tourist information centers at 174 rue Notre-Dame Est in Vieux-Montréal (corner of Place Jacques-Cartier; September–May, weekdays 9–1 and 2:15–5, weekends 9–5; June–August, daily 9–6) and at Dorval Airport (September–May, daily 1–8; June–August, daily 10–8). Tel. 514/871–1595 for both locations.

Consulates

United States (Complexe Desjardins South Tower, ground floor, Métro Place des Arts, tel. 514/281–1886).

United Kingdom (635 boul. René-Lévesque O, Métro Bonaventure, tel. 514/866–5863).

Emergencies

Dialing 911 will put you through to the **police, fire,** and **ambulance.**

Doctors and Dentists The U.S. Consulate cannot recommend specific doctors and dentists but does provide a list of various specialists in the Montréal area. Call in advance (tel. 514/281–1886) to make sure the consulate is open.

Dental clinic (tel. 514/324–4444) open 24 hours, Sun. emergency appointments only; Montréal General Hospital (514/937–6011); the Québec Poison Control Centre (800/463–5060); Touring Club de Montréal-AAA, CAA, RAC (514/861–7111).

Travel Agencies **American Express** (1141 boul. de Maisonneuve O, tel. 514/284–3300). **Thomas Cook** (1155 rue University, Suite 314, tel. 514/842–2541).

Opening and Closing Times

Banks are open weekdays from 10 to 4, with some banks open until 5 on weekdays and on Saturday morning. Many Montréal banks also have 24-hour banking-machine services.

Shops are open generally from 9 to 6 Monday to Wednesday, 9 to 9 Thursday and Friday, and 9 to 5 on Saturday. You'll find most retail stores closed on Sunday and many specialty service shops closed on Monday, particularly in predominantly French neighborhoods.

Guided Tours

Orientation **Gray Line** (tel. 514/934–1222) has eight different tours of Montréal and its environs, including Île Ste-Hélène, the Laurentians, and the Underground City. It offers pickup service at the major hotels, or you may board the buses at Info-Touriste (1001 Square Dorchester).

Aerocar/Murray Hill (tel. 514/937–5311) offers many different tours on buses departing from Square Dorchester (Métro Peel). You may buy tickets at major hotels or from Murray Hill personnel.

Boat Tours **Montreal Harbour Cruises** (tel. 514/842–3871) offers 1½-hour tours of the harbor on the MV *Concordia*, a 27-meter (88-foot) ship with a restaurant, two decks, and room for 290 passengers. Boats leave as often as six times a day from Victoria Pier at the foot of rue Berri in the Vieux-Port next to Vieux-Montréal (Métro Champs de Mars).

Calèche Rides Open horse-drawn carriages—fleece-lined in winter—leave from rue Notre-Dame between rue Bonsecours and rue Gosford, Square Dorchester, Place des Armes and rue de la Commune. An hour-long ride is $40 (tel. 514/844–1313 or 845–7995).

Exploring Montréal

Orientation

by Andrew Coe

Andrew Coe has written for the San Francisco Examiner *and other publications.*

When exploring Montréal, there's very little to remind you that it's an island. It lies in the St. Lawrence River roughly equidistant (256 kilometers, 160 miles) from Lake Ontario and the point where the river widens into a bay. For its entire length, the St. Lawrence is flanked by flat, rich bottomland for 48 kilometers (30 miles) or more on each side. The only rise in the landscape is the 233-meter (764-foot) Mont Royal, which gave

Montréal its name. The island itself is 51 kilometers (32 miles) long and 14 kilometers (9 miles) wide and is bounded on the north by the narrow Rivière des Prairies and on the south by the Fleuve St. Lawrence. Aside from Mont Royal, the island is relatively flat, and because the majority of attractions are clustered around this hill, most tourists don't visit the rest of the island.

Head to the Mont Royal Belvedere (lookout) for a panoramic view of the city. You can drive most of the way, park, and walk ½ kilometer (¼ mile) or hike all the way up from avenues Côte-des-Neiges or des Pins. If you look directly out—southeast—from the belvedere, at the foot of the hill will be the McGill University campus and, surrounding it, the skyscrapers of downtown Montréal. Just beyond, along the banks of the St. Lawrence, are the stone houses of Vieux-Montréal. Hugging the opposite banks are the îles Ste-Hélène and Notre-Dame (St. Helen and Notre-Dame islands), sites of La Ronde amusement park and Man and His World exhibition center (former Expo '67 site), respectively.

There are a host of attractions that you can see on all-day and half-day trips. The most popular are the zoo, aquarium, and amusement park complex on Île Ste-Hélène and the Olympic Stadium and its neighbor, the Botanical Garden. The 500 forested acres of Parc Mont-Royal are busy with joggers, strollers, and skaters all year. Beyond the city limits are l'Estrie and the Laurentians for day trips or weekends in the country.

Montréal is easy to explore. Street signs, subways, and bus lines are clearly marked and the instructions usually given in both French and English. The city is divided by a grid of streets roughly aligned east–west and north–south. (This grid is tilted about 40 degrees off—to the left of—true north, so west is actually southwest and so on.) North–south street numbers begin at the Fleuve St. Lawrence and increase as you head north. East–west street numbers begin at boulevard St-Laurent, which divides Montréal into east and west halves. The city is not so large that seasoned walkers can't see all the districts around the base of Mont Royal on foot.

Tour 1: Vieux-Montréal (Old Montréal)

Numbers in the margin correspond with points of interest on the Tour 1: Vieux-Montréal map.

The Fleuve St. Lawrence was the highway on which the first settlers arrived in 1642. Just past the island of Montréal are the Lachine Rapids, a series of violent falls over which the French colonists' boats could not safely travel. It was natural for them to build their houses just above the rapids, near the site of an old Iroquois settlement on the bank of the river nearest Mont Royal. In the mid-17th century Montréal consisted of a handful of wood houses clustered around a pair of stone buildings, the whole flimsily fortified by a wood stockade. For the next three centuries this district—bounded by rues McGill and Berri on the east and west, rue St-Antoine on the north, and the river to the south—was the financial and political heart of the city. Government buildings, the largest church, the stock exchange, the main market, and the port were there. The narrow but relatively straight streets were cobblestone and lined with solid, occasionally elegant, houses, office buildings, and warehouses—also made of stone. Exiting the city meant using one of four gates through the thick stone wall that protected against Indians and marauding European powers. Montréal quickly grew past the bounds of its fortifications, however, and by World War I the center of the city had moved toward Mont Royal. The new heart of Montréal became Dominion Square (now Square Dorchester). For the next two decades Vieux-Montréal, as it became known, was gradually abandoned, the warehouses and offices emptied. In 1962 the city began studying ways to revitalize Vieux-Montréal, and a decade of renovations and restorations began.

Today, Vieux-Montréal is a center of cultural life and municipal government, if not of commerce and politics. Most of the summer activities revolve around Place Jacques-Cartier, which becomes a pedestrian mall with street performers and outdoor cafés spilling out of restaurants. This lovely square is a good place to view the fireworks festival, and it's adjacent to the Vieux-Port exhibition grounds and the docks for the harbor cruises. Classical music concerts are staged all year long at the Notre-Dame Basilica, which possesses one of the finest organs in North America, and plays are staged in English by the Centaur Theatre in the old stock-exchange building. This district has six museums devoted to history, religion, and decorative and fine arts.

To begin your tour of Vieux-Montréal, take the Métro to the Place d'Armes station, beneath the Palais des Congrès convention center, and walk 1½ blocks south on rue St-Urbain to
1 **Place d'Armes.** In the 1600s, Place d'Armes was the site of battles with the Iroquois and later became the center of Montréal's "Upper Town." In the middle of the square is a statue of Paul de Chomedey, Sieur de Maisonneuve, the founder of Montréal. In 1644 he was wounded here in a battle with 200 Indians. Historians recently uncovered a network of tunnels beneath the square; they connected the various buildings, and one tunnel ran down to the river. These precursors of the Underground City protected the colonists from the extremes of winter weather and provided an escape route should the city be overrun. Unfortunately, the tunnels are too small and dangerous to visit. Calèches are available at the south end of the square.

2 The north side of the square is dominated by the **Bank of Montréal,** an impressive building with Corinthian columns (re-modeled by renowned architects McKim, Mead & White in 1905) that houses a small, interesting numismatics museum. *129 rue St-Jacques. Admission free. Open weekdays 10–4.*

The office building to the west of the square is the site of the old Café Dillon, a famous gourmet restaurant frequented by members of the fur traders' Beaver Club (*see* Dining, below). Two extremely important edifices form the south end of Place d'Armes: the Sulpician Seminary, the oldest building in Montréal, and the imposing Notre-Dame Basilica.

The first church called Notre-Dame was a bark-covered structure built within the fort in 1642, the year the first settlers arrived. Three times it was torn down and rebuilt, each time in a different spot, each time larger and more ornate. The enormous
3 (3,800-seat) neo-Gothic **Notre-Dame Basilica,** which opened in

Tour 1: Vieux-Montréal

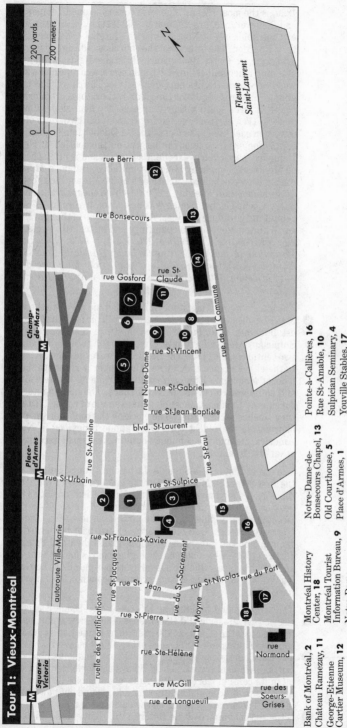

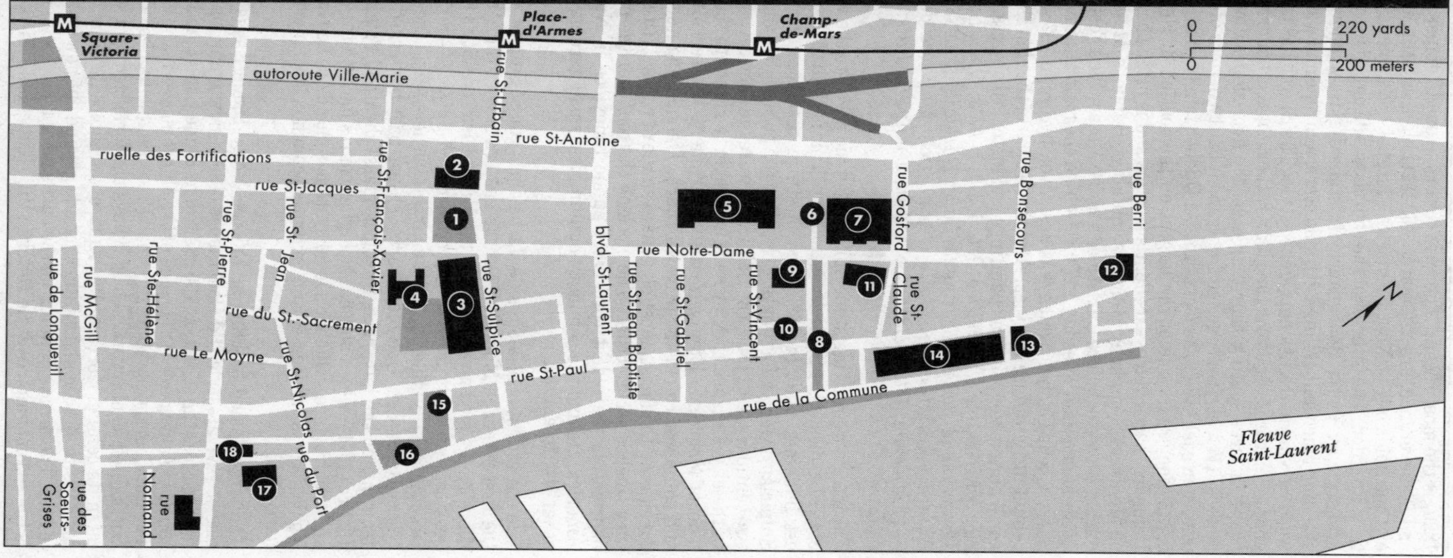

Bank of Montréal, **2**
Château Ramezay, **11**
George-Etienne Cartier Museum, **12**
Hôtel de Ville, **7**
Marché Bonsecours, **14**
Montréal History Center, **18**
Montréal Tourist Information Bureau, **9**
Notre-Dame Basilica, **3**
Notre-Dame-de-Bonsecours Chapel, **13**
Old Courthouse, **5**
Place d'Armes, **1**
Place Jacques Cartier, **8**
Place Royale, **15**
Place Vauquelin, **6**
Pointe-à-Callières, **16**
Rue St-Amable, **10**
Sulpician Seminary, **4**
Youville Stables, **17**

1829, is the most recent. The twin towers, named Temperance and Perseverance, are 227 meters (69 feet) high, and the western one holds one of North America's largest bells, the 12-ton Gros Bourdon. The interior of the church was designed in medieval style by Victor Bourgeau, with stained-glass windows, a stunning blue vault ceiling with gold stars, and pine and walnut wood carving in traditional Québec style. The church has many unique features: It is rectangular rather than cruciform in shape; it faces south rather than east; the floor slopes down 4 meters (1¼ feet) from back to front; and it has twin rows of balconies on each side. The Casavants, a Québec family, built the 5,722-pipe organ, one of the largest on the continent. Notre-Dame has particularly excellent acoustics and is often the site of Montréal Symphony concerts, notably, Handel's *Messiah* during the week before Christmas and the Mozart Plus Festival in the summer on Tuesday at 7 PM. Behind the main altar is the Sacre-Coeur Chapel, which was destroyed by fire in 1978 and rebuilt in five different styles. Also in the back of the church is a small museum of religious paintings and historical objects. *116 rue Notre-Dame O. Basilica: tel. 514/849–1070. Open Labor Day–June 24, daily 7–6; June 25–Labor Day daily, 7 AM–8 PM. Guided tours May–Oct. daily 9–4:30, Oct.–May weekdays, 9–4. Museum: tel. 514/842–2925. Admission: $1 adults, 50¢ children. Open weekends 9:30–4.*

The low, more retiring stone building behind a wall to the west
4 of the basilica is the **Sulpician Seminary.** This is Montréal's oldest building, built in 1685, and is still a residence for the Sulpician order (unfortunately closed to the public). For almost two centuries until 1854, the Sulpicians were *the* political power in the city, because they owned the property rights to the island of Montréal. They were also instrumental in recruiting and equipping colonists for New France. The building itself is considered the finest, most elegant example of rustic 17th-century Québec architecture. The clock on the roof over the main doorway is the oldest (pre-1701) public timepiece in North America. Behind the seminary building is a small garden, another Montréal first.

The street that runs alongside the basilica, **rue St-Sulpice,** was the first street in Montréal. On the eastern side of the street there's a plaque marking where the Hôtel-Dieu, the city's first hospital, was built in 1644. Now cross rue St-Sulpice—the Art Deco **Aldred Building** sits on the far left corner—and take rue Notre-Dame Est. One block farther, just past boulevard St-Laurent, on the left, rises the black-glass–sheathed **Palais de Justice** (1971), which houses the higher courts for both the city and the province. (Québec's legal system is based on the Napoléonic Code for civil cases and on British common law for criminal cases.)

The large domed building at 155 rue Notre-Dame Est is the
5 classic revival–style **Old Courthouse** (1857), now municipal offices. Across the street, at 160 rue Notre-Dame Est, is the **Maison de la Sauvegarde** (1811), one of the oldest houses in the city.
6 The Old Courthouse abuts the small **Place Vauquelin,** named after the 18th-century naval hero who is memorialized by a statue in its center. North of this square is **Champs de Mars,** the
former site of a colonial military parade ground but now a parking lot. The ornate building on the east side of Place Vauquelin
7 is the second empire–style **Hôtel de Ville** (City Hall, 1878). On

July 24, 1967, French President Charles de Gaulle stood on the central balcony of the hotel and made his famous *"Vive le Québec libre"* speech.

8 You are in a perfect spot to explore **Place Jacques-Cartier,** the heart of Vieux-Montréal. This two-block-long square opened in 1804 as a municipal market, and every summer it is transformed into a flower market. The 1809 monument at the top of the place celebrates Lord Nelson's victory at Trafalgar. At the western corner of rue Notre-Dame is a small building (1811), site of the old Silver Dollar Saloon, so named because there were 350 silver dollars nailed to the floor. Today it's the home of
9 the **Montreal Tourist Information Bureau** (*see* Important Addresses and Numbers, above). Both sides of the place are lined with two- and three-story stone buildings that were originally homes or hotels.

Time Out **Le St-Amable** (188 rue St-Amable, tel. 514/866–3471) features a Businessmen's Lunch weekdays from noon to 3 PM, but you don't have to be an executive or even be dressed like one to sample such classics as fresh poached salmon or grilled New Zealand lamb chops.

---

10 In the summer, the one-block **rue St-Amable** becomes a marketplace for local jewelers, artists, and craftspeople. From the bottom of Place Jacques-Cartier you can stroll out into the **Port of Montreal Exhibition Ground,** where from Winter Carnival through summer there is always something going on. At the foot of boulevard St-Laurent and rue de la Commune are the port's major summertime exhibitions: **Images du Futur** and **Expotec.** Here, you'll also find Montréal's new year-round **IMAX Super Cinema.**

Retrace your steps to the north end of Place Jacques-Cartier, then continue east on rue Notre-Dame. At the corner of rue St-
11 Claude on the right is **Château Ramezay** (1705), built as the residence of the 11th governor of Montréal, Claude de Ramezay. In 1775–76 it was the headquarters for American troops seeking to conquer Canada. Benjamin Franklin stayed here during that winter occupation. One of the most elegant colonial buildings still standing in Montréal, the château is now a museum, and it has been restored to the style of Governor de Ramezay's day. The ground floor is furnished like a gentleman's residence of New France, with dining room, bedroom, and office. *280 rue Notre-Dame E, tel. 514/861–3708. Admission: $2 adults, $1 senior citizens, 50¢ students and children under 16. Wheelchair visitors are advised to reserve 1 day in advance. Open Tues.–Sun. 10–4:30. Open Monday from June through August.*

At the end of rue Notre-Dame are two houses built by Sir George-Étienne Cartier, a 19th-century Canadian statesman.
12 They recently have been opened as the **George-Étienne Cartier Museum,** a showcase of decorative arts. Displays depict the daily life of Montréal's elite in that era. *458 rue Notre-Dame E, tel. 514/283–2282. Admission free. Open in summer, daily 9–5; rest of the year, Wed.–Sun. 10–5.*

One block back on rue Notre-Dame is rue Bonsecours, one of the oldest streets in the city. At the end of rue Bonsecours is
13 the small but beautiful **Notre-Dame-de-Bonsecours Chapel.**

Marguerite de Bourgeoys, who was canonized in 1983, helped found Montréal and dedicated this chapel to the Virgin Mary in 1657. It became known as a sailor's church, and small wood models of sailing ships are suspended from the ceiling just above the congregation. In the basement there is a small, strange museum honoring the saint that includes a story of her life modeled by little dolls in a series of dioramas. A gift shop sells Marguerite de Bourgeoys souvenirs. From the museum you can climb to the rather precarious bell tower (beware of the slippery metal steps in winter) for a fine view of Vieux-Montréal and the port. *400 rue St-Paul E, tel. 514/845–9991. Admission: $1 adults, 25¢ children. Chapel and museum open Tues.–Fri. 9–11:30 and 1–5, weekends 9 AM–11:30 PM.*

Double back and head west on rue St-Paul. The long, large,
14 domed building to the left is the **Marché Bonsecours** (1845), for many years Montréal's main produce, meat, and fish market and now municipal offices.

Rue St-Paul is the most fashionable street in Vieux-Montréal. For almost 20 blocks it is lined with fine restaurants, shops, and even a few nightclubs. Québécois handicrafts are a specialty here, with shops at 88, 136, and 272 rue St-Paul Est. In the basement of the **Brasserie des Fortifications,** a French restaurant at 262 rue St-Paul Est, you can see remnants of the stone wall that once encircled Montréal. **L'Air du Temps,** at 191 rue St-Paul Ouest, is one of the city's top jazz clubs. Nightly shows usually feature local talent, with occasional international name bands. Take rue St-Paul eight short blocks west of Place
15 Jacques-Cartier, and you will come to **Place Royale,** the site of the first permanent settlement in Montréal.

16 Behind the Old Customs House you will find **Pointe-à-Callières,** a small park that commemorates the settlers' first landing. A small stream used to flow into the St. Lawrence here, and it was on the point of land between the two waters that the colonists landed their four boats at its mouth on May 17, 1642. After they built the stockade and the first buildings at this site, the settlement was almost washed away the next Christmas by a flood. When it was spared, de Maisonneuve placed across on top of Mont Royal as thanks to God. A 1½-block walk down rue
17 William takes you to the **Youville Stables** on the left. These low stone buildings enclosing a garden were originally built as warehouses in 1825 (they never were stables). A group of businessmen renovated them in 1968, and the buildings now house offices, shops, and restaurants.

18 Across rue William from the stables is the **Montreal History Centre.** Visitors to this high-tech museum are led through a series of audiovisual environments depicting the life and history of Montréal. *335 Place d'Youville, tel. 514/872–3207. Admission: $2 adults, $1 senior citizens and children. Open daily 10–4:30, last show begins 3:30. Closed Mon.*

Tour 2: Downtown

Numbers in the margin correspond with points of interest on the Tour 2: Downtown Montréal map.

Downtown is a sprawling 30-by-8-block area bounded by avenue Atwater and boulevard St-Laurent on the west and east, respectively, avenue des Pins on the north, and rue St-Antoine on the south.

After 1700, Vieux-Montréal wasn't big enough for the rapidly expanding city. In 1701 the French administration signed a peace treaty with the Iroquois, and the colonists began to feel safe about building outside Montréal's fortifications. The city inched northward, toward Mont Royal, particularly after the English conquest in 1760. By the end of the 19th century, rue Ste-Catherine was the main commercial thoroughfare, and the city's elite built mansions on the slope of the mountain. Since 1960 city planners have made a concerted effort to move the focus eastward. With the opening of Place des Arts (1963) and the Complexe Desjardins (1976), the city center shifted in that direction. It hasn't landed on any one corner yet, although some Montréalers will tell you it's at the intersection of boulevard de Maisonneuve and rue University.

A major development of the last 30 years is the inauguration of the **Underground City,** an enormous network of passages linking various shopping and office complexes. These have served to keep the retail trade in the downtown area, as well as to make shoppers and workers immune to the hardships of the Canadian winter.

Our tour of downtown—unless you are hale of limb you may not be able to do all of it in a day—begins at the McGill Métro station. The corner of rue University and boulevard de Maisonneuve has recently been the center of intensive development. Two huge office buildings, **2020 University** and **Galleries 2001,** with malls at street and basement levels, rise from the north side of the intersection. The southwest corner, indeed the en-
19 tire block, is taken up by **Eaton,** one of the Big Three department stores in the city. Aside from many floors of mid-priced clothing and other merchandise, the real attraction of Eaton is the ninth-floor art deco dining room.

Time Out **Eaton le 9e** was modeled after the dining room of the luxury liner *Ile-de-France*, Lady Eaton's favorite cruise ship. Elegant pink-and-gray marble columns hold up the ceiling, and the walls are decorated with two pre-Raphaelite murals on culinary themes. The patrons are usually shoppers, of course, dining on pasta, fish, and meat dishes. The service is practical and fast; the decor's the thing. *677 rue Ste-Catherine O, tel. 514/284–8421. AE, MC, V. Open Mon.–Wed. 11:30–3, Thurs. and Fri. 11:30–3 and 5–7, Sat. 11:30–3. Closed Sun.*

Eaton is connected to **Les Terrasses** and the **Eaton Centre** shopping complex via passageways; it is connected as well to the McGill Métro and La Baie store.

20 Across rue University from Eaton stands **Christ Church Cathedral** (1859), the main church of the Anglican Diocese of Montréal. In early 1988 this building was a sight. Plagued by years of high maintenance costs and declining membership, the church fathers leased their land and air rights to a consortium of developers for 99 years. All the land beneath and surrounding the cathedral was removed, and the structure was supported solely by a number of huge steel stilts. The glass 34-story office tower behind the cathedral, **La Maison des Cooperants,** and the Place de la Cathédrale retail complex beneath it, are the products of that agreement.

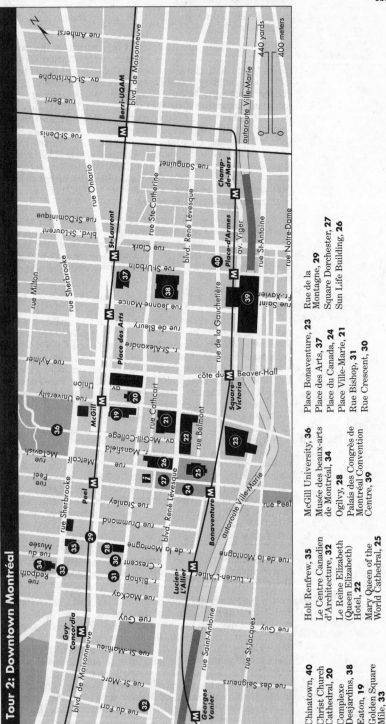

Tour 2: Downtown Montréal

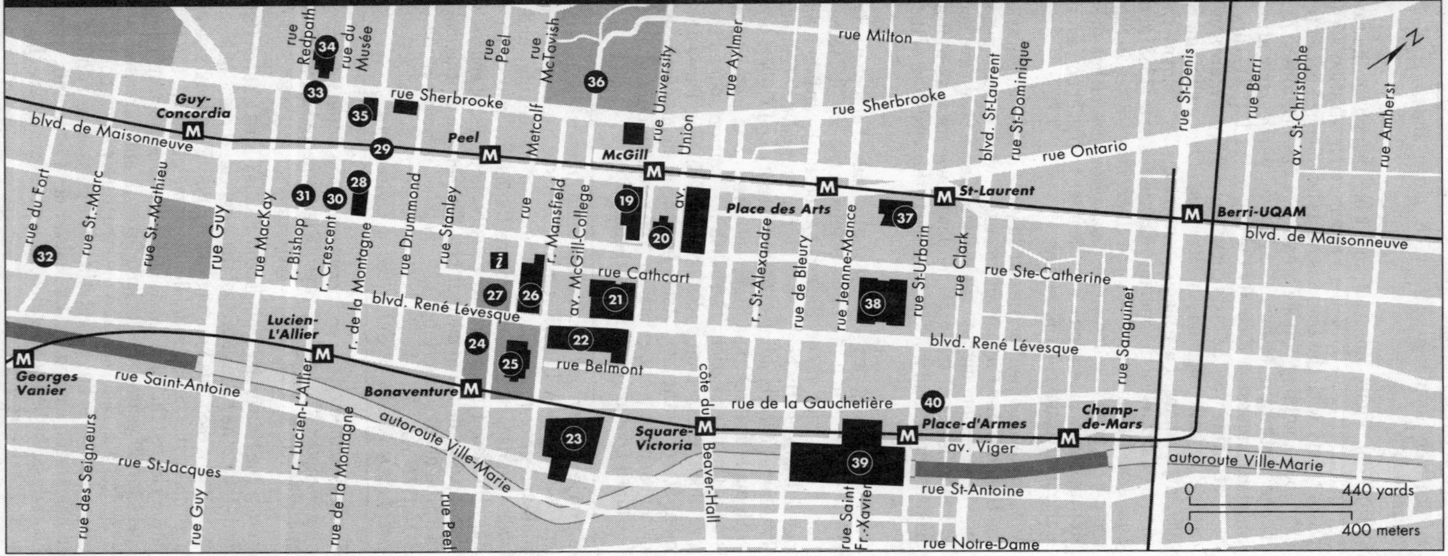

Chinatown, **40**
Christ Church Cathedral, **20**
Complexe Desjardins, **38**
Eaton, **19**
Golden Square Mile, **33**
Holt Renfrew, **35**
Le Centre Canadien d'Architecture, **32**
Le Reine Elizabeth (Queen Elizabeth) Hotel, **22**
Mary Queen of the World Cathedral, **25**
McGill University, **36**
Musée des beaux-arts de Montréal, **34**
Ogilvy, **28**
Palais des Congrès de Montréal Convention Centre, **39**
Place Bonaventure, **23**
Place des Arts, **37**
Place du Canada, **24**
Place Ville-Marie, **21**
Rue Bishop, **31**
Rue Crescent, **30**
Rue de la Montagne, **29**
Square Dorchester, **27**
Sun Life Building, **26**

21 **Place Ville-Marie** is an office, retail, and mall complex that signaled a new era for Montréal when it opened in 1962. It was the first link in the huge chain of the Underground City, which meant that people could have access to all the services of the city without setting foot outside. It was also the first step Montréal took to claiming its place as an international city. The labyrinth that is the Underground City now includes six hotels, thousands of offices, 30 movie theaters, more than 1,000 boutiques, hundreds of restaurants, and almost 15 kilometers (9.3 miles) of passageways.

From Place Ville-Marie head south via the passageways to-
22 ward **Le Reine Elizabeth (Queen Elizabeth)** hotel. You can
reach the **Gare Centrale (Central Railway Station)** just behind
the hotel. Trains from the United States and the rest of Canada
arrive here. Then follow the signs marked "Métro/Place Bona-
23 venture" to **Place Bonaventure,** the largest commercial building in Canada. On the lower floors there are shops and
restaurants, then come exposition halls and offices, and finally
the whole thing is topped by the Bonaventure Hilton International (*see* Lodging, below) and 2½ acres of gardens. From here
take the route marked "Place du Canada," which will bring you
to the mall in the base of the **Hôtel Château Champlain.** This
building is known as the Cheesegrater because of its rows and
rows of half-moon–shape windows (*see* Lodging, below). Our
exploration of this leg of the Underground City will end at
Windsor Station (follow the signs). This was the second railway
station built in Montréal by the Canadian Pacific Railway Company. Windsor Station was designed in 1889 by George Price, a
New York architect, with a massive rustic stone exterior holding up an amazing steel-and-glass roof over an arcade.

It's time for a bit of fresh air now, so exit at the north end of
Windsor Station and cross the street to the park known as
24 **Place du Canada.** In the center of the park there is a statue to
Sir John A. MacDonald, Canada's first prime minister. Then
25 cross the park and rue de la Cathédrale to the **Mary Queen of
the World Cathedral** (1894), which you enter on boulevard René-Lévesque. This church is modeled after St. Peter's Basilica
in Rome. Victor Bourgeau, the same architect who did the interior of Notre-Dame in Vieux-Montréal, thought the idea of the
cathedral's design terrible but completed it after the original
architect proved incompetent. Inside there is even a canopy
over the altar that is a miniature copy of Bernini's *baldacchino*
in St. Peter's. The massive gray granite edifice across boule-
26 vard René-Lévesque from the cathedral is the **Sun Life Building** (1914), at one time the largest building in Canada. During
World War II much of England's financial reserves and national
treasures were stored in Sun Life's vaults. The park that faces
the Sun Life building just north of boulevard René-Lévesque is
27 **Square Dorchester,** for many years the heart of Montréal. Until
1870 a Catholic burial ground occupied this block (and there are
still bodies buried beneath the grass), but with the rapid development of the area, the city fathers decided to turn it into a
park. The statuary of Square Dorchester includes a monument
to the Boer War in the center and a statue of the Scottish poet
Robert Burns near rue Peel.

A block north of Square Dorchester is rue Ste-Catherine, the main retail shopping street of Montréal. Three blocks west, at 1307 rue Ste-Catherine Ouest and rue de la Montagne, is

28 **Ogilvy,** the last of the Big Three department stores. The store has been divided into individual name boutiques that sell generally pricier lines than La Baie or Eaton. Most days at noon a bagpiper plays Scottish airs as he circumnavigates the ground
29 30 floor. **Rue de la Montagne (Mountain),** and **rues Crescent** and
31 **Bishop,** the two streets just west of it, constitute the heart of Montréal's downtown nightlife and restaurant scene. This area once formed the playing fields of the Montréal Lacrosse and Cricket Grounds, and later it became an exclusive suburb lined with millionaires' row houses. Since then these three streets between rues Sherbrooke and Ste-Catherine have become fertile ground for trendy bars, restaurants, and shops ensconced in those old row houses.

While you're in the vicinity, take in one of downtown's newest
32 attractions, **Le Centre Canadien d'Architecture (Canadian Centre for Architecture),** just four blocks west at rue St-Marc on rue Baile. The lifelong dream of its founding director, Phyllis Lambert (of the Bronfman fortune), the CCA opened in May 1989 and houses one of the world's premier architectural collections. *1920 rue Baile, tel. 514/939–7000. Admission free Thurs. eve. only to CCA members, ICOM-cardholders, children under 12, and general public; otherwise, $3 adults, $2 senior citizens and students. Open Wed. and Fri. 11–6, Thurs. 11–8, weekends 11–5. Group rates available. Reservation required.*

Now that you're in the mood for historic pursuits, backtrack to rues Ste-Catherine and Bishop. By walking two blocks north on rue Bishop to rue Sherbrooke, you enter a very different en-
33 vironment: the exclusive neighborhood known as the **Golden Square Mile.**

Directly across the street from the end of rue Bishop is the
34 **Musée des beaux-arts de Montréal (Montreal Museum of Fine Arts),** the oldest established museum in Canada (1860). The present building was completed in 1912 and holds a large collection of European and North American fine and decorative art; ancient treasures from Europe, the Near East, Asia, Africa, and America; art from Québec and Canada; and Indian and Eskimo artifacts. From June through October there is usually one world-class exhibition, such as the inventions of Leonardo da Vinci, or the works of Marc Chagall.

The Museum of Fine Arts is undergoing a massive expansion, with a new wing due to open in 1991. The museum has a gift shop, an art-book store, a boutique selling Inuit art, and a gallery in which you can buy or rent original paintings by local artists. *3400 av. du Musée, tel. 514/285–1600. Admission: permanent collection, $4 adults, $2 students, free 16 and under; visiting exhibitions, $7 adults, $3 students and senior citizens, $1 children 12 and under; audio guides, $3.50. Open Tues.–Sun., permanent collection 10–5, visiting exhibitions 10–7.*

Walking east on rue Sherbrooke brings you to the small and ex-
35 clusive **Holt Renfrew** department store, perhaps the city's fanciest, at the corner of boulevard de la Montagne (*see* Shopping, below). A few blocks farther east along rue Drummond stands the **Ritz-Carlton,** the grand dame of Montréal hotels. It was built in 1912 so the local millionaires' European friends would have a suitable place to stay. Take a peek in the elegant Café de Paris restaurant. It's Montréal's biggest power dining spot,

and you just might see the prime minister dining there. (For more on the Ritz-Carlton and its restaurants, *see* Lodging and Dining sections, below.) The Ritz-Carlton's only real competition in town is the modern and elegant **Hôtel Quatre Saisons (Four Seasons),** two blocks west at rues Sherbrooke and Peel. Just beyond this hotel on the other side of the street begins the
36 grassy **McGill University** campus. James McGill, a wealthy Scottish fur trader, bequeathed the money and the land for this institution, which opened in 1828, and is perhaps the finest English-language school of higher education in the nation. The student body numbers 15,000, and the university is best known for its medical and engineering schools.

Turn right on rue University and walk a block to the McGill Métro station. Take the train one stop in the direction of Honoré-Beaugrand to the Place des Arts station.

Montréal's Métro opened in 1966 with well-designed stations—many decorated with works of art—and modern trains running on quiet pneumatic wheels. Today there are 65 stations on four lines with 65 kilometers (40 miles) of track. The 759 train cars carry more than 700,000 passengers a day. When you exit at
37 **Place des Arts,** follow the signs to the theater complex of the same name. From here you can walk the five blocks to Vieux-Montréal totally underground. Place des Arts, which opened in 1963, is reminiscent of New York's Lincoln Center in that it is a government-subsidized complex of three very modern theaters. The largest, Salle Wilfrid Pelletier, is the home of the Orchestre Symphonique de Montréal (Montréal Symphony Orchestra), which has won international raves under the baton of Charles Dutoit. The Orchestre Métropolitain de Montréal, Grands Ballets Canadiens, and the Opéra du Québec also stage productions here.

38 While still in Place des Arts, follow the signs to the **Complexe Desjardins.** Built in 1976, this is another office building, hotel, and mall development along the lines of Place Ville-Marie. The luxurious Meridien Hotel (*see* Lodging, below) rises from its northwest corner. The large galleria space is the scene of all types of performances, from lectures on Japanese massage techniques to pop music, as well as avid shopping in the dozens of stores. The next development south is the **Complexe Guy-Favreau,** a huge federal office building named after the Canadian Minister of Justice in the early '60s. If you continue in a
39 straight line, you will hit the **Palais des Congrès de Montréal Convention Centre** above the Place d'Armes Métro stop. But if you take a left out of Guy-Favreau onto rue de la Gauchetière,
40 you will be in **Chinatown,** a relief after all that artificially enclosed retail space.

The Chinese first came to Montréal in large numbers after 1880, following the construction of the transcontinental railroad. They settled in an 18-block area between boulevard René-Lévesque and avenue Viger to the north and south, and near rues Hôtel de Ville and Bleury on the east and west, an area that became known as Chinatown, where there are many restaurants, food stores, and gift shops.

Tour 3: St-Denis, Prince Arthur, and North

Numbers in the margin correspond with points of interest on the Tour 3: St-Denis, Prince Arthur, and North map.

After a long day of fulfilling your touristic obligations at the historical sites and museums of downtown and Vieux-Montréal, it's good to relax and indulge in some primal pleasures, such as eating, shopping, and nightlife. For these and other diversions, head to the neighborhoods east and north of downtown. Our tour begins in the Latin Quarter, the main student district, then wends its way north.

The southern section of this area, around the base of rue St-Denis, was one of the city's first residential neighborhoods, built in the 19th century as the city burst the bounds of Vieux-Montréal. Then known as Faubourg St-Laurent, it was the home of many wealthy families. The lands to the north of present-day rue Sherbrooke were mostly farms and limestone quarries.

Our tour begins at the **Berri-UQAM** Métro stop, perhaps the most important in the whole city, because three lines intersect here. This area, particularly along **rue St-Denis** on each side of boulevard de Maisonneuve, is known as the **Latin Quarter** and is the site of the **Université du Québec à Montréal** and a number of other educational institutions. Rue St-Denis is lined with cafés, bistros, and restaurants that attract the academic crowd. On rue Ste-Catherine there are a number of low-rent nightclubs popular with avant-garde rock-and-roll types. Just west
41 of rue St-Denis you find the **Cinémathèque Québécoise,** a museum and repertory movie house. For $2 you can visit the permanent exhibition on the history of filmmaking equipment and see two movies. The museum also houses one of the largest cinematic reference libraries in the world. *335 boul. de Maisonneuve O, tel. 514/842–9763. Admission free; movies $2. Library open June–Aug., weekdays 12:30–4:30; Sept.–May, weekdays 12:30–5; museum and theater open Tues.–Sun. 5–8:30.*

Around the corner and half a block north on rue St-Denis
42 stands the 2,500-seat **Théâtre St-Denis,** the second-largest auditorium in Montréal (after Salle Wilfrid Pelletier in Place des Arts). Sarah Bernhardt and numerous other famous actors have graced its stage. It currently is the main site for the summertime concerts of the Montréal International Jazz Festival. On the next block north you see the Beaux Arts **Bibliothèque nationale du Québec** (1915), a library that houses Québec's official archives (1700 rue St-Denis; open Tues.–Sat. 9–5). If you have a lot of money and some hours set aside for dining, try **Les Mignardises** at 2035–37 rue St-Denis just south of rue Sherbrooke (*see* Dining, below).

Continue north on rue St-Denis past rue Sherbrooke. On the right, above the Sherbrooke Métro station, is the **Hôtel de l'Institut,** the hands-on training academy of the government *hôtel-*
43 *ier* school. To the left is the small **Square St-Louis,** once considered among the most beautiful in Montréal. Unfortunately, now it is a haven for neighborhood panhandlers and the growing numbers of homeless in the city, and as a result, the ambience has changed. In its heyday, this was the focal point of the community, and the surrounding neighborhood takes its name from the once grand square. Originally a reservoir, these blocks became a park in 1879 and attracted upper-middle-class families and artists to the area. French-Canadian poets were among the most famous creative people to occupy the houses back then, and the neighborhood is the home today for Mon-

Tour 3: St-Denis, Prince Arthur, and North

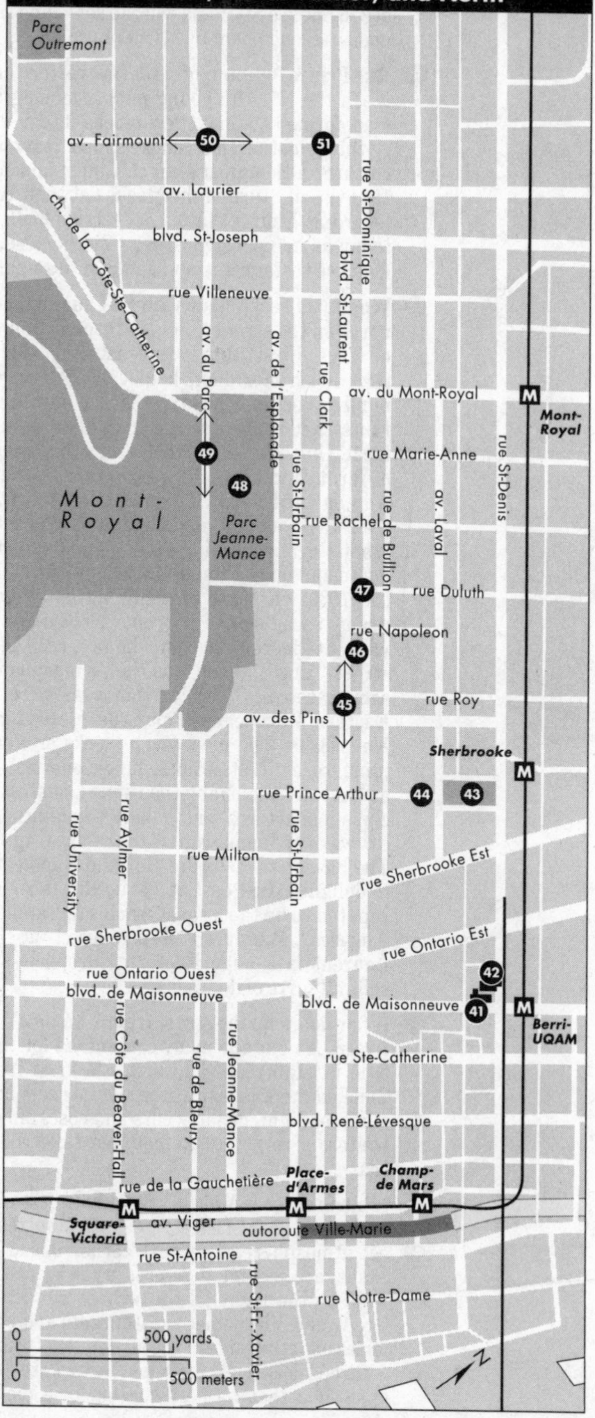

tréal painters, filmmakers, musicians, and writers. On the wall of 336 Square St-Louis you can see—and read, if your French is good—a long poem by Michel Bujold.

44 **Rue Prince Arthur** begins at the western end of Square St-Louis. In the '60s the young people moving to the neighborhood transformed the next few blocks into a small hippie bazaar of clothing, leather, and smoke shops. It remains a center of youth culture, although it's much tamer and more commercial. In 1981 the city turned the blocks between avenue Laval and boulevard St-Laurent into a pedestrian mall. Hippie shops live on today as inexpensive Greek, Vietnamese, Italian, Polish, and Chinese restaurants and *boîtes* of the singles-bar variety.

45 When you reach **boulevard St-Laurent,** take a right and stroll north on the street that cuts through Montréal life in a number of ways. First, this is the east–west dividing street; like the Greenwich meridian, boulevard St-Laurent is where all the numbers begin. The street is also lined with shops and restaurants that represent the incredible ethnic diversity of Montréal. Until the late 19th century this was a neighborhood first of farms and then of middle-class Anglophone residences. It was on boulevard St-Laurent in 1892 that the first electric tramway was installed that could climb the slope to Plâteau Mont-Royal. Working-class families, who couldn't afford a horse and buggy to pull them up the hill, began to move in. In the 1880s the first of many waves of Russian-Jewish immigrants escaping the pogroms arrived and settled here. Boulevard St-Laurent became known as The Main, as in "main street," and Yiddish was the primary language spoken along some stretches. The Russian Jews were followed by Greeks, Eastern Europeans, Portuguese, and, most recently, Latin Americans. The next seven blocks or so are filled with delis, junk stores, restaurants, luncheonettes, and clothing stores, as well as fashionable boutiques, bistros, cafés, bars, nightclubs, bookstores, and galleries exhibiting the work of the latest wave of "immigrants" to the area—gentrifiers and artists. The block between rues Roy and Napoléon is particularly rich in delights. Just east at 74 rue Roy is **Waldman's Fish Market,** reputed to be the largest wholesale/retail fish market in North America. **Warshaw's Supermarket** at 3863 boulevard St-Laurent is a huge Eastern European–style emporium that sells all sorts of delicacies.

46 A few doors up the street from Warshaw's is **Schwartz's Delicatessen.** Among the many contenders for the smoked-meat king title in Montréal, Schwartz's is most frequently at the top. Smoked meat is just about all it serves, but the meat comes in lean, medium, or fatty cuts and costs only $3 a sandwich. The waiters give you your food and take your money, and that's that.

A block north is **Moishe's Steakhouse** (*see* Dining, below), home of the best, but priciest, steaks in Montréal as well as the noisi-
47 est atmosphere. The next corner is **rue Duluth,** where merchants are seeking to re-create rue Prince Arthur. If you take a walk to the right all the way to rue St-Denis, you will find Greek and Vietnamese restaurants and boutiques and art galleries on either side of the street. A left turn on rue Duluth and
48 a three-block walk brings you to **Parc Jeanne-Mance,** a flat, open field that's a perfect spot for a picnic of delicacies pur-

chased on The Main. The park segues into the 2 wooded, hilly square kilometers (494 acres) of **Parc Mont-Royal.**

49 **Avenue du Parc** forms the western border of Parc Jeanne-Mance. To get there either cut through the park or take a left on avenue du Mont-Royal at the north end. No. 93 avenue du Mont-Royal Ouest is the home of **Beauty's,** a restaurant specializing in bagels, lox, pancakes, and omelets. Expect a line weekend mornings. Turn right and head north to **avenue Laurier.** All along this avenue, from Côte Ste-Catherine to boulevard St-Laurent, are some of the fanciest fur stores, boutiques, pastry shops, and jewelers in the city. For a quick chocolate eclair bracer or two, go to **Lenôtre Paris,** at 1050 avenue Laurier, a branch of the Parisian shop of the same name.

Time Out **La Petite Ardoise** is a casual, slightly arty café that serves soups, quiches, sandwiches, and more-expensive daily specials. The onion soup is lovingly overdosed with cheese, bread, and onions. Whether it's breakfast, lunch, or dinner, the best accompaniment for your meal is a big, steamy bowl of creamy café au lait. This café is a perfect place to take a breather from shopping. *222 av. Laurier O, tel. 514/495–4961. AE, DC, MC, V. Open 8 AM–midnight, later on weekends.*

The next three blocks of avenue du Parc form the heart of the Greek district. Try **Symposium,** at No. 5334, or the neighboring **Milos** at 5357 avenue du Parc (*see* Dining, below) for some of the best Greek appetizers, grilled seafood, and atmosphere you'll find in this hemisphere.

50 **Avenue Fairmount,** a block north of avenue Laurier, is the site of two small but internationally known culinary landmarks. The **Fairmount Bagel Factory,** at 74 avenue Fairmount O, claims to make the best bagels in the world.

Half a block east, on the corner of avenue Fairmount and rue
51 Clark, stands the famous **Wilensky's Light Lunch** (*see* Dining, below). Moviegoers will recognize this Montréal institution from *The Apprenticeship of Duddy Kravitz,* based on the Mordecai Richler novel of the same name. Lunch is all that's served here, and it certainly is light on the wallet. A couple of dollars will get you a hot dog or a bologna, salami, and mustard pretzel roll sandwich and a strawberry soda. Books are available for entertainment. The atmosphere is free.

Parks and Gardens

Numbers in the margin correspond with points of interest on the Olympic Park and Botanical Garden map.

Of Montréal's three major parks, **LaFontaine** is the smallest (the other two are Parc Mont-Royal and Île Ste-Hélène). Parc LaFontaine, founded in 1867, is divided into eastern and western halves. The eastern half is French style; the paths, gardens, and lawns are laid out in rigid geometric shapes. There are two public swimming pools on the north end, along rue Rachel. In the winter the park is open for ice-skating. The western half is designed on the English system, in which the meandering paths and irregularly shaped ponds follow the natural contours of the topography. Pedal boats can be rented for a paddle around one of two man-made lakes. Its band shell is the site of many free outdoor summertime concerts and performances by dance and theater groups. Take the Métro to the Sherbrooke station and walk five blocks east along rue Cherrier. *4000 Calixa-Lavallée, tel. 514/872–6211. Open 9 AM–10 PM.*

The giant, mollusk-shape **Olympic Stadium** and the tilted tower that supports the roof are probably the preeminent symbols of modern Montréal. Planning for the Olympic Stadium complex began in 1972, and construction in the old Parc Maisonneuve started soon afterward. The Olympics took place in 1976, but the construction has just been finished. Montréal authorities are nevertheless proud of what they have. The Olympic Park
52 53 includes the 70,000-seat **Olympic Stadium,** the **Olympic Tower,**
54 six swimming pools, the **Aréna Maurice-Richard,** and the Olympic Village. Tours of the entire complex leave from Tourist Hall at 12:30 and 3:30 in the off-season, more often from June to August (tel. 514/252–4737). During baseball season, you can see the Expos play. Perhaps the most popular visitor activity is a ride up to the tilted tower's observatory on the Funicular, the exterior cable car. The two-level cable car holds 90 people and takes two minutes to climb the 270 meters (890 feet) to the observatory, from which you can see up to 80 kilometers (50 miles) on clear days. The **Velodrome** was never profitable as a bicycle racing track and is being transformed into a natural-
55 sciences museum, the **Montreal Biodome.** When it opens, in 1992, it will be the second most important botanical garden in the world. If you've brought your swimsuit and towels, take a
56 dip at the **Aquatic Center** (tel. 514/252–4737 for hours). There is also a cafeteria and a souvenir shop on the grounds. You can reach the **Olympic Park** via the Pie-IX or Viau Métro stations (the latter is nearer the stadium entrance).

For a back-to-nature experience after all this technology, cross rue Sherbrooke to the north of the Olympic Park (or take the
57 free shuttle bus) to reach the **Montréal Botanical Garden** (closest Métro stop is Pie-IX). Founded in 1931, this garden is said to be one of the largest in the world. During the summer you can visit the 809,000 square meters (200 acres) of outdoor gardens—a favorite is the poisonous plants garden; the 10 exhibition greenhouses are open year-round. There are more than
58 26,000 species of plants here, including bonsai in the **Japanese**
59 **Garden.** The **Insectarium,** a bug-shape building, houses more than 130,000 insect specimens collected by Montréal entomologist Georges Brossard. *4101 rue Sherbrooke E, tel. 514/872–1400. Greenhouse admission: $3 adults, $1.50 senior citizens, handicapped, and children 5–7. Gardens open sunrise–sunset, greenhouses 9–6.*

Île Ste-Hélène (along with Île Notre-Dame, the former site of the Expo '67 World's Fair), opposite Vieux-Montréal in the middle of the St. Lawrence River, draws big crowds, particularly during the warm months. You can reach it via either the Victoria or Jacques-Cartier bridges, via the Métro to the Île Ste-Hélène station, or by city bus (summer only) from downtown. Île Ste-Hélène is a wooded, rolling park perfect for picnicking in the summer and cross-country skiing and ice-skating during the snow season.

La Ronde was created as part of the celebration. This world-class amusement park boasts a huge new roller coaster (the second-highest in the world), water slides with incredible drops, an international circus, Ferris wheels, boat rides, and rides,

Aquatic Center, **56**
Aréna Maurice-Richard, **54**
Biodome, **55**
Botanical Garden, **57**
Insectarium, **59**
Japanese Garden, **58**
Olympic Stadium, **52**
Olympic Tower, **53**

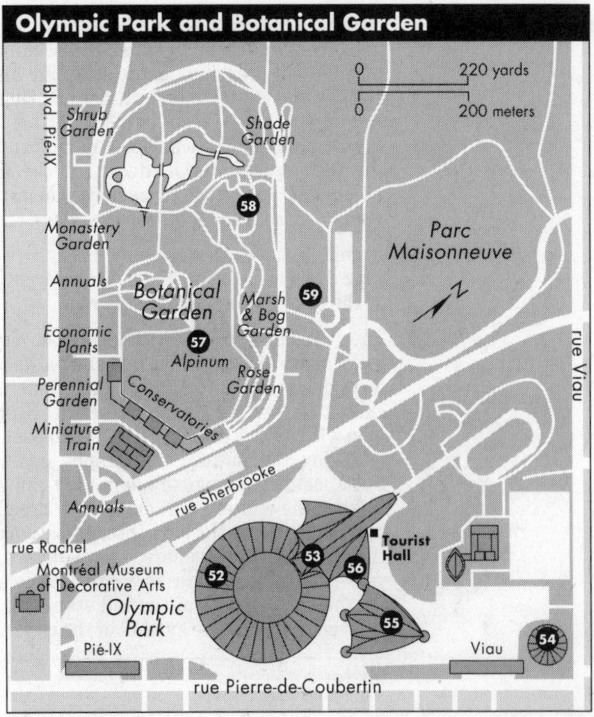

rides, rides. The Aqua Park shares the island with La Ronde and has 20 of its own thrilling slides and pools. A combined $22 pass for adults, $14 for teens, and $10 for children 4 to 11 is good for a day at the amusement park as well as the water slides. Both parks have the same schedule. There are also haunted houses, musical cabarets, Wild West shows, restaurants, snack bars, and the obligatory monorail and cable-car rides. La Ronde is also the site of the annual Benson & Hedges International Fireworks Competition running from the last week in May to mid-June on Wednesday and Saturday nights. *Île Ste-Hélène, tel. 514/872–6222 or 800/361–7178. Admission: $15 adults, $8 children (in-cludes all rides and entertainment), family and special Wed. rates available. Open May and early June, weekends only; mid-June–Labor Day, Sun.–Thurs. 11 AM–midnight, Fri.–Sat. 11 AM–1 AM.*

Admission to La Ronde allows access to the neighboring **Aquarium de Montréal.** Anyone who enjoys seeing marine life should stop in. The penguin tank is billed as the highlight, but there are also fascinating exhibits of tropical fish and local freshwater environments (see what you're having for dinner). The aquarium will move into the Biodome when it opens. *Tel. 514/872–4656. Admission: $2.50 adults, $1.25 children 5–17. Open summer, daily 10–8; off-season, 10–5.*

A stroll back along the north side of the island brings you to the **Old Fort** just under the Jacques-Cartier Bridge. This former British arsenal has been turned into the **David M. Stewart Museum** and a dinner theater called **Le Festin du Gouverneur.** The latter is a re-creation of a 17th-century banquet, complete with balladeers and comedy skits. In the military museum are displays of old firearms, maps, scientific instruments, uniforms, and documents of colonial times. During the summer the parade ground is the scene of mock battles—cannons and all—by the Compagnie Franche de la Marine and bagpipe concerts by the 78th Fraser Highlanders. *Tel. 514/861–6701. Admission: $3 adults; $2 senior citizens, students, and children. Open summer, daily 10–5; off-season, Tues.–Sun. 10–5.*

In mid-June, Île Notre-Dame is the site of the Molson Grand Prix du Canada, a top Formula I international circuit auto race at the Gilles Villeneuve Race Track.

The **Parc Mont-Royal,** the finest in the city, is not easy to overlook. These 494 acres of forest and paths at the heart of the city were designed by Frederick Law Olmsted, the celebrated architect of New York's Central Park. He believed that communion with nature could cure body and soul. The park is designed following the natural topography and accentuating its features, as in the English mode. You can go skating on Beaver Lake in the winter, visit one of the three lookouts and scan the horizon, or study the park interpretation center in the chalet at the Mont Royal belvedere. Horse-drawn transport is popular year-round: sleigh rides in winter and calèche rides in summer. On the eastern side of the hill stands the 30-meter (100-foot) steel cross that is the symbol of the city.

Shrines

St. Joseph's Oratory, on the northwest side of Mont Royal, is a Catholic shrine on a par with Lourdes or Fatima. Take the blue Métro line to the Côte-des-Neiges station, then walk three blocks uphill on the chemin de la Côte-des-Neiges. You can't miss the enormous church up on the hillside. Brother André, a member of the Society of the Brothers of the Holy Cross, constructed a small chapel to St. Joseph, Canada's patron saint, in 1904. Brother André was credited with a number of miracles and was beatified in 1982. His chapel became a pilgrimage site, the only one to St. Joseph in the world (St. Joseph is the patron saint of healing). Inspired by the miracles and Brother André's simple, devout life, believers began sending in offerings for a shrine. The construction of the enormous basilica began in 1924 and took 31 years. The dome is among the world's largest, and while the interior is of little aesthetic interest there is a small museum dedicated to Brother André's life, and many displays, including thousands of crutches discarded by the formerly crippled faithful. Carillon, choral, and organ concerts are held weekly at the oratory during the summer, and you can still visit Brother André's original chapel and tomb at the side of the massive basilica. *3800 chemin Queen Mary, tel. 514/733–8211. Open summer, daily 6:30 AM–9:30 PM; fall and spring, 8 AM–8:30 PM; winter, 8–5.*

Montréal for Free

The Saidye Bronfman Centre "hands-on" fine arts school's open-house activities, gallery exhibitions, and public affairs lectures (*see* Off the Beaten Track, below).

Musée d'art contemporain (*see* Off the Beaten Track, below).

Classical and pop concerts, dance performances, and theater at **Parc de LaFontaine,** rue Rachel.

Picnic in **Parc Mont-Royal,** sail miniature boats in its Beaver Lake during the summer, and skate on it during the winter (*see* Parks and Gardens, above).

Bicycle along Montréal's waterfront to the Lachine Canal, atop its mountain, or through the Vieux-Port (*see* Participant Sports, below).

Le Centre Canadien d'Architecture, Thursday evening (*see* Tour 2, above).

What to See and Do with Children

La Ronde's Amusement Park (*see* Parks and Gardens, above).

Images du Futur offers futuristic, interactive exhibitions. *Vieux-Port at boul. St-Laurent and rue de la Commune, tel. 514/849–1612. May 31–Sept. 24, daily noon–11 PM.*

IMAX Super Cinema offers films on a seven-story-tall screen. *Vieux-Port, Shed no. 7, tel. 514/496–IMAX for information, 514/522–1245 for tickets.*

Olympic Tower. Zoom up the "tallest-inclined-tower-in-the-world" on the funicular for a 50-mile panorama of Montréal and its environs. *4545 Pierre-de-Coubertin (Métro Pie-IX), tel. 514/252–8687, 10–10. Closed mid-Jan. to mid-Feb.*

The Botanical Garden's **Insectarium** (*see* Parks and Gardens, above).

Aquarium de Montréal on Île Ste-Hélène (*see* Parks and Gardens, above).

Dow Planetarium. The heavens are reproduced with the aid of a giant Zeiss projector on the inside of the planetarium's vaulted dome. *1000 rue St-Antoine, tel. 514/872–4530. Open Tues.–Sun. 12:30–8:30.*

At the Old Fort on Île Ste-Hélène, now the site of the **David M. Stewart Museum,** mock battles, military drills, military-history exhibitions, and bagpipe concerts take place all summer long (*see* Parks and Gardens, above).

Off the Beaten Track

Just two blocks west of Victoria and the Métro Côte-Ste-Catherine station is the **Saidye Bronfman Centre.** This multidisciplinary institution has long been recognized as a focus of cultural activity with the Jewish community in particular and with Montréal as a whole. The center was a gift from the children of Saidye Bronfman in honor of their mother's lifelong commitment to the arts. In fact, the Mies van der Rohe–inspired building was originally designed by Mrs. Bronfman's daughter, Montréal architect Phyllis Lambert. Accessible by car, just one block east of the Décarie Expressway and about four blocks north of chemin Queen Mary, the center is well worth the trip.

Open year-round, many of its activities, such as gallery exhibits, lectures on public and Jewish affairs, performances, and concerts, are offered free to the public. The center is home to the Yiddish Theatre Group, the only Yiddish company performing today in North America. The theater also presents English works, often by local playwrights. Many an artist has passed through the doors of the center's School of Fine Arts. *5170 Côte Ste-Catherine, tel. 514/739–2301; box office 514/739–7944. Closed Fri. from 2 PM, Sat., and Jewish holidays. Call for information and program schedule.*

Far from the Saidye Bronfman Centre, but equally accessible by car, Métro, and bus, is the original **Musée d'art contemporain de Montréal,** located at Cité du Havre on part of the former Expo '67 site. The museum's large permanent collection represents works by Québec, Canadian, and international artists in every medium. The museum often features weekend programs, with many child-oriented activities, and almost all are free. There are guided tours, though hours vary and groups of more than 15 are asked to make a reservation. *Open Tues.–Sun. 10–6. Donation. Weekdays, take MUTC's regular bus No. 168 from the McGill, Bonaventure, and Victoria Métro stations. Weekends, take the free Museum Blue Bus. Pickups and returns are made at the McGill and Bonaventure Métro stations.*

For something completely different, head one block east of Parc LaFontaine on rue Rachel. There stands a forgotten museum that is a must-see for those with a taste for the, well, slightly odd. The **Midget Palace** was purchased in 1913 and renovated by 92-centimeter-tall (3 foot) Phillipe Nicol as a home for him and his wife, the "Count and Countess of Lilliputian Royalty." It was later bought by Huguette Rioux, a midget and founder of the Canadian Midgets Association, who turned it into a museum and doll hospital. On either side of the entrance are stained-glass panels depicting midgets shaking hands over the caption, "Toward a New Future." Inside you can take a tour of eight rooms that have been shrunk for midget use. The doorknobs and the furniture, including a baby grand piano, have all been lowered, and the kitchen is replete with specially scaled-down appliances. Ms. Rioux conducts the tour. *961 rue Rachel E, tel. 514/527–1121. Admission: $3.50 adults, $2.50 senior citizens, handicapped, and children. Open Mon.–Thurs. 10–noon.*

Shopping

by Patricia Lowe

Montréalers *magasiner* (go shopping) with a vengeance, so it's no surprise that the city has 160 multifaceted retail areas encompassing some 6,200 stores. Between 1990 and this fall, some 650 new boutiques and retail outlets will have been added to this rough estimate.

Visitors usually reserve at least one day to hunt for either exclusive fashions along rue Sherbrooke or bargains at the Vieux-Montréal flea market. But there are specific items that the wise shopper seeks out in Montréal.

Montréal is one of the fur capitals of the world. Close to 85% of Canada's fur manufacturers are based in the city, as are many of their retail outlets: **Alexandor** (2025 rue de la Montagne); **Shuchat** (2015 de la Montagne); **Grosvenor** (400 boulevard de Maisonneuve O); **McComber** (440 boulevard de Maisonneuve O); **La Baie** (Square Phillips); and **Birger Christensen at Holt**

Renfrew (1300 rue Sherbrooke O) are a few of the better showrooms.

Fine English bone china, crystal, and woolens are more readily available and cheaper in metropolitan stores than in their U.S. equivalents, thanks to Canada's tariff status as a Commonwealth country. There are three **Jaeger** boutiques (Ogilvy downtown, Centre Rockland in the town of Mount Royal, and Centre Fairview in the West Island) selling traditional woolen sweaters, along with $700 pure-wool suits. Collectors of china and crystal will do well at any of the **Birks Jewellers** on Square Phillips or in shopping complexes and suburban shopping centers. With lower price tags, **Caplan Duval** (Côte-St-Luc's Cavendish Mall) offers an overwhelming variety of patterns.

Today, only dedicated connoisseurs can uncover real treasures in traditional pine Canadiana, but scouting around for Québec *antiquités* and art can be fun and rewarding, especially along increasingly gentrified rue Notre-Dame Ouest.

The Montréal area has six major retail districts: the city center (or downtown), Vieux-Montréal, Notre-Dame Ouest, the Plâteau Mont Royal–St-Denis area, the upper St-Laurent–Laurier Ouest areas of Outremont, and the city of Westmount.

Montréal stores, boutiques, and department stores are generally open from 9 or 9:30 to 6 Monday, Tuesday, and Wednesday. On Thursday and often on Friday, stores close at 9, Saturday at 5. A number of pharmacies are open six days a week until 11 PM or midnight; a few are 24-hour operations. Just about all stores, with the exception of some bargain outlets and a few selective art and antiques galleries, accept major credit cards. Buy your Canadian money at a bank or exchange bureau beforehand to take advantage of the latest rates on the dollar.

A Québec sales tax of 9% applies to all clothing purchases over $500 and shoes and boots over $125. The recently legislated federal GST tax adds 7% to all goods and services except groceries and essential medications, etc. However, there is still no Québec sales tax on books, home furnishings, or clothing under $500.

If you think you might be buying fur, it is wise to check with your country's customs officials before leaving to find out which animals are considered endangered and cannot be imported. Do the same if you think you might be buying Eskimo carvings, many of which are made of whalebone and ivory and cannot be brought into the United States.

City Center

Central downtown is Montréal's largest retail district. It takes in rue Sherbrooke, boulevard de Maisonneuve, rue Ste-Catherine, and the side streets between them. Because of the proximity and variety of shops, it's the best shopping bet for visitors in town overnight or over a weekend.

Faubourg Ste-Catherine

Several new or soon-to-open complexes have added glamour to the city center shopping scene. A good place to start is the **Faubourg Ste-Catherine,** Montréal's answer to Boston's Quincy Market. At the corner of rues Ste-Catherine Ouest and Guy, it is a vast bazaar housed in a former parking and auto-body garage abutting the Grey Nuns' convent grounds. Three levels of clothing and crafts boutiques, as well as food counters selling fruits and vegetables, pastry, baked goods, and meats, surround the central atrium of tiered fountains and islands of café tables and chairs. This is the place to pick up a $30 original Peruvian wall hanging or a fine French wine, also about $30, at the government-run **Société d'alcools du Québec.** Prices at most stores are generally reasonable here, especially if you're sampling the varied ethnic cuisine at any of the snack counters.

Les Cours Mont-Royal

Continuing east on Ste-Catherine, the *très* elegant **Les Cours Mont-Royal** dominates the east side of rue Peel between this main shopping thoroughfare and boulevard de Maisonneuve. This mall caters to expensive tastes, but even bargain hunters find it an intriguing spot for window shopping.

Place Montréal Trust

Just two blocks away, Place Montréal Trust at McGill College is the lively entrance to an imposing glass office tower. Shoppers, fooled by the aqua and pastel decor, may think they have stumbled into a California mall. Prices at the 120 outlets range from hundreds (for designs by **Alfred Sung,** haute couture at **Gigi** or **Rodier,** or men's high fashion at **Bally**) to mere dollars (for sensible cotton boys' T-shirts, or beef-and-kidney pies or minced tarts at the British dry goods and food store, **Marks & Spencer**). These imported goodies share the floor space with moderately ticketed ladies' suits, menswear, lingerie, and children's clothing. Marks & Spencer is a far cry from neighboring **Abercrombie and Fitch,** which stocks the offbeat and the outrageous, such as a fold-up miniature billiards table or a $5,995 toy sports car.

Les Cours Mont-Royal and this complex will have competition from the **Centre Eaton** and **Les Promenades de la Cathédrale.** All four of these centers will be linked to the Underground City retail network.

Always a favorite with visitors, the nearly 15-kilometer (9-mile) "city below" draws large crowds to its shop-lined corridors honeycombing between Les Promenades de la Cathédrale, Place Ville-Marie, Place Bonaventure, and Complexe Desjardins.

Les Promenades de la Cathédrale

Nestled between Eaton and La Baie department stores, this underground retail complex is already proving popular with Montréalers. Its unusual location makes it a sightseeing adventure as well. Connected to the McGill Métro and located directly beneath the stately and historic Christ Church Cathedral, a highlight (some say a travesty) of the retail mall's design is the replication of architectural details found in the cathedral above. The retail complex boasts some 150 stores, with many well-known international and Canadian chain stores among them.

Place Ville-Marie

Weatherproof shopping began in 1962 beneath the 42-story cruciform towers of Place Ville-Marie on boulevard René-Lévesque (formerly Dorchester Boulevard) at rue University. A recent renovation has opened Place Ville-Marie up to the light, creating a more cheerful ambience as well as adding stores.

Stylish women head to Place Ville-Marie's 125-plus retail outlets for the clothes: haute couture at **Lalla Fucci, Jacnel, Marie-Claire, Cactus,** as well as **Holt Renfrew's** branch store. Traditionalists will love **Heritage House** and **Aquascutum.** More affordable clothes shops include **Dalmy's, Gazebo, Reitman's,** and, for shoes, **Mayfair, Brown's, François Villon,** and **Cemi.**

Place Bonaventure From here it's an easy underground trip through Gare Centrale (the train station) to Place Bonaventure's mall beneath one of Canada's largest commercial buildings. It houses some 120 stores, ranging from the trendy (**Au Coton** and **Bikini Village**) to the exclusive (**Alain Giroux** boutique).

Complexe Desjardins Still in the downtown area but a bit farther east on boulevard René-Lévesque is Complexe Desjardins. It's a fast ride via the Métro at Bonaventure station; just get off at Place des Arts and follow the tunnels to Desjardins' multitiered atrium mall. Also home to the Meridien Hotel, Complexe Desjardins' opening coincided with the 1976 Summer Olympic Games and was an immediate hit. It is popular with a mainly French-speaking clientele, making it more typical of the city's cultural mix. Filled with splashing fountains and exotic plants, Desjardins exudes a Mediterranean joie de vivre, even when it's below freezing outside. Roughly 80 stores include budget outlets like **Le Château** for fashion and **Sarosi** for shoes, as well as the exclusive **Rodier of Paris,** where dresses start at about $150. A pleasant art gallery, **France-Martin,** on the lower level, features works by local and other Canadian painters.

Department Stores **Eaton** is the city's leading department store and part of Canada's largest chain. Founded in Toronto by Timothy Eaton, the first Montréal outlet appeared in 1925. It now sells everything—from the art decorating the top-floor restaurant entrance to zucchini loaves in the basement bakery. Floors in between sell Canadian crafts and souvenirs; Canadian designers as well as labels by Nipon and Ports International; fine furnishings and accessories in addition to the bargain-basement variety; microwaves, VCRs, the whole gamut of department store selections. The main restaurant is an unusual Art Deco replica of the dining room aboard the old *Île de France* ocean liner, once Lady Eaton's favorite cruise ship. Construction has been completed on the $120 million Eaton Centre, which incorporates the present store and the adjoining Les Terrasses labyrinth of boutiques.

The nearby sandstone building housing **La Baie** opened in 1891, although the original Henry Morgan Company that founded it moved to Montréal as early as 1843. Morgan's was purchased in 1960 by the Hudson Bay Company, which was founded in 1670 by famous Montréal voyageurs and trappers Radisson and Grosseilliers. For more than 150 years, Hudson Bay held the monopoly on Canada's fur trade, so it follows that this store's fur salon has a reputation for quality. La Baie is also known for its Hudson Bay red-, green-, and white-striped blankets and duffel coats. It also sells the typical department store fare. Its ground floor has undergone a dramatic renovation. It now features "boutique" shopping à la Ogilvy, in which the fashion-conscious will find the latest in jewelry and accessories from Lancel Handbags, Beverley Hamburg, Yves St-Laurent cosmetics, and Boutique 317 For Men, among others.

Exclusive **Holt Renfrew,** at 1300 rue Sherbrooke O, is also known for its furs. The city's oldest store, it was established in 1837 as Henderson, Holt and Renfrew Furriers and made its name supplying coats to four generations of British royalty. When Queen Elizabeth II married Prince Phillip in 1947, Holt's created a priceless Labrador mink as a wedding gift. Commoners, however, must be content with a brown-dyed blue fox for $14,750. Holt's also now carries the exclusive and pricey line of furs by Denmark's Birger Christensen, as well as the haute-couture and *prêt-à-porter* collections of perennial fashion favorite Yves St-Laurent (in a fabulously elegant new boutique devoted exclusively to the internationally lionized designer's designer).

Around the corner and two blocks down rue de la Montagne, at **Ogilvy** (1307 rue Ste-Catherine O), a kilted piper regales shoppers every day at noon. An institution with Montréalers since 1865, the once-homey department store has undergone a miraculous face-lift. Fortunately, it has preserved its delicate pink glass chandeliers and still stocks traditional apparel—Aquascutum, Jaeger, tweeds for men, and smocked dresses for little girls. Every Christmas its main window showcases a fantasy world of mechanized animals busy with their holiday preparations, as it has since Steiff of Germany first made the display for Ogilvy in 1947. Style-conscious customers snap up designs by Valentino, Jean Muir, Don Sayres, and Raffinati; Joan & David shoes; and the unusual dyed coats in the fur salon.

This area—bounded by rues Sherbrooke and Ste-Catherine, and rues de la Montagne and Crescent—also boasts antiques and art galleries as well as designer salons. Rue Sherbrooke is lined with an array of art and antiques galleries: **Waddington & Gorce** (No. 1504), featuring contemporary pieces; the **Petit Musée** (No. 1494), selling ancient *objets* and *bijoux* from the Orient, Egypt, and Greece: **Galerie Claude Lafitte** (No. 1480) showcases Canadian and Québec art; **Galerie D'Art Eskimau** (No. 1434), one of the country's largest galleries specializing in Eskimo sculpture; **Dominion Gallery** (No. 1438), known for introducing sculptor Henry Moore to Canada; and **Walter Klinkhoff** (No. 1200). Clotheshorses strolling rue Sherbrooke stop at **Brisson & Brisson** (No. 1472), featuring elegant styles and accessories for men; **Bruestle** (No. 1490), for tailored women's classics; **Les Gamineries** (No. 1458), outfitting fashionable children; **Ralph Lauren** (No. 1316), a house full of East Coast styles; **Ungaro** (No. 1430), high fashion by a top designer; **Bijouterie** (No. 1498); and recent arrival **Cartier** (at the corner of rues Sherbrooke and Simpson), where diamonds sparkle from showcase windows in the green marble facade.

Rue Crescent is a tempting blend of antiques, fashions, and jewelry boutiques displayed beneath colorful awnings: **André Antiques** (No. 2125), for fine furniture; **Ferroni** (No. 2145), known for English antiques; and **Laura Ashley** (No. 2110), two stories of romantic clothes, linens, and fabric. Head to **Olly de Hollande** (No. 2165) for colorful, avant-garde fashions from the Netherlands and **Neo-Nix** (No. 1260) for high-tech gifts, such as a stuffed bear that takes telephone messages and repeats them back to you.

Vieux-Montréal

The second major shopping district, historic Vieux-Montréal, can be a tourist trap; but a shopping spree there can be a lot less expensive and more relaxing than shopping downtown. Both rues Notre-Dame and St-Jacques, from rue McGill to Place Jacques-Cartier, are lined with low to moderately priced fashion boutiques, garish souvenir shops slung with thousands of Montréal T-shirts, and shoe stores. **Tripp Distribution & Importation** (389 and 21 rue Notre-Dame O) has bargains on Ralph Lauren (polo shirts for $25) and other labels; the store prefers cash to credit cards. Québec crafts are well represented at **Centre de Céramique de Bonsecours** (444 rue St-Gabriel), which sells and shows ceramics and sculptures by local artisans from noon to 5. **Desmarais & Robitaille** (60 rue Notre-Dame), a store specializing in religious objects and vestments, also has lovely handcrafted souvenirs, knits, and weavings.

For finer art, go to **Galerie St-Paul** (4 rue St-Paul E), selling limited edition prints, sculptures, and works by local and international artists; or **La Guilde Graphique** (9 rue St-Paul O), for prints. **Les Artisans du Meuble Québeçois** (88 rue St-Paul E) has an artistic selection of Québec-made crafts as well as silver, jewelry, and clothing. **Le Rouet Metiers d'Art,** which sells handcrafts, has its main store at 136 rue St-Paul Est.

Along the edge of Vieux-Montréal is Montréal's rejuvenated waterfront, the Vieux-Port, which hosts a sprawling flea market, the **Marché aux puces,** on Quai King Edward (King Edward Pier). Dealers and pickers search for secondhand steals and antique treasures as they prowl through the huge hangar that is open Wednesday through Sunday from spring through early fall.

Notre-Dame Ouest

The place for antiquing is the city's third shopping sector, beginning at rue Guy and continuing west to avenue Atwater (a five-minute walk south from the Lionel-Groulx Métro station). Once a shabby strip of run-down secondhand stores, this area has blossomed beyond its former nickname of Attic Row. It now has the highest concentration of antiques, collectibles, and curiosity shops in Montréal. Collectors can find Canadian pine furniture—armoires, cabinets, spinning wheels, rocking chairs—for reasonable prices here.

A westbound walk along this avenue takes in: **Portes & Vitraux Anciens du Grand Montréal** (No. 1500), which sells Canadian pine furniture and stained glass; **Danielle J. Malynowsky Inc.** (No. 1640), including Victorian and Chinese pieces with Canadiana; **Antiquités Marielle Moquin and Michelle Parent** (No. 1650), where silver tea services (sterling cream and sugar, $250) grace an inlaid buffet; **Martin Antiques** (No. 1732); **Antiquités Ambiance & Discernement** (No. 1654), blending old and new furniture designs; and **Antiquités G. M. Portal** (No. 1894), for more Canadian pine. Eclectic collections (barber poles and suits of armor) crowd together at **Deuxièmement** (No. 1880). The jumbly attics of **Basilières** (No. 1904) and **Gisela's** (No. 1960) are for old dolls and teddy bears.

Plateau–Mont Royal–St-Denis

Popular with students, academics, and journalists, this easterly neighborhood embraces boulevard St-Laurent, the longtime student ghetto surrounding the Prince Arthur mall, St-Denis and its Latin Quarter near the Université du Québec à Montréal campus, and the Plateau district. Plateau–Mont Royal–St-

Denis attracts a trendier, more avant-garde crowd than the determined antiquers along Notre-Dame.

Boulevard St-Laurent—dubbed "The Main" because it divides the island of Montréal into east and west—has always been a lively commercial artery. It was first developed by Jewish merchants who set up shop here in the early 1900s. Cutting a broad swath across the island's center, this long boulevard has an international flavor, with its mélange of stores run by Chinese, Greek, Slav, Latin American, Portuguese, and Vietnamese immigrants. Lower boulevard St-Laurent is lined with discount clothing and bric-a-brac stores, secondhand shops, electronics outlets, and groceries selling kosher meats, Hungarian pastries, Peking duck, and natural foods. Fashionable clothing shops join this colorful bazaar, though none has been as successful as the now-international **Parachute Boutique** (No. 3526), which began its career in Montréal.

While boulevard St-Laurent's personality is multiethnic, rue St-Denis's is distinctly French. (Both are lengthy arteries, so make use of Bus 55 for boulevard St-Laurent, Bus 31 and 30 along rue St-Denis.) More academic in makeup, its awnings shelter bookstores (mostly French), with **Librairie Flammarion Scorpion** (No. 4380) being one of the best. Rare- and used-book stores are scattered along the street from **Librairie Kebuk** (No. 2048) to **Librairie Delteil** (No. 7348). **Musique Archambault** (off rue St-Denis at 500 rue Ste-Catherine) caters to the city's music students. Bookstores are complemented by scattered art galleries (**Michel Tétrault,** No. 4260; **Morency,** No. 4340; **Art Select,** No. 6810) and antiques stores (**Antiquités Je Me Souviens,** No. 8254-A, and **Puces Libres,** No. 4240). The **Galerie Leport Tremblay** (No. 3979) sells unique furnishings and accessories. **Le Château** has one of its many trendy fashion boutiques at No. 4201; **Thalie** (No. 4203) has inexpensive, high-quality, and fashion-forward men's and women's knitwear; and Maurice Ferland's designs are available at **Un Brin d'Elle** (No. 4417). Denim sportswear by Canadian designers at **Revenge** (No. 3852) and international fashions at **Orphee** (No. 3997) are among a wide range of other boutiques. Modern furnishings, such as colorful art clocks for $85, brighten up the showroom at **Dixversions** (No. 4361). **Les Concepts Zone** (No. 4246) is known for its arty hand-blown martini glasses; **Millésimes** (No. 3901) stocks a variety of wine drinkers' goodies and crystal. **Le Sieur Duluth chapeaux, bijoux et accessoires** (No. 4454) is an absolute must for mad hatters of either sex. Many of the creations are designed in-house; custom orders are also accepted. And the array of ready-to-wear (or just waiting to be bought) hats, jewelry, and accessories will delight the eye.

Upper St-Laurent and Laurier Ouest

Upper boulevard St-Laurent (for our purposes, roughly from avenue du Mont-Royal north to rue St-Viateur), intersecting with avenue Laurier Ouest and climbing the mountain to rue Bernard, has blossomed into one of Montréal's chicest *quartiers* in recent years. It's not entirely surprising, given that much of this area lies within or adjacent to Outremont, traditionally the enclave for wealthy Franco-phone Montréalers, with restaurants, boutiques, nightclubs and bistros catering to the upscale visitor. In addition, the influx of a new generation of multiethnic professionals, artists, and entrepreneurs is making its mark on the area.

Upper boulevard St-Laurent now rivals St-Denis, the downtown, and Laurier Ouest as a cultural hot spot, and it is reminiscent of New York City's SoHo. Here you'll find the lusciously colored, butter-soft suede and leather fashions for men and women designed by Montréaler **Robert Krief** at his showroom storefront of the same name (No. 5226), as well as his more rugged "Western" leather and denim unisex fashions at his boutique, **Paris, Texas** (No. 5251). If those are too pricey, check out **Le Chateau's** own label—knockoffs of the latest designer styles and retro fashions at its two-floor boutique (No. 5160); **Trois & Un** (No. 5129) for sportswear; **Luna** (No. 5155) or **Le Lotus Blanc** (No. 5163) for soft, brightly colored cotton and rayon knit jersey wear; **Double Vé** (No. 5145) for Annie Coriat-Ropsard sportswear; and **Atout Fringues** (No. 5183) for NafNaf, Paris's latest casual wear.

Avenue Laurier Ouest, from boulevard St-Laurent to chemin de la Côte-Ste-Catherine—roughly an eight-block stretch, which you'll crisscross many times as ya (No. 5155) or **Le Lotus Blanc** (No. 5163) for soft, brightly colored cotton and rayon knit jersey wear; **Double Vé** (No. 5145) for Annie Coriat-Ropsard sportswear; and **Atout Fwall coverings at Griffe** (No. 92 O); French-Canadian pine antiques at **Boutique Confort** (No. 201 O); or unusual handcrafted ceramics and pottery at **Cache-Cache** (No. 1051 O).

Head-to-toe fashion choices for men and women of all ages—from haute couture to the internationally marketed same-as-everywhere fashions by Benetton (No. 1068 O)—can also be found on avenue Laurier Ouest. Canadian designers include **Les Tricots d'Ariane** (No. 207 O) for knits by Ariane Carle, and **Revenge** (No. 111 O) for Québécois rising designer stars Denommé-Vincent, Dagisco, Jean-Claude Poitras, and Alain Thomas.

The more culturally inclined can discover the reigning literary stars of Québec and French literature at **Librairie Lettre Son** (No. 1005 O) or Québec's contemporary artists at **Artes** (No. 102 O), devoted exclusively to promoting works in every medium by Québec's established and up-and-coming artistic talent.

Square Westmount and Avenue Greene

Visitors with time to shop or friends in the elegant residential neighborhood of Westmount, a separate municipality in the middle of the island of Montréal should explore Square Westmount and adjacent avenue Greene. Next door to downtown, these malls are on the Angrignon Métro line, easily accessible via the Atwater station, which has an exit at Square Westmount. Just follow the tunnel to this mall's 20 or so exclusive shops, including **Cacharel,** for Liberty prints; **Guy Laroche; Chacok,** for the avant-garde; **Lily Simon,** for French and Italian haute-couture, *prêt-à-porter,* and sportswear designer fashions; and **Marcelle de Paris.**

The square's plaza opens onto avenue Greene's two-block shopping area, which is lined with trees and flowers. Its redbrick row houses and even the renovated old post office are home to a wealth of boutiques and shops.

Sports and Fitness

The range of sporting activities available in Montréal is testament to Montréalers' love of the outdoors. With world-class skiing in the Laurentians less than an hour away and dozens of skating rinks within the city limits, they revel in winter. When the last snowflake has melted, they store away skis, poles, and skates and dust off their bikes, tennis rackets, and fishing poles. And year-round they watch the pros at hockey matches, baseball and football games, car races, and tennis tournaments.

Participant Sports

Bicycling The island of Montréal—except for Mont Royal itself—is quite flat, and there are more than 20 cycling paths around the metropolitan area. Among the most popular are those on Île Ste-Hélène, along rue Rachel, and in Angrignon and Vieux-Port parks. You can rent 10-speed bicycles at **Cycle Peel** (6665 rue St-Jacques, tel. 514/486–1148).

Parks Canada conducts guided cycling tours along the historic **Lachine Canal** (1825) every summer weekend. Tours leave from the corner of rues McGill and de la Commune at 10:30 AM, in English on Saturday, in French on Sunday. For more details, call 514/283–6054 or 514/872–6211.

Golf For a complete listing of the many golf courses in the Montréal area, call **Tourisme-Québec** at 514/873–2015.

Hunting and Fishing Québec's rich waters and forests are filled with fish and wildlife. Before you begin the chase you need to purchase the appropriate license from the Ministère des Loisirs, de la Chasse et de la Pêche or from an authorized agent. The lakes and rivers around Montréal teem with fish, and a number of guides offer day trips. For hunting you'll have to go farther afield, to the Laurentians or l'Estrie (*see* Chapter 11). For complete information, call **Tourisme-Québec** (tel. 514/873–2015).

Ice Skating There are at least 150 outdoor and 21 indoor rinks in the city. You'll probably find one in the nearest park. Call parks and recreation (tel. 514/872–6211). A few of the more popular outdoor rinks include:

Parc Angrignon. Night skating. 7050 boulevard de la Vérendrye.

Île Notre-Dame. Olympic rowing basin.

Parc LaFontaine. Rue Sherbrooke E at Calixa-Lavallée.

Parc du Mont-Royal. Night skating on Beaver Lake.

Jogging Montréal became a runner's city following the 1976 Olympics. There are paths in most city parks, but for running with a panoramic view, head to the dirt track in **Parc du Mont-Royal** (take rue Peel, then the steps up to the track).

Rafting Montréal is the only city in the world where you can step off a downtown dock and minutes later be crashing through Class V white water in a sturdy aluminum jet boat. The Lachine Rapids, just south of Vieux-Montréal, were responsible for the founding of Montréal. The roiling waves were too treacherous for the first settlers to maneuver, so they founded Ville-Marie, the forerunner of Vieux-Montréal. Modern voyageurs suit up for the 45-minute jet-boat trip in multiple layers of wool and rain gear, but it's nearly impossible to stay dry—or to have a bad time. *Lachine Rapids Tours Ltd. 105 rue de la Commune, Vieux-Montréal, tel. 514/284-9607. 5 trips daily, departing from Quai Victoria May–Sept., 10, noon, 2, 4, and 6. Trips are narrated in French and English and reservations are necessary. Rates: $32 adults, $24 teens 13–18, $14 children 6–12, $25 senior citizens.*

Skiing
Downhill For the big slopes you'll have to go northwest to the Laurentians or south to l'Estrie, an hour or two away by car. There is a small slope in Parc du Mont-Royal. Pick up the Ski-Québec brochure at the Tourisme-Québec offices.

Cross-country Trails crisscross most of the city's parks, including Notre-Dame and Île Ste-Hélène, Angrignon, Maisonneuve, and Mont-Royal.

Squash You can reserve court time for this fast-pace racquet sport at **Nautilus Centre St-Laurent Côte-de-Liesse Racquet Club** (8305 chemin Côte-de-Liesse, tel. 514/739–3654).

Swimming There is a large indoor pool at the **Olympic Park** (Métro Viau, tel. 514/252–4622) and another at the **Centre Sportif et des Loisirs Claude-Robillard** (1000 av. Emile Journault, tel. 514/872–6900). The free outdoor pool on Île Ste-Hélène is an extremely popular (and crowded) summer gathering place. Open June–Labor Day. The new city-run beach at Île Notre-Dame is the only natural swimming hole in Montréal (tel. 514/872–6211).

Tennis There are public courts in the Jeanne-Mance, Kent, LaFontaine, and Somerled parks. For details call Montreal Sports and Recreation (tel. 514/872–6211).

Windsurfing and Sailing Sailboards and small sailboats can be rented at **L'École de Voile de Lachine** (2105 boul. St.-Joseph, Lachine, tel. 514/634–4326) and the **Club Nautique de Pleine Air de Montréal** (Île Notre-Dame, tel. 514/872–6093).

Spectator Sports

Baseball The National League **Montreal Expos** play at the Olympic Stadium from April through September. For information, call 514/253–3434 or 800/351–0658; for credit card reservations, call 514/253–0700.

Cycling **La Classique Cycliste de Montréal** is a professional cycling competition through the LaFontaine, Mont-Royal, and Olympic parks held in early June (tel. 514/251–6955).

Le Tour de L'Île de Montréal has made the *Guinness Book of Records* for attracting a great number of participants for the past four years. More than 30,000 amateur cyclists participate in "North America's most important amateur cycling event" each June, wending their way 70 kilometers (38 miles) through the streets and parks of Montréal (514/251–6955).

In early August, **Le Grand Prix cyclistes** brings together professional cyclists from around the world to compete in this 200-kilometer (124-mile) cycling competition (tel. 514/879–1027).

Grand Prix The annual **Molson Grand Prix du Canada,** which draws top Formula 1 racers from around the world, takes place every June at the Gilles Villeneuve Race Track on Île Notre-Dame (tel. 514/392–0000 for tickets, tel. 514/392–9022 for information).

Hockey The **Montréal Canadiens,** winners of 23 Stanley Cups, meet National Hockey League rivals at the Forum (2313 rue Ste-Catherine O, tel. 514/932–6131) from October to April.

Marathon More than 12,000 runners do the grueling **Montréal International Marathon** each September through the streets of Montréal (tel. 514/879–1027).

Tennis The **Player's Challenge tennis championships** are held during the first two weeks of August on the courts of Jarry Tennis Stadium (rue Jarry and boul. St-Laurent, tel. 514/273–1515). The men compete in odd years, the women in even years.

Dining

by Josée Blanchette and Andrew Coe

Josée Blanchette is a restaurant critic for Montréal's French daily newspaper, Le Devoir, *and for Radio Canada (CBC French network). She takes a special interest in traditional Canadian and ethnic cooking.*

The promise of a good meal is easily satisfied in Montréal. Les Montréalais don't "eat out"; they "dine." And they are passionate about dining. The city has more than 7,000 restaurants of every price representing more than 35 ethnic groups. It has culinary institutions like Les Mignardises, Le Paris, and the Beaver Club, which emphasize classic cuisine and tradition. Delicatessens such as Briskets, Schwartz's, and Wilensky's are mainstays for budget dining. In between there are ethnic eateries featuring the foods of China, Greece, India, Morocco, and Italy. Then there are the ubiquitous inexpensive fast-food outlets and coffee shops. But above all, Montréal is distinguished by the European ambience of its restaurants. Catch a glimpse of the eateries' terraces from midday to 2 PM for a look at the hours that Montréal diners take most seriously. Each of the city's well-known bistros is more Parisian than the next. The challenge to dining in Montréal is choosing from among the thousands of restaurants and the varieties of cinexpensive fast-food outlets and coffee shops. But above all, Montréal is distinguished by the European ambience of its restaurants. Catch a glimpse of the eateries' terraces from midday to 2 PM for a look at the hours that Montréal diners take most seriously. Each of the city's well-known bistros is more Parisian than the next. The challenge to dining in Montréal is choosing from among the thousands of restaurants and the varieties of cuisine.

Many expensive French and Continental restaurants offer two options, which can be a blessing or a burden to your wallet. Either choice guarantees you a great meal. Instead of ordering à la carte—you select each dish—you can opt for the table d'hôte or the *menu de dégustation*. The table d'hôte is a complete two- to four-course meal chosen by the chef. It is less expensive than a complete meal ordered à la carte and often offers interesting special dishes. It also may take less time to prepare. If you want to splurge with your time and money, indulge yourself with the menu de dégustation, a five- to seven-course dinner executed by the chef. It usually includes, in this order, salad, soup, a fish dish, sherbet, a meat dish, dessert, and coffee or tea. At the city's finest restaurants, this menu for two and a good bottle of wine can cost $170 and last three or four hours. But it's worth every cent and every second.

Montréal restaurants are refreshingly relaxed. Although many of the hotel restaurants require a jacket and tie, neatness (no torn T-shirts and scruffy jeans) is appreciated in most of the other restaurants. Lunch hour is generally from noon to 2:30 and dinner from 6 to 11 or midnight. (Montréalers like to dine late, particularly on summer weekends.) Some restaurants are closed on Sunday or Monday. Since there is no consistent annual closing among Montréal eateries—some will take time off in August, while others will close around Christmas and January—call ahead to avoid disappointment.

Highly recommended restaurants in each price category are indicated by a star ★.

Category	Cost*
Very Expensive	over $30
Expensive	$20–$30
Moderate	$10–$20
Inexpensive	$5–$10

**per person without tax (10% for meals over $3.25), service, or drinks*

Chinese

Moderate **Cathay Restaurant.** Hong Kong investors, fearful of their city's future, are pouring money into Montréal's and other Chinatowns in North America. Among other businesses, they're opening slick, Hong Kong-style restaurants and competing with the older Chinese eateries. The consumer wins in these restaurant wars. The 15-year-old Cathay was remodeled and expanded in 1985, and is now the most popular and largest dim sum restaurant in the city. The two floors are both huge rooms with institutional dropped ceilings and the usual red and gold Chinese stage decorations. From 11 AM to 2:30 PM waitresses emerge from the kitchen pushing carts laden with steaming beef dumplings in bamboo steamers, spicy cuttlefish, shrimp rice noodles, bean curd rolls, and on and on. *73 rue de la Gauchetière O, Chinatown, tel. 514/866–3131. No reservations on weekends, so be prepared to wait on Sun. morning. Dress: casual. AE, DC, MC, V.*

Delicatessens

Inexpensive **Bens.** On the menu of this large, efficient deli, all the items with "Bens" in the name are red or are covered in red: "Bens Cheesecake" is smothered in strawberries; "Bens Ice Cold Drink" is the color of electric cherry juice; and the specialty, the "Big Ben Sandwich," is two slices of rye bread enclosing a seductive, pink pile of juicy smoked meat (Montréal's version of corned beef). According to Bens lore, the founder, Ben Kravitz, brought the first smoked-meat sandwich to Montréal in 1908. The rest, as they say, is history. A number of the walls are devoted to photos of celebrities who have visited Bens. The decor is strictly '50s, with yellow and green walls and vaguely art deco, institutional furniture. The waiters are often wise-cracking characters but are nonetheless incredibly efficient. Beer, wine, and cocktails are served. Bens motto: "But for life the Universe were nothing, and all that has life requires nourishment." *990 boul. de Maisonneuve O, downtown, tel. 514/ 844–*

Auberge le Vieux St-Gabriel, **13**
Beaver Club, **17**
Bens, **19**
Bocca d'Oro, **26**
Cathay, **16**
Chez Delmo, **15**
Katsura, **23**
La Chartreuse, **10**
La Sucrerie de la Montagne, **1**
Le Café de Paris, **21**
Le Lutetia, **22**
Le Mitoyen, **2**
Le Restaurant, **18**
Le Taj, **20**
Les Filles du Roy, **12**
Les Halles, **25**
Les Mignardises, **11**
L'Express, **8**
Milos, **4**
Moishe's, **7**
Pizzaiole, **3, 24**
Prego, **6**
Stash's, **14**
Wilensky's Light Lunch, **5**
Xuan, **9**

Montréal Dining

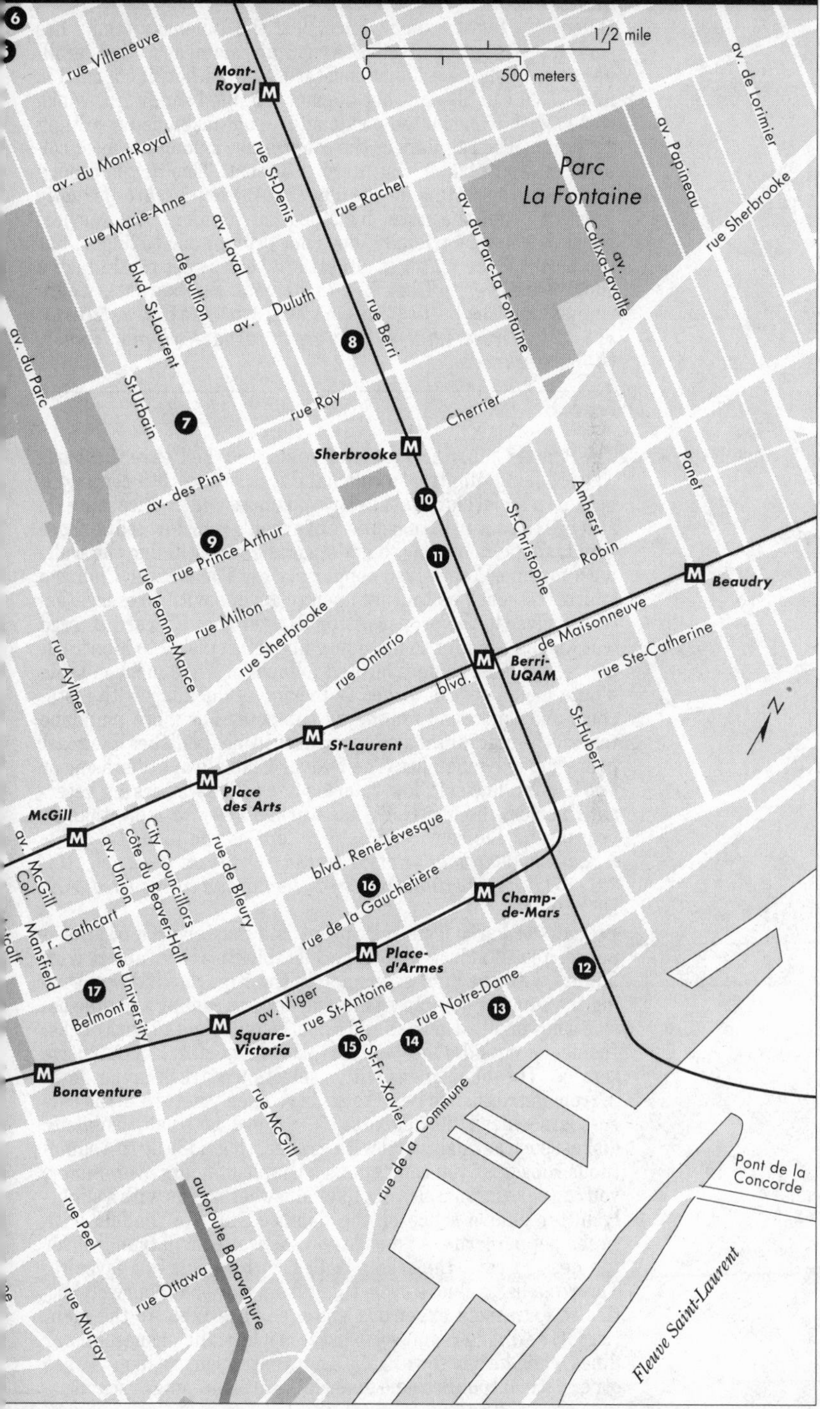
0
1/2 mile
0
500 meters
rue Villeneuve
Mont-Royal
av. du Mont-Royal
rue St-Denis
rue Marie-Anne
av. Laval
de Bullion
blvd. St-Laurent
av. du Parc
av. Duluth
rue Rachel
rue Berri
av. du Parc-La Fontaine
Parc La Fontaine
av. Calixa-Lavallé
av. Papineau
av. de Lorimier
rue Sherbrooke
St-Urbain
rue Roy
Cherrier
Sherbrooke
av. des Pins
rue Prince Arthur
rue Jeanne-Mance
rue Milton
rue Sherbrooke
rue Aylmer
rue Ontario
St-Christophe
Amherst
Robin
Panet
Beaudry
de Maisonneuve
blvd.
Berri-UQAM
rue Ste-Catherine
St-Hubert
St-Laurent
Place des Arts
McGill
av. McGill Col.
City Councillors
côte du Beaver-Hall
av. Union
rue de Bleury
blvd. René-Lévesque
rue de la Gauchetière
Champ-de-Mars
r. Cathcart
Mansfield
rue University
Belmont
Place-d'Armes
av. Viger
rue St-Antoine
rue Notre-Dame
Square-Victoria
rue St-Fr.-Xavier
Bonaventure
rue McGill
rue de la Commune
rue Peel
autoroute Bonaventure
rue Ottawa
rue Murray
Pont de la Concorde
Fleuve Saint-Laurent
N

1000. Reservations accepted. Dress: casual. MC, V. Closed Sun.

Wilensky's Light Lunch. Since 1932 the Wilensky family has served up its special: Italian-American salami on a Jewish roll, generously slathered with mustard. Served hot, it's a meal in itself. You can also get hot dogs or a grilled sandwich, which comes with a marinated pickle and an old-fashioned sparkling beverage. The regulars at the counter are among the most colorful in Montréal. A visit here is a must. This neighborhood haunt was the setting for the film *The Apprenticeship of Duddy Kravitz*, from the novel by Mordecai Richler. The service, which is not very friendly, does not prompt one to linger, but the prices make up for it. To satisfy your sweet tooth, take a short walk over to Chez L-G (5181 boul. St-Laurent), where you will find the best cookies in town. *5167 rue Clark, tel. 514/271–1247. Dress: informal. No credit cards. No liquor license. Closed weekends.*

French

Very Expensive

The Beaver Club. Early fur traders started the Beaver Club in a shack during Montréal's colonial days. In the 19th century it became a social club for the city's business and political elite. It still has the august atmosphere of a men's club devoted to those who trap: pelts of bear, buffalo, and beaver still line the walls with members' engraved copper plates. The Beaver Club is a gourmet French restaurant open to anyone with a reservation who arrives in the proper attire. Master chef Edward Merard was among the first to introduce nouvelle cuisine to Montréal, and he has a large and devoted following. The luncheon table d'hôte includes such dishes as terrine of duckling with pistachios and onion and cranberry compote. For more mundane tastes, the restaurant also specializes in meaty dishes like roast prime rib of beef au jus. The Beaver Club always offers one or two low-fat, low-salt, low-calorie plates. The waiters are veteran (Charles, the maître d', has worked here for more than 20 years), and the service is as excellent as the food. *La Reine Elizabeth, 900 boul. René-Lévesque O, downtown, tel. 514/861–3511. Reservations required. Jacket and tie required. AE, DC, MC, V.*

Le Café de Paris. This restaurant is a masterpiece of atmosphere. You sit at large, well-spaced tables in a room ablaze with flowers with the light streaming in the French windows. During the summer you can sit outside under a canopy and dine beside a flower-filled garden and a pool complemented with ducks. Inside or outside the waiters provide perfect, unobtrusive service. The menu opens with a selection of fresh caviar flown in from Petrossian in New York City. Then you turn to the seven-course menu de dégustation, a meal of small, exquisite dishes, such as quail salad with grapes, that adds up to a sumptuous repast. If you can't spend a couple of hours over dinner, you can choose from classics like calf sweetbreads with a slightly bitter endive sauce or the flambéed fillet of buffalo with green peppercorns. At meal's end the waiter will trundle over the dessert cart; the crème brûlée with raisins is a favorite. The wine list includes everything from reasonably priced bottles to extremely expensive vintages. The table to the right rear of the dining room as you enter is where the prime minister dines when he's in town. If he's not there, you are likely to see other national political and financial figures supping or schmoozing between tables. *Hôtel Ritz-Carlton, 1228 rue Sherbrooke O, tel. 514/842–4212. Reservations required. Jacket required at lunch and dinner. AE, MC, V.*

★ **Les Halles.** Definitely French, this restaurant took its name from the celebrated Parisian market immortalized by the pen of Émile Zola in *Le Ventre de Paris.* Its old-France character, enhanced by mirrors and typical bistro inscriptions, will give you the feeling of having gone from busy rue Crescent to even busier rue Montorgueil. However, dependable cuisine and tradition make Les Halles very efficient. The fussy waiters, with their white aprons and towels on their arms, seem to come straight out of a '40s French film. The wine cellar is exceptional and contains about 250 different bottles, from $11 for half a bottle to $475. The menu shows a lot of imagination without ignoring the classics: terrine of venison with a walnut sauce, fish stew with croutons, snails in all kinds of sauces, *plaice* (lemon sole) in cider, chicken *forestière,* and duck with foie gras in port sauce sit comfortably beside the chef's ventures into nouvelle cuisine, such as his lobster with ginger and coconut. The desserts are classic, delicious, and remarkably fresh. The Paris-Brest, a puff pastry with praline cream inside, is one of the best in town. *1450 rue Crescent, tel. 514/844–2328. Reservations advised. Dress: neat but casual. AE, DC, MC, V. Closed Sun.–Mon., Sat. lunch.*

Le Lutetia. This magnificent restaurant is worth a little detour, if only for the piano bar happy hour. The plethora of styles—rococo, renaissance, empire, fin de siècle, and baroque—is a spectacle in itself. This outrageously romantic restaurant is the perfect choice for a tête-à-tête by candlelight. The French cuisine, sometimes nouvelle, sometimes classic, is always served under a silver cover. Behind their glass partition, the cooks busy themselves and give the clientele an appetizing show, even at the busiest moments. The menu gastronomique changes each week according to the market and the seasons. À la carte half portions are available—which enables the diners to taste many dishes in one meal. Shrimp with fennel in puff pastry, ballotine of pheasant in a brioche dough, noisettes of veal *périgourdine* (with truffles), or medallion of beef with coarse mustard precede the cheese or the dessert cart. There is a very good wine list and champagne. *1430 rue de la Montagne, tel. 514/288–5656. Reservations advised. Dress: neat but casual. Terrace on the roof in summer. AE, CB, DC, MC, V.*

★ **Les Mignardises.** Chef Jean-Pierre Monnet used to run the kitchen at Les Halles. Now that he has his own place, his talents are given free range. Les Mignardises is considered the finest and certainly the most expensive restaurant in town. You enter via the bar and climb up one flight to the simple, elegant dining room decorated with copper pans hanging from the exposed-brick walls. The dining area holds only about 20 tables, so reservations are a must. If your wallet is full, you can choose the seven-course menu de dégustation ($58.95, or $71.50 if you allow the chef to choose the dishes for you). But if you're on a budget, it's still possible to enjoy a full meal. The three-course table d'hôte lunch menu allows you to sample delicious dishes like fish salad on gazpacho or marinated duck breast with vinegar sauce. The latter is sliced rare duck breast artfully arranged on a bed of oyster mushrooms with a slightly sweet vinegar sauce. The former is an appetizer of marinated raw salmon, tuna, and swordfish with tarragon and pink peppercorns on a light tomato gazpacho. Delicious potatoes sautéed with bouillon and onions in a little copper pot accompany the dishes. One of the house special desserts is crepes with honey ice cream. The presentation always takes a back seat to the taste. As you would expect, the wine list is large and pricey (the least expensive bottle is $24.50). The waiters and waitresses are prompt, knowledgeable, and friendly. *2035–37 rue St-Denis, near Berri and Sherbrooke métros, tel. 514/842–1151. Reservations required. Dress: casual, but no jeans or T-shirts. AE, CB, DC, MC, V. Closed Sun. and Mon.*

Expensive–Very Expensive

Le Restaurant. Le Quatre Saisons' management claims to have invented Montréal's version of "power" dining here. (The competition with the Ritz-Carlton continues.) Le Restaurant certainly has the power look. The choicest seats are on a raised circular platform, encircled by a white Hellenistic colonnade. They are comfortable, but very businesslike, executive chairs. In these impressive surroundings Québec's political and business leaders dine on first-class nouvelle cuisine. Many must suffer from high blood pressure, because the menu features "alternative cuisine" dishes with reduced salt, cholesterol, and calories. The fricassee of sweetbreads and prawns with lobster butter is not on this list. If you suffer from chronic low wallet weight, you can stop in for lunch and have the onion soup with a ham and cheese sandwich on French bread. Power breakfasts start at 7 AM. The standard of service here, as in the rest of the hotel, is high. The wine list is expensive and excellent, of course. *Le Quatre Saisons, 1050 rue Sherbrooke O, tel. 514/284–1110. Reservations required. AE, CB, DC, MC, V.*

Expensive

Auberge le Vieux St.-Gabriel. Established in a big stone house in 1754, this restaurant claims to be the oldest in America. The interior is lined with rough stone walls, and enormous old beams hold up the ceilings. In late 1987 it reopened with new owners who plan to expand both the menu and the dining space. At this writing the fare was hearty yet unadventurous French, with a bit of local Québecois flavor. The pea soup à la Canadienne is yellow and chunky rather than the American-style bland green puree. The perch fillets sautéed in dill butter are morsels of tender fish on top of mushy, overly rich creamed mushrooms. Other entrées include beef tenderloin with morels in a brandy and cream sauce and a terrine of rabbit with prunes and apples in a honey cream. If you're worried about your cholesterol, watch out. The restaurant seats close to 500 people, but you'd never guess it because there are so many separate dining rooms. *426 rue St-Gabriel, Vieux-Montréal, tel. 514/878–3561. Reservations advised. Dress: casual. AE, DC, MC, V. Closed Sun. except in summer.*

Moderate–Expensive
★

L'Express. The crowd is elbow to elbow, and the animated atmosphere is reminiscent of a Paris train station at this earnest establishment. L'Express has earned the title "best bistro in town." It is also the best-stocked. Popular media figures come here to be seen, a task made easier by the mirrored walls. The atmosphere is smoky, and the noise level at its peak on weekend evenings. The cuisine is always impeccable, the service is fast, and the prices are very good. L'Express has one of the best and most original wine cellars in town. Wine and champagne are available by the glass as well as by the bottle. The steak tartare with french fries, the salmon with sorrel, the calf's liver with tarragon, the first course of chicken livers with pistachios, or even the modest smoked salmon, are all marvelous year-round.

There are specials of the day to give the many regulars a change of pace. Jars of gherkins and fresh *baguettes*, cheeses aged to perfection, and quality eaux-de-vie make the pleasure last longer. *3927 rue St-Denis, tel. 514/845–5333. Reservations required. Dress: neat but casual. AE, CB, DC, MC, V.*

Greek

Expensive ★ **Milos.** Nets, ropes, floats, and lanterns—the usual cliché symbols of the sea—hang from Milos's walls and ceilings. The real display, however, is in the refrigerated cases and on the beds of ice in the back by the kitchen: fresh fish from all over the world; octopus, squid, and shrimp; crabs, oysters, and sea urchins; lamb chops, steaks, and chicken; and vegetables, cheese, and olives. In short, all the makings of your meal are there for you to inspect before you make your choice. The seafood is flown in from wholesalers in Nova Scotia, New York, Florida, and Athens. A meal can start out with chewy, tender, and hot octopus, or if you're adventurous, you might try the cool and creamy roe scooped from raw sea urchins. The main dish at Milos is usually fish—pick whatever looks freshest—grilled over charcoal and seasoned with parsley, capers, and lemon juice. It's done to a turn and is achingly delicious. The fish are priced by the pound, and you can order one larger fish to serve two or more. Don't be afraid to use your fingers: Hot towels are provided at the end. The bountiful Greek salad (enough for two) is a perfect side dish or can be a meal itself. For dessert you might try a *loukoumad* (honey ball), a deep-fried puff of dough doused in honey, chopped nuts, and cinnamon. The waiters are professional but not always knowledgeable about the whole array of exotic seafood available. Milos is a healthy walk from Métro Laurier. You can also take Bus 51 from the same Métro stop and ask the driver to let you off at avenue du Parc; Milos is halfway up the block to the right. *5357 av. du Parc, tel. 514/272–3522. Reservations required. Dress: casual. AE, MC, V.*

Indian

Expensive **Le Taj.** One of the rare Indian restaurants in town in which the decor and the music are appropriate. The cuisine of the north of India is honored here, less spicy and more refined than that of the south. The tandoori ovens seal in the flavors of the grilled meat and fish, the *nan* bread comes piping hot to the table, and behind a glass partition the cook retrieves the skewers with his bare hands from the hot coals just like an experienced fakir. There are a few vegetarian specialties on the menu; for example, the *taj-thali*, consisting of lentils, chili *pakoras*, *basmati* rice, and *saag panir*—spicy white cheese with spinach. The tandoori quail and the nan stuffed with meat go well together, as does a whole series of dry curries, from lamb to chicken and beef with aromatic rice. The desserts, coconut ice cream, or mangoes (canned) are sometimes decorated with pure silver leaves if the patron so desires. Other cultures, other mores! The tea scented with cloves is delicious; it cleans the palate, warms in winter, and cools in summer. *2077 rue Stanley, tel. 514/845–9015. Weekend reservations advised. Dress: neat but casual. AE, MC, V. Closed Sat. lunch.*

Italian

Expensive ★ **Prego.** European chic lives at Prego. So does excellent nouvelle Italian cuisine. The clientele looks old and wealthy and is outfitted in the latest fashions. They sit on *faux* zebra-skin chairs or black banquettes and watch the flames in the high-tech black kitchen (if they aren't watching themselves in the mirror). Every dish is relatively light and absolutely fresh. The *insalata caprese* is a simple, satisfying salad of tomatoes, basil, olive oil, and bocconcini cheese. Between courses you are given a small serving of sorbet; if you're lucky, it will be the tarragon sorbet with poppy seeds sprinkled in it. The linguine with tuna, tomatoes, and capers is warm, light, and redolent of summer, even on a winter night. An excellent main dish is *medaglione di vitello ai pistacchi* (veal with cream; pistachios; fresh fruits; and Frangelico, a hazelnut liqueur). Keep some room for dessert, because Prego serves one that should be in a hall of fame somewhere: *tiramisu* (a light cake with a filling of sweet, creamy mascarpone cheese and a chocolate icing dusted with cocoa). On the serving plate it sits next to a pool of sweet vanilla and chocolate *crème* in a sunburst design crowned with a single candied violet. It's a feast for the eyes and the mouth. The service and wine list are first-rate. *5142 boul. St-Laurent, 5 blocks from Métro Laurier, tel. 514/271–3234. Reservations required. Dress: neat but casual. AE, CB, DC, MC, V. Closed lunch.*

Moderate–Expensive **Bocca d'Oro.** This Italian restaurant next to Métro Guy has a huge menu offering a wide variety of appetizers, pastas, and veal and vegetarian dishes. One pasta specialty is *tritico di pasta*, which is one helping each of spinach ravioli with salmon and caviar, shells marinara, and spaghetti primavera. A good choice from the dozen or so veal dishes is scaloppine *zingara* (with tomatoes, mushrooms, pickles, and olives). With the dessert and coffee, the waiters bring out a big bowl of walnuts for you to crack at your table (nutcrackers provided). The two floors of dining rooms are decorated with brass rails, wood paneling, and paintings, and Italian pop songs play in the background. The staff is extremely friendly and professional; if you're in a hurry, they'll serve your meal in record time. *1448 rue St-Mathieu, downtown, tel. 514/933–8414. Reservations advised. Dress: neat but casual. AE, CB, DC, MC, V. Closed Sun.*

Moderate **Pizzaiole.** The wood-fired oven pizzas have had no respite since they started to appear in Montréal in the beginning of the 1980s. Pizzaiole, the pioneer in the field, is still by far the best. The two branches have somewhat adopted the same fresh decor emphasizing the brick oven, but the clientele and the ambience of the rue Crescent place are a bit younger. In both places, there are about 20 possible combinations, without counting the toppings and extras that personalize a pizza in no time at all. Whether you choose a simple tomato-cheese; a "Monalisa" with onions, ham, tomato, cheese, and eggs on crackling "half-dough" (actually half the weight of the regular pizza dough); one with smoked salmon, béchamel sauce, and capers; or a ratatouille on a whole-wheat crust, you'll find that all the pizzas are made to order and brought immediately to the table. The calzone, a turnover filled with a variety of meats and cheeses, is worth the trip. Try the thirst-quenching Massawipi beer from a local brewery, perfect with a pizza. As for the desserts, the chocolate terrine is delicious and easily shared by two people, but it is even better when eaten by one. *Two locations: 1446-A rue Crescent, tel. 514/845–4158; 5100 rue Hutchison, tel. 514/274–9349. AE, MC, V.*

Japanese

Expensive–Very Expensive

Katsura. This cool, elegant Japanese restaurant introduced sushi (Japanese raw fish) to Montréal and is the haunt of businesspeople who equate raw food with power. If you're with a group or just want privacy, you can reserve a tatami room closed off from the rest of the restaurant by rice-paper screens. Tatami are the straw mats you sit on (sans shoes) for a traditional Japanese dining experience. The sushi chefs create an assortment of raw seafood delicacies, as well as their own delicious invention, the Canada roll (smoked salmon and salmon caviar) at the sushi bar at the rear. Sushi connoisseurs may find some offerings less than top quality. The service is excellent, but if you sample all the sushi, the tab can be exorbitant. *2170 rue de la Montagne, downtown between Peel and Guy métros, tel. 514/849–1172. Reservations required, but you might get a seat at the sushi bar without them. Dress: neat but casual. AE, CB, DC, MC, V. Closed weekend lunch.*

Polish

Moderate ★

Stash's. This Montréal institution is also the preferred refuge for pilgrims and tourists visiting the Notre-Dame Basilica. A way to renew one's ties with the native Poland of the Pope, this unpretentious little restaurant offers a cuisine totally adapted to the hard winters of Québec. Pork, potatoes, and cabbage are the basis of this Eastern European cuisine, just as they were in Québec not so long ago. The soup of the day is generously served in a big bowl and accompanied with slices of buttered rye bread. More like a stew, it is a meal in itself. The specials of the day—stuffed cabbage, stuffed peppers, or goulash—share the bill with the à la carte dishes, either veal scallops topped with an egg or the famous pierogis stuffed with cheese or meat. The desserts also deserve an honorable mention and are a reminder of family cooking. *461 rue St-Sulpice, tel. 514/861–2915. Dress: casual. AE, MC, V.*

Québécois

Moderate–Expensive ★

Les Filles du Roy. This restaurant serves fine Québécois cuisine, a blend of 17th-century French recipes, North American produce and game, and some culinary tips picked up from Native Americans . . . with a lot of maple syrup poured over everything. The Trottier family opened Les Filles du Roy (the name refers to the women brought over to New France by Louis XIV to marry settlers) in an 18th-century stone mansion in 1964. If you want to go the native route—and you can eat excellent classic French cuisine as well—start with the "caribou," which is an eye-popping drink made of grain alcohol, sweet local wine, a dash of scotch, and Drambuie. The original recipe was concocted by hunters; it called for real caribou blood and homemade alcohol and provided warmth as well as vitamins. A traditional Québécois meal starts with an appetizer like Canadian-style pork and beans or pea soup. If you like sweet meat dishes, try the ham with maple syrup. More refined dishes using local game and produce include wild lake duck with blueberries and *cipaille du Lac St-Jean,* which is a combination of six different meats, some wild, in a pie crust with vegetables. A large variety of maple syrup desserts are available: *trempette au sirop d'érable* (pieces of bread that have been dipped in boiling maple syrup in a bowl of heavy cream), sugar pie, and *oeuf cuit dans le sirop d'érable* (an egg poached in maple syrup). The popular Sunday brunch, served from 11 to 3, attracts groups of Japanese tourists wolfing down the ham and maple-syrup dishes. The interior of Les Filles du Roy is all stone and wood, and the furniture looks authentic; the staff wears the usual colonial-era dress. The service is knowledgeable and friendly. *415 rue Bonsecours, 3 blocks from Métro Champs de Mars in Vieux-Montréal, tel. 514/849–3535. Reservations required. Dress: neat but casual. AE, DC, MC, V.*

Seafood

Expensive ★

Chez Delmo. This stretch of rue Notre-Dame is halfway between the courts and the stock exchange, and at lunchtime Chez Delmo is filled with professionals gobbling oysters and fish. The first room as you enter is lined with two long, dark, wood bars, which are preferred by those wishing a fast lunch. Above both are murals depicting a medieval feast. The back room is a more sedate and cheerful dining room. In either room the dining is excellent and the seafood fresh. A good first course, or perhaps a light lunch, is the seafood salad, a delicious mix of shrimp, lobster, crab, and artichoke hearts on a bed of Boston lettuce, sprinkled with a scalliony vinaigrette. The poached salmon with hollandaise is a nice slab of perfectly cooked fish with potatoes and broccoli. The lobsters and oysters are priced according to market rates. Chez Delmo was founded at the same address in 1910. The service is efficient and low-key. *211–215 rue Notre-Dame O, Vieux-Montréal, tel. 514/849–4061. Dinner reservations advised. Dress: neat but casual. AE, CB, DC, MC, V. Closed Mon. dinner, Sat. lunch, Sun.*

Steaks

Expensive ★

Moishe's. A paradise for carnivores, Moishe's is the last place to receive dietetic advice. The meat portions are as large as a pound, which will no doubt send your cholesterol level way up. Rib steak, T-bone, and filet mignon are all grilled on wood and presented with dill-scented pickles, cole slaw, and french fries or baked potato. The meat, imported from West Canada, is juicy and tender, marbled and delectable, and aged 21 days in the restaurant's cold chambers. Moishe's grouchy service, its white aluminum-siding exterior and dark interior (reminiscent of an all-male private club), and its tasteless desserts don't seem to frighten away the real meat eaters. For those with a smaller appetite, the portions can be shared, but it will cost you an additional $4 and the waiter's reproachful look. *3961 boul. St-Laurent, tel. 514/845–1696. Reservations required for parties of 3 or more. Dress: casual. AE, MC, V.*

Vietnamese

Moderate ★

Xuan. Near the pedestrian zone of rue Prince Arthur, this little restaurant strives to perpetuate real Vietnamese cuisine beyond the brochettes formula so popular with competitors. The owners lived in France for many years before settling in the province of Québec. They have included on the menu typical dishes, such as the Vietnamese crepe with vegetables and mint, the five-flavor stuffed quail, honey and citronella pork, and numerous soups at noontime that are hearty enough to be meals. The cold spring rolls in Hoisin sauce are particularly filling. For dessert, there is a delicious *assiette maison* (house plate) consisting of fruit puffs and rice-alcohol-scented ice cream, decorated with little Chinese umbrellas and flambéed in the French style. *26 rue Prince Arthur O, tel. 514/849–4923. AE, MC, V. Closed Mon.*

Tearooms

Inexpensive **La Chartreuse.** This tiny tearoom, in the Viennese tradition, has big surprises in store. On the counter are exhibited heavy and filling cakes, sparsely decorated but mouth-watering. *Nusstorte* with hazelnut butter cream, *Dobostorte* with chocolate layers and caramel icing, Sacher torte garnished with apricot jam, and Rigo Jancsi with chocolate ganache, fresh nuts and coffee syrup make your time at La Chartreuse well spent. One moment on the lips, forever on the hips! The coffee (there is no espresso or cappuccino for lack of the appropriate equipment) is served with liqueurs, chocolate, cinnamon, or cream (whipped or not). Mozart is played discreetly in the background. *3439 rue St-Denis, tel. 514/842–0793. Dress: casual. No credit cards. Open 4 PM–midnight. Closed Mon.*

Bagels

Bagel Factory (74 av. Fairmount O, tel. 514/272–0667).
The Bagel Place (1616 rue Ste-Catherine O, tel. 514/931–2827).
Bagel Shop (263 rue St-Viateur O, tel. 514/276–8044; 158 rue St-Viateur O, tel. 514/270–2972).

Chocolate

La Brioche Lyonnaise (1593 rue St-Denis, tel. 514/842–7017). This little café also serves pastries and coffee at chic tables in a dining alcove off the counter area and now has added a backyard terrace for summer dining. It is an enjoyable way to break a tour of St-Denis around teatime.
Léonidas (605 boul. de Maisonneuve O, tel. 514/849–2620; 5111 av. du Parc, tel. 514/272–3447).
Chocolat Heyez (Passage CN, Place Bonaventure, 1000 rue de la Gauchetière O, tel. 514/392–1480).
Lenôtre (1050 av. Laurier O, tel. 514/270–2702).

Restaurants near Montréal

Very Expensive **Le Mitoyen.** North of the city, in the small village of Ste-Dorothée (today part of the city of Laval), this great French restaurant leans resolutely in favor of nouvelle cuisine. People come from everywhere (mostly from Montréal) to taste the inventions of the self-taught chef. Meticulously decorated, this old house with the red roof is a haven for gourmands. Try the galette of smoked salmon, sweetbreads ragout with artichoke hearts, Guinea hen with sherry wine vinegar, or quail with juniper berries in puff pastry. All are heavenly. For dessert, the maple nougat glacé or the poached pears in red wine and pepper end the meal elegantly. *Place publique Ste-Dorothée,*

Laval (Rte. 15 N), tel. 514/689–2977. Reservations required. Dress: neat but casual. Closed Mon., and lunch daily (except for parties).

Expensive ★ **La Sucrerie de la Montagne.** On the road to Rigaud in the direction of Ottawa, maple syrup flows from carafes year-round and seasons the plates of pork and beans, *tourtière*, maple ham, omelet soufflés, and crepes cooked over wood fires at this old-fashioned sugar hut. Even the bread is baked on the premises in the old brick ovens fired with maple wood. Everything in this young maple grove is intended to re-create the atmosphere of the sugar season: from the sap flowing in the snow (in season) to the workhorses to men collecting the sap bucket by bucket. Pierre Faucher, the owner of this immense sugar cabin, who looks more like a lumberjack than a restaurateur, greets the Sunday passersby as well as the buses overflowing with Japanese tourists in the middle of July. The food is good, but do not buy the souvenir syrup here; you will find syrup as good in any grocery in Montréal for a lot less money. Complete meal: $25 for adults (tax and sleigh ride included). *300 rang St-Georges, Rigaud (Rte. 40, exit 17), tel. 514/451–5204. Reservations a must. Dress: informal. No credit cards.*

Lodging

On the island of Montréal alone there are 29,000 rooms available in every type of accommodation, from world-class luxury hotels to youth hostels, from student dormitories to budget executive motels. Keep in mind that during peak season (May–Aug.), it may be difficult to find a bed without reserving, and most, but not all, hotels raise their prices. Prices often drop from mid-November to early April. Throughout the year a number of the better hotels have two-night, three-day, double-occupancy packages that offer substantial discounts.

If you arrive in Montréal without a hotel reservation, the tourism information booths at either airport can provide you with a list of hotels and room availability. You must, however, make the reservation yourself. There are no information booths at the Voyageur bus terminal, but the Gare Centrale is directly behind Le Reine Elizabeth hotel.

The following list is composed of recommended lodgings in Montréal for various budgets. The rates quoted are for a standard double room in May 1990; off-season rates are almost always lower.

Highly recommended hotels in each price category are indicated by a star ★.

Category	Cost*
Very Expensive	over $150
Expensive	$120–$150
Moderate	$85–$120
Inexpensive	under $85

**All prices are for a standard double room, excluding an optional service charge.*

Downtown

Very Expensive ★

Bonaventure Hilton International. This 394-room Hilton—situated atop a Métro station, the Place Bonaventure exhibition center, and a mall crowded with shops and restaurants—is, first and foremost, a resort hotel, and it's 17 floors above the street. When you exit the elevator, you find yourself in a spacious reception area flanked by an outdoor swimming pool (heated year-round) and 2½ acres of gardens, complete with ducks. Also on this floor is a complex of three restaurants and a nightclub that features well-known international entertainers. Le Castillon is the flagship restaurant, known for its three-course, 55-minute businessman's lunch. On Sunday, Imperial Evening, the fare is Austro-Hungarian. All rooms have fully stocked mini-bars and black-and-white TVs in the bathrooms. The Bonaventure has excellent access to the Métro station of the same name beneath it and to all the shops at Place Ville-Marie through the Underground City. *1 Place Bonaventure, H5A 1E4, tel. 514/878–2332 or 800/445–8667. 394 rooms. Facilities: 3 restaurants, nightclub, health club with sauna, outdoor pool, rooftop garden, gift shop (hotel is located in a building with a shopping mall), and 24-hr room service. AE, CB, DC, MC, V.*

Le Centre Sheraton. In a huge 37-story complex well placed between the downtown business district and the restaurant streets of Crescent and Bishop, this Sheraton offers a wide variety of services to both the business and tourist crowds. It's also a favorite with international entertainment celebrities. There are three restaurants, five lounges, a nightclub, an indoor pool, a health club, and indoor parking for 600 cars. The elite, five-story Towers section is geared toward business travelers. The Sheraton caters to conventions, so expect to encounter such groups when you stay here. Though the decor is beige and unremarkable (once inside you could be in any large, modern hotel in any North American Métropolis), the location's the thing. *1201 boul. René-Lévesque O, H3B 2L7, tel. 514/878–2000 or 800/325–3535. 878 rooms. Facilities: 3 restaurants, 5 lounges, nightclub, health club with whirlpool and sauna, indoor pool, unisex beauty parlor, and gift shop. AE, CB, DC, MC, V.*

Le Château Champlain. In the heart of downtown Montréal, at the southern end of Place du Canada, Le Château Champlain is a 36-floor skyscraper with distinctive half-moon–shape windows. The decor of this Canadian Pacific hotel is formal, and there are only 20 rooms per floor. There are two restaurants and a coffee shop in the Place du Canada corridor in addition to the Caf' Conc' supper club, where can-can girls and featured acts entertain in a red-draped theater that resembles a Toulouse-Lautrec poster (imitations of the French café artist's works add to the decor). The rooftop Escapade offers hot and cold buffet fare for $29.50, $31 Friday and Saturday, along with heady panoramas of the city. You can work off the excesses of appetite at Le Spa, a health club with an exercise room, saunas, and a large indoor pool; a number of floors are reserved for nonsmokers. Underground passage ways connect the Champlain with the Bonaventure Métro station, the Bonaventure Hilton International, and Place Ville-Marie. *1 Place du Canada, H3B 4C9, tel. 514/878–9000 or 800/828–7447. 614 rooms. Facilities: 3 restaurants, lounge with entertainment, health club with*

Auberge de Jeunesse Internationale de Montréal, **13**
Bonaventure Hilton International, **20**
Château Versailles, **2**
Delta Montréal, **16**
Holiday Inn Crowne Plaza, **17**
Hôtel de la Montagne, **4**
La Citadelle, **18**
Le Baccarat, **15**
Le Centre Sheraton, **8**
Le Château Champlain, **9**
Le Grand Hôtel, **21**
Le Meridien, **22**
Le Nouvel Hôtel, **3**
Le Quatre Saisons (Four Seasons), **11**
Le Reine Elizabeth (Queen Elizabeth), **19**
Le Royal Roussillon, **23**
Le Shangrila Best Western, **10**
Lord Berri, **24**
McGill Student Apartments, **12**
Ramada Renaissance du Parc, **14**
Ritz-Carlton, **5**
Université de Montréal Residence, **1**
YMCA, **7**
YWCA, **6**

Montréal Lodging

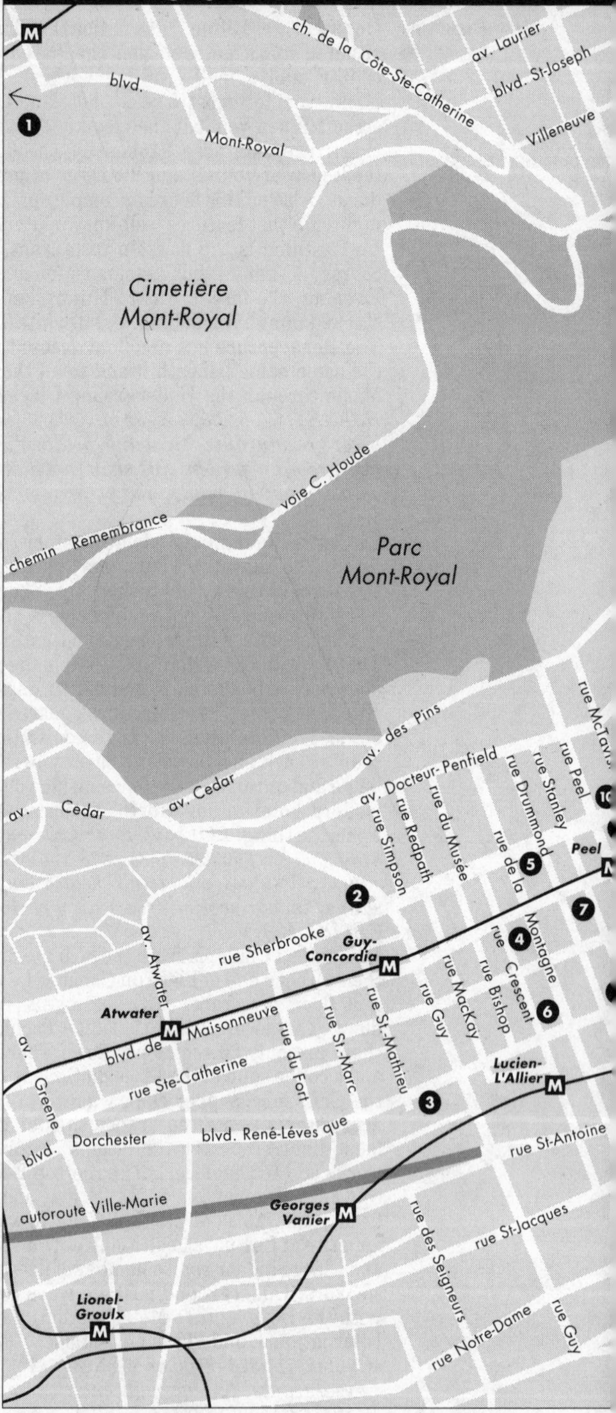

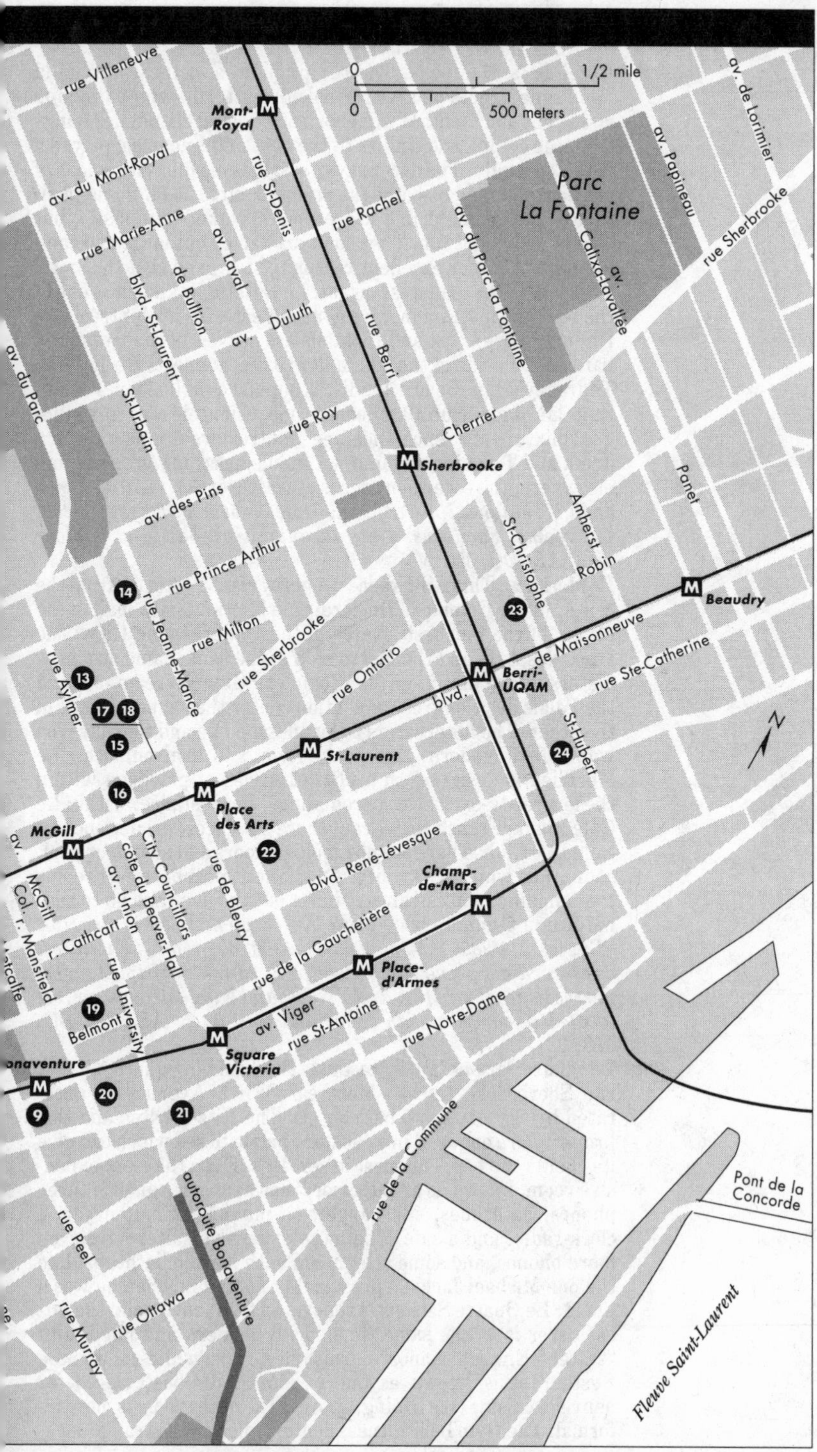
0
1/2 mile
0
500 meters
Mont-Royal
rue Villeneuve
av. du Mont-Royal
rue St-Denis
rue Marie-Anne
av. Laval
de Bullion
blvd. St-Laurent
av. Duluth
rue Rachel
av. du Parc La Fontaine
Parc La Fontaine
av. Calixa-Lavallée
av. Papineau
av. de Lorimier
rue Sherbrooke
rue Berri
av. du Parc
St-Urbain
rue Roy
Cherrier
Sherbrooke
av. des Pins
rue Prince Arthur
St-Christophe
Amherst
Panet
Robin
Beaudry
rue Jeanne-Mance
rue Milton
rue Sherbrooke
rue Ontario
de Maisonneuve
blvd.
Berri-UQAM
rue Ste-Catherine
rue Aylmer
St-Hubert
St-Laurent
Place des Arts
McGill
av. McGill Col.
City Councillors
côte du Beaver-Hall
av. Union
rue de Bleury
blvd. René-Lévesque
Champ-de-Mars
r. Cathcart
r. Mansfield
rue University
rue de la Gauchetière
Place-d'Armes
Belmont
av. Viger
rue St-Antoine
rue Notre-Dame
Square Victoria
onaventure
rue de la Commune
Pont de la Concorde
rue Peel
autoroute Bonaventure
rue Ottawa
rue Murray
Fleuve Saint-Laurent
9
13
14
15
16
17
18
19
20
21
22
23
24

sauna and whirlpool, large indoor pool, movie theater, and gift shops. AE, CB, DC, MC, V.

★ **Hôtel de la Montagne.** The reception area of the Hôtel de la Montagne greets you with a naked, butterfly-winged nymph rising out of a fountain. An enormous crystal chandelier hangs from the ceiling and tinkles to the beat of disco music played a little too loudly. The decor says Versailles rebuilt with a dash of art nouveau by a discothèque architect circa 1975. Some puritanical tastes might find it overdone ("Naked nymphs!"), but others will find it fun. The rooms are tamer but large and comfortable. Another excellent reason to stay in or visit this hotel is the food. The main restaurant, Le Lutetia, is known as one of the best and most innovative gourmet eateries in Montréal (*see* Dining, above). Tea and cocktails are served in the two lobby bars on each side of the hall, and a tunnel connects the hotel to Thursday's/Les Beaux Jeudis, a popular singles bar, restaurant, and dance club all rolled into one. Clientele is a truly bilingual mixture of French-speaking Montréalers stopping by for a drink and Torontonians in town on business. If you're staying elsewhere, the reception area is at least worth a visit. *1430 rue de la Montagne, H3G 1Z5, tel. 514/288–5656 or 800/361–6262. 132 rooms. Facilities: 2 restaurants, disco-bar, and outdoor pool. AE, DC, MC, V.*

Le Meridien. This Air France property rises 12 stories from the center of the Complexe Desjardins, a boutique-rich mall in the center of the plushest stretch of the Underground City. The Place des Arts and the Métro stop of the same name are mere meters in one direction, the Complexe Guy-Favreau mall and the Palais des Congrès convention center the same distance in the other. The hotel caters to businesspeople and tourists who want ultra-modern European style and convenience. Le Meridien is designed on a plan of circles of privilege within these already-exclusive surroundings. For instance, within Le Café Fleuri French restaurant there's a chicer, pricier enclave called Le Club. There are no-smoking floors and an indoor pool, sauna, and whirlpool facility. And if the atmosphere ever seems too confining, you can always burst out the door and go to Chinatown, a 5-minute walk away. *4 Complexe Desjardins, H5B 1E5, tel. 514/285–1450 or 800/543–4300. 601 rooms. Facilities: 3 restaurants, piano bar, indoor pool, sauna, whirlpool, guest passes to nearby YMCA and YWCA, and baby-sitting services; located in complex with shops and boutiques. AE, CB, DC, MC, V.*

★ **Le Quatre Saisons (Four Seasons).** The "Golden Square Mile" of rue Sherbrooke Ouest—Montréal's Fifth Avenue—is decorated by the city's two best hotels. The Ritz-Carlton and this property are engaged in a constant battle to see which can give its clients the best and most in services. Even the least expensive room, known as a "Superior," has amenities galore: three phones, bathrobes, silk hangers, a minibar, a hair dryer, a clock-radio, and a safe. The more expensive suites have even more phones, and some are graced with marble bathtubs, like the one Michael Jackson presumably floated in when he was a guest. Le Quatre Saisons is renovated frequently, and the latest decor is at the same time slickly modern and filled with "stately English manor" furnishings. The white-column Le Restaurant is known as one of Montréal's best places for nouvelle cuisine (*see* Dining, above). The other room is more informal. The GymTech Fitness center, filled with strange-looking machines, is available for guests' complimentary use, and there's also a heated, year-round outdoor pool. Le Quatre Saisons is one block from Métro Peel in the heart of Montréal's fanciest shopping district. *1050 rue Sherbrooke O, H3A 2R6, tel. 514/284–1110 or 800/332–3442. 302 rooms. Facilities: 1 restaurant, lounge, health club with whirlpool and sauna, outdoor pool, and 24-hr room service. AE, CB, DC, MC, V.*

Ramada Renaissance du Parc. The Ramada chain bought the old Hôtel du Parc in July 1987 and has made it the most luxurious of its four Montréal properties. Half a block away from the acres of greenery in Parc Mont-Royal, this Ramada's locale is prime. The hotel itself aims its services mainly at a corporate clientele. The rooms are large, and the decor is modern and well maintained. From the lobby you can descend to a shopping mall with many stores and movie theaters. The nightlife of rue Prince Arthur is six blocks away. *3625 av. du Parc, H2X 3P8, tel. 514/288–6666 or 800/228–9898. 455 rooms. Facilities: 2 restaurants, café-bar, lounge, nonsmoking floors, gift shop. AE, CB, DC, MC, V.*

★ **Le Reine Elizabeth (Queen Elizabeth).** If the Ritz-Carlton is a stately old cruise ship, then the Queen Elizabeth, also called Le Reine Elizabeth, is a battleship. Massive and gray, this Canadian Pacific hotel sits on top of the Gare Centrale train station in the very heart of the city, beside Mary Queen of the World Catholic Cathedral and across the street from Place Ville-Marie. The lobby is a bit too much like a railway station—hordes march this way and that—to be attractive and personal, but upstairs the rooms are modern, spacious, and spotless, especially in the more expensive Entrée Gold section. All the latest gadgets and other trappings of luxury are present. The Beaver Club (*see* Dining, above), the flagship restaurant, is such an institution that there is a small museum devoted to it on the lobby level. There's a cheaper restaurant, too, as well as four lounges. Conventions are a specialty here. *900 boul. René-Lévesque H3B 4A5, tel. 514/861–3511 or 800/268–9143. 1,045 rooms. Facilities: 4 restaurants, 2 bars/lounges, beauty salon, boutiques, gift shops. AE, CB, DC, MC, V.*

★ **Ritz-Carlton.** This property floats like a stately old luxury liner along rue Sherbrooke. It was opened in 1912 by a consortium of local investors who wanted a hotel in which their rich European friends could stay and indulge their champagne-and-caviar tastes. Since then many earth-shaking events have occurred here, including the marriage of Elizabeth Taylor and Richard Burton. Power breakfasts, lunches, and dinners are the rule at the elegant Café de Paris, and the prime minister and others in the national government are frequently sighted eating here. A less heady atmosphere prevails at the Ritz-Carlton's three other excellent restaurants. Guest rooms are a successful blend of Edwardian style—some suites have working fireplaces—with such modern accessories as electronic safes. Careful and personal attention are hallmarks of the Ritz-Carlton's service. Even if you're not a guest, stop by the Ritz's Hotel Courtyard for afternoon tea and to see the duck pond, a Ritz tradition since 1912. *1228 rue Sherbrooke O, H3A 2R6, tel. 514/842–4212 or 800/223–9868. 240 rooms. Facilities: 4 restaurants, piano bar, gift-shop, beauty salon, barber shop, and 24-hour room service. AE, CB, DC, MC, V.*

Le Shangrila Best Western. If you're a frequent traveler to Montréal, you may want to try something different: an Oriental-style hotel. The hotel's decor from reception to restaurant to rooms is modern with an amalgam of Korean, Chinese, Japanese, and Indian motifs and artwork. In addition to special corporate-class extras, such as a lounge for buffet breakfasts and snacks, there are also pluses for the fitness fanatic, including several new gym rooms. Alcove gyms, fitted out with mirrors, and rowing and other machines, let guests work out in the peace and quiet of their own rooms. There is a large Szechuan-style restaurant, Dynastie de Ming, on the lobby level. The Shangrila has 12 to 15 "health rooms," private rooms with exercise facilities. During the week the clientele is corporate, while on weekends most of the guests are tourists from the United States and Ontario. Le Shangrila is situated across the street from Le Quatre Saisons on rue Sherbrooke, one block from Métro Peel. *3407 rue Peel, H3A 1W7, tel. 514/288–4141 or 800/528–1234. 161 rooms. Facilities: café, restaurant, bar, gift shop, and salon. AE, CB, DC, MC, V.*

Expensive

La Citadelle. There's a small pack of hotels on rue Sherbrooke, all of them convenient to Place des Arts, shopping, and the financial district; the Citadelle, a Clarion Hotel property, is one of them. This relatively small business hotel offers four-star elegance in a low-key atmosphere and service, along with all the features of its better-known brethren: minibars, in-room movies, a small health club with an indoor pool, etc. There's also a passable French restaurant, C'est La Vie. *410 rue Sherbrooke O, WH3A 1B3, tel. 514/844–8851 or 800/263–8967. 180 rooms. Facilities: restaurant; lounge with entertainment; health club with Nautilus, sauna, and steam room; indoor pool; and gift shop. AE, CB, DC, MC, V.*

Delta Montreal. One of Montreal's newest hotels, the French-style Delta is making a bid to break into the ranks of Montréal's world-class hotels. Many of the spacious guest rooms have balconies and excellent views of the city. The Le Bouquet restaurant and the piano lounge are designed like 19th-century Parisian establishments, with dark wood paneling and brass chandeliers. The cuisine is Continental and not above trendy touches like grilling over mesquite. The Delta has the most complete exercise and pool facility in Montréal. There are indoor and outdoor pools, two international squash courts, an exercise room, a sauna, and a whirlpool. The innovative Children's Creative Centre lets your children play (under supervision) while you gallivant around town. *450 rue Sherbrooke O, H3A 2T4 (entrance off av du President-Kennedy), tel. 514/286–1986 or 800/268–1133. 458 rooms. Facilities: 24-hour room service, restaurant; jazz bar (which also serves lunch Mon.–Fri.); indoor and outdoor pools; health club with whirlpool, sauna, squash courts, aerobics classes; children's center; gift shop, pinball and video-game rooms. AE, CB, DC, MC, V.*

★ **Le Grand Hôtel.** Le Grand abuts the stock exchange; Place Bonaventure is half a block one way, the western fringe of Vieux-Montréal one block the other, and the Métro Square Victoria can be reached via an underground passage. In the midst of all this, Le Grand, a Hôtel des Gouveneurs property, rises above a stunning three-story atrium-reception area. It's yet another large, modern hotel attractive to meeting planners. Le Grand offers the usual health club and pool facilities, a more exclusive floor for higher-paying guests, and a shopping arcade on the underground level. Its most outstanding feature: the restaurants. The Tour de Ville on the top floor is the city's only revolving restaurant, and its bar has live jazz nightly. Chez Antoine is an art nouveau–style bistro with grilled meats a specialty. *777 rue University, H3C 3Z7, tel. 514/879–1370 or 800/361–8155. 737 rooms. Facilities: 2 restaurants, bar, health club with spa and steam room, aerobics classes, indoor pool, and gift shop. AE, DC, MC, V.*

Holiday Inn Crowne Plaza. The flagship of the Holiday Inn chain's downtown Montréal hotels, the Crowne Plaza could just as well have been plopped down in Las Vegas or Atlanta. On the other hand, one doesn't stay in Holiday Inns for originality of design. This hotel *does* sparkle: It was recently renovated from top to bottom and has the largest indoor pool of the city's hotels, in addition to a health club, café-restaurant, two bars. It has two suites, a penthouse, and two business floors. Popular for conventions, this hotel is near Métro Place des Arts, rue Sherbrooke shopping, and downtown. *420 rue Sherbrooke O, H3A 1B4, tel. 514/842–6111 or 800/465–4329. 487 rooms. Facilities: 24-hour room service, café-restaurant, 2 bars, indoor pool, health club with sauna and whirlpool, unisex beauty parlor, and gift shop. AE, DC, MC, V.*

Moderate

Le Baccarat. Completely renovated in 1988, this medium-size, medium-price hotel, next to the McGill campus, caters to the business trade. Exercise machines and a spa with sauna have been added, and the lobby was redone. The decor of the restaurant is Italianate, with lots of brass and marble and with bay windows overlooking the street. There's also a terrace for summer dining outdoors. The new chef presents Italian and Continental cuisine. Le Baccarat is handy to downtown business and shopping areas. *475 rue Sherbrooke O, H3A 2L9, tel. 514/842–3961 or 800/361–4973. 200 rooms. Facilities: restaurant and café. AE, CB, DC, MC, V.*

★ **Château Versailles.** This small, charming hotel occupies a row of four converted mansions in an excellent location on rue Sherbrooke Ouest. The owners have decorated it with many antique paintings, tapestries, and furnishings; some rooms have ornate moldings and plaster decorations on the walls and ceilings. Each room also has a full bath, TV, and air-conditioning. The reception area is designed to look like a European pension. Across the street, at 1808 rue Sherbrooke, the Villeneuve family has added a former apartment hotel as an annex to the original town houses. Called La Tour Versailles, it offers 107 larger, more spartan rooms, at the same reasonable price, and a restaurant. The staff is extremely helpful and friendly. The Versailles is unassuming, not too expensive, and classy. *1659 rue Sherbrooke O (near Métro Guy-Concordia), H3H 1E3, tel. 514/933–3611 or 800/361–3664. 177 rooms. Facilities: breakfast and tearoom in the Château, restaurant in the Tour. AE, MC, V.*

Le Nouvel Hôtel. The Nouvel Hôtel is what hotel managers like to call a "new concept"—in its four towers it has studios, suites, and 2½-room apartments. It's not very classy, but it's all new, brightly colored, and functional. Le Nouvel Hôtel is near the restaurant district, five or six blocks from the heart of downtown, and two blocks from the Guy-Concordia Métro station. *1740 boul. René-Lévesque O, H3H 1R3, tel. 514/931–8841 or 800/567–2737. 481 rooms. Facilities: restaurant, bar, gift shop, and outdoor pool. AE, DC, MC, V.*

Inexpensive

Lord Berri. Next to the Université du Québec à Montréal, the Lord Berri is a new, moderately priced hotel convenient to the restaurants and nightlife of rue St-Denis. It offers some of the services of its more expensive competition: minibars, in-room movies, and nonsmoking floors. The De La Muse restaurant serves good bistro food and is popular with a local clientele. The Berri-UQAM Métro stop is a block away. *1199 rue Berri, H2L 4C6, tel. 514/845–9236 or 800/363–0363. 154 rooms. Facilities: restaurant and gift shop. AE, DC, MC, V.*

Le Royal Roussillon. This hotel is adjacent to the Terminus Voyageur bus station (buses park directly beneath one wing of the hotel), and some of the bus station aura seems to rub off on the Roussillon; it's a little dingy. But if you're stumbling after a long bus ride and want somewhere to stay, *now*, the Roussillon's rooms are large and clean, the service is friendly, and the price is right. It's also handy to the Berri-UQAM Métro station. *1610 rue St-Hubert, H2L 3Z3, tel. 514/849–3214. 104 rooms. Facilities: restaurant. AE, DC, MC, V.*

YMCA. This clean Y is downtown, next to Peel Métro station. Book at least two days in advance. Women should book seven days ahead—there are fewer rooms with showers for women. Anyone staying summer weekends must book a week ahead. *1450 rue Stanley, H3A 2W6, tel. 514/849–8393. 331 rooms, 429 beds. MC, V.*

YWCA. Very close to dozens of restaurants, the Y is right downtown, one block from rue Ste-Catherine. *1355 boul. René-Lévesque, H3G 1P3, tel. 514/866–9941. 107 rooms. Facilities: recently renovated hotel and fitness facilities. Accepts women only. Men may use café. Rooms with sink or bath available. (Reserve for best choice.) Oct.–May, stay 7 nights, pay for 6. Café open 7:30 AM–7 PM. Pool, sauna, whirlpool, weight room, fitness classes—no extra charge for hotel guests. MC, V.*

McGill University Area

Inexpensive

Auberge de Jeunesse Internationale de Montréal. The youth hostel near the McGill campus in the student ghetto charges $9.50 for members, $12.50 for nonmembers, per night per person. Reserve early during the summer tourist season. *3541 rue Aylmer, H2X 2B9, tel. 514/843–3317. 112 beds. Facilities: rooms for 4–12 people (same sex); a few rooms available for couples and families. No credit cards.*

McGill Student Apartments. From mid-May to mid-August, when McGill is on summer recess, you can stay in its dorms on the grassy, quiet campus in the heart of the city. Nightly rates: $21 students; $28.50 nonstudents (single rooms only). *3935 rue University, H3A 2B4, tel. 514/398–6367. 1,000 rooms. Facilities: campus swimming pool and health facilities (visitors must pay to use them).*

Université de Montréal Area

Inexpensive

Université de Montréal Residence. The university's student housing accepts visitors from May 9 to August 22. It's on the other side of Mont Royal, a long walk from downtown and Vieux-Montréal, but there's the new Université de Montréal Métro stop right next to the campus. Nightly rates: $17 students; $27 nonstudents. *2350 boul. Édouard-Montpetit, H3C 3J7, tel. 514/343–6531. 1,171 rooms. Facilities: campus sports center with pool and gym (visitors must pay to use it). AE, MC, V.*

Bed-and-Breakfasts

Bed and Breakfast à Montréal. Founded in 1979, this is the oldest B & B agency in Montréal. Most of the more than 50 homes are downtown or in the elegant neighborhoods of Westmount and Outremont. Some of them can be quite ritzy. Others are less expensive, but all provide breakfast and a wealth of information about the city. Visitors who take a Gray Line tour get a 15% discount. *Contact: Marian Kahn, 4912 av. Victoria, Montréal H3W 2N1, tel. 514/738–9410. Single $30–$50, double $45–$100. "Unhosted" apartments also available, minimum 4-night stay, rates $90 and up. AE, MC, V accepted for deposits only; the balance must be paid with cash or traveler's checks.*

Downtown B & B Network. This organization will put you in touch with 75 homes and apartments, mostly around the downtown core and along rue Sherbrooke, that have one or more rooms available for visitors. These homes generally are clean, lovingly kept-up, and filled with antiques. The hosts generously dole out, with breakfast, recommendations about what to see and do during your stay in Montréal. Even during the height of the tourist season, this organization has rooms open. *Contact: Bob Finkelstein, 3458 av. Laval (at rue Sherbrooke), Montréal H2X 3C8, tel. 514/289–9749. Single $25–$40, double $35–$55. AE, MC, V.*

The Arts and Nightlife

When it comes to entertainment, Montréal has a superiority complex. It can boast of serious culture—symphony orchestras, opera, and dance companies. At the pinnacle of the High Art scene stands the Orchestre Symphonique de Montréal, led by Charles Dutoit, and l'Opéra de Montréal. The city is known for its adventurous theatrical companies; unfortunately for the English-speaking visitor, most presentations are in French. Montréal is also the home of a small group of filmmakers and the National Film Board who regularly bring home accolades from international festivals. On the low-life side of the tracks, the city is filled with all types of bars and clubs, including jazz and rock clubs, discos, cabarets, singles bars, and strip clubs. Puritanism is definitely not in fashion here. There are also a number of larger halls where international pop and rock stars regularly perform. Summer is the time for the most action—more events, bigger crowds, later hours—but if you visit during the off-season there's sure to be something going on.

The entertainment section of the *Gazette,* the English-language daily paper, is a good place to find out about upcoming events. The Friday weekend guide has an especially good list of all events at the city's concert halls, theaters, clubs, dance spaces, and movie houses. The "Best Bets" column goes beyond the listings to descriptions of the most interesting shows.

For tickets to major pop and rock concerts, shows, festivals, and hockey and baseball games, go to the individual box offices or call **Ticketron** (tel. 514/288–3651). Ticketron outlets are located in La Baie department store, in all Sears stores, and downtown at Phillips Square. Place des Arts tickets may be purchased at its box office underneath the Salle Wilfrid-Pelletier, next to the Métro station.

The Arts

Music The **Orchestre Symphonique de Montréal** has gained world renown under the baton of Charles Dutoit. When not on tour its regular venue is the Salle Wilfrid-Pelletier at the Place des Arts. The orchestra also gives Christmas and summer concerts in the Notre-Dame Basilica and pops concerts at the Arena Maurice Richard in the Olympic Park. For tickets and program information, call 514/842–2112. Also check the *Gazette* listings for its free summertime concerts in Montréal's city parks. Montréal's other orchestra, the **Orchestre Métropolitain de Montréal** (tel. 514/598–0870), also stars at Place des Arts most weeks during the October–May season. McGill University, at Pollack Concert Hall (tel. 514/398–4547) and Redpath Hall (tel. 514/398–4539 or 514/398–4547), is also the site of many classical concerts. The most notable are given by the **McGill Chamber Orchestra,** which also occasionally plays at Place des Arts with guest artists. **L'Opéra de Montréal,** founded in 1980, stages four productions a year at Place des Arts (tel. 514/521–5577).

The 20,000-seat **Montréal Forum** (tel. 514/932–6131) and the much larger Olympic Stadium are where rock and pop concerts are staged. More intimate concert halls include the **Théâtre St-Denis** (1594 rue St-Denis, tel. 514/849–4211) and the **Spectrum** (318 rue Ste-Catherine O, tel. 514/861–5851).

Theater French-speaking theater lovers will find a wealth of dramatic productions. There are at least 10 major companies in town, some of which have an international reputation. Best bets are productions at **Théâtre Denise Pelletier** (4353 rue Ste-Catherine E, tel. 514/253–8974), **Théâtre du Nouveau Monde** (84 rue Ste-Catherine E, tel. 514/861–0563), and **Théâtre du Rideau Vert** (4664 rue St-Denis, tel. 514/845–0267). Anglophones have less to choose from, unless they want to chance the language barrier. **Centaur Theatre,** the best-known English theatrical company, stages productions in the beaux arts-style former stock exchange building at 453 rue St-François-Xavier in Vieux-Montréal (tel. 514/288–3161). English-language plays can also be seen at the **Saidye Bronfman Centre** at 5170 chemin de la Côte Ste-Catherine. Michel Tremblay is Montréal's premier playwright, and all of his plays are worth seeing, even if in the English translation. Touring companies of Broadway productions can often be seen at the completely renovated and expanded **Théâtre St-Denis** on rue St-Denis (tel. 514/849–4211), as well as at Place des Arts (tel. 514/842–2112)—especially during the summer months.

Dance Traditional and contemporary dance companies thrive in Montréal, though many take to the road or are on hiatus in the summer. Among the best-known are **Ballets Classiques de Montréal** (tel. 514/866–1771); **Les Grands Ballets Canadiens,** the leading Québec company (tel. 514/849–8681); **Les Ballets Eddy Toussaint** (tel. 514/524–3749); **Montréal Danse** (tel. 514/845–2031); **LaLaLa Hum n Steps** (tel. 514/288–8266); **Les Ballets Jazz de Montréal** (tel. 514/875–9640); soloist **Margie Gillis** (tel. 514/845–3115); and **Tangente** (tel. 514/842–3532)—a nucleus for many of the more avant-garde dance troupes. When not on tour, many of these artists can be seen at Place des Arts or at any of the Maisons de la Culture (tel. 514/872–6211) performance spaces around town. Montréal's dancers have a brand-new downtown performance and rehearsal space, the Agora

Dance Theatre, affiliated with the Université de Montréal dance faculty (840 rue Chérrier E, tel. 514/525–1500). Check newspaper listings for details. Every other September (that is, in the odd years, such as 1991), the **Festival International de Nouvelle Danse** brings "new" dance to various venues around town. Tickets for this event always go quickly—such is the caliber of the companies that perform and the fanaticism of Montréal dance fans.

Nightlife

Bars and Clubs Elegant dinner-theater productions have revitalized Montréal's English theater. Prices range from about $12 for the show alone to more than $50 for the show and dinner (not including drinks—which can run up to about $6.50 each—tips, or tax). Enthusiasts find this a great excuse to dress up for a night on the town. Small, cabaret-type shows can be found at a few major hotels. **Le Caf' Conc'**, at the Château Champlain (tel. 514/878–9000), is a 19th-century French period piece, reminiscent of the theaters painted by Toulouse-Lautrec, which serves up a supper with a saucy can-can show and performances by guest artists. **La Diligence** (tel. 514/731–7771) has two dinner theaters and a solid reputation for presenting polished performances of popular productions—usually Broadway hits, as well as light musical comedies and plays in English. **The Csarda Dinner Theater** (3479 boul. St-Laurent) features Hungarian musical productions Saturday and Sunday nights (tel. 514/843–4346). **Le Festin du Gouverneur,** at the old fort on Île Ste-Hélène (tel. 514/879–1141), offers a unique dinner-theater experience. Light operatic airs are beautifully rendered as a merry 17th-century frolic in the military barracks mess hall is served up with copious amounts of food and drinks. Great for group outings. **The Foolhouse Theater Company** (tel. 514/483–5426) stages musical comedies, such as its local hit *Let's Go to the Ritz,* at various venues around town. Call for its latest show times and places.

Aside from full-fledged cabarets and dinner theater, most of the big hotels offer some kind of live entertainment, including music and dancing to live music between shows. The Ritz-Carlton (tel. 514/842–4212) has a ground-floor bar *(très élégant),* with a pianist in evening dress, at which you can nibble on smoked salmon. There is music and slow dancing at **Puzzle's Jazz Bar** in the Ramada Renaissance (tel. 514/288–3733), the Sheraton's **L'Impromptu** (tel. 514/878–2000), and the **Tour de Ville,** atop Le Grand Hôtel (tel. 514/879–1370).

Jazz Montréal has a very active local jazz scene. The best-known club is Vieux-Montréal's **L'Air du Temps** (191 rue St-Paul O, tel. 514/842–2003). This small, smoky club presents 90% local talent and 10% international acts from 5 PM on into the night. There's a cover charge Thursday through Saturday. If you like jazz and you're downtown, duck into **Biddle's** (tel. 514/842–8656), at 2060 rue Aylmer, where bassist Charles Biddle holds forth most evenings when he's not appearing at a local hotel. Bernard Primeau's Trio are weekend regulars and Montréal's own Oliver Jones can occasionally be found tickling the ivories on those rare occasions when he's in town. This upscale club is also a restaurant that serves ribs and chicken, so lick the bones clean and start drumming. There's a cover charge for the big acts. You also might try **Club Jazz 2080** (tel. 514/285–0007), at

2080 rue Clark, where jazz legend Sonny Greenwich can often be heard, or **Le Grand Café** (tel. 514/849–6955), at 1720 rue St-Denis. **Le Bijou** (tel. 514/288–5508), at 300 rue Lemoyne, is another sure bet. This popular jazz club in Vieux-Montréal has launched the career of many local jazz and rhythm-and-blues musicians. Montréal Festival jazz greats like Pat Metheny sometimes turn up for impromptu jam sessions.

Rock Rock clubs seem to spring up, flourish, then fizzle out overnight. **Club Soda** (tel. 514/270–7848), at 5240 avenue du Parc, the granddaddy of them all, sports a neon martini glass complete with neon effervescence outside. Inside it's a small hall with a stage, three bars, and room for about 400 people. International rock acts play here as well as local talent. It's also a venue for the comedy and jazz festivals. Open seven nights from 8 PM to 3 AM; admission ranges from nothing up to $20, depending. **Foufounes Electriques** (tel. 514/845–5484)—which translates as "electric buns"—at 97 rue Ste-Catherine Est in the Latin Quarter is the downscale, more avant-garde competitor of Club Soda. Foufounes is the center for the local band scene and also attracts up-and-coming acts from the United States. There's a "quiet" section for conversation and a "loud" section for music and dancing. Open weekdays 1 PM–3 AM, weekends 7 PM–3 AM; admission varies. Other clubs include **Studebaker's** (1255 rue Crescent, tel. 514/866–1101), the **American Rock Café** (2080 rue Aylmer, tel. 514/288–9272), **Déjà Vu** (1224 rue Bishop, tel. 514/866–0512), **Station 10** (2071 rue Ste-Catherine O, tel. 514/934–0484), **Secrets** (40 av. des Pins O, tel. 514/844–0004), and **Nuits Magiques** (22 rue St-Paul E, tel. 514/861–8143) in Vieux-Montréal.

Discos Montréalers are as into discos as you could imagine. The newest and the glitziest is **Metropolis** (tel. 514/288–5559), at 59 rue Ste-Catherine Est. The crowd is young, primarily French-speaking, and clad in black. This club is reminiscent of New York's Palladium in that the enormous space (a former theater where Sarah Bernhardt performed) has been given a complete workover by local architects, and it has high-powered light and sound systems. It's open Thursday through Sunday, and the admission is $5 unless a band is appearing. The more popular discothèques are **Le Business** (3500 boul. St-Laurent, tel. 514/844–3988), and the **Diamond Club** (1186 rue Crescent, tel. 514/866–4048).

Singles Bars Singles bars center on rues Crescent, Bishop, and de la Montagne. The two mainstays are **Thursday's**—the city's best-known—and the **Sir Winston Churchill Pub** at Nos. 1449 and 1459 rue Crescent. Emulators of the former are **Thirsty's** (1187 rue Bishop) and **Friday's** (636 rue Cathcart). The athletic set unwinds at **La Cage aux Sports,** not too far from the Forum, at 2250 rue Guy. Another bar scene takes place on rue Prince Arthur. The French-flavored **Vol de Nuit,** at No. 14, and **Du Côté de Chez Swann,** at No. 54, are the *classiest* joints there. Nearby, on boulevard St-Laurent, is **Lola's Paradise** (No. 3604)—a trendy, lively all-night hideaway conveying the glitz and glamour of the '30s. Bar service until 3 AM; it also serves dinner daily 5 PM–6 AM. **Le Keg** (25 rue St-Paul E) is known as a place for raucous carousing in Vieux-Montréal. A quieter, more sophisticated (and probably more expensive) evening can be had at one of the bars in the better hotels, the **Grand Prix Bar** in the Ritz-Carlton being the classiest.

5 Québec City

Introduction

by Alice H. Oshins

A New York–based freelance writer, Alice H. Oshins has written extensively on French Canada.

An excursion to French-speaking Canada is incomplete without a visit to Québec City, located in one of the most beautiful natural settings in North America. Don't be fooled by the fact that the area called la Vieille Ville (Old City) is only 1 square mile; it actually has a lot of ground to cover. This well-preserved part of town is a small and dense place, steeped in four centuries of history and French tradition. It is the only fortified city in North America, an attribute that led UNESCO to declare it a World Heritage Treasure site of "outstanding universal value," on par with the Taj Mahal and the Egyptian pyramids.

In 1535, French explorer Jacques Cartier first came upon what the Algonquin Indians called "Kebec," meaning "where the river narrows." New France, however, was not actually founded in the area of what is now Québec City until 1608, when another French explorer, Samuel de Champlain, recognized the military advantages of the location and set up a fort, making Québec City the oldest municipality in the province. The first settlement was established in the area today referred to as Place Royale. Twelve years later, to make the colony less vulnerable to attack from above, Champlain expanded its boundaries to the top of the cliff, to the site of present-day Château Frontenac.

During the early days of New France, the French and British fought for the control of the area. On September 13, 1759, the British army, led by General James Wolfe, scaled the colony's cliff and took the French troops, led by Général Louis-Joseph Montcalm, by surprise. The British defeated the French in a 20-minute battle on the Plains of Abraham, and New France came under English rule.

The British continued to expand upon the fortifications left by the French and built a wall encircling the city and a star-shape citadel, both of which still stand. The city remained under British rule until 1867, when the Act of Confederation united several Canadian provinces (Québec, Ontario, New Brunswick, and Nova Scotia) and designated Québec City the capital of the province of Québec, as it is today.

Despite the period of British rule, Québec City has remained a center of French-Canadian culture, with more than 95% of its 600,000 residents speaking French.

Essential Information

Arriving and Departing by Plane

Airports and Airlines

Québec City has one airport, **Quebec City International Airport,** located in the suburb of Sainte-Foy, approximately 19 kilometers (12 miles) from downtown. Few U.S. airlines fly directly to Québec City. You usually have to stop in Montréal or Toronto and take one of the regional or commuter airlines, such as Air Canada's **Air Alliance** (tel. 418/692–0770) or **Intair** (tel. 418/692–1031).

Between the Airport and Center City The ride from the airport into town should be no longer than 30 minutes. Most hotels do not have an airport shuttle, but they will make a reservation for you with a bus company. If you're not in a rush, a shuttle bus offered by Maple Leaf Tours (*see* below) is convenient and only half the price of a taxi.

By Bus **Maple Leaf Tours** (575 Arago O, tel. 418/687–9226) has a shuttle bus that runs from the airport to hotels and costs $7 one-way. The shuttle makes about seven trips to and from the airport every day except on weekends, when it runs less frequently. Stops include the major hotels in town, and any other hotel upon request. Reservations are necessary.

By Taxi Taxis are always available immediately outside the airport exit, near the baggage claim area. Some local taxi companies are **Taxi Québec** (975 av. 8ieme, tel. 418/522–2001) and **Taxi Coop de Québec** (496 av. 2ieme, tel. 418/525–5191), the largest company in the city. A ride into the city will cost approximately $20.

By Limousine Private limo service is expensive, starting at $50 for the ride from the airport into Québec City. Try **Service de Limousines** (1792 des Epinettes Rouges, Lac St. Charles, tel. 418/849–7473). Some of the local tour companies offer car service to the airport or act as a referral service. **Maple Leaf Tours** (575 Arago O, tel. 418/687–9226) has a private car service for about $45.

By Car If you're driving from the airport, take Route 540 (Autoroute Duplessis), to Route 175 (boulevard Laurier), which becomes Grande Allée and leads right to the Old City. The ride is about 30 minutes and may be only slightly longer (45 minutes or so) during rush hours (7:30 AM–8:30 AM into town and 4 PM–5:30 PM leaving town).

Arriving and Departing by Car, Train, and Bus

By Car Montréal and Québec City are connected by Autoroute 20 on the south shore of the St. Lawrence River and by Autoroute 40 on the north shore. On both highways, the ride between the two cities is about 240 kilometers (150 miles) and takes approximately three hours. I–87 in New York, I–89 in Vermont, and I–91 in New Hampshire connect with Autoroute 20. Highway 401 from Toronto also connects with Autoroute 20.

Driving northeast from Montréal on Autoroute 20, follow signs for Pont Pierre-Laporte (Pierre-Laporte Bridge) as you approach Québec City. After you've crossed the bridge, turn right onto boulevard Laurier (Route 175), which becomes the Grande Allée, leading into Québec City.

It is necessary to have a car only if you are planning to visit outlying areas. The narrow streets of the Old City leave few two-hour metered parking spaces available. However, there are several parking garages at central locations in town, with rates running approximately $6 to $9 a day. Main garages are located at City Hall, Place d'Youville, Complex G, Place Québec, Château Frontenac, Québec Seminary, rue St-Paul, and the Old Port.

Rental Cars Rental-car companies that serve Québec City include **Avis** (airport, tel. 418/872–2861; 3 Place Québec, tel. 418/523–0041), **Budget** (29 côte du Palais, tel. 418/692–3660), and **Hertz** (air-

Metropolitan Québec City Exploring *(Box Refers to Detail Map)*

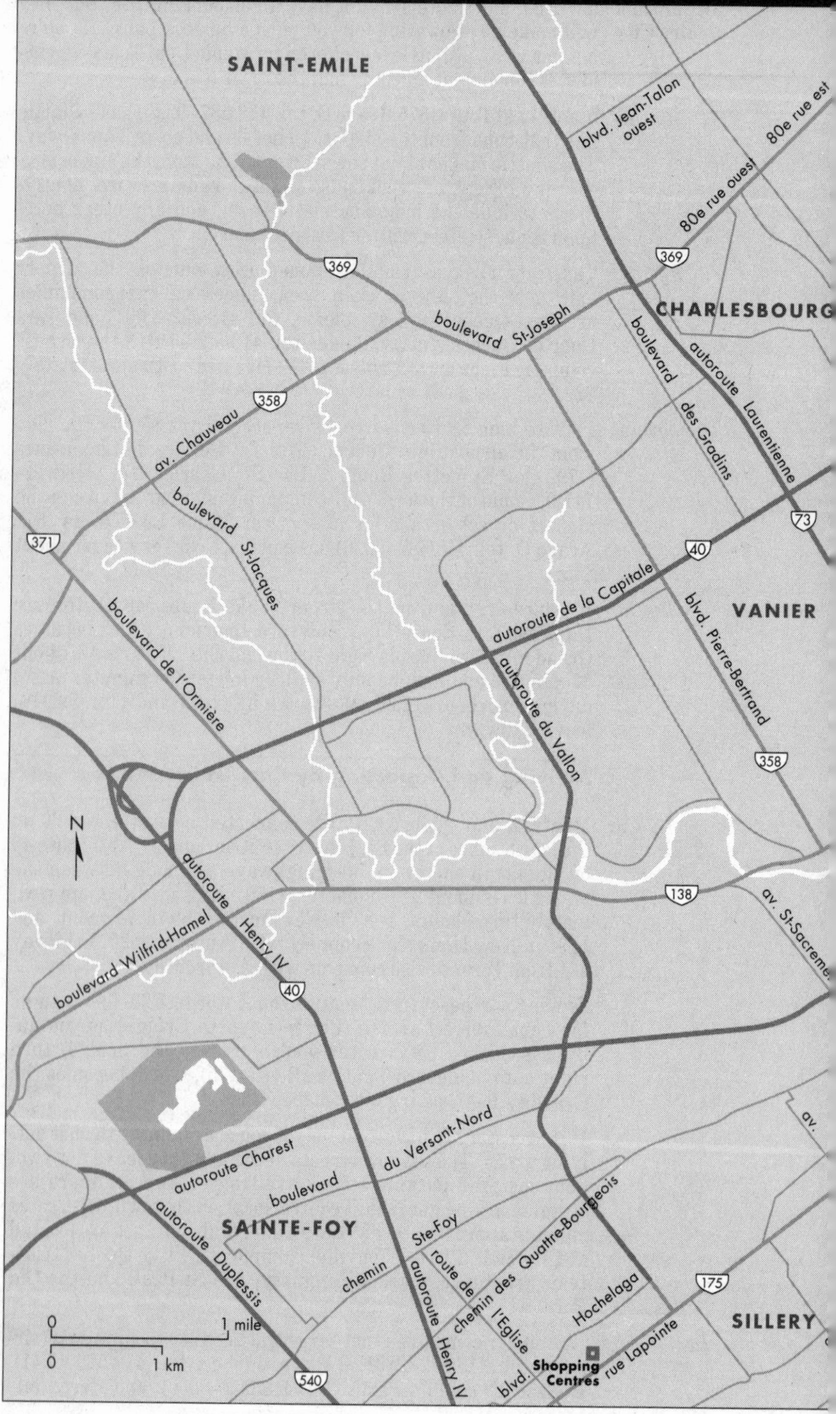
SAINT-EMILE
blvd. Jean-Talon ouest
80e rue est
80e rue ouest
369
369
CHARLESBOURG
boulevard St-Joseph
boulevard des Gradins
autoroute Laurentienne
358
av. Chauveau
boulevard St-Jacques
73
371
40
autoroute de la Capitale
VANIER
boulevard de l'Ormière
blvd. Pierre-Bertrand
autoroute du Vallon
358
N
autoroute Henry IV
138
av. St-Sacrement
boulevard Wilfrid-Hamel
40
av.
autoroute Charest
boulevard du Versant-Nord
SAINTE-FOY
autoroute Duplessis
chemin Ste-Foy
autoroute Henry IV
route de l'Eglise
chemin des Quatre-Bourgeois
Hochelaga
175
SILLERY
0
1 mile
0
1 km
540
blvd.
Shopping Centres
rue Lapointe

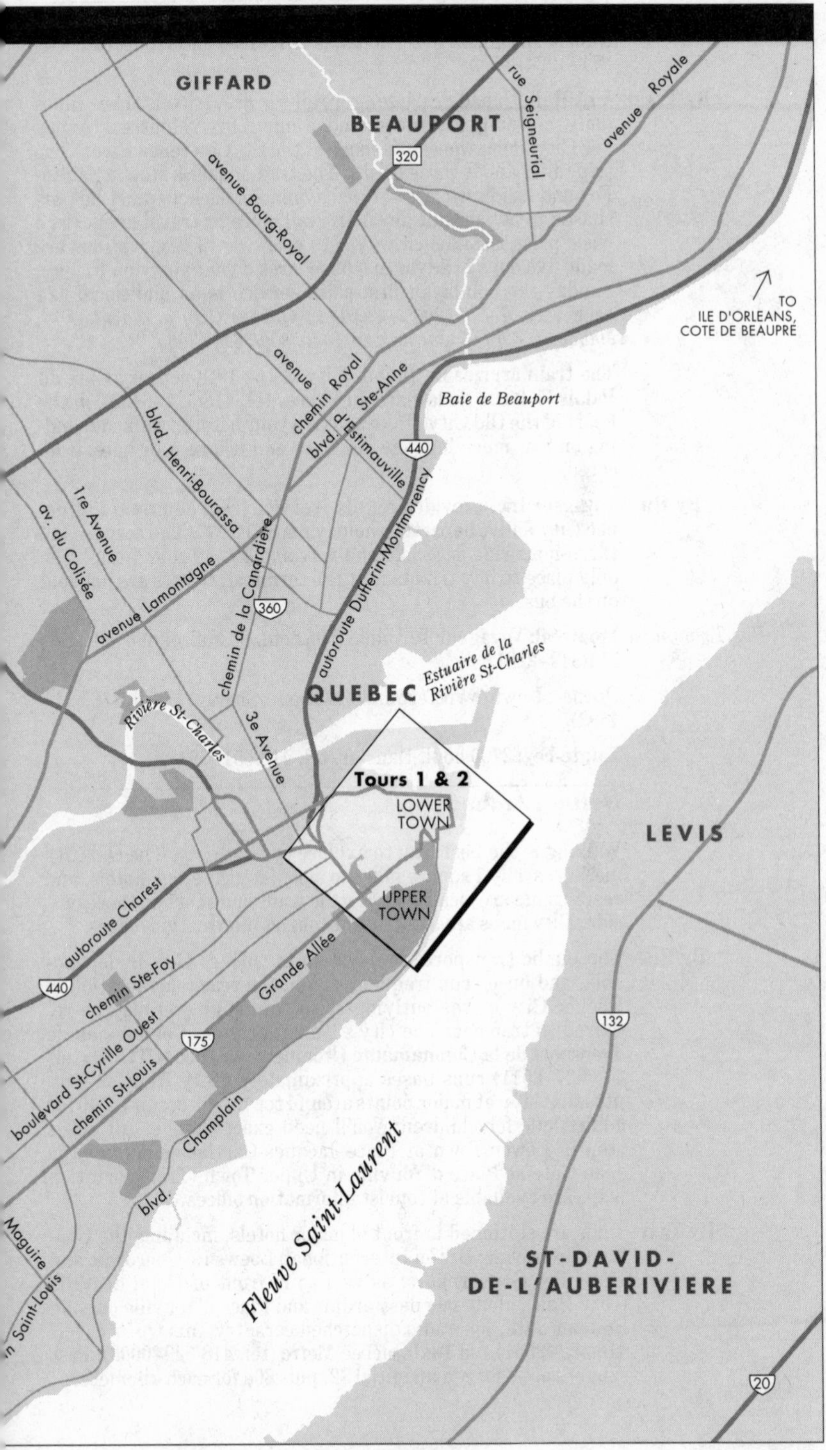
GIFFARD
BEAUPORT
320
rue Seigneurial
avenue Royale
avenue Bourg-Royal
TO ILE D'ORLEANS, COTE DE BEAUPRE
avenue
chemin Royal
blvd. Ste-Anne
Baie de Beauport
blvd. d'Estimauville
440
autoroute Dufferin-Montmorency
blvd. Henri-Bourassa
1re Avenue
av. du Colisée
avenue Lamontagne
chemin de la Canardière
360
Estuaire de la Rivière St-Charles
QUEBEC
Rivière St-Charles
3e Avenue
Tours 1 & 2
LOWER TOWN
UPPER TOWN
LEVIS
autoroute Charest
440
chemin Ste-Foy
Grande Allée
boulevard St-Cyrille Ouest
175
chemin St-Louis
Champlain
blvd.
Fleuve Saint-Laurent
132
Maguire
Saint-Louis
ST-DAVID-DE-L'AUBERIVIERE
20

port, tel. 418/871–1571; 44 côte du Palais, tel. 418/694–1224). **Tilden,** an affiliate of National, is located at the airport (tel. 418/871–1224).

By Train **VIA Rail,** Canada's passenger rail service, travels three times daily (morning, afternoon, and evening) from Montréal to Québec City along the south shore of the St. Lawrence River. The trip takes about three hours. The train makes a stop in Sainte-Foy and has first-class service available. Tickets must be purchased in advance at any VIA Rail office or travel agent. The basic price is $32 each way, $19 each way if reservations are made five days in advance (these fares do not apply on Friday, Sunday, or holidays); first-class service is an additional $24 each way. *Tel. 418/692–3940; in Québec City or Sainte-Foy, 800/361–5390; in Québec province, 800/361–5390.*

The train arrives in Québec City at the 19th-century **Gare du Palais** (450 rue de la Gare du Palais, tel. 418/524–6452), in the heart of the Old City. Take a taxi to your hotel or walk, depending on how much luggage you have and where your hotel is located.

By Bus **Voyageur Inc.** provides regular service from Montréal to Québec City daily, departing hourly 6 AM–11 PM. The cost for the three-hour ride is $26.20 one-way and $52.40 round-trip. The only place to buy tickets is at the terminal; tickets are not sold on the bus.

Bus Terminals **Montréal:** Voyageur Terminal (505 boul. de Maisonneuve E, tel. 514/842–2281).

Québec: Downtown Terminal (225 boul. Charest E, tel. 418/524–4692).

Sainte-Foy: 2700 boul. Laurier, tel. 418/651–7015.

Getting Around

Walking is the best way to explore Québec City. The Old City measures only 1 square mile, so most historic sites, hotels, and restaurants are located within the walls or a short distance outside. City maps are available at tourist information offices.

By Bus The public transportation system in Québec City is dependable, and buses run frequently: You can reach any location in Québec City or the outlying areas, although you may be required to transfer. The city's transit system, **Commission de Transport de la Communauté Urbaine de Québec (CTCUQ,** tel. 418/627–2511) runs buses approximately every 15 or 20 minutes that stop at major points around town. The cost is $1.40 for adults, 80¢ for children: You'll need exact change. All buses stop in Lower Town at Place Jacques-Cartier or outside St-Jean Gate at Place d'Youville in Upper Town. Transportation maps are available at tourist information offices.

By Taxi Taxis are stationed in front of major hotels, including the Château Frontenac; Hilton International; Loews Le Concorde; and Hôtel des Gouverneurs; as well as in front of Hôtel de Ville (City Hall), along rue des Jardins and Place d'Youville outside St-Jean Gate. For radio dispatched cars, try **Taxi Québec** (tel. 418/522–2001) and **Taxi Québec-Metro** (tel. 418/529–0003). Passengers are charged an initial $2, plus 80¢ for each kilometer.

By Limousine **Sec-Pro** (1975 boul. Charest O, Sainte-Foy, tel. 418/687-3311) and **Service de Limousines Québec** (1792 des Epinettes Rouges, Lac St. Charles, tel. 418/849-7473) have 24-hour service.

Important Addresses and Numbers

Tourist Information **Quebec City Region Tourism and Convention Bureau** has two tourist information centers:

Québec City: 60 rue d'Auteuil, tel. 418/692-2471. Open June-Aug., daily 8:30 AM-8 PM; Sept.-mid-Oct., daily 9-5; mid-Oct.-mid-Apr., weekdays 9-5; mid-Apr.-May, daily 8:30-6.

Sainte-Foy: 3005 boul. Laurier (near the Québec and Pierre-Laporte bridges), tel. 418/651-2882. Open June-Aug., daily 8:30 AM-8 PM; Sept.-mid-Oct., daily 8:30-6; mid-Oct.-mid-Apr., daily 9-5; mid-Apr.-May, daily 8:30-6.

Quebec Government Tourism Department: 12 rue Ste-Anne (Place d'Armes), tel. 418/643-2280 or 800/443-7000. Open daily 9-5; summer 8:30-7:30.

U.S. Consulate The consulate (2 Place Terrasse Dufferin, tel. 418/692-2095) faces the Governors Park near the Château Frontenac.

Emergencies **Police and fire,** tel. 418/691-6911; **provincial police,** tel. 418/623-6262.

Hospitals **Hôtel-Dieu Hospital** (11 côte du Palais, tel. 418/691-5042) is the main hospital inside the Old City; **Jeffrey Hale Hospital** (1250 chemin Sainte-Foy, tel. 418/683-4471) is opposite St. Sacrament Church.

24-hour Medical Service (tel. 418/687-9915).

24-hour Health Information (tel. 418/648-2626).

Distress Center (tel. 418/683-2153).

24-hour Poison Center (tel. 418/656-8090).

Dental Service 1175 rue Lavigerie, Room 100, Sainte-Foy, tel. 418/653-5412. Open Mon.-Tues., 8-8; Wed.-Thurs. 8-5, Fri. 8-3. In case of emergencies, call 418/656-6060.

Late-night Pharmacy **Pharmacie Lippens** (Les Galeries Charlesbourg, 4266 1ier av., north of Québec City in Charlesbourg, tel. 418/623-1571) is open daily 8 AM-midnight.

Road Conditions Tel. 418/643-6830.

Weather Tel. 418/872-2859.

English-language Bookstore **La Maison Anglaise** (33 boul. St.-Cyrille O, tel. 418/649-0339) has a large selection of books in English.

Travel Agencies **American Express Inter-Voyage** (1155 rue Claire-Fontaine, tel. 418/524-1414), located on the first floor of the Édifice La Laurentienne (Laurentian Building) behind the Parliament, is open weekdays 8:30-5.

Opening and Closing Times

Most banks are open Monday through Wednesday 10-3 and close later on Thursday and Friday. **Bank of Montreal** (Place Laurier, 2700 boul. Laurier, Sainte-Foy, tel. 418/525-3786) is open on Saturday. For currency exchange, **Banque d'Amérique**

(24 côte de la Fabrique, tel. 418/694–1937) is open weekdays 9–5:30, weekends 9–5. **Deak International** (615 Grande Allée E, tel. 418/529–1155) is open daily 9–5, during summer months 9–9.

Museum hours are typically 10–5, with longer evening hours during summer months. Most are closed on Monday.

Shopping hours are Monday through Wednesday 9:30–5:30, Thursday and Friday 9:30–9, and Saturday 9:30–5. Stores tend to stay open later during summer months.

During the winter, many attractions and shops change their hours; visitors are advised to call ahead.

Guided Tours

Orientation
By Bus

Gray Line offers guided bus tours. Tickets can be purchased at most major hotels or at the kiosk at Terrasse Dufferin at Place d'Armes. From November to April a pickup service from major hotels can be arranged by calling at least one hour in advance. Prices are $15–$34; half-price for children. *720 rue des Rocailles, tel. 418/622–7420. City tours year-round; others May–mid-Nov. and mid-June–mid-Oct.*

Maple Leaf Sightseeing Tours (575 Arago O, tel. 418/687–9226) offers guided tours in a minibus. Call for a reservation, and the company will pick you up at your hotel. Prices range from $16 to $49; reduced rates for children.

Visite Touristique de Québec (1576 av. du Parc, Sillery, tel. 418/653–9722) gives tours in a panoramic bus, costing $16–$49 adults; reduced rates for children.

Smaller companies offering tours include **La Tournée du Québec Inc.** (tel. 418/831–1385), **Fleur de Lys** (418/831–0188), and **Group Voyages Québec Inc.** (tel. 418/525–4585).

By Ferry

The **Québec-Lévis ferry** offers a 15-minute crossing of the St. Lawrence River to the town of Lévis. It leaves daily from the pier at rue Dalhousie across from Place Royale every half-hour from 6:30 AM until 6:30 PM, then hourly until 2:30 AM, and a final crossing at 3:45 AM. *Tel. 418/644–3704. Cost: $1 adults, 50¢ children and senior citizens.*

By Horse-drawn Carriage

Hire a *calèche* (horse-drawn carriage) on rue d'Auteuil, between the St-Louis and Kent gates, from **André Beaurivage** (tel. 418/687–9797). The cost is about $40 for a 45-minute tour of the Old City.

Special-interest
Boat Trips

Beau Temps, Mauvais Temps (991 rte. Prévost, Île d'Orléans, tel. 418/828–2275) offers two river cruises that stop to tour neighboring islands. Boats depart from the pier at Saint-François, on Île d'Orléans. The boat trip to Île-aux-Grues, offered Saturday, Sunday, and Monday, has two departures: at 9:30 AM and 2 PM. The cost is $49 for adults, $28 for children, including meal, tax, and service. The boat trip to Grosse-Ile, offered Sunday and Tuesday, has two departures, at 9:30 AM and 2 PM. The cost is $45 for adults, children under 12 not accepted. A light lunch is served.

Croisières AML Inc. (Chouinard Pier, 10 rue Dalhousie, tel. 418/692–1159) runs cruises on the St. Lawrence River aboard the M/V *Louis-Jolliet.* One- to three-hour cruises from May through mid-October cost $13.50–$19.75 for adults, $7–$10 for children.

Île d'Orléans **Beau Temps, Mauvais Temps** (991 rte. Prévost, Île d'Orléans, 418/828–2275) has guided tours of Île d'Orléans by bus, walking tours of the island's historic manors and churches, and trips to a maple-sugar hut (*see* Dining Chapter 11).

Walking **Baillairgé Cultural Tours, Inc.** (2216 chemin du Foulon, Sillery, tel. 418/658–4799), has a 2½-hour walking tour, "Québec on Foot," from late June through October 15 at 9:30 AM and 2 PM daily. Cost is $11 for adults, children under 12 free. The tour begins at the Musée du Fort and includes sights in both the Upper and Lower towns.

Exploring Québec City

Orientation

Québec City's split-level landscape is notable for having one part on the cape (Upper Town) and the other along the shores of the St. Lawrence River (Lower Town). Separating these two sections is steep and precipitous rock, against which were built the city's more than 25 *escaliers* (staircases). Today you can also take the *funiculaire* (funicular) to get from one level to the other.

The first two tours are in the oldest sections of town, while the third tour features sites outside the city walls.

Tour 1: Upper Town

Numbers in the margin correspond with points of interest on the Tours 1 and 2: Upper and Lower Towns map.

This tour takes you to the most prominent buildings of the city's earliest inhabitants, who came from Europe in the 17th century to set up political, educational, and religious institutions. Upper Town became the political capital of the colony of New France and, later, of British North America.

1 Begin this tour where rue St-Louis meets rue du Fort at **Place d'Armes.** For centuries, this square has been a meeting place for parades and military events. It is bordered by government buildings; at its west side, the majestic **Ancien Palais de Justice** (Old Courthouse), a Renaissance-style building from 1887, replaced the original 1650 courthouse.

To the south, at 17 rue St-Louis, is the colony's former treasury building, **Maison Maillou,** which has architectural traits typical of New France: a sharply slanted roof, dormer windows, concrete chimneys, shutters with iron hinges, and limestone walls.

You are now within a few steps east of Québec City's most cele-
2 brated landmark, **Château Frontenac** (1 rue des Carrières, tel. 418/692–3861), which was built as a hotel in 1893 and considered remarkably luxurious at that time: Guest rooms contained fireplaces, private bathrooms, and marble fixtures, and a special commissioner traveled to England and France in search of antiques for the establishment. The hotel was completed in 1925 with the addition of a 20-story central tower. Owned by Canadian Pacific Hotels, it has accumulated a star-studded

Antiques District, **24**
Basilique Notre-Dame-de-Québec, **9**
Cavalier du Moulin, **5**
Château Frontenac, **2**
Couvent des Ursulines, **6**
Église Notre-Dame-des-Victoires, **18**
Holy Trinity Anglican Cathedral, **7**
Jardin des Gouverneurs, **4**
Lévis-Québec Ferry, **21**
Maison Chevalier, **16**
Maison des Vins, **19**
Maison Louis-Jolliet, **14**
Maison Montcalm, **25**
Monastère des Augustines, **10**
Musée de la Civilisation, **22**
Musée du Fort, **13**
Parc de l'Artillerie, **26**
Parc Montmorency, **12**
Place d'Armes, **1**
Place de Paris, **20**
Place Royale, **17**
Rue du Trésor, **8**
Rue du Petit-Champlain, **15**
Séminaire de Québec, **11**
Terrasse Dufferin, **3**
Vieux-Port de Québec, **23**

Tours 1 and 2: Upper and Lower Towns

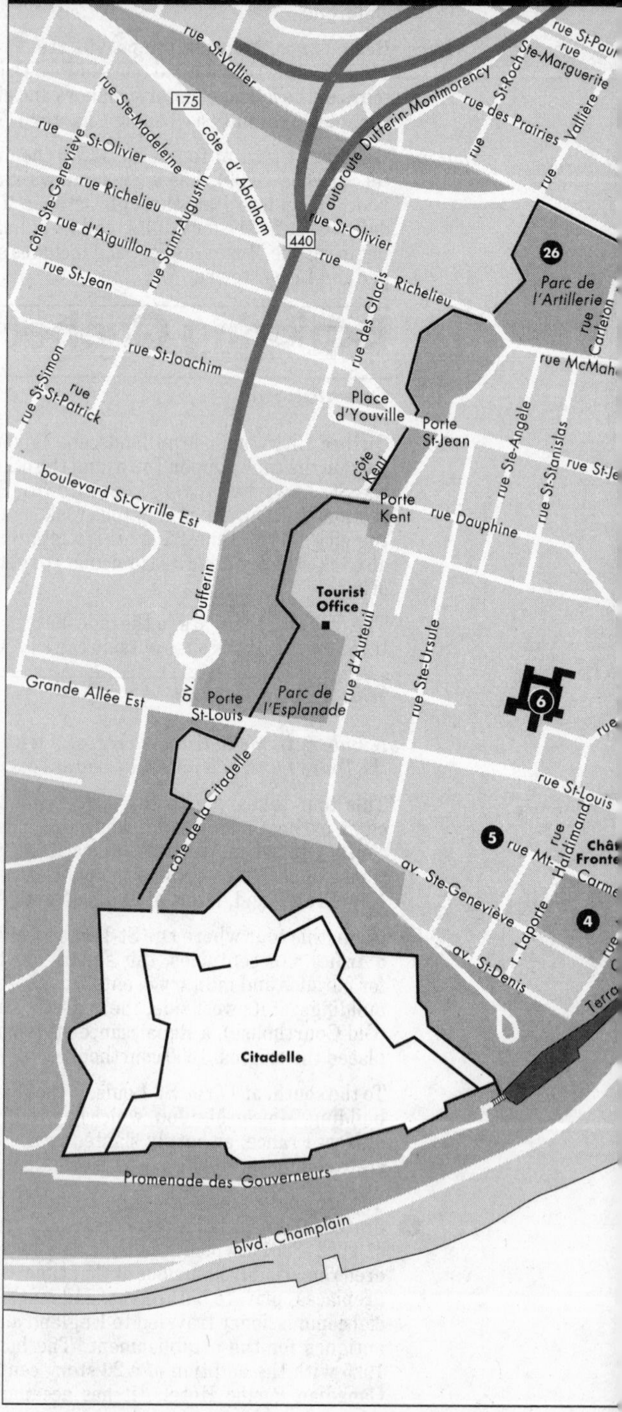

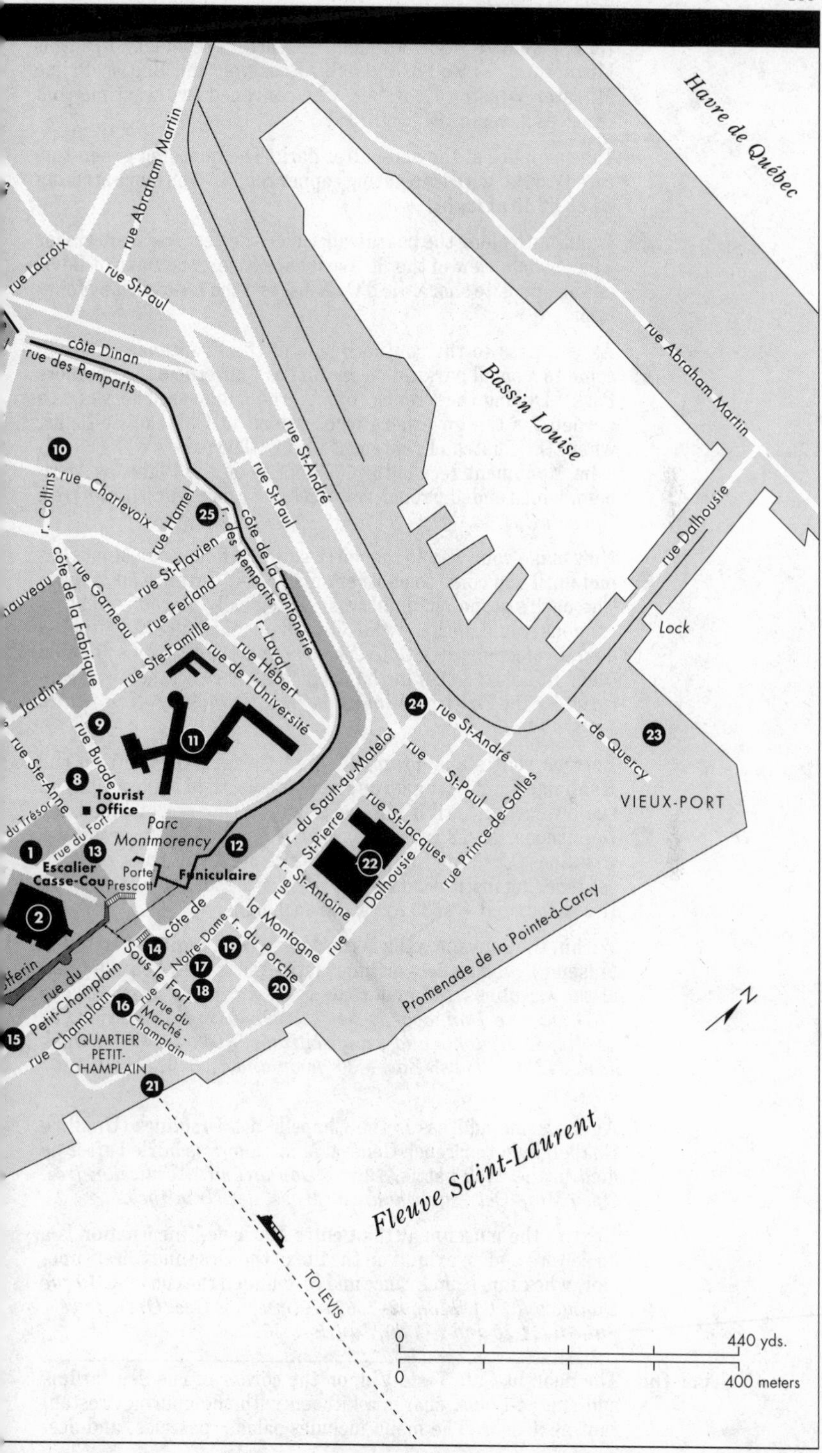
Havre de Québec
Bassin Louise
rue Abraham Martin
rue Lacroix
rue St-Paul
côte Dinan
rue des Remparts
rue St-André
rue St-Paul
rue Dalhousie
Lock
rue Collins
rue Charlevoix
rue Hamel
côte de la Canotonnerie
r. des Remparts
rue St-Flavien
rue Ferland
rue Garneau
côte de la Fabrique
rue Ste-Famille
r. Laval
rue Hébert
rue de l'Université
Jardins
rue Buade
rue Ste-Anne
Tourist Office
du Trésor
rue du Fort
Parc Montmorency
Escalier Casse-Cou
Porte Prescott
Funiculaire
r. du Sault-au-Matelot
rue St-André
r. de Quercy
VIEUX-PORT
rue St-Paul
rue Prince-de-Galles
r. St-Pierre
rue St-Jacques
r. St-Antoine
Dalhousie
côte de la Montagne
rue
r. du Porche
Notre-Dame
Sous le Fort
Promenade de la Pointe-à-Carcy
rue du Petit-Champlain
rue Champlain
rue du Marché Champlain
QUARTIER PETIT-CHAMPLAIN
Fleuve Saint-Laurent
TO LEVIS
N
0
440 yds.
0
400 meters
1
2
8
9
10
11
12
13
14
15
16
17
18
19
20
21
22
23
24
25

guest roster, including Queen Elizabeth, Madame Chiang Kai-shek, Ronald Reagan, and French President François Mitterrand, as well as Franklin Roosevelt and British Prime Minister Winston Churchill, who convened two wartime conferences here, in 1943 and 1944.

Take a glance at the hotel after dark. The imposing green-turreted castle, with its slanting copper roof, is even more striking when lit up at night.

3 Walk south along the boardwalk called the **Terrasse Dufferin** for a panoramic view of the St. Lawrence River, the town of Lévis on the opposite shore, Île d'Orléans, and the Laurentian Mountains.

As you pass to the southern side of the Frontenac, you will
4 come to a small park called **Jardin des Gouverneurs** (Governors Park). During the French regime, the public area served as a garden for the governors who resided in Château St-Louis, where the Château Frontenac is today. The park's Wolfe-Montcalm Monument recalls the 1759 battle on the Plains of Abraham, which ended French rule of New France. *Admission free. Open daily.*

Now make your way to the north side and follow rue Mont Car-
5 mel until you come to another small park, **Cavalier du Moulin.** The park's stone windmill was strategically placed so that its cannons could destroy the Cap-Diamant Redoubt (situated near Promenade des Gouverneurs) and the St-Louis Bastion (near St-Louis Gate) in the event that New France was captured by the British. *Admission free. Open May–Nov., daily 8 AM–9 PM.*

Retrace your steps down rue Mont Carmel, turn left on rue Haldimand and left again on rue St-Louis; then make a right on rue du Parloir until it intersects with a tiny street called rue
6 Donnacona. At 12 rue Donnacona, you'll find the **Couvent des Ursulines** (Ursuline Convent), the site of North America's oldest teaching institution for girls, which is still a private school. It was founded in 1639 by two French nuns.

Within the convent walls is the **Musée des Ursulines** (Ursuline Museum), which offers an informative perspective on 120 years of the Ursulines' life under the French regime, from 1639 to 1759. *12 rue Donnacona, tel. 418/694–0694. Admission: $2 adults, $1 students and senior citizens, $4.25 families. Open Jan. 3–Nov., Tues.–Sat. 9:30–noon and 1:30–5, Sun. 12:30–5:15.*

At the same address is the **Chapelle des Ursulines** (Ursuline Chapel), where French Général Montcalm was buried after he died in the 1759 battle. *12 rue Donnacona. Admission free. Open May–Oct., same hours as Musée des Ursulines.*

Next to the museum at the **Centre Marie-de-l'Incarnation** is a bookstore and an exhibit on the life of the Ursulines' first superior, who came from France and co-founded the convent. *10 rue Donnacona, tel. 418/692–1569. Admission free. Open Tues.–Sat. 10–11:30 and 2–4:30, Sun. 2–4:30.*

Time Out The neon-lit **Café Taste-Vin,** on the corner of rue des Jardins and rue St-Louis, shares a kitchen with the gourmet restaurant next door. The menu includes salads, pastries, and desserts. *32 rue St-Louis, tel. 418/692–4191. AE, DC, MC, V. Open 8 AM–11 PM.*

From rue Donnacona, walk north to rue des Jardins. Within a
7 few yards you'll see the **Holy Trinity Anglican Cathedral.** The land was originally given to the Recollet fathers (Franciscan monks from France) in 1681 by the king of France for a church and monastery. When Québec came under British rule, the Recollets made the church available to the Anglicans for services. Later, King George III of England ordered construction of the present cathedral, which was completed in 1804. It was the first Anglican cathedral outside the British Isles. *31 rue des Jardins, tel. 418/692–2193. Admission free. Open May–June, daily 9–5; July–Aug., daily 9–9; Sept.–mid Oct., weekdays 9–3.*

Continue north on rue des Jardins and turn right at rue Ste-Anne, a narrow, cobbled street lined with boutiques and restaurants. In the summer, this lively area buzzes from early in the morning until late at night. Stores stay open, artists paint, and street musicians entertain.

8 Turn left on **rue du Trésor,** where prints, paintings, and local artwork are displayed. Often the artist is on site to answer questions or discuss his or her work. This alley is active both day and night, especially in the summer.

At the bottom of rue du Trésor, turn left on rue Buade. When you reach the corner of côte de la Fabrique, you'll see the
9 **Basilique Notre-Dame-de-Québec** (Our Lady of Québec Basilica), with the oldest parish in North America, dating back to 1647. Despite its ornate interior, this basilica has a somber ambience perhaps attributed to the basilica's large and famous crypt, which was Québec City's first cemetery; more than 900 people are interred here, including 20 bishops and four governors of New France. Champlain is believed to be buried in the vicinity of the basilica. Archaeologists have been searching for his tomb for more than 40 years. *16 rue Buade, tel. 418/692–2533. Admission free. Open daily 7 AM–8 PM.*

The basilica marks the beginning of Québec City's Latin Quarter, which extends to the streets northwest of Québec Seminary (rue Buade, rue des Remparts, côte de la Fabrique, and côte du Palais) as far as rue St-Jean. This district was deemed the Latin Quarter because Latin was once a required language course at the seminary and was spoken among the students. Although Latin is no longer compulsory, and Québec Seminary-Laval University has moved out to a larger campus in Sainte-Foy, students still cling to this neighborhood.

Head down côte de la Fabrique and turn right when it meets rue Collins. The cluster of old stone buildings sequestered at
10 the end of the street is the **Monastère des Augustines de l'Hôtel-Dieu de Québec** (Augustine Monastery). The **Hôtel-Dieu Hospital,** connected to the monastery, was the first hospital north of Mexico and was founded in 1639. The **Musée des Augustines** (Augustine Museum), located on the first floor of the monastery, features a small exhibit of antique medical instruments used by the Augustines.

Upon request, the Augustines also offer guided tours of the chapel (1800) and the cellars used by the nuns as a hiding place beginning in 1659, during bombardments from the British. *32 rue Charlevoix, tel. 418/692–2492. Admission free. Open Tues.–Sat. 9:30–11:30 and 1:30–5, Sun. 2–5. Closed Mon.*

Time Out For a crusty white or whole-wheat croissant, try **Croissant Plus** (50 rue Garneau, tel. 418/692–4215).

Retrace your steps on rue Collins and côte de la Fabrique. When you reach rue Ste-Famille on the left, you will find the
11 wrought-iron entrance gates of the **Séminaire de Québec** (Québec Seminary). The seminary was founded in 1663 by François de Montmorency Laval, the first bishop of New France, to train priests of the new colony. In 1852 the seminary became Université Laval (Laval University), the first Catholic university in North America, which moved its campus to Sainte-Foy in 1946. *1 côte de la Fabrique, tel. 418/692–3981. Admission free. Open May 5–mid-Sept., daily 9:30–5:30.*

At this entrance (the seminary's west entrance) you'll find the small Roman-style **Chapelle Extérieure** (Outer Chapel). In 1950 a memorial crypt of Laval (the body has since been removed) was added here. *Admission free. Open May 5–mid-Sept., daily 9:30–5:30.*

Head north across the courtyard to the **Musée du Séminaire** (Seminary Museum). The museum focuses on the three centuries of the seminary's existence, until 1940, and houses paintings dating to the 15th century, scientific instruments used for research and teaching, and, in a former chapel, an exhibit of religious and secular antique silver. The museum also has a rare collection of Canadian money that was used in colonial times. *9 rue de l'Université, tel. 418/692–2843. Admission: $2 adults, $1 students and senior citizens, 50¢ children. Open June–Sept., Tues.–Sun. 10:30–5:30; Oct.–May, Tues.–Sun. 11–5. Closed Mon. year-round.*

Use the southeast exit at rue de l'Université to leave the semi-
12 nary and head south to côte de la Montagne, where **Parc Montmorency** (Montmorency Park) straddles the hill between Upper Town and Lower Town. This park marks the spot where Canada's first wheat was grown in 1618 and where the nation's first legislation was passed in 1694, in Lower Canada's first parliament. A monument stands to the first Canadian farmer, and another honors the father of the 1867 Confederation, Georges-Étienne Cartier.

On the south side of the park, walk across an arched bridge called **Porte Prescott** (Prescott Gate), which the British added to the three gates built by the French. However, in 1871 Prescott Gate was demolished because it was considered a hindrance to traffic; it was rebuilt in 1983.

Take the **Escalier Frontenac** (Frontenac Stairway) up to the north end of the Terrasse Dufferin. You may be out of breath, but the climb is worth it for the 30-minute recap on the six
13 sieges of Québec City at the **Musée du Fort** (Fort Museum). This museum's sole exhibit is a sound-and-light show with a model of 18th-century Québec that reenacts the region's most important battles. *10 rue Ste-Anne, tel. 418/692–2175. Admission: $3.50 adults, $2 students and senior citizens. Open summer, daily 10–6; fall, Mon.–Sat. 10–5, Sun. 1–5; winter, weekdays 11–3,*

Sat. 10–5, Sun. 1–5; spring, Mon.–Sat. 10–5, Sun. noon–5. Closed Dec.

As you exit from the museum, head southeast to the funicular booth along Terrasse Dufferin. Ride the funicular (75¢) to Lower Town to begin Tour 2.

Tour 2: Lower Town

Numbers in the margin correspond with points of interest on the Tours 1 and 2: Upper and Lower Towns map.

New France began to flourish in the streets of Lower Town along the banks of the St. Lawrence River. These streets became the colony's economic crossroads, where furs were traded, ships came in, and merchants established their residences.

Despite the status of Lower Town as the oldest neighborhood in North America, its narrow and time-worn thoroughfares have a new and polished look. Today, modern boutiques, restaurants, galleries, and shops catering to tourists occupy the former warehouses and residences.

Begin this tour on the northern tip of rue du Petit-Champlain at
14 **Maison Louis-Jolliet** (16 rue du Petit-Champlain, tel. 418/692–1132), which houses the lower station of the funicular and a souvenir shop. Built in 1683, this home was used by the first settlers of New France as a base for further westward explorations.

At the north side of the house is **Escalier Casse-cou** (Breakneck Steps), the city's first iron stairway. Its ambitious 1893 design was by Charles Baillairgé, a city architect and engineer, and it was built on the site of the original 17th-century stairway that linked the Upper and Lower towns during the French regime.

15 Head south on **rue du Petit-Champlain,** the city's oldest street, which retains its size from its days as the main street of a harbor village. In 1977 artists, craftsmen, and private investors decided to initiate a revival of the street; today it consists of pleasant boutiques and cafés (*see* Shopping, below).

Where rue du Petit-Champlain intersects with boulevard Champlain, make a U-turn to head back north. One block farther, at
16 the corner of rue du Marché-Champlain, you'll find **Maison Chevalier,** an annex of the ethnographic Musée de la Civilisation (Civilization Museum). The stone house was built in 1752, combined with two other buildings in 1959, and is now under renovation. It is scheduled to reopen in Spring 1991 with an exhibit of 18th-century furniture. *60 rue du Marché-Champlain, tel. 418/643–9689. Admission free. Open Tues.–Sun. 10–5. Closed Mon.*

East of Maison Chevalier, take rue Notre-Dame, which leads
17 directly to **Place Royale,** formerly the heart of New France. This cobblestone square is encircled by buildings that were once the homes of wealthy merchants.

The small stone church at the south side of the Place Royale is
18 the **Église Notre-Dame-des-Victoires** (Our Lady of Victories Church), the oldest church in Québec, dating back to 1688. It was built on the site of Samuel de Champlain's first residence, which also served as a fort and trading post. The church had to

be completely restored on two occasions: after a fire in 1759, and more recently in 1969. A scale model suspended from the ceiling represents *Le Brezé*, the boat that transported French soldiers to New France in 1664. Sunday Mass is at 8, 9:15, 10, 11, and noon. *Place Royale, tel. 418/692–1650. Admission free. Open May 15–Oct. 15, Mon.–Sat. 9–4:30, Sun. 7:30–4:30; Oct. 16–May 14, Tues.–Fri. 9–noon, Sat. 9–noon and 2–4:30, Sun. 7:30–1 and 2–3:30.*

19 Turn to the northwest corner of the square to the cool, dark, musty cellars of the **Maison des Vins,** a former warehouse dating back to 1689; here the Québec Société des Alcools sells more than 1,000 kinds of rare and vintage wines valued from $7 to $1,000. *1 Place Royale, tel. 418/643–1214. Admission free. Open Tues.–Wed. 9:30–5:30, Thurs.–Fri. 9–9, Sat. 9:30–5. Closed Sun. and Mon.*

20 On the east side of Place Royale, take rue de la Place, which leads to an open square, **Place de Paris,** a newcomer to these historic quarters. Looming at its center is a black and white geometric sculpture, positioned on the site where the first French settlers landed.

21 At this point of the tour you may conveniently catch the 15-minute **ferry to Lévis** (pronounced Lee-vee) on the opposite shore of the St. Lawrence River. The boat docks a block south on rue Dalhousie; we recommend you take the ferry for an unprecedented view of Québec City's skyline, with the Château Frontenac and the Québec Seminary high above the cliff. The view is even more commanding at night. For departure times and cost, *see* Guided Tours, above.

22 Continue north on the rue Dalhousie until you come to the **Musée de la Civilisation.** Wedged into the foot of the cliff, this spacious museum, with its striking limestone and glass facade, has been artfully designed to blend into the city landscape. Architect Moshe Safdie skillfully incorporated three historic buildings into the museum's modern structure: the house Estèbe, the site of the First Bank of Québec, and the Maison Pagé-Quercy. Many of the materials that were used to construct the newer portions of the museum are native to Québec Province. The building's campanile echoes the shape of church steeples throughout the city.

The museum, which opened officially in 1988, houses innovative, entertaining, and sometimes playful exhibits devoted to aspects of Québec's culture and civilization. Several of the shows, with their imaginative use of artwork, video screens, computers, and sound, appeal to both adults and children.

The museum features several temporary shows a year; its permanent exhibition, "Memoires" ("Memories"), considers both Québec's history and French-Canadian society today. This comprehensive display evokes domestic life in the early days of the cold, northern frontier by means of historic artifacts and music. Other sections of the exhibit touch upon key political events, local inventions, regional celebrations, and the opinions of Québécois on contemporary issues. Guides are available in the exhibition rooms. *85 rue Dalhousie, tel. 418/643–2158. Admission: $4 adults, $3 senior citizens, $2 students, under 16 free. Tues. free. Open June 24–Sept. 7, daily 10–7; Sept. 8–June 23, Tues., Thurs.–Sun. 10–5, Wed. 10–9. Closed Mon.*

From rue Dalhousie, head east toward the river to the
23 **Vieux-Port de Québec** (Old Port of Québec). The old harbor dates back to the 17th century, when ships first arrived from Europe bringing supplies and settlers to the new colony. At one time this port was among the busiest on the continent, but it saw a rapid decline after steel replaced wood and the channel to Montréal was deepened to allow larger boats to reach a good port upstream.

In 1984 the 72-acre port was restored with a $100-million grant from the federal government; today it encompasses several parks and the **Agora,** the city's largest open-air theater. At the northwest area of the port, an exhibition center, **Port de Québec in the 19th Century,** presents the history of the port in relation to the lumber trade and shipbuilding. *100 rue St-André, tel. 418/648–3300.*

The port's northwestern tip features the **Marché du Vieux-Port** (Farmer's Market), where farmers come from the countryside to sell their fresh produce. *Admission free. Open May–Oct., daily 8–8.*

24 You are now in the ideal spot to explore Québec City's **antiques district.** One block south from rue St-André, antiques boutiques cluster along the rue St-Pierre and rue St-Paul. In 1964 the low rent and commercial nature of the abandoned area attracted several antiques dealers. Today, numerous cafés, restaurants, and art galleries have turned this area into one of the town's more fashionable sectors.

Walk west along rue St-Paul and turn left onto a steep brick incline called côte Dambourges; when you reach côte de la Cantonerie, take the stairs back on the cliff to rue des Remparts. Continue approximately a block west along rue des Remparts until you come to the last building in a row of purple houses.
25 **Maison Montcalm** was the home of French Général Louis-Joseph Montcalm from 1758 until the capitulation of New France. A plaque dedicated to the general is situated on the right side of the house.

Continue west on rue des Remparts and turn left on rue de
26 l'Arsenal, which brings you to the **Parc de l'Artillerie** (Artillery Park). This National Historic Park is a complex of 20 military, industrial, and civilian buildings, situated to guard the St. Charles River and the Old Port. Its earliest buildings served as headquarters for the French garrison and were taken over in 1759 by the British Royal Artillery soldiers. *2 rue d'Auteuil, tel. 418/648–4205. Admission free.*

One of the three buildings you may visit is a former **powder house.** The building houses a detailed model of Québec City in 1808, built to convince British officials of the strategic importance of Québec, so that more money would be provided to expand the city's fortifications. *Open Apr.–Oct., Mon. 1–5, Tues.–Sun. 10–5; Nov.–Mar., weekdays 10–noon and 1–5.*

The **Dauphine Redoubt** served as a barracks for the French garrison until 1760, when it became an officers' mess for the Royal Artillery Regiment. When the British called their soldiers back to England in 1871, it became a residence for the Canadian Arsenal superintendent. *Open Apr.–Oct., daily 1–5. Closed Nov.–Mar.*

The **Officers' Quarters** building, a dwelling for Royal Artillery officers, is now a museum for children, with shows on military life during the British regime. *Open Apr.–Oct., daily 1–5. Closed Nov.–Mar.*

Tour 3: Outside the City Walls

Built at the city's highest point, the **Citadelle** (Citadel) is the largest fortified base in North America still occupied by troops. The 25-building fortress was intended to protect the port, prevent the enemy from taking up a position on the Plains of Abraham, and provide a last refuge in case of an attack. The facility includes the governor-general's residence, the officers' mess, five heavily fortified bastions, and the Cap-Diamant Redoubt (Cape Diamond Redoubt). If weather permits, you may witness the Changing of the Guard, an elaborate ceremony in which the troops parade before the Citadel in the customary red coats and black fur hats. *1 côte de la Citadelle, tel. 418/648–3563 and 418/648–5234. Guided tours only. Admission: $3 adults, $1 students. Free for children under 7 and handicapped persons. Open Mar.–Apr. and Oct., weekdays 9–4; May–mid-June and Sept., daily 9–5; mid-June–Labor Day, daily 9–7; Nov., weekdays 9–noon. Dec.–Feb., reservations are necessary. Changing of the Guard, mid-June–Labor Day, daily at 10. Tattoo, July–Aug., Tues., Thurs., Sat., and Sun. at 7 PM. Cannon fire from the Prince-de-Galles Bastion (Prince of Wales Bastion), daily at noon and 9 PM.*

The **Parliament Buildings,** which mark the area known as **Parliament Hill,** were erected between 1877 and 1884 and are the headquarters of the provincial government. A 30-minute guided tour of the Renaissance-style buildings (in both English and French) takes in the President's Gallery, the National Assembly Chamber, and the Legislative Council Chamber. *Corner of av. Dufferin and Grande Allée E, door 3, tel. 418/643–7239. Admission free. Guided tours Sept.–Nov. and Jan.–May, weekdays 9–4:30; June 24–Aug., daily 10–5:30. Closed Dec. and June 1–23.*

The "Grande Ouverture" of the just-renovated **Musée de Québec** (Québec Museum) is scheduled for Spring 1991. The original museum, erected in 1933, is doubling its exhibition space by incorporating a nearby abandoned prison, which dates to 1867. The museum has more than 15,000 traditional and contemporary pieces. *1 av. Wolfe-Montcalm, tel. 418/643–2150. Admission free. Open June 15–Sept. 14, daily 10–8:45; Sept. 15–June 14, Tues.–Sun. 10–5:45, Wed. until 10 PM. Closed Mon.*

Québec's tallest office building, **Anima G** (Complex G) has by far the best view of the city and the environs. An express elevator ascends to the observation gallery on top. *1037 rue de la Chevrotière, tel. 418/644–9841. Admission free. Open mid-Jan.–May and Sept.–mid-Dec., weekdays 10–4, weekends and holidays 1–5; June–Aug., weekdays 10–8, weekends and holidays 1–5. Closed mid-Dec.–mid-Jan.*

What to See and Do with Children

Aquarium du Québec (Québec Aquarium). The Québec City transit system, **Commission de Transport de la Communauté Urbaine de Québec (CTCUQ,** tel. 418/627–2511) runs buses here. *1675 av. du Parc, Sainte-Foy, tel. 418/659–5266. Admission: $3.50 adults, $1.75 children and senior citizens; Nov.–Apr. half-price. Open daily 9–5.*

Jardin Zoologique du Québec (Québec Zoological Gardens). The zoo is situated 11.3 kilometers (7 miles) west of Québec City on Route 73. If you don't have a car, **CTCUQ** (tel. 418/627–2511) runs buses here. *8191 av. du Zoo, Charlesbourg, tel. 418/622–0312. Admission: May–Oct., $5.50 adults, $2 children and senior citizens; Nov.–Apr., free weekdays, half-price weekends. Open May–Oct., daily 9:30–6; Nov.–Apr., daily 9:30–5.*

Parc Cartier-Brébeuf. Playgrounds and 9 kilometers (5½ miles) of walking paths are available. *175 rue de l'Espinay, tel. 418/648–4038. Admission free. Call for admission times.*

Parc de l'Artillerie (Artillery Park). The Officers' Quarters was a British colony from 1759 to 1867. *2 rue d'Auteuil, tel. 418/648–4205. Admission free. Open Apr.–Oct., daily 1–5. Closed Nov.–Mar.*

Parc du Porche. This playground has ladders and swings in a historic setting just outside Place Royale (between rue du Porche and rue de l'Union). *Admission free. Open daily.*

Shopping

Prices in Québec City tend to be on a par for the most part with those in Montréal and other North American cities, so you won't have much luck hunting bargains. When sales occur, they are usually listed in the French daily newspaper *Le Soleil.*

Stores are generally open Monday through Wednesday 9:30 to 5:30, Thursday and Friday until 9, and Saturday until 5. During the summer, shops may be open seven days a week, and most have later evening hours.

Shopping Centers

The mall situated closest to the Old City is **Place Québec** (5 Place Québec, tel. 418/529–0551), near the National Assembly. This multilevel shopping complex has 75 stores and is connected to the Hilton International. **Alimentation Petit-Cartier** (1191 av. Cartier, tel. 418/524–3682), located off Grande Allée and a 15-minute walk from St-Louis Gate, is a food mall for gourmets, with everything from utensils to petits fours.

Other shopping centers are approximately a 15-minute drive west along Grande Allée. The first mall is **Place Sainte-Foy** (2450 boul. Laurier, Sainte-Foy, tel. 418/653–4184). Next door is **Place Belle Coeur** (2600 boul. Laurier, Sainte-Foy, tel. 418/653–4169). Directly behind it is **Place de la Cité** (2635 boul. Hochelaga, Sainte-Foy, tel. 418/657–6920). Massive **Place Laurier** (2700 boul. Laurier, Sainte-Foy, tel. 418/653–9318), has more than 350 stores.

Quartier Petit-Champlain (tel. 418/692–2613) in Lower Town is a pedestrian mall with some 50 boutiques, local businesses, and restaurants. This popular district is the best area to find native Québec arts and crafts, such as wood sculptures, weaving, ceramics, and jewelry.

Specialty Stores

Antiques **Louis Zaor** (112 rue St-Paul, tel. 418/692–0581), the oldest store on rue St-Paul, is still the best place in the area to find excellent English, French, and Canadian antiques. The floor upstairs houses a fine collection of Québec wood furniture.

Art **Aux Multiples Collections** (69 rue Ste-Anne, tel. 418/692–1230; 70 rue Dalhousie, tel. 418/692–4434) features a good selection of Inuit art done by Canada's native people, as well as antique furniture and such accessories as sculpted wood ducks.

Galerie Christin (113 rue St-Paul, tel. 418/692–4471), one of Québec's finest galleries, displays work by new and better-known local artists.

Galerie Madeleine Lacerte (1 côte Dinan, tel. 418/692–1566), situated in Lower Town, features contemporary art and sculpture for sale.

Clothing **Boutique Amelia** (47 rue Sous Le Fort, tel. 418/692–2875) sells fashionable clothes and accessories at reasonable prices.

François and Hélène Cote (18½ and 20 Cul de Sac, tel. 418/692–3395) is a chic boutique with fashions for men and women.

La Maison Darlington (7 rue Buade, tel. 418/692–2268) carries well-made woolens, dresses, and suits for women by fine names in couture.

Louis Laflamme (Place Québec, tel. 418/523–6633) has a large selection of stylish men's clothes.

Fur Québec City is a good place to purchase quality furs at fairly reasonable prices. Since 1894, one of the best furriers in town has been **Jos Robitaille** (700 rue Richelieu, tel. 418/522–3288). The department store **J.B. Laliberté** (Mail Centre-Ville, tel. 418/525–4841) also carries furs.

Jewelry **Blanc d'Ivoire** (48 rue du Petit-Champlain, tel. 418/692–4425) specializes in ivory, with all pieces made at the store.

Sports and Fitness

For information about sports and fitness, contact **Quebec City Region and Convention Bureau** (60 rue d'Auteuil, Québec G1R 4C4, tel. 418/692–2471) or **Quebec City Bureau of Parks and Recreation** (1595 Monseigneur-Plessis, Québec G1M 1A2, tel. 418/691–6017).

Participant Sports

Bicycling, Jogging, and Cross-Country Skiing The 250-acre **Parc des Champs-de-Bataille** (Battlefields Park), (tel. 418/648–4071), with its panorama of the St. Lawrence River, is a favorite place to bike, jog, and cross-country ski. It is located at the south side of the city. Bicycles can be rented at **Location Petit Champlain** (92 rue du Petit-Champlain, tel. 418/692–2817).

Boating One of the best nearby resorts for canoeing, kayaking, and windsurfing is **Lac Beauport** (tel. 418/849–2821). Take Route 73 north of the city to Saint-Dunstan de Lac Beauport, then take exit 157, boulevard du Lac. Boats and boards can be rented at **Campex** (8 chemin de l'Orrée, Lac Beauport, tel. 418/849–2236).

Fishing Permits are needed for hunting and fishing in Québec. They are available from the **Ministry of Recreation, Hunting, and Fishing** (Place de la Capitale, 150 boul. St-Cyrille E, tel. 418/643–3127) and at Pascal (Place Laurier, 2700 boul. Laurier, Ste-Foy, tel. 418/653–9306).

Réserve Faunique des Laurentides (tel. 418/848–2422) is a wildlife reserve with good lakes for fishing, approximately 30 miles (48 kilometers) north of Québec City via Route 73.

Golf Reservations during summer months are essential. **Club de Golf Métropolitain** (4135 boul. Chauveau, tel. 418/872–9292) in Sainte-Foy, with nine holes, is one of the closest courses to Québec City. **Parc du Mont Sainte-Anne** (Rte. 360, C.P. 653 Beaupré, G0A 1E0, tel. 418/827–3778), a half-hour drive north of Québec, has one of the best 18-hole courses in the region.

Health and Fitness Clubs **Nautilus Plus** (3 Parc Samuel-Holland, Sainte-Foy, tel. 418/527–2577) is open to the public for $10. The health club features Nautilus equipment, cardiovascular machines, aerobics classes, an indoor pool, a sauna, and a whirlpool.

Hiking The **Parc Cartier-Brébeuf** north of the Old City, along the banks of the St. Charles River, has about 13 kilometers (8 miles) of hiking trails. For more mountainous terrain, head 19 kilometers (12 miles) north via Route 73 to **Lac Beauport.** For a description of **Battlefields Park,** *see* Bicycling, Jogging, and Cross-Country Skiing, above.

Skating The skating season runs December through March. There is a 3.8-kilometer (2.4-mile) stretch for skating along the **St. Charles River,** between the Samson and Marie de l'Incarnation bridges, January through March, depending on the ice. Rentals and changing rooms are nearby. *Skating hours: weekdays noon–10, weekends 10–10.*

Place d'Youville, just outside St-Jean Gate, has an outdoor skating rink. *Skating hours: weekdays noon–10, weekends 10–10.*

Skiing **Parc du Mont Sainte-Anne** (rte. 360, C.P. 400 Beaupré, G0A 1E0, tel. 418/827–4561) is the largest resort in eastern Canada, with more than 40 downhill trails. **Stoneham** (1420 av. Hibou, Stoneham, Québec, G0A 4PO, tel. 418/848–2411) is known for its long, easy slopes. Both resorts have night skiing.

A municipal bus service, **Skibus** (tel. 418/627–2511), is offered on Saturday and Sunday. It leaves from major bus stops in downtown Québec City and Sainte-Foy between 7:30 AM and 8:30 AM to ski areas in Lac Beauport and Stoneham, and returns once a day at 4:15. The cost is $3 each way.

Also *see* Bicycling, Jogging, and Cross-Country Skiing, above.

Tennis At **Montcalm Tennis Club** (901 boul. Champlain, Sillery, tel. 418/687–1250) there are four indoor and seven outdoor courts open daily 7–11.

Spectator Sports

Harness Racing Horse racing is on view at the racetrack **Hippodrome de Québec.** *C.P. 2053, Parc de L'Exposition, G1K 7M9, tel. 418/524–5283. Admission: $2 adults, $1 senior citizens, free for children under 16.*

Hockey A National Hockey League team, the Québec Nordiques, plays at the **Colisée de Québec** (Québec Coliseum). *2205 av. du Colisée, Parc de l'Exposition, tel. 418/523-3333 or 800/463-3333. Open Oct.-Apr.*

Dining

Québec City reveals its French heritage most obviously in its cuisine. You'll discover a French touch in the city's numerous cafés and brasseries and in the artful presentation of dishes at local restaurants. Most dining establishments usually have a selection of dishes à la carte, but you'll often find more creative specialties by opting for the table d'hôte, a two- to four-course meal chosen daily by the chef. At dinner, most restaurants will offer a menu de dégustation, a tastefully crafted five- to seven-course dinner of the chef's finest creations.

Although most visitors will find a gourmet meal in their price range, budget-conscious diners may want to try out the more expensive establishments during lunchtime. Lunch often costs about 30% less than dinner, and many of the same dishes are available. Lunch is usually served 11:30 AM through 2:30 PM; dinner, 6:30 until about 11 PM. You should tip about 15% of the bill.

Québec City is the best place in the province to sample French-Canadian cuisine, which is composed of robust, uncomplicated dishes that make use of the region's bounty of foods, including fowl and wild game (caribou, quail, venison), maple syrup, and various berries and nuts. Because Québec has a cold climate for a good portion of the year, it has a traditionally heavy cuisine with such specialties as *cretons* (pâtés), *tourtière* (a meat pie) and *tarte au sucre* (maple-syrup pie).

Highly recommended restaurants in each price category are indicated by a star ★.

Category	Cost*
Very Expensive	over $30
Expensive	$20-$30
Moderate	$10-$20
Inexpensive	under $10

**per person, excluding drinks, service, and 9% sales tax for meals over $3.25*

Very Expensive

★ **À la Table de Serge Bruyère.** This restaurant has put Québec on the map of great gastronomic cities. The city's most famous culinary institution serves classic French cuisine presented with plenty of crystal, silver, and fresh flowers, and with relentless attention to detail. Only one sitting is offered each night. Chef Serge Bruyère came to Québec City from Lyons, France. The menu de dégustation costs approximately $52; an extensive and pricey wine list starts at $23 and goes up to $1200. Specialties include scampi in puff pastry with fresh tomatoes, scallop stew with watercress, and duckling supreme with blueberry sauce.

(In 1984, Bruyère expanded inside the restaurant's old 1843 Livernois building and created a minimall with a European-style tearoom, a contemporary piano bar, and a gourmet food store—all serving gourmet treats from his celebrated kitchen. If À la Table de Serge Bruyère is out of your price range, **À la Petit Table** in the food mall is cheaper and less formal, with such dishes as seafood terrine and pork with estragon sauce.) *1200 rue St-Jean, tel. 418/694–0618. Reservations required. Jacket required. AE, DC, MC, V. No lunch weekends.*

Café de la Paix. An evening spent at this local favorite takes you back to a dining experience in Paris circa 1930. The tables could not get closer nor the lights dimmer amid the art deco extravagance of lamps in Venetian glass, wood sculpted in geometric patterns, and stained-glass windows. Included in the table d'hôte is a tasty pheasant with peaches. Salmon comes with four sauces: raspberry vinegar, hollandaise, tarragon, or mustard. The meat entrées, including filet mignon and leg of lamb, are also recommended. You choose your dessert from a cart; try the fresh fruit and the chocolate truffle cake. The service is prompt and attentive. Private dining rooms are available on the second floor. *44 rue des Jardins, tel. 418/692–1430. Reservations advised. Dress: neat but casual. AE, DC, MC, V. No lunch Sun. in winter.*

★ **Le Saint-Amour.** This restaurant has all the makings of a true haute-cuisine establishment without having a pretentious atmosphere. A light and airy atrium, with a retractable roof is used to good effect for summer dining. Chef Jean-Luc Boulay continues to educate himself by taking various courses in France; his studies pay off in the creation of such specialties as stuffed quails in port sauce and salmon with light chive mousse. Sauces here are light, with no flour or butter. The menu de dégustation has seven courses with a scrumptious house apple sherbet to cleanse the palate. Wines can be ordered by the glass to complement courses. The chef's true expertise shines when it comes to his diverse dessert menu. *48 rue Ste-Ursule, tel. 418/694–0667. Reservations advised. Dress: neat but casual. AE, DC, MC, V.*

Expensive

★ **Aux Anciens Canadiens.** Worth the price if you want to experience authentic French-Canadian cuisine, Aux Anciens Canadiens has four dining rooms with different themes. The recently decorated *vaisselier* (dish room) is bright and cheerful, with other room displays guns from the French regime. The hearty specialties include duck in maple glaze or lamb with blueberry wine sauce. The restaurant also serves the best caribou drink in town. (Caribou is a local beverage made with sweet red wine and whiskey; it is known for its kick.) *34 rue St-Louis, tel. 418/692–1627. Reservations advised. Dress: casual. AE, CB, DC, MC, V.*

L'Astral. This circular restaurant on the 29th floor of the Hôtel Loews Le Concorde revolves high above Battlefields Park and the Old City. The food is not the best in town, but the views are excellent. The modern and uninspired decor does not detract from the view, either; there's no room for anything besides the dining tables next to large windows and the vast buffet of salads, meat, and poultry dishes. Sunday brunch offers more than 45 items for $19.75; $6 for children under 12. *1225 Place Mont-*

Dining

À la Table de Serge Bruyère, **14**
Aux Anciens Canadiens, **19**
Café de la Paix, **18**
Chalet Suisse, **16**
Chez Temporel, **15**
L'Apsara, **8**
L'Astral, **2**
L'Echaudée, **25**
Le Cochon Dingue, **24**
Le Paris Brest, **4**
Le Saint-Amour, **9**
Pizzeria d'Youville, **11**
Restaurant au Parmesan, **20**

Lodging

Château de la Terrasse, **22**
Château Frontenac, **23**
Hilton International Québec, **6**
Hôtel Château Laurier, **5**
Hôtel Clarendon, **17**
Hôtel Loews Le Concorde, **3**
Hôtel Maison Sainte-Ursule, **10**
L'Auberge du Quartier, **1**
L'Auberge Saint-Louis, **21**
L'Hôtel du Vieux Québec, **13**
Manoir d'Auteuil, **7**
Manoir des Remparts, **26**
Manoir Victoria, **12**

Québec City Dining and Lodging

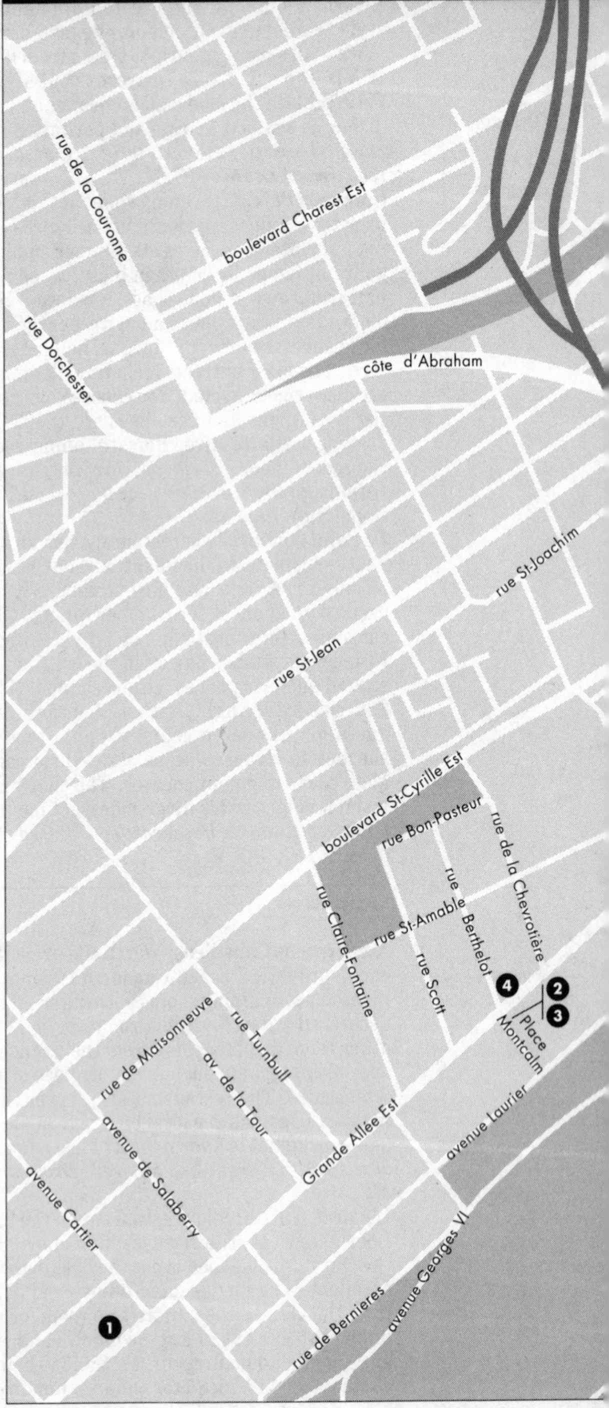

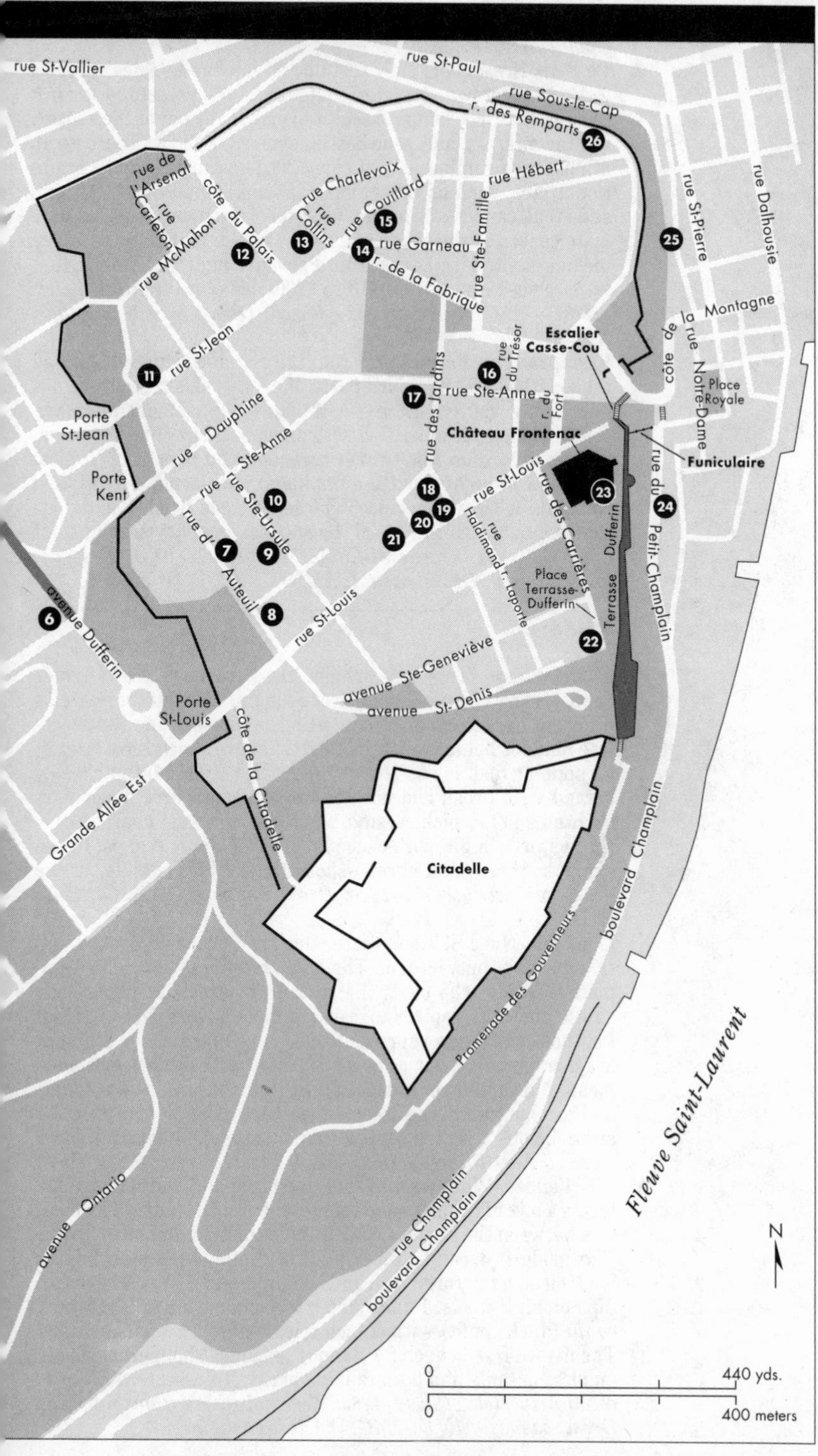
rue St-Vallier
rue St-Paul
rue Sous-le-Cap
r. des Remparts
rue de l'Arsenal
rue Carleton
côte du Palais
rue McMahon
rue Charlevoix
rue Collins
rue Couillard
rue Hébert
rue Garneau
r. de la Fabrique
rue Ste-Famille
rue St-Pierre
rue Dalhousie
côte de la Montagne
rue Notre-Dame
Place Royale
Escalier Casse-Cou
rue du Trésor
rue St-Jean
rue Ste-Anne
rue des Jardins
r. du Fort
Château Frontenac
Funiculaire
Porte St-Jean
rue Dauphine
rue Ste-Anne
Porte Kent
rue Ste-Ursule
rue d'Auteuil
rue St-Louis
rue Haldimand
r. Laporte
rue des Carrières
Terrasse Dufferin
rue du Petit-Champlain
Place Terrasse-Dufferin
avenue Dufferin
rue St-Louis
avenue Ste-Geneviève
avenue St-Denis
Porte St-Louis
côte de la Citadelle
Grande Allée Est
Citadelle
boulevard Champlain
Promenade des Gouverneurs
Fleuve Saint-Laurent
avenue Ontario
rue Champlain
boulevard Champlain
N
0
440 yds.
0
400 meters

calm, tel. 418/647–2222. Reservations advised. Dress: neat but casual. AE, DC, MC, V.

★ **Le Paris Brest.** This busy restaurant on Grande Allée serves a gregarious crowd attracted to its tastefully presented French dishes. Art Deco lamps, a sculpted mahogany bar at the center, frosted mirrors, and wine bottles shelved in the walls create an atmosphere reminiscent of early 20th-century France. Traditional fare, such as *escargots au Pernod* (snails with Pernod) and steak tartare, is offered with special touches, such as a tomato carved in the shape of a rose. Popular dishes served here include lamb with herbs from Provence and beef Wellington. Wine prices range from $18 to $200. *590 Grande Allée E, tel. 418/529–2243. Reservations advised. Dress: neat but casual. AE, DC, MC, V.*

Restaurant au Parmesan. From the red-and-white-checkered tablecloths to its standard pasta offerings, this restaurant has everything you expect in an Italian establishment and then some. Thousands of bottles with unusual shapes line the walls, and an accordion player will serenade you over such typical dishes as *gnocchi* (potato dumplings) with tomato sauce and tortellini with cream sauce. The service can be slow and inattentive, but with the jovial, boisterous crowd, you might not mind the wait. *38 rue St-Louis, tel. 418/692–0341. Reservations advised. Dress: casual. AE, DC, MC, V.*

Moderate

Chalet Suisse. This large chalet close to the Place d'Armes serves Swiss cuisine. Fondues are a mainstay, and there are 14 different ones to choose from, with the Gruyère and the chocolate fondues being two of the tastiest house specialties. Another popular dish is *raclette,* a Swiss dish with melted cheese, served with bread and potatoes as well as diverse flavorings, such as onions, pickles, and ham. The spacious chalet looms three stories high, with clichéd murals of alpine scenes. In the summer, there are umbrella-shaded café tables outside. *32 rue Ste-Anne, tel. 418/694–1320. Dress: informal. AE, CB, DC, MC, V.*

L'Apsara. Near St-Louis Gate, this restaurant serves innovative dishes from Vietnam, Thailand, and Cambodia. The Cambodian family who owns the restaurant excels at using both subtle and tangy spices to create unique flavors that are ideal for those seeking a reprieve from French fare. Good starters are *fleur de pailin* (a rice paste roll filled with fresh vegetables, meat, and shrimp) or *mou sati* (pork kebabs with peanut sauce and coconut milk). The assorted miniature Cambodian pastries are delicious with tea served from a little elephant container. *71 rue d'Auteuil, tel. 418/694–0232. Dress: casual. AE, MC, V.*

★ **L'Echaudée** (Whitewash). This chic black and white bistro attracts a mix of business and tourist clientele because of its location between the financial and antiques district in Lower Town. The modern decor features a stark dining area with menus written on a mirrored wall and a stainless-steel bar where you dine on high stools. Lunch offerings include *cuisse de carnard confit* (duck confit) with french fries and fresh seafood salad. The five-course brunch for Sunday antiques shoppers includes giant croissants and a tantalizing array of desserts. *73 Sault-au-Matelot, tel. 418/692–1299. Weekend reservations advised. Dress: casual. AE, DC, MC, V. Closed Sun. night.*

Inexpensive

★ **Chez Temporel.** Tucked behind rue St-Jean and côte de la Fabrique, this homey café is an experience *très Français*. The aroma of fresh coffee fills the air. The rustic decor incorporates wood tables, chairs, and benches, while a tiny staircase winds to an upper level. Croissants are made in-house; the staff will fill them with Gruyère and ham or anything else you want. Try the equally delicious *croque-monsieur* (grilled ham and cheese sandwich) and quiche lorraine. *25 rue Couillard, tel. 418/694–1813. No reservations. No credit cards. Open 7:30 AM–1:30 AM.*

Le Cochon Dingue (The Crazy Pig). Across the street from the ferry in Lower Town, this cheerful café with sidewalk tables and indoor dining rooms has artfully blended the chic and the antique. Café fare includes dependably tasty homemade quiches, thick soups, and such desserts as fresh raspberry tarte and maple-sugar pie. *46 boul. Champlain, tel. 418/692–2013. No reservations. Dress: casual. AE, MC, V. Open 7:30 AM–midnight.*

Pizzeria d'Youville. This restaurant located in the Latin Quarter has a pizza for everyone, with more than 25 combinations. Tasty pies are cooked in a wood oven and then heated by fire at your table. You can go beyond tomato sauce and cheese here, and try the Hawaiian pizza, with ham, cheese, and pineapple, or L'Amalfitana, which combines tomato sauce, cheese, shrimp, and garlic. Meat dishes, pasta, and salads are also offered on the menu. Its Latin Quarter location is one of Québec City's liveliest neighborhoods, perfect for an after-dinner stroll. *1014 rue St-Jean, tel. 418/694–0299. Reservations accepted. Dress: casual. AE, DC, MC, V.*

Lodging

Québec City has more than 35 hotels within its 1-square-mile radius. It is necessary to make a reservation during peak season, from May through September and for the Winter Carnival in February. During busy times, hotel rates are usually 30% above prices at other times of the year.

Highly recommended properties in each price category are indicated by a star ★.

Category	Cost*
Very Expensive	over $140
Expensive	$85–$140
Moderate	$50–$85
Inexpensive	under $50

**All prices are for a standard double room, excluding an optional service charge.*

Very Expensive

★ **Château Frontenac.** Towering above the St. Lawrence River, the Château Frontenac is indisputably Québec City's most renowned landmark. As a modern hotel, it can no longer claim to be the city's top-rated place to stay; nevertheless, the mystique of staying at "the château" is an enduring tradition. Its public rooms, from the intimate piano bar to its 700-seat ballroom, which is reminiscent of the Versailles Hall of Mirrors, have all the opulence of years gone by, while almost all the guest rooms offer excellent views. Last year, Canadian Pacific Hotels committed $50 million to modernize its rooms and facilities, keeping in mind the hotel's refined French Renaissance decor. The Frontenac has one of the finer restaurants in town, Le Champlain, where classic French cuisine is served by waiters dressed in traditional French costumes. The ground floor has several luxury shops and a restaurant, Le Café Canadien. *1 rue des Carrières, G1R 4P5, tel. 418/692–3861 or 800/268–9420. 530 rooms. Facilities: 2 restaurants and bar. AE, CB, DC, MC, V.*

★ **Hilton International Québec.** Just outside St-Jean Gate, the Hilton rises from the shadow of Parliament Hill as the city's finest luxury hotel. It has such spacious facilities and efficient services that it could easily cater exclusively to the convention crowd. Instead, it has adapted its renowned comfort and dependable service to tourists. The sprawling atrium lobby is flanked with a bar and an open-air restaurant, and it offers the added convenience of being connected with the mall, Place Québec. Ultramodern rooms with pine furniture feature tall windows so that rooms on upper floors afford fine views of the Old City. *3 Place Québec, G1K 7M9, tel. 418/647–2411 or 800/268–9275. 563 rooms, 30 suites. Facilities: outdoor pool, health club, sauna, whirlpool, and 2 restaurants. AE, CB, DC, MC, V.*

★ **Hôtel Loews Le Concorde.** When Le Concorde was built in 1974, the shockingly tall concrete structure went up with controversy because it was taking the place of 19th-century Victorian homes. Yet of all the modern hotels outside the city gates, tourists will probably find that Le Concorde occupies one of the most convenient locations for city touring and nightlife. Inside the hotel there's almost as much going on as at the cafés and restaurants along the nearby Grande Allée; Le Concorde offers the revolving restaurant L'Astral (*see* Dining, above), a sidewalk café, a bar, and a disco. Rooms have good views of Battlefields Park and nearly all have been redone in modern decor combined with traditional furnishings. Amenities for business travelers have expanded; one of the new VIP floors is reserved for female executives. *1225 Place Montcalm, G1R 4W6, tel. 418/647–2222 or 800/223–0888. 422 rooms. Facilities: 2 restaurants, heated outdoor pool, sauna, whirlpool, health club, bar, discothèque. AE, DC, MC, V.*

Manoir Victoria. This promising, new hotel is located in the heart of the Latin quarter, off St-Jean Street. Since it opened its doors in 1988, it has undergone extensive renovations, transforming the original 90-year-old Hotel Victoria into a modern-day manor. Don't be fooled by its conservative exterior: The hotel is larger and more elaborate than it appears. When completed, the $14 million project will include a discothèque connected to the hotel. Its spacious lobby with Greco-Roman pillars is furnished with white and blue sofas and the walls feature an exhibit of Québec art. The brightly decorated rooms are clean and comfortable but lack the view offered by some hotels. *44 côte du Palais, G1R 4H8, tel. 418/692–1030 or 800/463–6283. 144 rooms with private bath, 5 rooms with whirlpool bath. Facilities: bar, 2 restaurants, health club, indoor pool, beauty salon, parking. AE, DC, MC, V.*

Expensive

Hôtel Clarendon. Staying at the Clarendon is much like residing at the Château Frontenac, but on a smaller scale. You can immerse yourself in history by staying in a landmark, while you'll also be in the center of the Old City. The Clarendon is Québec City's oldest hotel, established in 1870. Since then, it has experienced one major renovation in 1930, which gave it its present stunning Art Deco design, influencing every aspect of the building—the lamps, banisters, doors, and reception area. The spacious rooms are decorated in blue and red hues. The Clarendon is known for its famous jazz bar, the city's oldest and still its finest. Its Victorian-style restaurant, Le Charles Baillargé, has live music six days a week. *57 rue Ste-Anne, G1R 3X4, tel. 418/692–2480. 135 rooms with private bath. Facilities: restaurant and bar. AE, DC, MC, V.*

L'Hôtel du Vieux Québec. Located on a secluded street in the Latin Quarter, this hotel has a brick exterior that gets lost amid the more striking historic structures around it. The establishment was once an apartment building and has the long-term visitor in mind. The interior design is also nondescript, featuring sparsely decorated but comfortable rooms done in earth tones. Most rooms have a full kitchenette with a stove, cabinets, a sink, and a refrigerator; all have cable TV. *8 rue Collins, G1R 4J2, tel. 418/692–1850. 27 units with private bath. AE, MC, V.*

★ **Manoir d'Auteuil.** Originally a private home, this lodging is one of the more lavish manors in town, artfully revamped at great taste and expense. An ornate sculpted iron banister wraps around four floors. Guest rooms feature lavish trimmings in mahogany and marble and blend modern design with precious Art Deco antiques. Each room differs in terms of shape and design; one room was formerly the residence's chapel, while another has become a duplex with a luxurious marble bathroom on the second floor. Some rooms look out to the wall between the St-Louis and St-Jean gates. *49 rue d'Auteuil, G1R 4C2, tel. 418/694–1173. 16 rooms with private bath. AE, MC, V.*

Moderate

Château de la Terrasse. While this four-story inn may not have the same charm as others in the city, it does have something that the others are lacking: This is the sole inn within the area that has a view of the St. Lawrence River. However, only half of the rooms face the river; others in the rear look out onto the backs of buildings. While the interior hints at having once possessed a refined and elegant decor because of its high ceilings and stained glass lining the large bay windows, the furnishings these days are plain and unremarkable. *6 Place Terrasse Dufferin, G1R 4N5, tel. 418/694–9472. 18 rooms with private bath. V.*

Hôtel Château Laurier. This medium-size hotel closely resembles a dormitory, which may explain why it attracts a youthful clientele. Located at one of the louder intersections in town, it has front doors that open up to the nightlife on Grande Allée. The lobby consists of couches clustered around a central television. Guest rooms are spacious, but some of the no-frills furnishings appear worn. Some rooms look out onto Parliament Hill, while the others, facing Grande Allée, may be noisy at night. *695 Grande Allée E, G1R 2K4, tel. 418/522-8108. 55 rooms with private bath. Free parking. AE, DC, MC, V.*

★ **L'Auberge du Quartier.** This small, amiable inn, situated in a house dating from 1852, will please those seeking moderately priced lodging with a personal touch. Proprietors Lise Provost and Pierre Couture are highly attentive to their guests' needs. The cheerful rooms, without phones or televisions, are modestly furnished but well-maintained; two of them have fireplaces. Rooms 5 and 8 are recommended to couples. A suite on the third floor can accommodate a family at a reasonable cost. This is one of the few inns in the area that offers a tasty Continental breakfast of warm croissants, homemade banana bread and preserves, strong coffee, and fresh fruits. A 20-minute walk west from the Old City, L'Auberge du Quartier is convenient to avenue Cartier and Grande Allée nightlife; joggers can use Battlefields Park across the street. *170 Grande Allée O, G1R 2G9, tel. 418/525-9726. 11 rooms with private bath, 2 rooms share bathroom. Free parking. AE, MC, V.*

L'Auberge Saint-Louis. This hotel is perfect for the traveler with convenience in mind; its central location on the main street of the city can't be beat. The inn features small rooms, tall staircases, and a lobby resembling a European pension. The newly decorated guest rooms contain comfortable but bare-bones furniture. The ultrabudget room on the fourth floor is just big enough for a bed. The service here is friendly and hospitable. Most guest rooms share floor bathrooms or have a semi-bathroom. *48 rue St-Louis, G1R 3Z3, tel. 418/692-2424. 22 rooms, 9 with private bath. MC, V.*

Inexpensive

★ **Hôtel Maison Sainte-Ursule.** Situated on a tiny street west of the Ursuline Convent, this well-kept hotel is a boon for the sophisticated yet economical traveler, with historic charm and reasonable prices all in one. The building, constructed in 1780, is typical of the architecture of New France, with dormer windows, small doors, and a slanting roof. Immaculate accommodations contain the old-fashioned basics, with sturdy and simple wood furniture; some rooms even have the original pint-size doors. Seven rooms are located in an annex in a private rear courtyard that becomes a garden in the summer. The amiable staff is eager to see that you are comfortable. *40 rue Ste-Ursule, G1R 4E2, tel. 418/694-9794. 15 rooms, 12 with private bath. AE, DC, MC, V. Closed in Jan.*

Manoir des Remparts. There's nothing fancy about this hotel, which is on a residential street bordering the north side of Québec City's natural cliff. But this manor offers just enough to attract the budget-conscious traveler: spacious and clean rooms with back-to-basics old-time furnishings. The halls are well-lighted and considered large for a residence in the Old City. Guest rooms have private baths or share a bath on the floor, but none have telephones or televisions. *3½ rue des Remparts, G1R 3R4, tel. 418/692-2056. AE, MC, V.*

Bed-and-Breakfasts

Quebec City Tourist Information (60 rue d'Auteuil, G1R 4C4, tel. 418/692-2471) has B&B listings.

Bed and Breakfast-Bonjour Québec (3765 boul. Monaco, G1P 3J3, tel. 418/527-1465). This agency has several B&Bs to choose from in or close to the Old City. Reserve in advance in the summer. Prices range from $30 for a single room to $50 for a double.

Hostels

Centre International de Séjour (19 rue Ste-Ursule, G1R 4E1, tel. 418/694–0755).

Service des résidences de l'Université Laval (Pavillon Parent, Local 1643, Université Laval, Sainte-Foy, Québec G1K 7P4, tel. 418/656–2921).

YWCA (855 av. Holland, G1S 3S5, tel. 418/683–2155). Accommodations are for women only, and reservations are suggested.

The Arts and Nightlife

For arts and entertainment listings in English, consult the *Québec Chronicle-Telegraph*, published on Wednesday. Each day in the French-language daily newspaper Le Soleil listings appear on a page called "Où Aller à Québec" ("Where to Go in Québec"). *Voilà Québec* and *Hospitalité Québec* are bilingual quarterly entertainment guides distributed free in tourist information areas.

The Arts

Dance **Grand Théâtre de Québec** (269 boul. St-Cyrille E, tel. 418/643–8131) presents a dance series with both Canadian and international companies. Dancers also appear at Bibliothèque Gabrielle-Roy, Salle Albert-Rousseau, and the Palais Montcalm (*see* Theater, below, for more information).

Film Most theaters present French films and American films dubbed in French. Two popular theaters are **Cinéma de Paris** (966 rue St-Jean, tel. 418/694–0891) and **Cinéma Place Charest** (500 du Pont, tel. 418/529–9745). **Cinéma Place Québec** (5 Place Québec, tel. 418/525–4524) almost always features films in English.

Music **L'Orchestre Symphonique de Québec** (Québec Symphony Orchestra) is Canada's oldest. It performs at Louis-Frechette Hall in **Grand Théâtre de Québec** (269 boul. St-Cyrille E, tel. 418/643–8131).

Bibliothèque Gabrielle-Roy (350 rue St-Joseph E, tel. 418/529–0924). Classical concerts are offered at the Auditorium Joseph Lavergne.

Theater All theater productions are in French. The following theaters schedule shows from September through April:

Grand Théâtre de Québec (269 boul. St-Cyrille E, tel. 418/643–8131). Classic and contemporary plays are staged by the leading local theater company, le Théâtre du Trident (tel. 418/643–5873).

Palais Montcalm (995 Place d'Youville, tel. 418/670–9011). This municipal theater outside St-Jean Gate features a broad range of productions.

Salle Albert-Rousseau (2410 chemin Ste-Foy, Sainte-Foy, tel. 418/659–6710). A diverse repertoire, from classical to comedy, is offered here.

Summer Theater **Agora** (120 rue Dalhousie, tel. 418/692–4540). The largest open-air amphitheater in the Old Port between the river and the customs building features variety shows, plays, and classical and contemporary music concerts.

Nightlife

The most popular spot in town is *Grande Allée*—an entire block lined with discothèques, pubs, restaurants, and cafés. It is always lively, especially in the summer. *Avenue Cartier*, more recent to the nightlife scene, offers quaint, artsy cafés and lively bars where patrons can dance. *Rue St–Jean* is another nightspot area featuring bars and clubs. Most bars and clubs stay open until 3 AM.

Bars and Lounges

Le Central (1200 rue St-Jean, tel. 418/694–0618). At this stylish piano bar at Serge Bruyère's restaurant's complex, you can order from the restaurant's sophisticated haute-cuisine menu.

Le Pub Saint-Alexandre (1087 rue St-Jean, tel. 418/694–0015). This popular English-style pub, formerly a men-only tavern, is a good place to look for your favorite brand of beer.

Disco

Le Tube Hi-Fi (139 rue St-Pierre, tel. 418/692–0257). A majestic old bank building in Lower Town now houses a glitzy discothèque with giant Greco-Roman columns, lasers, a dance floor, billiard tables, and video games.

Jazz

L'Emprise at Hôtel Clarendon (57 rue Ste-Anne, tel. 418/692–2480). The first jazz bar in Québec City is the preferred spot for enthusiasts. The Art Deco decor sets the mood for the Jazz Age rhythms.

Excursions from Québec City

Île d'Orléans

Île d'Orléans, discovered by Jacques Cartier in 1535, exemplifies the historic charm of rural Québec Province with its quiet, traditional lifestyle. A drive around the island will take you past stone churches that are among the oldest in the region and centuries-old houses amid acres of lush orchards and cultivated farmland.

The island, about 9 kilometers (5 miles) wide and 34 kilometers (21 miles) long, is now composed of six small villages. These villages have sought over the years to remain relatively private residential and agricultural communities; the island's bridge to the mainland was built only in 1935.

Important Addresses and Numbers

Beau Temps, Mauvais Temps has a tourist office located in Saint-Pierre. *991 rte. Prévost, tel. 418/828–2275. Open June–Aug., daily 8:30–7; Sept.–May, weekdays, 9–4.*

The island's Chamber of Commerce operates a tourist information kiosk situated at the west corner of côte du Pont and chemin Royal. *490 côte du Pont, St-Pierre, tel. 418/828–9411. Open June–Sept., daily 8:30–6; Oct.–Nov., weekdays 8:30–noon and 1–4:30, weekends 10–4; Dec.–May, weekdays 8:30–noon and 1–4:30.*

Medical Clinic

Centre Medical (1015 rte. Prévost, St-Pierre, tel. 418/828–2213) is the only medical clinic on the island.

Escorted Tours **Beau Temps, Mauvais Temps** (991 rte. Prévost, St-Pierre, Île d'Orléans, tel. 418/828–2275).

The Québec City touring companies that visit the island include **Maple Leaf Sightseeing Tours** (tel. 418/687–9226), **Gray Line** (tel. 418/622–7420), and **Visite Touristiques de Quebec** (tel. 418/653–9722).

Any of the offices of **Quebec City Region Tourism and Convention Bureau** can also provide information on tours and accommodations on the island.

Getting Around
By Car The only way to get to and around the island, unless you take a guided tour, is by car. The main road, chemin Royal (Route 368), extends 67 kilometers (40 miles) through all the island's six villages; street numbers along chemin Royal begin at No. 1 for each municipality.

From Québec City, take Route 440 (Dufferin-Montmorency Autoroute) northeast. After a drive of approximately 10 kilometers (7 miles) take the bridge, Pont de l'Île d'Orléans, to reach the island. Before you get to the island's only traffic light, turn right, heading west on chemin Royal, to begin the exploring tour below.

Exploring Île d'Orléans *Numbers in the margin correspond with points of interest on the Île d'Orléans map.*

Allow plenty of time to bask in the island's tranquil scenery. You'll want to stroll along the country roads and take time to observe the traditional French and English architecture of the homes.

Start heading west on chemin Royal to **Sainte-Pétronille,** the first village to be settled on the island. Founded in 1648, the community was chosen in 1759 by British General James Wolfe for his headquarters. With 40,000 soldiers and a hundred ships, the English bombarded French-occupied Québec City and Côte de Beaupré. This region is considered by many the island's most beautiful area.

On the left at 20 chemin Royal is the **Plante family farm,** where you can stop to pick apples (in season) or buy some of the island's fresh fruits and vegetables.

❶ Farther along on the right is the **Maison Gourdeau de Beaulieu House** (137 chemin Royal), the island's first home, built in 1648. Its thick walls and dormer windows are characteristic of Brittany architecture, but its sloping bell-shape roof, designed to protect buildings from large amounts of snow, is typically Québécois.

After you descend an incline, turn right beside the river on the
❷ tiny street called **rue Horatio-Walker,** named after the 19th-century painter known for his landscapes of the island. Around the corner are his home and studio, where exhibits of his paintings are held in the summer. Before the bridge to the mainland was built in 1935, rue Horatio-Walker was where people walked an ice path to reach the mainland in the winter. *13 rue Horatio-Walker. Open only upon reservation late-May–Oct. with Beau Temps, Mauvais Temps (tel. 418/828–2275).*

Continue on chemin Royal until you approach the village of
❸ Saint-Laurent, where you'll find the **studio of blacksmith Guy Bel** (2200 chemin Royal, tel. 418/828–9300). You can watch him

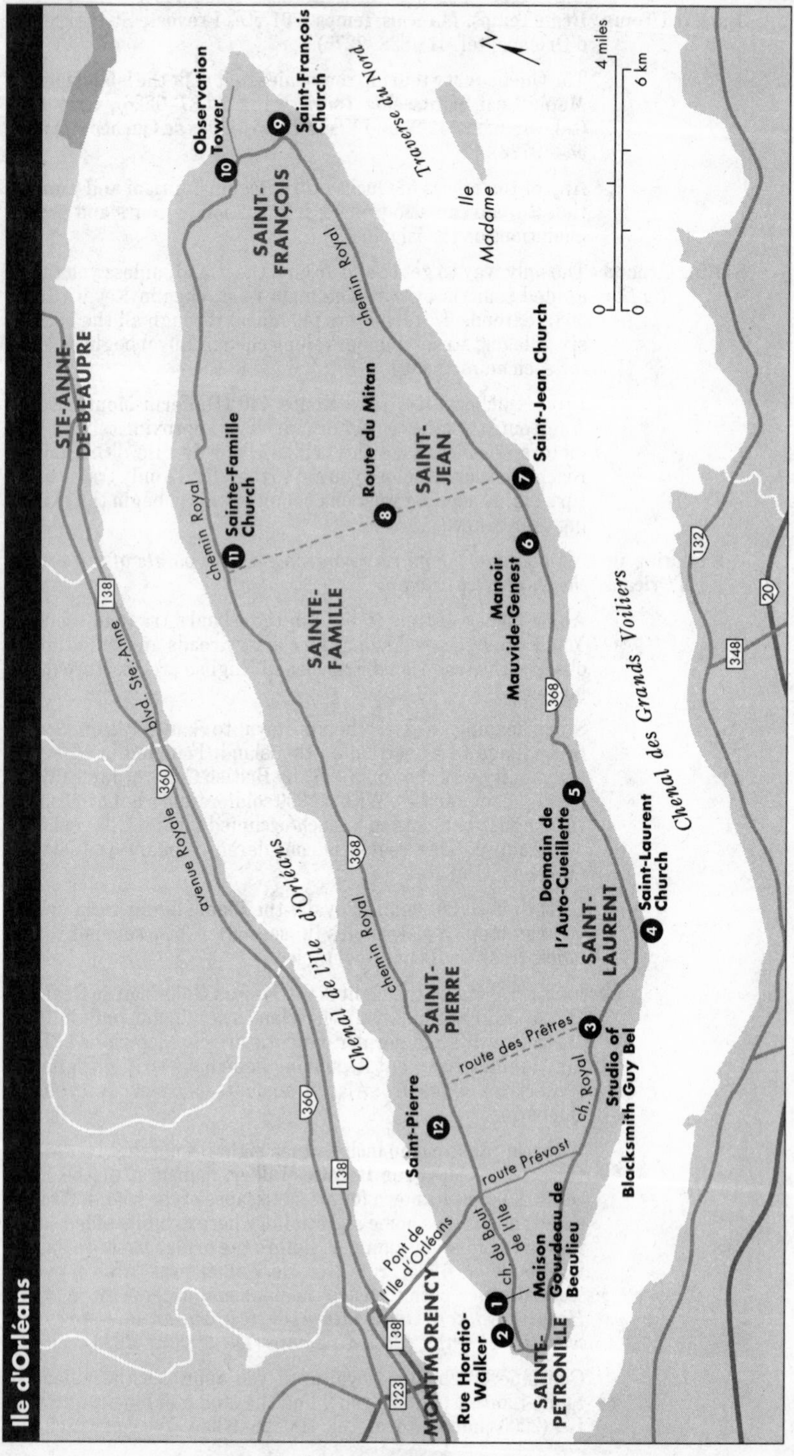
Ile d'Orléans
STE-ANNE-DE-BEAUPRE
MONTMORENCY
Pont de l'Ile d'Orléans
avenue Royale
blvd. Ste-Anne
Chenal de l'Ile d'Orléans
Chenal des Grands Voiliers
Traverse du Nord
Ile Madame
SAINTE-PETRONILLE
SAINT-PIERRE
SAINT-LAURENT
SAINTE-FAMILLE
SAINT-JEAN
SAINT-FRANÇOIS
1 Maison Gourdeau de Beaulieu
2 Rue Horatio-Walker
3 Studio of Blacksmith Guy Bel
4 Saint-Laurent Church
5 Domain de l'Auto-Cueillette
6 Manoir Mauvide-Genest
7 Saint-Jean Church
8 Route du Mitan
9 Saint-François Church
10 Observation Tower
11 Sainte-Famille Church
12 Saint-Pierre
ch. du Bout de l'Ile
route Prévost
ch. Royal
route des Prêtres
chemin Royal
138
323
360
368
132
20
348
0
4 miles
0
6 km
N

hard at work; his stylish candlesticks, mantels, and other ironworks are for sale.

Saint-Laurent, founded in 1679, is one of the island's maritime villages. Next to the village's marina stands the tall, inspiring
4 **Saint-Laurent Church,** built in 1860. A wood chapel houses a gallery where artists display their work in the summer. *1532 chemin Royal. Admission free. Open daily in summer only.*

You won't find better strawberries anywhere else in the prov-
5 ince than on Île d'Orléans. Pick your own at **Domaine de l'Auto-Cueillette** (211 chemin Royal), located in Saint-Laurent. You can buy an empty basket here for 25¢; a full basket of strawberries will cost about $4.

If you continue on chemin Royal, you'll come to **Saint-Jean,** a village whose inhabitants were once river pilots and navigators.

At 1451 chemin Royal is the village's most beautiful Normandy-
6 style manor, **Manoir Mauvide-Genest,** built in 1734. Most notable about this house is the degree to which it has held up over the years, in spite of its being targeted by English guns during the 1759 siege of Québec City. The house has an exhibit of French architecture and, downstairs, a French restaurant. *1451 chemin Royal, tel. 418/829–2630. Open summer only 10–5.*

7 At the opposite end of the village is **Saint-Jean Church,** a 1749-structure that bears a remarkable resemblance to a ship. The church's cemetery is also intriguing. The headstones, engraved in French, recall the tragedy of lives lost in these harsh waters. *Admission free. Open daily in summer.*

As you leave Saint-Jean, chemin Royal mounts the incline and
8 crosses **route du Mitan,** the most direct route from north to south. If you're running out of time and want to end the tour here, take route du Mitan, which brings you to Saint-Pierre and the bridge to the mainland.

When you come to 17th-century farmhouses separated by sprawling open fields, you know you've reached **Saint-Françcois,** a village with many *cabanes à sucre* (maple-sugaring huts), found along chemin Royal. Stop at a hut for a tasting tour; sap (maple sap turns into maple syrup when boiled) is gathered from the maple groves and boiled down so that, when poured on ice, it tastes like a delicious toffee. The maple season is late March through April, but these huts stay open year-round.

In Saint-François, the rue du Quai intersects with chemin Royal and leads to the quay where boats depart for excursions (*see* Escorted Tours, above).

9 Straight on chemin Royal is **Saint-François Church,** built in 1734. In 1988, a fatal car crash set the church on fire. Although it is in the process of being rebuilt, most of the interior treasures were lost.

The **1870 schoolhouse** next to the church is also worth seeing; here you can buy crafts and woven articles by artists living on the island. About a mile down the road is a picnic area with a
10 wood **observation tower** situated for perfect viewing of the majestic St. Lawrence. During the spring and autumn months, you can observe wild Canada geese here.

Head north on chemin Royal to reach **Sainte-Famille,** one of the island's earliest villages (1661). It has many stone houses dating to the French regime, and apple orchards and strawberry patches.

11 Take a quick look at **Sainte-Famille Church,** which, dating to 1749, is the only church to have three bell towers at the front. The church also holds a famous painting, *L'Enfant Jésus Voyant La Croix,* done in 1670 by Frère Luc (Father Luc), who was sent from France to decorate churches in the area. *Admission free. Open daily in summer.*

The next village situated on the north side of the island,
12 **Saint-Pierre,** was founded in 1679. It has long been the center of traditional farming industries and has a well-earned reputation for its butter and dairy products. Its 1717 church no longer is used for worship but is open to the public. *1243 chemin Royal. Admission free. Open daily in summer.*

If you continue west on chemin Royal, just up ahead is the bridge back to the mainland and Route 440.

Dining and Lodging

For price categories, *see* Dining and Lodging in Québec City, above.

Dining

La Goéliche. Although this rustic inn has a romantic dining room with windows overlooking the St. Lawrence River and a view of Québec City, the main reason to dine here is the good food. The menu is classic French and depends upon the fruits and vegetables in season. Lunch is more moderately priced. The evening's menu de dégustation features such specialties as quail with red vermouth and chicken with pistachio mousseline. The desserts, such as maple syrup mousse with strawberry syrup, have a regional flavor. *22 rue du Quai, Ste-Pétronille, tel. 418/828–2248. Reservations advised. Dress: neat but casual. AE, DC, MC, V. Open lunch and dinner in summer. Very Expensive.*

L'Atre. After you park your car, take a horse-drawn carriage to a 17th-century Normandy-style house furnished with Québécois pine antiques. True to the establishment's name, which means "hearth," all the traditional dishes are cooked and served from a fireplace. The menu emphasizes hearty fare, such as beef bourguignonne and tourtière and maple-sugar pie for dessert. *4403 chemin Royal, Ste-Famille, tel. 418/829–2474. Reservations required. Dress: neat but casual. AE, MC, V. Closed mid-Oct.–Apr. Expensive.*

Lodging

La Goéliche. This 1890 Victorian country inn stands just steps away from the St. Lawrence River in the village of Sainte-Pétronille. Québécois antiques decorate light and spacious rooms with original wood floors. Half the rooms look out across the river to Québec City. The rooms have no televisions, but they do have phones. *22 rue du Quai, Ste-Pétronille, G0A 4C0, tel. 418/828–2248. 16 rooms with private bath. Facilities: 2 restaurants. AE, DC, MC, V. Moderate.*

You can get to know the island by staying at one of its 30 bed-and-breakfasts. Reservations are necessary. A room for two is $40–$60. **Beau Temps, Mauvais Temps** (tel. 418/828–2275) is a referral service for these accommodations.

Côte de Beaupré

by Alice H. Oshins

First settled by French farmers, this fertile meadow is known as Côte de Beaupré (Beaupré Coast) and stretches 40 kilometers (25 miles) from Québec City to the famous pilgrimage site of Sainte-Anne-de-Beaupré. The impressive Montmorency Falls is located midway between these two points.

Tourist Information

Beaupré Coast Interpretation Center, housed in the old mill Petit-Pré, built in 1695, features displays on the history and development of the region. *7007 av. Royale, Château-Richer, tel. 418/824–3677. Admission free. Open mid-June–Aug., daily 9–noon and 1–5; Sept.–mid-Oct., weekdays 10–noon and 1–4 weekends 9–noon and 1–5.*

The offices of **Quebec City Region Tourism and Convention Bureau** (tel. 418/692–2471) can provide information on tours of the Beaupré Coast.

Getting Around

By Car

To reach Montmorency Falls, take Route 440 (Dufferin-Montmorency Autoroute) northeast from Québec City. Approximately 9.6 kilometers (6 miles) east of the city is the exit for Montmorency Falls. To drive directly to Sainte-Anne-de-Beaupré, continue northeast on Route 440 for approximately 29 kilometers (18 miles) and exit at Sainte-Anne-de-Beaupré.

An alternative way to reach Sainte-Anne-de-Beaupré is to take Route 360 or avenue Royale. Take Route 440 from Québec City, turn left at d'Estimauville, and right on boulevard des Chutes until it intersects with Route 360. Also called "le chemin du Roi" (the King's Road), this panoramic route is one of the oldest in North America, winding 30 kilometers (18.8 miles) along the steep ridge of the Beaupré Coast.

Escorted Tours

Québec City touring companies, such as **Gray Line** (tel. 418/622–7420) and **Maple Leaf Sightseeing Tours** (tel. 418/687–9226), offer day excursions along the Beaupré Coast, with stops at Montmorency Falls and the Sainte-Anne-de-Beaupré Basilica from April through November.

Exploring Côte de Beaupré

Begin this excurison with a visit to **Montmorency Falls.** The falls, which is actually 50% higher than the wider Niagara Falls, measure 83 meters (274 feet) in height. During very cold weather conditions, the falls' heavy spray freezes and forms a giant loaf-shape ice cone known to Québécois as the Pain du Sucre (Sugarloaf); this phenomenon attracts sledders and sliders from Québec City. A park in the river's gorge leads to an observation terrace; the top of the falls can also be observed from avenue Royale. *Admission free. Open daily.*

The monumental and inspiring **Basilique Sainte-Anne-de-Beaupré** (Saint-Anne-de-Beaupré Basilica) is located in a small town with the same name. The basilica has become a popular attraction as well as an important shrine: More than half a million people visit the site each year.

According to local legend, Saint Anne was responsible over the years for saving voyagers from shipwrecks in the harsh waters of the St. Lawrence. Tributes to her miraculous powers can be seen in the shrine's various mosaics, murals, altars, and church ceilings. Numerous crutches and braces posted on the back pillars have been left by those who have felt the healing powers of Saint Anne.

The present-day neo-Roman basilica, constructed in 1923, was the fifth church built on the site in honor of Sainte-Anne. The first was erected in the 17th century. The basilica, which is in the shape of a Latin cross, has 22 chapels, 18 altars, and 214 stained-glass windows. The windows tell a story of salvation through personages who were believed to be instruments of God over the centuries. *10,018 av. Royale, Ste-Anne-de-Beaupré, tel. 418/827–3781. Admission free. Open year-round. Reception booth open May, daily 8–5; June–mid-Sept., daily 8:00AM–9PM. Tours in summer, daily at 1 PM, start at the information booth (open mid-Apr.–mid-Oct.) at the southwest corner of the courtyard outside the basilica. Guided, off-season (mid-Sept.–Apr.) tours must be arranged in advance.*

Across the street from the basilica, on avenue Royale, is the **Commemorative Chapel,** built in 1878, on the location of the transept of a stone church built in 1676. The building's foundations and the church bell are remnants of the original chapel.

Northeast of the basilica stands the small **Scala Santa** (Chapel of the Holy Stairs). Erected in 1891, it features a replica of the stairs that Christ mounted before appearing before Pontius Pilate. *Both chapels: av. Royale, tel. 418/827–3781. Admission free. Open May–Oct., daily 8–5.*

West of the Scala Santa is the **Chemin de la Croix** (Way of the Cross). The path crosses a hill and is lined with 14 life-size, cast-iron figures installed between 1913 and 1946. *av. Royale. Open all day.*

To continue up the river coast through Charlevoix, *see* Chapter 11.

6 Vancouver

Introduction

by Terri Wershler

Terri Wershler, publisher of Brighouse Press, a regional book publisher, is also the author of The Vancouver Guide.

The reason people come to Vancouver is to be outdoors. Yes, there is the shopping, the galleries, and the history; but there is nothing *anywhere* to rival Vancouver's sea, mountains, and forests. The wilderness and ocean are within ¼ mile of downtown. And with 10 miles of sandy beaches and two 1,000-acre wilderness parks within reach of your hotel, Vancouver promises perfect atmosphere for every visitor. The mountains are a 15-minute drive from the classy boutiques and sidewalk cafés of Robson Street, superlative Asian restaurants, and five-star hotels.

Keep in mind that while you're soaking up the outdoors you might get a little wet. Rain is a way of life around here, so if you find yourself in four straight days of rain, grab your umbrella and rubber boots and carry on—you'll experience the real west coast.

Essential Information

Arriving and Departing by Plane

Airport and Airlines

International Airports

Vancouver International Airport is on an island about 14 kilometers (9 miles) south of downtown. The main terminal building has three levels: departures, international arrivals, and domestic arrivals; a small south terminal building services flights to secondary destinations within the province. **American Airlines** (tel. 800/433–7300), **Continental** (tel. 604/222–2442), **Delta** (tel. 604/682–5933), **Horizon Air** (800/547–9308), and **United** (tel. 604/683–7111) fly into the airport. The two major domestic airlines are **Air Canada** (tel. 604/688–5515) and **Canadian Airlines** (tel. 604/682–1411).

Other Facilities

Air BC offers 30-minute harbor-to-harbor service (downtown Vancouver to downtown Victoria) several times a day. Planes leave from near the Bayshore Hotel. Harbor-to-harbor service (Seattle to Vancouver) is run by **Lake Union Air** (tel. 800/826–1890). **Helijet Airways** (tel. 604/273–1414) has helicopter service from downtown Vancouver to downtown Victoria. The heliport is near Vancouver's Pan Pacific Hotel.

Between the Airport and Downtown

The drive from the airport to downtown is 20–45 minutes, depending on the time of day. Airport hotels offer free shuttle service to and from the airport.

By Bus

The **Airport Express** (tel. 604/266–0376) bus leaves the domestic arrivals level of the terminal building every 15 minutes, stopping at major downtown hotels and the bus depot. It operates from 5:30 AM until 12:30 AM. The fare is $6.75 one way or $11.50 round-trip.

By Taxi

There are taxi stands in front of the terminal building on the domestic and international arrivals levels. Taxi fare to downtown is about $20. Area cab companies are **Yellow** (tel. 604/681–3311), **Black Top** (tel. 604/681–2181), and **MacLures** (tel. 604/731–9211).

By Limousine

Limousine service from **Airlimo** (tel. 604/273–1331) costs about the same as a taxi to downtown: The current rate is about $21.

Arriving and Departing by Car, Ferry, Train, and Bus

By Car From the south, I-5 from Seattle becomes **Highway 99** at the U.S.–Canada border. Vancouver is a three-hour drive from Seattle. Avoid border crossings during peak times: holiday weekends, Friday evenings, Saturday mornings, and Sunday afternoons and evenings.

Highway 1, the **Trans-Canada Highway,** enters Vancouver from the east. If you enter the city after rush hour (8:30 AM), you should not have a problem with traffic.

By Ferry **BC Ferries** operates two major ferry terminals outside Vancouver. From Tsawwassen to the south (an hour's drive from downtown), ferries sail 38 kilometers (24 miles) to Victoria on Vancouver Island and through the Gulf Islands (the small islands between the mainland and Vancouver Island). From Horseshoe Bay (30 minutes north from downtown), ferries sail a short distance up the coast and to Nanaimo on Vancouver Island. Call (tel.604/685–1021) for departure and arrival times.

By Train The **VIA Rail** (tel. 800/665–8630) station is at Main Street and Terminal Avenue. VIA provides service through the Rockies to Banff. Passenger trains leave the **BC Rail** (tel. 604/984–5246) station in North Vancouver for Whistler and the interior of British Columbia. There is no longer Amtrak service from Seattle.

By Bus **Greyhound** (tel. 604/662–3222) is the biggest bus line servicing Vancouver. The **Vancouver bus depot** is at the corner of Dunsmuir and Cambie streets, a 10-minute walk from Georgia and Granville streets. **Quick Shuttle** (tel. 604/591–3571) bus service runs between Vancouver and Seattle four times a day.

Getting Around

By Car Although no freeways cross Vancouver, rush-hour traffic is not yet horrendous. The worst rush-hour bottlenecks are the North Shore bridges, the George Massey Tunnel on Highway 99 south of Vancouver, and Highway 1 through Coquitlam and Surrey.

By Subway Vancouver has a one-line, 22-kilometer (14-mile) rapid transit system called **SkyTrain** that travels underground downtown and is elevated for the rest of its route to New Westminster. Trains leave about every five minutes. Tickets must be carried with you as proof of payment. They are sold at each station from machines; correct change is not necessary. You may use transfers from Sky Train to Seabus and BC Transit buses (*see* below) and vice versa.

By Bus Exact change is needed to ride the buses: $1.25 adults, 65¢ for senior citizens and children 5–13. Books of 10 tickets are sold at convenience stores and newsstands; look for a red, white, and blue "Fare Dealer" sign. Day passes, good for unlimited travel after 9:30 AM, cost $3.75 for adults. They are available from fare dealers and any SeaBus or SkyTrain station.

By Taxi It is difficult to hail a cab in Vancouver; unless you're near a hotel, you'd have better luck calling a taxi service. Try **Yellow** (tel. 604/681–3311), **Black Top** (tel. 604/681–2181), or **MacLures** (tel. 604/731–9211).

Vancouver Exploring *(Boxes Refer to Detail Maps)*

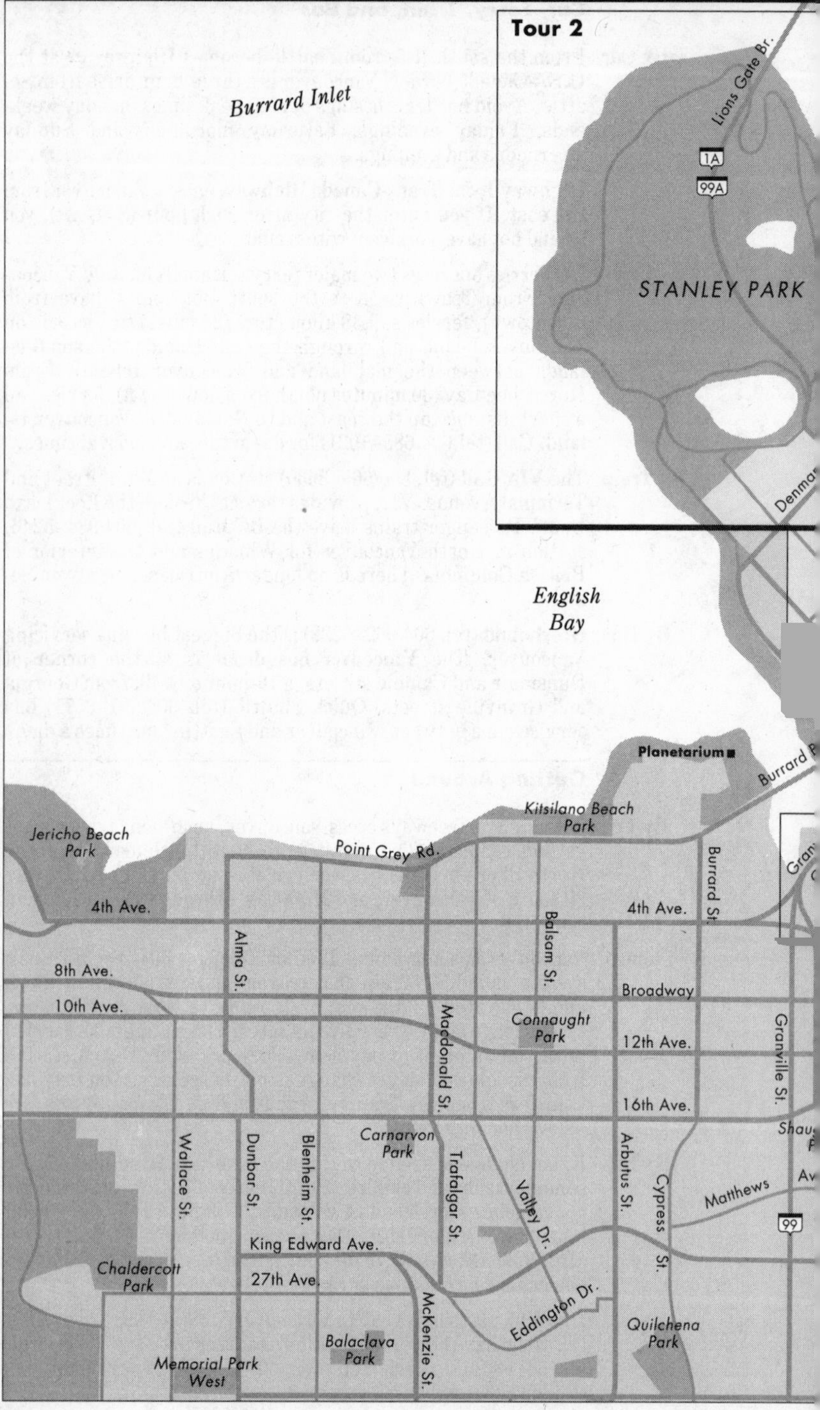

NORTH VANCOUVER
Burrard Inlet
0
1 mile
0
1 km
Pender St.
Georgia St.
Robson St.
Hastings St.
Dunsmuir St.
Burrard St.
Howe St.
Seymour St.
Powell St.
Cordova St.
Hastings St.
7A
Tour 1
Davie St.
Pacific St.
Richards St.
B.C. Place Stadium
Powell St.
Strathcona Park
Clark
Victoria
Terminal Ave.
Cambie Br.
False Creek
2nd Ave.
Tour 3
Quebec St.
Commercial
Broadway
7
Cedar Cottage Park
12th Ave.
Oak St.
Heather St.
16th Ave.
Clarke Park
Windsor St.
Knight St.
28th Ave.
Cambie St.
Manitoba St.
Main St.
Fraser St.
Victoria Dr.
King Edward
1A
99A
33rd Ave.
Queen Elizabeth Park

By SeaBus The **SeaBus** is a 400-passenger commuter ferry that crosses Burrard Inlet from the foot of Lonsdale (North Vancouver) to downtown. The ride takes 13 minutes and costs the same as the transit bus. With a transfer, connection can be made with any BC Transit bus or SkyTrain.

Important Addresses and Numbers

Tourist Information **Vancouver Travel Infocentre** (1055 Dunsmuir St., tel. 604/683–2000) provides maps and information about the city, and is open in summer, daily 8–6; in winter, Monday–Friday 9–5. A kiosk, located at Stanley Park in the Aquarium parking lot, is open mid-May–September, daily 10–6. The kiosk in Pacific Centre Mall is open daily in summer, Monday–Saturday 9:30–5, Sunday noon–5; in winter, Monday–Saturday 9–5. Eaton's department store downtown also has a tourist information counter that is open all year.

Embassies There are no embassies in Vancouver, only consulates and trade commissions: **United States** (1075 W. Georgia St., tel. 604/685–4311) and **United Kingdom** (800–1111 Melville St., tel. 604/683–4421). For a complete listing, see the Yellow Pages under consulates.

Emergencies Call 911 for **police, fire department,** and **ambulance.**

Hospitals and Clinics **St. Paul's Hospital** (1081 Burrard St., tel. 604/682–2344), a major downtown hospital, has an emergency ward. **Medicentre** (1055 Dunsmuir St., lower level, tel. 604/683–8138) is a drop-in clinic on the lower level of the Bentall Centre.

Dentist The counterpart to Medicentre is **Dentacentre** (1055 Dunsmuir St., lower level, tel. 604/669–6700), and is next door.

Late-night Pharmacy **Shopper's Drug Mart** (1125 Davie St., tel. 604/685–6445) is open until midnight every night except Sunday when it closes at 9 PM.

Road Emergencies **BCAA** (tel. 604/293–2222) has 24-hour emergency road service for members of AAA or CAA.

Travel Agencies **American Express Travel Service** (1040 W. Georgia St., tel. 604/669–2813), **Hagen's Travel** (210–850 W. Hastings St., tel. 604/684–2448), **P. Lawson Travel** (409 Granville St., tel. 604/682–4272).

Opening and Closing Times

Banks traditionally are open Monday–Thursday 10–3 and Friday 10–6, but many banks have extended hours and are open on Saturday, particularly in the suburbs.

Museums are generally open 10–5, including Saturday and Sunday. Most are open one evening a week as well.

Hours at **department stores** are Monday–Wednesday and Saturday 9:30–6, Thursday and Friday 9:30–9, and Sunday noon–5. Many smaller stores are also open Sunday. Robson Street and Chinatown are particularly good for Sunday shopping.

Guided Tours

Orientation **Gray Line** (tel. 604/681–8687), the largest tour operator, offers the 3½-hour Grand City bus tour year-round. Departing from the Hotel Vancouver, the tour includes Stanley Park, Chinatown, Gastown, English Bay, and Queen Elizabeth Park, and costs about $30. **City and Nature Sightseeing** (tel. 604/683–2112) accommodates up to 14 people in vans that run a 3½-hour City Highlights Tour for $25 (pick-up available from any downtown location). A short city tour (2½ hours) is offered by **Vance Tours** (tel. 604/222–1966) in their minibuses and costs $20.

North Shore tours usually include any or several of the following: a gondola ride up Grouse Mountain, a walk across the Capilano Suspension Bridge, a stop at a salmon hatchery, the Lonsdale Quay Market, and a ride back to town on the SeaBus. Half-day tours cost about $35 and are offered by **Landsea Tours** (tel. 604/687–5640), **1st Tours** (tel. 604/688–7246), **Gray Line** (tel. 604/681–8687), **City and Nature** (tel. 604/683–2112), and **Pacific Coach Lines** (tel. 604/662–7575).

Air Tours Tour the mountains and fjords of the North Shore by helicopter for $149 per person for 45 minutes: **Vancouver Helicopters** (tel. 604/683–4354) flies from the Harbour Heliport downtown. Or see Vancouver from the air for $49 for 20 minutes: **Harbour Air**'s (tel. 604/688–1277) seaplanes leave from beside the Bayshore Hotel.

Boat Tours The Royal Hudson, Canada's only functioning steam train, heads along the mountainous coast up Howe Sound to the coastal logging town of Squamish. After a break to explore, you sail back to Vancouver via the M.V. *Britannia*. This highly recommended excursion costs $42, takes 6½ hours, and is organized by **1st Tours** (tel. 604/688–7246). Reservations are necessary.

The **S.S. *Beaver*** (tel. 604/682–7284), a replica of a Hudson Bay fur-trading vessel that ran aground here in 1888, does two trips. One is the Harbour Sunset Dinner Cruise, a three-hour trip with a mesquite-grilled salmon dinner; the other is a day-time trip up Indian Arm with salmon for lunch. Each is about $35. Reservations are necessary.

Harbour Ferries (tel. 604/687–9558) takes a 1½-hour tour of the Burrard Inlet in a paddle wheeler. Including pick-up from a downtown hotel, the cost is $15.

Fraser River Tours (tel. 604/250–3458 or 604/584–5517) will take you on a 3½-hour tour of a fascinating working river—past log booms, tugs, and houseboats. The cruiser, *Atria Star*, leaves from Westminster Quay Market (a handy destination from downtown via SkyTrain) and costs $18.

Personal Guides **Fridge's Early Motion Tours** (tel. 604/687–5088) covers Vancouver in a Model-A Ford convertible. Minimum charge is $45 or $18 per person for an hour-long trip around downtown, Chinatown, and Stanley Park.

AAA Horse & Carriage (tel. 604/734–5115) will pick you up at your downtown hotel and take you for a ride in Stanley Park for $100 an hour.

Walking Pick up "A Self-Guided Walking Tour of Downtown Vancouver," published by Tourism Vancouver (Vancouver Travel Infocentre, 1055 Dunsmuir St., tel. 604/683–2000).

Exploring Vancouver

Orientation

The heart of Vancouver—which includes the downtown area, Stanley Park, and the West End high-rise residential neighborhood—sits on a peninsula bordered by English Bay and the Pacific Ocean to the west; by False Creek, an inlet on which you will find Granville Island, to the south; and to the north by Burrard Inlet, the working port of the city, past which loom the North Shore mountains. The oldest part of the city—Gastown and Chinatown—lies at the edge of Burrard Inlet, around Main Street, which runs north–south and is roughly the dividing line between the east side and the west side. All the avenues, which are numbered, have east and west designations.

Highlights for First-time Visitors

Chinatown, Tour 1: Downtown Vancouver

English Bay, Tour 2: Stanley Park

Granville Island, Tour 3: Granville Island

Robson Street (*see* Shopping, below)

Stanley Park, Tour 2: Stanley Park

Tour 1: Downtown Vancouver

Numbers in the margin correspond with points of interest on the Tour 1: Downtown Vancouver map.

You can logically begin your downtown tour in either of two
1 ways. If you're in for a day of shopping, amble down **Robson Street** (*see* Shopping, below), where you'll find any item from souvenirs to high fashions, from espresso to muffins.

2 If you opt otherwise, start at **Robson Square,** built in 1975 and designed by architect Arthur Erickson to be the gathering place of downtown Vancouver. The complex, which functions from the outside as a park, encompasses the Vancouver Art Gallery and government offices and courts that have been built under landscaped walkways, a block-long glass canopy, and a waterfall that helps mask traffic noise. An ice-skating rink and restaurants occupy the below-street level.

3 The **Vancouver Art Gallery** that heads the Square was a neoclassical-style 1912 courthouse until Erickson converted it in 1980. Notice some original details: the lions that guard the majestic front steps and the use of columns and domes are features borrowed from ancient Roman architecture. In the back of the old courthouse, a more modest staircase now serves as a speakers' corner. *750 Hornby St., tel. 604/682–5621. Admission: $2.75 adults, $1.25 students and senior citizens; free Thurs. eve. Open Mon., Wed., Fri., and Sat. 10–5, Thurs. 10–9, Sun. noon–5.*

4 Adjacent to the art gallery, on Hornby Street, is the **Hotel Vancouver** (1939), one of the last of the railway-built hotels. (The last one built was the Chateau Whistler, in 1989.) Reminiscent of a medieval French castle, this château style has been incorporated into hotels throughout every major Canadian city.

Tour 1: Downtown Vancouver

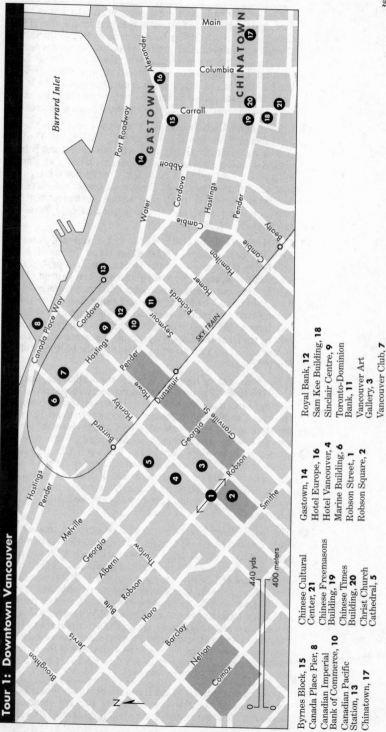

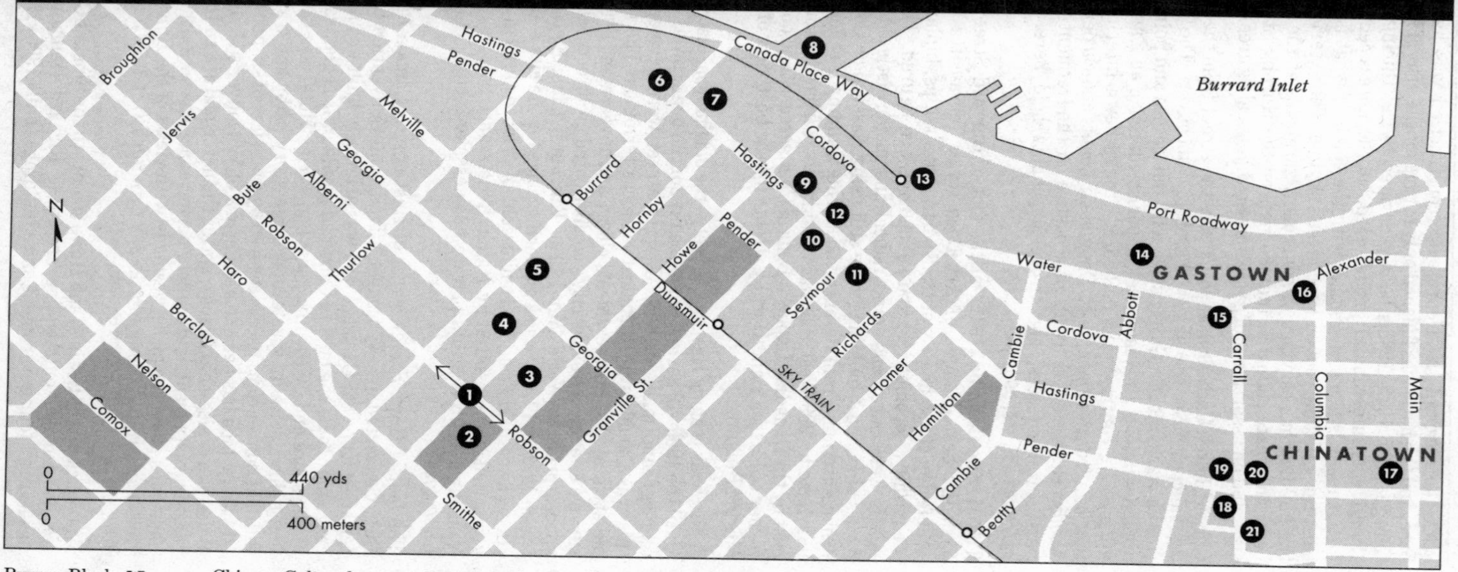

Byrnes Block, **15**
Canada Place Pier, **8**
Canadian Imperial Bank of Commerce, **10**
Canadian Pacific Station, **13**
Chinatown, **17**
Chinese Cultural Center, **21**
Chinese Freemasons Building, **19**
Chinese Times Building, **20**
Christ Church Cathedral, **5**
Gastown, **14**
Hotel Europe, **16**
Hotel Vancouver, **4**
Marine Building, **6**
Robson Street, **1**
Robson Square, **2**
Royal Bank, **12**
Sam Kee Building, **18**
Sinclair Centre, **9**
Toronto-Dominion Bank, **11**
Vancouver Art Gallery, **3**
Vancouver Club, **7**

With the onset of the Depression, construction was halted here, and the hotel was finished only in time for the visit of King George VI in 1939. It has been renovated twice: During the 1960s it was unfortunately modernized, but the more recent refurbishment is more in keeping with the spirit of what is the most recognizable roof on Vancouver's skyline. The exterior of the building has carvings of malevolent gargoyles at the corners, an ornate chimney, Indian chiefs on the Hornby Street side, and an assortment of grotesque mythological figures.

5 **Christ Church Cathedral** (1895), across the street from the Hotel Vancouver, is the oldest church in Vancouver. The tiny church was built in a Gothic style with buttresses and pointed arched windows and looks like the parish church of an English village. By contrast, the cathedral's rough-hewn interior is that of a frontier town, with Douglas-fir beams and carpenter woodwork that offers excellent acoustics for the frequent vespers, carol services, and Gregorian chants held here. *690 Burrard St., tel. 604/682–3848.*

6 The **Marine Building** (1931), at the foot of Burrard Street, is Canada's best example of Art Deco style. Terra-cotta bas-reliefs depict the history of transportation: airships, biplanes, steamships, locomotives, and submarines are figured. These motifs were once considered radical and modernistic adornments since most buildings were still using classical or Gothic ornamentation. From the east, the Marine Building is reflected in bronze by 999 West Hastings, and in silver from the southeast by the Canadian Imperial Bank of Commerce. Stand on the corner of Hastings and Hornby streets for the best view of the Marine Building.

A nice walk is along Hastings Street—the old financial district. Until the 1966–72 period, when the first of the bank towers and underground malls on West Georgia Street were developed, this was Canada's westernmost business terminus. The temple-style banks, businessmen's clubs, and investment houses survive as evidence of the city's sophisticated architectural ad-
7 vances prior to World War I. The **Vancouver Club,** built between 1912 and 1914, was a gathering place for the city's elite. Its architectural design is reminiscent of private clubs in England that were inspired by Italian Renaissance palaces. The Vancouver Club is still a private businessmen's club. *915 W. Hastings St., tel. 604/685–9321.*

8 The foot of Howe Street, north of Hastings, is **Canada Place Pier.** Converted into Vancouver's Trade and Convention Center after Expo 86, Canada Place was originally built on an old cargo pier to be the off-site Canadian pavilion. It is dominated at the shore end by the luxurious Pan Pacific Hotel (*see* Lodging, below), with its spectacular three-story lobby and waterfall. The convention space is covered by a fabric roof shaped like 10 sails, which has become a landmark of Vancouver's skyline. Below is a cruise-ship facility, and at the north end are an Imax theater, restaurant, and outdoor performance space. A promenade runs along the pier's west side with views of the Burrard Inlet harbor and Stanley Park. *999 Canada Pl., tel. 604/682–1070.*

9 Walk back up to Hastings and Howe streets to the **Sinclair Centre.** Vancouver's outstanding architect, Richard Henriquez, has knitted four government office buildings (built 1905–1939)

into an office-retail complex. The two Hastings Street buildings—the 1905 post office with the elegant clock tower and the 1913 Winch Building—are linked with the Post Office Extension and Customs Examining Warehouse to the north. Painstaking and very costly restoration involved finding master masons—the original terrazzo suppliers in Europe—and uncovering and refurbishing the pressed-metal ceilings.

Canada has a handful of old chartered banks; the oldest and
10 most impressive of these is the former **Canadian Imperial Bank of Commerce** headquarters (1906–1908) at Hastings and Granville streets; the columns, arches, and details are of typically
11 Roman influence. The **Toronto-Dominion Bank,** one block east, is of the same style, but was built in 1920.

Backtracking, directly across from the CIBC on Hastings
12 Street, is the more Gothic **Royal Bank.** It was intended to be half of a symmetrical building that was never completed, due to the Depression. Striking, though, is the magnificent hall, ecclesiastical in style reminiscent of a European cathedral.

13 At the foot of Seymour Street is the **Canadian Pacific Station,** the third and most pretentious of three CPR passenger terminals. Built 1912–14, this terminal replaced the other two as the western terminus for Canada's transcontinental railway. After Canada's railways merged, the station became obsolete until a 1978 renovation turned it into an office-retail complex and SeaBus terminal. Murals in the waiting rooms show passengers what kind of scenery to expect on their journeys across Canada.

From Seymour Street, pick up Water Street, on your way to
14 **Gastown.** Named after the original townsite saloon keeper, "Gassy" Jack Deighton, Gastown is where Vancouver originated. Deighton arrived at Burrard Inlet in 1867 with his Indian wife, a barrel of whiskey, and few amenities. A statue of Gassy Jack stands on the north side of Maple Tree Square, the intersection of five streets, where he built his first saloon.

When the transcontinental train arrived in 1887, Gastown became the transfer point for trade with the Orient and was soon crowded with hotels and warehouses. The Klondike gold rush encouraged further development until 1912, when the "Golden Years" ended. The 1930s–1950s saw hotels being converted into rooming houses and the warehouse district shifting elsewhere. The area gradually became unattended and rundown. Recently, however, both Gastown and Chinatown were declared historic areas and revitalization projects are underway.

15 The **Byrnes Block** building was constructed on the corner of Water and Carrall streets (the site of Gassy Jack's second saloon) after the 1886 Great Fire. The date is just visible at the top of the building above the door where it says "Herman Block," which was its name for a short time. The extravagantly detailed Alhambra Hotel that was situated here was luxury class for the time, at a cost of a dollar a night.

Tucked behind 2 Water Street is **Blood Alley** and **Gaoler's Mews.** Once the site of the city's first civic buildings—the constable's cabin and courthouse, and a two-cell log jail—today the cobblestone street with antique streetlighting is the home to architectural offices.

16 The **Hotel Europe** (1908–1909), a flatiron building at Powell and Alexander streets, was billed as the best hotel in the city, and was Vancouver's first reinforced concrete structure. Designed as a functional commercial building, the hotel lacks ornamentation and fine detail, a style unusually utilitarian for the time.

From Maple Tree Square, walk three blocks up Carrall Street
17 to Pender Street, where **Chinatown** begins. There was already a sizable Chinese community in British Columbia because of the 1858 Cariboo gold rush in central British Columbia, but the biggest influx from China occurred in the 1880s, during construction of the Canadian Pacific Railway, when 15,000 laborers were imported. The Chinese were among the first inhabitants of Vancouver, and some of the oldest buildings in the city are in Chinatown.

Even while doing the hazardous work of blasting the railbed through the Rocky Mountains, the Chinese were discriminated against. The Anti-Asiatic Riots of 1907 stopped growth in Chinatown for 50 years and immigration from China was discouraged by more and more restrictive policies, climaxing in a $500 head tax during the 1920s.

In the 1960s the city council was planning bulldozer urban renewal for Strathcona, the residential part of Chinatown, and freeway connections through the most historic blocks of Chinatown were charted. Fortunately, plans were halted and today Chinatown is an expanding, vital district fueled by investment from Vancouver's most notable newcomers—immigrants from Hong Kong. It is best to view the buildings in Chinatown from the south side of Pender Street, where the Chinese Cultural Center stands. From here you'll get a better view of important details that adorn the upper stories. The style of architecture typical in Vancouver's Chinatown is patterned on that of Canton, and won't be seen in any other Canadian cities.

The corner of Carrall and East Pender streets, now the western boundary of Chinatown, is one of the neighborhood's most his-
18 toric corners. Standing at 8 West Pender Street is the **Sam Kee Building,** recognized by *Ripley's Believe It Or Not!* as the narrowest building in the world. The 1913 structure still exists, with its bay windows overhanging the street and a basement that burrows under the sidewalk.

19 The **Chinese Freemasons Building** (1901) at 1 West Pender Street has two completely different styles of facades: The side facing Chinatown displays a fine example of Cantonese-imported recessed balconies; on the Carrall Street side, the standard Victorian style common throughout the British Empire is displayed. It was in this building that Dr. Sun Yat-sen hid for months from the agents of the Manchu dynasty while he raised funds for its overthrow, which he accomplished in 1911.

20 Directly across Carrall Street is the **Chinese Times Building,** constructed in 1902. Inside, there is a hidden mezzanine floor from which police officers could hear the clicking sounds of clandestine mah-jongg games played after sunset. Attempts by vice squads to enforce restrictive policies against the Chinese gamblers proved fruitless because police were unable to find the players who were hidden on the secret floor.

21 Planning for the **Chinese Cultural Center** and Dr. Sun Yat-sen Gardens (1980–87) began during the late-1960s; the first phase

was designed by James Cheng, a former associate of Arthur Erickson. The cultural center has exhibition space, classrooms, and meeting rooms. The **Dr. Sun Yat-sen Gardens** (*see* Parks and Gardens in Sports and Outdoor Activities, below), located behind the cultural center, were built by 52 artisans from Suzhou, the Garden City of the People's Republic. The gardens incorporate design elements and traditional materials from several of that city's centuries-old private gardens and are the first living classical Chinese gardens built outside China. As you walk through the gardens, remember that no power tools, screws, or nails were used in the construction. *Dr. Sun Yat-sen Gardens. 578 Carrall St., tel. 604/689–7133. Admission: $3 adults, $2 senior citizens and students, $6 family. Open May–Sept., daily 10–8; Oct.–Apr., daily 10–4:30.*

Tour 2: Stanley Park

Numbers in the margin correspond with points of interest on the Tour 2: Stanley Park map.

A 1,000-acre wilderness park just blocks from the downtown section of a major city is a rarity, but is one of Vancouver's major attractions. In the 1860s, due to a threat of American invasion, the area that is now Stanley Park was set aside as a military reserve (though it was never needed). When the City of Vancouver was incorporated in 1886, the council's first act was to request that the land be set aside for a park. In 1888 permission was granted and the grounds were named Stanley Park after Lord Stanley, then Governor-General of Canada (the same person after whom hockey's Stanley Cup is named).

An afternoon in Stanley Park gives you a capsule tour of Vancouver that includes beaches, the ocean, the harbor, Douglas fir and cedar forests, and a good look at the North Shore mountains. The park sits on a peninsula and along the shore is a 9-kilometer (5½-mile) long pathway called the seawall. You can walk or bicycle all the way around, or follow the shorter route, suggested below.

Bicycles are for rent at the foot of Georgia Street near the park entrance. Cyclists must ride in a counterclockwise direction and stay on their side of the path. A good place for pedestrians
22 to start is at the foot of Alberni Street beside **Lost Lagoon.** Go through the underpass and veer right to the seawall.

23 The old wood structure that you pass is the **Vancouver Rowing Club,** a private athletic club (established 1903), a bit farther
24 along is the **Royal Vancouver Yacht Club.**

25 About ½ kilometer (⅓ mile) away is the causeway to **Deadman's Island,** a former burial ground for the local Salish Indians and the early settlers. It is now a small naval training base called the HMCS *Discovery* that is not open to the public. Just ahead
26 is the **Nine O'Clock Gun,** a cannon-like apparatus that sits by the water's edge. Originally used to alert fishermen of a curfew ending weekend fishing, now it automatically signals every night at 9.

27 Farther along is **Brockton Point,** and its small but functional lighthouse and foghorn. The **totem poles,** which are situated more inland, make a popular photo spot for tourists. Totem poles were not carved in the Vancouver area; these were brought to the park from the north coast of British Columbia

Tour 2: Stanley Park

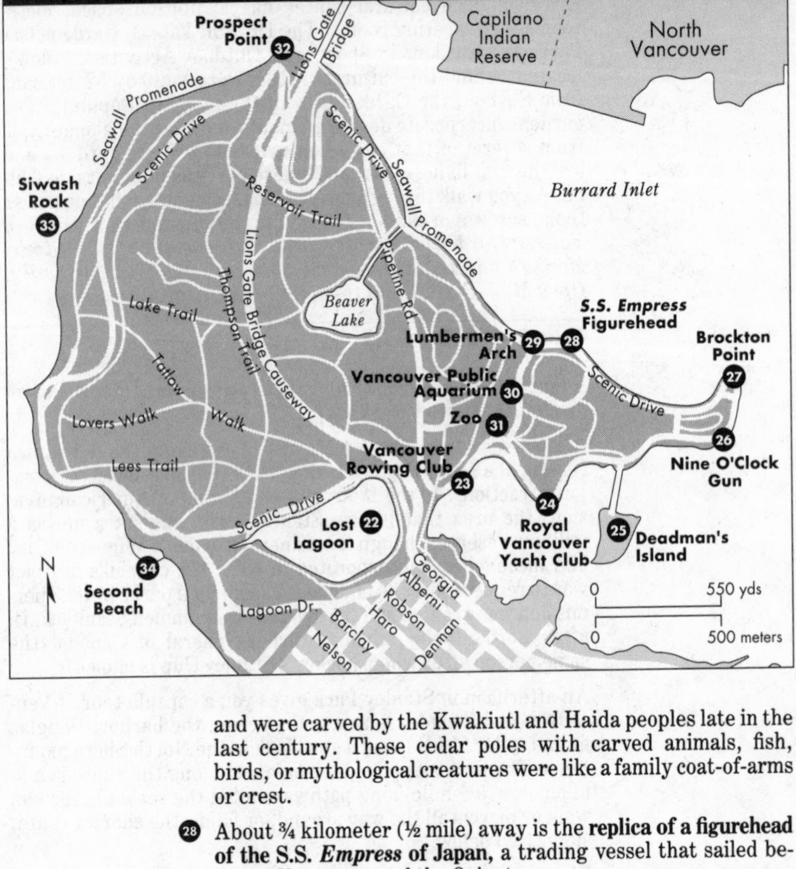

and were carved by the Kwakiutl and Haida peoples late in the last century. These cedar poles with carved animals, fish, birds, or mythological creatures were like a family coat-of-arms or crest.

28 About ¾ kilometer (½ mile) away is the **replica of a figurehead of the S.S. *Empress* of Japan,** a trading vessel that sailed between Vancouver and the Orient.

29 At kilometer 3 (mile 2) is **Lumberman's Arch,** a huge log archway dedicated to the workers in Vancouver's first industry. Beside the arch is an asphalt path that leads back to Lost Lagoon, for those who want a shorter walk. (This is about a third of the
30 distance.) This path also leads to the **Vancouver Public Aquarium,** with killer and beluga whale shows several times a day. Also part of this attraction is the humid Amazon rain-forest gallery, through which you can walk, with its piranhas, giant cockroaches, alligators, tropical birds, and jungle vegetation. Other displays show the underwater life of coastal British Columbia, the Canadian arctic and other areas of the world. The Clamshell Gift Shop next to the aquarium is the best spot in town for quality souvenirs and gifts, most with an emphasis on natural history. *Aquarium, tel. 604/682–1118. Admission: $7 adults, $6 senior citizens and youths, $4.50 children 5–12. Open daily in summer 9:30–8; daily in winter 10–5. Clamshell open July–Labor Day, daily 9:30–8; rest of year, daily 10–6.*

31 Next to the aquarium is the **Stanley Park Zoo,** a friendly place, easily seen in an hour or two. Except for the polar bears, most

of the animals are small—monkeys, seals, exotic birds, penguins, and playful otters.

About 1 kilometer (¾ mile) farther is the **Lions Gate Bridge—** the halfway point of the seawall. On the other side of the bridge
32 is **Prospect Point,** where you can see cormorants in their seaweed nests on the ledges along the cliffs. The large black diving birds are recognized by their long necks and beaks; when not nesting, they often perch atop floating logs or boulders. Another remarkable bird found along the shore in the park is the beautiful great blue heron. Reaching up to 4-feet tall with a wing span of 6 feet, the heron preys on passing fish in the waters here. The oldest heron rookery in British Columbia is in the trees around the zoo.

Continuing around the seawall you will come to the **English Bay** side and the beginning of sandy beaches. The imposing
33 rock just off shore is **Siwash Rock.** Legend tells of a young Indian who, about to become a father, bathed persistently to wash his sins away so that his son could be born pure, and for his devotion he was blessed by the gods and immortalized in the shape of Siwash Rock. Two small rocks, said to be his wife and child, are just up on the cliff above the site.

Time Out Along the seawall is one of Vancouver's best restaurants, the **Ferguson Point Teahouse.** Set on the great lawn among Douglas fir and cedar trees, the restaurant is the perfect stopover for a summer weekend lunch or brunch. If you just want a snack, a park concession stand is also at Ferguson Point.

The next attraction along the seawall is the large saltwater pool
34 at **Second Beach.** In the summer it is a children's pool with lifeguards, but during winter the pool is drained and skateboarders perform stunts. At the pool you can take a shortcut back to Lost Lagoon. To take the shortcut, walk along the perpendicular road behind the pool that cuts into the park. The wood footbridge that's ahead will lead you to a path along the south side of the lagoon and to your starting point at the foot of Alberni or Georgia street.

If you continue along the seawall, it will emerge out of the park into a high-rise residential neighborhood, the **West End.** You can walk back to Alberni Street along Denman Street where there are plenty of places to stop for coffee, ice cream, or a drink.

Tour 3: Granville Island

Numbers in the margin correspond with points of interest on the Tour 3: Granville Island map.

Granville Island was just a sandbar until World War I when the nearby creek was dredged for access to the sawmills that lined the shore. Sludge heaped on the sandbar gradually created the island that was then used to house supplies for the logging industry. In 1971 the federal government bought the island with an imaginative plan to refurbish it and introduce a public market, marine activities, and artisans' studios. The opposite shore of False Creek was the site of the 1986 World's Fair and is now part of the largest urban redevelopment plan in North America.

The small island is almost strictly commercial except for a small houseboat community. Most of the previously used industrial buildings and tin sheds have been retained, but are painted in upbeat reds, yellows, and blues. The government regulates the types of businesses that settle on Granville Island; only businesses involving food, crafts, marine activities, and the arts are permitted here.

Access on foot to Granville Island starts with a 15-minute walk from downtown Vancouver to the south end of Thurlow Street. From a dock behind the Vancouver Aquatic Center, the Granville Island Ferry leaves every six minutes for the short trip across False Creek to the Granville Island Public Market. These pudgy boats are a great way to see the sights on False Creek, but for a longer ride, go to the Maritime Museum (1905 Ogden St., tel. 604/737–2211) and catch the Aquabus. For more information call False Creek Ferries (tel. 604/684–7781).

Another option is to take a 20-minute ride on a BC Transit (tel. 604/261–5100) bus. Take a UBC, Granville, Arbutus, Cambie, or Oak bus from downtown to Granville and Broadway and transfer to the Granville Island bus No. 51. Parking is limited, but if you must take a car, go early in the week and early in the day to avoid crowds. Parking is free for only three hours; an alternative is to use the pay parking buildings on the island if you can find a space.

35 The ferry to Granville Island will drop you off at the **Granville Public Market**. Although there are a few good food stores outside, most stalls are enclosed in the 50,000-square-foot building. Since the government allows no chains, each outlet is unique, and most are of good quality. You probably won't be able to leave the market without a snack, espresso, or fixings for a lunch out on the wharf. Don't miss the charcoal-grilled oysters from **Sea-kist,** fish chowder or bouillabaisse from the **Stock Market,** fresh fudge at **Olde World Fudge,** or smoked salmon from the **Salmon Shop.** In the summer you'll see mounds of raspberries, strawberries, blueberries, and even more exotic fruits like persimmons and lychees. On the water side of the market is lots of outdoor seating. *Public Market. Tel. 604/261–5100. Open June–Aug., daily 9–6; closed Mon. Sept.–May except holidays.*

36 The **Granville Island Information Centre,** kitty-corner to the market, is a good place to get oriented with the island. Maps are available and a slide show depicts the evolution of Granville Island. Ask here about special-events days; perhaps there's a boat show, outdoor symphony concert, dance performance, or some other happening. *1592 Johnston St., tel. 604/666–5784. Open daily 10–6.*

Continue walking south on Johnston Street, along a clockwise loop of the island. Next is **Ocean Cement,** one of the last of the island's former industries; its lease does not expire until the year 2004.

37 Next door is the **Emily Carr College of Art and Design.** Just inside the front door, to your right, is the **Charles H. Scott Gallery.** This gallery hosts contemporary multi-media exhibits. *1399 Johnston St., tel. 604/687–2345. Open daily 11–5, Thurs. 11–8.*

Tour 3 : Granville Island

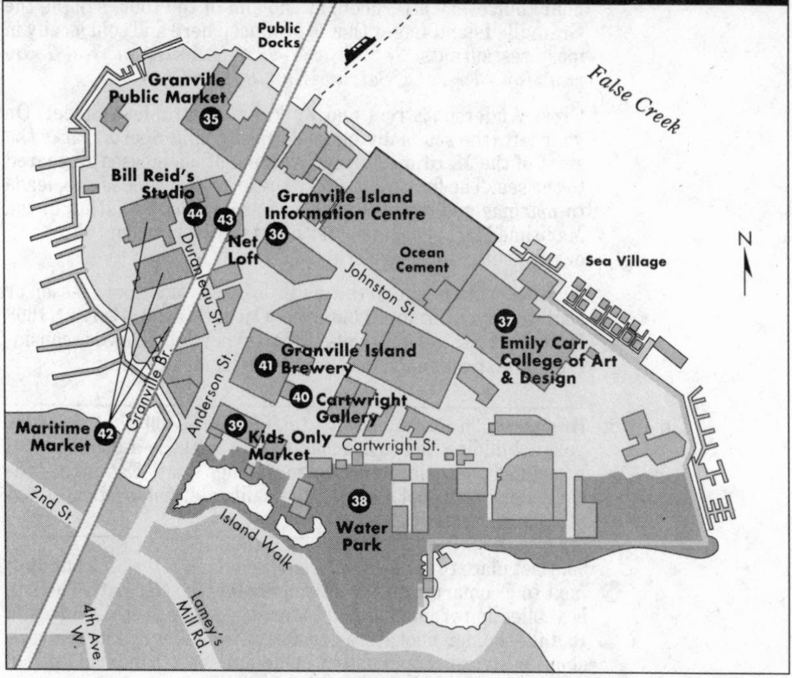

Past the art school, on the left, is one of the only **houseboat communities** in Vancouver; others have been banned by the city because of problems with sewage and property taxes. The owners of this community appealed the ban and won special status. Take the boardwalk that starts at the houseboats and continues partway around the island.

As you circle around to Cartwright Street, stop in Kakali at number 1249, where you can watch the process of making fine handmade paper from all sorts of materials like bluejeans, herbs, and sequins. Another unusual artisan on the island is the glassblower at 1440 Old Bridge Street, around the corner.

The next two attractions will make any child's visit to Granville Island a thrill. First, on Cartwright Street, is the children's
38 **water park,** with a wading pool, sprinklers, and a fire hydrant made for children to shower each other. A bit farther down, be-
39 side Isadora's restaurant, is the **Kids Only Market,** with two floors of small shops selling toys, arts-and-crafts materials, dolls, records and tapes, chemistry sets, and other sorts of kid stuff. *Water park. 1496 Cartwright St., tel. 604/689–8447. Admission free. Open June–Aug., daily 10–6. Kids Only Market. Admission free. Open June–Aug., daily 10–6; Sept.–May, Tues.–Sun. 10–6.*

40 Across from the Kids Only Market is the **Cartwright Gallery,** which hosts such temporary exhibits as native Indian and local crafts and intriguing traveling exhibits. *1141 Cartwright St., tel. 604/687–8266. Open Tues.–Sat. 10–5, Sun. 11–3.*

41 At the **Granville Island Brewery,** next door, you can take a half-hour tour every afternoon; at the end of the tour, sample the Granville Island Lager that is produced here and sold locally in most restaurants. *Tel. 604/688–9927. Admission free. Tours run Mon.–Fri. at 2; Sat. and Sun. at 1 and 3.*

Cross Anderson Street and walk down Duranleau Street. On your left, the scuba diving pool in **Adrenalin Sports** marks the
42 start of the **Maritime Market,** a string of businesses all geared to the sea. The first walkway to the left, Maritime Mews, leads to marinas and dry docks. There are dozens of outfits in the Maritime Market that charter boats (with or without skippers) or run cruise-and-learn trips.

Another way to take to the water is by kayak. Take a lesson or rent a kayak from **Ecomarine Ocean Kayak Center** (1668 Duranleau St., tel. 604/689–7575). Owner John Dowd is considered *the* expert on Pacific Northwest ocean kayaking.

Time Out **Bridges** (1696 Duranleau St., tel. 604/687–4400), in the bright yellow building that overlooks False Creek, is a good spot to have lunch, especially on a warm summer's day. Eat on the spacious deck that looks out on the sailboats, fishing boats, and other water activities.

The last place to explore on Granville Island is the blue building
43 next to Ecomarine on Duranleau Street, the **Net Loft.** The loft is a collection of small, quality stores—good places to find a gift to take home: bookstore, crafts store/gallery, kitchenware shop, postcard shop, custom-made hat shop, handmade paper store, British Columbian native Indian gallery, do-it-yourself jewelry store, and more reside here.

Behind Blackberry Books, in the Net Loft complex, is the
44 **studio of Bill Reid,** British Columbia's most respected Haida Indian carver. His *The Raven and the First Men* (which took five carvers more than three years to complete) is in the Museum of Anthropology (*see* Other Museums, below). Reid's Pacific Northwest Coast Indian artworks are world-renowned. Although you can't visit the studio, there are large windows through which you can look.

Since you have come full circle, you can either take the ferry back to downtown Vancouver, or stay for dinner and catch a play at the **Arts Club** (tel. 604/687–1644) or **Waterfront Theater** (tel. 604/685–6217).

Other Museums

The **Maritime Museum** traces the history of marine activities on the west coast. Permanent exhibits depict the port of Vancouver, the fishing industry, and early explorers; the model ships on display are a delight. Traveling exhibits vary, but always have a maritime theme. Guided tours are led through the double-masted schooner, the *St. Roch,* the first ship to sail in both directions through the treacherous Northwest Passage. A changing variety of restored heritage boats, from different cultures, are moored behind the museum and a huge Kwakiutl totem pole stands out front. *North foot of Cypress St., tel. 604/737–2211. Admission: $3 adults, $1 children, students, and* *senior citizens, $6 families; free Wed. eve. Open daily 10–5, Wed. 10–9. Access available by the Granville Island ferries.*

The **Museum of Anthropology,** focusing on the arts of the Pacific Northwest Indians, is Vancouver's most spectacular museum. Situated on the campus of the University of British Columbia, the museum is housed in an award-winning glass and concrete structure designed by Arthur Erickson. In the Great Hall are large and dramatic totem poles, ceremonial archways, and dugout canoes—all adorned with carvings of frogs, eagles, ravens, bears, and salmon. Also showcased are exquisite carvings of gold, silver, and argillite (a black stone found in the Queen Charlotte Islands). Masks, tools, and costumes from many other cultures are also displayed. *6393 N.W. Marine Dr., tel. 604/228–3825. Admission: $3 adults, $1.50 youths (13–18) and senior citizens, $1 children; free on Tues. Open Tues. 11–9, Wed.–Sun. 11–5.*

Science World is in a gigantic shiny dome that was built for Expo 86 for an Omnimax Theater—the world's largest dome screen. Science World is not a traditional museum, but is very much hands-on. Visitors are encouraged to touch and to participate in the theme exhibits. A special gallery, the Search Gallery, is aimed at younger children, as are the fun-filled demonstrations given in Center Stage. *1455 Québec St., tel. 604/687–7832. Admission to Science World: $6 adults, $4 senior citizens and children. Admission to Omnimax is the same; for admission to both you get a discount. Open daily 10–5.*

Vancouver Museum displays permanent exhibits that focus on the city's early history and native art and culture. Life-size replicas of an 1897 CPR passenger car, trading post, Victorian parlor, and a real dugout canoe are highlights. Also on the site are the Planetarium and Observatory (*see* Off the Beaten Track, below). *1100 Chestnut St., tel. 604/736–7736. Admission: $4 adults, $1.50 senior citizens and children. Open Tues.–Sun. 10–5.*

Vancouver for Free

Several public galleries and museums are free on certain days: The **Vancouver Art Gallery** (750 Hornby St., tel. 604/682–5621) is free on Thursday evenings; the **Maritime Museum** (1950 Ogden St., tel. 604/737–2211) is free Wednesday evenings for shanty-singing night; the **Museum of Anthropology** (6393 N.W. Marine Dr., tel. 604/228–3825) is free Tuesday.

Also free is the **Beatles Museum** (498 Seymour St., tel. 604/685–8841), with memorabilia from the early years of the Fab Four.

Learn about one important aspect of the history of Vancouver at the **B.C. Sugar Museum** (123 Rogers St., tel. 604/253–1131).

What to See and Do with Children

Stanley Park Zoo (*see* Tour 2: Stanley Park, above).

The **miniature steam train** in Stanley Park, just five minutes northwest of the aquarium, is a big hit with children as it chugs through the forest.

Splashdown Park (Hwy. 17, just before the Tsawwassen Ferry causeway, tel. 604/943–2251), 38 kilometers (24 miles) outside

Vancouver, is a giant water-slide park with 11 slides (for toddlers to adults), heated water, picnic tables, and minigolf.

Richmond Nature Park (No. 5 Rd. exit from Hwy. 99, tel. 604/273–7015), with its displays and games in the Nature House, is geared toward children. Guides answer questions and give tours. Since the park sits on a natural bog, rubber boots are recommended if it's been wet, but a boardwalk around the duck pond makes some of the park accessible to strollers and wheelchairs.

Maplewood Farms (405 Seymour River Pl., tel. 604/929–5610), a 20-minute drive from downtown Vancouver, is set up like a small farm, with all the barnyard animals for children to see and pet. Cows are milked every day at 1:15.

Kids Only Market (*see* Tour 3: Granville Island, above).

The Planetarium (1100 Chestnut St., tel. 604/736–3656), on the same site as the Vancouver Museum in Vanier Park, has astronomy shows each afternoon and evening, and laser rock music shows later in the night.

Science World (*see* Other Museums, above)

Off the Beaten Track

On the North Shore you can get a taste of the mountains and test your mettle at the **Lynn Canyon Suspension Bridge** (Lynn Headwaters Regional Park, North Vancouver, tel. 604/987–5922), which hangs 240 feet above Lynn Creek. Also on the North Shore is the **Capilano Fish Hatchery** (4500 Capilano Rd., tel. 604/987–1411), with exhibits about salmon.

If the sky is clear, the telescope at the **Gordon Southam Observatory** (1100 Chestnut St., in Vanier Park, tel. 604/738–2855) will be focused on whatever stars or planets are worth watching that night. While you're there, visit the planetarium on the site.

Shopping

Unlike many cities where suburban malls have taken over, Vancouver's downtown area is still lined with individual boutiques and specialty shops. Stores tend to be open every day and on Thursday and Friday nights.

Shopping Districts

The immense **Pacific Center Mall,** in the heart of downtown, connects Eaton's and The Bay department stores, which stand at opposite corners of Georgia and Granville streets. Pacific Center is on two levels and is mostly underground.

A new commercial center is developing around **Sinclair Center** (*see* Tour 1, above), which caters to sophisticated and upscale tastes.

On the opposite side of Pacific Center, stretching from Burrard to Bute streets, is **Robson Street**—the place for fashion-conscious clothing. Chockablock with small stores and cafés, it is Vancouver's liveliest street and provides many excellent corners for people-watching.

Two other shopping districts, one on **West 41st Avenue,** between West Boulevard and Larch Street, in Kerrisdale, and the other on **West 10th** from Discovery Street west, are both in up-scale neighborhoods and have quality shops and restaurants.

Fourth Avenue, from Burrard to Balsam streets, offers an eclectic mix of stores (from sophisticated women's clothing to surfboards and Jams), with an emphasis on sports shops.

In addition to the Pacific Center Mall, **Oakridge Shopping Center** at Cambie Street and 41st Avenue has chic, expensive stores that are fun to browse.

Ethnic Districts **Chinatown** (*see* Tour 1, above)—centered around Pender and Main streets—is an exciting and animated place for restaurants, exotic foodstuffs, and distinctive architecture.

Commercial Drive (around East 1st Avenue) is the heart of the **Italian community,** here called Little Italy. You can sip cappuccino in coffee bars where you may be the only one speaking English, buy sun-dried tomatoes, real Parmesan, or a home espresso machine.

The **East Indian shopping district** is on Main Street around 50th Avenue. Curry houses, sweet shops, grocery stores, and sari shops abound.

A small **Japantown** on Powell Street at Dunlevy Street is made up of grocery stores, fish stores, and a few restaurants.

Department Stores

The two biggest department stores in Vancouver, **Eaton's** and **The Bay,** are Canadian owned and located downtown and at most malls. The third, **Woodward's,** is a local chain and is found only in British Columbia and Alberta. The flagship store is in the Oakridge Shopping Center.

Flea Markets

A huge flea market (703 Terminal Ave., tel. 604/685–0666), with more than 300 stalls, is held Saturday, Sunday, and holidays from 8–4. This is easily accessible from downtown via SkyTrain.

Auctions

On Wednesday at noon and 7 PM, auctions are held at **Love's** (1635 W. Broadway, tel. 604/733–1157). **Maynard's** (415 W. 2nd Ave., tel. 604/876–6787) also has home furnishings auctions on Wednesday at 7 PM. Phone for times of art and antiques auctions.

Specialty Stores

Antiques A stretch of antiques stores runs along Main Street from 20th to 35th avenues. On 10th Avenue near Alma are a few antiques stores that specialize in Canadiana, including **Folkart Interiors** (3715 W. 10th Ave.), **Old Country Mouse Factory** (3720 W. 10th Ave.), and **Canada West** (3790 W. 10th Ave.). For very refined antiques, see **Artemis** (321 Water St.) in Gastown. For Oriental rugs, go to Granville Street between 7th and 14th avenues.

Art Galleries There are many private galleries throughout Vancouver. The best of them are: **Bau-Xi** (3045 Granville St., tel. 604/733–7011); **Buschlen-Mowatt** (1445 W. Georgia St., tel. 604/682–1234); **Diane Farris** (1565 W. 7th Ave., tel. 604/737–2629), **Equinox** (2321 Granville St., tel. 604/736–2405); and the **Heffel Gallery** (2247 Granville St., tel. 604/732–6505).

Books The best general bookstores are **Duthie's**, located downtown (919 Robson St.) and near the university (4444 W. 10th Ave.), and **Blackberry Books** (1663 Duranleau St.) on Granville Island.

Specialty bookstores include: **Banyen Books** (2671 Broadway) and **Banyen Sound** (2669 W. Broadway) for New Age books and cassettes, **The Travel Bug** (2667 W. Broadway) and **World Wide Books and Maps** (736 Granville St., downstairs) for travel books, **Vancouver Kidsbooks** (3083 W. Broadway), **Pink Peppercorn** (2686 W. Broadway) for cookbooks, **William McCarley** (213 Carrall St.) for design and architecture, **Graffiti Books** (3514 W. 4th Ave.) for visual and performing arts, **Manhattan Books** (1089 Robson St.) for books and magazines in French, **Siliconnections** (3727 W. 10th Ave.) for computer books, **Sophia** (725 Nelson St.) for books on the Orient, and **White Dwarf** (4374 W. 10th Ave.) for science fiction.

Most of the secondhand and antiquarian dealers such as **William Hoffer** (60 Powell St.) and **Colophon Books** (407 W. Cordova St., upstairs), are in the Gastown area. A block or two away are **McLeod's** (455 W. Pender St.), **Ainsworth's** (321 W. Pender St.), and **Bond's** (319 W. Hastings St.).

Children's Stores An unusual children's store worth checking out is **The Imagination Market** (528 Powell St.), an oddball warehouse-type store selling recycled industrial goods for arts and crafts materials. Here you can find barrels of metallic plastic, feathers, fluorescent-colored paper, buttons, bits of Plexiglas, and other materials by the bagful, which children can then use at a free drop-in workshop. **Einstein's** (4424 Dunbar St.) sells toys, games, crafts, and books relating to science. **Vancouver Kidsbooks** (3083 W. Broadway) has a huge selection of books and tapes.

Clothing

Men Several quality men's clothing stores are in the business district: **Edward Chapman** (833 W. Pender St.) has conservative looks; **E.A. Lee** (466 Howe St.) is stylish; **Leone** (757 W. Hastings St.) is ultra-chic; and **Polo Country** (375 Water St.) offers a casual line of Ralph Lauren.

A few blocks away, at Pacific Center, are **Harry Rosen** and **Holt Renfrew**, both on the upper level. If your tastes are traditional, don't miss **George Straith** (900 W. Georgia St.) in the Hotel Vancouver.

On Robson Street, a more trendy shopping area, are **Ralph Lauren** (No. 1123) and **Club Monaco** (No. 1153), for casual wear.

Outside downtown Vancouver there are two men's boutiques selling Italian imports: **Mondo Uomo** (2709 Granville St.) and **Boboli** (2776 Granville St.).

In Kerrisdale, two excellent men's clothing stores are **Finn's** (2159 W. 41st Ave.) and, across the street, **S. Lampman** (2126 W. 41st Ave.).

Women For women's fashions, visit **E.A. Lee** (466 Howe St.), **Wear Else?** (789 W. Pender St.), **Leone** (757 W. Hastings St.), and the more conservative **Chapy's** (833 W. Pender St.), all in the business district. Nearby is the casual **Polo Country** (375 Water St.).

On Robson Street, look for **Margareta** (No. 948), **Ralph Lauren** (No. 1123), **Alfred Sung** (No. 1143), **Club Monaco** (No. 1153), and a lingerie shop, **La Vie en Rose** (No. 1001). For shoes, try **Aldo** (No. 1016), **Pegabo** (No. 1137), and **Stephane de Raucourt** (No. 1024). Off Robson is **Morgan** (813 Hornby St.).

Two expensive and very stylish import stores in South Granville are: **Boboli** (2776 Granville St.) and **Bacci** (2778 Granville St.). Nearby, one of the largest and best shoe stores in town is **Freedman Shoes** (2867 Granville St.).

On the west side **Enda B.** (4325 W. 10th Ave.) and **Wear Else?** (2360 W. 4th Ave.) are the largest and best stores for high-quality fashions, but there's also **Bali Bali** for the more exotic (4462 W. 10th Ave.) and **Zig Zag** (4424 W. 10th Ave.) for fashion accessories.

Gifts Want something special to take home from British Columbia? The best places for quality souvenirs are the **Vancouver Art Gallery** (750 Hornby St.) and the **Clamshell Gift Shop** at the aquarium in Stanley Park. The **Salmon Shop** in the Granville Island Public Market will wrap smoked salmon for travel. Downtown, Haida and Salish Indian art is available at **Images for a Canadian Heritage** (779 Burrard St.). Near Granville Island is **Leona Lattimer** (1590 W. 2nd Ave.), where the inside of her shop is built like an Indian longhouse and is full of Indian arts and crafts ranging from cheap to priceless.

Records If you're shopping for classical music, try **A&B Sound** (556 Seymour St., upstairs) and **Sikora's Classical Records** (432 W. Hastings St.). For jazz, blues, and folk go to **Black Swan** (2936 W. 4th Ave.) and for rock, try **A&B Sound** and **Zulu** (1869 W. 4th Ave.).

Sports and Outdoor Activities

Participant Sports

Biking **Stanley Park** (see Tour 2 in Exploring Vancouver, above) is the most popular spot for family cycling. Rentals are available here from **Bayshore Bicycles** (1876 Georgia St., tel. 604/688–2453) or around the corner at **Stanley Park Rentals** (676 Chilco St., tel. 604/681–5581).

Another biking route is along the north or south shore of **False Creek.** Rent bikes at **Reckless Rider** (1840 Fir St., tel. 604/736–1605), near Granville Island.

Fishing You can fish for salmon all year in coastal British Columbia **Sewell's Landing Marina** (6695 Nelson St., Horseshoe Bay, tel. 604/921–7461) organizes a daily four-hour trip on Howe Sound or has hourly rates on U-drives. **Westin Bayshore Yacht Charters** (1601 W. Georgia St., tel. 604/682–3377) has a daily five-hour fishing trip; boats are moored five minutes from downtown Vancouver. **Tymac Charters** (north foot of Main St., tel. 604/681–4152) arranges charters or boat shares and supplies all gear.

Golf Lower Mainland golf courses are open all year. **Fraserview Golf Course** (tel. 604/327–3717), a spacious course with fairways well defined by hills and mature conifers and deciduous trees, is the busiest course in the country. Fraserview is also the most central, about 20 minutes from downtown. **Seymour Golf and Country Club** (tel. 604/929–2611), on the south side of Mt. Seymour, on the North Shore, is a semiprivate club that is open to the public on Monday and Friday. One of the finest public courses in the country is **Peace Portal** (tel. 604/531–4444), near White Rock, a 45-minute drive from downtown.

Health and Fitness Clubs Both the **YMCA** (955 Burrard St., tel. 604/681–0221) and the **YWCA** (580 Burrard St., tel. 604/683–2531) downtown have drop-in rates that let you participate in all activities for the day. Both have pools, weight rooms, and fitness classes; the YMCA has racquetball, squash, and handball courts. Two other recommended clubs are: **Chancery Squash Club** (202–865 Hornby St., tel. 604/682–3752) and **Tower Courts Racquet and Fitness Club** (1055 Dunsmuir St., lower level, tel. 604/689–4424), both with racquet courts, weight rooms, and aerobics.

Hiking **Pacific Spirit Park** is a 1,000-acre wilderness park, with 30 miles of hiking trails (*see* Parks and Gardens, below).

The **Capilano Regional Park,** (*see* Off the Beaten Track, in Exploring Vancouver, above), on the North Shore, provides a scenic hike.

Jogging The seawall around **Stanley Park** (*see* Tour 2 in Exploring Vancouver, above), is 9 kilometers (4 miles) and gives an excellent minitour of the city. A shorter run of 4 kilometers (2½ miles) in the park is around **Lost Lagoon.**

Skiing
Cross-Country The best cross-country skiing is at **Hollyburn Ridge** in Cypress Park (tel. 604/925–2704).

Downhill Vancouver is two hours away from **Whistler/Blackcomb** (Whistler Resort Association, tel. 604/685–3650; snow report, tel. 604/687–7507), one of the top ski spots in North America. (*See* Excursion 1: Whistler, below.)

There are three ski areas on the North Shore mountains, close to Vancouver, with night skiing. The snow is not as good as at Whistler and runs are generally used by novice, junior, and family skiers or those who want a quick ski after work. **Cypress Park** (tel. 604/926–6007; snow report, tel. 604/926–5612) has the most and the longest runs; **Grouse Mountain** (tel. 604/986–6262; snow report, tel. 604/980–9311) has extensive night skiing, restaurants, and bars; and **Mt. Seymour** (tel. 604/986–3444; snow report, tel. 604/986–2261) is the highest in the area, so the snow is a little better.

Water Sports
Kayaking Rent a kayak from **Ecomarine** (tel. 604/689–7575) on Granville Island (*see* Tour 3 in Exploring Vancouver, above).

Rafting The Thompson, the Chilliwack, and the Fraser are the principal rafting rivers in southwestern British Columbia. The Fraser River has whirlpools and big waves, but for frothing white water, try the Thompson and Chilliwack rivers. Trips range from three hours to several days. Some well-qualified outfitters who lead trips are: **Kumsheen** (Lytton, tel. 604/455–2296; in B.C., tel. 800/482–2269), **Hyak** (Vancouver, tel. 604/734–8622), and **Canadian River Expeditions** (Vancouver, tel. 604/736–9366).

Sailing Several charter companies offer a cruise-and-learn vacation, usually to the Gulf Islands. The five-day trip is a crash course teaching the ins and outs of sailing. The **Jib Set** (Granville Island, tel. 604/689–1477), **Sea Wing** (Granville Island, tel. 604/669–0840), **Pacific Quest** (Granville Island, tel. 604/682–2205), or **Blue Orca** (Granville Island, tel. 604/683–6300) offer this package.

Windsurfing Rental shops clustered on the west side of town include: **Surf City** (420 W. 1st Ave., tel. 604/872–8585), **The Windsurfing Shop** (1793 W. 4th Ave., tel. 604/734–7245), and at **Windsure** (Jericho Beach, tel. 604/224–0615). Boards can also be rented at **Jericho Beach** or **English Bay Beach** (Davie and Denman Sts.).

Spectator Sports

The **Vancouver Canucks** (tel. 604/254–5141) of the National Hockey League play in the Coliseum October–April. The **Canadians** (tel. 604/872–5232) play baseball in an old-time outdoor stadium in the Pacific Coast League. Their season runs April–September. The **B.C. Lions** (tel. 604/681–5466) football team scrimmage at the B.C. Place Stadium downtown June–November. Tickets are available from Ticketmaster (tel. 604/280–4444).

Beaches

An almost continuous string of beaches runs from Stanley Park to the University of British Columbia. Children and hardy swimmers can take the cool water but most others prefer to sunbathe; these beaches are sandy with grassy areas running alongside. Note that liquor is prohibited in parks and on beaches. For information on beaches, call the **Parks Department of the City of Vancouver** (tel. 604/681–1141).

Kitsilano Beach. Kits Beach, with a lifeguard, is the busiest of them all—transistor radios, volleyball games, and sleek young bodies are ever-present. The part of the beach nearest the Maritime Museum is the quietest. Facilities include a playground, tennis courts, heated saltwater pool (good for serious swimmers to toddlers), concession stands, and many nearby restaurants to cafés.

Point Grey Beaches. Jericho, Locarno, and Spanish Banks begin at the end of Point Grey Road. This string of beaches has a huge expanse of sand, especially in the summer and at low tide. The shallow water here is warmed slightly by the sun and the sand and so is best for swimming. Farther out, toward Spanish Banks, you'll find the beach becomes less crowded, but the last concession stand and washrooms are at Locarno. If you keep walking along the beach just past Point Grey, you'll hit Wreck Beach, Vancouver's nude beach. It is also accessible from Marine Drive at the university but there is a fairly steep climb from the beach to the road.

West End Beaches. Second Beach and Third Beach, along Beach Drive in Stanley Park, are large family beaches. Second Beach has a guarded saltwater pool. Both have concession stands and washrooms. Farther along Beach Drive, at the foot of Jervis Street, is Sunset Beach, a surprisingly quiet beach considering the location. A lifeguard is on duty, but there are no facilities.

Parks and Gardens

Dr. Sun Yat-sen Classical Chinese Garden (*see* Tour 1 in Exploring Vancouver, above).

Nitobe Garden is a small (2.4-acre) garden that is considered the most authentic Japanese garden outside Japan. The circular path around the park symbolizes the cycle of life and provides a tranquil view from every direction. In April and May cherry blossoms are the highlight, and in June the irises are magnificent. *1903 West Mall, Univ. of B.C., tel. 604/228–4208. Admission: $1 adults, 50¢ senior citizens and students, free Wed. and every day Oct. 11–Mar. 17. Open daily 10–dusk; phone for specific closing times.*

Pacific Spirit Park (W. 16th Ave., tel. 604/432–6350) is a 1,000-acre park that is bigger and more rugged than Stanley Park. Pacific Spirit's only amenities are 30 miles of trails, a few washrooms, and a couple of signboard maps. Go for a wonderful walk in the west coast woods—it's hard to believe that you are only 15 minutes from downtown Vancouver.

Queen Elizabeth Park has lavish gardens and lots of grassy picnicking spots. Illuminated fountains; the botanical Bloedel Conservatory, with tropical and desert zones and 20 species of free-flying tropical birds; and other facilities including 20 tennis courts, lawn bowling, pitch and putt, and a restaurant are on the grounds. *Cambie St. and 25th Ave., tel. 604/872–5513. Admission to conservatory: $2.30 adults, $1.15 senior citizens, $1.05 students, $4.60 family ticket. Open May–Sept., daily 10–9; Oct.–Apr., daily 10–5.*

Stanley Park (*see* Tour 2 in Exploring Vancouver, above).

Van Dusen Botanical Garden was a 55-acre golf course, but is now the grounds of one of the largest collections of ornamental plants in Canada. Native and exotic plant displays include the shrubbery maze and the rhododendrons in May and June. *5251 Oak St. at 37th Ave., tel. 604/266–7194. Admission: $3.75 adults, $2 senior citizens and youths (13–18), $7.75 family ticket. Open 10–dusk.*

Dining

by Eve Johnson

Eve Johnson writes about food and restaurants for the Vancouver Sun.

Among other allures, experiencing Vancouver's diverse gastronomical pleasures makes a visit to the city worthwhile. Restaurants appear throughout Vancouver—from the bustling downtown area to trendy beach-side neighborhoods—making the diversity of the establishment's surroundings as enticing as the succulent cuisine they serve. A new wave of Chinese immigration and Japanese tourism has brought a proliferation of upscale Chinese and Japanese restaurants, offering dishes that would be at home in their own leading cities. Restaurants featuring Pacific Northwest fare—including homegrown regional favorites such as salmon, accompanied by British Columbia and Washington state wines—have become some of the city's leading attractions.

Highly recommended restaurants in each price category are indicated by a star ★.

Category	*Cost
Very Expensive	over $41
Expensive	$31—$40
Moderate	$21—$30
Inexpensive	under $20

**per person, including appetizer, entree and dessert; excluding drinks, service, and sales tax*

American

Isadora's. Not only does Isadora's offer good coffee, a menu that ranges from samosas to lox and bagels, and children's specials, but there is also an inside play area packed with toys, and restrooms with changing tables accommodate families. In the summer, the restaurant opens onto Granville Island's waterpark, so kids can entertain themselves. Service can be slow, but Isadora's staff is friendly. *1540 Old Bridge St., Granville Island, tel.604/681–8816. Reservations required for 6 or more. Dress: casual. Closed dinner Mon. Sept–May. MC, V. Inexpensive.*

Nazarre BBQ Chicken. The best barbecued chicken in several hundred miles comes from this funky storefront on Commercial Drive. Owner Gerry Moutal massages his chickens for tenderness before he puts them on the rotisserie, then bastes them in a mixture of rum and spices. Chicken comes with roasted potatoes and a choice of mild, hot, extra hot, or hot garlic sauce. You can eat in, at one of four rickety tables, or take out. *1408 Commercial Dr., tel. 604/251–1844. No reservations. Dress: casual. No credit cards. Inexpensive.*

Cambodian/ Vietnamese

Phnom Penh Restaurant. A block away from the bustle of Keefer Street, the Phnom Penh is part of a small cluster of Southeast Asian shops on the fringes of Chinatown. Simple, pleasant decor abounds: arborite tables, potted plants, and framed views of Ankor Wat on the walls. Hospitable staff serves unusually robust Vietnamese fare including crisp, peppery garlic prawns fried in their shell and slices of beef crusted with ground salt and pepper mixed in the warm beef salad. *244 E. Georgia St., tel. 604/682–5777. No reservations for lunch; advised for dinner. Dress: casual. MC, V. Closed Tues. Inexpensive.*

Chinese

★ **Kirin Mandarin Restaurant.** Kirin, located two blocks from most of the major downtown hotels, presents attentively served Chinese food in posh, elegant surroundings. Live fish tanks set into the slate green walls remind one of aquariums displayed in a lavishly decorated home. Drawn from a smattering of northern Chinese cuisines, dishes include Shanghai-style smoked eel, Peking duck, and Szechuan hot-and-spicy scallops. *1166 Alberni St., tel. 604/682–8833. Reservations advised. Dress: neat but casual. AE, MC, V. Closed for 2 days, 15 days after Chinese New Year. Moderate.*

★ **The Pink Pearl.** In the world of Cantonese restaurants, biggest may very well be best: This 650-seat restaurant certainly wins the prize in this city. The huge, noisy room features tanks of live seafood—crab, shrimp, geoduck, oysters, abalone, rock cod, lobsters, and scallops. Menu highlights include clams in

Downtown Vancouver Dining

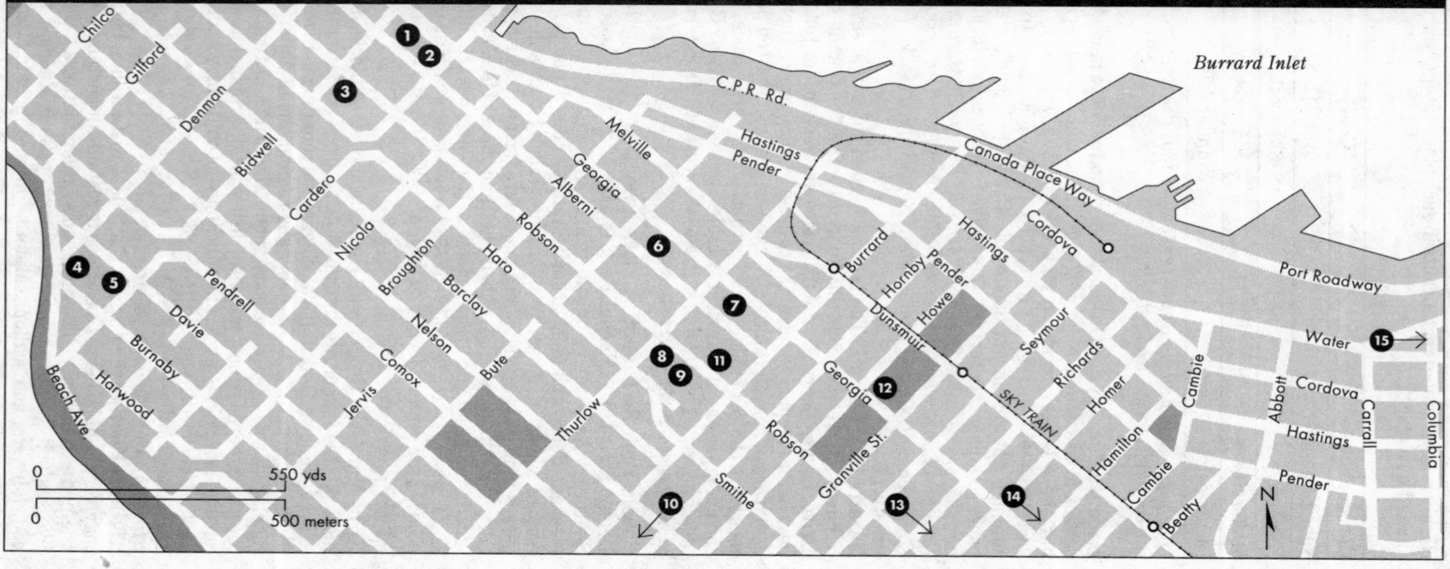

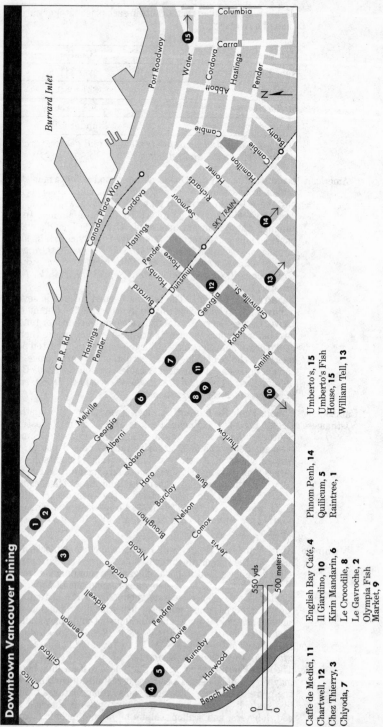

Caffe de Medici, **11**
Chartwell, **12**
Chez Thierry, **3**
Chiyoda, **7**
English Bay Café, **4**
Il Giardino, **10**
Kirin Mandarin, **6**
Le Crocodile, **8**
Le Gavroche, **2**
Olympia Fish Market, **9**
Phnom Penh, **14**
Quilicum, **5**
Raintree, **1**
Umberto's, **15**
Umberto's Fish House, **15**
William Tell, **13**

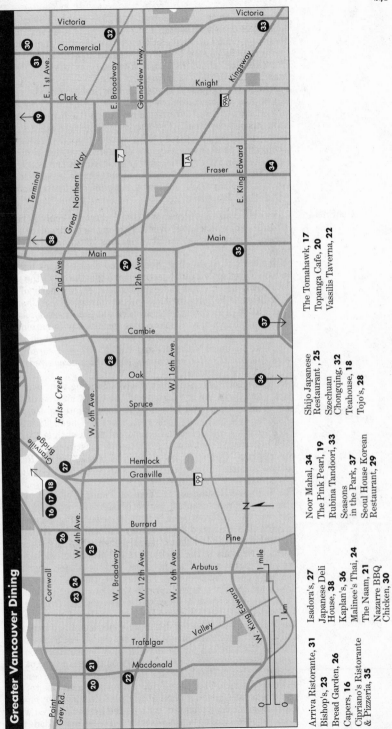

Greater Vancouver Dining

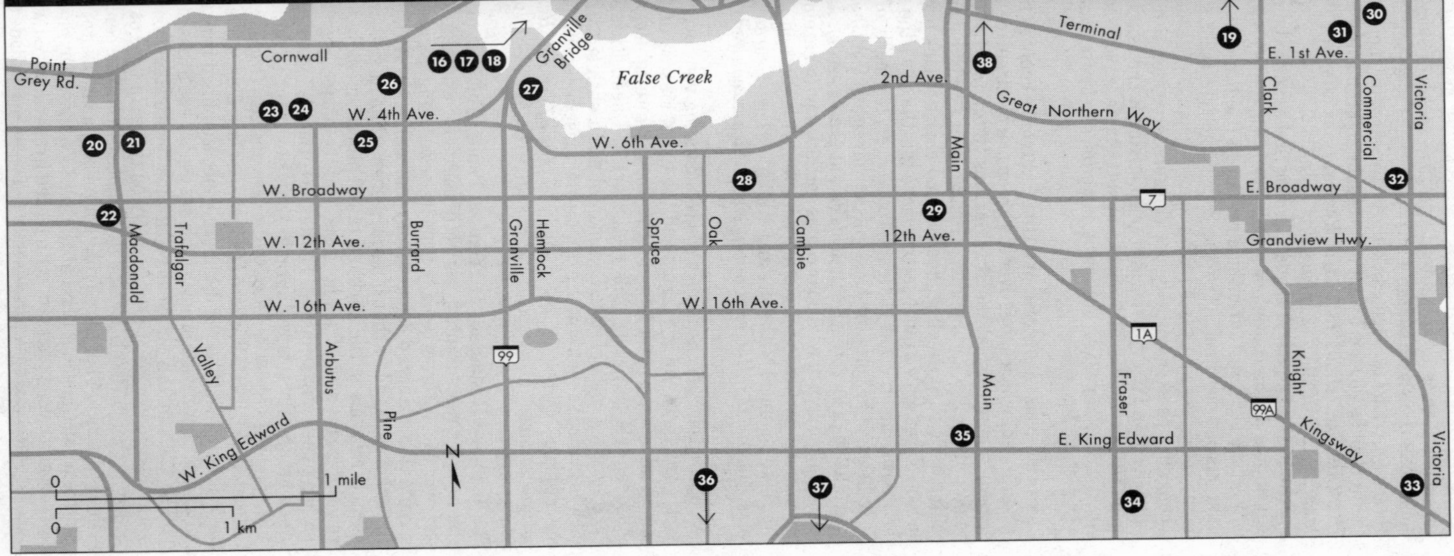

Arriva Ristorante, **31**
Bishop's, **23**
Bread Garden, **26**
Capers, **16**
Cipriano's Ristorante & Pizzeria, **35**
Isadora's, **27**
Japanese Deli House, **38**
Kaplan's, **36**
Malinee's Thai, **24**
The Naam, **21**
Nazarre BBQ Chicken, **30**
Noor Mahal, **34**
The Pink Pearl, **19**
Rubina Tandoori, **33**
Seasons in the Park, **37**
Seoul House Korean Restaurant, **29**
Shijo Japanese Restaurant , **25**
Szechuan Chongqing, **32**
Teahouse, **18**
Tojo's, **28**
The Tomahawk, **17**
Topanga Cafe, **20**
Vassilis Taverna, **22**

black bean sauce, crab sautéed with five spices (a spicy dish sometimes translated as crab with peppery salt), and Pink Pearl's version of crispy-skinned chicken. Arrive early for dim sum on the weekend if you don't want to be caught in the lineup. *1132 E. Hastings St., tel.604/253–4316. Reservations advised. Dress: casual. AE, MC, V. Inexpensive.*

★ **Szechuan Chongqing.** Although fancier Szechuan restaurants can be found, the continued popularity of this unpretentious white tablecloth restaurant in a revamped fried chicken franchise speaks for itself. Try the Szechuan-style fried green beans, steamed and tossed with spiced ground pork or the Chongqing chicken—a boneless chicken served on a bed of spinach cooked in dry heat until crisp, giving it the texture of dried seaweed and a salty, rich, and nutty taste. *2495 Victoria Dr., tel. 604/254–7434. Reservations advised. Dress: casual. AE, MC, V. Inexpensive.*

Continental

★ **Chartwell.** Named after Sir Winston Churchill's country home (a painting of which hangs over the green marble fireplace), the flagship dining room at the Four Seasons Hotel, (*see* Lodging, below), looks like an upperclass British men's club. Floor-to-ceiling dark wood paneling, deep leather chairs to sink back in and sip claret, plus a quiet setting make this the city's top spot for a power lunch. Chef Wolfgang von Weiser, (formerly of the Four Seasons in Toronto) cooks robust, inventive Continental food (although less creative than his recent predecessor). A salad of smoked loin of wild boar comes sprinkled with hazelnuts; the seafood pot au feu is served with fennel bread and aioli. Conclude the meal with Port and stilton. *791 W. Georgia St., tel. 604/689–9333. Reservations advised. Jacket required. AE, DC, MC, V. Expensive.*

Seasons in the Park. Seasons has a commanding view over the park gardens to the city lights and the mountains beyond. A comfortable room with lots of light wood, white tablecloths, and deep-pile carpeting, this restaurant in Queen Elizabeth Park serves a conservative Continental menu with standards such as grilled salmon with fresh mint and roast duck with Bing cherry sauce. *Queen Elizabeth Park, tel. 604/874–8008. Reservations advised. Dress: neat but casual. AE, MC, V. Closed Christmas Day. Expensive.*

★ **The Teahouse Restaurant at Ferguson Point.** The best of the Stanley Park restaurants is perfectly poised for watching sunsets over the water, especially from its newer wing, a glassed-in room that conveys a conservatory-like ambience. Although the teahouse has a less than innovative menu than its sister restaurant, Seasons in the Park, certain features, including the cream of carrot soup, duck in cassis, and the perfectly grilled fish don't need any meddling. For dessert, there's baked Alaska—a natural for this restaurant. *Ferguson Point in Stanley Park, tel. 604/669–3281. Reservations required. Dress: neat but casual. AE, MC, V. Closed Christmas Day. Expensive.*

The William Tell. Silver underliners, embossed linen napkins, and a silver flower vase on each table set the tone of Swiss luxury. The William Tell's 20-year reputation for excellent Continental food continues at new quarters on the main floor of the Georgian Court Hotel, located 10-minutes from the central business district. Chef Lars Trolle Jorgenson, a member of the gold-medalist Canadian team at the 1988 Culinary Olympics, offers locally raised pheasant with glazed grapes and red wine sauce, sauteed veal sweetbreads with red onion marmalade and marsala sauce, as well as the Swiss specialty *Buendnerfleisch* (paper-thin slices of air-dried beef). Professional and discreet service contribute to the restaurant's excellence. *765 Beatty St., tel. 604/688–3504 Reservations advised. Jacket required at dinner. AE, DC, MC, V. Expensive.*

English Bay Café. Downstairs, the English Bay Café is a noisy tapas bistro serving nachos, crabcakes, and other grazing food. Upstairs, in the more serious dining room, you'll find the chef's fondness for venison and racks of lamb. Regardless of the level, however, when you look out the windows, it's all the same: with English Bay just two lanes of traffic away, you're guaranteed a glorious view of the sunset. Both bars are substantial; the bistro offers a large choice of imported beers, while the upstairs features jalapeno-pepper martinis. Valet parking is available and well worth the money. *1795 Beach Ave., tel. 604/669–2225. Reservations required. Dress: casual downstairs; neat but casual upstairs. AE, DC, MC, V. Moderate.*

Deli/Bakery

The Bread Garden Bakery, Café & Espresso Bar. What began as a croissant bakery has taken over two neighboring stores, and is now the ultimate Kitsilano 24-hour hangout. Salads, smoked salmon pizzas, quiches, elaborate cakes and pies, giant muffins, and cappuccino bring a steady stream of the young and fashionable. The Bread Garden to Go, next door, serves over-the-counter, but you may still be subjected to an irritatingly long wait in line; things just don't happen fast here. *1880 W. 1st Ave., tel. 604/ 738–6684. No reservations. Dress: casual. DC, MC, V. Inexpensive.*

★ **Kaplan's Deli, Restaurant and Bakery.** Tucked into a mini-mall on Oak Street (the road that leads to the Tsawwassen ferries and Seattle), Kaplan's is the traveler's last chance for authentic Jewish deli food before boarding. Eat in at booths, or take your chopped liver, chopped herring, lox, and home-made corned beef with you. The bakery makes justly famous cinnamon buns. *5775 Oak St., tel. 604/263–2625. No reservations. Dress: casual. MC, V. Closed Jewish holidays. Inexpensive.*

East Indian

★ **Rubina Tandoori.** If one must single out the best East Indian food in the city, then Rubina Tandoori, 20 minutes from downtown, ranks as a top contender. The large menu spans most of the sub-continent's cuisines, and the especially popular *chevda* (East Indian salty snack,) gets shipped to fans all over North America. Maitre d' Shaffeen Jamal has a phenomenal memory for faces who frequent the restaurant. Non-smokers get the smaller, funkier back room with the paintings of coupling gods and goddesses; smokers get the big, upholstered banquettes in the new room. *1962 Kingsway, tel. 604/874–3621. Reservations advised on weekends. Dress: casual. AE, MC, V. Closed lunch Sun. Moderate.*

Noor Mahal. The only Lower Mainland restaurant that specializes in South Indian food, the Noor Mahal provides good-size portions at a reasonable price in authentic surroundings. The pink walls help to create the light and airy decor. Try a *dosa* for lunch: a lacy pancake made from bean, rice, and semolina flour, stuffed with curried potatoes, shrimp, or chicken. Owners Susan and Paul Singh double as staff so service can be slow and harried during busy periods. *4354 Fraser St., tel. 604/873–9263. Reservations advised on weekends. Dress: casual. AE, MC, V. Closed lunch Mon. and Tues. Inexpensive.*

French

★ **Le Gavroche.** Time has stood still in this charming turn-of-the-century house, where a woman dining with a man will be offered a menu without prices. Featuring classic French cooking, lightened—but by no means reduced—to nouvelle cuisine, Le Gavroche's menu also includes simple listings such as smoked salmon with blinis and sour cream. Other options may be as complex as smoked pheasant breast on a puree of celeriac, shallots, and wine with a light truffle sauce. The excellent wine list stresses Bordeaux. Tables by the front window promise mountains and water views. *1616 Alberni St., tel. 604/685–3924. Reservations advised on weekends. Jacket and tie advised. AE, DC, MC, V. Closed Dec. 24–Jan. 1. Expensive.*

Chez Thierry. This cozy bistro on the Stanley Park end of Robson Street adds pizzazz to a celebration: Owner Thierry Damilano stylishly slashes champagne corks with a sword on request. The country-style French cooking emphasizes seafood. Try watercress and smoked salmon salad; fresh tuna grilled with artichokes, garlic, and tomatoes; and apple tarte Tatin for dessert. During the week the intimate dining room promises a relaxing meal; on the weekend, however, with every one of the 16 tables jammed, the restaurant gets noisy. *1674 Robson St., tel. 604/688–0919. Reservations required on weekends. Dress: casual. AE, DC, MC, V. Closed lunch; Dec. 24–26. Moderate.*

★ **Le Crocodile.** Why do people want to sit packed tighter than sardines in this tiny bistro? Because chef Michael Jacob serves extremely well-cooked simple food at very moderate prices. His Alsatian background shines with the caramelly, sweet onion tart. Anything that involves innards is superb, and even old standards such as duck a l'orange are worth ordering here. The one flaw? A small, over-priced wine list. *818 Thurlow St., tel. 604/669–4298. Reservations required. Jacket advised. AE, MC, V. Closed lunch; Sat., Sun. Moderate.*

Greek

Vassilis Taverna. The menu in this family-run restaurant, located in the heart of the city's small Greek community, is almost as conventional as the decor: checked tablecloths and mandatory paintings of white fishing villages and the blue Aegean Sea. At Vassilis, though, even menu standards become memorable due to the flawless preparation. The house specialty is a deceptively simple *kotopoulo*, (a half-chicken, pounded flat, herbed, and charbroiled); the lamb fricassee with artichoke hearts and broad beans in an egg-lemon sauce is more complicated, though not necessarily better. Save room for a *navarino*, a creamy custard square topped with whipped cream and ground nuts. *2884 W. Broadway, tel. 604/733–3231. Reservations advised on weekends. Dress: casual. AE, DC, MC, V. Closed lunch Mon.; Sat. and Sun. Moderate.*

Health Food

Capers. Hidden in the back of the most lavishly handsome health food store in the Lower Mainland, Capers (open for breakfast, lunch, and dinner), drips with earth-mother chic: wood tables, potted plants, and heady smells from the store's bakery. Breakfast starts weekdays at 7, weekends at 8. Eggs and bacon? Sure, but Capers serves free-range eggs, and bacon without additives. Feather-light blueberry pancakes, crammed with berries star here. The view of the water compensates for service that can be slow and forgetful. *2496 Marine Dr., W. Vancouver, tel. 604/925–3316. No reservations. Dress: casual. MC, V. Inexpensive.*

★ **The Naam Restaurant.** Vancouver's oldest alternative restaurant is now open 24 hours, so those needing to satisfy a late-night tofu burger attack, rest easy. The Naam has left its caffeine-and-alcohol-free days behind, and now serves wine, beer, cappuccinos, and wicked chocolate desserts, along with the vegetarian stir-fries. Wood tables and kitchen chairs make for a homey atmosphere. On warm summer evenings, the outdoor courtyard at the back of the restaurant welcomes diners. *2724 W. 4th Ave., tel. 604/738–7151. Reservations required for 6 or more. Dress: casual. MC, V. Inexpensive.*

Italian

★ **Caffe de Medici.** It takes shifting gears as you leave the stark concrete walls of the Robson Galleria behind and step into this elegant restaurant with its ornate moulded ceilings, rich green velvet curtains and chair coverings, and portraits of the Medici family. But after a little wine, an evening's exposure to courtly waiters, and a superb meal, you may begin to wish the outside world conformed more closely to this peaceful environment. Although an enticing antipasto table sits in the center of the room, consider the *Bresaola* (air-dried beef marinated in olive oil, lemon, and pepper) as a worthwhile appetizer. Try the rack of lamb in a mint, mustard, and Martini & Rossi sauce. Any of the pastas is a safe bet. *1025 Robson St., tel. 604/669–9322. Reservations advised. Jacket advised. AE, DC, MC, V. Closed lunch Sat. and Sun. Expensive.*

Il Giardino di Umberto, Umberto's, Umberto's Fish House. First came Umberto's, a Florentine restaurant serving classic northern Italian food, installed in a century-old Vancouver home at the foot of Hornby Street. Then, next door, Umberto Menghi built Il Giardino, a sunny, light-splashed restaurant styled after a Tuscan house. This restaurant features braided breast of pheasant with polenta and reindeer filet with crushed peppercorn sauce. Finally up went Umberto's Fish House, on the other side of the original bright yellow house. Where Il Giardino attracts a regular young, moneyed crowd, Umberto's is more quiet and sedate. Umberto's Fish House, a flower-filled room with tile floors, is a top contender for having the best seafood in the city. Fish is treated either Italian style—rainbow trout grilled and served with sun-dried tomatoes, black olives, and pinenuts—or with a taste of the far east, as in yellow-fin tuna grilled with wasabi butter. *Il Giardino, 1382 Hornby St., tel. 604/687–2422. Umberto's, 1380 Hornby St., tel. 604/687–6316. Umberto's Fish House, 1376 Hornby St., tel. 604/ 687–6621. Reservations advised. Dress: neat but casual. AE, DC, MC, V. Closed lunch and Sun. (except Il Gardino). Moderate–Expensive.*

Arriva Ristorante. Commercial Drive Italian restaurants, like Chinese restaurants in Chinatown, are best looked at with a skeptical eye. The best of the breed are elsewhere, what's left is often found cranking out North Americanized travesties of the home country's food. Arriva is one Little Italy restaurant that's worth the drive, and a welcome find if you've spent the day shopping in Italian groceries. There's a version of spaghetti and meatballs on the menu, ziti with spicy squid sauce, and a fusili with wild game—"Bambi and Bugs Bunny"—as the waiters have affectionately coined it. The antipasto plate includes a heaping order of octopus, shrimp, roasted red peppers, cheese, sausage, and fat lima beans in a herby marinade. Don't miss the orange sherbet served in a hollowed-out orange for dessert. *1537 Commercial Dr., tel. 604/251–1177. Reservations ad-*

vised. Dress: casual. AE, MC, V. Closed lunch Sat. and Sun. Moderate.

Cipriano's Ristorante & Pizzeria. Formerly a Greek pizza parlor, Cipriano's has been transformed into an Italian restaurant, with green-white-and-red walls representing the Italian flag, Mama-mia!—inexpensive and hearty Italian food is the mainstay here, including good pizza, even better pasta, and the "Pappa" lasagna. *3995 Main St., tel. 604/879–0020. Reservations accepted. Dress: casual. V. Closed lunch. Inexpensive.*

Japanese ★ **Tojo's.** Hidekazu Tojo is a sushi-making legend here. His handsome blond-wood tatami rooms, on the second floor of a new green-glass tower in the hospital district on West Broadway, provide proper ambience for intimate dining, but Tojo's 10-seat sushi bar stands as the centerpiece. With Tojo presiding, this is a convivial place for dinner, and a ringside seat for watching the creation of edible art. Although Tempura and teriyaki dinners will satisfy, the seasonal menu is more exciting. In October, ask for *dobbin mushi*, a soup made from pine mushrooms that's served in teapot. In spring, try sushi made from scallops and pink cherry blossoms. *777 W. Broadway, No. 202, tel. 604/872–8050. Reservations advised on weekends. Dress: neat but casual. AE, MC, V. Closed Mon.; Dec. 24–26. Expensive.*

Chiyoda. The robota bar curves like an oversize sushi bar through Chiyoda's main room: on one side are the customers and an array of flat baskets full of the day's offerings; on the other side are the robata chefs and grills. There are 35 choices of things to grill, from squid, snapper, and oysters to eggplant, mushrooms, onions, and potatoes. The finished dishes, dressed with sake, soy, or *ponzu* sauce, are dramatically passed over on the end of a long wooden paddle. If Japanese food only means sushi and tempura to you, check this out. *1050 Alberni St., tel. 604/688–5050. Reservations accepted. Dress: casual. AE, MC, V. Closed lunch Sat. and Sun. Moderate.*

Shijo Japanese Restaurant. Shijo has an excellent and very large sushi bar, a smaller robata bar, tatami rooms, and a row of tables overlooking bustling Fourth Avenue. The epitome of modern urban Japanese chic is conveyed through the jazz music, handsome lamps with a patinated bronze finish, and lots of black wood. Count on creatively prepared sushi, eggplant *dengaku* topped with light and dark miso paste and broiled, and shitake *foil yaki*, (fresh shitake mushrooms cooked in foil with ponzu sauce). *1926 W. 4th Ave., tel. 604/732–4676. Reservations advised. Dress: casual. AE, MC, V. Closed lunch, Sat. and Sun. Moderate.*

Japanese Deli House. The least expensive sushi in town is served in this high-ceilinged room on the main floor of a turn-of-the-century building on Powell Street, once the heart of Vancouver's Japantown. Along with the standard sushi-bar menu, Japanese Deli House makes a pungent but tender hot ginger squid appetizer from baby squid caught off the Thai coast, and a geoduck appetizer in mayonnaise worth wandering off the beaten path for. Food is especially fresh and good if you can make it an early lunch: nigiri sushi and sushi rolls are made at 11 AM for the 11:30 opening. *381 Powell St., tel. 604/681–6484. No reservations. Dress: casual. No credit cards. Closed Mon. Inexpensive.*

Korean **Seoul House Korean Restaurant.** The shining star in a desperately ugly section of East Broadway, Seoul House is a bright restaurant, decorated in Japanese style, that serves a full menu of Japanese and Korean food. The best bet is the Korean Barbecue, which you cook at your table. A barbecue dinner of marinated beef, pork, chicken, or fish comes complete with a half dozen side dishes— *kim chee* (Korea's national pickle), salads, stir-fried rice, and pickled vegetables—as well as soup and rice. Service can be chaotic in this very popular restaurant. *36 E. Broadway, tel. 604/874–4131. Reservations advised. Dress: casual. MC, V. Closed lunch Sun. Inexpensive.*

Mexican

Topanga Cafe. Arrive before 6:30 or after 8 PM to avoid waiting in line for this 40-seat Kitsilano classic. The California-Mexican food hasn't changed much in the 12 years the Topanga has been dishing up fresh salsa and homemade tortilla chips. Quantities are still huge and prices are low. Kids can color blank menu covers while waiting for food; a hundred or more of the clientele's best efforts are framed and on the walls. *2904 4th Ave., tel. 604/ 733–3713. No reservations. Dress: casual. MC, V. Closed Sun. Inexpensive.*

Nouvelle

★ **Bishop's.** John Bishop established Vancouver's most influential restaurant five years ago, serving a variety of cuisines from northern Italian to nouvelle and East-West crossover. Penne with grilled eggplant, roasted peppers, and basil pasta cohabits the menu with marinated loin of lamb with ginger and sesame. The small white rooms—their only ornament some splashy, expressionist paintings—are favored by Robert de Niro when he's on location in Vancouver. *2183 W. 4th Ave., tel. 604/738–2025. Reservations required. Dress: casual. AE, DC, MC, V. Closed 1st week in Jan. Expensive.*

Thai

★ **Malinee's Thai.** The city's most consistently interesting Thai food can be found in this typically southeast Asian–style room, tapestries adorning the walls. The owners, two Canadians who lived several years in Thailand, can give you detailed descriptions of every dish on the menu. Steamed fish with ginger, pickled plums, and red chili sauce is on the regular menu; a steamed whole red snapper, marinated in oyster sauce, ginger, cilantro, red pepper, and lime juice is a special worth ordering when available. *2153 W. 4th Ave., tel. 604/737–0097. Reservations advised. Dress: casual. AE, DC, MC, V. Closed lunch Sat. and Sun.; Mon. Moderate.*

Pacific Northwest

Quilicum. Only a few blocks from English Bay, this downstairs "longhouse" serves the original Northwest Coast cuisine: bannock bread, baked sweet potato with hazelnuts, alder-grilled salmon and soap-berries for dessert. Try the authentic, but odd dish—oolichan grease—that's prepared from candlefish. Native music is piped in, and Northwest Coast masks (for sale) peer out from the walls. *1724 Davie St., tel. 604/681–7044. Reservations advised. Dress: casual. AE, MC, V. Closed lunch Sat. and Sun. Moderate.*

★ **The Raintree.** This cool, spacious restaurant offers a local menu and wine list; the latter won a 1988 award from the *Wine Spectator* for its British Columbia, Washington, and Oregon choices. Raintree bakes its own bread, makes luxurious soups, and has pumped-up old favorites such as a slab of apple pie for dessert. With main courses, which change daily depending on market availability, the kitchen teeters between willfully eccentric and exceedingly simple specials could include Queen Charlotte abalone and side-stripe shrimps stir fried with scallions and spinach in chamomile essence, or grilled lamb chops with a mint and pear puree. *Leon's Bar and Grill*, newly opened on the ground floor, stocks local beers and a respectable number of single malt scotches. The pub-food menu, under the direction of chef Rebecca Dawson, includes organic-beef burgers and vegetarian chili. *1630 Alberni St., tel. 604/688–5570. Reservations advised on weekends. Dress: casual. AE, DC, MC, V. Closed Dec. 24–26. Moderate.*

The Tomahawk. North Vancouver was mostly trees 65 years ago, when the Tomahawk first opened. Over the years, the original hamburger stand grew and mutated into part Northwest Coast Indian kitsch museum, part gift shop, and part restaurant. Renowned for its Yukon breakfast—five slices of back bacon, two eggs, hash browns, and toast—the Tomahawk also serves gigantic muffins, excellent french toast, and pancakes. The menu switches to burgers named after Indian chiefs for lunch and dinner. *1550 Philip Ave., tel.604/988–2612. No reservations. Dress: casual. AE, MC, V. Inexpensive.*

Seafood

Olympia Fish Market and Oyster Co. Ltd. Some of the city's best fish and chips are fried in this tiny shop located behind a fish store in the middle of the Robson Street shopping district. The choice is halibut, cod, prawns, calamari, and whatever's on special in the store, served with genuine, unfrozen, french fries. *1094 Robson St., tel. 604/685–0716. No reservations. Dress: casual. No credit cards. Inexpensive.*

Lodging

Lodging has become a major business for Vancouver, a fairly young city that hosts a lot of Asian businesspeople who are used to an above-average level of service. Although by some standards pricey, properties here are highly competitive, and you can expect the service to reflect this trend.

Highly recommended lodgings in each price category are indicated by a star ★.

Category	Cost*
Very Expensive	over $180
Expensive	$120–$180
Moderate	$80–$119
Inexpensive	under $80

**All prices are for a standard double room for two, excluding 10% provincial accommodation tax, 15% service charge, and 7% goods and services tax. Non-Canadians are eligible for a rebate on the goods and services tax paid for hotel accommodations.*

Very Expensive

Four Seasons. The 28-story hotel is adjacent to the Vancouver Stock Exchange and is attached to the Pacific Centre shopping mall. Standard rooms are not large; corner deluxe or deluxe Four Seasons rooms are recommended. Expect tasteful and stylish decor in the rooms and hallways that provide a calm mood despite the bustling hotel. A huge sun deck and indoor-outdoor pool are part of the complete health club facilities. Service is outstanding and the Four Seasons has all the amenities. The formal dining room, Chartwell (*see* Dining, above), is one of the best in the city. *791 W. Georgia St., V6C 2T4, tel. 604/*

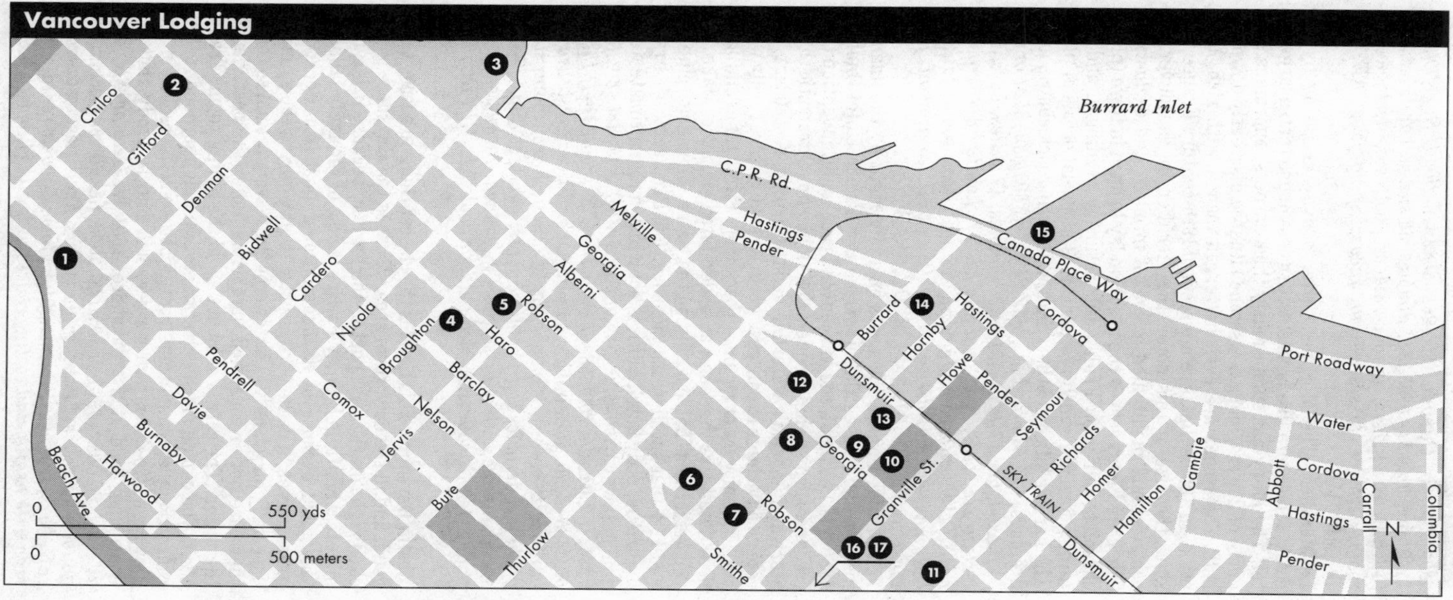

Abbotsford, **14**
Buchan Hotel, **2**
Delta Airport Inn, **17**
Delta Place, **13**
Delta River Inn, **16**
Four Seasons, **10**
Georgia Hotel, **9**
Hotel Vancouver, **8**
Hyatt Regency, **12**
The Kingston, **11**
Le Meridien, **6**
O'Doul's, **5**
Pan Pacific, **15**
Sylvia Hotel, **1**
Wedgewood Hotel, **7**
West End Guest House, **4**
Westin Bayshore, **3**

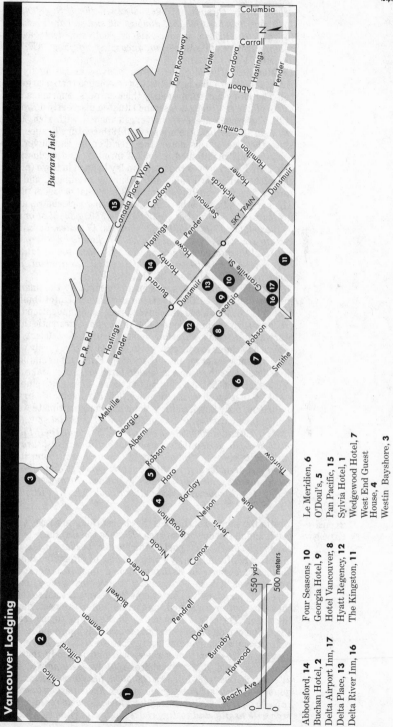

689–9333; in Canada, 800/268–6282; in the U.S., 800/332–3442; fax 604/684–4555. 317 doubles, 68 suites. Facilities: restaurant, café, bars, indoor-outdoor pool, sun deck, weight room, aerobics classes, sauna, Jacuzzi, ping-pong. AE, CB, DC, MC, V.

★ **Le Meridien.** The Meridien, given a five-star rating by the AAA, feels more like an exclusive guest house than a large hotel. The lobby has sumptuously thick carpets, enormous bouquets of flowers, and a newsstand situated discreetly down the hall. The rooms are even better, furnished with rich, dark wood, in a style that is reminiscent of 19th-century France. Despite the size of this hotel, the Meridien in Vancouver has achieved and maintained a level of intimacy and exclusivity. The **Café Fleuri** serves the best Sunday brunch in town (plus a chocolate buffet on Friday and Saturday evenings), and **Gerard,** a formal French restaurant, is a special-occasion place. The bar has lots of leather, dark wood, wingback chairs, and a fireplace. *845 Burrard St., V6Z 2K6, tel. 604/682–5511 or 800/543–4300, fax 604/682–5513. 350 doubles, 47 suites. Facilities: restaurant, café, bar, business center, handicapped rooms, health club with pool, Jacuzzi, sauna, steam room, tanning bed, masseur, hairdresser, weights, exercise equipment, joining apartment hotel. AE, CB, DC, MC, V.*

★ **Pan Pacific.** Canada Place sits on a pier right by the financial district and houses the luxurious Pan Pacific Hotel (built in 1986 for the Expo), the Vancouver Trade and Convention Centre, and a cruise ship terminal. The lobby has a dramatic three-story atrium with a waterfall, and the lounge, restaurant, and café all have huge expanses of glass, so that you are rarely without a harbor view or mountain backdrop. Earth tones and Japanese detail give the rooms an understated elegance. Make sure you get a room that looks out on the water. The health club has a $10 fee that's well worth the price. The Pan Pacific is a grand, luxurious, busy hotel, but it is not a pick for an intimate weekend getaway. *300–999 Canada Pl., V6C 3B5, tel. 604/662–3223; in Canada, 800/663–1515; in the U.S., 800/937–1515; fax 604/685–8690. 468 doubles, 40 suites. Facilities: 3 restaurants, bar, health club with indoor track, sauna, steam room, state-of-the-art aerobics equipment, weights, massage and Shiatsu, sports lounge with wide-screen TV, squash, racquetball, and paddle-tennis courts, heated outdoor pool. AE, CB, DC, MC, V.*

Expensive–Very Expensive

Westin Bayshore. This hotel is the closest thing to a resort that you'll find in the downtown area. Because the Bayshore is perched right on the best part of the harbor, because it is a five-minute walk from Stanley Park, because of the truly fabulous view, and because of its huge outdoor pool, sun deck, and grassy areas, it is the perfect place to stay during the summer, especially for a family. The tower is the newer section, so rooms there are better furnished, larger, and offer the best view of the water. The café is okay but avoid the dining room, Trader Vic's; you can do much better at several neighborhood restaurants. People commuting from Seattle via Lake Union Air (downtown-to-downtown service) will find it handy that the floatplanes land at the Bayshore. *1601 W. Georgia St., V6G 2V4, tel. 604/682–3377 or 800/228–3000; fax 604/687–3102. 481 doubles, 38 suites, 2 handicapped floors. Facilities: restaurant, café, bars, free shuttle service downtown, bicycle rentals, marina with fishing and sailing charters, health club with indoor* *and outdoor pools, Jacuzzi, sun deck, masseur, sauna, pool table. AE, DC, MC, V.*

Expensive **Delta Airport Inn.** It's not a view or a shoreline that make this place (five minutes from the airport) a resort, it's the facilities on the 12-acre site: three swimming pools (one indoor), four all-year tennis courts with a pro (matching list for partners), an outdoor fitness circuit, squash courts, aqua-exercise classes, outdoor volleyball nets, golf practice net, a play center for children, summer camps for 5- to 12-year-olds, and a playground. In spite of its enormity, the atmosphere is casual and friendly. There are two guest-room towers and a few low-rise buildings for convention facilities. The rooms are nothing special, but all the extras, and the hotel's close proximity to the airport, make it worthwhile. The Japanese restaurant is expensive and all show. *10251 St. Edwards Dr., V6X 2M9, tel. 604/278–9611; in Canada, 800/268–1133; in the U.S., 800/877–1133; fax 604/276–1122. 460 doubles, 4 suites. Facilities: restaurant, café, bar, free shuttle to airport and shopping center, meeting rooms. AE, CB, DC, MC, V.*

Delta Place. This 18-story hotel was built in 1985 by the luxurious Hong Kong Mandarin chain but was sold to Delta Hotels in 1987. The rates have gone down but the environment has not changed. The lobby is restrained and tasteful—one has to look for the registration desk. A slight Oriental theme is given to the deluxe furnishings and dark, rich mahogany is everywhere. Most rooms have small balconies and the studio suites are recommended since they are much roomier and only slightly more expensive than a standard room. The business center has secretarial services, work stations, cellular phones for rent, and small meeting rooms. The restaurant and bar are adequate and the location is perfect; the business and shopping district is a five-minute walk away. *645 Howe St., V6C 2Y9, tel. 604/687–1122; in Canada, 800/268–1133; in the U.S., 800/877–1133; fax 604/689–7044. 181 doubles, 16 suites. Facilities: restaurant, bar, squash and racquetball courts, lap pool, weight room. AE, DC, MC, V.*

Delta River Inn. This hotel, on the edge of the Fraser River, is two minutes from the airport. Rooms on the south side get the best view. Although renovations began in 1990, the River Inn still has a way to go to compete with others in the price range. The rooms do not have the style and pizzazz that some have. All the dark wood in the hotel gives it an out-of-date feel, but the hotel is convenient. The marina attached to the hotel organizes fishing charters. Food does not seem to be a priority with Delta. *3500 Cessena Dr., V7B AC7, tel. 604/278–1241; in Canada, 800/268–1133; in the U.S., 800/877–1133; fax 604/276–1975. 410 doubles, 6 suites. Facilities: jogging route, free shuttle to airport, shopping center, and extensive health club at the nearby Delta Airport Inn. AE, CB, DC, MC, V.*

★ **Hotel Vancouver.** The Hotel Vancouver, built in 1939 by the Canadian National Railway, is a grand old lady of the château-style hotels that appear in Canadian cities. It commands a regal position in the center of things across from the fountains of the art gallery. Standard rooms are nothing special, but are decorated in a more classic style than the Hyatt or the Four Seasons. But the hotel has a category called Entré Gold: two floors with all the extra services and amenities. Entré Gold suites have a luxurious amount of space, French doors, graceful wingback chairs, and fine mahogany furniture. The style and elegance of the Hotel Vancouver leaves its mark here. The hotel's restaurants and bars are adequate. *900 W. Georgia St., V6C 2W6, tel. 604/684–3131; in Ontario and Quebec, 800/268–9420; rest of Canada, 800/268–9411; in the U.S., 800/828–7447; fax 604/662–1937. 466 doubles, 42 suites, handicapped rooms. Facilities: 2 restaurants, 2 bars, two-line telephones, health club with lap pool, exercise machines, tanning bed, sun deck. AE, CB, DC, MC, V.*

Hyatt Regency. The 16-year-old Hyatt is in the midst of a badly needed $11-million renovation, but the location is still perfect. The Hyatt's standard rooms are the largest in the city, and are decorated in deep, dramatic colors and dark wood. Ask for a corner room with a balcony on the north or west side. The lobby, however, can't escape the feel of a large convention hotel. The Hyatt has two special features: Camp Hyatt and the Regency Club. The Camp Hyatt has organized evening activities for children. For a small fee, the Regency Club gives you the exclusivity of two floors accessed by keyed elevators, your own concierge, a private lounge with a stereo and large TV, complimentary breakfast, 5 PM hors d'oeuvres, and evening pastries. Robes and special toiletries are also in the Regency Club rooms. For a hotel restaurant, Fish & Co. is unusual in that the room is casual, the atmosphere fun, and the food good. The Gallery Lounge is one of the most pleasant in town. Health club facilities are available, they leave much to be desired. *655 Burrard St., V6C 2R7, tel. 604/687–6543 or 800/233–1234, fax 604/689–3707. 612 doubles, 34 suites. Facilities: restaurant, café, 2 bars, health club. AE, CB, DC, MC, V.*

O'Doul's. Set on a lively street with loads of shops and restaurants, this hotel is a five-minute walk from either the heart of downtown or Stanley Park. This is a great location if you're traveling with teenagers who want time on their own. It was built in 1986 in a long, low style and feels like a very deluxe motel. The rooms are what you'd expect from any mid-range hotel, with modern decor and pastel color schemes, but the place is very well maintained. The deluxe rooms (with king-size beds) face Robson Street, and are worth the price, especially off-season when rates plummet. *1300 Robson St., V6E 1C5, tel. 604/684–8461 or 800/663–5491, fax 604/684–8326. 119 doubles, 11 suites. Facilities: 3 telephones in every room, pool, Jacuzzi, steam rooms, exercise machines. AE, CB, DC, MC, V.*

★ **Wedgewood Hotel.** This hotel upholds a reputation for being a small, elegant hotel run by an owner who fervently cares about her guests. The intimate lobby is decorated in fine detail with polished brass, a fireplace, and tasteful artwork. All the extra touches are here, too: nightly turn-down service, afternoon ice delivery, dark-out drapes, flowers growing on the balcony, terry-cloth robes, and morning newspaper. No tour groups or conventions stop here; the Wedgewood's clients are almost exclusively corporate, except on weekends when it turns into a honeymoon retreat. Health facilities are next door at the excellent Chancery Squash Club. The lounge and restaurants couldn't be better. It's a treasure. *845 Hornby St., V6Z 1V1, tel. 604/689–7777 or 800/663–0666, fax 604/688–3074. 60 doubles, 33 suites. Facilities: 2 restaurants, bar, use of the adjacent Chancery Squash Club with 7 squash courts, weight room, aerobics, sauna, and whirlpool. AE, CB, DC, MC, V.*

Moderate

Abbotsford. For the businessperson looking for a bargain, this location is tops. The six-story, 70-year-old Abbotsford is the only moderately priced hotel in the business core, and the new renovations of the guest rooms and the lobby have made this accommodation even more agreeable. This is a basic accommodation but rooms are bright, clean, and functional. Standard rooms are very large but there is no room service and few amenities. Suites 310, 410, 510, and 610 have a harbor view. The bar, the **Bombay Bicycle Club,** is a favorite with businesspeople. *921 W. Pender St., V6C 1M2, tel. 604/681–4335 or 800/663–1700, fax 604/681–7808. 74 doubles, 11 suites. Facilities: restaurant, 2 bars, free parking. AE, CB, DC, MC, V.*

★ **Georgia Hotel.** Across from the Four Seasons, this hotel is a five-minute walk from the business district. This handsome 12-story hotel, built in 1927, has such Old-World features as an oak-paneled lobby, ornate brass elevators, and a subdued, genteel atmosphere. Although it's lacking in special amenities, the Georgia is a reliable and satisfactory deal. Rooms are small but well furnished, with nothing worn around the edges. Executive rooms have an almost-separate seating area. Rooms facing the art gallery have the best views. *801 W. Georgia St., V6C 1P7, tel. 604/682–5566 or 800/663–1111, fax 604/682–8192. 310 doubles, 4 suites. Facilities: restaurant, 3 bars. AE, CB, DC, MC, V.*

★ **West End Guest House.** The bright-pink exterior of this delightful Victorian house may throw you: The gracious front parlor with its early 1900s furniture is more indicative of the charm of the place. Most of the rooms are small but are extraordinarily handsome because of the high brass beds, antiques, gorgeous linen, and dozens of old framed pictures of Vancouver. All rooms have phones, TVs, and new bathrooms. There's a veranda for people-watching, and a back deck for sunbathing. A full breakfast is included and can be served in bed. The inn's genial hosts, Charles and George, have learned that it is the little things that make the difference, including an evening glass of sherry, duvets and feather mattress-pads, and a pantry where guests can help themselves to tea or snacks. The inn is in a residential neighborhood that is a 15-minute walk from downtown and Stanley Park and two minutes from Robson Street. This is a nonsmoking establishment. Call for restrictions. *1362 Haro St., V6E 1G2, tel. 604/681–2889. 7 rooms. Facilities: off-street parking. MC, V.*

Inexpensive

★ **Buchan Hotel.** The Buchan is a three-story 1930s building conveniently set in a tree-lined residential street a block from Stanley Park, a block from shops and restaurants on Denman Street, and a 15-minute walk from the liveliest part of Robson Street. The hallways appear a bit institutional, but the rooms are bright and clean. Furnishings, in good condition, consist of a color TV, and a wood-grained arborite desk and chest of drawers. The rooms are small and the bathrooms tiny. None of the rooms have phones and you have to park on the street, but with this location you probably won't use your car much. Rooms on the east side are brightest and overlook a park; front corner rooms are the biggest. **Delilah's,** a popular restaurant with an eclectic menu, is in the basement and is open for dinner. *1906 Haro St., V6G 1H7, tel. 604/685–5354. 60 rooms, 30 with private bath. Facilities: TV lounge, laundry room. AE, DC, MC, V.*

The Kingston. The Kingston is a small budget hotel in a location convenient for shopping. It is an old style, four-story hotel, with no elevator—the type of establishment you'd find in Europe. The spartan rooms are small, immaculate, and share a bathroom down the hall. All rooms have phones but no TVs. Rooms on the south side are brighter. Continental breakfast is included. *757 Richards St., V6B 3A6, tel. 604/684–9024. 60 rooms, 7 with bath. Facilities: sauna, coin-op laundry, TV lounge, free nighttime parking. AE, MC, V.*

★ **Sylvia Hotel.** Perhaps the Sylvia Hotel is the best bargain in Vancouver, but don't count on staying here June–August unless you've booked six months ahead. What makes this hotel so popular are its low rates and near-perfect location: about 25 feet from the beach, 200 feet from Stanley Park, and a 20-minute walk from downtown. Vancouverites are particularly fond of the eight-story ivy-covered brick building—it was once the tallest building in the West End and the first to open a cocktail bar in the city in 1954. It's part of the local history and was declared a protected heritage building in the 1970s. Rooms are unadorned and have basic plain furnishings that have probably been around for 20 years—not much to look at but the view and price make it worthwhile. Suites are huge and all have kitchens, making this a perfect family accommodation. There is little difference between the old and new wings. *1154 Gilford St., V6G 2P6, tel. 604/681–9321. 97 doubles, 18 suites. Facilities: restaurant, lounge, free parking. AE, DC, MC, V.*

The Arts and Nightlife

For information on events, look in the entertainment section of the *Vancouver Sun;* also, Thursday's paper has complete listings in the **"What's On"** column, and the **Arts Hotline** (tel. 604/684–ARTS). For tickets to major events, book through **Ticketmaster** (tel. 604/280–4444).

The Arts

Theater The **Vancouver Playhouse** (Hamilton St., tel. 604/872–6722) is the most established venue in Vancouver. The **Arts Club Theatre** (tel. 604/687–1644), with two stages on Granville Island (1585 Johnston St.) and performances all year, is the most active. Both feature mainstream theatrical shows. **Carousel Theater** (tel. 604/669–3410), which performs off-off Broadway shows at the **Waterfront Theatre** (1405 Anderson St.) on Granville Island, and **Touchstone** (tel. 604/687–8737), at the Firehall Theater (280 E. Cordova St.), are smaller but lively companies. The **Back Alley Theatre** (75 Thurlow St., tel. 604/688–7013) hosts **Theatresports,** a hilarious improv event. The **Vancouver East Cultural Centre** (1895 Venable St., tel. 604/254–9578) is a multipurpose performance space that always hosts high-caliber shows.

Music The **Vancouver Symphony Orchestra** (tel. 604/684–9100) and the **CBC Orchestra** (tel. 604/662–6000) play at the restored **Orpheum Theatre** (601 Smithe St.). Choral groups like the **Bach Choir** (tel. 604/921–8012), the **Cantata Singers** (no tel.), and the **Vancouver Chamber Singers** (no tel.) play a major role in Vancouver's classical music scene. The **Early Music Society** (tel. 604/732–1610) performs medieval, renaissance, and baroque music throughout the year, and hosts the summer concerts of the most important Early Music Festival in North America. Concerts by the **Friends of Chamber Music** (no tel.) and the

Vancouver Recital Society (tel. 604/736–6034) are always of excellent quality.

Vancouver Opera (tel. 604/682–2871) stages four productions a year, usually in October, January, March, and May at the **Queen Elizabeth Theatre** (600 Hamilton St.). Productions are high caliber with both local and imported talent.

Dance The **Dance Hotline** (tel. 604/872–0432) has information on upcoming events. Watch out for **Ballet BC's Dance Alive!** series, presenting visiting or local ballet companies (from the Kirov to Ballet BC), as well as the modern dance series, **Discover Dance.** Most performances by these companies can be seen at the Orpheum or the Queen Elizabeth Theater (*see* above). Local modern dance companies worth seeing are **Karen Jamison, Judith Marcuse,** and **Anna Wyman.**

Film Two theaters have distinguished themselves by avoiding the regular movie fare: **The Ridge** (3131 Arbutus St., tel. 604/738–6311), which generally plays foreign films; and **Pacific Cinémateque** (1131 Howe St., tel. 604/688–3456), which goes for even more esoteric foreign or art films. The **Vancouver International Film Festival** (tel. 604/685–0260) is held in September and October in several theaters around town.

Nightlife

Bars and Lounges **The Gérard Lounge,** (845 Burrard St., tel. 604/682–5511) at Le Meridien Hotel, is probably the nicest in the city because of the fireplaces, wingback chairs, dark wood, and leather. The **Bacchus Lounge,** (845 Hornby St., tel. 604/689–7777) in the Wedgewood Hotel is stylish and sophisticated. The **Gallery Lounge,** (655 Burrard St., tel. 604/687–6543) in the Hyatt, is a civilized bar, with lots of windows letting in the sun and views of the action on the bustling street. The **Garden Lounge,** (791 W. Georgia St., tel. 604/689–9333) in the Four Seasons, is bright and airy with greenery and a waterfall, plus big soft chairs you won't want to get out of. For a more lively atmosphere, try **Joe Fortes** (777 Thurlow St., 604/669–1940), or **Night Court,** (801 W. Georgia St., tel. 604/682–5566) in the Georgia Hotel.

The **English Bay Cafe** (1795 Beach Ave., tel. 604/669–2225) is the place to go to catch the sunset over English Bay. **La Bodega,** (1277 Howe St., tel. 604/684–8815), beneath the Chateau Madrid is a popular Spanish tapas bar.

Two bars on Granville Island catering to the after-work crowd are **Bridges** (tel. 604/687–4400), near the Public Market, and the upscale **Pelican Bay** (tel. 604/683–7373) in the Granville Island Hotel, at the other end of the island.

Music
Discos While discos come and go, lines still form every weekend at **Richard's on Richards** (1036 Richards St., tel. 604/687–6794) for live and taped Top-40 music.

Jazz A jazz and blues hotline (tel. 604/682–0706) gives you current information on concerts and clubs. The **Grunt Gallery** (209 E. 6th Ave., tel. 604/875–9516) is an informal, unlicensed club that features adventurous, contemporary jazz. **Carnegie's** (1619 W. Broadway, tel. 604/733–4141) and the **Alma Street Cafe** (2502 Alma St., tel. 604/222–2244), both restaurants, are more traditional venues with good mainstream jazz.

Rock The **Town Pump** (66 Water St., tel. 604/683–6695) is the main venue for local and touring rock bands. The **Soft Rock Cafe** (1925 W. 4th Ave., tel. 604/736–8480) is decidedly more upscale. There's live music, dinners, and weekend lineups. The **86th Street Music Hall** (750 Pacific Blvd., tel. 604/683–8687) serves up big-name bands.

Casinos A few casinos have been licensed recently in Vancouver and proceeds go to local charities and arts groups. Downtown there is the **Royal Diamond Casino** (535 Davie St., tel. 604/685–2340) and the **Great Canadian Casino** (2477 Heather St., tel. 604/872–5543) in the Holiday Inn.

Comedy **Yuk Yuks** (750 Pacific Blvd., tel. 604/687–5233) is good for a few laughs.

Excursion 1: Whistler

If you think of skiing when you hear mention of Whistler, British Columbia, you're thinking on track. Whistler and Blackcomb mountains, part of the Whistler Resort Association, are the two biggest ski mountains in North America; there's summer glacier skiing, the longest vertical drop in North America, and the most advanced lifts in the world. At the base of the mountains is Whistler Village—a small, pedestrianized community of lodgings, restaurants, pubs, gift shops, and boutiques. With more than 28 hotels arranged within a five-minute walk between the mountains, the site is a hot bed of activity. Culinary options within the village range from burgers to French, Japanese to deli cuisine; and nightly entertainment runs the gamut from sophisticated piano bars to casual pubs. During the day and into the evening T-shirt shops, gift stores, and fashion boutiques offer skiers a break from the slopes.

Adjacent to the area is the 78,000-acre Garibaldi Provincial Park, with dense mountainous forests splashed with hospitable lakes and streams. But even if you don't want to roam much farther than the village, there are five lakes for canoeing, fishing, swimming, and windsurfing, and many nearby hiking and mountain-bike trails.

In the winter, the village buzzes with skiers taking to the slopes in vibrantly colored attire, but as the scenery changes from winter's snow-white to summer's lush-green landscapes, the mood of Whistler changes, too. Things seem to slow down a bit, and the resort sheds some of its competitive edge and welcomes a more relaxed, slower-paced environment. Even the local golf tournaments and the triathlon are interspersed with Mozart and bluegrass festivals.

No matter what the season, though, Whistler Village is very accessible to the pedestrian. Anywhere you want to go within the resort is at most five minutes away, and parking lots are just outside the village. The bases of Whistler and Blackcomb mountains are also just at the edge; in fact, you can ski right into the lower level of the Chateau Whistler Hotel, and all 1,220 of the village's hotel rooms are less than 1,000 feet from the lifts.

Tourist Information

For advance information, contact the **Whistler Resort Association** (Box 1400, Whistler, B.C. V0N 1B0; in Whistler, tel. 604/932–3928; reservations, tel. 604/932–4222; in Vancouver, tel. 604/685–3650; in the U.S., tel. 800/634–9622). In Whistler Village an information booth at the front door of the Conference Center is open 8:30–8.

A provincial government **Travel Infocentre** (tel. 604/932–5528) is on the main highway, about a mile south of Whistler.

Guided Tours

Alpine Adventure Tours (tel. 604/932–2705) has a Whistler history tour of the valley and a Squamish day trip.

Caledon's Carriage Tours (tel. 604/932–3033) will tour you around the village in a horse and buggy.

Sea to Sky Tours (tel. 604/984–2224) offers a scenic day trip by BC Rail to historic Lillooet.

Arriving and Departing

By Car Whistler is 122 kilometers (75 miles) north of Vancouver, on Highway 99. The road can be treacherous in winter; snow tires are required by law; chains are advisable. Phone the Department of Highways (tel. 604/660–9775) for road conditions.

By Limo Service from downtown Vancouver and the airport to Whistler by **Airlimo** (tel. 604/273–1331) is $180 per car.

By Train **BC Rail** (tel. 604/984–5246) in North Vancouver has daily service to Whistler. The train leaves early morning for the 2½-hour trip and departs Whistler in late afternoon. There is free parking at the North Vancouver train station, or a shuttle bus will take you from the bus depot in downtown Vancouver to the station in North Vancouver. Tickets ($12 one way) are available at the station or from the conductor. In Whistler a shuttle bus will transport you the 3¼ kilometers (2 miles) from the train station to the village.

The scenery from the train is spectacular, but, since there's only one train, there's no flexibility with departure and arrival times. One option is to take the train up and the bus back. Several buses leave late in the day from Whistler Village, making it easier to accommodate your own agenda (*see* below).

By Bus **Maverick Coach Lines** (tel. 604/255–1171) has buses leaving every couple of hours from the bus depot in downtown Vancouver. The bus stops at Whistler Village and the fare is $11 one way. During ski season, the last bus leaves Whistler at 10 PM.

Perimiter Transportation (in B.C., tel. 800/663–4265; outside B.C., tel. 604/261–2299) has daily service, November–May, from Vancouver Airport to Whistler. Reservations are necessary; the ticket booth is on the arrivals level of the airport.

By Air **Canadian Helicopters** (in Vancouver, tel. 604/276–7670 or in Canada and western U.S., tel. 800/663–1151) runs daily service from Vancouver Airport or the downtown heliport to the base of Blackcomb for $235 round-trip.

Getting Around

By Car Although a car is not necessary in the village area, it will be necessary to explore some of the scenic spots along the highway.

Rental Cars: At Whistler you can rent a car from **Budget** (tel. 604/932–1236), located on Highway 99 just south of Whistler, or at **Avis** (tel. 604/938–1331) in Whistler Village.

By Taxi For taxi service in Whistler call **Sea to Sky Taxi** (tel. 604/932–8294) or **Whistler Taxi** (tel. 604/932–5455).

By Bus A free shuttle (tel. 604/932–3434) operates 8–5:30 from Whistler South to Whistler Village during ski season. **Whistler Transit** (tel. 604/932–2705) operates to and from residential neighborhoods and the village.

Festivals and Seasonal Events

During the summer, festivals and special events happen one after the other. For information phone the festival coordinator at the Whistler Resort Association (tel. 604/932–3928). The Mozart Festival, held in August, includes free outdoor activities and concerts, finishing with a performance by the Vancouver Symphony Orchestra on top of Blackcomb Mountain. You may see a brass quintet playing on a raft in Lost Lake, or a chamber group playing a dinner concert. There is also a two-day jazz festival in September; a country and blues festival in July; a Porsche rally held in mid-August; a triathlon held in late July, that draws top competitors from all over the world; a children's art festival in June; and summer-long street entertainment. All concerts are free except some classical music events.

Winter Activities

Skating Areas on the five lakes around Whistler are often cleared for skating. The only rentals are at the **KOA Kampground** (tel. 604/932–5181), a mile north of the village.

Skiing *Downhill* The vertical drops and elevation at **Blackcomb** and **Whistler** mountains are, perhaps, the most impressive features to skiers. Blackcomb has a 5,280-foot vertical drop (North America's longest); Whistler has a 5,020-foot drop. The top elevation is 7,494 feet on Blackcomb and 7,160 on Whistler.

Also enticing is that these mountains have the most advanced ski-lift technology, with lift capacity on Blackcomb being 23,850 skiers per hour; on Whistler, it is 20,395 per hour. Other reasons to ski here are the 85 marked trails on Blackcomb and 96 on Whistler; both mountains have an average of 450 inches of snow per year; and Blackcomb is open June–August for summer glacier skiing.

Lift tickets for Whistler or Blackcomb mountains are about $40 a day; three-day tickets for both mountains are about $120.

Rentals are available at **Blackcomb Ski and Sport** (tel. 604/932–3141), **Jim McConkeys Sport Shop** (tel. 604/932–2311), and **Village Ski Services** (tel. 604/932–3659). Some of these shops also rent clothing and snow boards.

Whistler Mountain Ski School (tel. 604/932–3141) and **Blackcomb Ski School** (tel. 604/932–3141) have learn-to-ski programs, group lessons, private lessons ($50 per hour), and mogul clinics, powder clinics, peak performance clinics, and, of course, children's lessons. Ski Esprit—a program run jointly by the two schools—provides three or four days of guided skiing with instructors who will help you with technique, take you to out-of-the-way places, videotape your runs, and organize races. All this is for $150 plus lift tickets.

Cross-Country Around the village the popular cross-country spots are the 15 kilometers (9.3 miles) of **Lost Lake Trails** (tel. 604/932–6436) or the **Whistler Golf Course,** which is perfect for beginners. Any of the logging roads in Garibaldi Park—especially around **Garibaldi Lake,** where there are warming shelters—and the trail to **Callaghan Lake** are used by cross-country skiers.

Heli-skiing **Canada Heli-Sports** (tel. 604/932–3512), **Tyax Heli-Skiing** (tel. 604/932–7007), and **Whistler Heli-Skiing** (tel. 604/932–4105) have day trips with up to four glacier runs or 12,000 vertical feet of skiing for experienced skiers; the cost is about $300.

Paragliding Imagine hang-gliding, but with a parachute and skis that give you a smooth lift-off and landing. Day courses are available from **Parawest** (tel. 604/932–7052) for $95.

Snowmobiling **Whistler Snowmobile Service** (tel. 604/932–4086) offers snowmobile rentals and has guided tours to Cougar Lake or Ancient Cedar Grove.

Summer Activities

Biking Mountain bike rentals by the hour are available from **Jim McConkey's Sport Shop** (tel. 604/932–2311), **Pumphouse Fitness Center** (tel. 604/932–1984), and **Blackcomb Ski and Sport** (tel. 604/932–3142). The shops have bike-trail maps that indicate routes and the degree of difficulty.

Lifestyles Adventure Company (tel. 604/932–4264) has a range of guided trips from two hours to five days. Their popular descent trip takes you and a bike up the chair lift, so that you can ride down Blackcomb Mountain. **Whistler Backroads Mountain Bike Adventures** (tel. 604/932–3111) has day trips to Brandywine Falls, Cougar Lake, and other destinations, depending on the degree of difficulty you choose.

Canoeing and Kayaking You'll see lots of canoes and kayaks at the many lakes and rivers near **Whistler.** If you want to get in on the fun, rentals are available at Alta Lake at both **Lakeside Park** and **Wayside Park.** Another spot that's perfect for canoeing is the **River of Golden Dreams,** either from Meadow Park to Green Lake or upstream to Twin Bridges. Kayakers looking for a thrill may want to try **Green River** from Green Lake to Pemberton. Call **Whistler Canoe Guides** (tel. 604/932–6615) or **Whistler Kayak Adventures** (tel. 604/932–6615) for equipment or guided trips.

Fishing **Green River Fishing Guides** (tel. 604/932–3474) will take care of anything you need—equipment, guides, or four-wheel-drive transportation. All five of the lakes around Whistler are stocked with trout, but the area around **Dream River Park** is one of the most popular fishing spots. Slightly farther afield, try **Cheakamus Lake, Daisy Lake,** and **Callaghan Lake.**

Golf Arnold Palmer designed the par-72 championship **Whistler Golf Course** (tel. 604/932–4544), which is said to be a "good four-iron shot from the village." The course is very scenic, fairly flat, and challenging for the experienced, but pleasant for beginners.

Hiking Covered chair lifts will take you up **Blackcomb Mountain** (tel. 604/932–3141) to take part in free guided nature walks. On **Whistler Mountain,** you can take the enclosed express gondola 4,000 feet up for a walking tour. Chair-lift fares are the same for both mountains: $12 adults, $6 senior citizens and children. Restaurants are at the top of both mountains. In the valley, some of the many hiking trails go to **Nairn Falls, Brandywine Falls,** or **Cheakamus Lake** in Garibaldi Park. Trail maps are available from the information booth at the Conference Center.

Heli-hiking **Tyax Heli-Skiing** offers heli-hiking day trips that take you for an alpine hike with a guide for $125.

Horseback Riding **Whistler Trail Riding** (tel. 604/932–6623) conducts one- and three-hour rides in the valley.

Swimming Beaches (without lifeguards) are at **Lost Lake Park, Alpha Lake Park, Wayside Park,** and **Rainbow Park.** Lost Lake is the smallest and warmest, and has a diving raft. Historic buildings of the first settlers in the valley have been left on the site at Rainbow Park. Grassy areas with picnic tables and washrooms are at each beach.

Tennis Covered courts are at the **Delta Mountain Inn** (tel. 604/932–1982), where same-day bookings can be made even if you're not a guest. Public outdoor courts are at the **Myrtle Philip Elementary School** (tel. 604/892–5228), **Alpha Lake Park, Whistler Creek, Meadows Park, Alpine Meadows,** and **Emerald Park.**

Windsurfing Rentals (tel. 604/932–1984) are available at **Lakeside Park** (tel. 604/932–3389) at Alta Lake. There are Thursday-night windsurfing races at Lakeside Park—just show up at 7 PM with your board.

Dining and Lodging

See Vancouver Dining and Lodging, above, for price categories.

Dining **Il Caminetto Di Umberto, Trattoria di Umberto, The Grill.** Umberto Menghi is Vancouver's best-known restaurateur because of his three fabulously successful Italian restaurants. Now there are three in Whistler. Il Caminetto and the Trattoria are in the village and The Grill is in Whistler Creek, a couple of miles south. Umberto offers home-style Italian cooking and specializes in pasta dishes like crab-stuffed cannelloni or a four-cheese lasagna, that mix well with the relaxed atmosphere. The Trattoria has a Tuscan-style rotisserie, featuring pasta served with a tray of chopped tomatoes, hot pepper, basil, olive oil, anchovies, and Parmesan so that you can mix it as spicy and flavorful as you like. The Grill's specialty is lean grilled beef and chicken, and Il Caminetto, perhaps the best restaurant in the Whistler area, is known for its veal, osso buco, and zabaglione. *Il Caminetto: 4242 Village Stroll, tel. 604/932–4442; Trattoria: Mountainside Lodge, tel. 604/932–5858; The Grill: Whistler Creek Lodge, tel. 604/932–3000. Reservations advised for dinner. Dress: neat but casual. AE, CB, DC, MC, V. Expensive.*

The Wildflower Cafe. Although this is the main dining room of the Chateau Whistler, it's an informal, comfortable restaurant.

Huge picture windows overlook the ski slopes and let in the bright sun reflected off the snow. The rustic look of the Chateau Whistler lobby continues in the Wildflower—more than 100 old wood birdhouses decorate the room, and chairs and tables have that farmhouse look. Although there is an à la carte menu that focuses on Pacific Northwest cuisine, the restaurant features a terrific breakfast, lunch, and dinner buffets that may include sweet potato–and-parsnip soup, barbecued salmon, smoked halibut, artichoke-and-mushroom salad, pepper salad, seafood pâté, pasta in a spicy tomato sauce, and cold meats. *Chateau Whistler Hotel, tel. 604/938–8000. Reservations advised for dinner. Dress: neat but casual. AE, CB, DC, MC, V. Expensive.*

Lodging Any accommodations, including pensions, can be booked through the Whistler Resort Association (tel. 604/932–4222). All pensions are outside the village, so if you don't have a car, pick one within walking distance.

Chateau Whistler. Whistler's most extravagant hotel is a large and friendly looking fortress, just outside the village. The hotel is built and run by Canadian Pacific Railway, and is the same style as the Banff Springs Hotel and the Jasper Park Lodge. The marvelous lobby is filled with rustic Canadiana, handmade Mennonite rugs, enormous fireplaces, and enticing overstuffed sofas. Floor-to-ceiling windows in the lounge, the health club, and the Wildflower Cafe overlook the base of Blackcomb Mountain. Skiers can ski from there right into the basement of the hotel. The standard rooms are called premier and are fairly small, but the suites are fit for royalty, with specially commissioned quilts and artwork, and are complemented by antique furnishings. Both the Wildflower Cafe (*see* Dining, above) and La Fiesta, a tapas bar, are very good choices for a meal. Look for summer rates that drop by 50%. *4599 Chateau Blvd., Box 100, V0N 1B0, tel. 604/938–8000, fax 604/938–2020. 303 doubles, 40 suites, handicapped rooms. Facilities: 2 restaurants, bar, indoor-outdoor pool, indoor and outdoor Jacuzzis, morning stretch classes for skiers, 3 covered tennis courts. AE, CB, DC, MC, V. Very Expensive.*

Pension Edelweiss. The Edelweiss is one of five charming and very European bed-and-breakfasts around Whistler, and is within walking distance from Whistler Village. Rooms have balconies and fireplaces and that crisp, northern European spic-and-span feel, in keeping with the Bavarian chalet style of the house. Each morning a different breakfast (included in room rate) is served: Scandinavian, American, French, German. For dinner, proprietor Ursula Morel serves fondue or raclette. Minimum stay in high season is three nights. *7162 Nancy Greene Way, Box 850, tel. 604/932–3641, fax 604/932–3776. 7 rooms, all with private bath. Facilities: sauna, transportation to lifts. MC, V. Inexpensive.*

Excursion 2: Mayne Island

Introduction

The Gulf Islands lie in the Gulf of Georgia, between Vancouver and Victoria. The southern islands Galiano, Mayne, Saturna, Pender, and Salt Spring (the most commercialized) are warmer, have half the rainfall of Vancouver, and are graced with smooth sandstone rocks and beaches. Marine birds are numerous, and ususual vegetation such as arbutus trees (a leafy evergreen with red peeling bark) and Garry oaks make the islands very different from other areas around Vancouver. Writers, artists, craftsmen, weekend cottagers, and retirees take full advantage of the undeveloped islands and their wildlife.

For a first visit to the Gulf Islands, make a stopover on Mayne, the most agricultural of the group. In the 1930s and 1940s the island produced vegetables for Vancouver and Victoria until the Japanese farmers who worked the land were interned during World War II. Mayne's close proximity to Vancouver and its manageable size (even if you're on a bicycle) make it accessible and feasible for a one- or two-day trip. A free map, published by the islanders, is available on the ferry or from any store on Mayne.

Arriving and Departing by Ferry

BC Ferry (tel. 604/685–1021 for recorded message; for reservations, 604/669–1211) runs frequent service from outside Vancouver and Victoria to the Gulf Islands. The trip to Mayne Island takes about 1½ hours, and a couple of sailings run each day. Call for a 24-hour recorded phone message of crossings. If you plan on taking a car, it is often necessary to make reservations a couple of weeks in advance, especially if you are traveling on the weekend. Go mid-week if possible.

Getting Around

By Bicycle Because Mayne Island is so small (20 sq km, or 8 sq mi) and scenic, it is great territory for a vigorous bike ride, though the small hills make it not-quite-a-piece-of-cake. Renting a bike in Vancouver is a good idea, unless the weather looks dodgy; then it would be worth taking a car. Some B&Bs have bicycles; ask for them to be set aside for you when making your reservation. A few bicycles are for rent at the island's only gas station (604/539–5411) at Miners Bay.

By Car The roads on Mayne Island are narrow and winding.

Exploring Mayne Island

Mayne Island saw its heyday around the turn of the century when passenger ships traveling from Victoria and Vancouver stopped over to enjoy Mayne's natural beauty. British and Japanese farmers had productive vegetable, dairy, and sheep farms, and late-19th-century wood houses, hotels, and a church still stand today among the newer A-frames, log cabins, and split-level homes. Although there is no real town in Mayne, except for a few commercial buildings and homes around Miners Bay, you will find eagles, herons, and rare ducks; sea lions and black-tail deer; quiet beaches, coves, and forest paths; and warm, dry weather in the summer.

Starting at the ferry dock at **Village Bay,** head toward Miners Bay via Village Bay Road. A small white sign on your left will indicate the way to **Helen Point,** previously an Indian reservation that has no inhabitants. Indian middens at Village Bay show that the island had been inhabited for 5,000 years by Cowichan Indians from Vancouver Island who paddled to

Mayne Island in dugout canoes. If you choose to go all the way to Helen's Point (about a two-hour, round-trip walk), you can look north across **Active Pass** (named for the turbulent waters).

If you continue on Village Bay Road, head toward **Miners Bay,** a little town about 2 kilometers (1.2 miles) away. This commercial hub has a post office, restaurant, health-food store, gas station, bakery (with espresso), a general store, and a secondhand bookstore. Look for the House of Taylor (tel. 604/539–5283), an arts-and-crafts gallery that features local works. Also, visit the **Plumbers Pass Lockup;** formerly a jail, it is now a minuscule museum with local history exhibits.

Time Out Stop at the **Springwater Lodge** (tel. 604/539–5521), built in 1892 and the oldest operating hotel in British Columbia. The deck of the Springwater overlooks the bay and is a fine place for a cold soda or beer on a sunny day.

From Miners Bay head east on Georgina Point Road. About a mile away is **St. Mary Magdalene Church,** which doubles as an Anglican and United church. If Pastor Larry Grieg is around, he'll show you the century-old building, but the cemetery next to the church is even more interesting. Generations of islanders—the Bennetts, Georgesons, Maudes, and Deacons—whose names are all over the Mayne Island map—are buried here. Across the road, a stairway leads down to the beach.

At the end of Georgina Point Road is the **Active Pass Lighthouse.** The grassy grounds, open to the public every day from 1 to 3, are great for picnicking. Bald eagles are often on the shore along with many varieties of ducks (waterfowl is most abundant in spring and fall).

Head back down Georgina Point Road a short way and turn left on Waugh Road, left on Porter Road, and right to the end of Edith Point Road. A path leads off into the woods to **Edith Point,** an hour's walk away. The path is a bit steep in parts—not recommended for small children—but the sunny smooth sloping sandstone at the point is a real enticement. Many of the beaches on Mayne are on the north or east side, but at Edith Point you can take advantage of the full southern exposure. If the tide is out, beachcomb your way back to your car.

From Edith Point Road, go back along Waugh Road a short distance to Campbell Bay Road. Take this to Fernhill Road (which becomes Bennett Bay Road), heading east to **Bennett Bay,** the island's most popular beach. Just past the junction of Bennett Bay and Wilkes roads, beyond the Marisol Cottages, a small green sign on the right indicates beach access. The beach is wide and long and the bay is shallow, so the water warms up nicely. (Don't expect washrooms or concession stands in the Gulf Islands.) The mountain looming in the distance is Washington state's Mt. Baker. The nicest part of the beach is to your left if you are facing the water.

The last stop on the tour is **Mount Parke,** which was declared a wilderness park in 1989. Access is from Village Bay Road, where you will see a timber archway naming Mt. Parke. Drive up as far as you can until you see the sign that says "No Vehicles Beyond This Point." It is then about a 15-minute walk to the highest point on the island and a stunning, almost 360-degree view of Vancouver, Active Pass, and Vancouver Island. You may be face-to-face with eagles using the updraft to maintain their cruising altitude.

Dining and Lodging

Dining

Five Roosters Restaurant. The Five Roosters is in an old house near Miners Bay, and along with the funky atmosphere there is warm, friendly service. It is the only restaurant on the island not associated with an inn and, apart from the deli and the pub, is the only place for a sit-down lunch. The seafood club sandwich is recommended. Breakfast, lunch, and dinner are served. *Village Bay Rd., tel. 604/539–2727. MC, V. Moderate.*

Dining and Lodging

Fernhill Lodge and Herb Farm. The lodge has built its reputation on friendly service, distinctive rooms, and historical dinners. Odds are the chef and owner, Brian Crumblehume, will be serving the Cleopatra, Chaucer, or Roman dinners. If you're not staying at the lodge, you must make a dinner reservation by 1 PM. Breakfasts are more traditional and are fabulous. They feature fresh-squeezed orange juice, freshly baked buns and muffins, good coffee, and eggs and sausages. In the summer, reserve in advance unless you're coming midweek. You have a choice of six rooms: the Jacobean, Oriental, Canadiana, farm house, 18th-century French, or Victorian. *Fernhill Rd., Box 140, V0N 2J0, tel. 604/539–2544. Facilities: bicycles, kayak, sauna under the trees, sun room, library, piano, herb garden. MC, V. Moderate.*

Lodging

Oceanwood Country Inn. This promising deluxe waterfront inn is scheduled to open by 1991. Eight units will be available; all will have a private bathroom and sitting area. Some rooms will have a fireplace or whirlpool bath. Northwest cuisine will head the menu in the dining room, which will welcome guests and islanders. Breakfast and afternoon tea is included in rates. *22 Dinner Bay Rd., V0N 2J0, tel. 604/539–5074. Facilities: library, games room, conference room, bicycles. MC. Expensive.*

Blue Vista Resort. The sizable '60s-style cabins, decorated with rumpus room–style family furnishings, are about 100 feet from the beach at Bennett Bay. This is the best family accommodation on the island, because units are complete with kitchens and there are no restrictions on pets. Owners Gerry and Naomi Daignault can also provide bicycles, barbecues, and a rowboat. *Arbutus Rd., V0N 2J0, tel. 604/539–2463. MC, V. Inexpensive.*

Gingerbread House. This is the first choice of all the B&Bs on the island. The lovely restored Victorian house overlooks Campbell Bay, and is near a trail that leads down to the beach. All of the rooms have a Victorian theme including antiques and floral wallpaper. The Honeymoon Room has a private bath with a clawfoot bathtub and French doors opening onto a private deck. Breakfast is different each day and can include smoked salmon quiche or strawberry waffles. *Campbell Bay Rd., V0N 2J0, tel. 604/539–3133. 4 rooms, 1 with private bath. MC, V. Closed Nov.–Feb. Inexpensive.*

7 Coastal British Columbia

Introduction

by Ray Chatelin

Travel writer Ray Chatelin is a columnist for Province, *and contributing editor to* Business Travel Management Magazine. *His articles have appeared in a wide variety of travel and music publications worldwide.*

After Québec and Ontario, British Columbia is Canada's third-largest province. Only one American state, Alaska, is larger in surface area and only 30 nations in the world are bigger. The province is four times the size of Great Britain; Japan would fit into British Columbia 2½ times; and you could put California, Oregon, and Washington into British Columbia and have enough room left over for Tennessee.

But size alone doesn't account for British Columbia's popularity as a vacation destination. Even easterners, content in the fact that Ontario and Québec form the industrial heartland of Canada, admit that British Columbia is the most spectacular part of the nation. British Columbians see the rest of the country as a collection of workers, trying to save enough money to eventually move west and settle. The rest of the country, on the other hand, view British Columbians as a bit hedonistic.

The province used to be very British and predictable, reflecting its colonial heritage, but no longer. Vancouver, for example, has become an international city whose relaxed lifestyle is spiced by a rich and varied cultural scene embracing large Japanese, Chinese, Italian, and Greek communities. Even Victoria, which clings with restrained passion to British traditions and lifestyles, has undergone an international metamorphosis in recent years.

No matter how modern the province, evidence of the earliest settlers, Pacific Coast Indians (Haida, Kwakiutl, Cowichan, Sooke, Salish, and others), who occupied the land for more than 12,000 years before the first Europeans arrived en masse in the late 19th century, remains.

But material proof of their heritage may not be enough for today's Native Indians who often face social barriers that have kept them from the mainstream of the province's rich economy. Although some have gained university educations and have fashioned careers, many are just now beginning to make demands on the nonnative population. In dispute are thousands of square miles of land claimed as aboriginal territory, some of which is located within major cities such as Vancouver, Prince George, and Prince Rupert.

Although the issue of ownership remains inconclusive, testimony of British Columbia's roots is apparent throughout the province, from small-town boutiques to big-city dining establishments. Native arts, such as wood-carved objects and silver-etched pendants, fetch top dollar from visitors and residents alike, and Native Indian restaurants prepare authentic culinary delights from traditional recipes.

Essential Information

Important Addresses and Numbers

Tourist Information

For information concerning the province write to **Tourism British Columbia** (Parliament Buildings, Victoria V8V 1X4). There are 140 **Travel Infocentres** across the province.

The principal regional tourist offices are: **Tourism Association of Southwestern B.C.** (304–828 W. 8th Ave., Vancouver V5Z

1E2, tel. 604/876-3088); **Tourism Association of Vancouver Island** (302-45 Bastion Sq., Victoria V8W 1J1, tel. 604/382-3551); **Okanagan-Similkameen Tourist Association** (104-515 Hwy. 97 S, Kelowna V1Z 3J2, tel. 604/769-5959); **High Country Tourist Association** (403-186 Victoria St., Kamloops V2C 5R3, tel. 604/372-7770); **North By Northwest Tourism** (3840 Alfred Ave., Smithers V0J 2N0, tel. 604/847-5227); **Rocky Mountain Visitors Association** (495 Wallinger Ave., Kimberley V1A 2Y5, tel. 604/427-4838); **Prince Rupert Convention and Visitors Bureau** (100 McBride St., Box 669 CMG, Prince Rupert V8J 3S1, tel. 604/624-5637); **Kootenay Country Tourist Association** (610 Railway St., Nelson V1L 1H4, tel. 604/352-6033); **Cariboo Tourist Association** (190 Yorston St., Williams Lake V2G 2V8, tel. 604/392-2226); **Peace River Alaska Highway Tourist Association** (10631-100th St., Fort St. John V1J 4J3, tel. 604/785-2544).

Emergencies Dial **911** in Vancouver and Victoria; dial **0** elsewhere in the province for **police, ambulance,** or **poison control.**

Hospitals British Columbia has hospitals in virtually every town, including: in Victoria, **Victoria General Hospital** (33 Helmscken St., tel. 604/727-4212); in Prince George, **Prince George Regional Hospital** (200 15th Ave., tel. 604/565-2000 or for emergencies, 604/565-2444); in Kamloops, **Royal Inland Hospital** (311 Columbia St., tel. 604/374-5111); in Kelowna, **Kelowna General Hospital** (2268 Pandosy St., tel. 604/762-4000).

Late-night Pharmacies All-night pharmacies are unknown in British Columbia, even in the largest cities, although some pharmacies do offer after-hours emergency numbers. Generally, emergency prescriptions can be filled through major hospitals. The following is a list of some pharmacies that could provide assistance: in Victoria, **McGill and Orme Pharmacies** (649 Fort St., tel. 604/384-1195); in Prince George, **Hart Drugs** (3789 W. Austin Rd., tel. 604/962-9666); in Kamloops, **Kipp-Mallery I.D.A. Pharmacy** (273 Victoria St., tel. 604/372-2531); in Kelowna, **Willits-Taylor Rexall Drugs** (387 Bernard St., tel. 604/763-7525).

Arriving and Departing by Plane

Airports and Airlines British Columbia is served by **Victoria International Airport** and **Vancouver International Airport**. Domestic airports are in most cities. **Air Canada** (tel. 604/688-5515) and **Canadian Airlines International** (tel. 604/279-6611) are the two dominant carriers. **Air B.C.** (tel. 604/688-5515) is the major regional line, and runs daily flights between Seattle and Victoria.

Arriving and Departing by Car, Bus, and Boat

By Car Driving time from Seattle to Vancouver is about 2½ hours. There are three main routes leading into British Columbia: through Sparwood, in the south, take Highway 3; from Jasper and Banff, in the central region, travel on Route 1 (Trans-Canada) or Highway 5; and through Dawson Creek, in the north, follow Highways 2 and 97.

By Bus **Greyhound** (tel. 604/662-3222) connects destinations throughout British Columbia with cities and towns throughout the Pacific North Coast.

By Boat There is year-round water service (closed Christmas) between Victoria and Seattle via the ***Victoria Clipper*** (tel. 800/888-2535).

Washington State Ferries (tel. in Sydney, 604/656–1531; in Seattle, 206/464–6400) cross daily, year-round, between Victoria and Anacortes, WA. **Black Ball Transport** (tel. 604/386–2202) operates between Victoria and Port Angeles, WA.

Getting Around

By Air

Queen Charlotte Islands **Trans Provincial Airlines** (tel. 604/637–5355) charters floatplanes between Sandspit, Masset, Queen Charlotte City, and Prince Rupert daily except Christmas, December 26, and New Year's Day.

Vancouver Island **Helijet** (tel. 604/273–1414) helicopter service is available from downtown Vancouver to downtown Victoria.

By Car Major roads in British Columbia, and most secondary roads, are paved and well-engineered. Mountain driving is slower, but more scenic. There are no roads on the coast once you leave the populated areas of the southwest corner near Vancouver.

Car Rentals Most major agencies, including **Avis, Budget,** and **Hertz,** service cities throughout the province (*see* Chapter 1).

By Bus **Greyhound** (tel. 604/662–3222) serves the area with hundreds of stops within the province.

North of Vancouver Island **Farwest Bus Lines** (tel. 604/624–6400) serves Prince Rupert, Terrace, Kitimat, Stewart, and Smithers.

Vancouver Island **Pacific Coach Lines** (tel. in Victoria, 604/385–5731; in Vancouver, 604/681–1161) operates service to Victoria from Vancouver. **Island Bus Lines** (tel. 604/385–4411 or 800/663–8390) serves the Vancouver Island area. **Maverick Coach Lines** (tel. 604/255–1171) services Nanaimo from Vancouver, via B.C. Ferries (*see* below).

By Ferry **B.C. Ferries** (tel. in Vancouver, 604/685–1021; in Victoria, 604/656–0757; in Nanaimo, 604/753–6626) has an efficient cross-strait ferry service from Tsawwassen and Horseshoe Bay to Vancouver Island (Victoria and Nanaimo), and the Gulf Islands. Ferries usually depart on the hour 7 AM–9 PM and can carry about 360 cars and 1,500 passengers. Ferries also run from Powell River, Campbell River, Comox, and Port McNeill to the Gulf Islands; and from Port Hardy to Prince Rupert, although schedules vary greatly. When traveling with car during summer months, expect a long line and delays. For schedule information call the numbers above for a 24-hour recorded message.

By Train **BC Rail** (in Vancouver, tel. 604/984–5246 or 604/631–3500; in Prince George, tel. 604/564–9080) travels from Vancouver to Prince George, with 10 stops in major towns and 22 more stops in small towns along the 463-mile route.

Vancouver Island **Esquimalt & Nanaimo Rail Liner** (450 Pandora Ave., Victoria V8W 3L5, tel. 604/383–4324), operated by Via Rail, travels from Victoria to Courtenay and returns. It leaves Victoria's Pandora Avenue Station daily at 8:15 AM, arrives in Courtenay by 12:50 PM, and departs 25 minutes later for a 5:45 PM return.

Guided Tours

Orientation The following operators offer familiarization tours throughout the province: **Great Escape Vacations** (103-10711 Cambie Rd., Richmond, B.C. V6X 3G5, tel. in Vancouver, 604/273–9100 or outside Vancouver, 800/663–2515); **Westours** (100 W. Harrison Plaza, Seattle, WA 98119, tel. 206/281–3535); **Maverick Coach Lines** (150 Dunsmuir St., Vancouver, B.C. V6B 1X1, tel. 604/255–1171 or 800/972–6300); and **Sea to Sky** (1928 Nelson St., N. Vancouver, B.C., V7V 2P4, tel. 604/984–2224).

Special-interest *Nature Tours* A few Vancouver Island–based companies that conduct whale-watching tours are: **Subtidal Adventures** (Box 78, Ucluelet V0R 3A0, tel. 604/726–7336), **Inter-Island Excursions** (Box 393, Tofino V0R 2Z0, tel. 604/725–3163), **Ocean Pacific Whale Charters Ltd.** (Box 590, Tofino V0R 2Z0, tel. 604/725–3919), **Subtidal Adventures** (Box 78, Ucluelet V0R 3A0, tel. 604/726–7336), and **Tofino Sea-Kayaking Company** (320 Main St., Tofino, VOR 2Z0, tel. 604/725–4222) will paddle you up the fjords of Clayoquot Sound.

Ecosummer Expeditions (1516 Duranleau St., Vancouver V6H 3S4, tel. 604/669–7741) runs ecological tours of the Queen Charlotte Islands.

Exploring Coastal British Columbia

Orientation

More than three-quarters of British Columbia's land area is mountainous: The Rocky Mountains run the length of the province cutting diagonally from the southeast to the northwest, flanked by a series of companion ranges. In the northeast corner is the Peace River region, the major flatland area in British Columbia, which covers about 137,700 square kilometers (85,000 square miles). The central interior is a high plateau with dense fir and spruce forests, and some of the largest cattle ranches in the world. In the Pacific is Vancouver Island, a region the size of Holland, having a mountainous spine that runs its length and breaks into long mountain fjords on its west coast—a wilderness area that's largely uninhabited, save for a sprinkling of small communities.

This chapter covers Vancouver Island, the west coast, the Queen Charlotte Islands, and the Okanagan Valley.

Highlights for First-time Visitors

Cathedral Grove Nature Park, Tour 3: North of Vancouver Island
Craigdarroch Castle, Other Points of Interest
O'Keefe Historic Ranch, Tour 4: Okanagan Valley
Pacific Rim National Park, Tour 2: Vancouver Island
Royal British Columbia Museum, Tour 1: Victoria

Tour 1: Victoria

Numbers in the margin correspond with points of interest on the British Columbia and Downtown Victoria maps.

1 For the most part, **Victoria** is a walker's city; most of its main attractions are located downtown or are a few blocks from the core. Attractions on the outskirts of downtown can easily be reached by bus or a short cab ride. In the summer you have the added option of horse-drawn carriages, bicycle, boat, or double-decker bus tours.

2 A logical place to begin this tour is at the **Visitors Information Centre,** located along the waterfront. Pick through numerous leaflets, maps, and tourism information concerning Victoria, Vancouver Island, ferries, entertainment, and accommodations. *812 Wharf St., tel. 604/382–2127. Open June–Sept., daily 9–9, Mar.-May, daily 9–5.*

3 Just across the way is the recently renovated **Empress Hotel,** a symbol both of the city and of the Canadian Pacific Railway. Originally opened in 1908, the hotel was designed by Francis Rattenbury, a renowned architect whose works dot Vancouver. The Empress is another of the great châteaus built by Canadian Pacific, the still-current owners who also built the Chateau Frontenac in Québec City, Chateau Laurier in Ottawa, and Chateau Lake Louise. The $55 million facelift has been a hot topic of discussion in traditional Victoria, though not all of the comments have been positive; criticism aside, the ingredients that made the 480-room hotel a tourist attraction in the past are still alive. Stop in for high tea—served at 3 PM—and partake of the set menu of honeyed crumpets, scones with cream and jam, finger sandwiches, and tea. The experience may lend to your appreciation of the lobby's high-beamed ceiling and wood floors. In the basement of the hotel is an informative collection of historical photos and items from the hotel's early days. *721 Government St., tel. 604/384–8111. Reservations required. Proper dress required; no jeans, shorts, or T-shirts.*

Also, in the north wing of the Empress is **Miniature World,** where small replicas of people, trains, and historical events are displayed. In the basement of the hotel is an informative historical collection of photos and items from the establishment's early days. *649 Humbolt St., tel. 604/385–9731. Admission: $6 adults, $5 children 12–17, $4 children under 12; children under 10 and disabled persons with escort free. Hours vary depending on season; call ahead.*

4 Just across the way is **Crystal Gardens.** Opened in 1925 as the largest swimming pool in the British Empire, this glass-roof building—now owned by the provincial government—is home to flamingos, macaws, 75 varieties of other birds, hundreds of blooming flowers, wallabies, and monkeys. At street level there are several boutiques and Rattenbury's Restaurant, one of Victoria's well-frequented establishments. *713 Douglas St., tel. 604/381–1213. Admission: $5.50 adults, $3.50 children 6–16 and senior citizens. Open daily 10–5:30.*

5 Cross Belleville Street to reach the **Royal British Columbia Museum,** where nature's effects on man are chronicled. Adults and children can wander for hours through the centuries, beginning with the present and going back 12,000 years. In the prehistoric exhibit, you can actually smell the pines and hear the

calls of mammoths and other ancient wildlife. Other exhibits allow you to explore a turn-of-the-century town, with trains rumbling past; in the Kwakiutl Indian Bighouse, the smell of cedar envelops you, while piped-in potlatch songs tell the origins of the genuine ceremonial house before you. Also explored in this museum are the industrial era, fur trading, pioneering, and the effects of modern history on native Indian cultures. *675 Belleville St., tel. 604/387–3014. Admission: $5 adults, $3 students and senior citizens, $2 children 6–18 and disabled persons, children under 5 free. Open Oct.–Apr., daily 10–5:30; May–Sept., daily 9:30–7.*

6 Heading Government Street is the **Legislative Parliament Buildings** complex. The stone exterior building, completed in 1897, dominates the inner harbor and is flanked by two statues: Sir James Douglas, who chose the location of Victoria, and Sir Matthew Baille Begbie, the man in charge of law and order during the gold-rush era. Atop the dome is a gilded statue of Captain George Vancouver, who first sailed around Vancouver Island; a statue of Queen Victoria stands in front of the complex; and outlining the building at night are 3,000 lights. *501 Belleville Ave., tel. 604/387–3046. Admission free. Tours run several times daily, and are conducted in 6 languages in summer and 3 in winter.*

Time Out On the north side of the inner harbor you'll find several fast-food outlets where you can grab a hamburger, hot dog, or sandwich for a picnic on the huge lawn in front of the Parliament Building.

Nearby, up the steps in front of the Legislative buildings and 2 blocks down Belleville Street is the old CPR Steamship Terminal, also designed by Rattenbury and completed in 1924. Today
7 it is the **Royal London Wax Museum,** housing 200 wax figures, including replicas of Queen Victoria, Elvis, Marilyn Monroe, and nearly 200 other life-size figures. *470 Belleville St., tel. 604/388–4461. Admission: $5.25 adults, $4.50 students and senior citizens, $2.50 children 5–12. Open Mar.-Dec., daily 9:30–5; Jan.–Feb., call ahead, as schedule varies greatly.*

8 Next to the wax museum is the **Pacific Undersea Garden,** where more than 5,000 marine specimens are on display in their natural habitat. You also get performing scuba divers and Armstrong the giant octopus. Unfortunately, there are no washrooms, and the site is not wheelchair accessible. *490 Belleville St., tel. 604/382–5717. Admission: $5.50 adults, $5 senior citizens, $4 children 12–17, $2.50 children 5–11. Open daily 9–5; closed Christmas. Shows run about every 45 minutes.*

A walk east on Belleville Street to Douglas Street will lead you
9 to the **Beacon Hill Park,** a favorite place for joggers, walkers, and cyclists. On the southern end of the park is **Findlayson Point,** the site of a fortified Indian village, though there's little visible evidence of the settlement. Between 1878 and 1892, the two cannons here protected the point against an expected Russian invasion that never took place.

10 From the park, pick up Douglas Street going north to **Bastion Square,** with its gas lamps, restaurants, cobblestone streets, and small shops. This is the spot James Douglas chose as the original Fort Victoria in 1841 and the original Hudson's Bay Company trading post. Today fashion boutiques and restau-

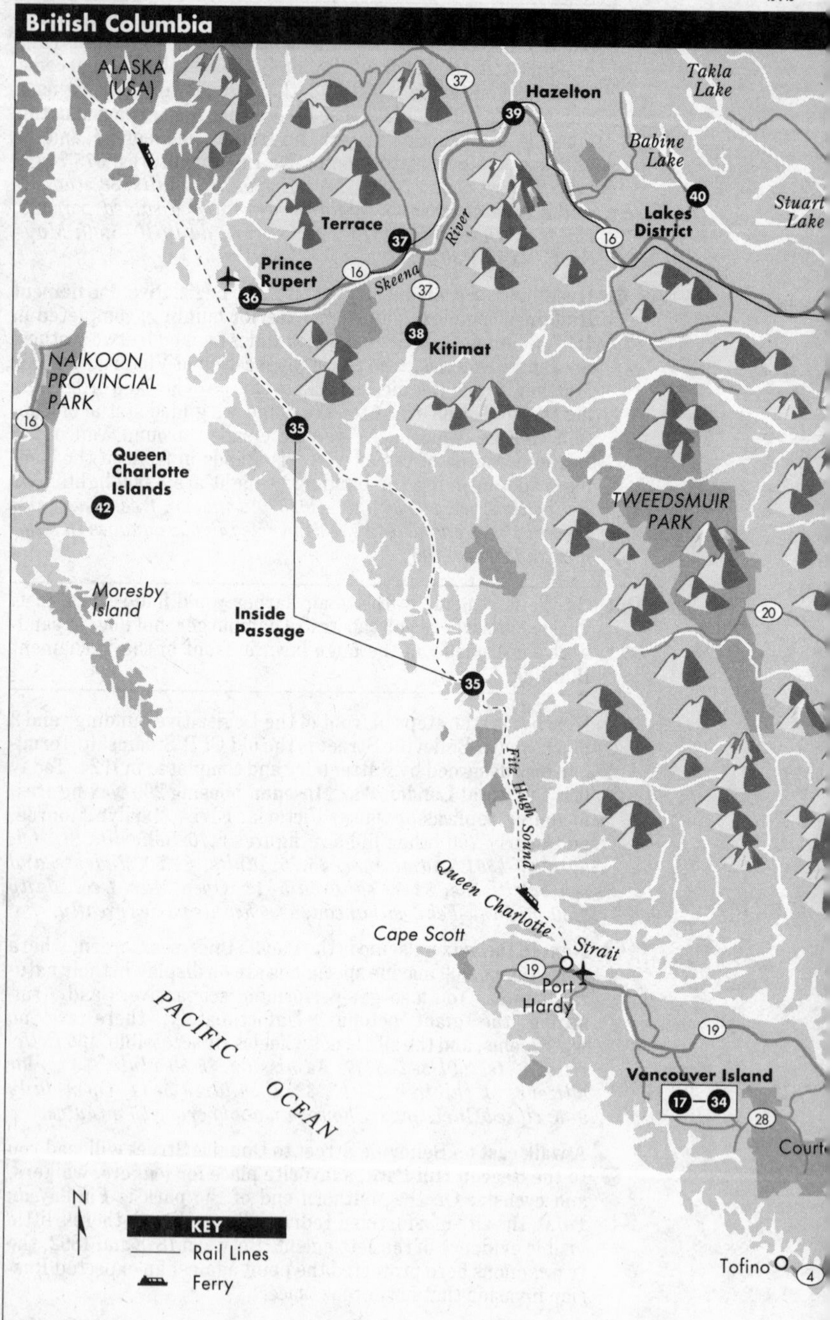
British Columbia
ALASKA (USA)
Hazelton
Takla Lake
Babine Lake
Stuart Lake
Lakes District
Terrace
Skeena River
Prince Rupert
Kitimat
NAIKOON PROVINCIAL PARK
Queen Charlotte Islands
TWEEDSMUIR PARK
Moresby Island
Inside Passage
Fitz Hugh Sound
Queen Charlotte Strait
Cape Scott
Port Hardy
PACIFIC OCEAN
Vancouver Island
17–34
Court
Tofino
KEY
Rail Lines
Ferry
N
0
100 miles
0
140 km
16
37
19
20
28
4
35
36
38
39
40
42

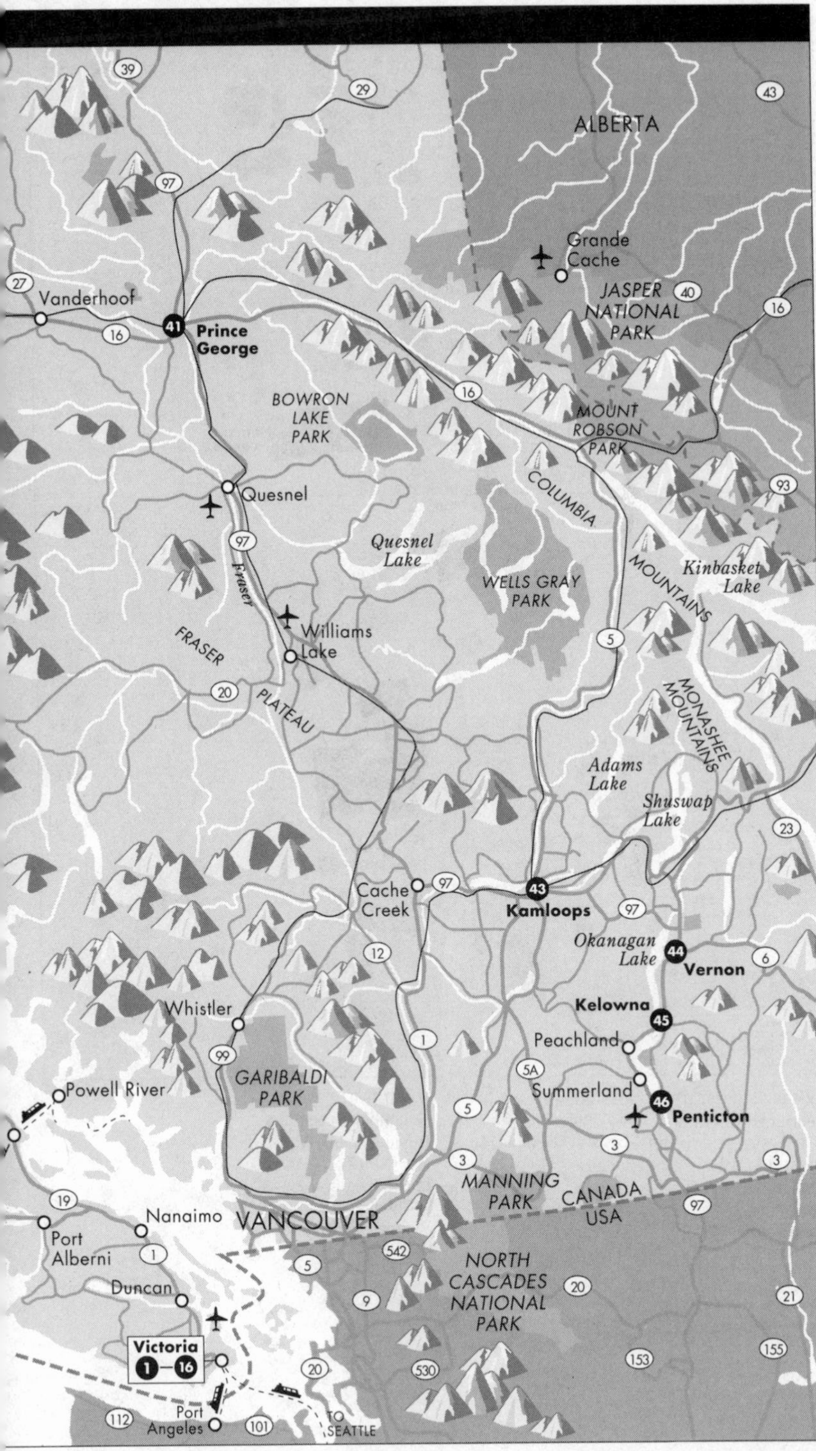
ALBERTA
Grande Cache
JASPER NATIONAL PARK
Vanderhoof
41 Prince George
BOWRON LAKE PARK
MOUNT ROBSON PARK
COLUMBIA MOUNTAINS
Quesnel
Quesnel Lake
WELLS GRAY PARK
Kinbasket Lake
Fraser
Williams Lake
FRASER PLATEAU
MONASHEE MOUNTAINS
Adams Lake
Shuswap Lake
Cache Creek
43 Kamloops
Okanagan Lake
44 Vernon
Kelowna 45
Peachland
Summerland
46 Penticton
Whistler
GARIBALDI PARK
Powell River
MANNING PARK
CANADA
USA
Nanaimo
VANCOUVER
Port Alberni
NORTH CASCADES NATIONAL PARK
Duncan
Victoria 1–16
Port Angeles
TO SEATTLE

Downtown Victoria

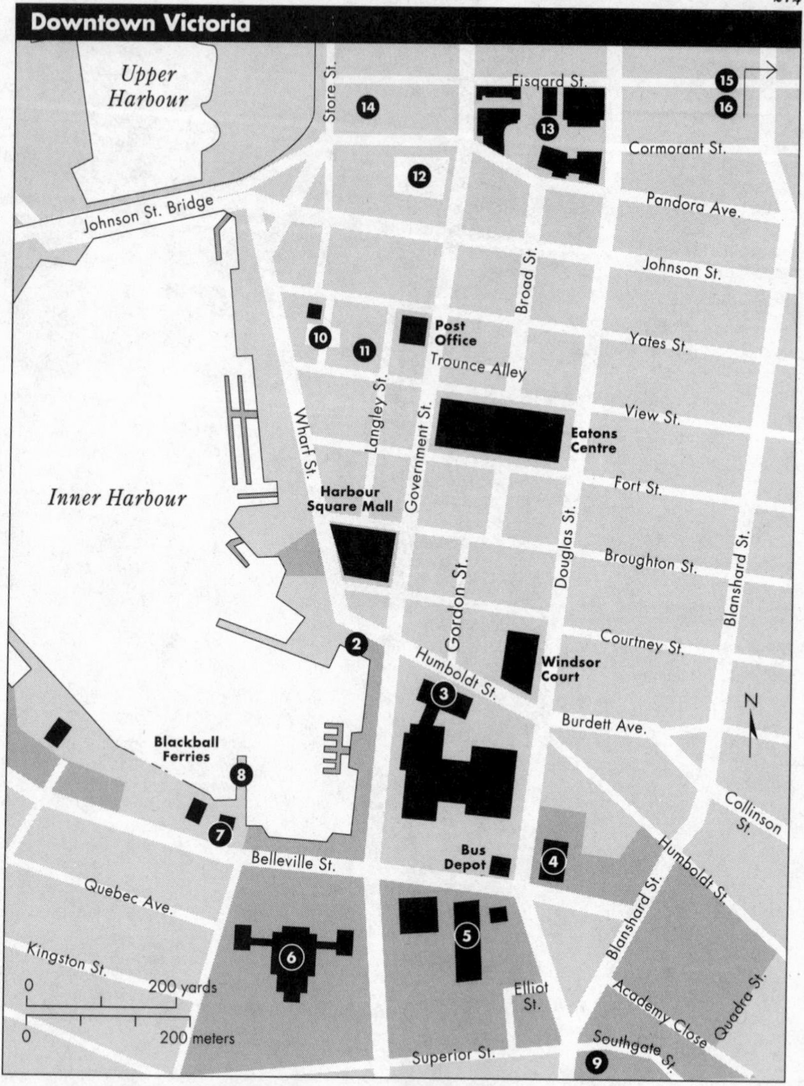

Bastion Square, **10**
Beacon Hill Park, **9**
Centennial Square/Old Town, **13**
Chinatown, **14**
Craigflower Farmhouse, **15**
Craigflower Schoolhouse, **16**
Crystal Gardens, **4**
Empress Hotel, **3**
Legislative/Parliament Buildings, **6**
Maritime Museum, **11**
Market Square, **12**
Royal British Columbia Museum, **5**
Royal London Wax Museum, **7**
Pacific Undersea Garden, **8**
Visitors Information Centre, **2**

rants occupy the old buildings. At the Wharf Street end of the square are some benches where you can rest your feet and catch a great view of the harbor. While you're here, you may want to stop in at what was Victoria's original courthouse, but is now
11 the **Maritime Museum of British Columbia.** Dugout canoes, model ships, Royal Navy charts, photographs, uniforms, and ships bells chronicle Victoria's seafaring history. A seldom-used 90-year-old cage lift, believed to be the oldest in North America, ascends to the third floor. *28 Bastion Sq., tel. 604/385–4222. Admission: $4 adults, $3 senior citizens, $1 children 6–18, children under 6 free. Open Sept. 16–June 16, daily 9:30–4:30; June 17-Sept. 15, daily 9:30–6:30; closed Christmas and New Year's Day.*

West of Government Street, between Pandora Avenue and
12 Johnson Street is **Market Square,** offering a variety of specialty shops and boutiques and considered one of the most picturesque shopping districts in the city. At the turn of the century this area—once part of Chinatown—provided everything a visitor desired: food, lodging, entertainment. Today the square, with its pre-1900's architecture restored to its original character, caters not only to shoppers but sightseers, too.

13 Bordering Pandora Avenue is **Centennial Square,** and the oldest part of Victoria. The buildings in the area date from about 1880 and 1890. The crown jewel in this collection is the refurbished three-story **Victoria City Hall,** originally constructed in 1878. The design incorporated high, arched windows and a clock tower was added in 1891. For the best view, walk up to Douglas Street to the front of the building. The facade masks modern government offices located inside.

A walk down nearby Fisgard Street, along Centennial Square,
14 will take you into one of the oldest **Chinatowns** in Canada. It was the Chinese who were responsible for building much of the Canadian Pacific Railway in the 19th century; and their influences still mark the region. Along the street, merchants display fragile paper lanterns, embroidered silks, imported fruits, and vegetables. **Fan Tan Alley,** situated just off Fisgard Street, holds claim not only to being the narrowest street in North America but also to having been the gambling and opium center of Chinatown, where mah-jongg, fantan, and dominoes games were played.

A 10-minute drive northeast of downtown Victoria will take
15 you to **Craigflower Farmhouse,** once the residence of Kenneth McKenzie, the overseer of one of the first farms established by the Hudson's Bay Company. The original structure—completed in 1856—and most of the furniture remain. *110 Island Hwy., tel. 604/387–4697. Admission: $3. Open May–Oct., daily 10–5; Nov.–Apr., Sun. 10–5.*

16 While at the farmhouse, ask for a tour of the **Craigflower Schoolhouse,** constructed 1854–55 from lumber supplied by the sawmill at the farm. Inside, the sloping door frames and tilting fireplace support the local legend that tells of drunken workers who built this one-room schoolhouse that operated until 1911. *2765 Admiral's Rd., no tel. Admission: $2. Tours given upon request at the farmhouse.*

Tour 2: Vancouver Island

Numbers in the margin correspond with points of interest on the British Columbia and Vancouver Island maps.

17 **Vancouver Island,** the largest island on the west coast, stretches 450 kilometers (280 miles) from Victoria in the south to Cape Scott, although 97% of the population live between Victoria and Campbell River (halfway up the island); 50% of them live in Victoria itself. Geographically, the differences between the east and west are impressive. The western side is wild, often inhospitable, with just a handful of small settlements. Virtually all of the island's human habitation is on the eastern coast where the weather is gentler and the topography is low-lying.

The cultural heritage of the island is Native Indian from the Kwakiutl, Nootka, and Coastal Salish groups. Native Indian art and cultural centers flourish throughout the region, especially in the lower section of the island. These centers enable visitors to catch a glimpse of contemporary Indian culture.

Mining, logging, and tourism are the important island industries. But environmental issues, such as logging practices by British Columbia's lumber companies, are becoming important to islanders—both native and non-native. Residents are working to reach a happy medium between the island's wilderness and its economy that is dependent on industrial development and tourism.

Beginning your driving tour from Victoria, travel up the eastern coast of Vancouver Island, toward Nanaimo, the mid-island B.C. Ferries terminal point. On your way you'll pass through
18 the town of **Duncan** (about 70 kilometers, or 43 miles, north of Victoria), home to the **Native Heritage Centre**, which opened in spring 1990. Covering 13 acres of land on the banks of the Cowichan River, the center features an Indian big house, interpretive dance presentations, an arts-and-crafts gallery that focuses on carvings and weaving traditions, and evenings of Potlatch entertainment complete with a barbecued salmon dinner. The center is still experiencing growing pains, so schedules may fluctuate; call ahead. *200 Cowichan Way, Duncan, tel. 604/746–8119. Admission: $5.50 adults, $3.75 children and senior citizens. Open May–Sept., daily 10–9; Oct.–Apr., call for schedule.*

Also in Duncan is the **B.C. Forest Museum.** More a park than a museum, the theme is "Man in the Forest," and it covers native Indian life from prehistory to the present. The attraction spans more than 40 hectares (100 acres), and includes indoor and outdoor exhibits and walking trails that detail the history of forestry in British Columbia. An original steam locomotive takes you from the entrance, over an old wood trestle bridge, to the main exhibit, which features logging and milling equipment. One of Duncan's main attractions is the Glass Castle, a home the superstructure of which is built entirely form glass bottles. Also, totem poles can be found in the center of the old town, and behind City Hall (corner of Kenneth and Craig streets) are two wood carvings; one is of a North American Indian, the other is of a New Zealand Maori donated by Duncan's sister city, Kaikohe. *RR 4 Trans-Canada Hwy., tel. 604/746–1251. Admission: $4.50 adults,*

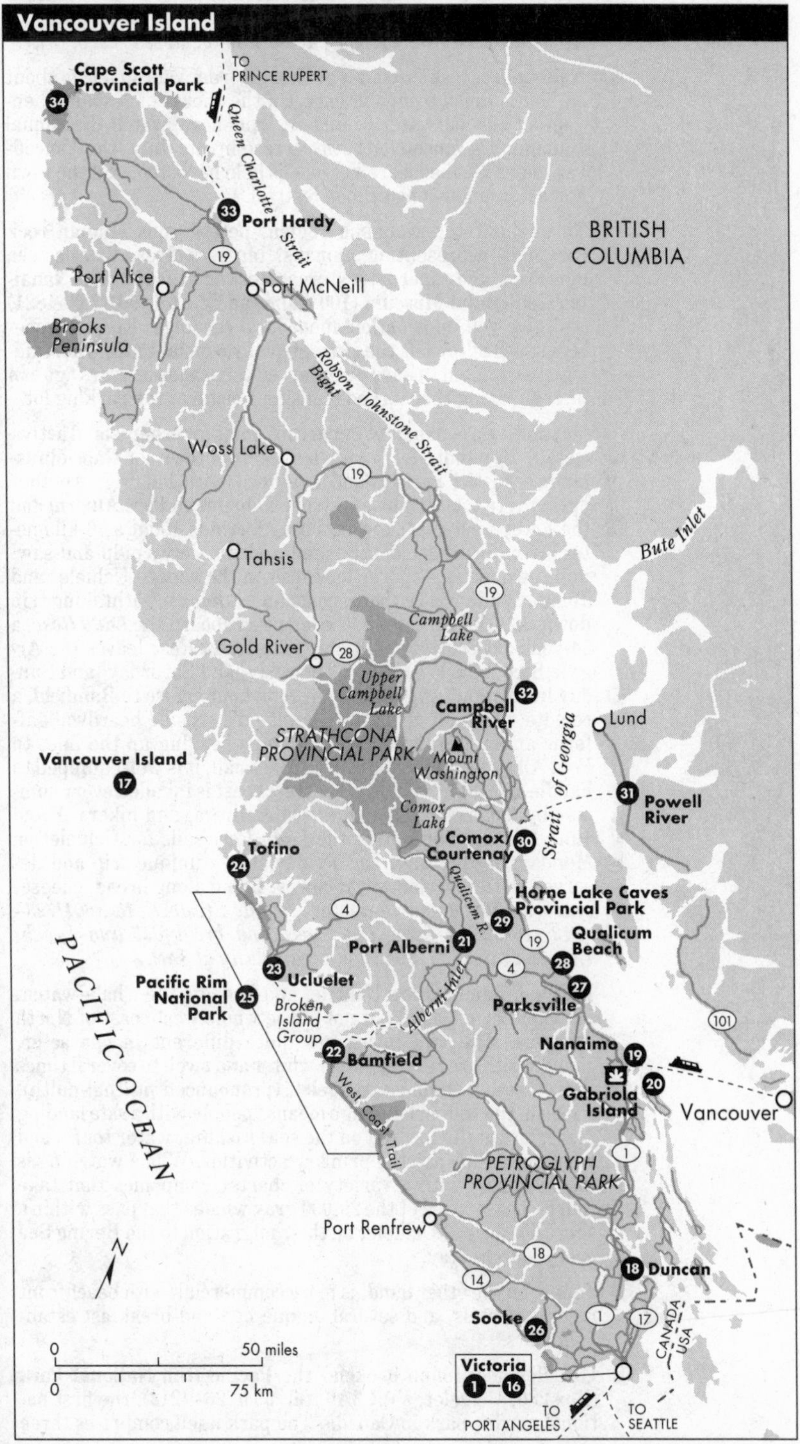
Vancouver Island
TO PRINCE RUPERT
Cape Scott Provincial Park
34
Queen Charlotte Strait
33 Port Hardy
BRITISH COLUMBIA
19
Port Alice
Port McNeill
Brooks Peninsula
Robson Bight
Johnstone Strait
Woss Lake
19
Bute Inlet
Tahsis
19
Campbell Lake
Gold River
28
Upper Campbell Lake
32
Campbell River
Lund
STRATHCONA PROVINCIAL PARK
Mount Washington
Strait of Georgia
Vancouver Island
17
31 Powell River
Comox Lake
Comox/ Courtenay 30
Tofino
24
Qualicum R.
Horne Lake Caves Provincial Park
29
4
Port Alberni 21
19
Qualicum Beach
28
PACIFIC OCEAN
4
27
23 Ucluelet
Pacific Rim National Park 25
Parksville
Broken Island Group
Alberni Inlet
101
22 Bamfield
Nanaimo 19
20
Gabriola Island
Vancouver
West Coast Trail
1
PETROGLYPH PROVINCIAL PARK
Port Renfrew
N
18
18 Duncan
14
Sooke
26
1
17
CANADA
USA
0
50 miles
0
75 km
Victoria
1 – 16
TO PORT ANGELES
TO SEATTLE

$3.50 senior citizens and children 13–18, $2 children 6–12. Open late-Apr.–early Sept., daily 9:30–6; closed rest of year.

19 **Nanaimo,** across the strait of Georgia from Vancouver, is about an hour's drive from Victoria. Off the shores of Nanaimo, engage in fine saltwater fishing or, from here, watch the annual Nanaimo-to-Vancouver bathtub race in mid-July; the Vancouver Island Shakespeare Festival is held here, too, and the town hosts a summer-long salmon festival.

Throughout the Nanaimo region, petroglyphs (Indian rock carvings) representing humans, birds, wolves, lizards, sea monsters, and supernatural creatures can be found. The **Nanaimo Centennial Museum** (100 Cameron St., tel. 604/753–1821) will give you information about local carvings. Eight kilometers south of town is the **Petroglyph Provincial Park,** where designs estimated to have been carved thousands of years ago can be seen, along the marked trails that begin at the parking lot.

Nanaimo is a convenient departure point for other island activi-
20 ties. A 20-minute ferry ride leaves from town for **Gabriola Island,** a rustic, rural island equipped with lodging. Another
option is to take Highway 4 from Nanaimo to Port Alberni and
21 the lower west-coast towns. **Port Alberni** is about a 70-kilome-
ter (44-mile) drive from Nanaimo and is mainly a pulp-and-saw-
mill town and a stopover for those on the way to Ucluelet and
Tofino. While you're there, consider taking a breathtaking trip
down the Alberni Inlet to the open sea aboard the ***Lady Rose***, a
54-year-old Scottish-built ship. The *Lady Rose* leaves the Argyle Street dock Tuesday, Thursday, and Saturday (and Sun-
22 day in July and August) for the four-hour cruise to **Bamfield,** a
remote village of about 200. Bamfield's seaside boardwalk affords an uninterrupted view of ships heading up the inlet to
Port Alberni. Oddly, for a place this small, it is well equipped to
handle overnight visitors. The west coast is invaded every summer by fishermen, kayakers, scuba divers, and hikers. From
June 1 to mid-September the *Lady Rose* sails for Ucluelet on
Monday, Wednesday, and Friday. It's a unique trip and de-
serves all the accolades it receives. Bring along bread, cheese,
and wine for added character. *Argyle St. dock, tel. 604/723–
8313. Bamfield fare: $30, including breakfast and lunch;
Ucluelet fare: $35. Sailings depart daily at 8AM.*

North of Bamfield are Ucluelet and Tofino—the whale-watching capitals of Canada, if not of the whole west coast of North
America. The two towns are quite different in character,
though both are relaxed in the winter and swell to several times
23 their sizes in summer. **Ucluelet,** (pronounced nu-chal-nulth),
which in the Indian language means "people with a safe landing
place," is totally focused on the sea. Fishing, water tours, and
whale watching are the primary activities. Whale watching is
big business, with a variety of charter companies that take
tourist boats to greet the 20,000 gray whales that pass within a
short distance of Ucluelet on their migration to the Bering Sea
every March–May.

24 **Tofino,** on the other hand, is more commercial, with beachfront resorts, motels, and several unique bed-and-breakfast establishments.

25 Ucluelet and Tofino bookend the **Pacific Rim National Park** (Box 280, Ucluelet, V0R 3A0, tel. 604/726–4212), the first national marine park in Canada. The park itself comprises three

separate areas—Long Beach, the Broken Group Islands, and the West Coast Trail. Each is designed to accommodate a specific interest.

Long Beach is an 11-kilometer (7-mile) strip of hard-packed white sand strewn with twisted driftwood, shells, and the occasional Japanese glass fishing float. Needless to say, the beach is a favorite spot during the summer and you often have to fight heavy traffic along the twisting 85 kilometers (53 miles) of Highway 4 from Port Alberni.

The 100 islands of the **Broken Group Islands** can be reached only by boat. Many boating tours are available from Ucluelet, which rests at the southern end of the park and at the entrance to the island group. The 100 islands are alive with sea lions, seals, and whales. The sheltered lagoons of Gibralter, Jacques, and Hand islands offer protection and good boating conditions, but go with a guide.

The third element of the park is the **West Coast Trail** that stretches along the coast from Bamfield to Port Renfrew. It can be traveled only on foot and takes an average of six days to complete. The 75-kilometer (44-mile) trail is for experienced hikers and follows part of the coast called the "Graveyard of the Pacific," so called because of the large number of shipwrecks that occurred there. After the SS *Valencia* ran aground in 1906, killing all the crew and passengers, the Canadian government constructed a lifesaving trail to help future victims of shipwrecks reach safe ground. The trail remains, with demanding bogs, steep slopes and gullies, cliffs (with ladders), slippery boardwalks, and insects. Although the difficult West Coast Trail presents many obstacles for hikers, the reward are the panoramic views of the sea, dense rain forest, sandstone cliffs with waterfalls, and wildlife that includes gray whales and seals.

26 Following Highway 14 from Port Renfrew you can reach **Sooke,** (26 miles, or 42 kilometers, west of Victoria), a logging, fishing, and farming community that's a very popular summer place for hikers and campers. The **Sooke Regional Museum and Travel Infocentre** is a worthwhile stop for information about the region. *2070 Phillips Rd., Box 774, V0S 1N0, tel. 604/642–6351. Admission free; donations accepted. Open summer, daily 9–7; winter, daily 9–5; spring, daily 9–6; closed Christmas.*

Time Out **Seventeen Mile House** (5196 Sooke Rd., Victoria, tel. 604/642–5942) is on the road to Sooke from Victoria. Stop here for English pub fare, a beer, or fresh local seafood. Built as a hotel, the house is an education in turn-of-the-century island architecture, as well.

If you choose to follow the eastern coastline from Nanaimo, in-
27 stead of heading off to Port Alberni, go on to **Parksville**—one of the east island's primary resort areas with lodges and waterfront motels catering to families, campers, and boaters. It's the entry to **Cathedral Grove Nature Park** (32 km, 20 mi west on Hwy. 4 to Port Alberni), long regarded by Indians as a sacred place. This stand of giant Douglas fir and western red cedar is one of the few remaining areas of its sort on the west coast. The tops of all the trees form a cathedral-like ceiling high above your head while the thick tree trunks, some as old as 800 years, rise as pillars from a forest floor of delicate fern. The park is

bordered by the highway that takes you into Port Alberni and eventually to the Pacific Rim National Park (*see* above).

28 Just 12 kilometers (7 miles) north of Parksville is **Qualicum Beach,** known largely for its salmon fishing and opportunities for beachcombing along the long, sandy beaches. The nonprofit **Old School House Gallery and Art Centre** (122 Fern Rd. W., tel. 604/752–6133) shows and sells the work of local artists and artisans.

Backtrack about a mile and head west off the highway and follow signs for about 8 kilometers (5 miles) to Horne Lake and the
29 **Horne Lake Caves Provincial Park.** Several of the caves are open at all times and vary in length and size from spacious chambers to small crawlways. Riverbend Cave has a total of 383 meters (1,259 feet) of mapped passages, but only guided access is allowed and must be arranged ahead of time. The upper third is spacious and accessible but lower sections require ladders, ropes, and some agility. Spelunking lessons and tours are offered for all levels, from beginner to advanced. *Tel. 604/248–3931. Fees for tours vary depending on ability level. Reservations required for tours.*

30 **Comox** and **Courtenay,** the twin cities of the island, are on the edge of **Strathcona Provincial Park,** and are commonly used as a base for anyone skiing Mt. Washington in the winter. Strathcona, the largest provincial park on Vancouver Island, encompasses **Mt. Golden Hinde,** at 2,200 meters (7, 218 feet) the island's highest mountain; and **Della Falls,** Canada's highest waterfall, reaching 440 meters (1,443 feet). The park's multitude of lakes and 161 campsites attract summer canoers, fishermen, and wilderness campers, and the **Strathcona Park Lodge and Outdoor Information Center,** well known for its wilderness-skills programs, provides information on the park's facilities. *Information Center, Hwy. 28, on Upper Campbell Lake, about 38 km (23 mi) west of Highway 19, Box 2160, Campbell River, V9W 5C9, tel. 604/286–3122.*

From Comox, you can take a 75-minute ferry east across the
31 Strait of Georgia to **Powell River,** a city extablished around the MacMillan pulp-and-paper mill, which opened in 1912. Renowned as a year-round salmon-fishing destination, the Sunshine Coast town has 30 regional lakes that offer exceptional trout fishing, as well. For information contact **Powell River Travelinfo Center** (6807 Wharf St., tel. 604/485–4701). Also from the twin cities, take the Lake Trail Road, turning right at Powerhouse Road, then follow the signs to the **Puntledge River and Hatchery** (Box 3111, Courtenay V9N 5N3, tel. 604/338–7444), where you can observe migrating fish.

32 **Campbell River,** a more commercial town than the others, is ringed by shopping centers that make it look like a free-zoned mess. But people don't come here for the aesthetics, they come for the fish; some of the biggest salmon ever caught on a line have been landed just off the coast of Campbell River. At the mouth of the town's namesake, you can vie for membership in Campbell River's Tyee Club, which would allow you to fish in a specific area, and possibly land a giant chinook. Requirements for membership in the club include registering and landing a tyee (a spring salmon weighing 30 pounds or more). Coho salmon and cutthroat trout are also plentiful in the river. *Travel Information Center, 1235 Island Hwy., Box 400, Campbell*

River, V9W 5B6, tel. 604/286–0764. Open June 25–Labor Day, daily 8–8; rest of year, Mon.–Fri. 9–5.

Pods of resident Orcas are nearby year-round in Johnstone Strait; and in one area, Robson Bight, they like using the beaches to rub against. Because of their presence, Robson Bight has been made into an ecological preserve: Whales must not be disturbed by human observers there. Gray whales migrate between Baja California and Alaska, traveling north in spring and south in fall. A few whales remain all summer near Vancouver Island but for certain results, you have to go in season.

33 Farther north is **Port Hardy,** the departure and arrival point for B.C. Ferries through the Inside Passage to Prince Rupert and the gateway to the Queen Charlotte Islands. If you choose to continue to the northernmost point on Vancouver Island, drive about 60 kilometers (about 37 miles) on logging roads to
34 reach **Cape Scott Provincial Park,** a wilderness camping region designed for well-equipped and experienced hikers. A network of trails carved through the wilderness by enterprising Danish colonists in the late 1800s has been rescued from encroaching rainforests. At Sand Neck, a strip of land that joins the cape to the mainland of the island, you can see both the eastern and western shores at once. Remnants of abandoned home sites, including rows of weatherbeaten wood fences, attest to the government's broken promise to settlers to provide access roads to markets so residents could sell crops, lumber, and fish.

Tour 3: North of Vancouver Island

Numbers in the margin correspond with points of interest on the British Columbia map.

35 Cruising the 274-nautical-mile **Inside Passage,** between Port Hardy on northern Vancouver Island and Prince Rupert, is a sail through sheltered marine highway that follows a series of natural channels behind protective islands along the green-and-blue shaded British Columbia coast. The undisturbed landscape of rising mountains and humpbacked islands has a prehistoric look that leaves an indelible impression.

After a short segment in the open ocean, the 410-foot MV *Queen of the North* ducks in behind Calvert Island into Fitz Hugh Sound. From there, its route is protected from ocean swells all the way through Finlayson and Grenville channels, which are flanked by high, densely wooded mountains that rise steeply, in places, from narrow channels. The *Queen of the North* carries 750 passengers and 157 vehicles, and takes an entire day to make the Port Hardy to Prince Rupert trip. The ship has plenty of deck space plus lounge areas, a self-serve cafeteria, and a satisfactory restaurant that offers a plentiful buffet. Sleeping rooms are included in the fare. Children can play in the Captain Kids Room. *British Columbia Ferry Corporation, 1112 Fort St., Victoria V8V 4V2, tel. 604/386–3431. Cost: one-way pedestrian Port Hardy–Prince Rupert, $68; with car, $142. Reservations required and advised for hotel accommodations at ports of call. Oct. 1–May 31 sailings are twice-weekly; June 1–Sept. 30 sailings daily, departing on alternate days from Port Hardy and Prince Rupert; departure time 7:30 AM, arrival time 10:30 PM. Schedule and fares subject to change.*

An alternative to the ferry cruise along the Inside Passage is to take the much more expensive luxury-liner cruises that sail along the B.C. coast (*see* Chapter 1) from Vancouver to Alaska. The ships cruise the waters that are inhabited with the occasional Orca, pods of dolphins, schools of fish, and throngs of birds that follow the ship.

36 **Prince Rupert,** the final stop on the B.C. Ferries route through the Inside Passage, is about 750 air kilometers (465 miles) northwest of Vancouver. It takes more than 20 hours to drive the 1,500 kilometers (936 miles) from Vancouver, and around the coastal mountains that make most of British Columbia's coastline inaccessible by vehicle. Prince Rupert has a mild but wet climate, so take an umbrella and rain gear.

The town lives off fishing, fish processing, logging, saw- and pulp-mill operations, and deep-sea shipping. It's also a place where British Columbia's cultural heritage is quite evident. The **Museum of Northern British Columbia** has one of the finest collections throughout the province of coastal Indian art, some artifacts dating back 10,000 years. Also featured are native artisans who carve totem poles in the carving shed and a 2½-hour boat tour of the harbor and Metlaktla Indian village. *1st Ave. and McBride St., Prince Rupert, tel. 604/624–3207. Admission: free; donations accepted. Open Sept–May, Mon.–Sat. 10–5; June–Aug., Mon–Sat. 9–9, Sun. 9–5.*

From Prince Rupert you can continue on to explore either the Alaskan Panhandle, interior British Columbia, or the Queen Charlotte Islands. If you wish to proceed north through the Alaskan waterways to Skagway, board the **Alaska Marine Highway System ferry** (tel. in Prince Rupert, 604/627–1745 or 800/642–0066), which docks alongside the *Queen of the North* in Prince Rupert. Alaska ferries travel this route daily in the summer; and on Tuesday and Friday from October to April.

To see interior British Columbia, take Highway 16. En route
37 38 you'll pass through or near such communities as **Terrace; Kiti-**
39 **mat** (on Highway 37, south of Highway 16); **Hazelton,** a town
40 surrounded by eight Indian villages; and the serene **Lakes Dis-**
41 **trict,** before coming to **Prince George** (Tourism Prince George, 1198 Victoria St., V2L 2L2, tel. 604/562–3700), British Columbia's third-largest city and the northern part of the province's hub. The province's focal point for east-west, north-south travel, the town is almost perfectly centered geographically.

The other choice from Prince Rupert is to visit the popular va-
42 cation destination, the **Queen Charlotte Islands,** or misty islands. Though once the remote preserve of the Haida Indians, the archipelago is now easily accessed by ferry. Though the Haida population at one time numbered high, today its numbers are few, making up about one-sixth of the total island population. Still, they're an important ingredient not only to the logging and fishing industries, but to tourism, as well. Haida elders lead tours—an essential service if you want to reach the isolated, abandoned villages. Though the region has become a popular tourist destination, limited accommodations make it necessary to reserve guest rooms well in advance.

The ***Queen of Prince Rupert*** (tel. in Prince Rupert, 604/624–9627) sails five times a week in June, and six times a week from July to October, and can easily accommodate recreational vehicles. Crossing the Hecate Strait from Prince Rupert to

Skidegate, near Queen Charlotte City on Graham Island takes about six hours. Schedules vary, so call ahead. The **MV *Kwuna,*** a B.C. Ferries ship, connects Skidegate Landing to Alliford Bay on Morseby Island, with 11 twenty-minute sailings daily. Access to smaller islands off Graham Island (the northernmost and largest of the group of 150) and Morseby Island is by boat or air, but plans should be made in advance through a travel agent.

In the Queen Charlottes, there are 150 kilometers (93 miles) of paved road, most of it on Graham Island, connecting Queen Charlotte City in the south to Masset in the north. The rest of the islands are laced with gravel roads, most of which can be accessed with any sturdy car or RV. The six islands that make up the biggest portion of the group are **Langara, Graham, Moresby, Louise, Lyell,** and **Kunghit,** with Graham the northernmost and largest. The rugged, rocky west coast of the archipelago faces the ocean, while the east coast has many broad sandy beaches. Throughout, the mountains and shores are often shrouded in fog and rain-laden clouds, adding to the mysteriousness of the islands.

Naikoon Provincial Park (tel. 604/557–4390), in the northeast corner of Graham, preserves a large section of the unique wilderness found here, where low-lying swamps, pine and cedar, lakes, beaches, trails, and wildlife combine to create an intriguing environment. The Haida people once occupied three major and five minor villages nearby. Take the 5-kilometer (3-mile) beach walk to the bow section of the old wooden shipwreck of the *Pezuta*, a 1928 hauling vessel once used by logging companies, but now a major tourist attraction.

Isolation from the mainland has given rise to subspecies of wildlife that are unique to the Queen Charlottes, including the largest black bears in the world and the world's largest concentration of the Peale peregrine falcon. Thus, the islands are sometimes called the Galapagos of the Northwest. Plan more than a day's stay on the islands so you can absorb the intrigue of these mysterious islands. *Queen Charlotte Islands Chamber of Commerce, Box 38, Masset V0T 1M0, tel. 604/626–5211.*

Tour 4: Okanagan Valley

Numbers in the margin correspond with points of interest on the British Columbia map.

The Okanagan Valley is a highland plateau between the Cascade range of mountains on the west and the Monashee mountains on the east. Dominating the valley is Okanagan Lake, a vacation hot-spot for tourists from the west coast and Alberta. In summer months it can be difficult to find accommodations.

The valley includes Penticton to the south, Kelowna in the middle, and Vernon at the north end. Between are the recreational and resort communities of **Summerland, Peachland, Westbank,** and **Oyama.** These communities situated along the lake are popular tourist destinations and have camping facilities, motels, and cabins. Favorite local lore attests to the legendary Ogopogo, a snakelike creature that inhabits the lake between Peachland and Summerland. Though small in size (only 3% of the province's total land mass), the area contains the interior's largest concentration of people. Kamloops, though not officially a part of the Okanagan, is a convenient passageway from Fraser Canyon and Thompson Valley.

The valley is the fruit-growing capital of Canada, producing apricots, cherries, pears, plums, apples, and peaches. A visit to the region from mid-April through early June promises to jolt to your senses, with the brightness of spring blossoms, and a sweet smell in the air that can't be found later in the summer.

43 **Kamloops,** 50 minutes northeast of Vancouver by air and 425 kilometers (260 miles) from Vancouver, is in the center of some of the best inland fishing to be found in British Columbia, and is not far from Adams River where each year millions of salmon migrate to their birthplace to breed. The **Adams River Salmon Run,** 65 kilometers (40 miles) east of Kamloops off the Trans-Canada Highway, is one of the biggest sockeye salmon runs in the world and one of the great natural wonders on the continent; it is also the base of British Columbia's entire fishing industry.

The river is protected by the **Roderick Haig-Brown Conservation Area** in its 11-kilometer (7-mile) run between Adams and Shuswap lakes. Salmon that have fought their way up the Fraser and Thompson rivers start arriving in Adams River in October. In a dominant run on the Adams River, once every four years, up to 200,000 visitors come to watch 2 million salmon jam into the creek to spawn.

Vernon, Kelowna, and Penticton, running south along Highway 97, like to believe each has a distinct personality, but local rivalries aside, this is actually one large unit. Okanagan Lake is their glue, offering recreational activities, lodging, and restaurants.

44 **Vernon** draws its economic strength more from forestry and agriculture and less from tourism than Kelowna or Penticton. The **O'Keefe Historic Ranch,** 10 kilometers (6 miles) north of Vernon, recalls the early cowboy days in the highland interior of British Columbia. The O'Keefe mansion is an 1876 log house that has a magnificent interior luxuriously furnished with original antiques that were considered the best of Canadian craftsmanship at the time. On the grounds, which now comprise 62 acres, there are a Chinese cooks' house, St. Ann's Church, a carriage shed, a blacksmith shop, a reconstructed general store, a cowboy's bunkhouse and a barn; all are preserved true to turn-of-the-century life. Also featured are a contemporary restaurant and gift shop. *9830 Hwy. 97, 12 km (8 mi) north of Vernon, tel. 604/542–7868. Admission: $4 adults, $3 senior citizens and children 13–18, $2 children 6–12; family and group rates available. Open July–Aug., daily 9–7; Easter–Thanksgiving, daily 9–5.*

45 **Kelowna** is the center of the valley's wine industry, with **Calona Wineries** (1125 Richter St., tel. 604/762–9144), British Columbia's oldest and biggest wine factory. Also around Kelowna are smaller, but more intimate wineries, including **Gray Monk Cellars** (1051 Camp Rd., 8 km, 5 mi west of Winfield, off Hwy. 97, tel. 604/766–3168), and **CedarCreek Estate Winery** (14 km, 8.5 mi south of Kelowna, off Hwy. 97, tel. 604/764–8866). Other wineries in the Okanagan Valley are Penticton's **Cartier Wines & Beverages** (2210 Main St., tel. 604/492–0621), the second-largest; **Gehringer Brothers** (4 km, 2.5 mi south of Oliver, off Hwy. 97, tel. 604/493–2287); and across the road

from Gehringer, about three minutes' walk, is the **Divino Estate** (Rd. 8 at Hwy. 97, tel. 604/498–3527).

46 **Penticton** is the most tourist-oriented of the three. While its winter population is about 25,000, its population in summer nears 130,000. Since Penticton is at the south end of the generally calm lake, boaters often spend the day just going from one end to the other. **Cathedral Provincial Park** (tel. 604/494–0321). 42 kilometers (26 miles) south of Penticton off Highway 3 and along the American border, features 81,500 acres of alpine meadows, jagged peaks, azure lakes, and rock formations carved by the wind into curious shapes. The park is a good spot from which to see such animals as mule deer, mountain goats, and California bighorn sheep; the hike into the main part of the park takes about six hours. Sixteen campsites and the Cathedral Park Resort are on the premises. The resort provides four-wheel-drive transportation into the park for a fee. Arrangements must be made ahead of time.

Other Points of Interest in British Columbia

Butchart Gardens, situated on the 130-acre Butchart estate, offers more than 5,000 varieties of flowers including Italian, Japanese, and English rose gardens. Once a limestone quarry, the grounds were transformed in 1904 when Canadian cement pioneer Robert Butchart began building bridges and walkways and planting shrubs and flowers on the 50-acre site. Also on the premises is a gift shop, teahouse, and restaurants. *800 Benvenuto Ave., Victoria, tel. 604/652–5256. Admission: $6.50 adults, $3 children 12–17, $1 children under 12. Prices and schedules vary greatly depending on time of year; call ahead.*

Craigdarroch Castle is a lavish mansion that was built as the home of British Columbia's first millionaire, Robert Dunsmuir, who oversaw coal mining for the Hudson's Bay Company (he died before the castle's completion in about 1890). Recently restored to its original condition, the castle features large stained-glass windows, intricately carved oak on the walls, and walnut, mahogany, cedar, and spruce paneling throughout its 39 rooms. The location offers a wonderful view of downtown Victoria from the fifth-floor tower; guided tours are given. *1050 Joan Crescent, Victoria, tel. 604/592–5323. Admission: $4 adults, $3 senior citizens and children. Open June 16–Aug., daily 9–7:30; Sept.–June 15, daily 10–5.*

Fable Cottage Estate, located 20 minutes from downtown Victoria, is 3½ acres of brightly flowered gardens with a 609-squaremeter (2,000-square-foot) thatched home that took 11 years to build. *Off Hwy. 17 on Marine Dr., Victoria, tel. 604/658–5741. Admission: $7.50 adults, $6.50 senior citizens, $4 children 13–17, $3 children 5–12. Open mid-Mar.–mid-Oct., daily 9:30–dusk.*

'Ksan, set in Interior British Columbia, 291 kilometers (180 miles) from Prince Rupert, is a re-created Gitskan Indian village. The brightly painted community of six longhouses is a replica of the one that stood on the same site when the first explorers arrived in the last century. Tribal houses are decorated with paintings, carved interior poles, and painted screens in traditional Northwest Coast Indian style. On Friday evenings, July through August, 'Ksan dancers perform traditional Indian dances and you can take a guided tour of several historic sites in the area. This is one of the few sites that provides understanding about Indian life before the advent of Europeans. A gift shop and museum are on the grounds. *Box 326, Hazelton, tel. 604/842–5544. Admission: $4.50 adults, $3 senior citizens, $2.50 students, $1.50 children 5–12. Open May–mid-Oct., daily 9–6; mid-Oct.–Apr., Mon–Fri. 9–5. Tours given in summer, on the hour.*

Scenic Drives From downtown Victoria, get on Dallas Road and follow the scenic route signs for a **marine drive around Victoria** that takes you past a residential area, along pebble beaches, and into the city's mansion area known locally as the Tweed Curtain, reflecting its house designs and residents' British lifestyles. The road continues past Beacon Hill Park (the street name changes to Beach Drive), Gonzales Point, through the township of Oak Bay, and past Uplands Park, with its stone-gate entrance leading to the huge estates of Uplands. After passing the east side of the University of Victoria, the route will eventually reach Sidney, from which you can take a ferry across to the mainland and head over to Vancouver.

The **Gold Rush Trail** is a 640-kilometer (400-mile) route along which the frontiersmen traveled in search of gold in the 19th and early 20th centuries. The interior British Columbia trail begins just below Prince George in the north, and extends to Lilooet in the south, but juts off at points in between. Following the route you can travel through Quesnel, Williams Lake, Wells, Barkerville, along the Fraser Canyon, and Cache Creek. Most towns and communities through which the trail passes have re-created villages, history museums, or historic sites that help to tell the story of the gold-rush era. For more information contact the **Cariboo Tourist Association** (Box 4900, Williams Lake V2G 2V8, tel. 604/392–2226, or in U.S. 800/663–5885).

What to See and Do with Children

Anne Hathaway's Cottage, tucked away in a unique English-village complex, is a full-size replica of the original thatched home in Stratford-Upon-Avon, England. The building and the 16th-century antiques inside are typical of Shakespeare's era. The Olde England Inn, on the grounds, is a pleasant spot for tea or a traditional English-style meal. You can also stay in one of the 50 antiques-furnished rooms, some complete with four-poster beds. *429 Lampson St., Victoria, V9A 5Y9, tel. 604/388–4353. Admission: $4.50 adults, $2.95 senior citizens and children 8–17, children under 8 free. Open June–Sept., daily 9–9; rest of year, daily 10–4. Guided tours leave from the Inn. From downtown Victoria, take the Munro bus to the door.*

Dominion Astrophysical Observatory, maintained by the National Research Council of Canada, has a 72-inch telescope that transmits pictures of planets, star clusters, and nebulae. A museum display around the inside of the domed building provides a quick lesson in astrophysics, and video monitors are set up for visitors' easy viewing. *Off W. Saanich Rd. (Hwy. 17), 16 km (10 mi) from Victoria on Little Saanich Mt., tel. 604/388–0001. Admission: free. Open Mon.–Fri. 9–4:30, Sat. 9–11 PM.*

Sealand of the Pacific. Featured at this aquarium are Orcas (killer whales), seals, and sea lions, with poolside shows every hour. The setting itself is an attraction, offering one of the finest views of the Strait of Juan de Fuca in the Victoria area. *1327 Beach Dr., Oak Bay, tel. 604/598–3373. Admission: $6 adults, $4.50 children 12–17, $2.50 children 5–11. Open June–Sept., daily 10–6; Sept.–May, daily 10–5; closed Mon. and Tues. in Nov., Jan., Feb.*

Shopping

Prince Rupert Native art is available at **Studio 9** (516 3rd Ave. W tel. 604/624–2366).

Queen Charlotte Islands The **Haida Gwaii** Indians carve valuable figurines from the hard, black slate called argillite that is found only on the islands. Their works can be found at the **Adams Family House of Silver** (tel. 604/626–3215), in Old Masset, behind the Haida Museum. Other island specialties are silk screen prints and abalone jewelry.

Vancouver Island Duncan is the home of Cowichan Indian wool sweaters, handknitted by the native Indians. A large selection is available from **Hills Indian Crafts** (tel. 604/746–6731) and **Big Foot Trading Post** (tel. 604/748–1153), both located on the main highway, about 1½ kilometers (1 mi) south of Duncan. Also check out **Modeste Mill** (tel. 604/748–8983), located in the Old Cowichan Band Cultural Centre.

Victoria Shopping in Victoria is easy. Virtually everything can be found in the downtown area, beginning at the Empress and walking north along Government Street. In succession you'll hit **George Straith Ltd.** (tel. 604/384–6912) for woolens; **Piccadilly Shoppe British Woolens** (tel. 604/384–1288) for women's woolens; **E.A. Morris Tobacconist, Ltd.** (tel. 604/382–4811) for unusual pipe tobacco blends; **Munro's Books** (tel. 604/382–2464), for the best selection of Victoriana in the city; **Roger's Chocolates and English Sweet Shop** (tel. 604/384–7021), for fine chocolates; and the **Gallery of the Arctic** (tel. 604/382–9012), for quality Inuit art.

The **Eaton's Centre** at Government and Fort streets is both a department store and a series of small boutiques, with a total of 170 shops and restaurants. A block farther are **Bastion Square** and **Windsor Court** for upscale boutiques.

At last count, Victoria had 60-plus **antiques shops** specializing in coins, stamps, estate jewelry, rare books, crystal, china, furniture, or paintings and other works of art. A right at Fort Street and a four-block walk will take you to **Antique Row** between Blanshard and Cook streets. The **Connoisseurs Shop** (tel. 604/361–4341), and **David Robinson, Ltd.** (tel. 604/384–6425), offer a wide selection of 18th-century pieces. You will also find antiques on the west side of Government Street near the **Old Town.**

Lower Johnson Street, near **Centennial Square,** has colorful and eclectic stores selling high-fashioned junk as well as the latest skiing and hiking apparel. **Market Square,** with three stories of specialty shops, is the focal point of Old Town.

Chinatown is marked by the red Gate of Harmonious Interest. On Fisgard Street shops offer merchandise and meals straight from the Orient. You must visit the little shops of **Fan Tan Alley,** a walkway between two buildings so small that two people have a difficult time passing without one giving way.

Sports and Outdoor Activities

Fishing British Columbia has about 4,350 miles of convoluted mainland coastline (much of it protected from the open ocean by islands), more than 6,000 lakes and 11,000 rivers and streams. Every year more than 750,000 fishermen net an average of 27 fish each and keep 17 of them. Of the 72 species of fish found in British Columbia, 22 are considered sport fish, including Chinook salmon, found in salt water, and rainbow trout that thrive in the freshwater lakes and rivers of interior British Columbia.

Freshwater An annual freshwater fishing license is $10 for Canadians. For a nonresident or non-Canadian, it's about $3.50 a day, $10 for three days, and $30 annually. A license is good through March 31, regardless of when it was purchased.

Saltwater A saltwater fishing license for six days costs $9 for Canadian residents and $13 for non-Canadians, and is available at virtually every fishing lodge and sporting goods outlet in the province. Annual licenses are about double that amount and are also good through March 31.

Golf There are more than 200 golf courses in British Columbia and the figure is growing quickly. The province is now an Official Golf Destination of the PGA Tour in Canada and of the American PGA tour. Greens fees are about $20–$35. The topography in British Columbia tends to be mountainous, and many courses have fine views as well as some of the most treacherous approaches to greens in Canada.

Victoria Area Though **Victoria Golf Club** (1110 Beach Dr., Victoria, tel. 604/598–4322) is private, it's open to other private-club members. This windy course is the oldest (built in 1893) in British Columbia and offers a spectacular view of the Strait of Juan de Fuca. **Uplands Golf Club** (3300 Cadboro Bay Rd., Victoria, tel. 604/592–1818) is a flat, semi-private course (it becomes public after 2), with a reciprocity policy. **Cedar Hill Municipal** (1400 Derby Rd., Victoria, tel. 604/595–3103) is a public course with up-and-down terrain. **Royal Oak Inn Golf Club** (4680 Lake Dr., Victoria, tel. 604/658–1433) is the newest nine-hole course in the area. **Gorge Vale Golf Club** (1005 Craigflower Rd., Victoria, tel. 604/386–3401) is a semiprivate course, but is open to the public. It has punitive traps and a deep gorge that eats up golf balls. **Glen Meadows Golf and Country Club** (1050 McTavish Rd., Sidney, tel. 604/656–3921), situated near the ferry terminal, is a semiprivate course that's open to the public at select times.

Okanagan Valley The Okanagan has a central tee-time booking service for out-of-town golfers that lists all of the Okanagan/interior British Columbia courses below. *Box 342, Westbank V0H 2A0, tel. 800/663–4732. Open May 15–Oct. 15, Mon.–Sat. 8–5.*

Gallaghers Canyon Golf Resort (4320 McCulloch Rd., Kelowna, tel. 604/861–4000) is one of the most challenging courses in British Columbia, with long, rolling and twisting fairways. **Kelowna Golf and Country Club** (1297 Glenmore Dr., Kelowna, tel. 604/763–2736) is a private club that favors straight drivers; visitors are welcome but advised to avoid weekends. **Osoyoos Golf and Country Club** (20th Ave., Osoyoos, tel. 604/495–7003) provides a green setting in the dry, parched hills; only two of the 12 par-fours on the course are under 350 yards. Visitors are welcome. **Penticton Golf and Country Club** (799 Eckhardt Ave., Penticton, tel. 604/492–8727) has 10 acres of water hazards, challenging traps, and bunkers; it is a private club that welcomes visitors. **Rivershore Golf Course** (Rivershore Dr., Kamloops, tel. 604/573–4622) is a Robert Trent Jones–designed course, and is British Columbia's longest at 7,007 yards. Visitors are welcome. **Salmon Arm Golf Club** (3400 Hwy. 97B, Salmon Arm, tel. 604/832–4727) welcomes visitors to its hilly terrain. **Shadow Ridge Golf Club** (3770 Bulman Rd., Kelowna, tel. 604/765–7777) is a relatively new course, set in a valley and surrounded by orchards. **Summerland Golf and Country Club** (2405 Mountain Ave., Summerland, tel. 604/494–9554) is slightly off the beaten track, but has two distinctly different nines with the front nine clear and the back nine cut through a pine forest. **Twin Lakes Golf Club** (Hwy. 3A, Kaleden, tel. 604/497–5359) has an on-site RV park.

Hunting

All hunters for game—moose, bear, mountain goat and sheep, caribou, deer, birds—need licenses. Of the 112 species of mammals that dwell in British Columbia, 74 of them are peculiar only to this province. Nonresidents of Canada are required to be accompanied by a licensed guide while hunting big game in British Columbia. More than 300 outfitters provide the service. Prices vary depending on species and length of trip, but equipment, including a tent, food, and transportation is usually part of the package. For more information contact the **B.C. Wildlife Branch** (Parliament Bldgs., Victoria V8V 1X5, tel. 604/387–9737).

Skiing

Cross-country

British Columbia has hundreds of kilometers of groomed cross-country (Nordic) ski trails in the provincial parks and the 31 cross-country resorts. Most downhill destinations have carved out Nordic routes along the valleys, and there are literally thousands of more trails in unmanaged areas of British Columbia.

For cross-country enthusiasts, **Manning Park Resort** (Manning Park V0X 1R0, tel. 604/840–8822) enroute to the Okanagan, east of Hope, is one of the finest in the province and is located about 200 kilometers (124 miles) west of Vancouver. It also has downhill facilities, which are just as popular as the Nordic program. On Vancouver Island, **Mt. Washington** (*see* below) has Nordic facilities.

Downhill

With more than half the province situated higher than 4,200 feet above sea level, downhill courses are abundant in the 34 major, and 20 smaller, community resorts.

On Vancouver Island, **Mt. Washington Ski Resort Ltd.** (Box 3069, Courtenay V9N 5N3, tel. 604/338–1386), with 39 runs and an elevation of 5,200 feet, is the largest ski area on Vancouver Island, and the third-largest in terms of visitors, in the province. Located in the Comox Valley, it's a modern, well-organized mountain with snowpack averaging 472 inches a year. It also has 30 kilometers (19 miles) of triple-set Nordic trails. Other island ski areas are **Forbidden Plateau** (2050 Cliffe Ave., Courtenay V9N 2L3, tel. 604/334–4744), located near Mt. Washington, with 12 runs and a fall of 1,150 feet; and **Mt. Cain** (Box 1225, Port McNeill V0N 2R0, tel. 604/949–7667), on the northern part of the island near the community of Sayward off Highway 19, with 16 runs and a fall of 1,500 feet.

The Okanagan Valley region, four hours east by car from Vancouver, or one hour by air, offers some of the best ski bargains in the province. **Big White Ski Resort** (Box 2039, Station R, Kelowna V1X 4K5, tel. 604/765-3101) is the highest ski area in British Columbia, though Whistler (*see* Excursion 1: Whistler in Chapter 6) has a longer free fall. The resort has 47 runs, hotels, restaurants, and, like Whistler, is in the process of rapidly expanding. **Silver Star Mountain Resorts Ltd.** (Box 2, Silver Star Mtn. V0E 1G0, tel. 604/542-0224), with 35 runs, offers well-lighted night skiing. The complete village at the base of the mountain has enough hotels to accommodate 650 people. **Apex Alpine** (Box 488, Penticton V2A 6K9, tel. 604/493-3200) has 36 runs and is the largest ski resort in South Okanagan. On-mountain condominiums—many for rent—can accommodate a total of 350 people.

Kootenay Country, a southeastern section of British Columbia that includes the Rockies, Purcells, Selkirks, and Monashees mountain ranges, features two major resorts: **Whitewater** (Box 60, Nelson V1L 5P7, tel. 604/354-4944), with 20 runs and a lot of powder skiing; and **Red Mountain Resorts** (Box 670, Rossland V0G 1Y0, tel. 604/362-7700), which spans two mountains and three mountain faces, and has 30 runs.

The resorts in the High Country reflect British Columbia's most diverse topographical area. At 3,100 feet of vertical drop, **Tod Mountain** (Box 869, Kamloops V2C 5M8, tel. 604/578-7222) has 47 runs. The failing of this resort is that the only on-mountain lodging facility is a B&B that accommodates up to 32 people. **Mt. Mackenzie** (Box 1000, Revelstoke V0E 2S0, tel. 604/837-5268) has 20 runs and offers deep-powder skiing. Revelstoke, located 5 kilometers (3 miles) from the base, has a wide selection of lodging.

Heli-skiing

Heli-skiing operators are often located at well-established resorts, taking clients into otherwise inaccessible deep-powder regions of the mountains. Others operate as independents and offer accommodations, dining, and recreational facilities in their deluxe lodges. Some offer Snowcat skiing, in which an enclosed all-terrain vehicle takes you into the wilderness areas.

In Kootenay Country, try **Kootenay Helicopter Skiing** (Box 717, Nakusp V0G 1R0, tel. 604/265-3121; in Alberta and the U.S., 800/663-0100). With accommodations at Nakusp Lodge, they run seven-day packages to and from Kelowna, Spokane, and Castlegar. **Great Northern Snowcat Skiing** (Box 2763, Salmon Arm V0E 2T0, tel. 604/832-9500) has three-, five-, and six-day packages to and from Revelstoke. Lodges are located at Trout Lake. **Selkirk Wilderness Skiing** (General Delivery, Meadow Creek V0G 1N0, tel. 604/366-4424) offers five-day packages (including remote lodging) to and from Nelson.

In the High Country, **Cat Powder Skiing** (Box 1479, Revelstoke V0E 2S0, tel. 604/837-9489) organizes two-, three-, and five-day packages that run into the Selkirks and on the upper slopes of Mt. MacKenzie in Revelstoke.

Dining and Lodging

Dining

Throughout British Columbia you'll find a variety of cuisines, from Victoria's numerous French and Continental restaurants and Vancouver Island's seafood places to interior British Columbia's wild game-oriented menus. Prices vary from location to location, but ratings reflect the categories listed on the dining chart.

Category	Cost*
Very Expensive	over $35
Expensive	$25–$35
Moderate	$15–$25
Inexpensive	under $15

**per person, excluding drinks, service, and GST tax (7%), in Canadian dollars*

Highly recommended restaurants in each price category are indicated by a star ★.

Lodging

The lodging possibilities across the region are as diverse as the restaurant menus. Accommodations range from bed-and-breakfast inns and rustic cabins to deluxe chain hotels. In the cities, especially, there is an abundance of accommodations, but once you get off the beaten track, guest rooms are often a rare commodity and may require advance booking.

Prices below are quoted in Canadian dollars.

Category	Cost*
Very Expensive	over $125
Expensive	$90–$125
Moderate	$50–$90
Inexpensive	under $50

**All prices are for a standard double room; excluding 7% GST tax. Prices are in Canadian dollars.*

Highly recommended lodgings in each price category are indicated by a star ★.

North of Vancouver Island

Prince Rupert
Dining

Smile's Seafood Café. If you don't mind walking among the fish-processing plants by the railway, you'll find this place a real change of pace. It has been a mainstay of Prince Rupert since 1935 and has succeeded because it provides small-town friendly service along with its seafood menu. Favorites include the fresh Dungeness Crab, halibut, and cod. *1 George Hills Way,* *tel. 604/624–3072. No reservations. Dress: casual. MC V. Moderate.*

Lodging **The Highliner Inn.** A modern highrise near the waterfront, this facility, located in the heart of the downtown shopping district and one block away from the airline terminal building, has a view of the harbor from the rooms' private balconies. *815 1st Ave. W., V8J 1B3, tel. 604/624–9060. 126 rooms; handicapped rooms available. Facilities: restaurant, lounge, convention facilities, beauty salon, shopping arcade. AE, DC, MC, V. Moderate–Expensive.*

Dining and Lodging ★ **Crest Motor Hotel.** It may surprise you to find a four-diamond AAA hotel in this small community, but this warm, modern hotel is probably the finest in the north. It's one block away from the two shopping centers, but is situated on a bluff overlooking the harbor. The pleasantly decorated Crest restaurant has brass rails, beam ceilings, and a waterfront view, and specializes in seafood; particularly outstanding are the salmon dishes. *222 1st Ave. W, V8J 3P6, tel. 604/624–6771 or in B.C. and Alberta, 800/663–8150. 102 rooms. Facilities: restaurant, lounge, coffee shop, convention-banquet facilities, cable TV, nightly entertainment. Reservations required for restaurant. Dress: casual but neat. AE, DC, MC, V. Moderate.*

Okanagan Valley

Kaleden *Lodging* **The Ponderosa Point Resort.** Located just north of Okanagan Falls, this 25-cabin resort rests along an 800-foot beach on Skaha Lake. The decks off of the one- and two- bedroom Pan Abodes offer a glorious view of the sun setting over the lake. The unpretentious rental cabins are clean, comfortable, homey, and all unique, as they're furnished by individual owners. Children can choose between the beach, the central grassy area, or the playground to while away the days. *319 Ponderosa Ave., Box 106, V0H 1K0, tel. 604/497–5354. 26 rooms. Facilities: boat rentals, tennis court, basketball, water skiing. No credit cards. Moderate–Expensive.*

Kamloops *Lodging* ★ **Lac le Jeune Resort.** This is the property that locals use when they want to combine the outdoors and sophisticated, modern surroundings. With 160 kilometers (99 miles) of cross-country skiing, a lake stocked with trout, and a restaurant that serves robust helpings, this is a good choice for an accommodation. The rustic, self-sufficient cabins are perfect for families because of their ample size and amenities, and pets are permitted. *Off Coquihala Hwy., 29 km (18 mi) southwest of Kamloops, Box 3215, Kamloops V2C 6B8, tel. 604/372–2722. 42 rooms. Facilities: restaurant, lounge, meeting room, gift shop, indoor whirlpool, sauna, boat rentals. AE, MC, V. Moderate.*

Kelowna *Dining* **Papillion.** This contemporarily furnished restaurant features a Continental menu that offers pasta, seafood, and steak. While seafood is not necessarily the specialty here, the salmon with hollandaise is superb and highly recommended. The wine list includes a wide selection of imported and local wines that work nicely with the meals. *375 Leon Ave., tel. 604/763–3833. Reservations advised. Dress: casual. AE, MC, V. Closed weekend lunch. Moderate.*

Lodging ★ **Lake Okanagan Resort.** This Five-Star Resorts and Hotels property is a popular, self-contained destination on the west side of Okanagan Lake. All rooms have their own kitchens and range in size from one-room suites in the main hotel to spacious three-room chalets situated around the 300 acres. The resort shows some signs of age, particularly in the worn floors; but functional, earth-tone furnishings, wood-burning fireplaces, and perfect views of the lake make this a good choice of accommodations. *Westside Rd., Box 1321, Station A, 17 km (10.5 mi) north of Kelowna, V1Y 7V8; tel. 604/769-3511 or 800/663-3273. 170 rooms. Facilities: restaurant, café, poolside lounge, 3 pools, par-3 9-hole golf course, 7 tennis courts, horse stables, summer childrens camp. AE, DC, MC, V. Expensive.*

★ **Gables Country Inn and Tea House.** Make reservations early for this B&B, but it'll be worth the time spent planning ahead. Set on Indian lands, surrounded by vineyards, and the sparkling waters of the inn is Lake Okanagan, only 15 minutes from downtown. The 19th-century Heritage house promises a garden-, mountain-, or lake view from every room; ask for the one with a private balcony overlooking the water. Breakfasts include homemade scones; fresh fruits; and cherry, plum, and peach jams made from fruit trees on the property. *2405 Bering Rd., Box 1153, V1Y 7P8; tel. 604/768-4468. 3 rooms. Facilities: garden, pool. No credit cards. Inexpensive.*

Merritt
Dining and Lodging ★ **Corbett Lake Country Inn.** The locals want to keep this one a secret, but not owner Peter McVey, a French-trained chef. His restaurant offers a different, fixed menu every night, but it will probably feature some sort of fish fresh from Lake Corbett. For a $25 fee, you can fish McVey's two privately stocked lakes, with no limit on trout, but any more than one becomes part of that night's menu. The six single cabins (with extra beds) and two duplexes are comfortable, but not plush. Small pets are allowed. *Off Hwy. 5A, 11 km (6.8 mi) south of Merritt, Box 327, V0K 2B0, tel. 604/378-4334. 8 cabins. Facilities: 2 stocked lakes; boat rentals; groomed, cross-country ski trails open all winter. Reservations required for restaurant. Dress: casual. No credit cards. Closed Mar.–Apr., Oct. 15–Dec. 23. Moderate.*

Penticton
Dining ★ **Granny Bogner's.** The decor in this mostly Continental restaurant is a bit contrived, with flowing lace curtains, Oriental rugs, wood chairs, cloth-covered tables, and waitresses adorned in long paisley skirts, conveying that this is a "homey" place. But the food is par excellence, with each order prepared meticulously to order. The poached halibut and roasted duck have contributed to the widely held belief that this is the best restaurant in the Okanagan. *302 Eckhardt Ave. W, tel. 604/493-2711. Reservations advised. Dress: casual. AE, MC, V. Closed lunch; Sun. and Mon.; Jan. Moderate–Expensive.*

Lodging **Coast Lakeside Resort.** On the shore of Okanagan Lake, the inn is both a peaceful retreat and right in the center of the action. For relaxation the waterfront offers reprieve, and the nearby Penticon Golf and Country Club invites a competitive round of golf. Vancouver businesspeople love this place because it provides comfort and convention facilities. Rooms are bright and airy, and half of them have lake views. *21 Lakeshore Dr. W, V2A 7M5, tel. 604/493-8221 or 800/663-9400. 204 rooms. Facilities: 2 restaurants, 2 tennis courts, 6 nearby golf courses, in-*

door pool, health club, sauna, Jacuzzi, game room. AE, DC, MC, V. Expensive.

Queen Charlotte Island For bed-and-breakfast information contact **Okanagan Bed and Breakfast** (Box 5135, Kelowna V1Y 8T9, tel. 604/768–4469).

Lodging **Singing Surf Inn.** Situated on Old Beach Road and convenient to air facilities, this inn, decorated with Native Indian art, is popular with just about every type of traveler. The area's largest accommodation is considered deluxe by local standards and features a restaurant that prepares simple seafood dishes. *1504 Old Beach Rd., Box 245, Masset, V0T 1M0, tel. 604/626–3318; fax 604/626–5204. 29 rooms. Facilities: lounge, car rental. AE, MC, V. Moderate.*

Spruce Point Lodge. This cedar-sided building, encircled by a balcony, attracts families and couples because of its inexpensive rates and down-home feel. Like most Queen Charlotte accommodations, this one is more rustic than luxurious and features locally made pine furnishings that go with the northern-woods motif. For the money you get a Continental breakfast and an occasional seafood barbeque, with a menu that depends on the daily catch. Kayakers and hikers on a budget should ask about the bunk room that's usually available at a low nightly rate. *609 6th Ave., Queen Charlotte City V0T 1S0, tel. 604/559–8234. 6 rooms. No credit cards. Inexpensive.*

Vernon
Lodging **Village Green Inn.** This hotel offers access to 3 golf courses and to the Silver Star Ski Resort, just 22 kilometers (14 miles) away. The bright, pleasant decor makes this reasonably priced hotel a good alternative to the hotels that line Highway 97. The rooms are spacious and the service is personal and friendly. *4801 27th St., V1T 4Z1, tel. 604/542–3321; fax 604/549–4252. 138 rooms. Facilities: restaurant, coffee shop, lounge, indoor and outdoor pools, sauna, Jacuzzi. AE, DC, MC, V. Moderate.*

Vancouver Island

Campbell River
Dining **Royal Coachman Inn.** This is another of those informal, blackboard-menu restaurants that dot the landscape of the island. The menu is surprisingly daring for what is essentially a high-end pub, and the inn draws crowds nightly, especially on Tuesday and Saturday (prime rib nights). The menu, however, changes daily, so if ribs aren't your favorite try one of the other specials. Come early for both lunch and dinner to beat the crowds. *84 Dogwood St., tel. 604/286–0231. No reservations. Dress: casual. AE, MC, V. Moderate.*

Lodging ★ **Painter's Lodge.** In business for more than 50 years, this is one of the region's major resorts. The wood-frame lodge was rebuilt in 1985, and is decorated with wood furnishings and old photos of award-winning catches. Most packages include guided fishing, but this resort, overlooking Discovery Passage, is appealing even to those who don't fish. *1625 MacDonald Rd., V9W 5C1, tel. 604/286–1102 or 800/663–7090. 62 rooms. Facilities: restaurant, lounge, pub, pool, gift shops, 2 golf courses, boats, fishing guides. AE, MC, V. Moderate–Expensive.*

Comox/Courtenay
Dining **The Old House Restaurant.** This split-character restaurant offers both formal and casual dining, in a restored turn-of-the-century pioneer home with large cedar beams and a stone fireplace. Upstairs, among linen and fresh flowers, you select from a Continental menu that's expensive but innovative, with

a delightful pepper steak leading as the house specialty. Downstairs, where it is decidedly more informal, you can get sandwiches, pastas, and salads. *1760 Riverside La., Courtenay, tel. 604/338-5406. Reservations advised upstairs; no reservations downstairs. Jacket and tie advised upstairs; casual downstairs. AE, DC, MC, V. Moderate–Expensive.*

Leeward Brew Pub. Owners Gil and Ron Gaudry have captured the Northwest coast ambience in this simple, bleached-wood pub. Between the four types of home-brewed beer and a menu that offers a wide range of seafood, pasta, Mexican dishes, and sandwiches, this weathered, intimate watering hole also serves as the perfect place for a casual, relaxed lunch or dinner. *649 Anderton Rd., Comox, tel. 604/339-5400. Reservations accepted except on Tues., Fri., and Sat. nights. Dress: casual. MC, V. Inexpensive.*

Lodging

★ **The Kingfisher Inn.** Situated among trees and set off the highway overlooking the Straight of Georgia, this hotel is five minutes south of Courtenay. The inn's solid furnishings, clean white-stucco walls, bright lobby with lots of greenery, and rooms with mountain- and ocean views offer a nice change from the majority of plain accommodations lining the main drag. *Site 672, RR 6, Courtenay V9N 8H9, tel. 604/338-1323. 30 units. Facilities: restaurant, lounge, 2 tennis courts, outdoor pool, sauna, whirlpool. AE, DC, MC, V. Inexpensive–Moderate.*

★ **The Greystone Manor.** This nonsmoking B&B, set in a 70-year-old house with period furnishings, looks right out on Comox Harbor. The antiques, wood stove, Laura Ashley–style wallpaper, and wood paneling add to the hospitable, cozy feel of this inn. Breakfast, which includes fresh fruit, muffins, fruit pancakes, or quiche, is enough to keep you filled most of the day. The proprietors take photos of their guests and send off copies. *4014 Haas Rd., Comox V9N 8H9, tel. 604/338-1422. 4 rooms. Facilities: garden, walking trails. No credit cards. Inexpensive.*

Nanaimo

Dining

★ **Old Mahle House.** This relaxed, homey place has a menu that includes fresh-caught prawns and other catches of the day. Twelve items adorn the regular menu, including a succulent carrot and ginger soup. Care to detail and the intimate setting of three country-style rooms make this one of the finest dining experiences in the region. *Cedar and Heemer Rds., tel. 604/722-3621. Reservations advised. Dress: casual but neat. MC, V. Closed lunch and Mon.–Tues. Moderate.*

The Grotto. A perennial favorite, The Grotto is a Nanaimo institution that specializes in a variety of seafood, including sushi. The restaurant is set against a waterfront background, and dining here is relaxed and casual. Try the burgers or the seafood platter—zum-zum—that's big enough for two. *1511 Stewart Ave., tel. 604/753-3303. Reservations accepted. Dress: casual. AE, MC, V. Closed lunch and Sun. Inexpensive.*

Lodging

★ **La Coast Bastion Inn.** This hotel is conveniently located in the middle of the downtown area, and is appealing to travelers because of its proximity to the ferry terminal. All rooms with balconies have views of the old Hudson's Bay fort and the ocean and are modernly furnished. The three eating/entertainment establishments located within the hotel make this a self-sufficient accommodation. *11 Bastion St., V9R 2Z9, tel. 604/753-6601 or 800/663-1144. 179 rooms. Facilities: restaurant,* *lounge, Irish deli/pub, gift shop, boutique, convention facilities, sauna, hot tub. AE, DC, MC, V. Moderate–Expensive.*

Big 7 Economy Hotel. For those who are looking for a simple, clean family-oriented place with few amenities, the Big 7 is the answer. The hotel is six blocks from the city-center, has rooms that can accommodate up to four people, and permits small pets. *736 Nicole St., V9R 4V1, tel. 604/754–2328. 58 units. Facilities: satellite TV. MC, V. Inexpensive.*

Dining and Lodging ★

Yellow Point Lodge. Yellow Point is a spit of land south of Nanaimo, east of Ladysmith, that has a series of luxurious rustic lodges of which this is the finest example. Rebuilt in 1985 after a fire destroyed the original, the lodge lost almost nothing in ambience and gained a great deal: Larger rooms have better facilities (many now have private baths). Situated on a rocky knoll overlooking the Stuart Channel, the hotel has 9 lodge rooms (open year-round) and beach cabins, field cabins, and beach barracks (closed mid-October to mid-April) for the hardy. Beach cabins can be private and include tree-trunk beds and wood-burning stoves; beach barracks are not as sound, and noises carry from unit to unit, but the location along the shore makes them popular. One hundred thirty-two acres of land for strolling make the lodge an estate experience. Three full meals and snacks are included in the tariff. *Yellow Point Rd., RR 3, V0R 2E0, tel. 604/245–7422. 50 rooms. Facilities: restaurant, 2 tennis courts, seawater pool, hot tub, sauna, windsurfing gear. MC, V. Expensive.*

Parksville
Dining

The Judge's Manor. The interior of this former judge's manor home reflects his love for fine antiques and warm surroundings. Today, the family-run restaurant (with a glorious ocean view) still conveys kindness, from the service to the carefully prepared dishes. Local and organic produce, venison, rabbit, and other game highlight the eclectic menu. Other tasty choices include loin-of-lamb medallions. *193 Memorial Ave., tel. 604/248–2544. Reservations accepted. Dress: casual but neat. AE, MC, V. Closed weekend lunch and Mon. Moderate.*

Lodging

Beach Acres Resort Hotel. For a family vacation, this collection of cottages set in the woods facing the Georgia Strait is both charming and practical. Each unit is a home away from home, with one or two bedrooms, living room, kitchen, and storage areas. In July and August, only stays for a minimum of a week are reserved. *1015 E. Island Hwy., V0R 2S0, tel. 604/248–3424; fax 604/248–6145. 60 cottages. Facilities: restaurant, indoor pool, sauna, whirlpool, playground, 3 tennis courts, health club. AE, DC, MC, V. Expensive.*

The Roadhouse Inn. This Swiss chalet is set on three acres, and is central to four of the region's golf courses. There are only a limited number of rooms, but all are comfortable. *1223 Smithers Rd., V0R 2S0, tel. 604/248–2912. 6 rooms. Facilities: restaurant. MC, V. Inexpensive.*

Port Hardy
Lodging

Glen Lyon Inn. All of the rooms have a full ocean view of Hardy Bay and, like most area motels, have clean, modern amenities. But perhaps the biggest bonus in a stay here is that this well-maintained inn is so close to the ferry terminal. *6435 Hardy Bay Rd., Box 103, V0N 2P0, tel. 608/949–7115; fax, 604/949–6415. 29 rooms. Facilities: restaurant, lounge, nearby marina, boat launch. AE, DC, MC, V. Moderate.*

Sooke
Dining and Lodging
★

Sooke Harbour House. This original 1931 clapboard farmhouse turned inn presents three suites, a new 10-room addition, and a dining room—all of which exude elegance. One of the finest restaurants in British Columbia, it is well worth the trip to Sooke, from Victoria. The fish is just-caught fresh, and the herbs, picked from some 200 varieties, are grown on the property. Four chefs sharing the kitchen guarantees an abundance of creative dishes. On a nice summer evening you may want to sit on the terrace, where you can catch a glimpse of the sea mammals that play by the spit of land in front of the restaurant. Equally exquisite are the romantic guest rooms, with natural-wood and white finishes adding to each unit's unique theme. Rooms range from the Herb Garden Room—decorated in shades of mint, with French doors opening onto a private patio—to the Longhouse Room, complete with Native American furnishings. All units, with fireplaces and either ocean- or mountain views, come with fresh flowers and a decanter of port, and some have wet bars that include herbal teas and cookies. Breakfast and lunch are included in your room rate. Hosts Frederica and Sinclair Philip have spent 12 years paying attention to details here. *1528 Wiffen Spit Rd., RR 4, V0S 1N0, tel. 604/642-3421. 13 rooms. Facilities: restaurant. Reservations required for restaurant. Closed lunch except for hotel guests. Dress: casual. MC, V. Hotel: Expensive–Very Expensive. Restaurant: Very Expensive.*

Ucluelet/Tofino
Dining

Whale's Tale. This is a no-frills, dark but warmly decorated place where mama's seafood cooking comes straight from the kitchen. The view isn't much but the building, set on pilings, shakes with a good gust of wind. The menu is highlighted by a variety of salmon and a nicely sautéed halibut. *1861 Peninsula Rd., Ucluelet, tel. 604/726-4621. Reservations accepted. Dress: casual. AE, MC, V. Closed lunch and Nov.–Jan. Moderate.*

★ **The Wickaninnish Restaurant.** Before the Canadian government acquired this wonderful, wood building for its interpretive center, it was indeed a wonderful lodge. The beach setting, combined with the restaurant's glass exterior and a stone-and-beam interior—accented by a stone fireplace—cannot be matched anywhere else in the area. It is run by the same people who make Painter's Lodge in Campbell River (*see* above) such a delight. Seafood is the primary experience here—especially the clam chowder—but if you take the veal in a red currant and mushroom sauce, you won't be disappointed. *On Long Beach, 16 km (11 mi) north of Ucluelet, tel. 604/726-7706. Reservations advised for parties of 7 or more. Dress: casual. AE, MC, V. Closed mid-Oct.–mid-Mar. Moderate.*

Lodging
★

Chesterman's Beach Bed and Breakfast. This is one of several small, romantic B&Bs located on the beach, but the front yard—which is the rolling ocean surf—makes this one unique. You can while away the hours just walking the beach, searching the tidal pools, or—during the right time of year—watching whales migrating by the front door. All of the self-contained suites in the main house are romantic, cozy, and unique; all have comfortable beds and a view of the beach. The separate, self-sufficient one-bedroom garden cottage offers no ocean view but accommodates up to four; it's a good option for a family vacation. Owner Joan Dublank makes hot muffins every morning. *1345 Chesterman's Beach Rd., Tofino V0R 2Z0, tel. 604/725-*

3726. 3 suites. Facilities: bikes, surfboards, beach. V. Moderate–Expensive.

Pacific Sands Beach Resort. Just a mile north of Pacific Rim National Park is this rustic resort with motel suites and individual one-bedroom cottages with fireplaces. The motel rooms are basic with modern furnishings, but with fireplaces seem cozier. Pacific Sands is close to Long Beach golf course and is on the ocean. *1421 Pacific Rim Hwy., Box 237, Tofino V0R 2Z0, tel. 604/725–3322. 58 rooms. AE, MC, V. Moderate–Expensive.*

Canadian Princess Fishing Resort. If old ships are to your liking, this converted survey ship has 30 comfortable, but hardly opulent, cabins. Each offers one to six berths, and all share washrooms; for something a bit more spacious, request the captain's cabin; or roomier than the ship rooms and complete with more contemporary furnishings are shoreside rooms. Promising an unusual experience, this spartan resort provides the bare necessities—mostly to scuba divers and fishermen, who flock here during the summer. *The Boat Basin, Box 939, Ucluelet V0R 3A0, tel. 604/726–7771 or 800/603–7090; fax 604/726–7121. 76 sleeping units. AE, MC, V. Inexpensive—Moderate.*

Victoria

Dining

Chez Daniel. One of Victoria's old standbys, Chez Daniel offers dishes that are rich, though the nouvelle influence has found its way into a few of the offerings. The interior, following a burgundy color scheme, seems to match the traditional rich, caloric cuisine. The wine list is varied and the menu has a wide selection of basic dishes: rabbit, salmon, duck, steak. This is a restaurant where you linger for the evening in the romantic atmosphere. *2522 Estavan Ave., tel. 604/592–7424. Reservations advised. Jacket advised. MC, V. Closed lunch and Sun. Expensive.*

★ **Larousse.** The menu in this artsy, waterfront restaurant includes an unusual combination of French cuisine with a definite Oriental touch. Soups are superb—particularly the lovage-and-sorrel combination—and such offbeat combinations as Indian or African creations with a French flair are featured on the seasonally changing menu. The breast of chicken in a spicy Senegalese peanut sauce, and *escalope de veau pandora* (cuts of veal in a rich Chinese-mushroom sauce) highlight the menu, but save room for the chocolate-and-orange cake, the special house dessert. Romantic atmosphere and fabulous food make Larousse the perfect place for an intimate evening out. *1619 Store St., tel. 604/386–3454. Reservations advised. Dress: casual. AE, MC, V. Closed lunch and Mon.–Tues. Expensive.*

★ **La Ville d'Is.** This seafood house is one of the best bargains in Victoria in terms of quality and price. Run by Michel Duteau, a Brittany native, the restaurant is cozy and friendly, with an outside café open May–October. An extensive, imaginative wine list features bottles from the Loire Valley that go well with the seafood, rabbit, lamb, and beef tenderloin specials. Try the *perche de la nouvelle aelande* (orange roughie in muscadet with herbs) or lobster soufflé for a unique taste. *26 Bastion Sq., tel. 604/388–9414. Reservations advised. Dress: casual. AE, MC, V. Closed Sun. and Jan. Expensive.*

Camilles. This restaurant is romantic, intimate, and one of the few West Coast–cuisine restaurants in Victoria. House specialties such as fish-and-flower terrine (salmon and red snapper layered with fresh flowers), chicken mango (boneless breast of chicken in a coconut mango sauce), and phyllo-wrapped salmon (fresh fillet of salmon in phyllo pastry) are all served in generous portions. Camilles also has an extensive wine cellar, uncommon in Victoria. *45 Bastion Sq., tel. 604/381–3433. Reservations advised. Dress: casual. AE, MC, V. Closed lunch and Sun.–Mon. Moderate.*

Chez Pierre. Established in 1973, this is the oldest French restaurant in Victoria; and the downtown location, combined with an intimate, rustic decor, creates a pleasant ambience. House specialties include canard à l'orange (duckling in orange sauce), rack of lamb, and British Columbia salmon. Although a tourist destination, this restaurant has managed to maintain its quality over the years. *512 Yates, tel. 604/388–7711. Reservations advised. Dress: casual. AE, MC, V. Closed lunch and Sun. Moderate.*

French Connection. Located in one of Victoria's Heritage homes, built in 1884, the restaurant has maintained the character of the time. From the outside, ornate details indicate the French tradition that you will find in the service and on the menu. The food is prepared with care, with an emphasis on the sauces. *512 Simcoe St., tel. 604/385–7014. Reservations required. Dress: casual. AE, MC, V. Closed lunch and Sun. Moderate.*

Monty's Pub and Restaurant. This is not your typical dark and dank pub, but it's quite popular with the Yuppie crew, who hang out in this San Francisco–like turn-of-the-century-style bar that offers several local brews that complement the pub-style fare. The restaurant features a brass ceiling from which hangs a half-size model of a Sopwith Camel biplane. *Century Hotel, 603 Pandora St., tel. 604/383–3351. Reservations accepted. Dress: casual. MC, V, Moderate.*

★ **Pagliacci's.** If you want Italian food, Pagliacci's is a must. Featured are quiches and veal, and chicken in marsala sauce with fettuccine. The pastas are freshly made in-house. The orange-color walls are covered with photos of Hollywood stars, so there's always something to look at here. *1011 Broad St., tel. 604/386–1662. No reservations. Dress: casual. MC, V. Moderate.*

Hungarian Village Restaurant. Tasty Hungarian standards such as goulash soup, chicken paprika, lamb, and pirogi served in generous portions are enhanced by romantic candlelight. The menu matches the robust Hungarian wines. *1550 Cedar Hill Cross Rd., tel. 604/477–3023. Reservations advised. Dress: casual. Closed weekend lunch. AE, MC, V. Inexpensive–Moderate.*

Koto. Like most Japanese restaurants in British Columbia, Koto maintains a high standard of freshness. What sets this place apart, however, are the unique dishes, particularly the tempura and sukiyaki selections. The atmosphere is authentic Japanese and private tatami rooms provide surroundings for an intimate evening. *510 Fort St., tel. 604/382–1514. Closed lunch Sun. Reservations advised. Dress: casual. AE, MC, V. Inexpensive–Moderate.*

Le Petite Saigon. This is a small, intimate café-style restaurant, offering a quiet dining experience with beautifully presented meals and a fare that is primarily Vietnamese, with a touch of French. The crab, asparagus, and egg swirl soup is a specialty of the house, and combination meals are a cheap and tasty way to learn the menu. *1010 Langley St., tel. 604/386–1412. Dress:*

casual. AE, MC, V. Closed Sat. lunch and Sun. Inexpensive–Moderate.

Rattenbury's. Located on the ground floor of the Crystal Garden, across from The Empress, this is a standard American steak-and-seafood house. Its attractions are its reasonable prices, casualness, and its convenient downtown location. The food is best described as robust and plentiful. *703 Douglas St., tel. 604/381–1333. Reservations advised. Dress: casual. AE, MC, V. Inexpensive–Moderate.*

Fuddruckers. Hamburgers are the specialty here, and are further complemented by the 25 topping choices and fresh-baked buns. Also on the menu are chicken, fish, steak, and items that go well with the particularly tasty fries. *787 Hillside Ave., tel. 604/386–4522. No reservations. Dress: casual. AE, MC, V. Inexpensive.*

Louie Louie's Diner. This on-the-waterfront eatery is a trip back into the 1950s, featuring mama's stick-to-the-ribs cooking and classic rock 'n' roll. For a hearty sandwich try the roast beef; burgers, salads, and blue-plate specials also appear on the menu. If you can, come just before dusk when you can get a nice view of the setting sun, the inner harbor, and Parliament buildings. *1001 Wharf St., tel. 604/382–1959. Reservations accepted. Dress: casual. AE, DC, MC, V. Inexpensive.*

Periklis. Standard Greek cuisine is offered in this warm, Taverna-style restaurant, but there are also steaks and ribs on the menu. On the weekends you can enjoy Greek and belly dancing, but be prepared for the hordes of people who come for the entertainment. *531 Yates St., tel. 604/386–3313. Reservations accepted. Dress: casual. AE, MC, V. Inexpensive.*

★ **Six-Mile-House.** This 1855 carriage house is a Victoria landmark. The brass, carved oak moldings, and stained glass, set a festive mood for the evening. The menu is constantly changing, but always features seafood selections and burgers. Try the cider or one of many international beers offered. *494 Island Hwy., tel. 604/478–3121. Reservations accepted. Dress: casual. MC, V. Inexpensive.*

★ **Wah Lai Yuen.** Although Chinatown seems to be offering less-interesting restaurants than before, this one has managed to maintain its character. It's a small corner of authenticity, combining Cantonese cuisine with wonderful baked goods including pork and curry beef buns. The portions are enormous and the price is right. *560 Fisgard St., tel. 604/381–5355. No reservations. Dress: casual. No credit cards. Closed Mon. Inexpensive.*

Lodging

The Bedford Hotel. This European-style hotel, located in the heart of downtown, is reminiscent of San Francisco's small hotels, with personalized service and strict attention to details. In keeping with the theme, rooms follow an earthen color scheme, and many have goose-down comforters, fireplaces, and Jacuzzis. Meeting rooms and small conference facilities are available also, making this a good businessperson's lodging. Continental breakfast and afternoon tea are included in the room rate. *1140 Government St., V8W 1Y2, tel. 604/384–6835 or 800/665–6500; fax 604/386–8930. 40 rooms. Facilities: restaurant, pub. AE, DC, MC, V. Very Expensive.*

★ **The Empress Hotel.** This is Victoria's dowager queen with a face-lift. First opened in 1908, it recently underwent a multimillion dollar renovation that has only enhanced its Victorian charm. In the renovation process, stained glass, carved archways, and hardwood floors were rediscovered and utilized effectively. Forty-six new rooms were added and the others were brought up to modern standards, something the hotel desperately needed. A new entrance has been constructed, in addition to the new rooms and re-landscaped grounds. The Empress dominates the inner-harbor area and is the city's primary meeting place for politicians, locals, and tourists. This is one of Victoria's top tourist attractions, so don't expect quiet strolls through the lobby. *721 Government St., V8W 1W5, tel. 604/384–8111 or 800/268–9411; fax 604/381–4334. 488 rooms. Facilities: 2 restaurants, 2 lounges, conference center, indoor pool, sauna, health club, in-room movies, cable TV, Christmas discount, family discount. AE, DC, MC, V. Very Expensive.*

★ **Hotel Grand Pacific.** This is a new hotel and one of Victoria's finest, with modern motifs and international service standards. Overlooking the harbor, and adjacent to the legislative buildings, the hotel accommodates business people looking for comfort, convenience, and great scenery; ask for a room that overlooks downtown, or the harbor. *450 Québec St., V8V 1W5, tel. 604/386–0450 or 800/663–7550; fax 604/383–7603. 149 rooms. Facilities: restaurant, lounge, sauna, whirlpool, fitness center, convention facilities, underground parking, indoor pool. AE, DC, MC, V. Very Expensive.*

Victoria Regent Hotel. Originally built as an apartment, this is a posh, condo-living hotel that offers views of the harbor or city. The outside is plain, with a glass facade, but the interior is sumptuously decorated with warm earth tones and modern furnishings; each apartment has a living room, dining room, deck, kitchen, and one or two bedrooms with bath. *1234 Wharf St., V8W 3H9, tel. 604/386–2211 or 800/663–7472; fax 604/386–2622. 50 rooms. Facilities: restaurant, free parking, limo service. AE, MC, V. Very Expensive.*

Executive House Hotel. In the heart of downtown, this all-facilities tower-style hotel is appealing to businesspeople because of the conference space and convenient downtown location. The hotel's posh lobby offers aesthetic delights, from the woven wall hangings to the comfortable leather couches. The tastefully decorated but functional rooms are comfortable, and some have kitchenettes; specialty suites on upper floors of the tower offer the best views of downtown and the Georgia Strait. *777 Douglas St., V8W 2B5, tel. 604/388–5111 or 800/663–7001; fax 604/385–1323. 179 rooms. Facilities: 2 restaurants, 2 lounges, pub, sauna, Jacuzzi, fitness facility, parking. AE, DC, MC, V. Expensive–Very Expensive.*

★ **Holland House Inn.** Two blocks from the inner harbor, legislative buildings, and ferry terminals, this nonsmoking, adult hotel has a sense of casual elegance. Some of the individually designed rooms have original fine art created by the owner, and some have four-poster beds and fireplaces. All rooms have private baths and all but one have their own balconies. A gourmet breakfast is served and included in room rates. You'll recognize the house by the picket fence around it. *595 Michigan St., V8V 1S7, tel. and fax 604/384–6644. 10 rooms. Facilities: lounge. AE, MC, V. Expensive–Very Expensive.*

★ **Laurel Point Inn.** This waterfront hotel has recently been given a new addition that has expanded this modern-design hotel to about double its original size. The contemporary style of this place is a refreshing change from the city's Victorian flavor.

Angular construction allows views of the harbor from all rooms, which are furnished modernly; the lounge on the ground floor is bright, with large windows and a panoramic view of the inner harbor. The Café Laurel serves the finest Sunday brunch in town. *680 Montréal St., V8V 1Z8, tel. 604/386–8721 or 800/663–7667; fax 604/386–9547. 202 rooms. Facilities: restaurant, 2 lounges, convention facilities, indoor parking, indoor pool, hot tubs, saunas. AE, MC, V. Expensive–Very Expensive.*

★ **The Beaconsfield Inn.** The Beaconsfield has a feel for Old World charm, despite that it was built in 1984. Dark mahogany wood appears throughout the house; fireplaces, down comforters, and some canopy beds and claw-foot tubs adorn the rooms, reinforcing the Victorian style of this residentially situated inn. An added plus is the guest library and conservatory/sun room. Full breakfast, with homemade muffins, and a cocktail hour (6–7 PM), with sherry, cheese, and fruit, are included in the room rates. *998 Humboldt St., V8V 2Z8, tel. 604/384–4044; fax 604/384–4044. 12 rooms. Facilities: library, Jacuzzi. MC, V. Expensive.*

Chateau Victoria. This 19-story hotel, situated across from Victoria's new Conference Centre, near the inner harbor and the Royal British Columbia Museum, promises wonderful views from its upper rooms and its rooftop restaurant. Following a Victorian motif, the rooms are warm and spacious, some with balconies or sitting areas and kitchenettes. *740 Burdett Ave., V8W 1B2, tel. 604/382–4221 or 800/663–5891; fax 604/380–1950. 175 rooms. Facilities: restaurants, lounge, indoor pool, courtesy vans to ferry, access to health club. AE, MC, V. Expensive.*

★ **Abigail's.** A Tudor country inn with gardens and crystal chandeliers, Abigail's is not only posh, but also conveniently located four blocks east of downtown. All guest rooms are lavishly detailed with a rose, peach, and mint color scheme. Crystal goblets in each room, down comforters, and Jacuzzis and fireplaces in some add to the luxurious atmosphere. There's a sense of elegant formality about the hotel, noticed especially in the guest library and sitting room, where you'll want to spend an hour or so in the evening relaxing. Breakfast, included in the room rate, is served from 8 to 9 in the downstairs dining room. *906 McClure St., V8V 3E7, tel. 604/388–5363; fax 604/361–1905. 16 rooms. MC, V. Moderate–Expensive.*

★ **Dashwood Manor.** One of those small, intimate places for which you're always on the lookout, Dashwood Manor is on the waterfront next to Beacon Hill Park and is truly a find. This Heritage Tudor mansion, built in 1912 on property once owned by Governor Sir James Douglas, offers panoramic views of the Strait of Juan de Fuca and the Olympic Peninsula. Three rooms in this B&B have fireplaces. In the afternoon, join the other guests for sherry or brandy, or relax in the small library. *1 Cook Rd., V8V 3W6, tel. 604/385–5517. 14 rooms. MC, V. Moderate–Expensive.*

Huntingdon Manor Inn. Just west of the legislative buildings, overlooking the inner harbor, is this Edwardian-style inn, located behind the most tourist-oriented area of the city. Extras such as champagne upon arrival and a roaring fireplace in the parlor make the place comfortable. Honeymooners get special attention when staying here. *330 Québec St., V8V 1W3, tel. 604/381–3456 or 800/663–7557; fax 604/381–3456. 116 rooms.*

Facilities: breakfast restaurant, lounge, Jacuzzi, laundry, valet service, whirlpool, sauna. AE, MC, V. Moderate–Expensive.

Oak Bay Beach Hotel. This Tudor-style hotel, located in Oak Bay, on the southwest side of the Saanich Peninsula, is well removed from the bustle of downtown. There's a wonderful atmosphere here, though; the hotel, situated oceanside, overlooks the Haro Strait, and catches the setting sun. The interior decor is as dreamy as the grounds, with antiques and flower prints decorating the rooms. The restaurant, Tudor Room by the Sea, is average, but the bar with its cozy fireplace is truly romantic. *1175 Beach Dr., V8S 2N2, tel. and fax 604/598–4556. 51 rooms. Facilities: restaurant, yacht for cruises, access to health club. AE, DC, MC, V. Moderate–Very Expensive.*

Best Western Emerald Isle Motor Inn. Near Butchart Gardens, ferries, and the airport, this motel is perfect for families because it's close to everything, and the kitchenettes enable guests to save the cost of eating out. The decor is beige and functional. *2306 Beacon Ave., Sidney V8L 1X2, tel. 604/656–4441 or 800/528–1234; fax 604/655–1351. 63 rooms; nonsmoking rooms available. Facilities: restaurant, free in-house movies, cable TV, Jacuzzis, sauna, health spa. AE, DC, MC, V. Moderate.*

Captain's Palace Hotel and Restaurant. This is a unique lodging, contained within three Victorian-era mansions, and located only one block from the legislative buildings. Once a one-bedroom B&B, it has expanded to 16 guest rooms and a restaurant. Rooms, decorated in florals and pastels, offer different extras: some have private baths with claw-foot tubs, others have balconies. Although the restaurant provides ample breakfasts, don't overlook offerings in the neighborhood for dinner. Ask about special honeymoon, holiday, and blossom-time packages. *309 Belleville St., V8V 1X2, tel. 604/388–9191; fax 604/388–7606. 16 rooms. Facilities: restaurant, money exchange, bicycles. AE, MC, V. Moderate.*

Courtyard Inn. Downtown, within three blocks of the Legislative buildings, this inn combines the old and the new with liberal use of cedar and warm paneling. The Old Bailey Pub, on the premises, is one of Victoria's favorite watering holes. *850 Blanchard St., V8W 2H2, tel. 604/385–6787; fax 604/385–5800. 64 rooms. Facilities: restaurant, lounge, pub, indoor pool, sauna, laundry. AE, DC, MC, V. Moderate.*

Admiral Motel. Located on the Victoria harbour and along the tourist strip, this motel is right where the action is, although it is relatively quiet in the evening. If you're looking for a basic, clean lodging, the Admiral is just that—nothing more, nothing less. Rooms are functional, and small pets are permitted. *257 Belleville St., V8V 1X1, tel. 604/388–6267. 29 rooms, 12 with kitchens. Facilities: cable TV, free parking, laundry. AE, MC, V. Inexpensive–Moderate.*

★ **Craigmyle Guest House.** In the shade of Craigdarroch Castle, about 1 mile from the downtown core, this lodge, built in 1913, has a special view of the castle. The rooms are quietly elegant and simple, with decor reminiscent of Laura Ashley prints; some units have shared bath. The Edwardian touches are best felt in the main lounge, where you'll find high ceilings and a huge fireplace. A hearty English-style breakfast, with home-made preserves, porridge, and eggs, is a main attraction here.

1037 Craigdarroch Rd., V8S 2A5, tel. 604/595–5411; fax 604/370–5276. 19 rooms, 15 with shared bath. MC, V. Inexpensive–Moderate.

The Arts and Nightlife

The Arts

Galleries **The Art Gallery of Greater Victoria** is considered one of Canada's finest art museums and is home to large collections of Chinese and Japanese ceramics and other art, and also to the only authentic Shinto shrine in North America. The gallery hosts about 40 different temporary exhibitions yearly. *1040 Moss St., Victoria, tel. 604/384–4101. Admission: $3 adults, $1.50 students and senior citizens, children under 12 free; free Thurs. after 5, though donations are accepted. Open Mon.–Wed., and Fri.–Sat. 10–5, Thurs. 10–9, Sun. 1–5.*

The Emily Carr Gallery houses artworks of the province's most famous painter—an Impressionist who made use of any materials available to her—and features, on a rotating basis, sketches and studies from the archive's collection. Documentary films, artifacts, journals, and memorabilia are shown also. Prints of Carr's work are available. *1107 Wharf St., Victoria, tel. 604/387–3080. Admission free. Open Sept.–May, Tues.–Sat. 10–4:30; June–Aug., Mon.–Sat. 10–4:30.*

Music The **Victoria Symphony** has a winter schedule and a summer season, playing out of the weathered **Royal Theatre and University Centre Auditorium** (805 Broughton St., Victoria, tel. 604/383–9711). The **Pacific Opera Victoria** performs three productions a year in the 800-seat **McPherson Playhouse** (3 Centennial Sq., tel. 604/385–0222), adjoining the Victoria City Hall. The **University of Victoria** (tel. 604/721–8480) has an active music and theater season with something going on virtually every day. The **Victoria International Music Festival** (tel. 604/736–2119) features internationally acclaimed musicians, dancers, and singers each summer from the first week in July through late August.

Theater Live theater activity includes the **Belfry Theatre** (1291 Gladstone Ave., Victoria, tel. 604/385–6815), **Phoenix Theatre** (tel. 604/721–8000) at the University of Victoria, **Victoria Theatre Guild** (805 Langham Ct., tel. 604/384–2141), **McPherson Playhouse** (3 Centennial Sq., tel. 604/386–6121).

In Prince George visit the **Prince George Playhouse** (2833 Recreation Place, tel. 604/563–8401). In Kelowna the **Sunshine Theatre Company** (1304 Ellis, tel. 604/763–4025) and the **Stagedoor Dinner Theatre** (1820 Benvoulin Ave., tel. 604/861–5555) stage productions.

In Kamloops call the **Sagebrush Theatre Company** (821 Munro St., tel. 604/372–0966) or the **Western Canada Theatre Company** (1025 Lorne St., tel. 604/372–3216) for schedule information.

Nightlife

Victoria After 8 PM, **Tudor House Hotel Pub** (533 Admirals Rd., tel. 604/382–1912) becomes a pub attracting the younger set. There's a dance floor and large screen for disco and video entertainment nightly.

Outside Victoria In cities and towns throughout British Columbia you'll find most live entertainment in major hotels or at local theater and music complexes.

8 The Canadian Rockies

Introduction

by Peter Oliver

Peter Oliver is a New York writer who covers sports, travel, and the outdoors. His articles have appeared in Backpacker, The New York Times, Skiing, *and many other publications.*

Comparing mountains is a subjective and imprecise business. Yet few would argue that the 640-kilometer (400-mile) stretch of the Canadian Rockies easily ranks as one of the most extravagantly beautiful ranges on earth. With little standing between the mountains and the Alberta prairie, the Rockies etch on the horizon an abrupt and stony line of chaotic grandeur that can be seen from 100 kilometers (60 miles) away. Behind the prairie, granite walls rise thousands of feet above evergreen forests and glacially carved basins.

The peak that best epitomizes the character of the Canadian Rockies is Mt. Robson, which, at 3,954 meters (12,931 feet), is the highest of them all. A colossus of tumbling glaciers and cliff walls, usually shrouded in storm clouds, Mt. Robson creates its own irascible climate zone: the rush of avalanches down its flanks has triggered wind blasts well over 320 kilometers (200 miles) an hour.

The Canadian Rockies, about 60 million years old, are relatively young as mountains go. The parallel ranges of the Columbia Mountains, just west of the Rockies, were first formed about 180 million years ago. Measured against the U.S. Rockies, the Rockies of Canada are not exceptionally high, either; elevations generally average 600 to 900 meters (about 2,000 to 3,000 feet) lower than those in Colorado, for example. Still, the Canadian Rockies *seem* higher, primarily because the tree line is lower. The tree line is the approximate elevation above which trees generally can't grow and the landscape becomes rocky, open, and often covered by snow and ice. In the Canadian Rockies, the tree line is at about 2,000 meters (6,500 feet) compared with Colorado tree lines that usually start above 3,000 meters.

But while glaciers in the United States have all but disappeared, they remain a common sight in Canada—in Glacier National Park in the Columbias, for example, more than 400 glaciers cover 10% of the park's territory. The pale glacial blue strikes a dramatic balance against the blue-gray granite, the deep green of fir, spruce, and larch forests, and the panchromatic sweep of wild flowers. The glacial melt also feeds high-mountain lakes with mineral-rich silt deposits that tint the waters emerald green and cobalt blue, colors that change with the moods of the weather and the seasons.

Recognizing early the exceptional natural beauty of the region, the Canadian government began shielding the area from human development and resource exploitation in the 1880s. In 1885, the government created a park preserve around the Cave and Basin Hot Springs in Banff. Two years later, Canada's first national park, Rocky Mountain Park (later Banff National Park) was officially established. Lands that would later become Yoho National Park and Glacier National Park in the Columbias were first set aside in 1886.

Today, approximately 25,000 square kilometers (roughly 10,000 square miles)—an area larger than the state of New Hampshire—are protected in seven national parks in the Rockies and the Columbias. Because they were protected early on, the parks of the Rockies—Waterton Lakes, Banff, Kootenay, Yoho, and Jasper—have remained relatively untouched by human development. The only significant clusters of human settlement are the town centers of Banff, Jasper, and Waterton Lakes, and the area around Lake Louise. Several thousand more square kilometers are also protected as wilderness areas and provincial parks, most notably Mt. Robson and Mt. Assiniboine provincial parks and Kananaskis Country.

The establishment of parks was a boon to wildlife, and today, it is virtually impossible to visit the national parks and *not* spot elk, mule deer, or bighorn sheep, especially in fall and winter. Human visitation, however, is another story. Two major roadways, Routes 1 and 93, as well as an extensive network of hiking trails and climbing routes, have made the wilderness of the Canadian Rockies remarkably accessible. Visitors taking advantage of its easy access have made Banff the most visited of Canada's national parks. June, July, and August are the months when most visitors come to the parks; it's also the time when lodging prices double. But the changing colors of fall (especially when contrasted against the early snows) attract leaf lovers into mid-October. And winter snows, most abundant in the Columbias, keeps skiers coming from December through April. Only the transitional months of April, late October, and November are quiet times.

That the Canadian Rockies have become such a popular attraction might well have amazed pioneers and prospectors a century and a half ago, when the mountains were formidable and unwelcome—a barrier rather than a thing of beauty. Working for trading companies, the Hudson's Bay Company and the North West Company, explorers searched for a route to the west, but the mountains hindered the prospects of trade and transportation. When word spread in the east of gold discoveries in southeastern British Columbia in the early 1860s, the mountains exacted a mortal toll among prospectors attempting the east–west crossing. In return, they yielded far less ore than had been hoped for.

The mountains treated railway builders no less cruelly a few years later; between 1885 and 1911, more than 200 people, almost all railroad workers, were killed in avalanches in the Rogers Pass area (now Glacier National Park). A single slide in 1910 killed 62 men. It is no wonder, then, that the completion of the Canadian Pacific Railroad (CPR) route through the Rockies and the Columbias is still championed today as one of the great feats of Canadian engineering and perseverance.

The arrival of the railroad also was instrumental in opening up the Canadian Rockies to tourism, and in a lucky marriage of public and private interests, Canadian Pacific helped encourage the national government to establish the parks that would attract tourists. Hoping to fill trains with outdoor-minded vacationers, CPR General Manager W.C. Van Horne, with great entrepreneurial verve, declared: "If we can't export the scenery, we'll import the tourists!" That's just what they did. The railroad company built its first hotel, the Banff Springs Hotel, in 1888. Others would follow, most notably the Lake Louise Chalet (to become Chateau Lake Louise) and the Jasper Park Lodge, as well as backcountry lodges.

The main reason people still come to the Canadian Rockies is to appreciate the mountainous outdoors. One quickly becomes fascinated by mountain-building dynamics—sedimentary compression, overthrust, glacial erosion, and so on. Although historical sites in the region are few, and cultural attractions fewer—even a movie theater is hard to find—the scenery has made this one of the world's great automotive touring regions, and in summer, Routes 1 and 93 are heavily trafficked with cars, recreational vehicles, and tour buses.

Sticking to the highways, however, is a needless exercise in self-deprivation. Hikes of no more than three or four kilometers (about 2 ½ miles) can lead to secluded lakes and basins of pristine, high-alpine splendor. Roadside trailheads are everywhere, and a number of trails are wide and gentle enough for wheelchair access. Horses, helicopters, mountain bikes, canoes, skis in winter—the modes of transportation for exploring the mountain outback are many, as are equipment-rental and guide services as well as backcountry guide books. (*See* Sports and Outdoor Activities, below.)

Many, too, are the moods of the weather. Summer temperatures typically range between the 60s and 80s, although the temperature tends to drop 5 to 10 degrees with every 300 meters (1,000 feet) of elevation gain. Mid-winter temperatures typically range between the teens and low 30s. However, snow in July is not uncommon at higher elevations, and warm Chinook winds that hit the eastern slopes in winter can raise temperatures into the 60s in January, as happened during the 1988 Winter Olympics. Even for summer months, it is advisable to pack a wool sweater, warm socks, and light gloves, especially if you plan to do much hiking, boating, cycling, or other outdoor activities. Weather can change quickly, and with it, temperatures. For half-day or longer hikes, it is always a good idea to pack a few light layers (e.g., a light sweater or sweatshirt) and a water-repellent windbreaker.

Essential Information

Important Addresses and Numbers

Tourist Information

The three major sources of tourism information are: **Travel Alberta** (15th floor, Box 2500, Edmonton, AB T5J 2Z4, tel. 800/ALBERTA), **Tourism British Columbia** (Parliament Bldgs., Victoria, BC V8V 1X4, tel. 800/663–6000), and **Parks Canada** (Information Services, Box 2989, Station M, Calgary, AB T2P 3H8, tel. 403/292–4401). Parks Canada information is also available at the **Parks Information Bureau** (Box 900, 224 Banff Ave., Banff, AB T0L 0C0, tel. 403/762–4256). Specify particular interests when requesting information; all the organizations have an extensive list of maps and publications.

For local information in Banff, contact the **Banff–Lake Louise Chamber of Commerce** (94 Banff Ave., Banff, AB T0L 0C0, tel. 403/762–3777); in Jasper, **Jasper Park Chamber of Commerce** (Box 98, Jasper, AB T0E 1E0, tel. 403/852–3858); in Kananaskis Country, **Kananaskis Country** (Suite 412, 1011 Glenmore Trail SW, Calgary, AB T2V 4R6, tel. 403/297–3362); in Waterton Lakes, **Waterton Lakes National Park** (Superintendent, Waterton Park, AB T0K 2M0, tel. 403/859–2262) or **Waterton Park Chamber of Commerce** (Box 55, Waterton Park, AB T0K 2M0, tel. 403/859–2203); in Revelstoke and Glacier Parks, **Mount Revelstoke and Glacier National Parks** (Park Superintendent, Box 350, Revelstoke, BC V0E 2S0, tel. 604/837–5155).

Emergencies Throughout Alberta and British Columbia **911** is the number for **police** or **ambulance.** For any extended trip into the backcountry, always register with the nearest park warden's office.

Arriving and Departing by Plane

Calgary is the most common gateway for travelers arriving by plane. Those who plan to visit only Jasper and northern park regions may prefer to use Edmonton as a gateway city. Both cities have international airports served by several major carriers; the Calgary flight schedule is somewhat more extensive.

Airports and Airlines **Calgary International Airport** and **Edmonton International Airport** serve the British Columbia Rockies region. (For airline information, *see* Arriving and Departing by Plane in Chapter 9.)

Air Canada and **Canadian Air** have daily flights to and from Cranbrook's airport, in central British Columbia; most of these flights connect with flights through Vancouver International Airport and the international airports in Calgary and Edmonton.

Arriving and Departing by Car, Train, and Bus

By Car Route 1, the Trans-Canada Highway, is the principal east–west route into the region. Banff is 128 kilometers (80 miles) west of Calgary on Route 1 and 858 kilometers (515 miles) east of Vancouver. The other major east–west routes are Route 16 to the north, the main highway between Edmonton and Jasper, and Route 3 to the south. The main routes from the south are Route 89, which enters Canada east of Waterton Lakes National Park from Montana, and Route 3, also from Montana, which provides access to the British Columbia Rockies.

By Train **VIA Rail** (tel. 800/361–3677), Canada's national rail company, offers service connecting Banff and Jasper with Calgary, Edmonton, and Vancouver. As a result of recent cuts in the VIA budget, service has been pared significantly on many Canadian routes. When using VIA services, call in advance to confirm schedule.

By Bus **Greyhound/Trailways** (call local listing) provides regular service to Calgary, Edmonton, and Vancouver, with connecting service to Jasper and Waterton Lakes. **Brewster Grayline** (tel. 800/661–1152) offers service between the Calgary International Airport and Banff, Jasper, and Lake Louise.

Getting Around

A fee is charged to all vehicles entering the national parks. A day pass is $3; a four-day pass, $6; and an annual pass, for any stay longer than four days, $20. You are permitted to leave and reenter the park for the duration of the pass without additional charge.

By Car Snow arrives early in fall and leaves late in spring. When traveling between October and April, stay informed of local road conditions, especially if you're traveling over mountain passes or along the Icefields Parkway. A few roads, such as Route 40 over Highwood Pass in Kananaskis Country, are closed during the winter.

Rental Cars Car-rental outlets are located at the Calgary and Edmonton airports, as well as in Banff, Jasper, and Cranbrook. Daily rentals for sightseeing are available, but should be reserved well ahead of time, especially in summer.

Guided Tours

Orientation *Bus Tours* **Brewster Transportation and Tours** (Box 1140, Banff, AB T0L 0C0, tel. in Banff, 403/762–2241; in Lake Louise, 403/522–3544; in Jasper, 403/852–3332; or 800/661–1152) offers half-day and full-day sightseeing tours of the parks. Prices start at about $12.

Tauck Tours (11 Wilton Rd., Westport, CT 06881, tel. 203/226–6911) and **Holland America Westours** (300 Elliot Ave. W, Seattle, WA 98119, tel. 206/281/3535) feature multi-day bus tours through the region. Some Tauck Tours include heli-hiking options.

Jasper Scenic Bus Tours (Box 1252, Jasper, AB T0E 1E0, tel. 403/852–5570) runs daily tours of the Jasper area. In winter, the company also packages cross-country skiing excursions around Maligne Lake with bus tours.

Boat Tours **Minnewanka Boat Tours** (Box 2189, Banff, AB T0L 0C0, tel. 403/762–3473) offers summer tours on Lake Minnewanka, near Banff.

Maligne Lake Scenic Cruises (626 Connaught Dr., Jasper, AB T0E 1E0, tel. 403/852–3370) runs half-day tours on Maligne Lake, near Jasper.

Scenic Boat Cruises (Box 126, Waterton, AB T0K 2M0, tel. 403/859–2362) offers half-day and full-day cruises of Waterton Lake, some with hiking options.

Auto Tours Audiocassette tapes for self-guided auto tours of the parks are produced by **Inc. Auto Tape Tours** and **Rocky Mountain Tape Tours.** Tapes can be rented or purchased at news or gift shops in Banff, Lake Louise, and Jasper.

Special-interest *Seasonal Tours* **Challenge Enterprises** (1300 Railway Ave., Box 2008, Canmore, AB T0L 0M0, tel. 403/678–2628) has a variety pack of tour options, including fishing, rafting, and cycling trips in summer, as well as snowmobiling, ice-fishing, and dogsledding tours in winter.

Kingmik Expeditions (Box 227, Lake Louise, AB T0L 1E0, tel. 604/344–7288) specializes in dogsledding tours, from half-day to five-day outings.

For hiking, mountaineering, or backcountry ski tours, **Banff Alpine Guides** (Box 1025, Banff, AB T0L 0C0, tel. 403/762–2791) organizes tours according to weather conditions. Bookings can be arranged for private groups. The **Canadian School of Mountaineering** (Box 723, Canmore, AB T0L 0M0, tel. 403/678–4134) offers tours and instruction for mountaineering (in summer and winter) and backcountry skiing.

In Waterton Lakes National Park, **Russell Guide Service** (Box 68, Waterton Park, AB T0K 2M0, tel. 403/627–3241) runs fishing and hiking tours, focusing on regional flora and fauna.

Bicycle Tours Several operators offer guided on-road and off-road bicycle tours. **Rocky Mountain Cycle Tours** (Box 1987, Canmore, AB T0L 0M0, tel. 403/678–6770) features one- to seven-day tours, both in the Banff area and in British Columbia. **Ride the Rockies Bicycle Touring** (Box 6866, Station D, Calgary, AB T2P 2E9, tel. 403/278–9823) offers trips ranging from one-day mountain bike tours in Kananaskis, to 12-day tours from Jasper to Waterton. **Glacier Cycle Mountain Bike Tours** (607 Patricia St., Jasper, AB T0E 1E0, tel. 403/852–4809) specializes in off-road tours in Jasper National Park from April through November.

Exploring the Canadian Rockies

Orientation

Most people who come to the Canadian Rockies arrive from the east, from Calgary, via Route 1. Because it is just more than an hour's drive west of Calgary, and because of the abundant lodging, dining, and shopping options, Banff is the logical first stop for most visitors. Many, however, continue on to Lake Louise, a half-hour's drive north of Banff.

From Banff, the most popular excursion is the scenic drive north, along the Icefields Parkway (Route 93), to Jasper, 280 kilometers (180 miles) away. Excursions into Yoho and Kootenay parks are not as common, primarily because services, especially in Kootenay, are almost nonexistent.

A sensible and economical option to using Banff as a base camp is to stay in Canmore, 40 kilometers (25 miles) east, where lodging is generally less expensive. Canmore is an excellent step-off point for those interested in exploring Kananaskis Country, the mountain ranges that stretch south of Banff. With fewer restrictions than the national parks, Kananaskis Country is popular with sportsmen—horseback outfitters, hunters, and fishermen.

Another economical option to staying in Banff is to find accommodations in the British Columbia Rockies. Inexpensive lodging is abundant in Radium Hot Springs, 128 kilometers (80 miles) west of Banff, at the southern edge of Kootenay National Park. Also, consider staying in Golden, on Route 1, 80 kilometers (50 miles) west of Lake Louise. These towns are good access points to the Columbia ranges as well as the Rockies, but they are certainly not as scenic as the townsites within the parks.

Waterton Lakes National Park, 354 kilometers (220 miles) to the south, is a rare side trip from Banff, with much of the drive along a relatively undistinguished route (though no drive in this part of the world really lacks scenery). People who visit Waterton Lakes generally make it their principal destination, or combine it with a vacation in Glacier National Park (not to be confused with Canada's park), the abutting park across the U.S. border in Montana.

Highlights for First-time Visitors

Banff Springs Hotel, Tour 1

Cave and Basin Hot Springs, Tour 1

Chateau Lake Louise, Tour 1

Icefields Parkway (between Bow Pass and Sunwapta Falls), Tour 2

Kananaskis Village, Tour 3

Kimberly, Tour 4

Maligne Lake, Tour 2

Tour 1: Banff and Lake Louise

Numbers in the margin correspond with points of interest on the Canadian Rockies and Banff maps.

1 **Banff** is a town of unlikely contrasts: Amid the bustle of commercialism, elk regularly graze on the town common; tour-bus sightseers carrying souvenir-stuffed bags mix on Banff Avenue (the main drag) with rugged outdoorspeople, among them some of the world's most accomplished mountaineers. For almost all who come to the Canadian Rockies, Banff is the central depot in their Canadian Rockies travel. The reason is simple: Except for Jasper and tiny Field in Yoho, Banff is the only town—and by far the largest—in the four contiguous parks.

Banff straddles a thin line between mountain resort town and tourist trap. It is certainly not a quaint little western outpost; except for the oft-photographed Banff Springs Hotel, its architecture is mostly modern, simple, and undistinguished. Because of the limitations that park regulations have set on expansion, Banff hasn't expanded in recent years but has instead compressed in on itself. This and the contrasting backdrop of surrounding wilderness make Banff the hub of hyperactivity during the summer.

The two points of reference that Banff explorers use are Banff Avenue and the Banff Springs Hotel. An amazing number of shops and restaurants have been crammed together on the half-
2 mile stretch of **Banff Avenue** that comprises the core of downtown. This is made possible because most of the shops are small and have been clustered together in about a half-dozen indoor walking malls.

The mix of shops consists of art galleries, clothing stores, photo stores, bookstores, and confectioners whose fudge and cookie output make Banff Avenue a mine field for anyone with a sweet tooth. Items sold in the galleries are of the sort you might expect—landscape paintings, native crafts, and wood carvings, ranging from trinkets to kitsch to genuine art. Except for a few stores in Jasper, this is pretty much where shopping begins and ends in the national parks.

Heading south, Banff Avenue crosses the Bow River over a
3 great stone bridge, ending in a T in front of the **Parks Information Office.** Here, you can pick up park trail maps and other materials concerning the area. *224 Banff Ave., tel. 403/762–4256. Open daily 8 AM–10 PM.*

The Canadian Rockies

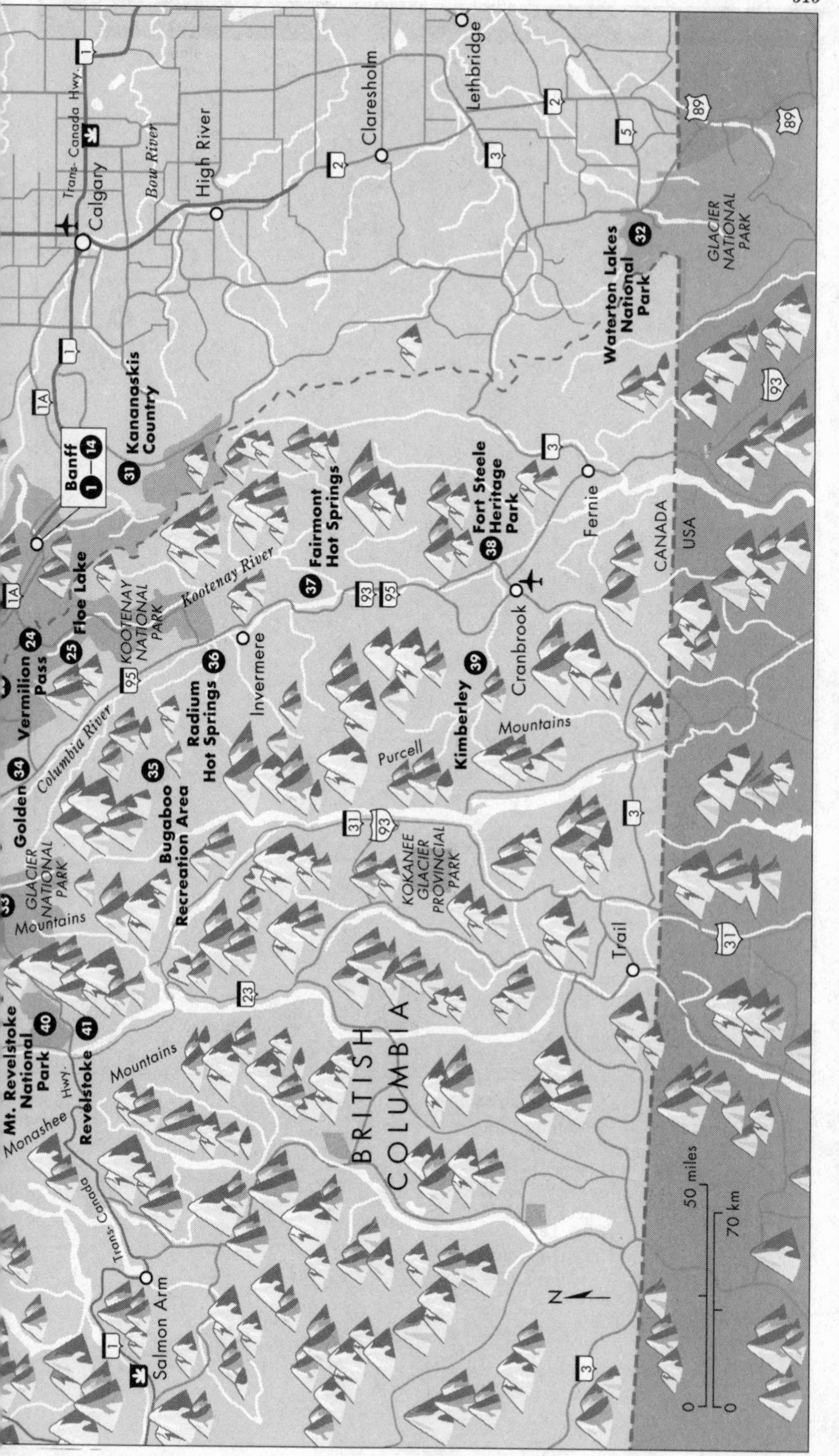
Calgary
Trans- Canada Hwy.
Bow River
High River
Claresholm
Lethbridge
Banff
1—14
31 Kananaskis Country
Waterton Lakes National Park 32
GLACIER NATIONAL PARK
Vermilion Pass 24
25 Floe Lake
KOOTENAY NATIONAL PARK
Kootenay River
37 Fairmont Hot Springs
Fort Steele Heritage Park 38
Fernie
CANADA
USA
Golden 34
Columbia River
35
Radium Hot Springs 36
Invermere
Cranbrook
Kimberley 39
Mountains
Purcell
GLACIER NATIONAL PARK
Mountains
Bugaboo Recreation Area
KOKANEE GLACIER PROVINCIAL PARK
Trail
Mt. Revelstoke National Park 40
Revelstoke 41
Hwy.
Monashee
Mountains
BRITISH COLUMBIA
Trans- Canada
Salmon Arm
N
0
50 miles
0
70 km
1
1A
2
3
5
89
93
95
31
23

Banff

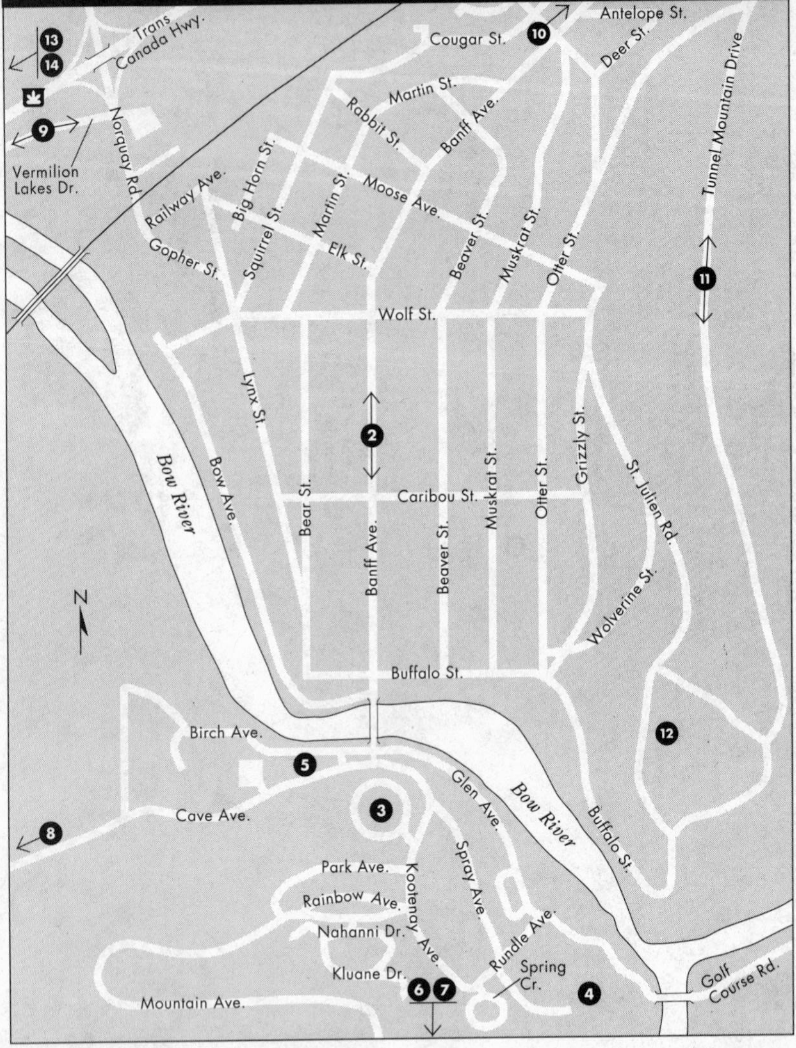

Banff Avenue, **2**
Banff Centre, **12**
Banff Springs Hotel, **4**
Buffalo Paddock, **10**
Cave and Basin Hot Springs, **8**
Chateau Lake Louise, **13**
Luxton Museum, **5**
Moraine Lake, **14**
Parks Information Office, **3**
Sulphur Mountain Gondola, **7**
Tunnel Mountain Drive, **11**
Upper Hot Springs, **6**
Vermilion Lakes Drive, **9**

4 A left turn leads to the **Banff Springs Hotel** (*see* Lodging, below), a year-round three-ring circus. Built in 1888, the hotel is easily recognized by its castle-like exterior, while inside the visitor can expect to get lost in the crazy-quilt network of restaurants, shops, salons, and ballrooms. Even renovators got confused; evidently, the hotel has a hidden room—one that was accidentally sealed off by an overzealous plasterer. It was left that way to add a chapter to the hotel lore.

5 A quick right will take you to the **Luxton Museum** where you can study native Canadian life through artifacts and wax-made figures in natural settings. *1 Birch Ave., Banff, tel. 403/762–2388. Admission: $2 adults, children under 12 free. Open daily 10–6.*

6 Take Mountain Avenue for one mile to **Upper Hot Springs** (tel.
7 403/762–2056) for a dip, or to the **Sulphur Mountain Gondola** for a vista. Views during the steep eight-minute ride to and from the summit are spectacular, but they are hardly private. The observation decks and short summit trails are well-visited, especially in summer.

A right turn at the Park Information Office leads 3.2 kilometers
8 (2 miles) to the **Cave and Basin Hot Springs.** Once considered sacred by the Stoney Indians, the springs were discovered by prospectors in 1883; they became the birthplace of the park system when they were given national park protection in 1885. Two interpretive trails provide good insight into the geology and plant life of the region.

Both the **Upper Hot Springs** and the **Cave and Basin Centre Pool** (Cave Ave., 2 km, or 1¼ mi, west of downtown Banff, tel. 403/762–4900) promise to be exhilarating. The Upper Hot Springs is more of a soak; Cave and Basin is more of a swim. Lockers, suits, and towels are available to rent at both.

Several short excursions are possible from the town of Banff.
9 **Vermilion Lakes Drive,** just off the west Banff exit from Route 1, offers one of the best opportunities for wildlife sightings: elk, bighorn sheep, muskrat, and the very occasional moose. Dur-
10 ing the summer, the **buffalo paddock,** near the east Banff exit from Route 1, is the place to go to see the animals.

11 On the other side of town, **Tunnel Mountain Drive** makes a scenic 3-mile loop. Two points of particular interest along the drive are the Hoodoos, fingerlike rock formations caused by erosion,
12 and the **Banff Centre** (St. Julien Rd., tel. 403/762–6300), *the* place in town and in the parks for the performing arts.

Most people traveling from Banff to Lake Louise take Route 1 for about 56 kilometers (35 miles) north along the Bow River. But if you aren't in a hurry, the two-lane Route 1A, running approximately parallel to Route 1, is the more scenic option. A few kilometers north of Banff, look for the turnoff to the ski area called **Sunshine Village.** The gondola that serves its slopes in winter also runs in summer, providing easy access for strolling around high-alpine meadows. Many active hikers and backpackers use the gondola to reach Mt. Assiniboine Provincial Park. Mt. Assiniboine has been called the "Matterhorn of the Canadian Rockies," and with good reason; it is the lookalike of its Swiss counterpart. *Sunshine Village Gondolas, exit Rte. 1, 8 km (5 mi) west of Banff, tel. 403/762–6500. Admission:*

$12 adults, $7 senior citizens, $5 children 7–12, children under 7 free. Open late June–early Sept., daily 9–8.

At the Lake Louise junction, a right turn leads to the Lake Louise ski area, one of the top three or four skiing sites in Canada. It was originally to be the site of the 1988 Olympic alpine skiing events, but concerns about the Olympic crowds' possible environmental impact on the park led instead to the development of Mt. Allen in Kananaskis Country for the Olympic events.

A left turn at the junction leads to what ostensibly is the center of Lake Louise: a crossroads, a train crossing, a few hotels, and a small shopping center just off Route 1. Almost all visitors zip
13 through town barely noticing it on their way to **Chateau Lake Louise** (another 6 kilometers, or 4 miles), one of the CPR hotels, built in 1923, that overlooks the blue-green lake and the Victoria Glacier. The extraordinary Alpine-style structure is as scenic as it is popular; camera shutters must certainly click thousands of times a day during the summer months. Canoe rentals are available at the boat house.

The château is also a departure point for several short, moderately strenuous, well-traveled hiking routes. The most popular hike (about 3.5 kilometers, or 2 miles) is to the small teahouse overlooking Lake Agnes. The tiny lake hangs on a mountain-cupped shelf that opens to the east with a distant view of the Bow River Valley. On a sunny day, you'll have plenty of company; tough it out on a rainy day, and you'll have the teahouse pretty much to yourself.

Time Out The **Lake Agnes teahouse** is a one-room café tucked onto a ledge overlooking the small lake and the waterfall that descends steeply from it. Fresh-baked goods and a variety of teas are a welcome reward for the short hike, and the view from the porch is fabulous.

A longer hike (about 6 kilometers, or 4 miles) leads to a larger teahouse/restaurant on the Plain of the Six Glaciers, at the edge of the Victoria Glacier moraine.

14 The other popular place to visit is **Moraine Lake,** 11 kilometers (7 miles) from the heart of Lake Louise. In an area dubbed the "Valley of the Ten Peaks," the lake reflects in deep blue the granite peaks that rise abruptly around it. Moraine Lake is one of the two main stops that tour buses make in Lake Louise (Lake Louise itself being the other), so, again, expect company.

Several moderate hiking trails lead from the lake into some spectacular country; a popular overnight hike is to trek over Sentinel Pass and through Paradise Valley to Lake Louise. For great views, the short (3-kilometer, or 1.9-mile) but steep hike from Moraine Lake to Larch Valley is well worth the effort. Canoe rentals are available from the office of Moraine Lake Cabins. *Moraine Lake Cabin Office, Box 70, Lake Louise, AB T0L 1E0, tel. 403/522–3733. Open June 1–Sept. 30.*

Tour 2: North and West of Banff

Numbers in the margin correspond with points of interest on the Canadian Rockies map.

Heading North Just north of Lake Louise, Routes 1 and 93 diverge. Route 93, the Icefields Parkway, continues northward for more than 230 kilometers (143 miles) to Jasper. Route 1 bears west over Kicking Horse Pass—named, according to local lore, after an unpleasant encounter between a pack animal and a member of an exploratory expedition in the mid-1800s—into Yoho National Park and British Columbia.

If possible, pick a clear day to drive the Icefields Parkway. The *only* thing to do along the parkway is to take in the scenery, whether through a car or bus window or from a hiking trail. As you drive north, the more dramatic scenery will be on your left. The peaks demarcate the Continental Divide; many of the great rivers of western Canada spring from the glaciers and ice fields along the divide. As a matter of definition, ice fields are essentially giant frozen lakes, while glaciers are the frozen rivers that extend from them. There are several viewpoints and short, well-marked hiking trails along the highway, providing not only breathtaking mountain views but also firsthand lessons in glacial dynamics.

15 The parkway begins a steady climb from the intersection of Routes 1 and 93, to **Bow Pass**, which, at 2,070 meters (7,880 feet), may be covered with snow as late as May and as early as September. On the north side of the pass is Peyto Lake; on the south side is Bow Lake, source of the Bow River that flows through Banff. Above Bow Lake hangs the edge of Crowfoot Glacier; to the south, across the lake, is the beginning of the Waputik Icefield. Around the lake are stubbly pines and underbrush—the tree line ends here and high-alpine country begins.

Time Out From Bow Pass, the road gradually descends past Peyto Lake to **Saskatchewan River Crossing.** Between Lake Louise and Jasper, this is the only place from fall to spring (except during the summer when you can refuel at the Icefield Centre; *see* below) where you can get food and refuel. Stop for the gas, but you'll be wise to bring a picnic lunch; the cafeteria food is overpriced and unimpressive.

The road descends from the crossing into the Northern Saskatchewan River valley. Three river systems diverge here—the Sasketchwan, Howse, and Misaya rivers. From several overlooks you can see the three river valleys and the glaciers that reach from the giant ice fields ahead. The Parker Ridge trail—a 3-kilometer (1.9-mile) loop north of the crossing—provides an excellent view of the Sasketchwan Glacier, whence the river of the same name begins.

Shortly, the road begins to climb again, in places along steep hairpin turns, toward Sunwapta Pass—the juncture of Banff and Jasper national parks. Wildlife abounds in this area, and is most visible in spring and autumn after a snowfall, when herds of bighorn sheep come to the road to lick up the salt used to melt snow and ice. Drive cautiously, though; the sheep's desire for salt tends to override their respect for traffic, and they move reluctantly from the highway to make room for passing vehicles.

After Sunwapta Pass, **Athabasca Glacier,** an extension of the Columbia Icefield, appears on your left. The Columbia Icefield, covering 325 square kilometers (125 square miles), is the largest mass of ice in subarctic North America. Well worthwhile is a trip onto the Athabasca Glacier, via buses (called snowcoaches) modified to drive on ice. Hikers can also walk onto the tongue of the glacier, but the going can be slow and chilly. *Bus tours: Brewster Tours, tel. 403/762–2241. Admission to buses June–Sept.: $14 adults, $7 children for 1-hr, 20-min. tour. Walking tours: tel. 403/852–4242. $20 for 5-hr walk, $15 for 3-hr walk; conducted mid-June–August.*

16 Across the highway, on your right, is the **Icefield Centre,** where you can get food, gas, and even lodging in the summer. The center also provides interpretive exhibits, including a model of the entire ice field, an audiovisual presentation, and guided walking tours. *125 km (75 mi) north of Lake Louise on Rte. 93, tel. 403/852–4242. Open Sept.–May, daily 9–5; June–Aug., daily 9–7.*

From Icefields Centre the highway descends gradually into Jasper National Park, leaving the glaciers, ice fields, and waterfalls behind. One point of interest along the way is
17 **Athabasca Falls,** where the Athabasca River is squeezed through a narrow gorge. The site is especially dramatic in early summer, when the river is swollen by the snow melt.

At Athabasca Falls there is a juncture: Route 93 continues ahead, while Route 93A bears left toward Mt. Edith Cavell, perhaps the most imposing peak in the park. From here you can pick up trails leading to Tonquin Valley, *the* most popular hiking area in the park, and Marmot Basin, which is particularly attractive to skiers. Twenty-four kilometers (15 miles) later the highways converge. Nearby, where Route 93 joins Route 16, you can catch the Yellowhead Highway, which reaches east 360 kilometers (225 miles) to Edmonton.

The town of Jasper is at the edge of a broad, open valley where the Athabasca and Miette rivers converge. The modest but attractive town first came into being in 1911 and 1912, with the arrival of the railroad. As you enter the town from the south
18 onto **Connaught Drive,** the main drag, train tracks run parallel on the right.

As you enter town you'll see on the left the stores, restaurants, and inexpensive motels that line Connaught Drive. Unlike in Banff, the shopping and dining in Jasper are low-key matters, because most people who come here use the town as a base for traveling elsewhere in the park.

Many people consider Jasper the preeminent backpacking area in North America. Multi-day loops of more than 160 kilometers (100 miles) are possible on well-maintained trails. However, day trips are much more common, especially around Mt. Edith Cavell, Pyramid Lake, Jasper Park Lodge, and Maligne Lake.

19 Attractions nearest to the town are the **Jasper Tramway,** 3 kilometers (1.9 miles) south of town off Route 93 on Whistlers Mountain Road. The tram rises 950 vertical meters (3,000 feet) on the steep flank of Whistlers Mountain, and you can take in stunning views from the summit of Mt. Robson (when clear) to the west and the Miette and Athabasca valleys which make the trip worth it. *Tel. 403/852–3093. Admission: $7 adults, $3.50 children. Open late March–mid-Oct.; call for times; hours vary throughout season.*

Time Out At the top of the summit, have a leisurely dinner on the glass-enclosed terrace of the **Tramway Dining Room,** (Continental cuisine, fully licensed). After a sunset meal, a short after-dinner hike, and glorious views, take the 11 PM (summer) tram back down to the bottom.

20 Another short, popular excursion is to **Pyramid** and **Patricia lakes,** just 4 kilometers (2½ miles) from town. Different sorts of boats can be rented from Pyramid Lake Bungalows (*see* Lodging, below), including canoes, kayaks, catamarans, and motorized surfboards. *Pyramid Ave., tel. 403/852–3536. Open mid-April–mid-Oct.*

A somewhat longer excursion will take you 30 kilometers (18 miles) to Maligne Lake, one of the largest glacier-fed lakes in the world. Follow Maligne Lake Road, which begins 3 kilometers (1.9 miles) east of town, off Route 16. You'll pass Maligne Canyon, where the Maligne River cuts a deep, narrow gorge through limestone bedrock; it is an impressive site, but the 4-kilometer (2½-mile) trail along the canyon can be crowded, so it's best saved for evening when the crowds thin out. The other point of interest along this road is **Medicine Lake,** whose water levels fluctuate dramatically at different times of year. At certain times, an underground drainage system completely empties the lake, and you can see a bed of glacial silt and residue.

21 **Maligne Lake,** 22 kilometers (14 miles) long, can be explored on a 1½-hour guided cruise or on a rented boat. Spirit Island, which earned its name because its beauty elevates the spirit of those who witness the sight, is a small outcropping in the middle of the lake, and is the main destination. Several hiking trails, some with brief, steep sections, lead to promontories offering panoramas of the lake and the surrounding mountain ranges. *Maligne Lake Tours, 626 Connaught Dr., tel. 403/852–3370. Open mid-May–Sept., daily 9–9.*

Eighty kilometers (50 miles) west of Jasper on Route 16 is tow-
22 ering **Mt. Robson.** First sighted by Hudson's Bay Company explorers about 1820, this peak was not successfully scaled until 1913, despite numerous attempts. Pick as clear a day as possible to go, though Mt. Robson's weather is notoriously bad, and it is a rare day that the summit is not encircled by clouds. A favorite backpacking trip on the mountain is the strenuous 18-kilometer (11-mile) hike to Berg Lake, through the wonderfully named Valley of A Thousand Falls. Berg Lake is no tranquil body of water; the grunt and splash of chunks of ice calving from Robson's glaciers into the lake are regular sounds in summer. The 5-kilometer (3-mile) hike to Kinney Lake, along the Berg Lake trail, is a good option for day hikers.

23 For an entirely different experience, spend a day at **Miette Hot Springs,** 58 kilometers (36 miles) from Jasper. Visitors come here to soak in naturally heated mineral waters originating from three springs that are some of the warmest waters in the Canadian Rockies. *Tel. 403/866–3750. $2 adults, $1.25 children; suit, locker, and towel rentals available. Open mid-May–early Sept., daily 8:30 AM–10 PM.*

Driving from Jasper, you are likely to notice scenery that's different from that to the west. As the Athabasca River widens along the flat flood plain, notice how the trees begin to thin out, a sign that you're moving into the drier climate of the prairie.

Heading West Smaller and less renowned than Banff and Jasper national parks are the less-visited siblings: Kootenay and Yoho national parks. **Kootenay National Park,** named after the Kootenai Indians who settled in the area, is 16 kilometers (10 miles) north of Banff, and is reached by bearing west on Route 93. The highway climbs steeply to
24 **Vermilion Pass,** where Banff and Kootenay parks meet. The atmosphere is eerie here. In 1968, a huge forest fire swept over thousands of acres, leaving only charred spars in its wake. Regeneration has begun, though; amidst the skeletons left by the fire, new growths have reached heights of 2–3 meters (6–10 feet).

Just beyond the Vermilion Pass summit is the trailhead for the Stanley Glacier trail, one of the fine choices for a day hike in the park. The trail climbs easily for 4 kilometers (2½ miles), through fire remnants and new growth, across rock debris and glacial moraine, ending in the giant amphitheater of the Stanley Glacier basin.

From the Stanley Glacier trailhead, Route 93 turns south, and on the right, the high, rocky ridge—the park's most predominant feature—can be seen. Among the popular hiking destina-
25 tions is **Floe Lake,** a 10-kilometer (6-mile) trek from the highway. The area surrounding the lake, a 1,000-meter-high (3,300-foot) dark limestone wall, characterizes the Kootenay terrain.

Along the 65-kilometer (40-mile) stretch from the intersection of Routes 1 and 93 to Radium Hot Springs (*see* Tour 4, below), the only service area is at Vermilion Crossing, the approximate halfway point. South of Vermilion Crossing, the mountains open up gradually, their flanks covered by thick stands of Douglas fir, as the Vermilion River joins with the wider Kootenay River. From there, the highway heads west, winding through the narrow limestone canyon cut by the Sinclair River before reaching the springs.

Farther north, along Route 1, **Yoho National Park** can be reached by continuing west on the highway at its intersection with the Icefields Parkway (Route 93), just north of Lake Louise. The park's name is an onomatopoeia derived from an Indian word that might translate to today's expression "awesome." Indeed, the park is awesome, featuring some of the most outstanding scenery in the Canadian Rockies.

Yoho is divided into two parts—the northern half, which includes Emerald Lake and the Yoho River Valley, and the southern half, for which Lake O'Hara is the physical and spiritual epicenter.

The two main accesses to the northern half are the Takakkaw
26 Falls road and the Emerald Lake Lodge road. The **Takakkaw Falls,** 254 meters (833 feet) high, are spectacular especially in the summer. But the falls are just a taste of what lies ahead for day hikers and backpackers. The Yoho River Valley, leading toward the pyramid-capped Yoho glacier, is bound on one side by the peaks of the President Range and, on the other, by the distant Wapta Icefield.

More enthusiastic hikers can also reach points throughout the
27 Yoho Valley from the vivid green **Emerald Lake** by taking well-marked trails. But those who come to this corner of Yoho can

also take an easy stroll around the lake, rent a canoe, or have a cup of tea at the teahouse by the lodge.

28 **Lake O'Hara,** Yoho's other half, is widely regarded as one of *the* places to go in the Canadian Rockies for outdoor enthusiasts. For summer, Lake O'Hara Lodge (*see* Lodging, below) is booked months in advance. You can take one of several moderately easy hikes from the lodge to high-alpine lakes above the tree line. The area is also popular among climbers. A lodge-run bus makes fast work of the several kilometers of forest-lined fire road between Route 1 and the lake, but it also makes the remote area more accessible to other people, too, therefore limiting your private wilderness experience.

29 Also in Yoho, the **Burgess Shale site,** halfway between the Takakkaw Falls road and the Emerald Lake Lodge road, contains the fossilized remains of 120 marine species dating back 530 million years. Burgess Shale was designated a World Heritage Site in 1981; reservations for guided hikes through fossil sites can be made through the Yoho Parks Information Centre (*Box 99, Field, BC V0A 1G0, tel. 604/343–6324*).

Three kilometers (1.9 miles) west of the border between Alberta and British Columbia, you come to the observation deck for
30 the **Spiral Tunnels,** train tunnels that make figure-eight loops on each side of Route 1. These were the engineering answer to the problem of getting trains up and down the steep grade of the Rockies' western slope. The tunnels wind in circles through the mountainside, allowing trains to climb and descend more gradually, as if on spiral stairs. Many trains use the tunnels, and Via Rail and CPR provide schedules so you can time your arrival to the roadside observation deck off Route 1 for when a train is passing through. Without a train, the tunnels simply look like holes in the mountainside; but when a train goes through, its engine can be seen coming from one tunnel, while its caboose can be seen entering the other, almost directly above the engine.

Tour 3: South of Banff

Numbers in the margin correspond with points of interest on the Canadian Rockies map.

Canmore and Kananaskis Country

Until Calgary was awarded the Olympics in 1988, the area immediately south of Banff—Canmore and Kananaskis Country—was generally the stomping ground of local folks from Calgary and Banff. While Canmore, just outside the park boundary, offered affordable housing for people living in Banff, Kananaskis Country, an hour's drive from Calgary and with fewer restrictions on horseback riding, snowmobiling, and hunting, was a popular weekend locale for folks from the city.

Then came the Olympics. When logistical problems forced planners to look from Banff and Lake Louise to other possible sites for Olympic events, Canmore and Kananaskis Country popped into the limelight. The **Canmore Nordic Centre** (*see* Sports and Outdoor Activities, below), for nordic skiing events, was built. In Kananaskis Country, a half-hour away, the Nakiska ski area on Mt. Allen was created, along with a nearby lodging complex—Kananaskis Village (*see* Lodging, below). Suddenly, Canmore and the 4,000-square-kilometer
31 (1,600-square mile) **Kananaskis Country** were on the interna-

tional travel map. *Box 1979, Canmore, AB T0L 0M0, tel. 403/678–2400. No trail fee; rentals available. Open dawn to dusk, with lights until 9:30.*

In character, post-Olympic Canmore is not radically different from its pre-1988 incarnation. The former coal-mining outpost remains a bedroom community for Banff workers, although now more park visitors also save money by staying in Canmore's less expensive lodgings. The attractive, boutique-lined Main Street and several good restaurants are indications that Canmore is no longer strictly a locals' town; it's become the regional center for the active outdoor life—with streets full of young, robust types who live for climbing, hiking, and mountain-biking in the summer, cross-country and alpine skiing in winter. Several outfitters, climbing schools, and guide services make their base in Canmore.

This does not, however, add up to a town of historic or scenic attractions. You can get a good meal here, or a place to bed down at a reasonable price, and you can zip around the tracks of the nordic center. Generally, Canmore is a place to think of, as local people do, as a base camp for going into the parks or Kananaskis Country.

The main highway through Kananaskis Country is Route 40 (closed in winter about 20 kilometers south, or 12 miles, of Kananaskis Village), also known as the Kananaskis Trail. The highway begins 23 kilometers (14 miles) east of Canmore, off Route 1, and climbs past Kananaskis Village and Nakiska, which appear on the right at about the 20-kilometer (12-mile) point. The Village, on a small plateau between the ski area and the twin 18-hole golf courses, is the only place in Kananaskis Country that offers hotel-style accommodations. Recreational vehicles and campgrounds—of which there are many—are the overnight choices of most visitors to the region.

The highway proceeds through **Peter Lougheed Provincial Park** (essentially a subsection of Kananaskis Country) and over Highwood Pass (2,208 meters, or 7,280 feet), the highest drivable pass in Canada. It then descends to join Route 541, east of Longview. Access to East Kananaskis Country, a popular area for horseback-riding trips, is via Route 66, which heads west from Priddis.

The mountains of Kananaskis Country are surprisingly different in climate from their neighbors in the parks. On the eastern slope of the Rockies, the Kananaskis mountains tend to get less precipitation, which often means snow-poor winters—a cause of controversy and occasional ridicule when Mt. Allen was chosen as the site for the Olympic ski area. Extensive snowmaking was the solution. Closer to the prairie, the Kananaskis mountains are also exposed to more wind, including the famed, warm chinooks, which have been known to sweep through in mid-winter, bearing temperatures exceeding 15°C (60° F).

Kananaskis Country has little of the glacial spectacle of the parks; its scenery is, in some ways, simpler, with thick pine forests and granite mountain peaks. Regularly modulating temperatures cause frequent snow and rock slides. Anyone interested in the power of sliding snow or rock should take a short drive on Route 40 south of Kananaskis Village, to see where the steep mountainsides are raked with one slide path after another.

As a multi-purpose area run by the Alberta provincial government, Kananaskis Country offers some advantages over the parks, but some disadvantages as well. On the plus side, there are more varieties of recreational activities in Kananaskis Country. For example, in the northeastern corner of the park (take Route 68 east from Route 40), a large area has been set aside for motorcycles, all-terrain vehicles, and snowmobiles—all machinery that are anathema in the parks. East Kananaskis Country, where pine forests mix with stands of aspen, has been divvied up for use by licensed horse-pack outfitters. Also, the provincial government has made special efforts to accommodate disabled visitors. **William Watson Lodge,** near the Kananaskis Lakes, is one of the rare lodges designed exclusively for disabled and handicapped people, as well as senior citizens. Access points have been built along Mt. Lorette Ponds north of Kananaskis Village to accommodate wheelchair fishermen, and many hiking trails near the village have been cut wide and gentle enough for wheelchair travel. *William Watson Lodge located 30 km (18 mi) south of Kananaskis Village on Rte. 40; for information write Kananaskis Country, Box 280, Cranmore, AB T0L 0M0, tel. 403/591–7222. Overnight and day-use facilities for seniors and handicapped people open Mon.–Fri. 8:30–4:30; cabin reservations available year-round.*

On the down side, wildlife does not flourish in Kananaskis Country, as it does in the parks, primarily because hunting is permitted in season; animals are much more cautious about human interaction here than they are in protected areas.

Finally, Kananaskis Country is not all free-range land for recreational enthusiasts. Forestry, gas, and ranching operations may restrict backcountry travel in some areas.

Waterton Lakes National Park
32

Geologically, **Waterton Lakes National Park** is the meeting of two worlds—the flatlands of the prairie and the abrupt upthrust of the mountains. Chief Mountain, the squared-off peak on the eastern end of the stand of mountains seen as you drive from the north, juts up from the prairie, dominating the horizon from the north and east. In this juncture of worlds, the park squeezes into a relatively small arena (525 square kilometers, 200 square miles) an unusual mix of wildlife, biota, and climate zones.

Take a drive up **Red Rock Canyon** (turning right before the town in Waterton), the bottom of which is covered with scrub pine and prairie grasses. Turn a few kilometers later, at the center of Waterton, onto the Akima Parkway, leading to **Cameron Lake,** and you'll find a land of high basins and glacially carved cirques, filled in summer with hundreds of varieties of alpine wildflowers, including about 22 varieties of wild orchids.

The common denominator in the park is wind. Although the mountains and canyon walls provide protection in some areas, the wind blows powerfully and regularly from the prairie, often at speeds of more than 50 kilometers (30 miles) an hour. Trees along the lakeside bear the evidence, as they grow at about an 80-degree angle, rather than straight up—in deference to the incessant wind.

Politically, too, Waterton represents a meeting of worlds. Although the park was officially established in 1895, it was joined in 1932 with Glacier National Park in Montana to form Waterton/Glacier International Peace Park—a symbol of friendship and peaceful coexistence between Canada and the United States. In fact, some services in the park, including the Prince of Wales Hotel, are under Glacier Park management in the United States.

Whether it is a pervading spirit of international peace or the long driving distance from Calgary (especially compared with the short Calgary–Banff drive), Waterton is a decidedly low-key place. Hiking, horseback riding, and boating are the main activities. The park is full of numerous short hikes for day-trippers and some longer treks for backpackers. Boats can be rented at the townsite for Upper Waterton Lakes or at Cameron Lake.

One of the most popular things to do is to take a two-hour cruise on Upper Waterton Lake from the townsite, south to **Goat Haunt,** where there are shelters, a ranger station, and a boat dock. From here, several short, easy hikes are possible before you return to Waterton; properly equipped overnighters can also camp out at Goat Haunt. (Because Goat Haunt is in the United States, travelers going to and from must clear customs.) *Shoreline Cruises Co., tel. 403/859–2362. Cruises run mid-May–mid-Sept.; call for schedules.*

Whatever the day's activity, turning in early is the order of things in Waterton. Except for reading and conversation, nightlife is virtually nonexistent. Most of Waterton turns in early for the season, too—from early October until mid-May, the park has all but closed up shop.

Because of Waterton's proximity to the U.S. border, and its bond with Glacier National Park, many visitors to the park come from the south. The common thing to do is to fly into Great Falls, Montana, and drive to Waterton via Routes 89, 17, and 6. Those who choose instead to drive the 264 kilometers (158 miles) from Calgary (via Routes 2, 3, and 6) have an interesting side trip worth considering.

Tour 4: The British Columbia Rockies

Numbers in the margins correspond with points of interest on the Canadian Rockies map.

"British Columbia (B.C.) Rockies" is in part a misnomer, for it is a term often used to designate an area that includes the mountain ranges of the Columbias, which are not a part of the Rocky Mountain chain. Roughly, the British Columbia Rockies encompass the area of southeastern British Columbia, immediately west of the four contiguous parks.

Keeping mountain ranges straight in this part of the world is a tricky business. In simple terms, southeastern British Columbia is defined by two main ranges: the Rockies to the east and the Columbias to the west. They are separated for most of their parallel run by the Columbia River Valley—or "trench," as it is often called. Wide and flat, the valley has an elevation that's surprisingly low, only about 600 meters (2,000 feet) on average.

The mountain range confusion is made even worse by the subdivision of the Columbias: to the north are the Cariboos, west of Jasper and Mt. Robson Parks; reaching south like three long talons from the Cariboos are (west to east) the Monashees, the Selkirks, and the Purcells. Finally, perhaps the best-known mountains of all—the Bugaboos—are only a few dramatic peaks in the Purcells, but are often thought of as encompassing the entire region.

In subtle and overt ways, the world of the British Columbia Rockies region is very different from that of the national parks. Perhaps the most obvious differences are the conspicuous lumber yards, mining pits, farms, and ranches—signs of development throughout the British Columbia Rockies that are not present in the industry-shielded parklands to the east. This physical evidence attests to minimally successful attempts made to mine gold, silver-lead ore, and other metals. The significant difference between the two ranges, however, is age. More than 100 million years older than the Rockies, the Columbias show the signs of their years: The effects of erosion are more in evidence, along with the more dramatic effects of upthrust and glaciation. This is not to suggest that the Columbias lack drama or beauty. The pyramidal peaks of Glacier National Park and the Bugaboo and Howser spires, rising in the Purcells like slender granite fingers from glacial beds, are sights as striking as anything in the four contiguous parks.

As the first ranges to capture storms moving from the west across the plains of interior British Columbia, the Columbias get much more rain and snow than do the Rockies. Annual precipitation in many areas exceeds 60 inches, and in the Monashees, the most westerly of subranges, annual snowfalls have exceeded 800 inches.

Such precipitation has helped to create the large, deep glaciers that add to the high-alpine beauty of the Columbias. Lower down, a rain-forest climate has contributed to a lush life of ferns, grasses, flowers, and shrubbery not found in the Rockies to the east. In winter, the deep snows have made the Columbias—particularly the Monashees—a must port-of-call for aficionados of deep-powder and helicopter skiing.

Of course, such extreme conditions can be hazardous, too. 33 **Rogers Pass,** the center of **Glacier National Park,** is a case in point. In the early 1900s avalanches claimed hundreds of lives of railway-construction workers, and continued to be a threat during highway construction in the 1950s.

Today, the Rogers Pass war against avalanches is both active and passive. Heavy artillery—105-mm howitzer guns—is used to shoot down snow buildups before they can become so severe as to threaten a major avalanche. (If traveling in the backcountry, be cautious of unexploded howitzer shells that pose a potential hazard.) That's the active battle; passive means of defense include train tunnels and long snow sheds along the highway that shield travelers from major slide paths.

The park's history is well documented at the **Rogers Pass Centre**—worth a visit whether you're staying in Glacier or just passing through. Open year-round, the center displays geology and wildlife and offers 30-minute movies on subjects ranging from avalanches to bears. *Tel. 604/837-6274, ext. 41. Admission free. Open daily 7 AM–9 PM.*

Not all of the British Columbia Rockies region is inundated by rain and snow. Storms tend to exhaust themselves in the

Columbias—the reason the Columbia River trench stays relatively dry. The annual precipitation in Golden is only about 500 millimeters (25 inches), less than half of what it is in Revelstoke, 148 kilometers (80 miles) west at the foot of the Monashees and the western extreme of the region discussed in this section.

For the most part, the towns of the Columbia River trench are
34 not beautiful, nor do they aspire to be. For example, **Golden**—a town best described as a service center—is the epitome of this plain-Jane character. Primarily a stopping-off point for anyone journeying elsewhere, Golden is a base for several river runners, outfitters, and guide services.

The 105 kilometers (63 miles) south from Golden to Radium Hot Springs, where Route 93 joins Route 95, across the rolling flood plain of the Columbia River, are relatively uneventful. To the right are the river and the Purcell Mountains; more immediately to the left are the Rockies, although the major peaks are hidden by the abrupt frontal ranges. Climbers and hikers should look for unpaved roads out of the towns of Spillimacheen and
35 Brisco that lead to the **Bugaboo Recreation Area.**

But for the tourist, the 90-kilometer (56-mile) stretch of Routes
36 93–95 from **Radium Hot Springs** to Kimberley is the main pod. The hot springs, 2 kilometers (1¼ miles) northeast of the Routes 93 and 95 junction on Route 93, are the town's longest-standing attraction, and the summer lifeblood for the numerous motels in the area. There is a large outdoor pool tucked beneath the walls of Sinclair Canyon. Lockers, towels, and suits are available to rent. *Jct. Rtes. 93 and 95, tel. 604/347-9615. Admission: $2 adults, $1.25 children 16 and under. Schedules vary with season; call ahead.*

However, sitting in the hot springs or hiking the short trails of Sinclair Canyon aren't the only things to do in this part of the world. Windermere and Columbia lakes—actually extra-wide stretches of the Columbia River—are popular among boatspeople and boardsailers. Golf is becoming a growing attraction, with several fine courses between Radium Hot Springs and
37 **Fairmont Hot Springs.** And a right turn at the Invermere intersection leads to **Panorama** (*see* Lodging, below), the year-round resort known best for skiing in winter, and to the **Purcell Wilderness,** a large area devoted to backcountry hiking, camping, and fishing.

After traveling south for about 60 kilometers (36 miles), the road splits; Route 93/95 continue southeast to Fort Steele, while Route 95A leads to Kimberley. The two routes rejoin again north of Cranbrook.

Fort Steele and Kimberley are historically significant because they are the home to many German and Swiss immigrants who arrived a century ago to work as miners and loggers. Southeastern British Columbia was not unlike the Tyrol region they had left, so it was easy to settle here. Later, a demand for experienced alpinists to guide and teach hikers, climbers, and skiers brought more settlers from the alpine countries, and Tyrolian influence is evident throughout southeastern British Columbia. Chalet-style buildings here are as common here as log cabin–style structures are in the national parks. Schnitzels and fondues appear on menus as often as burgers and fries.

38 **Fort Steele Heritage Park,** a reconstructed 19th-century mining outpost, is a step back to those silver-lead mining days. Its theater, millinery, barbershop, and dry-goods store breathe authenticity, helping to preserve the 1890s lifestyle. Plan a half-day or more; there is enough here to hold the interest of adults as well as children. *Ft. Steele, 16 km (10 mi) northeast of Cranbrook on Rte. 93/95, tel. 604/426–6923. Admission for 2 consecutive days: $5 adults, $3 children 13–18 and senior citizens, $11 children 6–12, children under 6 free, $10 family. Open year-round; Old West shows performed in the summer months.*

39 **Kimberley,** a cross between a quaint and a kitschy town, is rich with Tyrolian character. The Platzl ("small plaza," in German), a walking mall of shops and restaurants styled after a Bavarian village, is crowned by what is reputed to be the world's largest cuckoo clock. In the summer Kimberley plays its Bavarian theme to the hilt: Merchants dress up in lederhosen and dirndls, and promotional gimmicks abound.

Beyond Kimberley or Fort Steele, **Cranbrook** (28 kilometers, or 18 miles), primarily a service center, offers moderately priced gas, lodging, and food.

Returning to Golden, Route 1 continues west through Glacier and Mt. Revelstoke national parks. When the weather is clear, many of the glaciers can be seen from the highway. However, to fully appreciate Glacier, one must take to the trail. From the Illecillewaet Campground, a few kilometers west of the Rogers Pass Centre (off Route 1), several trails lead to good viewpoints and glacier tongues, offering good day-hiking opportunities. One of the best, although fairly strenuous, is the Asulkan Valley trail. In a 13-kilometer (8-mile) round loop, it crosses brooks and moraine, passes waterfalls, and yields views of the Asulkan Glacier and three massifs, called the Ramparts, the Dome, and Mt. Jupiter. A much easier hike is the 1.6-kilometer (1-mile) Loop Brook trail (6 kilometers, or 3½ miles, west of the Rogers Pass Centre), with views of the glaciers of Mt. Bonney.

Conceived primarily as a day-use park, the just 260-square ki-
40 lometer (100-square mile) **Mt. Revelstoke National Park** is another option. The park's principal attraction is the 26-kilometer (15½-mile) Summit Road to the top of the mountain, at 1,938 meters (6,395 feet) high. The gravel road begins from Route 1, two kilometers (1¼ miles) before the turnoff to the town of Revelstoke, and its last few kilometers may be closed off by melting snows until well into July. There are several easy hikes to follow from the summit parking lot, taking you past small lakes, views of the Selkirk and Monashee ranges, and mountain meadows full of wildflowers.

Shortly after the Summit Road turnoff is the junction with Route 23, which leads north to Mica Dam. Four kilometers (2½ miles) along this road is **Revelstoke Dam,** a large hydroelectric- and flood-control project. Lake Revelstoke, a reservoir created by the dam on the Columbia River, is a popular boating area in summer, primarily along its southern reaches. *Visitor Centre, tel. 604/837–6211. Self-guided tours free. Open March 14–July 14 and mid-Sept.–mid-Oct., daily 10–6; June 15–mid-Sept., daily 10–8.*

From Revelstoke Dam, Route 23 continues another 145 kilometers (90 miles) north to Mica Dam, the juncture of Revelstoke and Kinbasket lakes. Those who venture along this route are entering wild country—a world of wilderness canoeing, big fish, abandoned mining camps, and bears.

41 The town of **Revelstoke,** a skiers' headquarters in winter, is worth a brief side trip. In 1986, the town began to restore its downtown district, creating an attractive, authentic turn-of-the-century renovation that today houses modern shops, restaurants, and businesses.

What to See and Do with Children

Fort Steele Heritage Park (*see* Tour 4, above).

Luxton Museum (*see* Tour 1, above).

For those interested in natural phenomena, the **Rogers Pass Centre** (Glacier National Park, tel. 604/837–6274) offers exhibits and audiovisual presentations on glacial dynamics, avalanches, regional biota and wildlife, as well as exhibits on the construction of the trans-Canadian rail route.

Another museum well worth a visit is the **Frank Slide Interpretive Centre** (*see* off the Beaten Track, below).

The **Railway Museum** (1 Van Horne St. N, Canmore, tel. 604/489–3918), housed in restored Canadian Pacific Railway cars, presents a good picture of rail travel in the 1920s.

If you're visiting the Invermere area June through August, one of the best museums is the **Windermere Valley Pioneer Museum** (622 3rd St., tel. 604/342–9769), depicting the life of 19th-century pioneers.

Off the Beaten Track

A possible detour on the Calgary–Waterton trip is to continue for 60 kilometers (36 miles) on Route 3, past the turnoff for Route 6 to Waterton, until you reach **Crowsnest Pass.** In the early 1900s, Crowsnest Pass developed as a coal-mining community and was touted as "the Pittsburgh of Canada." From the outset, however, the coal-mining industry in Crowsnest Pass was ill-fated. In April of 1903, some 90 million tons of rock, from Turtle Mountain buried the town of Frank, killing 70 people. Then, in 1914, a massive mine explosion killed 189 people, and, a few years later, with the uncertainties of an impending war, the coal-mining industry all but collapsed. The story of the slide, and the history of coal-mining in the region, is well-recorded at the **Frank Slide Interpretive Center** (Crowsnest Pass, tel. 403/562–7388).

Head-Smashed-In Buffalo Jump is located 18 kilometers (11 miles) northwest of Ft. Macleod on Route 785 (off Route 2). It is considered one of the best-preserved examples of a site where Plains Indians herded buffalo to their death over a low cliff, and later harvested the meat and fur from the carcasses. As an archaeological site, it is not especially inspiring; it is, simply, a ledge in the middle of the rolling prairie. However, the museum at the site provides not only a fascinating explanation of the buffalo jump tradition, but also insight into the life and customs of the Plains Indians, particularly the Blackfoot. Guided walks and audio-video exhibits are presented. *Tel. 403/553–2731. Ad-*

mission free; donations accepted. Open summer, daily 9–8; Labor Day–May 15, daily 9–5.

Fernie, however, located on Route 3 between Cranbrook and Crowsnest, has a relatively undiscovered ski area that's worth a visit. *Box 788, Fernie, BC V0B 1M0, tel. 604/423–4655. Accommodations at ski area.*

Shopping

When shopping in the Canadian Rockies, you'll find the best selection in Banff, although Canmore may provide you with better bargains. The **Banff Springs Hotel,** and shops on **Banff Avenue,** have the usual souvenirs, as well as native crafts, sporting gear, landscape paintings, woolens, and outdoor wear.

Native Crafts One of the most authentic places to shop for authentic articles is the **Banff Indian Trading Post** (Birch and Cave Aves., tel. 403/762–2456). Also, the **Lake Louise Trading Company** (Lake Louise Rd., tel. 403/522–2333) sells eclectic native items, from baked goods to twig furniture.

Local Crafts On weekend afternoons, the **Guild Artists and Artisans Gallery,** in the **Canmore Library Building** (tel. 403/678–4255), gives visitors an opportunity to buy directly from the artists.

Several galleries in Banff, Canmore, and Jasper offer arts and crafts, including handmade jewelry and watercolor paintings. Among those in Banff (with the widest selection) worth checking out are the **Canadian House Gallery** (Caribou and Bean Sts., tel. 403/762–3757) and the **Banff Indian Trading Post** (Birch and Cave Aves., tel. 403/762–2456).

Sporting Goods For sporting gear, **Mountain Magic** (224 Bear St., Banff, tel. 403/762–2591) has four floors of hiking, climbing, skiing, running, and biking equipment, and a 30-foot indoor climbing wall for gear testing. Outdoor wear can be found in a number of stores in Banff.

Sports and Outdoor Activities

Biking Around Banff, the **Vermilion Lakes loop** and the strenuous **loop over Tunnel Mountain** are popular half-day bike tours. For a longer ride, **Route 1A** between Banff and Lake Louise is a good choice. Those seeking a good workout can test lungs and legs on the steep switchbacks leading up to **Mt. Norquay** ski area.

Mountain biking has become increasingly popular in the last four years. Although mountain bikes provide good access to the backcountry, they are restricted on many trails and in many areas. Check with the nearest park warden or bike store before heading off-road.

Bikes can be rented from **Spoke N' Edge** (315 Banff Ave., tel. 403/762–2854) or **Park and Pedal Bike Shop** (229 Wolf St., tel. 403/762–3191) in Banff. Bikes can also be rented from **Freewheel Cycle** (off Miete St., between Patricia and Giekie Sts., tel. 403/852–5380) in Jasper; in Revelstoke try **Revelstoke Cycle Shop** (118 MacKenzie Ave., tel. 604/837–2648) in Revelstoke.

Guided bike tours, on-road and off-road, are also offered by several operators (*see* Guided Tours in Essential Information, above).

Camping There are more than 40 public campgrounds within the national parks, not including backcountry sites for backpackers and climbers. Most operate on a first-come, first-served basis, though a few require reservations. The season generally runs from mid-May to October, although a few campgrounds are open year-round. Campground information is available from **Parks Canada** (Information Services, Box 2989, Station M, Calgary, AB T2P 3H8, tel. 403/859–2203) and from **Kananaskis Country** (Suite 412, 1011, Glenmore Trail SW, Calgary, AB T2V 4R6, tel. 403/297–3362).

Numerous privately run campgrounds, for which reservations usually can be made, offer sites outside park boundaries. Contact **Tourism B.C.** for its "Super Camping" publication, which lists more than 25 campgrounds in the Canadian Rockies region, or contact Parks Canada or Travel Alberta (*see* Important Addresses and Numbers in Essential Information, above).

Climbing Except for Waterton Lakes, where the rock is generally crumbly, the Canadian Rockies is one of the world's great climbing regions. Among the ascents considered to be classics are **Mt. Assiniboine,** the oft-dubbed "Matterhorn of the Rockies"; glacier-cloaked **Mt. Athabasca,** near Sunwapta Pass; and **Mt. Sir Donald,** in Glacier National Park. Outside the parks, a series of rock spires, known collectively as the **Bugaboos,** rises like rocket cones from glacial beds and are known among rock climbers the world over.

Climbing permits are required for activities within the parks and can be obtained at park warden offices. Except for very experienced mountaineers, guide and instruction services are essential for climbers in the Canadian Rockies.

The **Canadian School of Mountaineering** (629 10th St., Box 723, Canmore, AB T0L 0M0, tel. 403/678–4134) or **Banff Alpine Guides** (Box 1025, Banff, AB T0L 0C0, tel. 403/762–2791), catering to all ability levels, lead trips throughout the parks. Both organizations also conduct ski mountaineering tours in winter. Climbing gear can be rented at outdoor stores in Banff.

Climbers or backpackers interested in extended stays of more than three or four days might consider membership in the **Alpine Club of Canada** (Box 1026, Banff, AB T0L 0C0, tel. 403, 762–4481). The club maintains several mountain huts in the parks and leads hikes and climbs of varying difficulty.

Fishing The principal game fish in the Canadian Rockies is trout–cutthroat and rainbow being the most common varieties. The best fishing tends to be in streams, rivers, and lakes in the valleys, rather than in waters from glacial sources. The **Bow River** and the **lakes of British Columbia** are considered to have some of the best fishing in the region.

Fishing licenses are required and can be purchased at information centers and sports shops throughout the region. A seven-day license is $5; a yearly license, $10. For more information, contact the **Ministry of Environment & Parks** (Fish & Wildlife Branch, Parliament Bldgs., Victoria, BC V8V 1X5, tel. 604/387–4573). Separate licenses for fishing outside the parks are required and can be purchased at sporting goods stores, tackle shops, and marinas. A British Columbia license is good only in British Columbia; an Alberta license is good only in Alberta.

Travel Alberta and Tourism British Columbia (*see* Important Addresses and Numbers in Essential Information, above) can provide lists of outfitters and guides who offer half-day to week-long fly-in adventure services.

Golf The golf season is short, running from about mid-May through mid-October. Given the abundance of water in the region, golf courses are generally in excellent playing condition, with lush grasses and well-kept greens. If hole lengths seem long, keep in mind that at the elevation of Canadian Rockies courses (above 1,200 meters, or 4,000 feet), a golf ball tends to travel 10% farther than at sea level.

Canadian Rockies courses, situated on the relatively flat valley floors, are not difficult to walk for those so inclined; the mountains simply provide dramatic backdrops. However, all courses listed below offer full pro-shop services, including cart rentals. Most courses enforce a standard dress code, requiring shirts with collars and Bermuda-length shorts or long pants.

Greens fees range from $20 to $40 for 18 holes. Cart rentals range from $15 to $27.

Within the parks, the **Banff Springs Hotel** (tel. 403/762–2211, ext. 162) and the **Jasper Park Lodge** (tel. 403/852–3301) each has an 18-hole course. **Kananaskis Village** (tel. 403/591–7070) has two 18-hole courses.

The area between Golden and Kimberley in British Columbia is growing as a golfing hotbed. With two new courses built in the last three years, golfers in the region have more than a half-dozen 18-hole layouts and several 9-hole courses to choose from. Arrangements for golfing can be made through **Fairmont Hot Springs Resort** (tel. 604/345–6311 or 800/663–4979), with two courses on site; **Radium Hot Springs Resort** (tel. 604/347–9311), with one course on site; or **Panorama** (tel. 604/342–6941), which offers multicourse, multiday golf packages.

Hiking The four contiguous parks (Banff, Jasper, Kootenay, and Yoho) have 2,900 kilometers (1,750 miles) of hiking trails. In Waterton Lakes there are 183 kilometers (114 miles) of trails, with further access to more than 1,200 kilometers (750 miles) of trails in adjacent Glacier National Park in the United States. Kananaskis Country offers numerous hiking and backpacking opportunities (although water can be in short supply, especially in late summer and fall), while Revelstoke and Glacier parks in British Columbia are generally best for shorter day hikes.

The hiking season runs from mid-May to early November, depending on the latitude and elevation of the trail. Trails along the Icefields Parkway, where elevations are generally highest, tend to be passable only between June and September. The hiking season in Waterton Lakes Park, far to the south, tends to be longest. Though most trails are restricted to foot traffic, horses and mountain bikes are permitted in some areas. Check with the park warden for selected trails.

Backpackers are required to register with the nearest park warden for permits. There is generally no fee for the use of backcountry camp sites, although there is a fee for reservations, which can be made by contacting the park superintendent up to three weeks in advance. The park warden's office can also supply trail and topographical maps and information on current trail status.

The differences in hiking terrain among the four contiguous parks are not easily characterized. Anyone interested in hiking or backpacking should obtain one of several good books that describe various routes and route combinations. One of the best, *The Canada Rockies: Trail Guide*, by Brian Patton and Bart Robinson (Summerthought Ltd., $14.95), is available in most bookstores in Banff, Lake Louise, and Jasper.

Banff The trails of Banff tend to get the most traffic, especially in summer. Although there are several trails within and leading from Banff townsite, more interesting hikes tend to be north of town. The most popular day-hiking areas, being both accessible and scenic, are around **Lake Louise** and **Moraine Lake.**

Jasper **Jasper,** with the most extensive trail network (nearly 1,000 kilometers, or 600 miles), is popular for hikers seeking to get deep into the wilderness for several days at a time. **Tonquin Valley,** near Mt. Edith Cavell, is considered one of Canada's classic backpacking routes. Its high mountain lakes, bounded by a series of steep, rocky peaks known as the Ramparts, receive many visitors in the height of summer. Good day-hiking areas in Jasper are around **Maligne Lake** and **Mt. Edith Cavell.**

Kootenay The trail that best characterizes the hiking in Kootenay is the strenuous **Rockwall trail,** which runs along the series of steep rock facades that are the predominant feature of the park. **Floe Lake,** sitting at the base of a sheer, 1,000-meter (3,300-foot) wall is a trail highlight. Several long day-hike spurs connect the trail with Route 93.

Yoho Yoho is divided into two parts: the popular hiking arena around **Lake O'Hara,** dotted with high-alpine lakes, and the less-traveled **Yoho River valley,** terminating at the Yoho Glacier. Access to the Lake O'Hara region is somewhat restricted by the long, rather uneventful fire road from Route 1. Most hikers and climbers take the Lake O'Hara Lodge shuttle bus (*see* Lodging, below). Entry into the Yoho River valley is more immediate, either from Takakkaw Falls or from Emerald Lake.

Heli-Hiking Another way to experience high-Alpine hiking is by heli-hiking, a summer offspring of heli-skiing. Most of the climbing is done by helicopter; the hiking itself tends to be flat or even downslope. **Canadian Mountain Holidays** (CMH, Box 1660, Banff, AB T0L 0C0, tel. 403/762–4531), in conjunction with **Tauck Tours** (11 Wilton Rd., Westport, CT 06881, tel. 203/226–6911) offers heli-hiking tours for three to nine days, using CMH's relatively luxurious remote lodges in the Cariboo and Purcell ranges. **Golden Mountain Holidays** (Box 1932, Golden, BC V0A 1H0, tel. 604/348–2361) provides helicopter access to a series of three small chalets in the Esplanade Range, north of Golden. Both guided, catered tours and self-guided, noncatered tours are available.

Horseback Riding One of the most popular ways to experience the Canadian Rockies is on horseback. Horses are restricted from many trails within the national parks, but there are still some opportunities; among the most popular areas for pack trips within the parks is Tonquin Valley in Jasper. Restrictions are far fewer in Kananaskis Country, the provincial parks, and the British Columbia Rockies region.

Arrangements for hourly or daily rides, as well as riding instruction, can be made through the sports desks at the **Banff Springs Hotel, Chateau Lake Louise, Emerald Lake Lodge,** and **Jasper Park Lodge** (*see* Lodging, below). Other stables in the region include **Alpine Stables** (Box 53, Waterton Park, AB T0K 2M0, tel. 403/859–2462), **Boundary Stables** (Box 44, Kananaskis Village, AB T0L 2H0, tel. 403/591–7171), and **Brewster Stables** (Box 964, Banff, AB T0L 0C0, tel. 403/762–3872).

Multi-day pack trips are offered by dozens of guest ranches and outfitters throughout the region. Outfitters are licensed to operate within specific areas, so your choice of outfitter may be determined by the area you would like to ride in. Typically, trips include three meals a day and nightly accommodations in trailside tents. Riding experience isn't necessary, but it is recommended for longer trips. Trips may last from three to 10 days, with groups ranging in size from 6 to 10 people. Daily costs range between $80 and $120 a day. A few operators offer hunting, fishing, and hiking options. The pack season runs approximately from June through September.

Travel Alberta and Tourism B.C. can provide listings of guest ranches and outfitters in the region. In British Columbia, further information is also available from the **Guide-Outfitters Association** (Box 769, 100 Mile House, BC V0K 2E0, tel. 604/395–2438).

Rafting Rafting opportunities range from gentle floats along the Bow River near Banff to rollicking white-water rides on the Kicking Horse River near Golden. Most trips are half-day or full-day. For those seeking white water at its frothiest, June is the best month, when rivers are still swollen with the snow melt but not dangerously so.

Mirage Adventure Tours (Box 2338, Canmore, AB T0L 0M0, tel. 403/678–4919) specializes in trips on the Kananaskis River. In the Banff area, **Rocky Mountain Raft Tours** (Box 1771, Banff, AB T0L 0C0, tel. 403/762–3632) features trips on the Bow River and others. In the Jasper area, **Jasper Raft Tours** (Box 398, Jasper, AB T0E 1E0, tel. 403/852–3613) offers half-day float trips on the Athabasca. **Maligne River Adventures** (626 Connaught Dr., Jasper, AB T0E 1E0, tel. 403/852–3370) offers half-day white-water trips on the Maligne.

Alpine Rafting Company (Box 1409, Golden, BC V0A 1H0, tel. 604/344–5016) offers a variety of trips on the Kicking Horse and the Illecillewaet, between Glacier National Park and Revelstoke.

Skiing Winter remains an active time in the Canadian Rockies. There are 11 lift-serviced ski areas in the region, five of which are within an hour's drive of Banff. Cross-country opportunities are also plentiful, and many backcountry lodges are winterized and offer guide services for backcountry touring. Numerous tour operators—based both in the region and elsewhere—feature ski packages; Travel Alberta or Tourism B.C. can assist you in choosing a tour that best suits your interests, abilities, and budget.

Cross-Country **The Canmore Nordic Centre** (Box 1979, Canmore, AB T0L 0M0, tel. 403/678–2400) was the site of the 1988 Olympic nordic events. With 56 kilometers (36 miles) of groomed trails, the center features the most extensive groomed cross-country network in the region. Other groomed trails (and rental equipment) can be found near the **Banff Springs Hotel, Chateau Lake Louise, Jasper Park Lodge, Fairmont Hot Springs Resort,** and **Emerald Lake Lodge** (*see* Lodging, below).

Lake O'Hara Lodge, Mt. Assiniboine Lodge, and **Skoki Lodge** (*see* Lodging, below) are among several lodges that offer guided backcountry ski touring. The **Canadian School of Mountaineering** (Box 723, Canmore, AB T0L 0M0, tel. 403/ 678–4134) and **Banff Alpine Guides** (Box 1025, Banff, AB T0L 0C0, tel. 403/ 762–2791) also lead backcountry ski tours.

Downhill The three ski areas in the immediate Banff vicinity are **Lake Louise** (Box 5, Lake Louise, AB T0L 1E0, tel. 403/522–3555), **Mt. Norquay** (Box 1258, Banff, AB T0L 0C0, tel. 403/762–4421), and **Sunshine Village** (Box 1510, Banff, AB T0L 0C0, tel. 403/ 762–6500 or 800/661–1363). Lake Louise's terrain is large and varied; Mt. Norquay's is generally short and steep; Sunshine Village's terrain is mostly intermediate and above tree line.

Nakiska (Box 1988, Kananaskis Village, AB T0L 0M0, tel. 403/ 591–7777), about 45 minutes southeast of Banff, was the sight of the 1988 Olympic alpine events, and features wide-trail intermediate skiing. **Marmot Basin** (Box 1300, Jasper, AB T0E 1E0, tel. 403/852–3816), near Jasper, has a wide mix of terrain.

In the British Columbia Rockies, **Panorama** (Box 7000, Invermere, BC V0A 1K0, tel. 604/342–6941 or 800/663–2929) has the largest lift-serviced vertical rise (1,156 meters, or 3,800 feet) of any ski area in the region. **Fernie Snow Valley** (Box 788, Fernie, BC V0A 1M0, tel. 604/423–4655) and **Kimberley Ski Resort** (Box 40, Kimberley, BC V1A 2Y5, tel. 604/427–4881) have vertical rises of more than 2,000 feet. Sunshine Village, Nakiska, Panorama, Fernie Snow Valley, and Kimberley have on-mountain lodging and resort facilities.

Heli-skiing Heli-skiing has become increasingly popular in the region, and tours can be arranged through several operators on a daily or weekly basis. Daily tours start above $200 per person, and weekly packages (including meals and lodging) begin at about $2,500.

The original, and by far the largest, heli-skiing operator in the region is **Canadian Mountain Holidays** (*see* Heli-hiking, above). Reservations for CMH's services should be made several months in advance. Other weekly operators include **Mike Wiegele Helicopter Skiing** (Box 249, Banff, AB T0L 0C0, tel. 403/762–5548 or 800/661–9170), which operates out of Blue River in British Columbia, and **Selkirk Tangiers Heli-Skiing** (Box 1409, Golden, BC V0A 1H0, tel. 604/344–5016). Selkirk Tangiers also offers daily tours, as does **R.K. Heli-Ski** (Box 695, Invermere, BC V0A 1K0, tel. 604/342–6494), which operates out of the Panorama ski area.

Water Sports With an abundance of lakes and rivers in the region, watersport opportunities abound. However, the glacier-fed waters of the Canadian Rockies tend to be cold, even in midsummer. Whether you're waterskiing, board sailing, boating, or swimming, know the conditions and wear proper gear.

Boat and canoe rentals are available at **Lake Louise** and **Moraine Lake** in Banff National Park, at **Emerald Lake** and **Lake**

O'Hara in Yoho, and at **Pyramid Lake** in Jasper. However, the main centers of boating activity within the four contiguous parks are Lake Minnewanka in Banff and Maligne Lake in Jasper. In Banff, **Minnewanka Boat Tours** (Box 2189, Banff, AB T0L 0C0, tel. 403/762–3473) offers boat and canoe rentals; **Monod Sports** (111 Banff Ave., tel. 403/762–4571) offers sailboard rental and instruction. Boat rentals on Maligne Lake are available at the boat house by the **Maligne Lake Chalet** and through **Maligne Lake Scenic Cruises** (626 Connaught Dr., Jasper, AB T0E 1E0, tel. 403/852–3370).

Spray Lakes reservoir and Kananaskis Lakes are the main sites of boating activity in Kananaskis Country, and boat rentals are available through **Peregrin Sports** (Kananaskis Village, T0L 2H0, tel. 403/591–7555). Lake Invermere, in British Columbia, is popular among sailors, board sailors, and waterskiers, and is warm enough for swimming in the midsummer months. For information and equipment rentals, contact the **Invermere Information Centre** (Box 2605, Invermere on the Lake, BC V0A 1K0, tel. 604/342–6316). To the north, the long, dam-controlled Kinbasket and Revelstoke lakes give boaters, canoeists, and fishermen more of a wilderness experience. There are several boat ramps on the lakes but few services.

For sailors and board sailers who like strong winds, Waterton Lakes, with winds from the Alberta prairies often exceeding 50 kilometers (30 miles) per hour, is the place to be. The **Athabasca, Bow, Kicking Horse,** and **Maligne rivers** provide various levels of river-running challenges for canoeists and kayakers—from still water to white water (*see* Rafting, above).

Dining

Dining in the Canadian Rockies is, for the most part, a casual affair. Given the general mix of travelers to the region—families and active outdoorspeople—emphasis is on good food served in large quantities, at moderate prices. This is not the place for the traveler who expects haute service and cuisine; there are only a handful of top-caliber restaurants in the region. However, people who like fresh game and fish will not be disappointed. Trout, venison, elk, moose, quail, and other game are items that even modest dining establishments feature on their menus.

Highly recommended restaurants are indicated by a star ★.

Category	**Cost***
Very Expensive	over $20
Expensive	$16–$20
Moderate	$10–$15
Inexpensive	under $10

* *per person, excluding drinks, service, and sales tax*

Banff

★ **Le Beaujolais.** Elegantly decorated in a neoclassical style, this restaurant is strikingly out of place in casual Banff. The color scheme is a rich velvety red, and horse-scene oil paintings adorn the walls. The most successful menu items are traditional

French specialties: chateaubriand and trout fillets with fresh herbs. The wine cellar is lavishly and imaginatively stocked. *212 Buffalo St. at Banff Ave., tel. 403/762–2712. Reservations required. Jacket and tie required. AE, MC, V. Closed lunch. Very Expensive.*

Banff Springs Hotel. This hotel (*see* Lodging, below) houses 10 restaurants of varying formality and cuisine. In addition to a couple of coffee houses, and a German *stube* (parlor or chamber), there's also a grand dining room and a pasta restaurant. The best food, however, may be from the Samurai, a Japanese restaurant whose standards must be supreme to satisfy the hotel's large Japanese clientele. The Grapes Wine Bar, which serves a light-fare menu, including salads and cheeses, is tucked away in a small, quiet room on the mezzanine level. Big windows make for nice views here. The Alhambra, open in summer only, specializes in Spanish-style cuisine and flambé in a grottolike setting. In the Rob Roy Supper Club, waiters negotiate flambé carts around guests who come here to dance to live music. A hotel highlight in summer is the barbecue on the Red Terrace. The flavor of the traditional barbecue fare—steaks, corn on the cob, roast potatoes—seems greatly enhanced by the view of Rundle Mountain, the Bow River, and the hotel golf course. *Spray Ave., tel. 403/762–2211. Dining hours, dress codes, and reservation policies vary among restaurants. Dinner reservations in summer required at most restaurants. AE, DC, MC, V. Moderate–Very Expensive.*

Caboose. Situated in the railway depot, the Caboose is reminiscent of the bygone train era. Old train-engine, rail-car, and train-depot paraphernalia fill the dining room, while dim lighting adds to the spirit of nostalgia. The Continental dishes, served with salad, are good but basic: simply prepared prime rib, crab legs, beef, and salmon steaks. *Elk and Lynx Sts., tel. 403/762–3622. Reservations advised. Dress: neat but casual. AE, MC, V. Closed lunch. Expensive.*

Buffalo Mountain Lodge. An exposed, rough-hewn post-and-beam interior gives the dining room a comfortable likeness to a converted barn. This is a woodcraftsman's showcase, highlighted by the large polished wine cabinet that divides the dining and bar areas. The menu comprises fish, meat, and game dishes with sweet-tasting nouvelle sauces. The highlight is the imaginatively mixed shrimp-and-papaya salad. Buffalo Mountain is open for breakfast. *Tunnel Mountain Rd., tel. 403/762–2400. Reservations advised. Dress: neat but casual. AE, MC, V. Moderate–Expensive.*

★ **Giorgio's.** This is two restaurants in one: **La Pasta,** a casual spot, is located downstairs; **La Casa,** the more formal dining room, is upstairs. La Casa serves classic Italian fare with a romantic, dinner-under-the-eaves atmosphere. La Pasta, appealing to the local crowd, serves pizzas and pasta dishes in the dimly lit tavernlike room. *219 Banff Ave., tel. 403/762–5116 (La Casa); 403/762–5114 (La Pasta). Reservations advised for La Casa. Dress for La Casa: neat but casual; La Pasta, casual. No credit cards. Moderate (La Pasta)–Expensive (La Casa).*

Balkan Restaurant. The bright blue-and-white decor, with tile trim, cane-back chairs, and plants, evokes the Mediterranean. The menu offers classic Greek dishes, such as moussaka and souvlakia, as well as creative ethnic mixes, such as Greek chow mein (rice and veggies with feta cheese). Lunchtime can be crowded. *120 Banff Ave., tel. 403/762–3454. Reservations accepted. Dress: casual. AE, DC, MC, V. Moderate.*

Melissa's Missteak. Behindan ersatz German-beerhaus facade is an ersatz log-cabin interior. Upstairs, the lounge is true roadside-America, with popcorn, video games, and TV monitors. The restaurant serves decent food at fair prices, three meals daily, and the video games serve as a great diversion for children. Steaks are the predominant dinner-menu item, although deep-dish pizza is a house specialty. *218 Lynx St., tel. 403/762–5511. Reservations advised. Dress: casual. AE, MC. Moderate.*

★ **The Yard.** This busy, casual place is a favorite lunch spot, often attested to by the 15- to 20-minute wait for a table. In the summer, the outdoor patio, with parasol-topped picnic tables, is the preferred place, as opposed to the bright interior that's more like a spruced-up fast-food restaurant than a hot spot. Mexican food—tacos, burritos, huevos rancheros—and burgers are lunch fare. Such Cajun dishes as Louisiana shrimp show up on the dinner menu. *206 Wolf St., tel. 403/762–5678. No reservations. Dress: casual. AE, MC, V. Inexpensive–Moderate.*

★ **Joe Btfsplk's Diner.** It's either fun, camp, or overbearing, depending on your tastes. This restaurant is a re-created 50s-style diner, with red vinyl banquettes, chrome-trimmed tables, and waitresses dressed in vintage-50s attire. The menu is taken straight from a true-Americana cookbook: meat loaf and hash for lunch or dinner, eggs and biscuits for breakfast. Fresh-baked cookies and muffins, available for take-out, are the culinary highlight. *221 Banff Ave., tel. 403/762–5529. No reservations. Dress: casual. AE, MC, V. Inexpensive.*

Canmore

★ **Pepper Mill.** The small dining room is simply adorned with off-white walls, brown tablecloths, and cloth-covered hanging lamps. Reputed for its pepper steak, the restaurant offers well-prepared pasta dishes, as well. In summer, meals are also served on a deck in front, alongside a quiet Canmore side street. *726 9th St., tel. 403/678–2292. Reservations advised. Dress: neat but casual. MC, V. Closed lunch. Moderate–Expensive.*

Faro's. Colorful drawings of Canmore hung against white walls and blond-wood tabletops lend to a bright, casual environment. The menu offers pizzas and steaks, but Greek dishes, such as souvlaki and moussaka, are the house specialties. *8th St. and 8th Ave., tel. 403/678–2234. Reservations accepted before 5:30. Dress: casual. AE, MC, V. Moderate.*

★ **Martha's Cafe.** You get fresh-baked breads and good home cooking from this small, white-clapboard house on a Canmore back street. The big windows give a bright, airy atmosphere, and deck chairs and wood tables make dining here decidedly casual. In summer, dining on the outdoor deck is also an option. The menu leans toward vegetarian, with pasta being one of the best dinner bets, but there are plenty of good meat dishes, too. Fresh-baked breads make great lunch-time sandwiches, which can also be packed to go for picnics. Breakfast is served at 8 AM. *730 9th St., tel. 403/678–2101. No reservations. Dress: casual. AE, MC, V. Inexpensive–Moderate.*

Cranbrook

City Cafe. If you find yourself stuck for lunch in the fast-food world of Cranbrook, City Cafe will be a breath of fresh air. The flowered tablecloths, low ceilings, and pine banquettes give the small dining room a French-country-bistro air, especially in the morning, when breakfast is served. Sandwiches served on fresh, crusty French bread are tasty and very reasonably priced. *1015 Baker St., tel. 604/489–5413. Reservations advised. Dress: casual. MC, V. Inexpensive–Moderate.*

Invermere **Toby Creek Lodge.** The restaurant, part of a 1960s-era ski lodge, has cedar walls, lighting fixtures that look like upside-down buttercups, a slant-roof ceiling, and—in winter—a big roaring fire in the central fireplace. In the summer, the outside deck offers fresh air, though not much of a view. The food, alas, is fairly ordinary Continental fare, and often overcooked—something to keep in mind when ordering meat. Toby Creek is open for breakfast, too. *Panorama Resort, 18 km (11 mi) west of Invermere, tel. 604/342–6941. Reservations advised. Dress: neat but casual. AE, MC, V. Expensive.*

★ **Chalet Edelweis.** This cute little chalet really looks as if it could have been plucked and transplanted from a hillock in the Swiss countryside. The interior is refreshingly simple—a few blond-wood tables, scrubbed white walls, and a small bar. The atmosphere inspires you to try the fondue, but schnitzels and fettucine are also good. *934 7th Ave., tel. 604/342–3525. Reservations advised. Dress: casual. MC, V. Closed lunch. Moderate–Expensive.*

Jasper **Beauvert Room** and **Moose Nook.** For fancy dining and a wide-ranging Continental menu, the Beauvert Room is the place to go around Jasper. The huge dining room, whose main decor is stone pillars and hard angles, conveys a big-hotel–style ambience. Moose Nook, more intimate but retaining a modernistic coolness, has an imaginative, game-oriented menu that includes pheasant, reindeer, and buffalo steaks. Both restaurants are open for breakfast. *Jasper Park Lodge, 4 km (2½ mi) northeast of Jasper, off Rte. 16, tel. 403/852–3301. Reservations required. Jacket advised. AE, MC, V. Very Expensive.*

★ **Le Beauvallon.** When Jasperites go out for a special meal, this is often where they go. Upholstered chairs, blue tablecloths, and wood-trimmed crimson walls bring an air of elegance to this dining room. The menu has some seafood items, but meat dishes are featured, including lamb in pesto sauce and an elk/beef/pork mélange. The giant Sunday brunch buffet has epic feast potential for active outdoorspeople. Try Le Beauvallon for breakfast, too. *Chateau Jasper, 96 Giekie St., tel. 403/852–5644. Dinner reservations advised. Dress: neat but casual; jacket advised for dinner. AE, MC, V. Expensive–Very Expensive.*

★ **L'Auberge.** French cuisine is offered in this small mountain-lodge retreat with panoramic views of the Athabasca River. Weather permitting, meals are served on the porch in front, but traffic noise from nearby Route 93 may make indoor dining preferable. The menu is creatively assembled from French classics; highlights are brie baked in puff pastry (appetizer) and veal with wild mushrooms (entrée). Though no lunch is served, breakfast begins at 8 AM. *Near Becker's Chalets, 5 mi south of Jasper on Rte. 93, tel. 403/852–3535. Reservations advised for dinner. Dress: casual. AE, MC, V. Closed lunch and mid-Oct.–Apr. Expensive.*

L & W. Plants adorning the sloping greenhouse roof bring life to this otherwise ordinary hotel coffee shop. The menu is all over the lot—pizzas, Greek dishes, barbecued ribs—the common denominator being a salad bar. Dishes are adequately prepared, and the simplest—burgers and pizzas—are the best choices. Families come here for a decent meal at a reasonable price. Takeout and delivery service are available. *Hazel and Patricia Sts., tel. 403/852–4114. No reservations. Dress: casual. AE, MC, V. Moderate.*

Mountain View Cafe. This is a good place to pick up a morning cup of coffee or sandwiches for a picnic lunch. The café has a health-food store in the back and a deli counter up front. Though the emphasis is on health foods, you can still get an old-fashioned three-meat hero to eat in or take out. The tabbouleh salad is especially good. Browse through the store's book rack while waiting for your sandwich to be made. *606 Connaught St., tel. 403/852–4050. No reservations. Dress: casual. No credit cards. Inexpensive.*

Kananaskis Country

L'Escapade. In the evening, the atmosphere in L'Escapade is tastefully elegant and romantic, with such fine details as white tablecloths, real silver, and candlelight. The menu is main-stream French: caviar, seafood mousse, chateaubriand. Together, the fare and ambiance make this restaurant the most elegant in all the village. Breakfast is served. *Hotel Kananaskis, Kananaskis Village, Hwy. 40, tel. 403/591–7711. Reservations advised for dinner. Dress: neat but casual; jacket advised for dinner. AE, CB, DC, MC, V. Very Expensive.*

Kimberley

Gasthas am Platzl. With individually lit wood booths and waitresses dressed in dirndls, the restaurant is a none-too-subtle re-creation of a German bierstube. The menu goes right along with the furnishings: schnitzels and wursts are served, but non-German pasta dishes are also listed. *240 Spokane St., tel. 604/427–4851. Reservations advised. Dress: casual. AE, MC, V. Moderate–Expensive.*

★ **Chef Bernard's Kitchen.** Dining in this small, homey storefront on the Kimberley pedestrian mall is like dining in someone's pantry. The decor is alpine—with goat horns, cowbells, and photos adorning the walls. The menu is small but widely varied, including pastas and chateaubriand. *170 Spokane St., tel. 604/427–4820. Reservations advised. Dress: neat but casual. MC, V. Moderate.*

Lake Louise

★ **Post Hotel.** Here is one of the true epicurean experiences in the Canadian Rockies. The restaurant receives numerous commendations and awards, and with good reason. A low, exposed-beam ceiling and a stone hearth in the corner lend a warm, in-from-the-cold atmosphere; white tablecloths and fanned napkins provide an elegant touch. Venison and veal are specialties, and sauces and garnishes are Alpine-influenced; dark gravies and wild mushrooms are common. Homemade pastries and desserts cap off the meal; you can also order them for tea in the hotel lobby (*see* Lodging below). Breakfast is served. While the food is excellent, service can be stuffy. *200 Pipestone St., tel. 403/522–3989. Reservations advised. Jacket advised for dinner. AE, MC, V. Very Expensive.*

Chateau Lake Louise. A half-dozen restaurants in this hotel (see Lodging, below) present an array of options, from light snacking in the Alpine Lounge to night-on-the-town elegance in the Edelweiss Dining Room. Regardless of choice, dining inevitably defers to the view, brought into play by arced, 10-foot-high windows. The size of the Victoria Dining Room, with seating for more than 300, is nicely toned down by plush carpeting, upholstered chairs, and standing plants. The food and atmosphere are European hotel–style—croissants and jam for breakfast, Continental fare for lunch and dinner—with white cotton tablecloths, and polished silver. For simpler, less expensive, coffee shop–style eating throughout the day, there is the Poppy Room. Afternoon tea in the Lakeside Lounge could consist of fresh scones, pastries, or croissants—along with coffee and tea—served on high-tea silver. *Lake Louise Dr., tel. 403/522–3511, ext. 52. Dinner reservations required in summer for most restaurants. Dress: casual; jacket required for dinner in Edelweiss Dining Room. AE, DC, MC, V. Moderate (Poppy Room)–Very Expensive (Edelweiss and Victoria dining rooms).*

Laggan's Mountain Bakery and Deli. This six-table coffee shop is where the local work crews, mountain guides, and park wardens come for an early-morning muffin and a cup of coffee. Laggan's, in Sampson Mall, has excellent baked goods, especially the poppy-seed sweet breads. You might want to pick up a sandwich here for your drive north on the Icefields Parkway. *Samson Mall, off Rte. 1, tel. 403/522–2017. No reservations. Dress: casual. No credit cards. Inexpensive.*

Radium Hot Springs

Alte Liebe. The main cuisine is German, but it comes with an unusual twist—a touch of Japanese. This might be the only restaurant with Wiener schnitzel and salmon sushi on the same menu. The dining room has a German decor, but the place to sit on a nice evening is on the outdoor deck, with a panoramic view of the Radium Valley under the setting sun. *Madsen Rd. (turn off .5 km (or ⅓ mi) east of Rtes. 93 and 95 junction), tel. 604/347–9548. Reservations advised. Dress: neat but casual. No credit cards. Closed lunch and mid-Sept.–March. Moderate–Expensive.*

Revelstoke
★

One-Twelve. Housed in the Regent Inn (*see* Lodging, below), this restaurant is the real star of the British Columbia Rockies, where dinner is usually an ordinary affair. Lots of cedar, low ceilings, and an abundance of historic photos lend a warm atmosphere. Continental dishes, such as salmon, chicken Cordon Bleu, and beef brochette, are the basic fare, but the unrivaled king of the menu is the lamb broiled with rosemary and red wine. *Regent Hotel, 112 1st St. E, tel. 604/837–2107. Reservations advised. Dress: neat but casual. AE, MC, V. Expensive.*

Yoho
★

Emerald Lake Lodge. The dining room is a glass-enclosed terrace, with views of the lake through tall stands of evergreens. The furnishings are eclectic, some tables with upholstered chairs, some straight-backs, but all evoking an old-lodge atmosphere. Also eclectic is the menu, which mixes traditional Canadian/American fare—steaks, game, and fish—with nouvelle sauces like ginger-tangerine glaze. Excellent pastas and hamburgers are also available. For those who want a light meal in a more casual setting, salads, quiches, and baked cheeses are served around a giant stone hearth in the lounge area. The lodge serves breakfast also. *6 mi north of Field, tel. 604/343–6321. Reservations advised. Dress: neat but casual. AE, MC, V. Moderate–Expensive.*

Lodging

The hotels, inns, and lodges of the Canadian Rockies comprise an eclectic list, ranging from rustic, backcountry lodges without electricity or running water to standard roadside motels to hotels of supreme luxury. With just a few exceptions, however, they share one common trait—room rates that are considerably higher in the summer than during the rest of the year. The week between Christmas and New Year's often commands a higher rate as well. For this reason, flexibility in travel planning can mean considerable savings—a room that goes for $100 a night on September 15 may well drop to $50 on September 16. Lodgings are categorized according to their off-peak rates. High-season rate increases, if any, are noted within each listing.

Highly recommended lodgings are indicated by a star ★.

Category	Cost*
Very Expensive	over $120
Expensive	$80–$120
Moderate	$50–$79
Inexpensive	under $50

**All prices are for a standard double room (or an equivalent, where not applicable), are in Canadian dollars, and do not include a 5% room tax in Alberta or an 8% room tax in British Columbia.*

Banff **Banff Springs Hotel.** Built in 1888, this castlelike hotel was the beginning of Banff's tourism boom. The massive, stone-walled hotel has a seemingly endless maze of hallways and stairwells, huge sitting areas, and banquet rooms, complimented by lots of dark wood furnishings and chandeliers. The complexity of the hotel's floor plan, however, can be disorienting, and the lobby is surprisingly small—contributing to traffic jams during checkout time. The 829 guest rooms come in all shapes and sizes, with such old-hotel characteristics as high ceilings, rattling windows, and layers of cream-color paint. Refurbished bathrooms are a plus. The hotel caters to tour groups and conventioneers, making this ever-active lodge anything but a getaway mountain retreat. Rooms are not soundproof, and often the noises carry. *Spray Ave., Box 960, T0L 0C0, tel. 403/762–2211 or 800/268–9411. 760 rooms, 69 suites. Facilities: 10 restaurants, 24-hr room service, cable TV, shops, health club, 5 tennis courts, riding stables, golf course. Premium rates mid-May–mid-Oct. AE, DC, MC, V. Very Expensive.*

Banff Park Lodge. The high, slanted ceiling and dark-cedar paneling, in addition to the lean, modern, and unembellished style, exudes a Scandinavian feeling. On a quiet street in downtown Banff, the lodge is within walking distance of shops and restaurants. The rooms, recently spiffed up with new carpet and paint, are bright, with lots of beige and ecru. A few have large, in-room Jacuzzis, two giant steps from bedside. *217 Lynx St., Box 2200, T0L 0C0, tel. 403/762–4433 or 800/661–9266. 211 rooms, some with steam showers and Jacuzzis. Facilities: 2 restaurants, room service, whirlpool, sauna, indoor pool, shops, cable TV. Premium rates June–Sept. AE, DC, MC, V. Expensive.*

Banff Rocky Mountain Resort. Five kilometers (3 miles) east of Banff, this resort, with chalet-style buildings and numerous outdoor facilities, is the place for active people. Inside, rooms are bright, with white walls, wall-to-wall carpeting, and lots of blond-wood trim. Many rooms have fireplaces and kitchens with microwave ovens. *Banff Ave. and Tunnel Mountain Rd.,*

Box 100, T0L 0C0, tel. 403/762–5531 or 800/661–9563. 132 studio, 1-bedroom, and 2-bedroom units. Facilities: cable TV, 2 tennis courts, squash courts, weight room, games room, indoor pool complex, video service on premises, shuttle-bus service to and from Banff. Approximate 35 to 50% rate increase from mid-June–mid-Sept. and late–Dec. AE, DC, MC, V. Expensive.

★ **Buffalo Mountain Lodge.** Part of the Canadian Rocky Mountain Resorts group, along with Emerald Lake Lodge in Yoho and Deer Lodge in Lake Louise, this lodge is similar, in ambience and style. The lobby area, with lots of polished pine and exposed rough-hewn beams, is dominated by a large stone hearth with a buffalo head over the mantle. There is a main lodge, with lobby and restaurant; a new hotel/condo cluster built in 1987; and an older group of chalet buildings. Newer rooms are dressed in pastel shades and have small fireplaces, wicker chairs, and pine cabinetry. Older chalet units are larger, with two bedrooms, and are similarly decorated. Although the lodge sits high atop the road, on the outskirts of Banff, few rooms have views. *Tunnel Mountain Rd., Box 1326, T0L 0C0, tel. 403/762–2400 or 800/661–1367. 85 units, including hotel rooms, and 2-bedroom condos. Facilities: cable TV, hot tub, steam room. Approximately 60% rate increase mid-June–mid-Sept. and Christmas week. AE, MC, V. Expensive.*

Tunnel Mountain Chalets. Situated on Tunnel Mountain, above Banff village, many of the condominium-style units and modified A-frame cottages have terrific views of the Bow River Valley, and balconies and porches in some units bring the view even closer. Inside, however, brown-beige wall-to-wall carpeting and average-quality furnishings make the rooms look rather ordinary. Rooms in the condos and cottages have fireplaces and kitchens. *Tunnel Mountain Rd., Box 1137, T0L 0C0, tel. 403/762–4515 or 800/661–9193. 75 units. Facilities: satellite TV, indoor pool, whirlpools, saunas, steam rooms, barbecue facilities. AE, MC, V. Expensive.*

★ **Storm Mountain Lodge.** This is one of the original Canadian Pacific Railway backcountry lodges, built in 1922. Hardly backcountry today, it is on Route 93, just east of Vermilion Pass. The sitting area of the main, log cabin–style lodge is dominated by a large fireplace that is crowned by the head of a bighorn sheep. The dining area embodies the elegance of simplicity: straight-back wood chairs and white tablecloths on an enclosed porch with big glass windows overlooking the pass. Sleeping cabins, tucked in the woods, are smallish but cozy, made so by fireplaces, old lamps, and down comforters. *Rte. 93, 4.8 km (3 mi) west of Rte. 1 interchange. Box 670, T0L 0C0, tel. 403/762–4155. 12 cabins. Facilities: restaurant, lounge, hiking trails. Closed mid-Sept.-late-May. AE, MC, V. Moderate–Expensive.*

Castle Mountain Village. The Village, about halfway between Banff and Lake Louise, consists of three different chalet styles. The smallest—about 12 by 14 feet—have kitchens, bathrooms, and sleeping areas with fireplaces. Although cramped and on the dark side, they are also clean and quiet. Larger and newer pine-log chalets have two bedrooms and can sleep as many as six people. For four people, the large chalets are a comfortable, economic choice. Request a cabin with a view of Castle Mountain. *Rte. 1A between Banff and Lake Louise, Box 1655, T0L 0C0, tel. 403/762–3868. 21 chalets. Facilities: cable TV, conve-*

nience store, barbecue facilities. 35%–40% rate increases June–Oct. and Christmas week. Pets $10 extra. MC, V. Moderate.

High Country Inn. There is nothing fancy here—just clean, simple, comfortable motel rooms. The units are slightly more spacious than those in the Red Carpet Inn next door, wood-veneer furnishings are a little newer, and cedar-covered walls give some rooms a touch of regional character. Ask for a room in the back, away from heavy traffic running along Banff Avenue. *419 Banff Ave., Box 700, T0L 0C0, tel. 403/762–2236. 71 rooms. Facilities: restaurant, satellite TV, whirlpool. Premium rates May–mid-Sept. AE, MC, V. Moderate.*

Red Carpet Inn. Under the same management as the High Country Inn next door, Red Carpet offers one of the few moderately priced lodging options in downtown Banff. Like its neighbor, this motel is basically no-frills; the lobby is modestly adorned with a desk, an office, and a postcard stand. Motel-style rooms are small, but by Banff standards so are the prices that are slightly below those of the High Country Inn. Rooms in the front, on Banff Avenue, get traffic noise. *425 Banff Ave., Box 1800, T0L 0C0, tel. 403/762–4184. 46 rooms. Facilities: satellite TV, indoor pool, whirlpool. Premium rates May–mid-Sept. AE, MC, V. Inexpensive–Moderate.*

Canmore

Bow Valley Motel. Located in the center of Canmore, this two-story, few-frills motel is enhanced by the friendliness of its management and its close proximity to town. For those who put a premium on being able to walk to dining and shopping, this is the place to stay. Rooms are simply furnished with a wood-veneer bed, a dresser, a 12-inch TV, and not much more. Five rooms have kitchens. *610 8th St., Box 231, T0L 0M0, tel. 403/678–5085. 25 rooms. Facilities: cable TV. Premium rates June–Sept. AE, DC, MC, V. Moderate.*

Skiland Motel. Added in 1987, the newer section of this two-part motel is more attractive than the older. A slanting exposed-wood and rafter ceiling gives a chaletlike feel to an otherwise simple motel room. Rooms in the older section are clean and plainly furnished with vinyl furniture that is more convincingly a 1960s style than a Swiss chalet. Rooms are equipped with kitchenettes. *Hwy. 1A, Box 696, T0L 0M0, tel. 403/678–5445. 45 rooms. Steam room, playground, cable TV. Premium rates June–Sept. MC, V. Moderate.*

★ **Mt. Engadine Lodge.** Hiking and cross-country skiing trails begin out the back door of this backcountry lodge, where the mountains and lakes of Kananaskis Country are an immediate presence. The surroundings draw young and old, and most of the clientele come here to enjoy the outdoors. Wood is the lodge's main design feature, with cedar walls on the exterior and white-pine ceilings and furnishings inside. Rooms (dormitory-style as well as private) have a scrubbed simplicity to them, as do the common areas. Meals, served family-style, are included in the rate. The lodge operators are also backcountry guides, and hiking or skiing packages are available. *At Mt. Shark turn off on Spray Trail, 38 km (22 mi) south of Canmore. Box 1679, Canmore T0L 0M0, tel. 403/678–4080. Lodging for 28 persons in dorm-style, shared, and private rooms, all with shared baths. Facilities: restaurant, sun deck. Winter rates slightly higher than summer. MC, V. Inexpensive–Moderate.*

Fairmont Hot Springs

Fairmont Hot Springs Resort. With an extensive selection of activities from golf to heli-hiking, a vacation at this resort is like being at camp. In addition to the recreational facilities, Fairmont also has hot springs, a spa, and an airport. Rooms, available in condo villas and the main lodge, are familiarly furnished with contemporary decor, and many are wood-paneled. The low-slung, bungalow-style architecture is attractive. Some rooms are equipped with kitchens, and have balconies or patios. *Rte. 93/95, Box 10, Fairmont Hot Springs V0B 1L0, tel. 604/345–6311 or 800/663–4979. Lodging for 800 in 140 lodge rooms and 265 villa units, some with kitchens, patios, and/or balconies. Facilities: restaurants, lounge, snack bar, 2 golf courses, 2 tennis courts, heli-hiking, 4 pools, hot springs, spa, airport. Golf, ski and spa packages. AE, MC, V. Expensive.*

Panorama Resort. The resort, at the edge of the Purcell Wilderness, has a wide variety of accommodations and activities. The lodge at the base of the ski lifts is more casual, and conveys a college-dorm atmosphere, with its long hallways and doors that look as though they've been kicked a few times with ski boots. Inside, rooms are large, with yellow walls and lots of mirrors. The other accommodations are in condo villas that look to be part of a mountainside suburb. Attractively decorated, the villa rooms follow a light-brown-and-beige color scheme, and many rooms have fireplaces, patios, or balconies. Originally conceived as a winter resort, Panorama has a fine ski area and is adding other amenities that will appeal to summer visitors. Of these, an on-site golf course is in the works, to go with tennis, swimming, and hiking. *18 km (11 mi) west of Invermere. Box 7000, Panorama N0A 1T0, tel. 604/342–6941 or 800/663–2929. 355 lodge and condo units. Facilities: satellite TV, sauna, indoor and outdoor whirlpools, outdoor pool, tennis courts, skiing, heli-skiing. AE, MC, V. Moderate.*

Glacier National Park

Glacier Park Lodge. This modern, two-floor motel at the top of Rogers Pass offers ambience in the familiar Best Western format: wood-veneer tables and chairs, maroon wall-to-wall carpeting, and undecorated walls. The steep-sloping A-frame roof is a design concession to the heavy winter snows. Being the only lodging within Glacier National Park boundaries, the location is the main attraction. Situated on Highway 1, the lodge accommodates long-distance travelers with its 24-hr service station, 24-hour coffee shop, and gift shop. *The Summit, Rogers Pass, BC V0E 2S0, tel. 604/837–2126 or 800/528–1234. 51 motel-style rooms. Facilities: restaurant, 24-hr coffee shop, heated outdoor pool. AE, CB, MC, V. Moderate.*

Golden

Swiss Village. This is a combination motel and campground lodging, with a little more modern polish than some of its Golden neighbors. There is nothing special here, just basic motel rooms—bed, bathroom, TV—at a fair price. The RV sites have electrical set-ups and water. *Off Rte. 1, west end of Golden. Box 765, V0A 1H0, tel. 403/344–2276. 40 motel rooms, 10 RV sites. Facilities: satellite TV, whirlpool. AE, MC, V. Inexpensive.*

Invermere

★ **Delphine Lodge.** This is the sort of place for those seeking an out-of-the-way cubbyhole. Originally built in 1899, this hotel has been restored to its present bed-and-breakfast status. Big, lace-curtained windows shed lots of light on a living/dining area that is distinguished by its polished, wide-board floors, huge stone hearth, and antique straight-back chairs and wicker rockers. Handcrafted pine furnishings and down comforters fill the smallish, pastel-shaded bedrooms. Continental breakfast is served every morning. *Main St., 5 km (3 mi) from Invermere, Box 2797, V0A 1K0, tel. 604/342–6851. 6 rooms, 1 with private bath, 5 sharing 2 baths. V. Inexpensive.*

Jasper **Jasper Park Lodge.** Jasper's original resort, a lakeside compound northeast of town, hums with on-site recreational amenities, including guided activities. The main lodge, with a large window overlooking Beauvert Lake and the mountains, features polished-stone floors, carved totem-pole pillars, and high ceilings, that convey a cool, open-warehouse atmosphere. The rooms vary: Some are in a modern, hotel-room style; others have an exposed-log, rustic character, with fireplaces; but most are arranged in one-story cottages and all have brightly patterned down comforters on all the beds, and a porch, patio, or balcony. Breakfast and dinner at the lodge's restaurants, the Beauvert Room and Moose Nook (*see* Dining, above), are included in the room rate. *4 km (2½ mi) northeast of Jasper, off Rte. 16. Box 40, T0E 1E0, tel. 403/852–3301; in the U.S. 800/ 828–7747. 419 rooms. Facilities: 3 restaurants, satellite TV, golf course, 2 tennis courts, boating, bicycling, horseback riding, fishing. 40%–50% rate increase June–Sept. AE, CB, DC, MC, V. Very Expensive.*

Chateau Jasper. Big wood beams cantilevered over the front door of this two-story inn suggest a Scandinavian interior, but rooms are of the American motel–style with Colonial motif, most notable in the Colonial-style headboards. Burgundy carpets and low ceilings add coziness to largish rooms; some units have kitchen areas, though they are spare and in need of a facelift. The hotel's restaurant, Le Beauvallon, is excellent (*see* Dining, above). *96 Giekie St., T0E 1E0, St., tel. 403/852–5644. 121 rooms. Facilities: satellite TV, heated indoor parking, indoor pool, whirlpool, roof-top sun deck. Premium rates June–Sept. AE, MC, V. Expensive.*

Jasper Inn. A modern interpretation of chalet-style architecture, this inn has lots of oblique angles and hard edges, with sleek, low-slung furniture to match. This angular coolness is warmed by slanted cedar ceilings and red brick. During breakfast, the sky-lit dining area is as bright as the beach on a sunny day. Accommodations are arranged in a variety of ways, but living areas in condo-style units are particularly spacious. Most units have kitchenettes and fireplaces. *Giekie St. and Bonhomme Ave., Box 879, T0E 1E0, tel. 403/852–4461 or 800/661–1933. 124 units. Facilities: satellite TV, indoor pool, sauna, whirlpool, steam bath. Approximately 40% rate increase June–Sept. Children under 12 stay free in parents' room. AE, MC, V. Moderate–Expensive.*

Pyramid Lake Bungalows. Situated on the shores of active Pyramid Lake, this lodging is a great place for those who enjoy hiking, boating, horseback riding, and marvelous sunrises. Sixteen new units (built in 1988) in two log-cabin chalets are preferable to the older bungalows that are closer to the lake but more run-down. All units have kitchenettes. The restaurant is fair, but Jasper, a few kilometers down the road, has much to offer. *Pyramid Lake Rd., 5.6 km (4 mi) from Jasper. Box 388, T0E 1E0, tel. 403/852–3491. 18 units in 10 bungalows and 2 chalets. Facilities: satellite TV; beach with boat, canoe, and sailboard rentals. MC, V. Closed mid-Oct.–mid-May. Moderate.*

★ **Alpine Village.** Located 1 kilometer (⅔ mile) south of town, this is one of Jasper's bargains. Logs in many cabins are left exposed on interior walls, adding to the warm, rustic feeling of this family-run operation. Furnishings are garage-sale eclectic, and frilly throw cushions abound. Most units have fireplaces and sun decks; two-bedroom cabins have full kitchens. The Athabasca River and a view of distant Mt. Edith Cavell are just out front, although a small road must be crossed to get to the river. *Rte. 93A, 1 km (⅔ mi) south of Jasper. Box 610, T0E 1E0, tel. 403/852–3285. 42 units, including 1-room sleeping cabins and 2-bedroom cabins. 25%–35% rate increase, mid-June–mid-Dec. DC, V. Closed Nov.–Apr. Inexpensive–Moderate.*

Kananaskis Country

Kananaskis Village. This is the lodging village built for the 1988 Olympics, as the smell and look of newness attests. This full-service resort, sandwiched on a small plateau between the Nakiska ski area and two 18-hole golf courses, is tastefully designed and decorated. Accommodations are in three facilities—the Inn, the Lodge, and the Hotel. All surround an attractively landscaped, man-made pond that provides a nice lounging spot on a summer day. Of the three, the Inn is the most moderately priced, with log pillars and a redwood exterior inviting you into the motel-style rooms, some with private balconies (balconies facing west get the best sun), kitchenettes, or fireplaces. Larger, and more lavishly furnished, some rooms in the Lodge and Hotel have rosewood furnishings, ceramic-base lamps, and rustic wood armoires to hide TV sets. The hotel throws in special amenities, such as bathrobes and hair dryers, and some rooms have fireplaces and Jacuzzis. Several restaurants, skewed toward high-end elegance, offer food ranging from sushi to haute cuisine. The Peaks dining room in the Lodge, with floor-to-ceiling windows casting light on a dark wood motif, may have the nicest atmosphere for those seeking a fancy meal. *Hwy. 40, 28 km (17 mi) south of Rte. 1. Kananaskis Village T0L 2H0, tel. 403/591–7711 or 800/828–7447. Inn: 96 rooms. Lodge: 255 rooms and suites. Hotel: 69 rooms and suites. Facilities: 5 restaurants, satellite TV, indoor pool, sauna, whirlpool, health club, ski area, two 18-hole golf courses, stables nearby, shops, post office, heated indoor parking for the Lodge and Hotel. Lodge and Hotel: AE, CB, DC, MC, V; Inn: AE, MC, V. Expensive–Very Expensive.*

Kimberley

Rhinekastle Hotel. In keeping with downtown Kimberley's Bavarian theme, the hotel's exterior is very German, with exposed wood beams and stucco, and tinted, blown-glass windows. Large rooms have a small sitting area and are plainly furnished with dark brown wood-veneer furniture, including a bed, bureau, and TV. The restaurant serves good, reasonably priced food. Just a block from the Platzl, this is *the* hotel in Kimberley. *300 Wallinger Ave., V1A 1Z4, tel. 604/427–2266. Facilities: restaurant, lounge, cable TV. AE, MC, V. Moderate.*

Lake Louise

★ **Chateau Lake Louise.** There's a good chance that no hotel—anywhere—has a more dramatic view out its back door than this chateau. Terraces and lawns reach to the famous aquamarine lake, backed up by the Victoria Glacier. The impressive turn-of-the-century stone facade has a similarly grand interior, with lobby and sitting areas that convey a stadiumlike sense of spaciousness. A major renovation, begun in 1987, has been tastefully done. In the public areas, off-white walls, polished wood and brass, and burgundy carpeting blend well with the lake view, seen through large, horseshoe-shape windows. Guest rooms feature bright, floral-pattern wallpaper, neo-Colonial furnishings, and terraces. An all-out afternoon high tea in the Lakeside Lounge has become one of the hotel's great traditions. In spite of all the space, though, the hotel can become very crowded with bus tours, hikers, day-trippers from Banff, and hotel guests. *Lake Louise, AB T0L 1E0, tel. 403/572–3511 or 800/268–9411. 525 rooms and suites. Facilities: 6 restaurants, indoor pool, canoeing, riding stables, sauna, whirlpool, shops. AE, DC, MC, V. Very Expensive.*

★ **Post Hotel.** The location, next to the small shopping mall just off Highway 1, is rather ordinary, but the hotel makes up for it in other ways. A gold-colored wood dominates the decor, giving the hotel an atmosphere of muted elegance—a modern interpretation of the country-lodge concept. Rooms come in 13 different configurations, from standard doubles to units with sleeping lofts, kitchens, balconies, and fireplaces. The wood theme extends to the furniture, made of solid Canadian pine. Bathrooms are large, most equipped with whirlpool tubs. The restaurant (*see* Dining, above) is regularly rated as one of the best in the Canadian Rockies. *Box 69, T0L 1E0, tel. 403/522–3989 or 800/661–1586. 93 units. Facilities: cable TV, indoor pool, whirlpool. 25%–35% rate increase mid-May–mid Sept. and Christmas week. AE, MC, V. Expensive.*

Lake Louise Inn. This four-building complex offers a variety of accommodations, from motel rooms to two-bedroom condo units. Dark-wood paneling and fireplaces in some rooms are relief from an otherwise ordinary motel-style decor. Catch the morning sun in the wood-paneled lobby; and later, for a cozy setting, head up to the atticlike lounge. For economy-minded travelers, the Pinery, a separate 56-room building, offers spare but comfortable accommodations. A remodeling and addition of 36 rooms was scheduled to begin in late 1990. *210 Village Rd., Box 209, T0L 1E0, tel. 403/522–3791 or 800/661–9237. 186 rooms and condo units. Facilities: restaurant, pub with dance music, cable TV, indoor pool, sauna, whirlpool, exercise room, ski-area shuttle-bus service, multiday ski packages. AE, DC, MC, V. Moderate.*

Paradise Lodge & Bungalows. This lodge is only 2 kilometers (1¼ miles) down the access road from the lake, and, clearly, location and moderate prices are the features here. Six small rooms share baths upstairs in the log-cabin main lodge. The bungalows, or log-sided cabins (some with kitchenettes) are more rustic from the outside than from the inside. Set in a spruce and pine grove, rooms can be somewhat dark and cramped but are well maintained. *Box 7, T0L 1E0, tel. 403/522–3595 (summer), 403/522–3987 (winter). 6 lodge rooms with shared bath, 21 one- and 2-room cottages. Facilities: barbecue facilities, playground. Closed Oct.–mid-May. MC, V. Moderate.*

Radium Hot Springs

The Chalet. In a town where ordinary, interchangeable motels abound, the Chalet is a cut above—figuratively and literally. The hotel sits on a crest above town, and has several rooms with expansive views of the Columbia River Valley, though these units come at a premium. The decor is nothing special—lots of browns, navy blue, and wood veneer, but each room comes with a sitting area and minikitchen (microwave, refrigerator, sink), and many have balconies. This is a good, economical choice for a family with one or two small children. *Madsen Rd., Box 456, V0A 1M0, tel. 604/347–9305. 17 studios. Facilities: cable TV, Jacuzzi. 35% rate increase June–Aug. $8 additional for young children. AE, DC, MC, V. Moderate.*

Radium Hot Springs Resort. Although the architecture and style of this resort are undistinguished, the recreational facilities and activities bring to life this otherwise basic Best Western property. Rooms, decorated with bright colors and modern furnishings, are simple but functional; some have kitchens and wet bars. Breakfast in the main dining room is a good way to start the day, as the morning sun shines brightly through the big windows. *Off Rte. 93, south of Radium Hot Springs. Box 310, V0A 1M0, tel. 604/347–9311 or 800/528–1234. 90 hotel and condo units. Facilities: indoor pool, hot tub, sauna, whirlpool, exercise room, 2 tennis courts, squash court, racquetball court, golf, cross-country skiing, cable TV. Golf and ski packages available. 25% rate increase May– mid-Oct. and Christmas week. AE, MC, V. Moderate.*

Motel Tyrol. Among the group of motels along the 3-kilometer (1¾-mile) strip of Route 93 (between the Route 95 junction and the hot springs), this one stands out. Its exterior lives up to its name: a motel structure with vibrant Tyrolian touches—flower boxes, and walls painted with Tyrolian designs. The rooms are generally motel-style; they're small and on the dark side, but clean and comfortable; some have kitchens. *Rte. 93, Box 312, V0A 1M0, tel. 403/347–9402. 22 motel rooms. Facilities: satellite TV, heated pool, whirlpool. MC, V. Inexpensive–Moderate.*

Revelstoke

Regent Inn. The newly renovated inn mixes many styles: Colonial, with its brick-arcade facade; true Canadian, in its pine-trimmed lobby area and restaurant; and Scandinavian, in the angular, low-slung wood furnishings of the guest rooms. Rooms are on the large side, but have no spectacular views. The hotel is located downtown, in a revitalized, two-block area of Revelstoke, and is near several boutiques and restaurants. The hotel's own restaurant, One-Twelve, is the best of all (*see* Dining, above). *112 Victoria Rd., Box 450, V0E 2S0, tel. 604/837–2107. 40 rooms. Facilities: restaurant, club with live entertainment, cable TV, whirlpool. AE, MC, V. Moderate.*

Waterton Lakes

Bayshore Inn. As the name suggests, the two-story inn is on the lakeside, and rooms with balconies take full advantage of the setting. Indeed, the setting is the thing; otherwise, the inn's common areas and motel-style rooms are rather ordinary, although some have balconies and kitchenettes. A distinctive touch is the heart-shaped tubs in the three honeymoon suites. When the usual Waterton wind is mellow, the lakeside patio is a great spot for light meals and drinks. *Main St., Box 38, Waterton Park, AB T0K 2M0, tel. 403/859–2211. 70 rooms, including 2-bedroom and honeymoon suites. Facilities: restaurant, coffee shop, satellite TV, gift shop. AE, MC, V. Closed Oct.–Apr. Moderate–Expensive.*

★ **Prince of Wales Hotel.** Situated between two lakes, this property has a breathtaking view of a mountain backdrop from one direction, and a lake-and-prairie setting from another. Eaves, balconies, and turrets fantastically adorn this hotel, and it's crowned by a high steeple. The baronial, dark-paneled interior evokes the feeling of a royal Scottish hunting lodge. Expect creaks and rattles at night—the old hotel (built in the 1920s) is exposed to winds that often blow hard. *Waterton townsite.*

Write to: Mail Station 5570, Phoenix, AZ 85078, tel. 602/248-6000. 81 rooms. Facilities: restaurant. Children under 12 stay free in parents' room. MC, V. Closed mid.-Sept.–May. Moderate–Expensive.

★ **Kilmorey Lodge.** The 60-year-old inn with a log-cabin facade sits at the edge of the Waterton Lakes townsite. Rooms are steeped in country-cottage atmosphere, with pine-wood walls, Indian rug wall hangings, sloped floors, and homespun antique furnishings. Some rooms have additional sleeping or sitting areas. There is a full restaurant with decent food that serves three meals a day. This is the only lodging in Waterton Lakes that's open all year round. *Box 100, Waterton Park, T0K 2M0, tel. 403/859–2334 or 800/661–8069. 25 rooms. Facilities: restaurant. AE, MC, V. Moderate.*

Yoho

★ **Emerald Lake Lodge.** This is an enchanted place, set at the edge of a secluded, glacier-fed lake in Yoho National Park. It's a great spot for canoeing on the lake, hiking, cross-country skiing through miles of trails in the park. A sitting area in the main lodge has overstuffed chairs and small tables, and offers light meals served around a large stone hearth. There is also a full bar and an excellent restaurant that serves a mix of haute cuisine and nouvelle Canadian dishes on a glass-enclosed porch. Cottages surround the log-cabin main lodge. Guest rooms have fireplaces, and many have balconies with lake views. Soundproofing is the one drawback—you can hear your neighbors. *9.5 km (6 mi) north of Field, BC. Box 10, Field, BC V0A 1G0, tel. 604/343–6321 or 800/663–6336. 85 rooms in 24 2- and 4-room cottages. Facilities: restaurant, teahouse, bar, exercise room, sauna, outdoor hot tub, boat rentals. AE, MC, V. Expensive.*

Backcountry Lodges and Guest Ranches

Backcountry lodges have been an integral part of Canadian Rockies travel since the '20s. They vary considerably in terms of accommodations and accessibility: At the luxurious end are lodges with private rooms, private baths, full electricity, telephones, and restaurant-style dining; at the rugged extreme are lodges with bunk beds and kerosene lamps for evening light. A few are accessible by car in the summer, some can be reached only by hiking or by skiing in winter, and still others can be reached only by helicopter.

Surprisingly—given the difficulty of getting supplies to remote locations—meals served at most backcountry lodges tend to be excellent, no doubt improved by the fresh mountain air and appetites swelled by the active life of the backcountry. The lodges and ranches listed below are a sampling. Both Travel Alberta and Tourism B.C. can provide more complete lodge and ranch listings as well as descriptions. (*see* Important Addresses and Numbers in Essential Information, above).

Backcountry Lodges

Lake O'Hara Lodge. Secluded in the heart of one of the most scenic and popular hiking and climbing regions in the Canadian Rockies, this lodge is situated just west of Lake Louise. In summer, guests are ferried by a lodge-operated bus along an 11.25-kilometer (7-mile) fire road between Highway 1 and the grounds. In winter, guests must ski the distance. The lodge and lakeside cabins offer fairly luxurious backcountry living, including private rooms with baths and a restaurant that serves three meals a day (included in room rates). *Off Hwy. 1 in Yoho National Park. Box 55, Lake Louise AB T0L 1E0, tel. 604/343–6442 or 604/762–2118. 23 units in lodge and cabins. Facilities: hiking, climbing, canoeing. Reservations for high season should be booked several months in advance. Closed May, Oct., Nov. MC, V. Moderate–Expensive.*

Skoki Lodge. An 11-kilometer (6½-mile) hike or ski from the Lake Louise ski area, Skoki is the kind of backcountry lodge you must work to get to. The high-alpine scenery of Skoki Valley makes the travel well worthwhile, as does the small log-cabin lodge itself, built in 1930. The log walls, big stone fireplace, and mantel cluttered with old ski gear, make Skoki seem the epitome of backcountry coziness. So, too, do the rooms upstairs in the main lodge, with beds tucked tightly under the wood eaves. Don't expect such luxuries as private baths, running water, or electricity, but meals are included in the rates. *Box 5, Lake Louise, AB T0L 1E0, tel. 403/522–3555. Lodging in 22 guest rooms and cabins with wood-burning stoves and outdoor washrooms. Reservations must be made in advance. AE, MC, V. Inexpensive–Moderate.*

Guest Ranches

Homeplace Ranch. Just east of the Kananaskis Country foothills, the ranch is just as its name suggests: homey. It is secluded, several miles along gravel roads, surrounded by other working ranches. Bedrooms have tiny, private baths (unusual for ranch accommodations), and the small living/dining area is cluttered with books and magazines that provide good nightly reading, the principal evening activity. During the day, the activity is riding over the rolling land, aspen groves, and open meadows near the ranch. Also available are extended, multiday pack trips into Kananaskis Country. Meals, included in the guest rate, are served family style, and such is the homey atmosphere that you might find yourself wanting to pitch in and help with the cooking or the dishes. *Off Rte. 2, 10 km (6 mi) west of Priddis. R.R. 1, Box 6, Priddis, AB T0L 1W0, tel. 403/931–3245. Lodging for 12 in private rooms in ranch house. Packages, including pack trips, available. Moderate–Expensive.*

Kananaskis Guest Ranch. Set near the Bow River at the edge of Kananaskis Country, a main lodge with restaurant and lounge is surrounded by cabins and larger "chalets." Cedar walls and, in some units, cedar-beam ceilings, give a rustic flavor to two otherwise plain, double-bed bedrooms. The Donut Tent—a log-and-wood-roofed "tent" with a large hole in the middle, where bonfires are built for family-style barbecues—is the ranch's claim to fame. In addition to the obligatory horseback riding, the ranch also offers jet-boat trips on the Bow River. *Ranch office on Ranch Rd., from the Seebe–Exshaw exit on Rte. 1 east of Canmore, General Delivery, Seebe AB T0L 1X0, tel. 403/673–3737. Lodging for 50 in cabins and chalets. Facilities: dining room, lounge, souvenir shop, whirlpool. AE, MC, V. Closed Nov.–Apr. Inexpensive–Moderate.*

The Arts and Nightlife

The Arts

Most of the cultural activity in the Canadian Rockies is in and around Banff. Unquestionably, the hub of cultural activity is the **Banff Centre** (St. Julien Rd., tel. 403/762–6300). Presenting a performing-arts grab bag throughout the year, with pop and classical music, theater, dance, and film, the center peaks in summer with the two-month Banff Festival of the Arts.

Galleries and Museums Housed in Banff Centre is the **Walter J. Philips Gallery,** which focuses principally on works by Canadian artists and artists at the Banff Centre School of Fine Arts. *Tel. 403/762–6253. Admission: free. Open noon–5.*

Also in Banff, the **Whyte Museum** features art, photography, historical artifacts, and exhibits about life in the Canadian Rockies. *111 Bear St., tel. 403/762–2291. Admission: $2, children free. Open mid-May–mid-Oct., daily 10–6; off-season hours vary.*

The **Banff Park Museum** features wildlife displays, wildlife art, and a library on natural history. *93 Banff Ave., tel. 403/ 762–3324. Admission free. Open 10–6.*

Performing Arts The **Jasper Activity Centre** (303 Pyramid Ave., tel. 403/852–3381), hosts local troupes presenting theater, music, and dance productions throughout the year.

The **Jasper Summer Theatre** (Giekie and Miette Sts., tel. 403/ 852–5325) performs shows from June through August, at the Anglican Church Hall.

At the **Wild Horse Theater** (Fort Steele, BC V0B 1N0, tel. 604/ 426–6923), in Fort Steele, college presentations are staged from late June–mid-September.

Music During the summer months, Bavarian bands in Kimberley strike up with oompah music on the Platzl, especially when festivals are in swing. The **Old Time Accordion Championships,** in early July, is a Kimberley musical highlight.

In late summer, the Royal Canadian Mounted Police perform their precision **Musical Ride at Fort Steele** (tel. 604/426–6923).

Nightlife

Like many activities in the Canadian Rockies, nightlife, too, is an outdoor event. In summer darkness doesn't fall until after 10 PM, so an after-dinner hike, sail, or even nine holes of golf is possible.

For cocktails and socializing, the big hotels—the **Banff Springs Hotel, Chateau Lake Louise, Jasper Park Lodge,** and the **Lodge at Kananaskis**—have lounges or dining rooms with entertainment and dancing (*see* Lodging, above).

The **Works** (tel. 403/762–3311), a record-spinning discothèque at the Banff Springs Hotel, is a lively, jam-packed hot spot.
In Canmore, local folk kick back at **Sherwood House** (738 8th St., tel. 403/678–5211), which occasionally has live bands on weekends.

In Jasper, the **Athabasca Hotel's** nightclub (510 Patricia St., tel. 403/852–3351) features dancing to Top-40 music and live bands.

9 Manitoba Saskatchewan Alberta

Introduction

by Theodore Fischer

Theodore Fischer is senior editor for the Washington, D.C.-based magazine Export Today.

Between the wilds of western Ontario and the eastern slopes of the Rockies lie Canada's three prairie provinces—Manitoba, Saskatchewan, and Alberta. This is Canada's heartland: the principal source of such solid commodities as wheat, oil, and beef. These provinces are also home of a rich stew of ethnic communities that make the flat plains unexpectedly colorful and cosmopolitan.

The northern sectors (about two-thirds of Manitoba, one-third of Saskatchewan, and the northeast corner of Alberta) are part of the Canadian Shield—sparsely inhabited expanses of lakes and forests atop a foundation of Precambrian rock. To the south lie the prairies, vast plains of fertile soil mostly covered with fields of wheat. Some consider the landscape boring; we'll concede that it's monotonous but also stipulate that it's soothing, inspiring, and brimming with subtle variations in topography, agronomy, and rural architecture.

Certain historical threads are common to all three provinces. Dinosaurs roamed what was semitropical swampland 75 million years ago, and the first human settlers crossed the Bering Strait from Asia 12,000 years ago. European fur traders began arriving in the 17th century, and in 1670 the British Crown granted the Hudson's Bay Company administrative and trading rights to "Rupert's Land," a patch that incorporated the vast territory whose waters drained into Hudson Bay. A hundred years later, the North West Company went into direct competition by building outposts throughout the area. The fur trade produced a new group of people called the Métis, French-speaking offspring of Indian women and European traders who followed the Roman Catholic religion but adhered to a traditional Indian lifestyle.

The North West Mounted Police was established in 1873, six years after the formation of the Canadian government and three years after the Hudson's Bay Company had sold its western holdings to the new government. The Mounties' first chores included resolving conflicts between the Indians and American whiskey traders and overseeing the orderly distribution of the free homesteads granted by the Dominion Lands Act of 1872. The Mounties ultimately had to suppress the North West Rebellion—a revolt by Métis, who feared that incorporation into Canada threatened their traditions and freedom. Although the Métis eventually succumbed, and their leader, Louis Riel, was hanged in 1885, Riel is now hailed as a martyr of French-language rights and provincial autonomy, and a statue of him stands on the grounds of Manitoba's Legislature Building.

Railroads arrived in the 1880s and with them a torrent of immigrants seeking free government land. An influx of farmers from the British Isles, Scandinavia, Holland, Germany, Eastern Europe, and Russia (and especially the Ukraine), plus persecuted religious groups, such as the Mennonites, Hutterites, Mormons, and Jews, transformed the prairies into a rich wheat-growing breadbasket and cultural mosaic, if never exactly a melting pot, that is still very much in evidence today. Alberta and southwest Saskatchewan offered rich opportunities to cattle ranchers after the treaties were signed with the native Indians in the 1870s. In 1947, a big oil strike transformed

Edmonton and Calgary into gleaming metropolises full of "blue-eyed Arabs."

The people of the prairie provinces are relaxed, reserved, and irascibly independent. They maintain equal suspicion toward "Ottawa" (big government) and "Toronto" (big media and big business). To visitors, the people of this region convey a combination of Western openness and Canadian-style courtesy: no fawning, but no rudeness. Visitors also find exceptional outdoor recreational facilities—a spectrum of historical attractions that focuses on Mounties, Métis, dinosaurs, and railroads; excellent accommodations and cuisine at reasonable (but not low) prices; and quiet, crowdless expanses of extraordinarily wide open spaces.

Essential Information

Important Addresses and Numbers

Tourist Information

Manitoba

Travel Manitoba (Dept. 9036, 7th floor, 155 Carlton St., Winnipeg, Manitoba, R3C 3H8, tel. 204/945–3777 or 800/665–0040) distributes a free road map and several useful brochures. The office is open weekdays 8:30–4:30.

Manitoba Travel Information Centers are located just inside the Manitoba border along major routes. The centers are open mid-May through early September from 8 AM to 9 PM.

Saskatchewan

Tourism Saskatchewan (Saskatchewan Trade & Convention Centre, 1919 Saskatchewan Dr., Regina, Sask. S4P 3V7, tel. in Sask., 800/667–7538; in U.S. and Canada, 800/667–7191) can provide you with brochures and maps of attractions, accommodations, and parks inside and outside the province. The main office is open weekdays 8–7, Saturday 10–4.

Information centers are located in cities throughout the province, and in the summer along the Trans-Canada Highway.

Alberta

Travel Alberta (City Centre Bldg., 10155 102nd St. Dept. E, Box 2500, Edmonton, Alberta T5J 2Z4, Canada, tel. in Alberta, 403/427–4321; throughout Canada and continental U.S., 800/661–8888 or 800/222–6501) distributes extremely comprehensive and useful free promotional literature. The office is open weekdays 8:15–4:30.

Arriving and Departing by Plane, Bus, and Train

By Plane

Air Canada has direct or connecting service from Boston, New York, Chicago, San Francisco, and Los Angeles to Winnipeg, Regina, Saskatoon, Calgary, and Edmonton. Commuter affiliates serve other U.S. and Canadian destinations. U.S. airlines serving the prairie provinces include **Northwest** to Winnipeg; **America West, American, Continental, Delta,** and **United** to Calgary; **America West, American, Delta,** and **Northwest** to Edmonton.

By Bus

Greyhound (consult local directory) and local bus companies provide service from the United States, other parts of Canada, and throughout the prairie provinces.

By Train

There is no rail service between the United States and the Prairie Provinces.

Via Rail trains, (tel. 800/361–3677) connects eastern Canada and the west coast through Winnipeg–Regina–Calgary, and another line runs Winnipeg–Saskatoon–Edmonton.

Getting Around

By Car Two main east–west highways link the major cities of the prairie provinces. The Trans-Canada Highway (Route 1), mostly a four-lane divided freeway, runs through Winnipeg, Regina, and Calgary on its nationwide course. The two-lane Yellowhead Highway (Route 16) branches off the Trans-Canada Highway west of Winnipeg and heads northwest toward Saskatoon, Saskatchewan, and Edmonton, Alberta. Traveling north–south, four-lane divided freeways connect Saskatoon–Regina (Route 11) and Edmonton–Calgary (Route 2).

From the United States, interstate highways cross the Canadian border, and two-lane highways continue on to major prairie province cities. From Minneapolis, I–94, and then I–29, connects to Highway 75 at the Manitoba border south of Winnipeg. Driving distance between Minneapolis and Winnipeg is 691 kilometers (432 miles). A main route to Alberta is I–15 north of Helena, Montana, which connects to Highways 4, 3, and 2 to Calgary. Calgary is 690 kilometers (425 miles) from Helena; it's also 670 kilometers (419 miles) from Seattle, via the Trans-Canada Highway.

Winnipeg

With a population of just more than 600,000, Winnipeg ranks as Canada's seventh-largest city and the largest population center between Toronto and Calgary. Though geographically isolated, this provincial capital has become a center for both commerce and culture, boasting a symphony orchestra, ballet and opera companies, a lively theater scene, and a thriving community of local and native artists.

The first stop on the great Canadian land rush of the late 19th century, Winnipeg is still home to descendants of the original French and British settlers, and has distinct neighborhoods of Ukrainians, Jews, Italians, Mennonites, Hungarians, Portuguese, Poles, and Chinese. Unlike the boom-and-bust towns farther west, Winnipeg has enjoyed steady growth, with a diversified economy based on manufacturing, banking, transportation, and agriculture. Winnipeg looks like the cosmopolitan centers of midwest America—Minneapolis, Milwaukee, Chicago—with a downtown area filled with cast-iron buildings and established neighborhoods of older homes along curving, tree-lined streets.

Originally, buffalo-hunting Plains Indians were the only inhabitants of the area that was franchised by the British Crown to the Hudson's Bay Company. That was until Pierre Gaultier de Varennes established, in 1738, a North West Company fur-trading post at the junction of the Red and Assiniboine rivers. Lord Selkirk, a Scot, brought a permanent agricultural settlement in 1812; Winnipeg was incorporated as a city in 1873; and soon after, in 1886, the Canadian Pacific Railroad arrived, bringing a rush of European immigrants. Winnipeg boomed as a railroad hub, a center of the livestock and grain industries, and the principal market city of central Canada.

Manitoba

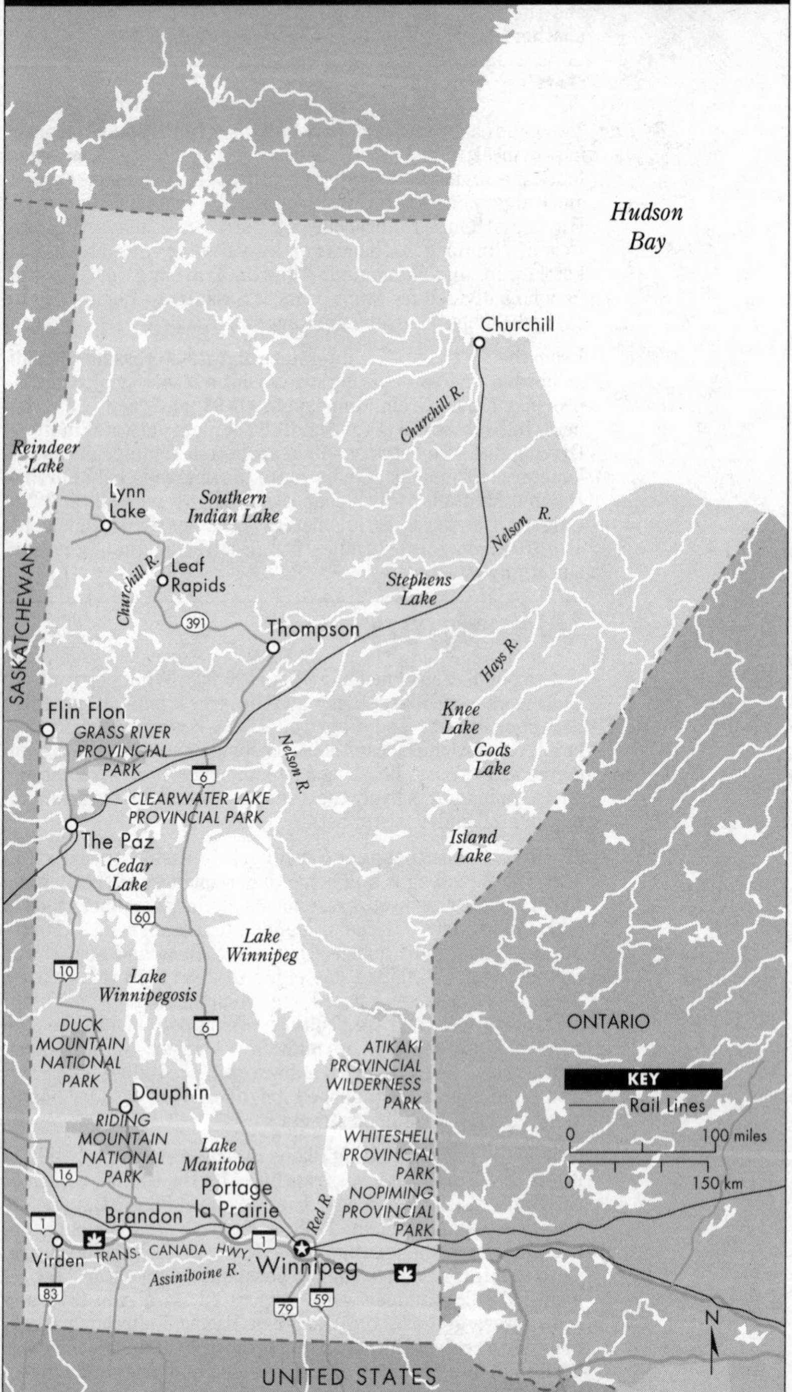
Hudson Bay
Churchill
Churchill R.
Reindeer Lake
Lynn Lake
Southern Indian Lake
Nelson R.
Leaf Rapids
Churchill R.
Stephens Lake
SASKATCHEWAN
391
Thompson
Hays R.
Flin Flon
GRASS RIVER PROVINCIAL PARK
Knee Lake
Nelson R.
Gods Lake
6
CLEARWATER LAKE PROVINCIAL PARK
The Paz
Island Lake
Cedar Lake
60
Lake Winnipeg
10
Lake Winnipegosis
DUCK MOUNTAIN NATIONAL PARK
6
ONTARIO
ATIKAKI PROVINCIAL WILDERNESS PARK
KEY
Rail Lines
Dauphin
RIDING MOUNTAIN NATIONAL PARK
Lake Manitoba
WHITESHELL PROVINCIAL PARK
0
100 miles
0
150 km
16
Portage la Prairie
NOPIMING PROVINCIAL PARK
Red R.
1
Brandon
1
Virden
TRANS-CANADA HWY.
Winnipeg
Assiniboine R.
83
79
59
N
UNITED STATES

Important Addresses and Numbers

Tourist Information The **Government Tourist Reception Office** (Broadway and Osborne St., tel. 204/945–3777 or 800/665–0040), housed in the Manitoba Legislature Building, is open May–Labor Day, daily 8:30 AM–9 PM; Labor Day–April, weekdays 8:30–4:30. **Tourism Winnipeg** (375 York Ave., 2nd floor, tel. 204/943–1970) is open weekdays 8:30–4:30.

Emergencies Dial 911 for **fire, police, ambulance,** or **poison control.**

Hospitals Emergency rooms are located at the **Health Services Centre** (820 Sherbrook St., tel. 204/787–3167 general emergency; tel. 204/787–2306 children's emergency); **Winnipeg Municipal Hospital** (1 Morley Ave., tel. 204/452–3411), and **Misercordia General Hospital** (99 Cornish Ave., tel. 204/788–8188).

Late-night Pharmacy **Nieman Pharmacies** (905 Corydon Ave., tel. 204/453–8331) is open until 11:30 PM.

Arriving and Departing by Plane

Winnipeg International Airport is served by Northwest, Air Canada, Canadian Airlines International, and several commuter airlines. Because the airport is only about 8 kilometers (5 miles) away, taxi fare downtown runs about $10. **Kidd Limousine Service** buses charge $7 for the ride. Some airport-area hotels provide complimentary airport shuttles.

Getting Around

By Bus The **City of Winnipeg Transit System** (tel. 204/284–7190) operates an extensive network of buses throughout the city and metropolitan area. Adult fare is $1 exact change ("loonies," or $1 coins preferred) for adults, 50¢ for seniors and children; transfers are free.

Free **Downtown Area Shuttle** (DASH) buses loop downtown and around the warehouse area weekdays 11–3: Look for DASH bus stops along Broadway, Main Street, Graham Avenue, King Street, and elsewhere.

By Taxi Taxis—relatively expensive by U.S. standards—can be found outside downtown hotels or summoned by phone. Car services are: **Unicity** (tel. 204/942–3366 or 204/942–7555), **Duffy's Taxi** (tel. 204/775–0101).

Guided Tours

Boat Tours Several lines ply the Red and Assiniboine rivers between May and mid-October. The **MS *Lady Winnipeg*** and **MS *River Rouge*** (tel. 204/669–2824) offer a variety of cruises (dining, dinner-dance, evening) from a dock at 312 Nairn Avenue, beside the Louise Bridge. The 179-foot **M.S. *Lord Selkirk*** (tel. 204/582–2331) has daily dinner and dance cruises, and Sunday afternoon excursions from Redwood Bridge, Redwood Avenue, and Main Street. The **MS *Paddlewheel Queen*** and **MS *Paddlewheel Princess*** (tel. 204/339–1696) combine cruises with double-decker bus tours from docks at 2285 Main Street.

Train Tours The **Prairie Dog Central Steam Train** (tel. 204/832–5259) plies a 58-kilometer (36-mile) route from the CNR St. James Station (1661 Portage Ave.) to Grosse Ile on Sunday, June–September.

Walking Tours Walking tours of the turn-of-the-century **Exchange District** begin at the Manitoba Museum of Man & Nature (190 Rupert Ave., tel. 204/774–3514) during July and August.

Exploring Downtown Winnipeg

Numbers in the margin correspond with points of interest on the Downtown Winnipeg map.

It's somewhat difficult to get one's bearings in Winnipeg. The downtown area is located just north of the junction of the Red and Assiniboine rivers, and its streets interconnect at skewed angles with the curving rivers, creating diagonal streets in all directions. Much of downtown Winnipeg is linked by a network of enclosed overhead pedestrian overpasses and underground concourses. The intersection of Portage Avenue and Main Street is the focal point of the city, with Portage Avenue (Hwy. 1) the principal artery heading west and Main Street (Hwy. 52) heading north. South of Winnipeg, the main drag is Pembina Highway (Hwy. 42). Streets in St. Boniface, east of the Red River, are labeled in French—evidence of the community's ethnic heritage.

Begin at the southeast corner of downtown Winnipeg at the tourist information center (*see* Important Addresses and Numbers, above), housed in the **Legislative Building.** The classic Greek–style structure made of local Tyndall stone contains the offices of Manitoba's premier, members of the cabinet, and the chamber where the legislature meets. The 240-foot dome supports Manitoba's symbol—Golden Boy, a gold-sheathed statue with a sheaf of wheat under his left arm and the torch of progress in his right hand. Along the grounds and gardens surrounding the riverside stand statues that celebrate Manitoba's ethnic diversity, including Scotland's Robert Burns, Iceland's Jon Sigurdson, Ukrainian poet Taras Ahevchenko, and Métis leader and "Father of Manitoba" Louis Riel. Walk east on Broadway and south on Carlton Street to **Dalnavert,** a Victorian gingerbread-style house built in 1895 for Hugh John MacDonald, the son of Canada's first prime minister. Costumed guides escort visitors around the premises. *61 Carlton St., tel. 204/943–2835. Admission: $2.50 adults, $2 senior citizens and students, $1 children. Open June–Aug., Tues., Wed., Thurs., and weekends 10–6; Sept.–May, Tues., Wed., Thurs., and weekends noon–5; Jan.–Feb., weekends noon–5.*

Back at the Legislature, head north on Osborne Street past the stately The Bay store (the legacy of the Hudson's Bay Company) to the **Winnipeg Art Gallery.** The gallery, which owns the world's largest collection of Inuit sculpture and art, also houses contemporary Canadian art and sculpture. *300 Memorial Blvd., tel. 204/786–6641. Admission free. Open Tues., Fri., and weekends 11–5; Wed., Thurs. 11–9; closed Mon.*

Turn east at the north end of the Winnipeg Art Gallery to Portage Avenue. The north side of Portage between Balmoral and Carlton streets is occupied by sprawling **Portage Place,** an indoor mall encompassing 120 stores (*see* Shopping, below).

Centennial Centre, **7**
Winnipeg Commodity Exchange, **5**
Dalnavert, **2**
Exchange District, **6**
Legislative Building, **1**
Portage Place, **4**
St. Boniface Cathedral, **8**
Winnipeg Art Gallery, **3**

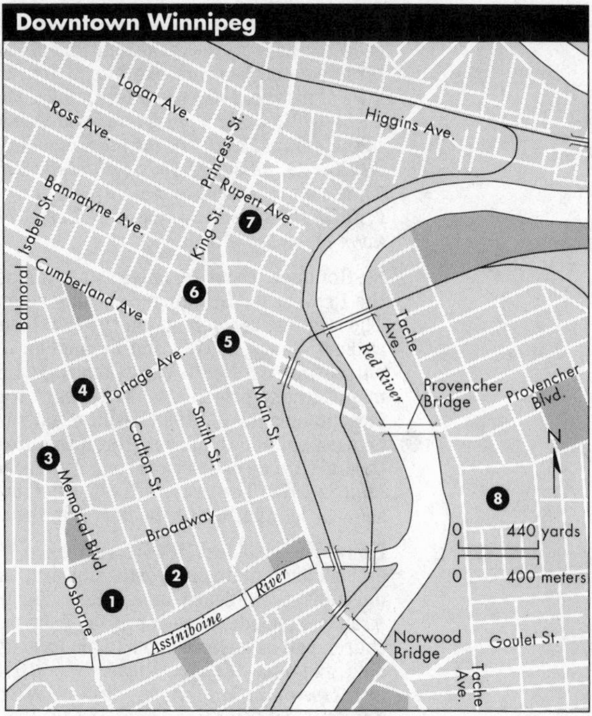

Time Out Winnipeg's oldest restaurant, the 1918 **Chocolate Shop** (268 Portage Ave., tel. 204/942–4855), serves generous sandwiches for lunch and more ambitious entrées at dinner time. Teacups and tarot cards are read from 1–9.

Continue east on Portage Avenue to Main Street, and what's reputed to be the windiest intersection in the world. Five floors **5** above the breeze, visit the **Winnipeg Commodity Exchange** and observe the controlled chaos of wild men (and a few women) involved in the buying and selling of grains, cooking oils, gold, and silver. *360 Main St., tel. 204/949–0495. Open weekdays 9:30–1:15.*

Below-ground is **Winnipeg Square,** an underground concourse with shops and fast-food stores. Emerge to street level on **6** the north side of Portage Avenue, and into the **Exchange District**—a concentration of renovated warehouses, banks, and insurance companies that were built during Winnipeg's turn-of-the-century boom period but now stand as a thriving nightlife spot. On Sunday, May–October, attention focuses on **Old Market Square Park** (King St. and Bannatyne Ave.), a new marketplace bursting with fresh produce, fish, crafts, and street performers.

7 Continue north on Main Street to Rupert Avenue and **Centennial Centre,** site of a concert hall, the **Manitoba Museum of Man and Nature,** and the dazzling **Manitoba Planetarium.** Exhibits at the museum focus on prehistoric Manitoba, local wildlife, the native peoples of the region, and the exploration of

Hudson Bay. Downstairs, the planetarium presents a variety of cosmic adventures in the multi-media **Star Theater,** and 60 interactive multisensory exhibits in Touch the Universe explain laws of nature. *190 Rupert Ave., tel. 204/943–3139 (museum), tel. 204/943–3142 (planetarium). Admission: museum $3, planetarium $3.50, "Touch the Universe" $2.50, all three $6.50 adults; $2, $2.50, $1.75, $4.50 students; $1.75, $1.75, $1.50, $3.50 senior citizens and children 4–12. Open mid-June–Sept. 2, daily 10–8; Sept. 2–mid-June Tues.–Thurs. 10–5, weekends noon–6, closed Mon.*

St. Boniface, about 1½ miles away, can be reached by crossing the Provencher Bridge and turning right onto Avenue Tache. The largest French community in western Canada was founded as Fort Rouge in 1783 and became an important fur-trading outpost for the North West Company. Upon the arrival of Roman Catholic priests, the settlement was renamed St. Boniface. Remnants of a 1908 basilica that survived a 1968 fire can
8 be seen outside the perimeter of the present **St. Boniface Cathedral** (Av. de la Cathedral and Av. Tache, tel. 204/233–7304), built in 1972. The grave of Louis Riel, the St. Boniface native son who led the Métis rebellion, is in the churchyard.

Housed in the oldest (1846) structure in Winnipeg and the largest oak log building in North America, the **St. Boniface Museum** tells the French and Métis side of Manitoba history. Artifacts include an altar crafted from papier-mâché, the first church bell in western Canada, and a host of innovative household gadgets. *494 Av. Tache, tel. 204/237–4500. Admission free. Open mid-May–Sept., daily 9–9; Sept.–mid-May, weekdays 9–5, weekends and holidays 10–5.*

Other Points of Interest

About 48 kilometers (30 miles) southeast of Winnipeg is the town of **Steinbach,** populated with nearly 10,000 pious and austere descendants of Mennonites who fled religious persecution in the Ukraine in 1874. Note the large number of automobile dealerships: Manitoban car buyers flock here because of the Mennonite reputation for making square deals.

In the **Mennonite Heritage Museum,** a 20-building complex, museum guides demonstrate blacksmithing, wheat grinding, and old-time housekeeping chores while conversing in the Mennonite Low German dialect. During the Pioneer Days festival in early August, everyone wears costumes and demonstrates homespun crafts. An authentic and extremely low priced restaurant serves Mennonite specialties, such as borscht, pirogies, and *ukrenky* (cheese or potato torte). *Hwy. 12, 2 km (1¼ mi) north of Steinbach, tel. 204/326–9661. Admission: $2 adults, $1 students and senior citizens, 75¢ children grades 1–6. Open May and Sept., Mon.–Sat. 10–5, Sun. noon–5; June–Aug., Mon.–Sat. 9–7, Sun. noon–7.*

Lower Fort Garry, built in 1830, is the oldest stone fort remaining from the Hudson's Bay Company fur-trading days. Nowadays, costumed employees describe daily tasks and recount thrilling journeys by York boat, the "boat that won the west." Beaver, raccoon, fox, and wolf pelts hang in the fur loft as a reminder of the bygone days. *Hwy. 9, 6.5 km (4 mi) south of Selkirk, tel. in Winnipeg, 204/983–6341; in Selkirk, 204/482–6483. Admission: $2.50 adults, $1 children 5–16. Grounds* *open year-round in daylight hours. Buildings open mid-May–Sept. 2, daily 9:30–6; Sept., weekends 9:30–6.*

Gimli, the largest Icelandic community outside the homeland, was once the center of the independent state of New Iceland. A giant Viking statue proclaims allegiance to the far-off island; the **Gimli Historical Museum,** on the Gimli harbor waterfront, preserves the ethnic heritage of early Ukrainian and Icelandic settlers and records the history of the Lake Winnipeg commercial fishing industry. *Hwy. 9, Gimli harbor area, tel. 204/642–5317. Admission: $1.25 adults, 75¢ children, $3 families, senior citizens free.*

National and Provincial Parks

Opening and closing times vary from park to park, although admission fees are generally uniform within the province. Unless otherwise noted, the daily rate is $3 per vehicle per day; $12 per vehicle per year.

Assiniboine Park, situated in Winnipeg along the river of the same name, encompasses 376 acres of cycling paths, picnic areas, playgrounds, a miniature railway, formal English and French gardens, a conservatory, and a cricket pitch. **Assiniboine Zoo,** also on the grounds, houses more than 1,200 species in reasonably natural settings. *Assiniboine Park and Zoo, tel. 204/888–3636. Admission free. Open year-round daily 10 AM–dusk.*

The Forks National Historic Site, at the junction of the Red and Assiniboine rivers, is where Winnipeg began 6,000 years ago. Today, the 56 acres host a playground, riverside promenade, small boat dock, and amphitheater. A marina, native center, all-season leisure center, and archaeological excavations are planned for the site. *At the confluence of the Red and Assiniboine rivers, tel. 204/983–2007.*

Grand Beach Provincial Park is on the eastern shore of Lake Winnipeg, the seventh-largest lake in North America. On summer weekends, crowds flock here from Winnipeg for the white powder sand, the grass-crowned 30-foot dunes, and a lagoon that makes birdwatchers' dreams come true. **Grand Marais** is the service area at the southern portal to the park. *Hwy. 12, 87 km (54 mi) northwest of Winnipeg, tel. 204/754–2212. Open May–Sept.*

Hecla Provincial Park, about a 2½-hour drive from Winnipeg, is a densely wooded archipelago named for the Icelandic volcano that drove the area's original settlers to Canada. The park is located on the central North American flyway, and 50,000 waterfowl summer here. **Moose Tower** is a good spot in the early morning and evening to view moose and other wildlife. The original 1880s Hecla Icelandic Fishing Village is restored near **Gull Harbour,** the tourist center of the park and site of the luxurious **Gull Harbour Resort** (tel. 204/475–2354), complete with a marina, hiking trails, and a devilishly difficult golf course. *Hecla Provincial Park. Hwy. 8, 175 km (109 mi) north of Winnipeg, tel. 204/378–2945. Open May–Sept.*

Spruce Woods Provincial Heritage Park encompasses, among rolling hills of spruce and basswood, the desertlike Spirit Sands, a 16-square-kilometer (10-square-mile) tract of cactus-filled sand dunes. Walk the self-guided trail through the dunes, but keep your eyes peeled for lizards and snakes! Your final destination will be **Devil's Punch Bowl,** a dramatic pit dug out by an underground stream. You can also tour the park in a horse-drawn covered wagon. *Hwy. 5, 180 km (114 mi) west of Winnipeg, tel. 204/827–2543. Open May–Sept.*

Whiteshell Provincial Park, a 1,620-square-kilometer (1,000 square-mile) tract on the edge of the Canadian Shield, encompasses 200 lakes that offer some of the best northern pike, perch, walleye, and lake trout fishing in western Canada. The **Falcon Lake** area has a shopping center, golf course, tennis courts, a very good beach, a sailing club, and top-grade accommodations in the 35-room **Falcon Lake Resort & Club** (tel. 204/349–8400). **Beaver Creek** trail is a short walk to wilderness denizens like beaver and deer. Farther on, **West Hawk Lake** (or Crater Lake)—formed a few thousand years ago by a falling meteor—is 365 feet deep and full of feisty smallmouth bass. Scuba divers love it. *Whiteshell Provincial Park. Hwy. 1E., 143 km (89 mi) from Winnipeg. Open daily 8 AM–11 PM.*

What to See and Do with Children

Assiniboine Park and Zoo (*see* National and Provincial Parks, above).

Fort Whyte Center for Environmental Education (1961 McCreary Rd., Winnipeg, tel. 204/895–7001) makes use of several cement quarries and the 200 acres of land around them to re-create the natural habitats of Manitoba's lakes and rivers. Self-guided nature trails and an interpretive center explain all.

Fun Mountain Water Slide Park (Rte. 1, east at Murdoch Rd., Winnipeg, tel. 204/255–3910), located about 13 kilometers (8 miles) east of downtown; it includes bumper boats, a mammoth hot tub, rides, and playground.

Manitoba Children's Museum (109 Pacific Ave., Winnipeg, tel. 204/957–0005), western Canada's first hands-on museum for children, shows them how to operate a grain elevator, put on a circus, understand their senses, and much more.

Manitoba Museum of Man and Nature/Planetarium (*see* Exploring Downtown Winnipeg, above).

Skinner's Wet N' Wild Waterslide Park (Hwy. 44, Lockport, tel. in Winnipeg, 204/477–0676; in Lockport, 204/757–2623) has four big slides, two kiddie slides, and many other damp attractions.

Regina

Originally named "Pile O'Bones," in reference to the remnants left by buffalo-hunting native tribes centuries ago, "Regina" was named after the Latin title of former Queen Victoria, the reigning monarch in 1882. It was at this time, when the railroad arrived, that the city became the capital of the North West Territories, and the Mounties made it their headquarters. When the province of Saskatchewan was formed in 1905, Regina was chosen as its capital. At the beginning of the 20th century, immigrants from the British Isles, Eastern Europe, and the Far East rushed in to claim parcels of the river-fed prairie land for $1 per lot. Oil and potash were discovered in the 1950s and

Saskatchewan

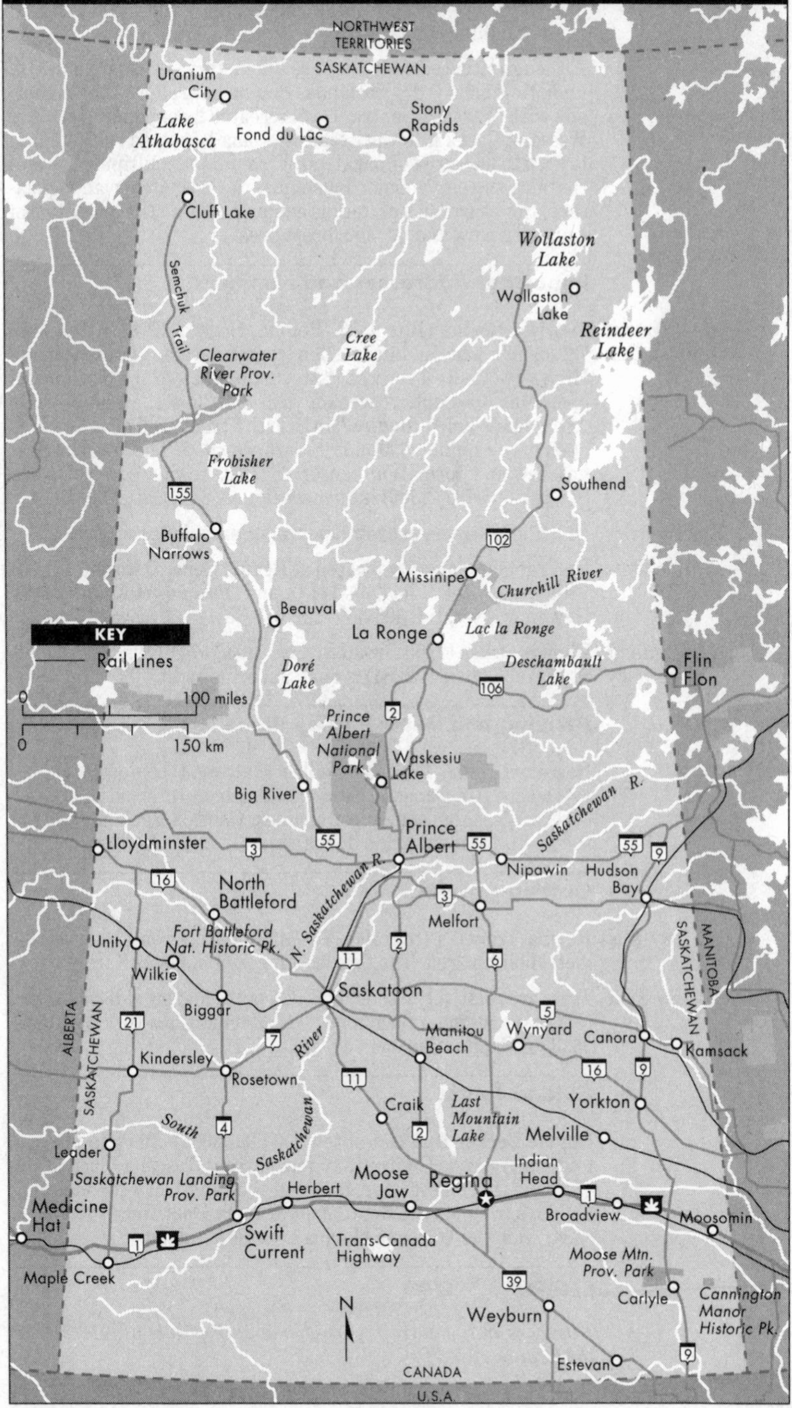
NORTHWEST TERRITORIES
SASKATCHEWAN
Uranium City
Lake Athabasca
Fond du Lac
Stony Rapids
Cliff Lake
Semchuk Trail
Wollaston Lake
Wollaston Lake
Reindeer Lake
Cree Lake
Clearwater River Prov. Park
Frobisher Lake
155
Buffalo Narrows
Southend
102
Missinipe
Churchill River
Beauval
La Ronge
Lac la Ronge
KEY
Rail Lines
Doré Lake
Deschambault Lake
Flin Flon
106
0
100 miles
0
150 km
Prince Albert National Park
2
Waskesiu Lake
Big River
Saskatchewan R.
Prince Albert
Lloydminster
3
55
55
55
9
Nipawin
Hudson Bay
N. Saskatchewan R.
16
North Battleford
3
Melfort
MANITOBA
SASKATCHEWAN
Fort Battleford Nat. Historic Pk.
Unity
Wilkie
2
11
6
Saskatoon
Biggar
5
ALBERTA
SASKATCHEWAN
21
7
River
Manitou Beach
Wynyard
Canora
Kamsack
Kindersley
Rosetown
16
9
11
Craik
Last Mountain Lake
Yorkton
South
Saskatchewan
4
2
Melville
Leader
Indian Head
Saskatchewan Landing Prov. Park
Herbert
Moose Jaw
Regina
1
Broadview
Medicine Hat
Moosomin
1
Swift Current
Trans-Canada Highway
Maple Creek
Moose Mtn. Prov. Park
39
Carlyle
Cannington Manor Historic Pk.
N
Weyburn
9
Estevan
CANADA
U.S.A.

1960s and Regina became a major agricultural and industrial distribution center, as well as the location of the world's largest grain-handling cooperative.

Although situated on 109 square kilometers (42 square miles) of undistinguished, dry flatlands, Regina has relieved the monotony with Wascana Centre. It was created by expanding meager Wascana Creek into the broad Wascana Lake and surrounding it with 2,300 acres of parkland. This unique multipurpose site contains the city's major museums, the Saskatchewan legislature, the University of Regina campus, plus all the amenities of a big-city park and bucolic forest preserve.

Important Addresses and Numbers

Tourist Information **Tourism Regina** (Box 3355, Regina, Sask. S4P 3H1, tel. 306/789–5099) has an information center on the Trans-Canada Highway (Route 1) on the eastern approach to the city, and is open May 15–Sept. 2, weekdays 8–8; 8:30–5 the rest of year. **"Streetcar Named Inquire,"** in Scarth Street Mall downtown, is open in the summer, Monday–Saturday 9–5. The **Tourism Saskatchewan** information center (Saskatchewan Dr. and Rose St., tel. 306/787–2300) is open weekdays 8–7, Saturday 10–4.

Emergencies Dial 911 for emergency **fire, police,** or **ambulance service.**

Hospitals Emergency rooms are located at **Regina General Hospital** (1140 14th Ave., tel. 306/359–4444) and **Pasqua Hospital** (4101 Dewdney Ave., tel. 306/359–2222).

Late-night Pharmacy **Pinders Drugs** (2160 Broad St., tel. 306/757–8100; 3992 Albert St. S, tel. 306/584–2284) is open until midnight.

Arriving and Departing by Plane

Regina Airport, located 5 miles southwest of downtown, is served by Air Canada, Canadian Airlines International, and several Canadian commuter airlines. Cabs charge about $6 for the 10- to 15-minute ride downtown.

Getting Around

By Bus **Regina Transit's** (tel. 306/777–7433) 19 bus routes serve the metropolitan area. The fare is $1 for adults, 60¢ children.

By Taxi Taxis are relatively expensive but easy to find outside major hotels or to summon by phone. Call **Regina Cabs** (tel. 306/453–3333) or **Capital Cab** (tel. 306/781–7777).

Guided Tours

Double Decker Bus Tours (tel. 306/522–3661) offers 45-minute tours of Wascana Centre that depart from Wascana Place (2900 Wascana Dr.) on the hour, between noon and 7 on weekends and holidays from May to September 2. **Ferry Boat Tours** (306/525–8494) from the Wascana Marina are also available.

Exploring Regina

Numbers in the margin correspond with points of interest on the Regina map.

Streets in Regina run north–south; avenues, east–west. The most important north–south artery is Albert Street (Rte. 6); Victoria Avenue is the main east–west thoroughfare. The Trans-Canada Highway (Route 1) bypasses the city to the south and east.

❶ Begin at the northwest corner of **Wascana Centre,** at the **Saskatchewan Museum of Natural History.** A time line traces local history from prehistory through the dinosaur era to today. Vivid dioramas depict the area's animal life in natural, sometimes violently realistic, settings. In June 1991 a new **Native Peoples Gallery** will highlight all aspects of native life with displays, tapes of Indian dances, holograms, and live performances. *College Ave. and Albert St., tel. 306/787–2815. Admission free. Open May–Sept. 2, daily 9–8:30; Sept. 3–Apr., daily 9–4:30.*

Continue south on Albert Avenue past **Speakers Corner,** where, similar to London's Hyde Park free speech is volubly expressed. Turn left on Legislative Drive, to the quasi-Ver-
❷ sailles–style **Legislative Building.** "The Ledge" was built in 1908–12, with local Tyndall stone on the exterior and an interior composed of 34 types of marble from all over the world. As you tour the Legislative Assembly Chamber, note the huge picture of Queen Elizabeth—a reminder that Canada retains a technical allegiance to the British Crown. *Legislature Dr., tel. 306/787–5357. Admission free. Open May 20–Sept. 2, daily 8–9; winter, daily 8–5. Free tours leave on the half-hour.*

Take Saskatchewan Road (west of the Legislature) south to the
❸ new location of the **Mackenzie Art Gallery,** which displays American and European works from the mid-19th century to the present. The popular Prairie Artists Series allows emerging Saskatchewan artists to display recent work. *3475 Albert St., tel. 306/522–4242. Admission free. Open Mon., Tues., Thurs., and weekends noon–6, Wed. noon–10; closed Mon.*

Continuing along Saskatchewan Drive, turn north on Avenue G
❹ and then east on Lakeshore Drive to the **Wascana Waterfowl Park Display Ponds,** a boardwalk constructed over a marsh and accompanied by display panels that help identify the more than 60 breeds of migrating waterfowl found here. *Lakeshore Dr., tel. 306/522–3661. Admission free. Open year-round daily 9–9; guided tours available (if there is a group) June–Sept. at 3.*

Return to Broad Street, cross the bridge to Wascana Drive, and
❺ head toward Winnipeg Street and the very new **Saskatchewan Science Centre,** now housed in the old SaskPower powerhouse. Hands-on exhibits encourage visitors to build bubbles, juggle hot-air balloons, make voice prints, and take apart human bodies; demonstrations of biological, geological, and astronomical phenomena take place on the hour. *Winnipeg St. and Wascana Dr., tel. 306/352–5811. Admission: $4 adults, $3 students, $2 senior citizens and children 3–13; $10 family pass. Open Tues., Wed., Sat. 10–5 (in summer, Thurs., Fri. 10–8, in winter, 10–5); Sun. and Mon. holidays 1–5; closed nonholiday Mon.*

Time Out **Invision** at the Science Center comprises an appropriately high-tech setting for old-fashioned sandwiches, tasty salads, pastries, beer, and wine. Museum admission is not necessary for access.

Government House, **6**
Legislative Building, **2**
Mackenzie Art Gallery, **3**
Royal Canadian Mounted Police Academy, **7**
Saskatchewan Museum of Natural History, **1**
Saskatchewan Science Centre, **5**
Wascana Waterfowl Park Display Ponds, **4**

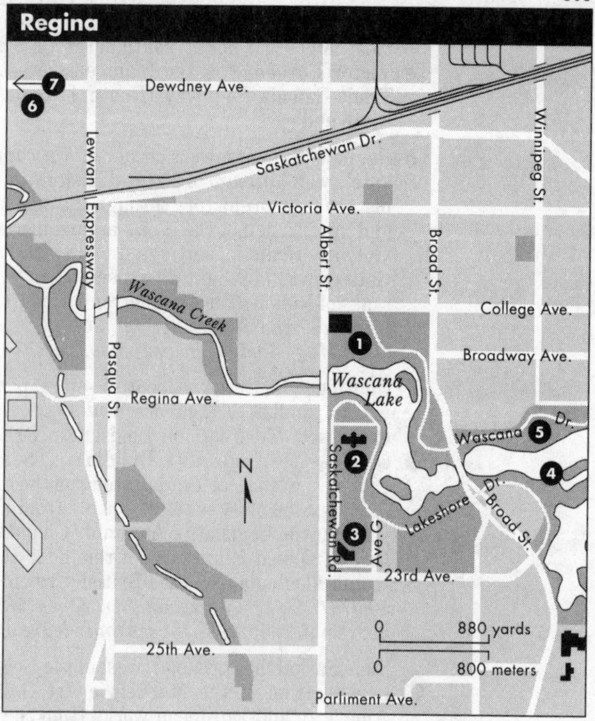

A car or bike will be necessary to continue the tour. Return to Broad Street and take it north to Dewdney Avenue, then head west to the **Government House.** Between 1891 and 1945 this was the lavish home of Saskatchewan's lieutenant governors. On Tuesday, Wednesday, and Friday nights in July and August, its old ballroom becomes the courtroom setting for "The Trial of Louis Riel." Riel, who led rebellions of the Métis against the new Canadian government in the 1870s and 1880s, was tried here (and ultimately hanged) for treason. *4607 Dewdney Ave., tel. 306/787-5726. Admission free. Open Sept.–June, Tues.–Sat. 1–4, Sun. 1–5; July–Aug., Tues.–Sun. 1–5.*

6

7 Continue west on Dewdney Avenue to the **Royal Canadian Mounted Police Academy,** the Mounties' only training center. Visitors can tour the grounds and nondenominational RCMP Chapel, a converted cookhouse originally built in 1883 and considered Regina's oldest building. Try to arrive about 12:45 weekdays for the stirring Sergeant Major's parade on Parade Square (in Drill Hall during winter and inclement weather). On the grounds is the **Centennial Museum,** featuring exhibits and mementos of the Mounties (originally the North West Mounted Police). The order's proud history is revealed by weaponry, uniforms, photos, and oddities, such as Sitting Bull's rifle case and tobacco pouch. A minitheater screens *Rose-Marie, Saskatchewan,* and other Mountie-theme flicks. *Dewdney Ave. W, tel. 306/780-5358. Admission free. Open June–Sept. 15, daily 8 AM–8:45 PM; Sept. 15–May, daily 8–4:45.*

Other Points of Interest

Cannington Manor Historic Park, just south of Moose Mountain Provincial Park (*see* National and Provincial Parks, below), preserves the 1880s lifestyles of this experimental aristocratic Victorian settlement. Abandoned after 15 years, what remains to be seen are the original manor house, church, shops, and a museum housed in the original schoolhouse. *Hwy. 603, 16 km (10 mi) northeast of Manor, tel. 306/787–9573. Admission fee. Open late-May–Sept. 2, daily 10–6.*

Moose Jaw, Saskatchewan's third-largest city (population 35,000), is a prosperous railroad and industrial center, renowned as a wide-open Roaring '20s haven for American gangsters. It is said that Al Capone visited here from Chicago, on the old Soo Line train. Today, Moose Jaw's most prominent citizen is Mac the Moose, an immense sculpture that greets travelers alongside the visitor information center (Rte. 1 east of Rte. 2, tel. 306/692–6414) on the Trans-Canada Highway.

A stop at the information center can direct you to other Moose Jaw attractions, including: the **Moose Jaw Wild Animal Park** (7th Ave. SW, tel. 306/691–0111), a log fortress that combines a zoo with an amusement park; the **Western Development Museum** (50 Diefenbaker Dr., tel. 306/693–6556), focusing on the air, land, water, and rail transportation; and **The Moose Jaw Art Museum** (Crescent Park, Athabasca St. and Langdon Crescent, tel. 306/692–3144), that features Indian art and small farm implements. While there, pick up *A Walking Tour of Downtown Moose Jaw* ($1.50), a guide to the city's notable and notorious landmarks.

National and Provincial Parks

Moose Mountain Provincial Park is 401 square kilometers (155 square miles) of rolling poplar and birch forest that forms a natural refuge for moose and elk and a wide variety of birds. A 24-kilometer (15-mile) gravel road accesses moose and elk grazing areas (best times: early morning and early evening). The park supplements wildlife experiences with beaches, golf, tennis, and riding horses. The Kenosee Inn (Kenosee Village, S0C 2S0, tel. 306/577–2099) is a 30-room accommodation on the park grounds. *Hwys. 9 and 209, tel. 306/577–2131. Admission: $5/day per car, senior-citizen drivers free. Open year-round.*

A 50-kilometer (31-mile) drive north on Highway 4, from Swift Current, will bring you to **Saskatchewan Landing Provincial Park** (tel. 306/375–2434). The 54-square-kilometer (21-square-mile) natural preserve is situated at the point where Indians and pioneers forded the South Saskatchewan River en route to northern Saskatchewan. The hills are full of Indian grave sites and tepee rings. Campsites, picnic facilities, and an interpretive center are on hand. *Hwy. 4, tel. 306/375–2434. Admission: $5/day per car, senior-citizen drivers free. Open year-round.*

What To See and Do with Children

RCMP Academy & Centennial Museum (*see* Exploring Regina, above).

Saskatchewan Museum of Natural History (*see* Exploring Regina, above).

Saskatchewan Science Centre (*see* Exploring Regina, above).

Tee Off Park (3310 Pasqua St., Regina, tel. 306/586–4585). This is a family-fun complex with year-round indoor miniature golf and, between June and September, a walk-through maze and kiddieland rides.

Saskatoon

Saskatchewan's largest city, Saskatoon (population 185,000) is nicknamed "City of Bridges" because seven spans cross the undeveloped riverfront that cuts the town in half diagonally. Saskatoon was founded in 1882 when a group of Ontario Methodists were granted 200,000 acres to form a temperance colony. Teetotalling Methodists controlled only half the land, however, and eventually the influence of the other "half" turned the town "wet." The coming of the railroad in 1890 made it the major regional transportation hub, but during the 20th century it became known for its three major resources: potash, oil, and wheat. One of Canada's fastest-growing cities, Saskatoon today is the high-tech hub of Saskatchewan's agricultural industry, and is also home to the University of Saskatchewan—a major presence in all aspects of local life.

Important Addresses and Numbers

Tourist Information The **Saskatoon Visitor & Convention Bureau** (310 Idylwyld Dr. N, Box 369, Saskatoon, Sask. S7K 3L3, tel. 306/242–1206) is open weekdays 8:30–4:30 year-round. In summer, information booths are set up at various points along the highway. **Tourism Saskatchewan** (122 3rd Ave. N, tel. 306/664–6240) is open weekdays 9–5:30.

Emergencies Dial 911 for **police, fire, ambulance, poison,** and **emergency** services.

Hospitals Emergency rooms include **City Hospital** (Queen St. and 6th Ave. N, tel. 306/242–6681) and **St. Paul's Hospital** (1702 20th St. W, tel. 306/382–3220).

Late-night Pharmacy **Pinders Drug** stores (2418 22nd St. W, tel. 306/382–5005; 602 Taylor St. E, at Broadway Ave., tel. 306/343–1608) are open until midnight.

Arriving and Departing by Plane

Saskatoon Airport, 7 kilometers (4½ miles) northwest of downtown, is served by Canadian Airlines International, Air Canada, and Canadian commuter carriers. Taxis to the downtown area cost about $8.

Getting Around

By Bus **Saskatoon Transit** (tel. 306/975–3100) buses offer convenient service to points around the city. The fare is 75¢ for adults and 40¢ for children.

By Taxi Taxis are plentiful, especially outside downtown hotels, but they are fairly expensive. For service call **United Cab** (tel. 306/652–2222) or **Saskatchewan Radio Cab** (tel. 306/242–1221).

Guided Tours

Heritage Tours (tel. 306/382–1911) offers guided bus tours of the city and outlying areas mid-May–August. **W.W. Northcote River Cruises** depart on the hour for 7-mile tours of the **South Saskatchewan River** (tel. 306/665–1818. Tours run May–Sept., weekends 1–4; June–Aug., daily 1–8).

Exploring Saskatoon

Numbers in the margin correspond with points of interest on the Saskatoon map.

Reasonably compact for a Western city, Saskatoon proper is easily accessible to drivers and cyclists. Idylwyld Drive divides the city into east and west; 22nd Street divides the city into north and south. The downtown area and the Spadina Crescent are located on the west side of the South Saskatchewan River.
1 Begin exploring at **Meewasin Valley Centre,** a small museum that traces Saskatoon history back to temperance-colony days. Meewasin is Cree for "beautiful valley" and this a fitting place to embark upon the **Meewasin Valley Trail,** a 15-kilometer (9-mile) biking and hiking trail along both banks of the beautiful South Saskatchewan River. *Meewasin Valley Centre, 402 3rd Ave. S, tel. 306/665–6888. Admission free. Open weekdays 9–5, weekends 10:30–6.*

Follow Spadina Crescent north along the river and past the
2 **Hotel Bessborough** (*see* Lodging, below), the most prominent old building in the Saskatoon skyline. A few blocks farther
3 north is the **Ukrainian Museum of Canada,** which celebrates—through photos, costumes, textiles, and of course the famous *pysanky* (Easter eggs)—the rich history of the Ukrainian peoples, who make up 10% of Saskatchewan's population. *910 Spadina Crescent E, tel. 306/244–3800. Admission: $1 adults, 50¢ children and senior citizens. Open mid-June–Aug., weekdays 10–4:30, Sat. 1–5, Sun. 1–8; Aug.–mid-June, 1–4:30, closed Sat. and Mon.*

From Spadina Crescent, head east over the river via the Uni-
4 versity Bridge to The **University of Saskatchewan,** which occupies a 2,550-acre site overlooking the river. Turn left into the campus at Bottomley Avenue and look for the **Place Riel Campus Centre** (Campus Dr., tel. 306/966–5788). Here, you can pick up a map that will help to orient you with the whereabouts of the **Biology Museum, Museum of Natural Sciences, Museum of Antiquities,** the **Observatory,** and the **Diefenbaker Centre** (tel. 306/966–3884), an art museum commemorating the Saskatchewan-bred (though Ontario-native) Canadian prime minister John G. Diefenbaker. Continue on Campus Drive to the **University Farm.** Note the 1909 stone barn, purported to be the most photographed building in Saskatchewan.

Exit the campus and head west on College Drive and then pick up University Drive, lined with grand old homes. University
5 Drive eventually becomes **Broadway Avenue,** the city's oldest business district and location of more than 150 shops, restaurants, and a cinema.

Broadway Avenue, **5**
Hotel Bessborough, **2**
Meewasin Valley Centre, **1**
Saskatoon Prairieland Exhibition Grounds, **7**
Ukranian Museum of Canada, **3**
University of Saskatchewan, **4**
Western Development Museum, **6**

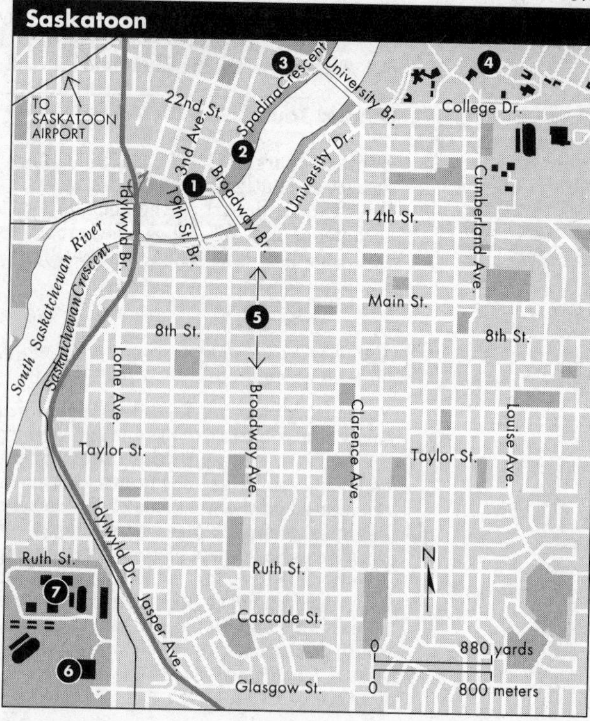

Time Out Unpretentious and entirely too small, **Calories** (721 Broadway Ave., tel. 306/665-7991) is a crowded but delicious place to stop for cheesecakes and pastries, ice cream, sandwiches, and superb coffee.

6 Take Broadway Avenue south to 8th Street; then head west to Lorne Avenue and south to the **Western Development Museum.** One of Saskatchewan's four such museums, the Saskatoon branch is called "1910 Boomtown" and re-creates early 20th-century life in the Canadian west. *2610 Lorne Ave. S, tel. 306/931–1910. Admission: $2.50 adults, $1.50 senior citizens, 75¢ preschool to 15. Open mid-May–mid-Sept., daily 9–9; winter, weekdays 9–5, weekends noon–5.*

7 The museum is part of the **Saskatoon Prairieland Exhibition Grounds** (tel. 206/931–7149), a vast plot that encompasses space for agricultural shows and rodeos, horse races, and Diefenbaker Park by the river.

To return to downtown Saskatoon, take the scenic route: Head north on Lorne Avenue, then east on Ruth Street to the river. Follow Henry Avenue, Taylor Street, and Saskatchewan Crescent past the fine old homes that overlook one of the prettier stretches of the South Saskatchewan River. Cross over the Idylwyld Bridge.

Other Points of Interest

Prince Albert, 141 kilometers (88 miles) north of Saskatoon, is Saskatchewan's fourth-largest city (population 34,000), the center of the lumber industry, and the self-proclaimed "Gateway to the North." It's a prosperous modern city straddling the North Saskatchewan River, and the most interesting attractions are downtown. Pick up a walking-tours pamphlet at the **Prince Albert Historical Museum,** housed in an old firehouse. *River St. and Central Ave., tel. 306/764–2992. Admission: $1.50 adults, $1 senior citizens and students, 50¢ children under 12. Open daily 10–6.*

The **Western Development Museum** in North Battleford, 138 kilometers (86 miles) northwest of Saskatoon, presents a re-created 1920s farming village, complete with homes, offices, churches, and a Mountie post. The museum also exhibits vintage farming tools, and provides demonstrations of agricultural skills used. *Hwys. 16 and 40, tel. 306/445–8033. Admission: $2.50 adults, $1.50 senior citizens, 75¢ children under 16. Open mid-April–Oct. and May 20–Sept. 2, daily 8–8; other times, daily 9–5.*

For a refreshing, revitalizing 24-kilometer (77-mile) getaway from Saskatoon, take Routes 16 and 365 southeast, to **Manitou Beach.** Fifty years ago the town of Manitou Beach was a world-famous spa nicknamed the "Carlsbad of Canada." The mineral water in Little Manitou Lake is said to be three-times saltier than the ocean and dense enough to make anyone float. Today, **Manitou Springs Mineral Spa** (open year-round) attracts vacationers, as well as sufferers of arthritis, rheumatism, and skin disorders, to the healing facility. *Hwy. 365, Manitou Beach, tel. 306/946–3949.*

National and Provincial Parks

Fort Battleford National Historic Park, established in 1876 by the North West Mounted Police, originated as a post to make the land safe for farming from local Indians and white fur traders. Costumed guides explain day-to-day life at the post, and an interpretive center displays weapons, vehicles, and souvenirs of the fur trade. *Central Ave., tel. 306/937–2621. Admission free. Open May–mid-Oct. and July–Aug., daily 10–6; other times, Mon.–Sat. 9–5, Sun. and holidays 10–6.*

Prince Albert National Park, 220 kilometers (137 miles) north of Saskatoon, encompasses nearly a million acres of wilderness and waterways and is divided into three landscapes: wide-open fescue grassland, rolling wooded parkland, and dense arboreal forest.

In addition to hiking trails, the park has three major campgrounds, with more than 500 sites, plus rustic campgrounds and primitive sites in the backcountry. Pick up maps and information at the visitor center in **Waskesiu Lake,** a townsite with restaurants, motels, and stores within the park.

The **Nature Centre,** located inside the visitor center, can help to orient you to plant and animal life of the area. Hiking along the marked trails, you have a good chance of spotting moose, deer, bear, elk, and red fox. Canoes, rowboats, and powerboats can be rented from Waskesiu Lake Marina. Lodging in Waskesiu Lake includes the Lakeview Hotel (Lakeview Dr., Box 26, S0J 2Y0, tel. 306/663–5311), a year-round accommodation. *Prince Albert National Park, off Hwy. 2, tel. 306/663–5322. Admission: $3/day per car; $6 for 4 days. Open year-round. Waskesiu*

Lake Visitor Center, Routes 263 and 264, tel. 306/663-5322. Open May-Sept., daily 8 AM-10 PM; Oct.-Apr. 1, weekdays 8-4:30.

What to See and Do with Children

Battlefords Superslide (King Hill, off Railway Ave., N. Battleford, tel. 306/445-0000) is a massive water park with 11 waterslides, pools, a hot tub, and game area.

Forestry Farm Park and Zoo (off Attridge Dr. in NE Saskatoon, tel. 306/975-3382) spotlights cold-weather denizens like deer, bear, and wolves. The park encompasses barbecue areas, nature displays, cross-country ski trails, and sports fields.

Kinsmen Park (Spadina Crescent and 25th St., Saskatoon, tel. 306/975-7529) is a riverside amusement park and a children's play village.

Western Development Museum (*see* Exploring Saskatoon, above).

Calgary

With the eastern face of the Rockies as its backdrop, Calgary's crisp concrete-and-steel skyline seems to rise from flat plains as if by sheer force of will. In fact, all the elements in the great saga of the Canadian West—Mounties, Indians, railroads, cowboys, oil—have converged to create a city with a brand-new face and a surprisingly traditional soul.

Calgary, Gaelic for "preserved pasture at the harbor," was founded in 1875 at the junction of the Bow and Elbow rivers as a North West Mounted Police post. The Canadian Pacific Railroad arrived in 1883, and ranchers established major spreads on the plains surrounding the town. Incorporated as a city in 1885, Calgary grew quickly, and by 1911 its population had reached 43,000.

Oil was first discovered in 1914, but it wasn't until the late 1960s that the industry exploded, with about 80% of Canada's oil companies and subsidiaries establishing headquarters here. Today, Calgary is a city of more than 647,000 (slightly larger than arch rival Edmonton), that combines Wild West geography with a mild West disposition. People are easygoing, slow-talking, and downright neighborly. Downtown is still evolving but Calgary ("Cal-gree" to locals) makes life nice by connecting most of the buildings with Plus 15, a network of enclosed walkways 15 feet above street level.

Important Addresses and Numbers

Tourist Information The main **Calgary Visitor Information Centre** (Burns Bldg., 237 8th Ave. SE, tel. 403/263-8510) is open daily 8 AM-9 PM in summer, varying hours the rest of the year. For information about other centers around Calgary, call the **Connect Info Line** (tel. 403/266-6328). **Travel Alberta** is located in McDougall Centre (455 6th St. SW, tel. 403/297-6574).

Emergencies Dial 911 for all emergencies; **police,** tel. 403/266-1234; **poison center,** tel. 403/270-1414.

Alberta

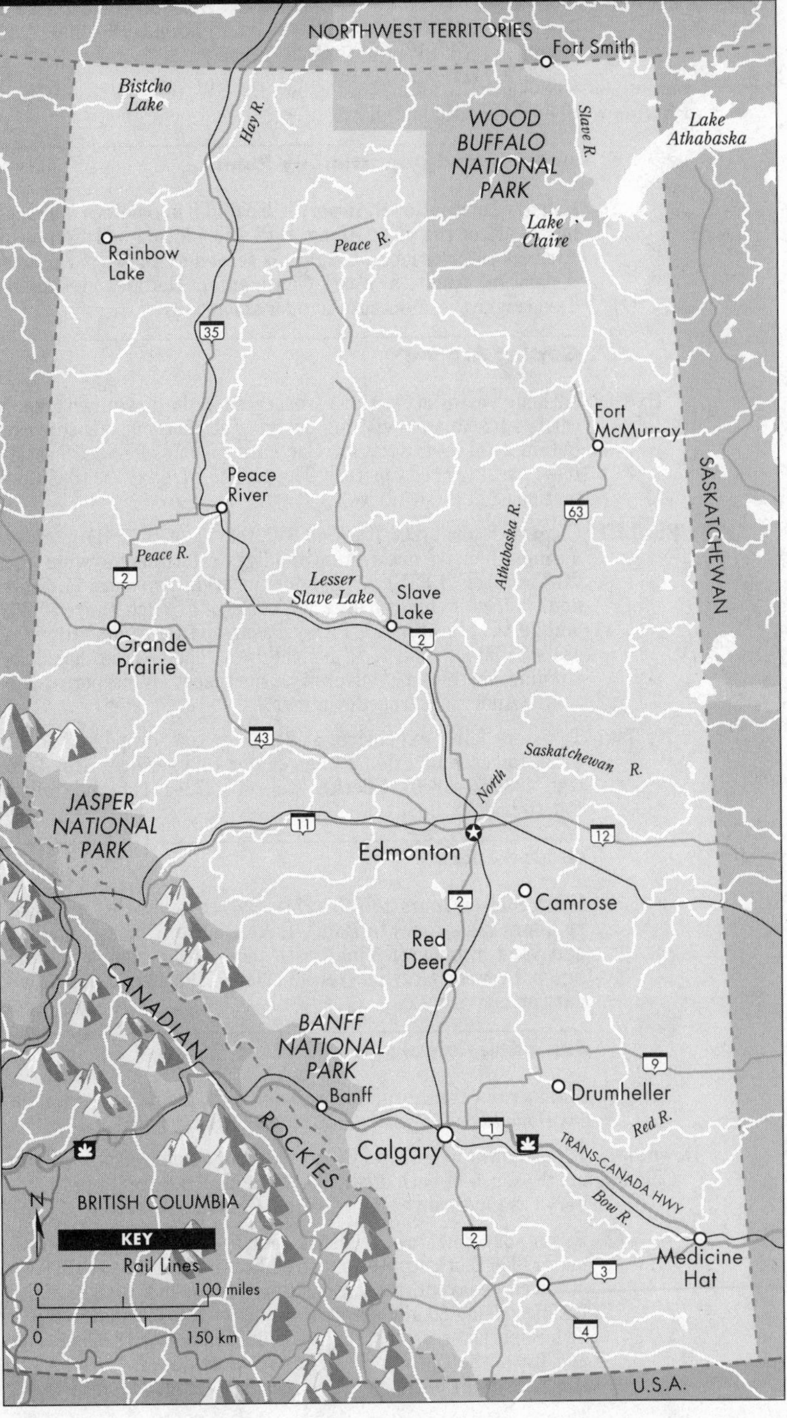

NORTHWEST TERRITORIES
Fort Smith
Bistcho Lake
Hay R.
WOOD BUFFALO NATIONAL PARK
Slave R.
Lake Athabaska
Lake Claire
Rainbow Lake
Peace R.
35
Fort McMurray
SASKATCHEWAN
Peace River
63
Athabaska R.
Peace R.
2
Lesser Slave Lake
Slave Lake
2
Grande Prairie
43
Saskatchewan R.
North
JASPER NATIONAL PARK
11
Edmonton
12
2
Camrose
Red Deer
CANADIAN ROCKIES
BANFF NATIONAL PARK
9
Drumheller
Banff
Red R.
1
Calgary
TRANS-CANADA HWY
Bow R.
BRITISH COLUMBIA
N
KEY
Rail Lines
0
100 miles
0
150 km
2
Medicine Hat
3
4
U.S.A.

Hospitals Emergency rooms are located at **General Hospital** (841 Centre Ave. E, tel. 403/268–9111), **Foothills Hospital** (1403 29th St. NW, tel. 403/270–1110), and **Alberta Children's Hospital** (1820 Richmond Rd. SW, tel. 403/229–7211).

Late-night Pharmacy The **Super Drug Mart** (504 Elbow Dr. SW, tel. 403/228–3338) is open daily until midnight.

Arriving and Departing by Plane

Calgary International Airport is located 8 kilometers (5 miles) northeast of the city. Along with Air Canada and Canadian Airlines International, Calgary is served by the U.S. carriers American, America West, Continental, Delta, and United. Taxis make the 30-minute trip for about $16.

Getting Around

By Car Although many attractions are located in the downtown area, a car is advisable for visiting outlying attractions. Visitors can obtain a three-day **Visitor Car Park** permit offering "hassle-free" parking at city meters. The permit is free at Visitor Information Centre (*see* above).

By Bus/LRT Calgary Transit (206 7th Ave. SW, tel. 403/276–7801) operates a comprehensive bus system and light rail transit system (the **"C-Train"** or **"LRT"**) throughout the area. Fares are $1.25 for adults; 75¢ for children over six; books of five tickets are $5.50, and 10 tickets $10. A CT Day Pass good for unlimited rides costs $3.50 for adults, $2 for children. The C-Train has lines running northwest (University), northeast (Whitehorn), and south (Anderson) from downtown.

By Taxi Taxis are fairly expensive, at $1.50 for the "drop" and about $1.20 for each additional mile. Major taxi services are: **Aero** (tel. 403/250–8800), **Checker** (tel. 403/272–1111), and **Yellow Cab** (tel. 403/250–8311).

Guided Tours

White Stetson Tours (tel. 403/274–2281) conducts City of Calgary Tours (plus tours to Banff, Lake Louise, Dinosaur Valley, and West Edmonton Mall) with pick-up by small vans and buses. **Brewster Grayline** (tel. 403/260–0719) offers tours of Calgary and environs.

Exploring Calgary

Numbers in the margin correspond with points of interest on the Downtown Calgary and Greater Calgary maps.

Downtown Calgary In the downtown Calgary grid pattern, numbered streets run north–south in both directions from Centre Street, and numbered avenues run east–west from Centre Avenue.

❶ Begin your downtown walking tour at **Calgary Tower,** a 190-meter (626-foot), scepter-shape edifice that affords great views of the city's layout, the surrounding plains, and the face of the Rockies rising 80 kilometers (50 miles) west. A flame on top is lit for special occasions; the revolving **Panorama Dining Room** and **Top of the Town Cocktail Lounge** provide refreshment. *9th Ave. SE and Centre St. S, tel. 403/266–7171. Admission: $3*

Calgary Tower, **1**
Calgary Centre for the Performing Arts, **3**
Devonian Gardens, **6**
Glenbow Museum, **2**
Municipal Building, **5**
Olympic Plaza, **4**
Stephen Avenue Mall, **7**

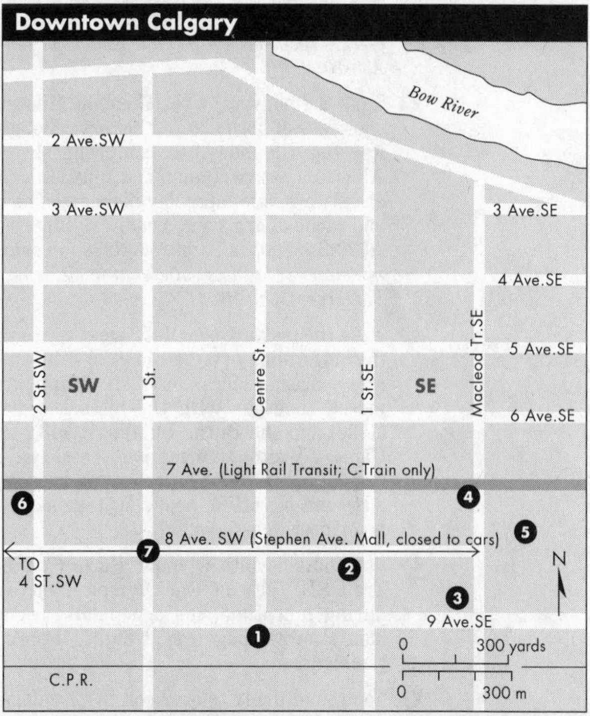

Alberta Science Centre Planetarium, **14**
Calgary Zoo, **10**
Canada Olympic Park, **15**
Canadian Forces Currie Barracks, **13**
Deane House, **9**
Fort Calgary, **8**
Heritage Park, **12**
Stampede Park, **11**

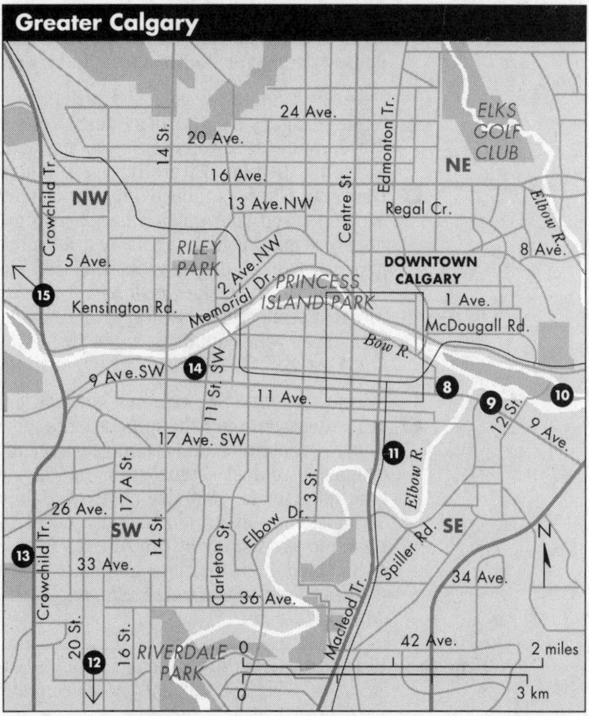

adults, $2 senior citizens, $2.25 children 13–17, $1.25 children 6–12. Open weekdays and Sat. 7:30 AM–11:30 PM, Sun. 7:30 AM–10:30 PM.

2 Take the pedway to the **Glenbow Museum,** Calgary's premier showcase of both art and history. Along with traveling exhibits, the Glenbow has comprehensive displays devoted to Alberta's native (Indian and Inuit) inhabitants, early European settlers, and later-day pioneers. The mineralogy collection and cache of arms and armor are superb. *130 9th Ave. SE, tel. 403/264–8300; tel. 403/237–8988 for exhibit information. Admission: $2 adults, 50¢ senior citizens. $1 children over 12; Sat. free. Open 10–6.*

3 Take the pedway over 1st Street SE to the **Calgary Centre for the Performing Arts** (tel. 403/294–7455), a complex of three theater spaces, a concert hall, and shopping area. The center was pieced together with the historic Calgary Public Building (1930) and the Burns Building (1913), which now houses the Calgary Visitor Information Centre (*see* Important Addresses and Numbers, above). Come at night for a performance (*see* The Arts and Nightlife, below) or take a one-hour walking tour at noon most weekdays.

4 Step outside into **Olympic Plaza** (7th Ave. SE and Macleod Trail SE), site of the Olympic medals presentation. Now, during lunchtime, it's a popular park space full of governmental brown-baggers; at night, there's a full slate of entertainment.

5 You're not likely to overlook the **Municipal Building** (8th Ave. SE and Macleod Trail), an angular mirror-walled structure that reflects city landmarks. One of the most stunning reflections is **City Hall,** a stately 1911 sandstone building that still houses the mayor's office and some city offices.

Seventh Avenue SE is closed to cars to make room for the C-Train, Calgary's light rail system. Hop on for a free ride (along 7th Avenue downtown only) to the center of the downtown shopping district. Literally, the top attraction of the area is
6 **Devonian Gardens,** above Toronto Dominion Square. The 2½-acre enclosed roof garden has 20,000 mostly tropical plants, nearly a mile of lush walkways, a sculpture court, and playground. Accessed by a glass-enclosed elevator just inside the 8th Avenue door, the Gardens has a reflecting pool that turns into a skating rink in winter and a small stage for musical performances year-round. *Between 2nd and 3rd Sts., and 7th and 8th Aves. SW. Admission free. Open daily 9–9.*

Seventh Avenue SE, between Macleod Trail and 4th Street SW
7 is a pedestrian-only shopping area called **Stephen Avenue Mall.** Shops, nightclubs, and restaurants occupy the ground floors of Calgary's oldest structures, mostly sandstone buildings erected after an 1886 fire destroyed almost everything older. To learn more about old Calgary, check out the historical photographs on display at the **Alberta Historical Resources Foundation** and pick up the pamphlet, *Stephen (8th) Ave. Mall walking tour. 102 8th Ave. SE, tel. 403/297–7320. Open weekdays 8:30–4:30.*

Time Out **17 Food Outlets** (304 Lancaster Bldg., Stephen Ave. Mall, 304 8th Ave. SW, tel. 403/266–2484) conglomerates purveyors of

Chinese, Indian, and Mexican dishes, pizzas, crepes, and quite a bit more. It's located on the second floor with seating overlooking the bustling mall.

Greater Calgary

You'll need a car to continue from here. Head on to **Fort Calgary,** at the confluence of the Bow and Elbow rivers, established in 1875 by the North West Mounted Police to subdue local whiskey traders who were raising havoc among the Indians. In the 40-acre park in the valley occupied by Fort Calgary, a line of stumps traces the outline of the original post, and an ultra-contemporary interpretive center traces the history of area Indians, Mounties, and white settlers. The **Deane House** (809 9th Ave. SE, tel. 403/269–7747), situated directly across the 9th Avenue Bridge, is the renovated 1906 post commander's house; it has free tours and a tearoom serving light meals. *Ft. Calgary Interpretive Centre, 750 9th Ave. SE, tel. 403/290–1875. Admission free. Open daily 9–5.*

Continue east on 9th Avenue, turn north on 12th Street, and cross the bridge to St. George's Island and the **Calgary Zoo,** with more than 1,400 animals, including 388 rare and endangered species, in plausibly natural settings. Polar bears and seals cavorting underwater are perennial crowd pleasers. The **Kinsmen's Children's Zoo,** part of the larger site, offers hands-on experiences with baby animals, and the adjacent Prehistoric Park displays dinosaur replicas in a bygone natural habitat. *1300 Zoo Rd. NE, tel. 403/262–8144. Admission: $5.50 adults, $3 senior citizens and youths 12–17, $2 children; $2.25 adults half-price and senior citizens free on Tues. Open 9 AM, closing times seasonally adjusted.*

Head south and west to Olympic Way and **Stampede Park** (17th Ave. and 2nd St. SE, tel. 403/261–0101), the focus each July of the world-famous Calgary Exhibition and Stampede (*see* Festivals and Seasonal Events in Chapter 1). Throughout the year the Roundup Centre, Big Four Building, and Agriculture Building host trade shows; the Olympic Saddledome has concerts and Calgary Flames hockey games; and the Grandstand is the site of Thoroughbred and harness racing (*see* Sports, below). Visitors can wander the grounds, take free one-hour tours of the **Saddledome** (tel. 403/261–0405), and visit the free **Grain Academy** in Roundup Centre, an interesting little museum that proudly proclaims itself "Canada's only grain interpretive centre." *Grain Academy in Stampede Park, tel. 403/263–4594. Admission free. Open weekdays 10–4, Sat. noon–4.*

Follow Macleod Trail past a strip of fast-food outlets, motels, and shopping centers and go west on Heritage Drive to **Heritage Park,** where more than 100 authentic structures from all over western Canada have been collected in a parklike setting beside Glenmore Reservoir. The "neighborhoods," inhabited by costumed staff, range from an 1850s fur-trading post to a 1910-era town. Steam trains, horse-drawn buses, and paddle-wheel steamers provide transportation, and North America's only antique amusement park re-creates bygone thrills. Theme snacks—sasparilla, beef jerky, fresh apple pie—abound. *1900 Heritage Dr. SW, tel. 403/255–1182. Admission: $5 adults, $4 senior citizens, $3.50 youth 12–17, $2.25 children 3–11. Open late-May–June, weekdays 10–4, week-*

ends 10–6; July–Sept. 2, daily, 10–6; Sept. 3–early Oct., weekends and holidays 10–5.

East along Glenmore Trail, turn north on Crowchild Trail to
13 reach the **Canadian Forces Currie Barracks** (4225 Crowchild Trail SW), site of two military museums in one building: **Lord Strathconas (Royal Canadian) Horse Museum** (tel. 403/242–6610) features an extensive collection of medals and weapons; **Princess Patricia's Canadian Light Infantry** (tel. 403/240–7901) displays memorabilia of a distinguished old regiment (founded in 1914) that fought in both world wars and joined with the United Nations peacekeeping forces. Note: Both museums are free, but you may need to show identification to enter the military base. *Bldg. B6, Currie Barracks, 4225 Crowchild Trail SW. Admission free. Horse Museum open weekdays 9–4, weekends 10–4; Infantry Museum open Tues.–Fri. and Sun. 10–4.*

Continuing north on Crowchild Trail, turn east on 9th Avenue
14 SW and then north again on 11th Street SW to the **Alberta Science Centre/Planetarium.** The Science Centre in the lower chamber has more than 35 hands-on exhibits of scientific marvels, such as holograms, frozen shadows, and laser beams; user-friendly demonstrations are given Friday–Sunday. Up in the planetarium, the 360-degree Star Chamber presents educational Star Shows with children's matinees on weekends, Laser Shows on Friday–Sunday nights. Imaginative combinations of special effects, magic tricks, and old-time show-biz make performances fascinating for all ages. *701 11th St. SW, tel. 403/221–3700. Admission: Science Centre, $2 adults and senior citizens, $1 children, free with Star Show ticket; Star Shows, $4 adults and senior citizens, $2 children; Laser Shows, $5. Open 1:30–9.*

Follow Crowchild Trail south to 16th Avenue NW (Rte. 1) and
15 then head west about 8 kilometers (5 miles) to **Canada Olympic Park,** site of the 1988 Winter Olympics and a year-round attraction. A one-hour bus tour goes over, under, around, and through the 70- and 90-meter ski jumps, bobsled, and luge tracks (in summer you have the option of walking down the slopes). In winter the slopes are open to the public (lessons available). Visitors can experience Olympic-size thrills on the one-minute Tourist Bobsleigh Ride ($100) and slightly briefer Tourist Luge Ride ($10); safety equipment is provided. Premises include a Calgary Visitor Information Centre, a day lodge with a cafeteria, and the **Olympic Hall of Fame,** a collection of Olympic memorabilia and video displays. The highlight here is the scarifying Ski Jump Experience where you strap on skis and make a simulated jump. *Trans-Canada Hwy. W (Rte. 1) at Bowfort Rd. NW, tel. 403/286–2632. Admission: Bus or self-guided tour, $6 adults, $3 senior citizens, students and children. Hall of Fame, $3 adults, $2 senior citizens, students and children. Tour and Hall of Fame, $8 adults, $4 senior citizens, students and children. Park open mid-June–Sept. 2, daily 7 AM–9 PM; Sept. 3–mid-June, daily 10–5; Hall of Fame open daily 8–8.*

What To See and Do with Children

Calaway Park (Rte. 1, 10 km, or 6 mi, west of Calgary, tel. 403/240–3822). The 20-ride amusement park supplements thrills with rock and children's shows, a petting farm, and 18 fast-food outlets.

Calgary Zoo (*see* Exploring Calgary, above).

Canada Olympic Park (*see* Exploring Calgary, above).

Heritage Park (*see* Exploring Calgary, above).

Off the Beaten Track

Museum of Movie Art. Far north of Hollywood, the mazelike museum claims to possess the world's largest collection (4,000) of movie posters. There are continuous video movies and a well-stocked poster shop. *#9, 3600 21st St. NE, tel. 403/250-7588. Admission $1. Open weekdays 9:30-5:30, Sat. 11-5.*

Edmonton

Lucky Edmonton is a recidivist boomtown that never seems to go bust. The first boom arrived in 1795 when the North West Company and Hudson's Bay Company both established fur-trading posts in the area. Boom II came in 1897 when Edmonton became principal outfitter on the overland "All Canadian Route" to the Yukon goldfields; as a result, Edmonton was named capital when the province of Alberta was formed in 1905. The latest and greatest of booms began on February 13, 1947, when oil was discovered in Leduc, 40 kilometers (25 miles) to the southwest. More than 10,000 wells were eventually drilled within 100 kilometers (62 miles) of the city and with them fields of refineries and supply depots. By 1965 Edmonton had solidified its role as the "Oil Capital of Canada."

More interesting is how wisely Edmonton has spread the wealth to create a beautiful and livable city. Shunning the uncontrolled development of some other oil boomtowns, Edmonton turned its great natural resource, the North Saskatchewan River Valley, into a 17-mile greenbelt of parks and recreational facilities. With a population of 576,000 in the city and 761,000 in the metro region, Edmonton is the largest northerly city in the Americas and the fourth-largest city in Canada. It is also Canada's largest city in land area—681 hectares (270 square miles). As the seat of the Alberta government and home to the University of Alberta, Edmonton's unusually sophisticated atmosphere has generated many fine restaurants and a thriving arts community. Its premier attraction, the West Edmonton Mall, is a year-round drawing card for shoppers and families, complete with facilities ranging from Fantasyland shopping center to a hotel, from a cinema complex to a water park.

Important Addresses and Numbers

Tourist Information The main office of the **Edmonton Convention and Tourism Authority Visitor Information Centre** (97th St. and Jasper Ave., tel. 403/988-5455 or 403/422-5505) is located downtown at the Edmonton Convention Centre. The office is open mid-May-September, daily 8:30-4:30; September-mid-May, weekdays 8:30-4:30. Other offices are open around Edmonton; for locations and times call the main office.

Emergencies Dial 911 for **police, fire, ambulance,** and **poison center.**

Hospitals Emergency rooms are located at the **Royal Alexandra Hospital** (10240 Kingsway Ave., tel. 403/477–4111) or **University of Alberta Hospitals** (8440 112th St., tel. 403/492–8822).

Dentists For 24-hour dental care, contact **Tridont Dental Service** (472 Southgate Shopping Centre, 111th St. and 51st Ave., tel. 403/434–9566 or 403/437–5716).

Late-night Pharmacy **Mid-Niter Drugs** (11408 Jasper Ave., tel. 403/482–1011) is open all night.

Arriving and Departing by Plane

Edmonton has two airports, though most international flights and long-haul domestic flights use **Edmonton International Airport.** Short-haul flights, mainly to neighboring provinces, use **Edmonton Municipal Airport,** just north of downtown. Along with the major Canadian airlines (Air Canada, Canada Airlines International, Wardair), Edmonton is served by American, America West, Delta, and Northwest.

Taxi rides from Edmonton International can be costly, but The Grey Goose Airporter (tel. 403/890–7234 or 403/463–7520) provides frequent service between the airport and major downtown hotels. Fare is $7 one-way, $12 round-trip. Grey Goose also provides service between Edmonton International and Edmonton Municipal Airport or West Edmonton Mall ($9 one-way/$15 round-trip).

Getting Around

By Bus/LRT Edmonton Transit (tel. 403/421–INFO) operates a comprehensive system of buses throughout the area and a light rail transit (**LRT**) line from downtown to the northeast side of the city. The fare is $1.25 for adults, 60¢ for senior citizens and children 6–16; transfers are free. Buses operate from 5:30 AM to 2 AM. The LRT is free in the downtown area (between Churchill and Grandin stations) weekdays 9–3 and Saturday 9–6. The **Downtown Information Centre** above Central LRT Station (100A St. and Jasper Ave.) provides free information, timetables, and maps, weekdays 9–5.

By Taxi Taxis tend to be costly: $1.90 for the first 125 meters (1/15 mile) and 10¢ for each additional 125 meters. Cabs may be hailed on the street but phoning is recommended. Call **Alberta Co-op Taxi** (tel. 403/425–8310), **Checker** (tel. 403/455–2211), **Wagon Taxi & Wheelchair Service** (tel. 403/438–4445), or **Yellow** (tel. 403/462–3456).

Guided Tours

From early May–early October three **Royal Tours** (403/424–8687) itineraries hit the high points of Edmonton. Day tours of the Alberta countryside are also offered. **Klondike Jet Boats** (tel. 403/451–4263) ply the North Saskatchewan River, May–October. **Landing Trail House** (tel. 403/931–3370 or 403/450–0267) offers customized horse-drawn carriage tours for $60 per hour.

Exploring Downtown Edmonton

Numbers in the margin correspond with points of interest on the Downtown Edmonton map.

The Edmonton street system is a straight grid with numbered streets running north–south and numbered avenues running east–west. Meeting at the center are 100th Street and 100th Avenue; Edmontonians often use the last digit or two as shorthand for the complete number: the Inn on 7th is on 107th Street; the 9th Street Bistro can be found on 109th Street. Edmonton's "Main Drag" is Jasper Avenue, which runs east–west through the center of downtown.

The city's striking physical feature, where most recreational facilities are located, is the broad green valley of the North Saskatchewan River, running diagonally northeast–southwest through the city center. The downtown area lies just north of the river, between 95th and 109th streets.

1 Start exploring downtown Edmonton from the top: at **Vista 33,** the 33rd floor of the **Alberta Government Telephone** (AGT) corporate headquarters. It's not the tallest building in town (that honor goes to ManuLife Place at 34 stories), but it's high enough for you to appreciate the South Saskatchewan River and to overlook 4,000 square kilometers (2,500 square miles) of (mostly flat) Alberta countryside. In addition to the view, Vista 33 includes the **AGT Man and Telecommunications Museum,** which traces the history of the telephone. *10020 100th St., tel. 403/493–3333. Admission: 50¢ adults and children, senior citizens and preschoolers free. Open daily 10–8.*

Walk north on 100th Street and turn right on Jasper beside the MacDonald Hotel, a grand old railroad hotel closed since 1983 but expected to reopen by mid-1991, after an extensive renova-
2 tion. Walk two blocks to the **Edmonton Convention Centre** (9797 Jasper Ave., tel. 403/421–9797), a most unconventional building filled with surprises. On street level the building houses the **Edmonton Tourism Visitor Information Centre** (*see* Important Addresses and Numbers, above), a repository of useful brochures and advice. It's all literally downhill from there, since the Centre has been built onto a slope with various terraced levels accessed by glass-enclosed escalators with great views of the North Saskatchewan River Valley. The Pedway Level houses **Canada's Aviation Hall of Fame,** with exhibits and artifacts from Canada's flying past. On Exhibition Level check out the **Canadian Country Music Hall of Honor,** actually a wall filled with plaques memorializing good old boys like Hank Snow, Wilf Carter, and Orval "The Canadian Plowboy" Prophet. *Hall of Fame, tel. 403/424–2458. Admission: $3 adults, $1 senior citizens, 50¢ students, children free, $7 families. Open Tues.–Thurs. 10–5, Fri. 10–8, weekends noon–5.*

Return to 99th Street and turn north to the **Civic Centre,** a six-block area that incorporates many of Edmonton's major institu-
3 tions; Civic Centre structures surround **Sir Winston Churchill Square.** The largest theater complex in Canada, the **Citadel Theatre** (*see* The Arts and Nightlife, below) houses five different theaters (plus workshops and classrooms) and an indoor garden with waterfall. Across 99th Street the **Edmonton Public Library** (7 Sir Winston Churchill Sq., tel. 403/423–2331)

Downtown Edmonton

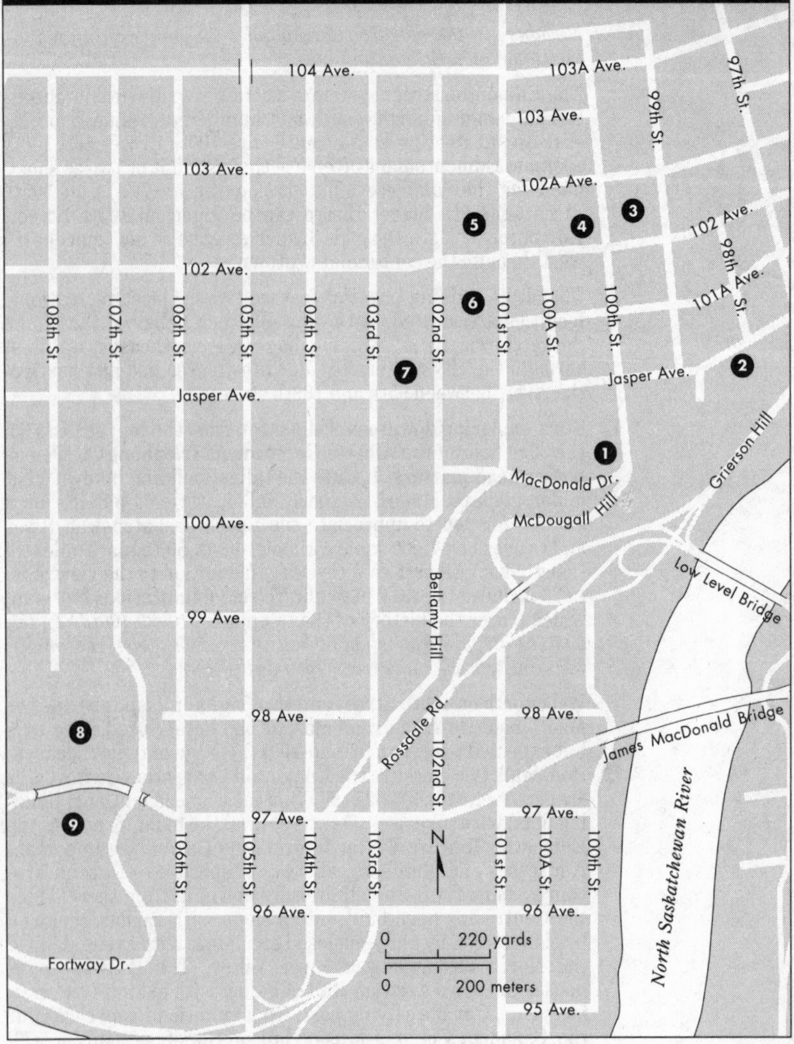

Alberta Government Centre, **8**
Alberta Legislature Building, **9**
The Bay, **7**
Eaton Centre, **5**
Edmonton Convention Centre, **2**
Edmonton Square, **4**
ManuLife Place, **6**
Sir Winston Churchill Square, **3**
Vista 33, **1**

augments books and art exhibits with a lively round of activities in the Children's Art Department.

As you cross 102nd Avenue, glance east at **Chinatown Gate,** a symbol of friendship between Edmonton and sister city Harbin, China; it spans the portal to Edmonton's meager Chinatown. In 1992 a **new City Hall** is scheduled for completion across the square from the **Edmonton Art Gallery,** site of more than 30 yearly exhibits of classical and contemporary art from Canada and the rest of the world. *2 Sir Winston Churchill Sq., tel. 403/422–6223. Admission: $2 adults, $1 senior citizens and youth, children free. Open Mon.–Wed. 10:30–5, Thur. and Fri. 10:30–8, weekends and holidays 11–5; free Thurs. after 4.*

Directly west of Churchill Square begins a maze of multi-level shopping malls, department stores, cinemas, and office buildings—all climatically controlled and interconnected by a network of tunnels and second-floor "pedways." Cross 100th
4 5 Street to enter **Edmonton Square;** head west to **Eaton Centre,** with a miniature golf course in the middle of the mall; south of
6 102nd Avenue are the shops of **ManuLife Place;** and on 102nd Street you'll find the domain of one of Canada's most powerful
7 institutions, **The Bay,** contemporary retail descendant of the Hudson's Bay Company (*see* Shopping, below).

Time Out For a change of scenery, exit briefly to **Boardwalk Market** (102nd Ave. and 103rd St., tel. 403/424–6297). The bright and airy renovated historic block encompasses an indoor-outdoor market with everything from Mongolian beef to steamed clams and pastries, all accompanied by a lively assemblage of street entertainers.

Emerging from The Bay on Jasper Avenue, enter the LRT station at 103rd or 104th Street for the ride to Grandin Station and
8 the seat of the Alberta government. The **Alberta Government Centre** (109th St. and 97th Ave.) encompasses several hectares of carefully manicured gardens and fountains highlighted by
9 the Government Greenhouse (tel. 403/427–7445). The **Alberta Legislature Building** is a stately 1912 Edwardian structure overlooking the river on the site of an early trading post. Frequent free tours of the building help to explain the intricacies of the Albertan and Canadian systems of government. *109th St. and 97th Ave., tel. 403/427–7362. Admission and tours free. Open May 20–Sept. 2, weekdays 9–8:30, weekends 9–4:30.*

Other Points of Interest

The **Muttart Conservatory** is one of the most important botanical facilities in North America. Separate greenhouses each contain flora of a different climate: arid, tropical, temperate. A show pavilion features special seasonal floral displays. *9626 96A St., tel. 403/428–5226. Admission: $3 adults, $1.75 senior citizens and youths, $1.25 children, $8.50 families. Open June–Aug., daily 11–9; Sept.–May, Sun. Wed. 11–9, Thur.–Sat. 11–6.*

The **Old Strathcona Historic Area** (the area surrounding 104th Street and 82nd Avenue) is a district of restored houses and shops built mainly when Strathcona Town amalgamated with Edmonton, in 1912. The low buildings and wide streets have a decidedly Old West air, and Old Strathcona is a good place to get out and wander. For a more determined exploration, pick up a walking tour map at the Old Strathcona Foundation. *8331 104th St., tel. 403/433–5866. Open weekdays 8:30–4:30.*

The **Provincial Museum of Alberta** hosts exhibits concerning paleontology, geological evolution, native crafts and life, and pioneer settlement. Displays of Canadian wildlife in near-natural settings are especially informative. *12845 102nd Ave., tel. 403/453–9100. Suggested donation: $2 adults, $5 families, senior citizens and children free. Open May 20–Sept. 2, daily 9–8; Sept. 3–May 19, Tues.–Sun. 9–5, Wed. 9–8, closed Mon.*

The **Edmonton Space Sciences Centre** explores the heavens with a stunning variety of high-tech techniques. Standing exhibits and a fascinating science shop are always of interest, but the star attractions include laser-light concerts and IMAX films of an appropriately celestial nature. *11211 142nd St., tel. 403/451–7722. Admission: exhibits free; IMAX or Star Theatre shows, $4 adults, $2 senior citizens and children under 14; Laser Show, $5 adults, $3 senior citizens and children; 2-theater package, $7 adults, $3.50 senior citizens and children. Open late June–Sept. 2, Sun.–Thurs. 10–10, Fri. and Sat. 10–10:30; Sept. 3–late June, Tues.–Sat. 10–10, Sun. noon–10, closed Mon.*

Fort Edmonton Park is home to an authentic re-creation of several periods in Edmonton history. There are a fur press and reenactments of shooting matches from the old Fort Edmonton days; blacksmith shops, saloons, and jails along 1885 Street; photo studios and a firehouse on 1905 Street; and relatively modern conveniences on 1920 Street. Horsewagon, streetcar, stagecoach, and pony rides are available; a farmers' market operates on summer Sundays. *Whitemud and Fox Drs., tel. 403/435–0755. Admission: $5 adults, $3.75 senior citizens and youth, $2.50 children 6–12, $15 families. Open mid-May–June, weekdays 9:30–4, weekends 10–6; July 1–Sept. 2, daily 10–6; Sept. 3–Thanksgiving (second Mon. in Oct.), Sun. and holidays 11–5; closed Thanksgiving–mid-May.*

West Edmonton Mall, acclaimed by the *Guinness Book of World Records* as the world's largest mall, is Edmonton's preeminent attraction. Its sheer magnitude and variety transform it from a mere shopping center to an indoor city with high-rent districts, blue-collar strips, and hidden byways waiting to be discovered. The credentials shout for themselves. There are 800 stores, including 11 major department stores, 19 movie theaters, and 110 places to eat, but the mall also contains: Fantasyland amusement park; an ice-skating rink; a replica of Columbus's ship the *Santa Maria;* an 18-hole miniature golf course; the Deep Sea Adventure submarine ride and dolphin show; the five-acre World Waterpark water amusement park; a luxury hotel (*see* Lodging, below); auto dealerships; a playhouse; a bingo parlor; a chapel; and much more. If you don't feel like walking the Mall, rent an electric scooter or hitch a ride on a rickshaw. *8770 170th St., tel. 403/444–5200. Attraction costs: Fantasyland, day pass—$15.95 adults, $6.75 seniors, $13.50 children 3–10, $39.95 families of up to 5, individual ride tickets 65¢ with rides costing 1–6 tickets. World Waterpark, day pass—$15.95 adults, $13.50 senior citizens and children 5–10, $39.95 families of up to 5. Deep Sea Adventure, $9.95 adults, senior citizens, children 3–10, $29.95 families. Open mid-June–Sept. 2,*

Mon.–Sat. 10–10, Sun. noon–8; Sept. 3–mid-June, Sun.–Thurs. noon–8, Fri. and Sat. 10–10.

What to See and Do with Children

Edmonton Space Sciences Centre (*see* Other Points of Interest, above).

Fort Edmonton Park (*see* Other Points of Interest, above).

Old Strathcona Model and Toy Museum (8603 104th St., tel. 403/433–4512) features playthings from the past.

Valley Zoo (134th St. and Buena Vista Rd., tel. 403/483–5511) is a small but imaginative zoo in riverside Laurier Park, that uses well-known storybook settings with exotic species.

William Hawrelak Park (off Groat Rd., just south of North Saskatchewan River, tel. 403/428–3559) invites children only—or adults in their company—to fish in this rainbow trout–stocked pond. Park includes paddleboats and adventure playground.

West Edmonton Mall (*see* Other Points of Interest, above).

Whitemud Drive Amusement Park (7411 51st Ave., tel. 403/465–1190) features go-carts, bumper-boats, miniature golf, and batting cages.

Wild Waters Waterslide Park (21415 103rd Ave., tel. 403/447–3900) offers lots of wet fun on the western edge of the city.

Shopping

Calgary
Malls and Shopping Districts

Calgary's premier shopping areas are located in the center of the downtown area. **Centre Four** consists of an interconnected network of department stores and malls, with 200 stores located along the 7th Avenue SW transit way between 1st and 5th streets SW. Directly to the south, the six-block stretch of 8th Avenue SW between 3rd Street SW and Macleod Trail SE has been turned into the traffic-free Stephen Avenue Mall.

Specialty Stores

Western Outfitters (128 8th Ave. SE, tel. 403/266–3656) and **Boot & Jean** (235 8th Ave. SE, tel. 403/264–4775 and Westbrook Mall, 1200 37th St. SW, tel. 403/240–0990) carries a full line of Western clothing. The **Alberta Boot Co.** factory outlet (614 10th Ave. SW, tel. 403/263–4623) specializes in footwear. **Cottage Craft Gifts** (6503 Elbow Drive SW, tel. 403/252–3797) has a large stock of authentic Indian and Inuit sculpture, carvings, and prints.

Edmonton
Malls and Shopping Districts

In the heart of **downtown,** between 100th and 103rd streets, is a complex of shopping centers (Eaton Centre, 120 stores; ManuLife Place, 65 stores; Edmonton Centre, 140 stores); and department stores (The Bay, Eaton's, Woodward's) connected by tunnels or second-level pedways. **West Edmonton Mall** (87th Ave. and 170th St.; *see* Other Points of Interest, above) has 800 retail establishments, including such department stores as Sears, The Bay, Eaton's, Woodward's, Zeller's, Ikea (furniture), and Canadian Tire. **Strathcona Square** (8150 105th St., tel. 403/424–6060) in the Old Strathcona Town (*see* Other Points of Interest, above) 1913-era post office has been converted into a cheerful market filled with restaurants, food stalls, and enticing boutiques. **High Street/124th Street** (along 124th and 125th streets between 102nd and 109th avenues) is an outdoor shopping area full of boutiques, bistros, bookstores, and galleries.

Regina
Malls

Cornwall Centre (11th Ave. and Saskatchewan Dr.), located downtown, is an indoor mall with more than 100 shops, including Eaton's and Sears. Indoor passages connect to the **Galleria** (11th Ave. and Saskatchewan Dr.), an indoor mall with more than 50 stores. Other major malls include **Northgate Mall** (Albert St. N and 9th Ave. N), with more than 80 stores, and **Southland Mall** (Albert St. S and Gordon Rd.), which also has more than 80 stores.

Art and Antiques

The **Strathdee Shoppes** (Dewdney Ave. and Cornwall St.) consists of arts, antiques, and specialty stores. The **Antique Mall** (1175 Rose St., tel. 306/525–9688) encompasses 28 antiques, art, and collectibles sellers. Also featuring arts and crafts are **Patchworks** (3026 13th Ave., tel. 306/522–0664), **Sarah's Corner** (1853 Hamilton St., tel. 565–2200), and **Saskatchewan Indian Arts & Crafts Corp.** (2431 8th Ave., tel. 306/522–5669).

Saskatoon
Malls and Shopping Districts

Midtown Plaza (22nd St. and 1st Ave., tel. 306/652–9366) and **Scotia Centre Mall** (123 2nd Ave., tel. 306/665–6120) are enclosed malls located downtown. The area around **Broadway Avenue,** between 8th and 12th streets east of the river, has 150 boutiques and services.

Specialty Stores

Trading Post Limited (226 2nd Ave. S, tel. 306/653–1769) carries an extensive and reasonably priced selection of Inuit and Indian crafts and Canadian foodstuffs—including Saskatoon berry products. Local crafts are also available at **Handmade House** (710 Broadway Ave., tel. 306/665–5542) and the **Homespun Craft Emporium** (212 3rd Ave. S, tel. 306/652–3585).

Winnipeg
Malls and Shopping Districts

Downtown shopping is dominated by **Portage Place** (Portage Ave. between Balmoral and Carlton Sts.) and **Eaton Place** (bounded by Graham Ave., Hargrave St., St. Mary Ave., Donald St.), two malls with numerous stores, fast-food joints, and movie theaters.

Across the Assiniboine River, the **Osborne Village** area (Osborne St. between River and Corydon Aves.) has 150 trendy boutiques and specialty shops, cafés, and crafts shops.

Art and Crafts

The **Crafts Guild of Manitoba** (183 Kennedy St., tel. 204/943–1190) features works by Manitoba carvers, weavers, and jewelers. **Northern Images** (Portage Pl., tel. 204/942–5501; Airport Executive Centre, 1780 Wellington Ave., tel. 204/788–4806) markets the work of the Inuit and Dene members of the NWT Co-operative, which owns the stores. For more Indian art, check out the **Great Canadian Indian Gallery** (75Albert St., tel. 204/942–1002) or **The Upstairs Gallery** (266 prints, drawings, wall hangings, and sculpture.

Sports

Participant Sports

Bicycling and Jogging
Calgary

Calgary has about 120 kilometers (75 miles) of bicycling and jogging paths, most of which wind along rivers and through city parks. Maps are available at **Visitor Information Centres** (*see* Important Addresses and Numbers in Calgary, above) and bike shops. Rent bikes at **The Bike Shop** (1321 1st St. SW, Calgary, tel. 403/264–0735) and **Sports Rent** (4424 16th Ave. NW, Calgary, tel. 403/292–0077).

Edmonton The North Saskatchewan River Valley is the longest stretch of urban parkland in Canada. For information about jogging and cycling trails call the **River Valley Outdoor Centre** (10125 97th Ave., Edmonton, tel. 403/428–3033).

Regina Wascana Place (2900 Wascana Dr., Regina, tel. 306/522–3661) provides maps of the many jogging, biking, and hiking trails in **Wascana Centre.** Rent bikes within Wascana Centre at the **Wascana Pool** (2211 College Ave., Regina, tel. 306/777–7921).

Saskatoon The **Meewasin Valley Trail** (tel. 306/665–6887) is a gorgeous 15.35-kilometer (9½-mile) biking and jogging trail along both banks of the South Saskatchewan River in Saskatoon.

Winnipeg Most public parks in Manitoba have marked biking and jogging paths. For routes, pick up maps from **Travel Manitoba** (*see* Important Addresses and Numbers in Essential Information, above). Bikes can be rented from **Ralf's Cycle & Sports** (1133 Henderson Hwy., Winnipeg, tel. 204/338–7278; 2071 Portage Ave., Winnipeg, tel. 204/885–4164).

Health and Fitness Clubs

Calgary Three **Leisure Centre** waterparks in Calgary have wave pools and waterslides, plus gymnasiums and training facilities; Southland and Family have racquetball and squash courts. *Village Square Leisure Centre, 2623 56st St. NE, tel. 403/280–9714; Family Leisure Centre, 11150 Bonaventure Dr. SE, tel. 403/278–7542; Southland Leisure Centre, 2000 Southland Dr. SW, tel. 403/251–3505. Rates and hours vary.*

Just south of downtown, the striking white-dome **Lindsay Park Sports Centre** (2225 Macleod Trail SW, Calgary, tel. 403/233–8619) encompasses a 50-meter natatorium, a 200-meter track, squash/racquetball courts, and weight room.

Edmonton The **Kinsmen Sports Centre** (9100 Walterdale Rd., Edmonton, tel. 403/428–5350) and **Mill Woods Recreation Centre** (7207 28th Ave., Edmonton, tel. 403/428–2888) have swimming pools and a variety of facilities for the entire family.

Regina The **Regina Sportplex** (1717 Elphinstone St., Regina, tel. 306/777–7156 for fieldhouse; tel. 306/777–7323 for aquatic center) encompasses a pool and diving well, 200-meter track, tennis and badminton courts, weight rooms, sauna, whirlpool, and drop-in aerobic and aquacize sessions.

Saskatoon The **Courtyard Racquet & Fitness Centre** (322 Saguenay Dr., Saskatoon, tel. 306/242–0010) has racquetball and squash courts, a weight room, aerobics classes, mini-golf, and beach volleyball in summer. The **Saskatoon Field House** (University of Alberta, 2020 College Dr., Saskatoon, tel. 306/975–3354) has tennis courts, weight room, gymnastics area, indoor track, fitness dance area, and drop-in fitness classes.

Winnipeg Drop-in rates and a full slate of classes and equipment are available at **Body Options** (1604 St. Mary's Rd., Winnipeg, tel. 204/255–6600) and **Bodyworks** (2 Donald St., Winnipeg, tel. 204/477–1691).

Spectator Sports

Baseball *Calgary* The **Calgary Cannons,** the Seattle Mariners' AAA Pacific Coast League affiliate, play April–August at **Foothills Stadium** (Crowchild Trail and 16th Ave. NW, Calgary, tel. 403/284-1111). Tickets for baseball and other team sports can be purchased from BASS outlets (tel. 403/270-6700).

Edmonton The **Edmonton Trappers** play AAA Pacific Coast League baseball April–August at **John Ducey Park** (10233 96th Ave., Edmonton, tel. 403/429-2934).

Curling *Regina* Check out this incredibly popular local sport at the **Curlodrome** (Exhibition Park, Lewvan Expwy. and 11th Ave., Regina, tel. 306/352-9809).

Football *Calgary* The **Calgary Stampeders** of the Canadian Football League play in **McMahon Stadium** (Crowchild Trail and 16th Ave. NW, Calgary, tel. 403/289-0258) June–October.

Edmonton The **Edmonton Eskimos** play Canadian Football League games June–October at the **Commonwealth Stadium** (11000 Stadium Rd., Edmonton, tel. 403/429-2881).

Regina The **Saskatchewan Roughriders** play a Canadian Football League schedule June–October at **Taylor Field** (2940 10th Ave., Regina, tel. 306/525-2181).

Winnipeg The Canadian Football League's **Winnipeg Blue Bombers** play June–October at **Winnipeg Stadium** (1465 Maroons Rd., Winnipeg, tel. 204/775-9751).

Hockey *Calgary* The **Calgary Flames** play National Hockey League matches October–April at the **Olympic Saddledome** (17th Ave. and 2nd St. SE, Calgary, tel. 403/261-0475) in Stampede Park.

Edmonton The **Edmonton Oilers** play National Hockey League hockey October–April at the **Northlands Coliseum** (118th Ave. & 74th St., Edmonton, tel. 403/471-2191).

Regina The **Regina Pats** play other World Hockey League (minor league) teams in the **Agridome** (Exhibition Park, Lewvan Expwy. and 11th Ave., Regina, tel. 306/781-9300).

Saskatoon The **Saskatoon Blades** play Western Hockey League (minor league) matches at **Saskatchewan Place** (3315 Thatcher Ave., Saskatoon, tel. 306/975-7800).

Winnipeg The **Winnipeg Jets** confront National Hockey League opposition between October and April at the **Winnipeg Arena** (1430 Maroons Rd., Winnipeg, tel. 204/772-9491).

Horse Racing *Calgary* There's racing year-round (except March) in **Stampede Park** (17th Ave. and 2nd St. SE, Calgary, tel. 403/261-0120); Thoroughbreds race April–May and September–November; trotters May–September and December–February.

Edmonton **Northlands Park** (112th Ave. and 74th St., Edmonton, tel. 403/471-7378) hosts harness racing from early March to mid-May and from mid-September through November. Thoroughbred racing occupies the summer months, mid-May through early September.

Regina **Queensbury Downs Raceway** (Exhibition Park, Lewvan Expwy. and 11th Ave., Regina, tel. 306/781-9310) hosts Thoroughbred or Standardbred racing year-round.

Saskatoon **Marquis Downs Racetrack** (Prairieland Exhibition Centre, enter on Ruth St., Saskatoon, tel. 306/242-6100) has Thoroughbred and harness racing early May–mid-October.

Winnipeg **Assiniboia Downs** (3975 Portage Ave. at Perimeter Hwy. W, Winnipeg, tel. 204/885-3330) hosts Thoroughbred racing May–November; trotters November–April.

Soccer
Calgary The **Calgary Strikers** of the Canadian Soccer League play a May–September schedule at **Mewata Stadium** (9th Ave. and 11th St. SW, Calgary, tel. 403/249-7566).

Edmonton The **Edmonton Brick Men** play Professional Canadian Soccer League matches June–September at **Clarke Stadium** (91st St. & Stadium Rd., Edmonton, tel. 403/429-2934).

Dining and Lodging

Dining

While places specializing in generous helpings of Canadian beef still dominate the scene, restaurants throughout the prairie provinces now tastily reflect the regions' ethnic make-up and offer a wide variety of cuisine to fit every price range.

Highly recommended restaurants in each price category are indicated by a star ★.

Category	Cost*
Very Expensive	over $25
Expensive	$20–$25
Moderate	$15–$19
Inexpensive	under $15

**three-course dinner, per person, excluding drinks, service, and 7% sales tax*

Lodging

Highly recommended lodgings in each price category are indicated by a star ★.

Category	Cost*
Very Expensive	over $150
Expensive	$75–$150
Moderate	$50–$74
Inexpensive	under $50

**All prices are for a standard double room, excluding 5%–7% service charge.*

Calgary

Dining
Very Expensive **Hy's Steak House.** This is where Calgary (and Edmonton, Winnipeg, Toronto, and elsewhere in Canada) goes for immense portions of charcoal-broiled steaks, fresh seafood, chicken, and

a huge selection of wines. Wood paneling and earthy decor are evidence of the sedate Victorian ambience. *316 4th Ave. SW, tel. 403/263-2222. Reservations advised. Jacket advised. AE, CB, DC, MC, V. Closed Sun.*

★ **Owl's Nest.** Plush armchairs and dark-wood booths express the subdued confidence of a restaurant long proclaimed the best in town. Standards are maintained, and all dishes are served with impeccable Continental flair. Alberta beef entrées are still ample and tender; British Columbia salmon is memorably fresh; the wine list is still exhaustive. *Westin Hotel, 320 4th Ave. SW, tel. 403/266-1611. Reservations advised. Jacket advised. AE, CB, DC, MC, V.*

Expensive

Green Street Café. This lively and unpretentious spot serves French-Italian-Cajun specialties in a three-level setting that's loaded with greenery inside and out. Menu highlights include veal medallions Danny Kaye and a pan-fried oyster dish with pecan pie for dessert. Come to the café for Sunday brunch, too. Upstairs bar features live jazz. *815 7th Ave. SW, tel. 403/266-1551. Reservations advised. Jacket advised. AE, MC, V. Closed Sat. lunch, Sun.*

Mama's. Just what you'd expect from a place called "Mama's": cheery red-and-white-check tablecloths; warm, friendly service; and large portions of tasty Italian food. The antipasto buffet—marinated eggplant, scallops, shrimp, squid, quail eggs, plus much more—is excellent. Veal dishes are the best entrée choices, and the wine list emphasizes Italian. *320 16th Ave. NW, tel. 403/276-9744. Reservations required. Jacket advised. AE, MC, V. Closed Sun.*

Moderate

Santorini Greek Taverna. This restaurant has an open patio that chimes with music and chatter. The northside spot transplants the Mediterranean to the northern plains. Stick with classic Greek specialties, such as moussaka, calamari, *taramasalata* (roe), dolmades (stuffed grape leaves), and *soutzoukakia* (beef sausage). Or order *mezethes*, and get a taste of a lot of things. *1502 Centre St. N, tel. 403/276-8363. No reservations. Dress: casual. AE, CB, DC, MC, V.*

Inexpensive

★ **Buzzards Wine Bar.** This lively European-style downtown café serves 70 wines by the bottle or glass and the exclusive home brew, Buzzard Breath Ale. Wine-theme prints and posters adorning the walls remind you of the tour original attraction to this place. However, fine food selections include various species of eight-ounce Alberta beef Buzzard Burgers, pub grub, and low-priced entrées, such as teriyaki chicken and fettucine Alfredo. In summer, dine out on the patio. *140 10th Ave. SW, tel. 403/264-6959. No reservations. Dress: casual. AE, CB, DC, MC, V.*

Silver Dragon. A Chinatown institution for more than 20 years, the huge L-shape dining room is mellowed out by soft carpeting and delicate Chinese paintings. The menu includes standard beef, pork, and poultry dishes but shines on concoctions of rock cod, crab, abalone, cuttlefish, and other seafood. Dim sum lunch is featured daily. *106 3rd Ave. SE, tel. 403/264-5326. No reservations. Dress: casual. AE, CB, DC, MC, V.*

Lodging

Very Expensive

Delta Bow Valley. The bright new 24-story high rise occupies a relatively quiet street on the southern edge of downtown. The pinkish lobby is sunny and full of lush foliage. Decent-size contemporary rooms, with rose-and-green furnishings, have good views on upper floors. For the brightest and most colorful units, request a room with a northern exposure. *209 4th Ave. SE, T2G 0C6, tel. 403/266–1980 or 800/268–1133. 400 rooms. Facilities: 2 restaurants, 2 lounges, indoor pool, saunas, exercise room, nonsmoking floors. AE, CB, DC, MC, V.*

Skyline Calgary. This is a business-class hotel with an incredibly convenient location in the heart of downtown. The warm, inviting lobby works well with the clean pastel-and-maroon-toned rooms. Surrounded by and connected to the convention center, Glenbow Museum, the Calgary Centre for Performing Arts, and the VIA train station, the hotel appeals to executive and leisure travelers. *110 9th Ave., T2G 5A6, tel. 403/266–7331 or 800/648–7200. 387 rooms. Facilities: 2 restaurants, 2 lounges, indoor pool, sauna, fitness club, racquetball arrangements at nearby club, nonsmoking floors. AE, CB, DC, MC, V.*

★ **Westin Hotel.** The luxury high rise in the midst of downtown connects to most other important structures via Calgary's Plus 15 pedway system. Renovated in 1987, the rooms—especially those in the Tower Section—are large and furnished with tasteful contemporary furniture, and are dominated by pastel peach tones and neutrals. Rooftop pool, poolside buffet, and sauna offers great city views and light breakfasts. Owl's Nest (*see* Dining, above) is among the best in town and Lobby Court features Fitness Buffet breakfasts. *320 4th Ave. SW, T2P 2S6, tel. 403/266–1611 or 800/228–3000. 525 rooms, including nonsmoking rooms. Facilities: 2 restaurants, 2 lounges, indoor pool, fitness club, sauna. AE, DC, MC, V.*

Expensive **Palliser.** The downtown area of every Canadian city has a grand old railroad hotel, and the Canadian Pacific Palliser (opened 1914) is Calgary's. The enormous lobby is paneled in dark wood and festooned with twinkling chandeliers. Guest rooms may have quirky shapes but all are newly renovated with classic furnishings, ornate moldings, and high ceilings. *133 9th Ave. SW, T2P 2M3, tel. 403/262–1234 or 800/828–7447. 404 rooms. Facilities: restaurant, bar, exercise room, nonsmoking floor. AE, CB, DC, MC, V.*

Moderate **Carriage House.** Located about 9.7 kilometers (6 miles) south of City Centre, this unique locally owned property has a lobby with fish tanks, caged songbirds, and a waterfall. Room decor is comfortably mismatched. Nighttime entertainment options include a disco/rock club, country-and-western saloon, and English pub. Guests get discounts at nearby Family Leisure Centre (*see* Sports and Fitness, above). *9030 Macleod Trail S, T2H 0M4, tel. in U.S. call collect, 403/253–1101; or 800/661–9566. 175 rooms, including nonsmoking rooms. Facilities: 3 restaurants, 3 bars, outdoor pool, sauna. AE, CB, DC, MC, V.*

★ **Prince Royal Inn.** This 28-story high rise has quite a lot going for it: downtown location, all-suite (studios, one- and two-bedrooms) accommodations with fully-equipped kitchens, free parking, free Continental breakfast, and health club. Large rooms with kitchens make it a great deal for families. *618 5th Ave. SW, T2P 0M7, tel. 403/263–0520 or in Canada, 800/661–1592. 300 suites. Facilities: restaurant, bar, health club with sauna, exercise equipment, convenience store, florist, dry cleaner, nonsmoking floors. AE, CB, DC, MC, V.*

Quality Inn Airport. This convenient and comfortable property is located on the northeast side of town a few minutes from Calgary International Airport. Bright rooms are large, have standard furnishings, and are tastefully decorated with a rose-

and-mauve scheme. *1250 McKinnon Dr. NE, T2E 7T7, tel. 403/230–1999 or 800/228–5151. 168 rooms, including nonsmoking rooms. Facilities: restaurant, bar, indoor pool, sauna, sun deck. AE, CB, DC, MC, V.*

Inexpensive **Relax Inns.** Like most units of Canada's first economy chain, the two Calgary properties have clean efficient rooms, indoor pools, family-style restaurants, and suburban locations. The design exudes taste and warmth; blues and maroons enhance the appeal of the modern furnishings. *Calgary Airport: 2750 Sunridge Blvd. NE, T1Y 3C2, tel. 403/291–1260 or 800/661–9563. 203 rooms; nonsmoking rooms available. Facilities: restaurant, indoor pool, games room. AE, CB, DC, MC, V. Calgary South: 9206 Macleod Trail S, T2J 0P5, tel. 403/253–7070 or 800/661–9563. 260 rooms. Facilities: restaurant, indoor pool, games arcade. AE, CB, DC, MC, V.*

Royal Wayne. A vaguely Tudor two-story structure in the Motel Village triangle on the northwest side, this accomodation features large, albeit somewhat garish, rooms. Local phone calls are free, and Andy's Spur Lounge is an attractively Western-type spot for drinks. Some kitchenette units are available for families. *2416 16th Ave., T2M 0M5, tel. 403/289–6651. 52 rooms. Facilities: restaurant, bar, outdoor pool. AE, CB, DC, MC, V.*

Edmonton

Dining
Very Expensive **La Boheme.** On the historic east side Gibbard Block, this restaurant is fittingly splendid. The cuisine is classic French, prepared with invention and served with solicitous care. The setting features Edwardian pressed-tin ceilings and a French provincial fireplace surrounded by Voltaire chairs. Specialties include lamb sausages, pâté maison, and daily concoctions of fresh fish. *6427 112th Ave., tel. 403/474–4693. Reservations advised. Jacket advised. AE, MC, V.*

★ **Unheardof Dining Lounge.** Hardly "unheard of" any longer, this is an extremely popular restaurant in an antiques-filled old house. The seven-course prix-fixe dinner changes weekly but is likely to feature game in autumn, poultry or beef the rest of the year. Dinners begin with a light pâté and are punctuated by surprising salads and refreshing sorbets. Desserts, especially the Danish cream-cheese cheesecake, are light and delicious. *9602 82nd Ave., tel. 403/432–0480. Reservations required, often far in advance. Jacket advised. AE, MC, V. Closed lunch Tues.–Sat.*

Walden's. Dine romantically outside in the sunny garden or within the raw cedar confines of the cozy dining room. The Continental menu spotlights flavorful Alberta beef—try it raw with seed mustard and black pepper—and fresh fish flown in daily from British Columbia. Other good bets include Alberta rabbit, lamb with mustard and garlic, and marinated salmon. The wine list features California; desserts are so-so. *10245 104th St., tel. 403/420–6363. Reservations advised for dinner. Jacket advised. AE, MC, V.*

Expensive **Bistro Praha.** The decor of table lamps and paintings of Praha (Prague) street scenes make this European-style café feel as homey as Grandma's living room. Background music is classical, clientele mainly urban young professional. The menu features Eastern European favorites like cabbage soup, Wiener schnitzel, and *natur schnitzel* (no breading). Rich selection of desserts and a choice from 12 brands of tea make it perfect for snacks. *10168 100A St. at Jasper Ave., tel. 403/424–4218. No reservations. Dress: casual. AE, CB, DC, MC, V.*

La Spiga. Admirable Northern Italian cuisine is served in a flower-filled 1913 home that feels more like Montréal than the western plains. Menu highlights include rack of lamb with grappa, breast of chicken with fresh tomato, and various renditions of veal. Portions are large and accompanied by fettucine; the wine list is long. *10133 125 St. at 102nd Ave., tel. 403/482–3100. Reservations advised. Jacket advised. AE, MC, V. Closed lunch and Sun.*

Moderate

Bourbon Street. This is actually an assemblage of moderately priced restaurants situated around a cul-de-sac on the main floor of West Edmonton Mall. "Exterior" decor features New Orleans street lamps and wrought-iron balconies. **Café Orleans** serves Cajun/Creole dishes such as jambalaya and oysters. **Sherlock Holmes** is an English pub with imported draft beer and dishes like Mrs. Hudson's Home Made Pies. **Albert's** has deli fare including the Montréal favorite, smoked meat. Other spots include **Zambelli's Pizza & Steak House, Pacific Fish Co.** (*see* below), and, for belly-up-to-the-bar drinking, the **Bourbon Street Saloon.** *West Edmonton Mall, 8770 170th St., Entrance 6. No reservations. Dress: casual. AE, MC, V.*

Pacific Fish Company. Three locations satisfy landlocked Edmonton's appetite for fresh seafood with daily fly-ins. Order oysters Rockefeller and whisky shrimp as appetizers, and anything charbroiled over mesquite turns out fine. Decor varies slightly, but count on the deck flooring, corrugated walls, and nets dangling overhead. *10020 101A Ave., tel. 403/422–0282; Argyll Plaza, 6258 99th St., tel. 403/437–7472; West Edmonton Mall, Bourbon St., Entrance 6, tel. 403/444–1905. Reservations advised. Dress: casual. AE, MC, V.*

Vi's. In summer, this old house has outdoor seating on a deck overlooking the river; in winter, tables are warmed by a blazing fire. All year the menu emphasizes the basics: hearty soups, fresh salads, extravagant sandwiches, and desserts—with special mention for chocolate pecan pie. Try Vi's for Sunday champagne brunch. *9712 111th St., tel. 403/482–6402. No reservations. Dress: casual. AE, MC, V.*

Inexpensive

★ **Chianti.** This extremely popular spot occupies part of the main floor of Strathcona Square, a converted post office in the lively Old Strathcona District. A mostly young crowd gathers for square meals featuring tasty shellfish appetizers, more than 20 varieties of pasta, a couple dozen veal dishes, and a discriminating selection of desserts. Be prepared to wait for seating on weekend evenings. *10501 82nd Ave. S, tel. 403/439–9829. No reservations. Dress: casual. AE, MC, V.*

Mongolian Food Experience. The "experience" is selecting from a vast buffet of raw meat (lamb, beef, turkey), vegetables (mushrooms, scallions, sprouts, cabbage), and exotic sauces and then having the chef barbecue it for you. Non-"experience" dishes, such as Szechwan beef, lemon chicken, and moo shoo pork, are also available. Decor is bright and unpretentious. *10160 100A St., tel. 403/426–6806; 12520 102nd Ave., tel. 403/452–7367. Reservations advised. Dress: casual. AE, MC, V.*

Lodging

Very Expensive

Fantasyland Hotel & Resort. This important component of massive West Edmonton Mall (*see* Other Points of Interest in Edmonton, above) has regular and theme rooms; the latter include: Victorian Coach Rooms, where guests sleep in hackney cabs; Roman Rooms, with classic round beds; Truck Rooms, where the bed is the back of a pick-up; and Polynesian Rooms, with catamaran beds and waterfalls. All theme rooms have Jacuzzis, and nontheme quarters are comfortable and tidy. *17700 87th Ave., T5T 4V4, tel. 403/444–3000 or 800/661–6454. 354 rooms, 125 theme rooms. Facilities: 3 restaurants; attached to shopping mall with 5-acre water park, miniature golf course, indoor amusement park, 800 shops. AE, CB, DC, MC, V.*

★ **Hilton International Edmonton.** Formerly the Four Seasons, and a Hilton International property since 1988, this financial-district luxury high rise connects by second-level passageways to five major office buildings and two shopping centers. Rooms, all with bay windows, convey sophistication, with marble table-tops, walnut furniture, and accents of brass—all complimented by the blue-and-grey color scheme. Mezzanine-level Patisserie serves a bargain Loonie Breakfast (coffee and muffin for a buck) and The Rose and Crown is is an authentic English pub, perfect for throwing darts and drinking draft beers. *10235 101st St., T5J 3E9, tel. 403/428–7111 or 800/268–9275. 314 rooms. Facilities: 4 restaurants, 2 lounges, indoor pool, whirlpool, saunas, access to exercise room and squash/racquetball courts, nonsmoking floors. AE, CB, DC, MC, V.*

Westin Hotel. The stunning brown block structure in the heart of downtown has large, comfortable rooms that are tastefully decorated with attractive artwork. The atrium lobby, with a decorative mobile, trees, and plants, conveys comfort and luxury; beige-and-pastel rooms, in keeping with the hotel's outward appearance, are equally sophisticated, down to the Caswell and Massey toiletries. The experienced staff, speak a total of 29 languages. The Carvery serves some of the finest beef in the downtown area. *10135 100th St., T5J 0Z1, tel. 403/426–3636 or 800/228–3000. 420 rooms. Facilities: 2 restaurants, 2 lounges, indoor pool, sauna, whirlpool, nonsmoking floors. AE, CB, DC, MC, V.*

Expensive

★ **Edmonton House.** The cylindrical design creates oddly shaped but large and comfortable one- and two-bedroom suites. All units have balconies with views of the skyline or river valley, and kitchens are fully equipped (down to a toaster). A small mezzanine-level convenience store supplies basic essentials. Free Continental breakfast is provided every morning. Weekend and long-term rates are available. *10205 100th Ave., T5J 4B5, tel. 403/424–5555 or 800/661–6562. 283 suites. Facilities: restaurant, lounge, indoor parking, shuttle service to mall, indoor pool, sauna, fitness center, games room, nonsmoking floors. AE, MC, V.*

Sheraton Plaza Edmonton. The renovated property on a quiet street a few blocks from downtown features a lobby and fair-size guest rooms with old-style flair: richly appointed, cherrywood furniture and a warm, cozy ambience. Some rooms have balconies, and almost all have MovieBars—a unit that includes TV, VCR, minibar, and snacks. A selection of videotapes is for rent in the lobby. Room rates include breakfast buffet. *10010 104th St., T5J 0Z1, tel. 403/423–2450 or 800/325–3535. 133 rooms. Facilities: restaurant, lounge, indoor pool, sauna, exercise room, nonsmoking floors. AE, CB, DC, MC, V.*

Moderate

Inn on 7th. Edmonton shorthand provides the name for this cheerful property on 107th Street. The foliage-filled lobby features Paul Bunyan–size easy chairs. A former Holiday Inn now run by the Courtyard Inn chain, this hotel caters to tourists, government employees, and Pacific Coast League baseball teams who play in nearby John Ducey Park. Rooms are comfortably modern; location is convenient but not stressful. *10001 107th St., T5J 1J1, tel. 403/429–2861 or 800/661–7327. 188 rooms. Facilities: restaurant, lounge, nonsmoking floors. AE, MC, V.*

West Harvest Inn. One of Edmonton's newest lodging establishments, this clean, modern three-story hotel catering to the family is on the western edge of town and is only five minutes away from West Edmonton Mall. Rooms in the new wing are slightly larger and more expensive than those in the older wing, but all are comfortable. Grainfield's family restaurant is located on the premises; Yian Chinese restaurant is next door. *17803 Stony Plain Rd. (Rte. 16), T5S 1B4, tel. 403/484–8000 or 800/661–6993. 162 rooms. Facilities: restaurant, lounge. AE, CB, DC, MC, V.*

Inexpensive

Relax Inn. Canada's home-grown budget chain operates two clean and functional motels (plus the spiffier, moderately priced Relax Inn–Edmonton International Airport). Relax Inn–West is located on the edge of town, not far from West Edmonton Mall; Relax Inn–South is on the road to the airport. *18320 Stony Plain Rd.; T5S 1A7; tel. 403/483–6031 or 800/661–9563; 227 rooms including nonsmoking rooms. 10320 45th Ave. S; T6H 5K3; tel. 403/436–9770; 222 rooms including nonsmoking rooms. Facilities: restaurant, lounge, indoor pool, whirlpool. AE, CB, DC, MC, V.*

YMCA of Edmonton. This Y is in an outstanding location: in the heart of downtown next door to the Hilton International and adjacent to Edmonton Centre shopping mall. Rooms are small and spare but carpeted and cheerfully furnished. Women and couples welcome; rates are \$20–\$30 a room. All facilities are available to overnight guests. *10030 102A Ave., T5J 0G5, tel. 403/421–9622. 113 rooms, 30 with bath. Facilities: cafeteria, indoor pool, fitness center, weight room, running track, racquetball courts. MC, V.*

Regina

Dining

Very Expensive

Jules. This bright, cheerful, and very sophisticated Art Deco spot in the Landmark Inn features European cuisine with a regional touch. Menu specialties include lobster; steak Diane; fillet de boeuf "Madagascar"; and a lamb dish, *carré d'agneau Canadienne.* The wine list is diverse and reasonably priced. *4150 Albert St., tel. 306/585–1880. Reservations advised. Jacket advised. AE, CB, DC, MC, V. Closed lunch and Sun.*

Expensive

C.C. Lloyd's. Locals esteem the fine service and casual elegance of the dining room in the downtown Chelton Inn. The decor evokes the atmosphere of Manhattan circa 1930, and the menu features international classics like veal Oscar, fillet of beef Madeira, shrimp Provençal, and a variety of tasty steaks. *1907 11th Ave., tel. 306/569–4650. Reservations advised. Jacket advised. AE, MC, V.*

★ **Mieka's.** Chef Mieka Wiens learned her craft at the Cordon Bleu; her art-filled walls and sleek contemporary furniture certainly reflect outside influence. The menus of this downtown café change with the season but always include imaginative combinations of fresh seafood and meat, local produce, spices, and liquors. There are also creative sandwiches, unusual salads, and a terrific cheesecake. A cookware shop is located on the premises. *1810 Smith St., tel. 306/522-6700. Reservations advised. Dress: casual. AE, MC, V. Closed Sun.*

Moderate **Bartleby's.** This good-time downtown "dining emporium and gathering place" is a veritable museum of western memorabilia, musical instruments, and old-time carnival games. Victorian lampshades and heavy leather armchairs further convey the whimsical tone. The menu features big sandwiches, western beef, and a local specialty, Saskatchewan pickerel. *1920 Broad St., tel. 306/565-0040. No reservations. Dress: casual. AE, MC, V. Closed Sun. dinner.*

Bukovina. A nondescript space alongside the Trans-Canada Highway is the setting for hearty meals from Saskatchewan's significant Ukrainian community. Specialties include *koubisi* pork and perogies, but lunch and dinner buffets offer a sampling of everything. The wine list is small but modestly priced. *1840 Victoria Ave. E, tel. 306/789-1822. No reservations. Dress: casual. MC, V.*

Inexpensive **Brewsters.** The copper kettle and shiny fermentation tanks are proudly prominent in Saskatchewan's first brew pub. Three home brews are always available, as are a large selection of imports and domestic beers. Menu consists of "pub grub" snacks, sandwiches, salads, and fish and chips. Promotional specials—25¢ chicken wings, $2.75 pints of Brewsters Beer—occur nightly. *Victoria East Plaza, 1832 Victoria Ave. E, tel. 306/761-1500. No reservations. Dress: casual. AE, MC, V.*

Lodging

Very Expensive **Ramada Renaissance.** The tallest building in Saskatchewan, Regina's newest and most luxurious hotel rises 25 stories over the city and is attached to the Saskatchewan Trade & Convention Centre. Rooms are furnished in subtle pastels and have modern amenities. The pool has a three-story waterslide, and there's a Tourism Saskatchewan information center in the lobby. *1919 Saskatchewan Dr., S4P 4H2, tel. 800/667-0400. 256 rooms, including nonsmoking rooms. Facilities: 2 restaurants, 2 lounges, indoor pool, waterslide, whirlpool. AE, CB, DC, MC, V.*

Expensive **Regina Inn.** A plant-filled lobby with a soothing fountain welcomes you into this modern downtown hotel. Most rooms, decorated with blues, grays, and browns, have balconies, and the local hot spot, the Original California Club discothèque, is on the ground floor. *1975 Broad St. at Victoria Ave., S4P 1Y2, tel. 306/525-6767 or 800/667-5954. 237 rooms. Facilities: 2 restaurants, 2 lounges, indoor parking, indoor pool, sauna, whirlpool. AE, MC, V.*

★ **Sheraton Centre.** The modern downtown property has a dramatic multi-level, sun-filled lobby that's graced by abundant foliage and a charming waterfall. A second-floor Oasis is the perfect setting for water-theme pastimes, such as a soothing soak in the whirlpool or, for the children, a dip in either the kiddie or standard pool. Rooms are airy and modernly furnished in light colors and dusty rose. *1818 Victoria Ave., S4P 0R1, tel. 306/569-1666 or 800/325-3535. 251 rooms. Facilities: 2 restaurants, lounge, pub, underground heated parking, indoor pool, sauna, whirlpool, games room. AE, CB, DC, MC, V.*

Moderate **Chelton Inn.** A bargain situated in the heart of downtown, Chelton Inn is an older property where rooms are modernized and downright huge. Rooms are spacious, with contemporary, light-wood furnishings to match earth tones. Service is particularly friendly, and the cuisine in C.C. Lloyd's (*see* Dining, above) is among the best in town. *1907 11th Ave., S4P 0J2, tel. 306/569–4600 or 800/667–9922. 56 rooms. Facilities: restaurant, coffee shop, lounge. AE, MC, V.*

★ **Landmark Inn.** This locally owned three-story property, on the south side, has large, modern rooms and a unique indoor-outdoor waterslide. Rooms, decorated in pastel greens and white, are light and airy and have modern furnishings. Jules (*see* Dining, above), a top restaurant, is on the premises. *4150 Albert St. (Hwy. 6), S4S 3R8, tel. 306/586–5363; in Saskatchewan 800/667–9811; elsewhere in Canada 800/667–8191. 188 rooms, including nonsmoking rooms. Facilities: 2 restaurants, lounge, pub, indoor pool, waterslide, sauna, whirlpool, games room. AE, CB, DC, MC, V.*

Inexpensive **Journey's End.** One of Canada's largest budget chains operates a tidy modern roadside property on the eastern edge of town. Earth tones, contemporary furnishings, and basic amenities make this a comfortable place to stay. Not many frills, but freebies include morning coffee, newspaper, and local phone calls. *3221 E. Eastgate Dr., S4N 0T0, tel. 306/789–5522 or 800/668–4200. 100 rooms. AE, CB, DC, MC, V.*

★ **Sandman Inn.** This easternmost outpost of a Vancouver-based budget chain has a mock-Tudor facade; average-size, well-furnished rooms; and Saskatchewan's largest private indoor pool. The poolside Showboat lounge offers dining and dancing to music of the '50s. *4025 Albert St. (Hwy. 6), S4S 3R6, tel. 306/586–2663 or 800/663–6900. 184 rooms. Facilities: 2 restaurants, lounge, indoor pool, whirlpool. AE, CB, DC, MC, V.*

Saskatoon

Dining

Very Expensive **R.J. Willoughby's.** The lush, tropical, pink-and-green color scheme of the Holiday Inn's main dining room is enhanced by copious groves of bamboo and foliage. The menu features Continental preparations plus "Sizzling Stone Cooking" of meat, fish, and veggies on a hot slab of granite. Entrées labeled with hearts have been approved by the Canadian Heart Foundation; breakfast augments the regular menu with a healthful "Fruit & Fibre Buffet." *Holiday Inn, 90 22nd St. E, tel. 306/244–2311. Reservations advised. Jacket advised. AE, CB, DC, MC, V.*

Expensive **St. Tropez Bistro.** This sophisticated dining establishment features intimate French-bistro decor, with blue-and-pink florals, candle-lit tables, outdoor café, and imaginative preparations that change daily. Veal, fish, pasta, quiche, crepes—and outstanding homemade bread are often offered. For dessert, the chocolate fondue is aces. The bistro is a short stroll from downtown hotels. *243 3rd Ave. S, tel. 306/652–1250. Reservations advised. Dress: casual. AE, MC, V. Closed Sun.*

Moderate **Lydia's.** Lydia's, occupying the main rooms in an old house on Broadway Avenue, has a split personality. The front room is an unpretentious setting for Ukrainian specialties like *nalysnyky* (crepes), *varenyky*, (mashed potato and Cheddar cheese boiled with butter and served with sour cream) and smoked sausage; the back room is the oak and stained-glass white-tablecloth venue for such exotic concoctions as "A Night in Hungary" (pork Tokany), "Ascent to the Carpathians" (Dijon veal), and

"A Visit to Bulgaria" (beef Gulyas). The wine list is small but inexpensive. *650 Broadway Ave., tel. 306/652–8595. Reservations advised. Dress: casual. MC, V.*

Saskatoon Station Place. The station is newly built, but the railroad cars and decorative antiques are fascinatingly authentic. The newspaper-style menu headlines Canadian prime rib and steaks, seafood, and Greek specialties, such as Greek ribs and souvlaki. *221 Idylwyld Dr. N, tel. 306/244–7777. Reservations advised. Dress: casual. AE, CB, DC, MC, V.*

Inexpensive

★ **Adonis.** By day such Middle Eastern dishes as falafel, hummus, and donair are served cafeteria-style. At night, tablecloths and candles transform the room into a romantic setting for couscous, dolmades, steak Andalousia, and other Mediterranean delights. It's one of Saskatoon's few outdoor cafés and a great place for breakfast. *101 3rd Ave. S, tel. 306/652–9598. No reservations. Dress: casual. AE, CB, DC, MC, V.*

Taunte Maria's. This is a Mennonite restaurant, which is to suggest a menu of hearty soups, huge farmer's sausages, coleslaw, potato salad, homemade bread, and noodles steeped in gravy. The decor, too, reflects the Mennonite tradition: simple, functional, and comfortable. *Try* to save room for Ho-Ho Cake (chocolate cake with chocolate icing) or bread-and-butter pudding. Taunte Maria's is convenient to the airport. *51st St. and Faithful Ave., tel. 306/931–3212. No reservations. Dress: casual. MC, V. Closed Sun.*

Lodging

Very Expensive

Ramada Renaissance. Saskatoon's newest luxurious property has a prime riverfront/downtown location and 18 floors of classically styled ample-size rooms (request a river view). Units are large and the peach, gray, and pastel colors make them bright and airy. The elaborate Waterworks Recreation Complex encompasses an indoor pool, whirlpool, sauna, and two three-story water slides. *405 20th St. E, S7K 6X6, tel. 306/665–3322 or 800/228–9898. 295 rooms, including nonsmoking rooms. Facilities: 2 restaurants, lounge, indoor pool, sauna, whirlpool, waterslides. AE, CB, DC, MC, V.*

Expensive

★ **Hotel Bessborough.** Saskatoon's grand old landmark, opened in 1935, looks like a French château and dominates the skyline from its riverfront setting. Rooms have quirky shapes and antique furniture but are complete with modern amenities. Front rooms are larger; rear rooms have river views. Delta Hotels acquired it in 1989, promising a major (and much-needed) facelift. What won't change are the gold-leaf details in the public areas, the gardens, or "The Castle's" role as Saskatoon's meeting place. *601 Spadina Crescent E, S7K 3GB, tel. 306/244–5521 or 800/667–8788. 230 rooms, including nonsmoking rooms. Facilities: 2 restaurants, 2 lounges, indoor and outdoor pools, sauna, whirlpool. AE, CB, DC, MC, V.*

Sheraton Cavalier. Located downtown opposite Kiwanis Park, this eight-story property features unusually large mauve-and-blue rooms that face either the city or the river, and an elaborate water-sports complex. The Top of the Inn is one of Saskatoon's top discothèques; the Barley Bin is a sophisticated but chummy pub. *612 Spadina Crescent E, S7K 3G9, tel. 306/652–6770 or 800/325–3535. 250 rooms, including non-smoking rooms. Facilities: 2 restaurants, pub, disco, 2 indoor pools, water slides, sauna, whirlpool, exercise room, games room. AE, CB, DC, MC, V.*

Moderate **Travelodge.** This sprawling property near the airport has themed its decor around the two flora-filled indoor pool complexes. Rooms come in a great variety of sizes and shapes; many have balconies overlooking the pool. The Aloha Gardens offers poolside dining; the Heritage Dining Room has medieval feasts. *106 Circle Dr. W, S7L 4L6, tel. 306/242–8881 or 800/255–3050. 219 rooms, including nonsmoking rooms. Facilities: 2 restaurants, lounge, pub, 2 indoor pools, water slides, sauna, whirlpools, games room. AE, CB, DC, MC, V.*

Inexpensive **Colonial Square Motel.** This pink-stucco, two-story motel opened in 1989 east of the river, along a fast-food strip. Rooms are furnished in pastel colors and have two queen-size beds or a double bed plus pull-out sofa. Across the parking lot is the Venice Pizza House and Lounge. *1301 8th St. E, S7H 0S7, tel. 306/343–1676 or 800/667–3939. 80 rooms, including nonsmoking rooms. Facilities: restaurant, lounge. AE, MC, V.*

★ **King George.** Situated in the center of downtown, opposite the transit mall, this older hotel welcomes seniors and anyone else looking for a bargain. Earth-toned rooms are large but a bit dreary; suites—some with wet bars—are terrific deals. Seniors get 30% off rooms and 15% off meals in several restaurants, including the entertaining Karl's Schnitzel Haus. *157 2nd Ave. N, S7K 2A9, tel. 306/244–6133. 104 rooms. Facilities: 2 restaurants, 2 lounges, bowling alley. AE, CB, DC, MC, V.*

Winnipeg

Dining

Very Expensive **Restaurant Dubrovnik.** The setting is a romantic Victorian town house, with seating on an enclosed veranda overlooking the Assiniboine River. An extensive menu blends Continental specialties, such as rack of lamb, breast of duck, and pheasant, with southern Yugoslavian dishes. Two good dishes to try are the *gibanica* (feta cheese in phyllo pastry) and the *muckalica* (pork, lamb, chicken and sausage casserole). A lengthy wine list is available. *390 Assiniboine Ave., tel. 204/944–0594. Reservations advised. Jacket required. AE, MC, V. Closed Sun.*

★ **Victor's.** Before Osborne Village was a fashionable locale, Winnipeg's power restaurant had already taken over the ground floors of a renovated apartment house. Downstairs, the natural brick walls and bentwood chairs offer an understated setting for such Continental specialties as breast of pheasant, bouillabaisse, and pepper steak. Upstairs, Joanna's is a more casual spot for drinks and some of Victor's dishes at greatly reduced prices. On either level, Joanna's poppyseed cake is a must for dessert. *100 Osborne St., tel. 204/284–2339. Reservations advised. Jacket advised. AE, CB, DC, MC, V. Closed Sun.*

Expensive **Amici.** The sophisticated and posh downtown *ristorante* is the local avatar of *cucina nuova*, the Italian version of nouvelle cuisine. Clever pastas and such dishes as roast quail on radicchio and chicken stuffed with goat cheese are served in a second-floor dining room that's divided by partitions of frosted glass. Downstairs, the Bombolini Wine Bar serves many of the simpler dishes at lower prices. *326 Broadway, tel. 204/943–4997. Reservations advised. Jacket advised for Amici; casual for Bombolini. AE, MC, V. Closed Sun.*

★ **Le Beaujolais.** This sophisticated, bright spot in the French St. Boniface district presents waiters in black tie; a softly lit ambience with French blue, coral, and burgundy decor; fresh-cut flowers; and a menu that combines classic French with lighter nouvelle cuisine. Salmon with basil or monkfish in red wine is the recommended seafood; tournedos with five peppers and rack of lamb are other entrée suggestions. Save room for dessert; after-theater menu served from 10 PM. *131 Provencher Blvd., tel. 204/237-6306. Reservations advised. Jacket advised. AE, CB, DC, MC, V.*

Oliver's Old Bailey. The erstwhile Exchange District headquarters of Great West Life Insurance, decorated with wood and leather, suggests a British gentlemen's-club ambience. Antique sideboards adorn the three upstairs dining rooms, where martinis and single-malt Scotch seem the only proper cocktails. The dinner menu stresses beefsteak, veal, and chicken dishes; lower-priced sandwiches are served for lunch. *185 Lombard Ave., tel. 204/943-4448. Reservations advised. Jacket and tie advised. AE, CB, DC, MC, V. Closed Sun.*

Moderate

★ **Bistro Dansk.** Wood tables, bright red chairs, and strains of classical music convey a cozy European air. Dinner entrée selections mingle Danish specialties like *frikadeller* (meat patties) and more expected Continental dishes like roast chicken. A less expensive lunch menu features a vast variety of open-face sandwiches. *63 Sherbrook St., tel. 204/775-5662. Reservations advised. Dress: casual. V. Closed Sun.*

Homer's. This unpretentious, good-time downtown place has been one of the city's favorite Greek restaurants for more than 20 years, with ionic columns and hanging grapevines setting the mood. Stick to modern Greek standards: souvlaki, moussaka, and excellent Greek desserts. Non-Greek dishes, served with french fries, are also available. *520 Ellice Ave., 204/788-4858. Reservations advised. Dress: casual. AE, MC, V.*

Mandarin. The Sargent Avenue Mandarin is a crowded, 12-table westside place with unique and reasonably exotic northern Chinese dishes. Complete "Gourmet Delight Dinners" include soup, dumplings, entrée and dessert. Only wine is served. The River Mandarin, a spin-off, has a slightly different menu, a calmer pace, and a full liquor license. *Mandarin, 613 Sargent Ave., tel. 204/775-7819; River Mandarin, 252 River Ave., tel. 204/284-8963. Reservations advised. Dress: casual. V.*

Picasso's. It may be named after a Spanish painter, but this is a Portuguese restaurant, featuring outstanding seafood. On the street level it's a bustling neighborhood café; upstairs, there's a subdued atmosphere where white tablecloths, candlelight, and soft music prevail. Try the salmon, or Arctic char; Portuguese favorites are paella, octopus stew, or steak Picasso. *615 Sargent Ave., tel. 204/775-2469. Reservations advised. Dress: casual. AE, CB, DC, MC, V.*

Inexpensive

★ **d'8 Schtove.** The name is Mennonite for "the eating room," and, true to its name, the menu features heavyweight servings of soup, salads, and Mennonite concoctions, usually involving meat, potatoes, onions, and vegetables. Try the *klopz* (ground-beef-and-pork meatballs) or *wrenikje* (cottage-cheese pierogies). The new south-side location is bright, immaculately clean, and looks spacious, although you may still have to wait for a table. Service is quick and friendly. *1842 Pembina Hwy., 204/275-2294. No reservations. Dress: casual. MC, V.*

Kelekis. This north-end shrine has purveyed legendary burgers, hot dogs, fries, and onion rings for almost 60 years. Decor includes a photo montage of family history and autographed celebrities' photos. Breakfast is served daily. *1100 Main St., tel. 204/582–1786. No reservations. Dress: casual. No credit cards.*

Osborne's Cafe. This crowded little basement spot in swinging Osborne Village features borscht and other hearty soups, an array of salads, and diverse dishes from around the globe, including Siberian *pelmeni* (dumplings), Danish quiche, and Greek moussaka. Beer and a brief list of wines from France, Hungary, and Canada are available. *106 Osborne St., tel. 204/475–9599. No reservations. Dress: casual. MC, V.*

Lodging

Very Expensive

Holiday Inn. Winnipeg's largest hotel, this Holiday Inn is 17 stories high and connects to the Convention Centre. Rooms, having recently undergone a major renovation, are decorated in pastels and have pleasant modern furnishings; some rooms overlook the skylighted pool. Ticker's lobby bar is a lively spot for a rendezvous. *350 St. Mary Ave., R3C 3J2, tel. 204/942–0551 or 800/465–4329. 392 rooms, including nonsmoking rooms. Facilities: 3 restaurants, lounge, cabaret, indoor and outdoor pools, sauna, whirlpool, exercise room. AE, CB, DC, MC, V.*

★ **Westin Hotel.** The top luxury hotel is located near Winnipeg's hub—Portage and Main streets—and is connected by the skywalk to office buildings and North Portage Mall. Large, newly restored rooms feature striking Colonial-style furniture. The 21st-floor rooftop indoor pool makes a dramatic setting for a swim. Chimes is a contemporary setting for light meals and dinner theater. *2 Lombard Pl., R3B 0Y3, tel. 204/957–1350 or 800/228–3000. 350 rooms nonsmoking rooms available. Facilities: 3 restaurants, 2 lounges, dinner theater, nonsmoking floor, indoor pool, sauna, whirlpool, fitness center. AE, CB, DC, MC, V.*

Expensive

Birchwood Inn. This bright and sumptuous modern property is located on the Trans-Canada Highway's western approach to Winnipeg, near the airport, race track, and shopping areas. Rooms are large, with modern earth-tone furnishings. Executive suites, decorated in blue and green, are a bit fancier than standard units. The atrium is a lush setting for a pool and poolside lounge. *2520 Portage Ave., R3J 0J9, tel. 204/885–4478 or 800/665–0352. 210 rooms. Facilities: 2 restaurants, lounge, indoor pool, sauna, exercise room. AE, MC, V.*

Hotel Fort Garry. Built in 1913 and known far and wide as the Grand Castle, the old railroad hotel has been resuscitated from near-bankruptcy and has resumed its role as one of Winnipeg's gathering places. Located on the south edge of downtown, near Union Station, the hotel and its hushed spacious lobby are furnished with inviting armchairs, original marble, brass, and crystal finishes. Large guest rooms still have classic dark-wood furnishings and floral wallpapers. *222 Broadway, R3C 0R3, tel. 204/942–8251 or 800/665–8088. 270 rooms. Facilities: 2 restaurants, lounge, cabaret. AE, CB, DC, MC, V.*

★ **Place Louis Riel.** This luxury-class bargain is a converted apartment building that has 245 contemporary suites with living rooms, dining areas, and fully-equipped kitchens. Though all rooms are up-to-date, the suites on the upper floors facing west are preferred because of their view of the Parliament Building. The supreme downtown location—adjacent to Eaton Place mall—is only one of the hotel's highlights. *190 Smith St., R3C 1J8, tel. 204/947–6961 or in Canada, 800/665–0569. 245* *suites. Facilities: restaurant/lounge, free parking. AE, CB, DC, MC, V.*

Relax Plaza. Positioned at the low end of our expensive range, this high-rise venture of Canada's oldest budget chain is in a strategically desirable location, next to the bus depot and adjacent to The Bay and Winnipeg Art Gallery. Rooms on the south side look out on the Legislative Building, and north-side rooms overlook the city. Guest rooms have subdued modern furnishings in either neutral or pastel colors. *360 Colony St., R3B 2P3, tel. 204/786–7011 or 800/661–9563. 157 rooms, including nonsmoking rooms. Facilities: restaurant, indoor pool, whirlpool. AE, CB, DC, MC, V.*

Moderate

★ **Charter House.** Half the refurbished rooms in this five-story low-rise on the south side of downtown have balconies. Furnishings are contemporary motel-style, and the atmosphere is quite friendly. The Rib Room is a popular moderately priced place for dinner. *330 York Ave., R3C 0N9, tel. 204/942–0101 or in Manitoba, 204/942–0101 or 800/782–0175. 90 rooms. Facilities: 2 restaurants, lounge, outdoor pool. AE, MC, V.*

Gordon Downtowner. There's nothing fancy here, but it's a good deal on the edge of downtown a block from the Portage Place mall. Most rooms are decorated in dusty rose with grey carpeting. Two-room suites, modernly furnished, are the best bargains. *330 Kennedy St., R3B 2M6, tel. 204/943–5581. 40 rooms. Facilities: restaurant, pub, free parking. AE, MC, V.*

Marlborough Inn. The rooms of this ornate old (1914) Gothic structure in the Financial District are large, but furnishings could use refreshing. Try to avoid rooms facing the unsightly inner core. Flander's Cafe has vaulted ceilings, a stained-glass window, and acceptable breakfasts and lunches. *331 Smith St., R3B 2G9, tel. 204/942–6411. 143 rooms. Facilities: 2 restaurants, lounge. AE, CB, DC, MC, V.*

Inexpensive

Assiniboine Gordon Inn on the Park. The two-story hotel and motor inn is adjacent to a park on the west side, not far from the airport. Rooms are modern and large, albeit somewhat overwrought with masculine dark wood and bold designs. *1975 Portage Ave., R3J 0J9, tel. 204/888–4806. 47 rooms. Facilities: restaurant, lounge, disco. AE, MC, V.*

Journey's End. This is a reliable choice for an inexpensive, south-side lodging. The rooms are an adequate size and are furnished in contemporary style, with rose or beige carpets and either dusty-rose or earth-tone accessories. There's no charge for local phone calls, and morning coffee is free. *3109 Pembina Hwy., R3T 4R6, tel. 204/269–7390 or 800/268–0405. 80 rooms. AE, MC, V.*

The Arts and Nightlife

Tickets for events at the Calgary Centre for the Performing Arts, Jubilee Auditorium, and Olympic Saddledome are available at BASS ticket outlets at Calgary Centre box office, The Bay, Sears, or by telecharge (tel. 403/270–6700 or 403/266–8888). In Edmonton, BASS ticket outlets are located in Edmonton Centre, Citadel Theatre box office, Champions in West Edmonton Mall, and Sears stores, or call 403/451–8000 to telecharge tickets to most events.

The Arts

Theater
Calgary Calgary's showcase theater facility is the **Calgary Centre for the Performing Arts** (205 8th Ave. SE, Calgary, tel. 403/294-7455), with three modern auditoriums in two contiguous historic buildings. Productions by resident Alberta Theatre Projects (ATP) of principally Canadian playwrights are highly recommended. More than 20 local companies use the stage of the **Pumphouse Theatre** (2140 9th Ave. SW, Calgary, tel. 403/263-0079). The **University of Calgary Theatre** (Reeve Theatre, 2500 University Drive NW, Calgary, tel. 403/220-4900) features classic and contemporary works.

Edmonton Edmonton has 13 professional theater companies. The paramount facility is the glass-clad downtown **Citadel Theatre Complex** (99th St. and 101A Ave., Edmonton, tel. 403/425-1820) where four theaters mingle esoteric works and classics. **Northern Light Theater** (Kaasa Theatre, Jubilee Auditorium, 118th Ave. and 74th St., Edmonton, tel. 403/471-1586) takes chances that usually succeed.

Regina On a theater-in-the-round stage inside the old Regina City Hall, the **Globe Theatre** (1801 Scarth St., Regina, tel. 306/525-9553) offers six classics and contemporary Saskatchewan work from September to May. **Theatre Regina** (Performing Arts Centre, 1077 Angus St., Regina, tel. 306/565-2277) presents lighthearted original productions.

Saskatoon Saskatoon's oldest professional theater, **25th Street Theatre Centre** (420 Duchess St., Saskatoon, tel. 306/664-2239) produces mostly works by Canadian playwrights during the October-May season. **Persephone Theatre** (2802 Rusholme Rd., Saskatoon, tel. 306/384-7727) presents six plays and musicals a year. The **Saskatoon Gateway Players** (709 Cumberland St., Saskatoon, tel. 306/653-1200) presents five productions October-April. **Nightcap Productions** (tel. 306/653-2300) offers "Shakespeare on the Saskatchewan" in a riverside tent in July and August, and midnight improvisational comedy at the Broadway Theatre (715 Broadway Ave., Saskatoon, tel. 306/652-6556).

Winnipeg One of Canada's most acclaimed regional theaters, the **Manitoba Theatre Centre,** produces serious plays from many sources on the 785-seat **Mainstage** (174 Market Ave., Winnipeg, tel. 204/942-6537), and more experimental work in the **MTC Warehouse Theatre** (140 Rupert Ave., Winnipeg, tel. 204/942-6537). The **Prairie Theatre Exchange** focuses on local playwrights in an attractive facility in the Portage Place Mall (Portage Ave. and Carlton St., Winnipeg, tel. 204/942-5483).

Music and Dance
Calgary **Calgary Philharmonic Orchestra** (tel. 403/294-7420) concerts, chamber groups, and a broad spectrum of music and dance shows are performed in the 1,755-seat Jack Singer Concert Hall in the **Calgary Centre for the Performing Arts** (205 8th Ave. SE, Calgary, tel. 403/294-7455). The larger **Jubilee Auditorium** (1415 14th Ave. SW, Calgary, tel. 403/297-8000) hosts the Alberta Ballet company and a variety of classical music, opera, dance, pop, and rock concerts. Concerts are also performed at **University of Calgary Theatres** (2500 University Dr. NW, Calgary, tel. 403/220-4900).

Edmonton The **Edmonton Opera** (tel. 403/482-7030), **Edmonton Symphony Orchestra** (tel. 403/428-1414), and **Alberta Ballet Company** (tel. 403/438–4350) all perform in the **Northern Alberta Jubilee Auditorium** at the University of Alberta (87th Ave. and 114th St., Edmonton, tel. 403/427–9622).

Regina Two theaters in the **Saskatchewan Centre of the Arts** (Wascana Centre, 200 Lakeshore Dr., Regina, tel. 306/565–0404) are venues for the Regina Symphony, pop concerts, dance performances, and Broadway musicals and plays. **Regina Modern Danceworks** (1100 Broad St., Regina, tel. 306/359–3183) presents contemporary productions.

Saskatoon The **Saskatoon Symphony** (tel. 306/665–6414) performs an October–April season at **Centennial Auditorium** (35 22nd St. E, Saskatoon, tel. 306/644–9777). When the symphony isn't in concert, the 2,003-seat auditorium hosts ballet, rock and pop concerts, comedians, musical comedies, and opera. The **Mendel Art Gallery** (950 Spadina Crescent E, Saskatoon, tel. 306/975–7610) has a regular concert program, and the **Saskatoon Jazz Society** performs in its permanent space, **The Basement** (245 3rd Ave. S, Saskatoon, tel. 306/652–1421).

Winnipeg Winnipeg's principal venue for serious music, dance, and pop concerts is the magnificent 2,263-seat Centennial Concert Hall in the **Manitoba Centennial Centre** (555 Main St., Winnipeg, tel. 204/956–1360). From September–mid-May it is the home of the **Winnipeg Symphony Orchestra** (tel. 204/947–1148); the **Royal Winnipeg Ballet** (tel. 204/956–0183) performs there in October, December, March, and May; and the **Manitoba Opera Association** (tel. 204/942–7479) presents three operas a year—in November, February, and May. Throughout the year, pop concerts use the Centre.

The **Winnipeg Art Gallery** (300 Memorial Blvd., tel. 204/786–6641) features jazz, blues, chamber music, and contemporary groups. The **Westend Cultural Centre** (586 Ellice Ave., tel. 204/775–1055) is a downtown venue for blues, folk music, and dance. For contemporary dance and new music, check out **Le Rendez-Vous** (768 Av. Tache, tel. 204/452–0229) in St. Boniface. Other performance spaces include **Pantages Playhouse Theatre** (180 Market Ave. E, tel. 204/986–3003) and the **Winnipeg Convention Centre** (375 York Ave., tel. 204/ 956–1720).

Film
Winnipeg In Winnipeg, the best places to find imports, art films, oldies, and midnight cult classics are at **Cinemathèque** (100 Arthur St., Winnipeg, tel. 204/942–6795) and **Cinema 3** (585 Ellice Ave., Winnipeg, tel. 204/783–1097). The **WAG** (Winnipeg Art Gallery, 300 Memorial Blvd., Winnipeg, tel. 204/786–6641) also has a cinema series.

Edmonton Edmonton's **Metro Cinema** (NFB Theatre, Canada Place, 9700 Jasper Ave., Edmonton, tel. 403/425–9212) presents classics, imports, and brave new films on weekend nights. The **Edmonton Film Society** screens an ambitious program at a theater in the **Provincial Museum of Alberta** (12845 102nd Ave., Edmonton, tel. 403/427–1730). The **Princess Theatre** (10337 Whyte Ave., Edmonton, tel. 403/433–5785), an old-time movie house in Old Strathcona district presents revivals, experiments, and foreign films.

Nightlife

Bars and Clubs
Calgary
Loose Moose (2003 McKnight Blvd. NE, Calgary, tel. 403/291–5682) features competitive "Theatresports" and all sorts of fun and games.

Edmonton
The **Rose & Crown** English-style pub in the Hilton International (10235 101st St., Edmonton, tel. 403/428–7111) is a popular downtown gathering place with dart boards and a huge selection of beers. **Elephant & Castle Pubs** are pleasant watering holes in downtown Edmonton's Eaton Centre (tel. 403/424–4555) and the West Edmonton Mall (tel. 403/444–3555).

Regina
Caper's, in the Ramada Renaissance (1919 Saskatchewan Dr., Regina, tel. 306/525–5255), is where local movers and shakers mingle with visitors from the convention center next door.

Winnipeg
Hy's Steak Loft (216 Kennedy St., Winnipeg, tel. 204/942–1000) is convenient for cocktails and has a late-evening piano bar. The abundant **Rorie Street Marble Club** (65 Rorie St., Winnipeg, tel. 204/943–4222) is the contemporary hot spot of the young crowd. A most convincingly British pub in the Exchange District is **The King's Head** (120 King St., Winnipeg, tel. 204/957–1479).

Saskatoon
One Up (410 22nd St. E, Saskatoon, tel. 306/244–0955) is a civilized rooftop place with great river views. Saskatoon's businesspeople interface with traveling executives at **Caper's Lounge** (405 20th St. E, Saskatoon, tel. 306/665–3322) in the Ramada Renaissance.

Casinos
Calgary
In Calgary, play blackjack, roulette, and wheel of fortune at **River Park Casino** (1919 Macleod Trail S, Calgary, tel. 403/269–6771), **Cash Casino Place** (4040B Blackfoot Trail SE, Calgary, tel. 403/287–1635), and **Frontier Casino** at the top of Big Four in Stampede Park.

Edmonton
Roulette, blackjack, and wheel of fortune action usually takes place in Edmonton between noon and midnight daily except Sunday at the **Casino ABS Downtown** (10161 112th St., Edmonton, tel. 403/428–6679), **Casino ABS South** (7055 Argyll Rd., Edmonton, tel. 403/466–0199), and at the **Mayfair Hotel** (10815 Jasper Ave., Edmonton, tel. 403/484–0821).

Comedy
Calgary
The Calgary outpost of **Yuk Yuk's** (Blackfoot Inn, 5940 Blackfoot Trail, Calgary, tel. 403/258–2028), Canada's comedy chain, has name performers from Canada and the United States. **Punchlines** (239 10th Ave. SE, Calgary, tel. 403/269–6669) has comedians and Wednesday-night open mikes.

Edmonton
Edmonton boasts two branches of **Yuk Yuk's** (7103 78th Ave. and 9663 101A Ave., Edmonton, tel. 403/425–1855).

Regina
Regina's **Yuk Yuk's** (806 Idylwyld Dr. N, tel. 306/244–9857) presents cutting-edge comedy. More sedate literary readings by candlelight take place at the **Victorian Dining Room** (243 21st St. E, Regina, tel. 306/244–0060).

Winnipeg
Yuk Yuk's (108 Osborne St., tel. 204/475–YUKS), in a large Osborne Village basement, in Winnipeg, presents raunchy comedy, certain to offend everyone. Try also **Rumors Comedy Club** (2025 Corydon Ave., Winnipeg, tel. 204/488–4520) or the **Comedy Oasis** (531 St. Mary's Rd., Winnipeg, tel. 204/231–1463), just for laughs.

Music
Calgary

Calgary's **Sparky's Diner** (1006 11th Ave. SW, Calgary, tel. 403/244–4888) presents a pleasing array of blues, rock, folk, and big-band performers. The Casablanca-style **Cafe Calabash** (107 10A St. NW, Calgary, tel. 403/270–2266) has live jazz every night but Sunday. **Cover to Cover** (738 11th Ave. SW, Calgary, tel. 403/262–1933) also features jazz musicians. For Western sights and sounds, head for **Ranchman's** (9311 Macleod Trail S, Calgary, tel. 403/253–1100) or the **Longhorn Restaurant & Dance Hall** (9631 Macleod Trail S, Calgary, tel. 403/258–0528). **Dickens Pub** (9th Ave. and 9th St. SW, Calgary, tel. 403/265–4200) is the premier spot for high-energy music and dancing. Dance to Top–40 high-tech at **Raffles** (5940 Blackfoot Trail SE, Calgary, tel. 403/252–2253).

Edmonton

The **Sidetrack Cafe** (10333 112th St., Edmonton, tel. 403/421–1326) features top-name entertainers, big-screen telecasts of sports events, Variety Night on Sunday, and the Monday night Comedy Bowl. **Yardbird Suite** (10206 86th Ave., Edmonton, tel. 403/432–0328) is Edmonton's premier jazz showcase. **Club Malibu** (10310 85th Ave., Edmonton, tel. 403/432–7300) blasts out Top-40 hits in a converted armory. **Goose Loonies** (6250 99th St., Edmonton, tel. 403/438–5571) has two levels of lights, lasers, and loudness. **Cook County Saloon** (8010 103rd St., Edmonton, tel. 403/432–0177) has mellow honky-tonk ambience and country-and-western music.

Regina

The **Original California Club** (Regina Inn, Victoria Ave. and Broad St., Regina, tel. 306/525–6767) is the city's liveliest discothèque. **W.H. Shooters** (2075 Broad St., Regina, tel. 306/525–3525) features Canadian and American country-and-western bands. Relax English-style with darts and ale and music at **Formerly's,** in the Hotel Saskatchewan (2125 Victoria Ave., Regina, tel. 306/522–7691).

Saskatoon

See top rock groups at **Bud's On Broadway** (817 Broadway Ave., Saskatoon, tel. 306/244–4155) and **Amigos** (632 10th St. E, Saskatoon, tel. 306/652–4912). **Top of the Inn** (612 Spadina Crescent, Saskatoon, tel. 306/652–6770), atop the Sheraton Cavalier, has great river views and the city's hottest dance floor. The **Artful Dodger** (100–119 4th Ave. S, Saskatoon, tel. 306/653–2577) is a pub with live entertainment. Go out to **Texas T** (3331 8th St. E, Saskatoon, tel. 306/373–8080) for country sights and sounds around the city's largest dance floor.

Winnipeg

Country-and-western music fans flock to Winnipeg's **Golden Nugget** (1155 Main St., Winnipeg, tel. 204/589–6308) and the **Palomino Club** (1133 Portage Ave., Winnipeg, tel. 204/772–0454). The hardest-rocking places in town are **Circuit** (611 rue Archibald, Winnipeg, tel. 204/231–2111), **Spectrum** (176 Fort St., Winnipeg, tel. 204/943–6487), and the **Albert** (48 Albert St., Winnipeg, tel. 204/943–8750). Good rock 'n' roll dancing can be found at **DeSoto's** (171 McDermott Ave., Winnipeg, tel. 204/943–4444). A more sedate dance floor comes alive after 9 PM in **Windows Lounge** in the Sheraton Winnipeg (161 Donald St., Winnipeg, tel. 204/942–5300).

Excursions

Excursion from Calgary: Southern Alberta

Head east on the Trans-Canada Highway (Route 1) out of Calgary and enter the vast Canadian prairie of seemingly endless expanses of flat country in every direction. About 30 kilometers (19 miles) east of Calgary, turn north on Highway 9 and drive 70 kilometers (43 miles) to **Drumheller,** a town that mined coal until oil and natural gas were discovered in the late 1940s. The small town is situated in the rugged valley of the Red Deer River, where millions of years of wind and water erosion exposed the "strike" that produced what amounts to present-day Drumheller's major industry: dinosaurs.

The barren lunar landscape of stark badlands and eerie rock cylinders (called hoodoos) may seem an ideal setting for the herds of dinosaurs that stalked the countryside 75 million years ago, but in fact, when the dinosaurs were here the area had a semitropical climate and verdant marshlands not unlike the Florida Everglades. You learn this and more geological and paleontological history of Alberta at the **Tyrell Museum of Paleontology.** Participate in hands-on exhibits and meet the local hero, Albertosaurus, a smaller, fiercer version of Tyrannosaurus Rex that was the first dino discovered around here. *Hwy. 838, 6 km (4 mi) northwest of Drumheller, tel. 403/823–7707; in Calgary, 403/294–1992. Suggested admission: $2 adults, $1 children, $5 families. Open May 20–early Oct., daily 9–9; early Oct.–mid-May, Tues.–Sun. 10–5.*

Capitalizing on its rich paleontological past, Drumheller has a number of dinosaur-related businesses. **Reptile World** (Hwy. 9, tel. 403/823–TOAD) boasts a crowd-pleasing collection of poisonous snakes; the **Homestead Antique Museum** (Hwy. 838, tel. 403/823–2600) packs 4,000 Indian artifacts, medical instruments, period clothing, and other items of Canadiana into a roadside quonset hut; **Ollie's Rock & Fossil Shop** (off Hwy. 575, tel. 403/823–6144) depicts life-size dinosaurs in a badlands setting and sells a vast selection of fossils, bones, rocks, and petrified wood. No visit to Drumheller is complete without a family portrait beside the comic-book Tyrannosaurus Rex guarding the Highway 9 bridge over the Red Deer River.

Continuing the dinosaur tour of Alberta requires a 142-kilometer (90-mile) drive south from Drumheller on Highway 56. Go east on the Trans-Canada Highway (Route 1), north at Brooks on Highway 873, east on Highway 544, and follow the signs to **Dinosaur Provincial Park,** a 15,000-acre park encompassing Canada's baddest badlands. Soft sedimentary rock was deposited by 72-million-year-old rivers and sculpted into starkly fascinating shapes by melting waters of the Ice Age that occurred a mere 14,000 years ago. Incessant wind, water, and frost erosion have exposed one of the world's most important collections of fossilized bones. Roads access some *in situ* fossil sites; two looped interpretive trails lead to more, with guided tours on weekends. During summer, 90-minute bus tours explore backcountry areas from which visitors are otherwise restricted. The cacti bloom from June through August. The **Tyrell Museum of Paleontology Field Station** in the park offers a concise orientation to the prehistoric world. Note: Since concessions are limited, bring a lunch to eat in one of the picnic areas. *Hwy. 551, Patricia, 48 km (30 mi) northeast of Brooks, tel. 403/378–4587. Admission: $1.50 per person, children under 6 free. Tyrell Field Station open May 20–Sept. 2, daily 9–9 winter, Wed.–Sun. 10–5.*

Time Out Throughout the year the **Patricia Water Hole** (Main St., tel. 403/378–4647) in the Patricia Hotel is the renowned Wild West setting for Alberta beefsteak, with all the trimmings and 100% buffalo burgers (buffalo steaks available with 24-hour notice).

Medicine Hat lies about 95 kilometers (60 miles) southeast of Patricia on the Trans-Canada Highway. Roadside views consist of small well pumps and storage tanks amid endless expanses of "prairie wool," principally spear and blue grama grass. There is much local lore concerning the origin of the name Medicine Hat, but one legend tells of a battle waged between Cree and Blackfoot Indians; the Cree fought bravely until their medicine man deserted, losing his headdress in the South Saskatchewan River. The site's name, "Saamis," meaning "medicine man's hat," was later translated by white settlers into Medicine Hat.

Medicine Hat is a prosperous and scenic city built on high banks overlooking the South Saskatchewan River. Alberta's fifth-largest city's wealth derives from vast deposits of natural gas below, some of which gets piped up to fuel quaint gas lamps in the turn-of-the-century downtown area. Prosperity is similarly communicated by the striking glass-sided **Medicine Hat City Hall.** *1st St. SE and 6th Ave. SE, tel. 403/529–8100. Open weekdays 8:30–4:30. Guided group and self-guided tours available.*

But Medicine Hat's greatest achievement was turning the land alongside the South Saskatchewan River and Seven Persons Creek into parkland and environmental preserves interconnected by 15 kilometers (9⅓ miles) of walking, biking, and cross-country ski trails. Detailed trail maps are available at the **Tourist Information Centre** (8 Gehring Rd. SW, tel. 403/527–6422). Other Medicine Hat attractions include a half-mile of falling water at **Riverside Waterslide** (Hwy. 1 and Power House Rd., tel. 403/529–6218) and **Echo Dale Regional Park** (Holsom Rd. off Hwy. 3, tel. 403/529–6225), the riverside setting for swimming, boating, fishing, a 1900s farm, and an historic coal mine.

For a side trip out of Medicine Hat, take Highway 1 east and Highway 41 south for the 70-kilometer (43-mile) drive to **Cypress Hills Provincial Park.** Alberta's second-largest provincial park, Cypress Hills is a 200-square-kilometer (77-square-mile) oasis of hills and tall lodgepole pines. Elkwater Townsite provides a full complement of services. The park is contiguous to Cypress Hills Provincial Park, Saskatchewan (*see* Excursion from Regina, below), which also has accommodations and visitor amenities. *Visitor Centre, Elkwater Townsite, tel. 403/893–3833. Open late June–Sept. 2. Administration Bldg., tel. 403/893–3777. Open weekdays 8:15–4:30.*

Head west out of Medicine Hat toward **Lethbridge** on Crowsnest Highway (Rte. 3). Lethbridge, Alberta's third-largest city, is an 1870s coal boomtown that is now the center of agriculture, oil, and gas. The main attraction, **Fort Whoop-Up,** part of the **Indian Battle Park,** is a reconstruction of a southern Alberta whiskey fort. Along with weapons, relics, and a 15-minute audiovisual historical presentation, Fort Whoop-Up has wagon-train–ride tours of the river valley and other points of local historical interest. *Indian Battle Park, Whoop-Up Dr. and Oldman River, tel. 403/329–0444. Fort Whoop-Up admission free. Open late-May–Labor Day, daily 10–8; Labor Day–late-May weekdays, noon–4, weekends noon–5.*

Henderson Lake Park, 3 kilometers (2 miles) east on the other side of downtown Lethbridge, is filled with lush trees, a golf course, baseball stadium, tennis courts, a swimming pool, and a 60-acre man-made lake. Alongside the lake, **Nikka Yuko Japanese Gardens** is a tranquil setting for manicured trees and shrubs, miniature pools and waterfalls, a teahouse, and pebble designs constructed in Japan and reassembled alongside Henderson Lake. *Henderson Lake Park, Mayor Magrath Dr. and S. Parkside Dr., tel. 403/320–3020; Gardens, tel. 403/328–3511. Admission: $2 adults, $1 seniors and students, children under 12 free. Open mid-May–mid-June, daily 9–5; mid-June–Aug., daily 9–8; Sept.–early Oct., daily 9–5.*

Travel west along Highway 3 for 50 kilometers (31 miles) to **Fort Macleod.** Southern Alberta's oldest settlement, the installation was founded by the Mounties in 1874 to maintain order among the farmers, Indians, whiskey vendors, and ranchers beginning to settle here. The wood-frame buildings (pre-1900) and the more-recent sandstone-and-brick buildings have established this as Alberta's first historic area. For information about guided and self-guided tours, visit the information booth (tel. 403/553–2500) beside Fort Macleod Museum. An authentic reconstruction of the 1874 fort, **Fort Macleod Museum** grants almost equal exhibitory weight to settlers, Indians, old North West Mounted Police, and today's Royal Canadian Mounted Police. *25th St., tel. 403/553–4703. Admission: $3 adults, $2.50 seniors, $1 students 13–18, 50¢ children 6–12. Open May–June 14 and Sept. 3–Oct. 15, daily 9–5; June 15–Sept. 2, daily 9–7.*

Dining For rates, *see* Dining and Lodging chart, above.

Lethbridge **Cafe Martinique.** Located in the El Rancho Motor Hotel, this locally renowned fine dining spot puts the emphasis on aged steaks and chateaubriand made with tender Alberta beef. Live music and dancing take place most nights. Try the El Rancho coffee shop for less expensive, more informal meals. *526 Mayor Magrath Dr., tel. 403/327–5701. Reservations advised. Jacket advised. AE, CB, DC, MC, V. Expensive.*

Sven Eriksen's Family Restaurant. The homey colonial-style place features hearty and tasty versions of Canadian prairie standards like chicken, seafood, and an especially good prime rib. "Family Restaurant" label notwithstanding, there's a full bar. *1715 Mayor Magrath Dr., tel. 403/328–7756. Reservations advised, especially on weekends. Dress: casual. AE, MC, V. Moderate.*

Lodging *Lethbridge* **Lethbridge Lodge Hotel.** This modern-day lodge has great Oldman River views and a pleasant tropical courtyard. *320 Scenic Dr., T1J 4B4, tel. 800/661–1232 or 403/328–1123. 190 rooms, including nonsmoking rooms. Facilities: restaurant, lounge, indoor pool, whirlpool. AE, MC, V. Moderate.*

Park Plaza Hotel. This comfortable hotel is a good bargain within walking distance of Henderson Lake Park. *1009 Mayor Magrath Dr., T1K 2P7, tel. 403/328–2366. 64 rooms, including* *nonsmoking rooms. Facilities: restaurant, lounge. AE, MC, V. Inexpensive.*

Medicine Hat **Medicine Hat Lodge.** Situated on the edge of town adjacent to a shopping mall, this hotel has several rooms with inward views of the indoor pool, whirlpool, and huge curving water slide. The Atrium Dining Room serves fine Continental meals. J.D.'s is a hotel country-and-western spot. *1051 Glen Dr. SE, T1B 3T8, tel. 403/529–2222 or 800/661–8095. 190 rooms, including nonsmoking rooms. Facilities: 2 restaurants, 2 lounges, indoor pool, whirlpool, waterslide, steam room. AE, CB, DC, MC, V. Moderate.*

Excursion from Regina: Swift Current to Cypress Hills Provincial Park

West of Regina, the Canadian West begins as the square townships and straight roads of the grain-belt prairie farms gradually give way to the arid rolling hills of the upland plains ranches.

The Trans-Canada Highway skirts the edge of the Missouri Coteau—glacial hills that divide the prairie from the dry western plain—on its way west to **Swift Current** (174 kilometers, or 108 miles). The West begins at Swift Current (population 16,000), which cultivates the image during Frontier Days Stampede and rodeo (*see* Festivals and Seasonal Events in Chapter 1). Further depicting Swift are the exhibits at the **Swift Current Museum,** where pioneer and Indian artifacts and exhibits of local natural history are displayed. *105 Chaplin St., tel. 306/778–2775. Admission free. Open July–Aug., daily 2–5, 7–9; June and Sept.–Oct. 15, weekends and Mon. 2–5, Tues.–Fri. 7–9; Oct. 15–May, Sun. and Mon. 2–5.*

Along the next 128-kilometer (80-mile) stretch of the Trans-Canada Highway, the road skirts the southern edge of **The Great Sand Hills.** These desertlike remnants of a huge glacial lake now abound with such native wildlife as pronghorn antelope, mule deer, coyote, jackrabbit, and kangaroo rats. Heading south on Highway 21 will bring you into **Maple Creek,** a self-styled "old cow town," with a number of preserved Old West storefronts. Saskatchewan's oldest museum, the **Old Timer's Museum,** features pictures and artifacts of Mounties, early ranchers, and Indians. *218 Jasper St., tel. 306/662–2474. Admission: $2 adults, $1 seniors, 50¢ children. Open daily 10–5.*

Time Out It doesn't look like much from the outside, but inside the **Commercial Hotel** (Pacific Ave., tel. 306/662–2673) is a haphazardly preserved specimen of an Old West hotel and saloon. The bar, restaurant, and lobby are adorned with trophies of local game. This is a class joint, or so indicates the sign that warns "Your Shoes Must Be Cleaned" for admittance to the hotel.

Drive south on Highway 21 for another 27 kilometers (17 miles) to **Cypress Hills Provincial Park.** Cypress Hills consists of two sections, a Centre Block and Western Block, which are about 25 kilometers (16 miles) apart and separated by non-park land. The larger Western Block abuts the border with Alberta and is connected to Alberta's Cypress Hills Provincial Park (*see* Excursion from Calgary, above). Within the Centre Block, the Cypress Hills plateau, rising more than 4,000 feet above sea level, is covered with spruce, aspen, and lodgepole pines that were erroneously identified as cypress by early European explorers. From Lookout Point you have a 50-mile-range view of Maple Creek and the Great Sand Hills beyond. In addition to the wildlife and flora that abound in the park, there is Cypress Four Seasons (*see* Lodging, below) resort, complete with a golf course, tennis courts, campgrounds, riding stables, and a full complement of winter sports. Maps are available at the Administrative Building near the park entrance. *Cypress Hills Provincial Park, Hwy. 21, tel. 306/662–4411. Admission: $5/day per car, senior drivers free. Open year-round.*

A rough gravel road connects the Cypress Hills Centre Block plateau with the Western Block plateau. During wet weather, take Highway 21 north to Maple Creek and Highway 271 southwest to the Western Block.

The two blocks share the same plant life, animal life, and scenic vistas, but the Western Block also encompasses **Fort Walsh National Historic Park.** The original fort was built by the Mounties in 1875 to establish order between the "wolfers" (whiskey traders) and the Assiniboine Indians. Fort Walsh remained the center of local commerce until its abandonment in 1883. Today, free bus service is available between the **Visitor Reception Centre** and the reconstructed fort itself, Farwell's Trading Post, and a picnic area. No private vehicles are permitted beyond the parking area. *Ft. Walsh, Hwy. 271, 55 km (34 mi) southwest of Maple Creek, tel. 306/667–2645. Admission free. Open mid-May–mid-Oct., daily 9–6.*

Dining

For rates, *see* Dining and Lodging chart, above.

Cypress Hills

Cypress Four Seasons Resort. Located within the Centre Block of Cypress Hills Provincial Park, the restaurant of the resort is a bright and woodsy place with picture windows overlooking the forest. The standard Canadian fare is more successful than the Chinese dishes on the menu. *Box 1480, Maple Creek, tel. 306/662–4477. No reservations. Dress: casual. MC, V. Moderate.*

Swift Current

Wong's Kitchen. This longtime area favorite features fine Canadian food and an even better Oriental menu: dry garlic ribs are the star attraction. Count on live entertainment nightly. *Hwy. 1, S. Service Rd., tel. 306/773–6244. Reservations advised. Dress: casual. AE, MC, V. Expensive.*

Lodging

Cypress Hills

Cypress Four Seasons Resort. It's not part of the Four Seasons chain, but the rooms here are new, comfortable, modern, and right in the middle of a lodgepole pine forest. Either pastel or earth tones adorn the rooms that are contemporary with basic amenities. *Box 1480, Maple Creek, S0N 1N0, tel. 306/662–4477. 35 rooms; cabins and condos. Facilities: restaurant, lounge, indoor pool, whirlpool. MC, V. Moderate.*

Swift Current

Horseshoe Lodge. It's conveniently situated along the Trans-Canada Highway service road, yet the rooms still have fine views of the surrounding countryside. The cocktail lounge is a popular meeting spot, and the restaurant features solid Canadian cooking. *Mobile Rte. 35 Hwy. 1E, S9H 3X6, tel. 306/773–4643. 49 rooms. Facilities: 2 restaurants, lounge, outdoor pool. AE, CB, DC, MC, V. Inexpensive.*

Excursion from Winnipeg: Western Manitoba, The Grain Belt

East of Winnipeg you enter Manitoba's Grain Belt, thousands of acres of exceptionally fertile black loam prairie soil covered principally with wheat, barley, and oats but irrigated enough to produce market garden crops like onions, carrots, tomatoes, potatoes, cabbage, corn, and sunflowers. The first settlers, Scottish and Irish immigrants who arrived in the early 19th century under the sponsorship of Lord Selkirk, laid out river lots along the Assiniboine River and named them after Scottish and French saints. Today's visitors can get into the Grain Belt spirit by staying at—and maybe pitching in on the chores at—a working farm or ranch. For information, request the booklet "Manitoba Farm Vacations" from Travel Manitoba (tel. 800/665–0040).

Head west out of Winnipeg on Portage Avenue (Highway 1). At the junction of Highway 26 in St. François Xavier you can't miss the striking **White Horse Statue.** According to legend, an Indian maiden and her Cree bridegroom attempted to escape the arrows of a rejected Sioux suitor who was riding a white horse. The suitor caught and killed them, but local tribes insist the horse escaped with the maiden's soul to haunt the plains forever.

Continuing west on Highway 1 across serious wheat country, the first major town is **Portage la Prairie,** so named because fur traders carrying canoes between the Assiniboine River to the south and Lake Manitoba to the north would rest here. The principal mid-town attraction is **Island Park and Crescent Lake,** which surrounds a deer and waterfowl sanctuary that has a large captive flock of Canada geese. *Jct. Saskatchewan Ave. and Royal Rd., tel. 204/857–7778. Admission free.*

Fort la Reine Museum and Pioneer Village, whose original fort was built in 1738 and was base of operations for French-Canadian explorer Gaultier de la Verendrye, is situated on the edge of town. Today, the installation depicts 19th-century pioneer life, with shops, a log homestead, and a circa-1890 "Farm of the Century" home. *Rte. 1 and Yellow Quill Trail, tel. 204/857–3259. Admission: $1 adults, 75¢ children under 12. Open May–mid-Sept., weekdays 8–6, weekends 10–6.*

Fifty kilometers (31 miles) farther west on Highway 1 is Austin, distinguished by the **Manitoba Agricultural Museum.** With more than 500 machines, the museum houses the largest collection of working vintage farm equipment in Canada. **Homesteader's Village,** on the same site, is a re-created 1890 prairie hamlet, circa 1890. *On Rte. 34, 2.5 km (1½ mi), south of Rte. 1, tel. 204/637–2354. Admission: $2 adults, children under 12 free. Open mid-May–mid-Oct., daily 10–6.*

Dining and Lodging

For rates *see* Dining and Lodging chart, above.

Although there are no lodgings in Austin, there are some in Portage la Prairie, 45 kilometers (28 miles) east of town.

Portage la Prairie

Manitoba Inn. Portage la Prairie's top lodging option is a modern and fully-equipped spot on the southwest fringe of the city. The dining room is one of the city's best bets. *Hwy. 1 and Yellowquill Trail, Box 867, R1N 3C3, tel. 204/857–9791. 63* *rooms. Facilities: 2 restaurants, lounge, indoor pool, sauna. AE, CB, DC, MC, V. Moderate.*

Midtown Motor Inn. This comfortable heart-of-downtown bargain offers rooms and a couple of good spots to eat and drink any time of the day. *177 Saskatchewan Ave. W, R1N 0P5, tel. 204/857–6881. 20 rooms. Facilities: 2 restaurants. AE, CB, DC, MC, V. Inexpensive.*

10 Ontario

Introduction

Ontario is an old Iroquois word meaning "shining waters." The province contains 156,670 square kilometers (68,490 square miles) of fresh water—one quarter of all there is in the world. The waters of the St. Lawrence Seaway and the Great Lakes bound Ontario for a thousand miles on its populous and affluent southern rim. Here its waterways are plied by hulking ocean tankers, lake cruisers, and pleasure craft. But the majority of Ontario's lakes are blue expanses crossed by the occasional lone canoe.

The sheer immensity of Ontario (an area of almost a half-million square miles) makes it hard to discern a character. Inside one political boundary you will find frontier mining towns like South Porcupine, the gentle pastoral scenery of Kitchener's Mennonite farm communities, flashing neon sophistication of midtown Toronto, and gray stone conservatism of townships around Kingston.

The scenery varies tremendously and so do the people. Ontario, with 9 million people, is the most populous province in English Canada. It's home to wealthy industrialists, Indian and Métis trappers, celebrated artists, solitary bush pilots, WASP gentry, and immigrants of all colors and creeds. It has more Germans than Nuremberg, more Italians than Florence, more blacks than Bermuda. The province is as big as two Texases, three Japans, or France, Germany, and Italy combined. As a traveler in a province this big and this diverse, the best you can do is scratch the edges and marvel at the rest—like the first explorers who glimpsed its vastness more than three and a half centuries ago.

In this chapter, we cover the most frequently visited sites in the southern part of the province. Toronto is covered in Chapter 3.

Essential Information

Important Addresses and Numbers

Tourist Information

Ontario

Ontario Travel (Queen's Park, Toronto M7A 2E5, tel. 416/965–4008, in English; 416/965–3448, in French; or 800/668–2946), a division of the Ministry of Tourism and Recreation, can supply information and maps for the entire province. For a free copy of the *Ontario Accommodation Directory*, call 800/668–2746. The provincial government also operates numerous **Travel Information Centres** (open mid-May to Labor Day 8–8, Labor Day to mid-May 8–4:30) throughout the province. All the information centers are open daily; call 800/668–2746.

Ottawa

For information on Ottawa, contact the **Canada's Capital Visitors and Convention Bureau** (222 Queen St., 7th floor, Ont. K1P 5V9, tel. 613/237–5158).

Niagara Falls

Contact the **Niagara Falls, Canada Visitor and Convention Bureau** (4673 Ontario Ave., Niagara Falls L2E 3R1, tel. 416/356–6061).

There is also an **Information Center** (tel. 416/358–3221) at the corner of Highway 420 and Stanley Avenue. You'll see the big

TRAVEL ONTARIO sign shortly after you leave Queen Elizabeth Way, heading east into Niagara Falls.

Niagara-on-the-Lake Festival schedules, lists of hotels and restaurants, and a Historic Guide are available from the **Shaw Festival** (Box 774, Niagara-on-the-Lake, Ont. L0S 1J0, tel. 416/468–2153 or from Toronto 416/361–1544). Also contact the **Chamber of Commerce** (153 King St., Box 1043, tel. 416/468–4263).

Windsor Information on Windsor attractions is available at the **Convention and Visitors Bureau of Windsor, Essex County, and Pelée Island** (80 Chatham Street East, tel. 519/255–6530), weekdays 8:30–4:30.

Emergencies Dial 911 for **fire, police** or **ambulance** service anywhere in Ontario. The main hospital in Ottawa is **General Hospital** (tel. 613/737–7777).

Arriving and Departing by Plane

Airports and Airlines Toronto, the area's major city, is served by **American, Eastern,** and many international carriers, such as **KLM, Air France, El Al,** and **Alitalia** (*see* Chapter 3). Ottawa's Uplands International Airport has direct flights from New York on **Eastern** (tel. 800/327–8376); **Canadian Airlines International** (tel. 800/387–2737), and **Air Canada** (tel. 800/872–0487); and from Toronto via **Canadian Pacific** (tel. 800/733–5491) and **Air Canada.**

The closest airport to Niagara Falls is **Buffalo International Airport. Niagara Scenic Bus Lines** (tel. 716/648–1500 or 416/282–7755) operates a shuttle service from the airport to both the American and Canadian Niagara Falls. Fares are about $8.25 one-way.

Arriving and Departing by Car, Train, and Bus

By Car The **Trans-Canada Highway** links Ottawa with Montréal from the east and goes west through Sault Ste. Marie, Thunder Bay, and into Manitoba. **Highway 7** is the central route between Ottawa and Toronto. From Michigan in the southwest, the **Macdonald–Cartier Highway** (Route 401) connects Windsor, London, Toronto, and Kingston. From New York State, **Queen Elizabeth Way** connects Fort Erie and Niagara Falls with Hamilton and Toronto; an international bridge connects Rooseveltown, New York, to Cornwall, Ontario, from which Highway 401 runs southwest along the shore of Lake Ontario to Toronto. For 24-hour road condition information anywhere in Ontario (especially helpful in the winter), call 416/235–1110.

By Train Ontario is served by cross-Canada **Via Rail** (tel. 800/361–3677) service and connects with **Amtrak** (tel. 800/872–7245) service at Windsor (Detroit) and Fort Erie (Buffalo). VIA Rail operates frequent trains between Toronto/Montréal and Ottawa's modern station at the southeastern end of town (2000 Tremblay Rd., tel. 613/238–8289).

By Bus **Voyageur Lines** (tel. 613/238–5900) offers hourly service from Montréal to Ottawa and frequent service from Toronto, including some express buses. **Greyhound Lines** (check your local phone book) links Ontario with neighboring provinces and the United States.

Getting Around Ottawa

By Taxi Major cab lines, such as **Blue Line** (tel. 613/238–1111) and **Diamond** (tel. 613/235–1821), provide adequate citywide service.

By Bus There are two bus systems in Ottawa, the **Rideau-Carleton Regional Transit Commission** and **La Commission de Transport de la Communaute Regionale de l'Outaouais;** a bus loop joins Ottawa, Hull, and the two systems. Tickets must be purchased in specially designated neighborhood stores, or a cash fare is required. A **Visipass** gives you unlimited rides on buses for one day for $3 adults, $7 family. For schedule and fare information and a public transportation map, call 613/741–4390.

Guided Tours

Ottawa *City Tours* **Gray Line Sightseeing** (tel. 613/748–4426) uses buses on its 50-kilometer (30-mile) sightseeing circuit leaving from Confederation Square from mid-April through October. Gray Lines' two-hour National Capital Tour takes in Parliament Hill, the Central Experimental Farm, Hog's Back Falls, and various embassies, and provides a quick orientation for those who then want to strike out on their own. **Ottawa-Carleton Transportation Commission** (tel. 613/741–4390) runs seven daily coach tours of the capital that last from two to five hours. Tours run mid-April–October.

Boat Tours **Paul's Boat Lines** (tel. 613/733–5186) conducts 75-minute cruises of the Rideau Canal and 90-minute cruises on the Ottawa River, both available in English or French, from mid-May to mid-October. Riverboats can be boarded below the Bytown Museum; canal boats dock across from the National Arts Centre. **Ottawa Riverboat Company** (tel. 613/232–4888 or 613/778–2092) has two-hour cruises on the Ottawa River and shuttle service between the Montebello Hotel and the Chateau Laurier Hotel in Ottawa.

Niagara Falls **Double Deck Tours** are exactly that: A double-decker bus tours the Falls and environs. During the high season, the buses operate every 30 minutes from 9:30 AM, visiting many of the major points of interest. Although the complete tour lasts 90 minutes, you may get off at any stop and grab another bus later in the day. *Tel. 416/295–3051. Cost: $16 adults, $8 children 6–12. A more complete tour lasting 5 hours costs twice as much. Meet at the Maid of the Mist building; no reservations required.*

The following all have air-conditioned limos: **Bluebird Tours** (4357 River Rd., tel. 416/356–5462), **Honeymoon Motel Tours** (4943 Clifton Hill, tel. 416/357–4330), and **Niagara Clifton Scenic Tours** (5876 Victoria Ave., tel. 416/357–0923).

Niagara Helicopters (Victoria Ave. at the river, tel. 416/357–5672) let you see the Falls at an unforgettable angle. *Major credit cards accepted. Departures Feb.–Dec., 9 AM–sunset.*

Winery Tours takes you on a 30-minute walk through the wine cellars, followed by a wine tasting. The tours are free, but the bottles at the recently expanded retail wine shop are most decidedly not. *4887 Dorchester Rd., off Hwy. 420, tel. 416/357–2400. Tours May–Oct., Mon.–Sat. 10:30, 2, and 3:30; Nov.–Apr., 2 only.*

Niagara-on-the-Lake The **Niagara Foundation** visits local homes and gardens every spring. Phone the Chamber of Commerce (tel. 416/468–2325).

Hillebrand Estates Winery (Hwy. 55, Niagara Stone Rd., tel. 416/468–7123) offers free tours, followed by a free sampling of their award-winning products.

A much larger, more established firm is **Inniskillin Wine,** which offers tours and has numerous displays that illustrate the wine-making procedure inside a 19th-century barn. *Off the Niagara River Pkwy., just south of town, tel. 416/468–2187. Tours June–Oct. daily 10:30 and 2:30; Nov.–May, weekends 2:30.*

Stratford **Stratford Tours Inc.** arranges a variety of tours, including dining and theater. *Box 45, Stratford N5A 6S8, tel. 519/271–8181.*

The Avon Historical Society (tel. 519/271–5140) conducts charming one-hour tours of the city, July 1–Labor Day, daily except Sunday at 9:30 AM. Meet at the tourist information booth at Lakeside Drive and Ontario Street.

Exploring Ontario

Orientation

Our exploration of the province begins in Ottawa and its sister city across the Ottawa River, Hull. Tour 2 travels along the St. Lawrence River and the northern shore of Lake Ontario; Tour 3 threads around the lakes north of Toronto. Tour 4 begins at Niagara Falls, below Lake Ontario, and heads west of Toronto to Windsor, across the river from Detroit, Michigan.

Highlights for First-time Visitors

Canadian Museum of Civilization, Hull, Tour 1: Ottawa and Hull

Changing of the Guard in front of Parliament Hill, Ottawa, Tour 1: Ottawa and Hull

Horseshoe Falls, Niagara Falls, Tour 4: Niagara and West to Windsor

National Gallery of Canada, Ottawa, Tour 1: Ottawa and Hull

Shakespeare Festival, Stratford, Tour 4: Niagara and West to Windsor

Shaw Festival, Niagara-on-the-Lake, Tour 4: Niagara and West to Windsor

Tour 1: Ottawa

In 1858 Queen Victoria astounded Canada by choosing Bytown, a backwoods lumbering town, to be the capital of the new Dominion. Typically, her compromise site pleased neither French-Canadians (who were arguing for Québec City) nor the English (who supported Kingston and Toronto). At any rate Bytown was renamed Ottawa, an Indian word meaning "a place of buying and selling." The name is perhaps a caution to the city's thousands of federal politicians and civil servants.

From a remote village with a population of 7,500 at the time of Confederation, "Westminster in the wilderness" has blossomed into a lively cosmopolitan capital of over 800,000 people. (The verb *blossom* is in Ottawa's case quite literal: the city is full of gardens and parks.) Parliament recesses for the summer, but politics remains the city's driving force. Indeed, the real Ottawa is inaccessible to tourists. It includes a humming gossip network, strategic tables in certain restaurants such as the Château Grill and Les Saisons in the Westin Hotel, and parties in the private homes of Rockcliffe. Still, Ottawa has charms for the apolitical tourist, too. Every May, to commemorate Canada's hospitality toward the exiled Dutch royal family during World War II, the government of Holland sends 3 million tulips, 600,000 daffodils, and a half million crocuses to paint Confederation Square, the banks of the Rideau Canal, and Parliament Hill. In late August the Central Canada Exhibition brings a horse show, a grandstand show, and a midway to town. In winter, skaters swarm on the Rideau Canal, Parliament Hill is floodlit on frosty nights, theater goers glitter in the foyer of the National Arts Centre, and skiers escape to the snowy slopes of the Gatineau Hills.

Numbers in the margin correspond with points of interest on the Lower Ontario Province and Downtown Ottawa maps.

1 The natural place to begin a walking tour of **Ottawa** is on
2 **Parliament Hill,** a 150-foot promontory overlooking the Ottawa River. Designed by architects Thomas Fuller and Chilion Jones, the neo-Gothic **Parliament Buildings** were opened in 1866. The **Peace Tower,** in the center block of the complex, is a 291-foot-high neo-Gothic structure that replaced the original Centre Block after it was gutted by fire in 1916. Ten-foot gargoyles project from each corner of the tower under the four-faced clock. Inside there's a monument to Canada's war dead, a lookout, and a 52-bell carillon. The 22,400-pound Bourdon Bell strikes the hour. Every summer day in front of the Peace Tower—weather permitting—the 30-minute-long changing of the guard ceremony is performed, at 10 AM, complete with pipes, drums, bear-skin hats, and the flashing red coats of the Governor General's Foot Guards and the Canadian Grenadier Guards of Montréal.

To the sides of the Peace Tower and Centre Block are the East and West blocks, their copper roofs oxidized blue-green above gray sandstone. Both are part of the original complex, having partially escaped the fires that devastated the Centre Block. Above the doorway of the **East Block**'s main (150-foot-high) tower are carved the coats of arms of Upper Canada and Lower Canada, which united to form the Confederation of Canada in 1867. On the western facade a carriage porch of cut freestone stands out from the building. At the northern end of the East Block is the entrance to the prime minister's office. The Senate, the House of Commons, and the office of the leader of the opposition are all located in the **Centre Block.** Austere, dignified, the limestone-and-oak hall of the House of Commons is the scene of the debates of Canada's 282 elected members of Parliament. The public is welcome to observe House debates and Question Period (usually the liveliest part of the proceedings), which take place daily when the House is in session. In the Centre Block's blazing gold-and-crimson Senate Chamber the governor-general (the Queen's representative in Canada) reads the speech from the Throne at the opening of each session of Parliament. The Centre Block also houses the library (completed 1876) with its

Lower Ontario Province

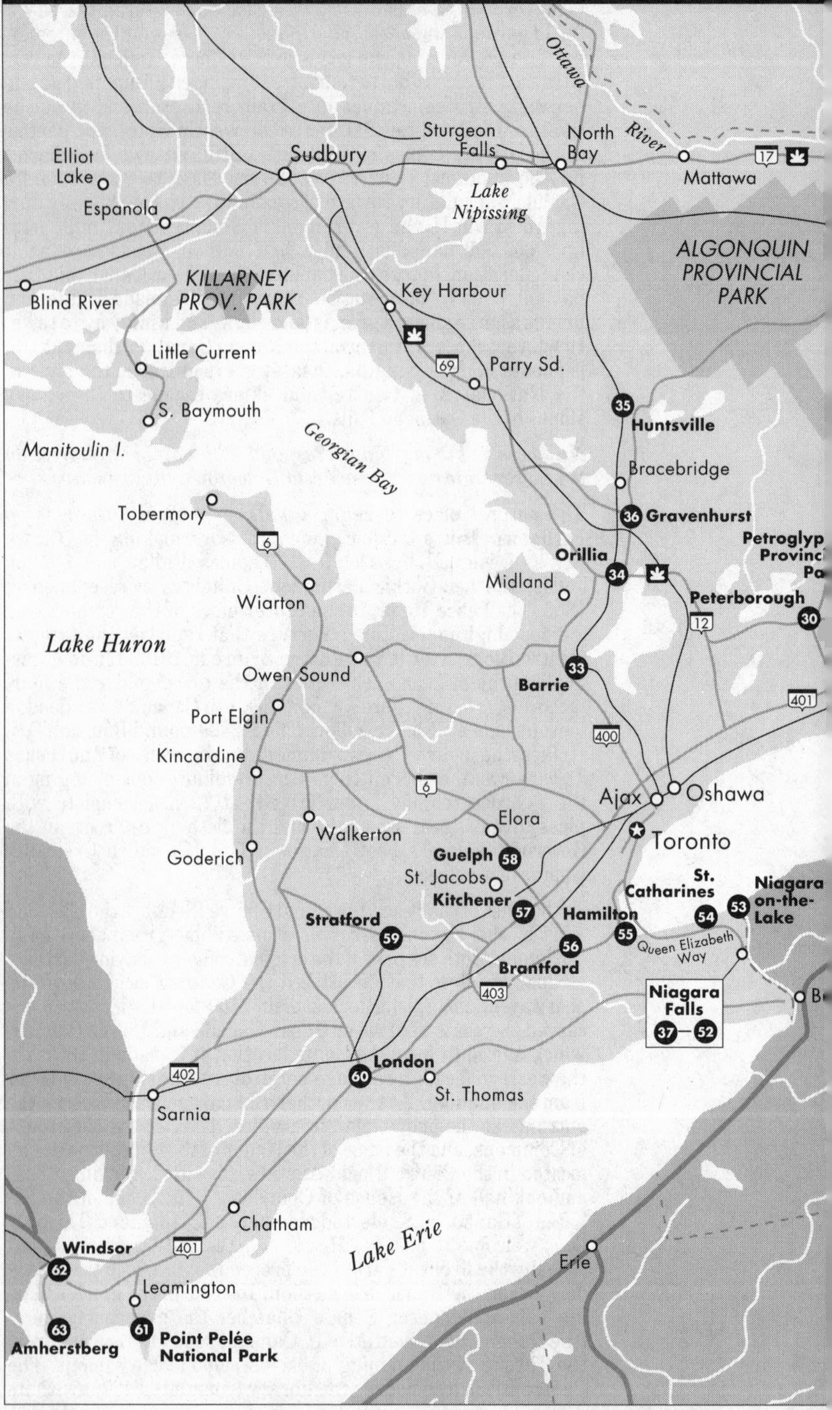

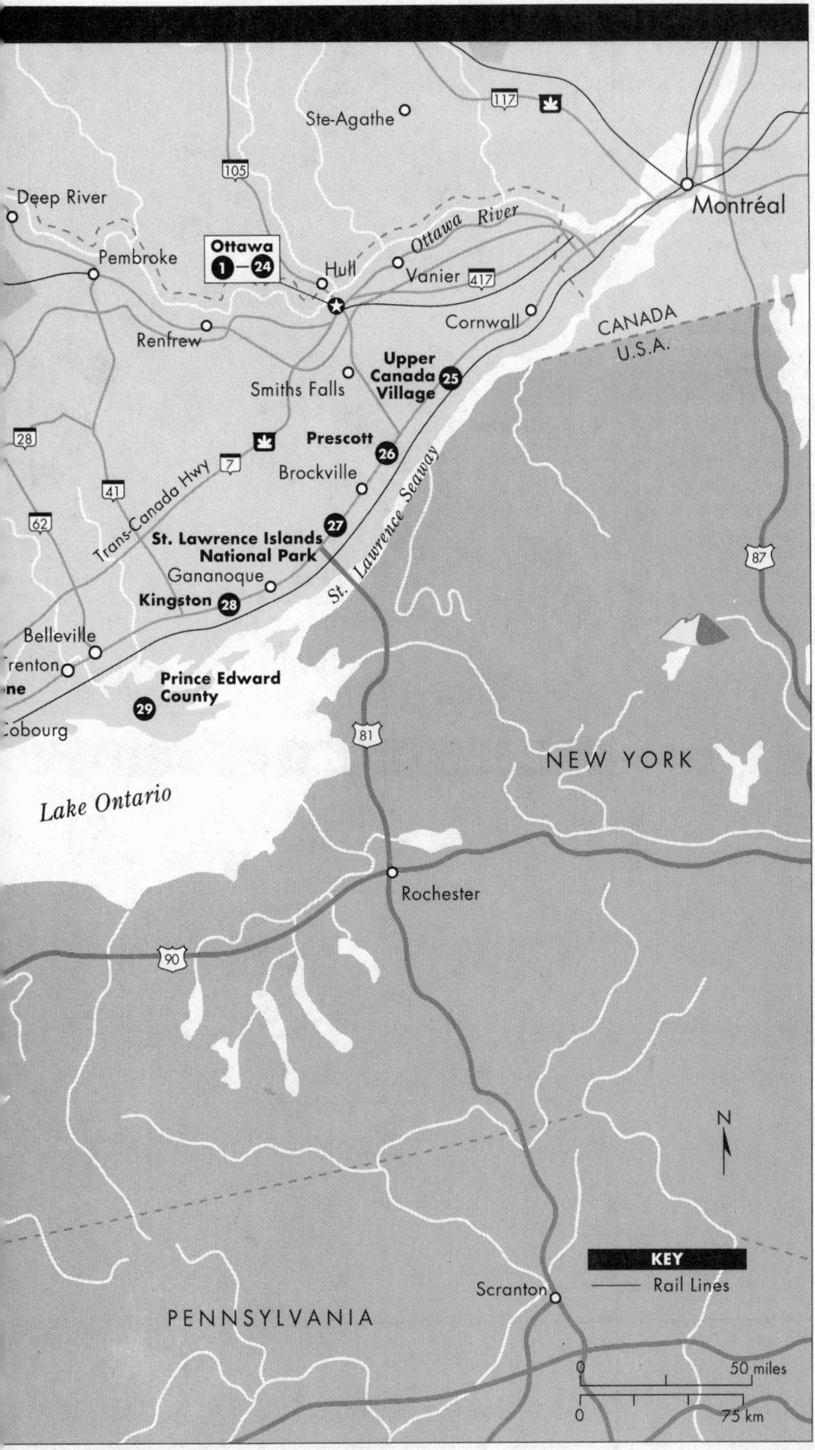
Ste-Agathe
117
105
Deep River
Montréal
Ottawa River
Ottawa
1–24
Pembroke
Hull
Vanier
417
Renfrew
Cornwall
CANADA
U.S.A.
Upper Canada Village
25
Smiths Falls
28
Prescott
26
Trans-Canada Hwy
7
Brockville
41
62
St. Lawrence Seaway
27
St. Lawrence Islands National Park
87
Gananoque
Kingston
28
Belleville
Trenton
Prince Edward County
29
Cobourg
81
NEW YORK
Lake Ontario
Rochester
90
N
KEY
Rail Lines
Scranton
PENNSYLVANIA
0
50 miles
0
75 km

Bytown Museum, **11**
Byward Market, **14**
Canadian Ski Museum, **15**
Canadian War Museum, **19**
Château Laurier, **12**
Confederation Square, **8**
Currency Museum, **3**
National Arts Centre, **9**
National Gallery of Canada, **17**
National Library, **5**
National Postal Museum, **6**
Nepean Point, **18**
Notre Dame Basilica, **16**
Parliament Hill, **2**
Rideau Canal, **10**
Rideau Centre, **13**
Royal Canadian Mint, **20**
Sparks Street Mall, **7**
Supreme Court, **4**

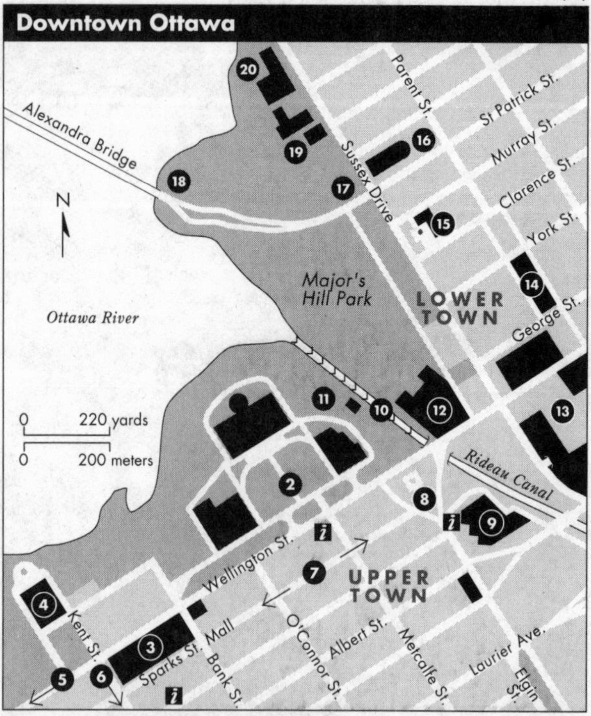

Canadian Museum of Civilization, **24**
Prime Minister's Residence, **22**
Rideau Falls, **21**
Rideau Hall, **23**

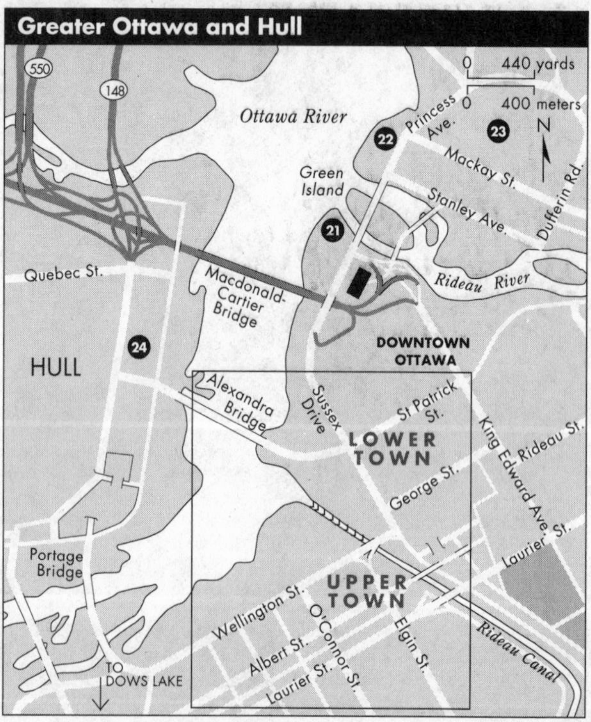

rich paneling, echoing 132-foot dome, and white-marble statue of Queen Victoria. Commons Committee meetings are held in the **West Block,** which also houses the offices of members of parliament. *Tel. 613/992–4793. Open summer, daily 9–8:30, winter, daily 9–4:30. Free 40-min. tours given in English or French; register at white tent near the building.*

Around the Peace Tower stretch Parliament Hill's 29 acres of brilliant lawn. The **Eternal Flame** in the center symbolizes Canadian unity. It is rumored to have gone out six times since it was first lit, in Canada's centennial year, 1967. All coins tossed in the surrounding fountain are given to charity. The grounds of Parliament Hill abound in statues. Among the more notable figures here immortalized are two fathers of Confederation who were assassinated: behind the Centre Block's northwest corner is George Brown, the Toronto journalist who founded the *Globe* (now the *Globe & Mail*, Canada's national newspaper). Brown was a reformer who helped shape the Liberal Party. He also championed runaway slaves who wished to settle in Canada. He died in 1880, after an employee whom Brown had dismissed from the newspaper shot him. Diagonally across from Brown is the Irish-born Thomas D'Arcy McGee, another political reformer, who drew the wrath of the Irish-immigrant Fenian group for criticizing their tactics. One Fenian, acting on his own, shot McGee in 1868. The statue of Sir Wilfred Laurier, Canada's first Francophone (French-speaking) prime minister, can be found in the extreme east corner of the grounds. At the southeast corner of Centre Block is the statue of the hard-drinking visionary, Sir John A. Macdonald, Canada's first prime minister.

Turn right on Wellington Street and walk past Bank Street to
3 the **Bank of Canada,** inside which is the **Currency Museum,** displaying examples of money from ancient times to the present. *Wellington St., tel. 613/782–8914. Admission free. Open Apr.–Sept., Mon.–Sat. 10:30–5, Sun. 1–5; Oct.–Mar., Tues.–Sun. 10:30–5.*

4 Turn right on Kent Street to the **Supreme Court.** Here the public can watch Canada's highest court make final and far-reaching decisions on constitutional, criminal, and civil cases. *Kent and Wellington Sts., tel. 613/995–4330. Free 20-min. tours leave every ½ hour, weekdays 9–5; reservations required.*

At the end of Wellington Street is the **Garden of the Provinces,** flanked by **St. Peter's Lutheran Church,** and **Christ Church Ca-**
5 **thedral.** Across from the garden are the **Public Archives** and the **National Library** (with 400,000 volumes and 100,000 more in micro-copy). The rounded bronze form of a Henry Moore sculpture stands in the foyer; the etched-glass windows on the first floor were created by John Hutton, who fashioned the windows of Coventry Cathedral in England. Books, films, paintings, watercolors, engravings, photographs, and maps are on display. *395 Wellington St., tel. 613/992–3052. Admission free. Open daily 9–9.*

Turn down Kent Street, heading away from the river, to visit
6 the **National Postal Museum.** Old photographs, old mailbags and pouches, ornate brass letter-scales, hand-canceling hammers, and a priceless collection of stamps make this an intriguing place to browse, even for nonphilatelists. An old general store and post office, circa 1885, have been reconstructed here,

right down to the weathered floorboards, tin boxes of medicinal herbs, glass jars, crocks, and earthenware. At the counter of the store you can buy the latest-mint stamps, first-day covers, and postcards. If you mail one from the store's Victorian mailbox, it will receive the special Postal Museum cancellation. *365 Laurier Ave. W, tel. 613/995–9904. Admission free. Open Tues., Thurs.–Sat. 9–5; Wed. 1–5.*

7 Now head back toward Parliament Hill via **Sparks Street pedestrian mall,** where rock gardens, fountains, sculpture, and café
tables have replaced automobiles, bringing thousands of
browsers and tourists to shop on balmy summer days. Emerg-
8 ing from the Sparks Street Mall, you'll face **Confederation
Square,** and the dense, heroic bronze figures of **Canada's War
Memorial.** Unveiled by King George VI in 1939, it commemorates the 66,655 Canadian dead of World War I. Ironically, the memorial was completed on the eve of World War II. The 70-foot-high sculpture is the work of Vernon March.

Adjacent to the square stands the three-theater complex of the
9 **National Arts Centre,** focus of the city's cultural life. Here you can enjoy dinner before a ballet or symphony in the 2,300-seat opera theater, hear drama in an 800-seat thrust-stage theater, or see something more avant-garde in the 300-seat experimental studio. Music, dance, and two resident (French and English) drama companies play here. The National Arts Centre Orchestra is a 45-member symphony conducted by Franco Mannino. The Arts Centre also features a pleasant waterside café, where on winter days you can watch the unusual but typically Ottawan sight of briefcase-carrying civil servants skating to work along the Rideau Canal.

10 The **Rideau Canal** winds through the heart of the city and falls
to the Ottawa River below Parliament Hill. The 3½-mile-long
Queen Elizabeth Driveway that follows the course of the canal
features cycle paths, shady spots to stop and gaze over the water, and, in May, Ottawa's famous tulips. Beside Parliament
Hill is a deep gorge, where eight manual locks can lift boats 79
feet up from the Ottawa River to the canal. Follow the steps
11 down the gorge to **Bytown Museum,** housed in an 1827 commissariat store that is Ottawa's oldest stone building. Most of its 3,500 artifacts relate to the building of the Rideau Canal, the development of Ottawa, and the personal history of Colonel By, an engineer in charge of the building of the canal. *Tel. 613/234–4570. Admission: $2 adults, $1 students and senior citizens, 50¢ children. Open Apr.–Nov., daily 10–4. Closed holidays.*

Climb back up to Wellington Street and take the bridge across
12 the canal. On your left is **Château Laurier,** one of Canada's
grand old hotels, which looks like an oversized, gray-turreted
baronial castle (*see* Lodging, below). Ahead of you, at the cor-
13 ner of Rideau Street and Sussex Drive, is the **Rideau Centre,** a
two-level modern complex containing some 200 stores.

You are now in **Lower Town,** as Ottawans call the section of the
city that lies across the canal from Parliament Hill. One block
past Sussex Drive, between York and George streets, is
14 **Byward Market,** a lively market, where since 1846 local farmers
have hawked cheeses, pickles, fresh produce, and cut flowers.

Our tour continues up Sussex Drive, where the original Georgian and Victorian shopfronts have been restored to house boutiques, art galleries, and cafés. On the second floor of the

historic stone building between Clarence and Murray streets is
15 the **Canadian Ski Museum,** where you'll see ancient skis and vintage photographs of skiers. *457A Sussex Dr., tel. 613/233–5832. Admission: $1 adults, 50¢ children 9–16. Open Tues.–Sat., daily 12–4. Closed holidays.*

16 **Notre Dame Basilica** (1841–46) stands on the corner of Sussex Drive and St. Patrick Street. The wood decorations inside were executed by Philippe Parizeau, who also worked on the National Library. *Tel. 613/236–7496. Tours free. Open daily 9–noon, 1:30–4:30.*

17 Across Sussex Drive is the new home of the **National Gallery of Canada,** a glass cathedral complex designed by Israeli-Canadian architect Moshe Safdie. Exhibits inside emphasize the work of Canadian artists, including Tom Thomson and the Group of Seven. *380 Sussex Dr., tel. 613/990–1985. Admission: $4 adults, $3 senior citizens and students. Closed Mon. during winter.*

If you turn left off Sussex Drive toward Alexandra Bridge,
18 you'll find yourself at **Nepean Point,** a small public park with a big beautiful view that encompasses the odd duality of the capital's character. Behind you, on an imposing bluff rising out of the Ottawa River, are the gray spires and distinguished blocks of Parliament Hill. Across the river is a tangle of industrial buildings and neon: Hull, Québec, which for a long time was, frankly, the most interesting part of Ottawa, Ontario. A statue of Samuel de Champlain, the French explorer, geographer, and governor of New France, gazes across the city from Nepean Point.

If you continue north on Sussex Drive, you soon pass on your
19 left the **Canadian War Museum.** Some of the specimens here date back 300 years, to the French-Indian bush wars. Displays include photos, maps, flags, models, a Sopwith Camel airplane, Indian clubs, and one of the finest medal collections in the world. *330 Sussex Dr., tel. 613/992–2774. Admission: $2 adults; $1 children, students, and senior citizens; $5 family. Open daily 9:30–5.*

20 Next door stands the **Royal Canadian Mint,** which produces all of Canada's coin currency. The mint also has a good display of historic coinage. *320 Sussex Dr., tel. 613/993–3500. Admission and tour free, by appointment only, weekdays except holidays.*

Numbers in the margin correspond with points of interest on the Greater Ottawa and Hull map.

You may want to use a car or bicycle to continue along Sussex Drive as it skirts the Ottawa River above limestone bluffs. Monumental institutional architecture gives way to the elegant leafy streets of Rockcliffe Park, the home of many governmental officials, embassies, and official residences. Past the
21 Macdonald Cartier Bridge you'll come to **Rideau Falls.** *Rideau* is French for *curtain,* and the double falls here form a striking curtain of water. In the 19th century, this was a major industrial site of water-powered textile and lumber mills, foundries, and breweries.

22 The **prime minister's residence** (24 Sussex Dr.) is a gray-stone mansion built in 1868. It was acquired by the government in 1943 and Prime Minister Louis St. Laurent became its first prime-ministerial occupant, in 1950.

23 Government House (**Rideau Hall**), the official residence of the governor-general, is across a park from the prime minister's residence, on MacKay Street. Built in 1838, it has its own ballroom, skating rink, and cricket pitch.

Cross the river on either the Macdonald Cartier Bridge or the Alexandra Bridge to visit **Hull.** Ottawa's relationship with Hull is symbiotic, for Ottawa has traditionally relied on the Québec lumbering town to alleviate its burdens of state—and in fact Hull still has many of the capital's finest French restaurants and liveliest nightclubs. Spurred by the city's raunchy reputation and relatively high crime rate, Hull is cleaning up its taverns.

24 While in Hull you may enjoy a visit to the **Canadian Museum of Civilization,** in its sweeping new complex designed by Canadian Métis architect Douglas Cardinal. The historical and anthropological exhibits inside provide a wealth of information. *100 Laurier St., Hull, Québec, tel. 819/776–7000. Admission: $4 adults, $3 senior citizens and students; children under 15 free. Admission free on Thurs. Open Tues.–Sun. 9–5, Thurs. 9–9.*

Tour 2: Heritage Highway

Most of Ontario's first French, English, and Loyalist settlers entered the province from the southeast. You can retrace some of their routes on southern Ontario's Heritage Highways. Highway 2, parallel to Highway 401, is smaller than the cross-Ontario freeway but more picturesque. It's the original 19th-century route that linked Québec and Kingston to "Muddy York" (Toronto) in the west.

Numbers in the margin correspond with points of interest on the Lower Ontario Province map.

From Ottawa Route 31 leads southeast about 75 kilometers (45 miles) to Highway 2. Go a few miles east, past Morrisburg, to
25 reach **Upper Canada Village,** a faithful re-creation of an Ontario community in the early 1800s. When the construction of the St. Lawrence Seaway flooded some riverside communities, the historic buildings were moved to the site of the Battle of Crysler's Farm, a dramatic military engagement in 1813. There is no echo of musketry today, however, in the peaceful, mid-19th-century Upper Canadian town that has been re-created at Crysler's Farm. You can tour the site by horse-drawn boat, ox-cart, or on foot, and visit a general store, church, tavern, or schoolmaster's house. In most of the more than 40 buildings there are costumed guides waiting to answer your questions. *Hwy. 2 East, tel. 613/537–2200. Admission: $7.25 adults, $5.50 students, $3.75 senior citizens, $2.50 children 6–12, children under 6 free. Open May 15–Oct. 15 daily, 9:30–5.*

Head west on Highway 2 about 40 kilometers (25 miles) to
26 **Prescott.** Here you can visit **Fort Wellington and the Old Lighthouse** (both of which saw action in the War of 1812), now restored and open to the public. Canadian, American, and French regiments perform period drills dressed in period costume in mid-July. You can also visit Prescott's old wood chapel (the Blue Church, built 1845). In its cemetery are the graves of many early settlers, including Barbara Heck, founder of Methodism in North America. *Fort Wellington and the Old Lighthouse, 370 Vankoughnet St., tel. 613/925–2896. Admission*

free. Open May 15–Aug., daily 10–6; Sept.–Oct. 15, daily 10–5; Oct. 16–May 14 by reservation only.

A scenic stretch of the highway leads to Brockville (named after Sir Isaac Brock, hero of the War of 1812), an entry point to
27 the **St. Lawrence Islands National Park,** which consists of 17 islands and some 80 rocky islets strung along 80 kilometers (50 miles) of Lake Ontario's coast. The mainland base is at **Mallorytown Landing,** about 25 kilometers (15 miles) past Brockville. At the park headquarters at the landing, there's a swimming beach, playground, and half-hour nature trail, as well as the Brown's Bay wreck exhibit, displaying a resurrected sunken 19th-century gunboat. There are plenty of docking facilities around the islands if you've brought your own boat; you can rent boats at Brockville, or take a boat tour from Rockport, Gananoque, or Ivy Lea through the Thousand Islands. *Box 469, RR 3, Mallorytown Landing, tel. 613/923–5241 or 613/923–5443. Park open year-round, campgrounds mid-May–mid-Oct.*

28 The city of **Kingston,** solid and enduring like the gray limestone of which it is built, was founded in 1673 by Count Frontenac, the governor of New France. There is a real spirit of Upper Canadian colonialism about the city. Martello towers (structures similar to those the British erected to guard the coasts of their other colonies) guard the harbor. Situated at the point where the Rideau Canal system and Lake Ontario join the St. Lawrence River, Kingston is very much a harbor town. In 1976 it was the site of the XXI Olympiad's yachting events. In late August the former Olympic site becomes the site of North American training regattas. Its 19th-century naval glory is recalled at the old shipbuilding yards (now on Royal Military College grounds), at the century-and-a-half-old Rideau Canal locks at Kingston Mills, and by the bright sails and riggings of the pleasure craft clustered in the city's harbor.

At **Old Fort Henry,** once the principal military stronghold of Upper Canada, you can see a splendid display of infantry, cavalry, artillery, and naval equipment. Muzzle-loading cannon, cast in 1874, blast salutes; and red-coated army cadets execute the traditional changing of the guard. *Hwy. 2 and 15, tel. 613/542–7388. Admission: $2.50 adults, $1 senior citizens, $1.25 children 6–18, children under 6 free. Open Wed.–Sun., daily 10–4. Closed holidays.*

Canada's **Royal Military College** features a museum with a fine weapons collection (housed in a Martello tower). *Hwy. 2 and 15, tel. 613/541–5010. Admission free. Open July–Sept., daily 10–5; Oct.–June, tours arranged by appointment.*

Bellevue House, a Tuscan-style villa, was once the home of Canada's first prime minister, Sir John A. Macdonald. *35 Center St., tel. 613/545–8666. Admission free. Open May–Nov., daily 9–6, Dec.–Apr., daily 10–5.*

Don't leave Kingston without dropping by the **Pump House Steam Museum,** housed in an imposing pile of Victorian limestone on the waterfront. It has the biggest working-order steam exhibit in the world. *23 Ontario St., tel. 613/546–4696. Admission: $2 adults, $1.50 senior citizens and students. Open July 15–Oct., daily 10–5; Mar.–July 14, daily 9–5.*

An hour's drive southwest on Highway 2 will bring you to **Belleville**, where you can cross a bridge to the out-of-the-way
29 pastoral countryside of the **Prince Edward County Peninsula.** Much of the peninsula was settled by German refugees from the American Revolutionary War. Still in use in the county center of **Picton** (population 4,300) is the original Greek revival courthouse, built in 1832, where Sir John A. Macdonald once practiced law. The Prince Edward County Peninsula is rich in historic sites; it also offers some beautiful lakeside campsites, like the breezy dunes of Sandbanks and North Beach provincial parks (18 kilometers, or 11 miles, west of Picton).

Another hour or so past Belleville is **Cobourg** and its neighboring city, **Port Hope,** both rich in architecture, particularly the 19th-century mansions of the wealthy Americans who summered here. Turn north from Highway 2 up Highway 28, traveling through the Great Pine Ridge and Kawartha Lakes
30 vacation regions, to come to **Peterborough,** a university town of 61,000 people. Besides the intricate modern architecture of Trent University, Peterborough offers the Kawartha Downs standard-bred racetrack, the second highest hydraulic lift locks in the world (on the Trent-Severn Waterway), and the annual Peterborough Summer Festival (aquatic events, music, and theater, in early July). On Saturday morning pick up some fresh fruit and baked goods at the local farmers' market, in Morrow Park. Rare pioneer homespun cloth, toys, photos, fossils, and an animated model of the Trent-Severn Waterway are only part of the collection of the **Peterborough Centennial Museum.** *Armour Hill (above lift lock), tel. 705/743–5180. Admission: $2.50 adults, $2 senior citizens and students, $1 children 6–12, children under 6 free, $5 families. Open late-May–mid-Oct., weekdays 9–5, weekends 10–5; late-Oct.–mid-May, weekdays 9–5, weekends noon–5.*

31 South of Peterborough, in **Keene,** you can visit 14 restored pioneer buildings at **Land Pioneer Village,** on the shore of the Indian River. *RR 3, tel. 705/295–6694. Admission: $4.25 adults, $3.50 senior citizens, $2.75 students, $2 children under 12, $11 family. Open mid-May–mid-Oct, weekdays 11–5, Sat. 1–5, Sun. 1–6.*

Also in Keene, picnickers mingle with archaeologists at the **Serpent Mounds Provincial Park.** Here a mysterious six-foot-high man-made mound snakes across the landscape; archaeological exhibits help visitors appreciate the park's Indian burial mounds. A campsite overlooks Rice Lake. *RR 3, tel. 705/295–6879. Admission: $5 per vehicle. Open mid-May–mid-Oct., daily.*

32 On Highway 28 north of Peterborough, in Woodview, **Petroglyphs Provincial Park** preserves prehistoric Indian paintings of unusual black symbols on the white rock. Hiking trails lead to a waterfall. *Tel. 705/877–2552. Admission: $5 per vehicle. Open mid-May–June, daily 9–5; July–Aug. 10–6; Sept.–mid-Oct. 9–5.*

Tour 3: North of Toronto to the Lakes

Numbers in the margin correspond with points of interest on the Lower Ontario Province map.

North on Route 400 from Toronto some 75 kilometers (45 miles)
33 you'll come to **Barrie,** a thriving city of 49,000 situated on the shores of Lake Simcoe. In winter it attracts ice fisherman and, at its Winter Carnival, ice motorcyclists, dog sledders, and other winter-sport sensation seekers. The town offers straw-hat theater at the Gryphon Theater, floodlit harness racing at Barrie Raceway, and lakeside regattas.

34 At the turn of the century **Orillia,** Barrie's sister city, at the junction of Lakes Simcoe and Couchiching, was a flourishing resort drawing regular vacationers from as far away as Memphis, Tennessee. Humorist Stephen Leacock immortalized Orillia's golden years in *Sunshine Sketches of a Little Town,* still recommended reading for ramblers through small-town Ontario. You can visit Leacock's summer home, a white colonial-style house off Highway 12B, from June to September in Orillia.

North of Orillia the gentle landscape changes to the granite-and-pine scenery of the Canadian Shield. You are in Muskoka, a resort region whose population triples in summer. Among Muskoka's sights are **Santa's Village** (at Bracebridge, open all summer); the 40-foot totem pole on **Canoe Lake** (a memorial to artist Tom Thomson, who disappeared here half a century ago);
35 and **Muskoka Pioneer Village** at **Huntsville** (Box 2082, Brunel Rd., tel. 705/789–7576; admission $4 adults, $2.75 senior citizens, $2.25 students; open July–mid-Oct., daily 10–5).

36 **Gravenhurst,** a holiday town on Lake Muskoka, is the birthplace of Norman Bethune, a Canadian doctor who treated Mao Tse-Tung's army of peasant revolutionaries and became a hero in the Peoples' Republic of China. Visitors from China make pilgrimages to Bethune's birthplace. North American visitors to Gravenhurst are attracted by summer theater at its restored Opera House, by lakeside Sunday evening concerts, and by cruises aboard the S.S. *Segwun.*

Tour 4: Niagara and West to Windsor

Numbers in the margin correspond with points of interest on the Lower Ontario Province and Niagara Falls maps.

Southeast of Toronto, near the border with New York State, is the popular Niagara area. West of Toronto, the Macdonald-Cartier Highway (401) leads through the cities of Kitchener and London to Windsor, just across the border from Detroit, Michigan.

37 Cynics have had their field day with **Niagara Falls,** calling it everything from "water on the rocks" to "the second major disappointment of American married life" (Oscar Wilde).

Others have been more positive. Missionary and explorer Louis Hennepin, whose books were widely read across Europe, first described the falls in 1678 as "an incredible Cataract or Waterfall which has no equal." Nearly two centuries later, novelist Charles Dickens wrote, "I seemed to be lifted from the earth and to be looking into Heaven. Niagara was at once stamped upon my heart, an image of beauty, to remain there changeless and indelible."

The Falls alone—with a combined flow of close to 11.5 million gallons per second—are obviously worth the 75-minute drive from Toronto, the 30-minute drive from Buffalo, New York, or whatever time it takes to come from anywhere else. It is, after all, the greatest waterfall in the world, by volume. Over 10,000 years ago—long before the first "My Parents Visited Niagara Falls and All They Got Me Was This Lousy T-Shirt" T-shirts—the glaciers receded, diverting the waters of Lake Erie northward into Lake Ontario. (Before that time, they had drained south; such are the fickle ways of nature.) There has been considerable erosion since that time: More than seven miles in all, as the soft shale and sandstone of the escarpment have been washed away. Wisely, there have been major water diversions for a generating station (in 1954) and other machinations (1954–1963), which have spread the flow more evenly over the entire crestline of the Horseshoe Falls. The erosion is now down to as little as one foot every decade, so you needn't rush your visit.

There's some interesting history to the rest of the area, as well. The War of 1812 had settlers on both sides of the river killing one another, with the greatest battle taking place in Niagara Falls itself, at Lundy's Lane (today, the name of a major street, with a Historical Museum on the site of the battle). Soon after, at the Treaty of Ghent, two modest cities of the same name arose on each side of the river—one in the United States, the other in Canada.

The city of Niagara Falls, Ontario, is quite easy to picture: To the west, running north–south (and eventually east, around Lake Ontario and up to Toronto), is Queen Elizabeth Way. To the east is the Niagara River and the glorious Falls.

38 ***Maid of the Mist*** boats are surely an unforgettable experience; they sail right to the foot of the Falls, and you'll be thankful for the raincoats they give out and for the exciting trip itself. *Boats leave from the foot of Clifton Hill St. Tel. 416/358–5781. Cost: $8 adults, $4.50 children 6–12. Daily from mid-May to late-Oct. From late June through Labor Day, trips leave as often as every 15 minutes, from 9:45 to 7:45; off-season boats leave every 30 minutes weekdays from 9:45 to 5:45; weekends 9:45–4:45.*

39 At **Table Rock Scenic Tunnels,** you don a weatherproof coat and boots, and an elevator takes you down to a fish-eye view of the Canadian Horseshoe Falls and the Niagara River and a walk through three tunnels cut into the rock. *Tours begin at Table Rock House, in Queen Victoria Park. Tel. 416/358–3268. Cost: $5 adults, $4 senior citizens, $2.50 children 6–12. Open mid-June–Labor Day 9 AM–11 PM; 9–5 the rest of the year. Closed Dec. 25.*

40 **Skylon** overlooks the Falls and is more than just a tower; there are amusements for children, entertainment, and shops. Rising 775 feet above the Falls, it does, indeed, have the best view of both the great Niagara and the entire city. There is also an indoor/outdoor observation deck and a revolving dining room. *Tel. 416/356–2651. Admission: $6 adults, $5 senior citizens, $3.50 children 6–18. Open 8:30 AM–1 AM. Go when the Falls are illuminated, especially during the Winter Festival of Lights.*

41 The **Niagara Spanish Aerocar** (the Whirlpool Aerocar) is a cable car that carries you high over the Niagara Gorge—and back, one hopes—on a 1,650-foot-long cable. Far, far below, you watch the river and Whirlpool Basin. *Located on River Rd.,*

Niagara Falls

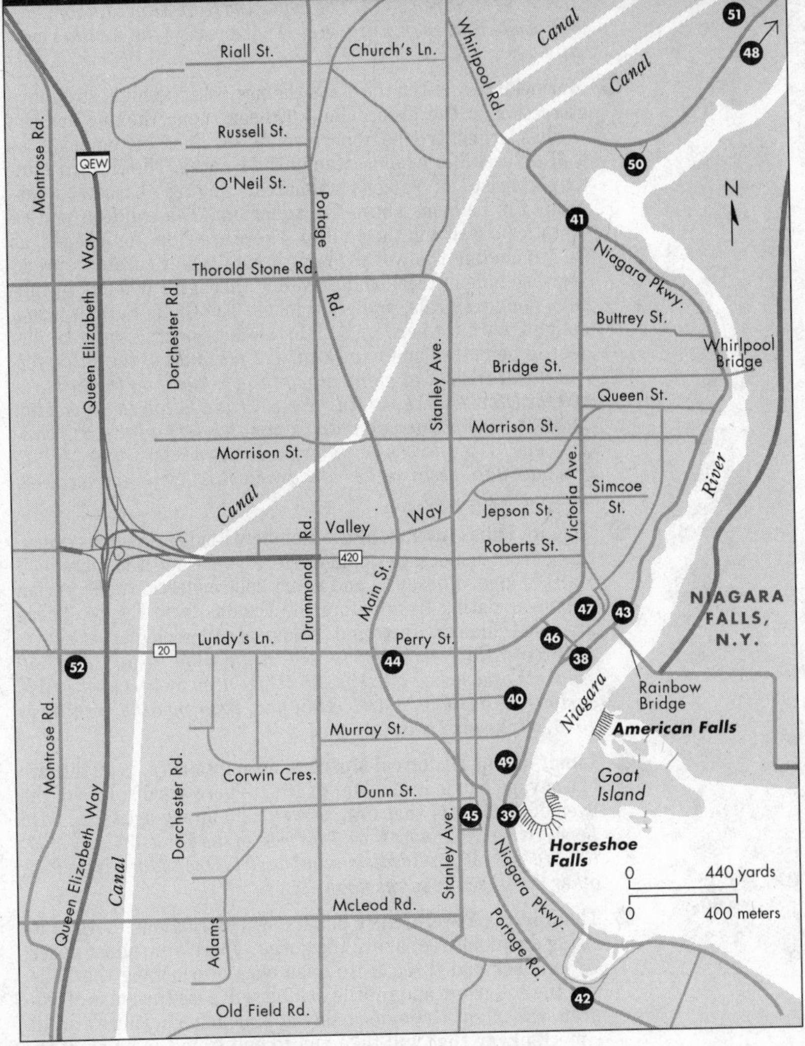

Clifton Hill, **46**
Floral Clock, **48**
Lundy's Lane Historical Museum, **44**
Maid of the Mist, **38**
Maple Leaf Village, **47**
Marineland, **42**
Minolta Tower-Centre, **45**
Niagara Falls Museum, **43**
Niagara Glen Nature Area, **50**
Niagara Parks School of Horticulture, **51**
Niagara Spanish Aerocar, **41**
Queen Victoria Park, **49**
Skylon, **40**
Table Rock Scenic Tunnels, **39**
Whitewater, **52**

about 2 mi north of the Falls, tel. 416/354–5711. Cost: $4 adults, $2 children 6–12. The ride runs from June–Labor Day, 9–9, and from then until mid-October when the weather permits.

42 **Marineland** is, after the Falls themselves, the highest quality attraction in the area. The 4,000-seat aqua theater has the world's largest troupe of performing sea lions and dolphins, as well as two killer whales, Kandu and Nootka. The Hot Air Fantasy consists of various animated, singing characters suspended in balloons above the aquarium. The children will be ecstatic (and so will the adults). There are rides for all ages, as well, including the world's largest steel roller coaster, spread over one mile of track and traveling through 1,000 feet of tunnels, double spirals, and giant loops. The Game Farm is also a delight, with its herd of buffalo, sloth of bears, and over 400 deer to be petted and fed. *Located 1 mi south of the Falls; follow the Marineland signs along the parkway by the falls, or exit the QEW at McLeod Rd. (Exit 27) and follow the signs; tel. 416/356–9565. Admission: approximately $18 adults, $13 children ages 4–9 and senior citizens. In the winter, prices fall to less than half, because the rides are closed. Open summers 9–6, off-season 10–4:30.*

43 **Niagara Falls Museum,** at the Rainbow Bridge, includes everything from schlock to quality. Here you'll find the Daredevil Hall of Fame, dinosaurs, and a very solid collection of Egyptian mummies dating from before the Exodus from Egypt. There are also Indian artifacts and zoological and geological exhibits. *5651 River Rd., tel. 416/356–2151. Admission: $5 adults, $3.50 students and senior citizens, $2.50 children 5–10. Open June–early Oct., daily 8:30 AM–midnight; other months, weekdays 10–5, weekends 11–5.*

44 **Lundy's Lane Historical Museum,** dating to 1874, is on the site of a savage battle in the War of 1812. There are displays of the lives of settlers of that era, as well as military artifacts. *5810 Perry St., a little more than 1 mi west of the Falls, on Hwy. 420; tel. 416/358–5082. Admission: about $1. Open May–Nov. 9–4; other months, weekdays noon–4.*

45 The **Minolta Tower-Centre** has its own attractions, beyond its rising about 665 feet above the gorge. There's an indoor observation deck and three more open ones overlooking the Falls, and the aquarium and reptile exhibit will ease the pains of children who might be denied a day at Marineland. There's an Incline Railway that will take you to and from the brink of the Falls, and its Top of the Rainbow dining rooms have won at least four restaurant awards during this decade. *6732 Oakes Dr., tel. 416/356–1501. Admission to exhibits or tower: $5 adults, $3.50 children 5–18 and senior citizens. Combination tickets: $7 adults, $6 children or senior citizens. Tower open summers 9 AM–midnight, other times: 10–10. Admission to aquarium and reptile exhibit: $4.25 adults, $3 senior citizens and students. Open May–Nov.*

Children, and adults with great patience, will get a kick out of
46 **Clifton Hill** (tel. 416/356–2299), where you can visit the Movieland Wax Museum, The Haunted House, The House of Frankenstein, The Funhouse, The Guinness Museum of World Records, Louis Tussaud's Waxworks, Ripley's Believe It or Not Museum, and the Super Star Recording Studio, where you can

make a tape/video of your fabulous voice/face. This is tourism at its most touristy.

47 **Maple Leaf Village** is a 350-foot observation tower with rides, games, shops, shows, and one of the largest Ferris wheels in captivity. This is where you'll find—if you dare—the That's Incredible Museum and The Elvis Presley Museum. *Clifton Hill and Falls Ave., at the Canadian terminus of the Rainbow Bridge; tel. 416/357–3090. Prices vary for various rides; admission to the village itself is free. Attractions are open mid-June–Labor Day 10 AM–midnight. The tower is open year-round.*

48 The **Floral Clock** is less than 10 kilometers (6 miles) north of the Falls, along River Road. Nearly 20,000 plants that bloom from earliest spring to late autumn make up one of the world's biggest, bloomin' clocks. Chimes ring every quarter-hour, and it actually keeps the right time. *Admission free.*

49 **Queen Victoria Park** (tel. 416/356–4699) runs along the Niagara River for 38 kilometers (24 miles). The Niagara Parks Greenhouse has four major horticultural displays each year, and there is an outdoor fragrance garden for the visually handicapped.

About 6.4 kilometers (4 miles) due north of the Falls, along the
50 Niagara Parkway, you can visit the **Niagara Glen Nature Area,** another free and most attractive attraction. You can actually work your way down to the gorge observing the plant life. And
51 just a bit north, along the parkway, is the **Niagara Parks School of Horticulture,** with 100 acres of free exhibits. *Tel. 416/ 356–8554.*

52 **Whitewater** is a water park with everything from mini-slides and mini-pools to five giant slides and a wave pool. *7430 Lundy's Lane at the QEW; tel. 416/357–3380. Open mid-May–mid-September, daily 9AM–11:30 PM. Special rates*

Numbers in the margin correspond with points of interest on the Lower Ontario Province map.

53 Since 1962, **Niagara-on-the-Lake** has been considered the southern outpost of fine summer theater in Ontario—the Shaw Festival. But offering far more than Stratford, its older theatrical sister to the north, this city is a jewel of Canadian history, architectural marvels, remarkable beauty, and, of course, quality theater. Though the town of 14,000 is worth a visit at any time of the year, it's most attractive from late April to mid-October, when both the Shaw Festival and the flowers are in full bloom.

Being located where the Niagara River enters Lake Ontario has both its advantages and disadvantages. Because of its ideal placement, it was settled by Loyalists to the British Crown, who escaped north when most other Americans opted for independence. Soon after, it was made the capital of Upper Canada by John Graves Simcoe. When the provincial parliament was later moved to York—today, Toronto—it changed its name from Newark to Niagara. But that, too, was wisely changed since it was continually confused with a more spectacular town of the same name, just 19 kilometers (12 miles) to the south.

The downside of its location came in the War of 1812 when the Americans came calling, but not as tourists. They captured nearby Fort George in 1813, occupied the town itself that summer, and burned it to the ground that December. The fort is now open for touring mid-May to October. Like so many other heritage sites in Ontario, it is staffed by people in period uniform, who conduct tours and reenact 19th-century infantry and artillery drills.

Some of Niagara-on-the-Lake's best days were in the 1850s, when it was connected to Toronto by steamer and to Buffalo, New York, by train. But that era soon passed with the opening of the Welland Canal and the transfer of the county seat to St. Catherines. It remained a sleepy town until the last quarter-century, when the plays of George Bernard Shaw and his contemporaries began to be performed in the Court House. Today, Niagara-on-the-Lake is one of the best-preserved 19th-century towns on the continent, with many neoclassical and Georgian homes still standing proudly—and lived in, too.

The three theaters used by the Shaw Festival do indeed present quality performances—the 10 productions in the summer of 1990 ranged from epics to murder mysteries, musicals to comedies, even lunchtime theater—but what's also special is the abundance of orchards and flower gardens, sailboats, and the utterly charming town of Niagara-on-the-Lake.

This is a very small town that can easily be explored on foot. Queen Street is the core of the commercial portion of this thriving mini-opolis. Walking east along that single street, with Lake Ontario to your north, you encounter many pleasures.

At **209 Queen** is the handsome Richardson-Kiely House, built circa 1832 for a member of Parliament, with later additions at the turn of the century. At **187 Queen** is an 1822 house, with later Greek Revival improvements. At **165 Queen** is an 1820 beauty, once lived in by a veteran of the Battle of Lundy's Lane, which took place in Niagara Falls in 1814. The house at **157 Queen,** built in 1823, is still occupied by descendants of the Rogers-Harrison family, prominent since the early 19th century in church and town affairs. **McClelland's West End Store** (106 Queen St.) has been in business on this same site since the War of 1812, and with good reason: Its local jams and cheeses are top notch. The huge "T" sign means "provisioner."

Across the street, but facing Victoria Street, is **Grace United Church,** built as recently as 1852. (It began as a congregation of "Free" Presbyterians, who later sold it to the Methodists.) Also at the corner of Queen and Victoria streets is the **Royal George Theater,** one of the three showcases of the Shaw Festival.

The **Court House,** on the next block, still going east, served until 1969 as the municipal offices of the town of Niagara; it recently underwent an award-winning restoration. It is another of the three theaters of the Shaw Festival.

Across the street (5 Queen St.) is the **Niagara Apothecary,** built in 1820 and moved here in 1866. The oldest continuing pharmacy in Upper Canada, it was restored in 1971. Note the exquisite walnut fixtures, crystal pieces, and rare collection of apothecary glasses. *Admission free. Open mid-May–Labor Day, daily noon–6.*

Behind the Apothecary is the **Masonic Hall,** also known as the Old Stone Barracks. It went up in 1816, possibly from the rubble of the town after the War of 1812. It still houses the first Masonic Lodge in Upper Canada, and some experts believe that the first meeting of the first Parliament of Upper Canada took place on this site in 1792, when it was used as a church as well.

Continue along Queen Street to Davy Street, and turn right (south) for two blocks. At 43 Castlereagh Street is the **Niagara Historical Society Museum,** one of the oldest and most complete museums of its kind in Ontario, with an extensive collection relating to the often colorful history of the Niagara Peninsula from the earliest Indian times through the 19th century. *Tel. 416/468–3912. Admission: $2 adults, $1 students, 50¢ children under 12. Open May–Oct., daily 10–5; Jan.–Feb., weekends only 1–5. Mar.–Apr. and Nov.–Dec., daily 1–5.*

Two blocks east, and a few steps north, is the handsome **Shaw Festival Theatre.** Just beyond it, on a wide stretch of parkland, is **Fort George National Historic Park.** Built in the 1790s to replace Fort Niagara, it was lost to the Yankees during the War of 1812. It was recaptured after the burning of the town in 1813, and largely survived the war, only to fall into ruins by the 1830s. It was reconstructed a century later, and visitors can explore the officers' quarters, barracks rooms of the common soldiers, the kitchen, and more. *Tel. 416/468–4257. Admission: $2 adults, $1 children 5–16, senior citizens free, $6 families. Open mid-May–late June, 9–5; July 1–Labor Day, 10–6; Labor Day–Nov., 10–5.*

54 **St. Catharines,** in the heart of Canada's fruit belt and major wine-producing region, celebrates the harvest with the 10-day Niagara Grape and Wine Festival, at the end of September. An old city, it was originally settled by the Loyalist troops of Butler's Rangers, who disbanded here in 1784. Loyalist nostalgia for Britain is also recalled in the Royal Canadian Henley Regatta, North America's largest rowing regatta, which is hosted by St. Catharines in early August. The city has its attractions throughout the year, among them the locks of the Welland Canal and **Rodman Hall Art Gallery** of graphics, sculpture, and tapestries. *109 St. Paul Crescent, tel. 416/684–2925.*

The **St. Catharines Historical Museum** (343 Merritt St., tel. 416/227–2978) displays prints and relics from the War of 1812, as well as photos and models relating to the construction of the Welland Canal.

55 **Hamilton** is Canada's steel capital. The city's spectacular entrances—over the Burlington Skyway from the north or via the Royal Botanical Gardens on the south—make Hamilton proper look gritty and industrial by contrast. But Hamilton is a tough, vital city with strong traditions. Chief among them is steel manufacturing; the flaming stacks of the Stelco and Dofasco plants dominate the bay area. Football—the Canadian variety—is also a prominent feature of Hamilton life, and you can visit the **Canadian Football Hall of Fame** (City Hall Plaza, tel. 416/528–7566).

Surprisingly, Hamilton is also known for sweeping expanses of parks. The Royal Botanical Gardens, in the city's north end, are comprised of 2,000 acres of garden and parkland. Strollers stop for refreshment at the Tea House overlooking the rock garden. Nearby, the marshes and gullies of Cootes Paradise provide a sanctuary for wildlife. On Tuesday through Saturday the Central (farmers') Market bustles with local produce. Hamilton is also proud of its glittering performing-arts center, Hamilton Place, home of the Hamilton Philharmonic Orchestra, and its boutique-and-restaurant shopping area, Hess Village.

Dundurn Castle, built between 1832 and 1835 by a pre-Confederation Canadian prime minister, Sir Allan Napier McNab, has gardens where in summer you can enjoy concerts and children's theater. *York Blvd., tel. 416/522–5313. Admission: $3.25 adults, $2.25 senior citizens, $2 students, $1.25 children. Open June 2–Labor Day, daily 11–4; mid-Sept.–June 1, daily 1–4. Closed Christmas and New Year's Day.*

56 **Brantford,** west of Hamilton on Highway 403, is named after Joseph Brant, the Loyalist Mohawk chief who brought members of the Six Nations Confederacy into Canada after the American Revolution. Brantford's other famous son is Alexander Graham Bell, whose homestead is a national historic site. Canadians claim he invented the telephone and made his first long-distance calls here in southern Ontario. *Tel. 519/756–6220. Admission free. Open Jun–Aug., daily 10–6; Sept.–May, Tues.–Sun. 10–5.*

At the **Brant County Museum,** learn about the history of the Six Nations Loyalist Indians whom Joseph Brant led to Canada after the Revolutionary War. The museum also illustrates the lives of Alexander Graham Bell, the Mohawk poetess E. Pauline Johnson, and novelist Thomas B. Costain. *57 Charlotte St., tel. 519/752–2483. Admission: $1 adults, 75¢ senior citizens and students, 50¢ children under 14, children under 6 free. Open Tues.–Fri. 9–5, Sat. 1–4; also open Sun. 1–4, May–Aug.*

North of Brantford via Route 24 are the twin towns of
57 **Kitchener** and **Waterloo.** Original German settlers have left their stamp on the towns. Kitchener's 10-day Oktoberfest is an annual beer-drinker's bonanza. The **Seagram Museum**—a showcase of the wine and spirits industries—is an architectural gem. *57 Erb St. W, tel. 519/885–1857. Admission free. Open Tues.–Fri. 11–8, weekends 11–5.*

More sober influences also appear in this region of Ontario. Here live many of Canada's Amish and Mennonites. Strict Mennonites still drive horse-drawn buggies; conveniences of all kinds are antithetical to their defiantly self-sufficient way of life. The baked goods, delicious preserves, and handicrafts of the Mennonite women are plied at the **Kitchener Farmers' Market** (25 Frederick St.) on Saturday.

58 **Guelph,** an old, gray-stone, university and manufacturing town northeast of Kitchener, is dominated by the spires of its Church of Our Lady Cathedral (modeled after the Cathedral of Cologne). Guelph has a waterfowl park, historical exhibits in the **Guelph Civic Museum** (6 Dublin St. S, tel. 519/836–1221), and the stone cottage where World War I poet John McCrae (who wrote "In Flanders Field") was born (108 Water St., tel. 519/836–1482). *Admission for McCrae House and Civic Museum is the same: $1.50 adults, $1 senior citizens and students, 50¢ children under 12; combination tickets for both sites available. Both are open daily 1–5 except holidays.*

Just north of Guelph is **Elora,** a picturesque village clinging to the sides of a limestone gorge. Many of its 19th-century shops have become antiques and crafts stores.

Ever since July 1953, when one of the world's greatest actors, Alec Guinness, joined with probably the world's greatest Shakespearean director, Tyrone Guthrie, beneath a hot, stuffy 59 tent in **Stratford,** a backward little town about 90 minutes from Toronto, the Stratford Festival has been one of the most successful, most widely admired theaters of its kind in the world.

The origins of the town of Stratford are modest. After the War of 1812, the British government granted a million acres of land along Lake Huron to the Canada Company, headed by a Scottish businessman. When the surveyors came to a marshy creek, they named it "Little Thames" and noted that it might make "a good mill-site." It was later christened Stratford, which purportedly means a narrow crossing. The year was 1832, 121 years before the concept of a theater festival would take flight and change Canadian culture forever.

In 1904, an insurance broker named Tom Orr transformed Stratford's riverfront into a park. He also built a formal English garden, where every flower mentioned in the plays of Shakespeare—monkshood to sneeze worse, bee balm to bachelor's button—blooms grandly to this day. When Tyrone Guthrie compared an aerial photograph of Stratford's park with a photo of the park in Stratford-on-Avon, England, he was stunned to find the two nearly identical.

Then came Tom Patterson, a fourth-generation Stratfordian born in 1920, who looked around; saw that the town wards and schools had names like Hamlet, Falstaff, and Romeo; and felt that some kind of drama festival might save his community from becoming a ghost town. (The diesel was coming in, and all the steam-engine repair shops that had kept Stratford alive for generations were soon to close down.)

The story of how he began in 1952 with $125 (a "generous" grant from the Stratford City Council), tracked down the directorial genius Tyrone Guthrie and the inspired stage and screen star Alec Guinness, obtained the services of the brilliant stage designer Tanya Moiseiwitsch, and somehow pasted together a world-class theater festival in a little over one year is almost unbelievable.

The early years also brought giants of world theater to the tiny town of about 20,000: James Mason, Siobhan McKenna, Alan Bates, Christopher Plummer, Jason Robards, Jr., and Maggie Smith. But the years also saw an unevenness in productions, a dreadful tendency to go for flash and glitter over substance, and a focus on costumes and furniture rather than on the ability to speak Shakespeare's words with clarity and intelligence. Many never lost faith in the festival; others, such as Canada's greatest critic, the late Nathan Cohen of the *Toronto Star,* once bemoaned that "Stratford has become Canada's most sacred cow." Sacred or not, Stratford's offerings are still among the best of their kind in the world, with at least a handful of productions every year that put most other summer arts festivals to shame. Be warned that due to the great faithfulness of the stage to its Shakespearean original, it is imperative to have seats that are fairly central in the audience; otherwise, words and even whole speeches can be lost.

There is also a traditional proscenium stage, the **Avon,** where *All's Well That Ends Well*, T. S. Eliot's *Murder in the Cathedral,* and the musical *Irma La Douce* have recently been presented. Connoisseurs of more daring theater—as well as the budget-conscious—should not miss **The Third Stage,** a more recent space that allows plays in the round and in experimental modes. In the last few years, *Twelfth Night* and *King Lear* were seen here. This is often the most exciting place to see plays, so don't panic if you can't get seats at the two larger theaters.

The Gallery Stratford has regular exhibits of local and Inuit art, as well as design sketches and costumes of the present year's productions. *54 Romeo St., just northeast of Festival Theatre; tel. 519/271–5271. Admission is nominal during the Festival's run; free at other times. Open late May–early Sept., Mon. 10–5, Tues.–Sun. 10–8. Closed Mon. and shorter hours the rest of the year.*

There are many tasteful shops in the downtown area, including antiques stores, arts and crafts studios, galleries, and new and rare bookshops.

The **Festival Theatre** (55 Queen St.) and the **Avon Theatre** (99 Downie St.) are open from early May to early November. They have evening performances Tuesday–Saturday, with matinees Wednesday, Saturday and Sunday. Tickets $20–$40. Rush seats are as little as one-third the cost. **The Third Stage** (Lakeshore Dr.) has a shorter season, from late May to early September. Prices are always under $20.

Meet the Festival is a series of informal discussions with members of the company. *Kiwanis Centre, next to the Third Stage. Admission free; no reservation required. July–Aug., Wed. and Fri., 11–noon.*

Thirty-minute **post-performance discussions** take place at the Festival Theatre Tuesday and Thursday nights, late June to early September. *Meet at Aisle 2, Orchestra Level, after the performance. Admission free; no reservations required.*

Backstage tours are offered Sunday morning from mid-June to mid-November. Tours depart from the Festival Theatre every 15 minutes from 9 AM to 10:30 AM. Admission: $5 adults, $2.50 students and senior citizens. Book in advance through the Festival Box Office, although some tickets are usually available at the door.

60 Southwest of Stratford, back on Highway 401, is **London,** a city of about 270,000. Chosen by Colonel (later Lieutenant Governor) John Graves Simcoe as Upper Canada's future capital, it has turned instead into an academic, industrial, and commercial center. Despite its white-collar, conservative reputation, London contains a surprising range of attractions—including a turn-of-the-century opera house that now houses a first-rate theater, and a respected regional art gallery (421 Ridout St., tel. 519/672–4580). The river—named the Thames, of course—is cruised by paddle-wheel boats. London's Fanshawe Park, with its dam, reservoir, and Pioneer Village, offers swimming, hiking, golfing, and sailing along the banks of the Thames. The **Labatt Pioneer Brewery** (150 Simcoe St., tel. 519/663–5050, admission free, open June-Aug., daily 11–5) shows early methods of beer making.

Some 150 kilometers (90 miles) southwest along Highway 401 61 turn south on route 77 to reach **Point Pelée National Park,** the southernmost point in mainland Canada, at about the same latitude as Chicago. A sandspit jutting into Lake Erie, the six-square-mile park is noted for its spring and autumn bird migrations and for Monarch butterfly migrations, in which millions of the insects stop on their way to Mexico each autumn.

Begin your visit at the Visitors Centre, four miles south of the entrance. It has bird-watching and wildlife exhibits, a small reference library, and displays on the formation of the park and the natural history of the region. An information desk posts a long up-to-date list of bird sightings, and a small theater presents natural-history films and audiovisual programs. About two-thirds of the park is marshland, the rest is forested, though there are open fields remaining from early attempts at farming. The outer edges of the peninsula are ringed with sand-and-pebble beach. The main beaches—Northwest, Black Willow, West, and East Point—have changing houses and beach patrols.

Among the short hiking trails is the 1.6-kilometer **Marsh Boardwalk,** part of which is floating. A 45-foot observation tower provides a bird's-eye view of the marsh. The **Tip Trail,** 0.8 kilometers on boardwalk, is an excellent bird-watching route and, in September, is the best area for viewing the Monarchs. *Daily admission fee $4 (Canadian) per car charged to enter Point Pelée National Park Apr.–Labor Day, free rest of year. Park is open daily 6 AM–10 PM, and opens an hour earlier for bird-watchers late Apr.–late May. Visitors Centre hours reduced in winter. Shuttle tram operates Apr. and June–Labor Day 9–9; May 6 AM–9 PM; Sept. 8–8; Oct. 8–8. For additional information contact Superintendent, Point Pelée National Park, RR 1, Leamington, N8H 3V4, tel. 519/322-2365.*

62 Like Detroit, **Windsor** is an industrial city—Ford, GM, Chrysler, and Champion Spark Plugs have manufacturing plants here, and the Hiram Walker Distillery is the third largest in Canada. Yet it is known as the City of Roses and is famous for its miles of riverfront parks and gardens. **Dieppe Gardens,** named in memory of members of the Essex Scottish Regiment who fell during the assult on Dieppe, France, in 1942, is set in the heart of the city and affords a view of the Detroit skyline. It is a favorite spot for downtown workers to eat lunch, and bands frequently perform for the crowd. To the east along the river is **Coventry Gardens,** with a large computer-controlled floating fountain. Away from the river, **Jackson Park** (south on Ouellette Ave.) has a six-acre garden displaying more than 12,000 roses in 450 varieties surrounding a World War II veterans memorial.

The newly renovated **Art Gallery of Windsor,** housed in a former brewery, has 15 areas presenting changing displays of contemporary and historic art from across Canada and abroad. The permanent collection of more than 3,000 paintings, graphics, and sculptures highlights achievements of Canadian artists from the 18th century on. *445 Riverside Dr. W, tel. 519/258-7111. Admission free. Open Wed. and Sat. 11–5, Thurs. and Fri. 11–9, Sun, 1–5.*

The **Hiram Walker Historical Museum** is named after the distiller who, in 1858, established the first large-scale industry on the

Canadian shore. Collections include Indian artifacts, firearms, tools, household items, glassware, maps, and newspapers; a reference library holds many original documents relating to the history of southwestern Ontario. *254 Pitt St. W, tel. 519/253–1812. Admission free. Open Tues.–Sat. 10–5, Sun. 2–5. Closed holidays.*

Willistead Manor, a mansion built in 1906 by Edward Chandler Walker (Hiram's son), is a 40-room Tudor-style mansion designed by the Detroit architect Alfred Kahn and set in a 15-acre park. Carved paneling is found throughout, as are Carrera marble fireplaces. The manor is used for public and private cultural, business, and social events. *1899 Niagara St., tel. 519/255–6545. Admission: $1.75 adults, $1.25 senior citizens, 75¢ children. Open 1st and 3rd Sun. 1–4 PM Sept.–Nov. and Jan.–June.; Dec., Sun. 1–6 and Wed. 7–9 PM; July–Aug., Sun.–Wed. 1–4.*

Farmers, butchers, and bakers from southwestern Ontario bring their fresh produce and goods to sell at the **Windsor City Market,** which has more than 500 stalls. *Chatham St. E. between McDougall and Market Sts., tel. 519/255–6260. Open 6 AM Mon.–Sat., most active Wed. and Sat.*

About 30 kilometers (18 miles) south of Windsor on Route 18, in
63 **Amherstberg,** the **North American Black Historical Museum** has a permanent exhibit on the Underground Railroad as well as displays on black origins in Africa, the years of slavery, and settlement and emancipation in North America. *277 King St., tel. 519/736–5433. Admission: $1 adults, 50¢ senior citizens and children under 17, $3 family. Open Wed.–Fri. 10–5, weekends 1–5.*

What to See and Do with Children

African Lion Safari. Lions, tigers, cheetahs, black bears, elephants, white rhinos, and zebras make this astonishingly uncommercial wildlife park truly special. Drive your own car or take an air-conditioned tram over a 6-mile safari trail. In addition to six large game reserves, there's a birds-of-prey flying demonstration, a parrot show, an elephant round-up, and even an *African Queen*–style boat that cruises past birds and primates. *Safari Rd., near Cambridge (take Hwy. 401 west from Toronto to Hwy. 6 and drive south), tel. 519/623–2620. Admission: $11.95 adults, $9.95 children 13–17, $7.95 children 3–12 and senior citizens. Open Apr.–late-Oct., weekdays 10–4, weekends and holidays 10–5.*

Marineland, Niagara Falls. *See* Tour 4, above.

Museum of Canadian Scouting. Displays here include old photos, insignia, and other memorabilia on the life of Lord Baden-Powell and the scouting movement in Canada. *1345 Baseline Rd., Ottawa, tel. 613/225–2770. Admission free. Open Mon.–Fri. 9–4:30.*

National Museum of Science and Technology. Interactive exhibits bring the laws of physics, meteorology, and astronomy to life; locomotives, vintage cars, and model ships are also on display. *1867 St. Laurent Blvd., Ottawa, tel. 613/991–3044. Admission: $4 adults, $3 senior citizens and students, $1 children 6–15, children under 6 free, $8 family. Admission free on Tues. Open mid-May–mid-Oct., Sat.–Tues. 9–6, Wed.–Fri. 9–8;*

late-Oct.–early May, Tues.–Wed. and Fri.–Sun. 9–5, Thur. 9–8.

Storybook Gardens. Miniature trains and Old MacDonald's Farm are some of the features at this amusement park. *929 Springbank Dr., Springbank Park, London, tel. 519/661–4757. Admission: $3.50 adults, $2.40 senior citizens, $1.90 children under 15. Open May–Aug., daily 10–8; Sept.–mid-Oct., daily 10–4.*

Shopping

Though it is not known as a shoppers's city, **Ottawa** has many museum shops and galleries that specialize in Indian and Inuit crafts, as well as antiquarian shops featuring historical pieces and good antiques. **Rideau Centre,** at Rideau and Sussex streets, features more than 200 stores, including The Bay, Ogilvy's, and Eaton's department stores. **Byward Market,** on York Street (*see* Exploring, above), is a good place to buy cheese, produce, and cut flowers. **John Coles** at the Astrolabe Gallery (90 Sparks St., tel. 613/234–2348) is a good source for 19th-century prints of the Parliament Buildings or antique maps of North America. **Ufundi Gallery** (541 Sussex Dr., tel. 613/232–3957) combines Canadian painting, sculpture, and ceramics with ethnic jewelry and African carvings and furniture. Look for the monumental Japanese-inspired ceramics by the two-person team, Doucet-Saito. **Snow Goose** (83 Sparks St., tel. 613/232–2213) specializes in Indian and Inuit crafts, which can be priced in the thousands of dollars, though a pair of irresistible Inuit children's woolen boots appliqued with seals and birds can be under $20.

In **Niagara Falls,** most shops offer tacky touristy fare, such as T-shirts and miniature totem poles. In **Hamilton,** Hess Village is the premiere shopping area. **Windsor** is a magnet for shoppers from Detroit; best buys are British imports, jewelry, china, and furs. Look for stores along Ouellette Avenue, the main street downtown, along Pelissier Street a block west, and on Erie and Wyandotte streets, which cross Ouellette Avenue.

Some of the best antiques are to be found at family-owned roadside stalls in **Cobourg, Peterborough, Marmora, Hastings,** and **Belleville.** Sunday flea markets in **Burlington, Aberfoyle,** and **Hamilton** can be another good source of antiques.

Sports and Outdoor Activities

Cycling Ottawa offers some 65 miles of bicycle paths. On Sunday, **Queen Elizabeth Driveway** and **Colonel By Drive** are closed to traffic until noon for cyclists.

Hiking The 680-kilometer (430-mile) **Bruce Trail** stretches along the limestone Niagara escarpment from the orchards of Niagara Falls to the cliffs and bluffs at the end of the Bruce Peninsula extending into Lake Huron. Contact the Bruce Trail Association, Box 857, Hamilton, L8N 3N9. For day hikes, try the **Grand Valley Trail,** which runs 128 kilometers (80 miles) between Elora and Brantford (contact Grand Valley Trail Association, Box 1233, Kitchener, N2G 4G8). The **Rideau Trail** runs

406 kilometers (241 miles) along the Rideau Canal from Kingston to Ottawa; access points from the highway are marked with orange triangles (contact Rideau Trail Association, Box 15, Kingston, K7L 4V6).

Skiing Ontario offers more than 400 slopes for downhill skiing. Some of the best are just north of Toronto: **Blue Mountain Resorts** in Collingwood, Ontario (tel. 416/869–3799), the **Caledon Ski Club** in Caledon (tel. 416/453–7404), **Glen Eden Ski Area** in Milton (tel. 416/878–5011), **Hidden Valley** in Huntsville (tel. 705/789–2301), **Hockley Valley Resort** in Orangeville (tel. 519/942–0754), and **Horseshoe Valley** in Barrie (tel. 705/835–2790). Phone 416/963–2992 for daily reports on lifts and surface conditions.

Dining and Lodging

Dining

Not so many years ago, when you asked for a dinner suggestion in Ottawa, you'd be directed across one of the bridges to Hull. But it's no longer necessary to go to Québec to eat well, now that the capital can claim several top-caliber restaurants.

In Stratford there is a certain inevitable mania to dining. Everyone arrives in a great rush at 6 PM, eats rather quickly, and is at the theater for curtain time. All three of the major players (The Church, sold in the summer of 1988; Rundles; and The Old Prune) tread the fine line between haste and grace, and they do so with enormous generosity of spirit.

Niagara Falls offers mainly fast foods, faster foods, and fastest foods, with a handful of modest exceptions. You'll find all your old family friends—the King (of the Burger), the Baron (of Beef), Harry (of Char Broil fame), the Colonel (still frying that greasy, finger-lickin' chicken), and Mr. Ronald McDonald, whom we sense needs no introduction whatsoever. Still, there are respectable restaurants at rather moderate prices, considering what a tourist mecca this place is.

The food in Niagara-on-the-Lake is not at the level of the finest dining in Toronto, or even of Stratford, but meals are usually decent, and served in romantic, century-old surroundings.

Windsor's large multicultural population has established ethnic restaurants serving French, Italian, Turkish, Greek, Mexican, and Asian cuisine. In summer the downtown area is dotted with outdoor cafés.

Highly recommended restaurants in each price category are indicated by a star ★.

Category	Cost*
Very Expensive	over $50
Expensive	$35–$50
Moderate	$15–$35
Inexpensive	under $15

**per person, excluding drinks, service, and 10% sales tax*

Lodging

Hotels in Ottawa tend to be more expensive, and book up earlier, than those in the rest of the province, so reservations are recommended, especially in the summer. If a B&B appeals to you, you'll find a number of choices in the capital. **Ottawa Bed and Breakfast** (Box 4848, Station E, Ottawa K1S 5J1, tel. 613/563–0161) can provide a list.

There are so many hotels and motels in and around Niagara Falls that you can take your pick from almost any price range, services, or facilities. Heart-shape bathtubs, waterbeds, heated pools, Jacuzzis, baby-sitting services—the choice is yours. For B&Bs in the area, contact the **Niagara Region Bed & Breakfast Service** (2631 Dorchester Rd., Niagara Falls, L2J 2Y9, tel. 416/358–8988). Prices fall by up to 50% between mid-September and mid-May, and less expensive packages for families, honeymooners, and others are common.

There are few accommodations in Niagara-on-the-Lake, but the ones that are here have unusual charm. For a list of area B&Bs contact the **Niagara-on-the-Lake Bed & Breakfast Association** (Box 1515, Niagara-on-the-Lake L0S 1J0, tel. 416/358–8988).

Because Stratford is not a hotel city, visitors with the most savvy like to stay at B&Bs. Write to the **Stratford and Area Visitors' and Convention Bureau** (38 Albert St., Stratford N5A 3K3, tel. 519/271–5140) and ask for the latest *Discover Stratford Guide*.

Highly recommended lodgings in each price category are indicated by a star ★.

Category	Cost*
Very Expensive	over $100
Expensive	$75–$100
Moderate	$35–$75
Inexpensive	under $35

**All prices are for a standard double room, excluding 10% service charge.*

Barrie
Dining

Maude Koury's Steak House. Established in 1968, this renovated house offers a varied menu and atmosphere. The front of the building bears a resemblance to the U.S. White House, with imitation 16th-century Doric columns and a striking white facade. There are four dining rooms, each with its own distinctive personality. Specialty dishes include steaks, lobster tails, and spare ribs. *126 Collier St., tel. 705/706–6030. Reservations advised. Dress: casual. AE, DC, MC, V. Closed Sun. and holidays. Moderate.*

Lodging

Journey's End. This hotel is part of a chain where fast, efficient service is a priority. The name comes from the home-away-from-home feeling the chain offers in its lodgings. Clean rooms and good service keep people coming back. *75 Hart Dr., L4N 5M3, tel. 705/722–3600. 60 rooms. AE, DC, MC, V. Inexpensive.*

Bracebridge
Dining

Inn At The Falls. Located in a small-town setting overlooking the Muskoka River and Bracebridge Falls, this Victorian inn exudes traditional old-fashioned hospitality and charm. Enjoy a meal in the pub while listening to live entertainment, or eat in the main dining room that overlooks the bay. Steak-and-kidney pie is a specialty. *17 Dominion St., tel. 705/645–2245. Reservations advised. Dress: casual. AE, MC, V. Closed holidays. Moderate.*

Dining and Lodging

Tamwood Resort. One of the longest log buildings in Canada, this resort near Lake Muskoka offers many diversions for a varied clientele. Whether you enjoy outdoor activity or a quiet stay at a relaxing cottage, you will find it here. There are three settings to choose from: standard rooms, superior rooms with whirlpools, and genteel cottages. The main dining room is made of solid logs with a large granite fireplace in the middle. *RR 1, P0B 1C0, 705/645–5172. 34 rooms. Facilities: restaurant, lounge, indoor pool, whirlpool, 3 tennis courts, paddle boats, canoes. MC, V. Closed Sept. 30–May 14. Expensive.*

Hamilton
Dining

Old Country Restaurant. The only restaurant within miles that uses an open pit for cooking, this Yugoslavian establishment goes all out to convey an "old country" atmosphere. Watch your meal being prepared over the fireplace in the main dining room or enjoy the view out on the patio. Lamb, pork, and chicken, and stews are the specialties. *1360 King St., tel. 416/547–2572. Reservations not required. Dress: casual. AE, MC, V. Moderate.*

Kingston
Dining

Chez Piggy. Originally a livery stable, built in 1810, this restaurant offers a relaxed, casual atmosphere along with eclectic cuisine. Because seven chefs from different parts of the world work here, the menu runs toward Continental. Salads are fresh, and breads and desserts are made on the premises. *68R Princess St., tel. 613/549–7673. Reservations not required. Dress: casual. Closed Monday. AE, MC, V. Moderate.*

Canoe Club Bar and Grill. Located in the Prince George Hotel, built in 1809 and one of Kingston's oldest landmarks, this friendly restaurant has something for everyone. The selection is diverse, with jerk pork and tandoori chicken the favorites; seafood, chicken, and pasta dishes are also offered. Notice the 60-foot rowing scull (built for Olympic rowers in 1950) hanging from the ceiling. *200 Ontario St., tel. 613/549–5440. Reservations not required. Dress: casual. AE, MC, V. Inexpensive.*

Lodging

The Prince George. On Lake Ontario, this 181-year-old hotel is full of character and offers a friendly, cozy atmosphere. All the rooms are decorated in Victorian style, with replicas of 19th-century antiques. Rooms at the front of the hotel overlook Lake Ontario. Continental breakfast is included in the price of the room. *200 Ontario St., K7L 2Y9, tel. 613/549–5440. 30 rooms, 2 suites. Facilities: restaurant, lounge, nightclub, sauna. AE, MC, V. Moderate.*

Kitchener
Dining

La Galleria. Located in the Walper Terrace Hotel, this award-winning Italian restaurant offers exquisite dining and an engaging atmosphere. Among the variety of reasonably priced dishes, try the *scallopine alla marsala* (scallops of veal topped with mushrooms and marsala sauce), or the filet mignon served with mushrooms. Many couples come to this local favorite to get engaged. *1 King St. W, tel. 519/745–4321. Reservations not* *required. Dress: casual. AE, MC, V. Closed holidays. Moderate.*

Lodging

Valhalla Inn. An old-Scandinavian atmosphere, in-house pastry chef, and warm hospitality greet you at this lodge located in downtown Kitchener and connected by skywalk to the Market Square shopping mall. A wonderful playground for the sports minded, this inn has a bowling alley, a pool hall, and a miniature golf course. *King St., Box 4, N2G 3W9, tel. 519/744–4141. 203 rooms. Facilities: dining room, bar, fitness center, banquet room. AE, DC, MC, V. Moderate.*

Walper Terrace Hotel. Located in the heart of downtown Kitchener, close to the famous Kitchener Farmers Market, this renovated 110-year-old Victorian hotel has many of its original features. *1 King St. W, tel. 519/745–4321. 112 rooms. Facilities: 2 restaurants, lounge, valet service. AE, DC, MC, V. Moderate.*

Leamington
Dining

Tropicana Restaurant. Featuring Greek and Canadian food, it is known for its chicken and ribs, Greek bread, and pizza. Steaks and seafood specials are also on the menu, and there is dining on an outdoor patio in season. *2311 Erie St. S, tel. 519/326–6071. Reservations advised. Jacket and tie advised for dinner. AE, MC, V. Moderate*

London
Dining

The Mug House. Sumptuous homemade pasta (veal Parmesan is the local favorite) and fresh Greek salads are the specialties at this family-style restaurant. Depending on your mood, you may dine upstairs in a quiet family setting or downstairs in a noisy and cheerful atmosphere. Check out the flower pots that surround the upstairs dining room. *1544 Dosdas St., tel. 519/453–9355. Reservations not required. Dress: casual. AE, DC, MC, V. Closed Sunday. Moderate.*

Niagara Falls
Dining

Capri Restaurant. One of the better Italian places in the area, the Capri offers ethnic dishes as well as steak and seafood. Its most popular dish is a huge Maritime Platter, piled high with lobster, shrimp, scallops, salmon, and more, at about $60 for two. There are three rooms, and the owner has won the "Restaurateur of the Year Award" several times. *5438 Ferry St. (Hwy. 20), less than 1 km (½ mi) from the Falls, tel. 416/354–7519. AE, MC, V. Moderate.*

Hungarian Village Restaurant. Family-owned for a half-century, it offers classic Eastern European dishes, as well as traditional Hungarian specialties—and a "famous Gypsy trio from Budapest" entertains in the evenings. There are three rooms, one of them more elegant and formal than the others. *5329 Ferry St. (Hwy. 20), tel. 416/356–2429. Reservations advised for weekends. AE, DC, MC, V. Moderate.*

Reese's Country Inn. A real cut above the other restaurants in the area, if a bit off the beaten track, it offers international cuisine in a country setting, complete with an open patio, fresh flowers, fireplace, and greenhouse. The most popular meal is rack of lamb. They recently added Sunday brunch and dinner. *3799 Montrose Rd. (Exit 32B from the QEW, then west almost 1 km—½ mi—on Thorold Stone Rd. and north on Montrose Rd.), tel. 416/357–5640. Jacket and tie advised. Reservations advised. AE, MC, V. Moderate.*

Rolf's Continental Dining. The French and German menu features rabbit, fillet of lamb, Dover sole, and chateaubriand. Meals are served in three small rooms in an old house, with candlelight, fresh flowers, and sparkling china. The full-course "early dinner," served between 5 and 6, costs about $15 a person. *3480 Main St., tel. 416/295–3472. Reservations advised. Dress: casual. MC, V. No lunch; closed Mon. Moderate.*

Lodging

Michael's Inn. Located by Rainbow Bridge, there's a view of the Falls from several balconies. *5599 River Rd., L2E 3H3, tel. 416/354–2727. 130 rooms with bath. Facilities: restaurant, wading pool, heated indoor pool, sauna, whirlpool, water beds, theme rooms, baby-sitting service, golf and tennis nearby, tours. AE, MC, V. Very Expensive.*

Old Stone Inn. Its charm comes from the renovated mill at its heart. Many suites have fireplaces. No charge for children under 14. *5425 Robinson St., L2G 7L6 (near Skylon Tower), tel. 416/357–1234. 114 rooms with bath. Facilities: restaurant, baby-sitting service, outdoor pool, whirlpool. AE, MC, V. Very Expensive.*

Lincoln Motor Inn. A pleasant landscaped courtyard gives this motor inn an intimate feeling. The Falls are within walking distance. Connecting family suites sleep up to a dozen. *6417 Main St., L2G 5Y3, tel. 416/356–1748. 57 rooms with bath. Facilities: restaurant, heated pool, heated outdoor whirlpool spa, baby-sitting service, beach, golf nearby. AE, MC, V. Expensive.*

Quality Inn Fallsway. Located very near the Falls on nicely landscaped grounds with patio. Pets allowed. *4946 Clifton Hill, Box 60, L2E 6S8, tel. 416/358–3601. 265 rooms with bath. Facilities: restaurant, lounge, indoor and outdoor pool, baby-sitting service, golf nearby, whirlpool. AE, MC, V. Expensive.*

Canuck Motel. Located a few blocks from the Falls, this motel has fancy tubs, water beds, and yet a family atmosphere. Housekeeping units are available. It was recently remodeled and enlarged. *5334 Kitchener St., L2G 1B5, tel. 416/358–8221. 79 rooms with bath. Facilities: heated outdoor pool, baby-sitting service, golf nearby. AE, MC, V. Moderate.*

Vacation Inn. Only two blocks from the Minolta Tower, this hotel offers easy access to the bus terminal and highways. Some rooms have water beds. *6519 Stanley Ave., L2G 7L2, tel. 416/356–1722. 95 rooms with bath. Facilities: restaurant, heated outdoor pool. AE, MC, V. Moderate.*

Alpine Motel. This is a disarmingly small place, set back from the road. Rooms have refrigerators, and housekeeping units are available. *7742 Lundy's La., L2H 1H3, tel. 416/356–7016. 10 rooms with bath. Facilities: heated outdoor pool, patio, golf nearby. MC, V. Inexpensive.*

Detroit Motor Inn. It's five miles to the Falls along Highway 20, but the spacious grounds, reasonable rates, and family facilities help make up for the drive. No pets. *13030 Lundy's La., L2E 6S4, tel. 416/227–2567. 38 rooms with bath or shower. Facilities: coffee shop, lounge, heated pool, miniature golf, playground. AE, MC, V. Inexpensive.*

Niagara-on-the-Lake

Dining

The Luis House—Bella's Great Food. This family-owned restaurant features seafood and prime ribs. The ambience is homey. *245 King St., tel. 416/468–4038. Dress: casual. Reservations advised. AE, MC, V. Expensive.*

The Oban Inn. This is an elegant country inn where you can lunch on the patio and enjoy a superior view of the lake. The fare is standard—steak, beef, duck, and lobster—with a very solid Sunday brunch. The fresh poached salmon is popular in the summer. Fresh-cut flowers are from the inn's own gardens. *160 Front St., tel. 416/468–2165. Dress: casual. Reservations required. AE, DC, MC, V. Expensive.*

The Prince of Wales Hotel. Continental cuisine is served in a handsome Victorian setting. Lamb, fresh Atlantic salmon, and pickerel are the summer specialties. The luncheon buffet and Sunday brunches offer good value. *6 Picton St., tel. 416/468–3246. Dress: casual. Reservations required. AE, MC, V. Expensive.*

Angel Inn. This is an English dining pub, located in the oldest operating inn in town. Specialties are steak, duck, and seafood, with an emphasis on the latter. Lots of antiques make this a handsome place to dine. *224 Regent St., tel. 416/468–3411. Reservations advised. Dress: casual. AE, MC, V. Moderate.*

Buttery Theatre Restaurant. Meals are served on a cozy terrace. On Friday and Saturday, there's a 2½-hour feast, "Henry VIII," that will have you looking like him when you finish. *19 Queen St., tel. 416/468–2564. Dress: casual, but jacket advised for dinner. Reservations advised. AE, MC, V. Moderate.*

Lodging

Pillar & Post Inn. This hotel, six long blocks from the heart of town, was built early in the century and restored in 1970. Most rooms have wood-burning fireplaces, hand-crafted pine furniture, and patchwork quilts. Wake up to free coffee and a newspaper. *48 John St., Box 1011, L0S 1J0, tel. 416/468–2123. 91 rooms with bath. Facilities: restaurant, baby-sitting service, hair dryers in rooms, outdoor pool, sauna, whirlpool, tennis, golf nearby. AE, MC, V. Expensive.*

Prince of Wales Hotel. First built in 1864, this charming Victorian hotel is in the heart of town and has been tastefully restored. Deluxe and superior rooms are worth the extra price. The Prince of Wales Court, adjacent to the main hotel, has many larger, newer rooms at higher prices. *6 Picton St., L0S 1J0, tel. 416/468–3246 or from Toronto 800/263–2452. 104 rooms with bath, some with fireplaces; housekeeping units available. Facilities: restaurant, lounge, coffee shop, heated indoor pool, saunas, whirlpool, health club, tennis courts, baby-sitting service, massage, golf nearby. AE, MC, V. Expensive.*

★ **Queens Landing.** Also called the Inn at Niagara-on-the-Lake, this remarkable property is a welcome addition to an old town that has had no new places in a long while. The owner—who also runs the Pillar & Post—has obtained antique furnishings and installed fireplaces in 78 rooms and Jacuzzis in 44 rooms. Located at the mouth of the Niagara River, right across from historic Fort Niagara, the views are knockout. And, unlike other century-old country inns of this lovely town, Queen's Landing has a superb indoor swimming pool, lap pool, and even a fully equipped exercise room. *Cnr. Melville and Bryon Sts., Box 1180, L0S 1J0, tel. 416/468–2195. 137 rooms. Facilities: dining room, lounge, lap pool, indoor pool, whirlpool, exercise facilities, baby-sitting service, 24-hour room service, tennis and golf nearby. AE, DC, MC, V. Expensive.*

The Oban Inn. Built about 1824 for a sea captain from Oban, Scotland, it was restored in 1963. The charming inn, centrally located, has broad verandas and beautifully manicured gardens. It also enjoys a waterfront view. Pets are allowed. *160 Front St., Box 94, L0S 1J0, tel. 416/468–2165. 23 rooms with bath; housekeeping units and rooms with fireplaces available. Facilities: restaurant, pub, patio bar, baby-sitting service, golf nearby. AE, MC, V. Moderate–Expensive.*

Moffat Inn. This is a charmer, with individually appointed rooms, some with original 1835 fireplaces, outdoor patios, brass beds, and wicker furniture. Enjoy breakfast fritters on the outdoor patio. *60 Picton St., L0S 1J0, tel. 416/468–4116. 22 rooms with bath. Facilities: restaurant, baby-sitting service, golf nearby. AE, MC, V. Moderate.*

The Angel Inn. Each of the 10 rooms has antiques and beds with canopies. Built in 1823, this English-style inn even claims to have a resident ghost. *224 Regent St., L0S 1J0, tel. 416/468–3411. 12 rooms with bath. Facilities: restaurant, English tavern, golf nearby. AE, MC, V. Inexpensive.*

Ottawa/Hull

Dining

★ **Le Soupcon.** The decor is a mixture of chrome, black, and icy pastels, and the food is imaginative nouvelle: Guinea hen in a gin and lemon sauce and Canadian lamb with mint-flavored pistou are typical offerings. *408 Rideau St., Ottawa, tel. 613/594–8808. Reservations advised. AE, DC, MC, V. Closed Sun. and Mon. Expensive.*

The Mill Dining Lounge. Originally built in 1850 as a lumber mill, this restaurant has solid stone walls that are 2 feet thick; parts of the lumber mill burned down in 1901, and in 1963 it was renovated into the restaurant. This open, airy establishment's forte is prime rib, but try the fried chicken or the roasted lamb, too. *555 Ottawa River Pkwy., Ottawa, tel. 613/237–1311. Reservations required. Dress: neat but casual. Free parking. AE, MC, V. Expensive.*

★ **Café Henry Burger.** Established in 1922, this is one of Hull's most illustrious restaurants and it serves beautifully presented seasonal fare inside, and more informal fare on the terrace. The location, directly across the street from the Canadian Museum of Civilization, is ideal: The smoked breast of chicken with asparagus salad and a glass of wine on the terrace are a good antidote to museum fatigue. *69 Laurier St., Hull, tel. 819/777–5646. Reservations advised. Jacket and tie required. AE, DC, MC, V. Moderate.*

Lodging

★ **Château Laurier.** It's old, gracious, and very much a Canadian institution. The large, airy rooms have recently been refurnished, but the dark paneled lobby has been allowed to retain its nostalgic elegance. Right beside Parliament Hill and the Rideau Canal, the hotel has an indoor pool, boutiques, and lounges with entertainment. *1 Rideau St., K1N 8S7, tel. 613/232–6411. 450 rooms. Facilities: restaurant, lounges with entertainment, indoor pool, sauna, health club, shops, indoor parking. AE, CB, MC, V. Very Expensive.*

Ottawa Westin. Located in the heart of downtown and connected by walkway to both the Rideau Centre and the Ottawa Congress Centre, this four-star, business-oriented hotel offers contemporary luxury. All rooms are soundproof and feature individual climate control and stocked refrigerators, among other amenities. *11 Colonel By Dr., Rideau Centre, K1N 9H4, tel. 613/560–7000 or 800/228–3000. 475 rooms, 37 suites. Facilities: 3 restaurants, 2 bars, nightclub, 24-hour room service, indoor pool, health club, hot tub, sauna, 3 squash courts, indoor parking. AE, DC, MC. Very Expensive.*

Lord Elgin. Though the rooms have recently been renovated and made larger, this hotel has not lost its warm and comfortable ambience. The staff pride themselves on their quality service and their ability to make you feel at home. *100 Elgin St., K1P 5K8, tel. 613/235–3333. 305 rooms. Facilities: restaurant, lounge, room service. AE, DC, MC, V. Moderate.*

Journey's End. Efficient, friendly service draws guests to this modern, no-frills hotel located amid downtown's many attractions. The hotel offers an excellent view of the Parliament buildings. *1252 Michael St., K1J 7T1, tel. 613/744–2900. 69 rooms. AE, DC, MC, V. Inexpensive.*

Peterborough
Dining and Lodging

Red Oak Inn. This contemporary inn offers 183 comfortably furnished, individually climate-controlled guest rooms—some with a splendid view of the Otonabee River. Enjoy the solarium, with a heated pool and tropical garden, and the warm hospitality of the restaurant and lounge. *100 Charlotte St., tel. 705/743–7272. 183 rooms. Facilities: sauna, whirlpool, heated pool, gift store, valet, free underground parking. AE, D, MC, V. Expensive.*

St. Jacobs
Dining

The Stone Crock. For a cozy atmosphere and fine dining in the country, this family-style restaurant, which was a store during the 19th-century, is just right. Just outside of St. Jacobs, this local favorite offers a menu and style of cooking borrowed from the Mennonites. The cabbage rolls and pork Schnitzel are known for miles around; desserts are baked in-house. *41 King St., tel. 519/664–2286. Reservations advised. Dress: casual. MC, V. Closed holidays. Moderate.*

Stratford
Dining

★ **Rundles.** The terrace overlooks Lake Victoria, the windows stream with summer light, the napkins, the lamps, and the funny wood mobiles are a cheerful chorus of summer colors. Rundles and The Church are equally expensive (about $100 for dinner for two with a modest wine), and in past years, while Rundles had its growing pains, The Church has seemed the better deal. But Rundles has splendidly, deliciously matured. There are some who snicker at the trendiness of a menu that features peppers, goat cheese, eggplant, cabbage, and wild mushrooms, all the culinary catchphrases of the '80s. But Rundles is doing it so beautifully that one would be a fool to say no. The roasted red-pepper and eggplant terrine is a stunner, a savory layer cake iced in black-olive puree. Perfectly grilled salmon sits on mustardy *beurre blanc*. Pink roast lamb is scented with rosemary and served with a fine surprise of cabbage and white beans. The cold poached lobster comes with zingy red-pepper sauce; the duck melts in your mouth. *9 Cobourg St., tel. 519/271–6442. Dress: casual. Reservations required weeks in advance. AE, MC, V. No lunch Tues.; closed Mon. Very Expensive.*

The Old Prune. This could be considered a junior Rundles—a little cheaper and a little less mastery in the kitchen. The Old Prune's vocabulary is like Rundles: goat cheese and peppers, raw fish, the grill rather than the oven, mustard and garlic rather than butter and cream. The ideas are fine, but Rundles does it with more flavor. But this is also a charmer: delightful to look at, with gray walls and exotic flowered tablecloths, theatrical prints on the walls, and perfect posies scattered on the Royal Albert teacups. It does a good job with light meals, quiches, terrines, pâtés, and salads. *151 Albert St., tel. 519/271–5052. Reservations advised weeks in advance. Dress: casual. MC, V. No lunch Tues.; closed Mon. Moderate.*

Lodging

Festival Inn. An Old-English atmosphere has survived modernization and the installation of Jacuzzi water beds in some rooms. Located on the eastern outskirts of town, just a brief ride to the theater. *1144 Ontario St., Box 811, N5A 6W1, tel. 519/273–1150. 151 rooms with bath. Facilities: restaurant, coffee shop, baby-sitting service, tennis, indoor pool, whirlpool, golf nearby. AE, MC, V. Expensive.*

Queen's Inn. Built in 1914 to replace an earlier inn that was destroyed by fire, this 30-room inn has been gutted and turned into an elegant, if still quite small, hotel. The walls are a pleasant two-tone gray and white; the large, curved windows and bright, floral chintz sofas will charm any visitor. The dining room can be quite inventive, and next door stands a "brewpub," where homemade beer is sold only on the premises. *161 Ontario St., N5A 3H3, tel. 519/271–1400. 30 rooms with bath. Facilities: lounge. AE, MC, V. Expensive.*

★ **Raj Guest House.** This is a beautiful and exotic place near the city center, furnished with antiques and Anglo-Indian arts from the British Raj period. Rooms vary from deluxe with whirlpool to smaller, less expensive rooms. Rates include full English breakfast. *123 Church St., N5A 2R3, tel. 519/271–7129. 14 rooms with bath. Facilities: guest lounge, outdoor area. No credit cards. Expensive.*

23 Albert Place. This late 19th-century hotel was completely redecorated several years ago. It is conveniently located in the heart of the downtown shopping area, just a few hundred yards from the Avon Theatre. Suites and minisuites are available, and pets are allowed. *23 Albert St., N5A 3K2, tel. 519/273–5800. 34 rooms with bath. Facilities: restaurant, coffee shop, baby-sitting service, golf nearby. AE, MC, V. Moderate–Expensive.*

Majer's Motel. This motel sits on landscaped grounds, a good distance from the highway. No pets. *Hwys. 7 and 8, about a mile east of the city, RR4, N5A 6S5, tel. 519/271–2010. 31 rooms with bath. Facilities: coffee shop, outdoor pool, golf nearby. MC, V. Moderate.*

Swan Motel. This motel is in a quiet country setting on generous grounds, just one mile south of the Avon Theatre. *1482 Downie St. S, RR2, N5A 6S3, tel. 519/271–6376. 19 rooms with bath. Facilities: outdoor pool, baby-sitting service, golf nearby. MC, V. Inexpensive.*

Stratford General Hospital Residence. Students, or those traveling on a very tight budget, pay less than $20 a night for a single room. It's modern, bright, and serviceable. *Housekeeping Supervisor, Stratford General Hospital Residence, 130 Youngs St., N5A 1J7, tel. 519/271–5084 or 271–2120, ext. 586. Facilities: access to lounges, kitchenettes, laundry facilities, and parking. No credit cards. Inexpensive.*

Windsor
Dining

★ **Mason-Girardot Alan Manor.** One of Windsor's notable restaurants, features Turkish and Continental cuisine in six dining rooms in a restored 1865 manor. Specials include Sheftalia kebab, fillet of sole Meunière, steak Diane, and unusual desserts. *3203 Peter St. (no restaurant sign), tel. 519/253–9212 or 519/973–9536. Reservations advised. Jacket and tie advised. AE, MC, V. No lunch Sat. Closed Sun. and Mon. Moderate.*

Chez Vin's. This intimate place features lobster, linguine and beef satay, among other dishes. There is an extensive wine list. *26 Chatham St. W, tel. 519/252–2801. Reservations advised. Jacket and tie advised. MC, V. Closed lunch. Moderate.*

The Old Fish Market. This is Windsor's original seafood restaurant, featuring fresh fish and shellfish, oysters on the half-shell, clams, and mussels. Nonseafood items are also available. There is a maritime atmosphere and decor. *156 Chatham St. W, tel. 519/253–2670. Reservations advised. Dress:*

casual. AE, DC, MC, V. Closed lunch weekends. Moderate.

Milano Restaurant and Tavern. This is a favorite luncheon haunt of auto bosses that offers Italian cuisine served in its chandeliered Verdi and LaScala rooms. There are pasta and veal specialties, flaming coffee, and daily specials. *1520 Tecumseh Rd. E, tel. 519/254–5125. Reservations advised. Jacket and tie advised. AE, DC, MC, V. Inexpensive–Moderate.*

Wong's Eatery. This is an outstanding Oriental restaurant featuring Szechuan, Cantonese, and Hong Kong cuisine. *1457 University Ave. W, tel. 519/252–8814. Reservations advised. Dress: casual. AE, DC, MC, V. Inexpensive.*

Lodging

Ivy Rose Motel. This hotel prides itself on its eclectic selection of rooms. Whether you want to sleep in a waterbed or a canopy bed, you are sure to find it here in this business-oriented motel just 10 minutes from the city. *2885 Howard Ave., N8X 3Y4, tel. 519/966–1700. 91 rooms. Facilities: restaurant, outdoor pool, children's playground. AE, DC, MC, V. Moderate.*

The Arts

Ottawa

Ottawa is a cultural center with its fine selection of museums and excellent music, dance, and drama presentations at the **National Arts Center.** The city is particularly lively in February during the **Winterlude** festival (*see* Tour 1: Ottawa and Hull in Exploring Ontario, above), in May for the **Festival of Spring,** and in July when it celebrates **Festival Ottawa.** From late June to early July **Canada Canoe Festival** recalls the colorful past of the Ottawa River.

The Shaw Festival

The festival in Niagara-on-the-Lake began modestly back in the early 1960s with a single play and an unpromising premise: To perform the plays of George Bernard Shaw and his contemporaries. Fortunately, Shaw lived into his 90s, and his contemporaries included nearly everyone of note for nearly a century. The Shaw season now runs from April into October and includes close to a dozen plays. (Box office tel. 416/468–2172 or from Toronto 416/361–1544). Tickets in the Festival Theatre run from $20 to nearly $45; in the Court House and Royal George, from $18 to $35. Lunchtime Theatre, usually a one-act play, costs less than $14 per seat during its July and August run. Half-price tickets are available at the Five Star Ticket Booth, near the Eaton Centre in Toronto, and there are always half-price rush seats available on the day of the performance, on sale at the Festival Theatre Box Office. There are performances in all three theaters Tues.–Sun. evenings, and matinees on Wed., Fri., Sat., and Sun.

The Stratford Festival

In Stratford, The Shakespeare Festival's season runs from early May to early November, with performances at three theaters: the Festival, the Avon, and the Third Stage. The Festival stage replicates Shakespeare's Globe Theatre; the Avon has a traditional proscenium stage; and the Third Stage is a theater-in-the-round where the drama is more experimental and the ticket prices somewhat cheaper. Although performances of Shakespeare's plays dominate the offerings at the Festival, the other two houses complement this with a range of works by other playwrights.

For tickets and information from late February 1991, phone from Toronto, tel. 416/363-4471; from Detroit, 313/964-4668; from elsewhere 519/273-1600. Or write the Festival Theatre, Stratford N5A 6V2.

11 Québec Province

Introduction

Among the provinces of Canada, Québec is set apart by its strong French heritage, a matter not only of language but of customs, religion, and political structure. Québec covers a vast area—almost ⅙ of Canada's total—although the upper three-quarters is only sparsely inhabited. Most of the population lives in the southern cities, especially Montréal (*see* Chapter 4) and Québec City (*see* Chapter 5). Outside the cities, however, you'll find serenity and natural beauty in the province's innumerable lakes, streams, and rivers, in its farmlands and villages, in its great mountains and deep forests, and in its rugged coastline along the Gulf of St. Lawrence. Though the winters are long, there are plenty of winter sports to while away the cold months, especially in the Laurentians, with its many ski resorts.

Québec's recent threats to secede from the Canadian union are part of a long-standing tradition of separatism. The first European to arrive in Québec was French explorer Jacques Cartier, in 1534; another Frenchman, Samuel Champlain, arrived in 1603, determined to build French settlements in the region, and Jesuit missionaries followed in due course. Louis XIV of France proclaimed Canada a crown colony in 1663, and the land was allotted to French aristocrats in large grants called *seigneuries*. As tenants, known as *habitants*, settled upon farms in Québec, the Roman Catholic church took on an importance that went beyond religion. Priests and nuns also acted as doctors, educators, and overseers of business arrangements between the habitants and between French-speaking fur traders and English-speaking merchants. An important doctrine of the church in Québec was *survivance*, the survival of the French people and their culture. Couples were told to have large families, and they did—families of 10 or 12 children were the norm.

Although the British won control of Canada in the French and Indian War, in 1763, Parliament passed the Quebec Act in 1774, which ensured the continuation of French law in Québec and left provincial authority in the hands of the Roman Catholic church. In general, the law preserved the traditional Québecois way of life. Tensions between Québec and English-speaking Canada accelerated throughout the 20th century, however, and in 1974 the province defiantly proclaimed French its national language. In 1990 the Meech Lake Accord, which would have made special provisions to keep Québec officially under the Canadian constitution, was rejected by Québec voters, nearly precipitating a constitutional crisis. At press time (January 1991) the final vote had still not been cast, and secession remained a distinct possibility.

Being able to speak French can make your visit to the province more pleasant—you can by no means count on the locals speaking English, even as a second language. If you don't speak French, arm yourself with a phrase book or at least a knowledge of some basic phrases. It's also worth your while to sample the hearty traditional Québecois cuisine, for this is a province where food is taken seriously.

Essential Information

Important Addresses and Numbers

Tourist Information
Québec

Tourism Québec (Case Postale 20000, Québec City G1K 7X2, tel. 514/873–2015, toll-free from the Montréal area; from Québec, Canada, or the United States, 800/363–7777) can provide information on provincial tourist bureaus throughout the province.

The Laurentians

The major tourist office is the **Maison du Tourisme des Laurentides** at Saint-Jérôme, just off the Autoroute des Laurentides 15 at exit 39. *14142 rue de Lachapelle, R.R. 1, St-Jérôme J7Z 5T4, tel. 514/436–8532. Open year-round, daily 9–5.*

You can also get information at **Infotouriste** (Square Dorchester, Montréal, tel. 514/873–2015 or 800/361–5405). Year-round regional tourist offices are located in the towns of Carillon, L'Annociation, Mont-Laurier, Mont-Tremblant, Saint-Antoine, Saint-Eustache, Saint-Sauveur-des-Monts, Saint-Jovite, Sainte-Adèle, and Sainte-Agathe-des-Monts. Seasonal tourist offices (mid-June–Labor Day) are also located in Labelle, Lachute, Morin-Heights, Notre-Dame-du-Laus, Piedmont, Saint-Adolphe-Howard, and Val David. The paper also prints a column, **"The Snow Report,"** which appears daily throughout the ski season.

L'Estrie

In Montréal, information about l'Estrie is available at **Infotouriste** (*see* above). Year-round regional provincial tourist offices are located in the towns of Bromont, Granby, Lac-Brome, Lac-Mégantic, Magog, Sherbrooke, Stanstead Plain, Sutton, and Thetford Mines. Seasonal tourist offices (June–Labor Day) are also located in Asbestos, Ayer's Cliff, Black Lake, Coaticook, North Hatley, Lac-Brome, La Patrie, Mansonville, Notre-Dame-des-Bois, Richmond, and Sutton. For lodging information, contact: **Association Touristique de l'Estrie** (2338 rue King O, Sherbrooke, PQJ1 1C6, tel. 819/566–7404).

Arriving and Departing by Plane

Most airline arrivals will be into either of Montréal's airports (Mirabel or Dorval) or Québec City's airport (*see* Chapters 4 and 5).

Arriving and Departing by Car, Train, and Bus

By Car

The major highways are Autoroute des Laurentides 15, a six-lane highway from Montréal to the Laurentians; Autoroute 10 East from Montréal to l'Estrie; U.S. 91 from New England, which becomes Autoroute 55 as it crosses the border to l'Estrie; and Highway 138, which runs from Montréal along the north shore of the St. Lawrence River.

By Train

Regular **Via Rail** passenger service connects all the provinces with Montréal and Québec City, as well as limited service to the Gaspé Peninsula.

By Bus

Most major bus lines in the province connect with **Voyageur** (tel. 514/842–2281).

Lower Québec

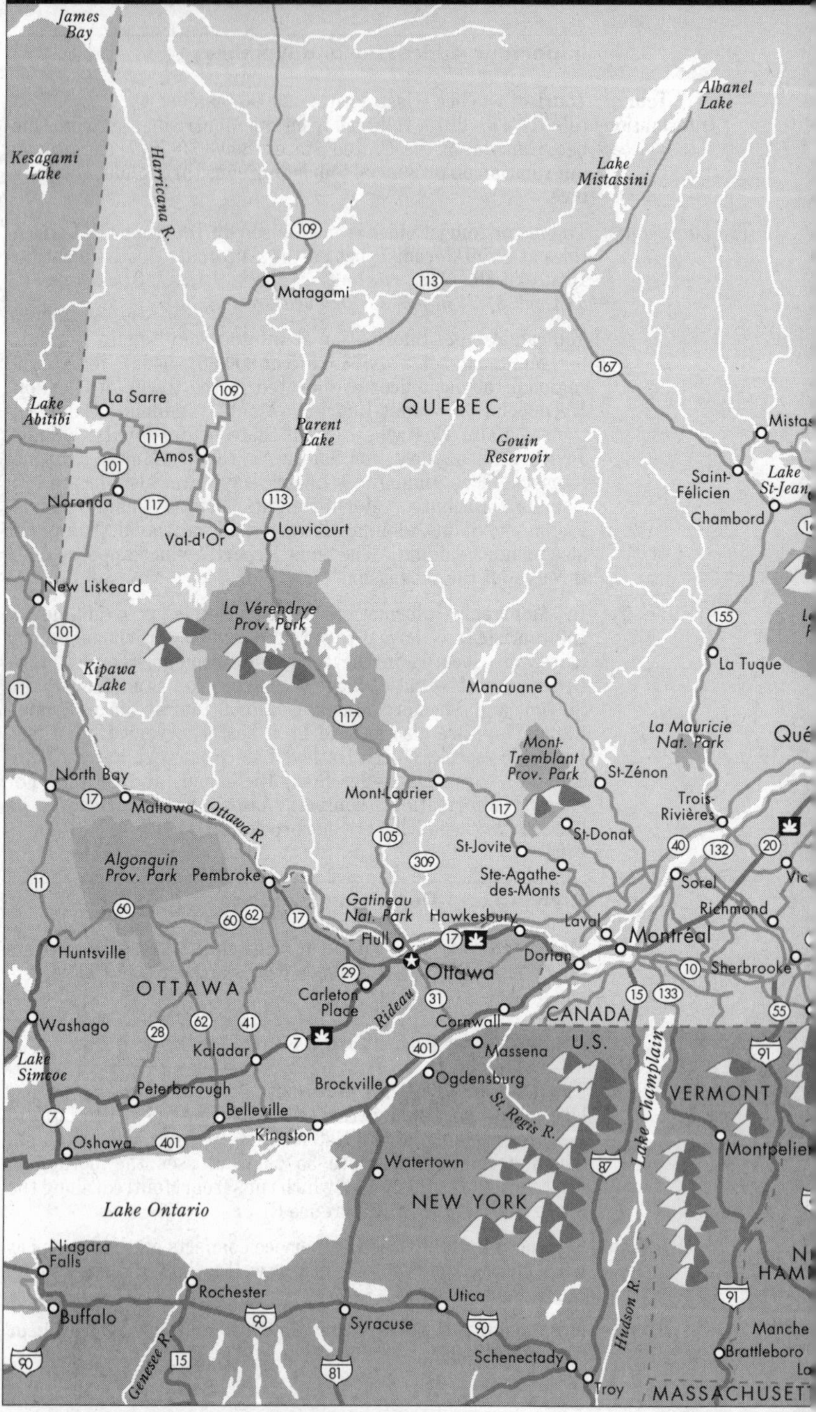

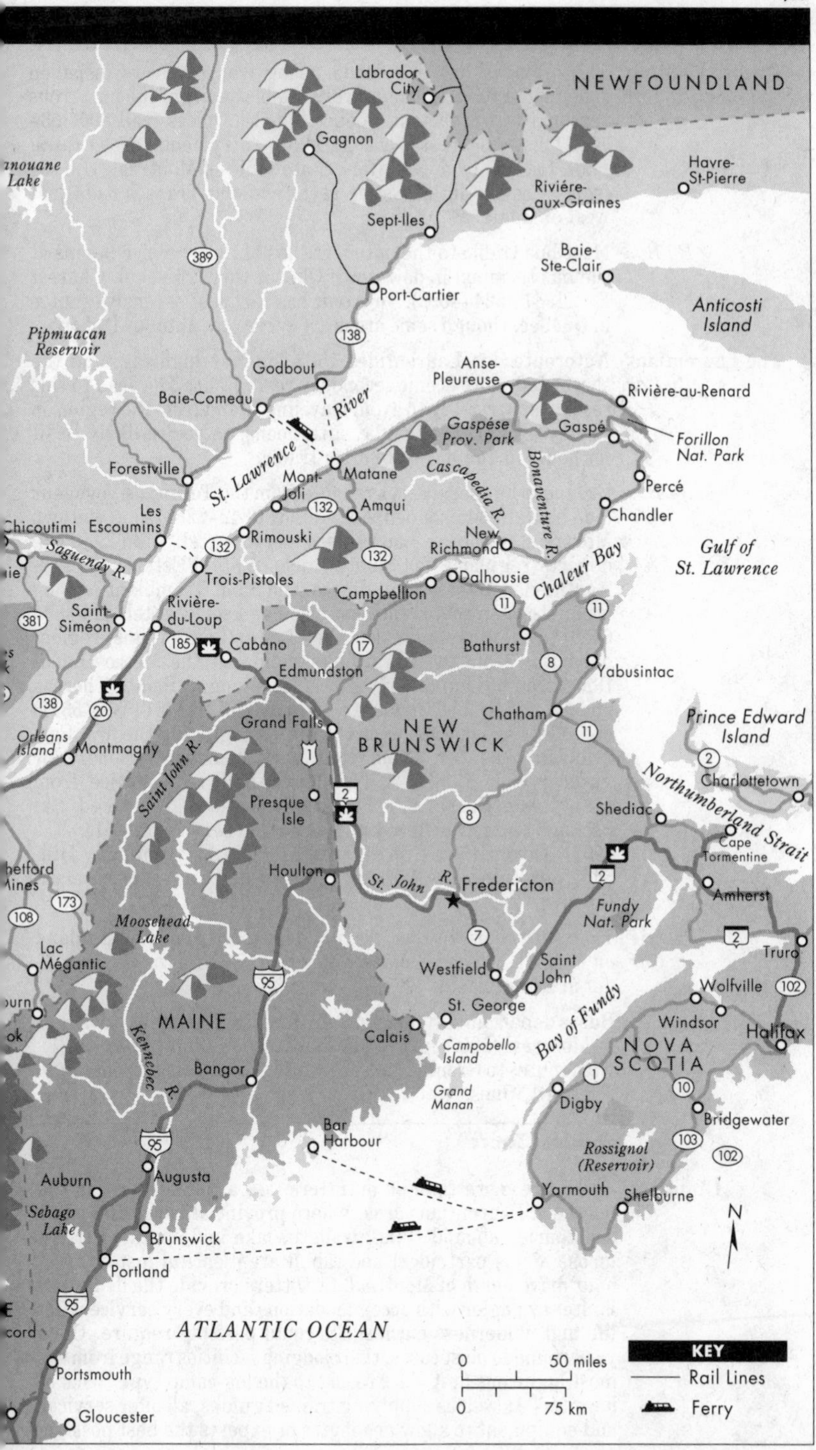
NEWFOUNDLAND
Labrador City
Gagnon
Havre-St-Pierre
Rivière-aux-Graines
Sept-Iles
Baie-Ste-Clair
Port-Cartier
Anticosti Island
Pipmuacan Reservoir
Godbout
Anse-Pleureuse
Rivière-au-Renard
Baie-Comeau
St. Lawrence River
Gaspése Prov. Park
Gaspé
Forillon Nat. Park
Forestville
Mont-Joli
Matane
Cascapedia R.
Bonaventure R.
Percé
Amqui
Chandler
Les Escoumins
Chicoutimi
Rimouski
New Richmond
Gulf of St. Lawrence
Saguenay R.
Trois-Pistoles
Dalhousie
Chaleur Bay
Campbellton
Saint-Siméon
Rivière-du-Loup
Cabano
Bathurst
Yabusintac
Edmundston
Chatham
Prince Edward Island
Grand Falls
NEW BRUNSWICK
Orléans Island
Montmagny
Charlottetown
Saint John R.
Northumberland Strait
Presque Isle
Shediac
Cape Tormentine
Houlton
St. John R.
Fredericton
Amherst
Fundy Nat. Park
Moosehead Lake
Truro
Lac Mégantic
Westfield
Saint John
Wolfville
St. George
Windsor
MAINE
Calais
Campobello Island
Bay of Fundy
Halifax
NOVA SCOTIA
Kennebec R.
Bangor
Grand Manan
Digby
Bridgewater
Bar Harbour
Rossignol (Reservoir)
Augusta
Auburn
Yarmouth
Shelburne
Sebago Lake
Brunswick
Portland
ATLANTIC OCEAN
Portsmouth
Gloucester
0 50 miles
0 75 km
KEY
Rail Lines
Ferry
N

Getting Around

Québec Province
By Car The province has fine roads, along which drivers insist on speeding. Free road maps are available at any of the numerous seasonal or permanent Québec Tourist Offices (call 800/363-7777 for the nearest location). Major entry points are Ottawa/Hull, U.S. 87 from New York State south of Montréal, U.S. 91 from Vermont into l'Estrie area, and the TransCanada just west of Montréal.

By Bus Most bus traffic to the outer reaches of the province begins at the bus terminal in downtown Québec City (255 boul. Charest E, tel. 418/524–4692). **Voyageur** has the most extensive routes in Québec, though some areas are served by **Autobus Dupont.**

The Laurentians
By Car Autoroute des Laurentides 15, a six-lane highway, and the slower but more scenic secondary road, Route 117, lead to this resort country. Try to avoid traveling to and from the region on Friday evenings or Sunday afternoons, as you're likely to sit for hours in bumper-to-bumper traffic.

By Bus Frequent bus service is available from the Terminus Voyageur (505 boul. de Maisonneuve E, tel. 514/842–2281) in downtown Montréal. **Limocar Laurentides'** service (tel. 514/629–9595) departs regularly for Sainte-Adèle, Ville d'Esterel, Sainte-Agathe-des-Monts, Saint-Jovite, and Mont Tremblant, among other stops en route. Limocar also has a service (tel. 514/383-6410) to the Basses Laurentides (Lower Laurentians) region, departing from the Laval bus terminal at the Métro Henri-Bourassa stop in north Montréal, stopping at Sainte-Thérèse and Saint-Jérôme. In winter, **Murray Hill** (tel. 514/937–5311) operates a private ski express service beginning the first Saturday in December, which requires advance reservations. **Tour Autocar** (tel. 514/476–2514) runs a daily ski service from Dorval and Mirabel airports; no reservations are needed. Ski package tours are offered by **Aerocar** ski service (tel. 514/397-9999), **Limocar** ski express (tel. 514/842–4281), **Murray Hill,** and **Tour Autocar.** All package tours require advance reservations.

L'Estrie
By Car Take Autoroute 10 East from Montréal or from New England on U.S. 91, which becomes Autoroute 55 as it crosses the border at Rock Island.

By Bus Buses depart almost hourly, daily from the Terminus Voyageur in Montréal (505 boul. de Maisonneuve E, tel. 514/842–2281), with routes to Granby, Lac-Mégantic, Magog, Sherbrooke, and Thetford Mines.

Guided Tours

Outfitters There are more than 60 outfitters (a.k.a. innkeepers) in the northern Laurentians area, where provincial parks and game sanctuaries abound. Pike, walleye, lake and speckled trout, moose, deer, partridge, and rabbit are plentiful just a three-hour drive north of Montréal. Outfitters provide the dedicated hunter or angler with accommodations and every service wildlife and wilderness enthusiasts could possibly require. Open year-round in most cases, their lodging facilities range from the most luxurious first-class resort to the log-camp type "back of beyond." As well as supplying trained guides, all offer services and equipment to allow neophytes or experts the best possible hunting and fishing in addition to boating, swimming, river rafting, windsurfing, ice-fishing, cross-country skiing, hiking, or just relaxing amid the splendor of this still spectacularly unspoiled region.

Outfitters recommended by the Laurentian tourist association include **Pourvoirie des 100 Lacs Nords** (tel. 514/659–4155), run by Claude Lavigne; **Club de Chasse et Pêche du Lac Beauregard** (tel. 819/425–7722) in Saint-Jovite; and **Club des Guides** (tel. 819/597–2486) at Lac-du-Cerf, run by Raymond Webster. Before setting off into the wilds, consult the Association des Pourvoyeurs du Québec (Québec Outfitters Association, 2900 boul. St-Martin O, Laval, H7T 2J2, tel. 514/687–0041) or ask for its list of outfitters available through tourist offices.

Don't forget: Hunting—which is strictly regulated, particularly for moose and deer—and fishing require a permit, available from the regional offices of the Ministère du Loisir, de la Chasse et de la Pêche (C.P. 22,000, Rosemont G1K 7X2, tel. 514/374–2417) or inquire at any Laurentians sporting-goods store displaying an "authorized agent" sticker.

Special-interest
Whale-watching

The St. Lawrence estuary is a habitat for 10 whale species, from white belugas that stay year-round to 140-ton blue whales that arrive late in May. Graduate-student marine biologists assigned to Montréal's Zoological Society accompany four popular weekend trips from Montréal, one each in July and September and two in August. Contact **Montréal Zoological Society** (2055 rue Peel, Montréal H3A 1V4, tel. 514/845–8317).

Croisières Navimex Canada, Inc. (25 Pl. Marché Champlain, Suite 101, Québec City G1K 4H2, tel. 418/692–4643) offers three-hour whale-watching cruises ($30 for adults) and 4½-hour dinner-cruises on the Saguenay Fjord ($40 for adults). Cruises depart from either Baie-Ste-Catherine or Tadoussac.

Industrial

Blessed with abundant natural resources, Québec exports hydroelectric power. Three **Hydro-Québec power stations** are open for visitors daily from mid-June to late August. Admission is free but children under the age of 14 are not allowed on tours. Contact the public relations department (tel. 819/372–3630) to schedule a tour at the Gentilly, Shawinigan, or La Tuque power station.

The **Laurentides Satellite Earth Station** (Weir, near Morin Heights, tel. 891/687–3241) is open for public tours from mid-June to Labor Day daily from 10 to 4:40, between Labor Day and Thanksgiving weekends only.

The exhibits at the province's eight **forestry education centers** in the Laurentians explain the business of forestry. Contact the Ministry of Energy and Resources (Education Service, CP 390, St-Faustin J0T 2G0, tel. 819/326–1606).

Exploring Québec

Orientation

There are two major attractions beyond the city limits of Montréal: l'Estrie (formerly the Eastern Townships), where city folk retreat in summer, and Les Laurentides (the Laurentians), where they escape in winter. Les Laurentides are characterized by thousands of miles of unspoiled wilderness and world-famous ski resorts, while l'Estrie has rolling hills and farmland. As major vacation areas in both winter and summer, they offer outdoor activities on ski slopes and lakes and in their provincial parks. The two other regions worth exploring are Charlevoix, often called the Switzerland of Québec because of its landscape, and the knobby Gaspé Peninsula, where the St. Lawrence River meets the Gulf of St. Lawrence.

Highlights for First-time Visitors

Basilica of Ste-Anne-de-Beaupre, Ste-Anne-de-Beaupre, Tour 3: Charlevoix

Bonaventure Island and its gannet colony, off Perce, Tour 4: The Gaspe Peninsula

Cross-country skiing in Les Laurentides, Tour 1: Les Laurentides

Jardin Zoologique de Granby, Granby, Tour 2: L'Estrie

"Sugaring off" at a sugar shack in Les Laurentides, Dining

Theatre du lac Brome, Knowlton, Tour 2: L'Estrie

Whale-watching in the St. Lawrence Seaway, Guided Tours

Tour 1: Les Laurentides

Avid skiers might call Montréal a bedroom community for the Laurentians; just 56 kilometers (35 miles) to the north, they are home to some of North America's best-known ski resorts. The Laurentian range is ancient, dating to the Precambrian era (600,000 years ago). These rocky hills are relatively low, worn down by glacial activity, but they include eminently skiable hills, with a few peaks above 2,500 feet. World-famous Mont Tremblant, at 3,150 feet, is the tallest.

The **P'tit Train du Nord** made it possible to easily transport settlers and cargo to the Upper Laurentians. It also opened them up to skiing by the turn of the century. Before long, trainloads of skiers replaced settlers and cargo as the railway's major trade. The Upper Laurentians soon became known worldwide as the No. 1 ski center in North America—a position that it still holds today. Initially a winter weekend getaway for Montréalers who stayed at boarding houses and fledgling resorts while skiing its hills, the Upper Laurentians began attracting an international clientele, especially with the advent of the Canadian National Railway's special skiers' train, begun in 1928. (Its competitor, the Canadian Pacific Railway, jumped on the bandwagon soon after, doubling the number of train runs bringing skiers to the area.)

Soon, points north of Saint-Jérôme began to develop as resort areas: Saint-Sauveur-des-Monts, Saint-Jovite, Sainte-Agathe-des-Monts, Mont Tremblant, and points in between became major ski centers.

Roads north of Saint-Jérôme weren't kept open in winter before the end of World War II, so travel by car was virtually impossible and very hazardous. However, an intrepid few had already penetrated deep into the Upper Laurentians' wilderness, staking out their claims for prime resort locations. The founders of **Gray Rocks Inn** in Saint-Jovite were the grandparents of them all. Nearly a hundred years ago, so the story goes, New Yorker George Ernest Wheeler fell for one Lucile Aldridge of Chicago. Though her family promised her a life of luxury if she would forgo marrying Wheeler, Aldridge spurned her family's offer and set out with him for the wilds of Québec, lured by the tales of lumber fortunes. In 1906, their lumber stake went up in smoke, literally. But the enterprising couple decided to open a wilderness retreat for city folk.

Gray Rocks Inn—named after the granite boulders of the Canadian Shield on which it stood—opened on the shores of Lac Ouimet. By 1938, the by-then gentrified country inn was attracting an international clientele, including movie stars flown in by the Wheelers' eldest son. Ever the innovator, Gray Rocks was the first resort to hire professional ski instructors. The Snow Eagle Ski School celebrated its 50th anniversary in 1988. Granddaughter Lucile Wheeler, who began skiing at the age of two under the tutelage of Tyrolean cousins Hermann Gadner and Hans Falkner, became North America's first champion skier and Canada's first Olympic medalist in the sport. Other Olympians have trained there since but not one has yet surpassed her international accomplishments.

Another pioneer who helped build the Laurentians' reputation for skiing was the late legendary cross-country skiing champion, Norway native "Jackrabbit" Herman Smith Johannsen. He began his Canadian trailblazing career in this region in 1918. A devout missionary for skiing, he considered it not only a sport but also a philosophy of life. Among his converts were members of the Red Birds Ski Club, all graduates of McGill University. In 1928, they established one of the first ski clubs at Saint-Sauveur-des-Monts on Hill 70—the central part of Mont Saint-Sauveur. Their award-winning exploits and championing of the sport made Hill 70 one of the Laurentians' early ski centers. Here both downhill and slalom races were introduced, and competitions were held annually. Competitors who couldn't fit into the "sleigh taxis" coming from Saint-Sauveur's nearby train station would ski the half-mile trip to the site.

Johannsen also opened up the famous Maple Leaf Trail linking Shawbridge (Prévost) to Mont Tremblant between 1932 and 1935. Before his death in 1987 at the age of 111, he personally participated in expanding the Laurentians network of cross-country ski trails, which today cover about 1,000 kilometers (625 miles). Inducted into the Temple de la renommée du ski des Laurentides (Laurentian Hall of Ski Fame) in 1982 at the age of 107, he continues to be celebrated by lovers of the sport.

The Upper Laurentians also began to grow as a winter haven for prominent Montréalers, who traveled as far north as Sainte-Agathe-des-Monts to establish private family ski lodges. A number of these properties continue to be preserved in their rustic turn-of-the-century wilderness settings. Proud of their heritage, these families consider their retreats a privilege to maintain, spending as much time there as possible year-round and enjoying the same outdoor pursuits as their forebears, though with considerably more ease.

Accessible only by train until the 1930s, when the highway was built, these were used primarily as winter ski lodges. But once the road opened up, cottages became year-round family retreats. Today, there is an uneasy alliance between the long-time cottagers and resort-driven entrepreneurs. Both recognize the other's historic role in developing the UpperLaurentians, but neither espouses the other's cause. At the moment, commercial development seems to be winning out. A number of large hotels have added indoor pools and spa facilities, and efficient highways have brought the country closer to the city—45 minutes to Saint-Saveur, 1½ to 2 hours to Mont Tremblant. Montréalers can drive up to enjoy the fall foliage or engage in spring skiing and still get home before dark. The only slow periods are early October, when there is not much to do, and June, when there is plenty to do but also a lot of black flies.

Les Basses Laurentides

The Laurentians are actually divided into two major regions, les Basses Laurentides (the Lower Laurentians) and les Hautes Laurentides (the Upper Laurentians). But don't be fooled by the designations; they don't signify great driving distances.

The Lower Laurentians start almost immediately outside Montréal. Considered the birthplace of the Laurentians, this area is rich in historical and architectural landmarks. Beginning in the mid-17th century, the governors of New France, as Québec was then called, gave large concessions of land to its administrators, priests, and top-ranking military, who became known as *seigneurs*. In the Lower Laurentians, towns like Terrebonne, Saint-Eustache, Lac-des-Deux-Montagnes, and Oka are home to the manors, mills, churches, and public buildings these seigneurs had built for themselves and their *habitants*—the inhabitants of these quasi-feudal villages.

Numbers in the margin correspond with points of interest on the Laurentians map.

Two of the most famous seigneuries are within an hour of Montréal: **La Seigneurie de Terrebonne,** on l'Île-des-Moulins, is about
1 20 minutes from Montréal; La Seigneurie du Lac-des-Deux-Montagnes, in St-Scholastique, is 40 minutes from Montréal. You reach Terrebonne by taking boulevard Pie-IX in Montréal to the bridge of the same name. From the bridge take Highway 25 North. Exit at Terrebonne to Highway 440.

Governor Frontenac gave the land to Sieur André Daulier in 1673. Terrebonne was maintained by a succession of seigneurs until 1832, when Joseph Masson, the first French-Canadian millionaire, bought it. He and his family were the last seigneurs de Terrebonne; their reign ended in 1883.

Today, Terrebonne offers visitors a bona fide glimpse of the past. Now run by the Corporation de l'Île-des-Moulins rather than a French aristocrat, the seigneurie's mansions, manors, and buildings have all been restored. Take a walk through Terrebonne's historical center and then stop at the **centre d'interprétation historique de Terrebonne Museum.** It features a large collection of artifacts from the life and times of Joseph Masson and his family. There is also the Île-des-Moulins art gallery, which presents exhibitions of works by local artists, a year-round theater presenting English and French plays as well as musical matinees and outdoor summer shows. Most activities are free. *Corner boul. des Braves and rue St-Pierre, tel. 514/471-0619. Admission free. Open daily 10–8, summer only.*

The Laurentians

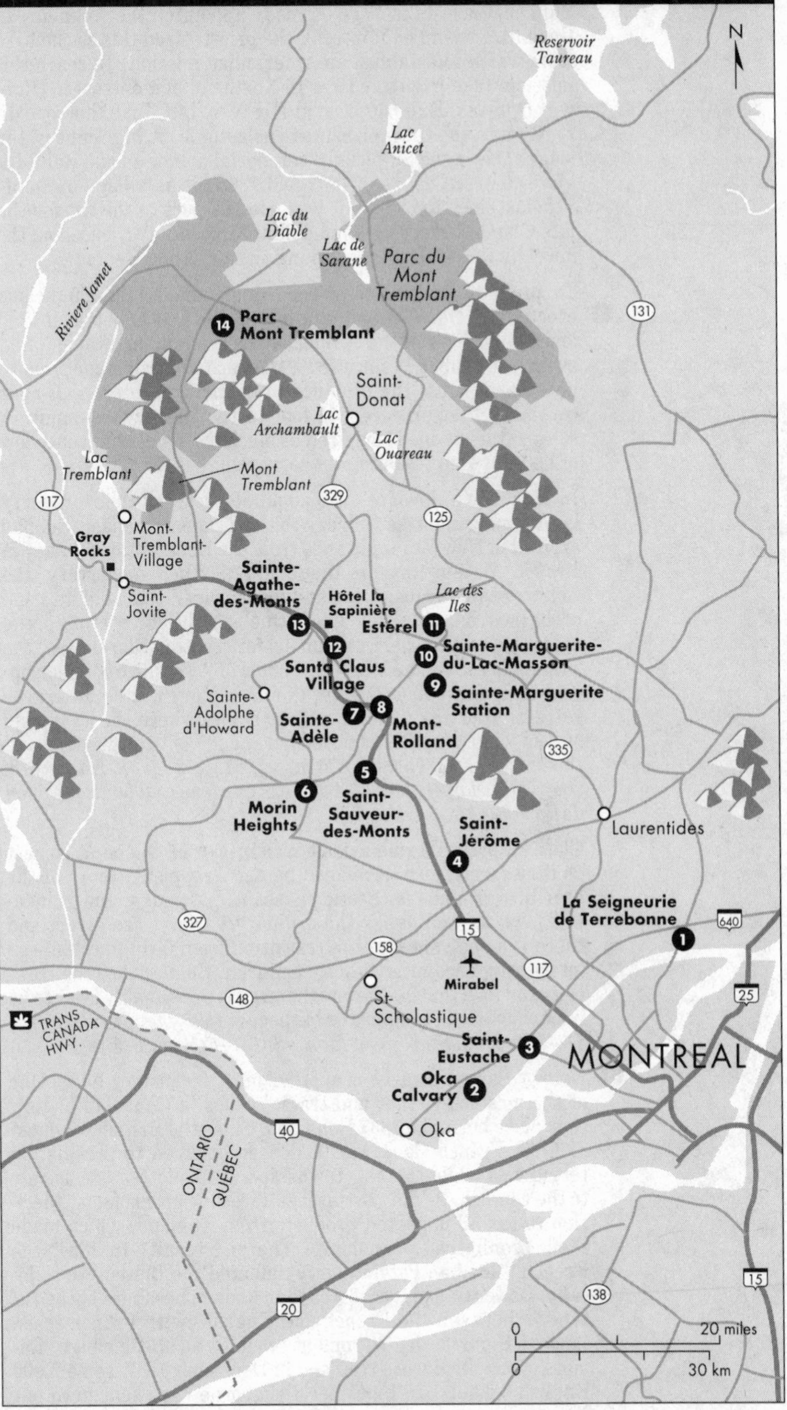

Reservoir Taureau
N
Lac Anicet
Lac du Diable
Lac de Sarane
Parc du Mont Tremblant
Riviere Jamet
14 Parc Mont Tremblant
131
Saint-Donat
Lac Archambault
Lac Ouareau
Lac Tremblant
Mont Tremblant
117
329
125
Mont-Tremblant-Village
Gray Rocks
Saint-Jovite
Sainte-Agathe-des-Monts
Hôtel la Sapinière
Lac des Iles
13
Estérel 11
12
10 Sainte-Marguerite-du-Lac-Masson
Santa Claus Village
9 Sainte-Marguerite Station
Sainte-Adolphe d'Howard
Sainte-Adèle 7
8 Mont-Rolland
335
5
6 Morin Heights
Saint-Sauveur-des-Monts
Saint-Jérôme
Laurentides
4
La Seigneurie de Terrebonne
1
640
327
15
158
Mirabel
117
148
St-Scholastique
25
TRANS CANADA HWY.
Saint-Eustache 3
MONTREAL
Oka Calvary 2
Oka
40
ONTARIO
QUÉBEC
138
15
20
0
20 miles
0
30 km

La Seigneurie du Lac-des-Deux-Montagnes was allotted to the Sulpician priests in 1717. Already appointed the seigneurs of the entire island of Montréal, the priests used this as the base from which to establish an Amerindian mission. To reach this mission, take Highway 13 or 15 North out of Montréal to Highway 640 West Exit 640 West at Highway 148. Take this road directly into the town of Saint-Scholastique. A highlight of the seigneurie is the Sulpicians' seignorial manor on rue Belle-Rivière, erected between 1802 and 1808 in the village of Saint-Scholastique. Recently, it was used as part of the set for the late Claude Jutra's acclaimed film, *Kamouraska,* based on the novel by Québec's prize-winning author, Anne Hébert.

❷ To promote piety among the Amerindians, the Sulpicians erected the **Oka Calvary (Stations of the Cross)** between 1740 and 1742. Three of the seven chapels are still maintained, and every September 14 since 1870, Québécois pilgrims congregate here from across the province to participate in the half-hour ceremony that proceeds on foot to the Calvary's summit. A sense of the divine is inspired as much by the magnificent view of Lac-des-Deux-Montagnes as by religious fervor.

In 1887, the Sulpicians gave about 865 acres of their property located near the Oka Calvary to the Trappist monks, who had arrived in New France in 1880 from the Bellefontaine Abbey in France. Within 10 years they had built their monastery, the **Abbaye cistercienne d'Oka,** and transformed this land into one of the most beautiful domains in Québec. The abbey is one of the oldest in North America. Famous for creating Oka cheese, the Trappists established the Oka School of Agriculture, which operated up until 1960. Today, the monastery is a noted prayer retreat. Tour the miller's modest home, where the Trappists stayed when they first arrived here, and visit the gardens and the chapel. *1600 chemin d'Oka, tel. 514/479–8361. Admission free. Chapel open daily 4 AM–9 PM; gardens and boutique open daily 9:30–11:30 and 1–4.*

Close by is the **ferme avicole d'Oka,** one of Québec's largest poultry farms, also developed by the Trappists. Tours of the breeding grounds for exotic pheasant, partridge, and guinea-hen fowl, as well as for the ordinary variety, are given, and there is a slide show of the transition from farm to table—an interesting encounter for city children. Bonuses are the fresh eggs and fowl that can be bought on site, presumably later to be roasted over the campfire or barbecue. *1525 chemin d'Oka, tel. 514/479–8394. Store open Mon.–Sat. 1–5, Sun. 1–5.*

❸ Nearby **Saint-Eustache** is another must for history buffs. One of the most important and tragic scenes in Canadian history took place here: the 1837 Rebellion. Since the British conquest of 1760, French Canadians had been confined to preexisting territories while the new townships were allotted exclusively to the English. Adding to this insult was the government's decision to tax all imported products from England, which made them prohibitively expensive. The end result? In 1834, the French Canadian Patriot party defeated the British party locally. Lower Canada, as it was then known, became a hotbed of tension between the French and English, with French resistance to the British government reaching an all-time high. Rumors of rebellion were rife, and in December 1837, some 2,000 English soldiers led by General Colborne were sent in to put down the "army" of North Shore patriots by surrounding the village of Saint-Eustache. Jean-Olivier Chénier and his 200 Patriots took refuge in the local church, which Colborne's cannons bombed and set afire. Chénier and 80 of his comrades were killed during the battle, and more than 100 of the town's houses and buildings erected during the seignorial regime were looted and burned down by Colborne's soldiers. Even today, traces of the bullets fired by the English army cannons are visible on the facade of Saint-Eustache's church at 123 rue St-Louis. Most of the town's period buildings are open to the public. Note especially **Manoir Globenski** and **Moulin Légaré,** the only water mill still in operation in Canada. For a guided tour or for a free brochure that gives a good walking-tour guide, visit the town's Arts and Cultural Services Center (235 rue St-Eustache, tel. 514/472–4440).

Time Out Before heading north, stop at **Pâtisserie Grande-Côte** (367 chemin de la Grande-Côte, tel. 514/473–7307) to sample the wares of St-Eustache's most famous bakery and pastry shop.

Les Hautes Laurentides 4

Rivaling Saint-Eustache in Québec's historic folklore is **Saint-Jérôme,** founded in 1830. Today a thriving economic center and cultural hub off Route 117, it first gained prominence in 1868 when Curé Antoine Labelle became pastor of this parish on the shores of Rivière du Nord. Of legendary stature, this charismatic priest was instrumental in the colonization of St-Jérôme and points beyond in what are now known as the Upper Laurentians. Messianic in his mission, Curé Labelle devoted himself to opening up northern Québec to French Canadians. Between 1868 and 1890, he founded 20 parish towns—an impressive achievement given the harsh conditions of this vast wilderness. But his most important legacy was the famous P'tit Train du Nord railway line, which he persuaded the government to build in order to open Saint-Jérôme to travel and trade.

Not surprisingly, he is still fervently admired by the Québecois, and many monuments and roads in Saint-Jérôme and elsewhere bear his name: boulevard Labelle, the municipality of Labelle, the Papineau-Labelle wildlife reserve, and the statue of Curé Labelle in Parc Antoine-Labelle facing Saint-Jérôme cathedral.

Follow Saint-Jérôme's **promenade,** a 4-kilometer-long (2½-mile) boardwalk alongside the Rivière du Nord from rue De Martigny bridge to rue St-Joseph bridge for a walk through the town's history. Descriptive plaques en route highlight episodes of the Battle of 1837. The **Centre d'exposition du Vieux-Palais** housed in St-Jérôme's old courthouse exhibits shows focusing on the town's history. The museum also houses a permanent art exhibit, offers some activities for children, and hosts concerts. *185 rue du Palais, tel. 514/432–7171. Admission free. Open Tues.–Fri. noon–5, Sun. 1–5.*

Saint-Jérôme's **Parc régional de la Rivière-du-Nord** (1051 boul. Industriel, tel. 514/431–1676) was created as a nature retreat. Paths throughout the park lead to the spectacular Wilson Falls *(chutes, en français).* Rain or shine, the Pavillon Marie-Victorin is open daily, with summer weekend displays and workshops devoted to nature, culture, and history.

The resort vacation area truly begins at Saint-Sauveur-des-Monts (Exit 60) and extends as far north as Mont Tremblant.

Then it turns into a wilderness of lakes, some with private chalets and fishing camps, and forests best visited with an outfitter. Laurentian guides planning fishing and hunting trips are concentrated around Saint-Donat near Parc Mont Tremblant.

To the first-time visitor, the hills and resorts around Saint-Sauveur, Sainte-Marguerite Station, Morin Heights, Val Morin, and Val David, up to Sainte-Agathe, form a pleasant hodgepodge of villages, hotels, and inns that seem to blend one into another.

5 **Saint-Sauveur-des-Monts,** exit 60 off the Autoroute, is the focal point for area resorts. During the past decade this town has grown so swiftly that vacationers who once camped on its outskirts say they barely recognize it.

The surrounding ski hill complexes of Mont-Habitant and Mont-Saint-Sauveur offer ever-increasing condo developments, lodges, hotels, motels, and inns at the foot of, or just a mile or so from, mountain slopes. Mont-Habitant alone features two 40-room and six 100-room lodges in addition to 125 motel rooms. Mont-St-Sauveur's slopes are dotted with modern condo units.

Despite all this development, Saint-Sauveur has managed to add more than 60 good restaurants and a shopping mall without totally ruining its character. It has gone from a 1970s sleepy Laurentian village of 4,000 residents that didn't even have a traffic light to a thriving year-round town attracting some 30,000 cottagers and visitors on weekends. Its main street, rue Principale, once dotted with quaint French restaurants, now boasts *brochetteries* and sushi bars, and the narrow strip is so choked in summertime by cars and tourists that it has earned the sobriquet "Crescent Street of the North." Residents here once won the battle against a McDonald's opening. Now the parking lots of major franchise fast-food eateries are always packed.

The gleaming white spires of **Saint-Sauveur Church** still dominate rue Principale, but Saint Francis of the Birds has not been so lucky. Built in 1951 with support from Montréal's Molson family, this sturdy, rustic log church with its fine stained-glass-window portraits of the Laurentian countryside no longer offers the worshiper or visitor a secluded and peaceful spiritual retreat. Where only two years ago its immediate neighbors were modest chalets dotting the forest, today the empty, bankrupt Delta Hotel complex sits in the church's backyard. However, classical concerts can still be heard in the church every Tuesday evening during July and August (tel. 819/227-2663).

But for those who like their vacations—winter or summer—lively and activity-filled, Saint-Sauveur is *the* place where the action rolls nonstop. In winter, skiing is the main thing. (Mont-Saint-Sauveur, Mont Avila, Mont Gabriel, and Mont Olympia all offer special season passes and programs, and some ski-center passes can be used at more than one center in the region.) From Mont-Saint-Sauveur to Mont Tremblant, the area's ski centers (most situated in or near Saint-Sauveur, Sainte-Adèle, Sainte-Agathe, and Saint-Jovite) offer night skiing—a perk for Montréalers and town residents who are fanatical about cramming as much skiing as possible into each season. All boast ski instructors—many are members of the Canadian Ski Patrol Association.

Mont-Saint-Sauveur is the new site of the **Pepsi Celebrity Ski Invitational,** in which Hollywood celebrities compete on and off the hills in this annual charity fund-raiser. It attracts at least 10,000 skiing and nonskiing stargazers to the popular weekend events held in mid-March.

Just outside Saint-Sauveur, the $7 million Mont-Saint-Sauveur **Aquatic Park** (tel. 514/871–0101 or 800/363–2426) and tourist center (exits 58 or 60) will keep children happy with slides, wave pools, snack bars, and more. Its latest attraction is the $1.7 million man-made "Colorado" rafting river, which follows the natural contours of the steep hills. The nine-minute ride requires about 12,000 gallons of water to be pumped per minute.

6 Nearby in **Morin Heights,** there's a new spin on an old sport at **Ski Morin Heights** (exit 60, Autoroute 15 N, tel. 514/226–1333 or 800/363–2527), where snowboarding is the latest craze. Likened to surfing a big wave, riding a skateboard down a hill, or windsurfing on a white-capped lake, snowboarding demands similar skills and dexterity, not to mention the fearlessness of the lionhearted. Nonetheless, it is carefully supervised by Ski Morin Heights' instructors. Would-be snowboarders are required to pass a test by the center's ski patrol. Although it doesn't have overnight accommodations, Ski Morin Heights boasts a 44,000-square-foot chalet with a full range of hospitality services and sports-related facilities. Eateries include the Après-Vous Pub and cafeteria, a new 300-seat restaurant (pizza and deli food are the specialties), and La Croissanterie for fresh croissants, Danish pastries, and muffins. Après-ski activities include Mardi Gras Pub nights and a new health club for those over age 18. Season ski-pass holders get reduced rates for club membership, which includes use of the international-size squash courts, gym with exercise equipment, Jacuzzi, and sauna.

There's also a large nursery on-site and special ski lesson programs for children age 3 and up. The nursery slope school emphasizes the fun of skiing with these youngsters. A Disneyland theme quickly wins over the most shy preschoolers, who are soon happily greeting ski instructors dressed as Mickey Mouse, Donald Duck, and Roger Rabbit as they advance through their lessons in Looney Toon station, encountering new toys, tunnels, and ski tracks en route.

The town's architecture and population reflect its English settlers' origins. Most residents are English-speaking. Morin Heights has escaped the overdevelopment of Saint-Sauveur but still offers the visitor a good range of restaurants, bookstores, boutiques, and crafts shops to explore. During the summer months, windsurfing, swimming, and canoeing on the area's two lakes are popular pastimes. The most recent addition, now entering its fifth season to popular and critical acclaim, is **Théâtre Morin Heights** (tel. 514/226–5863) whose productions are presented at Ski Morin Heights during the summer months. Popular musicals, lighthearted comedies, mysteries, and children's plays are in the repertoire. Run by a dedicated coterie of Morin Heights residents on a volunteer basis, the theater falls into the "highly professional amateur group" category. Ticket reservations are a must, especially since the theater offers a dinner-show package for only $25 per person. Both parts of the package have won kudos consistently.

In the summer holiday-goers head for the region's golf courses (two of the more pleasant are 18-hole links at Sainte-Adèle and Mont Gabriel), campgrounds at Val David, Lacs Claude and Lafontaine, and beaches; in the fall and winter, they come for the foliage as well as alpine and nordic skiing.

7 The busy town of **Sainte-Adèle** is full of gift and Québec-crafts shops, boutiques, and restaurants. It also has an active nightlife, including a few discos. The town locals are a dynamic bunch who participate wholeheartedly in the special events held year-round. Take the **Défi sur Neige** (tel. 514/229–2921), for example—held annually in early September, thanks to the modern miracle of snow machines. This two-day festival features acrobatic, downhill, and cross-country skiing competitions up and down the town's main streets.

Just as much of a rave with adults and children are the **Super Splash** ice slides, which are converted to water slides in the summer. *1791 boul. Ste-Adèle, tel. 514/229–2909. 2 giant ice slides for adults, 3 for children. Admission to ice slide: Mon.–Thurs., adults $7.50, children under 13 $6.50; Fri.– Sun. adults $9, children under 13 $7.50. Open Dec. 15–April, 9AM–10PM. Admission to water slide: $15 adults, $12 children. Open June–Sept.*

Sainte-Adèle is also the site of Tennis Canada's annual international tournament (tel. 514/229–3555) in early July, when 200 competitors from 15 countries vie for the championships and upgrading of their ranking for the international circuit.

A couple of miles north on Highway 117, the reconstructed **Village de Seraphin's** 20 small habitant homes, grand country house, general store, and church recall the settlers who came to Sainte-Adèle in the 1840s. This award-winning historic town also features a train tour through the woods. *Tel. 514/229–4777. Admission: $6.50 adults, $3 children 5–11. Open late-May–early Oct., daily 10–4:45.*

8 In **Mont-Rolland, Station touristique de Mont Gabriel** offers superb skiing, primarily for intermediate and advanced skiers. Most popular runs are the Tamarack and O'Connell trails for advanced skiers, the Obergurgl for intermediates. Mont Gabriel is also the annual site of the Free-Style World Cup Ski Championships (tel. 514/229–3547), in which more than 200 athletes from 20 countries compete every January. The on-site lodge, **Auberge Mont Gabriel** (*see* Lodging, below) has six-night ski-week packages (including all breakfasts and dinners, as well as unlimited day and night skiing available). Weekend ski packages are also available; ski lessons for both are extra. *Autoroute 15, exit 64, Mont-Rolland J0R 1G0, tel. 514/861–2852.*

Aside from the usual outdoor activities common to the Laurentians, Mont-Rolland's summer theater presents lighthearted entertainment for the whole family. Comedy, musicals, children's theater, and even circus acts may be part of the lineup. Your best bet is to check local newspapers or call **Théâtre de Mont-Rolland** (2525 chemin de la Rivière, tel. 514/229–5171).

9 **Sainte-Marguerite Station** is home to the large family-style **Alpine Inn** (*see* Lodging, below).

10 Neighboring community **Sainte-Marguerite-du-Lac-Masson** celebrated its 125th anniversary in 1990. The town's Service

des Loisirs (tel. 514/228–2543) is the place to call for details about events, and cruises and skating on Lac-Masson.

11 The permanent population of the town of **Estérel** is a mere 83 souls. But visitors to **Ville d'Estérel,** a 135-room resort at Autoroute 69, near Sainte-Marguerite Station, swell that number into the thousands. Founded in 1959 on the shores of Lac Dupuis, Fridolin Simard bought this 5,000-acre domain from Baron Louis Empain. Named Estérel by the baron because it evoked memories of his native village in Provençe, Ville d'Estérel soon became a household word for holiday vacationers in search of a first-class resort area. (For more details, *see* Lodging, below).

12 Children know **Val David** for its **Santa Claus Village.** *Tel. 819/ 322–2146. Admission: adults $6, children 2–12 $3. Open late May–early Oct.*

Home to Passe-Montagne, a leader in outdoor adventure tours, Val David is a rendezvous for mountain climbers, ice scalers, dogsledders, hikers, and summer or winter campers. For equipment rentals and other information, contact the Maison du Tourisme des Laurentides (tel. 514/436–8532). Val David also has three campgrounds, all along Route 117: La Belle Étoile, Camping Laurentien, and Le Montagnais.

Val David is also a haven for artists, many of whose studios are open to the public. Most of their work is for sale. **Les Créateurs associés** (2495 rue d'Église, tel. 819/322–2043) boutique and art gallery features a wide range of artisan handicrafts. **Atelier Bernard Chaudron, Inc.** (2449 chemin de l'Île, tel. 819/322–3944), sells hand-shaped and hammered lead-free pewter objets d'art.

About 96 kilometers (60 miles) from Montréal, overlooking Lac
13 des Sables, is **Sainte-Agathe-des-Monts,** the largest commercial center for ski communities farther north. This lively resort area attracts campers to its spacious **Camping Ste-Agathe** (Rte. 329, CP156, Sainte-Agathe-des-Monts J8C 383, tel. 819/326–5577), bathers to its municipal beach, and sailors to its lake cruises on the ***Alouette*** (tel. 819/326–3656) touring launch. Sailing is the favorite summer sport, especially during the "24 heures de la voile" sailing competition (tel. 819/362–0457) each Canada Day weekend in July.

Skin-diving is also popular here, with local headquarters for equipment rentals, guides, etc., at the **Centre de plongée sousmarine** (124 rue Principale, tel. 819/326–4464).

But mountain-climbing may be one of the best ways to view the scenery of the Upper Laurentians. The Fédération québécoise de la montagne (4545 rue Pierre-de-Coubertin, C.P. 1000, Succursale M, Montréal H1W 3R2, tel. 514/252–3004) can give you information about this, as can the region's tourist offices.

Also popular is the summertime festival "Le Nord en fête" (tel. 819/425–0457), which takes place for two weeks in late July and early August under the Big Top on the shores of Lac des Sables. Six months later, the town celebrates "L'hiver en Nord" (tel. 819/326–0457), a four-month festival of sports competitions, tournaments, and entertainment every weekend from mid-December to mid-March.

About 1 kilometer (½ mile) north of Sainte-Agathe-des-Monts is the **Village du Mont-Castor**, an attractive re-creation of a turn-of-the-century Québecois village; more than 100 new homes have been built here in the traditional fashion of full-length logs set *pièce sur pièce* (one upon the other).

Farther north lie two of Québec's best-known ski resorts, Gray Rocks and Mont Tremblant Lodge, now part of Station Touristique de Mont Tremblant (*see* Lodging, below). Mont Tremblant is also car-racing country. Racing champion Jackie Stewart has called Mont Tremblant "the most beautiful race-track in the world." Though Stewart didn't win the Canadian Grand Prix at Mont Tremblant in 1970 (his car fell apart), he did win a Can-Am race there in 1971 and came back in 1972 to win the Canadian Grand Prix. Nowadays, the **Formula 2000 "Jim Russell Championships"** of the Canadian Car Championships (tel. 819/425–2739) take place here on weekends in June, July, August, September, and October, as do three of the eight stock-car races for the **Rothmans-Porsche Turbo Cup.**

The mountain and the hundreds of square miles of wilderness
14 beyond it comprise **Parc Mont Tremblant.** Created in 1894, this was once the home of the Algonquin Indians, who called this area Manitonga Soutana, meaning "mountain of the spirits." Today it is a vast wildlife sanctuary of more than 500 lakes and rivers protecting some 230 species of birds and animals, including moose, deer, bear, and beaver. In the winter, its trails are used by cross-country skiers, snowshoers, and snowmobile enthusiasts. Moose hunting is allowed in season, and camping and canoeing are the main summer activities. There are three campgrounds with a total of 719 sites: Lac Monroe (which also has a park reception center), Lac Chat, and Lac Lajoie. In addition there are approximately 20 cottages for rent. Other park reception centers are in Saint-Donat and Saint-Come (tel. 819/688–2281).

Tour 2: L'Estrie

Numbers in the margin correspond with points of interest on the L'Estrie map.

L'Estrie (before Bill 101, known as the Eastern Townships) refers to the area in the southeast corner of the province of Québec, bordering Vermont and New York State. Its northern Appalachian hills, rolling down to placid lakeshores, were first home to the Abenaki Indians, long before "summer people" built their cottages and horse paddocks here. The Indians are gone, but the names they gave to the region's recreational lakes remain—Memphremagog, Massawippi, Mégantic.

L'Estrie, known as the garden of Québec, was left largely unsettled by the early French colonists, who, save for a few trappers, concentrated on northern Québec.

L'Estrie was initially populated by United Empire Loyalists fleeing the American War of Independence and, later, the newly created United States of America, to continue living under the English king in British North America. It's not surprising that l'Estrie is reminiscent of New England with its covered bridges, village greens, white church steeples, and country inns. They were followed, around 1820, by the first wave of Irish immigrants—ironically, Catholics fleeing their country's union with Protestant England. Some 20 years later the potato famine sent more Irish pioneers to the townships.

L'Estrie became more Gallic after 1850, as French Canadians moved in to work on the railroad and in the lumber industry, and later to mine asbestos at Thetford. Around the turn of the century, English families from Montréal and Americans from the border states discovered the region and began summering at cottages along the lakes. During the Prohibition era, the area attracted even more cottagers from the United States. Lac Massawippi became a favorite summer resort of wealthy families whose homes have since been converted into gracious inns, including the Manoir Hovey and the Hatley Inn.

Today the summer communities fill up with equal parts French and English visitors, though year-round residents are primarily French. Nevertheless, the locals are proud of both their Loyalist heritage and Québec roots. They boast of "Loyalist tours" and Victorian gingerbread homes, and in the next breath, direct visitors to the snowmobile museum in Valcourt, where, in 1937, native son Joseph-Armand Bombardier built the first *moto-neige* in his garage. (Bombardier's inventions were the basis of one of Canada's biggest industries, supplying New York City and Mexico City with subway cars and other rolling stock.)

Over the last two decades, l'Estrie has developed from a series of quiet farm communities and wood-frame summer homes to a thriving all-season resort area. In winter, skiers flock to nine downhill centers and 26 cross-country trails. By early spring, the sugar huts are busy with the new maple syrup. L'Estrie's southerly location makes this the balmiest corner of Québec, notable for its spring skiing. In summer, boating, swimming, sailing, golfing, and bike riding take over. And every fall the inns are booked solid with "leaf peepers" eager to take in the brilliant foliage.

15 **Granby,** about 80 kilometers (50 miles) from Montréal, is considered to be the gateway to l'Estrie. This town is best known for its zoo, the **Jardin Zoologique de Granby.** It houses some 1,000 animals from 200 species. Two of its newest inhabitants, rare snow leopards, have won the zoo recognition from the International Union for the Conservation of Nature. The Granby pair are on loan from Chicago's Lincoln Park Zoo and New York's Bronx Zoo. The complex includes amusement park rides and souvenir shops as well as a playground and picnic area. *347 rue Bourget, tel. 514/372-9113. Admission: $8 adults, $5.50 senior citizens, $4.75 children 5–17, $2 children 1–4. Open May–Oct., daily 10–5.*

Granby is also gaining repute as the townships' gastronomic capital. Each October, the month-long Festival Gastronomique attracts more than 10,000 *gastronomes* who use the festival's "gastronomic passport" to sample the cuisines at several dining rooms. To reserve a passport, write: *Festival gastronomique de Granby et région, 650 rue Principle, Granby J2G 8L4 tel. 514/378-7272.*

The **Yamaska** recreation center on the outskirts of town features sailboarding, swimming, and picnicking all summer, and cross-country skiing and snowshoeing in winter.

L'Estrie (Eastern Townships)

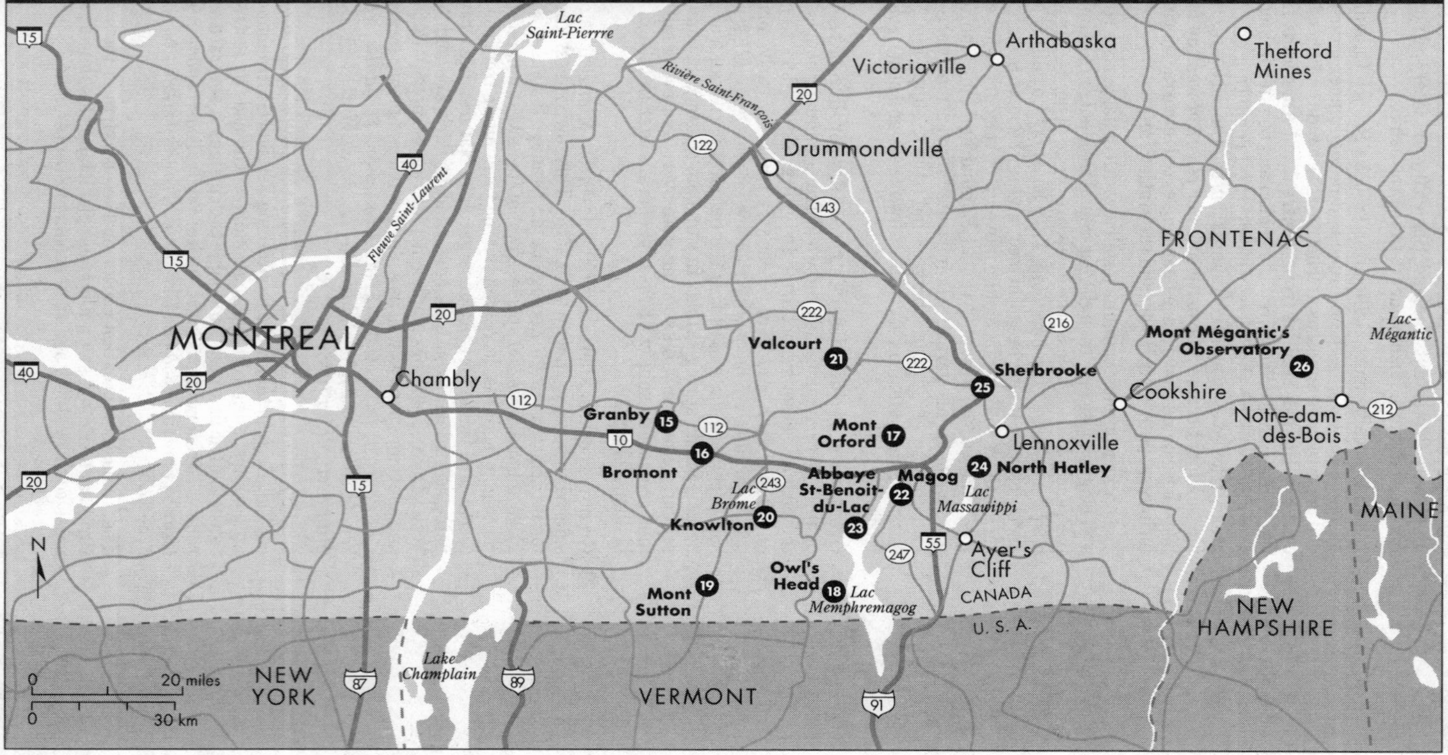

In the past two decades, l'Estrie has developed into a scenic and increasingly popular ski center. Although it is still less crowded and commercialized than the Laurentians, it boasts ski hills on four mountains that dwarf anything the Laurentians have to offer, with the exception of lofty Mont Tremblant. And, compared with Vermont, ski pass rates are still a bargain.

16 **Bromont,** closest to Montréal, is as lively at night as during the
day. It offers the only night skiing in l'Estrie and a slope-side
disco, **Le Debarque,** where the action continues into the night
17 après-ski. **Mont Orford,** located at the center of a provincial
park, offers plenty of challenges for alpine and cross-country
18 skiers, from novices to veterans. **Owl's Head** has become a mecca for skiers looking for fewer crowds on the hills. It also boasts
a 4-kilometer (2.4-mile) intermediate run, the longest in
l'Estrie. Aside from superb skiing, Owl's Head offers tremen-
dous scenery. From the trails you can see nearby Vermont and
Lac Memphremagog. (You might even see the lake's legendary
sea dragon, said to have been sighted some 90 times since
19 1816.) As it has for decades, **Mont Sutton** attracts the same diehard crowd of mostly Anglophone skiers from Québec. It's also
one of the area's largest resorts, with trails that plunge and
wander through pine, maple, and birch trees slope-side. **Sutton**
itself is a well-established community with crafts shops, cozy
eateries, and bars (La Paimpolaise is a favorite among skiers).

Bromont, Orford, and Sutton are active all summer as well. Bromont and Orford are *stations touristiques* (tourist centers), meaning that they offer a wide range of activities in all seasons—boating, camping, golf, horseback riding, swimming, tennis, water parks, trail biking, canoeing, fishing, hiking, cross-country and downhill skiing, snowshoeing, etc. A water-slide park (tel. 514/534-2200)—take exit 78 off Autoroute 10—and a large flea market (weekends from May to mid-November) offer pleasant additions to horseback riding.

20 Along the shore of Lac Brome is the village of **Knowlton,** a pleasant place to shop for antiques and gifts. In summer check to see what's playing at Knowlton's popular **LacBrome Theater** (*see* The Arts, below). In winter many Montréalers come here to ski at **Glen Mountain** (off Route 243, tel. 514/243-6142).

21 **Valcourt** is the birthplace of the inventor of the snowmobile, so it follows that this is a world center for the sport, with more than 1,500 kilometers (1,000-plus miles) of paths cutting through the woods and meadows. The **Musée Joseph-Armand Bombardier** displays this innovator's many inventions year-round. *1001 boul. Joseph-Armand Bombardier, tel. 514/532-2258. Admission: $4 adults, $2 senior citizens and students, children under 6 free. Open daily 10-5:30.*

Every February, Valcourt holds a snowmobile festival with races and demonstrations, including the **Grand Prix Labatt snowmobile race** (tel. 514/372-7272). Maps outlining scenic routes are available through l'Estrie tourist associations (tel. 819/566-7404).

South of Mont Orford at the northern tip of Lac Memphremagog, a large body of water reaching into northern Vermont, lies
22 the bustling resort town of **Magog,** which celebrated its cente-
nary in 1988. A once sleepy village, the town has grown into a
four-season resort destination. Two sandy beaches, great bed-
and-breakfasts, hotels and restaurants, boating, ferry rides,

bird-watching, sailboarding, aerobics, horseback riding, and snowmobiling are just some of the activities offered.

Stroll along Magog's **rue Principale** for a look at boutiques, art galleries, and crafts shops with local artisans' work. Other shops are spread throughout the town's downtown, where the streets are lined with century-old homes and churches, some of which have been converted into storefronts, galleries, and theaters.

Magog is lively after dark, with a variety of bars, cafés, bistros, and great restaurants to suit every taste and pocketbook. **La Brise discotheque** (tel. 819/847–0313) is a popular hangout. The more sedentary may find **La Source's** (tel. 819/843–0319) array of cheeses, pâtés, and Swiss chocolates irresistible.

23 Near Magog is the **Abbaye St-Benoit-du-Lac.** To reach St-Benoit from Magog, take the road to Austin and then follow the signs for the side road to the abbey. This abbey's slender bell tower juts up above the trees like a Disneyland castle. Built on a wooded peninsula in 1912 by the Benedictines, the abbey is home to some 60 monks, who sell apples and apple cider from their orchards as well as distinctive cheeses: Ermite, St-Benoit, and ricotta. Gregorian masses are held daily. Check for those open to the public (tel. 819/473–7278). The abbey is also known as a favorite retreat for some of Québec's best-known politicians; they abandon the thrust-and-cut of their secular concerns for spiritual rejuvenation.

24 One of the pastimes of **North Hatley** crosses language barriers easily. The town on the tip of Lac Massawippi is home to **The Pilsen,** Québec's earliest micro-brewery, which gives group tours by reservation (tel. 819/842–4259). If you prefer to sample the local brew in a more social setting, head for **The Pilsen Pub** (tel. 819/842–2971), which has great pub food, loads of atmosphere, and a convivial crowd year-round. The avant-garde **Piggery** theatre is based in North Hatley (*see* the Arts, below).

25 The region's unofficial capital and largest city is **Sherbrooke,** named in 1818 for Canadian Governor-General Sir John Coape Sherbrooke. Founded by Loyalists in the 1790s, and located along the St-François River, it boasts a number of art galleries, the **Musée des Beaux-Arts de Sherbrooke** (1300 boul. Portland; admission free; open Sun.–Fri. 1–5 PM), and the historic **Domaine Howard,** headquarters of the townships' historic society, which conducts city tours from this site weekdays from June to September.

For a more cosmic experience, continue from Sherbrooke along
26 Route 212 to **Mont Mégantic's Observatory.** Both amateur stargazers and serious astronomers are drawn to this site, located in a beautifully wild and mountainous part of l'Estrie. The observatory is at the summit of l'Estrie's second highest mountain (3,601 feet), whose northern face records annual snowfalls rivaling any in North America. The observatory is a joint venture by l'Université de Montréal and l'Université Laval. Its powerful telescope allows resident scientists to observe celestial bodies 10 million times smaller than the human eye can detect. There's a welcome center on the mountain's base, where amateur stargazers can get information about the evening celestial sweep sessions, Thursday through Saturday. *Notre-Dame-des-Bois, tel. 819/888–2822. Open late June–Labor Day, daily 10–6.*

Tour 3: Charlevoix

Numbers in the margin correspond with points of interest on the Charlevoix map.

Stretching along the St. Lawrence River's north shore east of Québec City from Sainte-Anne-de-Beaupre to the Saguenay River, Charlevoix embraces mountains rising from the sea and a succession of valleys, plateaus, and cliffs cut by waterfalls, brooks, and streams. The roads wind into villages of picturesque houses and huge tin-roof churches.

New France's first historian, the Jesuit priest François-Xavier de Charlevoix, gave his name to the region. Charlevoix (Sharle-**vwah**) was first explored by Jacques Cartier, who landed in 1535, although the first colonists didn't arrive until well into the 17th century. They developed a thriving shipbuilding industry, specializing in the sturdy schooner they called a *goelette*, which they used to haul everything from logs to lobsters up and down the coast in the days before rail and paved roads. Shipbuilding has been a vital part of the provincial economy until recent times, though wrecked and forgotten goelettes are visible from many beaches in the region.

Charlevoix begins about 33 kilometers (20 miles) east of Québec
27 City, in the tiny town of **Sainte-Anne-de-Beaupre.** Each year more than a million pilgrims visit the region's most famous religious site, the **Basilica of Sainte-Anne-de-Beaupre** (Québec's patron saint), which is dedicated to the mother of the Virgin Mary (*see* Chapter 5).

Only 8 kilometers (5 miles) beyond the pilgrimage center is the
28 **Cap Tourmente Wildlife Preserve,** where more than 100,000 greater snow geese gather every October and May. Other parts of the region offer whale-watching cruises, and you can often spot whales, seals, and dolphins, on occasion, from ferries and on land, so nature-lovers are encouraged to bring their binoculars. *St-Joachim G0A 3X0, tel. 418/827–3776.*

In fact, the region is a haven for anyone who enjoys being active in the outdoors, including hikers, joggers, cyclists, and, in particular, skiers. Charlevoix has three main ski areas, with excellent facilities for both the downhill and cross-country skier.
29 **Parc du Mont-Sainte-Anne,** outside Québec City, is on the
30 World Cup downhill ski circuit; **Mont Grand Fonds** has 13 slopes
31 and 135 kilometers (84 miles) of cross-country trails; and **Le Massif** is a three-peak ski resort that boasts the province's highest vertical drop (762 meters or 2,500 feet). At Le Massif, you take a 30-minute bus ride to the top and a guide leads you through powder snow to the beginning of your run. *For information on Parc du Mont-Ste-Anne,* see *Chapter 5; Mont Grand Fonds, 1000 Chemin des Loisirs, La Malbaie, tel. 418/665–4405; Le Massif, Rte. 138, tel. 418/435–3593.*

32 **Baie-St-Paul,** Charlevoix's earliest settlement after Beaupre, is popular with hang-gliding fans and artists. You will find artisans working in old habitant houses. Here, the high hills circle a wide plain holding the village beside the sea. Many of Québec's greatest landscapists portray the area, and their work is on display year-round at the **Centre d'Art Baie-St-Paul** (4 boul. Faford, tel. 418/435–3681). Recently the center has garnered a reputation in North America as a major regional arts center promoting the area's own talent, as well as provid-

Charlevoix

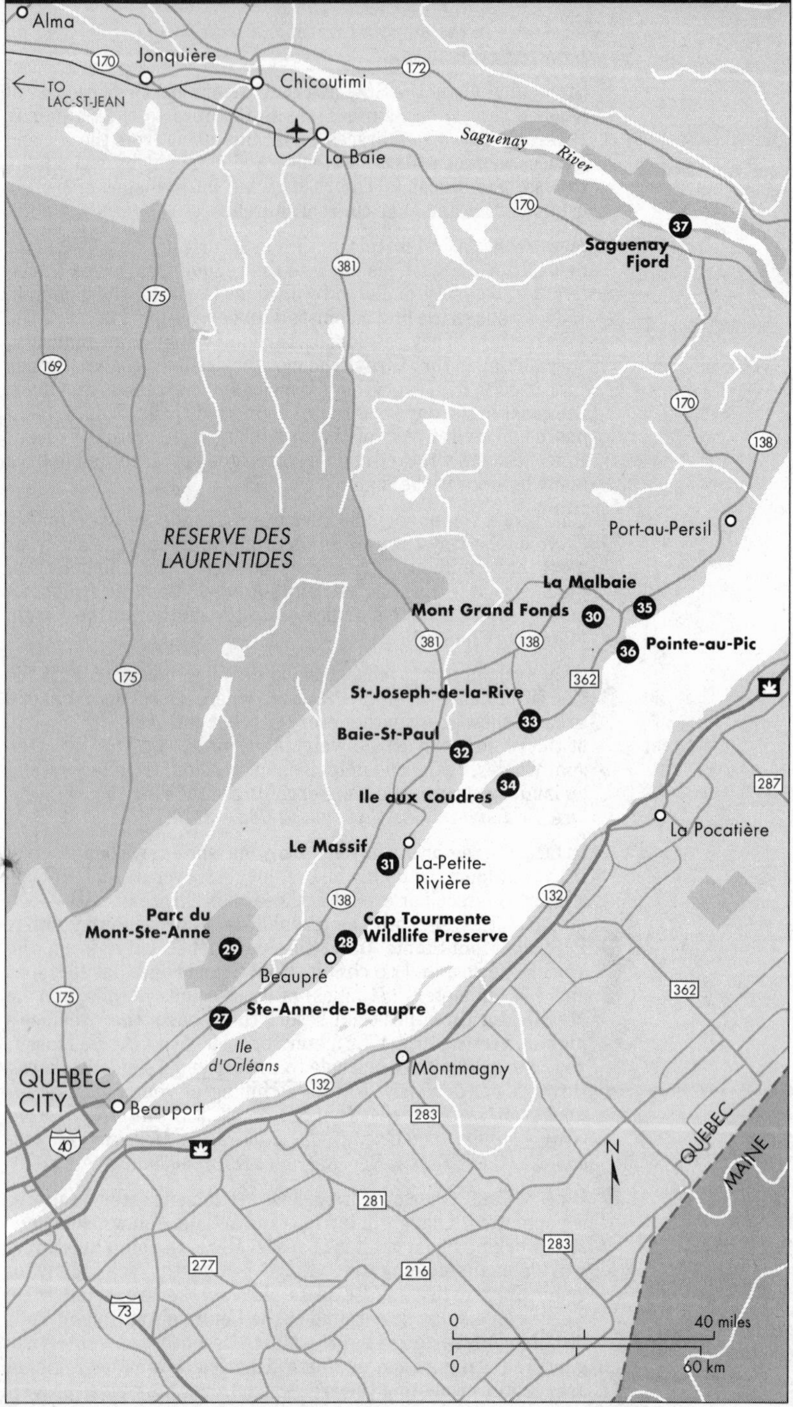

Alma
170
Jonquière
172
TO LAC-ST-JEAN
Chicoutimi
La Baie
Saguenay River
170
37
Saguenay Fjord
381
175
169
170
138
Port-au-Persil
RESERVE DES LAURENTIDES
La Malbaie
Mont Grand Fonds
30
35
381
138
36
Pointe-au-Pic
175
362
St-Joseph-de-la-Rive
33
Baie-St-Paul
32
34
Ile aux Coudres
287
La Pocatière
Le Massif
31
La-Petite-Rivière
138
132
Parc du Mont-Ste-Anne
29
Cap Tourmente Wildlife Preserve
28
Beaupré
175
362
27
Ste-Anne-de-Beaupre
Ile d'Orléans
QUEBEC CITY
Beauport
Montmagny
132
283
40
QUEBEC
MAINE
N
281
283
277
216
73
0
40 miles
0
60 km

ing those just starting out with wider exposure while they study their crafts. At town-center, **Maison Otis,** an 1858 stone house, has been converted into what many consider the area's finest inn/restaurant (*see* Lodging, below).

From Baie-St-Paul, you can take the open, scenic coastal drive (Rte. 362) or the faster Route 138 to **Pointe-au-Pic, La Malbaie,** and **Cap-a-L'Aigle.** This section of Route 362 has memorable views of rollings hills—green, white, or ablaze with fiery hues, depending on the season—meeting the broad expanse of the "sea" as the locals like to call the St. Lawrence estuary.

33 A secondary road leads sharply down into **St-Joseph-de-la-Rive,** with its line of old houses hugging the mountain base on the narrow shore road. The town is host to peaceful inns and inviting restaurants, such as l'Auberge Sous les Pins, which means "inn under the pines." Nearby Papeterie St-Gilles produces unusual handcrafted stationery, using a 17th-century process. The small **Charlevoix Musée** commemorates the days of the St. Lawrence goelettes. From St-Joseph you can catch a ferry to 34 **Île aux Coudres,** an island where Jacques Cartier's men gathered *les coudres* (hazelnuts) in 1535. Since then, the island has produced many a goelette, and former captains now run several small inns. Larger inns feature folk-dance evenings. Many visitors like to bike around the 16-kilometer (10-mile) island taking in inns, windmills, and old schooners, as well as boutiques selling paintings and local handicrafts, such as household linen.

Continuing on Route 362, you will come to one of the most elegant and historically interesting resorts in the entire province. 35 **La Malbaie** was known as Murray Bay in an earlier era when wealthy Anglophones summered here and in the neighboring villages of Pointe-au-Pic and Cap-a-l'Aigle. The regional museum—**Musée Laure-Conan**—traces its history as a vacation spot in a series of exhibits and is developing an excellent collection of local paintings and folk art. *1 chemin du Havre, Point au Pic, tel. 418/665–4411.*

Once called the "summer White House," this area became popular with both American and Canadian politicians in the late 1800s when Ottawa Liberals and Washington Republicans partied decorously through the summer with members of the Québec judiciary. William Howard Taft built the first of three 36 summer residences in **Pointe-au-Pic** in 1894, when he was the American Civil Governor of the Philippines. He became the 27th president of the United States in 1908, and later chief justice of the Supreme Court. Locals still fondly remember the Tafts and the parties they threw in their elegant summer homes. Interestingly, they refer to Americans, as they do all English-speaking people, as "les Anglais."

Now many Taft-era homes serve as handsome inns, guaranteeing an old-fashioned coddling, with extras like breakfast in bed, gourmet meals, whirlpools, and free shuttles to the ski areas in winter. Many serve lunch and dinner to nonresidents, so you can tour the area going from one gourmet's delight to the next. The cuisine, as elsewhere in Québec, is genuine French, rather than a hybrid invented for North Americans.

The road, the views, and the villages continue all the way up to Baie-Ste-Catherine, which shares the view up the magnificent 37 **Saguenay Fjord** with the small town of **Tadoussac.** Jacques Cartier made a stop at this point in 1535, and it became an important meeting site for fur traders in the French Territory until the mid-19th century. Whale-watching excursions and cruises of the fjord now depart from Tadoussac, as well as from Chicoutimi, farther up the deep fjord. As the Saguenay River flows from Lake St-Jean south toward the St. Lawrence it has a dual character: between Alm and Chicoutimi, the once rapidly flowing river has been turned into hydroelectric power; in its lower section, it becomes wider and deeper and flows by steep mountains and cliffs, en route to the St. Lawrence. The white beluga whale breeds in the lower portion of the Saguenay in summer, and in the confluence of the fjord and the seaway are many marine species, which attract other whales, such as pilot, finback, humpback, and blues. Day-and half-day cruises from Chicoutimi operate daily June–September (tel. 418/543–7630); other trips leave from Hotel Tadoussac (tel. 418/235–4421).

Tour 4: The Gaspé Peninsula

Numbers in the margin correspond with points of interest on the Gaspé Peninsula map.

Jutting into the stormy Gulf of St. Lawrence like the battered prow of a ship, the Gaspé Peninsula remains an isolated region of unsurpassed wild beauty, an area where the land ends. Sheer cliffs tower above broad beaches, and tiny coastal fishing communities cling to the shoreline. Inland rise the Chic-Choc Mountains, eastern Canada's highest, the realm of woodland caribou, black bear, and moose. Townspeople in some Gaspé areas speak mainly English, though *Gaspésiens* speak slightly Acadian-accented French.

Jacques Cartier landed on the Gaspé in 1534, but it wasn't until the early 1800s that the first settlers arrived. Today, the area still seems unspoiled and timeless, a blessing for travelers dipping and soaring along the spectacular coastal highways or venturing on river-valley roads to the interior. Geographically, the peninsula is among the oldest lands on earth. A vast, mainly uninhabited forest covers the hilly hinterland. Local tourist officials can be helpful in locating outfitters and guides to fish and hunt large and small game. The Gaspé's four major parks—**Port Daniel, Forillon, Causapscal,** and **Gaspé Park**—cover a total of 2,292 square kilometers (885 square miles).

Take the Trans-Canada Highway northeast along the southern shore of the St. Lawrence River to just south of Rivière-du-Loup, where you pick up the 270-kilometer (150-mile) Route 132, which hugs the dramatic coastline. At Ste.-Flavie, follow the southern leg of Route 132. Windsurfers and sailors enjoy the breezes around the Gaspé; there are windsurfing marathons in **Baie des Chaleurs** (at Carleton) each summer.

The Gaspé was on Jacques Cartier's itinerary—he first stepped ashore in North America in the town of Gaspé—but Vikings, Basques, and Portuguese fisherfolk came long before. The area's history is told in countless towns en route. Acadians, displaced by the British from New Brunswick in 1755, settled
38 39 **Bonaventure; Paspébiac** still has a gunpowder shed built in the
1770s to help defend the peninsula from American ships; and
40 United Empire Loyalists settled **New Carlisle** in 1784.

The largest colony of gannets in the world summers on the
41 Gaspé's **Bonaventure Island,** off Percé. The most famous sight in

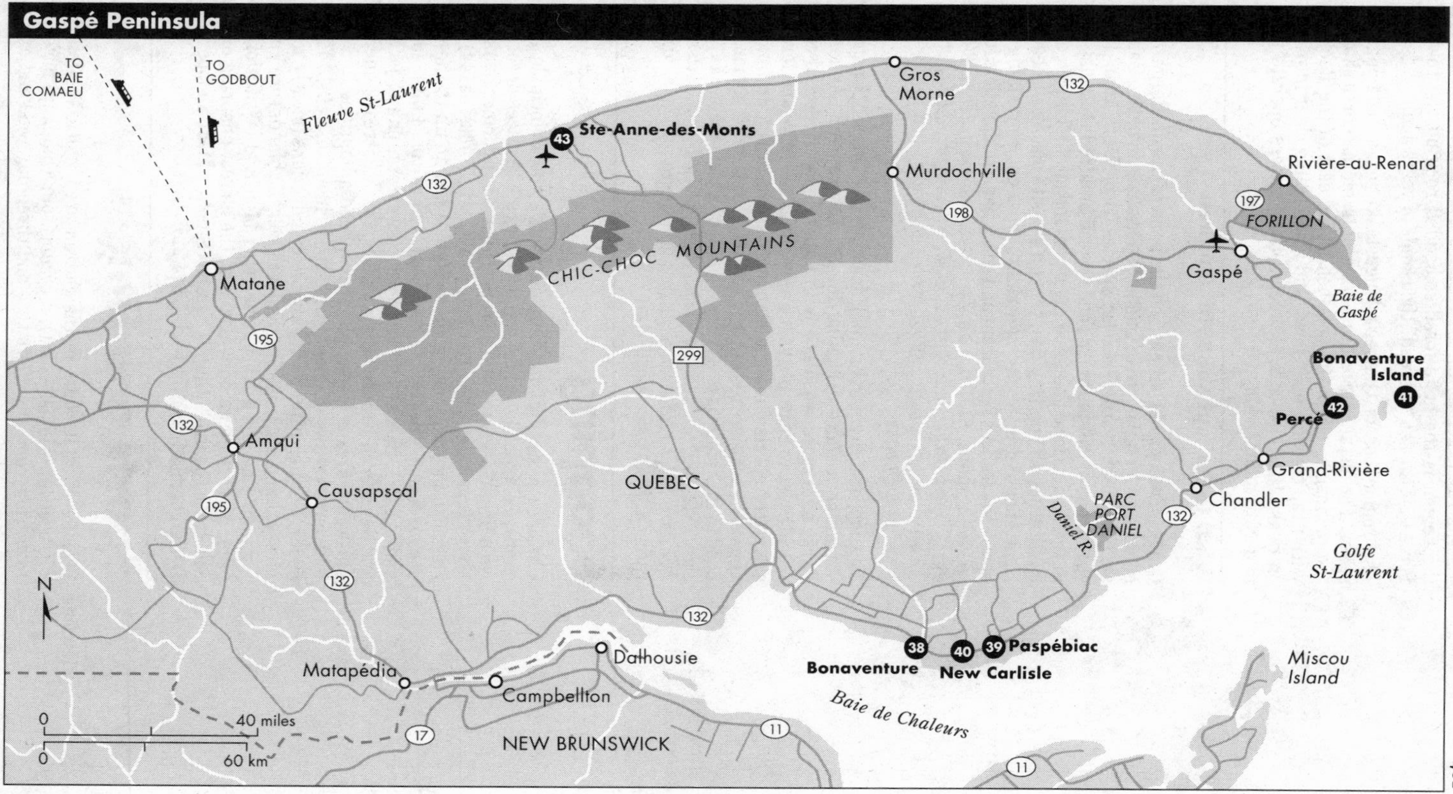
Gaspé Peninsula
TO BAIE COMAEU
TO GODBOUT
Fleuve St-Laurent
Gros Morne
132
Ste-Anne-des-Monts
43
Murdochville
198
Rivière-au-Renard
197
FORILLON
Gaspé
Baie de Gaspé
Bonaventure Island
41
42
Percé
Grand-Rivière
Chandler
Golfe St-Laurent
Matane
CHIC-CHOC MOUNTAINS
195
299
Amqui
Causapscal
QUEBEC
PARC PORT DANIEL
Daniel R.
Matapédia
Campbellton
Dalhousie
38
Bonaventure
40
New Carlisle
39
Paspébiac
Miscou Island
Baie de Chaleurs
17
11
NEW BRUNSWICK
0
40 miles
60 km
N

the region is the huge fossil-embedded rock off the town of
42 **Percé** that the sea "pierced" thousands of years ago.

The region boasts Québec's longest ski season and highest
43 peaks. For instance, **Ste-Anne-des-Monts,** on the north shore of the peninsula, offers the only heli-skiing east of the Rockies, with deep powder, open bowl, and glade skiing clear into June on peaks that rise to 2,700 feet. Other centers operate from mid-November to May.

What to Do and See With Children

Quebec Zoological Gardens, on the bank of the du Berger River, 11.3 km (7 mi) north of Québec, specializes in native Canadian fauna but features exotic species also. More than 1,000 specimens of 250-plus birds and several hundred mammals live in the 30 developed acres of the woodland site. Children especially enjoy the petting zoo, though the site also has a sea-lion show, horse-drawn carriage rides, cross-country skiing and snowshoe trails, a restaurant and snack bar, and handicraft and souvenir shops. *8191 ave du Zoo, Charlesbourg, tel. 418/622–0312. Open May– Oct., daily 9:30–6; Nov.–Apr., daily 9:30–5. Admission: $5 adults; $2 children, students, and senior citizens; family pass $10.*

The modern circular building housing the **Québec Aquarium** stands on a cliff overlooking the St. Lawrence in Aquarium Park, a terraced woodland with unparalleled river and countryside views. Featured at the aquarium are native and foreign saltwater species, marine mammals and reptiles, and nature films. The seals are fed at 10:15 AM and 3:15 PM daily; humans can head to the cafeteria (open year-round) or a picnic table. *1675 du Parc, Ste-Foy, tel. 418/659–5264. Open daily 9–5. Admission: $3 adults; $1.50 children, students, and senior citizens; family rate, $6. Half-price Nov.–Apr.*

Shopping

Consider a stroll along Saint-Sauveur's rue Principale amid shops, fashion boutiques, and outdoor café terraces decorated with bright awnings and flowers. Housed in a former bank, **La Voute Boutique** (239B rue Principale, tel. 514/227–4144) carries such international labels as Byblos and an up-to-the-minute all-season selection of coordinates in cotton, knits, suede, and leather, plus sequined dresses, sweaters, pants, jackets, and suits from France, Italy, and Spain. Montréal's queen of knitwear, Ariane Carle, has also opened a boutique in Saint-Sauveur, **Tricots d'Ariane** (248 rue Principale, tel. 514/227–6666). Her beautifully fluid knitwear collections (mostly woven jersey, linen, cotton, silks, and wool-acrylic blends) are known for their timeless quality. One other Montréal institution has recently arrived in Saint-Sauveur, the newest offspring of rue Sainte-Catherine's **Dunn's Famous Smoked Meat Shoppes and Delis** (chemin Lac Milette, tel. 514/227–1881).

Sports and Fitness

Bicycling Cycling is at its best in the Sutton area, with **Velotour de l'Estrie** (tel. 514/538–2361), a cycling tour company, based in town. The company offers two- and three-day weekend excursion packages for bicycling throughout l'Estrie. The tours begin and end in Sutton, with overnight stops at the area's inns (breakfast and dinners included).

Deltaplaning If white-water rafting isn't adventure enough, there is always deltaplaning, in which man and machine become one. The **Vélidelta au Mont Christie School** (C.P. 631, Mont-Rolland J0R 1G0, tel. 514/229–6887) offers lessons on free-flying, flight simulation, plus the more advanced tricks of the trade you'll need to earn the required deltaplane pilot's license—flight maneuvers, speed, and turns. Equipment is provided. You can choose a half-day initiation lesson, one-day flying lesson, or four-day course.

Horseback Riding As the former Olympic equestrian site, **Bromont** is horse country, and every mid-July it holds a riding festival (tel. 514/534–3255).

River Rafting The Rivière Rouge in the Laurentians rates as one of the best in North America, according to expert river rafters, so it's not surprising that this river has spawned a miniboom in the sport. Just an hour's drive north of Montréal, the Rouge cuts across the rugged Laurentians through rapids, canyons, and alongside beaches. From April through October, the adventurous can experience what traversing the region must have meant in the days of the voyageurs and *coureurs du bois*, though today's trip, by comparison, is much safer and more comfortable.

Four companies specializing in white-water rafting are on-site at the trip's departure point near Calumet. (Take Rte. 148 past Calumet; turn onto chemin de la Rivière-Rouge until you see the signs for the access road to each rafter's headquarters.) **Aventures en eau vive** (tel. 819/242–6084), **Nouveau Monde** (tel. 514/733–7166), **Propulsion** (tel. 514/382–0553), and **W-3 Rafting** (tel. 514/638–3437) all offer four- to five-hour rafting trips. All provide transportation to and from the river site, as well as guides, helmets, life jackets, and, at the end of the trip, a much-anticipated meal. Most have facilities on-site or nearby for dining, drinking, camping, bathing, swimming, hiking, and horseback riding. Propulsion even offers helicopter transportation. The only prerequisite: You must weigh at least 88 pounds (40 kilograms).

Skiing With the longest vertical drop (2,131 feet) in Eastern Canada, **Mont Tremblant** offers a wide range of ski trails. Beginners favor the 5-kilometer (3-mile) Nansen trail, while intermediate skiers head for the steeply sloped Flying Mile and Beauchemin runs. Experts choose the challenging Duncan and Expo runs on the mountain's north side. Mont Tremblant is a favorite ski destination of former Canadian Olympic Ski Jumping Team member Horst Bulau, who likes the variety of hills (33 trails in all), great snow conditions, and accommodations packages. Five-time World Cup downhill racer and former Canadian National Alpine Ski Team member Laurie Graham can also be found on the slopes.

In L'Estrie the larger downhill slopes include **Mont Brome** in Bromont (site of the 1986 World Cup) with 26 trails, **Mont Orford** with 35, **Owl's Head** with 25, and **Mont Sutton** with 54. The steepest drop, one of 853 meters (2,800 feet), is at Orford. All four resorts feature interchangeable lift tickets so skiers can test out all the major runs in the area. Call Ski East, tel. 819/566–7404.

L'Estrie's 26 cross-country trails are peaceful getaways. Trails at Bromont crisscross the site of the 1976 Olympic equestrian center. Three inns—Le Manoir Hovey, Auberge Hatley, and the Ripplecove Inn (*see* Dining and Lodging, below)—offer the **Skiwippi**, a week-long package of cross-country treks from one inn to another. The network covers some 32 kilometers (20 miles) of l'Estrie.

Dining

Whether you enjoy a croissant and espresso at a sidewalk café or order *poutine*, a streetwise mix of homemade french fries (*frites*) from a fast-food emporium, you won't soon forget your meals in Québec. There is no such thing as simply "eating out" in the province, as restaurants are an integral slice of Québec life.

Outside of Montréal and Québec City, you can find both good value and classic cuisine. Cooking in the province tends to be hearty, with such fare as cassoulet, *tourtières* (meat pies), onion soup, and apple pie heading up menus. In the Laurentians, chefs at some of the finer inns have attracted international followings. Local blueberries and maple syrup find their way into a surprising number of dishes.

Early reservations are essential. Monday or Tuesday is not too soon to book weekend tables at the best provincial restaurants. If you have any doubt about acceptable dress at a restaurant, call ahead. Jacket and tie are still the rule at many first-rate restaurants, even in summer.

Granby and its environs is one of Québec's foremost regions for traditional Québecois cuisine, here called *la fine cuisine estrienne*. Specialties include mixed-game meat pies like *cipaille* and sweet, salty dishes like ham and maple syrup. Actually, maple syrup—on everything and in all its forms—is a mainstay of Québecois dishes. L'Estrie is one of Québec's main maple-sugaring regions.

In addition to maple sugar, cloves, nutmeg, cinnamon, and pepper—the same spices used by the first settlers—have never gone out of fashion here, and local restaurants make good use of them in their distinctive dishes. The full country experience of l'Estrie includes warm hospitality at lodges and inns in the area as well.

Highly recommended restaurants in each price category are indicated by a star ★.

Category	**Cost***
Very Expensive	over $40
Expensive	$20–$40
Moderate	$10–$19
Inexpensive	under $10

**per person, excluding drinks, service, and sales tax (10% for meals over $3.25)*

Ayer's Cliff **The Ripplecove Inn.** This inn vies with the Hatley and Hovey inns for best in the region. Its dining, accommodations, and service are consistently excellent. Ripplecove's dining room is an award winner. Its English-pub style dining offers a combination of classical and nouvelle cuisine with such dishes as confit de canard Lac Brome followed by *rable de lapin* (rabbit served with honey sauce), topped off by a sublime dessert such as au chocolat arabica (a mousse laced with coffee flavor). Rooms have an antique feel. Family cottages are also available. *700 chemin Ripplecove, Box 246, J0B 1C0, tel. 819/838–4296. 26 rooms. Facilities: winter skating rink, groomed cross-country ski trails, wet-bar boat that cruises Massawippi. Reservations advised Fri. and Sat. nights. Dress: casual. AE, MC, V. Closed 2 weeks in November. Very Expensive.*

Magog **Auberge de l'Étoile.** This popular restaurant in Magog serves three meals a day in casual surroundings. (The restaurant is part of a motel with 26 units facing the lake. A double room costs $80–$95.) *1133 rue Principale O, tel. 819/843–6521. Reservations advised. AE, MC, V. Moderate.*

Notre-Dame-des-Bois **Aux Berges de l'Aurore.** This tiny bed-and-breakfast is situated at the foot of Mont Mégantic. The draw here is the inn's cuisine. The four-star restaurant features a five-course meal with ingredients supplied from the inn's huge fruit, vegetable, and herb garden, as well as wild game from the surrounding area: boar, fish, hare, and quail. It has been attractively furnished by its owners, Michel Martin and Daniel Pepin, and is closed most of the winter, from January 2 until April 1. It is near an observatory, and a lake and golf course are a 20-minute drive away. *Chemin de l'Observatoire, tel. 819/888–2715 J0B 2E0, 4 rooms. Moderate.*

St-Sauveur-des-Monte **Auberge Saint-Denis.** This classic Québec inn has earned the title of "Relais Gourmand" for its cuisine. Don't eat and run . . . it is one of the nicer places from which to base a Laurentian visit. *61 St-Denis, J0R 1R4, tel. 514/227–4602. 42 rooms, all with fireplace, some with Jacuzzi. Breakfast served daily; reservations advised for dinner. Dress: neat but casual. AE, MC, V. Very Expensive.*

Ste-Adèle ★ **L'Eau à la Bouche.** A consistent award winner in gastronomic circles the restaurant picked up Québec's 1988 *Ordre du mérite de la restauration*, the top award among the Laurentians region's auberge/restaurants for its superb marriage of nouvelle cuisine and traditional Québec dishes. Nonetheless, such superb supping doesn't come cheaply: L'Eau à la Bouche is one of the region's most expensive restaurants. However, the care and inventiveness of chef-proprietor Anne Desjardins, who opened the Bavarian-style restaurant nine years ago with her husband, Pierre Audette, is extraordinary. Such dishes as *chèvre* cheese tart, saddle of rabbit with onions, *baluchon* of lobster and scallops, roast partridge stuffed with oyster mushrooms in a cream sauce, *pavé* of dark chocolate with English cream or *cachette* of rhubarb and strawberries, leave dinner guests clamoring for more. *3003 boul. Ste-Adèle, Rte. 117, tel. 514/ 229–2991. Reservations required. Dress: neat but casual. AE, MC, V. No lunch. Very Expensive.*

Restaurant Les Cent-Ciel. Though there are no accommodations here, the French cuisine prepared by chef Pascal Lemonnier (originally from Paris) rivals that of L'Eau à la Bouche. House specialties include pork tenderloin, fish, and seafood in such delectable concoctions as *rillette de saumon fumé* (fresh and smoked salmon marinated in wine, shallots, and lemon and served with pickled baby onions and capers), and *filet de porc dijonnais à la crème. 430 chemin Ste-Marguerite, tel. 514/229–4164. Reservations suggested. AE, DC, MC, V. No lunch. Moderate–Expensive.*

Ste-Agathe ★ **Chatel Vienna.** Run by Eberhards Rado and his wife, who is also the chef, this moderately priced Austrian restaurant offers Viennese and other Continental dishes served up in a lakeside setting. House specialties include *Gulvas Suppe mit spaetzli* (goulash soup with dumplings) and *Bauernschmaus* (mixed plate of German and Swiss sausages, roast pork, sauerkraut, and potatoes). Meals are accompanied by hot spiced wine, Czech pilsner beer, or dry Austrian and Alsatian white wines. *6 rue Ste-Lucie, tel. 819/326–1485. Expensive.*

Chez Girard serves up moderately priced, excellent French cuisine in an auberge on the shores of Lac des Sables. *18 rue Principale O, tel. 819/326–0922. Dress: casual. Reservations advised. AE, MC, V. Expensive.*

Ste-Margarite **La Clef des Champs.** This family-owned hillside restaurant is well-known for its gourmet French cuisine, a charming alternative to even the most superbly prepared hotel fare. *875 chemin Ste-Marguerite, tel. 514/229–2857. Reservations advised. Dress: casual. AE, MC, V. Closed Easter week. Moderate.*

Sherbrooke **Restaurant Au P'tit Sabot.** This restaurant recently won an award for the best local-style eatery in the region. Among the many provincial dishes are wild boar, quail, and bison. *1410 King St. O, tel. 819/563–0262. Reservations advised. Dress: casual. AE, MC, V. Expensive.*

Sugar Huts

Every March the combination of sunny days and cold nights causes the sap to run in the maple trees. Sugar huts *(cabanes à sucre)* go into operation boiling the sap collected from the trees in buckets (now, at some places, complicated tubing and vats do the job). The many commercial shacks scattered over the area host "sugaring offs" and tours of the operation, including the tapping of maple trees, boiling vats, etc. and *tire sur la neige*, when hot syrup is poured over cold snow to give it a taffy consistency just right for "pulling" and eating. A number of cabanes offer hearty meals of ham, baked beans, and pancakes, all drowned in maple syrup. It's best to call before visiting any of these cabanes: **Erablière Robert Lauzier,** chemin Audet, Ayer's Cliff, tel. 819/838–4433; **Bolducs,** in Cookshire on Route 253, tel. 819/875–3167, and 525 chemin Lower, tel. 819/875–3022. **Ski Montjoye** is a new resort that has early spring sugaring-off parties around its 15-room inn on Route 108, North Hatley, tel. 819/842–8309.

Lodging

Weary travelers have a full spectrum of accommodation options in Québec: from large resort hotels in the Laurentians and Relais et Châteaux properties in L'Estrie, to shared dormitory space in rustic youth hostels near the heart of Gaspé. For information on camping in the province's private trailer parks and campgrounds, write for the free publication "Québec Camping," available from Tourisme Québec, Box 20,000, Québec City, Québec G1K 7X2. Inquiries about camping in Québec's three national parks should be directed to Parks Canada, Information Services, 3 Buade St., Box 6060, Haute Ville, Québec City, Québec G1R 4V7. **Agricotours** (525 ave. Viger, Montréal, Québec, H2L 2P1), Québec farm-vacation association, can provide lists of guest farms in the province.

Highly recommended lodgings in each price category are indicated by a star ★.

Category	Cost*
Very Expensive	over $100
Expensive	$50–$100
Moderate	$35–$49
Inexpensive	under $35

**All prices are for a standard double room, excluding 10% service charge.*

Baie-St-Paul ★ **Auberge la Maison Otis.** Situated in the center of the village, this inn offers calm and romantic accommodations in three buildings, including an old stone house. Chef Bernard Petan specializes in nouvelle cuisine and summer lunches are served amid flowers on an outdoor terrace. Some of the 30 country-style rooms have whirlpools, fireplaces, and antique furnishings; all are air-conditioned and have private bath, TV, and radio. Skiing and ice skating is nearby. *23 rue St-Jean-Baptiste, G0A 1B0, tel. 418/435–2255. 27 rooms, 3 suites. Facilities: restaurant, piano bar, lounge, pool, health center, and sauna. MC, V. Expensive–Very Expensive.*

Bromont **Le Château Bromont Resort Spa.** At this European-style resort spa you can receive therapeutic massages, algotherapy, electropuncture, algae wraps, facials, and aroma therapy. The Atrium houses an indoor pool, hot tubs, and a sauna. There are also outdoor hot tubs, squash, racquetball, tennis courts, and a Nautilus-equipped gym. After your workout, head for the château's dining room, Les Quatres Canards, where "cuisine sauvage" is created by chef Norman Rivard. (There is also a special spa menu offered.) Its L'Equestre Bar, named for Bromont's equestrian interests, features a cocktail hour and live entertainment. *90 rue Stanstead, J0E 1L0, tel. 514/534–3433. 154 rooms. Facilities: spa, indoor pool, sauna, gym, lounge, restaurant. AE, MC, V. Expensive.*

Cap-à-l'aigle ★ **Auberge la Pinsonnière.** The location, commanding a view of Murray Bay on the St. Lawrence, and the finely appointed bedrooms make this property special. An atmosphere of country luxury prevails. *124 rue St-Raphael, La Malbaie, G0T 1B0, tel. 418/665–4431. 26 rooms, 4 suites. Facilities: restaurant, indoor pool, private beach. AE, MC, V. Very Expensive.*

Eastman **Centre de Sante Eastman.** This four-season resort offers respite to the bone-weary and bruised skier. Holistic spa treatments include massage (Swedish and shiatsu) and gentle gymnastic workouts. *712 chemin Diligence, J0E 1P0, tel. 514/297–3009. 16 rooms. Dining room. Packages include 3 meals. MC, V. Moderate.*

Estérel **Ville d'Estérel.** The hotel features a private 18-hole golf course, beach, marina, swimming pool, tennis courts, and downhill skiing facilities. If this all-inclusive resort were in the Caribbean, it would probably be run by Club Med, given the nonstop activities. In particular, its sports complex and convention facilities make it a busy resort. *boul. Fridolin Simard, Estérel, tel. 514/228–2571 or 800/363–3623. All-inclusive packages available. AE, DC, MC, V. Very Expensive.*

Île aux Coudres ★ **Hotel Cap-aux-Pierres.** Located on Coudres Island in the St. Lawrence River, this hotel provides top-notch accommodations in both a traditionally Canadian main building and a motel section (open summer only). About a third of the rooms afford river views, and all feature color TV and telephones. The restaurant serves a mix of Québec standards and nouvelle cuisine, and entertainment includes folk dancing on Saturday evening. *220 rue Principale, La Baleine, G0A 2A0, tel. 418/438–2711 or 800/463–5250. 98 rooms, 1 suite. Facilities: dining room, bar, fireplace lounge, indoor and outdoor heated pools. AE, DC, MC, V. Very Expensive.*

Lennoxville **Bishop's University.** If you're on a budget this is a great place to stay. The prices can't be beat and the location near Sherbrooke is good for touring. The university's grounds are lovely, with a river cutting through the campus and its golf course. Much of the architecture is reminiscent of stately New England campuses. Visit the university's 132-year-old chapel and also look for the butternut tree, an endangered species in l'Estrie. *College St., J1M 1Z7, tel. 819/822–9651. 513 beds. Facilities: sports complex with Olympic-size indoor pool, 4 outdoor tennis courts. No credit cards. Inexpensive.*

Magog **Club Azur.** This is a Club Med–type condo facility that is perfect for family ski trips. There are activities for children, as well as tennis courts and indoor and outdoor pools. For the summertime it is a convenient two-minute walk from the beach. *81 Desjardins, J1X 3W9, tel. 819/847–2131 or 800/567–3535. 190 rooms. Facilities: restaurant, bistro, saunas, tennis courts, recreation complex, convenience store, day-care center. AE, MC, V. Expensive.*

O'Berge du Village. Half of this condo complex is on a time-share basis, while the other condos are run like a hotel. There is a casual outdoor restaurant. An indoor pool and a more elaborate restaurant have been added. *262 rue Merry S, J1X 3L2, tel. 819/843–6566 or 800/567–6089. 113 rooms. AE, MC, V. Moderate.*

Matane **Auberge des Gouverneurs.** Built in 1975, this seaside motor inn is well equipped with recreational facilities and offers many rooms with an ocean view. Located near the dock of the ferry for Baie Comeau, it's a good choice for visitors who have come to ski, fish, or hunt. All rooms have telephone and color TV. *250 av. DuPhare E, G4W 3N4, tel. 418/566–2651. 72 rooms, 2 suites. Facilities: restaurant, lounge, heated pool, tennis court, sauna, exercise room, parking facilities. AE, DC, MC, V. Expensive.*

Mont Rolland **Auberge Mont Gabriel.** This resort is worth a stay—overnight or for longer. This deluxe resort located on a 1,200-acre estate offers superb dining. Tennis, ski-week and weekend packages are also available, as is the Modified American Plan (MAP). *Autoroute 15, exit 64, Mont Rolland J0R 1G0, tel. 514/229–3547. 159 rooms. Facilities: Indoor/outdoor pools, tennis. AE, MC, V. Very Expensive.*

Mont Tremblant ★

Station Mont Tremblant Lodge. Only 90 minutes from Montréal, on 14-kilometer (9-mile) long Lac Tremblant, this is the northernmost resort that is easily accessible in the Upper Laurentians. The partying is lively in the winter, with lots of après-ski bars in the hotel and the immediate area. In summer, guests swim, windsurf, and sail. Mont Tremblant Lodge has a nine-hole golf course, and horseback riding and tennis are also available. *Lac Tremblant, J0T 1Z0, tel. 819/425–8711 or 800/567–6761. 231 rooms. AE, DC, MC, V. Very Expensive.*

Cuttle's Tremblant Club. Across the lake from Station Mont Tremblant Lodge is this hotel and condominium complex that uses the mountain for its skiing. Built as a private retreat in the 1930s by a wealthy American, the original large log-cabin lodge is furnished in Colonial style, with wood staircases and huge stone fireplaces. The rustic but comfortable main lodge has excellent facilities and a dining room with four-star gourmet cuisine. Both the main lodge and the deluxe condominium complex (fireplaces, private balconies, kitchenettes, and split-level design de rigueur), built just up the hill from the lodge, offer magnificent views of Mont Tremblant and its ski hills. Bordering Lac Tremblant, summer activities include swimming, fishing, boating, tennis, golf, and an indoor pool and exercise facility. *Chemin Lac Tremblant N, J0T 1Z0, tel. 819/425–2731. 67 rooms. AE, MC, V. Expensive–Very Expensive.*

Auberge Villa Bellevue. This equally venerable and less-expensive alternative to Gray Rocks (*see* below) is on Lac Ouimet. Run by the Dubois family for more than three generations, this inn has made its reputation as a family resort—so much so that accommodations for children are free if they share a room with their parents. (Meal plans are also scaled down accordingly: for children age 3–10 the cost is about $50, and for children 11–14 the cost is about $65 for vacation packages.) In winter, weekend packages include transportation to nearby Mont Tremblant, baby-sitting services, and a full program of children's activities. Accommodations range from hotel rooms to chalets and condominiums. In summer, special tennis-school packages for adults and children are available. Sailing, windsurfing, water-skiing, and lounging about on the outdoor terrace lakeside are other possible summer pastimes at Villa Bellevue. The indoor swimming pool and fitness center offer nonskiers plenty of physical activity during the winter without stepping outdoors. *845 Principale, J0T 1Z0, tel. 819/425–2734 or 800/567–6763. 108 rooms. AE, DC, MC, V. Closed mid-Oct.–Thanksgiving, mid-Apr.–mid-May. Expensive.*

Auberge du Coq de Montagne. This auberge has earned a favorable reputation for its owners, Nino and Kay Faragalli. Moderately priced, this cozy family-run inn is touted for its friendly service, great hospitality and modern accommodations. Kudos have also been garnered for the great Italian cuisine served up nightly, which also draws a local crowd, so reservations are a must. Situated on Lac Moore, year-round facilities and activities on-site or close by include canoeing, kayaking, sailboarding, fishing, badminton, sauna, exercise room, tennis, horseback riding, skating, and skiing. *324 chemin Principale, Lac Moore, J0T 1Z0, tel. 819/425–3380 or 819/425–7311. 27 rooms. MC, V. Moderate.*

North Hatley ★

Le Manoir Hovey. This inn is acclaimed for its gastronomic delights as well as for its accommodations. It is a former private estate dating to 1899. Reserve ahead for the dining room, where you can expect such dishes as scallop mousseline with essence of clam and tarragon, or lamb trilogy—three cuts of lamb braised with a light sauce of *morilles* (morels). Its rooms are elegantly furnished, some featuring four-poster beds and fireplaces. *Box 60, J0B 2C0, tel. 819/842–2421. 35 rooms. AE, MC, V. Very Expensive.*

Auberge Hatley. Gourmet cuisine is the main attraction at this country inn. Its dining room was named the top restaurant in Québec in the third annual Ordre du Merite de la restauration awards in 1988. A member of the Relais & Châteaux, it is home to award-winning chef Guy Bohec. After eating one of his fine meals, guests sleep it off in one of the 21 charmingly decorated rooms in this 1903 country manor. *Box 330, J0B 2C0, tel. 819/842–2451. 24 rooms, some with Jacuzzi and fireplace. Facilities: 4-star restaurant. AE, MC, V. Closed last 2 weeks in Nov. Expensive–Very Expensive.*

Orford **Auberge Estrimont.** An exclusive complex in cedar combining hotel rooms, condos, and larger chalets, it is close to ski hills, riding stables, and golf courses. Every room, whether in the hotel or an adjoining condo unit, has a fireplace and private balcony. *44 av. de l'Auberge, Box 96, Orford-Magog, J1X 3W7, tel. 819/843–1616 or 800/567–7320. 84 rooms. 70 2- and 4-bedroom condominium units and chalets. Facilities: indoor/outdoor pools, 2 tennis courts, health-care center, cross-country ski trails. AE, MC, V. Very Expensive.*

Perce **La Normandie Hotel/Motel.** All but four rooms of this decade-old split-level motel face the ocean, with views to Perce Rock and Bonaventure Island; and the location, in the center of town, puts shops and restaurants within walking distance. The brand-new third floor has larger rooms done in pastel colors. A more rustic, piney style prevails on lower floors. *Rte. 132, G0C 2L0, tel. 418/782–2112. 45 rooms. Facilities: restaurant, lounge, beach and municipal pool nearby, sauna. AE, DC, MC, V. Closed mid-Oct.–Apr. Expensive.*

La Bonaventure-Sur-Mer Hotel. Though the decor is motel standard, the waterfront location with views to Perce Rock and Bonaventure Island makes this place stand out. The older section is a big hotel building renovated two years ago. Some motel units offer kitchenettes. *Centre Hwy. 132, G0C 2L0, tel. 418/782–2166. 90 rooms. Facilities: dining room, solarium, private beach, water sports. AE, DC, MC, V. Closed Nov.–May. Moderate–Expensive.*

La Côte Surprise Motor Hotel. Most of the rooms of this recently renovated motel have views of Perce Rock and the village. Decor is the same standard-motel style in motel and second-floor hotel units, but the private balconies and terraces are a plus. *367 Rte. 132, G0C 2L0, tel. 418/782–2166. 36 rooms. Facilities: dining room, snack bar, lounge, parking. AE, DC, MC, V. Closed Oct.–mid-June. Moderate– Expensive.*

Ste-Adèle **Le Chantecler.** This Montréaler favorite on Lac Rond is nestled at the base of a mountain with 22 downhill ski runs. Skiing is the obvious draw—trails begin almost at the hotel entrance. (It's the official training site of the National Alpine Ski Teams.) Summer activities include tennis, golf, and boating. An indoor pool and spa, as well as a beach, make swimming a year-round possibility. *Box 1048, J0R 1L0, tel. 514/229–3555, or in Quèbec, 800/363–2420. 295 rooms. AE, DC, MC, V. Very Expensive.*

L'Eau à la Bouche. This 26-room auberge has received kudos for superb service, luxurious appointments, and first-class status as an intimately scaled resort, perfect for weekend getaways or business retreats. Its restaurant is a draw in itself (*see* Dining, above). The auberge faces Le Chantecler's ski slopes, so skiing is literally at the door, as is a golf course. Tennis, sailing, and horseback riding are nearby. Package rates are available. *3003 boul. Ste-Adèle, J0R 1L0, tel. 514/229-2991, 514/229-4151, or 800/363-2582. 26 rooms. Facilities: heated pool, whirlpool, flower garden terrace, wine cellar, handicapped facilities. Some suites with fireplaces. AE, DC, MC, V. Expensive-Very Expensive.*

The Auberge Swiss Inn. This authentic Swiss-style chalet exudes coziness, from the wood-paneling and fireplace lounge to the individually decorated rooms. *796 rte. St-Adolphe, J0R 1H0, tel. 514/226-2009. 10 rooms. Facilities: restaurant, canoeing, cross-country skiing, lounge, videos. AE, MC, V. Inexpensive.*

Pension Ste-Adèle en Haut Bed and Breakfast. For those whose pocketbooks are not inclined to the deluxe, this pension is a good alternative. This European-style B&B is located in a charming house. Inexpensive, cozy, and intimate, it has five rooms for overnight accommodations, B&B-style or dinner included. *151 rue Lesage Ste-Adèle, J0R 1L0, tel. 514/229-2624. 5 rooms. No credit cards. Inexpensive.*

Ste-Agathe

Auberge du Lac des Sables. A favorite with couples, this inn offers a quiet, relaxed atmosphere in a country setting with a magnificent view of Lake des Sables. Enjoy the view from your balcony or from the dining room, where you can indulge in an all-you-can-eat buffet brunch. All rooms have contemporary decor, with queen-size beds and color TVs. *230 St-Venant, Box 213, Ste-Agathe J8C 3S3, tel. 819/326-7016. 40 rooms. Facilities: whirlpool, dining room, fireplace. MC, V. Expensive-Very Expensive.*

Ste-Jovite

Gray Rocks. The oldest ski resort in the Laurentians, it was founded by the Wheeler family more than three generations ago. A sprawling wood hotel with modern chalets and units, it overlooks Lac Ouimet. Gray Rocks has its own private mountain ribboned by 18 ski runs. The winter ski weeks and weekends, including cross-country, are good value for the money, as are the summer tennis packages. Gray Rocks also runs the more intimate Auberge le Château with 36 rooms farther along on Route 327 North. *Rte. 327 N, Ste-Jovite, J0T 2HQ, tel. 819/425-2771 or 800/567-6767. 252 rooms. Facilities: 22 clay tennis courts, tennis school, riding stables, marina, La Spa fitness center with hot tubs, indoor swimming pool, sports-medicine clinic, children's activity programs, private airstrip and seaplane anchorage, gourmet restaurant. AE, MC, V. Full winter ski package available. Expensive.*

Ste-Marguerite

Alpin Inn. This a log cabin main house with separate chalets for rent. Surrounded by rolling ski hills and manicured grounds, it features good dining, golf (CPGA pro for lessons), a putting green, swimming pools (indoor and out), skating rink, and one of the Laurentians' most scenic cross-country ski trails. The social director organizes folksy summer barbecues around the pool and there are two-night packages available. *Chemin Ste-Marguerite, J0T 2K0, tel. 514/229-3516 or 800/363-2577. 102 rooms. AE, V. Very Expensive.*

Sutton

Auberge La Paimpolaise. This auberge is located right on Mont Sutton, 50 feet from the ski trails. *615 Maple St., J0E 2K0, tel. 514/538-3213. 29 rooms. AE, MC, V. Moderate.*

Auberge Schweizer. This lodge operates year-round. They have their own farm, and guests feast on home-cooked meals with vegetables straight from the garden. The lodge is surrounded by a lake and a pond for swimming as well as some hiking trails. Ski trails are nearby. In addition to the standard accommodations, the Auberge has a three-bedroom apartment with bath and living room; a two-bedroom chalet, each with private bath and powder room; and a three-bedroom chalet with one bath and a playroom. All the chalets have kitchens as well as washers and dryers. *357 Schweizer Rd., J0E 2K0, tel. 514/538-2129. V. Moderate.*

Auberge Le Refuge. In contrast to the area's many resorts, this small inn operates as a B&B during the winter season. *33 rue Maple, J0E 2K0, tel. 514/538-3802. 12 rooms. Closed summer Mon.-Wed. AE, MC, V. Inexpensive.*

Val David

Hôtel la Sapinière. Canada's first member of the French association of fine country hotels, the Relais & Châteaux, this homey, dark-brown frame hotel with its bright country flowers provides comfortable accommodations but is best known for its fine dining room and wine cellar. Under chef Marcel Kretz, who makes occasional TV appearances touting a certain brand of coffee, it has become one of Québec's, if not Canada's, better restaurants. In peak season, nonhotel diners should make reservations a week or two in advance. La Sapinière is a major convention center, catering to government summits and high-level meetings. *1244 chemin de la Sapinière, J0T 2N0, tel. 819/322-2020 or 800/567-6635. 70 rooms. AE, DC, MC, V. Moderate.*

The Arts

Lac Brome

The Lac Brome Theatre (tel. 514/243-0361 or 800/363-7079) is an English summer theater troupe that presents a three-play season of classic Broadway and West End hits. So successful has founding artistic director and British expatriate Emma Stevens been in galvanizing local community support and summer resident attendance that the company moved into a renovated, 200-seat, $250,000, air-conditioned theater. Located behind Knowlton's popular pub of the same name, the theater was a gift from Knowlton Pub owner Gerry Wood. Discounted theater tickets are available if visitors book the special B&B packages offered at local inns. Inquire when making reservations in Lac Brome.

Lac Massawippi

L'Association du Festival du Lac Massawippi presents an annual antiques and folk-arts show (tel. 819/842-4380) each July. The association also sponsors concerts, exhibitions, and poetry readings at various venues throughout the town year-round.

Lennoxville

Lennoxville's **Centennial Theatre and Consolidated-Bathurst Theatre** at Bishop's University (tel. 819/822-9692 or 819/822-9600) presents a roster of international, Canadian, and Québecois jazz, classical, and rock concerts, as well as dance, mime, and children's theater. Jazz greats Gary Burton, Carla Bley, and Larry Coryell have appeared here, as have classical artists like the Amsterdam Guitar Trio and the Allegri String Quartet.

Magog **Theatre Le Vieux Clocher** (64 rue Merry N, tel. 819/847–0470) presents summer pop and rock concerts, as well as French plays.

North Hatley **The Piggery** reigns supreme in l'Estrie cultural life. Housed in a former pig barn in North Hatley on the shores of Lac Massawippi, the Piggery is renowned for its risk taking, often presenting new plays by Canadian playwrights and even experimenting with bilingual productions. An attractive on-site restaurant serves country suppers and picnic fare indoors and out before the 8 PM curtain. *Box 390 North Hatley, J0B 2C0, tel. 819/842–2191 or 842–2431. Reservations required. Season runs June–Aug.*

Orford Orford's regional park is the site of an annual arts festival highlighting classical music, pops, and chamber orchestra concerts. For the past 39 summers, some 300 students have come to the **Orford Arts Center** to study and perform classical music. Canada's internationally celebrated Orford String Quartet originated here. Lately, Festival Orford has expanded to include jazz and folk music. Budding musicians rub shoulders and trade notes at master classes and in public performances with such big name artists as jazz pianist Oliver Jones and the inimitable folksinging duo, Kate and Anna McGarrigle. The center also welcomes artisans during its summer art exhibitions. Musicians give concerts in the gracefully designed concert hall or in the park, where they often practice while seated among the outdoor sculptures. *Orford Arts Center, Box 280, Magog J1X 3W8, tel. 819/843–3981 or in Canada from May to Aug., 800/ 567–6155.*

Sutton Sutton is also home to the visual and performing arts. **Arts Sutton** (7 Academy, tel. 514/538–2563) is a long-established mecca for the visual arts. Aside from exhibitions of work by renowned Québec artists, the center also runs summer workshop sessions in many media, with many of the seasonal instructors drawn from the Saidye Bronfman Centre's faculty members.

Arts and Music Sutton (tel. 514/596–1729) also offers intensive workshops in dance, music, and theater, which culminate in public performances.

12 Nova Scotia

Introduction

by Colleen Thompson

An award-winning international travel writer who specializes in the Atlantic Provinces, Colleen Whitney Thompson is the author of New Brunswick Inside Out *and a regular contributor to the travel sections of dozens of magazines and newspapers.*

Nova Scotia's not really an island—it's attached by a narrow neck of land to New Brunswick—but it has that mystical island feeling. It's often said that it resembles a lobster in shape. That's totally in keeping with its image as a kingdom of the sea.

A lot of its charm is the effect of two different geographical areas. West of Halifax, the lobster body is a land of apple blossoms, legends of Evangeline, sturdy little ship building towns, photogenic fishing villages, and the sandy beaches of the south shore.

East of Halifax, the real island part of the province, Cape Breton, is a giant claw with precipitous highland cliffs and roads that roll merrily and often from scenic height down to hidden cover to make it one of the most attractive drives of the east coast.

To the north the other claw reaches back toward New Brunswick, its Northumberland Strait beaches warm and inviting, its small towns offering everything from harness racing to coal mining exploring.

Sprinkle all this with good restaurants, abundant seafood, unique history, and you'll find yourself in a magical land of giants, giantesses, and fortresses, bagpipes and Gaelic, lobster and inventors, enticing mountain resorts, bustling Acadian or Loyalist villages by the sea, and a lively, cosmopolitan capital that is one of Canada's prettiest.

Pleasure sailors often settle here. They're lured by the fact that no part of the province is farther than 35 miles from the sea and a good part of the coast is protected by Prince Edward Island and New Brunswick, not to mention large inland lakes and the lovely, deeply indented coastline.

"I can be at the top of the World Trade Center, covering up my computers at five o'clock," says one Halifax office worker, "and twenty minutes later, I'm out on the harbor sailing toward the sun."

When residents feel that way, it's no wonder tourists have been flocking to this province for years. Its reputation as a vacation paradise is richly deserved. Good roads lead from Maine and Quebec through New Brunswick to the Nova Scotia border. Large car-carrying ferries operate from Digby in Saint John, NB, and from Bar Harbor and Portland, Maine, directly to Nova Scotia's shores.

For years tourism has been big business. For some families it has freed younger members from following the hard coal-mining life of their fathers, although, as in other maritime provinces, the flow of young people to richer provinces with higher pay scales has been intense. Still, despite the influx of visitors each summer, Nova Scotia has remained miraculously unspoiled. Genuine "old salts" haunt the wharves at Lunenburg. Honest-to-goodness fishermen man lobster boats at Cheticamp, and even in Halifax, a city of convention centres and posh hotels, the people in all facets of the hospitality industry are refreshing and amiable.

Nova Scotians also have access to some of the finest educational opportunities in the Atlantic provinces with several universities of note, Dalhousie Medical School among them.

Residents are mainly well educated, well traveled and gregarious. Still, in a thriving capital like Halifax, it is often surprising to open the largest daily paper of the province to find front page coverage of local road construction or a new sewage system on a Halifax street while you have to search for news of the world. As I mentioned, Nova Scotia is more like an island. But that's part of its charm.

Essential Information

Important Addresses and Numbers

Tourist Information The **Nova Scotia Department of Tourism and Culture** (Box 456, Halifax, Nova Scotia B3J 2R5, tel. 902/424–5000; in Canada, 800/565–7166; in continental U.S. except Maine, 800/341–6096; in Maine, 800/492–0643) can provide information on sights, accommodations, and transportation.

Halifax The **Nova Scotia Tourism Information Centre** (Old Red Store at Historic Properties, tel. 902/424–4247), and **Tourism Halifax** (Old City Hall, Duke and Barrington Sts., tel. 902/421–8736) are open mid-June–Labor Day daily from 9–7:30, rest of the year, weekdays 9–4:30.

Emergencies Dial 911 for **fire, police** or **ambulance** service anywhere in Nova Scotia. Victoria General (tel. 902/428–2110) is Halifax's major **hospital.**

Arriving and Departing by Plane

Airports and Airlines **Air Canada** (tel. 800/872–0487) provides regular, daily service to Halifax and Sydney, Nova Scotia, from New York, Boston, Toronto, Montréal, and St. John's, Newfoundland. **Canadian Airlines International** (tel. 800/527–8499) has service to Halifax via Toronto and Montréal. **Air Nova** and **Air Atlantic** provide regional service with flights to Toronto, Montréal, and Boston.

The **Halifax International Airport** is 40 kilometers (25 miles) northeast of downtown Halifax.

Arriving and Departing by Car, Ferry, Train, and Bus

By Car The Trans-Canada Highway (Route 104) will lead you to Nova Scotia by the overland route, through New Brunswick, entering the province at Amherst; to reach Halifax pick up Routes 2/102 at Truro. Most highways in the province lead to Halifax/Dartmouth. Highways 3/103, 7, 2/102, and 1/101 terminate in the twin cities.

To get to Cape Breton Island from mainland Nova Scotia, drive across the Canso Causeway, which is part of the Trans-Canada Highway.

By Ferry You can reach Nova Scotia by one of six car-ferry connections from Maine, New Brunswick, Prince Edward Island, and Newfoundland. **Marine Atlantic** (tel. 800/341–7981) sails from Bar Harbor, Maine, and **Prince of Fundy Cruises** (tel. 800/341–

7450) sails from Portland, Maine. From Saint John, New Brunswick, to Digby, Nova Scotia, ferry service is provided by **Marine Atlantic** (in New Brunswick tel. 800/565–9470).

By Train **Via Rail** provides service to Nova Scotia from stations across Canada; **Amtrak** from New York City makes connections in Montréal. For information and reservations, contact any Via Rail ticket office (tel. 800/561–3952) in Canada or Amtrak (tel. 800/USA–RAIL) in the United States.

By Bus **Greyhound** (consult telephone directory for local number) from New York, and **Voyageur Inc.** (tel. 613/238–5900) from Montréal, connect with **SMT** (tel. 506/458–6009) in New Brunswick. From there service is on **Acadian Lines Limited** (tel. 902/454–9321) in Nova Scotia.

Getting around Halifax

Walking or biking are excellent ways to get around and see the city, especially on weekdays when parking in the downtown area can be a problem.

By Taxi Rates begin at about $1.30 and increase based on the mileage and time engaged. A crosstown trip should be $4–$5 depending on traffic. Hailing a taxi on the street can be difficult, so the best bet is to call a taxi service.

By Bus The **Metropolitan Transit Commission** (tel. 902/426–6600) bus system covers the entire Halifax/Dartmouth area. The base fare is 75¢ and exact change is necessary.

By Ferry The **Dartmouth Ferry Commission** (tel. 902/464–2336) runs two passenger ferries from the George Street terminal in Halifax to the Portland Street terminal in Dartmouth from 6 AM–midnight on an hourly and half-hourly schedule. The fare for a single crossing is 50¢.

Guided Tours

City Tours Both **Gray Line Sightseeing** (tel. 902/454–9321) and **Metropolitan Transit Commission** (tel. 902/421–6620) have coach tours of Halifax, each lasting about two hours. The Gray Line tour picks up passengers at the major hotels and the Acadian Lines terminal on Almon Street.

Boat Tours **Halifax Water Tours** (tel. 902/423–7783 or 902/425–1271) operates an excellent two-hour, narrated cruise of Halifax Harbor and the Northwest Arm from mid-June through October. Tours leave from Privateer's Wharf up to four times a day in the height of the season and cost $6 for adults, $2 for children.

A 143-foot replica of the famous Nova Scotia sailing schooner, ***Bluenose II*** (tel. 902/422–2678 or 902/424–4247) departs from Privateer's Wharf on a two-hour harbor sail most of July, August, and September. The cost is $9 adults, $4.50 senior citizens, and $4 children.

Exploring Nova Scotia

Highlights for First-time Visitors

Cape Breton Highlands National Park, Tour 7: Cabot Trail

Evangeline Trail, Tour 2

Fortress Louisbourg National Historic Park, Tour 8: Marconi Trail

Halifax Citadel National Historic Park, Tour 1: Halifax and Dartmouth

Historic Properties, Tour 1: Halifax and Dartmouth

Peggy's Cove, Tour 3: Lighthouse Route

Pictou's Scottish heritage, Tour 5: Sunrise Trail

Sherbrooke Village, Tour 6: Marine Drive

Tour 1: Halifax and Dartmouth

Numbers in the margin correspond with points of interest on the Nova Scotia and Halifax maps.

1 Pretty and cosmopolitan, **Halifax** is one of Canada's jolliest cities as well as the largest in the maritime provinces. Most Atlantic Canada residents, it is said, wish to live in Halifax at one time in their lives, but in the maritime fashion few get around to doing so. Still, the Nova Scotian capital manages to draw outsiders, particularly those who like a lively city atmosphere without the stress of a truly large metropolis. The Old Town clock, located at the base of Citadel Hill and donated by time-conscious Prince Edward, son of King George III, in 1803, serves to remind Halifax workers that there is work to be done. So does the ear-splitting cannon blast that reverberates from the hill each day at noon.

2 We begin our tour where the city itself began—at the **Citadel,** the star-shaped fort first built in 1749 by Lord Cornwallis as a military base to protect the British colony. Set on a hill overlooking the Halifax peninsula and the harbor beyond, the Citadel is now a national historic park containing the fourth fortress built on this site, in 1861. Kilted soldiers drill on the grounds, and the **Army Museum** on site depicts the history of Colonial warfare. *Halifax Defense Complex, Box 1480, tel. 902/426–5080. Admission: $2 adults, $1 children, senior citizens free. Open mid-June–early Sept., daily 9–6; mid-Sept.–early June, grounds open 9–5 (admission free).*

3 Beside the Citadel on Summer Street is the **Nova Scotia Museum,** whose exhibits focus on the social and natural history of Nova Scotia. "Touch and feel" exhibits make this a good place to bring kids. *1747 Summer St., tel. 902/429–4610. Admission free. Open mid-May–Oct., Mon., Tues., Thurs., Sat. 9:30–5:30, Wed. 9:30–8, Sun. 1–5:30; Nov.–early May, Tues., Thurs., Sat. 9:30–5, Wed. 9:30–8, Sun 1–5.*

4 The **Halifax Public Gardens,** 18 acres of color in the heart of the city, is a favorite spot for relaxation for visitors and Haligonians. Landscaped originally in 1753, these gardens are among the oldest on the continent. In addition to trees and shrubs from every corner of the globe, there are fountains, a bandstand, and a large pond with various water birds. One corner has been set aside as a children's area. *Open mid-May–mid-Nov., 8–sundown.*

If you turn right on Spring Garden Road you can visit the cam-
5 pus of **Dalhousie University,** which has a fine art gallery and

performing-arts center (the Rebecca Cohn Auditorium, tel. 902/424–2298). If you turn left on Spring Garden Road from the gardens, you'll head downhill toward the harbor. At Barrington
6 Street you'll pass **St. Mary's Basilica,** reputed to have the highest granite spire in the world. Turn left on Barrington Street to
7 see **St. Paul's Church,** the oldest surviving building in Halifax (built 1749) and the oldest Protestant church in Canada. One
8 block east, on Granville Street, you'll find **Province House,** the oldest existing legislative building in Canada (built 1819). Charles Dickens called it "a gem of Georgian architecture." Nova Scotia's legislature still meets here. *Tel. 902/424–5982. Admission free. Open July–Aug., weekdays 8:30–6, Sat. 9–4, Sun 10–4; Sept.–June, weekdays 8:30–4:30.*

9 Across the street is the **Art Gallery of Nova Scotia,** which features work by Canadian and Nova Scotian artists. *1740 Hollis St., tel. 902/424–7542. Admission: $2. Open Mon.–Wed., Fri. 9–5:30; Thurs. 9–9; weekends noon–5:30.*

Proceed up Granville Street past Duke Street. On your left will
10 be **Scotia Square,** an ultramodern shopping-office-apartment-
11 hotel complex. On your right, you'll enter the **Historic Properties** area, whose cobblestone streets give you an idea of what Halifax looked like in the 1800s.

In the early 1960s the Historic Properties area was slated for demolition to make way for a superhighway along the waterfront. A successful campaign by civic groups saved the area from the wrecker's ball, and the city of Halifax, which owns most of the property, called for redevelopment plans to restore the buildings to their original appearance on the exterior, while retaining commercially usable interiors. Shops, restaurants, and offices are housed today in 12 restored buildings, which have nooks and crannies in interesting locations, arches and odd-shape windows, stucco and wood beams—all of those beautiful "useless" architectural appendages that modern designers often banish from their functional steel-and-glass buildings.

The block of North American Renaissance buildings on Granville Street, between Duke and Buckingham streets, was constructed after the great Halifax fire of 1859, which razed the area. Designed by Toronto architect William Thomas, the buildings were not built at the same time, but all exhibit a common theme and exterior format. Some of the storefronts that remain were fabricated of cast iron and were probably designed by James Bogardus, an American inventor known for his work with cast iron. The only way to tell if the structures are metal is to test them with a magnet. Although many of the extravagant architectural details of the 1870s have been obliterated by time, the original elegance may still be seen in the tall windows and storefront designs. This part of Granville Street is now a pedestrian area.

The **Privateer's Warehouse** is a stone building that housed the cargoes captured by Nova Scotia schooners serving as privateers; captured ships and cargoes were auctioned off by the Admiralty. **Privateer's Wharf,** on the waterfront at the south end of the Historic Properties, is the docking place for the schooner
12 ***Bluenose II,*** which carries passengers into the harbor July through August for three two-hour sailings daily. *Tel. 902/422–2678. Admission: $14 adults, $7 children and senior citizens.*

Nova Scotia
NEW BRUNSWICK
PRINCE
Borden
Cape Torment
Northumberlan
Amherst
Oxford
Springhill
Trans-Canada Hwy.
Chignecto Game Sanctuary
Great Village
Parrsboro
Cape Blomidon
Minas Basin
Maitland
St. John
Bay of Fundy
Minas Channel
Wolfville
Hantsport
Mount Uniacke
Evangeline Trail
Berwick
Windsor
Kingston
Three Mile Plains
Annapolis Royal
Middleton
Ross Farm
Port Royal
Bridgetown
Upper Sackville
Middle Sackville
Lower Sackville
Digby
St. Margarets Bay
Dartmo
Chester
Easte
Digby Neck
Bear River
Mahone Bay
Peggy's Cove
Herring Cove
Tiverton
KEJIMKUJIK NATIONAL PARK
Lunenburg
Halifax
Westport
Brier Island
TOBEATIC WILDLIFE MANAGEMENT AREA
Lake Rossignol
Milton
Brooklyn
Liverpool
TO BAR HARBOR (MAINE)
Yarmouth
Shelburn
TO PORTLAND (MAINE)
Lockeport
Woods Harbour
Barrington
TO TANCOOK ISLAND

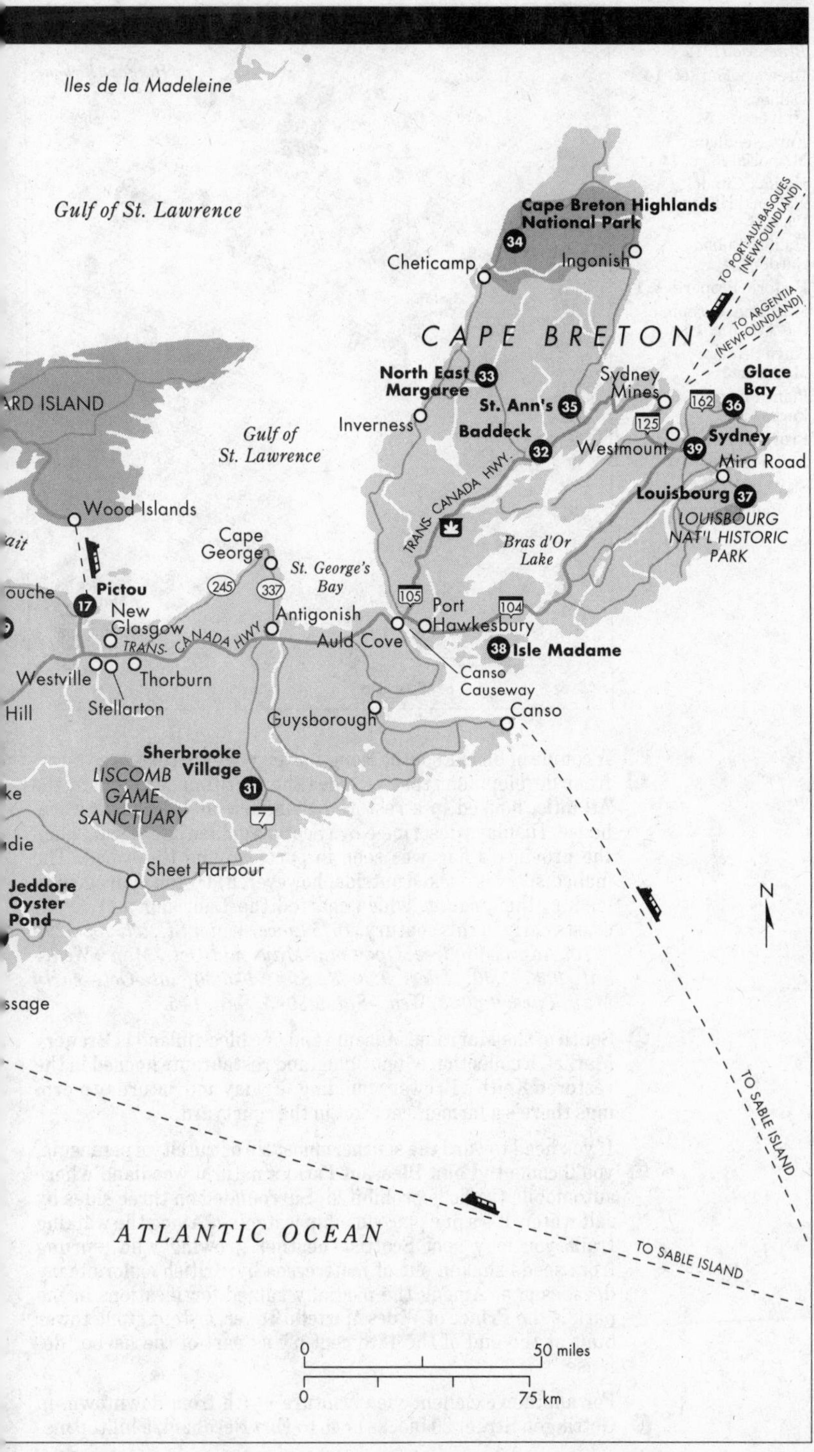
Iles de la Madeleine
Gulf of St. Lawrence
Cape Breton Highlands National Park
34
Cheticamp
Ingonish
TO PORT-AUX-BASQUES (NEWFOUNDLAND)
TO ARGENTIA (NEWFOUNDLAND)
CAPE BRETON
North East Margaree
33
St. Ann's
35
Sydney Mines
Glace Bay
36
162
125
Inverness
Baddeck
32
Westmount
39
Sydney
Mira Road
Louisbourg
37
LOUISBOURG NAT'L HISTORIC PARK
ARD ISLAND
Gulf of St. Lawrence
TRANS CANADA HWY.
Bras d'Or Lake
Wood Islands
Cape George
St. George's Bay
245
337
105
104
Pictou
17
ouche
New Glasgow
TRANS. CANADA HWY
Antigonish
Port Hawkesbury
Auld Cove
38
Isle Madame
Westville
Thorburn
Stellarton
Canso Causeway
Hill
Guysborough
Canso
Sherbrooke Village
31
LISCOMB GAME SANCTUARY
7
Sheet Harbour
Jeddore Oyster Pond
N
ssage
TO SABLE ISLAND
ATLANTIC OCEAN
TO SABLE ISLAND
0
50 miles
0
75 km

Art Gallery of Nova Scotia, **9**
Bluenose II, **12**
Brewery Market, **14**
Dalhousie University, **5**
Fort Needham Memorial Park, **16**
Halifax Citadel National Historic Park, **2**
Halifax Public Gardens, **4**
Historic Properties, **11**
Maritime Museum of the Atlantic, **13**
Nova Scotia Museum, **3**
Point Pleasant Park, **15**
Province House, **8**
Scotia Square, **10**
St. Mary's Basilica, **6**
St. Paul's Church, **7**

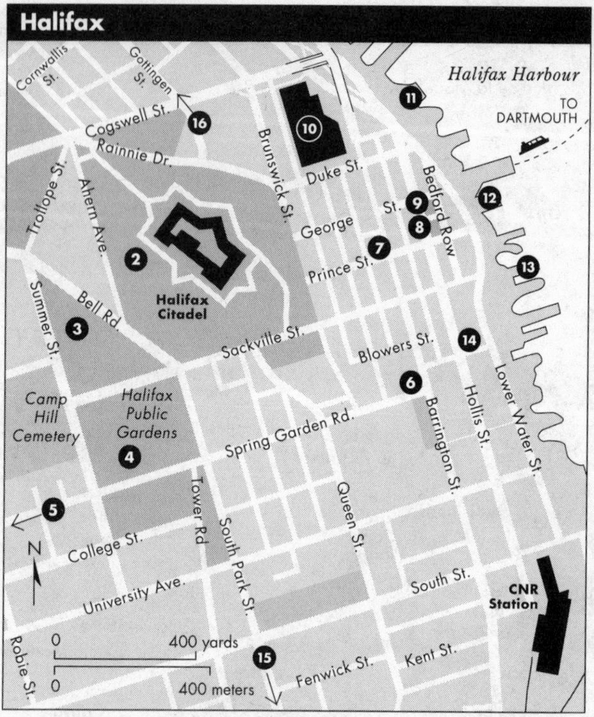

A couple of blocks south, along Lower Water Street, is a waterfront development that includes the **Maritime Museum of the**
13 **Atlantic,** housed in a restored chandlery and dockside warehouse. Displays describe Nova Scotia's golden age of sail, when the province's flag was seen in ports around the world. The main display is docked outside, however: a 900-ton hydrographic ship, the *Acadia*, which charted the Labrador and Arctic coasts early in this century. *1675 Lower Water St., tel. 902/429–8210. Admission free. Open mid-May–mid-Oct., Mon., Wed.–Sat. 9:30–5:30, Tues. 9:30–8, Sun. 1–5:30; late-Oct.–early May, Tues. 9:30–8, Wed.–Sat. 9:30–5, Sun. 1–5.*

14 South of the Maritime Museum and one block inland is **Brewery Market,** a collection of boutiques and restaurants housed in the restored Keith's Brewery building. Friday and Saturday mornings there's a farmer's market in the courtyard.

If you head toward the southernmost tip of the city's peninsula,
15 you'll come to **Point Pleasant Park,** a natural woodland where automobile traffic is prohibited. Surrounded on three sides by salt water, it's a fine place for ship watching. Along the walking trails you may spot Scottish heather growing wild, sprung from seeds shaken out of mattresses by British sailors many decades ago. Among the partially ruined fortifications in the park is the **Prince of Wales Martello Tower,** a stout stone tower built at the end of the 18th century as part of the harbor defense.

For another excellent view venture north from downtown up
16 Gottingen Street 20 blocks or so to **Fort Needham,** a hilltop me-

morial park that offers a panoramic view of the area devastated in the Great Halifax Explosion, on December 6, 1917. The explosion, the largest single man-made blast prior to the atomic bomb, was caused when a munitions ship collided with another vessel in the harbor. Two thousand fatalities were recorded, 10,000 more people suffered serious injuries, 25,000 were left homeless, and the shock wave was felt in the town of Truro, more than 60 miles away.

Tour 2: Evangeline Trail

Numbers in the margin correspond with points of interest on the Nova Scotia map.

The 278-kilometer (189-mile) drive from Mount Uniacke, near Halifax, to Yarmouth takes about 3½ hours (8 hours with two excursions). This route is clearly posted with trailway mark-
17 ers, as are the other routes described below. Starting at **Mount Uniacke,** you'll come upon **Uniacke House,** 1812–1815. With an imposing veranda and most of its furniture original to the house, the building is a grand example of late-Georgian architecture in the province. *Rte. 1, tel. 902/866–2560. Admission free. Open mid-May–mid-Oct., Mon.–Sat. 9:30–5:30, Sun. 1–5:30.*

Before driving from Windsor to Digby (through the apple-orchard-dotted **Annapolis Valley** where some of the earliest French settlements flourished), take a detour north from
18 Route 1 on Route 358 to **Cape Blomidon** for a view of four counties from the bluff. Return to Route 1 and continue west toward Annapolis Royal. Turn right just before crossing the Annapolis Causeway, to reach **Port Royal National Historic Park,** the first permanent European settlement north of the Gulf of Mexico. Here, in 1605, French explorers Samuel Champlain and Sieur de Monts established their *habitation,* or trading post, which stood until Virginia raiders scattered the French and leveled the buildings, in 1613. The rebuilt compound is an exact replica, constructed without nails. *Tel. 902/532–2898. Admission free. Park open year-round; buildings open mid-May–mid-Oct., daily 9–6.*

Drive east to Route 1 and cross the causeway into **Annapolis**
19 **Royal,** where you should stop to see **Fort Anne,** the scene of continuing French-British conflict for supremacy over the province. The 18th-century officers' quarters are reconstructed, although the earthworks and stone powder-magazine are original. *Tel. 902/532–5197. Admission free. Open mid-May–mid-Oct., daily 9–6; mid-Oct.–mid-May, weekdays 9–5. Closed holidays.*

A second excursion, along Digby Neck on Route 217, with two ferries, is to **Westport,** on Brier Island, one of the richest grounds for whale-watching in the North Atlantic.

Tour 3: Lighthouse Route

This rugged coastal tour along the South Shore, from Halifax to Yarmouth, covers 470 kilometers (275 miles) and takes up to 7 hours to drive, depending on whether you take the fast Route 103 or hug the winding shore on Route 3 and take side excursions. Early fishing and shipbuilding ports abound, but none is
20 more picturesque than **Peggy's Cove,** near Halifax: it is one of

the most photographed villages in Canada. It possesses one of the dozen or so lighthouses to be seen on this route and is North America's only post-office lighthouse (open Apr.–Nov.). Its postal cancellation shows an image of—what else?—a lighthouse.

Continue west through **Chester,** a favorite summer resort town with back and front harbors, go on to Chester Basin, turning off
21 onto Route 12 north. You'll soon reach **Ross Farm,** a living museum illustrating advances in agriculture from 1600 to 1925. Wear comfortable shoes or boots and old clothes. *Rte. 12, New Ross, tel. 902/689–2210. Admission: $2 adults, 50¢ children 4–14, $5 families. Open mid-May–mid-Oct., daily 9:30–5:30; late-Oct.–early May by appointment.*

Returning along Route 12, back to the Lighthouse Route, you'll once again be traveling along a scenic coastal highway. Stop at
22 **Lunenburg,** whose **Fisheries Museum of the Atlantic** is aboard two former fishing vessels and a one-time rumrunner. (Privately run sailing tours of Lunenburg Harbour aboard the *Timberwind*, a 35-foot gaff-rig schooner, operate from the museum mid-June to Labor Day.) *Blue Nose Dr., tel. 902/634–4794. Admission: $2 adults, 50¢ school-age children. Tours: $1.50. Open mid-May–mid-Oct., daily 9:30–5:30.*

Driving south, you'll come to **La Have,** where you can visit the **Fort Point Museum,** a former lighthouse-keeper's house (admission free; open June–Aug., daily 10–6; Sept., weekends 1–5). Farther down the coast you pass through **Shelburne,** settled by Loyalists escaping from the American Revolution. Some of the world's greatest yachts have been built here. (You can charter your own sailboat, large or humble, with or without crew, along this route.)

23 On the southern tip of Nova Scotia stop at the **Barrington Woolen Mill Museum,** where you will be shown how wool is woven into bolts of twills and flannels, blankets, and suitings. *Rte. 3, tel. 902/637–2185. Admission free. Open mid-June–Sept., Mon.–Sat. 9:30–5:30, Sun. 1–5:30.*

24 An appropriate ending to this marine tour is the **Yarmouth County Museum and Archives,** with its outstanding collection of 19th-century portraits of merchant ships built locally or commanded by Yarmouth sailors. *22 Collins St., tel. 902/742–5539. Admission: $1 adults, 50¢ students, 25¢ children under 14, $2.50 family. Open June–mid-Oct., Mon.–Sat. 9–5, Sun. 1–5; mid-Oct.–June, Tues.–Sat. 2–5.*

Tour 4: Glooscap Trail

Starting at Windsor (take Route 102 from Halifax, then Route 101), this 394-kilometer (246-mile) trail, named after the Micmac Indian warrior god, runs along the Minas Basin and Bay of Fundy to Amherst, just across the border from New Brunswick. This 7½-hour drive encircles the site of the world's highest tides. An early landmark is the **William Lawrence House** in
25 **Maitland.** The Victorian house, designed for a prosperous shipbuilder in 1870, overlooks the site where the largest clipper ship ever built in Canada was launched, in 1874. *Rte. 215, tel. 902/261–2628. Admission free. Open mid-May–mid-Oct., Mon.–Sat. 9:30–5:30, Sun. 1–5:30.*

26 Heading east around Cobequid Bay you are soon in **Truro.** For one of the best vantage points from which to view the twice-daily Bay of Fundy tidal bore (the first gushing wave of the incoming high tide), follow Tidal Bore Road off Route 102 to the Palliser Restaurant, in the Tideview Motel. (Call 902/426–5494 for a schedule of high tides at Truro and other locations in the province.) The water level quickly rises after the bore, reaching the highest point about an hour later.

Following the northern shore of Minas Basin brings you to
27 **Parrsboro,** where the **Geological Museum** displays local fossils and the agate, amethyst, and other minerals that are found on nearby beaches. **Partridge Island,** just south of Parrsboro, is a prime spot for mineral gathering. *Geological Museum, 1 Eastern Ave., tel. 902/254–3814. Admission free. Open mid-May–mid-Oct., daily 9–9.*

28 A branch of the trail runs north to **Springhill,** the site of several tragic mining disasters: Descend into a mine shaft at the **Springhill Miners' Museum.** *Tel. 902/597–3449. Admission: $3 adults, $2 children. Open June, daily 10–5; July–Aug., daily 8–8; Sept.–mid-Oct., daily 10–5.*

Also in Springhill, the **Anne Murray Centre** documents the life and career of the Springhill-born country singer, with gold records, awards, and other memorabilia. *Main St., tel. 902/597–8614. Admission: $4.50 adults, $3.50 senior citizens, $3 students, $2 children. Open mid-May–mid-Oct., daily 10–7.*

The final leg of the trail follows Chignecto Bay to Amherst, taking you through **Joggins,** where you can see fossilized palm trees in the cliffs.

Tour 5: Sunrise Trail

This 208-kilometer (129-mile) route along the Northumberland Strait from Amherst west to Mulgrave takes you through a fog-free playland of rolling hills and sandy beaches (65% of Nova Scotia's beaches are here). This shore is the warmest in the province: the water reaches 80°F in summer. The area retains a strong Scottish influence; **Pictou** (where the first Scottish settlers arrived, in 1773) and **Antigonish** host week-long Highland festivals every summer, and **Pugwash** has bilingual street signs in English and Gaelic.

Around the middle of the four-hour drive, head south off the
29 trail at Brule onto Route 326 to the **Balmoral Grist Mill** at **Balmoral Mills.** One of the oldest operating mills in the province, dating from 1860, it produces stone-ground flours and meals that visitors may purchase. A pleasant picnic ground overlooks the millpond and falls. *Tel. 902/657–3016. Admission free. Open May–mid-Oct., Mon.–Sat. 9:30–5:30, Sun. 1–5:30.*

Rejoining the trail you'll go through Pictou and New Glasgow to reach **Cape George,** the one mountainous segment of the drive. Approaching Mulgrave you'll skirt **Canso Causeway,** the gateway to Cape Breton Island, which passes over one of the deepest man-made, ice-free ports in the world.

Tour 6: Marine Drive

This 400-kilometer (250-mile) drive from Dartmouth to Canso follows the Atlantic coast, twisting and turning with every bend of the south shore as it passes thick inland forests and tiny fishing villages. This is an important center for fishing and fish processing, with **Canso** the closest mainland point to the North Atlantic fishing grounds. The views of the ocean are spectacular all along this curvy drive; allow 10–11 hours for the trip.

For an introduction to the life of a typical Nova Scotia inshore fisherman from 1890 to 1920, visit the **Fisherman's Life Muse-**
30 **um** at **Jeddore Oyster Pond,** just east of Dartmouth. *Tel. 902/889–2053. Admission free. Open mid-May–mid-Oct., Mon.–Sat. 9:30–5:30, Sun. 11–5:30.*

About two-thirds of the way to Canso, follow the markers in-
31 land to **Sherbrooke Village,** on Route 7, a restoration of a 19th-century lumbering-and-gold-mining community. The inhabitants of the village still live in their homes within the museum, and all of the buildings are staffed by costumed residents working at their trade. There are 25 buildings on their original sites, including a doctor's house and office, and a hotel that now functions as a restaurant. *Rte. 7, tel. 902/522–2400. Admission: $2 adults, 50¢ children. Open mid-May–mid-Oct., daily 9:30–5:30.*

The salmon and trout fishing is excellent in the rivers and streams of the forests along Marine Drive, especially in **St. Mary's River** near Sherbrooke. Some of the best smoked salmon in North America can be purchased here on the Atlantic coast.

Tour 7: Cabot Trail

Considered one of the greatest scenic marine drives in the world, this 296-kilometer (184-mile) trail, one of four on Cape Breton Island, loops through the Cape Breton Highlands, starting and ending at Baddeck, on the north shore of Bras d'Or Lake, a vast interior sea. The trip takes five hours.

32 **Baddeck** is the resort town Alexander Graham Bell chose for his summer home, and he is buried here. Although the estate is still used by the family and is not open to the public, you can spot it from the roof garden of the **Alexander Graham Bell Museum** nearby. Bell's genius went beyond inventing the telephone, and the museum documents all his experiments: in sound, aeronautics, medical technology, even sea transportation. He also invented the hydrofoil, and the remains of the original vessel are on display. *Chedbucto St., tel. 902/295–2069. Admission free. Open July–Sept., daily 9–9; Oct.–June, daily 9–5.*

Many drivers prefer to follow the trail in a clockwise direction.
33 Proceeding from Baddeck, stop at **North East Margaree,** where the **Margaree Salmon Museum** explores the remarkable life cycle of the Atlantic salmon and houses a collection of fishing paraphernalia used on the Margaree River in search of the fighting fish. *Tel. 902/248–2848. Admission: 50¢ adults, 25¢ children. Open mid-June–mid-Oct., daily 9–5.*

Continue to the Acadian community of **Chéticamp,** notable for locally made hooked rugs and other handwork.

The trail rings the northern and eastern boundaries of the for-
34 ests of **Cape Breton Highlands National Park,** with its sheer cliffs dropping into the sea. Outstanding panoramas abound, especially overlooking Aspy Bay; heading south after Black

Brook Cove to Ingonish; and going down Cape Smoky. The park is 950 square kilometers (376 square miles), with numerous rivers providing good fishing, excellent hiking and nature trails, camping (including a trailer park), and an 18-hole championship golf course ($17 per day, $85 weekly). A number of beaches on the eastern coast offer excellent swimming. *Tel. in winter 902/285–2691, in summer 902/285–2535. Admission: $4 per vehicle per day, $9 for 4-day pass, $25 for annual pass. No charge for vehicles passing through on Cabot Trail. Camping fee: $8.50–$13 per day.*

After Cape Smoky the trail skirts the Gaelic Coast, past sever-
35 al Scottish fishing villages. Stop to visit the **Gaelic College** at **St. Ann's** (tel. 902/295–3411), where the Scottish language and arts are taught and preserved. During the summer, students perform at regularly scheduled daytime and evening *ceilidh* (*kay*-lee), or entertainments. The college also hosts special festivals, and visitors may sit in on practice sessions of traditional Scottish music.

Tour 8: Marconi Trail

The 55-kilometer (34-mile) coastal route from Glace Bay to Louisbourg takes an hour to drive without stopping, but Fortress Louisbourg requires at least half a day to visit.

Mining coal has long been a way of life in Cape Breton. Part of
36 the Three Mine Tour in the **Glace Bay** area, the **Miners Museum** displays a 200-year history of mining in the area. Visitors can walk into the Ocean Deeps Colliery, and the adjoining Miner's Village has a replica of the company store and housing. *Quarry Point, tel. 902/849–4522. Admission including mine tour: $4.50 adults, $2.75 children, $2.25 students. Open June–Labor Day, daily 10–6; mid-Sept.–May, weekdays 9–4.*

Also in Glace Bay, the **Marconi Museum** is situated on the spot where in 1902 Guglielmo Marconi transmitted the first transatlantic wireless message. *Timmerman St., tel. 902/564–2730. Admission free. Open mid-June–Labor Day, daily 10–6.*

37 The trail culminates in **Fortress Louisbourg,** the most ambitious restoration project ever undertaken in Canada. The original fortress, constructed by the French between 1720 and 1745, was the focal point of the struggle between the French and English until its total destruction by the English in 1760. Buildings open to the public within the garrison (including the quarters of the governor, officers, and soldiers stationed here) are occupied by "animators" in period costume, who also roam the complex. Furnishings are either original to the period or are meticulously researched copies. A park bus takes visitors from the interpretive center to the fortress proper. *Rte. 22, Louisbourg, tel. 902/733–2280. Admission June–Sept.: $6 adults, $3 children, free for senior citizens and children under 5, $15 family. Open July–Aug., daily 10–6; May, June, Sept., Oct., daily 9:30–5; Nov.–Apr. by appointment.*

Tour 9: Fleur-de-lis Trail

This 160-kilometer (100-mile) drive takes 3½ hours to complete, starting at Port Hawkesbury, on Cape Breton Island near the Strait of Canso, and ending at the industrial city of Sydney.

About 60% of the trail takes you along the low, curvy eastern
coast of the island, through some of the oldest fishing villages in
North America. Soon after leaving Port Hawkesbury the trail
38 crosses the bridge to **Isle Madame,** an Acadian area for 400
years. **Little Anse** is a particularly picturesque fishing village.
In **Arichat,** another Isle Madame village, you can visit **Le Noir
Forge,** a restored 18th-century stone blacksmith shop with
working forge. *Tel. 902/226–2800. Admission free. Open mid-June–mid-Sept., weekdays 9–5, Sat. 10–3.*

Back on Cape Breton Island proper you'll soon come upon **St.
Peters Canal,** dug in 1854 to link Bras d'Or Lake with the Atlantic. A park on the east side overlooks the canal and is a perfect
spot for picnicking as you watch the pleasure craft negotiate
the locks. After Fourchu the trail cuts north, inland past
39 Gabarus Lake, to Marion Bridge and into **Sydney.** Stop by the
Cossitt House, built in 1787, which is the oldest house in the
city. *75 Charlotte St., tel. 902/539–1572. Admission free. Open mid-May–Oct., Mon.–Sat. 9:30–5:30, Sun. 1–5:30.*

Tour 10: Ceilidh Trail

This 107-kilometer (67-mile) drive goes along the west coast of Cape Breton Island from Port Hastings, at the Canso Causeway, to Margaree Harbour. A pretty introduction to the highlands of Cape Breton, the route takes 1½–2 hours to drive.

Soon after leaving Port Hastings you'll pass through **Creignish,** on St. George's Bay, one of several traditional Scottish villages on the trail. **Port Hood** and **Mabou** are charming fishing ports and were well known shipbuilding centers in the 19th century. The scenery becomes more dramatic as you climb the coastal cliffs of the **Mabou Highlands** perched over the Northumberland Strait. The trail connects with the Cabot Trail at **Margaree Harbour.**

Shopping

Halifax There are several specialty shopping districts in the city. The **Spring Garden Road** area features traditional goods, particularly British imports. The newer and more exquisite area is the oldest part of Halifax—the **Historic Properties** and **Barrington Inn complex**—where fine crafts are on sale at such shops as **Pewter House, Nova Pine,** and **The Eskimo Gallery.** The **Plaid Place** (1903 Barrington Pl.) has a dazzling array of tartans and Highland accessories. One block away in the **Scotia Square** complex is the city's main downtown mall for day-to-day items.

Yarmouth If you plan to make a kilt or anything else out of Nova Scotian tartan, stop at **Yarmouth Wool Shoppe** (352 Main St., tel. 902/742–2255) near the ferry.

Elsewhere in Nova Scotia Nova Scotia's shopping centers tend to be uninspiring and not all that different from those in other parts of Canada or in the United States. The largest mall in the province is MicMac Mall, in Dartmouth, off the A. Murray Mackay Bridge. On Route 4 in Sydney you'll find the Woolco Shopping Center.

For a uniquely Nova Scotian experience spend some time browsing through one of the province's antiques stores or try to track down some of its interesting craftspeople. Antiques stores proliferate all over the province, especially in **Cape Bret-**

on. And in the shops of craftspeople throughout the province you'll find everything from blacksmithing in East Dover and silversmithing in Waverly, to leaded glass hanging ornaments in Purcells Cove, hooked rugs in Cheticamp, wood toys in Middletown, pewter in Wolfville, pottery in Arichat, and apple dolls in Halifax. To help you sort out the various crafts and their regions, request a copy of the *Handcraft Directory* from the Nova Scotia Department of Culture, Recreation, and Fitness (Box 864, Halifax, NS B3J 2V2, tel. 902/424-4061) or the Department of Tourism (*see* Important Addresses and Numbers in Essential Information, above).

Sports and Fitness

Canoeing **Canoe** route information is available from the Nova Scotia Government Bookstore (Box 637, 1 Government Pl., Halifax, NS D3J 2T3). The publication *Canoe Routes of Nova Scotia* is available from Canoe Nova Scotia (Box 3010 South, 5516 Spring Garden Rd., Halifax, B3J 3G6, tel. 902/425-5450) for $9.25.

Cycling **Bicycle Nova Scotia** (5516 Spring Garden Rd., Box 3010, Halifax B3J 3G6, tel. 902/425-5450) conducts a variety of two-wheeling excursions around the province.

Golf Nova Scotia and Cape Breton have 38 golf courses as well as driving ranges and miniature golf courses. One of Canada's finest courses is at the **Digby Pines Resort,** in Digby (*see* Lodging, below).

Spectator Sports

Hockey Halifax is the home of the American Hockey League Nova Scotia Voyageurs, a farm team of the Montréal Canadiens. The team plays more than 20 home games from November to April. For information, call 902/453-4015.

Beaches

The island is one big seashore: the warmest beaches are found on the Northumberland Strait shore and include **Heather Beach, Caribou,** and **Melmerby,** all in provincial parks. South-shore beaches include those at **Queensland Provincial Park, Kejimkujik National Park, Shelburne/the Islands Provincial Park,** and **Rissers's Provincial Park.** In the Annapolis Valley it's **Ellenwood Lake Provincial Park** and **Lake George Provincial Park.** On the Eastern Shore try **Lawrencetown, Martinique Provincial Park, Clam Harbour Provincial Park, Taylor Head Provincial Park,** and **Tor Bay Beach.** Cape Breton beaches include those at **Dominion Provincial Park, East Bay, Port Hood,** and **Inverness.**

National Parks

Nova Scotia has two national parks: **Cape Breton Highlands National Park** (*see* Tour 7, above) and **Kejimkujik National Park,** in the interior of the western part of the province. Essentially a wilderness area with many lakes, Kejimkujik offers well-marked canoe routes into the interior with primitive campsites. Nature trails are marked for hikers, boat rentals are available, and there's freshwater swimming. One precaution: check for dog ticks after hiking in the deep woods. *Box 36, Maitland Bridge, Annapolis County, B0T 1N0, take Hwy. 8 between Liverpool and Annapolis Royal, tel. 902/242–2770. Admission: $4 per vehicle per day, $9 for 4-day pass, $25 for annual pass. Camping fee: $8.50–$13 per day.*

Dining and Lodging

Dining

Many of Halifax's restaurants are set in refurbished historic homes or other restored quarters. The menu almost always centers on seafood, including Malpeque oysters, Fundy lobster, and Digby scallops, though considering the city's proximity to some of the world's best fishing grounds, there should be more high-quality fish available. Only in expensive restaurants will a jacket be required; dress in all other restaurants is casual.

Highly recommended restaurants in each price category are indicated by a star ★.

Category	Cost*
Very Expensive	over $50
Expensive	$35–$50
Moderate	$15–$34
Inexpensive	under $15

**per person, excluding drinks, service, and 10% sales tax on meals more than $3.*

Lodging

Accommodations in Halifax/Dartmouth are generally comfortable and reservations are necessary year-round. Reservations can be made by calling the toll-free numbers of the Nova Scotia Department of Tourism (*see* Important Addresses and Numbers in Essential Information, above). Expect to pay quite a bit more in the capital district than elsewhere in the province. For those on a budget, look into a hostel or bed-and-breakfast option.

Highly recommended lodgings in each price category are indicated by a star ★.

Category	Cost*
Very Expensive	over $80
Expensive	$65–$80
Moderate	$45–$65
Inexpensive	under $40

**All prices are for a standard double room; excluding 10% service charge.*

Halifax/Dartmouth

Dining

★ **Clipper Cay.** This restaurant gets the prize for the best location in the city: overlooking Privateer's Wharf and the entire harbor. Request a table with a window view and order smoked salmon. The downstairs eatery, The Cay Side, serves lunch—seafood, of course—outside on the wharf in the summer. *1869 Upper Water St., Halifax, tel. 902/432-6818. Reservations advised. AE, DC, MC, V. Expensive.*

Ryan Duffy's. Steaks are the specialty at this atmospheric spot, where you select your own, though you can also choose from Japanese or Mexican menus. *5640 Spring Garden Rd., Halifax, tel. 902/421-1116. Reservations advised for dining room but not necessary for grill. AE, DC, MC, V. Expensive.*

The Five Fishermen. Near the Historic Properties downtown, this restaurant is set in an old school building where Anna of *The King and I* once taught music. Today, fresh fish is served here in a nautical atmosphere. Try the bouillabaisse. *1740 Argyle St., Halifax, tel. 902/422-4421. Reservations advised. AE, DC, MC, V. No lunch. Moderate.*

★ **Old Man Morias.** Authentic Greek specialties at this renovated Halifax town house include lamb on a spit and moussaka. *1150 Barrington St., Halifax, tel. 902/422-7960. Reservations advised. AE, DC, MC, V. Closed Sun. Moderate.*

The Birmingham Street Grill. This popular, often crowded bistro serves an upscale menu that features good pasta and seafood. The chrome-and-black interior has art-deco flair. *5511 Spring Garden Rd., Halifax, tel. 902/420-9622. Reservations advised. AE, MC, V. No lunch Sun. Inexpensive.*

The Golden Unicorn. Innovative Chinese food here incorporates Szechuan, chow mein, and the chef's creative ability. Especially tasty are the chicken dishes (try the special Unicorn chicken). Opt for a table on the patio in summer. *5657 Spring Garden Rd., Halifax, tel. 902/423-3888. Inexpensive.*

Lodging

Chateau Halifax. This central first-class Canadian Pacific hotel offers large, pretty rooms in a perfect location, near Scotia Square and Historic Properties. There's a good dining room and a lively bar. *1990 Barrington St., Scotia Sq., Halifax B3J 1P2, tel. 902/425-6700. 279 rooms, 21 suites. Facilities: restaurant, coffee shop, lounge with live entertainment, pool, sauna. AE, CB, DC, MC, V. Very Expensive.*

Citadel Halifax. Situated at the base of Citadel Hill, but still within walking distance of the action, this property attracts a business clientele. Rooms with a harbor view are recommended, though they will cost more than those without. It offers free parking, which is an asset in car-clogged Halifax. *1960 Brunswick St., Halifax B3J 2G7, tel. 902/422-1391. 261 rooms, 6 suites. Facilities: restaurant; cable TV movies; indoor pool; fitness center with sauna, whirlpool, and exercise room. AE, DC, MC, V. Very Expensive.*

Delta Barrington. This traditional-style hotel was built in 1979 using the original granite from the facade of an entire city block. It has a prime downtown location and the rooms are spacious. All-weather walkways connect the hotel to Scotia Square shops. *1875 Barrington St., Halifax B3J 3L6, tel. 902/429-7410. 200 rooms, 1 suite. Facilities: restaurant, lounge, piano bar, sauna, whirlpool, and pool. AE, CB, DC, MC, V. Very Expensive.*

Holiday Inn–Halifax Centre. This first-class property overlooks the Citadel, 1 kilometer (½ mile) from Scotia Square. *1980 Robie St., Halifax B3H 3G5, tel. 902/423–1161. 228 rooms, 3 suites. Facilities: restaurant, piano bar, pool, sauna, whirlpool, gift shop, free parking. AE, CB, DC, MC, V. Very Expensive.*

Prince George Hotel. Connected by underground tunnel to the World Trade and Convention Center, the Prince George is a new (1986), luxurious addition to the downtown accommodations roster. It is near the harbor and business districts. *1725 Market St., Halifax B3J 3N9, tel. 902/425–1986 or 800/565–1567. 208 rooms, 3 suites. Facilities: restaurant, café, 2 lounges, pub, pool, whirlpool, fitness center, concierge, children's playroom, roof deck and gardens. AE, CB, DC, MC, V. Very Expensive.*

Sheraton Halifax. Located in the charming Historic Properties in the heart of the business and shopping district, this elegant Sheraton features the Cafe Maritime restaurant and has an indoor pool with a summer sun deck, whirlpool, sauna, exercise room, and docking space for yachts. *1919 Upper Water St., Halifax B3J 3J5, tel. 902/421–1700 or 800/325–3535. 332 rooms, 24 suites. Facilities: 24-hr room service, concierge, shops, meeting facilities, skywalk to shopping and office complexes. AE, DC, MC, V. Very Expensive.*

Halliburton House Inn. You'll find antiques-filled rooms in this beautifully renovated town house of 1820. Enjoy the free breakfast in your room, free afternoon tea, and the pretty public rooms, as well as the delicious food in the inn's dining room. *5184 Morris St., Halifax B3J 1B3, tel. 902/420–0658. 33 rooms, 2 suites. Continental breakfast included in rate. AE, MC, V. Expensive.*

Holiday Inn. There are no surprises at this chain hotel, but the location is convenient: next to the Angus Macdonald Bridge. All rooms are air-conditioned and have color TV with movies; some have minibars. *99 Wuse Rd. at MacDonald Bridge, Dartmouth B3A 1L9, tel. 902/463–1100. 197 rooms, 6 suites. Facilities: restaurant, lounge, gym, sauna, outdoor pool, parking. AE, CB, DC, MC, V. Moderate.*

Journey's End Motel. Located on the main highway on the Dartmouth side of the Narrows, this new chain motel offers clean, modern, no-frills rooms. *456 Windmill Rd. (Rte. 7), Dartmouth B3A 1J7, tel. 902/463–9900. 81 rooms. AE, DC, MC, V. Moderate.*

Keddy's Halifax Hotel. Located about 15 minutes west of downtown, in the lake-studded Armdale neighborhood, this is a quite adequate chain hotel. Some rooms have kitchenettes. *20 St. Margaret's Bay Rd. (Rte. 3), Halifax B3N 1J4, tel. 902/477–5611. 125 rooms. Facilities: pool, sauna. AE, DC, MC, V. Moderate.*

Around the Mainland

Annapolis Royal
Lodging

Royal Anne Motel. Rebuilt in 1989 to accommodate more clientele and to upgrade facilities, this modern, no-frills motel offers clean rooms at reasonable prices. Enjoy the pleasant surroundings in a quiet country setting by taking a walk on the 20 acres of land the motel sits on. *400 Annapolis Royal, B0S 1A0, tel. 902/532–2323. 30 rooms. Facilities: whirlpool, sauna, conference room. AE, DC, MC, V. Moderate.*

Antigonish
Dining

Lobster Treat Restaurant. Located on the Trans-Canada Highway, this ordinary-looking restaurant has some nice surprises inside. Because of a relaxed atmosphere and a varied menu, including a separate one for the children, families like to frequent this restaurant. *241 Post Rd., tel. 902/863–5465. Reservations advised in summer. AE, DC, MC, V. Closed Jan. Moderate.*

Chester
Dining

The Galley. Decked out in nautical bric-a-brac and providing a spectacular view of the ocean, this restaurant has a menu that features seafood. Smoked salmon and mussel dishes are the local favorites, but save room for the homemade blueberry pie. *Hwy. 3, on the Marina, tel. 902/275–4700. Reservations advised. AE, MC, V. Closed Dec. 16–St. Patrick's Day. Inexpensive.*

Digby
Dining and Lodging

The Pines Resort Hotel. An elegant resort with fireplaces, sitting rooms, a colossal dining room, and a view of Digby harbor, this hotel offers myriad amenities. Seafood with a French touch is served daily, and there is live entertainment in the lounge nightly. *Box 70, Shore Rd., B0V 1A0, tel. 902/245–2511. 90 rooms in main lodge, 60 in cottages. Facilities: restaurant, lounge, tennis, outdoor pool, golf. AE, DC, MC, V. Closed Oct. 15–May 30. Expensive.*

Lorneville
Dining and Lodging

Amherst Shore Country Inn. Located at Lorneville, 20 miles from Amherst on Route 366, this superb inn has 5 rooms in-house and 2 seaside cottages with fireplaces. The food is incredible; four-course dinners are served in one daily seating, at 7:30 PM (reservations required). *Rte. 366, B4H 3X9, tel. 902/667–4800. 7 rooms. Facilities: restaurant. AE, DC, MC, V. Closed winter. Expensive.*

Lunenburg
Lodging

Bluenose Lodge. This 125-year-old mansion has 9 large bedrooms and offers a full complimentary breakfast, featuring treats such as freshly baked muffins, stewed rhubarb, and quiche. You can also partake of deep-sea fishing excursions, arranged by the lodge. *Box 339, 10 Falkland St., B0J 2C0, tel. 902/634–8851. 9 rooms. MC, V. Closed Nov.–mid-May. Inexpensive.*

New Glasgow
Lodging

Peter Pan Motel. Clean rooms and good hospitality keep people coming back to this motel. One of the few lodgings in the area that stay open all year, this motel is a good buy. *390 Marsh St., B2H 4S6, tel. 902/752–8327. 52 rooms. Facilities: dining room, bar, outdoor pool. AE, DC, MC, V. Moderate.*

Wolfville
Dining and Lodging

Blomidon Inn. Rooms at this elegant 19th-century sea-captain's mansion, restored in 1981, are uniquely decorated in authentic Colonial and Victorian fashion. The dining room serves local cuisine cooked in traditional style, using fresh seasonal produce. Complimentary tea is served every day at 4 PM. *127 Main St., B0P 1X0, tel. 902/542–2291. 27 rooms. Facilities: dining room, conference room, tennis court. MC, V. Closed Dec. 24–26. Expensive.*

Yarmouth
Dining and Lodging

Manor Inn. With superior rooms and good food in pleasant surroundings, this Colonial mansion on Highway 1 is a nice find. There are three settings to choose from: a lakeside cottage, the main estate, or the more secluded side wing. Steak and lobster are the specialties in the dining room. *Box 56, Rte. 1, B0W 1X0, tel. 902/742–2487. 54 rooms. Facilities: 2 dining rooms, 2 bars, whirlpool, heated pool, tennis court, fireplaces. Reservations required for restaurant. AE, DC, MC, V. Moderate.*

Cape Breton Island

Baddeck *Lodging* **Inverary Inn Resort.** These pleasant accommodations are found along the island's scenic central drive. With waterfront access, the property offers boating and swimming. The nearby village will keep you busy, yet the resort is tranquil. Some units are efficiencies or cottages. Families will appreciate the on-site children's playground. *Box 190, B0E 1B0, tel. 902/295–2674. 125 rooms. Facilities: restaurant, tennis, sauna. AE, DC, MC, V. Expensive.*

Iona *Dining* **Highland Heights Inn.** The rural surroundings, the Scottish home-style cooking served near the dining room's huge stone fireplace, and the unspoiled view of the lake are nice substitutes for being in the Scottish Highlands. Enjoy the salmon (or any fish in season), fresh-baked oat cakes, and homemade desserts. *Box 19, Rte. 223, tel. 902/725–2360. AE, MC, V. Moderate.*

Margaree Valley *Lodging* **Normaway Inn.** This secluded, 1920s inn is nestled in the hills of the river valley, on a 250-acre property. Many of the cabins have wood-burning stoves. Take advantage of the recreation barn and the nightly traditional entertainment—square dances and the like. The inn is known for its country gourmet food, all prepared on the premises. The owners will organize salmon-fishing trips. *Box 326, Egypt Rd., B0E 2C0, tel. 902/248–2987. 9 rooms, 17 cabins. Facilities: restaurant, tennis, bicycles. AE, MC, V. Closed Oct. 16–May. Moderate.*

Northeast Margaree *Lodging* **Heart of Hart's Tourist Farm.** This 100-year-old rural farmhouse on Cabot Trail is within walking distance of the village. Hot homemade oatmeal and Red River cereal are a favorite part of the full breakfast that is included in the room rate. Salmon- and trout-fishing trips can be arranged. *Northeast Margaree, D0E 2H0, tel. 902/248–2765. 5 rooms. No credit cards. Inexpensive.*

Sydney *Dining* **Joe's Warehouse.** For excellent food in the heart of town, stop here, where the specialties include local seafood and prime rib. Dress is casual and the atmosphere fun. After dinner head downstairs for live music and dancing at Smooth Herman's. *424 Charlotte St., tel. 902/539–6686. AE, MC, V. Moderate.*

Lodging **Sydney Mariner Hotel.** This hotel is excellently situated, on the bay beside the yacht club and close to the center of town. The attractively decorated guest rooms have all the amenities, and each has a view of the harbor. The intimate dining room specializes in seafood and Continental cuisine. *300 Esplanade, B1P 6J4, tel. 902/562–7500. 152 rooms. Facilities: restaurant, lounge, indoor pool, sauna, fitness center. AE, DC, MC, V. Expensive.*

The Arts and Nightlife

The Arts

Theater Halifax's premier professional theater group performs at the **Neptune Theater** (Sackville St., tel. 902/429–7300). The **Mulgrave Road Co-Op Theatre** (tel. 902/533–2092) is a small but active professional company performing all over the maritime provinces, producing original plays based on local history.

Among the best of Nova Scotia's thriving amateur companies are the **Kipawa Show Boat Company** (tel. 902/542–3500), which performs in Wolfville on summer weekends, and **Theatre Antigonish** (tel. 902/867–3954), which performs in Antigonish.

Music Live concerts and musical presentations are held in Halifax at the **Rebecca Cohn Auditorium** (6101 University Ave., tel. 902/494–2646) and the **Metro Centre** (Brunswick and Duke Sts., tel. 902/451–1202).

Nightlife

The multilevel entertainment center in Historic Properties, **Privateer's Warehouse** (tel. 902/422–1289), is a popular nighttime hangout. At the ground-level Lower Deck tavern you can quaff a beer to the strains of an accordionist or enjoy jazz riffs at the Middle Deck on the second floor. There is a cover for both decks and they are packed on weekends, so get there early.

Other popular Halifax night spots include **Bistro Too** (1770 Market St., tel. 902/420–9494), which presents live jazz on weekends; **Cheers** (1743 Grafton St., tel. 902/421–1655), with bands and entertainment nightly; and **Le Bistro Café** (South Park St., tel. 902/423–8428 or 902/423–8024), where you can listen to classical guitar.

13 Prince Edward Island

Introduction

Cradled on the waves of the Gulf of St. Lawrence, off the coasts of New Brunswick and Nova Scotia, Prince Edward Island has enchanted people for nearly 2,000 years. From about A.D. 100, the Micmac Indians canoed from the mainland across Northumberland Strait for summers of fishing. French explorer Jacques Cartier, on sighting the island in 1534, called it "the fairest land 'tis possible to see!" When the British took possession more than 200 years later, Edward, Duke of Kent, was impressed enough to give it his name. But those who live there and those who visit know it simply (and fondly) as "the Island."

The island is naturally beautiful. The red sandstone cliffs of the southern coastline, topped by rich green fields and trees, give summer visitors arriving by ferry across Northumberland Strait their first impressions of the lasting beauty of the province. The north shore, with its white, silky sand beaches, and the immaculate communities that form part of the gently rolling inland landscape, offer a contrasting beauty.

Prince Edward Island offers visitors a broad range of activities and attractions. Not surprisingly, many of them relate to water. There is sportfishing, boardsailing (wind surfing), boating, and other water sports on inland and coastal waters. The island's 1,760 kilometers (1,100 miles) of coastline offer 800 kilometers (500 miles) of Class A beaches, huge sand dunes, and some of the warmest salt water north of Florida.

What the visitor will find most distinctive are the historic and personal elements: the enduring French Acadian influence; the vestiges of Micmac, English, and Scottish settlements; vacation farms that offer visitors the unique experience of sharing accommodations—and chores—of their farm family hosts; homes/studios of the many local craftsmen (some of whom provide free demonstrations of their craft), where travelers can stop awhile and talk with the artisans and, of course, buy their works; the serenity of the low inland hills; and, above all, there is an essentially rural island personality that sets Prince Edward Island apart from similar but more commercial holiday destinations.

One of the most popular attractions is Green Gables House, which served as the setting for Lucy Maud Montgomery's well-known novel, *Anne of Green Gables*. Situated at Cavendish, in the center of the Island's north shore, the house should be visited by devotees of the book and other works by the author, although in other respects it is an unremarkable Island farmhouse. Nearby, Green Gables Post Office is the island's most popular center for stamps and postmarks during the summer.

Essential Information

Important Addresses and Numbers

Tourist Information For prices and information before your trip, contact the **Prince Edward Island Department of Tourism and Parks,** Visitor Services Division, Box 940, Charlottetown, PEI C1A 7M5, tel. 902/368–4444 or 800/565–0267. The government maintains 10 **Visitor Information Centers (VICs)** on the island and two VICs on the mainland—one at Aulac, New Brunswick, and one at Caribou, Nova Scotia. The main VIC is in Charlottetown (Rte. 1, tel. 902/368–4444). It is open daily mid-May through Oct.; weekdays Nov. to mid-May. Call ahead for exact hours. Other VICs are as follows: Bordon Ferry Terminal (Rte. 1, tel. 902/855–2090); Brackley Beach (Rte. 15, tel. 902/672–2259); Cavendish (Rte. 13, tel. 902/963–2639); Pooles Corner (Rtes. 3 and 4, near Montague, tel. 902/838–2972); Portage (Rte. 2, tel. 902/859–3125); Souris (Rte. 2 E, tel. 902/687–3238); Stanhope (Rte. 25, tel. 902/672–3329); Wilmot (Rte. 1A, near Summerside, tel. 902/436–2511); and Wood Islands (Rte. 1, tel. 902/962–2015). Municipal information centers operate in Kensington and New London. ***Dial-the-Island*** reservations/information service (tel. 800/565–7421) can answer questions about Prince Edward Island and handle any details of a trip to the island. The service is available year-round, but can only be called from the Maritime Provinces. Once you're on Prince Edward Island, a network of two-way radios at VICs can provide travel assistance.

Emergencies **Police and fire,** dial 0.

Hospitals **Queen Elizabeth Hospital,** Charlottetown, tel. 902/566–6200.

Arriving and Departing by Plane

Charlottetown Airport is 5 kilometers (3 miles) north of town and is served by the following airlines: **Canadian Airlines International** (tel. 800/387–2737) has flights from Boston, Toronto, Montréal, and Halifax daily. **Air Canada** (tel. 800/776–3000) has one-stop Moncton service from Toronto, as well as flights from Boston and New York.

Arriving and Departing by Ferry

Two car-ferry services operate regularly between Prince Edward Island and the mainland. **Marine Atlantic** ferries (Box 250, North Sydney, NS, B2A 3M3, tel. 902/748–8376) sail between Cape Tormentine, New Brunswick, and Borden, Prince Edward Island. There are regular daily crossings year-round between 6:30 AM and 1:30 AM; call ahead to check the departure schedule. The crossing takes about 45 minutes and costs about $3 per person, or $7 per car. The second service, **Northumberland Ferries** (54 Queen St., C1A 7L3, tel. 902/485–6580) sails between Caribou, Nova Scotia, and Wood Islands, Prince Edward Island, from May to mid-December. There are hourly crossings in summer; call ahead to check exact schedules. The crossing takes about an hour and 15 minutes, and costs about $4 per person, or $11 per car. For both ferries, plan to arrive early and expect long lines during the peak summer season. Neither service takes reservations.

Getting Around

By Car There are more than 5,440 kilometers (3,880 miles) of paved roads in the province to make exploration easy, including the three scenic drives called Lady Slipper Drive, Blue Heron Drive, and Kings Byway. The routes loop around western, central, and eastern Prince Edward Island, each following the coastline of the Island's three major land divisions formed naturally by the bays and rivers. Most highways are paved, with some short stretches of smooth red clay. With few exceptions, roads are evenly surfaced and well maintained for comfortable drives.

Guided Tours

Charlottetown **Abegweit Sightseeing Tours** (157 Nassau St., Charlottetown, PEI, C1A 2X3, tel. 902/894–9966) uses a double-decker London-style bus for a one-hour tour of old and new Charlottetown. Six sightseeing tours are conducted daily; $5 adults, $1 children under 10.

Regional Tours **Gulf Tours** (Kensington RR 1, PEI, C0B 1M0, tel. 902/886–2526 or 902/836–5418) has various tours; some packages include lodging.

Charlottetown

Sheltered on an arm of Northumberland Strait, Prince Edward Island's only city is named for the stylish consort of King George III. Charlottetown is a city of generous, gingerbread-clad clapboard houses and imposing trees. It is often called "the Cradle of Confederation," a reference to the 1864 conference held there that led to Canada's unification.

Charlottetown has no smokestack industry, in the traditional sense; its main activities center on government, tourism, and private commerce. While new suburbs were springing up around it, the core of Charlottetown remained unchanged and the waterfront was restored to recapture the tempo and appearance of earlier eras. Today, the waterfront includes the Prince Edward Hotel and Convention Centre, several informal restaurants, and handicraft and retail shops. You can easily explore the small downtown on foot in a couple of hours, more if you combine sightseeing with shopping and relaxing at a sidewalk café for a pizza or local seafood.

Exploring Charlottetown

Numbers in the margin correspond with points of interest on the Prince Edward Island and Charlottetown maps.

1 **Charlottetown's** historic red-brick core is the setting for the
2 modern concrete **Confederation Centre of the Arts,** opened in 1964 as Canada's national tribute to the Fathers of Confederation. Funded and maintained by contributions from all the provinces, the center houses a 1,100-seat theater, an art gallery, a library, art workshops, a children's theater, a memorial hall, and a gift shop that offers an assortment of Canadian crafts. From June to October the Confederation Centre's Charlottetown Summer Festival offers excellent professional theater, including the annual musical adaptation of *Anne of Green Gables. Queen St. between Grafton and Richmond Sts., tel. 902/566–2464; box office 902/566–1267. Open mid-June–Sept., daily 8 AM–9 PM; rest of the year, daily 9–5. 30-min guided tours July and Aug.*

3 Next door, on Richmond Street, is the Georgian-style **Province House,** which is the meeting-place of the provincial legislature. The three-story sandstone building, completed in 1847, contains the **Confederation Chamber,** where representatives of the 19-century provinces met to forge a union. This room, re-

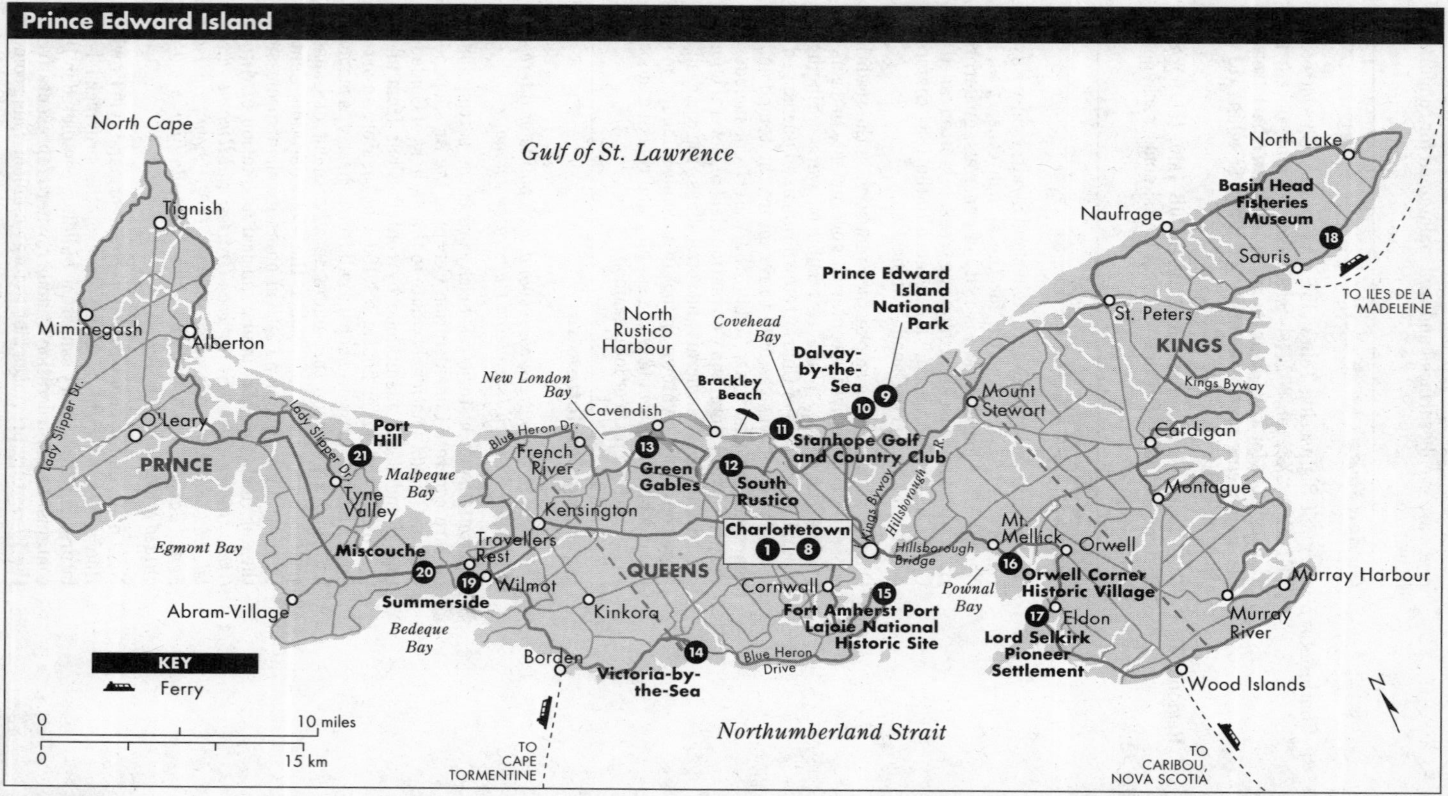

Prince Edward Island
North Cape
Gulf of St. Lawrence
Tignish
Miminegash
Alberton
O'Leary
Lady Slipper Dr.
PRINCE
Port Hill
21
Tyne Valley
Malpeque Bay
Egmont Bay
Miscouche
20
Summerside
19
Travellers Rest
Wilmot
Abram-Village
Bedeque Bay
New London Bay
Blue Heron Dr.
French River
Kensington
Cavendish
13
Green Gables
North Rustico Harbour
Brackley Beach
Covehead Bay
12
South Rustico
11
Stanhope Golf and Country Club
Dalvay-by-the-Sea
10
9
Prince Edward Island National Park
Charlottetown
1—8
QUEENS
Kinkora
Borden
14
Victoria-by-the-Sea
Blue Heron Drive
Cornwall
15
Fort Amherst Port Lajoie National Historic Site
Kings Byway
Hillsborough R.
Hillsborough Bridge
Mount Stewart
Pownal Bay
Mt. Mellick
16
Orwell Corner Historic Village
Orwell
17
Eldon
Lord Selkirk Pioneer Settlement
Wood Islands
Murray River
Murray Harbour
Montague
Cardigan
Kings Byway
KINGS
St. Peters
Naufrage
North Lake
Basin Head Fisheries Museum
18
Sauris
TO ILES DE LA MADELEINE
TO CARIBOU, NOVA SCOTIA
TO CAPE TORMENTINE
Northumberland Strait
KEY
Ferry
0
10 miles
0
15 km
N

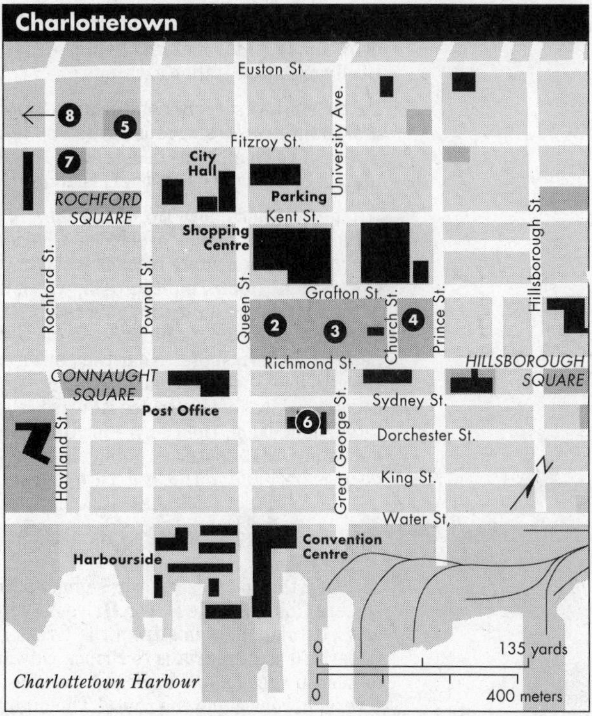

stored to its 1864 condition, and the legislative chamber are open to the public. Displays and a slide presentation portray the historic meeting. *Richmond St., tel. 902/566–7626. Admission free. Open July–Labor Day, daily 9–8; June and Labor Day–mid-Oct., daily 9–5; mid-Oct.–May, weekdays 9–5. Note: When provincial legislature is in session, certain rooms are closed to the public.*

4 Two churches near Province House are especially noteworthy. **St. Paul's Anglican Church** (east of Province House) was erected in 1747, making it the oldest Protestant church on the island. Its baptismal register includes the name of Margaret Gordon, sweetheart of author Thomas Carlyle and heroine of his masterpiece *Sartor Resartus*.

5 **St. James Presbyterian Church,** better known as "the kirk," has impressive stained-glass windows and relics from the island of Iona, one of the earliest Christian sites in Scotland. A block of granite resting on a marble slab embedded in the north wall of the kirk came from St. Mary's Cathedral on Iona. An intriguing legend involves the church. On the day when the ship *Fairy Queen* went down in Northumberland Strait in 1853, the kirk was empty, but the kirk's bell, so the story goes, was heard to toll many times. A townsman who heard it claimed that he saw three barefoot women disappear through the locked doors of the kirk. Later it was learned that three female members of the congregation had been lost in the wreck.

6 South of Province House stands **St. Dunstan's Basilica** (Great George St.), the seat of the Roman Catholic diocese in the prov-

ince. Not only is it one of the largest edifices of its kind in eastern Canada, but it contains an impressive altar, and many beautifully executed Italian carvings.

7 In the northwest corner of Rochford Square is **St. Peter's Cathedral,** built in 1879 and consecrated by the Lord Bishop of Nova Scotia. The chapel was designed in 1888 by W.C. Harris, with murals by his famous brother, islander Robert Harris.

At the southernmost tip of the city is the beautiful 40-acre
8 **Victoria Park,** which overlooks Charlottetown Harbor. Set on a hill between white birches is the impressive white colonial **Government House,** built in 1835, which is the official residence of the province's lieutenant governors. The cannons of **Fort Edward,** built in 1805 to defend the harbor mouth, still line the park's southern shore. Near the park's entrance **Beaconsfield,** the gracious Victorian mansion designed by W. C. Harris, contains the offices of the Prince Edward Island Museum and Heritage Foundation, the Centre for Genealogical Research, and a bookstore that features publications about the island. *Park open year-round, daily sunrise to sunset.*

Blue Heron Drive

Circling the island's center segment and roughly outlining Queens County, Blue Heron Drive is 190 kilometers (114 miles) long. It takes its name from the Great Blue Heron, a stately waterbird that migrates to Prince Edward Island each spring to nest in the shallow bays and marshes; you are likely to see several herons along the route. The highway marker is a white square with a blue border and a blue heron in the center.

From Charlottetown, Blue Heron Drive winds through farmland to the North Shore fishing villages, spectacular beaches of Prince Edward Island National Park and the Cabot Provincial Park, through Anne of Green Gables country, and along the south shore with its red sandstone seascapes and historic sites.

Arriving and Departing by Car and Ferry

By Car From Charlottetown, take 15 north to Route 6 at Cavendish, then follow the blue heron sign counterclockwise onto Route 19.

By Ferry The ferry service from Cape Tormentine, New Brunswick, docks at Borden, Prince Edward Island. From the ferry dock, turn west onto Route 10 to join the drive at Reads Corner. The service from Cape Tormentine takes about 45 minutes. There are numerous daily crossings from 6:30 AM to 1:30 AM.

Exploring Blue Heron Drive

Numbers in the margin correspond with points of interest on the Prince Edward Island map.

9 **Prince Edward Island National Park** stretches for about 40 kilometers (25 miles) along the north shore of the island on the Gulf of St. Lawrence. The jagged coast is softened by sandbars and fine beaches. Follow the **Gulf Shore Road** for views of the beaches and cliffs—especially Orby Head—and walks in the dunes. The park **Visitor Centre** in Cavendish provides a slide presentation and exhibits. The park has a few primitive

campsites. *24 km (15 mi) north of Charlottetown, tel. 902/672-2211. Park open daily; Visitor Centre open June–Oct., daily 9–8.*

10 At the eastern end of the park is **Dalvay-by-the-Sea,** built in the 1890s as a summer home by an oil magnate. The park now operates the house as a resort lodge (*see* Lodging, below).

Time Out The dining room of **Dalvay-by-the-Sea** (tel. 902/672–2048) specializes in fresh seafood, homegrown vegetables, and an old tradition: a dessert called Blueberry Grunt.

11 A few kilometers west of Dalvay, off Route 6, along beautiful Covehead Bay, is the **Stanhope Golf and Country Club.** Its course is among the island's longest, most challenging, and most scenic.

12 Moving westward, you pass Brackley Beach and then come to **South Rustico,** on Route 243. The town sits on a peninsula on Rustico Bay, its miniature collection of Victorian houses gathered around a dainty church. One of Canada's first cooperative banks—now a national historic site and museum—was founded here.

13 Continue along Gulf Shore Drive and follow the signs to **Green Gables,** the little green and white house where Lucy Maud Montgomery lived with her grandparents after the death of her parents. In 1908 she published *Anne of Green Gables,* one of the most popular children's books ever written. It is the story of a young orphan girl adopted by a strict but kindly brother and sister who live on a farm called Green Gables on the outskirts of Avonlea, Prince Edward Island. Once described by Mark Twain as "the sweetest creation of child life ever written," this story has so caught the imagination of its readers that thousands visit Green Gables every summer from as far away as Japan. The house is organized to reflect the story. *Near Cavendish, in Prince Edward Island National Park, tel. 902/963–2675. Open May–June 23, daily 9–5; June 24–Sept.1, daily 9–8; Sept. 2–Nov. 1, daily 9–5. Off-season tours are available through Parks and People Cooperative Association (tel. 902/894–4246).*

14 On the other side of the island is **Victoria-by-the-Sea,** a small fishing port that also harbors antiques and handicrafts shops and live summer theater in the historic Victoria Playhouse.

15 Completing the circle of Queens County, you can visit **Fort Amherst Port Lajoie National Historic Site,** opposite Charlottetown, the site of the French fort at Port La Joie, established in 1720. The British renamed it Fort Amherst later in the 18th century. *32 km (20 mi) south of Charlottetown on Rte. 19 at Rocky Point, tel. 902/675–2220. Open June–Labor Day, daily 10–6.*

Kings Byway

The Kings Byway is named after Kings County, which constitutes the eastern end of the province. The drive is 375 kilometers (225 miles) long and passes historic areas, farming regions, and scenic shore points.

Arriving and Departing by Car and Ferry

By Car From Charlottetown, take Route 1 east across Hillsborough Bridge and follow the purple crown Kings Byway signs. From Cavendish and the National Park area, take Route 6 east and follow Kings Byway in a clockwise direction.

By Ferry The ferry from Caribou, Nova Scotia, to Wood Islands, Prince Edward Island, lands visitors about 1.5 kilometers (1 mile) from Kings Byway. Turn east or west at Wood Islands. There are numerous daily sailings from May to mid-December. (*See* Arriving and Departing by Ferry in Essential Information, above.)

Exploring Kings Byway

Numbers in the margin correspond with points of interest on the Prince Edward Island map.

The Kings Byway heads south from Charlottetown through agricultural country.

16 **The Orwell Corner Historic Village** re-creates a 19th-century rural settlement in the form of a living farm museum. The historic site contains a combined store and post office, a school, a church, a farmhouse, and barns. Farming is done by 19th-century methods. *Tel. 902/651–2013. Open mid-May–mid-Oct. Hours vary; call before visiting. Admission: $2.50 (includes guided tour).*

17 **Lord Selkirk Pioneer Settlement,** in Lord Selkirk Provincial Park, is a re-creation of an early 19th-century settlement of Scots Highlanders who had lost their lands in the enclosure movement. Financed by Thomas Douglas, Lord Selkirk, the crofters underwent great privations before they finally established a thriving community in Canada. A small crafts shop sells replicas of the settlers' handiwork. *10 km (6 mi) south of Orwell on Rte. 1, Eldon, tel. 902/659–2427. Open late-June–early-Sept., daily 8–6. Admission: $2.50.*

18 The **Basin Head Fisheries Museum** overlooks the Gulf of St. Lawrence and is surrounded by rolling sand dunes where you can experience the "singing sands" (so-called because the sand squeaks loudly when you walk on it). The museum was established in 1973 to preserve the heritage of the island's inshore fishermen. Equipment, artifacts, and exhibits illustrate how their small boats were used and the types of fish they caught. The displays include a boat shed, an aquarium, a smokehouse, a fish-box factory, and fishermen's sheds. *Box 248, Souris, PEI C0A 2B0, tel. 902/357–2966. Admission: $2.50 adults, children under 12 free. Open mid-June–Labor Day, daily 9–5; Labor Day–mid-Sept., weekdays 9–5.*

Lady Slipper Drive

Taking its name from the delicate Lady Slipper Orchid, which is the province's official flower, this drive swoops past the red sandstone cliffs and silver sand dunes and rolls through the meadows of the narrow indented western end of the island. The region encircled by the drive is made up of small and very old villages (with the exception of Summerside, the largest Prince Edward Island community designated as a town, and second in size to Charlottetown), still adhering to a more traditional way of life. This western region is the home of the Island's Acadians, descendants of the original French settlers. In addition to the strong Acadian presence, Micmac Indians, farms, Irish moss, and oysters are pronounced influences in the region.

Arriving and Departing by Car

From Charlottetown, take Route 2 to Summerside and continue to the tiny village of Traveller's Rest. From there follow the red signs showing the silhouette of a lady slipper orchid.

Exploring Lady Slipper Drive

Numbers in the margin correspond with points of interest on the Prince Edward Island map.

Begin your tour at the Lady Slipper Visitor Information Center (tel. 902/436–2511) at **Wilmot,** on Route 1A, 2 kilometers (1¼ miles) east of Summerside. The staff at the information center can answer questions and help with reservations. Pro-
19 ceed to **Summerside,** the area's chief community and the center of this rich agricultural area. The eight-day Summerside Lobster Carnival is held every July. Actually a combination fair and festival, the carnival has exhibits of livestock, agriculture, and handicrafts, as well as parades; beauty contests; harness racing; a midway; and the regional specialty, lobster suppers.

From Summerside, follow the Lady Slipper signs on Route 1A
20 to St. Eleanors, then turn west on Route 2 to **Miscouche** and the **Acadian Museum of Prince Edward Island.** The artifacts in its collection predate the 19th century and include household and farm implements, as well as other domestic items. The red stone monument behind the museum stands over a collective Acadian grave transferred from River Platte in 1839. *Box 159, Miscouche, C0B 1T0. tel. 902/436–4017. Admission: $2 adults, $1 children 6–17. Open early Sept.–mid-June, weekdays 8–4; mid-June–Aug., weekdays 9:30–5, Sun. 1–5.*

About 35 kilometers (22 miles) north and west of Summerside
21 along the drive, in **Port Hill**, you'll find the Green Park Shipbuilding Museum and Historic House. Originally the home of James Yeo, Jr., this neo-classical 19th-century mansion, restored and open to visitors, is topped by a cupola, from which Yeo observed his nearby shipyard through a spyglass. The modern museum building on the site details the history of the shipbuilder's craft. *Rte. 12, Port Hill, tel. 902/831–2206. Admission: $2.50. Open mid-June–Labor Day, daily 9–5.*

Shopping

Handcrafted items have been valued by Prince Edward Island inhabitants since colonial days. The island's craftspeople excel at jewelry making, wood carving, pottery, enameling, leatherwork, quilting, and weaving, to name a few of the crafts. Full information on outlets and types of crafts is provided by the **PEI Craftsmen's Council, Inc.** (156 Richmond St., Box 1573, Charlottetown, PEI C1A 1H9, tel. 902/892–5152) or from the **PEI Visitors Information Centre** (*see* Important Addresses and Numbers in Essential Information, above). Shopping malls are open Monday–Saturday, 10–10. Other stores throughout the province are generally open 9–5 or 5:30, with many staying open until 9 on Friday. Country stores generally open earlier and close later.

The **Island Craft Shop** (156 Richmond St., Charlottetown) has a wide selection of island crafts and is open July and August, Monday–Saturday 9–8, rest of the year, Monday–Saturday 9–5.

Along Lady Slipper Drive look for turned bird's-eye maple-wood products at the **Leavitts' Maple Tree Craft Shop** (Alberton), which is open Monday–Saturday 8–5.

Dining

Plain, wholesome, home-cooked fare is a matter of course on Prince Edward Island. The service is friendly—though a little pokey at times—and the setting is informal everywhere but Charlottetown. Seafood is superb anywhere on the island, with top honors being given to lobster and any dish using local produce. Unless noted, there is no need to make a reservation or to wear a jacket and tie.

The lobster supper, an island tradition, should be sought out when touring the North Shore. Popular places for lobster suppers are New London, New Glasgow, St. Ann's Church in Hope River, Fisherman's Wharf in North Rustico, and Stanhope Beach Lodge.

Highly recommended restaurants in each price category are indicated by a star ★.

Category	Cost*
Very Expensive	over $35
Expensive	$25–$35
Moderate	$15–$24
Inexpensive	under $15

**per person, excluding drinks, service, and 10% sales tax*

Brackley Beach
Expensive
★

Shaw's Hotel and Cottages. This 1790s hotel offers fine home cooking in an elegant, family-oriented country environment. Lobster is served twice weekly, and the grand Sunday night buffets draw people from near and far to sample dishes including fresh salmon, seafood casserole, home-baked breads, and a variety of popular desserts, such as cheesecake and fresh berries in season. *Rte. 15, tel. 902/672–2022. Reservations advised. AE, MC, V. Closed Oct.–May and lunch.*

Cavendish
Inexpensive

Fiddles 'n Vittles. Here's a great place to take the family for dinner. Lively, friendly, and ocean rustic, with fishnets decorating the dining room, the restaurant specializes in fresh-fried fish and seafood. *Bay Vista Motor Inn, RR1, Breadalbane, tel. 902/963–3003. AE, DC, MC, V. Closed mid-Sept.–mid-June.*

Charlottetown
Very Expensive
★

The Griffon Room. This cozy dining room of the Dundee Arms Motel and Inn has a working fireplace and is filled with antiques, copper, and brass. In this comfortable elegance you can enjoy all-natural French-Continental cuisine; the restaurant prides itself in using no artificial additives or preservatives and on cooking only with fresh and natural ingredients. Fresh seafood is served year-round, with fresh salmon, scallops, and crab available all winter. Specialties include rack of lamb, Chateaubriand, and poached or grilled fillet of salmon in a light lime-dill sauce. *Dundee Arms Motel and Inn, 200 Pownal St., tel. 902/892-2496. AE, MC, V.*

Expensive ★ **Claddagh Room Restaurant.** You'll find some of the best seafood in Charlottetown at the Claddagh Room. The "Galway Bay Delight," one of the Irish owner's specialties, is a savory combination of fresh scallops and shrimp sautéed with onions and mushrooms, flambéed in Irish Mist, and doused with fresh cream. A pub upstairs features live Irish entertainment every night in summer and on weekends in winter. *131 Sydney St., tel. 902/892-9661. AE, DC, MC, V.*

Moderate **Queen Street Cafe.** Soft recordings of the music of Ella Fitzgerald and Louis Armstrong add to the intimacy of this small restaurant. The changing menu of only home-cooked food features whatever ingredients are fresh and in season. Chicken Kiev, seafood salad with mustard vinaigrette, and rum-raisin tart are among the favorites, and the seafood chowder is rumored to be the best on the island. *52 Queen St., tel. 902/566-5520. DC, MC, V.*

Cornwall
Moderate **Bonnie Brae.** Welcoming and comfortable, this restaurant offers fresh seafood and steaks, as well as Swiss specialties created by the Swiss owner/chef. The nightly all-you-can-eat lobster buffet in summer is guarnateed to satisfy any appetite—but leave room for the chef's light European desserts. *Centennial Rd., off Trans-Canada Hwy., tel. 902/566-2241. AE, DC, MC, V.*

Grand Tracadie
Expensive **Dalvay-by-the-Sea.** Choose a table by the island-stone fireplace or dine with a lake view on the enclosed terrace. The menu of this elegant Victorian dining room includes island lobster, curried scallops, poached halibut, peppercorn steak, and filet mignon—all served with fresh vegetables. Desserts are baked on the premises by the restaurant's pastry chef; "Blueberry Grunt," a sweet dumpling with blueberry sauce, is the Dalvay's own traditional specialty dessert and should not be missed. *Rte. 6, near Dalvay Beach, tel. 902/672-2048. Reservations advised. AE, MC, V.*

Kingsboro
Expensive **Seabreeze Motel.** People come from miles away for the seafood chowder at this motel restaurant. From lone travelers to families with children, all can relax in the down-home country environment over fried clams; steak; a lobster roll; or the Sunday buffet, with ham, turkey, seafood casserole, scalloped potatoes, and more. The fresh fruit pies, made with seasonal fruits, and the coconut-cream pie are too tempting to resist. *Hwy. 16, tel. 902/357-2371. AE, MC, V.*

Lodging

Prince Edward Island offers a variety of accommodations, from hotels, motels, cottages, and lodges, to farms that take guests. Lodgings on the north coast in summer should be booked early. Check the free *PEI Visitor Guide* (Department of Tourism, Box 940, Charlottetown, PEI, C1A 7M5) for a complete listing.

Highly recommended lodgings in each price category are indicated by a star ★.

Category	Cost*
Very Expensive	over $75
Expensive	$55–$75
Moderate	$40–$54
Inexpensive	under $40

**All prices are for a standard double room, excluding 10% provincial sales tax.*

Brackley Beach
Very Expensive
★ **Shaw's Hotel and Cottages.** Each room is unique in this 1790s hotel, with antique furnishings, floral-print wallpapers, and hardwood floors. Half of the cottages have fireplaces. Here you'll find comfortable country elegance. Guests can choose to include in their room rate a home-cooked breakfast and dinner in the Shaw's dining room (*see* Dining, above). *Rte. 15, C0A 2H0, tel. 902/672–2022. 40 units, including 18 cottages and 2 suites. Facilities: cocktail bar; sailboats, windsurfing, beach nearby. AE, MC, V. Closed late-Sept.–May.*

Cavendish
Expensive
Bay Vista Motor Inn. This clean, friendly motel caters to families. Parents can sit on the outdoor deck and admire the New London Bay view, while keeping an eye on their children in the motel's large playground. Almost all of the rooms have views of the bay. The Fiddles 'n Vittles restaurant is a great place to eat with the family (*see* Dining, above). *RR 1, Breadalbane, C0A 2H0, tel. 902/963–2225; in winter, RR 1, North Wiltshire, C0A 1Y0, tel. 902/675–3238. 30 units, including 2 motel efficiencies. Facilities: restaurant, outdoor heated pool, playground; boating, deep-sea fishing, golf nearby. AE, MC, V. Closed late-Sept.–mid-June.*

Charlottetown
Very Expensive
Best Western Machlauchlan's Motel. This is one of the many good motels in the Best Western motel chain. Two convenient apartment suites have a bedroom, living room, kitchen, and bathroom. *238 Grafton St., C1A 1L5, tel. 902/892–2461. 149 units, including 2 suites. Facilities: dining room, lounge, indoor pool, sauna, Jacuzzi; laundry facilities nearby. AE, DC, MC, V.*

★ **The Charlottetown.** This classic five-story red-brick hotel with white pillars and a circular driveway is just two blocks from the center of Charlottetown. Recently redecorated, the rooms and public areas offer the latest amenities while retaining the hotel's classic, old-fashioned stature, with well-detailed, antique-reproduction furnishings. *Kent and Pownal Sts., Box 159, C1A 7K4, tel. 902/894–7371. 109 rooms, including 2 suites. Facilities: dining room, lounge with entertainment, room service, meeting rooms, indoor pool, sauna, whirlpool, parking. AE, DC, MC, V.*

Dundee Arms Motel and Inn. Depending on your mood, you can choose to stay in either a 1960s motel or a 1904 inn. The motel is simple, modern, and neat; the inn is homey and furnished with brass and antiques. The Griffon Room, the inn's dining room, serves internationally acclaimed cuisine (*see* Dining, above). Continental breakfast is included in motel and inn rates. *200 Pownal St., C1A 3W8, tel. 902/892–2496. 18 rooms, including 2 suites. Facilities: restaurant, pub. AE, MC, V.*

Inn on the Hill. This inn is comfortable and convenient: Rooms are contemporary and spacious, and the inn is near the center of Charlottetown, one block from the train station. *150 Euston St., Box 1720, C1A 7N4, tel. 902/894–8572. 48 units, including 8 suites. Facilities: dining room, lounge, parking. AE, DC, MC, V.*

★ **Prince Edward Hotel and Convention Centre.** Two-thirds of this 10-story hotel's rooms overlook the newly developed Charlottetown waterfront. Part of the Canadian Pacific chain of hotels and resorts, the Prince Edward has all the comforts and luxuries one needs in a hotel and conference center—from Jacuzzis in some suites to a grand ballroom. Guest rooms are modern and decorated in warm pastels. The lobby is a bright, open, two-story atrium complete with a waterfall above the front desk. *18 Queen St., Box 2170, C1A 8B9, tel. 902/566–2222 or 800/828–7447. 211 rooms, including 33 suites. Facilities: 3 restaurants, lounge with nightly entertainment, heated indoor pool, whirlpool, sauna, Nautilus equipment; golf, tennis, waterskiing, horseback riding nearby. AE, DC, MC, V.*

Inexpensive

Court Bed & Breakfast. In a residential area 2 kilometers (1.2 miles) from the center of town, this two-story townhouse with a welcoming red door has been a B&B for five years. This is a place for people who don't want to have to pay for a lot of extra amenities and fancy facilities that they don't use. For truly reasonable rates, you get a large, simple, comfortable room and a full, hearty breakfast—including ham, eggs, bacon, muffins, and fresh fruit in season. And after a talk during breakfast with the owner (a 30-year Charlottetown resident), you'll be the best-informed tourist in town. *68 Hutchinson Ct., tel. 902/894–5871. 2 rooms with shared bath. No credit cards. Closed early Sept.–May 1.*

Grand Tracadie
Very Expensive

★ **Dalvay-by-the-Sea.** Just within the borders of the Prince Edward Island National Park, this Victorian house was built in 1896 as a private summer home. Now a popular inn (and a highly acclaimed restaurant), Dalvay-by-the-Sea offers elegant but homey rooms furnished with original and reproduction antiques. Guests can sip drinks or tea on the porch while admiring the inn's gardens, Dalvay Lake, or the dunes of the nearby beach. Breakfasts and dinners in the dining room (included in the room rates) are exceptional (*see* Dining, above). *Rte. 6, near Dalvay Beach, Box 8, C0A 1P0; tel. 902/672–2048, in winter 902/672–2546. 31 rooms in main house and 2 cottages. Facilities: restaurant, lounge, 2 tennis courts, driving range, canoes, rowboats, windsurfing. AE, MC, V. Closed mid-Sept.–mid-June.*

Montague
Moderate

Lobster Shanty North. With roses growing outside the windows of its weathered-wood exterior, and old fishnets draped around the barn-board walls of the dining room, this hotel is truly charming. All of the rooms have picture windows and open onto a deck overlooking the wandering Montague River. *Main St., Box 158, C0A 1R0, tel. 902/838–2463, 11 rooms. Facilities: restaurant, lounge; golf, clam digging, swimming nearby. AE, MC, V.*

North Rustico
Moderate

St. Lawrence Motel. Families can stay comfortably here in one-, two-, or three-bedroom housekeeping units. The motel is in a pleasant spot—inside the Prince Edward Island National Park overlooking the Gulf of St. Lawrence. *Hunter River RR2, C0A 1N0, tel. 902/963–2053; in winter: 125 Donahue Rd., North*

Granby, CT 06060, tel. 203/653–2706. 15 units. Facilities: recreation room, golf range; deep-sea fishing and beach nearby. MC, V. Closed mid-Oct.–mid-May.

O'Leary *Expensive–Very Expensive* **Rodd's Mill River Resort and Conference Center.** With activities ranging from night skiing and tobogganing to golfing, this is truly an all-season resort. With so much to do here, don't forget to sightsee. Ask about family-package weekends, offered year-round. *Box 399, C0B 1V0, tel. 902/859–3555; 80 rooms, including 3 suites. Facilities: dining room, 2 bars, 2 heated indoor pools, golf course, pro shop, tennis court, 2 squash courts, fitness center with whirlpool and sauna, games room, gift shop, parking, canoeing, windsurfing, bike rental, lighted ice-skating rink, toboggan run, cross-country skiing. AE, DC, MC, V. Closed Nov.–early Dec., Apr.*

Summerside *Expensive* **Best Western Linkletter Inn.** Another of the Best Western chain, this motel has standard modern comforts and is conveniently located within walking distance of Summerside's shops and beaches. *311 Market St., C1N 1K8, tel. 902/436–2157. 107 rooms, including 2 suites. Facilities: restaurant, lounge, parking; golf, tennis, beach nearby. AE, D, DC, MC, V.*

Moderate–Expensive **Quality Inn Garden of the Gulf.** Close to downtown Summerside, this motel is a clean and convenient place to stay. The 9-hole golf course on the property slopes to Bedeque Bay. *618 Water St. E, C1N 2V5, tel. 902/436–2295. 83 rooms, including 6 suites. Facilities: restaurant, coffee shop, lounge, heated outdoor pool, 9-hole golf course. AE, DC, MC, V.*

Moderate **Glade Motor Inn & Cottages.** Conveniently located 10 minutes from the Borden Ferry terminal, this property has comfortable, generic motel rooms, one- and two-bedroom cottages, and one four-bedroom "house" that can accommodate up to eight people. What's different about the place is that it is set on a 300-acre farm, with horseback riding and nature trails. Kids get free rides in the corral. *Box 1387, C1N 4K2, tel. 902/436–5564. 33 units. Facilities: restaurant, lounge, heated outdoor pool, horseback riding, nature trails. AE, MC, V. Closed late-Sept.–mid-June.*

The Arts

The highlights of the province's summer season are the productions of the **Charlottetown Festival,** which take place from June through October at the Confederation Centre of the Arts. Two full-scale musicals play in repertory six nights a week, along with the perennial favorite, *Anne of Green Gables*. Special art exhibitions are presented in the Centre's art gallery, one of Canada's premiere museums. The permanent collection features the country's largest assemblage of paintings by Robert Harris (1848–1919), Canada's foremost portrait artist. For information and tickets to the festival, write: Confederation Centre of the Arts, Box 848, Charlottetown, PEI, C1A 7L9.

14 New Brunswick

Introduction

by Colleen Thompson

Not long ago, at dawn on the bank of the Miramichi River, I stood on a cottage veranda with a resident of Blackville, watching the mirror surface of the water ripple as a run of shad arrowed toward the sea. With a coal-red glory rarely equaled anywhere else, the sky blazed and the river streamed toward the sun like a lava flow, bubbled occasionally by a jumping salmon.

"Fish won't be biting this early."

The comment was laconic but it had the conviction of being in the very best possible place on earth.

New Brunswick is where the great Canadian forest, sliced by sweeping river valleys and modern highways, meets the sea. It's an old place in New World terms, and the remains of a turbulent past are still in evidence in some of its quiet nooks. Near Moncton, for instance, bees gather nectar and wild strawberries perfume the air of the grassy slopes of Fort Beausejour, where one of the last minor battles for possession of Acadia took place—the English finally overcoming the French. The dual heritage of New Brunswick (35% of its population is Acadian French) provides added spice. Within a 400-kilometer (250-mile) drive from north to south, you can vacation in both Acadian and Loyalist regions, making New Brunswick a bargain—two vacations for the price of one.

More than half the province is surrounded by coastline—the rest nestles into Québec and Maine, creating slightly schizophrenic attitudes in border towns. The dramatic Bay of Fundy, which has the highest tides in the world, sweeps up the coast of Maine, around the enchanting Fundy Isles at the southern tip of New Brunswick and on up the province's rough and intriguing south coast. To the north and east, the gentle, warm Gulf Stream washes quiet beaches.

For years this Cinderella province has been virtually ignored by tourists who whiz through to better known Atlantic destinations. New Brunswick's residents can't seem to decide whether this makes them unhappy. Money is important in the economically depressed maritime area where younger generations have traditionally left home for higher paying jobs in Ontario and "The West." But no one wishes to lose the special characteristics of this still unspoiled province by the sea.

This attitude is a blessing in disguise to motorists who leave major highways to explore 2,240 kilometers (1,400 miles) of spectacular seacoast, pure inland streams, pretty towns and historical cities. The custom of hospitality is so much a part of New Brunswick nature that tourists are perceived more as welcome visitors than paying guests. Even cities often retain a bit of naiveté. It makes for a charming vacation but don't be deceived by ingenuous attitudes. Most residents are products of excellent school and university systems, generally travel widely, live in modern cities and are well versed in world affairs.

New Brunswick is still largely unsettled—85 percent of the province is forested lands. Inhabitants have chosen the easily accessible area around rivers, ocean, and lakes, leaving most of the interior to the pulp companies. In fact, the view from a plane will make you think that New Brunswick is still an unspoiled wilderness with little sign of civilization. But its towns and cities, some of the first to be founded on the continent, have emerged through centuries as cultured centers of learning and government, their respect for the past as acute as their awareness of the future.

Essential Information

Important Addresses and Numbers

Tourist Information **Tourism New Brunswick** (Box 12345, Fredericton E3B 5C3, tel. 506/453–2377 or 800/561–0123; in New Brunswick, 800/442–4422) can provide information on the 15 provincial tourist bureaus and municipal information centers throughout the province. Also helpful are information services of major cities: **Fredericton** (tel. 506/452–9500); **Moncton** (tel. 506/853–3333); and **Saint John** (tel. 506/658–2990).

Emergencies Dial 911 for medical emergencies and police.

Hospital **Dr. Everett Chalmers Hospital** (Priestman St., Fredericton, tel. 506/452–5400).

Arriving and Departing by Plane

Canadian Airlines International (tel. 800/426–7000) and **Air Canada** (tel. 800/776–3000) both have flights into Saint John, Fredericton, and Moncton. **Air Nova** and **Air Atlantic** are regional carriers that fly direct between Saint John and Boston.

Arriving and Departing by Car Ferry, Train, and Bus

By Car Ferry There are car ferries from Prince Edward Island and Nova Scotia. **Marine Atlantic** (tel. 902/794–7203) has a car-and-passenger ferry from Digby, Nova Scotia, which takes 2½ hours. For reservations in the United States, call 800/341–7981; in Maine, tel. 800/432–7344.

By Train Regular **Via Rail** passenger service from Moncton to Montréal and Halifax connects via ferry to Prince Edward Island and Newfoundland. The rail line does not pass through Fredericton, but buses take passengers from Fredericton Junction the last 30 miles to the city.

By Bus **SMT** (tel. 506/458–6009) within the province connects with most major bus lines.

Getting Around

By Car New Brunswick has an excellent highway system with numerous facilities. The only map you'll need is the free one given out at the tourist information centers listed above. Major entry points are at St. Stephen, Houlton, Edmundston, and Cape Tormentine from Prince Edward Island, and Aulac from Nova Scotia.

Guided Tours

Boat Tours **Fundy Isle Marine Enterprises** (tel. 506/529–3688) and **Romeo's Marine** in Shediac (tel. 506/532–6444) offer waterborne excursions. In the Caraquet and Fundy area there are numerous boat tour operators; request information from Tourism New Brunswick. On Deer Island or St. Andrews try **Cline Marine** (tel. 506/747–2287 or 506/529–4188).

In Fredericton **Pioneer Princess** (tel. 506/488–5588) embarks on riverboat tours and dinner cruises from the Lighthouse.

City Tours **Heritage Tour Guide Service** (856 George St., Fredericton E3B 1K7, tel. 506/459–5950) provides step-on guides for bus tours of Fredericton, and a walking guide is available at City Hall on Queen Street. **Calithumpians-Walking Guides** (tel. 506/459–1975) also offer tours of Fredericton.

Special-interest More than 240 species of seabirds nest on Grand Manan Island, and the island is a paradise for painters, nature photographers, and hikers, not to mention whale-watchers. Any of these activities can be arranged by calling **Tourism New Brunswick** at 800/561–0123. **Covered Bridge Bicycle Tours** (Box 693, Main Post Office, Saint John E2L 4B3, tel. 506/849–9028) offers bike tours.

Exploring New Brunswick

Orientation

Our exploration of New Brunswick is broken down into four areas: a tour of the city of Fredericton, a tour of the Saint John Valley ending at the city of Saint John, a tour of the Fundy Coast, and a jog north to the windswept Acadian Peninsula.

Highlights for First-time Visitors

Acadian Village, Grand Anse, Tour 4: Moncton and the Acadian Peninsula

Beaverbrook Art Gallery, Tour 1: Fredericton

Campobello Island, Tour 3: The Fundy Coast

Fundy National Park, Tour 3: The Fundy Coast

Kings Landing, Prince William, Tour 1: Fredericton

Kouchibouquac National Park, Acadian Peninsula, Tour 4: The Acadian Peninsula

Market Square and Market Slip, Saint John, Tour 2: Saint John River Valley

Moncton's Tidal Bore and Magnetic Hill, Tour 4: Moncton and the Acadian Peninsula

Tour 1: Fredericton

Numbers in the margin correspond with points of interest on the New Brunswick and Fredericton maps.

❶ The small inland city of **Fredericton** spreads itself on a broad point of land jutting into the Saint John River. Its predecessor, the early French settlement of Ste-Anne's Point, was established in 1642, during the reign of the French governor, Villebon, who made his headquarters at the junction of the Nashwaak and the Saint John rivers. Settled by Loyalists and named for Frederick, second son of George III, the city serves as the seat of government for New Brunswick's 710,900 residents. From the first town plan, the wealthy and scholarly Loyalists set out to create a gracious and beautiful place, and thus even before the establishment of the University of New Brunswick, in 1785, the town served as a center for "liberal arts and sciences."

Fredericton's streets are shaded by leafy plumes of ancient elms. Downtown Queen Street runs parallel with the river, and its blocks enclose historic sites and attractions. Most major highlights are within walking distance.

The **Military Compound** (including officers' quarters, parade grounds, guardhouse, and enlisted men's barracks) makes up two major Queen Street blocks. The buildings have been restored and are partly open to the public. Authentic redcoats stand guard and act as guides; in summer a changing-of-the-guard ceremony takes place at 11 and 7. *503 Queen St., tel. 506/453-3747. Admission free. Open June 15–Sept. 4, daily 10–5, Fri. 10–9. Closed Sept. 5–June 14.*

2 Officer's Quarters houses the **York-Sunbury Historical Museum,** displaying mementos of the past, including Indian artifacts (the local tribes were the Micmacs and the Malicetes) and replicas of early Acadian rooms, 19th-century Fredericton homes, and area history. It also contains the shellacked remains of one of Fredericton's legends, the puzzling Coleman Frog. This giant frog, allegedly discovered in nearby Killarney Lake by late hotelier Fred Coleman, supposedly weighed 42 pounds soaking wet at the time of its death (by a dynamite charge set by unorthodox fishermen). Coleman had the frog stuffed and displayed it for years in the lobby of his hotel. Take a look and judge for yourself—the frog just keeps on smiling. *Officer's Sq., Queen St., tel. 506/455-6041. Admission: $1 adults, 50¢ senior citizens and students, $2.50 family. Open May–Aug., Mon.–Sat. 10–6, Sun. 12–6; Sept.–Apr., Mon., Wed., Fri. 11–3, Sat. 12–4.*

Just a block or so east along the same street, at the intersection where Queen Street becomes Waterloo Row, you'll come to the
3 **Christ Church Cathedral,** one of Fredericton's prides. Completed in 1853, the gray stone building is an excellent example of decorated Gothic architecture and the first new cathedral foundation built on British soil since the Norman Conquest. Inside you'll see a clock known as "Big Ben's little brother," the test-run for London's famous timepiece, designed by Lord Grimthorpe.

The late Lord Beaverbrook, former New Brunswick resident and multimillionaire British peer and newspaper magnate, who began life as Max Aitken, showered gifts upon his native
4 province. Near the cathedral you'll find the **Beaverbrook Art Gallery,** displaying works by many of New Brunswick's noted artists. Salvador Dali's gigantic canvas *Santiago el Grande,* bought especially for the gallery's opening in 1959 by Beaverbrook's friend, Sir James Dunn, also a New Brunswick native, is worth more than a passing glance. There are also canvases by Reynolds, Turner, Hogarth, Gainsborough, the Cana-

New Brunswick

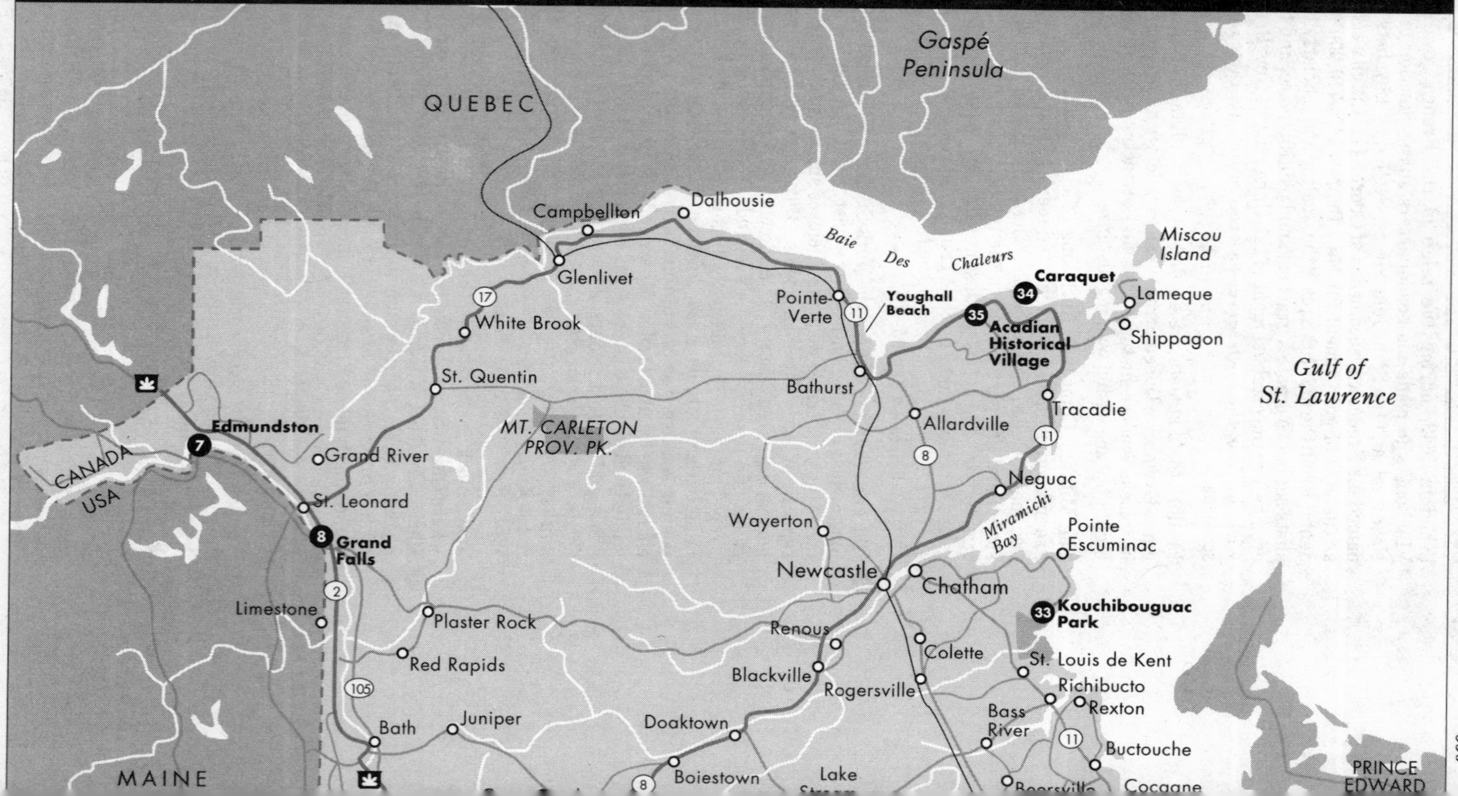

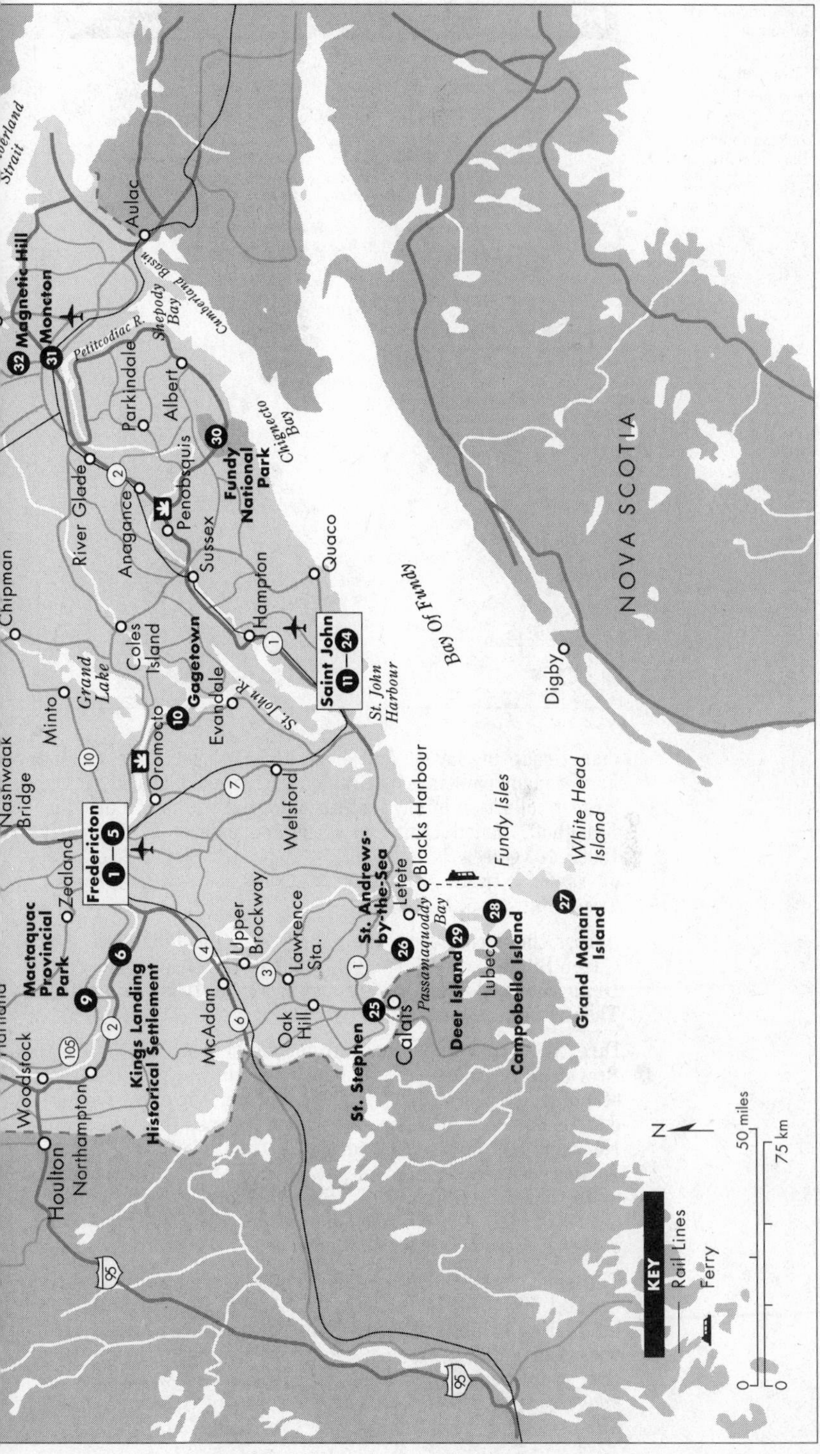
Strait
Aulac
Magnetic Hill
Moncton
Cumberland Basin
Petitcodiac R.
Shepody Bay
Parkindale
Albert
Chignecto Bay
Fundy National Park
River Glade
Anagance
Penobsquis
Sussex
Chipman
Quaco
Hampton
Coles Island
Grand Lake
Minto
Saint John
11—24
St. John Harbour
Bay Of Fundy
Gagetown
Evandale
St. John R.
Oromocto
Nashwaak Bridge
Fredericton
1—5
Welsford
NOVA SCOTIA
Digby
Zealand
Mactaquac Provincial Park
Kings Landing Historical Settlement
Upper Brockway
Lawrence Sta.
McAdam
Oak Hill
St. Andrews-by-the-Sea
Letete
Blacks Harbour
Passamaquoddy Bay
Fundy Isles
White Head Island
Deer Island
Lubec
Campobello Island
Grand Manan Island
St. Stephen
Calais
Woodstock
Northampton
Houlton
KEY
Rail Lines
Ferry
N
50 miles
75 km
0
0

Beaverbrook Art Gallery, **4**
Christ Church Cathedral, **3**
Provincial Legislature, **5**
York Sunbury Historical Museum, **2**

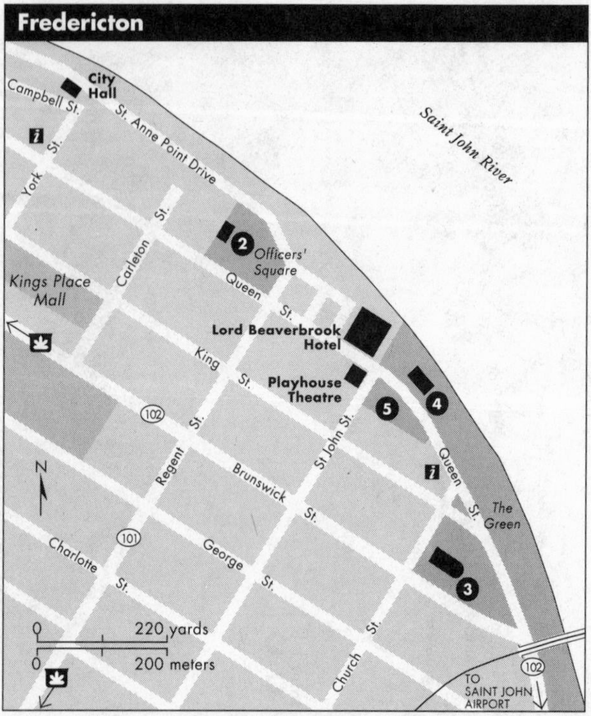

dian Group of Seven, and even Andy Warhol. The gallery houses many paintings by Graham Sutherland and also has the largest collection in any institution of the works of Cornelius Krieghoff, famed Canadian landscape painter of the early 1800s. *703 Queen St., tel. 506/458–8545. Admission: $3 adults, $2 senior citizens, $1 students. Open Sun.–Mon. noon–5, Tues.–Sat. 10–5.*

Across the corner from the gallery sits **The Playhouse** (686 Queen St., tel. 506/458–8344), a gift of the Beaverbrook and Dunn Foundation to the city and province. It is the home of Theatre New Brunswick.

Directly across the street from the gallery is the 1880
5 **Provincial Legislature.** In its legislative library, past the freestanding spiral staircase, you'll find a rare copy of the Domesday Book, the first census ever commissioned (by William of Normandy in 1087—this edition is from 1783) and a four-volume 1834 set of the priceless king-size Audubon bird books, more than 3 feet high, containing 435 hand-colored pictures. *Queen St., tel. 506/453–2338. Admission free. Open weekdays 8:15–5. Closed Dec. 24–26, Jan. 1.*

The small **National Exhibition Center** (Queen and Carleton Sts., tel. 506/453–3747) often has excellent displays of local art or interesting exhibits of other types. Upstairs, the **New Brunswick Sports Hall of Fame** might surprise you with the scope of area sportspeople. *503 Queen St., tel. 506/453–3747. Admission free. Open Sept.–Apr., weekdays noon–4:30, Sat. 10–5, Sun. 1–5; May–Aug., daily 10–5. Closed Dec. 25, Jan. 1.*

Continue east on Waterloo Row, turn south at University Avenue, and you'll arrive at the **University of New Brunswick** campus. Be prepared to climb—the buildings are scattered over a fairly steep hill. Established in 1783, and thus ancient by Canadian standards, it was originally called the College of New Brunswick, and later Kings College.

Tour 2: The Saint John River Valley to Saint John

Numbers in the margin correspond with points of interest on the New Brunswick map.

To understand New Brunswick's background and history, visit
6 **Kings Landing,** located about 23 miles west of Fredericton on the Trans-Canada Highway. This reconstructed village—55 buildings, including homes, inn, forge, store, church, school, working farms, and sawmill—illustrates life in the central Saint John River Valley between 1790 and 1870. Winding country lanes, creaking wagons, old houses, and freshly baked bread pull you back a century or more. The costumed staff is friendly and informative. The Tap Room of Kings Head Inn is a congenial spot to try a draft of cold beer or a mug of frosty cider; the restaurant upstairs serves tasty, old-fashioned traveler's fare. After lunch you can head for the barn that houses the Kings Theatre, which mounts light-hearted entertainment from "mellerdrama" to a humorous take-off on Chekhov. *Box 522, Fredericton, tel. 506/363–5805. Admission: $7 adults, $5 senior citizens, $4 students, $14 family. Open June, Labor Day–mid-Oct., daily 10–5; July–Aug., daily 10–6.*

The Saint John River forms 75 miles of the border with Maine and rolls down to the city of Saint John, New Brunswick's largest and Canada's oldest city. Gentle hills of rich farmland and the blue sweep of the water make this a pretty drive. The Trans-Canada Highway (Highway 2) follows the banks of the river for most of its winding, 250-mile course.

At the northern end of the valley, near the border with Québec, you will find yourself in the mythical Republic of Madawaska. In the early 1800s the narrow wedge of land was coveted by Québec on one side and New Brunswick on the other; the United States claimed it as well. Seeking to retain it for New Brunswick, Governor Sir Thomas Carleton found it easy to settle with Québec. He rolled dice all night with the governor of North America at Québec, who happened to be his brother. Sir Thomas won at dawn—by one point. Settling with the Americans was more difficult. The border had always been disputed, and even the lumbermen engaged in combat. Finally, in 1842, the British flag was hoisted over Madawaska county. One old timer, tired of being asked to which country he belonged, replied, "I am a citizen of the Republic of Madawaska." So began the republic, which exists today with its own flag (an independent eagle on a field of white) and a coat of arms.

7 **Edmundston,** the unofficial capital of Madawaska, has always depended on the wealth of the deep forest around it. Even today, Edmundston looks to the Fraser Company paper mill as the major source of employment in town. It was in these woods that the legend of Paul Bunyan was born, when the feats of a strong young Madawaskan were embroidered. Tales spread to Maine and even to the west coast. The Foire Brayonne festival

(which includes lumberjack competitions, folk dancing, handcraft exhibits, and pancake-eating contests) is a popular event, held annually, during the last week of July. In winter the whole province enjoys the slopes of Mt. Farlagne.

8 About 50 kilometers (30 miles) downriver, at **Grand Falls,** the Saint John throws itself over a high cliff, squeezes through a narrow rocky gorge, and emerges as a wider river. The result is a magnificent cascade, whose force has worn strange round wells in the rocky bed, some 16 feet in circumference and 30 feet deep. Take the Gorge Walk ($2 charge) where you'll see the holes and the magnificent stream up close. According to Indian legend, a young maiden named Malabeam led her Iroquois captors to their deaths over the foaming cataract rather than guide them to her village. When enough old boats are available during the town's annual Potato Blossom Festival, Malabeam's courage is commemorated by sending flower-filled crafts over the falls. Local history is depicted at the **Brand Falls Historical Museum.** *209 Sheriff St., tel. 506/473–3667. Admission free. Open July–Aug., Mon.–Sat. 9–5, Sun. 2–5; Sept.–June, by appointment.*

Although Grand Falls is largely French-speaking, the language of the valley becomes English as you move down the river. The Trans-Canada Highway is intriguingly scenic, but if you're looking for less-crowded highways and typical small communities cross the river to Route 105 at Hartland, via the **longest covered bridge** in the world—1,282 feet in length. Many of New Brunswick's covered bridges have been destroyed over the years, but the Department of Transportation is now seeking to protect the 78 or so that still exist.

If you prefer to stay on the Trans-Canada Highway you'll come to quiet **Woodstock,** population 5,068, named for a novel by Sir Walter Scott. The town is most lively during its Old Home Week celebrations, in July, although harness racing at Connell Park, with pari-mutuel betting, is a big draw all summer. The **Old Courthouse** (built in 1833)—once a coaching stop, a social hall, a political meeting place, and the seat of justice for the area—has been carefully restored.

Time Out Between Woodstock and Meductic, look for good German food at **Heino's Restaurant,** in the John Gyles Motel (junction Route 2 and Trans-Canada Highway).

---

9 At **Mactaquac Provincial Park** cars line up, sometimes all night, to claim the first empty camp lot in the morning. There are 300 campsites, supervised recreation, two beaches, two marinas, an 18-hole golf course, and a licensed lodge with dining room. Several other privately owned campsites are located in the area. Mactaquac is a pond created by the flooding of the upper Saint John River, as far up as Woodstock, when the hydroelectric dam was built. *Hwy. 105 and Mactaquac Dam, tel. 506/363–3011. Admission: $3 per vehicle summer, free in off-season. Open May 15–Sept. 2, 24 hrs.; Sept. 2–Nov. 30, 8–6; Dec. 1–May 14, 8–11.*

From Fredericton to Saint John you have a choice of two routes. Route 7 cuts away from the river to run straight south for its fast 68 miles. Route 102 leads along the Saint John River through engaging communities. You make your decision at **Oromocto,** the site of the Canadian Armed Forces Base, **Camp**

Gagetown, the largest military base in Canada (Prince Charles completed his helicopter training here). An interesting military museum within the base is open to the public. *Tel. 506/422–2630. Admission free. Open July 1–Aug. 30, weekdays 9–5, weekends 12–5; Sept. 1–June 30, weekdays 8:30–4, closed weekends.*

10 **Gagetown,** one of New Brunswick's pleasant historic communities, bustles with artisans' studios and the summer sailors who tie up at the marina. The gingerbread-trimmed **Tilley House** takes you back to Canada's beginnings. Once the home of Sir Leonard Tilley, one of the Fathers of Confederation, it is now a museum. *Front St., tel. 506/488–2966. Admission: $1 adults, 25¢ students. Open June–Sept. 15, daily 10–5.*

From Gagetown you can ferry to Jemseg and continue to **Grand Lake Provincial Park** (tel. 506/385–2919), which offers freshwater swimming off sandy beaches. At Evandale you can ferry to Belleisle Bay and the beautiful **Kingston Peninsula,** with its mossy Loyalist graveyards and pretty churches.

11 By the time you reach **Saint John** you'll be aware that New Brunswick is old, but here you'll begin to feel just how ancient the province is. The oldest incorporated city in Canada, with the special weather-beaten quality of any port city, Saint John is sometimes referred to as a blue-collar town because so many of its residents work for the Irving Oil interests. But its genteel Loyalist past is still to be seen in grand old buildings, ladies who take tea at the old Union Club, and the beautifully restored downtown harbor setting.

The city has spawned many of the province's major artists—Jack Humphrey, Millar Brittain, Fred Ross—along with such Hollywood notables as Louis B. Mayer, Donald Sutherland, and Walter Pidgeon. There's also a large Irish population that emerges in a jubilant Irish Festival every March. In July Saint John's Loyalist Days, with costumed residents re-enacting the landing of the Loyalists, is also a crowd pleaser.

In 1604 two Frenchmen, Samuel de Champlain and Sieur de Monts, landed here on St. John the Baptist Day to trade with the natives. Nearly two centuries later, in May of 1785, 3,000 Loyalists escaping from the Revolutionary War poured off a ship to found a city amid the rocks and forests. From those beginnings Saint John has emerged as a thriving industrial port city, a tribute to its hardy Loyalist forebears (they were so fiercely loyal to the British Crown, they even laid out King Square in the design of the old Union Jack).

Up until a few years ago the buildings around Saint John's waterfront huddled together in forlorn dilapidation, their facades crumbling and blurred by a century of grime. A recent surge of civic pride brought a major renovation project that reclaimed old warehouses and made them part of an enchanting waterfront development.

Numbers in the margin correspond with points of interest on the Downtown Saint John and Greater Saint John maps.

You can easily explore Saint John's town center and harbor area
12 on foot. Get your bearings on **King Street,** the town's old main
street, which is paved with red brick and lit with old-fashioned
13 lamps. King Street connects **Market Slip** on the waterfront
with King Square at the center of town.

King Square, **18**
King Street, **12**
Loyalist Burying Grounds, **17**
Market Slip, **13**
Market Square, **14**
Old City Market, **15**
Old Courthouse, **19**
Old Loyalist House, **16**
Trinity Church, **20**

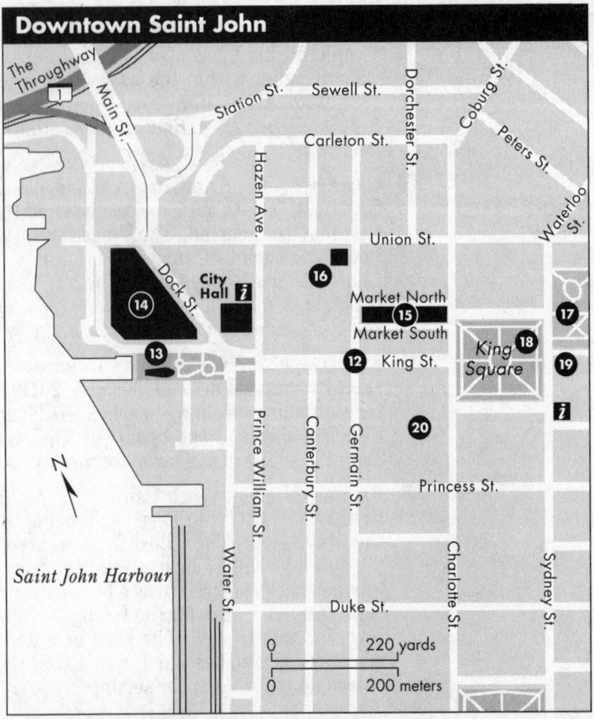

Carleton Martello Tower, **24**
Fort Howe, **21**
New Brunswick Museum, **22**
Reversing Falls Rapids, **23**

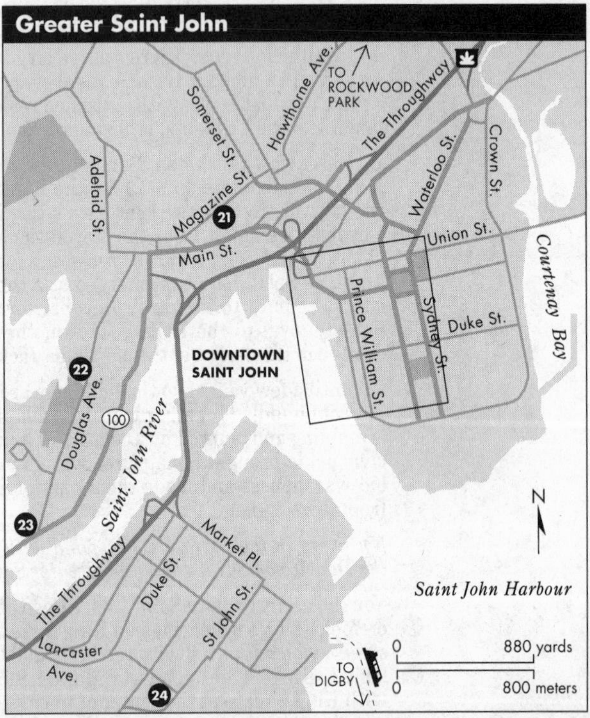

At Market Slip, where the Loyalists landed in 1783, and the ad-
14 joining **Market Square** you can while away a morning among the shops, historic displays, and cafés (some with outdoor dining in summer). Market Slip is the site of **Barbour's General Store** (tel. 506/658–2939), a fully stocked 19th-century shop redolent of the past: inside are the scents of tobacco, pickles, smoked fish, peppermint sticks, and the unforgettable tang of dulse, the edible seaweed. Beside the store is an **1800s Red School House,** and over toward Market Square is the **Ocean Hawk II,** the tugboat-turned-tourist-information-center, where you can watch the sun set from the deck. Skywalks and underground passages lead from Market Square to City Hall, the new Delta Hotel, and Brunswick Square, an adjoining shopping mall.

Stroll up King Street to Germain Street, turn left, and walk up
15 to the block-long **Old City Market,** built in 1876, which offers a variety of temptations, including red fresh-cooked lobster, great cheeses, dulse, inexpensive snacking, and the friendly chatter of the marketplace.

16 The **Old Loyalist House,** built in 1810 by Daniel David Merritt, a wealthy Loyalist merchant, retains its past beauty with authentic period furniture and eight fireplaces. *120 Union St., tel. 506/652–3590. Admission: $2 adults, 25¢ children. Open Mon.–Sat. 10–5, Sun. 2–5, or by appointment.*

Follow Union Street away from the harbor to Sydney Street
17 and turn right to visit the **Old Loyalist Burial Grounds.** At one
18 corner, in adjacent **King Square,** you'll find a strange mass of metal on the ground. It is actually a great lump of melted stock from a neighboring hardware store that was demolished in Saint John's Great Fire of 1877, in which 115 buildings were destroyed.

19 At the corner of King and Sydney streets is the **Old Courthouse.** Its spiral staircase, built of tons of unsupported stone, ascends seemingly by miracle for three stories.

20 Walk around the south side of King Square to visit **Trinity Church** (115 Charlotte St., tel. 506/693–8558). It dates to 1877, when it was rebuilt after the Great Saint John Fire. Inside, over the west door, note the coat of arms, a symbol of the monarchy, rescued from the council chamber of the colony at Massachusetts Bay. The coat of arms was deemed a worthy refugee and set in its place of honor in the church.

If you have a car, drive north from downtown on Prince William
21 Street to Main Street; in a park on your right you'll find **Fort Howe** (Rockland Rd. and Magazine St., tel. 506/658–2990). The reconstructed fortress sits atop a cliff overlooking the harbor and affords fine views from its walls. It is believed to be near the site of Fort LaTour, a French stronghold resolutely defended by Madame La Tour from her absent husband's fur-trading rival. Finally surrendering on the condition that the lives of her men would be spared, the unfortunate woman was betrayed and forced to watch them all put to death. She died shortly after, of a broken heart it is said—a romantic fate befitting her former profession as star of the Paris stage.

Main Street soon crosses Douglas Avenue; turn left to reach
22 two of the city's most notable attractions. First is the **New Brunswick Museum.** The first museum to be built in Canada, it is still recognized as one of the best of its size. You'll see the

figurehead from the bad-luck ship built in Saint John's famous shipyards—a ship that is said to have killed a man on every voyage. Along with impressive artifacts, there are costumes, a collection of dolls, some Egyptian relics, an impressive art gallery, and native animals displayed in natural surroundings. *277 Douglas Ave., tel. 506/693–1196. Admission: $2 adults, 50¢ students, senior citizens free. Open May–mid-Oct., daily 10–5; mid-Oct.–Apr., Tues.–Sun. 10–5.*

23 Continue west on Douglas Avenue to reach the **Reversing Falls Rapids,** touted by all tourist brochures as a sight no one should miss. Actually, you *should* see it, though more for its interest than its beauty. Now somewhat tarnished by the effluent of a pulp mill on the bank and occasionally blanketed by a less-than-sweet stench from the same mill, this phenomenon is nevertheless worth a look. It's actually a series of rapids and whirlpools at which, twice a day, the Fundy Tides attempt to push the river water back upstream. When the tide ebbs, the river once again pours over the rock ledges and the rapids appear to reverse themselves. A tourist information center here offers an excellent, free film on the falls.

Cross the river on Bridge Road to **West Saint John.** Make a right on Lancaster Avenue and proceed to Charlotte Street, where
24 you can't miss the **Carleton Martello Tower.** Like Fort Howe, this is a great place to survey the harbor. The tower was built in 1810 as a precaution against American attack. Costumed guides point out 8-foot-thick walls and pose for photographs. *Charlotte Ext. W, tel. 506/636–4011. Admission free. Open July–Aug., 9–8; Sept.–June, 9–6.*

Tour 3: The Fundy Coast

Numbers in the margin correspond with points of interest on the New Brunswick map.

Bordering the chilly and extravagantly tidal Bay of Fundy is some of New Brunswick's loveliest coastline. A tour of the region will take you from the border town of St. Stephen, through tiny fishing villages and past rocky coves, to Fundy National Park, where the world's most extreme tides rise and fall twice
25 daily. **St. Stephen,** on the Maine border, is a mecca for chocoholics, who converge on the small town during the Chocolate Festival held the first week in August. Choctails and chocolate puddings, cakes, and complete meals should come as no surprise when you realize that it was here that the chocolate bar was invented. Sample Ganong's famed hand-dipped chocolates at the factory store, **The Chocolatiere.** *73 Milltown Blvd., tel. 506/466–6437. Open July 1–Aug. 31, weekdays 9–8, Sat. 9–5, Sun. noon–5; Sept. 1–June 30, daily 9–5. Closed Dec. 25, Jan. 1.*

A small side trip along Ledge Road will take you to **Crocker Hill Gardens,** a tranquil oasis of herbs, dried flowers, irresistible potpourris, carved decoys, and comfortable garden seats. From here you can shout across the St. Croix River to friends in Maine. *209 Sheriff St., tel. 506/466–4251. Admission free. Open July–Aug., Mon.–Sat. 9–5, Sun. 2–5; Sept.–June, by appointment.*

26 Take Route 127 off Route 1 to **St. Andrews,** one of North America's prettiest and least spoiled resort towns. Long the summer

place of the affluent (mansions ring the town), St. Andrews retains its population of fishermen, and little has changed in the past two centuries. Of the town's 550 buildings 280 were erected before 1880; 14 have survived from the 1700s. Some Loyalists brought their homes with them piece by piece from Castine, Maine, across the bay, when the war didn't go their way.

Pick up a walking-tour map at the tourist information center on Water Street and follow it through the pleasant streets. Particular gems are the **Court House** and **Greenock Church.** The church owes its existence to a remark someone made at an 1822 dinner party about the "poor" Presbyterians not having a church of their own. Captain Christopher Scott, who took exception to the slur, spared no expense on the building, which is decorated with a carving of a green oak tree in honor of Scott's birthplace, Greenock, Scotland.

The **Ross Memorial Museum** features a fine antiques collection. *188 Montague St., tel. 506/529-3906. Admission free. Open June 15–Sept. 30, Mon.–Sat. 10–4, Sun. 1:30–4:30; Oct. 2–June 14, by appointment.*

A drive up Joe's Point Road takes you to the **Huntsman Marine Museum,** which houses marine life and displays. *Brandy Cove Rd., tel. 506/529-8895. Admission: $3.50 adults, $3 senior citizens, $2.50 children under 17. Open May–June, daily 10–4:30; July–Aug., daily 10–6; Sept.–Oct. 7, daily 10–4:30. Closed Oct. 8–Apr. 30.*

Back on Route 1 is **St. George,** a pretty town with some excellent B&Bs; one of the oldest Protestant graveyards in Canada; and a fish ladder running up the side of a dam.

The Fundy Isles—Grand Manan, Deer Island, and Campobello—are havens of peace that have lured mainland escapees for
27 generations. **Grand Manan Island,** largest of the three, is also farthest away (about two hours by car from Black's Harbour); you might see spouting whales, sunning porpoises, or a rare puffin on the way. Circular herring weirs dot the coastal water, and fish sheds and smokehouses lie beside long wharfs that reach out to bobbing fishing boats. Place names are romantic—Swallowtail, Southern Head, Seven Days Work, and Dark Harbour. It's easy to get around—only about 20 miles of road lead from the lighthouse at Southern Head to the one at Northern Head. A living encyclopedia of birds, Grand Manan attracted John James Audubon in 1831. The puffin is the island's symbol. Whale-watching expeditions can be booked at the Marathon Hotel and the Compass Rose, and scuba diving to old wrecks is popular.

Connected to Lubec, Maine, by an international bridge,
28 **Campobello Island** may be approached from the other side by toll ferry from Deer Island. Neatly manicured, preening itself in the bay, Campobello Island has always had a special appeal to the wealthy and the famous. It was here that the Roosevelt family spent their summers. The home of Franklin Delano Roosevelt, former president of the United States, is now maintained as a lovely museum in his honor. Located in the center of Roosevelt International Park, a joint project of the Canadian and American governments, **President Roosevelt's home** was the setting for the movie *Sunrise at Campobello. Roosevelt*

Park Rd., tel. 506/752–2922. Admission free. Open May 15–Oct. 15, daily 10–6. Closed Oct. 16–May 14.

The island's **Herring Cove Provincial Park** has camping facilities and a 9-hole golf course.

29 An easy, 20-minute, free ferry ride from Letete near St. George brings you to **Deer Island** for a relaxing visit. You'll enjoy exploring the fishing wharves such as those at **Chocolate Cove.** The world's largest lobster pound is at **Northern Harbour,** and you can walk through an interesting park at **Deer Point,** where you can catch a toll ferry to nearby Campobello. If you listen carefully, you may be able to hear the sighing and snorting of "the Old Sow," the second largest whirlpool in the world. If you can't hear it, you'll be able to see it, just a few feet off shore. Exploring the island takes only a few hours; it's 7½ miles long, varying in width from 3 miles to a few hundred feet at some points. West Isles World, an excellent B&B, also offers whale-watching and island tours.

After returning from the Fundy Isles to the mainland, proceed east along coastal Route 1. If you have the time, dip down to the peaceful, hidden fishing villages of **Maces Bay, Dipper,** and **Chance Harbour,** all much the same as they have been for centuries. At Dipper Harbour, you can rent sea kayaks or buy a lobster roll to munch on the long sun-warmed wharf.

30 Drive east through Saint John along a scenic stretch of Route 1 to Route 114, which angles south to the 80-square-mile **Fundy National Park.** Stand on a sandstone ledge or dark-sand beach and watch the bay's phenomenal tide rise or fall. *Box 40, Alma E0A 1B0, tel. 506/887–2000. Admission: June 22–Sept. 3, $4; Sept. 4–June 2, free.*

Alma is the small seaside town that services the national park. Here you'll find fresh lobster and sticky buns to die for. Past Alma the coast road to Moncton winds by covered bridges and along rocky coasts, with photogenic stops such as **Hopewell Cape,** home of the famous giant flowerpots, rock formations carved by the Fundy Tides.

Tour 4: Moncton and the Acadian Peninsula

Numbers in the margin correspond with points of interest on the New Brunswick map.

31 A friendly town, often called the Gateway to Acadia because of its mix of English and French and its proximity to the Acadian shore, **Moncton** has a pretty downtown anchored with wisely placed malls that keep business booming.

This city has long touted two natural attractions, the Tidal Bore and the Magnetic Hill. Be prepared to be disappointed. In days gone by, before the harbor mouth filled with silt, the **Tidal Bore** was indeed an incredible sight, a high wall of water that surged in through the narrow opening of the river to fill red-mud banks to the brim. It still moves up the river, and the moving wave is worth waiting for, but it's nowhere near as lofty as it used to be, except sometimes in the spring when the tides are very high. Bore Park on Main Street is the best viewpoint; viewing times are posted there.

32 **Magnetic Hill,** north of town just off the Trans-Canada Highway, is a hill that creates an optical illusion. If you park your car

in neutral at the designated spot, you'll seem to be coasting up hill without power.

Among Moncton's notable man-made attractions is the **Acadian Museum,** at the University of Moncton, which has a remarkable collection of artifacts reflecting 300 years of Acadian life in New Brunswick. *Clemeng and Cormier Aves., tel. 506/858–4088. Admission free. Open June 1–Sept. 30, weekdays 10–5, weekends 1–5; Oct. 1–May 31, Tues.–Fri. 1–4:30, weekends 1–4. Closed Mon., holidays.*

Turn northeast along the coast from Moncton to the salty shores of unique Acadian communities such as **Shediac, Cocagne, Buctouche,** and **Rexton,** which offer long warm sandbars, lobster feeds, lighthouses, weathered wharves, and sea-stained churches. Friendly Acadians make this trip a joy;
33 and the white, dune-edged beaches of **Kouchibouguac National Park** are among the finest on the continent. *Tel. 506/876–2443. Admission: $4 per vehicle. Open daily 8–8.*

Route 11 continues north to the Miramichi River and the fabled **Miramichi region** of lumberjacks, fishermen, and "come all ye's." Celebrated for its salmon rivers and the ebullient nature of its residents (Scottish, English, Irish, and a smattering of French and Indian), this is a land of stories, folklore, and lumber kings. Pleasant towns and villages of sturdy wood homes dot the banks of Miramichi Bay at **Chatham** and **Newcastle** (where the politician and British media mogul Lord Beaverbrook grew up and is buried). At **Doaktown** (south of Newcastle on Route 8), the **Miramichi Salmon Museum** (tel. 506/365–7787) provides a look at the endangered Atlantic salmon and at life in noted fishing camps along the rivers.

The **Woodmen's Museum** of Boiestown (in the exact center of the province) is housed in what looks like two giant logs, and portrays a lumberman's life. *Tel. 506/365–4431. Closed winter.*

Return to Newcastle and swing north and east on Route 11 to
34 **Caraquet,** on the Acadian Peninsula. The town is perched along the Baie des Chaleurs, with Québec's Gaspé Peninsula beckoning across the inlet.

The *pièce de résistance* of the Acadian Peninsula is, without
35 doubt, the **Acadian Historical Village,** 10 kilometers (6 miles) west of Caraquet on Route 11, near Grand Anse. As Kings Landing reflects the early English settlement, the Village Historique re-creates the lives of early Acadians between 1780 and 1890. A walk through the settlement is one of those unusually peaceful experiences of a summer day. A chapel bell tolls, ducks waddle and quack under a footbridge, wagons creak, and the smell of hearty cooking wafts from cottage doors. Costumed staff act as guides, and a restaurant serves old-Acadian dishes. *Tel. 506/727–3467. Admission: $7 adults, $4.25 children, $15 family. Open June–mid-Sept., daily 10–6.*

Shopping

New Brunswick is famous for its crafts, and the *Directory of New Brunswick Craftsmen & Craft Shops* provides comprehensive listings of potters, weavers, glassblowers, jewelers, and carvers throughout the province. Get a copy from Tourism New Brunswick (Box 12345, Fredericton, E3B 5A6, tel. 800/561–0123).

Fredericton Mammoth crafts markets are held occasionally in town and every Labor Day weekend in Mactaquac Park. **Aitkens Pewter** (81 Regent St.) and **Pewtercraft** (582 Brunswick St.) offer beautiful pewter hollowware, goblets, belt buckles, jewelry, and authentic reproductions of ancient folk dishes. After browsing, you can sample ice cream or a snack on Aitken's back porch. **Shades of Light Studio and Gift Shop** (Regent St.) features stained glass and other local crafts.

Excellent men's shoes can be bought at **Hartt's Shoe Factory** (York St.); **The Linen Closet** (King St.) sells laces, exquisite bedding, and Victorian nightgowns.

Gagetown **Flo Grieg's** on Front Street carries superior pottery. **Claremont House B&B,** on Tilley Road, displays unusual batik items and copper engravings. **Loomcrafters** is a good choice for handwoven items.

Moncton Five spacious malls and numerous pockets of shops in downtown Moncton help to make it the best place to shop in New Brunswick. Among the crafts to look for are the yarn portraits of La Sagouine, "the old sage" of Buctouche. The sayings of the old Acadian woman as she does her daily chores were made famous in Antonine Maillet's novel *La Sagouine*.

St.-Andrews-by-the-Sea This "veddy British" town has many places to buy English and New Brunswick woolens, English bone china, and marvelous wool yarn, among them **The Sea Captain's Loft, Cottage Craft,** and **Saint Andrews Woollens.** Collectibles, and rare and out-of-print books are sold at the **Pansy Patch,** a stunning old home across from the Algonquin Hotel. On Water Street, the main shopping strip, head to **La Baelein** for quality crafts, **Trading Post** for antiques, and **Tom Smith's Studio** for fine pottery.

Saint John The little antiques stores and crafts shops provide the best shopping in Saint John. They are sprinkled throughout the downtown area. **Prince William Street** has interesting browsing in excellent antiques shops and crafts boutiques. **Brunswick Square** and **Market Square** in the new harborfront have airy shopping with many top-quality boutiques. **Old City Market,** between Charlotte and Germaine streets, bustles six days a week and always stocks delicious local specialties, such as maple syrup and lobster.

St. Leonard A visit to the studio and store of the **Madawaska Weavers,** whose handwoven items are known the world over, is a must. Handsome skirts, stoles, and enchanting ties are some of the items on sale.

Sports and Fitness

Fredericton The Saint John River makes Fredericton an ideal place for sailing, wind surfing and boating of all kinds. Sculling is popular from the **Aquatic Center** (Woodstock Rd., tel. 506/458–5513), and sailboarding. Harness racing is a major event (May to October) at the **Fredericton Exhibition Grounds,** on Smythe Street.

Saint John Saint John has year-round harness racing, golf courses, tennis courts, and several good beaches. The **Aquatic Center,** a legacy from the Canada Games, is a world-class facility for all kinds of water sports; it has slides, swinging ropes, an Olympic-size pool, a warm-up pool, whirlpools, and a café. *Next to City Hall, tel. 506/642–7946. Admission: $3.50 adults, $2.50 children. Open daily 6:30 AM–10 PM.*

Fishing Crisscrossed with rivers, the province is a fisherman's heaven, offering Atlantic silver salmon, speckled trout, and black and striped bass. Said to offer the best bass fishing in North America, the province starts its season in mid-May with the Big Bass Tournament at Mactaquac, upriver from Fredericton. The Miramichi, the Restigouche, and the Nashwaak Rivers are prized by sport fishermen the world over.

Dining and Lodging

Dining

Although there are not a lot of choices for fine dining in New Brunswick, a few good restaurants exist, and families will find plenty of quality food in many outlets. A number of gourmet restaurants have popped up in Saint John in recent years—so there is hope that the dining scene will improve provincewide.

In the spring, once the ice has left streams and rivers, a provincial delicacy, the fiddlehead fern, is picked from the shores. Eaten as a vegetable (boiled, drenched with lemon, butter, salt, and pepper) fiddleheads have something of an artichoke taste, and go well with spring's bony fish, shad, and gaspereaux. Silver salmon, once a spring staple when set nets were allowed, is still available but quite costly. Most salmon served in restaurants is farm reared. Lobster, a favorite maritime dish, is available in most restaurants, but is not always cheap. The custom of the residents is to buy it fresh from the fishermen or shore outlets and devour it in huge quantities. Because of the cool waters, shellfish is especially tasty. Look for oysters, scallops, clams, crab, and mussels. And be sure to try the purple seaweed called dulse that the residents eat like potato chips. To be truly authentic, accompany any New Brunswick–style feast with hearty Moosehead beer, brewed in Saint John and one of the province's well-known exports.

Dress is casual everywhere except at the Expensive and Very Expensive listings, and, unless noted, no reservations are needed.

Highly recommended restaurants in each price category are indicated by a star ★.

Category	Cost*
Very Expensive	over $40
Expensive	$20–$40
Moderate	$10–$19
Inexpensive	under $10

**per person, excluding drinks, service, and 11% sales tax*

Lodging

New Brunswick has a number of officially designated Heritage Inns—historically significant establishments built in the last century. Many have antique china and furnishings or other charming touches, and their accommodations run the gamut from elegant to homey.

Hotels and motels in and around Saint John and Fredericton are adequate with friendly service. Accommodations in Saint John are at a premium in the summer, so reserve ahead to ensure a place to stay.

Highly recommended lodgings in each price category are indicated by a star ★.

Category	Cost*
Expensive	over $60
Moderate	$45–$60
Inexpensive	under $40

**All prices are for a standard double room, excluding 10% service charge.*

Campbelltown
Dining and Lodging
★

Aylesford Inn. Truly a find, near the Québec border and Sugarloaf Provincial Park, this friendly inn housed in a Victorian mansion has guest rooms handsomely furnished with Eastlake and Canadian-pine antiques. The gift shop sells crafts made by the owners. Large gardens and verandas offer views of the river. Excellent dinners are served to guests (quail and frogs' legs are featured entrées), and full breakfasts are included in the room rate. Nonguests are welcome for afternoon tea. *8 MacMillan Ave., E3N 1E9, tel. 506/759–7672. 7 rooms, 1 with bath. Facilities: dining room, croquet. AE, MC, V. Moderate.*

Campobello Island
Lodging

Owens House. This particularly charming historic house is now a B&B. A full hot breakfast is served, and there's a beach nearby. *Welshpool, E0G 3H0, tel. 506/752–2977. 9 rooms. No credit cards. Inexpensive.*

Caraquet
Dining and Lodging

Hotel Paulin. The word *quaint* really fits this property. There are pretty rooms, a bathroom down the hall, and an excellent small dining room specializing in fresh fish cooked perfectly. *143 Blvd. St. Pierre, tel. 506/727–9981. 10 rooms with shared bath. Facilities: restaurant. MC, V. Inexpensive.*

Deer Island
Dining and Lodging

45th Parallel Motel and Restaurant. Deer Island has only one motel, and it's a clean, comfortable, tastefully furnished one with water views from many rooms. A full breakfast is included, and for lunch or dinner you can get everything from lobster to pizza at the informal restaurant. Pets are welcome. *Fairhaven, Deer Island E0G 1R0, tel. 506/747–2231. 10 rooms. Facilities: restaurant, 3 rooms have kitchenettes. V. Moderate.*

West Isles World B&B. This white frame house overlooks the cove and offers three snug rooms with an informal country feel; the big upstairs bedroom has a water view. The owners will arrange whale-watching cruises for you. A full breakfast is included in the room rate, and other meals are served on request. *Lord's Cove, E0G 2J0, tel. 506/747–2946. 4 rooms, 1 with bath. No credit cards. Moderate.*

Fredericton

Dining

Benoit's. Fredericton's top-of-the-line restaurant features excellent French cuisine served in an art deco dining room. JC is the genial host, and seafood (try the "feast for two") is well prepared. *536 Queen St., tel. 506/459–3666. AE, DC, MC, V. No lunch Sat.; closed Sun. Expensive.*

Luna Steakhouse. Specialties include huge Caesar salad, garlic bread, escargots, and brochettes. In fine weather you can dine on an outdoor terrace. *168 Dundonald St., tel. 506/455–4020. AE, DC, MC, V. Moderate.*

Mei's Chinese Restaurant. The Szechuan dishes served here include dumplings, hot or mildly spiced. This is a neighborhood restaurant, with lots of casual congeniality in a small, happily decorated room. *74 Regent St., tel. 506/454–2177. AE, MC, V. No lunch weekends. Moderate.*

Bar B Q Barn. Special children's menus and barbecued ribs and chicken are the standards; the daily blackboard lists plenty of other full-course dinner specialties, such as salmon, scallops, and chili. This is a popular, attractive spot, great for winding down, and the bar serves fine martinis. *540 Queen St., tel. 506/455–2742. AE, MC, V. Inexpensive–Moderate.*

Lodging

Howard Johnson Motor Lodge. On the north side of the river and at the north end of the Princess Margaret Bridge, this HoJo's has a terrace bar in a pleasant interior courtyard overlooked by balconies from all the rooms. Guest-room decor is standard for the chain. *Trans-Canada Highway, Box 1414, tel. 506/472–0480. 117 rooms. Facilities: restaurant, bar, indoor pool. AE, DC, MC, V. Expensive.*

Lord Beaverbrook Hotel. A central location is this modern, seven-story hotel's main attraction, although a major renovation early in 1991 may spruce things up a bit. When last visited, guest rooms were adequately furnished; some have Jacuzzis or minibars. The food in the main dining room is forgettable. There are a couple of lively bars downstairs. *659 Queen St., E3B 5G2, tel. 506/455–3371. 175 rooms. Facilities: 3 restaurants, bar, indoor pool, nonsmoking rooms. Expensive.*

Auberge Wandlyn Inn. Just off the Trans-Canada Highway, this hotel is away from the downtown area but close to three shopping malls, many restaurants, and theaters. The guest rooms are no-frills, but the family-oriented dining room is pretty, and there's a cozy bar. *58 Prospect St. W, Box 214, E3B 4Y9, tel. 506/452–8937. 116 rooms. Facilities: restaurant, bar, pool. AE, DC, MC, V. Moderate.*

Carriage House Bed and Breakfast. This heritage mansion has lovely bedrooms. Breakfast is served in a sunny, glass-walled room. *230 University Ave., E3B 4H7, tel. 506/452–9924. 7 rooms, 2 with bath. MC, V. Moderate.*

Happy Apple Acres Bed and Breakfast. This B&B offers friendly atmosphere in a country setting. Besides the full breakfast that is included in the room rate, dinner can be arranged for guests, and the cooking is excellent. *Highway 105 (7 mi n. of Fredericton), RR 4, E3B 1A1, tel. 506/472–1819. 3 rooms with bath. MC, V. Inexpensive–Moderate.*

Grand Manan Island
Lodging

The Marathon Inn. Perched on a hill overlooking the harbor, this gracious mansion built by a sea captain offers newly renovated guest rooms furnished with antiques. Meals are served in the restaurant (breakfast and dinner are included in the room rate), and whale-watching cruises can be arranged. *Box 129, North Head, E0G 2M0, tel. 506/662–8144. 28 rooms, 15 with bath. Facilities: restaurant, bar, pool, tennis. MC, V. Expensive.*

Compass Rose. Lovely guest rooms are available in the two old houses that have been combined into this small inn. It's conveniently near the ferry landing, and whale-watching tours can be arranged. Breakfast is included in the room rate. *North Head, E0G 3K0, tel. 506/662–8570. Moderate.*

Ludlow
Lodging

Pond's Chalet Resort. You'll get a traditional fishing-camp experience here, in a lodge and chalets set among trees overlooking a salmon river. *Ludlow (near Boiestown), E0C 1N0, tel. 506/369–2612. 10 rooms in lodge, 8 camps. Facilities: dining room. AE, DC, MC, V. Moderate.*

Moncton
Dining

Cy's Seafood Restaurant. This favorite for seafood, decorated in dark wood and brass, has been serving generous portions for decades. Though renowned for its seafood casserole, the restaurant also offers reliable scallop, shrimp, and lobster dishes. You can see the Tidal Bore from the windows. *170 Main St., tel. 506/857–0032. AE, DC, MC, V. Moderate.*

Fisherman's Paradise. In spite of the enormous dining area (more than 350 tables), this restaurant serves memorable à la carte seafood dishes, in an atmosphere of candlelight and wood furnishings. The children's menu and down-home specials such as lobster bake make this a good spot for families. *375 Dieppe Blvd., tel. 506/859–4388. AE, MC, V. Moderate.*

Lodging
★

Hotel Beausejour. Moncton's finest and one of the nicest places to stay in the province, the hotel is decorated in Acadian style. The downtown location is convenient. Besides the standard guest rooms, there are some luxury concierge rooms. Staff in 18th-century costume lend a pleasant ambience to the main dining room, L'Auberge; the other restaurant is more formal. *750 Main St., tel. 506/854–4344. 317 rooms. Facilities: 2 restaurants, bar, outdoor pool, access to health club. AE, MC, V. Expensive.*

The Crystal Palace. Moncton's newest hotel is unique: there are theme rooms (want to be Ali Baba for a night?) and, for gears families, an indoor pool and a miniature wonderland of rides, midway stalls, coin games, food booths, and boutiques. Champlain Mall is across the street. *499 Paul St., tel. 506/858–8584. 119 rooms. Facilities: restaurant, indoor pool. AE, DC, MC, V. Moderate–Expensive.*

Newcastle
Lodging

Wharf Inn. Here in Miramichi country, the staff is friendly and the restaurant serves excellent salmon dinners. This low-rise modern building has two wings; guest rooms in the executive wing have extra amenities. *Jane St., tel. 506/622–0302. 70 rooms. Facilities: restaurant, patio lounge, indoor pool. AE, DC, MC, V. Moderate.*

Sackville
Lodging

Marshlands Inn. In this white clapboard inn, a welcoming double living room with fireplace sets the informal, country atmosphere. Bedrooms are furnished with sleigh beds or four-posters, but they also have modern touches such as air-conditioning and in-room telephones. *Box 1440, E0A 3C0, tel. 506/536–0170. 21 rooms, 14 with bath. Facilities: restaurant. AE, DC, MC, V. Moderate–Expensive.*

St. Andrews
Lodging

Algonquin Hotel. The wrap-around veranda of this grand old hotel overlooks wide lawns. Bellmen wear kilts. The dining room is noted for its buffets, and meals can be pleasant here if the staff is in the mood. *Rte. 127, E0G 2X0, tel. 506/529–8823. 193 rooms. Facilities: restaurant, bar, pool, golf, tennis. AE, MC, V. Closed winter. Expensive.*

★ **Pansy Patch B & B.** Across the street from the Algonquin Hotel is this Norman-style farmhouse, built in 1912, distinguished by a turret and steep roofs. The guest rooms are appointed with antiques and have views of the water. The owners also operate an antiques shop and bookshop on the property. Full breakfast is included in the room rate. *59 Carleton St., E0G 2X0, tel. 506/529–3834. 4 rooms with shared bath. AE, MC, V. Closed mid-Oct.–mid-May. Expensive.*

Saint John
Dining

La Belle Vie. Dine in the drawing rooms of a lovely Second Empire–style mansion, where you'll note examples of trompe l'oeil near the ceiling. The cooking is traditional French; try the lobster bisque. *325 Lancaster Ave., tel. 506/635–1155. Reservations advised. AE, DC, MC, V. Expensive.*

Turn of the Tide. Overlooking the harbor, this large hotel dining room is decorated with antiques. Although the dining is pleasant at all times, the best meal of the week is the Sunday buffet, with a long table full of dishes from the exotic to the tried-and-true. Fill your own crepes for dessert. *Hilton Hotel, Market Sq., tel. 506/693–8484. Reservations advised. AE, DC, MC, V. No lunch Sat. Expensive.*

Café Creole. Creole and Cajun food, spicy or not, is prepared by Deadra, a student of Paul Prudhomme. The small, attractive dining room is well situated to let you watch the life of Saint John pass by. Lunch can be downright cheap. *14 King Sq., tel. 506/633–8091. AE, MC, V. No dinner Sun. Moderate–Expensive.*

Grannan's. Seafood is featured in this nautically decorated restaurant, and the desserts here are memorable. Dining spills over onto the sidewalk in summer, and there are three lively bars connected to the restaurant. *Market Sq., tel. 506/634–1555. AE, DC, MC, V. No lunch Sun. Inexpensive–Moderate.*

Incredible Edibles. Here you can enjoy down-to-earth food—biscuits, garlic-laden hummus, salads, pastas, and desserts—in cozy rooms or, in summer, on the outdoor terrace. They also serve a good cup of coffee. *177 Prince William St., tel. 506/633–7554. AE, MC, V. Closed Sun. Inexpensive–Moderate.*

Reggie's. This popular spot near Brunswick Square begins serving breakfast at 6 AM. Later in the day specialties include chowders, bagel burgers, and lobster rolls. The restaurant closes at 6 or 7 PM, so come early if you want dinner. *26 Germain St., tel. 506/657–6270. MC, V. Inexpensive.*

Lodging

Delta Brunswick Inn. This lively new hotel atop Brunswick Square has a good, moderately priced dining room and banquet-and-convention facilities. *39 King St., E2L 4W3, tel. 506/648–1981. 255 rooms. Facilities: restaurant, bar, pool, children's center. AE, DC, MC, V. Expensive.*

Saint John Hilton. Part of the Market Square complex, the smallest Hilton in the world is furnished in Loyalist decor; guest rooms overlook the harbor or the town. Mellow antiques furnish corners of the dining room and the medieval-style Great Hall, which hosts banquets. Adjoining the 12-story property are shops, restaurants, bars, and a library. *1 Market Sq., E2L 4Z6, tel. 506/693–8484 or 800/361–6140. 197 rooms. Facilities: restaurant, bar, pool. AE, DC, MC, V. Expensive.*

★ **Shadow Lawn Country Inn.** This atmospheric village inn is located in an affluent suburb with tree-lined streets and palatial houses, 10 minutes from Saint John. Tennis, golf, horseback riding, and a yacht club are nearby. The inn has eight old-fashioned bedrooms, some with fireplaces. Besides breakfast for guests (not included in the room rate), the dining room is open to the public for a set-menu dinner by reservation only; specialties include beef Wellington and seafood brioches. Predinner sherry is served in the mahogany-panel bar. *Box 41, Rothesay Rd., E0G 2W0, tel. 506/847–7539. 8 rooms with bath. DC, MC, V. Moderate–Expensive.*

Shediac
Dining and Lodging

★ **Chez Françoise.** This lovely old mansion with a wrap-around veranda has been decorated in Victorian style, with hardwood floors and antiques; an annex across the street contains several guest rooms as well. Front rooms enjoy water views. The dining room, open to the public for lunch and dinner, serves excellent traditional French cuisine with an emphasis on seafood. *93 Main St., tel. 506/532–4233. 10 rooms in main house, 6 with bath; 10 rooms in annex, 4 with bath. Facilities: restaurant. AE, MC, V. Closed Jan. 1–Easter. Inexpensive–Moderate.*

The Arts and Nightlife

The Arts

Theatre New Brunswick performs in the Playhouse in Fredericton (686 Queen St., tel. 506/458–8344). Top musical groups, noted professional singers, and performers usually appear here or at the **Aitken Center,** on the University of New Brunswick campus.

Nightlife

Fredericton

Folk singers (usually not terribly good) are featured at the **River Room** in the Lord Beaverbrook Hotel (loud); the **Cosmopolitan Club** (King St.) sometimes presents great jazz and also has a back room for the younger crowd; The **Chestnut Inn,** on York Street, has dining and live (usually country or folk) music. Try **The Lunar Rogue** (King St.) and the **Hilltop** (Prospect St.) for good pub food.

Saint John

Taverns and lounges, usually with music of some kind, provide a lively nightlife. For quiet conversation with a "Play it, Sam" background, try the **Brigantine,** in the Hilton. Lively **Grannans,** in Market Square, has several bars and theme nights during summer. **O'Leary's,** on Princess Street, is good for Saint John Irish fun; **Checkers,** in Keddy's Motel, is the place for dancing; go to **Sherlock's,** at the foot of King Street, for a young, congenial crowd.

French Vocabulary

Words and Phrases

	English	*French*	*Pronunciation*
Basics	Yes/no	Oui/non	wee/no
	Please	S'il vous plait	seel voo play
	Thank you (very much)	Merci (beaucoup)	mare-**see** (boh-**koo**)
	You're welcome	De rien	deh ree-**en**
	That's all right	Il n'y a pas de quoi	eel nee ah pah deh kwah
	Excuse me, sorry	Pardon	pahr-**doan**
	Sorry!	Désolé(e)	day-zoh-**lay**
	Good morning/afternoon	Bonjour	bone-**joor**
	Good evening	Bonsoir	bone-**swar**
	Goodbye	Au revoir	o ruh-**vwar**
	Mr.(Sir)/ Mrs.(Ma'am)	Monsieur/madame	meh-see-**ur**/mah-**dahm**
	Miss	Mademoiselle	mad-mwah-**zel**
	Pleased to meet you	Enchanté(e)	on-shahn-**tay**
	How are you?	Comment allez-vous?	ko-men-tahl-ay-**voo**
	Very well, thanks	Très bien, merci	tray bee-**en**, mare-**see**
	And you?	Et vous?	ay voo?
Numbers	one	un	un
	two	deux	dew
	three	trois	twa
	four	quatre	**cat**-ruh
	five	cinq	sank
	six	six	seess
	seven	sept	set
	eight	huit	wheat
	nine	neuf	nuf
	ten	dix	deess
	eleven	onze	owns
	twelve	douze	dues
	thirteen	treize	trays
	fourteen	quatorze	ka-**torz**
	fifteen	quinze	cans
	sixteen	seize	sez
	seventeen	dix-sept	deess-**set**
	eighteen	dix-huit	deess-**wheat**
	nineteen	dix-neuf	deess-**nuf**
	twenty	vingt	vant
	twenty-one	vingt-et-un	vant-ay-**un**
	thirty	trente	trahnt
	forty	quarante	ka-**rahnt**
	fifty	cinquante	sang-**kahnt**
	sixty	soixante	swa-**sahnt**

	seventy	soixante-dix	swa-sahnt-**deess**
	eighty	quatre-vingts	cat-ruh-**vant**
	ninety	quatre-vingt-dix	cat-ruh-vant-**deess**
	one hundred	cent	sahnt
	one thousand	mille	meel
Colors	black	noir	nwar
	blue	bleu	blu
	brown	brun	brun
	green	vert	vair
	orange	orange	o-**ranj**
	pink	rose	rose
	red	rouge	rouge
	violet	violette	vee-o-**let**
	white	blanc	blahnk
	yellow	jaune	jone
Days of the Week	Sunday	dimanche	dee-**mahnsh**
	Monday	lundi	lewn-**dee**
	Tuesday	mardi	mar-**dee**
	Wednesday	mercredi	mare-kruh-**dee**
	Thursday	jeudi	juh-**dee**
	Friday	vendredi	van-dra-**dee**
	Saturday	samedi	sam-**dee**
Months	January	janvier	jan-**vyay**
	February	février	feh-vree-**ay**
	March	mars	mars
	April	avril	a-**vreel**
	May	mai	may
	June	juin	jwan
	July	juillet	jwee-**ay**
	August	août	oot
	September	septembre	sep-**tahm**-bruh
	October	octobre	oak-**toe**-bruh
	November	novembre	no-**vahm**-bruh
	December	décembre	day-**sahm**-bruh
Useful Phrases	Do you speak English?	Parlez-vous anglais?	par-lay vooz ahng-**glay**
	I don't speak French	Je ne parle pas français	jeh nuh parl pah fraun-**say**
	I don't understand	Je ne comprends pas	jeh nuh kohm-prahn **pah**
	I understand	Je comprends	jeh kohm-**prahn**
	I don't know	Je ne sais pas	jeh nuh say **pah**
	I'm American/British	Je suis américain/anglais	jeh sweez a-may-ree-**can**/ ahng-**glay**
	What's your name?	Comment vous appelez-vous?	ko-mahn voo za-pel-ay-**voo**
	My name is . . .	Je m'appelle . . .	jeh muh-**pel** . . .
	What time is it?	Quelle heure est-il?	kel ur et-**il**
	How?	Comment?	ko-**mahn**
	When?	Quand?	kahnd

	How much is it?	C'est combien?	say comb-bee-**en**
	It's expensive/cheap	C'est cher/pas cher	say sher/pa sher
	A little/a lot	Un peu/beaucoup	un puh/bo-**koo**
	More/less	Plus/moins	ploo/mwa
	Enough/too (much)	Assez/trop	a-**say**/tro
	I am ill/sick	Je suis malade	jeh swee ma-**lahd**
	Please call a doctor	Appelez un docteur	a-pe-lay un dohk-**tore**
	Help!	Au secours!	o say-**koor**
	Stop!	Arrêtez!	a-ruh-**tay**
	Fire!	Au feu!	o fuw
	Caution!/Look out!	Attention!	a-tahn-see-**own**
Dining Out	A bottle of . . .	une bouteille de . . .	ewn boo-**tay** deh
	A cup of . . .	une tasse de . . .	ewn tass deh
	A glass of . . .	un verre de . . .	un vair deh
	Ashtray	un cendrier	un sahn-dree-**ay**
	Bill/check	l'addition	la-dee-see-**own**
	Bread	du pain	due pan
	Breakfast	le petit déjeuner	leh pet-**ee** day-zhu-**nay**
	Butter	du beurre	due bur
	Cheers!	A votre santé!	ah vo-truh sahn-**tay**
	Cocktail/aperitif	un apéritif	un ah-pay-ree-**teef**
	Dinner	le dîner	leh dee-**nay**
	Dish of the day	le plat du jour	leh pla do **zhoor**
	Enjoy!	Bon appétit!	bone a-pay-**tee**
	Fixed-price menu	le menu	leh may-**new**
	Fork	une fourchette	ewn four-**shet**
	I am diabetic	Je suis diabétique	jeh swee-dee-ah-**bay-teek**
	I am on a diet	Je suis au régime	jeh sweez o ray-**jeem**
	I am vegetarian	Je suis végétarien (ne)	jeh swee vay-jay-ta-ree-**en**
	I cannot eat . . .	Je ne peux pas manger de . . .	jeh nuh puh pah mahn-**jay** deh
	I'd like to order	Je voudrais commander	jeh voo-**dray** ko-mahn-**day**
	I'd like . . .	Je voudrais . . .	jeh voo-**dray**
	I'm hungry/thirsty	J'ai faim/soif	jay fam/swahf

Is service/the tip included?	Est-ce que le service est compris?	ess keh leh sair-veess ay comb-**pree**
It's good/bad	C'est bon/mauvais	say bon/mo-**vay**
It's hot/cold	C'est chaud/froid	say sho/frwah
Knife	un couteau	un koo-**toe**
Lunch	le déjeuner	leh day-juh-**nay**
Menu	la carte	la cart
Napkin	une serviette	ewn sair-vee-**et**
Pepper	du poivre	due **pwah**-vruh
Plate	une assiette	ewn a-see-**et**
Give me . . .	Donnez-moi . . .	doe-nay-**mwah**
Salt	du sel	dew sell
Spoon	une cuiller	ewn kwee-**ay**
Sugar	du sucre	due **sook**-ruh
Waiter!/Waitress!	Monsieur!/ Mademoiselle!	meh-see-**ur** /mad-mwah-**zel**
Wine list	la carte des vins	la cart day **van**

Index

Personal Itinerary

Departure *Date*

Time

Transportation

Arrival *Date* *Time*

Departure *Date* *Time*

Transportation

Accommodations

Arrival *Date* *Time*

Departure *Date* *Time*

Transportation

Accommodations

Arrival *Date* *Time*

Departure *Date* *Time*

Transportation

Accommodations

Personal Itinerary

Arrival *Date* *Time*

Departure *Date* *Time*

Transportation

Accommodations

Arrival *Date* *Time*

Departure *Date* *Time*

Transportation

Accommodations

Arrival *Date* *Time*

Departure *Date* *Time*

Transportation

Accommodations

Arrival *Date* *Time*

Departure *Date* *Time*

Transportation

Accommodations

Personal Itinerary

Arrival *Date* *Time*

Departure *Date* *Time*

Transportation

Accommodations

Arrival *Date* *Time*

Departure *Date* *Time*

Transportation

Accommodations

Arrival *Date* *Time*

Departure *Date* *Time*

Transportation

Accommodations

Arrival *Date* *Time*

Departure *Date* *Time*

Transportation

Accommodations

Personal Itinerary

Arrival *Date* *Time*

Departure *Date* *Time*

Transportation

Accommodations

Arrival *Date* *Time*

Departure *Date* *Time*

Transportation

Accommodations

Arrival *Date* *Time*

Departure *Date* *Time*

Transportation

Accommodations

Arrival *Date* *Time*

Departure *Date* *Time*

Transportation

Accommodations

Addresses

Name

Address

Telephone

Name

Address

Telephone

Name

Address

Telephone

Name

Address

Telephone

Name

Address

Telephone

Name

Address

Telephone

Name

Address

Telephone

Name

Address

Telephone

Name

Address

Telephone

Name

Address

Telephone

Name

Address

Telephone

Name

Address

Telephone

Name

Address

Telephone

Name

Address

Telephone

Name

Address

Telephone

Name

Address

Telephone

Fodor's Travel Guides

U.S. Guides

Alaska
Arizona
Boston
California
Cape Cod
The Carolinas & the Georgia Coast
The Chesapeake Region
Chicago
Colorado
Disney World & the Orlando Area
Florida
Hawaii
Las Vegas
Los Angeles
Maui
Miami & the Keys
New England
New Mexico
New Orleans
New York City
New York City (Pocket Guide)
Pacific North Coast
Philadelphia & the Pennsylvania Dutch Country
Puerto Rico (Pocket Guide)
The Rockies
San Diego
San Francisco
San Francisco (Pocket Guide)
The South
Texas
USA
The Upper Great Lakes Region
Vacations in New York State
Vacations on the Jersey Shore
Virgin Islands
Virginia & Maryland
Waikiki
Washington, D.C.

Foreign Guides

Acapulco
Amsterdam
Australia
Austria
The Bahamas
The Bahamas (Pocket Guide)
Baja & the Pacific Coast Resorts
Barbados
Belgium & Luxembourg
Bermuda
Brazil
Budget Europe
Canada
Canada's Atlantic Provinces
Cancun, Cozumel, Yucatan Peninsula
Caribbean
Central America
China
Eastern Europe
Egypt
Europe
Europe's Great Cities
France
Germany
Great Britain
Greece
The Himalayan Countries
Holland
Hong Kong
India
Ireland
Israel
Italy
Italy 's Great Cities
Jamaica
Japan
Kenya, Tanzania, Seychelles
Korea
Lisbon
London
London Companion
London (Pocket Guide)
Madrid & Barcelona
Mexico
Mexico City
Montreal & Quebec City
Morocco
Munich
New Zealand
Paris
Paris (Pocket Guide)
Portugal
Rio de Janeiro
Rome
Saint Martin/ Sint Maarten
Scandinavia
Scandinavian Cities
Scotland
Singapore
South America
South Pacific
Southeast Asia
Soviet Union
Spain
Sweden
Switzerland
Sydney
Thailand
Tokyo
Toronto
Turkey
Vienna & the Danube Valley
Yugoslavia

...t Journal Guides to Business Travel

International Cities
The Pacific Rim
USA & Canada

...'s Flashmaps ...w York
...dor's Flashmaps Washington, D.C.
Shopping in Europe
Skiing in North America
Smart Shopper's Guide to London
Sunday in New York
Touring Europe